THE VOYAGE OF DISCOVERY

A HISTORICAL INTRODUCTION TO PHILOSOPHY

|||

SECOND EDITION

William F. Lawhead

University of Mississippi

WADSWORTH

TM

THOMSON LEARNING

Australia • Canada • Mexico • Singapore • Spain
United Kingdom • United States

WADSWORTH

THOMSON LEARNING™

Publisher: Eve Howard
Philosophy Editor: Peter Adams
Assistant Editor: Kara Kindstrom
Editorial Assistant: Chalida Anusasananan
Marketing Manager: Dave Garrison
Marketing Assistant: Adam Hofmann
Print/Media Buyer: Barbara Britton
Permissions Editor: Joohee Lee

Production Service: The Book Company
Text Designer: Wendy LaChance
Photo Researcher: Myrna Engler
Copy Editor: Jane Loftus
Cover Designer: Yvo Riezebos
Cover Image: Shinichi Eguchi/Photonica
Compositor: Thompson Type
Cover and Text Printer: R. R. Donnelley, Crawfordsville

Printed in the United States of America
1 2 3 4 5 6 7 05 04 03 02

For permission to use material from this text, contact us by:
Web: http://www.thomsonrights.com
Fax: 1-800-730-2215
Phone: 1-800-730-2214

Wadsworth/Thomson Learning
10 Davis Drive
Belmont, CA 94002-3098
USA

For more information about our products, contact us:
Thomson Learning Academic Resource Center
1-800-423-0563
http://www.wadsworth.com

International Headquarters
Thomson Learning
International Division
290 Harbor Drive, 2nd Floor
Stamford, CT 06902-7477
USA

UK/Europe/Middle East/South Africa
Thomson Learning
Berkshire House
168-173 High Holborn
London WC1V 7AA
United Kingdom

Asia
Thomson Learning
60 Albert Street, #15-01
Albert Complex
Singapore 189969

Canada
Nelson Thomson Learning
1120 Birchmount Road
Toronto, Ontario M1K 5G4
Canada

Library of Congress Cataloging-in-Publication Data
Lawhead, William F.
  The voyage of discovery: a historical introduction to philosophy / William F. Lawhead.—2nd ed.
      p. cm.
  Includes bibliographical references and index.
  ISBN 0-534-52022-7
  1. Philosophy—History. I. Title.

B72.L375 2001
190—dc21   2001023776

CHRONOLOGICAL LIST OF PHILOSOPHERS

THE ANCIENT PERIOD

Thales	c. 624–545	B.C.
Anaximander	c. 610–545	B.C.
Anaximenes	c. 580–500	B.C.
Pythagoras	c. 570–495	B.C.
Xenophanes	c. 570–478	B.C.
Heraclitus	c. 540–480	B.C.
Parmenides	c. 515–450	B.C.
Anaxagoras	500–428	B.C.
Empedocles	c. 495–435	B.C.
Zeno the Eleatic	c. 490–430	B.C.
Protagoras	c. 490–420	B.C.
Gorgias	c. 483–375	B.C.
Socrates	c. 470–399	B.C.
Democritus	c. 460–360	B.C.
Plato	c. 428–348	B.C.
Aristotle	384–322	B.C.
Pyrrho	c. 360–270	B.C.
Epicurus	341–270	B.C.
Zeno the Stoic	c. 336–264	B.C.
Epictetus	c. 50–138	
Plotinus	205–270	

THE MIDDLE AGES

Augustine, Saint	354–430
Boethius	c. 480–524
Erigena, John Scotus	c. 810–877
Anselm, Saint	1033–1109
Avicenna	980–1037
Al-Ghazali	1058–1111
Abelard, Peter	1079–1142
Averroës	1126–1198
Maimonides, Moses	1135–1204
Aquinas, Saint Thomas	1225–1274
Eckhart, Meister	c. 1260–1327
Scotus, John Duns	c. 1266–1308
Ockham, William of	c. 1280–1349

THE MODERN PERIOD

Erasmus, Desiderius	1466–1536
Copernicus, Nicholas	1473–1543
Luther, Martin	1483–1546
Bacon, Francis	1561–1626
Galileo	1564–1642
Hobbes, Thomas	1588–1679
Descartes, René	1596–1650
Pascal, Blaise	1623–1662
Spinoza, Benedict (Baruch)	1632–1677
Locke, John	1632–1704
Newton, Sir Isaac	1642–1727
Leibniz, Gottfried	1646–1716
Berkeley, George	1685–1753
Voltaire	1694–1778
Hume, David	1711–1776
Rousseau, Jean Jacques	1712–1778
Kant, Immanuel	1724–1804
Bentham, Jeremy	1748–1832
Hegel, Georg W. F.	1770–1831
Schopenhauer, Arthur	1788–1860
Comte, Auguste	1798–1857
Mill, John Stuart	1806–1873
Darwin, Charles	1809–1882
Kierkegaard, Søren	1813–1855
Marx, Karl	1818–1883
Engels, Friedrich	1820–1895
Dostoevsky, Fyodor	1821–1881
Nietzsche, Friedrich	1844–1900

THE CONTEMPORARY PERIOD

Peirce, Charles S.	1839–1914
James, William	1842–1910
Freud, Sigmund	1856–1939
Husserl, Edmund	1859–1938
Bergson, Henri	1859–1941
Dewey, John	1859–1952
Whitehead, Alfred North	1861–1947
Russell, Bertrand	1872–1970
Einstein, Albert	1879–1955
Wittgenstein, Ludwig	1889–1951
Heidegger, Martin	1889–1976
Carnap, Rudolph	1891–1970
Ryle, Gilbert	1900–1976
Sartre, Jean-Paul	1905–1980
Beauvoir, Simone de	1908–1986
Quine, Willard V. O.	1908–2000
Ayer, A. J.	1910–1989
Austin, John	1911–1960
Foucault, Michel	1926–1984
Derrida, Jacques	1930–
Rorty, Richard	1931–

To the memory of my mother, Cecelia Lawhead,
and that of
my father, James Lawhead,
and to Pam, Joel, and Andy

BRIEF CONTENTS

CONTENTS

PART II
THE MIDDLE AGES 109

P R E F A C E

This book has grown out of my thirty years of teaching the history of Western philosophy. I love to teach this subject. I have found that the history of philosophy develops students' critical thinking skills. After journeying with the course for awhile and following the point and counterpoint movements of the great historical debates, students begin to show a flare for detecting the assumptions, strengths, problems, and implications of a thinker's position. Furthermore, the history of philosophy provides students with an arsenal of essential terms, distinctions, categories, and critical questions for making sense out of the barrage of ideas they encounter in history, literature, psychology, politics, and even on television.

One reward of teaching philosophy is to see students develop new confidence in themselves on finding a kindred spirit in one or more of the great minds of history, who agree with their own assessment of what is fallacious or sound. By exposing students to unfamiliar viewpoints that are outrageous, fascinating, perplexing, hopeful, dangerous, gripping, troubling, and exhilarating, the history of philosophy helps them gain a renewed sense of childlike wonder, teaching them to look at the world with new eyes. Finally, throughout the history of philosophy, students often find ideas that are liberating and challenging, leading them down exciting paths that were not even on their conceptual maps when they started the course. I hope that this book will be an effective navigator's guide to such intellectual journeys.

GOALS THAT GUIDED
THE WRITING OF THIS BOOK

After many years of teaching a course, a professor begins to get a sense of the "ideal" textbook. For me, an effective history of philosophy text should achieve the following goals:

1. Make the ideas of the philosophers as clear and accessible as possible to the average person. A student-friendly philosophy text will not read like an encyclopedia article, which contains dense but terse summaries of factual information.

2. Provide strategies for sorting out the overwhelming mass of contradictory ideas encountered in the history of philosophy.

3. Find the correct balance between the competing concerns of (a) technical accuracy versus accessibility and (b) breadth of scope versus depth of exposition.

4. Communicate the fact that philosophy is more than simply a collection of opinions on basic issues. Understanding a philosopher's arguments is just as important as the philosopher's conclusions.

5. Encourage the reader to evaluate the ideas discussed. The history of philosophy should be more than the intellectual equivalent of a wine-tasting party, where various philosophers are "sampled" simply to enjoy their distinct flavors. Although that is certainly one of the delights of studying philosophy, and should be encouraged, assessing the strengths and weaknesses of a philosopher's ideas is equally important.

6. Make clear the continuity of the centuries-long philosophical conversation. A course in the history of philosophy should not be like a display of different philosophical exhibits in glass cases. For me, the guiding image is philosophy as a big party where new conversations

are continually starting up, while the themes of previous conversations are picked up and carried in different directions as new participants join the dialogue.

DISTINCTIVE FEATURES OF THIS TEXT

• *The Introduction provides tools for studying philosophy.* It (1) motivates the study of philosophy's history, (2) provides criteria for evaluating philosophical claims, (3) discusses procedures for analyzing arguments, and (4) surveys the main types of philosophical questions. In addition, an important section on "A Strategy for Reading Philosophy" presents a four-step approach for reading philosophy that takes the student from the acquisition of facts about a philosopher's position, then into exploratory and critical inquiries, and finally to a personal engagement with that position.

• *A consistent structure is used.* For consistency and ease of comparison, the majority of chapters follow the same basic pattern:

1. The life and times of the philosopher

2. The major philosophical task that the philosopher tried to accomplish

3. Theory of knowledge

4. Metaphysics

5. Moral and political philosophy (when relevant)

6. Philosophy of religion (when relevant)

7. Evaluation and significance

• *Analysis of philosophical arguments is provided.* To emphasize that philosophy is a process and not just a set of results, I discuss the intellectual problems that motivated a philosopher's position and the reasons provided in its support. The book analyzes twenty-three explicitly outlined arguments of various philosophers, providing models of philosophical argumentation and analysis. In addition, I informally discuss numerous other arguments throughout the book.

• *The evaluation of ideas is stressed.* Most of the chapters end with a short evaluation of the philosophy discussed. These evaluations, however, are not presented as decisive "refutations" of the philosopher, which would relieve the reader of any need to think further. Instead, the evaluations have been posed in terms of problems needing to be addressed and questions requiring an answer. Whenever possible, I have made this section a part of the historical dialogue by expressing the appraisals given by the philosopher's contemporaries and successors.

• *The significance of the ideas is emphasized.* The conclusion of each chapter also indicates the immediate and long-term significance of the philosopher's ideas and prepares the reader for the next turn in the historical dialogue. It makes clear the ways in which philosophical ideas can lead robust lives that continue far beyond their author's time.

• *The philosophers are related to their cultural contexts.* Each major historical period (Greek, early Christian to medieval, Renaissance and Reformation, Enlightenment, the nineteenth century, and the twentieth century) is introduced with a brief chapter discussing the intellectual social milieu that provides the setting for the philosophies of that era. The questions addressed are: What were the dominant concerns and assumptions that animated each period in history? How did the different philosophers respond to the currents of thought of their time? How did they influence their culture?

• *Diagrams.* Fifteen diagrams and two tables provide visual representations of the elements of various philosophers' ideas.

• *Glossary.* A glossary is provided in which key terms used throughout the book are clearly and thoroughly defined. Words appearing in boldface in the text may be found in the glossary.

• *Questions for review and reflection.* At the end of each chapter are two lists of questions. The questions for understanding are more factual and enable the readers to review their understanding of the important ideas and terms. The questions for reflection require the readers to engage in philosophy by making their own evaluations of the philosopher's ideas, as well as working out their implications.

 • *Instructor's Manual.* In addition to the usual sections containing test questions and essay questions, this manual provides suggested topics for research papers, tips for introducing and motivating interest in each philosopher, chapter-by-chapter topics for discussion, and the contemporary implications of each philosopher's ideas.

SUGGESTED WAYS TO USE THIS BOOK

This book may be used with students who are already familiar with the leading issues and positions in philosophy and who now need to place these ideas in their historical context. However, since it does not assume any previous acquaintance with the subject, it may also be used to introduce students to philosophy for the first time, through the story of its history. I have tried to make clear that philosophy is an ongoing conversation, in which philosophers respond to the insights and shortcomings of their predecessors. Nevertheless, the chapters are self-contained enough that the instructor may put together a course that uses selected chapters. For example, the chapter on Aquinas could be used as representative of medieval philosophy and Descartes used to represent the modern rationalists (skipping Spinoza and Leibniz). In the case of chapters that discuss a number of philosophers, only certain sections could be assigned. For example, to get a quick but partial glimpse of the wide range covered by analytic philosophy, the students could read only the sections on the early and later Wittgenstein. Although skipping over key thinkers is not ideal, teaching is a continual battle between time constraints and the desire to cover as much material in as much depth as possible.

The *Instructor's Manual* contains objective and essay questions that may be used in making up tests. In addition, Part 1 contains more reflective questions for discussion and essay assignments. I would encourage the instructor to make use of these questions in class in order to emphasize that philosophy is not just a list of "who said what" but that it also involves the evaluation and application of the great ideas. Furthermore, because the students will have some of these topics and others posed as questions for reflection at the end of each chapter, they can be asked to have thought about their response to these questions prior to their discussion in class.

ABOUT THE SECOND EDITION

I am gratified by the responses to the first edition of *The Voyage of Discovery* that I have received from professors using the book, from students who have been introduced to philosophy and its history through it, as well as from interested readers around the world who read it for personal enrichment. This second edition continues to have the distinctive features that so many enjoyed in the first edition and that have been highlighted in the previous sections of this preface. The subtitle has been changed to *A Historical Introduction to Philosophy* to communicate the fact that the book is intended to be used to introduce readers to philosophy for the first time as well as to provide a comprehensive survey of Western philosophy. Besides some changes that have been made to aid in clarity and ease of reading, this current edition ends each chapter with questions to aid the reader to study the material and to engage in philosophical reflection on the ideas. Some of these questions have been taken from the essay and discussion questions in the *Instructor's Manual.* Nevertheless, over fifty percent of the essay questions in the *Instructor's Manual* remain unique to it. This edition is now available in two formats. As before, there is the one-volume edition that covers philosophy from the early Greeks to the contemporary period. New to the second edition is an alternative format that divides the book into four paperback volumes, corresponding to the four parts of the book. This makes it much more economical for the instructor to use parts of the book for courses that emphasize only particular time periods.

I hope that everyone who uses this book will find it both profitable and interesting. I encourage both professors and students to share with me their experience with the book as well as suggestions for improvement. Write to me at: Department of Philosophy, University of Mississippi, University, MS, 38677-1848. You may also e-mail me at: wlawhead@olemiss.edu.

ACKNOWLEDGMENTS

From the initial, tentative outline of this book to the final chapter revisions, the manuscript has been extensively reviewed both by instructors who measured its suitability for the classroom and by scholars who reviewed its historical accuracy. Their comments have made it a much better book than the original manuscript. I take full responsibility, of course, for any remaining shortcomings.

I am indebted to the following reviewers of this second edition: Jim Friel, State University New York—Farmingdale; John Longenay, University of Wisconsin—Riverside; Scott Lowe, Bloomsburg University; Michael Potts, Methodist College; and Blanche Premo-Hopkins, University of South Carolina—Aiken.

I also want to thank the reviewers of the first edition for their contributions: William Brown, Bryan College; Jill Buroker, California State University at San Bernardino; Bessie Chronaki, Central Piedmont Community College; Vincent Colapietro, Fordham University; Teresa Contrell, University of Louisville; Ronald Cox, San Antonio College; Timothy Davis, Essex Community College; Michelle Grier, University of San Diego; Eugene Lockwood, Oakton Community College; Michael Mendelson, University of California at San Diego; William Parent, Santa Clara University; Anthony Preus, State University of New York at Binghamton; Dennis Rothermel, California State University at Chico; James D. Ryan, Bronx Com-

munity College; James Spencer, Cuyahoga Community College; K. Sundaram, Lake Michigan College; Ken Stikkers, Seattle University; Robert Sweet, University of Dayton; Howard Tuttle, University of New Mexico; Jerome B. Wichelms, Jefferson Community College.

My thanks to the many people at the Wadsworth Publishing Company who played a role in the book's production. In particular, I appreciate the encouragement and support I received from Peter Adams, my editor.

The acknowledgments would be incomplete if I did not express my thanks to those individuals who have been particularly supportive throughout my career. My first exposure to philosophy was under the instruction of Arthur Holmes, my undergraduate chair, who ignited my love for the history of philosophy. The late Irwin C. Lieb guided me throughout my career as a graduate student, first as my professor, then as my department chair, and finally as graduate dean. Years of team teaching with David Schlafer, my former colleague, provided exciting lecture performances that have influenced what and how I teach. I have benefited from good philosophical discussions with present and past colleagues, particularly Michael Harrington, Michael Lynch, Louis Pojman, and Robert Westmoreland. I also need to thank the many bright students who taught me how to teach.

This book is dedicated to my parents, James and Cecelia Lawhead, who first introduced me to the two dimensions of philosophy, love and wisdom; to my wife, Pam, who knows that love sometimes means being close and sometimes it means giving space; and to my sons, Joel and Andy, who taught me how much I do not know.

William Lawhead

Introduction:
A Brief Tour Guide
to Philosophy

Philosophy Is Not an Optional Experience in Your Life!

PHILOSOPHICAL IDEAS
IN UNLIKELY PLACES

A number of strange ideas about philosophy float around our culture. Many people think of philosophy as an optional enterprise—just a detached, erudite hobby for the intellectually elite or the socially disabled. For example, someone once defined the philosopher as "a person who describes the impossible and proves the obvious." With equal disdain, some view the history of philosophy as a dusty museum, filled with the outdated relics of bygone eras. However, the history of philosophy is more of a living presence than we may realize. If you listen carefully, you will find philosophical assumptions, questions, and themes hidden within everyday conversations. See if you can find the philosophical issues that are latent within the following scenarios:

1. Two six-year-olds, Margie and Natasha, are arguing over a sand castle at the beach. Natasha says, "You can't play with my sand castle. I worked hard to build it, so it is mine!" Margie replies, "The sand belongs to everyone. You can't own it. Besides, we aren't at school so there are no rules. I can do anything I want. If you don't let me play with this sand castle, I'll bop you on the head." Natasha retorts, "You do that and my big sister will rearrange your nose."

2. Professor Linda Perry, a behavioral psychologist, has been studying hardened criminals to see what events in their childhood caused them to develop antisocial personalities. On her way to church, she begins to wonder if her own religious, moral, and career choices are also the inevitable result of previous causes and the built-in features of her personality.

3. Dr. Gregory Clark, an astronomer, calculates that if the expansion rate of the universe had been one-billionth of a percent larger or smaller, the universe would not have been able to sustain life. This leads him to wonder if such a finely tuned and delicately balanced system might not be the result of an intelligent design. Then again, he thinks, maybe

it is just a lucky break produced out of the blind interaction of random, physical events.

4. B. F. Skinner, an experimental psychologist, claims that all our behavior, including the acquisition of language, is the product of experience. According to his theory, a baby learns language as a result of receiving approval for reproducing the sounds of her parents' speech. However, Noam Chomsky, a noted linguist, argues that a child could not learn language unless the mind was already equipped at birth with an inner structure that is capable of organizing the data of the baby's linguistic experience.

5. Carlos Williams says to his twelve-year-old son, "You shouldn't have broken your promise to help with the school fundraiser. What if everyone broke their promises whenever they pleased? No one would ever trust another's promises."

6. Andrew says, "Professor Doreen Thompson doesn't seem to care about whether we learn or not. I hope I never get another teacher like her." Susan replies, "You call her a teacher! She's not a *real* teacher. A real teacher would be concerned about her students and would work hard to help them understand the lesson."

7. Senator Dale Malone argues, "There is too much sex and violence on TV. We don't allow factories to poison the air we breathe. But people's minds are just as important as their bodies. We must protect the public from this moral pollution." Senator Julie Freeman replies, "I agree, there is a lot of trash on TV. However, in a free society, we cannot censor any form of expression for this would restrict the free flow of ideas. In the end, the truth could become a victim of this suppression."

In each of these cases, philosophical issues lurk in everyday events. More important, each speaker, whether he or she realizes it or not, is expressing the position of one or more of the philosophers discussed in this book. Let's go back over each scenario and identify the philosopher whose ideas were present:

1. Natasha holds to John Locke's theory of property. Locke would partially agree with Margie that the sand on a public beach belongs to everyone, but only when it is in its natural state. However, he would support Natasha's right to the sand castle. When a person mixes her labor with nature, he said, the product she creates is her property. In contrast, Margie sides with Thomas Hobbes. He said that without a governing authority, there are no rules. In the absence of civil laws, everyone has a right to everything and there can be no private property. For this reason, we need to make social agreements, Hobbes said. Otherwise (as Natasha and Margie are about to demonstrate), we will be in a continual state of war and life will be "solitary, poor, nasty, brutish, and short." (See Chapters 14 and 19.)

2. Professor Perry is wrestling with the question of whether our choices are free or are determined by causes acting on us. Thomas Hobbes, among others, would say that our behavior is the inevitable result of causes in our environment. Gottfried Leibniz believed that all our actions necessarily follow from our given character. In contrast, René Descartes and Jean-Paul Sartre would say that our choices are genuinely free because the human will is an island of freedom within the surrounding world of causally determined natural events. (See Chapters 14, 15, 17, and 33.)

3. If Dr. Clark decides that there is design in the world that requires an explanation, then he is agreeing with one of Thomas Aquinas's arguments for the existence of God. If he decides that the evidence of design is inconclusive, then he is adopting the skeptical position of David Hume. (See Chapters 21 and 11.)

4. This scenario summarizes a real-life debate between two actual scientists concerning cognition and the acquisition of language. Skinner's position is a version of empiricism (the claim that all our knowledge comes from experience). He stands in a long philosophical tradition that begins in the modern period with John Locke and David Hume. Chomsky's position is an example of rationalism.

This is the claim that prior to experience, the mind contains a certain innate, rational content such as the principles of logic. Chomsky's ideas have affinities with those of historical rationalists such as Plato, René Descartes, and Gottfried Leibniz. (See Chapters 4, 15, 17, 19, and 21.)

5. In chastising his son for breaking a promise, Mr. Williams was presenting one of Immanuel Kant's arguments concerning our moral duties. Kant said that we must always ask if we could make the rule we are acting on one that we could consistently wish everybody to follow. (See Chapter 22.)

6. In suggesting that Professor Thompson is not "really" a teacher, despite her title, Susan is echoing Plato's view. Plato believed that ultimate reality consists of perfect ideals of each kind of thing and that particular individuals, such as Professor Thompson, participate in those perfect forms to greater or lesser degrees. (See Chapter 4.)

7. Senator Malone agrees with Plato that the good society is one that makes its citizens as good as possible. If artistic productions can ennoble us, they can also degrade us. So, the legislator must protect society from art, literature, and music that would make people worse human beings. Senator Freeman is supporting the position of John Stuart Mill that individual liberty and freedom of expression are essential to a good society. (See Chapters 4 and 28.)

Once you learn about the history of philosophy and keep your ears tuned, you can hear the voices of these great philosophical figures in everyday conversations, in newspaper editorials, in advertising, and wherever people express their opinions, their hopes, fears, ideals, and values. There are two reasons why the ideas of past philosophers pop up in contemporary contexts. First, these philosophers dealt with issues that are so fundamental to human experience that everyone must face them. Hence, since we are all asking many of the same questions, it is not surprising that the average person's thought would trace the same paths that others have explored. Second,

there is often a direct connection between the way people think today and the thoughts of the great philosophers of history. Although Plato, for example, has been dead for over two thousand years, his ideas are still alive. That is because they have seeped deeply into our Western tradition and have shaped people's way of thinking down through the centuries. Whether or not you have ever read Plato or have even heard of him, some of his ideas are alive and active in structuring the way in which you think about the world. I hope that it will begin to be clear why philosophy is not an optional experience in your life. We are continually engaged with philosophical ideas and assumptions, whether we know it or not. We can work at doing philosophy well, or we can do philosophy in a sloppy, haphazard manner, but we cannot opt out of doing philosophy altogether.

WHY IDEAS ARE LIKE COLDS

The fact that a philosopher's ideas can influence us without our knowing it raises an important issue. We acquire most of our beliefs, concepts, values, and attitudes unconsciously. In other words, we "catch" our beliefs and values the way that we catch a cold. When you wake up coughing with a stuffy head and congestion, you know you have a cold. However, you usually do not know when or how you caught the cold (unless, of course, a very close friend had it the week before). What happened is that the cold virus was floating around in your environment, and you simply breathed it in and now it is part of your internal system. Similarly, ideas and values are floating around in your culture. You simply absorb them, without thinking about them, but now they are *your* beliefs and *your* values. By studying philosophy historically, you will be able to (1) get a clearer picture of your own beliefs, (2) understand their origins, and (3) see what strengths and weaknesses others have discovered in them. In this way you will be in a better position to decide whether you want to consciously hold these beliefs or not. Hence, studying the history of philosophy is like reading a consumer's magazine to find out about other people's experiences with a product you are thinking of buying.

Another way to look at it is to say that studying philosophy is a way to develop intellectual muscles. You cannot become strong and physically fit by squeezing marshmallows or lifting blocks of Styrofoam. We develop our muscles by pitting them against something that offers resistance. Similarly, as long as we surround ourselves with people and books whose ideas are comfortable and like our own, we remain intellectually flabby. The philosophers discussed in this book present ideas that are challenging, unfamiliar, and, perhaps, zany and outrageous at times. Nevertheless, they also provide arguments why you should adopt their conclusions. By engaging your intellectual muscles with their arguments, you will develop the skills of critically analyzing others' ideas as well as articulating and defending your own. These skills can be generalized and applied to other courses and careers.

Although I have stressed the practical benefits of studying philosophy, it is important to add that the study of ideas can be rewarding in itself. When a reporter asked mountain climber George Mallory why he risked his life and went to such great expense to be the first person to climb Mount Everest, his terse reply was, "Because it's there." The best reason for working through a significant thinker's philosophy is not that it will train your mind for law school (although it will do that), but because "it's there." Like mountains, philosophical ideas contain challenges, beauty, mysteries, majesty, and drama that we can appreciate for their own sake, beyond any practical utility they may have.

What Is Philosophy, Anyway?

COMMONPLACE NOTIONS OF PHILOSOPHY

People often think of philosophy as simply one's general outlook on life. For example, a football coach once said that his philosophy was "It's not whether you win or lose but how you play the game." However, another coach said that "Winning is not the most important thing—it's the *only* thing." Companies sometimes express their philosophy in advertisements: "Our corporate philosophy is 'Providing reliable products with good service.'" Certainly, a number of philosophical issues are contained in these statements. What is the role of sports and competition in human life? Does the end justify the means? What does "*good* service" mean? Who decides whether it is good or not? However, the notion of "philosophy" latent in these pronouncements falls short of how the term is properly understood. Each of these people stated their beliefs, but offered no justification for them. Besides being a general outlook or policy, philosophy is the attempt to provide arguments or good reasons for our conclusions. As stated in the first section, we all have philosophical beliefs that we acquired from our cultural environment. However, we have not yet begun to do philosophy until we begin the task of clarifying, evaluating, and justifying our beliefs as well as examining them in the light of opposing viewpoints.

PHILOSOPHERS AND LOVERS

Perhaps it is time to give a more straightforward presentation of philosophy. We could define philosophy as

> The human attempt to systematically study the most fundamental structures of our entire experience in order to arrive at beliefs that are as conceptually clear, experientially confirmed, and rationally coherent as possible.[1]

Each term in this definition is significant. However, it is particularly important that we understand what it means to say that philosophy is a "human *attempt*" to take on a task we never can complete. What this means is that we are never finished with philosophy, and it is never finished with us, and our most dearly held and fundamental ideas are never without the need for modification and improvement. This is difficult to accept, because we like closure, finality, and quick solutions. We live in a world of thirty-minute television dramas, lightning-speed computers, instant coffee, and microwave meals. However, it is helpful to compare the search for philosophical understanding to cultivating a meaningful relationship. The minute two people decide that they have figured out their relationship and do not need to work at it anymore, the relationship has grown stale. In both relationships and philosophy, there are always new problems to face and old problems to address in new ways. Appropriately, the term *philosopher* literally means "a *lover* of wisdom."* The qualities that make one a successful lover or philosopher are similar. Successful lovers never tire of exploring the facets of one another's personality. Likewise, the successful philosopher endlessly desires to explore new ideas and undiscovered dimensions of old ideas. Hence, the search to understand our friend or to philosophically comprehend our experience is a quest that is always ongoing and never completed. However, this does not mean that we cannot make progress along the way.

PHILOSOPHICAL CRITERIA

I have said that philosophy, in the fullest sense of the word, is the activity of evaluating and justifying our beliefs and those of other people. How do we go about doing this? The definition just given contains three criteria for evaluating our own and others' ideas. Stated in abbreviated form to make them easy to remember, they were clarity, confirmation, and coherence. There may be others, but certainly these three are the most basic. We can use these criteria to evaluate the individual claims made by a philosopher as well as to assess a philosophy as a whole package. In a later section, we will apply these criteria to the evaluation of arguments.

Conceptual clarity is the first criterion that we should apply to a philosophy. Concepts and words are the vehicles of ideas. But if our vehicles are not

*The English word *philosophy* is derived from the Greek words *philia* ("love") and *sophia* ("wisdom"). As far as we can tell, Pythagoras, the well-known philosopher and mathematician, was actually the first person to call himself a *philosopher*. It was Socrates and Plato who popularized the word.

well tuned, we won't make much progress. Here are two controversial claims and the sorts of questions we need to ask to make the claims clear.

1. *"Computers have now attained the status of being genuine thinking machines."* What is the criterion for "thinking" that is being assumed here? Is following an input with the correct output all that there is to thinking? Can there be thinking without consciousness?

2. *"The only thing in life that people value is pleasure."* What does the speaker mean by "pleasure"? Do intellectual enjoyments count as pleasure, or only physical sensations? In what way does it make sense to say that a political martyr or a person who makes sacrifices for others is pursuing pleasure?

Experiential confirmation is the second test that a philosophy must pass. Since the purpose of philosophy is to clarify our experience, a philosophy will not be adequate unless it "fits" experience. This means that the philosophy must not conflict with any well-established facts and that it will be supported by experience as well as make our experience more intelligible. However, a large-scale philosophical theory usually cannot be supported or refuted by a single experience, as can the simple claim "this lump of sugar is soluble in water." Instead, this experiential criterion asks us to decide how adequately a philosophy interprets the broad range of human experience. We also measure scientific theories against experience. There is a difference between scientific and philosophical theories in how this test is applied, however. Typically, scientific theories let us generate testable consequences. If an experiment turns out as the scientific theory predicted, the theory has received some degree of experiential support. In contrast, philosophical theories are too general to be tested experimentally in this way. Their purpose is to provide the best interpretation of the experiences common to humanity rather than to predict specific, new physical events.

We can use one of Socrates' doctrines to illustrate the application of this test. Socrates argued that if we *know* what is good, we will naturally *do* what is good. From this he concluded that if someone does what is wrong, it must be because that person is ignorant of what is truly good. However, many would agree with Aristotle that "this view plainly contradicts the observed facts." Our common, human experience suggests that we often know what is good but fail to do it because of a weak will.*

Rational coherence is the third criterion. Minimally, this criterion requires that a philosophy not contain a contradiction or that it not conflict with itself. Even if a philosophy does not contain an explicit contradiction in terms of what the philosopher directly says, it may fall to the charge of incoherence, nonetheless. We may find a contradiction in an unstated assumption that the philosopher makes or in a conclusion that logically follows from his or her central claims. For example, skeptics make the claim that "there is no absolute truth and if there were, we could not know it." However, Socrates and Augustine battled the skeptics in their own times by pointing out that skepticism contradicts itself. The skeptics assert, "we cannot know what is true," but in making this claim we must assume they believe that "the skeptical philosophy is true." For this reason, their critics claim the skeptics' position undermines itself. A more subtle application of the coherence criterion recognizes that a philosophy may be free of outright logical contradictions and still its claims might not "hang together" very well. For example, the theist maintains that God is loving and all powerful at the same time that innocent people in our world suffer. Likewise, some philosophers claim that all our behavior and choices are determined by psychological causes not under our control while maintaining that we are morally responsible for our actions. To avoid the charge of incoherence, both the theist and the determinist have some hard work to do. They must show that the apparent conflicts

can be resolved and the disparate ideas in their systems can be successfully woven together into a harmonious whole.

We have given examples of how these three criteria have been used to critique common philosophical positions. One should not assume from these brief discussions, however, that these positions have been decisively refuted and are now sitting on the trash heap of philosophical history. Later in this book, we will see the ways in which proponents of each position have sought to evade the charges against them.

ASSESSING ARGUMENTS

Although these three criteria will take us a long way in assessing a philosophy as a whole, we need to pay special attention to evaluating arguments. In setting forth a philosophical position, philosophers usually employ a number of arguments to establish the main pillars of their philosophy. However, an author may fail to clearly lay out his or her arguments. In this case it may take some rooting around and restating of the main points to extract a precisely formulated argument. Nevertheless, there are probably arguments to be found. Even philosophers who have a reputation for being "irrationalists" usually try to show that they have plausible grounds for rejecting reason.

An argument consists of one or more statements called the "premises," which are used as evidence, grounds, or reasons for asserting another statement, called the "conclusion." There is a temptation to fall victim to what has been called the "bottom line" syndrome. This involves simply responding positively or negatively to the author's conclusion without analyzing whether or not the philosopher has provided good reasons for believing the conclusion. But this defeats a major goal of philosophy—to see whether our beliefs or those of others are justified. For example, St. Anselm provided an argument, called the "ontological argument," that had the conclusion "God exists." However, although Gaunilo, a contemporary of Anselm and a fellow Christian, agreed with the conclusion of the argument, he criticized the reasoning

*Defenders of Socrates point out that he evades this objection once we understand the special way he uses the terms "*knowing what is good.*"

that Anselm used to reach this conclusion. It is important to realize that in demonstrating that an argument is flawed, we have not proven that the author's conclusion is false. We have merely shown that the reasons the author has given us supporting that conclusion do not guarantee its truth. Nevertheless, if the only arguments that can be found to support a conclusion are bad arguments, there is no reason to suppose the conclusion is true.

It would take a whole book on logic to discuss all the techniques for analyzing arguments, so a few words on the topic will have to suffice. There are two basic questions to ask about an argument:

1. Are the premises acceptable?
   a. Are they clear?
   b. Are they plausible?
2. Do the premises provide adequate support for the conclusion?

The first question examines the clarity and plausibility of the premises. The second question asks about the acceptability of the form of reasoning. An argument provides good reasons for believing its conclusion only if the answer to both questions is yes.

Answering question 1 requires two steps: (a) Apply the criterion of clarity to each premise to make sure they each make a meaningful claim. (b) Decide if it is likely that each premise is true, according to objective standards. If not, then explain what problems it contains. To do this you must consider why the author believes each premise to be true. There are several possibilities. The author may be claiming that the premise is (1) a logical truth, (2) a definition, (3) based on experience, or (4) established by a previous argument. The truth of a premise must be evaluated on the basis of the type of claim that is being made.

If an argument has one or more false premises, then it cannot provide grounds for believing the conclusion. However, even if all the premises are true, this alone does not make an argument a good one. Consider this argument:

All U.S. Presidents are famous.

George Washington is famous.

Therefore, George Washington is a U.S. President.

Even though both the premises and the conclusion of this argument are true, it is not a convincing argument. Many people are famous but are not Presidents. So, it does not follow, from the fact that Washington is famous, that he is a U.S. President. Hence, in addition to question 1 concerning the premises, we have to ask question 2 and examine the form of reasoning employed.

Logicians have developed many specialized techniques for answering question 2. However, a simple way to approach the question is to ask yourself, "How easy would it be to imagine that all the premises were true at the same time the conclusion was false?" This will indicate how strongly the premises support the conclusion. In terms of the form of the reasoning, two kinds of arguments are acceptable. First, if it is absolutely impossible for the premises of an argument to be true and the conclusion false, then we say the argument is **deductively valid** (or simply "valid"). A valid argument with true premises is called a **sound argument**. The second type of acceptable reasoning is an argument in which the premises make the conclusion highly probable. We say this sort of argument is **inductively strong** (or simply "strong"). A strong argument with true premises is a **cogent argument**. A cogent argument does not absolutely guarantee the conclusion (as does a sound argument), but it does give us good reasons for believing the conclusion. In contrast, the more possibilities there are of the premises being true and the conclusion false, the weaker the argument.

We can illustrate these techniques for evaluating arguments by applying them to a concrete example. Consider the following argument:

(A) The majority of people throughout human history have believed in God.

(B) Therefore, God must exist.

Question 1 for evaluating arguments asks if the premises are acceptable. First 1a, apply the criterion of clarity to the premises. What does the author mean by "God" in premise (A)? If a culture believes that the trees contain spirits, does this constitute "belief in God"? Many of the world's great religions (versions of Buddhism, Confucianism, and Taoism, for example), believe in an *impersonal* spiritual dimension they call the "Undefinable One." Does this qualify as "belief in God"? There are a wide variety of conflicting religious conceptions throughout the world. Hence, the fact that there is no singular definition of "God" that people in all societies and ages would agree on makes it doubtful that premise (A), as stated, expresses a meaningful or unambiguous claim. If a premise is not clear, it is impossible to go on to step 1b to decide if the premise is true or not.

Question 2 asks if the premises adequately support the conclusion. In the present argument, the premises do not support the conclusion. Simply reporting what people believe to be the case, even a very large number of people, is not sufficient evidence to support a conclusion about the nature of reality. Even if the whole human population believed there was a God, everyone could still be mistaken. In analogous cases, large numbers of people throughout history have held mistaken beliefs about astronomy, the causes of disease, or the nature of reproduction.

Adding this second premise to the argument,

(A') If the majority of people believe there is a God, then God must exist.

would make the argument valid. However, although the two premises logically imply the conclusion, there is no reason to believe that the second premise (A') is true. So the argument fails on step 1b of our evaluation process.

Although any theistic philosopher would obviously accept the conclusion that "God exists," and many would say that this conclusion can be demonstrated, even most theists would agree that this particular argument does not support the conclusion. Again, philosophy is concerned not only with our beliefs but also with the rational support we can provide for these beliefs.

Becoming an Active Reader: Tactics and Strategies

PHILOSOPHY, BIKE RIDING, AND BASEBALL CARDS

Beginning to study philosophy is closer to learning how to ride a bike than to memorizing facts out of an encyclopedia. Apart from the detailed analogies that could be made between beginning philosophers and bike riders in terms of wobbling, falling off, and getting back on again, the main similarity is that they are both engaged in an activity. The physics formula for keeping one's balance on a bike is as follows: turn the bicycle into a curve which is proportional to the ratio of the imbalance divided by the square of the speed. Obviously, sitting in your armchair and learning that formula will not teach you how to ride a bike. Similarly, philosophy is something we do, not something we learn. It is a skill we can develop of thinking about things in a rational way. This book can help you develop that skill by making it possible for you to observe and learn from those who have practiced it throughout the centuries. To switch metaphors, reading the history of philosophy is different from collecting baseball cards, where we simply sort the different figures into categories and read the facts about them on the back of the card. As the next paragraph will make clear, learning facts about philosophers is only the threshold of philosophy itself.

A STRATEGY FOR READING PHILOSOPHY

To be an engaged reader, a systematic strategy is helpful. To help you *focus* on the philosophers and movements you study, keep in mind the five letters of the word *FOCUS*. They stand for Facts, Outlook, Critique, and Undergoing Self-examination. These activities alternate between objective and subjective approaches to a particular philosophy. We will explain each in turn.

Facts. As you are beginning to get acquainted with each philosopher, you will first want to know the answers to basic questions about that thinker such as where, what, why, and who. Using Plato as an example, you will want to find out

1. *Where* was Plato located within the cultural, intellectual movements of his time?

2. *What* problems was Plato trying to solve? *What* methods did Plato use to attack the problems? *What* solutions did he offer?

3. *Why* did Plato think his solutions were good ones? (What were his arguments?)

4. *Who* influenced Plato, and *whom* did he influence in turn?

These sorts of questions involve an *objective* consideration of Plato's philosophy.

Outlook. Try to sympathetically enter into Plato's outlook on the world. How does the world look when we see it through the lenses of Plato's philosophy? How would your outlook on life be different if you adopted Plato's viewpoint? What would Plato say about the news media today? What would be his opinion on current controversies in the world, in our nation, and on your campus? What questions would you ask Plato if you could call him up on the phone? This approach requires a *subjective* identification with the philosopher.

Critique the Philosopher's Ideas and Arguments. This is one of the most important and most difficult stages of reading philosophy. It's easy to get dazzled by the multiplicity of perspectives and see the history of philosophy as simply a kaleidoscope of changing, competing positions. The word *critique* does not mean to simply criticize. It comes from a Greek word that means "to separate" or "sift." Critiquing a philosopher means probing his or her ideas to find out where

they are solid and where they cannot support the weight they are supposed to bear. Here the three criteria mentioned earlier (clarity, experiential confirmation, and rational coherence) come into play. In addition, keep the following considerations in mind. Look for the strong points in the philosophy. How does the philosophy illuminate important features of human experience? What questions does it answer better than any other approach? Which of the philosopher's arguments seem impregnable? Also, look for the weak points. What data does the philosophy ignore or contradict? (This includes scientific data as well as the broad data of ordinary human experience.) What problems does the philosophy create that it cannot solve? How does it stand up to alternative approaches? Does the philosopher answer possible criticisms? What are the questionable assumptions in the philosopher's premises? What are the weak points in the philosopher's reasoning? Critically evaluating a philosophy is another kind of *objective* approach to it.

Undergo Self-Examination. Thus far, you have examined the philosopher's ideas; now let his or her ideas examine yours. The poet W. H. Auden once said that an important book is one that reads us, not the reverse. Likewise, the twentieth-century philosopher Martin Heidegger said that instead of asking what we can do with philosophy, we should ask what philosophy can do with us. Socrates said that "the unexamined life is not worth living." Søren Kierkegaard, one of the nineteenth-century founders of the movement of existentialism, once wrote in his diary, "There are many people who reach their conclusions about life like schoolboys: they cheat their master by copying the answer out of a book without having worked the sum out for themselves." This last stage of reading philosophy is a matter of "working out the sum for yourself." Having understood and evaluated a philosophy, what are you going to do with it? What challenges does it pose for your current beliefs? How would you answer the questions that the philosopher has posed? Does this philosophy offer any insights that you need to incorporate into your own view of the world? Has this philosophy changed you in any way? Why or why not? These questions, of course, involve a *subjective* engagement with the philosopher's ideas.

A General Map of the Terrain

Philosophy is like a tennis match where thought bounces back and forth between perplexing questions and the various philosophers' attempts to provide well-grounded answers to those questions. These questions fall into several categories. It is important that you become familiar with these divisions of philosophy and their names so that you can keep track of what sorts of questions a particular philosopher is trying to answer. Take note that these are not the labels for specific philosophical positions, but they represent the main issues that philosophers argue about and problems that specific philosophies try to solve. The following headings represent the three main areas of philosophy. Under each heading is a representative, but not exhaustive, list of questions that fall within that area.

Epistemology (the theory of knowledge)

- What is truth?
- What is knowledge?
- Does reason tell us about the world?
- What are the limits of reason?
- How reliable is sensory experience as a source of knowledge?
- Are there ways of arriving at the truth apart from the intellect (for example, faith or intuition)?

Metaphysics (the theory of reality)

- What is ultimately real?
- Are there other kinds of reality besides the physical world?
- How many different kinds of reality are there?
- What is the mind?
- How is the mind related to the body?
- Are we free or determined?

Ethics

- What makes an action right or wrong?
- Are there any absolute or objective moral principles?
- Are moral judgments based on knowledge, feelings, or intuition?
- Does morality depend on religion?

Most philosophical questions fall within one of the above topics. However, in addition to these three main areas, several, more specialized topics are frequently discussed throughout this book.

Logic (the study of the principles of reasoning)

Social and Political Philosophy

- What is the ideal political state?
- What is the purpose of the state?
- What makes a government legitimate?
- What are the proper limits of a government's power?
- Is civil disobedience ever justified? Under what conditions is it justified?

Philosophy of Religion

- Is there a God?
- Can the existence of God be proven? How?
- What is the nature of God?
- What is the relationship between faith and reason?
- Is there life after death?

Finally, in addition to these topics, other areas in philosophy raise philosophical questions about specific disciplines. These topics are discussed in this book only if they are central to a particular philosopher's thought. These additional areas of philosophy include philosophy of art (aesthetics), philosophy of education, philosophy of history, philosophy of language, philosophy of mathematics, philosophy of law, philosophy of psychology, philosophy of science, and so on.

Questions for Understanding

1. In what way do we acquire our ideas the way we catch a cold? Why is this bad? How might a study of the history of philosophy remedy this?

2. How is philosophy like a relationship?

3. What is the literal meaning of the term *philosopher*?

4. What are the three criteria for evaluating a philosophy?

5. What are the two questions to ask about an argument?

6. What is meant by the following terms: *deductively valid, sound argument, inductively strong, cogent argument*?

7. What are the four strategies for reading philosophy symbolized by the letters FOCUS?

8. What are the three main areas of philosophy? What are some of the questions that fall under each heading?

Questions for Reflection

1. Find examples in real life similar to the seven scenarios at the beginning of this chapter where people are discussing philosophical issues without really realizing it. By the way, what makes something a "philosophical issue"?

2. Ask friends who have not taken a philosophy course what the term "philosophy" means. How do these uses of the term compare with the way philosophy is used in this chapter? Do you think the term is misused in any of these cases?

3. Examine your own beliefs and values to find examples of when you acquired some of them unconsciously, as the book puts it "in the way one catches a cold." If you come to realize that you have acquired some beliefs or values in this way, in what ways does it or doesn't it change your attitude toward them?

4. State some philosophical claim that you believe. Provide a really weak argument for believing this claim. Now, provide what you think is a good argument for the same claim. What is it about the arguments that makes one weak and the other strong?

5. Choose one or more of the philosophical questions listed at the end of this chapter. Consider the ways in which these philosophical questions arise in or are relevant to disciplines other than philosophy. For example, in what ways is the question "Are we free or determined?" relevant to psychology or criminal trials? As another example, in what ways do ethical questions arise in the fields of business, law, or medicine?

Note

1. I am indebted to a former colleague of mine, David Schlafer, for most of the wording of this definition as well as for portions of its exposition in the following paragraph.

THE ANCIENT PERIOD

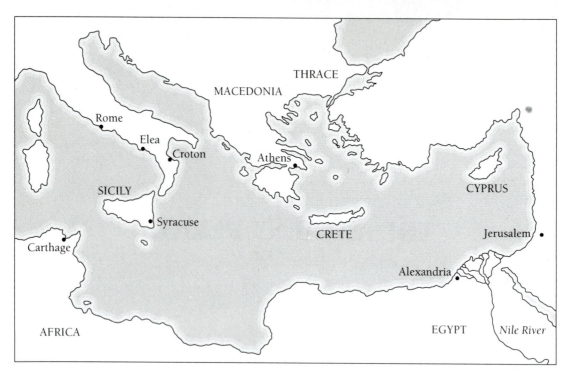

THRACE
MACEDONIA
Rome
Elea
Croton
Athens
SICILY
CYPRUS
Syracuse
Jerusalem
Carthage
CRETE
Alexandria
AFRICA
EGYPT
Nile River

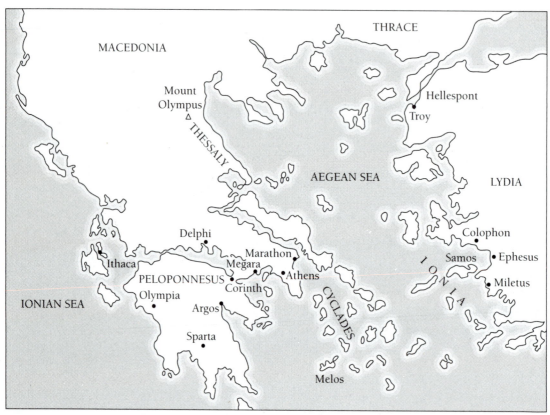

THRACE
MACEDONIA
Mount
Olympus
Hellespont
Troy
THESSALY
AEGEAN SEA
LYDIA
Delphi
Colophon
Marathon
Samos
Ephesus
Ithaca
Megara
IONIA
PELOPONNESUS
Corinth
Athens
Miletus
IONIAN SEA
Olympia
Argos
CYCLADES
Sparta
Melos

1

The Greek Cultural Context:
From Poetry to Philosophy

It was May 28, 585 B.C., and the sun beat down unmercifully as the six-year battle between the Medes and the Lydians waged on fiercely on the west coast of Asia Minor. Suddenly, a shroud of darkness began to cover the battlefield. Puzzled, the warriors on both sides lowered their weapons and looked up to the sky, where they discovered a black void where the sun had once stood. Was this a sign from the gods? Would worse calamities follow? Not wanting to know the answers to these questions, the soldiers of both armies threw down their arms and fled. Prudence, not military might, won the battle that day. However, in this same region a middle-aged merchant and engineer, who would later be known as a sage, was also looking upward. In contrast to the warriors, his face was not contorted with fear but sported a knowing smile as he nodded approval at the cosmic event. Who was this wise man, and why was he the only one to welcome the darkness of the sun?

The sage in question was named Thales. Many ancient sources consider Thales the first philosopher in Western history. One of the most notable achievements attributed to Thales is his predic-

tion of this solar event. Scientists calculate that an eclipse did occur on May 28, 585 B.C., and we can assume this was the one that gave Thales his fame. He surely did not predict the date exactly, but possibly he knew enough astronomy to pick the correct month. Given all this, does Thales belong in a book on the history of astronomy? What possible connection could there be between his prediction and the birth of Western philosophy? To understand the significance of his prediction, we must back up to see what preceded it.

The Role of the Poets

The story of philosophy begins with poetry. The poets held a central position in Greek culture. They were not only tellers of interesting tales in flowery language (it is questionable whether any good poetry is only that). Instead, the poets developed, preserved, and conveyed the historical, scientific, and religious truths of the time. They were concerned with history, because their tales gave an account of the past and how various traditions, races, and cultures came to be. Furthermore, they

3

When the philosopher Thales predicted a solar eclipse in 585 B.C., he demonstrated that the world exhibits a consistent, natural order that our minds can understand.

attempted to answer cosmological questions by speaking about the origins, structure, and workings of the universe. Hence, they explained the causes that lay behind thunderstorms, abundant crops, drought, health, and sickness. They also served an important religious function. The poets told the stories of the gods, and their accounts were taken to be authoritative. The Greeks thought that the poets were inspired by the Muses. These were the goddesses of literature and the arts. "Inspired" means "breathed into." Hence, to the Greeks, the poets were inspired or filled with a divine spirit no less than the biblical writers in the Christian tradition. Finally, all this served an ethical function. By explaining how great heroes triumphed or fell, how the universe worked, and how human destiny was controlled by the gods and fate, the poets helped make clear what course people should take in life and what actions were appropriate or improper, advantageous or ruinous.

The poets explained the world through myths. Many people think of myths as simply fanciful and false stories. They are more than this, however. They represent the attempt to explain the unfamiliar and mysterious in terms of what is familiar and observable. They are symbolic expressions of how the deepest concerns of human life fit into a large-scale picture of the cosmos. The primary model of explanation available to pre-scientific people was that of human motives and actions. Hence, their Greek gods were very human. They acted according to their purposes and aims. However, they were also anthropomorphic in the sense that they were driven by passion, lust, petty jealousies, were easily offended, vengeful, deceitful, played favorites, in short, their enormous power was equaled only by their raging immaturity. The Greek gods had a division of labor: there was a separate god for each area of life—war, love, trade, hunting, and agriculture. Both the favorable and the unfortunate events in life were attributed to the anger or the goodwill of this or that god. In short, even though they seem like extravagant fantasies to us, the myths of the poets tried to provide a comprehensive view of the world and the individual's place in it.

THE NATURAL ORDER ACCORDING TO HOMER

To set the stage for philosophy, it is worth looking at the most important Greek poet, Homer.* His authority within Greek culture is underscored by the fact that later philosophers found it important either to defend or to criticize his views. One of the earliest Greek philosophers, Xenophanes (about 570–478 B.C.), explains that he criticizes Homer because "All at first have learnt according to Homer."[1] Homer's poems suggest several broad conceptions about the nature of the universe. First, what order we find in nature (the pattern of the seasons, for example) is the product of the

---

*The Homeric poems *The Iliad* and *The Odyssey* were originally songs that were passed on orally from generation to generation. We believe they were put in written form sometime in the eighth century B.C. Because of tradition, we attribute them to a blind bard known as Homer. But scholars suspect that they are actually the product of more than one poet.

steady purposes and aims of the gods. However, nature is sometimes unpredictable, because the gods are fickle and impulsive. A devastating earthquake or a sudden storm, for example, is caused by the god Poseidon, but they do not fit into any long-term, rational purpose of his that would make his initiation of these events intelligible.

Second, the Homeric gods are a far cry from the omnipotent deity of the Judeo-Christian tradition. Not only can they be thwarted by other gods, including their own family members, but they are subject to such forces as fate or necessity. Although the fates are sometimes presented as several personal beings, their actions are usually so unintelligible and unpredictable that the human mind cannot penetrate their mysteries. Thus, from our standpoint, the collection of forces called *fate* is more a principle of randomness than it is a law of nature.

THE MORAL IDEAL ACCORDING TO HOMER

The Homeric notion of virtue is quite a bit different from that found in later moral traditions. Homer's virtues were the virtues of the warrior-hero and can be summarized under the heading of *excellence*. Excellence was defined in terms of success, honor, power, wealth, moderation, and security. Homer's heroes may be called on to look after the welfare of others and to take risks to meet the demands of loyalty. However, these moral duties are always for the sake of preserving one's honor and status, not because of the outcome for others.

Homer's conception of the gods was consistent with this picture. The gods' interests revolved around their own honor and status. They sat up on Mount Olympus, looking down on the spectacle of human affairs like spectators at the chariot races. Although the gods were able to suffer frustration, no one doubted that their lives were basically happy. Thus, when a mortal aspired to be godlike, this had more to do with enhancing his or her own status than it did with concern for others. When it came to their interaction with mortals, the gods did not reward virtue and punish evil as much as they expressed favoritism and reacted

negatively when annoyed. Flattery, bribery, cajoling, and coaxing worked as well to win the gods' favor as did moral goodness. Service to the gods was motivated not by their goodness but by their power. Consequently, all interactions between mortals and the gods was, for both sides, solely a matter of calculating self-interest.

Homer's account of Zeus, however, provides some exceptions to this general picture. Zeus was the supreme god among Homer's collection of deities. Although he was stronger than all the rest and they looked to him for advice and approval, he still was limited both by external forces and his own personality flaws. Nevertheless, we sometimes get glimpses of his concern to see justice prevail within human affairs. He becomes angry at the moral wrongs that mortals inflict on one another.[2] Homer's near contemporary, the eighth-century (B.C.) poet Hesiod, develops this line of thought even further. According to Hesiod, Zeus directs the other gods to measure humans' actions against a universal law of justice. As Hesiod states in his *Works and Days*,

> The deathless gods are never far away;
> They mark the crooked judges who grind down
> Their fellow-men and do not fear the gods.[3]

In these sorts of passages, the will of the gods takes on the character of a uniform, moral order operating in the world. This picture provided fertile soil for developing the notion of an impersonal natural order, independent of the gods' will.

CONFLICTS WITHIN HOMER'S PICTURE

To simplify and summarize, Homer and the other poets established four notions of world order: (1) Some events in the world are caused by purposeful, though frequently capricious, human or divine agents. (2) There is an element of randomness in the world such that some events are as purposeless as the throw of a pair of dice. (3) The fates represent an unyielding, amoral order in the world to which both mortals and the gods, including Zeus, are subject. (4) In some passages, the gods respond to a moral order and judge mortals by a standard of objective justice. Unfortunately, Homer does not make clear what happens when two or more of these forces conflict.

Despite the crudeness of Homer's picture of the universe, it provided a starting point for Greek scientific and philosophical thought.[4] It did this in two ways. First, the conflicts between his principles cry out for a more coherent view of the world. An inconsistent answer is no answer at all. Second, his last two principles (fate and justice) suggest a new sense of order that would lead beyond the Homeric myths. The notion of fate as an inescapable causal order is, in spite of its superstitious colorings, the predecessor of the notion of impersonal, natural laws. Also the idea that Zeus sometimes lays aside petty, personal interests and is concerned with justice, points toward the development of objective, ethical principles. Nevertheless, what we find in Homer are at best the seeds of theoretical thought. Only when these seeds break through the soil of mythological thought and rise above the darkness in which they took root will the fruits of philosophy begin to appear.

The Birth of Western Philosophy

Traditionally, the birth of Western philosophy has been located in the sixth century B.C. The problem is, to say *when* Western philosophy began requires an understanding of *what* philosophy is. However, to ask, "What is philosophy?" is to raise a philosophically controversial question. Hence, when and where one locates the birth of philosophy within a culture will depend on how narrowly or broadly one defines "philosophy." There are strains of philosophy in the poetry of Homer and Hesiod, and there are remnants of traditional, mythical thought throughout Greek philosophy. However, everyone agrees that Western philosophy did not leap into being from out of nowhere. Transitions in the history of thought are rarely that abrupt and do not arise from a vacuum. Historically, philosophy emerged within Western civilization the same way it emerges within our personal lives. Becoming philosophical is a gradual process in which cultures and individuals learn to look at the world in

a new way by becoming self-conscious and critical. Although we cannot pinpoint the birth of Western philosophy the way we can a solar eclipse, we can point to significant landmarks on the continuum from mythological tales to fully aware, self-critical philosophical thought.

To return to the solar eclipse, Thales' prediction was a significant event in the story of philosophy because it represented a new concept of order. If Thales was able to predict this natural phenomenon, it meant that he realized (unlike many of his contemporaries) that events in the world were neither the result of the irrational and unpredictable will of the gods, blind chance, nor the work of a largely inscrutable fate. Instead, Thales realized that such events were the product of a consistent, impersonal, natural order that can be studied and made the basis of generalizations and predictions. This raised the question of what this order must be like that allows the world to be open to rational inspection and understanding.

As with any philosopher, Thales owed an intellectual debt to many sources. In his time, the Greeks benefited both economically and intellectually from their trade with other cultures. Because of the thriving commercial life of their coastal cities, they were in touch with the leading centers of civilization: Egypt and Phoenicia; Lydia, Persia, and Babylon. Thales, no doubt, acquired much of his knowledge about mathematics from the Egyptians and his knowledge of astronomy from the Babylonians. It is quite possible that his philosophical speculations about the universe were nourished by the traditions of the different cultures around him. Furthermore, the suggestions in Homer's and Hesiod's myths that Zeus applies a consistent rule of justice to the world may have inspired Thales to search for an impersonal order in nature.

Although Thales applied and continued some of the ideas of his predecessors, he brought to these materials the spark of a new way of thinking. This new style of thought was that of original, theoretical inquiry. Rather than appealing to tradition or the stories of the gods to support his conclusions, he sent his opinions out into the world to stand or fall on their own merits. Thales' contemporaries and successors produced a whirl of questions, arguments, theories, and critical dialogue, making clear that a new way of answering questions and resolving disputes was emerging in Western history. From the womb of this spirit of inquiry and argument, both science and philosophy were brought to birth.

Outline of Classical Philosophy

From its early beginnings with Thales to its end in the Middle Ages, classical philosophy went through a number of distinct phases. This development is briefly summarized in the following outline:

1. *Cosmological Period* (585 B.C. to the middle of the fifth century B.C.)—Chapter 2
   - Concerned with external nature
   - Wanted to know what is fundamentally real

2. *Anthropological Period*—Chapter 3
   - Concerned with human-centered issues
   - Asked questions about knowledge and conduct
     a. Sophists (fifth century B.C.)—skeptical and practical
     b. Socrates (470–399 B.C.)—concerned to find objective knowledge and values

3. *Systematic Period*—Chapters 4 and 5
   - Concerned to develop a comprehensive, philosophical system
   - The first to raise all the basic questions of philosophy
     a. Plato (427–347 B.C.)
     b. Aristotle (384–322 B.C.)

4. *Post-Aristotelian or Hellenistic-Roman Philosophy* (320 B.C.–A.D. 529)—Chapter 6
   - Concerned with individualistic, practical issues
   - Metaphysical concerns subordinated to ethical concerns
     Cynicism, Epicureanism, Stoicism, Skepticism, Neoplatonism

Questions for Understanding

1. Why were the poets so important in ancient Greek culture?

2. What was Homer's view of the order of the world?

3. What was Homer's view of the moral order?

4. How did Thales' approach to understanding the world differ from that of Homer?

5. What were the four main stages in ancient Greek philosophy? What were the primary concerns of each stage?

Questions for Reflection

1. Homer provides accounts of the nature of the world, morality, and the meaning of human life. Given the account of philosophy in the introductory chapter of this book, in what sense were Homer's views philosophical and in what sense were they not?

2. Are most people in our contemporary society more like the ancient poets or are they more like Thales? In other words, do people tend to base their beliefs more on tradition and popular opinions or on critical thinking? Why is this? What are the strengths and weaknesses of each approach?

3. In this chapter we have examined philosophical thinking in its infancy. In an analogous sense, what sorts of philosophical questions came to your mind when you were a child? When in your life did you, like Thales, first begin to critically examine some of the traditional beliefs you had taken for granted up until then?

Notes

1. Quoted in John Burnet, *Early Greek Philosophy*, 4th ed. (New York: Meridian Books, 1930), 118.

2. See Homer, *Iliad* 16.384–393.

3. Hesiod, *Works and Days* in *Hesiod and Theognis*, trans. Dorthea Wender (New York: Penguin Classics, 1973), 66.

4. For the points made in this section, I am indebted to Terence Irwin's discussion in Chapter 2 of his *Classical Thought*, A History of Western Philosophy:1 (Oxford, England: Oxford University Press, 1989).

2

Greek Philosophy Before Socrates

THE MILESIAN PHILOSOPHERS

Thales

We have already encountered Thales in Chapter 1. He was the Greek philosopher who predicted the solar eclipse. He is also considered by many ancient authorities to be the first Western philosopher. The dates of his life are only approximate, but most scholars place him somewhere between the years 624 and 545 B.C. His native city of Miletus was a thriving Greek seaport in Ionia, on the western coast of Asia Minor. Because of their geographical location, Thales and his two successors are called the Milesian philosophers (and sometimes the Ionians). Miletus was a city noted for its commerce, wealth, and cosmopolitan ideas. Because the trading industry put them in contact with other countries, many Milesians were receptive to new ideas and the city was the perfect breeding ground for fresh perspectives.

Thales had a very practical mind. Besides predicting the eclipse, stories abound that he solved a number of engineering problems for the military and invented navigational instruments and techniques. However, it was not his technological achievements that earned him his place in history. He is important for understanding the Western intellectual heritage because he set in motion an ongoing debate about the ultimate nature of things. Many theories of these early thinkers may seem as much an example of early science as they are of philosophy. This is not surprising, for the disciplines were not clearly distinguished, as they are today. What we call *science* was considered to be "natural philosophy" for most of human history. Even today, a student receiving the highest degree in chemistry will get a Ph.D., which is a "doctor of philosophy" degree. This period represents both the birth of science and of philosophy because these early thinkers embarked on the quest for universal principles and rationally defensible theories rather than simply making observations and collecting data.

THALES' QUESTION

Thales' concern was to find the unity that underlies all the multiplicity of things in our experience. This is sometimes called the problem of "the one and the many." We encounter many things in the world: fish, sand, trees, stars, grapes, storms, rocks, and plants. But what unifies it all? Why do we consider this a *universe*, not a *multiverse*? What basic principle accounts for all this? What fundamental "stuff" underlies everything we find in the world? This is the primary issue that occupies all the Pre-Socratic philosophers.

THALES' ANSWER

The answer Thales gave, Aristotle tells us, is that water is the source of all things.* At first this answer may seem naive and improbable. However, before we criticize any of these early philosophers, we must remember that we stand on top of some twenty-five hundred years of philosophical speculation and scientific discoveries. Hence, these early attempts to answer these questions are remarkable in their originality and cleverness. Aristotle speculates that Thales reasoned from the fact that water is essential to life and the seeds of all things are moist to the conclusion that water is the fundamental element. Additional reasons may have occurred to Thales to support his conclusion that everything is transformed water. For example, liquid water can be transformed into a gas (steam), and it also can be changed into a solid (ice). Furthermore, water comes from the air in the form of rain and returns back to the air as mist. When water evaporates from a dish, it leaves a sediment (apparently turning into earth), while digging down into the earth will lead us to water. Finally, living in Miletus and being surrounded by water may have made it seem probable to Thales that everything comes from water. Although we don't know what Thales' real arguments were, the fact that his immediate successors offered rational support for their theories makes it likely that Thales did too.

THE PROBLEM OF CHANGE

Some further issues are involved in Thales' speculation. If water is the one permanent and basic substance, what causes the changes in water's appearance that transforms it into all the other things in our experience? This is the question of "permanence and change" or "being and becoming." A possible answer can be found in Thales' claim that all things are "full of gods." Contrary

*Aristotle could be considered the first systematic historian of philosophy. He was born close to 250 years after Thales and is discussed in Chapter 5.

to appearances, it is likely that he was not reverting to a naive theological explanation here. He noticed, for example, that magnetic stones have the power to move iron. He considered this power to be an animate, causal agent in a seemingly inert stone. Thus, he seemed to believe that the principle of animation and change resides in things themselves. However, the only vocabulary he had for expressing this was to say that things are alive and divinely animated in some fashion.

THALES' SIGNIFICANCE

We can summarize Thales' impact and contribution in terms of several key points. First, Thales' position was an early example of metaphysical monism. **Monism** is the name for any position that claims there is only one principle of explanation. His is a metaphysical monism because he is claiming that reality can be explained by one principle (water). Thales' immediate successors adopted this assumption without questioning it. They continued to look for the one principle that explains everything, and only differed with Thales on the details of what this is. Second, Thales assumed that this one principle is a material substance. This is called **material monism**. Again, this assumption went unquestioned for quite a while. Third, Thales made a contribution in the questions he asked. The turning points in the development of human thought are to be found in original questions as much as in insightful answers. Thales asked some practical questions, such as "What will the olive harvest be like?" However, when he asked, "What is the ultimate substance underlying all the appearances?", this question had no immediate, practical payoff. It represented a search for theoretical understanding for its own sake. Such a quest opens doors that the more practical questions never will.

Finally, Thales is a key figure in the history of thought because of the nature of his answers. The important point here is not his claim that water is the ultimate substance. After all, his contemporaries discarded this answer. What is important is that he did not appeal to tradition or authority for his answer nor did he simply spew forth opinions. He put forth a theory that others could examine and debate, and he provided rational grounds for his speculations. Thales made the first serve in the history of philosophical exchanges. It was up to his successors to return the shot. Arthur Koestler once said that the history of thought is full of barren truths and fruitful errors. Thales' theory is obviously an example of a fruitful error. His contemporaries did not accept his answer, but it set in motion the philosophical dialogue that continues on even in our own time.

Anaximander

Anaximander's dates are approximately 610 to 545 B.C. He was a younger contemporary of Thales and, perhaps, the latter's student. He was well known in Miletus and published a book on the evolution of the world. At the same time, significantly, prose was emerging as a form of literature to rival that of poetry. This shows that the way people made sense out of the world was shifting.

ANAXIMANDER'S QUESTION

Anaximander took up the task of his teacher by addressing the question "What is the single, basic stuff that is fundamental to all other things?" Notice that he also absorbed Thales' assumption that the key to the universe would be a *single* type of entity. Anaximander was not satisfied with his teacher's solution, however. Water is just another particular thing that we find in the world along with earth, air, and fire. How can one kind of thing explain all the other things? It is a contradiction to suppose that something that is clearly not water (for example, fire) really is water. Whatever is fundamental and universal cannot have the particular properties water has. Water itself needs to be explained. Thus, with Thales' pupil the process of philosophical criticism begins.

ANAXIMANDER'S ANSWER

According to Anaximander, the ultimate reality must be an eternal, imperishable source from which all things are made and to which all things return. This ultimate ground of all being is the *Apeiron*, which means the Boundless, the Infinite, or the Indefinite. It is without any internal boundaries or divisions and is a space-filling, dynamic mass. It is infinite in time, otherwise there would have to be something more fundamental that produced it. Furthermore, it is indefinite in quantity. The Boundless can be thought of as a reservoir from which all things and their qualities are produced. But what are the properties that describe it? Is it cold? No, Anaximander would say, for then it could not produce the property of heat. Is it wet? No, for then it could not produce the property of dryness. Since it contains or produces all specific properties, it itself cannot be identified with any one of them. Hence, it is undefinable, since we can only define things that have specific properties.

THE PROBLEM OF CHANGE

Anaximander has a much more developed theory of change than did his teacher. He says the world is made up of warring opposites (cold versus heat, night versus day). Since they are opposites, one cannot give birth to the other, but they must all come from something else more fundamental. Therefore, change is the process of various qualities separating out from and returning to the primordial substance. Originally, everything was part of the whirling mass of the Boundless, and in the act of creation the different qualities were flung out from it much as particles are separated out from a solution in a centrifuge. This whirling motion explains how the planets originally received their motion. Through this process all the warring opposites such as hot and cold, wet and dry were produced. Combinations of these qualities produced the objects in our experience. For example, from the combination of cold and wet came the earth and clouds. From the hot and dry came a ring of fire that enclosed the whole. This burst into smaller rings of fire, creating the heavenly bodies. From the warm and the wet came life. Interestingly, Anaximander included a primitive evolutionary theory in his account of the world, claiming that all life forms, including humans, originally came from the sea.

Anaximander gave a very modern answer to the age-old problem: What does the earth rest on? His answer was that it rests on nothing. Since the earth is the center of a spherical universe, it has no reason to go one way or another. Since any direction is equally attractive, it stays where it is. Anaximander recognized that from the standpoint of the universe as a whole, there can be no absolute directions of up or down.

The universe is an everlasting motion made up of the cycle of creation and destruction. This is the first philosophical account in the Western tradition of the cyclical view of history (a common theory among the Greeks). Although he is attempting to give a natural explanation of things, he retains the notion of a moral force in the universe as did his poetic predecessors. He uses the principle of justice to explain the world cycle. Since everything "borrowed" its existence from the Boundless, it must return the loan. Hence, everything ultimately returns to its original source.

ANAXIMANDER'S SIGNIFICANCE

Anaximander's first contribution was the fact that his theory moves in the direction of a more abstract mode of thought. This may seem like a deficiency, but actually it is not. We cannot imagine the Boundless, nor see it, nor feel it. Similarly, however, neither can we imagine nor directly sense most of the forces and particles that our contemporary physicists talk about. By going beyond Thales' crude principle of water, Anaximander frees reason to think about that which transcends our everyday experience. Second, he began the process of philosophical criticism. He learned from Thales but found his solutions inadequate. Therefore, he contributed to philosophical progress by building on his predecessor while improving the latter's theory. Third, Anaximander addressed more seriously the problem of change and tried to give a more detailed and adequate explanation of it. Fourth, with his principle of justice he struggled to articulate an early version of a natural, scientific law. True, he still characterized it as a moral law (a relapse back to a poetic, anthropomorphic view of things). Nevertheless, it was an impersonal princi-

ple that operated independently of the caprice of the gods, making it more scientific in character.

Anaximenes

Anaximenes' dates are hard to pin down, but he was active around 545 B.C., making him a younger contemporary of Anaximander and the third member of the Milesians or Ionians. He is said to have written a book, but it has not survived. Nevertheless, his contemporaries say that it had a simple, unpretentious style, and it seems to have been more scientific in tone and less poetic than the work of his predecessors.

ANAXIMENES' QUESTION

As with his fellow Milesians, Anaximenes is concerned primarily with the question "What is the basic substance that is the foundation of all reality?" He agrees with Anaximander that the basic reality must be eternal, unlimited, and singular. However (continuing the process of philosophical criticism), he finds his colleague's answer to be inadequate. To say that the basic reality is the Boundless is not to say much at all. If there is a basic substance, we must be able to say something about it if we know that it is there at all. Thus, using the criterion of clarity, Anaximenes has the task of finding a less vague and more convincing answer to the fundamental question.

ANAXIMENES' ANSWER

The answer he gives is simple: the basic reality is *air*. He may have come to this theory on the basis of several observations. First, air is much more pervasive than water, so it is a better candidate for the fundamental substance. Second, air is central to all nature. It is necessary for the existence of fire and can be found in water and in the earth. Third, he may have noticed that water falls when not supported, but air is self-supporting. Therefore, water cannot support the earth as Thales claimed. However, since air can support itself, it can conceivably support the heavenly bodies as well, just as a light breeze can float a leaf. Finally, air sustains life. It is the primary difference between the living and the dead. Anaximenes believed the soul was identical to air. When we breathe our last breath and then expire, air (which is the soul) leaves the body.

THE PROBLEM OF CHANGE

Anaximenes accounted for the process of change by two principles that produce changes in the density of the basic substance. One is *rarefaction* (or expansion), and the other is *condensation* (or compression). For example, extremely rarified air becomes warm and eventually becomes fire. As air becomes increasingly condensed, it becomes colder and successively changes into wind, water, earth, and finally stone. Not content to simply throw out opinions, Anaximenes provided the first recorded scientific experiment to provide evidence for his claims. He observed that when you open your mouth wide and blow on your hand, your breath will feel warm. But when you close your mouth as if you were going to whistle and blow on your hand, your condensed breath feels cold. Hence, by appealing to the quantitative changes produced by rarefaction and condensation, he believes we can account for all qualitative changes in the world.

ANAXIMENES' SIGNIFICANCE

Anaximenes' contributions are twofold. First, he showed that we must temper abstract thought with conceptual clarification. If the ultimate reality is indefinite, as Anaximander claimed, then we cannot know much about it and this concept explains very little. Second, Anaximenes treated the problem of change more explicitly and adequately than his predecessors. Instead of simply saying that all things contain the principle of change, as Thales seemed to conclude, or that some cosmic moral principle accounts for the world process, as Anaximander claimed, Anaximenes tries to give an explanation that has some degree of scientific basis.

Summary of the Milesians' Methods

None of these first three philosophers directly address the problem of how we obtain knowledge about the world. Nevertheless, they do illustrate the beginning emergence of epistemological and methodological concerns. Thales' and Anaximenes' positions could be viewed as examples of a primitive empiricism. **Empiricism** is the position that claims that sense experience is the best way to arrive at knowledge. Since they took observable substances (water and air) to be ultimate, they obviously were concerned that their theories stick close to what we can see and touch. In contrast, Anaximander's position might be seen as a crude and early version of rationalism. **Rationalism** claims that reason is the best method for obtaining knowledge. Since Anaximander's Boundless cannot be sensed but is postulated sheerly on the basis of a rational argument, his philosophical method differs from that of his two colleagues. Although the terms *empiricism* and *rationalism* are too precise to describe these early theories correctly, these philosophies contain seeds of an issue that will become very important in all philosophy from Plato to our century.

Summary of the Milesians' Metaphysics

Although they differed on the details, the Milesians were similar in many respects. First, the Milesians introduced the problem of appearance versus reality. They all agreed on how the world *appears* to be, but what they wanted to know was "What is reality ultimately like?" Water, the Boundless, and air were their respective attempts to answer this question. Second, despite their differences all three Milesians assumed they could explain everything in the universe, without exception, on the basis of a *single* principle. Third, they each assumed this monistic principle was a physical substance of some sort. Although later philosophers questioned these assumptions, the Milesians made the first attempt to reduce the multiplicity of nature to a simpler unity. Finally, they all had something to say about how change occurs. For Thales, change was sheer spontaneous transformation, because things were "full of gods." Anaximander explained change as the separation of qualities out of the reservoir of the Boundless. Anaximenes accounted for most changes with the processes of rarefaction and condensation. Despite their innovative brilliance, these answers were but halting attempts to deal with problems that would require a much more developed treatment by later philosophers.

PYTHAGORAS AND HIS SCHOOL

|||

Pythagoras: Mathematician and Mystic

The Pythagorean movement was begun by a philosophical, mathematical, religious mystic by the name of Pythagoras. Most people are familiar with him as the alleged discoverer of the Pythagorean theorem. However, we know very little about him apart from various tales and legends that developed around him. The best we can tell, he lived somewhere between 570 and 495 B.C. Born on the island of Samos, near the Ionian coast, he eventually migrated to Croton in southern Italy, where he founded a religious community that was open to both men and women. Many of his followers believed that Pythagoras was divine. For this reason, it is hard to separate his thoughts from those of his followers, since they tended to attribute all their ideas to their founder. Although spurious works were written in his name, it is generally thought that he did not produce any books. Instead, he passed on his teachings orally, along with a vow of secrecy. The Pythagorean religious community combined the Greek scientific spirit with religious mysticism. Hence, it functioned both as a school of mathematics and a religious order. The movement was a hardy one, lasting about two hundred years. The sect died out in the late fourth century B.C., but remnants of Pythagorean thought continued on into the Christian era.

PHILOSOPHY AND SALVATION

For the Pythagoreans, the goal of religion was purification, and the goal of purification was the salvation of one's soul. They believed that the soul was immortal and that after death it migrates into another body, possibly an animal's body. The only way to achieve release from this "wheel of birth" and the prison of the body was to purify the soul. They did this through various purification rites, resulting in an ascetic life filled with many taboos and dietary restrictions. Most important, Pythagoras taught that the soul achieved purity through an intellectual process of obtaining philosophical wisdom. Pythagoras is thought to be the first to call himself a "philosopher," which literally means "a lover of wisdom." The "right way of life" required harmony with the universe, and this implied the need to understand it. For the Pythagoreans there was no division between religion and science or between worship and the intellect. Their intellectual life was on one continuum with their religious worship.

REALITY IS MATHEMATICAL

The Pythagoreans taught that there was an order and unity to the cosmos and that it was mathematical in nature. Hence, numbers lie at the base of reality. In fact, they believed numbers have a reality of their own. This notion may seem strange to the average person. But consider the fact that numbers have objective properties that must be discovered. They are not something that we invent or make up. According to the Pythagoreans, mathematical points produce lines, conjunctions of lines create plane figures, and multiple plane figures form solids. Hence, from mathematical points we can understand our entire universe. We can reason about lines and planes without thinking of physical bodies, but we cannot understand physical objects without understanding the lines and planes embedded within them.

The Pythagoreans thought that music provided clues to the mathematical nature of the universe. In Greek music the three major tone intervals are the octave, the fourth, and the fifth. The Pythagoreans discovered that the differences between musical tones are functions of exact numerical ratios. When a string is doubled in length, the sound it makes is an octave lower. Two strings whose lengths are in a ratio of 4 to 3 make sounds four notes apart. Lengths in the ratio of 3 to 2 produce sounds a fifth apart. The physical material of the strings does not matter as long as the mathematical properties follow the correct pattern. If numbers are the basis of music, perhaps they are the basis of everything else, the Pythagoreans reasoned. Further considerations reinforced this speculation, for according to their crude measurements, the distances between the planets were in the same proportion as the notes in a musical scale. They called this "the harmony of the spheres." Furthermore, they taught that the body is healthy when all its parts are acting in harmony, as in a well-tuned musical instrument. Hence, music, astronomy, medicine, and all existence seemed to be controlled by mathematical ratios.

The Pythagoreans saw the universe as governed by a continual conflict between order and disorder. They summarized this in the "table of opposites":

Order	Disorder
Limit	Unlimited
Odd	Even
One	Many
Right	Left
Male	Female
Rest	Motion
Straight	Crooked
Light	Darkness
Good	Evil
Square	Oblong

Since the two columns represent two sorts of forces in the universe, this is a type of **metaphysical dualism**. Since one side is identified with good and the other with evil, this is also a moral dualism. The placement of male and female in this scheme of oppositions speaks volumes about the typical Greek male's attitude toward women. Although the two lists represent an eternal conflict between two fundamental forces, it seemed to the Pythagoreans that harmony had the edge over chaos. The battle between rational order and chaos also takes place within our own souls. The soul takes on the form of whatever it contemplates. Therefore, by studying the mathematical harmony of the universe, our souls will become like that order and we will achieve an inner harmony. Furthermore, since mathematics weans us away from the senses and the physical world (which was thought to be the soul's prison), pursuing the life of the mind can be a spiritually purifying and liberating activity.

The Pythagoreans' Significance

The Pythagoreans were innovative in several ways. First, they realized that metaphysical theory has a bearing on one's life. Whereas previous philosophers such as Thales focused on theoretical issues for their own sake, the Pythagoreans believed philosophy was not merely a matter of intellectual curiosity but a way of life. Hence, this is the first time we see individual, ethical concerns appearing in philosophy. Second, Pythagoras emphasized form over matter. Instead of trying to understand the universe in terms of a basic, material element, he sought to understand it in terms of its mathematical order. Hence, he gave mathematics a more exalted task than simply calculating the size of a grape orchard. Although he may have learned many of his mathematical ideas from the Mesopotamians and Egyptians, Pythagoras helped advance the study of mathematics. Viewing nature as a vast mathematical order was an amazing achievement. Pythagoras is said to be the first to apply the term *cosmos* (which means "order," "fitness," "beauty") to the universe. Without the revival of this Pythagorean perspective, modern science never would have gotten off the ground. In the seventeenth century, the astronomer Galileo followed the Pythagoreans when he said that the book of the universe "is written in the mathematical language" and if one doesn't understand its symbols "one wanders in vain through a dark labyrinth."[1]

XENOPHANES

The Destroyer of Myths

Xenophanes was born in Colophon, a little over forty miles north of Miletus. Although his exact dates are only approximate, we do know he lived a long life and probably lived from 570 to 478 B.C. He fled to Italy when the Persians conquered Ionia in 546 B.C. There and in Sicily, he spent most of his life wandering about, supporting himself by reciting his own poetry and speaking at banquets. Although he was a contemporary of Pythagoras, the two philosophers differed greatly in spirit. Xenophanes was said to be irreverent and cynical and was famous for his sharp, satirical wit. He enjoyed criticizing and mocking his contemporaries and predecessors. Among his targets were the theological myths of Homer and Hesiod, the glorification of athletes in his time, and the decadent vanity of people in his culture. Although he was famous because of his rational theology, he was also a serious student of physical nature. He dabbled in astronomy and meteorology and deduced conclusions about the changes in the earth and the origins of life from the fossil record. Although, as always, a good deal of information about him comes from ancient secondary sources, we are fortunate to have some fragments of his own writings.

Theory of Knowledge

Although Xenophanes has only a few brief remarks to make about the nature of knowledge, he is significant for being the first philosopher thus far who directly addresses the issue. In a significant passage, Xenophanes asserts, "If God had not made yellow honey, men would think figs were much sweeter" (G38; 1.401).[2] In other words, sense perception is relative. What we consider sweet (or heavy, or tall) may depend on what else in experience contrasts with it. This bespeaks an epistemological sophistication on Xenophanes' part that was rare at the time. In another passage he claims,

Certain truth has no man seen, nor will there ever be a man who knows [from immediate experience] about the gods and about everything of which I speak; for even if he should fully succeed in saying what is true, even so he himself does not know it, but in all things there is opinion. (G34; 1.395)

Here he is making an important contrast between knowledge and opinion. Some later Greeks thought he was expressing **skepticism** (the view that knowledge is unattainable). However, Xenophanes clearly does not mean to say that all opinions are equal in value or even worthless. Instead, he is providing a helpful corrective to the extreme dogmatism of his philosophical predecessors. Although humans can never have perfect knowledge or total certainty, through careful investigation we can achieve a close approximation of the truth. Hence, Xenophanes advised (presumably about his own teachings), "Let these things be believed as resembling the truth" (G35; 1.396).

Philosophy of Religion

Xenophanes' major contribution was in his philosophical theology. Previous philosophers had simply ignored the gods of popular religion, but Xenophanes subjects them to philosophical criticism. His criticisms are threefold. First, he says that his contemporaries used mythological explanations to explain events when natural explanations would suffice. For example, many Greeks thought the rainbow was really the radiant goddess Iris (the messenger to the other gods). However, as Xenophanes explains in his typical iconoclastic manner, "She whom men call Iris also is a cloud, purple and red and yellow to behold" (G32; 1.392).

Second, he deplored the immorality of the traditional gods: "Homer and Hesiod have ascribed to the gods all deeds that among men are a reproach and disgrace: Thieving, adultery, and mutual deception" (G11; 1.371). Third, he ridiculed the poets for creating the gods in their own image:

Men suppose that gods are brought to birth, and have clothes and voice and shape like their own. (G14; 1.371)

But if oxen and horses or lions had hands, or could draw and fashion works as men do, horses would draw the gods shaped like horses, and lions like lions, making the bodies of the gods resemble their own forms. (G15; 1.371)

Although most of his points are negative, Xenophanes does offer some positive theological claims of his own:

God is one . . . in no way like mortals either in body or in mind. . . . He sees as a whole, perceives as a whole, hears as a whole. . . . Always he remains in the same place, not moving at all . . . but without toil he makes all things shiver by the impulse of his mind. (G23 25; 1.374)

In contrast to the anthropomorphic polytheism of the Greek poets, Xenophanes presents a vision of one eternal and unmovable god. At times, it is true, he speaks of the gods in the plural. But this is generally thought to be simply a flippant concession to the popular figure of speech. Having said this, however, it would be a mistake to identify his position with Judeo-Christian monotheism. For Xenophanes, the deity is not beyond the cosmos but is identical with it. Reality is a god–cosmos unity.

Xenophanes' Significance

Xenophanes' position evokes two crucial questions: (1) What sense does it make to say the universe is divine? In other words, is Xenophanes doing any more than tagging the universe with the three-letter label of "God"? (2) How can an unmoving god be identical with a moving and changing world? Although these are serious questions, to be aware of these problems would require a level of philosophical precision not possible at this time, even for such an innovative thinker as Xenophanes. More positively, he contributed to the philosophical conversation in two ways. He raised crucial, epistemological questions, and he attempted to construct a rational theology that did not simply take for granted the traditional answers.

HERACLITUS

|||

The Lover of Paradoxes

Heraclitus was an Ionian Greek who was born into a noble family in Ephesus. He was well familiar with the philosophers we have already discussed, because his hometown was 25 miles up the coast from Miletus, close to Pythagoras's native island of Samos and Xenophanes' Colophon. He lived his entire life in and about Ephesus and was said to be in his prime around 500 B.C. His exact dates are unclear, but the period from 540 to 480 B.C. is as good a guess as any.

Heraclitus did not seem to be a very pleasant person, for he had a proud, arrogant, and contemptuous mind, which he employed to produce critical and dogmatic sayings. Although his attitude was very aristocratic, he stubbornly refused the honors bestowed on him by society, including an inherited position of religious and political distinction. His harsh disposition and utter disdain for humanity (both the common folk and his philosophical contemporaries) guaranteed that he would attract no disciples in his lifetime. He thought most people were no better than cattle. Nevertheless, even if he lived a lonely and withdrawn life, his writings and sayings seemed to have provoked a good deal of discussion among later generations.

Although the amount of material we have from him exceeds that of many early Greeks (over a hundred fragments), he has the reputation of being one of the most difficult philosophers to interpret. What is worse, there is every reason to believe he wanted it that way. He delighted in throwing out paradoxes and aphorisms (terse, pithy statements) rather than developing a patient, continuous line of argument. For this reason, the ancients called him "the Dark One," "the Riddler," "the Obscure." Although his style does not conform to the philosophical ideal of clarity, Heraclitus represents an interesting stage in the history of thought in that he put forth some dramatically innovative alternatives.

Reason Is the Path to Knowledge

According to Heraclitus, wisdom is the goal of philosophy. However, we cannot obtain wisdom by acquiring factual information, but by seeing the hidden meaning behind the appearances. According to Heraclitus, the world comes to us in the form of a riddle. "Reality loves to conceal itself" (G123; 1.418). The secret to reality is found by understanding the **Logos**. This very important Greek word is so rich in meaning that it is difficult to translate. Briefly, the Greek word *logos* means "statement" or "discourse," but it also refers to "reason" or "the rational content of what is spoken."* However, logos is not limited to what goes on in our minds—it also suggests the rational order or structure of the world itself. Fragment 2 gets to the heart of Heraclitus's point: "One must follow what is common; but although the Logos is common, most men live as if they had a private understanding of their own" (G2; 1.425). Thus, this universal, rational order is available to all, but most people prefer to follow their individual, idiosyncratic opinions. In our contemporary culture, we often hear that everyone has their own, personal opinion and one opinion is just as good as another. But Heraclitus would not accept this. We could imagine him saying,

*The notion of "rational discourse" comes out in many English words that were derived from the word *logos*, such as "logic," "geology," "psychology," and "biology."

If we are all rational and calculate 6 + 5, we should all get the same answer. Only a company of fools would come up with different, personal answers. On any issue there is but one truth, not many.

The key to wisdom, then, is searching out the principle of reason that lies hidden within the universe and within our own souls.

Reality as Change and Conflict

THE PRIMACY OF CHANGE

What is it that we must understand about reality that will give us wisdom about life? The Milesians sought for the one, material substance, the fundamental "stuff" that was permanent throughout all the changing appearances. For them, permanence was fundamental and change was a secondary phenomenon. According to Heraclitus, however, they had it all backward. He asserted that change is ultimate and most of our experiences of stability and permanence are merely how things *appear* to be. Heraclitus critiqued our tendency to divide the world into separate and distinct *things*. We talk of coins, fish, olives, rocks, and many particular things, but these are not what is ultimate. To focus in on a very ordinary example, we commonly talk about "the weather" with our acquaintances. This noun gives us the impression that we are referring to some distinct object. However, we know that "the weather" is really a collection of many different, interacting processes: high and low pressure fronts, humidity, temperature, precipitation, wind direction and velocity, and so on. Heraclitus suggested that all the "objects" we talk about are really a collection of processes.

Heraclitus used the metaphor of a river to make his point. Although scholars are divided on what his exact words were, he said something to the effect that "you cannot step into the same river twice." In one sense, the river may seem to be the same over time. We can identify it by name, such as "the Mississippi River." However, in another sense, while the name remains the same, the waters are constantly changing and we are not dealing with the same physical entity.

One writer in the first century A.D. quoted Heraclitus as saying, "We step and do not step into the same rivers, we are and are not" (G49a; 1.490). This suggests that *we* are like that river, constantly changing and never staying the same. For example, when I look at my high school picture taken in the 1960s, I recognize that person as being *me*. Yet in another sense, I am not the same person. Besides the fact that my hair is grayer and thinner, many of my values and beliefs are different. Even though there is some resemblance physically and psychologically, a good deal of change also has occurred. In another passage, Heraclitus makes the same point by saying, "The sun is new every day" (G6; 1.484). The problem of continuity within change later became such a problem that Aristotle made it one of the major issues in philosophy.

THE UNITY OF OPPOSITES

Going along with his emphasis on change, Heraclitus puts forth the thesis of "the unity of opposites." He gives us abundant evidence of this from common experience. For example, different aspects of the same thing can have opposite characteristics. The pen moves in a straight line across the page when we are considering the sentence, but it moves in a crooked line when we are considering the forming of individual letters. Some opposites are merely different stages in one, continuous process. In this sense, night and day are one (G57; 1.442), and hot and cold are relative qualities that coexist on the same continuum (G126; 1.445). Heraclitus taught not only that there is a unity of opposites, but also that the conflict between opposites is good. For example, he suggests that the bow and lyre show there is harmony in conflict (G51; 1.439). The bow leaning against the wall appears stable and passive. However, the illusion of stability results from the balanced opposition of forces. Only if they maintain their tension or conflict is the bow usable. If the force of the bent bow overpowers the weakened string, it snaps, and the power is unleashed, but in a chaotic, uncontrolled way. Similarly, a lyre can produce music only if there is tension in the strings.

FIRE

Heraclitus, ever the riddler and poet, adds to the river and war metaphors yet another puzzling image to capture the nature of reality. Whereas the Milesians debated whether the world is fundamentally water or air, Heraclitus says it is an everlasting *fire*. "This world-order, the same for all, none of the gods nor of men has made, but it was always and is and shall be: an ever-living fire, which is being kindled in measures and extinguished in measures" (G30; 1.454). It is not clear whether he meant this literally as an alternative to the answers of previous philosophers or whether he meant it in a more figurative sense. Either way, the image of a fire does capture a large portion of Heraclitus's vision of the world. A fire is a process rather than a substantial object. It is constantly changing yet remains the same. Finally, fire transforms everything it touches. Substances are fed into the fire and are changed into something else. Yet although things change, there is a balance to nature and the total amount of reality remains the same.

LOGOS AGAIN

Like Xenophanes, Heraclitus has nothing but disdain for popular religion. He ridicules those who pray to statues, saying that this confused piety "does not understand what gods and heroes really are" (G5; 1.472). Yet despite his harsh, critical mind, Heraclitus had a profound and passionate religious vision of his own. Throughout the changing world, one thing does not change. However, it is not a "thing"; it is the principle or law of change itself. Thus, although the river is in constant flux, the law that governs its flowing is constant. Like the Pythagoreans, he seeks the ultimate unity not in the physical things that are ordered, but in the rationality of that order. These are the beginnings of the concept of a physical law. He identifies this ultimate unity with the Logos or the rational order of the world. However, it is an active rationality, for Heraclitus says that "everything comes to pass in accordance with this Logos" (G1; 1.419). Furthermore, he advises people that if they will listen not to him but to the Logos, they will discover all things are one (G50; 1.425). He clearly identifies the Logos with the ever-living fire, for both have the attributes of a singular divinity. The fire "will come and judge and convict all things" (G66; 1.455). Although he speaks of "the gods" in typically Greek fashion, he believes there is one supreme deity over them all. Like Xenophanes' deity, Heraclitus's god is immanent and identified with the order of nature. "God is day and night, winter and summer, war and peace, satiety and hunger . . . but he changes just as fire, when it is mingled with perfumes, is named according to the scent of each" (G67; 1.444).

Moral and Social Philosophy

As we have seen, Heraclitus believes the conflict of opposites is necessary and good. In his mind, those who prefer stability and peace are "tender-minded" individuals (whom he despises), while those who relish change and strife are "hard-headed" realists. Pythagoras thought that harmony is a blending of opposites and a diminishing of differences. But Heraclitus believes harmony and justice can only come about when opposites sharply conflict. "One must know that war is common, and justice strife, and that all things come about by way of strife and necessity" (G80; 1.447). Heraclitus's outlook is alive in our own day among those who believe that a balance of equal destructive power among the supernations will ensure world stability and peace. Furthermore, our advocate system of law illustrates his point that "justice is strife." Through the conflict of two opposing lawyers, we believe truth and justice will emerge.

Heraclitus introduces the notion that the civil law is a reflection of the divine law, which foreshadows the Stoics' and the medievals' position: ". . . all human laws are nourished by one, the divine, . . ." (G114; 1.425). However, he balances off this thought with another one: "To God all things are fair and good and just, but men have supposed some unjust and some just" (G102; 1.413). This seems to suggest there is no real distinction between good and evil in this world. In other words, Heraclitus seems to be saying, "Whatever *is*, is good" (a problematic conclusion at best).

Heraclitus's Significance

Despite the obscurity of some of his broad, sweeping generalizations, Heraclitus made several contributions. First, like Pythagoras, he sought for the unity of reality not in a material substance but in a formal pattern. Second, he developed further the notion that a universal rationality pervades the universe that our finite minds can understand. This approach encouraged scientists and philosophers to understand this order. Third, he was the most comprehensive philosopher thus far, because he addressed the issues of epistemology, metaphysics, ethics, politics, and theology.

PARMENIDES AND THE ELEATICS

‖‖

Parmenides: The Rigorous Rationalist

Parmenides was born and lived in Elea, a city on the western coast of Italy. He founded a movement known as the Eleatic school of philosophy, which was named after his hometown. His birthdate is estimated to be about 515 B.C. and he probably lived until sometime after 450 B.C. Legend has it that he was influenced by a Pythagorean as a young man. His dates indicate that he was a younger contemporary of Heraclitus, whose work he seems to have known and criticized. In a dialogue named after Parmenides, Plato says that the philosopher—

"very distinguished looking" at 65—and his disciple Zeno visited Athens for a festival. There, according to Plato's report, he met the young Socrates. Although some have doubted this account, most scholars rely on it for Parmenides' dates.

At first glance, Parmenides' ideas will seem implausible and even absurd. Even though most philosophers did not accept his conclusions, he is considered one of the most influential of the Pre-Socratics. Parmenides uses logic more powerfully than any thinker thus far. In spite of his unacceptable conclusions, his style of reasoning accounts for his influence in the development of philosophy.

Reality Is Unchanging

Parmenides' starting point is the essence of simplicity. His position can be distilled into the claim "Whatever exists, *exists*, and there is nothing apart from that which exists." That is difficult to argue with! However, Parmenides squeezes some very startling conclusions from that obvious truth. We can summarize his first argument in this way:

(1) Anything we can think or speak about either exists or doesn't exist.

(2) Anything that doesn't exist is nothing.

(3) We cannot think or speak about nothing.

(4) So, we cannot think or speak about what doesn't exist.

(5) Therefore, anything we can think or speak about exists.

The first premise presents two mutually exclusive alternatives. The second premise is true by definition. So far, we may see no problem in granting Parmenides these points. However, the third and fourth premises are the controversial ones, and yet they are the key to all of Parmenides' metaphysics. Why can't we think about nothing—premise (3)? Parmenides' reasoning seems to be that all thought requires an object. If I really were thinking about sheer nothingness, my thought would have no content and would not be a thought. What about

premise (4)? It certainly seems possible to think about things that don't exist. For example, I can think about a hamburger stand on Mars. Parmenides would point out, however, that I am not thinking about nothing. I am thinking about Mars and a hamburger stand existing there, even if what I am picturing is inaccurate. It only appears to be the case that we can talk about what does not exist, for to talk about "what is not" is to talk about nothing. But if we are talking about nothing, we are merely tossing words around and speaking nonsense.

In premise (1) Parmenides only pretended it was really possible to think and speak about what does not exist. He did so only to lead us to see the absurdity of attempting it. Parmenides' position is a very rigorous rationalism. He claims that anything that can be the object of rational thought is identical to what exists and anything that cannot be thought cannot exist. For example, if I construct a mathematical proof to show that all the angles of any triangle add up to 180 degrees, I will always find that reality is consistent with this conclusion. And when I realize that the notion of "a round square" is unthinkable, I will be certain that nothing like that could ever exist.

For Parmenides, the fundamental reality of Being can be spoken of as the "what is" or "the One." He sometimes simply refers to this as "It," meaning everything and anything. However, note that he never refers to it as "God." From this initial argument, Parmenides draws out a number of logical consequences:

1. *Being is uncreated.* Parmenides uses what will come to be known as the "principle of causality." If Being began at some point or was created, it would either have to come from (a) something or (b) pop into being from nothing. But if Being is all there is, then condition (a) could not be true, for there could be no other cause from which Being came into existence. Furthermore, Being could not have come from *nothing*, because that does not exist and could not cause anything. So condition (b) cannot be true either. Parmenides also uses what later philosophers called the "principle of

sufficient reason." There must be a reason why Being appeared when it did and not, say, three minutes ago. But if nothingness precedes Being, there could be no reason for Being to come into existence at one time as opposed to another. Hence, Being cannot have an origin.

2. *Being is unchangeable and imperishable*. If it could change, what could it change into? It could not change into Being, because it is that already. Hence, if it ever changed or was destroyed, it would have to become nothing. But is this conceivable? No, for Parmenides has previously shown that non-Being cannot exist or be thought. It appears that Parmenides' Being is timeless, since time requires moments coming to be and passing away into nothingness. But if there can be no creation or destruction, there cannot be time as we know it. All of reality is like the eternal objects of mathematics. We cannot ask about circularity and the number 2, "How old are they?" or "What will they be like in the future?"

3. *Being is one and is indivisible*. If Being is a plurality or is divided, what could mark the divisions within it? If the thing marking the division is Being, this is the same as what is being divided. If something is continuous, it can have no divisions. To use an analogy, trying to divide a pool of water into two parts with another quantity of water would be useless. We would still end up with one quantity of water. Yet if the division is not made up of *what is*, then it must be nothing—in which case it is not a division at all.

4. *Being is motionless*. Motion would require empty space. But since empty space would necessarily contain nothing (which cannot be something that exists), there can be no motion.

5. *Being is a finite body*. Parmenides assumes the material monism of the Milesians and conceives of his Being as a physical body. He also assumes it is finite, because the Greeks were very nervous about the concept of an infinite quantity. They thought that anything infinite would be indefinite and incomplete. Since Being is homogenous and evenly distributed throughout the universe, Parmenides compares it to a perfectly round sphere.

Reason Versus the Senses

How could Parmenides possibly believe all this? Our common sense tells us we live in a world of changing, plural objects. Does he really want to deny what our senses so clearly tell us about the world? Parmenides' answer is that we have a basic choice to make. We have, on the one hand, the world as it appears to our senses. On the other hand, we have a description of reality that his logical arguments present. Which source of knowledge should we trust? With regard to the first alternative, he cautions, "Let not habit born of much experience force thee along this way, to ply a heedless eye and sounding ear and tongue" (G7, 2.21). Instead, we are to "judge by reason" (*logos*) the controversial conclusions he puts forth. When we see a magician pull a rabbit out of a previously empty hat, our senses tell us that Being came from non-Being. However, our reason vetoes the senses and tells us this is only an appearance. Parmenides asks us to do this with all our sense experience. He is, without a doubt, the most uncompromising rationalist in the history of philosophy. His position raised to prominence the question "What roles do sense experience and reason play in coming to know reality?" Other philosophers do not necessarily agree with his conclusions, but serious thinkers had to come to terms with his arguments.

Zeno of Elea: Coming to Parmenides' Defense

Parmenides was the object of a great deal of ridicule because of his outrageous conclusions. However, he had a very able defender in a disciple who was twenty-five years younger. Zeno of Elea (approximately 490–430 B.C.) wrote a book in which he produced a barrage of arguments (perhaps close to fifty of them) to refute his master's critics. His arguments are so extremely clever and penetrating that countless twentieth-century mathematicians and logicians have spent a great deal of time and ink trying to get to the bottom of them. The main strategy Zeno uses is to adopt the position of Parmenides' critics. From there he shows that one or more conclusions logically follow. However, the conclusions turn out to contradict one another or to be patently absurd. This type of argument has been called *reductio ad absurdum* or "reducing to an absurdity." The collection of these arguments have been labeled "Zeno's Paradoxes." A few examples will illustrate his technique.

1. *Arguments Against the Senses.* If we drop a small millet seed on the ground, it will make no noise. However, if we drop a bushel of millet seeds, they will make a thud. Either (1) millet seeds do not make a sound when dropped, or (2) millet seeds do make a sound when they are dropped. Which of the two experiences are we to believe? If condition (1) is true, then our senses deceived us when we heard a sound. If condition (2) is true, then our senses deceived us when we did not hear a sound. Either way, the senses are unreliable.

2. *Arguments Against Plurality.* Zeno is said to have offered forty arguments to show that the notion of plurality is full of paradoxes. To take the simplest argument, let's suppose numerous objects exist. They each must have some particular size. But any one of these objects can be infinitely divided into multiple parts and this leads, Zeno argues, to an absurdity. For example, take a 6-foot board. We can saw it in half, and then we can take each one of these pieces and saw them in half again, and do this repeatedly. In principle (although not in practice), we could divide each piece an infinite number of times. However, if the original board contained an infinite number of parts, each having some magnitude, then the original board must have been infinitely large. Since this conclusion is absurd, it must mean that the starting assumption—that there are multiple, divisible objects—is absurd also.

3. *Paradoxes of Motion.* Zeno produced four arguments to show that motion is impossible. The easiest to describe is called "the racecourse." Let us suppose a runner tries to run from the starting point A to a distant goal Z. Before he can get from

A to Z, he must first traverse half the distance. But before he can get halfway, he must first cross half that distance, and so on. At any given point in the race, his immediate goal is a certain distance that can be divided in half and this length can itself be divided into an infinite number of points. Since he always has an infinite number of points to cross, which will take an infinite amount of time, the poor runner will not be able to get anywhere at all. Therefore, contrary to our uncritical beliefs, it is impossible to make any rational sense out of motion.

Before we dismiss Zeno with a disgusted wave of the hand, it is worth pointing out that all great advances in human thought have gone against entrenched common sense. It is not immediately obvious to the senses that the earth is in motion, nor are some of the theories of present-day physicists any more palatable to common sense than Parmenides' conclusions. Nevertheless, while most philosophers have been sure that there is something wrong with Zeno's arguments, it has been hard to find agreement on where the problem lies. Contemporary analyses of the arguments have depended on the revolutionary work on infinite sets done by the mathematician Georg Cantor (1845–1918).

Evaluation and Significance of the Eleatics

A major problem in the Eleatics' arguments is that they confused grammar, logic, and metaphysics. This caused them to make fallacious leaps from language to reality. For example, they thought it was contradictory to say, "There *is* nothing." The problem was that the Greeks at this stage of philosophy could not conceive that a word might have more than one meaning. However, "to be" can have at least three meanings:

1. To exist—"There *is* a God."
2. Identity—"The butler *is* the murderer."
3. The attribution of a quality—"John *is* tall, and Mary *is* tall."

However, the early Greeks often confused these three uses of "is." For example, the fact that John and Mary are both tall does not imply that the two people are identical. Similarly, although it is true that "a unicorn is a one-horned beast," this does not mean that such a beast exists, just as the claim "there is nothing in the refrigerator" does not mean that *nothing* is some *thing* that exists. Plato attempted to clear up some of these points in his dialogue called the *Sophist*.

In spite of their problems, we must not overlook the Eleatics' positive contributions: (1) They were the first to reflect on the logical implications of words and concepts. (2) They had the courage to follow their assumptions to their logical conclusions, even though they seemed counterintuitive. Science cannot advance unless people are willing to forsake the obvious, the immediate, and the commonsensical. (3) They were very influential, even if in a negative way. The rigor of Parmenides' arguments forced Plato and Aristotle to wrestle with them to lay these problems to rest. The Eleatic philosophy is another example of a fertile error, for their philosophy was so cleverly argued yet so outrageous that it provoked hard thinking.

THE PLURALISTS

The Pluralists' Task

Parmenides showed what happens when we start with monism and consistently work out all its implications. It seemed clear to the philosophers who analyzed Parmenides' arguments that he and his followers must have started off in the wrong direction if they ended with the conclusion that the world of sense experience is one, massive illusion and that change does not really occur. The remedy, offered by a group of philosophers we call the *pluralists*, was to reject the starting point of radical monism.

Empedocles (495–435 B.C.)

Empedocles, a native of Sicily, was known as a philosopher, religious mystic, poet, and magician. Although he agreed with Parmenides that there can be no *absolute* creation or destruction of reality, Empedocles claimed there is *relative* change. In postulating both change and permanence, he achieved a compromise between Heraclitus and Parmenides. However, contrary to the Eleatics, he postulated that there is not one thing that is permanent but four things: earth, air, fire, and water. These are the eternal "root" substances or elements, and all change is explained as the combination and

separation of these permanent elements. He even worked out some of the details of how this might come about. For example, bone consists of two parts earth, two parts water, and four parts fire.*

However, this explanation of the composition of things is not enough to explain the world of our experience. Empedocles realizes we need a separate set of principles to explain change and motion. On the one hand, we find the world consists of certain unified objects such as chairs, trees, stones, and so forth. We need something to explain how the individual elements combine and stick together: a *principle of unification*. On the other hand, the world is not one, giant unity, as Parmenides thought. It is composed of individual objects. Furthermore, even these smaller unities disintegrate and break down into their separate components. Therefore, we also need a *principle of individuation*. Empedocles was insightful in realizing that both principles were essential.

According to Empedocles, *love* is the principle of unity and *strife* is the principle of individuation. The interaction of these two opposing forces results in a continual amount of flux in the world.

---

*We might suppose that if Empedocles had been familiar with our method of symbolizing chemical compounds, he would designate bone as $E_2W_2F_4$!

The present world is in an intermediate stage between total unity and separation. Concerning the direction in which it is headed, Empedocles was a pessimist. He says, "Things are becoming worse." Even though he speaks of these forces as deities, he also thinks of them as materialistic forces, for he says, "Love and strife run through all things like quicksilver." Many Greeks at this time still had difficulty imagining any other kind of reality except large material objects and very fine material objects. Notice that the forces that control the physical universe are moral forces (love and hate). Even though the Greek philosophers of this period had moved away from the fantastic stories of the gods controlling all events, their explanations were still tinged with a heavy dose of anthropomorphism.We may smile at some of their primitive notions until we realize how hard it is to escape the use of metaphors in describing the world. In contemporary physics, the notions of love and strife find their way into our talk of subatomic particles "attracting" and "repelling" one another.

Empedocles had three other theories worth mentioning. First, he denied that there could be empty space. He understood motion as one clump of matter moving between other clumps of matter, much like a fish moving through water. Although the Pythagoreans had postulated empty space, the notion that a void (nonbeing) could exist was difficult to accept at this time. Second, in terms of the written records we have, he developed the first theory of sense perception. According to his account, when particles of matter fly off an object and strike our sense organs, perception occurs. Thus, when you see a red tomato, this is the result of red particles from the tomato actually contacting your eyeballs. Finally, he proposed a theory of evolution based on a crude version of what we now call the "law of natural selection." He imagined that once there were random products of nature that consisted of creatures with heads of cattle and branches for arms and other fantastic combinations. For obvious reasons, these could not function very successfully, and so they died off and their species became extinct. The species that now exist are those whose random arrangements of bodily parts that were most advantageous for survival.

Anaxagoras (500–428 B.C.)

Anaxagoras was an Ionian who moved to Athens and became a part of the intellectual circle surrounding Pericles, a major political figure of this time. Anaxagoras had a hardheaded, naturalistic approach to the world that is best illustrated by two stories. First, we are told that he was exiled from Athens on charges of impiety for promoting the heresy that the sun was a white-hot stone and not a deity. Then there is the story of a one-horned ram that was given to Pericles. A soothsayer proclaimed that this unusual creature was a sign from the gods and predicted that if either Pericles or Thucydides possessed it, they would be victorious in battle. Anaxagoras was unimpressed and swiftly dissected its skull, finding that the lack of two horns was caused by a brain tumor. It was a natural phenomenon, not a miraculous sign, he explained.

Anaxagoras carried pluralism one step further. Instead of four elements, he said that every kind of thing has its own element. Thus, there is an indefinite number of elements or "seeds" (*spermata*). There are seeds for grass, bone, hair, gold, mud, and so on. How is it that when we eat food it becomes part of our bodies and is converted into flesh, bone, hair, and blood? The answer is that the particles of these things were already in the food to begin with. Thus, everything is in everything. When we see grass, the grass elements predominate in it and so that is all we see. However, if the cow eats grass and produces milk and the horse eats grass and it produces muscle, then bits of milk and muscle must be mixed in with the grass elements.

Anaxagoras introduced Mind (or *Nous*) as the source of motion and the principle of order. *Nous* does not create the world but is a free, spontaneous, active, perfect, and all-knowing force. Although this is the beginning of a vague dualism of mind and matter, in the final analysis *Nous* comes out to be merely a kind of rarefied matter.

EVALUATION OF ANAXAGORAS

There are several problems in Anaxagoras's philosophy: (1) He leaves us without any sort of unified explanation of reality. An extreme pluralism that claims there is an element for every kind of thing loses all explanatory value. Explanations are supposed to make the world simpler and more unified, not hand it back to us as diverse as when we first began. (2) Both Socrates and Aristotle point out that Anaxagoras brings in *Nous* or Mind only when mechanical explanations fail. Thus, it is an emergency principle that is called in only to fill in the blanks in our knowledge. Despite these problems, his principle of Mind led philosophers to ask what else besides matter is necessary to explain the world.

DEMOCRITUS AND THE ATOMISTS

The founder of the Atomist movement is thought to be a philosopher by the name of Leucippus, but we know very little about him. Therefore, Democritus (460–360 B.C.) is our source for most of the Atomists' ideas.* He was a younger contemporary of Anaxagoras who wrote on physics, epistemology, metaphysics, ethics, and history, besides being ranked highly as a mathematician.

Being

According to the Atomists, two principles explain reality: atoms and the void. Notice that by making the void or empty space a component of being, the Atomists disagree with Parmenides, for they are claiming that what-is-not *does* exist! Atoms have several features. First, they are indivisible, eternal, and unchanging (making them almost small editions of Parmenidean Being). However, they are infinite in number (the unlimited expanse of space allows this). Second, there are quantitative differences between them (they come in various sizes and shapes). Third, they are qualitatively alike or neutral (they have no color, taste, temperature, or odor).

Becoming

Change was understood as a result of the differing relationships between the atoms. Democritus's ar-

gument concerning change is as follows: (1) There is no up or down in any absolute sense, and, therefore, motion is directionless. (2) It follows that atoms do not have weight in any absolute sense.[†] (3) Since there is no natural, final resting place for the atoms, the motion of atoms is eternal (like dust particles dancing in the sunlight). Aristotle was not satisfied with this answer and complained, "They lazily shelved the question of the origin of motion."

The World of Appearances

The world we see about us can be explained on the basis of the previous principles: (1) the motion of the atoms and their geometrical properties produce (2) various interactions and combinations that produce (3) all the qualities found in sense experience. For example, solid matter results when atoms that have rough surfaces or hooks become interlocked. Liquids are made up of spherical atoms with smooth surfaces that continually roll over one another. Sweet-tasting substances are made up of smooth atoms, while bitter herbs, of course, are made up of atoms with sharp points that irritate our mouth atoms. For Democritus, there is no ordering principle in the world. What patterns there seem to be are simply products of the material properties of atoms and the chance collisions that result from their motions.

---

*Democritus is not truly a Pre-Socratic, because he was a younger contemporary of Socrates.

[†]We now know he is right. As space travel illustrates, weight is a relative property.

Theory of Knowledge

Democritus's epistemology follows from his materialism. He has an emanation theory of perception in which atoms from objects fly off and collide with our sense organs. The motion from this impact is then transmitted to our material soul atoms, and we experience an image of the original object. However, if this is true, then the senses do not give us direct knowledge of the world. They only produce certain appearances within us. Lemons taste bitter, while honey tastes sweet. Apples appear to be red, and water appears to be blue. However, these experiences are really produced by the objective spatial qualities of the atoms and the subjective effects of their impact on our sense organs. This is why the same food can taste different to different people. The colors, smells, and tastes we experience are not the real properties of the objects out there. For this reason, Democritus asserts there are two kinds of knowledge:

Trueborn	Bastard
Objective	Subjective
Things as they are	Things as they appear
Atoms and	Qualities: colors,
the void	sounds, smells,
	tastes, textures

What Democritus calls "bastard knowledge" is really sense experience. Thus, to know the true nature of things, reason must penetrate beneath the sensory appearances to discern the quantitative nature of the atoms. The implications of this distinction reverberated all the way into the modern age. In the seventeenth century, Galileo and Descartes made the same distinctions in terms of primary and secondary qualities. For both Democritus and these seventeenth-century mechanists, the world as viewed by the poet, the artist, or our unrefined senses is subjective. Only the world as given to us by scientific and mathematical reason is real. However, this epistemology caused some problems for Democritus. Sense experience gives us only appearances, but reason has no materials to work except those provided by the senses. Thus, according to one account, Democritus has the senses taunting reason: "Wretched mind, do you take your evidence from us and then throw us down? That throw is your overthrow" (G145; 2.460). In despair Democritus concludes, "In reality we know nothing, for truth is in the depths" (G117; 2.460).

Ethics

Democritus started with an attempt to develop a hardheaded scientific view of the world. However, he was also well aware that this had implications for all of life. His writings on morality seek to work this out consistently. As he says in one passage,

> Equanimity comes to men through proportionate pleasure and moderation in life. Excesses and defects are apt to change and cause great disturbances in the soul. Those souls which are moved over great distances have neither stability nor equanimity.[3]

The key term here is "moved." He is attempting to provide ethical advice on the basis of physics. His theory is based on three assumptions:

1. All experience is produced by the movement of atoms.

2. The good life is one in which this experience is pleasing.

3. Tranquility of the soul (gentle motions) is more pleasing than all the pleasures of the body (large-scale motions).

This view is known as "prudent hedonism." **Hedonism** is the theory that pleasure is the only value in life. What other sort of ethics could a materialist have but one that reduced ethical values to material, physiological motions? However, it is a *prudent* hedonism because he realizes that not all pleasures are worthy of being pursued. As far as our ultimate destiny is concerned, the Atomists theorized that the soul is only a bundle of very fine atoms. Since this compound (and hence the person) disperses at death, there is no personal immortality. Therefore, living our life here and now with as much joy and as little trouble as possible is the only goal we need worry about.

Significance of the Atomists

Plato ignored the Atomists and Aristotle rejected them because they found that an atomistic, mechanistic materialism was inadequate to explain the world. However, the Atomists' metaphysics and moral philosophy were revived in the Hellenistic period, mainly through the teachings of the Epicureans. Atomism as a foundation for science was reborn in the sixteenth and seventeenth centuries and virtually remained unchanged until the nineteenth century. Hence, we will defer any evaluation of their thought until we look at these later outworkings of their theory.

Summary of the Pre-Socratics

The philosophers that preceded Socrates set philosophy in motion by offering arguments for their theories and by criticizing one another. Although their arguments are not always cogent, they *did* present reasons for their positions as well as for the refutations of their contemporaries. This was a great advance over previous explanations of the universe, which simply relied on the noncritical transmission of the mythical and poetic traditions of the culture. However, along with their insights came a number of problems. The wide range of conflicting opinions that developed during this period would lead the next group of philosophers to be very skeptical about whether we could ever arrive at any truths that were more than simply personal opinions. These developments also made philosophers realize that more work needed to be done on the foundations of knowledge.

Questions for Understanding

1. What was Thales' basic question? What was his answer? What reasons might he have had to support his position?
2. How does Thales explain change?
3. What is metaphysical monism? Why could Thales' position be called "material monism"?
4. What does Anaximander mean by the Apeiron?
5. How does Anaximander explain change?
6. What is the basic substance according to Anaximenes?
7. According to Anaximenes, what two principles explain change?
8. What points of agreement were there among the Milesians?
9. In what sense did the Pythagoreans combine philosophy and religion?
10. What did the Pythagoreans mean when they said reality is mathematical? Why did they believe this?
11. Why are the Pythagoreans called metaphysical dualists?
12. What was the Pythagorean view of the soul?
13. In what ways were the Pythagoreans innovative?
14. What was Xenophanes' view of knowledge?
15. In what ways did Xenophanes' views differ from the typical Greek view of the gods?
16. According to Heraclitus, what is the Logos? Why is it important?
17. Why did Heraclitus say "you cannot step into the same river twice"? How does this represent his basic view of reality?
18. What does Heraclitus mean by the "unity of opposites"?
19. What does the image of fire symbolize in Heraclitus's philosophy?
20. What are the main themes in Heraclitus's moral and social philosophy?
21. Why does Parmenides believe reality is unchanging?
22. What are some examples of Zeno's paradoxes? How does he use them to defend Parmenides' philosophy?
23. According to Empedocles, what substances are fundamental?
24. What two principles does Empedocles use to explain change?
25. What is Anaxagoras's view of the basic elements?

26. What does Anaxagoras mean by Nous?

27. According to Democritus and the atomists, what two principles explain reality?

28. How does Democritus use the geometrical properties of atoms to explain the properties of the objects of everyday experience?

29. How does Democritus use his theory of atoms to explain knowledge? What features of reality are objective and what features are subjective?

30. What sort of account does Democritus give of ethics?

31. What is hedonism?

Questions for Reflection

1. If you were living during the time of the Pre-Socratics, which of their philosophies would you think was most plausible? Which would seem the least plausible. Why?

2. The Pre-Socratics' greatest contribution was not their answers, but their questions. What were some of the questions they raised that were particularly innovative, important, and that we still ask today?

Notes

1. Quoted in Edwin A. Burtt, *The Metaphysical Foundations of Modern Physical Science*, rev. ed. (Garden City, NY: Doubleday Anchor Books, 1932), 75.

2. Quotations of the Pre-Socratic philosophers are from W. K. C. Guthrie, *A History of Greek Philosophy*, vols. 1 and 2 (Cambridge, England: Cambridge University Press, 1962). This is abbreviated in the text with the letter "G." The first number of the reference is the fragment of the particular philosopher's work being quoted. The second set of numbers represents the volume and page in Guthrie where the quote can be found.

3. Quoted in John Mansley Robinson, *An Introduction to Early Greek Philosophy* (Boston: Houghton Mifflin, 1968), 220.

3

The Sophists and Socrates

THE SOPHISTS

Skepticism and the Keys to Success

In the fifth century, while philosophers from Parmenides to Democritus were debating traditional questions about physical nature, a major juncture or turning point in the history of philosophy was emerging. To understand this change in direction, we need to look at what was happening to the culture during this century. By this time, the city-state of Athens had risen to become the commercial, intellectual, and artistic center of Greek culture. This period was rich with advances in medicine, architecture, art, poetry, and drama. Furthermore, Athenian democracy came to birth as a new form of political governance. For these reasons, this century is known as the Golden Age of Greece. Ironically, the flood of social and political changes brought with them a moral and cultural malaise. As the century wore on, the old ideal of respect for the Athenian laws, religion, and customs began to disintegrate. Writing in the latter third of the century, after the outbreak of the Peloponnesian War, the historian Thucydides described a society that had lost its moorings:

The common meaning of words was turned about at men's pleasure; the most reckless bravado was deemed the most desirable friend; a man of prudence

and moderation was styled a coward; a man who listened to reason was a good-for-nothing simpleton.[1]

Likewise, in his play *Medea,* Euripides mourned the changes that had taken place in his culture:

Life, life is changed and the laws of it o'ertrod. . . .
Man hath forgotten God. . . .[2]

At least four causes produced these changes: (1) Respect for the culture's authorities (the poetic traditions concerning the gods) declined. This resulted in the loss of a metaphysical foundation for values. (2) Increased contact with different cultures, customs, and laws led to the conclusion that most beliefs and standards once thought to be universal and absolute were actually relative to the local culture. (3) The rise of democratic lawmaking made it difficult to assume the divine origins of one's society. Furthermore, the democratic spirit led to a new sense of individualism and opened up new opportunities for personal power and success. (4) The plurality of opinions among the philosophers and scientists concerning the nature of reality led to the skeptical conclusion that no one can ever know the truth. All this caused a loss of interest in metaphysical questions. Taking its place was an increased interest in the more practical concerns of individuals and their culture.

Into this philosophical turmoil stepped a group of educators called the Sophists. With the decline of the old aristocracy, political leadership was no longer a result of one's birth. One could now rise to power by winning the favor of the crowd and by prevailing in the judicial system. Accordingly, the Sophists offered guidance in practical matters to the rising class of politicians. Many of them traveled from town to town, offering their instruction for a fee. When the Sophist Protagoras was asked what a student would learn from him, he is said to have replied, "The proper care of his personal affairs, so that he may best manage his own household, and also of the state's affairs, so as to become a real power in the city, both as a speaker and man of action."[3]

The word "Sophist" is derived from the Greek word *sophia*, which means "wisdom."* Originally it had a neutral meaning and meant something like "professor." After Socrates' quarrels with the Sophists, however, they came into disrepute, and many people used the word as a term of abuse. For example, Plato referred to them as "shopkeepers with spiritual wares."[4] Aristotle complained that the training provided by Sophists such as Protagoras was a "fraud" because it taught the skill of "making the worse argument seem the better."[5] In their defense, we should note that most of our information on them comes from prejudiced sources.

In its worst forms, the Sophists' philosophy could be summed up in two words: *skepticism* and *success*. **Skepticism** is the claim that true knowledge is unattainable. When the thinkers of the fifth century looked back over their own, brief philosophical history, the jumble of conflicting opinions gave credibility to skepticism. Thales was refuted by Anaximander, who was refuted by Anaximenes. Heraclitus said everything is changing, and Parmenides said everything is permanent. It seemed as though no one really knew. So all truth is relative, claimed the Sophists. Likewise, all values and standards are relative. What is "truth," "justice," or "moral goodness"? According to many of the Sophists, they are just sounds we make.

The second main theme of the Sophists was that achieving success is the goal in life. If knowledge is impossible, then it is useless to seek for what you can't find. Instead, one should just try to get along. The Sophists taught that you should not ask of an idea, "Is it true?" Instead, you should ask, "Will advocating this idea help me?" Don't ask of an action, "Is it right?" Instead, you should ask, "Will performing this action be advantageous to me?" To the success-driven young people of Athens, the search for truth gave way to the marketing of one's opinions. The search for moral correctness gave way to promoting one's interests. Accordingly, the Sophists taught the skills of rhetoric, debate, public speaking, and persuasion.

An important issue to the Sophists was the distinction between *physis* and *nomos*. *Physis* is commonly translated as "nature" and refers to the features of the world that are independent of human traditions and decisions. Appropriately, our word "physics" is derived from it. *Nomos*, in contrast, refers to that which is based on human customs or conventions. The fact that Americans hold their fork in their right hand when eating and Europeans keep it in their left hand is a matter of *nomos*. However, the fact that eating is necessary to sustain life is a matter of *physis*. An important application of this distinction is found in the question "Are the laws of morality simply a matter of *nomos* (human convention), or can we find their basis in *physis* (the natural order of things)?" All the Sophists agreed that traditional morality was based only in convention or *nomos*. The conservatives among them said success was to be gained in accepting the morality of one's society. However, those with a more cynical bent said we should give lip service to conventional morality but should not allow it to limit our behavior.

PROTAGORAS

The first and most famous of the Sophists was Protagoras. His dates are in dispute, but most believe he was born in the early part of the fifth century B.C. (probably not later than 490) and may have

*Our English words *sophomore* and *sophisticated* share this same root.

died around the year 420 B.C. He became famous for his assertion "Man is the measure of all things, of those that are that they are, of those that are not that they are not." Two interpretations have been given of this slogan: (1) each individual person provides his or her own standard for interpreting things, or (2) society as a whole is the measure of all things. Under either interpretation, he expresses a radical humanism and relativism that says there is no standard other than those that individuals or societies invent. Actually, Protagoras seems to have embraced both alternatives. As we will see, he affirmed an individualistic subjectivism with respect to perception and a social subjectivism with respect to ethics.

Protagoras accepted without question the thesis that our only contact with the world is through perception. From this he drew the conclusion that everything is relative to the individual. To me the wind may feel warm, but to you it may seem cold. There is no correct answer here, for however it *seems* to you, that is the way it *is* (to you), and no one can say you are wrong. In his brief slogan, Protagoras swept away with a flourish all the debates of the previous philosophers. The cosmologists (such as Parmenides) were trying to find out how reality truly is, apart from how it appears to be. Protagoras argued that we can make no such distinction.* All we have are appearances and individual opinions. Hence, all beliefs are equally true.

Such a radical individualism would seem to lead to moral and social anarchy. However, Protagoras surprises us with a rather conservative position on ethics. Even though moral judgments are purely relative and a product of convention, society's traditions and laws are as good as any. Therefore, we should uphold and follow the traditions of our particular society because a peaceful and orderly society is good. As he is reported to have taught, "Whatever practices seem right and laud-

able to any particular state are so, for that state, so long as it holds by them."[6] No doubt, he would have approved of the advice "When in Rome do as the Romans do." Therefore, he comes down on the side of *nomos* (convention), since it is all we have to guide our lives. Protagoras believed that even though it is useless to worry about whether an idea is true or not, he thought it obvious that some ideas are better or more expedient than others. Therefore, our humanly invented standards can be given a pragmatic justification by virtue of the fact that they seem to work for our good.†

His skepticism led him to dismiss the possibility of theoretical discussions of theology:

> *Concerning the gods I am unable to discover whether they exist or not, or what they are like in form; for there are many hindrances to knowledge, the obscurity of the subject and the brevity of human life.*[7]

Nevertheless, he thought traditional religion should not be abandoned. Although he was not sure the gods existed, he did seem assured they should be worshiped. Religious belief was an integral part of the civilized society and political community of his time. Therefore, belief in the gods is necessary for social stability. Once again, his interests were practical and not theoretical.

GORGIAS

The Sophist Gorgias is thought to have lived over a hundred years, from around 483 to somewhere around 375 B.C. He was led to his skepticism by Zeno's arguments and even seems to have adopted the latter's style and method. Having given up on the pursuit of truth, he also gave up philosophy and became a teacher of rhetoric. His book was titled *On the Non-Existent or On Nature*, which seems to be a parody of the title *On Nature or the Existent*, which is thought to be the name Parmenides gave to his own book. Here, Gorgias appears to be following the advice he gave his students, which was "to destroy an opponent's seriousness by laughter."[8]

---

*In referring to "things that are and things that are not" in the "Man is the measure" formula, Protagoras may have been referring to Parmenides' discussion of Being and non-Being. Thus, in contrast to the Eleatics' teachings, Protagoras is saying that what exists and what doesn't exist is simply a matter of individual or social opinion.

†F. C. S. Schiller, one of the founders of the twentieth-century movement of pragmatism, called himself a disciple of Protagoras.

Whereas Protagoras argued that "everything is true," Gorgias delighted in proving that "nothing is true." Accordingly, he argued for three outrageous theses:

1. Nothing exists.
2. If anything exists, it is unknowable.
3. If it is knowable, it cannot be communicated.

We have a report of the arguments he provided for these conclusions, but they are too lengthy to reproduce here. It is not clear whether he meant these arguments to be regarded seriously, or whether he was showing off his rhetorical skills and offering a parody of Parmenides and the entire cosmological tradition. Nevertheless, it does seem that the point of each one of his theses is to promote a cynical skepticism. With the first conclusion, he is showing that rational argument is limited. Parmenides argued that Being exists, but Gorgias attempts to show that it is just as easy to argue that nothing exists. Hence, reason can prove anything and metaphysics is impossible. The second thesis implies that reason and experience are inadequate to tell us about the world. Thus, knowledge is impossible. The third thesis claims that human language is inadequate and each of us is trapped within our own subjective world of impressions. Nevertheless, according to Gorgias, a skilled rhetorician can reason to any conclusion. Persuasion, not truth, is the goal of discourse.

ANTIPHON

A distinction is often made between the earlier Sophists and the later ones. The earlier ones, such as Protagoras, tended to be more conservative. They endorsed *nomos* since, in the absence of any real knowledge, it is better for us to simply stick with the conventions of our society. The later Sophists, however, saw the laws of society (*nomos*) as being in tension with the laws of nature (*physis*) and said we are better off following nature. A good example of this viewpoint is found in Antiphon, a contemporary of Socrates. He argues that we naturally seek what is advantageous to us. We are all subject to the law of self-preservation. However, this law was not passed by any human legislators but is a law of nature itself. If we violate this law, the penalty is death, and, unlike human courts, nature's penalties follow swiftly and automatically:

> *Most of the things which are just by law are hostile to nature. . . . But life and death are the concern of nature, and living creatures live by what is advantageous to them and die from what is not advantageous; and the advantages which accrue from law are chains upon nature, whereas those which accrue from nature are free.*[9]

The problem is that many of the conventional laws work against the law of nature. For example, society tells me I cannot attack a malicious enemy except in self-defense. However, nature dictates that it is in the interest of my self-preservation to strike first. Consequently, Antiphon offers the following moral policy:

> *A man will be just, then, in a way most advantageous to himself if, in the presence of witnesses, he holds the laws of the city in high esteem, and in the absence of witnesses, when he is alone, those of nature.*[10]

Further cynical sentiments were expressed by Thrasymachus (represented in Plato's *Republic*) and Callicles (in Plato's *Gorgias*). Thrasymachus emphasized the sociological fact that those people who have the most power are in a position to dictate what we will call just or not. Hence, since morality is just a matter of social convention, then "justice" will be whatever serves the interests of the powerful. Callicles stressed that not only *will* the interests of the stronger persons prevail, but that they *should* prevail. In other words, the laws of nature dictate that "might makes right."

EVALUATION AND SIGNIFICANCE OF THE SOPHISTS

Socrates and Plato provided the negative critique of the Sophists. In brief, they said that: (1) The Sophists overemphasized the accidental, subjective, and personal elements in knowledge and conduct. (2) They failed to realize that objective standards are inescapable, for they are required for any judgment—including critical ones. (3) The Sophists claimed to teach success in life, but never examined this concept. Hence, they were uncritical in their criticisms.

Even if we agree with these criticisms of the Sophists, the perspective of history shows that they did make some positive philosophical contributions: (1) They raised critical questions in epistemology, ethics, and politics that had been ignored or taken for granted by their predecessors. (2) The Sophists focused on questions concerning human affairs (knowledge, values, and actions) and thereby expanded the range of philosophy beyond merely cosmological concerns. (3) They provided a "philosophical weeding service" by undercutting beliefs that were naively based on dogma and tradition. (4) The corrosive skepticism of the Sophists and their ethical relativism forced later philosophers to think more carefully about the foundations of knowledge and values. Thus, the Sophists, along with their opponent Socrates, represented a transitional stage to the more systematic philosophies of Plato and Aristotle. (5) The Sophists' study of language and argument contributed to the development of logic, rhetoric, and grammar. (6) They were a progressive force against entrenched tradition. Because they traveled about, they could look beyond the boundaries of the much too provincial city-states. Furthermore, their critique of blind faith in tradition led to more practical political solutions in the form of Panhellenism or a greater sense of unity between the Greek states. (7) Finally, the problems evoked by the Sophists' skepticism were a motivating force behind Socrates' philosophical quest. Hence, his reaction to them produced one of the most influential philosophies in human history. We now turn to this philosophical giant that occupied the body of an eccentric little man.

SOCRATES (470–399 B.C.)

Socrates on Trial

The year is 399 B.C. In the Athenian courtroom, the crowd murmurs as the former sculptor turned marketplace philosopher makes his way to the center of the room to face his accusers. To the unfeeling spectators, the defendant seems to be physically unimpressive as the light shines off his bald head and a disheveled and worn garment hangs awkwardly on his seventy-year-old, short and stocky frame. It would be a humorous scene except for the solemnity of the occasion. The "criminal" is Socrates, and he is arguing for his life before an Athenian jury made up of five hundred citizens, chosen at random. The charges are "Socrates is guilty of corrupting the youth, and of believing not in the gods whom the state believes in, but in other new divinities."[11] Although he is initially a comical figure, one's assessment of him changes when he begins to speak. He addresses the charges while weaving in the details of his life. The twinkle in his eye almost makes us forget that capital charges hang over him. As his voice increases in its intensity and urgency, we have a sense that it is not this aged philosopher that sits in judgment, but that the court and the citizens of Athens are on trial. How they make their decision will reveal both their own character and that of their society. The defendant speaks:

> Athenians, I hold you in the highest regard and affection, but I will be persuaded by the god rather than you. As long as I have breath and strength I will not give up philosophy and exhorting you and declaring the truth to every one of you whom I meet, saying, as I am accustomed, "My good friend . . . are you not ashamed of caring so much for the making of money and for fame and prestige, when you neither think nor care about wisdom and truth and the improvement

of your soul?" If he disputes my words and says that he does care about these things, I shall not at once release him and go away: I shall question him and cross-examine him and test him. If I think that he has not attained excellence, though he says that he has, I shall reproach him for undervaluing the most valuable things, and overvaluing those that are less valuable. This I shall do to everyone whom I meet, young or old, citizen or stranger. . . . For I spend my whole life in going about and persuading you all to give your first and greatest care to the improvement of your souls, and not till you have done that to think of your bodies or your wealth.[12]

And now, Athenians, I am not arguing in my own defense at all, as you might expect me to do, but rather in yours in order [that] you may not make a mistake about the gift of the god to you by condemning me. For if you put me to death, you will not easily find another who . . . clings to the state as a sort of gadfly to a horse that is large and well-bred but rather sluggish because of its size, so that it needs to be aroused. It seems to me that the god has attached me like that to the state, for I am constantly alighting upon you at every point to arouse, persuade, and reproach each of you all day long. You will not easily find anyone else, my friends, to fill my place; and if you are persuaded by me, you will spare my life.[13]

Apparently the majority did not appreciate Socrates' role as a gadfly in their midst, stinging them out of their complacency, for the vote of the jury was 280 votes for conviction and 220 votes for acquittal. Socrates spent the next thirty days in prison, discoursing with his friends and awaiting his execution. When the day arrived, he was surrounded by his weeping friends as he drank the poison hemlock and went to a quiet and peaceful death.

Having looked at the circumstances that brought about his death, what do we know about his life? Socrates was born in 470 B.C. in Athens. Unlike Plato, his student, he came from humble economic circumstances. His father was a sculptor and his mother a midwife. Socrates was eccentric in manner and appearance, yet he had a captivating effect on people. Even his friends testify that his clothes were always rumpled and that his walk was like the strut of a pelican. Nevertheless, he was physically robust. Although he rarely drank, he could consume enormous quantities of wine without getting drunk. He was in his seventies when he died, and he left behind a wife and three children; the oldest was a young man, and the youngest was still in arms.

Once a friend of his asked the oracle of Delphi if there was anyone wiser than Socrates. The priestess replied there was not. Socrates was speechless, for he was aware of his own, considerable ignorance. Deeply puzzled, he set about to clear up this riddle. His goal was to find someone wiser than he was, and thus prove that the oracle was mistaken. First he sought out a politician who had a reputation for being wise. As he says in his own words,

When I conversed with him I came to see that, though a great many persons, and most of all he himself, thought that he was wise, yet he was not wise. Then I tried to prove to him that he was not wise, though he fancied that he was. By so doing I made him indignant, and many of the bystanders. So when I went away, I thought to myself, "I am wiser than this man: neither of us knows anything that is really worth knowing, but he thinks that he has knowledge when he has not, while I, having no knowledge, do not think that I have. I seem, at any rate to be a little wiser than he is on this point: I do not think that I know what I do not know."[14]

Like a man obsessed, he sought out other politicians, and then poets, and finally skilled craftsmen, all of whom were well respected in Athens, in search of someone wiser than him. But the results were always the same as in the first case. Finally, he realized that he was better off with his honest ignorance than were the pompous leaders with their shallow and smug "wisdom."

This experience was the turning point in his life as a philosopher. Henceforth, he felt compelled by a divine calling to seek knowledge by questioning his contemporaries. Accordingly, he walked the streets of Athens questioning them on everything from politics to poetry. For Socrates, philosophy was not just a detached discussion of ideas but was a passionate search for wisdom that affected every area of life.

THE SOURCES OF SOCRATES' THOUGHT

Since Socrates believed that philosophy was best done in conversation and not by writing books, he never set down his ideas in print.* Accordingly, everything we know about Socrates comes to us by way of the writings of Plato and other contemporaries. It is particularly problematic to decide when Plato is giving us a faithful transcription of Socrates' ideas and when he is simply using the figure of Socrates as a mouthpiece for his own philosophy. While scholars differ on this issue, the most common opinion is that Plato's earliest dialogues are intended to represent the historical Socrates.[†] Likewise, it is commonly concluded that the voice of Socrates in the remaining dialogues represents Plato's philosophical maturity and contains his original philosophical reflections.[‡] These distinctions are based on the different styles that appear in each period of Plato's writings.

Socrates' Task: Exposing Ignorance

We are told that Socrates studied under the Sophist Prodicus, but because of poverty could only take the cheap course and not the more complete one.[15] Nevertheless, the more he became familiar with the teachings of the Sophists, the more he was troubled by their "schools for

success." He thought that they were both intellectually mistaken and morally harmful. These smooth-talking rhetoricians had never honestly sought after genuine knowledge, yet they presumed to instruct people in worldly success. Socrates worried that the people of Athens, under the influence of the Sophists, were mistaking false images and shadows for reality. It was as though the Sophists were selling people maps of the fictional land of Atlantis and claiming that these would help their customers to find their way around Greece. Learning from the Sophists how to speak smoothly and persuasively was dangerous to society and to oneself if one merely spouts eloquent errors.

Socrates was convinced that one could act only on the basis of the truth or, at least, our most carefully examined opinions. We must know *what* knowledge is available, *how* we can obtain it, and *why* it is true. To Socrates, the people in his society were ignorant of the one thing it is most important to know: how to conduct their lives or "tend" their own souls. Only one thing is worse than having cancer, and that is having cancer but not knowing it. If we know we have the disease, we can seek treatment. For Socrates, ignorance is a disease of the soul. It prevents the soul from functioning properly. The problem was that the people of Athens were inflicted with a multiple ignorance. They were ignorant and did not know it. So, Socrates was like a pathologist, he was trying to make people aware of their condition. Some were able to accept the diagnosis and seek for intellectual and spiritual health, while others were too vain to face the painful truths about themselves.

Socrates' Method

SOCRATIC QUESTIONING

Socrates' method for leading people to knowledge was so effective that it has become one of the classic techniques of education commonly known as the "Socratic method" or "Socratic questioning." Plato later referred to this method as **dialectic**. It is a conversational method that proceeds by means

---

*The importance of dialogue to Socrates is illustrated by his complaint that eloquent orators and books are alike in that they provide massive amounts of information, "but if one asks any of them an additional question, . . . they cannot either answer or ask a question on their own account." Plato, *Protagoras* 329a, trans. W. K. C. Guthrie, in *Collected Dialogues of Plato*, ed. Edith Hamilton and Huntington Cairns (New York: Bollingen Foundation, 1961).

[†]These are *Apology, Crito, Euthyphro, Laches, Charmides, Ion, Hippias Minor, Lysis, Euthydemus,* and, to some extent, the *Protagoras* and *Gorgias*.

[‡]These include the middle dialogues (*Meno, Hippias Major, Cratylus, Phaedo, Symposium, Republic*) and the late dialogues (*Parmenides, Phaedrus, Theaetetus, Sophist, Statesman, Timaeus, Philebus, Laws*).

of a series of questions and answers in which the inadequacy of the pupil's successive answers are exposed, progressively leading both the pupil and the teacher to answers that have greater clarity and refinement. The most powerful feature of the method is that instead of simply being given information, the pupils discover for themselves their own ignorance and are skillfully led to discover the truth on their own.

For Socrates, the method was employed to arrive at an understanding of the most important concepts in human life. He was scandalized by the fact that the leading figures in his society loved to hold forth in political speeches or orations in the law courts, using terms such as *wisdom, justice, goodness,* or *virtue.* Yet, when questioned by Socrates, they could not explain what these terms meant. How do we debate or resolve these issues unless we know what we are talking about or what it is we are seeking? Typically, Socrates' method of questioning moved through the following six stages.

1. Socrates meets someone on the street or at a party and begins a conversation with him. Soon Socrates steers the conversation into an area that has some philosophical significance. The genius of Socrates was his ability to find the philosophical issues lurking in even the most mundane of topics.

2. Socrates then isolates a key term on which the discussion hinges and that needs clarification before the conversation can proceed. Thus, the question is posed "What is *X*?" where *X* refers to some property or category. For example, in the *Charmides* the issue is temperance, in the *Laches* it is courage, in the *Lysis* it is friendship, in the *Euthyphro* it is piety, in the *Meno* it is virtue, in the *Symposium* it is love, and in the *Republic* it is justice.

3. Socrates then complains that he is ignorant and confused about the issue and begs the help of his companion in clearing up the matter. Typically, this feeds the arrogance and the smugness of his companion, causing the person to confidently put forth a definition of *X.*

4. Socrates then thanks him profusely for his assistance but says that he needs just one or two more points to be clarified. This leads to an examination of the definition and the discovery that it is inadequate.

5. Typically, the subject then produces another definition that improves on the earlier one. This leads back to step 4, and on close examination the definition is once again found to fail.

6. Steps 4 and 5 are repeated several times until the "victim" realizes that he doesn't really know what he is talking about. Typically, the dialogues end either when Socrates' companion finds some excuse for ending the conversation so that he can get out of Socrates' spotlight or the two agree that they need to seriously continue their search for a solution.

SOCRATES' METHOD OF ARGUMENT

Although a few of his arguments are a little thin, Socrates' methods for disposing of inadequate definitions and theories are fascinating examples of philosophical analysis. Basically, there are three ways that he attacks a definition. First, he sometimes finds a structural flaw in the definition. Sometimes the problem is that it is circular, as in "Justice is what a just person does." Another structural flaw is that a part is identified with the whole, as when justice is used to explain virtue when it is really only an aspect of virtue. Finally, a definition fails structurally when a mere list of examples is offered instead of the defining property that is common to them all. For example, Euthyphro seeks to define piety (or obligation) to Socrates by pointing out that his own actions of taking his own father to court are pious. To this Socrates replies,

> I did not ask you to tell me one or two of all the many pious actions that there are; I want to know what is characteristic of piety which makes all pious actions pious. . . . Well, then, explain to me what is this characteristic, that I may have it to turn to, and to use as a standard whereby to judge your actions and those of other men, and be able to say that whatever action resembles it is pious, and whatever does not, is not pious.[16]

Second, Socrates attacks his companion's position by employing the form of argument we now call *reductio ad absurdum* (or "reducing to an absurdity"). To use this technique, you begin by assuming that your opponent's position is true and then you show that it logically implies either an absurd conclusion or one that contradicts itself or other conclusions held by the opponent. If we can deduce a clearly false statement from a proposition, this is definitive proof that the original assumption was false. Plato provides a good example of this Socratic technique in his masterpiece, the *Republic*.[17] The Sophist Thrasymachus puts forth the cynical thesis that

(1) Justice means doing what is in the interest of those in power. (Thrasymachus's definition)

Socrates then elicits the following corollary to the definition from Thrasymachus:

(2) To be just is to obey the laws of those in power. (inference from thesis 1)

Next, Socrates has him agree to the common-sense observation that

(3) Those in power can make mistakes. (observation)

From this, the following two inferences may be drawn:

(4) Those in power may mistakenly make laws that are *not* in their own interest. (inference from 3)

(5) To obey such laws is not to act in the interest of those in power. (inference from 4)

Finally, Socrates elicits a contradiction:

(6) Therefore, to be just is to do what is in the interest of those in power. (paraphrase of 1)

and

To be just is to do what is *not* in the interest of those in power. (inference from 2 and 5)

Third, Socrates frequently uses the method of counterexample to show that a definition is either too narrow or too broad. In other words, if his opponent is defining some term X, Socrates shows that the definition of X excludes cases that clearly should be called X or he will show that the definition includes cases that are not examples of X. In his discussion with Socrates, Meno puts forth the definition that the virtuous (or excellent) person is the one that has the capacity to govern.[18] However, Socrates points out that while it makes sense to talk of a virtuous child, a child does not have the capacity to govern others. Thus, the definition is too narrow. Furthermore, he points out that the original definition should have said, "The virtuous person is the one who has the capacity to govern *justly*." Otherwise, the definition would allow us to include tyrants among the company of just people. Hence, the first definition was also too broad.

A typical response of those that were the target of this Socratic analysis was given by Nicias (an Athenian general and admirer of Socrates):

> *Anyone who is close to Socrates and enters into conversation with him is liable to be drawn into an argument, and whatever subject he may start, he will be continually carried round and round by him, until at last he finds that he has to give an account both of his present and past life, and when he is once entangled, Socrates will not let him go until he has completely and thoroughly sifted him.*[19]

Some of Socrates' contemporaries compared him to a stingray that leaves its victims numb from its sting, and others said he was like the legendary Daedalus, who could make statues move, just as Socrates makes one's firmly held convictions move and slip away.[20]

Young people flocked around Socrates to see him prick the pretentious, inflated opinions of their smug, pompous leaders. Of course, this did not earn him the favor of the establishment. However, if he often appears to play the part of the classroom smart aleck, it is not hard to believe that he had a genuine love for those he examined. Despite his skill at intellectual gamesmanship, truth—not the humiliation of his opponents—

was his goal. Nevertheless, the process of finding the truth is often unpleasant. If ignorance is like a disease, then pain is sometimes a necessary accompaniment to the healing process. At times, Socrates seems like a chess master who can see the conclusion of the game several moves ahead of his opponent. However, even if Socrates knows where the argument is leading, it would do no good to simply announce the answer to his partner, for Socrates realizes that this will not be effective in the person's life until he discovers it for himself. Much of the time, however, Socrates does not seem to know where the conversation will lead, for some of the intellectual dead ends they discover were the result of suggestions made by Socrates himself. He often insists that he is exploring territory that is as unfamiliar to him as it is to his dialogue partner.[21]

If Socrates' companions rarely get the final answer to their questions, he does not leave them unchanged, for he has forced them to examine their own lives, beliefs, and intellectual poverty. One of his opponents, Callicles, expressed the effect of Socrates on him in this way:

> Tell me, Socrates, are we to consider you serious now or jesting? For if you are serious and what you say is true, then surely the life of us mortals must be turned upside down and apparently we are everywhere doing the opposite of what we should.[22]

Although Socrates rarely arrives at firm answers, he does perform a weeding service. Confused ideas must be uprooted to prepare the soil for healthy intellectual fruits to grow. Even the answers Socrates rejects contain some truth in them, for they draw us closer to the goal. Rather than being like a skin that is peeled off and disposed of to get at the fruit, the initial answers of Socrates and his companions are more like rough approximations that need to be refined.

Socrates' Theory of Knowledge

Aristotle credits Socrates with making two contributions to philosophy: inductive arguments and universal definitions.[23] Inductive arguments, as Socrates employed them, reason from information about *some* examples of a class to general conclusions about *all* members of that class. In trying to understand justice, for example, Socrates examines several cases in which we would call a particular individual's actions just and when we would not. On Socrates' view, when we apply a universal term like *justice* to a number of different, particular examples, one of two things is occurring. One possibility is that the term has a different meaning each time it is applied. For example the word *bank* does not mean the same thing when applied to a financial institution as it does when applied to the edge of a river. But if there was never any common meaning between two applications of a term, then language would break down completely. The second possibility, then, is that the word *justice* refers to some quality or property that is found in all genuine cases of justice. If two actions performed by different people at different times are both just, it is because they share something in common. Socrates believes that the word *justice* refers to a common quality each time it is used and that it can be captured in a universal definition.

In searching for universal definitions, Socrates assumes that particular things can be grouped into certain natural and, hence, nonarbitrary categories. He further assumes that our universal concepts and definitions both allow us to identify the kind of thing something is, as well as to evaluate how well it fulfills its purpose. For example, if I say that "Holmes is a teacher" I am not only identifying the group to which he belongs but also a set of ideals or criteria for evaluating him. Plato later treats these common qualities uniting things as substantial realities, capable of existing independently of the particular things that exemplify them. However, Socrates does not offer us a full-fledged metaphysical theory as much as an attempt to unearth the assumptions and necessary conditions underlying our speech and actions.

To understand Socrates' view of the nature of knowledge and how it is to be obtained, it is important to note that he calls himself "the midwife of ideas."[24] A midwife does not bear a baby herself but merely helps another in the labor of bringing a baby to birth. Thus, Socrates claims that he does not have answers or wisdom to give but can help others find the truth within themselves. A conclusion that can be drawn from this metaphor is that Socrates believed the truth was not something to be found outside of us, through the senses. On the contrary, we already possess the truth, it is deep within us and written on our souls. All we need is assistance in discovering the truth within and bringing it to the light of day. This later became known as the doctrine of **innate ideas** and became one of the dominant theses within the rationalist theory of knowledge. The midwife analogy falls short on one point. Each biological baby is a unique individual. However, Socrates believed that when we pursue his method of dialectical questioning, we would all find within us one set of identical truths and moral virtues. In other words, the innate knowledge he is helping others discover is presumed to be the same for everyone.

Socrates' Metaphysics

As was mentioned earlier, we will not find much in Socrates that falls under the heading of metaphysics. He was too concerned with the more concrete problems of human life to engage in theoretical speculations about the nature of reality. Plato would take up the task of developing the metaphysical underpinnings of Socrates' philosophy. Nevertheless, Socrates did touch on metaphysical topics, particularly in his discussion of the soul.

THE HUMAN SOUL

For Socrates, the most important task in life is to care for one's soul. In many previous Greek accounts, the *psyche* (which we translate as "soul") was the breath of life, while the body was identified with the real person. The soul accompanied the body like a shadow, was useless apart from the body, and had no connection with the thoughts or emotions of the person. After death the soul was thought to exist as a kind of ghost that could be summoned back to prophesy or to take vengeance on the living. However, the soul was not really identified with the original person in many early Greek accounts.

Socrates reversed this picture of the relationship of the soul and the body. For him, the soul was the true self and the body was now merely thought to be its accompaniment.* The body is an instrument that the person uses in negotiating with the physical world. To care for the body and to pursue riches and fame while failing to attend to the soul is like spending all our time and resources polishing our shoe while our foot is infected and rotting from neglect. An excellent soul is well-ordered, has wisdom, and maintains control over the emotions and bodily desires. One must be careful not to read too much theological content into Socrates' notion of the soul. As Gregory Vlastos says,

> The soul is as worth caring for if it were to last just twenty-four more hours, as if it were to outlast eternity. If you have just one more day to live, and can expect nothing but a blank after that, Socrates feels that you would still have all the reason you need for improving your soul; you have yourself to live with that one day, so why live with a worse self, if you could live with a better one instead?[25]

Is the soul immortal for Socrates? In some of his remarks, Socrates seems undecided about this issue. Most of the time, however, he is confident that people survive physical death. For example, a humorous but telling remark occurs in the dialogue *Phaedo*. The very practical Crito asks Socrates, "How shall we bury you?" To which Socrates answers, "As you please, only you must catch me first, and not let me escape you." Thereon he explains that the dead body they will be left with is something quite different from the real Socrates whose immaterial self will swiftly escape both the prison walls and the confines of the body to dwell in "the happiness of the blessed." Even if many of the arguments in this dialogue are Plato's, the playful, quick wit and philosophical punch of the preceding remark are characteristically Socratic. This issue brings into sharp relief the problem of the relationship between the person (including the soul or the

---

*Socrates' account of the soul had many predecessors, such as the Pythagorean philosophy, for example. Nevertheless, Socrates' version is historically important for the powerful way it stated that the body is not the real person.

mind) and the physical body. Plato addresses the problem, and it remains one of the central problems in philosophy.

Ethics and the Good Life

VIRTUE AND EXCELLENCE

The concern of ethics is to determine how we ought to live our lives. In the *Crito* Socrates asserts that the most important goal for humans is not just living but "living well."[26] For Socrates, "living well" is an ethical notion, for it involves some notion of human excellence. Accordingly, in this same passage he asserts that "living well and honorably and justly mean the same thing." To understand how to live justly, therefore, we must understand what constitutes our perfect end or what standard of excellence we should be trying to fulfill. The Greeks used the word *arete* to capture this. It is usually translated into English as "virtue." In our time, to say that someone is "virtuous" suggests that they are very pious or, perhaps, sexually pure. However, for the Greeks the word had a much broader meaning. If something had "virtue," this meant it was good at a particular task or had a certain sort of excellence or fulfilled its function well. Thus, the virtue of a knife is its ability to cut things. The virtue of a racehorse is to run very fast. The virtue of a shoemaker is the skill of making high-quality shoes. While the shipbuilder, the wrestler, the physician, the musician each have a particular kind of virtue related to their specific task, Socrates is concerned with the question "What does it mean to be a virtuous human being?" In other words, being fully human is a task or a skill in itself. Just as we evaluate the knife in terms of the end or function of knives, so we can evaluate people in terms of the appropriate end or function of a human being. By speaking about a good person in the same way he speaks about a good knife, Socrates makes clear that morality arises out of nonmoral, naturalistic considerations. Morality is not something disclosed to us in a religious revelation, nor alien to our deepest interests or our fundamental nature. Instead, he argues that being moral boils down to being successful at the art of living. However, it will become clear that his notion of "success" is quite different from that of the typical Sophist.

Understanding this viewpoint shows us how Socrates would answer the question "Why be moral?" Socrates' view (which was the typical Greek view) is that since being virtuous means fulfilling our nature, it is the only thing that can guarantee our happiness. We will find little disagreement from any Greek moral theorist that happiness is the one end that all people pursue and that it is the one end that needs no justification. Hence, for the Greek, morality would never require a sacrifice of our own interests in the name of duty, because the very purpose of all morality is self-fulfillment. However, for Socrates, this does not mean that life should be lived selfishly. In fact, he claims that it is better to suffer a wrong than to inflict it.[27] Since he went to his death rather than violate his moral principles, it is obvious that he does not equate the good life with simply experiencing pleasure and also that he has a very complex notion of what constitutes one's real interest. The problem is that we can be mistaken about what is truly the good life. In being unjust or pursuing our bodily appetites, we may think we are serving our best interests. However, according to Socrates, in the process of living this way our soul is becoming corrupted and nothing is more miserable than a diseased soul.[28]

KNOWING AND DOING

At this point the link between morality and knowledge becomes clear. Socrates' position is sometimes called "ethical intellectualism," because of the role he thinks the intellect plays in our moral life. According to Socrates, knowledge and virtue are one. Without knowledge, all other virtues (temperance, justice, courage) are useless and may lead to harm.[29] A well-intentioned judge who is ignorant of the law and of the circumstances of the case will not mete out justice. Someone who is courageous because they are ignorant of the danger at hand, will act foolishly. There is not only a necessary unity between the virtues and knowledge, but there is also a unity among all the virtues themselves. Someone who is brave but unjust might end up being a dangerous tyrant. Each virtue requires the others. Plato will adopt all these conclusions and will consistently defend them throughout all his writings.

If every person naturally pursues his or her own good, and being virtuous is what is our good, then it follows that the wise person who *knows* what is right, will *do* what is right. In other words, *to know the good is to do the good*. The person who has learned the art of medicine is a physician. The person who knows what justice is, will be just.[30] The corollary is the startling claim that *no one chooses to do evil knowingly*. "For myself I am fairly certain that no wise man believes anyone sins willingly or willingly perpetrates any evil or base act. They know very well that all evil or base action is involuntary."[31] This view strikes many people as being counterintuitive, for our own moral experience of yielding to temptation seems to count against its truth. For this reason, Socrates' position was criticized by many of his contemporaries. Euripides, for example, a Greek playwright and contemporary of Socrates, had one of his characters proclaim, "By teaching and experience we learn the right but neglect it in practice, some from sloth, others from preferring pleasure of some kind or other to duty."[32]

Although many find Socrates' view implausible, maybe some things can be said in support of it. In the early part of the twentieth century in the United States, there was a notorious bank robber by the name of Willie Sutton. Supposedly a reporter asked him, "Why do you rob banks, Willie?" The criminal replied impatiently, "Because that's where the money is." This illustrates Socrates' point perfectly. The thief believes that money is the supreme good in life. If that is true, then it logically follows that one ought to do whatever is necessary to obtain the supreme good. If banks are where the money is, then robbing banks is good. Hence, the problem with the thief is that he is pursuing false values. He is mistaken about what is truly good. Socrates would argue that it would be inconceivable that anyone could say, "This is not a good goal and it will be harmful to me and make me unhappy, but I choose it nevertheless."

The key to making sense out of Socrates' claim that knowing the good is sufficient for doing the good is to realize that, for him, knowledge is more than simply having information or assenting to certain facts. On the contrary, true knowledge is identical to wisdom. One cannot be a wise person and a moral infant. For Socrates' formula to make sense, we must assume that the person is in the grip of a real personal conviction and that reason controls his or her soul. Moral knowledge is like the art of medicine: it involves practice, skill, and experienced judgment, and not just the acquisition of facts. I may know that pizza is bad for me because I have high cholesterol and high blood pressure. But if I choose to eat it, it is because my intellect is clouded and confused by my physical appetites, and for the moment I think that the immediate pleasure is what is good for me. Nevertheless, Aristotle was not convinced by Socrates' arguments. The former believed that it is possible for moral weakness and an insufficiently developed character to let us do wrong even when we know it is wrong. He complains that Socrates' view "plainly contradicts the observed facts."[33]

Political Philosophy

We will not find a well-developed political theory in Socrates. This task would be taken up later by Plato. Nevertheless, Socrates does express a number of convictions about our proper relationship to the state. Foremost among these was his distrust of popular democracy. Since he ties competence in any task to having the appropriate sort of knowledge, it follows that ruling the state requires a special sort of knowledge that only a few will have. We would not entrust our medical care to the vote of the inexperienced crowd. Similarly, Socrates taught, we should not choose public officials by casting lots or by a popular vote as was common in that time. Only those who have philosophical wisdom are competent to rule. Obviously, this doctrine did not endear him to the popular leaders of Athens.

Generally, Socrates took a very conservative stance toward the laws of society, saying that they merit our total obedience. In the scene described by Plato in the *Crito*, Socrates' friend Crito visits him in prison and tries to persuade him to avoid his unjust punishment by escaping. However, Socrates refuses to do this and, thereby, reveals to us some of his political theory. He argues that we only have two options if we disagree with the laws of our country. We can either try to persuade our legislators to change the laws, or we can register our dissent by lawfully leaving the country and revoking our citizenship.[34] Even though he had been unjustly condemned by his enemies who were administering the law, Socrates believed that if he subverted their decision he would be trampling on the laws themselves and thus wrongfully encouraging disrespect for the state.[35] The principle that guides him is that it is always wrong to return injustice for injustice. Or, as we might say, "Two wrongs do not make a right." When we commit injustice, we are corrupting our own souls and are only ending up worse than before. As he says, "It is a much harder thing to escape from wickedness than from death."[36]

In his trial, Socrates made one exception to his principle of unconditional obedience to the law. Arguing before the jury, he made it clear that he would refuse to obey any order to give up philosophizing, even if obedience would mean that he would be acquitted and disobedience would mean death.[37] However, he saw this situation as different from illegally escaping from prison. His principle in the trial was that his personal god had commanded him to do philosophy and obedience to this god took precedence over the state. Also, continuing to do philosophy would benefit the state, by showing where it was wrong. Finally, continuing to philosophize would still show respect for the law because, even though it would challenge the edict of the court, its public nature would demonstrate a willingness to accept the legal consequences. By contrast, escaping from prison would be an attempt to evade the law by doing an end run around it.

We can find in Socrates two notions of political philosophy in germinal form that became important later in history. The first is an implicit notion of the **social contract theory** of political

obligation. This theory claims that our relationship to the government is a contractual one. We have a tacit agreement that the state will provide certain services for us and, in return, we will fulfill our agreed-on obligations to the state. Accordingly, Socrates argued that we ought to always keep our just agreements. By living seventy years in Athens, he had benefited from the nurture and protection of the state. At any time, he could have left and moved to Sparta or Crete, but he chose to stay. Therefore, even though he disagreed with the judgments of the state in his case, he still felt an obligation to abide by its laws.[38]

The second sort of political theory that appears in Socrates is built around the notion of natural law. The term **natural law** in moral and political theory refers to the claim that there is a universal moral law that can be known through reason and experience. It is not created by governments. On the contrary, governments are deemed just by natural law theorists only to the extent that their civil laws conform to the natural law. Socrates believed that the laws of his society conformed to this universal standard of justice. However, even though his trial was legal in terms of its procedures, he claimed that his verdict was unjust. He could say this because he believed that there were laws above the laws of society. For this reason he imagined these universal laws saying to him that he was "a victim of the injustice, not of the laws, but of men."[39]

Socrates' Legacy

In terms of the doctrinal legacy of Socrates' thought, he influenced the ethical theories of a number of schools. Included among these are the Megarians, the Cyrenaics, and the Cynics (this latter group is discussed in a later chapter). Plato, of course, was the disciple who developed Socrates' insights into a full-blown philosophical system. Having mentioned these movements, however, it is important to note that Socrates is one of those rare individuals in the history of thought whose contribution lay less in his doctrines than in his personality. To be sure, there are plenty of intellectual fruits in Socratic philosophy for scholars to pick apart under their analytic microscopes. Nevertheless, the Socratic dialogues always seem to end abruptly before any definitive conclusions are nailed down. Instead, what he primarily gave us was the paradigm of the philosophical life—the passion to know, the conviction that everything else paled in importance compared to the search for wisdom, and the commitment to follow one's questions wherever they may lead. The history of philosophy took a decisive turn with Socrates. The early Greek thinkers primarily sought to know external nature. Although Socrates acknowledged that there was some value in this, he taught that there was a much more important goal in life. This was nothing less than achieving self-knowledge. To be sure, the Sophists also turned away from questions about the cosmos to focus on the human situation. However, Socrates was able to do this while avoiding the dead ends of their uncritical relativism, subjectivism, skepticism, and cynicism.

In the temple of Apollo at Delphi, where Socrates first understood his mission, was the inscription "Know thyself." This became the motto by which Socrates lived his life. However, Socrates never claimed to have this knowledge but merely the dialectical method of questioning that would lead each person toward this goal. For him, all philosophy began with the confession of ignorance. Only then would we be cleansed of the comfortable and familiar ideas that lead to intellectual and spiritual apathy. In the closing moments of his trial, he left us with the words that have become the driving conviction behind the philosophical journey: "An unexamined life is not worth living."[40]

Questions for Understanding

1. What four causes produced cultural changes in fifth-century Greece?

2. Who were the Sophists? What were the main themes of their philosophy?

3. What distinction is represented by the terms *physis* and *nomos*? How did the Sophists apply this distinction to morality?

4. What did Protagoras mean by saying "man is the measure of all things"?

5. What was Protagoras's view of ethics and religion?

6. What were Gorgias's three theses? What was his point in making these assertions?

7. What position did Antiphon, Thrasymachus, and Callicles take on justice and the laws of society?

8. What did Socrates finally conclude about the oracle of Delphi's claim that he was the wisest person in Athens?

9. According to Socrates, what is the "disease" that can inflict the soul?

10. What is the Socratic method?

11. Why was Socrates so concerned with definitions?

12. What is a *reductio ad absurdum* argument? How does Socrates use it against Thrasymacus?

13. What are innate ideas? How does this notion relate to Socrates' description of himself as a "midwife of ideas"?

14. What is Socrates' view of the soul?

15. Why did Socrates claim that no one chooses to do evil knowingly?

16. Why did Socrates argue that it would be wrong for him to escape from prison even though he considered his sentence to be unjust?

Questions for Reflection

1. What is wisdom? Why did Socrates consider it to be the most important goal in life? Was he correct about this? In what ways are you pursuing wisdom or not pursuing it in your life? What persons in history do you think were wise? Why?

2. Who would Socrates identify as the Sophists in our day?

3. Do you agree or disagree with Socrates' statement that "to know the good is to do the good"? Why?

4. Was Socrates correct in claiming that being moral or living up to the highest standards of human excellence is necessary for happiness and fulfillment?

5. Do you agree or disagree with Socrates' claim that morality is objective and not a matter of subjective opinion as the Sophists thought? Why?

6. Is it ever morally justified to break the law? If so, under what conditions? Assuming that Socrates' sentence was unjust, do you agree with his reasons for not escaping from prison?

Notes

1. Thucydides, *History of the Peloponnesian War*, bk. 3, line 82, quoted in Frank Thilly and Ledger Wood, *A History of Philosophy*, 3rd ed. (New York: Holt, Rinehart and Winston, 1957), 55.

2. Euripides, *Medea*, trans. Gilbert Murray, in *Ten Greek Plays*, ed. Lane Cooper (New York: Oxford University Press, 1940), 326.

3. Quoted by Plato in *Protagoras* 318e, trans. W. K. C. Guthrie, in *Collected Dialogues of Plato*, ed. Edith Hamilton and Huntington Cairns (New York: Bollingen Foundation, 1961).

4. Plato, *Protagoras* 313c.

5. Aristotle, *Rhetoric* 2:24, section 9, trans. W. Rhys Roberts, in *The Basic Works of Aristotle*, ed. Richard McKeon (New York: Random House, 1941), 1431.

6. Quoted by Plato in *Theaetetus* 167c, trans. F. M. Cornford, in *Collected Dialogues of Plato*.

7. Quoted in W. K. C. Guthrie, *A History of Greek Philosophy* (Cambridge, England: Cambridge University Press, 1969), 3:234.

8. Ibid., 3.194.

9. Antiphon, quoted in John Mansley Robinson, An Introduction to Early Greek Philosophy (Boston: Houghton Mifflin, 1968), 251.

10. Ibid., 250–251.

11. Plato, *Apology*, trans. F. J. Church, trans. rev. Robert D. Cumming, in *Euthyphro, Apology, Crito* (Indianapolis: Bobbs-Merrill, Library of Liberal Arts, 1956), 29.

12. Ibid., 35–36.

13. Ibid., 37.

14. Ibid., 26.

15. Plato, *Cratylus* 384b.

16. Plato, *Euthyphro* in *Euthyphro, Apology, Crito*, 7.

17. Plato, *Republic* 338c–339d.

18. Plato, *Meno* 71e–73d.

19. Plato, *Laches* 187e–188a, trans. Benjamin Jowett, in *Collected Dialogues of Plato*.

20. Plato, *Meno* 80a and *Euthyphro* 11b-d.

21. Plato, *Meno* 80c, *Charmides* 165b, 166c-d, and *Protagoras* 348c.

22. Plato, *Gorgias* 481c, trans. W. D. Woodhead, in *Collected Dialogues of Plato*.

23. Aristotle, *Metaphysics* 13:4.

24. Plato, *Theaetetus* 149–151.

25. Gregory Vlastos, "Introduction: The Paradox of Socrates," in *The Philosophy of Socrates*, ed. Gregory Vlastos (Garden City, NY: Anchor Books, Doubleday, 1971), 5–6.

26. Plato, *Crito* 48b.

27. Plato, *Gorgias* 469b.

28. Plato, *Gorgias* 479b.

29. Plato, *Meno* 88a-89a.

30. Plato, *Gorgias* 460b.

31. Plato, *Protagoras* 345e; cf. *Meno* 78a.

32. Euripides, *Hippolytus*, trans. E. P. Coleridge, line 380, in *The Complete Greek Drama*, ed. Whitney J. Oates and Eugene O'Neill, Jr. (New York: Random House, 1938), 1:773–774.

33. Aristotle, *Nicomachean Ethics* 7.1, trans. W. D. Ross, in *The Basic Works of Aristotle*.

34. Plato, *Crito* 52a, 51d.

35. Ibid., 50b–c.

36. Plato, *Apology* 39a.

37. Ibid., 29c–d.

38. Plato, *Crito* 49e–52e.

39. Plato, *Crito* 54b, in *Euthyphro, Apology, Crito*, 65.

40. Plato, *Apology* 38a.

4

Plato: The Search for Ultimate Truth and Reality

Plato's Life: From Student to University President

When Socrates was put to death, his student Plato was not quite thirty. The politically motivated death of his mentor may have been the turning point in Plato's life. As a result of his friendship with Socrates, he had taken up the elderly philosopher's challenge to pursue wisdom in his own life by facing hard questions. At Socrates' trial, Plato and three friends offered to pay a substantial fine to the court as an alternative to the death penalty. But to Plato's dismay, this attempt to change the court's mind failed and his brilliant teacher's life came to a tragic end. Plato's feelings, no doubt, were the same as those he attributes to Phaedo when Socrates breathed his last breath: "Such was the end . . . of our friend, who was, I think, of all the men of our time, the best, the wisest, and the most just." Because of these events, many questions haunted Plato: "What kind of society was it that could not tolerate a Socrates in its midst? What kind of society ought we to have if philosophical wisdom is to prevail in human affairs?" Consequently, he spent the rest of his life trying to answer these questions.

Plato had not always planned a career as a philosopher. Born in 428 or 427 B.C. into an aristocratic Athenian family, he was educated and groomed to become a great political leader. After Socrates' death, however, he decided to devote all his energies to philosophy. Initially, he traveled for a while. Some think he may have made it as far as Egypt. Whether this is true or not, we do know he went to Italy in 388 and to the city of Syracuse in Sicily. On returning to Athens, he founded a school, the first university in the Western world. Plato's school was called the Academy, having been located outside the city walls in a grove sacred to the hero Academus. Nine hundred years later, the institutional heir of Plato's school was still operating, and its fame lives on today, signified by the fact that "the Academy" and "academics" are still terms used to refer to higher education.

Plato spent the remainder of his life teaching and directing the Academy as well as writing philosophical works. Among the most famous of his works was the *Republic*. In this book he argued that society would never be just unless people with philosophical vision became rulers or rulers acquired philosophical wisdom. In 368 and again

45

in 361, he tried to realize this goal by returning to Syracuse in response to the request to educate Dionysius the Younger, the young ruler who had inherited the throne. Sadly, Plato's mission failed, for the ruler was too committed to tyranny and little interested in philosophy. On his second visit, the two did not get along at all, and Plato barely escaped with his life. Plato returned to the Academy, where he continued to teach until he died suddenly but peacefully around 348 or 347 B.C.

Plato's Task: Making Philosophy Comprehensive

Following in the steps of his teacher Socrates, Plato had an intense interest in ethical questions. However, Socrates' fate also taught him that good people will not survive unless society itself is transformed. Therefore, political philosophy was also a major concern in Plato's works. But Plato puts these issues into a much broader context than Socrates ever did. If goodness and justice are sheerly a matter of convention, as the Sophists claimed, then it is useless spending much time thinking about them. However, Plato believed that the answers to our ethical and political questions could be found in an adequate understanding of the nature of reality itself. Therefore, he devoted a substantial portion of his philosophical energies on metaphysical questions. However, we must establish the foundations of knowledge before we can make any progress with the other philosophical issues. Previous philosophers have had brief skirmishes with the problems of epistemology, but Plato was the first to make an all-out assault on these problems.

Theory of Knowledge: Reason Versus Opinion

To understand Plato's theory of knowledge, we first have to understand three positions that he rejects. He was concerned first with the relativism of the Sophists. Contrary to their emphasis on personal or cultural opinion, Plato believed that

our lives and societies must be founded on knowledge and that this knowledge must be universal (true for all people at all times). Second, he tried to disabuse us of our confidence in sense experience. The sort of knowledge we need must be eternal and unchangeable, and we cannot find that in experience. Finally, he argued that knowledge is more than true belief, for it must be grounded in rational insight.

REJECTION OF RELATIVISM

In the dialogue *Theaetetus*, he critically examines the claim of Protagoras the Sophist that "man is the measure of all things." This is a very concrete way of expressing the position of relativism. There is some initial plausibility to this position. For example, the same wind may seem chilly to one person and pleasant to a more warm-blooded person (Th 151e–152c).[1] If you say it is chilly *to you*, you cannot be mistaken about this judgment, and it would be very boorish of me to insist that you are wrong. Each person's opinion about how the wind appears to him or her is equally correct. Protagoras, of course, does not limit his claim to matters of comfort but applies the same sort of argument to all judgments, including judgments about morality. Plato, however, finds the relativist's position flawed. First of all, the position refutes itself. In the *Theaetetus* (171a,b), Plato gives this exchange between Socrates and the mathematician Theodorus:

> *Socrates*: Protagoras, for his part, admitting as he does that everybody's opinion is true, must acknowledge the truth of his opponents' belief about his own belief, where they think he is wrong.
>
> *Theodorus*: Certainly.
>
> *Socrates*: That is to say, he would acknowledge his own belief to be false, if he admits that the belief of those who think him wrong is true?
>
> *Theodorus*: Necessarily.

In other words, relativists do not really believe all opinions are equally true. Relativists believe they are *correct* and their opponents are *wrong* in their opinions about knowledge. Protagoras proposed to teach people what they needed to know and even expected them to pay him generous sums of money for this knowledge. But once the relativists have claimed that their opinions are better than others, they have abandoned their relativism.

Socrates goes on in the dialogue to point out that everyone recognizes a difference between wisdom and ignorance and between true belief and false belief. Suppose your physician believes your foot is broken, and you believe it is not. Does that mean it is true for your physician that your foot is broken, but equally true for you that it is not? Who would have the best opinion on whether a wine will turn out sweet or dry—the keeper of the vineyard or a flute player? Who could best tell if a musical score will be melodious or not—a musician or a gymnastics coach? (Th 178c–e). Plato's point is that not all opinions are of equal value.

REJECTION OF SENSE EXPERIENCE

The second position Plato rejects is one that would later be called *empiricism*. Empiricists claim that we derive all our knowledge from sense experience. However, Plato provides several reasons why we can never derive true knowledge from the data of the five senses. First, sense perception only gives us the world of constant change that Heraclitus described. In this realm we can never say with confidence what is true because it is always in flux. Hence, what is true at one time will become false at a later time. The minute I say, "The coffee in this cup is hot," it has already begun to cool, and shortly my description will no longer be correct. Furthermore, all claims about the sensory world are relative to the perceiver. The coffee I consider hot may seem tepid to you. Similarly, our perceptions are relative to the circumstances. For example, lukewarm coffee seems hot in comparison to iced tea but cool in comparison to boiling water. The dress that looked black inside the store now looks dark blue in the sunlight. If we were limited to sense experience, then the relativism of Protagoras would be inescapable. I could say only what seems to be the case or how things appear to me

and not what is definitely true. Hence, for Plato, the so-called knowledge gained from perception is too fleeting and ephemeral to take seriously.

Plato's second problem with sense experience follows from his conviction that the object of knowledge must be something universal that we can capture in an unchanging description or definition. However, if language only referred to the constantly changing particulars in the physical world, then the meaning of our terms would be in flux and language would not function. Hence, we achieve understanding through universal concepts. To clarify what Plato is saying here, let's perform some thought experiments. First, what would you call the object in Figure 4-1? Most likely, you would say it is a circle. However, Plato says that is incorrect. More accurately, it is an *attempt* to represent a circle. Why isn't it a true circle? Well, if you looked at it through a powerful magnifying glass, you would see that the line is somewhat jagged. The particles of ink are not all equidistant from the center. Furthermore, the line has a width that could be measured in minute fractions of an inch. Also, the line has depth, for it is made up of a layer of ink imposed on the paper. Finally, the ink can fade or the paper can burn, changing or destroying the printed figure. However, the points forming a true circle are perfectly equidistant from the center, have neither width nor depth, and cannot change or be destroyed. The figure is a fairly close approximation of a circle, but it is not a genuine circle. The point is that we cannot see true circularity; we can only know it conceptually, with the mind. This is why mathematicians do not need laboratories to make their discoveries. They use reason and not the senses to study their objects. If you saw a mathematician

FIGURE 4-1

cutting out cardboard circles and *then* measuring them, you would know this person did not really understand what mathematics is all about.

Let's try another thought experiment. Compare the different nations of the world in terms of the amount of justice they exhibit. Or compare the quantity and quality of justice in the United States during the era of slavery with the degree of justice in our present laws and institutions. How are you able to perform this comparison? Can you see justice with your eyes? What color is it? How tall is it? How much does it weigh? Clearly, these questions can apply to physical things, but it is meaningless to describe justice in terms of observable properties. We can see the actions of people and say that those actions exhibit justice or injustice. But we cannot literally see justice itself. Microscopes and telescopes help us to see features of the physical world that the naked eye cannot see. However, there are no "justice scopes" or "justice meters" that will make justice visible.

Furthermore, no nation is perfectly just. We have never seen an example of perfect justice in human history, only frail, human attempts to approximate it. Therefore, our concept of perfect justice could not have come from our experience. Nations differ in the degree of justice they manifest. Individual nations can change in the direction of becoming more just or more unjust. Nations, like all other particular things, are constantly changing. According to Plato, however, the standard of justice itself does not change. Only if that standard is singular and constant can we evaluate the moral changes in a nation. For such reasons, Plato agrees with Heraclitus that the eyes and ears are poor witnesses if they are not informed by the understanding that only reason can bring.

Plato is convinced that if justice is not something fixed that transcends the physical world, then the Sophists are right in saying that moral qualities such as justice are merely sounds or puffs of air. We can put Plato's position into the following argument form:

(1) Either justice is something real and objective, or it is a mere word.

(2) If the second alternative is true, then our moral judgments have no value. There is no real difference between Hitler and a saint except certain sounds we conventionally apply to them.

(3) But statement 2 is absurd. There *is* a difference between Hitler and a saint.

(4) So justice is something real and objective.

(5) That which is real must be either physical or nonphysical.

(6) Clearly, justice cannot be physical.

(7) Therefore, justice must be something real, objective, and nonphysical.

KNOWLEDGE IS NOT TRUE BELIEF

Finally, Plato insists on a very firm distinction between knowledge and belief. Beliefs can be either true or false, but knowledge must always be true. Could we then say that knowledge is the same as true belief? Plato does not think so. For example, let's suppose I believe that at this present moment the U.S. President is telephoning the governor of California. However, I have no grounds for this belief. It is just an arbitrary guess. Nevertheless, it *could* be a true belief by virtue of a fortunate coincidence. Clearly, we would not want to dignify such a lucky guess with the title of "knowledge." We could also imagine that a child has memorized the Pythagorean theorem and knows how to apply it. But if he (or she) does not understand the rational grounds for the truth of this theorem, then it is merely a secondhand true opinion, according to Plato. Even if the child had memorized the proof for this theorem, if he did not fully understand the logic of the proof, he still would not have knowledge. To be knowledge, it must be grounded in some sort of rational insight. For this reason Plato says,

> For true opinions, as long as they remain, are a fine thing and all they do is good, but they are not willing to remain long, and they escape from a man's mind, so that they are not worth much until one ties them down by (giving) an account of the reason why. . . . That is why knowledge is prized higher than correct opinion, and knowledge differs from correct opinion in being tied down.[2]

UNIVERSAL FORMS ARE THE BASIS OF KNOWLEDGE

Following Socrates' method, Plato is honing in on the correct understanding of knowledge by eliminating inadequate conceptions. From what has been said so far, Plato clearly believes that genuine knowledge is

1. Objective

2. Unavailable to the senses

3. Universal

4. Unchanging

5 Grounded in a rational understanding

Having made a strong distinction between the here-and-now realm of sense experience and the unchanging realm of rational knowledge, Plato goes on to show that they are intertwined in a special way. He says that the world of sense experience is not one of total flux or pure individuality. We find that particulars fall into a number of stable, universal categories. If this were not so, we could not identify anything nor talk about it at all. For example, Tom, Dick, Susan, and Jane are all distinct individuals, yet we can use the universal term "human being" to refer to each of them. In spite of their differences, something about them is the same. Corresponding to each common name (such as "human," "dog," "justice") is a **Universal** that consists of the essential, common properties of anything within that category.* Circular objects (coins, rings, wreathes, planetary orbits) all have the Universal of Circularity in common. Particular objects that are beautiful (roses, seashells, persons, sunsets, paintings) all share the Universal of Beauty. Particulars come into being, change, and pass away but Universals reside in an eternal, unchanging world. The rose grows from a bud, becomes a beautiful flower, and then turns brown and ugly and fades away. Yet the Universal of Beauty remains eternally the same.

Plato uses a number of terms to refer to these constants within experience. He calls them "Universals" because they are what is common to all the particulars in a certain category. Sometimes, he refers to "Justice Itself" (or "Beauty Itself" or "Goodness Itself"). Plato uses these terms to suggest that he is talking about the purest embodiment of the quality in question. For example, Justice Itself differs from the deficient, limited versions of justice we experience in human affairs.

Plato frequently uses the term "Ideas" (as in the "Idea of Justice," the "Idea of Goodness") to talk about the objects of knowledge. Hence, this whole discussion concerns what is sometimes called Plato's "theory of Ideas." This wording captures the sense that Plato is referring to nonphysical entities. The Idea of Humanity, for example, transcends the flesh-and-blood individuals that make up the human race. Unfortunately, however, the English term "idea" also refers to the subjective contents of one's mind. In this sense of the term, your ideas no longer exist if you become unconscious. Platonic Ideas, however, are realities that exist independently of the minds that know them. In Plato's account, if there were no circular objects, and no one ever thought of circularity, the objective, geometrical properties of circularity would still exist, waiting to be discovered. Fortunately, Plato uses another term for the Ideas, which can be translated as "Forms." Since this does not have the misleading associations of the former term, we will refer to Plato's account as the "theory of Forms" from now on. Be aware that the "Form" of something does not necessarily refer to its shape. If we are talking about the Form of Triangularity, then shape is a necessary aspect of it. Obviously, however, the Form of Justice has nothing to do with shape.

KNOWLEDGE COMES THROUGH RECOLLECTION

In the dialogue named after him, a young man by the name of Meno confronts Socrates with a paradox used by some of the Sophists to show that the search for knowledge is impossible. Meno states the dilemma in this way:

How will you look for something when you don't in the least know what it is? How on earth are you going

---

*Henceforth, I will capitalize terms such as "Universal," "Form," and "Justice" that Plato uses in a special, technical sense.

to set up something you don't know as the object of your search? To put it another way, even if you come right up against it, how will you know that what you have found is the thing you didn't know?[3]

In other words, if we are seeking the meaning of justice, we either know it or we don't. If we already know what it is, we don't need to seek it, but if we don't know what justice is, how will we recognize it when we find it? The answer that Plato gives is that both horns of the dilemma are true; we both know the universal Forms and we don't know them. First, we know them because they are imprinted on the soul. In other words, we have **innate knowledge** of what is ultimately true, real, and of intrinsic value. Plato believed that before the soul entered the body, we were directly acquainted with the Forms, but on entering the physical world we forgot this knowledge. This explains the second half of the dilemma—why we feel as though we don't have this knowledge. Nevertheless, this knowledge of the Forms is still there, waiting to be recovered through the process of *recollection*. When Plato talks about the pre-existence of the soul, he does so in myths and stories, recognizing that we cannot have detailed scientific knowledge of these states of affairs. The important point, however, is that gaining an understanding of what life is all about is more similar to remembering something than to discovering new data. We have all had the experience of coming to understand clearly something for the first time only to realize that we had sort of known it all along but had not grasped it at the level of full, conscious awareness. It is this sort of experience that Plato thinks illustrates the nature of knowledge. Certain truths are available to the rational mind and can be known independent of sense experience.

How do we trigger this recollection of the Forms? Plato's answer is that we do so by engaging in the sort of dialectical questioning that Socrates initiated. In the *Meno* Socrates converses with an uneducated slave boy who comes to recognize a geometrical truth when Socrates, the intellectual midwife, assists him by means of a series of questions. In the *Phaedo* Socrates argues that we can have a notion of such things as Absolute Justice, Beauty, Goodness, and Equality, even though we

have never seen any of these with our eyes. Sense experience and Socrates' method of dialectical questioning cannot give us knowledge of the Forms, for this is already in our possession. Instead, they remind us of what we dimly knew but could not consciously apprehend.

PLATO'S DIVIDED LINE

Ironically, even though Plato was disdainful of the world of the senses, some of the most revealing passages he provides for understanding his theory of knowledge use concrete images. One of his most famous symbols is his account of the divided line. Plato asks us to imagine the following:

> *Take a line divided into two unequal parts, one to represent the visible order, the other the intelligible; and divide each part again in the same proportion, symbolizing degrees of comparative clearness or obscurity. (R 6.509d–e)*

In his description of the divided line, Plato correlates the degrees or levels of knowledge with the different levels of reality. Although our interest in this section is in Plato's theory of knowledge, it is impossible to separate this from what he also believes about reality. Accordingly, Plato seeks to demonstrate that epistemology and metaphysics parallel each other. As we go up the ladder of awareness, our cognitive state more nearly approximates genuine knowledge. Similarly, the objects corresponding to the higher levels of awareness are more fully real. A diagram of the divided line is shown in Figure 4-2.

As is clear from the figure, the journey of the human mind along the vertical line from 1 to 2 passes through several modes of awareness that correspond to various levels of reality. The continuum from total ignorance (A) to pure knowledge (D) is divided into two main cognitive states, those of opinion and of knowledge. These correspond to the two main levels of reality, which are the visible (or physical) world (A' and B') and the intelligible world (C' and D'). However, each of these divisions is further divided. The lowest level of opinion could be called imagination or conjecture (A). This epistemological state corresponds

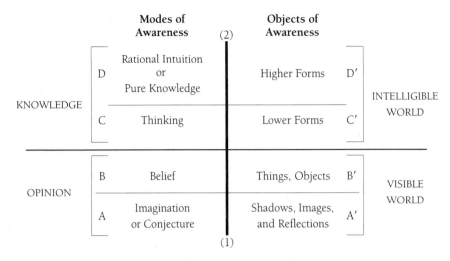

FIGURE 4-2 Diagram of Plato's divided line

to borderline "realities" such as shadows, images, reflections, optical illusions, dreams, and fantasies. Mistaking a desert mirage for water would be an obvious example of a person at this level of cognition and reality. Similarly, someone becoming emotionally involved in the lives of the soap opera characters on television, taking them to be real people, would be another example. However, we can be deceived not only by physical images but also by images created with clever words. Hence, those people who believe the slick rhetoric of a Sophist politician and his false images of what justice is about are trapped at the lower level of the line. They are confusing a distorted shadow of Justice with the real thing.

The second level (B) is that of commonsense belief. In terms of reality, it corresponds to the realm of natural objects as well as cultural objects. A person who recognizes individual horses or particular nations that practice justice but does not see these as imperfect representations of the Ideal Horse or of Perfect Justice is at this level. Such a person can have true opinions, but he (or she) does not have knowledge. This is because he does not understand the reason why things are this way and sees only particulars but not the Forms. There is a ratio here. The reflection of the horse in the water (segment A') is to the physical horse (seg-

ment B') as the entire world of visible things (A' and B') is to the intelligible world (C' and D').

When we have attained the third level (C), we have begun to find our way into the realm of knowledge. It is a transitional stage to the higher realm of awareness and represents the sort of reasoning employed in mathematics and the special sciences. This realm of cognition has two characteristics. First, the mind uses objects in the visible world as a means to arrive at an understanding of the intelligible world. For example, Plato says that the student of geometry uses diagrams and drawings of triangles to prove various theorems. But the visible lines he draws are really not the objects of his knowledge. It is the pure Form of Triangularity he is studying. Second, knowledge at this level is fragmented and based on assumptions that are taken to be self-evident. To be perfected, such knowledge will ultimately have to be derived from a nonhypothetical first principle.

In the final stage (D), the mind soars beyond all assumptions and sensory crutches to a rational intuition of the pure Forms. These Forms are the ultimate principles that we use to derive all subsidiary and specialized knowledge. The final destination of this process of dialectic is the apprehension of "the first principle of the whole." It needs no further explanation or justification and everything else depends on it. Plato calls this ultimate source of knowledge and reality "the Good" (R 7.508e, 518c). The only way we can describe it is by means of an analogy. Think of the Good as the sun, Plato says. The sun makes possible the existence of all living things and enables us to see them. Similarly, the Good is the source of the being and reality of all things and, like the light of the sun, enables our minds to see the truth. The knowledge discovered here cannot be put into words, because the Good is the transcendent source of all partial truths that words can convey. We can only encounter it "after a long period of attendance on instruction in the subject itself and of close companionship, when, suddenly, like a blaze kindled by a leaping spark, it is generated in the soul and at once becomes self-sustaining" (L 7.341c–d). Later Christian Platonists will identify Plato's Good with God. It is important to understand, however, that Plato's Good is an impersonal, rational principle that is the foundation of reality, but it is not a benevolent, anthropomorphic deity.

Metaphysics: Shadows and Reality

THE REALITY OF THE FORMS

Plato's attempt to work out Socrates' insights drove him to pursue their metaphysical foundations. Plato shared Socrates' concern to capture universal concepts in carefully constructed and rationally derived definitions. However, Socrates never had much interest in metaphysics. So he never paid much attention to the question of what sort of reality these Universals or Forms have. Plato, however, argued that if the Forms are the true objects of knowledge, then knowledge must be of something real. Therefore, the Forms must be objective, independently existing realities. What does the mathematician study when she reasons about the geometrical properties of circles? She doesn't examine the circular hoops, rings, or wheels she finds in experience. Instead, with her mind she contemplates the eternal Form of Circularity itself. Circular objects can be changed or destroyed, but what the mathematician studies cannot be changed.

If the Forms are real, then where do they exist? The question is meaningless because "where" and "when" questions apply only to spatiotemporal objects. You cannot ask, for example, where the multiplication tables exist. True, we have them in our minds and write them on our blackboards. But if our minds forgot them and the copies were destroyed, the truths in the multiplication tables would still endure. We did not invent them, but we *discovered* them. Hence, they do not depend on our minds for their existence. Every science and every craft accomplishes its task with reference to the Forms. The biologist studies frogs but is not interested in simply this or that particular frog for its own sake. Instead, the biologist seeks to know what is universally true about all frogs. He seeks to understand the Form characteristic of frogs. Similarly, the carpenter has a familiarity with the Form of Chairness and the Form of Tableness and seeks to instantiate these in his wood.

THE PROBLEM OF CHANGE

Plato was also driven to metaphysics by the unsolved problems that previous philosophers left behind. Looming large among these problems was the problem of change. Like a pebble in one's shoe, it was a constant irritant in Greek philosophy that refused to go away. There is a paradox about change. When you visit relatives whom you've not seen since you were very young, they may say, "My, how you have changed!" But what are they saying? Obviously, they are saying you are different from the way you were. However, you are not different from your younger self in the way you are different from your sister. In some sense you are the same person. You are the same, and you are not the same. Both Heraclitus and Parmenides sought to dissolve the paradox of change with extreme solutions. Heraclitus said that everything in the world of experience is changing and permanence is merely an illusion. Parmenides and his fellow Eleatics eliminated the problem by claiming that permanence is fundamental and change is merely an appearance.

Although their positions were diametrically opposite, both assumed monism, the claim that reality is essentially one sort of thing. If the Hera-clitean position is correct, then knowledge is impossible because there is nothing stable about the world that we could know. Yet Parmenides' solution is not satisfactory either, because change is obviously a fact of life. Plato believes that they are both wrong and they are both right. They are wrong in their monism, because they too quickly assume that all reality is one sort of thing. However, they are each right in describing one-half of the total picture. Plato was a genius at synthesizing the insights of his predecessors. He adopted their insights but modified them to eliminate their weaknesses.

In seeking a compromise between Heraclitus and Parmenides, Plato embraces **metaphysical dualism**, the claim that there are two completely different kinds of reality. His solution is to propose that there is a world in constant flux, at the same time there is a world that is eternal and unchanging. The world of flux is the physical world that we encounter in sense experience. Because it is constantly changing, we cannot have rational knowledge of it. The world that is eternal and unchanging is a nonphysical reality. It is not located in space or time. Plato sometimes refers to this as the "intelligible world" because only this reality is intelligible to reason.

THE RELATIONSHIP OF PARTICULARS TO THE FORMS

At this point, Plato faces the problem of all dualisms. Once you have separated reality into two different realms, how do you understand the relationship between them? For Plato, the universe is not a democracy, for these two kinds of reality are not equal. The physical world is less real than the world of Forms and depends on the higher world. The reality that transcends experience produces whatever order and reality we find in the world of experience.

It sounds strange to us to hear talk about "degrees of reality." After all, doesn't common sense tell us a thing either *is* or *is not* real? Even Parmenides, that great opponent of common sense, would agree. But according to Plato, the objects

of sensation occupy a gray area between the real and the unreal. Maybe it would help to examine some ways in which Plato's notion of degrees of reality finds its way into common experience and ordinary conversation. If we find ourselves stuck with a counterfeit $20 bill, we obviously have *something* in our wallet. Insofar as it is a piece of paper, it has as much reality as any paper does. However, as an example of legal currency it is not a *real* dollar bill. The counterfeit bill is only an imitation of the genuine article. If we have a photograph of someone we love, it is a kind of reality because it sits on our dresser and evokes warm memories within us. But, unfortunately again, it is not the *real* person, only a representation of them. What fascinates us about the picture is that it shares in some of the reality of the person we love. It was directly derived from the person and bears his or her image. Similarly, reflections in a mirror or shadows have some reality, but they are only vague images of something more substantial than they are. To use Plato's term, the photograph and the reflected images *participate* in the realities they represent. The better the picture, the more fully it participates in the real object and represents the features of the original.

Thus far, we have been comparing two physical objects, one of which is a copy of or derived from something else. These examples illustrate Plato's point that something is a lower level of reality if it depends on something else for its existence and bears the image of that higher reality. However, because these examples are confined to the physical world, they do not fully capture Plato's point. To better illustrate his position, let's look at some examples that compare a physical reality with a nonphysical, perfect, reality. I once overheard a frustrated student who had been given the runaround by an unfeeling, inefficient, college bureaucracy in her attempts to register for courses. Her comment was "This is *unreal!*" Plato would say she was comparing the spatiotemporal events in her experience with the way things ought to be. The vision of a humane, caring college, known only with her mind, was the standard against which she compared the present, deficient institution she was experiencing. As a result of this comparison, her school was so far from what a real college should be that she described it as "unreal." We tend to think of ideals as imaginary objects that exist only in our daydreams. But according to Plato, the ideal of a college genuinely serving its students constitutes what a *real* college is. The institutions you and I know are more or less real college communities to the degree that they approximate this higher reality.

Let us look at a second example. We frequently use the term "inhuman" to describe tyrants such as Adolf Hitler. Now, a very dull biologist might respond, "Oh, no, you're wrong—Hitler was human. He had two lungs, a four-chambered heart, the correct sort of chromosomes." But this person would have missed the point. To say Hitler was inhuman has nothing to do with what we would discover in an autopsy. For Plato, to be fully human depends not so much on physical characteristics as it does on one's nonphysical features such as the condition of one's soul, the degree of a person's rationality, and one's values.

We could contrast Hitler with a notable humanitarian such as Dr. Bill Walsh. Walsh was an American cardiologist who quit a lucrative medical practice in the 1960s to start a medical relief organization called Project HOPE. With donated money, supplies, and volunteer labor, he converted a former naval ship into the SS *HOPE*, a hospital ship that sailed all over the world, bringing medical treatment and training to needy people. In terms of Plato's philosophy we could say Walsh was more fully a real human being because of his exemplary moral qualities. Compared to him, Hitler was subhuman. Although he was a great humanitarian, Walsh could have only a partial hold on what it means to be human. According to Plato, no earthly, physical being (human or otherwise) ever attains the perfect reality of its Form, for to be physical is always to be limited, deficient, and changing. Accordingly, we could say Hitler was but a shadow of what a human is, whereas someone such as Bill Walsh is like a very clear photograph. He's not the full reality itself, but a very good likeness of it.

We can now summarize the relationship between particulars and their Forms. First, the Forms are the *cause* of the existence of particular things, analogous to the way a statue causes its shadow. Second, physical objects *resemble* their Forms, analogous to the way a photograph is the likeness of the person. Third, particular objects *participate* in their Forms. Compare the three shapes in Figure 4-3. Obviously, the one on the right participates in the Form of Circularity more fully than the other two. We might describe the middle one as "sort of a circle" because there is some likeness. However, the one on the left falls quite a bit short of the ideal circle. In fact, it falls so short of any recognizable Form that it would be hard to describe. Similarly, if we were to rank humans according to their participation in the Form of Humanity, Adolf Hitler would be on the left, the average person somewhere in the middle, and a saintly person would represent the fullest participation in the Form. Fourth, as the previous examples illustrate, Forms represent the *standards of evaluation* we use to judge particulars as excellent or deficient. Engineers evaluate ball bearings in comparison to the Perfect Sphere, and horse breeders judge their stock in comparison to the Ideal Horse. Finally, the Forms make particulars *intelligible*. Try to describe a close friend. No matter how unique they may be, you must resort to a list of universal qualities to say anything about them (for example, "tall," "brilliant," "female," "athletic"). Without the Forms we could not think, speak, or make sense out of anything.

THE ALLEGORY OF THE CAVE

Plato spells out his theory of knowledge and reality in the Allegory of the Cave, one of the most striking stories in the history of Western literature (R 7.514a–521b) (See Figure 4-4 on page 56). In the story, there is a group of prisoners that have lived all their life in the bottom of a cave where they have been chained so that they can only see the back wall of the cave. Behind them, some unnamed men parade statues of animals and other objects in front of a fire. However, the prisoners cannot see the fire or the artificial objects. They can only see the shadows projected on the wall, and consequently they believe these to be the sum

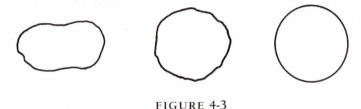

FIGURE 4-3

total of reality. Now imagine that one of these prisoners was liberated. At first the sight of the wooden objects would be confusing and the fire would hurt his eyes. He would be inclined to think that the familiar shadows were the true reality and that what he is seeing now are frightening illusions.

Now if he were dragged up to the opening of the cave and out into the sunlight, he would be even more amazed. The light of the sun would be even more disorienting than that of the fire. Eventually, however, he would become accustomed to this new level of reality. He would see real animals, trees, flowers, and stars for the first time and would realize that these colored, three-dimensional objects are more real than the shadows or even the wooden replicas in the cave. He would now see how pathetic is the life of those in the cave, for their vision of reality is limited to the shadows. Plato imagines they have a practice of awarding prizes and honors to those who are most skillful at recognizing and anticipating particular shadows. However, these honors are worthless to one who has encountered the fuller realities. Plato asks, "Would he not . . . far sooner 'be on earth as a hired servant in the house of landless man' or endure anything rather than go back to his old beliefs and live in the old way?" If this man would return to the cave, he would be the subject of ridicule, for his eyes would no longer be accustomed to the darkness and it would be difficult for him to discern the shadows as well as the prisoners. Furthermore, his former friends would think he had gone mad when he talked of the green grass, the glassy lakes, and the bright sunlight. Finally, Plato says, "If they could lay hands on the man who was trying to set them free and lead them up, they would kill him."

Plato makes several applications of this allegory. First, with respect to metaphysics, the story represents Plato's theory of the levels of reality. The shadows are imperfect representations of the wooden puppets, but these in turn are themselves just copies of real animals, trees, flowers, and so on. Hence, the cave world represents the physical world, a world made up of different levels of copies and images. The land above represents the realm of the Forms, the realities that are only imperfectly represented down below. Finally, the sun represents the Good, that supreme Form that gives life and intelligibility to everything else. In terms of epistemology, the story shows that simply accumulating more and more knowledge of the shadows will not produce understanding. What is required is a new perspective, a higher vision of the genuine realities. Hence, Plato says,

> Education is not what it is said to be by some, who profess to put knowledge into a soul which does not possess it, as if they could put sight into blind eyes. On the contrary, our own account signifies that the soul of every man does possess the power of learning the truth and the organ to see it with; and that, just as one might have to turn the whole body round in order that the eye should see light instead of darkness, so the entire soul must be turned away from this changing world, until its eye can bear to contemplate reality and that supreme splendour which we have called the Good. (R 7.518c)

Just as the person who has climbed up out of the cave is the only one that can really understand the shadows for what they are, so the person with wisdom is one who has mentally gone beyond the physical world and understood the Forms that make all things intelligible. The man in the story

FIGURE 4-4 This diagram of Plato's Allegory of the Cave represents a chained prisoner whose only reality is (A) the shadows, which are projected by (B) replicas of objects, and (in the upper left corner) the steep and rugged passage out of the cave to the upper world. If the prisoner follows this route, he will encounter (C) the world of real objects and (D) the sun. These levels correspond to the modes of awareness and levels of reality on the divided line depicted in Figure 4-2.

who had knowledge of the higher reality and returned back to the cave to free the others obviously represented Socrates (or any other person with the correct philosophical vision). He was misunderstood by the cave dwellers and thought to have gone mad because he was accustomed to living in the other world. Nevertheless, he felt an obligation to try to free the others, even at the cost of his own life.

Moral Theory

AGAINST RELATIVISM

As with much of his philosophy, Plato's discussion of morality is set in contrast to those of the Sophists, the antagonists of his beloved teacher, Socrates. Recall that the Sophists taught that we base our moral norms either on subjective, personal opinions or social conventions. However, if this is all there is to morality, then ethical values will be arbitrarily decided by whoever in society is the most persuasive. In the worst scenario, whoever in society is most powerful will determine its ethical values. Since, according to the Sophists, there are no higher standards of morality beyond convention, it would be impossible to evaluate or criticize the morality of a particular society. Hence, we could not find fault with the Nazi regime when they slaughtered multitudes of innocent men, women, and children, because this simply reflected the values and laws of their society at that particular time. Neither could we say that a humanitarian such as Mother Teresa, who cared for the poor and dying, was morally superior to Hitler. On the Sophist's view, we would have to say that these two people are morally equal in that they each sincerely pursued their own subjective moral code and both received the approval of their society.

Plato, of course, would point out that these conclusions indicate that something is deeply mistaken about moral relativism and subjectivism. Plato's general approach will be to maintain that ethics is just as objective a science as mathematics. In mathematics we explore the nonphysical Forms of Circularity, Triangularity, Equality, and so on. Similarly, in ethics we are concerned with such things as the Forms of Justice and the Good. This may seem like a very big leap. It seems relatively easy to arrive at and agree on the objective properties of a circle. However, even Plato would acknowledge that it is very difficult to get people to agree on a definition of moral goodness. Plato would respond, no doubt, that consensus is not a criterion of truth. The history of science makes clear that it is not unusual for the majority of people to be mistaken. Nevertheless, since mathematical and scientific issues in themselves do not impinge on our ethical choices, it is easier for people to perceive the truth in these areas. With morality, however, our bodily appetites, our irrational desires, and the shadow world of false values persistently cloud our vision and tempt us away from the truth. Therefore, we find less agreement about ethical issues, but this does not prove there are no right answers and wrong answers.

Plato persists in maintaining that if there are not objective, ethical Forms, then the Sophists are right and all moral terms are simply sounds and puffs of air that do not refer to anything real. In this case, human life would be comparable to being adrift in the middle of the ocean with no navigational maps, no compass, no guiding stars, no rudder, and no power. We would have no sense of direction in life and would be tossed about by the waves of our irrational desires and blown here and there by the arbitrary winds of power and persuasion in our society.

WHY BE MORAL?

A large part of Plato's moral theory revolves around the discussion of justice. For Plato, this was a very broad notion. It included a large part

of what we think of when we hear the word *justice*. Hence, it refers to a fair, decent, and correct ordering of society and its transactions. In this sense, we could say that the laws of a society, a judicial decision, or a business deal is just. But in Plato's philosophy the term also refers to the quality within a person who has a well-ordered soul. In this sense, a just person is the truly moral person. The parallel between the just (or well-ordered) individual and the just (or well-ordered) society is important to Plato. As we will see when we discuss his political philosophy, he believes that the principles of moral theory and of political theory are identical.

Justice receives Plato's fullest treatment in the *Republic*. Plato first gives a hearing to the voices of his skeptical and cynical peers, who question why we should even be concerned with justice. Accordingly, the question is raised, "Why be morally good?" In other words, what is the point of being a morally good person? Why should we prefer the just life over a life of pleasure and uncaring self-interest? To lay the groundwork for this discussion, Glaucon (one of the characters in the dialogue) sets out three categories of things that are good. First, some things are good for their own sake and not for their consequences. These would be simple pleasures, such as enjoying a sunset. Second, some things we value both for their own sake *and* for their consequences, such as knowledge and health. Third, some burdensome things we value *only* for their consequences. For example, no one enjoys going to the dentist, but the benefit of having healthy teeth is worth the pain. In which category should we place justice (or moral goodness)? Glaucon points out that most people would place it in the third category. It is "one of those things, tiresome and disagreeable in themselves, which we cannot avoid practicing for the sake of reward or a good reputation" (R 2.358a). Socrates, however, claims the just life falls into the second category. It is the highest sort of good, "a thing which anyone who is to gain happiness must value both for itself and for its results."

To make his point more forcefully, Glaucon tells the story of the magic ring. According to legend, a shepherd by the name of Gyges found a ring that gave him the magic power to become invisible at will. Glaucon asks whether anyone possessing such power would have the moral strength to resist the temptation to steal, kill, commit adultery, or engage in any immorality they desired, if they knew that they could never be caught or identified? To expand on this thought experiment, Glaucon then asks us to imagine two men. One is perfectly unjust or evil, and the other is perfectly just. However, the evil man (being very clever) manages to fool his society and maintains a spotless reputation while committing the worst crimes imaginable. In contrast, the society totally misunderstands the good man. Although he is perfectly just, his society wrongly inflicts him with an evil reputation and persecutes and torments him because of it. Under these circumstances, what would be the point of being just? Wouldn't it be better to be the evil man, who is admired and praised by his peers and receives all of society's rewards? We could expand on Glaucon's question and ask, "What if there were no afterlife or heaven to reward us for good behavior?" Don't these considerations make it clear that the only point of being a good person, the only value that justice has, is the good reputation and the external benefits it brings us (either in this life or the next)? Glaucon summarizes his speech by confronting Socrates with the following challenge:

> You must not be content merely to prove that justice is superior to injustice, but explain how one is good, the other evil, in virtue of the intrinsic effect each has on its possessor, whether gods or men see it or not. (R 2.367e)

Although these questions concerning the value of the just life are raised early in the *Republic*, Plato takes most of the book to provide an answer to Glaucon's challenge. To make clear why being a just person is a goal worth pursuing, Plato thinks it necessary to first give an account of human nature. In doing this, his approach to ethics is typically Greek. He does not begin by setting out a list of dos and don'ts. Instead, he examines what sort of creatures we are and from that extracts what moral goodness is and why it is life's most important pursuit.

MORALITY AND HUMAN NATURE

From his theory of Forms, it should be clear that the universe for Plato is not a chaotic hodgepodge of random objects and processes. Instead, it has a built-in, purposive, rational structure underlying it. According to Plato, we can understand anything in nature in terms of the Form that determines its function. To understand any type of thing, therefore, we must understand what constitutes its perfect end: what standard of excellence it is trying to fulfill. Hence, it would not be too far off the mark to say that for Plato, we derive moral principles from a correct understanding of human psychology.

For Plato, the essential core of the person is his or her *psyche*. This is usually translated as "soul." However, we must be careful not to read too much traditional religious content into that term. Whenever the word *soul* appears, it is best to think of it as referring to the "self." If we examine our own, inner experience, Plato says, we will find that the soul is not completely unified. We find inner conflicts and competing forces warring within us. This suggests that several types of elements or faculties are at work within the soul. Although Plato refers to the different "parts" of the soul, we should not think of these in the same way we think of the parts of an engine. Instead, we might think of them as different kinds of desires, or principles of action, or different types of psychological drives.

To illustrate these divisions, he asks us to imagine a thirsty man who has a desperate craving to drink, but refrains from doing so (perhaps because he knows the water is polluted). This shows that at least two conflicting forces are at work in a person. The first group of drives are the appetites or the appetitive part of the person. These are associated with our bodily needs and desires, such as the desire for food, drink, and sex. The appetites pull us in the direction of physical gratification and material acquisition. However, there is also the more reflective, rational part of the soul, which sometimes vetoes the urgings of the appetites. This is the voice of reason within us. This element also has desires, but these are rational desires. It is the source of the love of truth and the desire to understand. It might seem as though the struggle between these two forces is enough to explain human behavior. However, Plato finds a third element within the soul. This is the "spirited" part of us. The term *spirit* here has no religious connotations. It is used in the same sense that we talk of a spirited horse. This is the willful, dynamic, executive faculty within the soul. The spirited part expresses itself in anger, righteous indignation, ambition, courage, pride, or assertiveness. It is the source of the desire for honor, respect, reputation, and self-esteem. The spirit is associated with the passions or the emotions. It is distinct from the other two drives because we can be moved by anger or by moral fervor, when these are neither physiological drives nor the products of reflective reason. The spirit is a motive force, but it receives its direction from the other two faculties. It can follow the commands of either the appetites or the reason.

The appetites are the lowest and the most dangerous of our desires. They are the voice within us that says, "I want, I want," without regard for the consequences. For example, we may feel the desire for sexual gratification even though, under the circumstances, it would be harmful and irrational to follow through on this. However, if our reason is not in control, the spirit's desire for self-esteem and its pride may cause it to conspire with the appetites, leading us into an unfortunate situation. In contrast, my appetitive part may crave a gluttonous dessert, while my reason (the highest part of the soul) tells me this would not be good. In the midst of this struggle, a third voice within me may express disgust and anger with myself saying, "How can I be such a pig?" This is the spirited part, the intermediate element, reinforcing the pull of reason.

In the *Phaedrus*, Plato captures the dynamic structure of his psychology with a striking image. He presents the picture of a man driving a chariot with two horses (P 246a– b). The charioteer is the rational element of the soul, continually having to control the appetites and the spirited element. The one horse (the spirited element) is eager to obey. He is "a lover of glory, but with temperance

and modesty; one that consorts with genuine renown, and needs no whip, being driven by the word of command alone." The other horse (the appetites) is eager to take control. He continually seeks to run wild and pull the chariot off its path into destruction. He is "crooked of frame, a massive jumble of a creature, . . . consorting with wantonness and vainglory; shaggy of ear, deaf, and hard to control with whip and goad" (P 253d–254e). Only when reason tightly controls the reins can the other two elements be led to pull the person in the appropriate direction.

With this brief account of human psychology in place, Plato can now begin to apply it to the issues of morality. For Plato, there were four primary moral virtues: wisdom, courage, temperance, and justice. Each finds its place within the different elements of the soul. If reason is in control of the person and guides the other parts of the soul, the person possesses the virtue of *wisdom*. Like a military commander or an orchestra director, reason has an understanding of the whole picture and helps the others play out their appropriate roles. Like a parent or a physician, reason knows what is genuinely good for its charges.

If the spirited part subordinates itself to the counsel of reason and applies its energy, ambition, and assertiveness toward the right goals, then the person manifests the virtue of *courage*. The healthy spirit holds fast to the commands of reason and ignores the pulls of pain and pleasure. With the virtue of courage, the spirited element finds its sense of glory only in doing what is right, it fears only what is genuinely fearful, and bravely confronts all enemies of truth and goodness. It does not waste its passions on petty quarrels but rises in anger only at what is morally base.

If the appetites control and moderate their desire for pleasure and subordinate themselves to the two higher elements, then the person has the virtue of *temperance* or self-control. Notice that although Plato tends to downplay the importance of the body, he does not think the ideal is an ascetic denial of the body's needs altogether. If a person, for example, was so obsessed with the desire to study the history of philosophy that she turned a deaf ear to her body's need for sleep or food, this would not be an example of wisdom. Temperance, then, does not mean complete denial of the body's needs and desires, but a sense of balance and self-mastery.

Finally, where does *justice* fit in? It is an overarching virtue that is present when all the other elements have achieved their correct balance within the person. The just person is one who possesses wisdom, courage, temperance and in whom each element plays its proper role and maintains its proper place. Late in the *Republic* Plato uses yet another dramatic analogy to make clear the value of a well-balanced or just soul. He imagines that inside each human is a smaller person who represents the voice of reason. There is also a lion (the spirited part) and a wild, many-headed beast (the appetites). To say that immorality pays and that there is no point in doing right is like saying,

> It pays to feed up and strengthen the composite beast and all that belongs to the lion, and to starve the man till he is so enfeebled that the other two can drag him whither they will. . . . On the other hand, to declare that justice pays is to assert that all our words and actions should tend towards giving the man within us complete mastery over the whole human creature, and letting him take the many-headed beast under his care and tame its wildness, like the gardener who trains his cherished plants while he checks the growth of weeds. He should enlist the lion as his ally, and, caring for all alike, should foster their growth by first reconciling them to one another and to himself. (R 9.588e–589b)

The Socrates of the dialogue adds that a good action "tends to subdue the brutish parts of our nature to the human—perhaps I should rather say to the divine in us." In contrast, evil actions "enslave our humanity to the savagery of the beast" (R 9.589c–d).

Although the single-minded pursuit of pleasure is the obsession of the appetites and must be put aside to seek justice, Plato believes that the highest sort of pleasure and happiness accompanies the attainment of moral goodness. The person in whom wisdom and justice find their home knows the physical pleasures and allows them their proper place. Such a person also knows the

pleasures of honor and reputation and enjoys them to the proper degree. However, out of all the pleasures, "the sweetest will belong to that part of the soul whereby we gain understanding and knowledge, and the man in whom that part predominates will have the pleasantest life" (R 9.583a).

In the preceding passages, Plato, through the voice of Socrates, has made clear the nature of human psychology and the effects that justice and injustice have on our inner selves. Justice constitutes the health and well-being of the soul. Much like physical health, justice is a condition in which all the various elements of the person are balanced and in the right order. In contrast, wickedness is like a cancer of the soul. It is an inner abnormality, deformity, weakness, or a fatal disease that has taken over the person. A character in the dialogue sums up Plato's moral philosophy thus:

> People think that all the luxury and wealth and power in the world cannot make life worth living when the bodily constitution is going to rack and ruin; and are we to believe that, when the very principle whereby we live is deranged and corrupted, life will be worth living so long as a man can do as he will, and wills to do anything rather than to free himself from vice and wrongdoing and to win justice and virtue? (R 4.445a–b)

At the beginning, the question "Why be just or morally good?" seemed like a serious question. But after Socrates has laid out the options, it is like asking, "Why be in control of my life instead of being a slave? Why not be ravaged by the beasts and wild desires within me? Why be in the correct relationship to reality? Why be healthy instead of diseased?" When the question about the value of morality is asked in these ways, we can only reply as did Socrates, "It is a ridiculous question."

Political Theory

THE THREE DIVISIONS IN SOCIETY

The move from Plato's moral theory to his political theory is an easy one. In fact, the two topics are intertwined in the *Republic*. We have separated them only for ease of exposition. When Socrates runs into difficulties explaining the nature of the just life, he suggests they switch to a discussion of the just society since society is like an individual person "written large" (R 2.368d-e). In other words, the principles of psychology and political science are the same. The soul of the individual person is a miniature version of the structure of society and society could be viewed as the individual person projected on a large screen. However, the relationship between the two is deeper than that of simply having a parallel structure. Plato believes it is impossible to live the good life or to be a fulfilled individual apart from the state. Furthermore, a good society is only possible if the people in power are good and live by the light of philosophical reason. The good person and the good society depend on each other. This contrasts with Christian thought, where morality is often viewed as the solitary journey of the individual soul in relationship with God. Plato has a strong bias against individualism, unlike our modern age. There is no place in his society for hermits, rugged individualists, or people who march to the beat of a different drummer. For Plato, the state is like an organism in which each part finds its life in relationship to the whole. In the body it is impossible for an organ such as the heart to be healthy if poisons are circulating in the system or if the organ is severed from the rest of the body. Similarly, in human affairs, persons are organically related to each other and to the whole of society. Our fortunes rise and fall together.

For Plato, the most functional state is built around a division of labor. It is foolish for me to take the time to make my own shoes, because there are skilled workers who are much better at it than I. However, Plato expands this rather obvious point into a whole political philosophy that is highly critical of democracy. For him, politics is a science that should be left to the experts no less than with any craft, skill, or science. To elaborate on one of Plato's medical analogies, if you wanted to know whether you needed open-heart surgery, you would not put it to a democratic vote among your friends, your banker, or your automobile mechanic. Instead, you would seek the wisdom of

physicians who are experts on this matter. Similarly, when it comes to formulating the policies and laws that govern the state, the democratic majority represents those least likely to make an informed decision. If we are concerned with the health of the body, we yield to the advice of the experts. So, when we are concerned with the health of the state, we should similarly seek out those who have the necessary wisdom to govern. These experts must have a vision of the Good. They must know what constitutes true knowledge. Just as a navigator must understand the stars and be able to use them to guide a ship through the vast ocean, so our political rulers must be able to navigate the ship of state by means of a vision of the Forms and the Good. Who else would these political navigators be but those with philosophical wisdom?

> Unless either philosophers become kings in their countries or those who are now called kings and rulers come to be sufficiently inspired with a genuine desire for wisdom; unless that is to say, political power and philosophy meet together . . . there can be no rest from troubles . . . for states, nor yet, as I believe, for all mankind; nor can this commonwealth which we have imagined ever till then see the light of day and grow to its full stature. (R 5.473)

If justice in the individual soul is the balanced harmony of all the elements in the person, under the sovereignty of reason, then justice in the state will have the same structure. Corresponding to the three elements within the individual, therefore, there are three kinds of people within society. Each kind has its appropriate role to play within the state. The first kind of people are the *producers*. These provide the necessities of life and all its material and economic goods or services. This includes such groups as farmers, shoemakers, carpenters, and general laborers. It also includes shopkeepers, importers, and bankers. The second group is originally called the *guardians*. They are concerned with the welfare of society as a whole and protect it from both its external and internal enemies. Eventually, those trained to be guardians will be divided into two further groups based on their abilities. The one group is called the *auxiliaries*. They correspond to our police and military personnel, as well as to the other federal agents and administrators that support and enforce the policies of the rulers. The third and highest group retains the title of *guardians*, and its members are the ultimate rulers of the state. They are a select group, distinguished by their intelligence and philosophical wisdom. Their job is to establish the policies and laws within the society. Since the producers are concerned with material acquisition and physical comfort, they correspond to the appetitive part of the soul. The auxiliaries are those people who are ambitious, assertive, and desire honor. They manifest the spirited element of the soul. The guardians or rulers, of course, represent reason. The parallel structure of the individual and the state is now complete.

We will now make a more detailed examination of each role within society. It is tempting to suppose that the lowest class, the producers, correspond to the Marxist proletariat and suffer all the oppression and deprivation that we usually associate with the underclass. However, Plato's class structure defies all our usual notions of class divisions. Notice that the lower class in Plato's society includes not only the workers but merchants, physicians, businesspeople, and bankers as well. In other words, it includes those whom we would rank in the middle to upper classes in our society.

Ironically, the people in the lower class, for Plato, are afforded the most freedom and economic gain. They can live their lives as they wish, within the bounds of the law. They can marry whom they wish, can own property, and can acquire all manner of personal wealth and luxury, as long as society does not become unbalanced with too much wealth and too much poverty. Furthermore, the power and leadership roles in society are not apportioned in terms of family name, social origins, or gender. Plato thinks it entirely possible that the daughter of a mechanic will be blessed with the intelligence and aptitude to serve as a ruler. And the son of a ruler may turn out to be best suited to be a fisherman. Plato also recognizes that superior women are as equally qualified as their male counterparts to be rulers. This was quite radical for his time, because women were not very highly esteemed in Greek society

and were mainly relegated to domestic roles. However, Plato realized that intelligence and skill in ruling have nothing to do with gender. Thus, Plato's society is a meritocracy (a society based on merit alone). However, a social mobility is possible in his meritocracy that goes far beyond that of most societies that have ever existed. Nevertheless, just as the son of a superior flute player is likely to inherit natural musical abilities, so the offspring in each social class are likely to inherit the skills and abilities of their parents and thus play the same role within the state.

The lower class has the most freedom and physical comfort; the two higher classes (the auxiliaries and the guardians) live very regulated and austere lives. In the early years of life, the children of all classes are subjected to rigorous testing and observation and those with superior abilities and aptitudes are selected. Plato would have been delighted at the battery of intelligence tests and psychological diagnostic instruments our age has developed, since these sorts of instruments are crucial to his social planning.

Plato's *Republic* stands as one of the great classics in utopian literature. The idealism of his vision is inspiring, but most people would agree with Glaucon's complaint that such an ideal community exists nowhere on earth. To this Plato has Socrates reply,

> No . . . but perhaps there is a pattern set up in the heavens for one who desires to see it and, seeing it, to found one in himself. But whether it exists anywhere or ever will exist is no matter; for this is the only commonwealth in whose politics he can ever take part. (R 9.592)

THE DECLINE OF THE IDEAL STATE

Plato was well aware that this ideal society is a very fragile accomplishment. In fact, he calculated the forces that would cause it to fall apart. From the stage of an intellectual aristocracy (which was his ideal) the state could degenerate into a timocracy. This would occur if the rulers come to love honor and ambition rather than the good of society. Thus, the spirited element would take precedence over the rational part. Such rulers will be wary of intellectuals and will be more interested in the glories of war than in peace. The desire for honor could easily degenerate into a desire for wealth. The government would now become an oligarchy or plutocracy in which the wealthy few held the power. As the rulers became richer, the rest of society would become poorer, and the one unified country would now be divided into two groups with opposite interests. Once the passion for wealth is unleashed, then the self-discipline necessary for the ideal state will disintegrate. Finally the dissatisfaction of the powerless poor will reach a turning point, and the rulers will be overthrown and a democracy will result.

Plato has a very dismal view of democracy, for in such a state, "liberty and free speech are rife everywhere; anyone is allowed to do what he likes" (R 8.557b). Instead of the country being run by those who are most competent, a democratic public "will promote to honour anyone who merely call himself the people's friend" (R 8.558b). According to Plato, each of the various forms of government tends to shape its citizens after its own image. By making an idol out of equality and failing to recognize distinctions between people's abilities, a democratic government will encourage a personal stance toward life in which people will believe that "one appetite is as good as another and all must have their equal rights" (R 8.561c).

Plato believes that democracy is unstable, both as a political system and as an organizational principle of the soul, for if we treat every interest and desire equally, then there will be war between them for supremacy. As the different factions lobby for their interests, the ruler will give heed to whichever voice is the loudest and will gratify the masses at the expense of the rich. As the tensions mount, the people will rally around a leader who promises to champion their interests and will anoint him (or her) with power. But to consolidate his power, he will need to suppress all who might challenge it: the courageous, the proud, the intelligent, and the rich. Soon the state will degenerate into a despotism or a tyranny. In seeking to gratify their lust for money and pleasure, the people will have given themselves over to an un-

principled ruler whose only goal is power. Similarly, the democratic individual who gives free reign to all his passions instead of ranking them from better to worse, will find himself the victim of one master passion. Democracy, both as a political ideal and personality type, will lead to political and psychological bondage.

Plato's Cosmology: Purpose and Chance

Just as a society cannot exist unless there is order, so, Plato believes, the universe could not exist without a principle of order governing it. In his *Philebus*, he refers to the regular motion of the heavenly bodies as evidence of a "wonderous regulating intelligence."[4] For this reason, Plato rejects the Atomists' theory that the world is solely the product of chance collisions of moving particles. But what is a more plausible account? He provides his answer in the *Timaeus*, a work that was enormously influential throughout later eras in history. Before setting out his theory, Plato acknowledges (as do physicists today) that it is extremely difficult to arrive at a consistent and precise account of the origins of the universe. The best we can do, he says, is to construct a highly probable theory or "likely story."

Plato starts from the premise that "everything that becomes or is created must of necessity be created by some cause" (Tm 28a). Since the universe is so vast and complex, its cause must be immeasurably powerful and intelligent. This supreme cause is referred to as God or the Demiurge (meaning "Craftsman"). However, unlike the Judeo-Christian account, Plato's God is not omnipotent and does not create the cosmos out of nothing.* Instead, he is like a human craftsman who creates an article out of pre-existing materials by following a blueprint. The raw material the Demiurge works with is completely formless and chaotic, while the "blueprint" consists of the eternal Forms. Like a

---

*For the ancient Greek philosophers, the notion that anything could come out of nothing was unintelligible.

sculptor shaping a mass of clay, the Demiurge imposes the Forms on the malleable matrix of spatial "stuff," which is called the Receptacle.[†] Why did the Demiurge desire to bring order out the chaos? Plato explains that

> He was good, and the good can never have any jealousy of anything. And being free from jealousy, he desired that all things should be as like himself as they could be. (Tm 29e–30a)

The Divine Craftsman's motive is like that of the philosopher whose love of the Forms motivates him or her to bring the Forms to bear on the body of government. Hence, philosophers imitate God by extending the order and excellence of their own souls into the world.[5]

Since the Demiurge imparts some of its nature into the universe, Plato speaks of the created universe as a "living creature." Because it is an organic whole and not a hodgepodge of matter in motion, the universe is harmonious and all its elements work together. Furthermore, it consists of a visible body and an invisible soul, accounting for both its material and purposeful nature. The cosmic soul mediates between the eternal realm of the Forms and the Demiurge, and the changing, perishing physical world. The Demiurge did not create every object in the world directly, but having sowed the seed, he allowed the creative, rational powers of the cosmic soul to carry on the task of creation.

A significant feature of this narrative is that Plato explains the universe in terms of a purposeful order that permeates it. An explanation in terms of a purposeful or a goal-directed order is known as a **teleological explanation**. If I ask "Why are you sitting there?" you do not answer the question by talking about the physiology of your bones and muscles that enable you to sit. Instead, I want to know your goal or purpose for being there. Similarly, Plato thinks that explaining the universe by simply referring to its material elements is insufficient.[6] The order in the world exhibits purpose that points to a mind behind it all.[‡]

Those measures of beauty, goodness, and order found in the world are the result of the Forms and the Demiurge's activity. Plato explains the presence of disorder in the world by postulating an element of chance in the raw material from which the world is fashioned (the Receptacle). Plato calls this chaotic force "necessity" or the "variable cause" (Tm 47e,48a). For Plato, "necessity" is not related to logic, for it is the opposite of mind or rationality. Instead, it is a purposeless, random cause. Hence, while faulting the Atomists for ignoring the presence of purpose and intelligence in the cosmos, Plato did concede that some things just happen through blind chance. The world as we know it came about through a struggle or negotiation between the rational power of the Demiurge and the irrational, unruly nature of the raw materials. The mind of the Demiurge "persuaded necessity to bring the greater part of created things to perfection" and "through necessity made subject to reason, this universe was created" (Tm 48a).

The thesis that the material aspect of the world is basically irrational has three implications. First, matter resists the imposition of order, making the complete perfection of the physical universe a metaphysical impossibility, even for the God-like Demiurge. Second, this ingredient of chance or randomness in the physical world prevents us from making it fully intelligible or understanding it to the degree that we do mathematical objects. Third, since only beauty, goodness, and order come from the Forms, the intrinsic irrationality of matter and its continuous deviation from the Divine order is the source of all evil, both in humanity and nature.

Evaluation and Significance

Although almost every one of Plato's philosophical claims has been subjected to critical scrutiny,

---

[†]Scholars are divided as to whether Plato believes that the world began with an actual creative event or whether the creative production of the world is an ongoing eternal process.

[‡]Following Plato's example, Aristotle developed a teleological (purposeful) account of the universe. Similarly, Thomas Aquinas (thirteenth century A.D.) used the teleological nature of the universe as an argument for God.

his theory of the Forms has received the most attention. Since this theory is central to his view of knowledge, ethics, and politics, it will be worthwhile to take a closer look. The theory is a testimony to Plato's greatness as a philosopher, for he anticipated most of the major objections to his account of the Forms. He discusses three significant problems in his dialogue titled the *Parmenides.** The first problem concerns the question "Are there Forms of everything?" Plato has discussed the Forms of Beauty, Justice, Goodness, and other exalted concepts, but the Parmenides of the dialogue asks if there are Forms of hair, mud, filth, and disgusting things as well. Since these objects exist in the physical world, have definite properties, and can be discussed, it seems to follow that we understand them only because of the Forms they represent. Yet this admission would detract from the notion that the Forms represent ideals of perfection. Surely there can be no standards of excellence for disgusting objects. The second problem concerns the relationship between the Forms and particulars. How does the one Form of Humanity distribute itself over many particular individuals? Is the Form divided among the particulars like a birthday cake? Since a Form cannot be broken into smaller chunks, this answer will not do. Does the whole Form reside in each particular? This would deny the transcendence of the Forms that was so important to Plato. The Socrates of the dialogue replies that the sunlight is one, single light, yet it covers and illuminates everything without itself being diminished. Parmenides counters with a similar analogy of one sail spread over a number of people. He points out that, strictly speaking, only a fraction of the sail covers each person. Therefore, this analogy brings us back to the problematic position of each person participating in only a fraction of the Form of Humanity.

The third problem has been given the name "the Third Man Argument." According to Plato's philosophy, we identify Harry and Robert as both

males because they both participate in the same Form. But if the Form of Man is responsible for what is common between Harry, Robert, and all other men (the first level), then what accounts for their similarity to this universal Form of Man (the second level)? We would have to posit a Super-Form of Man (a Third Man) to explain what they have in common with the first Form. Obviously, this process would go on forever and so nothing ever gets explained.

Some have said that Plato's whole problem started when he made the realm of the Forms completely separate from the physical world of particulars. Once this dualism is in place, then it becomes hard to bridge the chasm between the world we live in and the transcendent world of Forms. Furthermore, by making the Forms so detached from the here and now, he seemed to downgrade the value of our individual, earthly existence. Individual things have value and meaning only in so far as they represent the universal, abstract Forms. To make matters worse, Plato's otherworldliness diminishes the value of the natural sciences. Science, as we think of it, studies physical nature. But to Plato, the physical aspect of the world is messy, changing, and unintelligible. Only when we contemplate the eternal Forms do we achieve knowledge. Plato's student, Aristotle, later took these problems as his agenda and tried to extract what was of value in his teacher's theory while avoiding its difficulties.

Despite some of the problems that Plato never resolved, his theory of the Forms turned out to be one of the most profound and far-reaching ideas in the history of thought. For this reason the philosopher and historian Alfred North Whitehead has said that "the safest general characterization of the European philosophical tradition is that it consists of a series of footnotes to Plato."[7] Although this may be somewhat of an overstatement, it is still true that the story of Western intellectual history is unintelligible without an understanding of Plato. Philosophers can be divided into two groups according to whether they find Plato's theory illuminating or an unfortunate mistake. In either case, philosophers through the centuries have inevitably found it necessary to come to terms with Plato's thought.

*The historical Parmenides never encountered Plato's theory. His character is used in this account as means of raising these issues with the character of Socrates.

Questions for Understanding

1. How does Plato argue against relativism?

2. What problems does Plato have with the view that knowledge is based on sense experience?

3. Why would Plato say that it is impossible to draw a circle?

4. Why is knowledge something more than simply having true beliefs?

5. Summarize Plato's requirements for genuine knowledge.

6. What are Universals or Forms according to Plato?

7. Why does he think there must be such Forms?

8. According to Plato, what is innate knowledge, and how do we acquire it?

9. Draw Plato's Divided Line. Explain the different modes of awareness and how they relate to the different objects of awareness.

10. What is the Good in Plato's system and what is its relationship to the world and knowledge?

11. Why does Plato believe the Forms are real and not simply ideas in our heads?

12. How does Plato explain change?

13. What is metaphysical dualism?

14. What are the various ways Plato explains the relationship between the Forms and particular things?

15. Explain what Plato means when he says there are degrees of knowledge.

16. Explain the various points Plato is making in the Allegory of the Cave.

17. What is moral relativism and why does Plato reject it?

18. What is Glaucon's view of the nature of morality?

19. What are the parts of the soul? How does each one function?

20. Given Plato's view of human psychology, what does this tell us about how to live well?

21. What is Socrates' and Plato's answer to the question "Why be moral?"

22. What are the three divisions in society, and how do they relate to Plato's theory of human nature?

23. What is the ideal society according to Plato?

24. What sorts of changes would cause a decline in the perfect society?

25. Why is Plato opposed to democracy?

26. What is the Demiurge in Plato's view of the universe? What is its function? How is it similar to and different from the Judeo-Christian view of God?

27. What is a teleological explanation?

28. What are some problems in Plato's theory of the Forms?

Questions for Reflection

1. Develop your own argument for or against Plato's thesis that the nature of Justice is objective and independent of what subjective notions we have of it. Furthermore, argue for or against his view that Justice is something real even though it is not physical.

2. Thinking about Plato's Allegory of the Cave, what are the shadows in our society? When have you had the experience of discovering that something you thought was important was really a shadow? What caused you to discover this?

3. Argue for or against Glaucon's view of morality.

4. Do you think Socrates and Plato give a satisfactory reason for being moral? Why?

5. Would you like to live in Plato's ideal society? Why or why not?

6. Would Plato be happy or unhappy with our current culture? Why?

7. In what ways is Plato's view of the world and human life similar to and different from traditional religious views with which you are familiar?

Notes

1. Unless indicated otherwise, references to Plato's works will be made in the text using the following abbreviations:

L   *Letters*, trans. L. A. Post, in *Collected Dialogues of Plato*, ed. Edith Hamilton and Huntington Cairns (New York: Bollingen Foundation, Pantheon Books, 1961). References will be made using the numbers of the letter and section.

P   *Phaedrus*, trans. R. Hackforth, in *Collected Dialogues of Plato*. References are made using the section numbers.

R   *The Republic of Plato*, trans. Francis MacDonald Cornford (London: Oxford University Press, 1941). References are made using the book and section numbers.

Th   *Theaetetus*, trans. F. M. Cornford, in *Collected Dialogues of Plato*. References are made using the section numbers.

Tm   *Timaeus*, trans. Benjamin Jowett, in *Collected Dialogues of Plato*. References are made using the section numbers.

2. Plato, *Meno* 98a, in *Five Dialogues: Euthyphro, Apology, Crito, Meno, Phaedo,* trans. G. M. A. Grube (Indianapolis: Hackett, 1981), 86.

3. Plato, *Meno* 80d, trans. W. K. C. Guthrie, in *Collected Dialogues of Plato*, ed. Edith Hamilton and Huntington Cairns (New York: Bollingen Foundation, Pantheon Books, 1961), 363.

4. Plato, *Philebus* 28d–e, trans. R. Hackforth, in *Collected Dialogues of Plato,* 1106.

5. Terence Irwin, *Classical Thought,* A History of Western Philosophy:1 (Oxford: Oxford University Press, 1989), 112.

6. *Phaedo,* 98c–e.

7. Alfred North Whitehead, *Process and Reality: An Essay in Cosmology* (New York: Harper Torchbooks, Harper & Brothers, 1957), 63.

5

Aristotle:
Understanding the
Natural World

Aristotle's Life: Biologist, Tutor, and Philosopher

After Sparta's defeat of Athens at the end of the Peloponnesian War in 404 B.C., the Greek city-states were gradually torn apart by continual conflict. As Greece became weaker and fragmented, the nearby empire of Macedonia became stronger until the Greek city-states were conquered by Philip of Macedon in 338. From Macedonia would later come the military genius of Alexander the Great (Philip's son), who would conquer the known world at that time. But this province would also produce the philosophical genius of Aristotle, whose ideas would conquer vast expanses of intellectual territory. Alexander's kingdom would eventually crumble, but in the twentieth century, after the passage of over twenty-three hundred years, Aristotle's ideas still maintain their hold on significant portions of the philosophical landscape.

Aristotle was born in 384 B.C. in the Macedonian town of Stagira. Following a long family tradition, Aristotle's father, Nicomachus, was a physician to Amyntus II, the king of Macedonia. It is not unlikely that the scientific, empirical flavor

of Aristotle's philosophy, his attention to detail, and his skills at classifying and analyzing the features of nature were inspired by his father's profession. Around age eighteen, Aristotle sought out the best education offered in his day and became a student in Plato's Academy in Athens. He studied and taught there with Plato for twenty years until the latter's death around 348. Plato was succeeded by his nephew, Speusippos, a mathematician who single-mindedly pursued the mathematical side of Plato's teachings. Whether or not Aristotle was repelled by this new emphasis, we can only speculate. We do know anti-Macedonian feelings were emerging in Athens, making it an uncongenial atmosphere for Aristotle. Consequently, Aristotle left the Academy and Athens. He spent several years traveling around the Greek islands, doing research in marine biology. In 342 he was summoned to the Macedonian court by King Philip, who had been a prince in Aristotle's childhood. The philosopher was asked to become a tutor to thirteen-year-old Alexander, the royal heir. A few years later, Aristotle's student inherited the empire and realized his father's dream of extending its dominion to the boundaries of the known world. According to one story, Alexander instructed his troops to collect biological specimens and send them back to his former tutor while they were on military expeditions to the remote corners of the world.

In 335 Aristotle returned to Athens and founded his own school and research institute, which became a rival to the Academy. It was named the Lyceum because it was near the temple of the god Apollo Lyceus. For the next twelve years he directed the scientific research there and wrote most of his major works. The research in the Lyceum ranged over a wide variety of fields, including natural science and history. It contained an extensive library, a museum, and both live and preserved collections of plants and animals.

When Alexander the Great died in 323, a wave of anti-Macedonian rage swept through Athens. Aristotle feared that his associations with Alexander would put him in danger. Remembering the fate of Socrates, but feeling no need to be a martyr, Aristotle fled the city "lest the Athenians should sin twice against philosophy." He died the following year. We have a copy of his will that underscores his reputation for having a generous and affectionate nature. In it, he refers to his happy family life and provides for the future of his wife, children, and servants. He had married a woman named Herpyllis after the death of his first wife, Pythias. While expressing affection for Herpyllis, he requested to be buried next to Pythias.

Plato and Aristotle

Focusing on Aristotle provides an interesting case study of the way in which philosophical ideas develop. To understand his agenda, we need to understand the relationship between his vision of philosophy and that of his teacher, Plato. On the one hand, the impact of Plato on his most famous disciple could never be erased. Throughout his philosophical writings, Aristotle sought to give more coherent and satisfactory solutions to the problems his teacher addressed. Soon after his teacher's death, Aristotle praised him as a man "whom bad men have not even the right to praise, and who showed in his life and teachings how to

be happy and good at the same time."[1] On the other hand, Aristotle was a powerful, independent, and innovative thinker. He was not content simply to repeat the ideas of his beloved teacher. He cautiously modified some of them and vigorously refuted and rejected others. In his work on ethics, he tenderly expresses the necessity of following the truth even if it means painfully dismissing ideas introduced by Plato, his close friend:

> It would perhaps be thought to be better, indeed to be our duty, for the sake of maintaining the truth even to destroy what touches us closely, especially as we are philosophers or lovers of wisdom; for, while both are dear, piety requires us to honour truth above our friends. (NE 1.6)[2]

Initially, the most striking difference between the two thinkers seems to be their style and temperament. The sorts of words that are commonly used to describe Plato are *idealistic, inspiring, otherworldly, perfectionist*. In contrast, Aristotle is described as *realistic, scientific, this-worldly,* and *pragmatic*. Although some of these contrasts are based on differences in the content of their philosophies, many are responses to their writing style. However, due to a historical accident, the obvious stylistic differences in their publications are misleading. We know that Plato gave technical lectures to advanced philosophy students in the Academy. However, there is no written record of these. Instead, the only manuscripts of Plato we have are his dialogues, which were designed to make his philosophy popular among a lay audience. Although these rank as some of the greatest works in world literature, they give us only a one-sided view of Plato's style. In contrast, all we have of Aristotle's works are his technical writings. We are told Aristotle also wrote some very elegant dialogues, but these have not been preserved for us. Many of the works that endured were detailed lecture notes not intended for publication. Consequently, they lack the grace and literary flourish of Plato's conversational writings. Nevertheless, the reader who is willing to work through Aristotle's careful arguments will find that they contain, as the philosopher Schopenhauer said, a sort of "brilliant dryness."[3]

© Bettmann/CORBIS

In this detail from Raphael's School of Athens, *the artist subtly depicts the philosophical differences between Plato and Aristotle. Plato is pointing upward to the transcendent world of Forms, while Aristotle is gesturing toward the here-and-now world of nature.*

Beyond these literary differences, there are a number of other more substantive differences between the two thinkers. It has been said that everyone is either a Platonist or an Aristotelian. Although we should not ignore their similarities, the two thinkers present us with different visions of the world and different convictions as to how it should be approached. Some people, because of their temperament or philosophical convictions, tend to be more sympathetic to Plato's speculative flights toward the ideal reality that transcends the mundane, here-and-now world. Others find Aristotle's down-to-earth approach—carefully cataloguing and analyzing the world as we experience it—to make more sense. The late-eighteenth-century poet Goethe described Plato's philosophy as a tongue of flame shooting up to heaven and

Aristotle's philosophy as a pyramid built on a broad, earthly base that rises systematically to its highest point. To see their differences, note that Plato often looks to mathematics as his model of knowledge. Mathematics deals with perfect, ideal entities such as circles, which can most fully be understood by reason and not through the senses. This model characterizes his approach to everything from art to politics. Aristotle, however, favored the science of biology. Biology involves reasoning about entities that are given to us in concrete experience. The world the biologist studies is a world that is constantly changing, and understanding these changes is an important part of the science. At some point, the biologist goes beyond the individual real specimens in her laboratory to formulate the universal characteristics, principles, and laws the specimens exemplify. Nevertheless, all universal knowledge arises out of and is used to make sense of the changing world of particulars.

Whether one takes mathematics or biology as the paradigm of knowledge will affect how one goes about doing philosophy. For this reason, Aristotle's method and conclusions differ greatly from Plato's. For example, Plato approaches political life by setting out a vision of the ideal society. Plato argues that anything less than this will be inferior. Consequently, he predicts the various stages of deterioration that will occur if there is any deviation from the perfect ideal. When confronted with the obvious complaint that it is unlikely this perfect state will ever exist, Plato has Socrates counter that it does not matter. We must still think in terms of perfection, he says. By way of contrast, Aristotle supported his political philosophy with a survey of some 158 constitutions of actually existing states. He arranged these in a series of general categories and examined which political structures work best in which circumstances. Although he concludes that some societies are clearly better than others, Aristotle never gives us one formula that all societies must follow. Both the similarities and the differences between Plato and his student indicate that Aristotle's philosophy was driven by the struggle to preserve what was of value in Plato's system while avoiding its shortcomings.

Theory of Knowledge: Finding Universals Within Particulars

ARISTOTLE'S APPEAL TO EXPERIENCE

We will begin our exploration into Aristotle's philosophy with his theory of knowledge. This starting point is appropriate, for Aristotle's all-consuming passion is to know and to understand the world in which he lived. Furthermore, he believes that such a project is intrinsic to being a member of the human species. He begins his *Metaphysics* by optimistically asserting that "All human beings by nature desire to know." He gives us a clue as to his basic orientation by claiming that the evidence that we desire to know is found in "the delight we take in our senses; for even apart from their usefulness they are loved for themselves." Hence, the source of knowledge is found in our immersion in sense experience. If we employ the correct method, we will rise from the level of sense data to theoretical or scientific knowledge. However, "science" is a much broader word for Aristotle than for us today, who associate it with laboratories filled with test tubes and spectrometers. For Aristotle, "science" means, quite simply, rational discourse. When we truly know something, we can say what it is and why it is the way it is. A person who knows the ultimate causes and principles governing things has wisdom.

Aristotle has quite a different view of science from Plato. For Plato, there could be no science of the physical things that our senses reveal because they are changing and too imperfect. Aristotle, however, says that knowledge begins with a study of particular things. Thus, he thinks it is a mistake to study an abstract quality in isolation from its concrete exemplifications. For example, "Musicalness cannot exist unless there is someone who is musical" (M 5.11). In other words, if we want to study "musicalness" we had better take a close look at musicians and what they do. Again, he says that a doctor does not attempt to cure the Form of Man but only individual men, such as Callias and Socrates (M 1.1). Plato urged his students to turn away from the realm of particulars,

but Aristotle says that someone who is full of theory but lacks experience of the relevant particulars is deficient in his or her knowledge. Knowledge, therefore, begins with experience of particular things. But this alone does not tell the whole story. Having knowledge is more than having sensations and more than simply being familiar with a collection of individual facts. The dog experiences the smells, the textures, and the tastes of things in its experience (such as its stash of bones), but does not have genuine knowledge. Science goes beyond knowledge of particular facts to show how these particular facts follow from more fundamental truths.

To understand how Aristotle conceives of science, we can contrast an artist's, a gardener's, and a scientist's interest in a tree. The artist revels in the individuality and particularity of the tree. She is fascinated with the play of colors in its leaves, the particular twists and turns of its limbs, and the unique textures of its bark. However, her acquaintance with this particular tree lacks the sort of generality necessary for scientific knowledge. The gardener has somewhat more knowledge, because he knows what fertilizers make trees flourish and how to prune them to increase their fruit. We could call this "recipe knowledge." It has the form "If you do this, then that will happen." He has a knowledge of what works, but doesn't fully understand why it works. Now, when the scientist tries to understand a tree, she is not interested in *this* particular tree as such. She wants a general understanding of trees in terms of their universal characteristics. To understand what is essential to being a tree, she mentally sifts out what is irrelevant and what is unique to this particular case. In Aristotle's terms, the scientist abstracts the essence of the tree from its accidental features. Furthermore, the scientist is not content to simply know what works. She wants to be able to account for how each fact fits into a system of facts and to understand the causes for each. For Aristotle, a scientific account shows that a particular fact could not be other than it is.

True scientific knowledge, then, is not a catalogue of facts. It inquires into the universal nature of things and finds the necessary connections among them. This requires a knowledge of the ultimate principles from which particular facts can be derived. This establishes what seems an extraordinarily high goal for science. Today's scientists are content with knowledge of probabilities. For Aristotle, however, the structure of true science is like that of geometry. It consists of necessary truths demonstrated from self-evident axioms and definitions that compose a complete deductive system.

LANGUAGE, THOUGHT, AND REALITY

One of Aristotle's fundamental convictions is that the structures of language, thought, and reality are the same. He never doubts that we do have knowledge and that the structures of human knowledge are congruent with the structures of reality. How else could our minds ever come to know or understand nature if there were not some sort of affinity between them? When we reason from one proposition to another proposition, we are not simply going from one mental item to another. Instead, we are going from one piece of information about the world to other facts that are true of the world. We need to add language to this harmonious picture. How could we even begin to speak about the world unless there is an affinity between language and reality? Thus the structure of language (in Aristotle's case, the Greek language) more or less divides reality at its joints. Language is important because knowledge does not consist of a mute, mystical insight but in the ability to discourse intelligently about the world. Language must have the same structure as thought, for how else could we put our thoughts into words?

THE ESSENTIAL CATEGORIES

Given this conviction, the task is now to uncover the basic structures of language, thought, and reality. According to Aristotle, the way we understand things is revealed by the sorts of assertions we can make about anything. These will reveal not only the categories of our thought and language but the categories of reality as well. In his most complete account, Aristotle gives us a list of ten categories.

For purposes of exposition, we can view them as ten kinds of questions we can ask about something (see Figure 5-1).

The first category of substance is unique among all the others that follow after it. Substances are individual things such as Socrates, Mount Olympus, Fido the dog, or the tree in my backyard. Substances have the characteristic that "they are the entities which underlie everything else, and . . . everything else is either predicated of them or present in them" (C 5). We can ask, "Where is Socrates?" "What is he like?" or "What is he doing?" The answers to the last two questions might be "Socrates is bald" and "Socrates is talking." Socrates is the subject that is the locus of many different properties and activities. However, the reverse is not the case. We could not say "Talking is Socrates." Furthermore, while Socrates would still exist whether or not he was bald or talking, baldness and talking cannot exist unless they are present in some subject or another. Hence, substances are defined by the role that they play in statements. They are the subject of assertions to which predicates (or the other nine categories) are applied. They are also distinguished by the role they play in reality. They have independent existence while the other categories can only exist insofar as they are present in some substance.

THE DISCOVERY OF LOGIC

To be more than a mere list of facts, science must employ reasoning. This is a process by which we acquire new information from information that we already have. However, for reasoning to be useful it must follow a procedure that guarantees that true information will always yield more true information and never a false conclusion. Aristotle was the first person to discover the rules of reasoning that we now call logic. His work on logic was so complete that very few modifications were made to it until the late nineteenth century.

Aristotle's logic concerned the ways in which we reason about the relationships between categories. We can make four kinds of assertions about the relationship between two categories. For example, we can say (1) "All students are poets,"

Questions	Typical Answers	Categories
1. What is it?	(a tree, a man)	Substance
2. How large is it?	(30 ft. or 6 ft. tall)	Quantity
3. What is it like?	(cone-bearing, wise)	Quality
4. How is it related?	(double, half, greater)	Relation
5. Where is it?	(in the Grove)	Place
6. When does (did) it exist?	(yesterday, today)	Time
7. What position is it in?	(leaning, sitting)	Position
8. What condition is it in?	(flowering, clothed)	State
9. What is it doing?	(growing, talking)	Action
10. How is it acted on?	(being burned, being arrested)	Passivity

FIGURE 5-1 Aristotle's ten categories

or (2) "No students are poets," or (3) "Some students are poets," or (4) "Some students are not poets." These different kinds of individual statements can be related together to form arguments. In an **argument**, the arguer claims that one set of statements, the premises, provide reasons for believing another statement, the conclusion. One of the most common forms of arguments, and the form that Aristotle analyzed, is the syllogism. A syllogism is an argument that is composed of two premises that lead to a conclusion. For example, we could argue that

All mothers are females.

Some parents are not females.

Therefore, some parents are not mothers.

This is a *valid* argument, which means that the conclusion necessarily follows from the premises. Thus, if the premises are true, the conclusion will always be true. Aristotle's great genius was in realizing that the validity of the reasoning does not depend on the content but on the structure of the argument. Thus he showed we could replace the category terms with symbols and the argument would still be valid. This was the first attempt in history to represent reasoning by means of symbols. Reduced to its skeletal structure, the preceding argument reads

All P are M.

Some S are not M.

Therefore, some S are not P.

In this argument, if you consistently substitute any other terms in place of the original ones and if the premises are true, this form of argument will always give you a true conclusion. However, Aristotle showed that some forms of reasoning are not valid. They do not reliably lead you from true information to a true conclusion. Consider this argument:

All mothers are parents.

Some parents are professors.

Therefore, some mothers are professors.

In this particular example, the premises are both true and the conclusion *happens* to be true. Nevertheless, the conclusion does not follow logically from the premises. This can be shown by substituting the word "fathers" for "professors." You will find that the premises are still true, but now the argument allows you to reason to a false conclusion. If this can occur, we say the argument is *invalid*. Just as the relationship between form and content is important in logic, so the relationship between form and content (or matter) plays an important role in Aristotle's metaphysics.

FIRST PRINCIPLES

Aristotle points out that not everything can be deductively demonstrated. If we insisted on demonstrating everything, we would end up in an infinite regress. So before we can deductively prove anything, we must start with premises or axioms that stand on their own two feet and do not depend on anything else. Aristotle calls these the "first principles." How do we arrive at these first premises for all knowledge? Are our first premises simply assumed by a sort of leap of faith? This would make them arbitrary and would not yield scientific and necessary knowledge. Then are the first principles innate, as Socrates and Plato thought? Again, Aristotle rejects this alternative because he finds it absurd to suppose that we possess detailed and certain knowledge from birth but are unaware of it.

Aristotle's answer is found in a twofold process of induction and intuition. Through induction we become acquainted with the universal and necessary features within the changing world of particulars. He says that sense experience leaves its traces within memory. Numerous sense perceptions of the same sort strengthen each other in memory, and a knowledge of the similar and universal qualities begins to emerge. Aristotle gives us this pictorial image of the process: "It is like a rout in battle stopped by first one man making a stand and then another, until the original formation has been restored" (PA 2.19). In other words, from an early age we are besieged with a booming, buzzing barrage of sensations. Initially, our minds are as confused as an army being overwhelmed in battle. Some of these sensations remain in memory, however, and the similar ones reinforce each other. An intelligible order begins to reveal itself as each universal takes its stand in the mind. Like soldiers holding their ground and then advancing to conquer new territory, the universals expand our understanding to greater and greater levels of generality. For example, we experience Tom, Dick, Susan, and Jane. We perceive their unique qualities, and we also experience their similarities. The mind can then extract the universal "human" from its particular examples. Through a similar process, we form the concepts of "dog," "lizard," "deer," and so forth. From this "stand" the mind advances to the universal of "animal" and eventually to the most fundamental universals that are found in all existing things whatsoever (such as substance, quality, relation, place).

Although it is clear how induction can enable us to make generalizations in this way, it is not clear how induction alone can give us necessary first principles. Here is where intuition comes in. Aristotle is convinced that the world consists of a rational order. Experience alone cannot demonstrate this order to us, but can acquaint us with it. However, only through a sort of intellectual intuition do we really "see" the universal and necessary truths that are the foundation of all genuine knowledge. For example, adding two apples and two apples, then two oranges and two oranges, may trigger the intellectual insight that $2 + 2 = 4$. This universal and necessary mathematical truth is not based on the changing world of apples and oranges. However, the concrete experiences provoked the intellectual intuition. For Aristotle, then, intuition is an additional step beyond the process of induction. Whereas Plato described the act of intuiting universals as a kind of "recollection" of knowledge already latent within the soul, the more empirical Aristotle refers to it as an act of "recognition." Hence, the mind has the power to recognize, or come to know for the first time, universal truths that are lurking within experience.

Two main classes of first principles are revealed in this process. There are the unique, fundamental principles and definitions of each particular science. Most of Aristotle's examples here are taken from mathematics with its self-evident axioms and definitions. However, he thinks that physics, medicine, ethics, and any other special science is likewise based on intuitively discovered and necessary principles. The second class of first principles are the laws of logic. These are fundamental to any sort of reasoning, no matter what its subject. The supreme principle among these is what is commonly called the "law of non-contradiction." It may be formulated as "A cannot be both B and Not-B." Others are the "law of excluded middle": "A must either be B or Not-B," and the "law of identity": "A is A." Notice that for Aristotle these principles describe both the laws of thought and the nature of reality itself, since he assumes that there will always be a correlation between the structure of rational thought and the structure of reality.

Metaphysics: Understanding the Here-and-Now World

CRITIQUE OF THE PLATONIC FORMS

The examination of the principles that are the common foundation for every science are what Aristotle called "first philosophy." The most complete discussion of this topic is in his book *Metaphysics*. We now use the term "metaphysics" to refer to the area of philosophy concerned with the nature of reality. However, this label is the result of a historical accident. A later editor of Aristotle's manuscripts did not know what to call a certain collection of monographs, so he labeled them as the writings that come after (*meta*) Aristotle's *Physics*.

To understand Aristotle's metaphysics, it is important to see how his approach differs from Plato's. Recall that Plato had a very severe dualism in which reality consisted of two worlds. The world of the Forms was nonphysical, eternal, unchanging, and known only by reason. The world of our everyday experience was material, temporal, constantly changing, and known through the senses. The first world, according to Plato, is what is ultimately real, whereas the world of our experience is like a collection of shadows. Aristotle has some very sharp criticisms of the Platonic Forms and tries to replace them with a radically revised theory of how universals and particulars are related.

Here are some of the main criticisms that Aristotle offers in his *Metaphysics* (M 1.9):

1. The Forms are useless. They have no explanatory power. Instead of explaining the natural world, Plato's theory creates a second world, thereby doubling the number of things that require explanation. Instead of bringing some unity to the multiplicity of things in experience, it complicates matters by introducing more multiplicity.

2. The Forms cannot explain change or the movement of things within our experience. "Above all one might discuss the question what on earth the Forms contribute to sensible things. . . . For they cause neither movement nor any change in them." In many passages, Plato presents change as a symp-

tom of the irrationality and imperfection of the physical world, and he was less interested in it than he was in what was eternal and permanent. For Aristotle, however, our lives are lived in a changing world, and we need to make some sense out of it. Hence, he complains that if the unchanging Forms are the basis for all explanation, then "the whole study of nature has been annihilated."

3. The Forms cannot be the essence or substance of things if they are separated from them.

4. It is not clear what it means for particulars to "participate" in the Forms. To say that the Forms are patterns and that particulars share in them "is to use empty words and poetical metaphors."

5. Also, Aristotle uses the Third Man Argument that was introduced in the chapter on Plato. If the relationship between two men is explained by means of the Form of Man, then do we need yet another Form to explain the similarity between the individual man and the Form of Man? If so, then this process would never end, for we would have Forms explaining Forms forever (M 1.9, 11.1).

For such reasons, Aristotle does not believe that the Platonic theory of Forms can be salvaged. Despite of his great respect for Plato, Aristotle harshly concludes, "The Forms we can dispense with, for they are mere sound without sense; and even if there are such things, they are not relevant to our discussion" (PA 1.22).

Despite Aristotle's rejection of the Platonic version of the Forms, we must not suppose that Aristotle does away with them altogether. With Plato, he still believes there are universal forms that are objective and that constitute the essences of things in the world. It is because of these forms that we are able to have knowledge. Furthermore, Aristotle agrees that the order in reality can only be explained by reference to the forms.*

---

*To avoid confusing Aristotle's concept of the forms with Plato's, we shall adopt the convention of capitalizing the word (*Form*) only when it refers to Plato's theory.

SUBSTANCE: THE KEY TO REALITY

Having dismissed Plato's extreme dualism, where does Aristotle locate the forms? To answer this question, he turns to the only reality we have—the natural world around us. For Plato's picture of *transcendent* Forms, Aristotle substitutes the notion of *immanent* forms. The forms can only be the cause and explanation of things if they are an intrinsic part of things. There is no abstract Form of "Tableness" apart from this world. There are only individual tables, each exhibiting the form that identifies something as a table. Hence, for Aristotle, the fundamental reality is the collection of substances we find in our everyday experience. We saw previously that substance was the key category in his account of propositions and thinking. Now he argues that it is the fundamental category in reality itself. The phrase "is bald, pot-bellied, and short" makes no sense until we supply the grammatical subject "Socrates." Similarly, baldness and the other qualities can have no existence apart from their inherence in some actually existing metaphysical substance such as a particular, individual person. Substances, then, are the fundamental unit of reality.

To understand any individual substance, I must understand two things about it. First, I must understand the individual's *whatness*. If I say, "What is that?" the answer might be "Socrates." But now if I say, "What is Socrates?" the answer might be "a rational animal," "a Greek," "a philosopher," "a short and bald man," and so on. This list would be a number of properties found in Socrates. But notice that these are all common or universal properties that also characterize other particulars. Although universal properties are important, they do not capture what is particular or unique about an individual substance. Socrates is a rational animal, but so are you; Socrates was a Greek, but so were Thales and Heraclitus. Particular substances, therefore, must be composed of more than just their universal features. How do we account for the particularity of particular things? To do this, we have to refer to their *thisness*. Socrates is this particular Greek, standing there in his slovenly toga and occupying a specific amount of space (the northeast corner of the marketplace of Athens) at a particular time (June 6, 420 B.C.). Even though there may be many bald, short, rational, Greek philosophers, Socrates is a unique exemplification of these properties.

FORM AND MATTER

These two aspects of individual substance can be captured by the notions of *form* and *matter*. The "whatness" of something refers to its form. Its "thisness" is its matter. The easiest way to see how these two features work together to constitute individual realities is to consider a simple object such as a coffee cup. We can answer the question "What is it?" because we recognize that the object has a particular form. In this case, it is an object that is cylindrical, about three inches in diameter, with a closed bottom and an open top, which is used to drink coffee. Even though many such objects are mass-produced with the same form, its matter lets us identify *this* cup as an individual reality of its own because it is this particular piece of formed ceramic sitting on my breakfast table.

This particular example may lead us to suppose that form and matter refer to physical shape and physical matter alone. However, certain subtleties in Aristotle's account must be understood. Broadly speaking, an object has the form it has because of a particular purpose or function it serves. The form constitutes an object's essence. The **essence** of something is the set of qualities that make it the sort of thing it is. Typically, the essence of a thing is what a dictionary definition attempts to describe. For example, the essence of a coffee cup is to hold coffee so that we can drink from it. Hence, even if an object had the physical shape of a cup but was made from soluble materials, it might be a decoration or an item in a practical joker's inventory, but it wouldn't really be a coffee cup. A coffee cup has an open top because its function is to serve beverages, whereas a juice bottle has a secure cap because its function is to store and transport beverages. Similarly, a legal brief has a particular form unique to it. However, in this case its form cannot be simply characterized by its physical characteristics. A rectangular sheet of paper with words on it physically characterizes the manuscript of a children's story as easily as it does a legal brief. Hence, the form of a legal document is better characterized by its style, its vocabulary, and its purpose. A manuscript for a children's story may look physically similar to the legal brief, but it will have a different literary form because it serves a different function. It will begin with "Once upon a time . . ." and will have a style that enlivens the imagination rather than a logical organization that establishes some abstruse legal conclusion.

Similarly, we must view matter in a broader way. Matter, as we have indicated, is the principle of individuation. It is what distinguishes the individual members of a class that share the same form. Matter may also be described as a collection of possibilities from which something else may be actualized. A pine board is an example of formed matter. But it can be stacked with other boards in a pile to become the matter for a bonfire. These same boards could be nailed together to form a bookcase. Although the boards are distinct substances in themselves, they can become the matter for a new kind of entity to be realized. Hence, if the same formed matter has a different form imposed on it, it will become a different kind of object. To use a more subtle example, an airplane disaster (which has its own "whatness" and "thisness") could itself become the matter for either a news report, a TV drama, a historical account, or a lawsuit. In each case, the same "matter" can be formed or organized in new ways to fulfill different functions. The flip side of this is that a form by itself does not give us a substantive object until it inheres in some sort of matter. The carpenter's diagram is not yet a bookcase. It suggests how the matter of lumber should be formed to produce a bookcase. Similarly, the general form of a TV drama is a mere abstraction without the matter of the characters and some sequence of events for its realization.

In summary, every individual substance is made up of two dimensions, its form (whatness) and its matter (thisness). We may discuss each dimension separately, but this is always an abstraction. They are not two parts of a substance the way that the legs and the seat are two parts of a stool.

We do not find bare matter to which form is added as an additional ingredient. However, one piece of formed matter can be the basis for a new object if it is reorganized by means of a different form.

POTENTIALITY AND ACTUALITY

The concepts of matter and form can be used to understand the reality of individual substances. However, this does not tell us the whole story. It is obvious that all earthly things (whether they are human artifacts or natural objects) come into being and undergo change or development. Let us take a particular individual substance—an acorn, for example. We could analyze the acorn as having its own, unique matter (this particular hunk of organic stuff nestled between two tufts of grass). We could also focus on its form (the qualities that make it like all other acorns). But according to Aristotle (and I think we would have to agree with him here), we do not fully understand what we have in our hands if this is all we know about it. Only when we understand its potential to become an oak tree do we know what it is.

Aristotle describes the stages that a changing, developing individual goes through as *potentiality* changes to *actuality*. Potentiality is associated with matter. The acorn on the ground is not a tree but it contains this possibility. In contrast, actuality is associated with form. The actual oak tree that results comes from the form guiding its process of development. In becoming first the sapling and then the tree, the acorn loses the form that originally made it an acorn. But part of what makes it an acorn is its capacity to take on these other forms that were potentially there. For this reason, the acorn cannot become a tomato. The tomato's form was not part of the acorn's potentiality. To understand the process of potentialities becoming actualities, we have to look more closely at Aristotle's theory of change.

UNDERSTANDING CHANGE

To understand a changing world, Aristotle says, we must understand the causes that operate in the world. According to Aristotle, four kinds of causes explain why a particular event happens or why something is the way it is. Since Aristotle uses the word *cause* in a much broader sense than we do today, these four causes may be best thought of as four different aspects that go into the explanation of any individual thing. The first thing we may want to know about something is (1) the *material cause* or its matter. For example, Aristotle says a hunk of bronze is the material cause of a statue. In the case of the oak, the material cause is the organic material of the acorn. Next, we need to know (2) the *efficient cause*. This is the origin of the process that produced the article in question. In the case of the statue, this would be the sculptor and his tools. For the tree, the action of moisture, the nurturing soil, and sunlight actualize the acorn's potential. Thus far, these two causes or modes of explanation seem roughly consistent with our modern scientific view of the world. We tend to think of nature as being made up of material objects being acted on by a set of forces.

For Aristotle, however, the most important part of the story is yet to be told. To explain something, we also need to know its (3) *formal cause*. This is the essence of the item, the form being actualized in its matter, that which makes it the sort of thing it is. Thus, when the sculptor begins his work, he has the form in mind as he works with the bronze. The form at work in the acorn causes it to grow into a tree and not a tulip. For Aristotle, the most important aspect of something was (4) *the final cause*. This is the end or purpose or function it is to fulfill. For an artificial object such as a statue, its purpose may be to depict the likeness of someone. A natural object such as an acorn is a growing entity that points toward its fulfillment in the tree that bears its own acorns.

We can imagine Aristotle's four-cause analysis being applied by an archeologist. Let's suppose that in one of her digs in South America, an archeologist runs across what seems to be some sort of implement. She will seek to know its material cause (silver), for this will tell her something about it. She will also want to know the efficient cause that produced it (Inca artisans). Next, she

might try to decide if it is a knife or a household decoration. This would be a search for the formal cause. Assuming that it is a knife, she then needs to figure out if it was used for religious rituals or hunting or cooking (its final cause). Only if she can answer these four kinds of Aristotelian questions has she fully understood the artifact.

The development of something from its beginnings to its final culmination is a process that involves several stages. The baby grows into the toddler and the toddler into the child on into the adolescent who then becomes an adult. At each stage, some potentiality is actualized (involving some or all of the four causes), but this then provides the potential for further stages to be actualized until the final end is realized. Each stage has its own matter and form. We may say that the 16-year-old is a model teenager. But though she has achieved excellence at this stage of her life, the form of the teenager will pass away and be replaced by the form of the adult. Thus, all change is the process of a particular matter successively being shaped by different forms until the final stage is reached.

TELEOLOGY

Aristotle's theories give us a picture of nature as a collection of dynamic processes all pointing to the fulfillment of various ends. This purposeful, goal-oriented structure that Aristotle attributes to the universe is called **teleology**. This comes from the Greek word *telos*, which means end or goal.* This does not mean that the acorn striving to grow into the oak is consciously trying to achieve that end. Nor, for Aristotle, does it mean that any other conscious intentions are at work in nature. Nevertheless, acorns grow into oaks, they do not become cabbages. The essence of each kind of substance includes its inner drive to behave or develop in a certain way. Aristotle uses the word *entelechy* to describe the end stage of a process,

---

*In the *Timaeus*, Plato used the notion of teleology to account for the origin and nature of the cosmos as a whole.

meaning the full actualization of a thing's form.[†] The entelechy of an acorn is the oak tree, for the oak does not go on to realize a further end other than to produce more acorns.

GOD: THE UNMOVED MOVER

Nature is a busy drama of restless, changing entities. Everywhere we look potentialities are being actualized, creating new potentialities, and every process is directed toward some end. What is the origin of all the activity of nature? Matter by itself, according to Aristotle, is merely a bundle of potentialities. It needs some other force to actualize its potential. We can imagine the universe with all the heavenly bodies suspended in space but completely motionless. They would have the potential to move but this potential must be actualized by something else. Hence, for Aristotle, motion is something that always requires an explanation. What he is looking for is not some temporally first cause that sets things moving, for he believed the universe and the motions of the heavenly bodies are eternal. For Aristotle, as for all the Greeks, the notion that the entire universe had an absolute beginning and was created out of nothing made no sense. Instead, the universe, for him, is like a flower that has eternally been moving to face the sun. Even if the flower had always existed, its eternal motion would require an eternal sun to continually sustain its life and motion.

If Aristotle is correct about what has been said thus far, then a very basic strand within the universe must account for the motion of everything else. However, this source of motion cannot itself be in motion, for then something else would have to sustain its motion. This would lead to an impossible infinite regress. Aristotle calls this fundamental cause the *Unmoved Mover*. There are several important points to understand about his Unmoved Mover. First, although it seems to be Aristotle's version of God, it is not a transcendent, anthropomorphic, personal God such as we find

in the Judeo-Christian tradition. Aristotle's God no more loves or performs acts of the will than does the law of gravity. To care for something is to have an emotional life, which makes you vulnerable to and affected by what you love. If the Unmoved Mover is the source of all motion, it cannot be emotionally affected by or moved by other things. Second, since the Unmoved Mover is not itself in motion, it cannot be an efficient cause. In other words, it cannot cause motion the way a batter does by hitting a ball. So how can it move other things? Aristotle's answer is that it operates as the final cause. It is the source of the teleology in the universe. In seeking to be fully complete, all things (unconsciously) desire to be like the Unmoved Mover. Different parts of nature strive for actuality in their own way. The plant seeks fulfillment when it works its way up through the ground. You and I attempt to know as much as possible and to realize all our potentialities. This drive toward actuality, which is present in every being, is like the power of love. You can be in love with someone and that love can affect everything you do. You try to improve yourself for the sake of the one you love or rearrange your schedule so that you can be near him or her. However, this does not mean that the one you love is similarly affected by you. The person may be completely unaware of your existence. Similarly, nature is moved by God, while he remains unmoved. Since all things in nature are moved by their innate love of God, Aristotle literally believes that "love makes the world go round"!

Finally, the Unmoved Mover must be the highest sort of reality. Everything else is full of potentiality that has not yet been realized. We are incomplete and always on the way, and thus our lives are never finished. But something that is a pure actuality does not need to change, for by its nature it is already complete. What then does the Unmoved Mover do? If it is the highest sort of reality, it must be engaged in the most valuable sort of activity. For Aristotle, this supreme activity is thought. Although the rest of nature blindly pursues its ends, human beings are capable of rational thought, making them the highest sorts of

---

[†]"Entelechy" translates the philosophically rich Greek word *entelecheia*—having (*echō*) its purpose (*telos*) within (*entos*).

creatures in nature. By extrapolation, the highest form of being in the universe must be one that is engaged in the highest form of rational thought. However, God cannot think about the particulars of the changing world, for this would introduce fragmentation and change into the heart of his being. Instead, the object of his thought must be undivided and eternal. "Therefore it must be of itself that the divine thought thinks (since it is the most excellent of things), and its thinking is a thinking on thinking" (M 12.9). The only analogy we can have of this singular, undivided intellectual vision would be that of a mathematician contemplating the whole of a mathematical proof instead of focusing on its individual steps. Aristotle's theology was influential throughout all antiquity, especially because of his impact on the Stoic and Neoplatonic philosophers. Furthermore, even though it may appear that this view of God is in tension with elements of the biblical tradition, it was very influential with the medieval theologians, particularly Thomas Aquinas.

Ethics: Keeping Things in Balance

Aristotle's most complete work on ethics is called the *Nicomachean Ethics* (which refers to the name of both his father and his son). It stands as one of the great classics of moral philosophy and is still influential. Aristotle does not pretend to offer us a radically novel ethical theory. He thought it would be absurd that no one in the history of the human race had ever discovered what it means to be morally good. We have abundant examples of good people who serve as models for the rest of us. Hence, we already have a sense of the character traits and moral principles that produce human excellence. This approach contributes to both the strengths and the weaknesses of Aristotle's moral theory. On the positive side, the whole of his ethical writings are characterized by a sort of down-to-earth, commonsense approach that captures the moral intuitions that we bring to philosophy. Yet adhering too closely to the moral wisdom of our society can blind us to the limitations and prejudices of our particular age and culture. Aristotle's acceptance of slavery and his

exclusion of women from political life are examples. Therefore, people who are sympathetic to Aristotle's overall perspective must separate his universal insights from what is culturally relative.

In Aristotle's view, ethics constitutes a body of objective knowledge. In this sense it is a science of correct conduct that guides us toward the goal of achieving human excellence. Aristotle agreed with Plato on this point. Both believed that for an individual in a particular set of circumstances there is a morally correct way of acting. Since morality is a matter of knowing, internalizing, and applying objective principles, it is possible to be mistaken in our moral opinions and objectively delinquent in our behavior. Plato had a very extreme interpretation of this point, for he believed that ethical principles were like mathematical principles. Aristotle, however, did not think that ethical theory can be as exact a science as mathematics. When we begin applying universal principles to the conduct of concrete human beings, we run into all the ambiguities and fine shades of gray that characterize the human situation. For this reason, he starts out the *Nicomachean Ethics* by explaining,

> *Our discussion will be adequate if it has as much clearness as the subject-matter admits of, for precision is not to be sought for alike in all discussions, any more than in all the products of the crafts . . . for it is the mark of an educated man to look for precision in each class of things just so far as the nature of the subject admits.* (NE 1.3)

HAPPINESS

Aristotle begins his book on ethics by observing that all human action aims at some end. Now some ends are merely instrumental. We pursue them only so that we can achieve other goals. For example, a student may stay up late studying for a statistics exam. She does this to pass the course, and she aims at this end to complete an accounting degree. This goal has value because it enables her to get a good job, and this has value because it enables her to earn money, and so on, and so on. However, this string of instrumental goals cannot go on forever or there would be no point to the whole process. All intermediate goals must ultimately aim at some final good we desire for its own sake. The most important task in life, then, is to determine what this chief and final good might be.

The answer is easy enough: the final goal of all human activity is *happiness*. The Greek term Aristotle uses is *eudaimonia*. This should not be confused with pleasure but is best thought of as meaning "well-being" or "living well" or "having a life worth living." You can ask about everything else someone does, "Why are you doing that?" But the question "Why are you trying to achieve happiness?" is absurd and cannot be given an answer because happiness is the final goal of all that we do and requires no further justification. Aristotle recognizes, however, that this does not get us very far, for there are many different opinions on this topic. Different people associate living well with pleasure, wealth, honor, and a wide variety of things. Accordingly, Aristotle admits that "to say that happiness is the chief good seems a platitude and a clearer account of what it is is still desired" (NE 1.7).

As we saw in his metaphysics, the purpose or function of something constitutes its real nature. Moreover, this will constitute its virtue or the standard of its excellence as well. The good carpenter is one who fulfills the purpose of carpentry, which is construction. The good eye is one that fulfills its function of seeing. Accordingly, becoming a good human being or finding personal fulfillment (which are basically the same for Aristotle), means fulfilling the end of being human. What can this be? It must be something unique and special to human beings that we do not share in common with other creatures. For this reason, Aristotle cautions that we will go astray if we equate happiness with pleasure. People who do that are "preferring a life suitable to beasts" instead of what would be the appropriate fulfillment for human beings (NE 1.5). Toward the end of his book, he concludes,

> *Happiness, therefore, does not lie in amusement; it would, indeed, be strange if the end were amusement, and one were to take trouble and suffer hardship all one's life in order to amuse oneself. For, in a word,*

everything that we choose we choose for the sake of something else—except happiness, which is an end. Now to exert oneself and work for the sake of amusement seems silly and utterly childish. (NE 10.6)

Having said that pleasure does not equal happiness, Aristotle points out that a minimal amount of pleasure is an ingredient in the good life. "Those who say that the victim on the rack or the man who falls into great misfortunes is happy if he is good, are, whether they mean to or not, talking nonsense" (NE 7.13). The same is true of all other "external goods." The lack of such resources as friends, health, and sufficient material support take the luster from happiness. Finally, while pleasure is not the goal of human life, it accompanies the life that is morally excellent.

> *The lovers of what is noble find pleasant the things that are by nature pleasant; and virtuous actions are such, so that these are pleasant for such men as well as in their own nature. Their life, therefore, has no further need of pleasure as a sort of adventitious charm, but has its pleasure in itself.* (NE 1.8)

We now come back to the question "What is the purpose of human life?" Aristotle answers this question in one of the most central passages of his *Ethics*: "We state the function of man to be a certain kind of life, and this to be an activity or actions of the soul implying a rational principle, and the function of a good man to be the good and noble performance of these" (NE 1.7). Several points in this passage need to be emphasized. First, we do not *give* ourselves a purpose. The end of human life is something that is *given to us* by nature and makes up the essence of our humanity. It distinguishes the kinds of beings we are from rocks, plants, beasts, and computers. Second, this passage emphasizes that the purpose of human life is found in a sort of performance or activity that exhibits excellence. Happiness is not a passive state we achieve, but it characterizes what we do and how we do it. Aristotle adds the qualification "in a complete life." As he explains, "One swallow does not make a summer, nor does one day; and so too one day, or a short time, does not make a man blessed and happy" (NE 1.7). Just as one winning game does not make an athlete a champion, so one noble act or one happy moment does not make a person's life excellent.

Third, the preceding description of the purpose of human life also stresses that it entails a life lived according to a certain plan or strategy that is furnished by reason. Thus, the good life involves both thinking and doing. This is because we are rational beings, as well as beings that feel, desire, and act. Hence, the road to happiness involves two dimensions. You must rationally judge what are the right principles to follow, and your appetites, feelings, and emotions must be disciplined to follow those rules. This requires two kinds of human excellence. These are *intellectual virtue* (or excellence of intelligence) and *moral virtue* (or excellence of character). A good life cannot be had if either of these is neglected.

Under the heading of intellectual virtue, the two main categories are philosophic wisdom and practical wisdom. Philosophic wisdom is purely theoretical and is achieved by understanding the unchanging structure of reality. Practical wisdom is the intellectual virtue required to be moral, for it is the rational understanding of how to conduct one's daily life. Aristotle points out, however, that something more is needed besides intellectual excellence. "For we are inquiring not in order to know what virtue is, but in order to become good, since otherwise our inquiry would have been of no use" (NE 2.2). What is needed is moral virtue or the ability to balance one's desires and emotions.

Aristotle begins by first discussing moral virtue. For us, this might be the whole of ethics, but for Aristotle it is just one ingredient in the good life. He describes virtue (or human excellence) as

> a state of character concerned with choice, lying in a mean, i.e., the mean relative to us, this being determined by a rational principle, and by that principle by which the man of practical wisdom would determine it. (NE 2.6)

Each term in this definition is analyzed in the sections that follow.

VIRTUE IS A STATE OF CHARACTER

First, he speaks of virtue as "a state of character." By this he means that a morally good person is not simply one who performs morally right actions but one who has developed a habit or disposition to do what is right. We can imagine someone who tells the truth on his income tax form—but only after he struggles with the temptation to cheat. By contrast, the truly moral person is one who tells the truth readily, happily, and without such a struggle. Hence, a well-formed character manifests itself not only in what we do but in our motives, our desires, our likes and dislikes. For this reason, Aristotle says that a good person "delights in virtuous actions and is vexed at vicious ones, as a musical man enjoys beautiful tunes but is pained at bad ones" (NE 9.9).

Although the intellectual virtues can be acquired by being taught, the moral virtues can only be acquired through practice, much as we acquire a skill. Thus, developing a moral character is more like learning how to play the piano or drive a car than it is like learning history. Aristotle criticizes philosophers (he may have been thinking of Socrates here) who think that being moral is simply a matter of knowing the good. He says that such theorists are like "patients who listen attentively to their doctors, but do none of the things they are ordered to do. As the latter will not be made well in body by such a course of treatment, the former will not be made well in soul by such a course of philosophy" (NE 2.4).

If moral virtue is a matter of *knowing how* to make moral decisions and not just *knowing that* certain things are true, then "we become just by doing just acts, temperate, by doing temperate acts, brave by doing brave acts" (NE 2.1). At first this may seem like a vicious circle. How can we do just acts unless we are already just? The answer is that when we learn a new skill, whether it is piano playing or being a moral person, we receive instructions from a parent or a teacher. They tell us what to do and we model our behavior after theirs. Eventually, through a process of repetition, the external actions become more or less effortless and are internalized in the form of dispositions. In the case of piano playing, the mature musician does not need the teacher to place her fingers where they are to go. She looks at the music and instantly responds. In the case of morally mature people, their parents do not have to remind them to tell the truth, for they do so by habit.

VIRTUE IS CONCERNED WITH CHOICE

Aristotle stresses that being moral involves choice of a certain kind. For example, suppose I swerve my car when driving down the street because I am testing out my new tires, but while doing so I unknowingly avoid hitting a small child. My avoiding the child was good, but it was by accident. In another case, suppose I take care of an aged aunt only because I hope to inherit her fortune. Again, this is a good action, but it is done for a despicable reason. In neither case can I be praised for being a virtuous person, for being moral involves knowing what is good and choosing it for its own sake.

Furthermore, for an action to be a genuine choice and thus capable of moral praise or blame, the action must be voluntary. Aristotle clarifies the notion of voluntary action and moral responsibility by looking at cases in which an action is not voluntary. He thinks that there are two classes of involuntary action or actions for which we are not morally responsible. These are all actions that are done under compulsion or out of ignorance. When an action is done under compulsion, the action originates in some external force operating on me. For example, if I slip on a rug or am pushed and break your favorite vase, I am not blameworthy for this because I did not choose to act as I did. However, there are some gray areas. Let's suppose I am forced to do an immoral act, because my family is being threatened with torture. Aristotle calls cases like this "mixed" cases. On the one hand, I voluntarily moved my own body to perform the act. On the other hand, because I was acting out of fear, it was an action I preferred not to do and my moral responsibility is diminished.

When am I acting out of ignorance? Aristotle says that I am not free of blame simply because I am ignorant of what is right or wrong. To say, "I didn't know that murder is wrong," does not relieve me of blame. However, if I am ignorant of certain relevant facts through no fault of my own, I am excused. Suppose that in good faith I offer someone what I think is water, not realizing his enemy has poisoned it. Here, my action is unfortunate but not blameworthy. However, there are limits here. In some cases my ignorance is the result of my own negligence. For example, I should check to see if a gun is loaded before I play with it, and a physician should check for possible allergic reactions before prescribing a medicine.

To further refine the notion of excusable ignorance, Aristotle makes a distinction between "acting *in* ignorance" and "acting *by reason of* ignorance." If I stab someone while drunk or in a blind rage, I may genuinely not realize what I was doing. However, although I am acting in ignorance, the ignorance was self-inflicted because I allowed myself to become drunk or never developed the character trait of self-control. When I act by reason of ignorance, there is something that, regrettably, I did not know, but for which I cannot be blamed.

VIRTUE AND THE MEAN

Next, Aristotle says that virtue is choice "lying in a mean." This became known as his famous "doctrine of the mean." The "mean" referred to here is the intermediate position between two extremes or vices. He observes that moral virtue is "concerned with passions and actions, in which excess is a form of failure, and so is defect, while the intermediate is praised and is a form of success" (NE 2.6). In other words, the virtuous person is one who finds the correct balance or the mean between the extremes. This emphasis on moderation was not new in Aristotle, for it had been a standard Greek ideal going back to Homer and the poets. Nevertheless, Aristotle gives it his own distinctive formulation.

The notion of virtue being a mean can best be explained by looking at a few examples based on

Activity	Vice (excess)	Virtue (mean)	Vice (deficit)
Confidence in Facing Danger	Rashness	Courage	Cowardice
Enjoying Pleasure	Self-indulgence	Temperance	Being puritanical
Giving of Money	Vulgarity	Generosity	Stinginess
Truth Telling About Oneself	Boastfulness	Self-honesty	Self-deprecation

FIGURE 5-2 Aristotle's analysis of virtue as the mean between extremes

Aristotle's discussion. For each kind of activity, there is a correct character trait that is the balance between the extremes of too much and too little (see Figure 5-2).

Aristotle points out that this analysis in terms of the mean does not apply to all feelings and actions. For example, we would not want to say that a good person is one who does not commit too much cruelty, nor too little cruelty, but just the right amount. Obviously, some feelings and actions are by their nature simply evil, and no amount of moderation will make them good. Examples he provides are feelings such as spite, shamelessness, and envy, and actions such as adultery, theft, and murder (NE 2.6).

UNIVERSAL PRINCIPLES AND RELATIVE APPLICATIONS

Fourth, Aristotle has said that virtue entails finding the "mean relative to us." Hence, the mean will not be the same for every individual under all circumstances. The genius of Aristotle's ethics is his recognition that universal and objective principles have relative applications for different people and within different circumstances. To use a nonmoral example, everyone ought to follow the general rule "Eat nutritious and well-balanced meals." Even though this principle applies equally to all persons, the specific diet it dictates for a 250-pound football player will differ from that of a 110-pound clerk. Notice that Aristotle is definitely not saying that the principles governing action are simply a matter of subjective opinion. I may feel that my new fad diet is good for me when it is actually robbing my body of essential nutrients and doing more harm than good. In the case of a moral virtue such as courage, we may praise the courage of a young child who overcomes his terror of the water and sticks his face in the water. It would not be an act of courage for a professional lifeguard to do this. Similarly, a widow who gives a dollar to charity when this is a substantial portion of her living expenses is exhibiting the virtue of generosity. However, if she inherits a million dollars, then giving a dollar under these circumstances would be exhibiting the vice of stinginess.

THE MEAN DETERMINED BY PRACTICAL WISDOM

Obviously, the mean is not identical to a mathematical average. If giving all my money to a charity is excessive and giving none is stingy, it does not follow that giving away half of my life savings is the correct amount to give. Even if we know the correct moral principles, how do we know what is right to do in a specific case? Aristotle can only say that it is "determined by a rational principle, and by that principle by which the man of practical wisdom would determine it" (NE 2.6). It is at this point that moral virtue links up with the intellectual virtue of practical wisdom. A person who has moral virtue will know which goals are the right ones for human life (the balance among her various desires and emotions). But she also needs practical wisdom to know how to achieve those goals. This involves the intellectual activity of deliberating correctly. Aristotle offers very little else in the way of guidance except to say that practical wisdom "is concerned not only with universals but with particulars, which become familiar from experience" (NE 6.8). Hence, though practical wisdom is an intellectual virtue, the person who has learned how to make decisions from practical experience is most likely to exemplify this form of wisdom.

In summary, the morally good person is one who carefully follows reason, desires to do the right thing, has a well-formed character, knows the proper goals in human life, can estimate how to achieve those goals in practice, and probably the one who has the most experience in making tough, moral decisions. Being ethical is more like learning how to keep one's balance on a bicycle than like calculating mathematical results. When we first learn how to ride the bicycle, we make a number of mistakes and fall down. Eventually, however, we can feel the correct point of balance. You cannot give someone a formula for doing this; he or she must learn it from experience. As Aristotle says,

> Both fear and confidence and appetite and anger and pity and in general pleasure and pain may be felt both too much and too little, and in both cases not well; but to feel them at the right times, with reference to the right objects, towards the right people, with the right motive, and in the right way, is what is both intermediate and best, and this is characteristic of virtue. (NE 2.6)

THE BEST FORM OF LIFE

Aristotle has argued that happiness is achieved by living in accordance with our nature, by fulfilling what it means to be human. But since human nature is multidimensional, it is reasonable to assume that the highest and most satisfying form of happiness is linked to what is the very best within us. There is no question, Aristotle believes, that the activity of contemplation fits this description. Aristotle lists several reasons for this conclusion. First, reason is that part of us that most fully expresses our humanity. Second, we can engage in reason continuously, in the midst of life's other engagements. Third, rational contemplation is a self-sufficient activity, for we can engage in it on our own. Apart from life's basic necessities, we do not need other people, equipment, or anything external for this activity. Fourth, it is the one activity we engage in for its own sake and not for the tangible results it brings. Finally, contemplation imitates the activity of God, the Unmoved Mover.

Evaluation and Significance

In the period of philosophy following Aristotle, many philosophers abandoned his metaphysics for the materialism of the Epicureans and Stoics and the otherworldliness of the Neoplatonists. Nevertheless, he was rediscovered in the Middle Ages, where his authority was so respected he was referred to simply as "the Philosopher." Because his system served as the foundation for the science, philosophy, and theology of the medieval thinkers, the early modern philosophers and scientists attacked his thought as being responsible for all the intellectual ills of the past. A system that views the changes in nature as the result of substances striving to fulfill their final ends will not pay close attention to the material and efficient causes that are so important to modern science. Consequently, the modern period came about when Aristotle's authority was abandoned and new ways of conceiving nature emerged. Not until the nineteenth and twentieth centuries did interest revive in a modernized Aristotelianism.

PART ONE: THE ANCIENT PERIOD

Some of the criticisms of Aristotle's system will be discussed when we examine the rise of modern science. Yet even his critics cannot detract from his extraordinary accomplishments. Among other things, he gave birth to the science of logic and did his job so well that no major modifications to his work were made for more than two thousand years. His was the first systematic work on ethics and is still a prominent theory in ethics today. Western culture would not have been the same without him. The Christian doctrines developed in the Middle Ages were expressed in Aristotelian categories. Many passages in Dante, Chaucer, Shakespeare, and Milton presume a knowledge of Aristotle's conception of the universe. Furthermore, his influence on traditional literary criticism has been formidable. However, it would be wrong to consider him a dusty museum piece, notable because of his influence over thinkers long dead. His ideas do not retain the supreme authority over intellectual life they once enjoyed, but they are still alive and well in many regions of contemporary philosophical thought.

Questions for Understanding

1. What are some differences between Plato's and Aristotle's style of doing philosophy?

2. According to Aristotle, what is the relationship between language, thought, and reality? What considerations might count in favor of his view and what count against it?

3. How do Aristotle's categories serve to explain both thought and reality? Do you think his view is plausible? Are there any changes, additions, or deletions you would make to his list of categories?

4. What is the relation between form and content in Aristotle's logic? How does he go on to use this distinction in describing reality?

5. What are first principles? How do we arrive at them? What role do they play in knowledge?

6. Why does Aristotle reject Plato's view of the Forms? How is Aristotle's view of form similar to and different from Plato's view?

7. What is Aristotle's view of substance? How does this result in a different view of reality than Plato's?

8. What does Aristotle mean by potentiality and actuality? What role do they play in his view of the world?

9. How does he use the notions of form and matter to explain the nature of things?

10. What are the four kinds of causes? Why does Aristotle think that we can never understand something completely without them?

11. What is teleology? What are some examples Aristotle could use to demonstrate that it is at work in nature?

12. What is the Unmoved Mover? Why does Aristotle believe in it? How is it similar to and different from traditional notions of God with which you are familiar?

13. Why does Aristotle distinguish happiness and pleasure?

14. Given that happiness is the goal of human life, how does Aristotle think that this is best achieved?

15. What does Aristotle mean by virtue? What are the two kinds of virtue?

16. How is moral virtue acquired? Can it be taught? What are its various dimensions?

17. What is the doctrine of the mean? What role does it play in deciding what to do and what sort of persons we should be?

18. What is practical wisdom?

19. In the final analysis, what is the best form of life according to Aristotle?

Questions for Reflection

1. Plato and Aristotle give two different visions of the nature of reality and how to approach our lives. Which one do you think is the most plausible? Why?

2. Construct your own examples to illustrate Aristotle's view that everything is made up of form and matter.

3. Use Aristotle's notions of potentiality and actuality and his theory of the four causes to describe the general outline of your own life from infancy to your present stage.

4. Many would say that modern science has reduced Aristotle's four causes to just two: material causes and efficient causes. How might Aristotle argue that our explanations are insufficient without the other two causes?

5. Aristotle argues that everything has an essence, a form, or a general nature and, hence, that everything in the world has a natural purpose. Do you agree with this? Do you think it is true of human beings? What would be the implications of accepting or rejecting this thesis with respect to human beings?

6. In what ways is moral virtue an objective quality and in what ways is it relative to each individual and his or her circumstances?

7. List examples of people in our contemporary culture who you consider to be excellent role models. To what degree do they fit Aristotle's model of a virtuous person? Do you agree with his description of what human life should be? In what ways might his account be criticized?

8. If you were a parent (perhaps you are) and an Aristotelian, what concrete means would you use to train your child to be an excellent human being?

9. Aristotle thinks that moderation is the key to the virtuous life. Do you think this is true? Can you think of any good people, people who made society better, who were more extreme than moderate? What would Aristotle say about these cases?

10. Aristotle believes that the life of contemplation is the best life. What are his reasons for saying this? Explain why you agree or disagree with his conclusion.

Notes

1. Quoted in Frederick Copleston, *A History of Philosophy*, vol. 1, pt. 2 (Garden City, NY: Image Books, Doubleday, 1962), 9.

2. All quotations from Aristotle's works are from *The Basic Works of Aristotle*, ed. Richard McKeon (New York: Random House, 1941). References to specific works will use the following abbreviations:

   C   *Categories*, trans. E. M. Edghill. (References are to chapter number.)

   M   *Metaphysics*, trans. W. D. Ross. (References are to book and chapter numbers.)

   NE   *Nicomachean Ethics*, trans. W. D. Ross. (References are to book and chapter numbers.)

   PA   *Posterior Analytics*, trans. G. R. G. Mure. (References are to book and chapter numbers.)

3. Arthur Schopenhauer, *The World as Will and Idea*, trans. R. B. Haldane and J. Kemp (London: Routledge & Kegan Paul, 1883), 2:21.

6

Classical Philosophy
After Aristotle

The Transition to Hellenistic and Roman Philosophy

The deaths of Alexander the Great in 323 B.C. and of Aristotle in 322 B.C. mark the end of the Hellenic period, an era in which Greek civilization was primarily self-contained. These dates also mark the beginning of the Hellenistic (that is, "quasi-Greek") period during which Greek civilization blended with other cultures, especially those of Egypt and the Near East. This was followed by the Roman period, which began when the Romans conquered the Hellenistic states during the second and first centuries B.C. Although the Romans triumphed militarily, the Hellenistic tradition triumphed culturally. Recognizing the richness of the philosophy, literature, and art of the region, the Romans absorbed its culture and passed it on to western Europe. The Roman period finally came to an end around the middle of the sixth century A.D. with the collapse of the empire.

To understand the philosophies that emerged during the Hellenistic period, we have to view them against the background of the overwhelming social changes taking place at this time. The first factor that influenced the philosophies of this period was the dramatic change in the political life of Greece. The wars between the Greek city-states had left them exhausted, both physically and spiritually. The result was that the small, comfortable, democratic communities of Greece were now caught up into a succession of military empires. To the Greek citizen, these events were overwhelming, and it seemed that history was beyond human control. To citizens living in the time of Socrates, Plato, and Aristotle, participation in one's city-state offered opportunities for personal fulfillment. However, when the Greek states lost their independence, people felt alienated from the distant and powerful government. Their proud sense of civic duty gradually changed into a grudging compliance with the laws of the empire. A second factor shaping the philosophy of this period was the fact that the social conditions Socrates reacted against still remained. There were no integrating values to produce social cohesion. The old institutions had failed, and popular religion was declining. The gods of the city-state seemed impotent, and blind fate seemed to be in charge.

These factors tended to produce an individual-istic, practical approach to philosophy. The philosophies of this age competed in offering solutions to the problems of living. There was little interest in theoretical concerns for their own sake. Instead, people wanted to know, What is most worthwhile in life? What is left to strive for? What do I need to know to best shape my life? They were searching for some form of escape from the dismal events of the day and were longing for personal peace and rest for their weary, alienated souls.

Although the Hellenistic philosophers dealt with metaphysical issues, they were interested primarily in practical, ethical concerns. For them, theoretical knowledge only had value if it gave them some insight into how to make their individual lives more liveable. Hence, many of the philosophical concerns of traditional Greek philosophy went by the wayside. We find some bursts of originality in this period, but the philosophers were mainly content to piece together any ideas of their predecessors that seemed to work. Seven philosophical movements were prominent in this period. Because they met deep-seated human needs, many of them became very popular and lasted a long time. The first two movements will only be mentioned briefly here. First, there were the Academics who carried on Plato's school. After Plato's death the school strayed far from the vision of its founder. In its middle period it even fell into the hands of the Skeptics. Second, there were the Peripatetics (this was the name of Aristotle's school). They were primarily devoted to empirical observation and science, but lacked some of the integrating vision of Aristotle.

The next four schools were very popular. These were Cynicism, Epicureanism, Stoicism, and Skepticism. These four philosophies have left their impact on our ordinary language: *cynical*, *epicurean*, *stoical*, and *skeptical* describe different types of people or particular stances toward life. Neoplatonism, the final and seventh movement, was a religious mysticism. It offered escape from the burdens of this world by means of religious enlightenment. We will now discuss each of these last five philosophies in turn.

Cynicism

The movement known as Cynicism actually began in the Socratic era, but the Cynics are important to this time period for their influence on the Stoics. The founding of the movement can be traced to Antisthenes (about 445–365 B.C.), who started out as a student of the Sophist Gorgias but later became a devoted disciple of Socrates. He considered himself the true spiritual heir of Socratic teaching, which made him a rival of Plato.

Cynicism is more of a stance toward life than a carefully worked-out philosophy. The Cynics' main interest was the opposition of nature and convention, a theme they borrowed from the Sophists. The Cynics glorified doing what is natural and repudiating all of society's conventions, claiming they were artificial and tyrannical. They taught that happiness is found in virtue and that virtue is attained by setting oneself free from all earthly possessions and pleasures. The Cynic Antisthenes said that he would rather fall victim to madness than to desire. The key to life is to stick with what is natural—namely, to cherish only your native mental and spiritual possessions—for all else is worthless. External and physical possessions such as wealth, reputation, freedom, and pleasure are not of value, nor are poverty, shame, loss of freedom, illness, and death thought evil. They taught that there is one God, who is best served by practicing virtue. Organized religion, with its temples, priests, prayers, rituals, and fantastic stories was vigorously condemned as a human invention. The Cynics' commitment to otherworldliness and freedom from fleeting desires was a model for the Stoics and, later, the Christians.

The Cynics made every effort to unsettle the conventional values of a society they thought corrupt and artificial, including carrying on their sexual and biological functions in public. They were insulting in their manners and squalid in appearance, wearing their trademark tattered poncho and leather pouch. Traveling from town to town, they preached in the streets, usually condemning the folly of the human race. The most famous and outlandish Cynic was Diogenes of

Sinope (412 to 323 B.C.). He called himself the dog and admired the animals for their ability to stick with the bare essentials.* The stories about Diogenes abound. It is said he once roamed around at noonday with a lantern, announcing that he was looking for an honest man. Supposedly Alexander the Great was charmed by him. A well-known story relates that when Alexander made his grand entrance into Corinth, he came on Diogenes sunning himself on the street. Moved by Diogenes' miserable condition, the ruler asked him if he could grant him any royal favors, to which the Cynic replied, "Stand out of my light." Such stories reflect the contemporary meaning of cynicism. However, the Cynics' more extreme behaviors should not be allowed to eclipse the highly spiritual and admirable ethical concerns at the core of their outlook.

Although Diogenes was a contemporary of Aristotle, he had the spirit of the Hellenistic age. Diogenes lacked the optimism and contentment with his society that we find in Aristotle. Instead, a world weariness and a longing for escape through resignation, independence, and the pursuit of personal virtue characterized the philosophies of this era. His disciple Crates passed on the best features of Cynicism to the Stoics. They carried on the Cynics' concern for virtue, independence from worldly cares, and liberation from the narrow confines of one's culture while leaving behind the latter's more abusive characteristics.

Epicureanism

Epicurus (341–270 B.C.) was born seven years after Plato's death. By the time he had reached his mid-thirties, he had achieved fame for the philosophy and the way of life that he taught. He purchased a garden at the edge of Athens where he created a very close-knit philosophical commune. The Garden (as the school was called) attracted many followers and was open to all people, the

community being made up of both men and women, and included children, slaves, soldiers, and courtesans as well as prominent citizens. Epicurus was noted for his warm affection for his followers, who in turn were deeply devoted to him. After his death, his followers at the Garden gladly carried out the request in his will that they hold a monthly feast in his memory and yearly celebrate his birthday. Epicureanism proved a very attractive philosophy, and with missionary zeal its adherents made so many converts that the philosophy rapidly permeated the Greek-speaking world. The successors of Epicurus made very few changes to his doctrines, because the philosophy was taught by means of a catechism (a form of memorized teachings common among religious groups). Even though his writings took up over three hundred scrolls, only three letters and several fragments have survived.

EPICUREAN METAPHYSICS

For Epicurus, the whole point of philosophy is to heal the soul and enable us to live a happy life. He is accordingly disdainful of theoretical speculations, whether in philosophy or the sciences, unless they serve practical human needs. He is reported to have said,

> Empty is the argument of the philosopher by which no human disease is healed; for just as there is no benefit in medicine if it does not drive out bodily diseases, so there is no benefit in philosophy if it does not drive out the disease of the soul. (I&G 66)[1]

The condition of the soul he hopes to cure is the psychological turmoil that robs us of a happy life. This sense of unrest is generated by false beliefs about what is true and valuable in life. Consequently, he intended his metaphysics to serve as an antidote to what troubles us. The first thing we need to realize, according to Epicurus, is that reality is made up of an infinite number of atoms continually moving in an infinite void. With his atomistic predecessor Democritus, he believed that these atoms vary in size and shape. However, he differed with Democritus on one crucial point. Since atoms are material, Epicurus concluded that

---

*The name Cynic means "canine" and may have been a term of abuse by opponents, or it may have referred to Diogenes' self-proclaimed nickname. Another theory is that the name comes from the Cynosarges, a place where Antisthenes taught.

they each must have weight. It follows from this, he reasoned, that their natural motion is to move downward through infinite space like cosmic rain. However, as they fall, some atoms randomly swerve to the side. This spontaneous deviation from their paths causes the atoms to collide and combine into groups. This accounts for the changing collections of large-scale objects such as rocks, trees, stars, and people.

If we start with material atoms as the fundamental reality, what implications for human life follow? Clearly, we must be collections of atoms in motion. The soul, or the seat of all our thoughts, emotions, and values, is really a material entity made up of very fine atoms collected together in the body. However, because the atoms can spontaneously deviate from their mechanically determined paths, the Epicureans believed that not everything is determined or predictable. Therefore, they concluded, there is some room in a materialistic universe for free will after all.

ETHICS AND PLEASURE

If the purpose of metaphysics is to provide us with a guiding vision for life, what sort of ethical theory could be developed out of an atomistic materialism? Certainly there could be no place in this universe for any nonphysical values such as Plato described. All values must be based on the way in which atoms impinge on our sense organs and create experiences of pleasure and pain. Epicurus believed that it was simply a psychological fact that the pursuit of pleasure motivates all human action. This claim is called **psychological hedonism**. As he puts it, "pleasure is the starting-point and goal of living blessedly"(LM, I&G 24). Every action you perform can be explained in terms of the pursuit of either physical or psychological pleasure. What other explanation could there be, Epicurus asks, but that you do things because you want to do them, and you want to do them because they make life more pleasant?

If this is the correct theory about human behavior, then any ethical advice about what we ought to do must be based on it. Accordingly, Epicurean philosophy identifies the notions of good and evil with pleasure and pain. Most people would say that pleasure is good. However, the Epicurean claim is that *only* pleasure is good. This position is called **ethical hedonism**. Thus, for Epicurus, the pursuit of pleasure both describes human behavior (psychological hedonism) and prescribes what is ultimately of value in human life (ethical hedonism). All moral philosophies say, "Pursue the good and avoid evil." According to Epicureanism, however, this translates into "Pursue pleasure (good) and avoid pain (evil)." If we stress the first part of the formula ("pursue pleasure") it leads to imprudent hedonism. Epicurus, however, thought the good life would be one that achieved repose, tranquillity, or quietude. Hence, the goal of wisdom is *ataraxia* or freedom from care. For this reason, he stressed the last part of the formula ("avoid pain"). If this is the overriding concern, then clearly not every pleasure is worthy of being pursued. The physical pleasures of promiscuous sex, rich foods, and strong drink are only momentary pleasures and tend to bring some form of pain in their wake (disease, emotional turmoil, poor health, hangovers). Only mental pleasures and friendship are enduring and produce tranquillity.

In a letter to a correspondent named Menoeceus, Epicurus catalogues the kinds of desires available to us:

> One must reckon that of desires some are natural, some groundless; and of the natural desires some are necessary and some merely natural; and of the necessary, some are necessary for happiness and some for freeing the body from troubles and some for life itself. (LM, I&G 24)

We may picture the desires structured as in Figure 6-1. Examples of each of these desires are as follows:

- Groundless (not rooted in nature)
  —Fame, material luxuries (jewelry, designer clothes)
- Natural, but unnecessary
  —Sex, delicious foods
- Natural and necessary
  —For happiness: wisdom, friendship

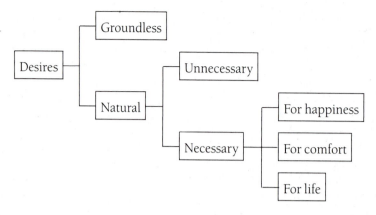

FIGURE 6-1 Epicurus's classification of desires

—For comfort: adequate clothing

—For life: water, food

It should be clear from what has been said, that Epicurus has gotten bad press. The label *epicurean* is often associated with the philosophy "Eat, drink, and be merry." Obviously, however, his ethics could not be further away from this vision of life. Epicurus says that the following characterizes the life of the happy person:

Prudence

Self-sufficiency

Sober reasoning

Honor

Justice

Wisdom

Health of the body

Peace of mind

Plain food

Accordingly, the disciples of the Garden lived very frugal and austere lives and placed a great emphasis on friendship as the supreme form of pleasure. Although the Epicureans lived very virtuous lives, it is important to realize that they did not consider moral virtue to be a matter of excellence, something to be pursued for its own sake. In the final analysis, virtue is a means to the end of individual pleasure. Epicurus says, "One must honour the noble, and the virtues and things like that, *if* they produce pleasure. But if they do not, one must bid them goodbye" (I&G 50).

EPICUREAN SOCIAL PHILOSOPHY

In the individualistic tenor of Epicurus's ideas, there is little social philosophy. He advises that the civil laws are based on human conventions and expediency and should be obeyed only because this will make our lives more peaceful. However, he cautioned people against involvement in politics, for this can only burden us with responsibilities, create enemies, and lead to personal unrest. Accordingly, Epicurus says that the wise must "free themselves from the prison of . . . politics" (I&G 31). He summed up his social philosophy in these words: "The purest security is that which comes from a quiet life and withdrawal from the many" (I&G 27).

RELIGION AND DEATH

One disease of the soul Epicurus seeks to heal is the fear produced by superstitious myths concerning the gods and our fate after death. Consistent with his belief that immaterial substance is unintelligible, Epicurus asserts that the gods have material bodies. Nevertheless, they are immortal, for their bodies consist of a different sort of atoms from the rest of nature. The point of the Epicurean teaching about the gods is to assure us that they are too aloof and preoccupied with their own pleasure to bother themselves with the problems of this world or to cause trouble for us. Ironically, the gods themselves seem to be adherents of the Epicurean philosophy:

> They spend their time in such a manner that nothing can be conceived which is more blessed or better supplied with all kinds of good things. For a god is idle, is entangled with no serious preoccupations, undertakes no toilsome labour, but simply rejoices in his own wisdom and virtue, being certain that he will always be in the midst of pleasures which are both supreme and eternal. (I&G 41)

If the gods are too peaceful to be capable of either gratitude or anger we do not have to worry about appeasing them or being punished by them. When we understand this, we can live our lives as autonomously and serenely as the gods.

Even if we don't have to worry about the gods, doesn't the fear of death still haunt us, robbing us of all our hard-won tranquillity? Again Epicureanism offers us peace of mind with the following argument: if we exist, then death does not; and if death exists, then we do not. In either case we will never literally experience death, for death is simply the moment when the soul atoms disperse into the air with our last breath and our ability to experience pain or anguish ceases. Epicurus gives the following advice in a letter:

> Get used to believing that death is nothing to us. For all good and bad consists in sense-experience, and death is the privation of sense-experience. Hence, a correct knowledge of the fact that death is nothing to us makes the mortality of life a matter of contentment, not by adding a limitless time [to life] but by removing the longing for immortality. (LM, I&G 23)

THE SIGNIFICANCE OF THE EPICUREANS

Although the Epicureans lived an admirable lifestyle, they considered that virtue was valuable only for its egoistic consequences. We are to be

virtuous because it makes life more pleasant and is to our advantage. One should be just only to avoid the consequences of one's evil actions being exposed. However, what if someone decides that the discomfort of social rebuke pales in comparison to the pleasures of being greedy and unfair? It would be difficult for an Epicurean to say that such a decision was morally wrong if it genuinely did maximize pleasure.

The tensions in Epicurean moral philosophy become apparent when we look at Epicurus's attitude toward friendship. Consistent with his principles, he says that "friendship comes to be because of its utility" and continually links it with the pleasure it brings us (I&G 35). But such passages make the Epicurean sound like a scheming, calculating, self-serving opportunist who makes friends and uses them for the pleasure they make possible. However, as with so many philosophers, the character of Epicurus was better than the ethical principles he espoused. By all accounts he showed kindness and generosity toward others that went beyond any personal payoff these actions may have brought. We are told that "Epicurus assembled . . . large congregations of friends which were bound together by a shared feeling of the deepest love" (I&G 47). He even says that friendship may require that you sacrifice your life for a friend. The problem is that the Epicurean ethics of pleasure clearly is an egoistic hedonism. This view implies that my friendships are valuable only for what pleasure I get out of them. In contrast, Epicurus says that "every friendship is worth choosing for its own sake" (I&G 30). This would imply that other things besides pleasure (such as friendship) are intrinsically valuable. If we embrace this doctrine, we must abandon the fundamental thesis of hedonism.

In conclusion, the individualism and withdrawal that lie at the heart of Epicureanism characterized the Hellenistic period. By way of contrast, the elaborate social philosophies of Plato and Aristotle indicate that they thought the good life was to be found in involvement in political life and in the attempt to make the state better. The Hellenistic philosophers, however, despaired over the possibility of meaningful involvement in society beyond one's intimate circle of friends. Clearly, Epicureanism met the needs of the age, for it spread very rapidly and lasted as an organized movement until the fourth century A.D. Although it no longer exists in this form, it is not hard to find people today whose lifestyles consciously or unconsciously follow the Epicurean ideals.

Stoicism

Stoicism developed about the same time that Epicurus founded his school. The Stoic philosophy developed into a formidable rival that competed with the hedonism of Epicurus for the minds of the Greek and Roman populace. The popularity and influence of these two systems indicate that they touched on real needs in their culture even though they provided different answers to the problems. We find them prevalent even in the Christian era, in the account of the Apostle Paul speaking to both groups in Athens (Acts 17).

Stoicism was founded by a philosopher named Zeno (who lived about 336 to 264 B.C.).* He journeyed from his native city of Citium (located in Cyprus) to Athens, where he founded a school. Zeno lectured on a porch or open colonnade. Accordingly, the name of the school comes from the Greek word *stoa*, which means "porch." He attracted many followers in Greece and Rome. He was widely admired for his moral earnestness, and the Athenians gave him official honors.

We will not be able to cover all the facets of Stoic thought, because they made contributions in so many different fields. For example, they developed a detailed empiricist philosophy of knowledge. Furthermore, the Stoics made a number of original contributions in the discipline of logic. They developed a logic of propositions that anticipated modern propositional logic and that went beyond the logic of categories that Aristotle had formulated. Building on their system, they founded our traditional science of grammar. However, it was their metaphysics and the ethical theory based on

it that made them famous. To introduce their ideas in these last two fields, let's briefly compare and contrast the Stoics with the Epicureans.

COMPARISON OF EPICUREANISM AND STOICISM

The Epicureans and the Stoics had a great deal in common: (1) they built enormously popular philosophies, yet they still attempted to provide rational justifications for their beliefs; (2) they were both concerned with logic and physics, but emphasized the relevance of these fields to practical ethics; (3) both were materialistic in their metaphysics and empiricists in their epistemology; and finally (4) both advised us to act according to nature (by "nature," referring to both the cosmos and human nature). However, in the details of this latter point their positions diverged, because they had different conceptions of the cosmos and human nature. For the Epicureans, the universe was mechanistic and governed by blind chance. For the Stoics, however, the universe was purposeful and governed by a benevolent, divine plan. According to the Epicureans, humans are basically pleasure-seeking organisms whose highest good is to pursue pleasure. Thus virtue has value only if it helps us achieve this end. For the Stoics, character, virtue, self-discipline, and the fulfillment of duty have value in themselves. Their ethical outlook was influenced by Socrates' life and death and by his confidence that no real harm can come to a person whose life is based on virtue and eternal values. The Epicureans built their social philosophy on enlightened self-interest and expressed disdain for involvement in larger social concerns. Accordingly, the attention they gave to social virtues such as justice was motivated by individualistic, prudential concerns. The Stoics, however, taught that we should subordinate our selfish interests to fulfillment of more universal ends and developed a social philosophy emphasizing that all humanity constitutes one great community or family.

STOIC METAPHYSICS

Like the Epicureans, the Stoics embraced materialistic monism or the claim that all reality is material.

*This Zeno should not be confused with the pupil of Parmenides who proposed the famous paradoxes.

The philosophy of Stoicism received its name from the Stoa (meaning porch) where its founder Zeno lectured.

However, unlike their rivals they did not believe there was any room for chance in the scheme of things. The realm of matter obviously includes the crasser sorts of stuff that make up things such as rocks and wood. However, when they came to discuss God and the human soul, as well as all the forms and forces operating in the world, they consistently concluded that these entities were also material. These sorts of beings are made up of very fine matter. Accordingly, they frequently used *pneuma* (the word for breath or wind) to describe these very subtle but still material realities.

As opposed to the Epicureans' universe of material particles governed by blind chance, the Stoics' universe was teleological (purposeful) and permeated by the divine. The Stoics used multiple names such as Zeus, God, Nature, Order, Universal Reason, Fate, Destiny, and Providence as interchangeable terms to refer to the same, fundamental reality. Unlike the impersonal or uncaring gods of Aristotle and Epicurus, the Stoic divinity is benevolent and just. He guides all things by his wisdom to realize the perfect, most beautiful, and good outcome. Although there is an aspect of God that is transcendent, he also diffuses himself throughout the world and assumes its form. Showing their indebtedness to Heraclitus, the Stoics taught that God is the Logos, or the rational principle pervading everything. He is immanent in the world as its creative and guiding force. Again drawing on Heraclitus, they said that the Logos takes the form of an all-permeating cosmic fire. The fiery vapor manifests itself in the flaming spheres in the heavens, in the warmth and vitality of plants and animals, and as rational thought in the soul of humans. Although the world is material, it is a continuum, like a field of force, or a diffused vapor, instead of the discrete particles of the

Epicureans. Thus, the world is one, living, divine body, and the Logos is its soul and reason. Little sparks of the divine fire, the *logoi*, are dispersed throughout the world like seeds to guide the growth and development of each thing.

But this God is not a free personality or free creator, for the process of nature flows from his substance with a rigid necessity. Hence, the Stoics believed there was no chance or contingency in the universe. Everything in the world is determined down to the smallest detail, and events could not be any other way than they are. However, because this logical determinism is an expression of a benevolent, divine providence, it is not cold, blind, and impersonal. Instead, it nurtures and fulfills our deepest human needs.

Human beings are sparks of the divine fire. Hence each individual is a microcosm or a miniature version of the universe. Our individual reason is identical with the universal world reason. This is why our finite minds can know the cosmos. After death, our souls endure until the end of the world, when they return to God along with everything else. At this point the Stoics disagreed among themselves. Cleanthes (around 331–232 B.C.) hypothesized that the afterlife applied to all souls, whereas Chrysippus (around 280–207 B.C.) claimed it was attained only by the virtuous souls.

An obvious problem arises for any philosophy that claims every detail of the world serves a benevolent, divinely ordered purpose. How does one reconcile this belief with the problem of evil? Sometimes the Stoics blamed human wickedness. However, corrupt human choices can only explain such evils as crimes and wars; they cannot account for natural evils such as disease, earthquakes, and famines. To this problem the Stoics offered two kinds of solutions. The first answer was to assert that if we could see the cosmos as a whole, we would see that the world really is perfect, beautiful, and good. Some things appear evil only because of our limited perspective. For example, if we focused narrowly on the dark shadows in a painting and did not see the lighter colors, we would not appreciate the beauty of the painting. The second answer claimed that some evils are the necessary means for realizing the good. For example, bitter medicine may produce health. Painful exercise may produce a muscular body. The Stoics pointed out that the existence of evil is essential to the production of virtue. Without vice and suffering to struggle against, there could not be courage, patience, or fortitude. In the final analysis, no matter how severe physical evil may be, it cannot affect the human character, which alone has intrinsic value.

ETHICS AND RESIGNATION

The Stoics agreed with Aristotle that the highest good for human beings is a life in accord with reason. Happiness is found in living a rationally self-determined life. The Stoics' ethics is tied in with their metaphysics, for the goal in life is to make one's mind a microcosm of the order in the universe. But how do I achieve rational control over my life? The first answer is, I must be free from all passion. If my emotions control me, then I am their victim and am not living a rationally self-determined life. The second answer is to tie my happiness only to what I can control. The search for such things as fame, wealth, pleasure, or the love of another person puts external events in control of my happiness. Furthermore, if every event in the universe is determined, then I cannot change the inevitable. The one thing I can control is my attitude toward life. I must welcome every event as the expression of God's will and as an essential part of the harmonious, beautiful scheme of things. In submitting my will to the will of the universe, I do not spend my life thrashing against the irresistible tide of necessity, but serenely go with the flow. If my happiness is based on the pursuit of virtue and an inner serenity, then I am in charge of my life:

> And this very thing constitutes the virtue of the happy man and the smooth current of life, when all actions promote the harmony of the spirit dwelling in the individual man with the will of him who orders the universe. (S 112)[2]

Zeno and Chrysippus used the following illustration:

Suppose a dog to be tied to a wagon. If he wishes to follow, the wagon pulls him and he follows, so that his own power and necessity unite. But if he does not wish to follow, he will be compelled to anyhow. The same is the case with mankind also. Even if they do not wish to follow, they will be absolutely forced to enter into the fated event. (S 109–110)

Epictetus (around A.D. 50–138) made the same point, saying, "Ask not that events should happen as you will, but let your will be that events should happen as they do, and you shall have peace" (S 135). Underscoring this sentiment, he quotes a prayer written by Cleanthes:

Conduct me, Zeus, and thou, O Destiny,
Wherever your decrees have fixed my lot.
I follow cheerfully, and, did I not,
Wicked and wretched, I must follow still.[3]

According to the Stoics, you and I are free as long as we act on basis of logical thought. Otherwise, we will be governed by our impulses like the brutes. Plato and Aristotle had a low view of the emotions but thought they were acceptable if they could be moderated and controlled by reason. The Stoics, however, thought that moral evil was the result of our passions and sought to eliminate them altogether. According to Chrysippus there are basically four kinds of emotions, each based on a false judgment:

Emotion	Object of the Mistaken Judgment
Pleasure	A present good
Desire	A future good
Grief	A present evil
Fear	A future evil

However, if all things that happen are inevitable and part of the beautiful plan of the universe, then it is irrational to be aroused by these emotions. To experience these sorts of emotions toward the events in my life is as irrational as regretting the necessary order of the multiplication tables or either desiring or fearing a change in them.

Because they disdained the emotions, the Stoic ideal of life was "apathy." This term should not be understood as listlessness but rather as the freedom from passion or the refusal to be upset by anything that happens. Even today we still say, "Be stoical" or "Be philosophical," when we are advising people to be content with what life brings their way. These slang expressions testify to how deeply the Stoics have influenced our cultural traditions. Consistent with their philosophy, the Stoics taught that death is not an evil and was not to be feared. It is a natural and inevitable part of being human. The Stoics were even willing to hasten its arrival when appropriate, finding no shame in an honorable suicide. The story is told that when Zeno tripped and injured his foot, he took this as a sign from God that his life had reached its appointed end. So he dutifully killed himself.

Initially, the Stoics did not acknowledge any degrees of virtue or vice. One was either perfectly virtuous or, like the rest of humanity, a fool and a reprobate. However, the later Stoics were more flexible and tried to broaden the appeal of their philosophy by acknowledging that some people were neither perfectly virtuous nor entirely bad, but were on their way to being wise. This tendency to make concessions was also illustrated by their modification of the doctrine concerning "indifferents." An indifferent is any external thing that does not affect the moral virtue or the happiness of the wise person. The list of indifferents would include health, pleasure, beauty, wealth, as well as disease, pain, ugliness, and poverty. But if these are all neutral, why choose health over sickness? The Stoics compromised with common sense by saying that while these things do not contribute to nor detract from our happiness, some indifferents can be classified as "preferences" or "advantages." It is permissible to pursue them as long as we do not pin our happiness to them.

STOIC SOCIAL PHILOSOPHY

Some may find the Stoics' view of the world to be quaint but antiquated. However, their social philosophy turned out to be an enduring and important contribution to the foundations of Western civilization. It is significant that many of the Stoics before the Christian era were from outside

Greece. By the time Stoicism developed, Athens had lost its role as the hub of culture. This led to a more international perspective and avoided some of the Athenian provincialism that pervaded Plato's and Aristotle's political theories. When Zeno was asked what his city was, he replied that he was "a citizen of the cosmos." The Cynics' emphasis on rising above the narrow conventions of one's society had an influence here. The Stoics taught that each individual is part of the larger whole of humanity and must be concerned with more than one's narrow self-interest. Their metaphysics implied that all rational beings, even slaves and foreigners, had a spark of the divine fire. Their metaphor of the fatherhood of God suggested that we are his children and the entire human race is one great family. Hence, gender, wealth, race, or social class ceased to have significance in the Stoic social philosophy. Whereas the Epicureans withdrew from politics, the Stoics emphasized our civic duties. It is our job to make society image the rationally ordered universe and reflect the justice and benevolence of God.

THE ROMAN STOICS

The Romans are noted for their innovations in engineering and politics but less so for their philosophies. They were content to borrow their philosophical conceptions from the work done by the Greeks. The Stoic philosophy was particularly appealing to them because of its notion that all people belong to one universal community, governed by one standard of justice—exactly the kind of universal state the Romans were trying to develop. For a time, it became the semiofficial philosophy of the Roman political establishment. Although a few Romans were suspicious of philosophy, the Stoics' emphasis on resignation made them popular with the established order. It is not a philosophy that encourages activists or revolutionaries. The Romans helped popularize Stoicism by downplaying its more severe elements and developing its practical aspects. To make it more coherent with the Roman context, they emphasized the virtues associated with civic duty more than the ideal of apathy. The universal ap-

peal of Stoicism is illustrated by the fact that its Roman phase attracted first a Roman lawyer (Cicero), then one of Nero's prime ministers (Seneca), as well as one of Nero's slaves (Epictetus), and even a Roman emperor (Marcus Aurelius Antoninus).*

An important contribution of the Roman Stoics was their application of the Stoic notion of natural law to Roman legal theory. All proponents of the **natural law theory** in ethics believe that nature is not only ruled by physical laws but that it is permeated by a moral order as well. This unwritten natural law is a moral code that applies to all people no matter what their culture. Thus, Cicero distinguished two kinds of laws. First, some laws are merely local, human inventions. Second, the natural moral order constitutes a universal law. All of us are subject to this second law by virtue of the fact that we all share in the divine reason. It is "the law above the law," and our human civil codes are valid and just only if they conform to the natural law. The opening paragraph of the American Declaration of Independence indicates the lasting influence of this theory, stating that people have inalienable rights "to which the laws of nature and of nature's God entitle them."

The Romans also developed the Stoic ethics of duty. Before Stoicism, Greek ethical theory placed very little emphasis on the notion of duty. Generally, even the most exalted, altruistic ethical advice was intimately tied up with one's own self-interest and the pursuit of the good life. The Stoics, however, gave duty and obligation a new importance. They taught that we must do some things simply because they are right. This emphasis is eloquently captured in Marcus Aurelius's comment: "Have I done something for the general interest? Well then I have had my reward."[4] Although he was a Roman emperor, his Stoicism extended his sense of loyalty far beyond the Roman Empire to embrace the whole human population: "But my nature is rational and social; and my city and country, so far as I am Antoninus, is Rome,

---

*Their dates are: Cicero (106–43 B.C.), Seneca (c. 4 B.C.–A.D. 65), Epictetus (c. A.D. 50–138), Marcus Aurelius (A.D. 121–180).

but so far as I am a man, it is the world."[5] Marcus Aurelius was the last great teacher of Stoicism, for it lost its hold on people as Christianity came into prominence. However, its voice was not completely silenced—many of its doctrines found their way into Christian thought.

THE SIGNIFICANCE OF THE STOICS

One of the most significant by-products of the Stoic philosophy was that it brought into focus the problem of freedom and determinism. Its critics claim that a fundamental incoherence lies at the heart of this philosophy. If the universe is determined down to the last detail, how can humans be free? If everything that happens is necessary and good, then how can any human actions or thoughts be bad? Yet the Stoics believed we are free and advise us that we can make good choices and bad choices, that we can harbor appropriate attitudes and wrong attitudes. However, given the deterministic Stoic metaphysics, it is hard to understand why human attitudes are not a part of the necessary order of nature and therefore beyond our control. It would be unfair to criticize the Stoics for not resolving this issue in their time, for it remains one of the most controversial problems in philosophy today.

Others have criticized Stoicism because of its ideal of apathy. Critics say that it purchases tranquillity at the expense of our normal and appropriate human emotions. If a child is suffering, the Stoics would say it is our duty to do what we can to alleviate her pain. However, if we are not successful, we should not feel grief or pity, because everything that happens is as it was meant to be. Seneca says that pity is not a virtue but "a mental defect." Expounding on this, he says,

Pity is the sorrow of the mind brought about by the sight of the distress or sadness caused by the ills of others which it believes come undeservedly. But no sorrow befalls the wise man. (S 128)

For this reason Bertrand Russell says that there is "a certain coldness in the Stoic conception of virtue. Not only bad passions are condemned, but all passions."[6]

Stoicism had a continuous history of about five hundred years. Even while it declined as a philosophical movement, the Christian tradition was taking up many of its ideals. The Stoic outlook comforted the Christians, who were suffering persecution and trying to endure a cruel and corrupt government. Both the Stoics and the Christians felt the freedom that comes from a serene detachment, because they realized that the pains of this world were but insignificant specks on the face of eternity and even the worst of evils would find some purpose in the beautiful tapestry of cosmic history that God is weaving. As with the Epicureans, some people today live out the Stoic ideal, whether or not they call it by that name.

Skepticism

The Skeptics looked with scornful amusement at the quarrels between their contemporaries the Epicureans and the Stoics. The latter two philosophies were merely the latest additions to the long parade of human opinions. The Skeptics complained that both their rivals assumed what they had no basis for assuming: the competence of human reason to know reality. The Skeptics found no basis for such an extravagant claim. The term "skeptic" comes from the Greek *skeptikos*, which means "inquirers." The Skeptics prided themselves on their ability to inquire into the foundations of our beliefs as well as on having the honesty to face the fact that there are no foundations.

Skeptical thought had been around since the early Greeks and was a prominent part of the Sophists' teachings. However, in the Hellenistic period, it received a new burst of energy from Pyrrho of Elis (360–270 B.C.). By at least the first century B.C., Pyrrhonism became a synonym for Skepticism. Pyrrho never wrote anything, but we have accounts of his views from other writers in his tradition. Pyrrho declared that sense experience cannot give us knowledge. To do so, our sense data must agree with their objects. But if we can never get outside of sensation, how could we ever know this? Furthermore, rational argument cannot give us knowledge either, because for every argument there is a counterargument and the two opposing positions cancel each other out.

Because problems arise with all our sources of knowledge, the Skeptics concluded that we cannot know the real nature of things. Hence, all we can confidently talk about are appearances. You can say, "The honey *appears* to me to be sweet" but not "The honey *is* sweet." The prudent approach is always to suspend judgment and assume nothing at all. The same advice holds for moral judgments. We cannot know anything for sure, so stop striving for absolute moral truth, they said. Consequently, a serene apathy and indifference characterize the wise person. What you do not know, you do not have to worry about. The Skeptics favored a social conservativism. Since we cannot know what is good or bad in itself, we might as well leave such judgments to the consensus of law and tradition.

ACADEMIC SKEPTICISM

The power of the Skeptical movement is signaled by the fact that its seeds took root within Plato's Academy. Arcesilaus (roughly, 316–242 B.C.) headed the Academy about the time when Zeno was inaugurating Stoicism. Arcesilaus was influential in turning the Academy toward Skepticism, a course that it would take for about two hundred years. His leadership was passed on to Carneades (who lived about 214–129 B.C.). Carneades was considered one of the most brilliant philosophers of his century. The Academic Skeptics complained that the Academy had lost the Socratic spirit of inquiry and had settled into a comfortable dogmatism. This may seem a strange turn for the Academics to take, since Plato himself was confident we could know the Forms and fought against the skepticism of the Sophists. However, the Academic Skeptics selectively chose those elements from the Platonic tradition that they liked. For example, they emphasized that Socrates said he knew nothing and that the Socratic dialogues always ended without establishing any definite conclusions. The Skeptics used Plato's skeptical arguments against the senses and noted that in

the *Timaeus* he said that physics is merely a "likely story."[7]

The Skeptics never tired of attacking the "dogmatism" of both the Epicureans and the Stoics. They both based knowledge on the senses, which the Skeptics argued can only give us appearances. However, the Stoics thought that some sense impressions were so indubitable the mind could not help but assent to them. The Skeptics had an easy job demonstrating that in dreams and hallucinations, we are presented with false images that are also convincing. In a wholesale fashion, the Skeptics undercut any search for a criterion of truth, for any principle we can come up with will itself need justification; that is, it will need a criterion for determining that it should be our guiding principle. They did not make the mistake of dogmatically asserting that nothing can be known. Instead, they merely asserted that we *appear* to be without knowledge. Thus, with admirable consistency, they suspended judgment on whether, in the final analysis, Skepticism is true.

In 156–155 B.C. Carneades represented Athens as an ambassador to Rome along with a Stoic and an Aristotelian. In between doing business, they gave public lectures. This was the first exposure the Romans had to philosophy, and Carneades' speeches attracted the most interest. On the first day he argued in favor of justice and eloquently commended its practice to the Romans. The next day, he argued the opposite position, using equally brilliant rhetoric to downgrade justice. This two-faced arguing was a favorite method of the Skeptics for undermining those who thought we have reasons for any positive opinion.

The Stoics vigorously attacked these views. They claimed that a consistent Skepticism would lead to the suspension of not only judgment but of all activity, paralyzing human life. Carneades tried to respond to these attacks by modifying the Skeptical thesis and arguing that even though we do not have certainty, we can have probability, which is all we need for meaningful action. Reportedly, Carneades said that "the wise man will employ whatever apparently plausible presentations he meets with, provided there is nothing which opposes its plausibility, and thus will every plan of life be governed" (I&G 171). This compromise won him the disdain of both the Stoics and the later Pyrrhonic purists within his own tradition.

THE REVIVAL OF PYRRHONIAN SKEPTICISM

The purists among the Skeptics believed that the Academic Skeptics had taken a wrong turn because they were not skeptical enough. For example, the purists complained that the notion of probability was suspect, for the ability to distinguish the probable from the improbable requires a good deal of knowledge. These more strict Skeptics called themselves "Pyrrhonists" in honor of the movement's founder. The members of this group delighted in formalizing Skepticism in terms of various groups of principles. For example, Agrippa claimed that Skepticism rests on five pillars: (1) *Disagreement*—on any issue, not everyone will agree. (2) *Infinite regress*—to resolve disagreements, we must find reasons for our conclusions, but these reasons need justification, so then we need justifications for our justifications, and so on, and so on. (3) *Relativity*—things are perceived differently in different circumstances. (4) *Hypothesis*—if we try to solve the regress problem by taking some statement as an axiom or an indubitable starting point, anyone can come along and say its contrary is self-evident. Hence, the starting point of every proof is groundless and arbitrary. (5) *Circular reasoning*—all arguments that avoid the first four problems will end up, in one way or another, assuming what we are trying to prove. Later Skeptics reduced the whole arsenal of arguments to two simple theses: nothing is self-evident, and nothing can be proved. As with all the philosophies of this time, the Skeptics' tightly reasoned arguments had one goal: personal peace. If we cannot know anything, then we cease to worry about whether or not we have the truth. We are free of the struggle to distinguish truth from falsehood and good from bad. We can just accept what appears to be the case and what our customs and laws tell us to do. This was expressed well by Sextus Empiricus, a physician who lived about the turn of the third century A.D.: "Therefore, he who suspends judgment about everything which is subject to opinion reaps a harvest of the most complete happiness" (I&G 238).

THE SIGNIFICANCE OF SKEPTICISM

As a close-knit movement, Skepticism died out in the third century A.D. The Skeptics could not answer the objection that it makes no sense to offer arguments unless we have some data to serve as the starting point of our reasoning. But this implies that at least we do have reasons to believe our premises are true. However, although they had no positive conclusions to offer, the Skeptics did contribute to philosophy. Skepticism of all varieties makes philosophy self-critical and keeps it honest and free of dogmatism. Furthermore, they set the agenda for later philosophers. Their successors had to either accept their arguments and live with the consequences or come up with an epistemology that survived all skeptical attacks. Thus, they inspired a good deal of work in epistemology. For example, St. Augustine wrote *Against the Academics* to lay the Skeptics' arguments to rest. In the beginning of the modern period, philosophers revived skeptical arguments and used them either as a foil for their own philosophies or as a weapon against their opponents. Descartes used skeptical doubt as a method for finding which beliefs were certain beyond all question. Berkeley sought to avoid skeptical conclusions by claiming that there was no reality beyond the appearances. Some religious philosophers found it a helpful critique of the pretensions of human reason, claiming that since reason cannot answer our questions, we are driven to faith and revelation. Worth mentioning here are Erasmus, Pascal, Montaigne, and Bayle. In the seventeenth century, the legacy of Skepticism seemed to have had some effect on the rise of modern science. If we cannot know the real essences of things, philosophers said, then we should not let ourselves be distracted by abstruse metaphysical perplexities. Instead, we should be content with an empirical study of the world of appearances.

By the time of its decline, Skepticism had not offered peace but only confusion. Traditional certitudes and the gods of Mount Olympus were no longer credible, but Skepticism offered nothing positive in return. Simply following religious and social traditions without conviction as some Skeptics urged, did not seem satisfactory. People in this age sought for something to cling to and, for many, faith filled this longing. Consequently, various religious philosophies based on Asian thought became popular. Eventually, Christianity emerged as a powerful cultural force, providing its own answers to the needs of the time.

Plotinus and Neoplatonism

When we reach the last vestiges of Greek thought in the Christian era, we find that a full circle has been made. Greek philosophy ends where it began—in religion. The conditions that caused this development are understandable. The third century A.D. represented the most dismal period in Roman history. Emperors rose to power by bribing the army, and assassination was the most common way to remove those in power. The Roman army was weakened by corruption and discord, and the barbarians chipped away at the territories in the north and the east. War and disease decimated the population, while corruption, exorbitant taxes, and diminished resources threw the empire into financial chaos.

In response to these depressing events, people felt a thirst for a better world and some sort of hope that they could pin to eternity far above the chaotic events of human history. People longed not simply for the Greek vision of the good life, but for a decidedly religious notion of salvation, to be found in a mystical absorption into God. Some found the answer in a revival of Platonic otherworldliness. Hence, there arose not just a Platonic philosophy of religion, but a genuinely religious philosophy. This new, religious Platonism (or Neoplatonism as it later came to be called) drew from all the nonmaterialistic and re-

ligious doctrines of earlier systems. Its sources were primarily Pythagorean, Aristotelian, Stoic, and, of course, Platonic.

The founder of Neoplatonism was Plotinus (A.D. 205–270). Raised in a provincial town in Egypt, he journeyed in his late twenties to Alexandria to study philosophy. Alexandria was a cosmopolitan city where Greek culture from the West and mystery religions from the East mixed freely. He sought out Ammonius Saccas, a famous teacher, and spent time under his instruction.* When Plotinus was forty, his journeys brought him to Rome, where he opened a school. He developed a large following that included several physicians, a poet, several women, and many members of the Senate. He even found favor with the Emperor Gallienus and his wife. Plotinus gained a reputation as a spiritual counselor and, although numerous people frequented him for advice, he never turned anyone away. Although continually in weak health, he had a powerful but gentle and affectionate spirit. We are told he never would reveal his birthday, because he did not want it celebrated. Instead, he invited friends to celebrations on the birthdays of Socrates and Plato. Although he never married, he took orphaned children into his house and became their guardian. After his death, his manuscripts were edited by his faithful disciple Porphyry. Porphyry divided them into six groups of nine called the *Enneads*.†

THE ONE

For Plotinus, those things that have the most reality are those with the most unity. Accordingly, the highest being is what he calls "the One." It is wholly transcendent, beyond all thought and being, and incomprehensible. To think about or describe it would be possible only if we could attribute properties to it. But to have distinguishable properties would mean that it was composed of parts. Thus, the source of all properties is be-

---

*Ammonius is said to have been raised as a Christian but later reverted to Greek religion.
†From the Greek word *ennea*, meaning "nine."

yond any of them and totally without any sort of plurality. It is engaged in neither thought, willing, nor any other conscious activity, for all these imply some sort of duality. Plotinus uses numerous names to refer to the One, such as God, the Good, First Existent, the Absolute, the Infinite, and the Father.

Although it does not consciously act, the being of the One is so full that it overflows and all things emanate from it, while the One itself remains the same. Plotinus borrows the metaphor of the sun from Plato to illustrate this. The sun sheds its light on all things but remains undiminished in the process. Similarly, an object may have its image reproduced in a mirror while being unaffected by this duplication. Thus, the One is like an eternal sun producing eternal light. However, this does not result from a conscious decision to create, for the world proceeds from the One by necessity.

INTELLECT

The first emanation from the One is *Nous*, which can be translated as Intellect, Intellectual Principle, Divine Mind, or Spirit. It is eternal and free of all imperfection. As with the One, Intellect is indivisible in the sense that it cannot be dissolved into parts. Yet, unlike the One, it has distinguishable aspects. These aspects are the knower and the objects of its knowledge. The Intellect intuits two objects: the One and itself. In knowing itself, it knows that it contains the whole of the Platonic Forms. However, it does not know them one after another but intuits the whole collection in one, eternal and unified vision. At this point, Plotinus goes on to differ from Plato, for he claims that there are not only Forms of universals but also Forms of individuals. Hence, there is not only a Form of Humanity, but a Form of Socrates as well. Thus, each individual is given an eternal value and status in the Divine Mind.

SOUL

Eternally emanating from Intellect is a third reality called Soul. It, too, is eternal and nonphysical. It functions as the mediator between the spiritual realm and the world of the senses and makes the cosmos like one, living organism. According to Plotinus, Soul has two aspects. The higher part looks to Intellect and remains untouched by what is beneath it, while the lower part descends to generate the sensible world and replicate its own vision of the Forms within it. However, it no more consciously wills to create the world than the magnet wills to radiate its magnetic field and order the iron filings around it. Because it is the principle of life, growth, order, and movement in the universe, Plotinus says that it can be identified with Nature. The world of physical beings it generates corresponds to all the possible forms of Being contained in Intellect.

Individual human souls are aspects of the World Soul. Plotinus says our souls are like the light from the sun, which shines into each individual house. Each house seems to have its own light but all of it is really the manifestation of one sun (E 4.3.4).[8] Human souls duplicate the structure of the World Soul in that the higher element within us belongs to the realm of Intellect and the lower element is involved with the body. Our souls existed prior to their union with the body, which occurs through a sort of descent from the realm of the spirit. The soul survives the death of the body and is reincarnated, but does not retain its memories.

THE MATERIAL WORLD

So far, we have three primary realities, a hierarchical trinity made up of the One, Intellect, and Soul. However, the Soul is always restless and desires to exercise its powers. Hence, from the Soul comes the final emanation, which is the realm of matter. However, the production of the material realm is not a creative act that happens at some point in time. As with all the higher emanations, the generation of the realm of matter is a necessary and eternal process. This final emanation, however, cannot be considered a fourth kind of reality, for Plotinus believes that matter is nonbeing. His metaphor of the sun helps clarify this point. The sun sends forth rays of light. But the further they get from their source, the dimmer they become, until the light diminishes into total darkness. Similarly, the One radiates being and goodness, but just as darkness is a privation of light, so matter is a privation of all that is real and good.

Following the Platonic model, Plotinus says that what goodness or intelligibility physical objects have is attributed to the dim reflections of the intelligible world that we see in them. But the mixture is never a happy combination, for matter corrupts everything that it touches. So, even though matter receives illumination from Soul, it "darkens the illumination, the light from that source, by mixture with itself, and weakens it" (E 1.8.14).

THE PROBLEM OF EVIL

Not surprisingly, passages in Plotinus suggest that matter is the source of evil. These passages taken by themselves would underscore Plotinus's otherworldliness and lead to a devaluing of the physical. There are even suggestions that the production of the physical world was a tragic mistake (E 1, 1.8.5–6). But he adds confusion to this pessimistic view of matter by also giving us an optimistic outlook on the physical world. First, he argues that since the physical realm is the last stage in the long chain of necessary emanations from the source of all goodness, it must share in the goodness of its source. This process creates all the possible degrees of being, graded from the more perfect to the less perfect. This produces the greatest amount of variety and thus results in the richest sort of world (E 4.8.6). Second, Plotinus argues that anything short of God necessarily falls short of his perfect goodness. Thus, to have a world at all means that some imperfections will exist (E 3.2.5). The world has as much goodness as any material realm could possibly attain, for "what other fairer image of the intelligible world could there be?" (E 2.9.4). Third, the cosmos is like a beautiful painting or a well-written play. Each part has its appropriate role to play in the whole. But if we focus exclusively on only one part, we will miss this. The worst parts of the universe can be used by God to serve the good, even though the reasons for them cannot be discerned by us (E 2.3.18). Even the moral wickedness of those around us serves to get our attention and gives us a greater appreciation for the beauty of virtue (E 3.2.5).

THE WAY OF ASCENT

In his more negative passages, Plotinus frequently talks of the descent of the human soul into the body as a "fall" into the inferior and lower part of the universe. The cause of this is our audacity and desire to be autonomous (E 5.1.1). Agreeing with Plato, he says that the more we focus on our bodies, the senses, and our own individuality, the more we are caught, buried in a cave, ignorantly engaged with our own chains, and alienated from the Whole. The soul is naturally made to fly in the spiritual realm but it becomes distracted, causing it to fall to earth and abandon its wings (E 4.8.4). Yet, at the same time, we are never completely lost, because despite this fall we remain metaphysically a part of the higher realm (E 4.8.8). Evil, then, is not a reality that pulls us down. It is our own willfulness that turns us away from the Good. Evil does not exist for the perfect soul that always turns toward the intellect. Only those souls blinded by their passions and seduced by the material world are affected by the darkness and privation of evil (E 1.8.4).

Plotinus did not develop his philosophy simply to obtain metaphysical knowledge for its own sake, but to show the way to salvation. We can find freedom from our chains and peace for our restless souls if we stay aloof from the body, ignore its seductive songs, and focus on the spirit. Salvation is achieved by traveling through several stages. First, we must purify ourselves through intellectual and moral discipline. Like Plato, Plotinus thought that learning to see the forms in particulars would point us in the right direction. For example, seeing beauty in ourselves and in the things and people around us will leave us nostalgic for the true source of all beauty that we have abandoned. As Plotinus puts it so beautifully,

> Go back into yourself and look; and if you do not yet see yourself beautiful, then, just as someone making a statue which has to be beautiful cuts away here and polishes there and makes one part smooth and clears another till he has given his statue a beautiful face, so you too must cut away excess and straighten the crooked and clear the dark and make it bright, and never stop "working on your statue" till the divine glory of virtue shines out on you. (E 1.6.9)

The next stage is to engage in philosophical dialectic, in which we more fully come to understand the eternal intelligible world. The final stage is a mystical and ecstatic union with God. This experience is beyond all language and discursive thought. Plotinus's description of this experience is eloquent and moving:

> When we do look to [the One], then we are at our goal and at rest . . . as we truly dance our god-inspired dance around him.
>
> And in this dance the soul sees the spring of life, the spring of intellect, the principle of being, the cause of good, the root of the soul; . . . There the soul takes its rest and is outside evils because it has run up into a place which is clear of evils. . . . And if anyone does not know this experience, let him think of it in terms of our loves here below, and what it is like to attain what one is most in love with, and that these earthly loves are mortal and harmful and loves only of images, and that they change because it was not what is really and truly loved nor our good nor what we seek. But there is our true love, with whom also we can be united. . . . There one can see both him and oneself as it is right to see: the self glorified, full of intelligible light—but rather itself pure light—weightless, floating free, having become—but rather, being—a god.[9]

We can achieve this experience in isolated moments within this life. According to Porphyry, Plotinus was united to God in this way on four occasions during the six years they were friends. However, we always suffer from the hinderance of the body. The good news is that we look to a future state in which this union is permanent and continuous. The goal of Plotinus's philosophy was summed up in his last words as he lay dying, "Try to bring back the god in you to the divine in the All!"[10]

THE SIGNIFICANCE OF NEOPLATONISM

The movement of Neoplatonism continued on more than three and a half centuries after the death of Plotinus. The school in Rome seems to have come under the direction of Porphyry (whose life is dated about A.D. 232–305). Furthermore, there were schools in Syria, Asia Minor, Athens, and Alexandria that followed this philosophy. In Athens, it was introduced into Plato's Academy by Plutarch in the latter half of the fourth century and was carried forward and developed there by his successor Proclus.*

Plotinus never said much about Christianity, although he does criticize the pseudo-Christian Gnostics for suggesting that Plato's grasp of ultimate reality was incomplete. However, his disciple Porphyry and other Neoplatonists were decidedly anti-Christian. Nevertheless, Neoplatonism was attractive to a number of Christian thinkers and became very important in shaping the form that Christianity took in the Middle Ages. Origen (about A.D. 185–254), an early Church theologian, was a student of Plotinus's teacher Ammonius. Following the pattern of Plotinus, Origen arranged the three persons of the Holy Trinity in a hierarchy and suggested that through sin, pre-existent human souls "descended" into bodies.† St. Augustine based his Christian philosophy on Plotinus's interpretation of Plato's philosophy. Augustine said that with only a few changes in their doctrines, the Platonic philosophers such as Plotinus would become Christians. Boethius (A.D. 480–525), a Roman Christian influenced by Neoplatonism, translated one of Porphyry's books on Aristotle into Latin. Around A.D. 500 emerged a work that was claimed to have been written by Dionysius, one of the Apostle Paul's converts. However, it was really written by a Neoplatonist in the sixth century. Because the medieval theologians did not know it was a forgery, it was very influential in introducing Neoplatonic themes into theology and in fueling Christian mysticism. The official presence of Greek philosophy and Neoplatonism in the West came to an end in A.D. 529 when the Christian Emperor Justinian closed all the pagan schools of philosophy in Athens. However, because of the influence of Neoplatonism on Christian thought, a seed was

---

*Plutarch of Athens is not the same person as the famous biographer of the same name who lived in the first century.

†Later, Origen's view of the Trinity was condemned as heretical, for the official position was that the three persons were coequal.

planted that would allow Greek philosophy to remain alive in the West.

Questions for Understanding

1. What were some of the social conditions that
   influenced the change in philosophy after
   Aristotle?

2. What were some characteristics the various
   Hellenistic philosophies held in common?

3. In what ways was the philosophy of the Cynics in ancient Greece similar to or different
   from the meaning of the word "cynicism" as
   we use it today?

4. How did the Epicureans account for free will
   in a materialistic universe?

5. In what ways is the Epicureans' ethical theory based on their metaphysics?

6. What is the difference between psychological hedonism and ethical hedonism?

7. Contrary to popular conceptions, the Epicureans' philosophy did not say we should
   live a life of unrestrained pleasure. How so?

8. In what ways did the Epicureans distinguish
   between different sorts of desires? Which desires ought we to pursue?

9. Why did the Epicureans not say much about
   social philosophy?

10. What was the Epicurean view of religion?

11. Why should we not fear death, according to
    the Epicureans?

12. In spite of their differences, in what ways
    were the Epicurean and the Stoic philoso-
    phies similar?

13. What differences were there between Epi-
    curean and Stoic metaphysics? How did this
    lead to differences in their ethics?

14. According to the Stoics, what is the relation
    between God and nature?

15. How did the Stoics reconcile their view of
    God with our experience of evil?

16. What did the Stoics mean and what did they
    not mean when they said that the ideal of life
    is "apathy"?

17. Since the Stoics preached the value of resig-
    nation, why would they prefer health over
    sickness?

18. What were the Stoics' contributions to social
    philosophy?

19. Why was Stoicism attractive to the Romans?
    What contributions did the Roman Stoics
    make to legal, social, and ethical philosophy?

20. Why were the Skeptics disdainful of both
    Epicureanism and Stoicism?

21. What were the various forms of Hellenistic
    Skepticism? How did they differ?

22. What did the Skeptics mean by "suspending
    judgment"? Why did they believe that this
    was the key to a happy life?

23. According to Agrippa, what are the five pil-
    lars of Skepticism?

24. In what ways is Neoplatonism related to the
    thought of Plato?

25. What roles do the notions of the One, Intellect,
    and Soul play in Neoplatonic metaphysics?

26. Why does Plotinus use the sun as his
    metaphor of what is fundamentally real?

27. How do the Neoplatonists address the prob-
    lem of evil?

28. What is the "way of ascent" in Plotinus's
    philosophy?

Questions for Reflection

1. Consider the five philosophies of Cynicism,
   Epicureanism, Stoicism, Skepticism, and Neoplatonism. For each philosophy in turn, imagine that you were a dedicated follower of that
   philosophy. How would you approach life differently under each philosophy? How would it
   affect your career, your relationships, your involvement in society, your conception of yourself and life's meaning?

2. Each of these philosophies claimed to offer
   practical guidance for life. Which one do you
   think is most plausible and satisfying?

3. Of all the Greek philosophies, Stoicism was
   one of the most attractive ones to the early
   Christians. Why do you suppose this is so?

4. While you may not agree with all the teachings of the various philosophies discussed in this chapter, for each one, list what you consider to be its positive contributions.

5. For each of the five philosophies discussed in this chapter, explain what you believe is its greatest shortcoming.

Notes

1. Quotations from the Epicurean tradition and the Skeptics are taken from *Hellenistic Philosophy: Introductory Readings*, trans. and ed. Brad Inwood and L. P. Gerson (Indianapolis: Hackett, 1988). References are cited in the text using the abbreviation "I&G" and the page numbers of this collection. The abbreviation "LM" is used to indicate quotations from Epicurus's well-anthologized *Letter to Menoeceus*.

2. Quotations from the Stoics that are cited in the text are taken from Greek and Roman Philosophy after Aristotle, ed. Jason L. Saunders (New York: The Free Press, 1966). References to this book use the abbreviation "S" and refer to the page numbers of this anthology.

3. Cleanthes, quoted by Epictetus in *The Enchiridion*, 52, trans. Thomas Wentworth Higginson, in *Epictetus: Discourses and Enchiridion* (Roslyn, NY: The Classics Club, Walter J. Black, 1944), 352.

4. Marcus Aurelius, *Meditations* 9.4, in *The Stoic and Epicurean Philosophers*, ed. Whitney J. Oates (New York: Modern Library, Random House, 1940), 571.

5. Marcus Aurelius, 6.44, in Oates, 533.

6. Bertrand Russell, *A History of Western Philosophy* (New York: Clarion, Simon & Schuster, 1945), 255.

7. Plato, *Timaeus* 29c–d.

8. Quotations from Plotinus's *Enneads* are taken from *Plotinus*, trans. A. H. Armstrong, 7 vols. (Cambridge, MA: Harvard University Press, 1966–1988). This work is referenced in the text using the abbreviation "E." The number following this stands for both the volume number of the translation and the number of the Ennead. The last two numbers refer to the treatise and section numbers of Plotinus's work.

9. Plotinus, *Enneads*, vol. 7, Ennead 6, chap. 9, 8–9.

10. Quoted by Porphyry in *On the Life of Plotinus and the Order of His Books*, 2, in *Plotinus*, vol. 1.

P | A | R | T

II

THE MIDDLE AGES

7

Cultural Context:
The Development
of Christian Thought

The Encounter Between
Greek and Christian Thought

In the preceding chapters, we have followed the stream of ancient Greek philosophy. Now we must backtrack and pick up another stream that crosses the previous one, mingles with its waters, carries forward some of its energy, and becomes one of the most powerful forces in Western history. This second cultural-intellectual stream is that of Hebraic thought and the Christian religion, which arose out of it. The impact Christianity has made on world history is signified by the fact that the standard method of dating historical events identifies them as either B.C. or A.D. These abbreviations stand for "before Christ" and *Anno Domini* or "in the year of the Lord." The rise of Christianity is an important turning point in the story of philosophy, for it overlapped with the decline of the Roman Empire and of Greco-Roman or Hellenistic philosophy. From very tenuous beginnings, it went on to dominate the intellectual life of Western Europe.

Initially, there were many differences between the Greek tradition and Judeo-Christian thought.

The Greeks tended to be polytheists, whereas the Jews and the Christians believed in one, supreme God. The gods of the Greeks were limited. On most accounts, they were subject to Fate. Typically, the deities in these philosophical systems were not sovereign over the world. Plato's creator (the Demiurge) had to consult the pre-existing Forms when imposing order on a pre-existing matter. Aristotle's deity was not transcendent but was immanent in the world. In contrast, the God of the Judeo-Christian tradition is all-powerful and transcendent. He created the world out of nothing and rules over it according to his sovereign will. Furthermore, Plato's ultimate principle, the Good, was impersonal, as was Aristotle's Unmoved Mover. The God of the Bible, however, was personal and had a loving concern for his creation.

Christianity presented itself as a revealed religion. Building on their Hebraic roots, the Christians claimed that God had spoken and revealed himself to us through the Old Testament prophets, in the person of Jesus of Nazareth, and in the Gospels and Epistles of the New Testament. Whereas the Greeks sought for truth and ultimate reality, the Christian message was that truth and

111

ultimate reality (in the person of God) was searching for us. The ancient Greeks talked of the Logos, the principle of order and reason that permeates the universe. Capitalizing on this tradition, John began his Gospel by proclaiming that the Logos was identical to God and that in Jesus the Logos took on human form and dwelled among us. For Christian thinkers, human history was to be understood in terms of the themes of sin, grace, salvation, and eternal life. However, these were not viewed as a series of philosophical doctrines but as moments in the individual's spiritual journey. Although many Christian intellectuals tried to show that their faith could hold its own with the best of Greek philosophy, they did not share the Greeks' confidence that philosophical reason alone could solve the deep problems of human life.

The first-century Christians faced four immediate concerns that left little time or energy for philosophical speculation. First, they had to prepare for the second coming of Jesus. Jesus' disciples and the Apostle Paul both had the impression that Jesus would return to earth in their lifetime.[1] Since time was short and nothing earthly was of lasting value, there was no point in engaging in long-term intellectual projects. Second, the early Church had to survive persecution. For the Romans, religion was a concern of the state. Only if all its citizens made sacrifices to the gods of the state would the country prosper. Besides refusing to pay homage to the pagan gods, the Christians proclaimed that Christ, not the emperor, was lord over all the earth. Hence, to be a Christian in the Roman Empire was treasonous and a capital crime. Although the intensity of the persecution rose and fell with each different emperor, it did not completely end until the reign of Constantine the Great, the first Christian emperor, who ruled from A.D. 305 to 337.

Third, the Christians felt an urgent need to evangelize the world and spread the good news. Their goal was not to promote a set of theoretical ideas but to save people's souls by reconciling them to God. Initially, this diminished their interest in theoretical speculation. The fourth immediate concern was to fight the heresies that abounded at this time. There were many alternative versions of Christian teaching, each claiming to be the authentic version of Christian truth. Some of these were really Greek religious philosophies that were given a Christian veneer, others were simply alternative interpretations of the New Testament theology. The result was a massive confusion that threatened to drag the new religion down with the weight of controversy.

Despite these four urgent problems, Christians gradually found that they could not ignore philosophy. After several generations passed, it became increasingly clear that Jesus' return to earth was not imminent. Hence, Christians began to turn to longer-term tasks such as Christianizing their culture. The most significant development was that Christianity broadened out from its Jewish background. This shifted the focus from trying to reconcile the new faith with the Jewish tradition, to trying to reconcile the faith with the Greek tradition. By the end of the second century, Christianity had penetrated the upper classes and began to attract intellectuals in the Roman Empire. The minds of many of these educated converts had been nurtured in the soil of Greek philosophy. Hence, Christian thinkers had to come to terms with Greek ways of thinking by formulating their doctrines in the categories of Greek philosophy and by showing that their faith was intellectually respectable. For these reasons, the original task of evangelization came to be supplemented by that of apologetics. "Apologetics" is a term derived from Athenian legal procedures. It refers to the art of making a reply or providing a defense of one's position. Because Christianity was "on trial" before the court of Greek culture and philosophy, Christian thinkers sought to make the best case possible for it, using the weapons of philosophy itself. Similarly, since many of the heresies arose out of philosophy, Christian thinkers discovered they needed to "fight fire with fire." Hence, the task of rebutting false doctrines required both logical arguments and a greater clarification of the true teachings. Accordingly, Christian thinkers used the tools of Greek philosophy to support their position and to achieve conceptual precision.

The Problem of Faith and Reason

One of the first problems that Christian thinkers had to face was the relationship between faith and reason. This issue was a major concern in the early centuries of the Church, continued to be debated during the medieval period, and remains a source of lively discussion among philosophers of religion in the twentieth century. The problem was virtually without precedent in the history of philosophy up to this point. For the Greeks there was no problem. They had only one principle to guide their thinking: philosophical reason. The Greeks did not have any divine revelation in the form of sacred scriptures, for most of their religious notions were transmitted through their poets and tradition. However, the philosophers either rejected these traditions or downplayed their importance. What little they did retain from popular religion they made conform to the dictates of their philosophical systems. Likewise, the Jewish tradition had no problem with faith and reason. The Jews also avoided the problem by adhering to only one side of the dichotomy, but in their case it was faith. Their communal stories of God's faithfulness to his people made philosophical grounds for belief seem superfluous.

As Greek ways of thinking began to displace the Jewish influences on Christianity, Christian thinkers found themselves having to answer attacks from philosophers without, resolve controversies within, and satisfy the Greek thirst for a systematic worldview. The problem was that they were presented with two sources of information—revelation and philosophical reason. This situation raised several questions: Is Christian belief rational? What is the relationship between faith and reason? Can one coherently embrace both routes to the truth? If faith and reason lead to conflicting conclusions, how do we resolve the quarrel between them? Should a person of faith dabble in the speculations of pagan philosophers in the first place?

The problem was intensified by the fact that the philosophical tradition provided mixed data. The Christians found much in Greek philosophy

repugnant. In addition to their differing conceptions of the nature of deity, noted earlier, a number of other problems arose. For Plato, individuals find their fulfillment not in relating to a divine creator but through exercising their autonomous reason. Plato also believed in reincarnation, a doctrine incompatible with the biblical account of the afterlife. As for Aristotle, his system did not allow for any notion of individual immortality. And the Epicureans taught that the pursuit of pleasure and not obedience to God was the goal of life. In death, according to Epicurus, the soul disintegrates with the body and there is no afterlife. Yet Christians found much to admire in Greek philosophy. Socrates and Plato did believe that the soul was an immortal, spiritual entity identical with the real person and that eternal, spiritual realities were more important than the transitory, physical world. Aristotle helpfully provided arguments for the existence of God and stressed that there was a built-in purpose to everything. The Stoics saw the cosmos as full of order, harmony, benevolence, and beauty that was directed toward the fulfillment of a divine purpose. For them, adjusting one's life to the will of God was the key to the good life.

Similarly, the biblical tradition provided mixed data. On the negative side, the Apostle Paul's first letter to the Corinthians proclaims that the wisdom of the world is foolishness in the eyes of God and that the gospel of Christ appeared foolish to the pagan world. Furthermore, Paul warned, "Make sure that no one traps you and deprives you of your freedom by some secondhand, empty, rational philosophy based on the principles of this world instead of on Christ."[2] But despite these negative points, the biblical tradition also provided a number of bridges to Greek thought. When Paul spoke to a group of Epicureans and Stoics, he said that he was providing fuller knowledge of the same God that they were already worshiping. He even went so far as to quote Stoic writers to support his theology.[3] Paul also said that even though the Greeks did not have biblical revelation, they still knew about God through his creation and had the moral law "engraved on their hearts."[4]* Furthermore, the Book of Proverbs sings praises to Wisdom in a way that even Socrates would approve. Finally, the prologue to the Gospel of John speaks of the Divine Logos and thus provided a conceptual link with Heraclitus and the Stoics. Given this mixed data, the future of Greek philosophy within the Christian tradition hung on whether or not the differences or the similarities between the two systems would be emphasized. A brief look at three Christian thinkers—Justin, Clement, and Tertullian—will provide a glimpse of how these issues were addressed.

JUSTIN MARTYR

Justin was born in Samaria around A.D. 100 to pagan parents. A passionate intellectual, he journeyed throughout the Middle East and Italy searching for a truth to embrace. He tells us that he enthusiastically tried Stoicism, Aristotelianism, and Pythagoreanism in turn, but these disappointed him and left him unsatisfied. Finally, he was attracted to Platonism, which made a lifelong impact on him. However, on encountering Christianity he found that even Platonic philosophy, the spiritual highpoint of Greek thought, fell short of what the gospel of Christ had to offer. Impressed by the consistency and courage of the Christians in the face of death, he became a convert and an articulate defender of the new religion. He suffered a martyr's death in Rome around A.D. 165, along with his associates.

Justin was cheerfully optimistic about the harmony between Christianity and Greek philosophy. To those wary of philosophy he says that the best of philosophy is "the greatest possession, and most honorable before God, to whom it leads us and alone commends us; and these are truly holy men who have bestowed attention on philosophy."[5] To

*Christian philosophers such as Thomas Aquinas later justified their attempts to prove the existence of God by appealing to Paul's remarks in this passage. Also, Christian Platonists such as Augustine cited the statement that there are truths written in the human heart.

Christianity's intellectual critics he asserts that the Christian gospel and the best in pagan philosophy do not compete, but point to the same truth:

> If, therefore, on some points we teach the same things as the poets and philosophers whom you honour, and on other points are fuller and more divine in our teaching, and if we alone afford proof of what we assert, why are we unjustly hated more than all others?[6]

Justin illustrates his claim by pointing out that Plato and the Scriptures agree that our souls have a special affinity to God, that we are morally responsible for our actions, and that there is a time of reckoning in the world to come. Furthermore, Justin claims that the Good in Plato's *Republic* is clearly the same as the God of the Bible. Working from historically spurious information, Justin assumes that Socrates and Plato had so much of the truth because they were acquainted with the Pentateuch (the first five books of the Old Testament). But in addition to this, John's Gospel tells us that the Logos (Christ) gives light to all humankind. That is why, Justin says, both the Greeks and non-Greeks were able to discover fragments of God's truth apart from the Bible, because they possessed "seeds" of the Divine Reason (the "Spermatic Logos"). Accordingly, Justin says Socrates and Plato, along with Abraham, were "Christians before Christ," because they followed the Divine Reason within them. In this way, both Greek philosophy and the Old Testament were preparatory phases that found their culmination in Christianity. Educated people need not choose between Christianity or their intellectual heritage, because all truth is God's revealed truth whether it comes through the mouth of the prophets or is implanted in pagan philosophers by the Divine Logos.

CLEMENT OF ALEXANDRIA

Born of pagan parents around A.D. 150, Clement became a Christian through the influence of his teacher Pantaenus, a converted Stoic. Clement had a very broad-minded ecumenical spirit in his approach to Greek philosophy. He seemed to be quite familiar with the ancient texts in the history of philosophy and quotes them abundantly in support of his points. In his work *The Stromata*, he makes an impassioned argument for Christians to respect the treasures of Greek thought. Quoting Psalms 29:3, "The Lord is on many waters," Clement speculates that this includes the waters of Greek philosophy and not just those of the biblical tradition.[7] Arguing this point, he states that all truth is *one* and all wisdom is from the Lord. If we find words of wisdom in Plato, then this is from God no less than the words of the prophets. Hence, fragments of God's eternal truth have found their way even into pagan philosophy.[8] Clement is saying, in so many words, that it is foolish for Christians to reinvent the wheel. If Plato has good arguments for the immortality of the soul, then we can use his work and don't need to duplicate his efforts. Clement sees philosophy as a gift of divine providence and compares the Old Testament law with philosophy. The first was given to the Jews and the second to the Greeks, and God used both sources of wisdom to prepare hearts and minds for receiving the message of Jesus.[9]

Philosophy, Clement says, can even be a helpful tool for understanding Scripture.[10] Philosophy teaches us the skills of logic, the value of clear definitions, the analysis of language, and the ability to formulate demonstrations, all of which will lead us to truth. To diminish the impact of Paul's warning against "empty, rational philosophy," Clement emphasizes Paul's qualification that he is referring to philosophies that are "based on the principles of this world instead of Christ." Clement concludes, then, that Paul was not branding all philosophy as alien to Christianity, but only those schools such as Epicureanism that abolished providence and deified pleasure.[11]

Despite his claims that Greek philosophy is a kind of divine revelation, Clement does make some negative comments about it. As with many of the early Christian writers, he believes the Greeks stole many ethical and theological ideas from the Hebrews.[12] Furthermore, he always insists that Greek philosophy gave us only fragmentary and partial truths, whereas the Christian revelation gives us the fuller picture. Finally, too much attention to philosophy can entangle us in irrelevant quarrels:

> But those who give their mind to the unnecessary and superfluous points of philosophy, and addict themselves to wrangling sophisms alone, abandon what is necessary and most essential, pursuing plainly the shadows of words.[13]

However, philosophy pursued for its own sake can be enjoyable and profitable for the Christian, but only if we see it as a dessert that tops off the main meal.[14] Despite some of these negative comments, the portions of Clement's position that had the most lasting influence can be summed up in these words of his:

> Philosophy is not, then, the product of vice, since it makes men virtuous; it follows, then, that it is the work of God, whose work it is solely to do good. And all things given by God are given and received well.[15]

TERTULLIAN

Not all Christians were as optimistic about the possibility or desirability of a philosophically informed Christian faith. The most famous example of the negative position was a writer by the name of Tertullian. He was born around A.D. 160 to pagan parents in the North African city of Carthage. In the midst of a successful career as a trial lawyer in Rome, he became a Christian convert in 193, when he was moved by the courage of Christians who were being put to death for their faith. Tertullian's passionate personality and his polemical courtroom style shine throughout all of his writings. One recent historian has described Tertullian as

> brilliant, exasperating, sarcastic, and intolerant, yet intensely vigorous and incisive in argument, delighting in logical tricks and with an advocate's love of a clever sophistry if it will make the adversary look foolish, but a powerful writer of splendid, torrential prose.[16]

Whereas Justin and Clement delight in the Christian truths they find in the Greeks, Tertullian only grudgingly admits that sometimes

ound the truth. For example, he
the philosophers agree with the
he Logos, the divine Word and
, created the universe.[17] However, while
philosophers became inflated with pride in their
own reason, their truths are not the result of spiritual insight but rather of dumb luck, much like a
sailor happening to find his way in a storm:

> Of course we shall not deny that philosophers have
> sometimes thought the same things as ourselves.. . . .
> It sometimes happens even in a storm, when the
> boundaries of sky and sea are lost in confusion, that
> some harbour is stumbled on (by the labouring ship)
> by some happy chance; and sometimes in the very
> shades of night, through blind luck alone, one finds
> access to a spot, or egress from it.[18]

On the whole, however, he has little use for philosophy. Christ tells us, "Seek and ye shall find."
However, rather than this sanctioning the sort of
seeking that characterizes philosophy, it tells us
that when we have found the truth (the Gospel of
Christ) "nothing else is to be believed, and therefore nothing else is to be sought."[19] He is troubled
by the way that heresies arise out of philosophy
and lumps them both with the worst of company:
"It has also been a subject of remark, how extremely frequent is the intercourse which heretics
hold with magicians, with mountebanks [quacks],
with astrologers, with philosophers; and the reason is, that they are men who devote themselves
to curious questions."[20] Tertullian describes the
Apostle Paul's meeting with philosophers in
Athens as an encounter with "huckstering wise-
acres."[21] He also has great iconoclastic fun ridi-
culing the revered figure of Socrates and the
philosopher's famous deathbed scene.[22]

Finally, Tertullian's most famous dismissal of
the project that Justin and Clement called for is
the following passage:

> What indeed has Athens to do with Jerusalem? What
> concord is there between heretics and Christians? . . .
> Away with all attempts to produce a mottled Chris-
> tianity of Stoic, Platonic, and dialectic composition!
> We want no curious disputation after possessing
> Christ Jesus, no inquisition after enjoying the gospel!
> With our faith, we desire no further belief. For this is

> our [victorious] faith, that there is nothing which we
> ought to believe besides.[23]

In other words, just as Athens (the intellectual
center of philosophy) and Jerusalem (the spiritual
home of Christianity) are separated by hundreds
of miles geographically, so pagan philosophy and
the Christian Gospel are miles apart spiritually
and can never meet.

Nothing is known of Tertullian after the date
of his last literary work in the year 220. Nevertheless, he has made his place in history as the
most forceful religious veto to the project of reconciling faith and philosophy. To be charitable,
we can try to understand his concern with the
way that alien philosophical ideologies were
muddying the waters of Christian theology. Nevertheless, his attempts to build a dam separating
the philosophical and biblical traditions failed.
We cannot underestimate the importance of writers such as Justin and Clement in arguing for the
importance of Greek philosophy for Christian
thought. Certainly, the shape of Western Christianity and intellectual history would have been
different if the medievals had not seen the value
of preserving the Greek philosophical tradition.*

Challenging Heresies and Clarifying Orthodoxy

One of the philosophical issues facing the early
Church was how to express the rather poetic theology of the Hebraic tradition in terms that would
be clear and acceptable to the Greek mind. The
Greek tradition with its taste for fine, logical distinctions forced Christian thinkers to give more
rigorous and refined definitions of their central
concepts. For the early believers, it was enough to
say that God was in Christ reconciling the world
to himself and that Jesus was filled with the Spirit
of God. But questions arose concerning exactly
what was being said in the previous sentence and

---

*There is still controversy today over the extent to which
philosophical categories introduced distortions into Christian
theology.

what was not being said. It did not help matters that the culture presented a spectrum of religious philosophies each vying for influence within the Church. Orthodoxy (which literally means "right belief") had to be separated from dangerous or false opinions. The Greek word *heresy* originally meant "choice" or "opinion." However, it now came to mean "incorrect opinion." Four main positions were condemned as heresies: Gnosticism, Manichaeaism, Arianism, and Pelagianism.

GNOSTICISM

The Gnostics consisted of a dozen or more sects in the second century that developed an interpretation of the new religion in which they substituted knowledge (*gnosis*) for faith. The Gnostics considered themselves superior to the rabble (including ordinary Christians) because they had an esoteric and secret body of knowledge that was revealed only to them. Gnosticism was a bizarre blend of Babylonian astrology, Egyptian cults, Persian religion, Greek mystery cults, Neo-Pythagoreanism, Neoplatonism, and Stoicism, mixed with Jewish and Christian doctrines. Actually, Gnostic sects were around long before the birth of Christianity, but it is their mingling with Christian thought that interests us here.

The Gnostics taught a pseudo-Christian mythology in which multiple deities, angels, archangels, and other spiritual beings emanated and descended from the one, supreme God. They viewed reality in terms of an extreme dualism between spirit and matter. They considered the God of the Old Testament to be an evil God who arose to become the rival of the God of Light. This dark force was called the Demiurge and was thought to have created the kingdom of evil and darkness that was identical to the world of matter. The Demiurge created the human race in an attempt to capture portions of the good, divine spirit within the physical prison of the body.

Christ was one of the highest spirits. He foiled the scheme of the Demiurge by entering into a human body (some say he merely took on the appearance of being physical). Only the spiritual elite who could comprehend the secret doctrines could escape their bondage to the material world and return to the Kingdom of Light. Because the physical world was considered evil, most of the Gnostics preached asceticism (a style of life that denies the value of anything in the physical world). A few sects, however, consisted of wanton libertines. They believed that the spirit and the body were so separate that anything that happened to the body (such as sexual promiscuity) could not affect the spirit. Some even believed that satiating physical desires would destroy their hold over people, and thus the spirit would triumph over the designs of the Demiurge.

THE MANICHAEAN HERESY

Manichaeism was founded by a third-century Iranian prophet named Mani. It could be considered an offshoot of Gnosticism because the two systems have much in common. The major difference is that the Gnostics believed that evil came into being from one of the emanations of the supreme deity, whereas the Manichaeans believed that the God of Light and the God of Darkness had existed as rivals from all eternity. Thus, they taught an extreme metaphysical dualism in which two equal but opposite forces continually struggled for dominance. One appeal of their teachings was that they did not have to explain how evil originated in a universe ruled by an all-powerful and all-good God. Their answer was that the good God was simply limited in his powers. Like the Gnostics, they believed matter was evil, created by the forces of darkness to imprison human souls. Hence, salvation was to be found by rising above involvement with the physical world through an ascetic denial of such things as meat, wine, marriage, and property. The Manichaeans sought to synthesize all religions by claiming that Buddha was the revelation of God to India, Zoroaster the prophet for Persia, Jesus the divine prophet to the West, and Mani the prophet for the present age. Obviously, Christians objected to this denial of the uniqueness of the Christian religion. Manichaeism proved a very popular and widespread religion. Augustine was a Manichaean for thirteen years before becoming a Christian, after which he became one of the most forceful critics of Manichaeism.

In summary, the two pseudo-Christian movements of Gnosticism and Manichaeism are significant for several reasons. First, they illustrate the confusing mixture of philosophical schools and mystery religions prominent at this time. All preached some form of personal salvation. By synthesizing elements from all the religious and philosophical movements of the age, these two movements became very appealing. Second, they promoted a spiritual-physical dualism, which resulted in the depreciation of the physical world. Although Gnosticism and Manichaeism were declared heresies, some of their dualism crept into the writings of the early Church theologians. Even though Christians taught that God created the physical world and declared it was good and that Christ came to earth in a physical body, a very strong element of spiritual-physical dualism and asceticism persisted throughout the Middle Ages.

Third, the way in which these pseudo-Christian philosophers perverted Christian teachings led some theologians to be suspicious of all philosophies, and these heresies fueled the anti-intellectual wing of Christianity. Finally, the confusions caused by such heresies showed Christian intellectuals the need to pursue the conceptual clarification of Christian theology.

THE NATURE OF GOD AND THE ARIAN HERESY

In the fourth century, a crisis within the Church forced Christian theologians to further clarify their doctrines. Christians proclaimed there was one God at the same time that they talked of three, equally divine persons (the Father, Son, and the Holy Spirit). The Son was identified with Jesus of Nazareth. The Son was also called the Logos, using terminology found in both the New Testament and Neoplatonism, and entailing all the latter's complications concerning the relationship of God to the Logos. From the very beginning, the problem posed by trinitarian theology was to understand how there could be both one

God and three divine persons. Several extreme answers emerged to solve this riddle. On the one hand, some said that these were simply different manifestations of the one divinity, much as "the husband of Martha Washington" and "the first President of the United States" both designate George Washington. This collapsed the distinction between Jesus and the Father and seemed to imply that God the Father died on the cross. Another answer was that the three persons are related to the divine substance, the same way three distinct human persons all partake of the essence of human nature. However, this implied a sort of polytheism and contradicted the biblical tradition that there is only one God. Some solved the tension by denying that Jesus was divine at all. Others denied that he was human. In the attempt to relate three persons and one God, every logical permutation was advocated.

The controversy came to a head in the opposition of two major factions. Athanasius, who later became Bishop of Alexandria, led a party that asserted God manifested himself in three persons who shared the same divine substance. Thus the Son was of the same substance as the Father. His opponent Arius, a well-educated Alexandrian cleric, took the parental metaphor literally and claimed that the Son was created by the Father and that the two were not the same. Facing civil disorder, the Christian Emperor Constantine tried to resolve the controversy by calling a general council of bishops to meet in Nicea in 325 to settle the matter once and for all. The two spokesmen presented their cases, but the party Athanasius led was in the majority and his position prevailed, becoming the official orthodoxy, while the Arians were formally denounced and declared heretics. These proceedings produced the famous Nicene Creed (a version of which people still recite in many churches today as the official statement of Christian belief).

This did not end the matter, however. The controversy raged on for several centuries as emperors of various theological persuasions lent their support to one side or the other. The radical Arians claimed that the Son's essence is unlike (*anomoios*, in Greek) the Father's, while the Nicene formula insisted that the two were of the same being (*homoousios*). Eventually, the supporters of the Nicene Creed and their more moderate opponents found they could compromise by agreeing that the Son and the Father were of "similar substance" (*homoiousios*). This issue may seem rather abstruse, because the difference between the various positions was often very subtle and their terminology differed by a matter of only a few letters. However, these thinkers felt the purity of the faith, the divine truth, and even one's salvation were at stake on this issue. When argument failed, riots and bloodshed took its place. More debates arose over the similar question of how Christ could be both human and divine and how these two natures combined in one individual. The conflict over Arianism continued for over fifty years, and it took several Church councils to settle the issues once and for all. Even when the official position was clarified, orthodoxy had to walk a narrow tightrope to keep from falling into one heresy or another.

The philosophical significance of these issues is that they illustrate the impact of Greek philosophy on Christian thought. The Nicene Creed answers the Arian controversy by stating that Christ was "begotten, not made, being of one substance with the Father." Notice that the philosophical category of "substance" occurs in this formula. The term is never used this way in the New Testament to refer to what Christ shares with the Father. Instead, it is being used in the technical sense familiar to Greek metaphysics. In this way, Greek philosophical distinctions played a large role in defining theological problems and in setting out opposing positions. Similarly, Platonic concerns about how particulars "participate" in universals lurked behind debates over whether and how Jesus participated in the divinity of the Father. This Greek philosophical background forced Christian theologians to face these issues in a particular way. We can only speculate whether and how these issues would have been addressed if Christianity had developed in a different cultural context.

THE PROBLEM OF FREE WILL AND SIN: THE PELAGIAN HERESY

The next major controversy was provoked by a British monk named Pelagius, who settled in Rome in the early years of the fifth century. He became concerned about the doctrine of original sin. According to this teaching, when Adam (the first man) disobeyed God, the result was that sin entered into the human race. Consequently, everybody since then has inherited a sinful nature and is a slave to sin. For this reason, it is said, Christ had to come and save us from our helplessness and bondage to sin. However, God is sovereign and only extends his grace or help to those whom he will. The rest remain victims (willingly, perhaps) of their own, corrupt natures. However, Pelagius believed that this teaching led to moral apathy. If, through no fault of my own, I am born with a sinful nature and cannot resist sinning, then why should I try to avoid the unavoidable? To Pelagius, this sort of thinking pulls the rug out from underneath any notion of moral responsibility and makes the struggle to be good apparently useless. In contrast, he sincerely believed that the correct Christian position was to assert human moral freedom. He insisted that we can resist sin and make correct moral choices without outside help. That sinfulness seems the norm for humanity is because Adam cursed his race with a bad example that was passed down to each succeeding generation. So where does God fit into the Pelagian picture? The answer is that God sent Jesus to live a life of perfect love. His teachings and example help us decide to will the good. However, with or without his work in our lives, our capacity for freedom remains the same. Augustine made Pelagianism one of his targets, and this controversy helped shape much of Augustine's theology and, thereby, much theology for centuries to come. The Church eventually condemned Pelagianism as a heresy because it overemphasized human moral autonomy and tended to make divine grace and Christ's redemptive death superfluous. Yet although Pelagianism was officially put to rest, religious philosophers still wrestle with the problem of reconciling God's sovereignty with human freedom. Furthermore, the problem of how to balance the determinants on human behavior with moral responsibility continue to vex religious and secular philosophers alike.

The Future Agenda: A Christian Philosophical Synthesis

As we have seen, most of what could be called Christian philosophy during the first few centuries had a negative agenda. Christian thinkers were trying to defend their faith from philosophical attacks and were trying to straighten out the confusions of theological heresies. As Christian thought began to seep into the culture and become more secure, the more positive task of working out a Christian philosophical worldview became the next stage in the development of Christian thought. What was needed was a comprehensive view of the world and human life as seen by the light of Christian truth. In addition to tackling the core philosophical questions in epistemology, metaphysics, and ethics, Christian thinkers in the centuries to come developed philosophical perspectives on physical nature, the state, law, history, art, and psychology.

Because of its Hebraic roots, Christianity did not originally have anything that a Greek or Roman would recognize as a well-articulated philosophy. Hence, it became necessary for Christian thinkers to borrow the philosophical tools and weapons of the pagans. (Augustine compared this to the Israelites stealing the goods of the Egyptians as they left for the promised land.) Christians naturally turned to the most spiritual-minded of the Greek philosophies for their resources. Accordingly, Christian thinkers in the Middle Ages drew primarily on Platonism and Neoplatonism, along with elements borrowed from the Stoics for the foundations of their thought. However, in the latter part of the medieval period, Aristotelian philosophy emerged as another important resource for Christian thought. The chapters covering Augustine to Aquinas will examine these attempts to fulfill the Greek philosophical agenda within a Christian context.

Questions for Understanding

1. In what ways did Greek thought differ from Christian thought?

2. What were four factors that delayed the growth of philosophical thought among the early Christians?

3. Why did many first- and second-century Christian thinkers find that philosophy was unavoidable?

4. What is the problem of faith and reason? How did this problem arise in Christian thought?

5. Why did Justin Martyr believe that there could be harmony between Christianity and Greek philosophy?

6. What was Clement of Alexandria's view of the relationship between faith and reason?

7. Why did Tertullian have such a dim view of philosophy?

8. Why were the following movements condemned as heresies? Gnosticism, Manichaeaism, Arianism, and Pelagianism.

Questions for Reflection

1. Using Justin Martyr and Clement of Alexandria as your models, imagine how you would explain to someone why a person of religious faith should study philosophy.

2. Imagine that Tertullian's view of philosophy had prevailed in Western Christendom. What would be the effects of this?

3. Suppose that you were either a medieval (a) Christian, (b) Muslim, or (c) Jew. Which Greek philosophers would you find to be most helpful in developing a philosophy consistent with your faith? Why?

Notes

1. Mark 13:24–30, 1 Thessalonians 4:16–17.

2. Colossians 2:8 (The Jerusalem Bible).

3. Acts 17:28.

4. Romans 1:19–20, 2:14–15.

5. Justin Martyr, *Dialogue with Trypho*, chap. 2, in *The Ante-Nicene Fathers*, vol. 1, ed. Alexander Roberts and James Donaldson (reprint ed., Grand Rapids, MI: Eerdmans, 1956), 195.

6. Justin Martyr, *Apology I*, in Roberts and Donaldson, 169.

7. Clement of Alexandria, *The Stromata*, bk. 6, chap. 8, in *The Ante-Nicene Fathers*, vol. 2, ed. Alexander Roberts and James Donaldson (reprint ed., Grand Rapids, MI: Eerdmans, 1962), 495. Subsequent references list the book and chapter numbers followed by the page number of this edition.

8. Ibid., 1:13, 313.

9. Ibid., 1:5, 305.

10. Ibid., 1:9, 309–310.

11. Ibid., 1:11, 311.

12. Ibid., 2:18, 365; 5:14, 465.

13. Ibid., 6:18, 518.

14. Ibid.

15. Ibid., 6:17, 517.

16. Henry Chadwick, *The Early Church* (Harmondsworth, England: Penguin, 1967), 91.

17. Tertullian, *The Apology*, chap. 21, in *The Ante-Nicene Fathers*, vol. 3, ed. Alexander Roberts and James Donaldson (reprint ed., Grand Rapids, MI: Eerdmans, 1956), 34. Subsequent references to Tertullian's works cite the chapter of the original work and the page number of this edition.

18. Tertullian, *A Treatise on the Soul*, chap. 2, 182.

19. Tertullian, *On Prescription Against Heretics*, chap. 9, 247–248.

20. Ibid., chap. 43, 264.

21. Tertullian, *A Treatise on the Soul*, chap. 3, 183.

22. Ibid., chap. 1, 181–182.

23. Tertullian, *On Prescription Against Heretics*, chap. 7, 246.

8

St. Augustine:
Philosophy in the Service of Faith

AURELIUS AUGUSTINE IS ONE OF THE MOST influential writers in the history of the Christian Church. He stood at one of the major crossroads in history, the transition from the Hellenistic period to the Middle Ages. Understanding his thought is essential to understanding the Middle Ages, for he influenced medieval thought for a thousand years. He was a prolific writer, producing 118 treatises on various theological topics. However, he is important not only because he had a great impact on theology and philosophy, but also because two of his major works have made him an important figure in the history of literature. Many consider his *Confessions* the greatest spiritual autobiography of all time. The personal voice in Augustine's writings stands out in a time when most works were commentaries and objective, detached treatises. His *City of God* is noted for being the first philosophy of history. Its style is equally innovative, for he does not merely provide a description of historical events but uses them to tell a story. However, after Augustine people paid little attention to the problem of history until the eighteenth century. At this time, the intellectuals of the French Enlightenment used historical nar-

ratives to support their faith in secular progress. Working from a more theistic perspective, Giambattista Vico (1668–1744), an Italian philosopher, social theorist, and devout Catholic, made history the central theme of his philosophy. In the nineteenth century, the philosophy of history occupied the center stage in the works of such figures as Hegel, Comte, Marx, and Nietzsche.

Augustine's Life: From Passionate Pleasure to a Passionate Faith

Augustine was born in A.D. 354 in North Africa. His father, Patricius, was not a Christian (although he became one on his deathbed). However, Monica, Augustine's mother, was a devout Christian who was later declared a saint. He was a bright student and excelled in the study of the Latin classics. Seeking the best possible education for him, his parents sent him to Carthage in 370 to study rhetoric. Carthage was the most prominent city in North Africa at this time, and must have been overwhelming for a young man of sixteen. Not only was it the center of government, but it also offered all the distractions, entertainments, and vices often associated with a port city. While there, he lived with a mistress for ten years and fathered an illegitimate son by her.

Always seeking spiritual and intellectual fulfillment, Augustine fell under the influence of the Manichaean religious cult. He was impressed by their rational presentation of truth, for they seemed to have the only reasonable answer as to why there is evil in the world, if a good God exists. As we saw in the previous chapter, the Manichaeans believed that there are two competing powers in the world, one good and the other evil. Since these opposing powers are in an eternal struggle for supremacy, this explains why we find both good and evil in the world. Human beings are a prime example of this struggle. Our souls are that part of us that participates in the power of goodness and light. They are at war with our bodies, which are products of the evil and dark force. Besides the intellectual attractions of this view, it also gave Augustine the comfort that his true self, his soul, was essentially good and his passions and sensual desires could be blamed on an outside cause. However, these spiritual struggles did not dilute his worldly ambitions. He pursued a successful career teaching rhetoric and literature, even winning a prize for his poetry. After nine years he became disillusioned with Manichaean thought. Faustus, the master teacher of Manichaean doctrines, paid a visit to Carthage. Seeking him out for answers to his questions, Augustine was dismayed to find out that he was a pompous simpleton.

Eventually, Augustine went to Rome to further his career and to seek better students. By this time he had adopted skepticism as his philosophical outlook. In 384 he ended up in Milan as a professor of rhetoric. At the request of Augustine's mother, he was befriended by St. Ambrose, the Bishop of Milan. Although he was impressed by the bishop's Christianity, Augustine's passions were so strong that he could not bring himself to change his lifestyle. His continual struggle against his lusts is vividly illustrated by his honest prayer to God: "Grant me chastity and continence, but

St. Augustine in his study. With Plato, Augustine believed that eternal truths could be found by searching inward. However, Augustine added that reason is not a neutral instrument but is affected by the orientation of our hearts, our passions, and our spiritual openness.

not yet" (C 8.7.17).[1] Giving up on any pretentions to moral purity, he took another mistress.

He began to read the Neoplatonists, including Plotinus, in earnest. Their teachings inspired him to turn inward and to seek after spiritual reality. He says that the Platonists gave him a glimpse, as though from a mountaintop, of the homeland of peace, but it was the writings of the apostle Paul that showed him the way to it (C 7.21.27). Augustine was moved when he heard of the Christian conversion of the great teacher Victorinus, a renowned translator of the Neoplatonists and Aristotle's logic, who was honored with a statue in the Roman Forum. Augustine was amazed that a man having such a reputation for scholarship could have the courage to publicly profess his Christian faith.

In the summer of 386, Augustine's constant inner turmoil eventually led him to the point of his own conversion. He wandered out into a garden and paced around in a state of extreme agitation. Within him, a voice said, "Let it be now" (C 8.11.25). However, he also heard the voice of his lustful passions say, "Are you getting rid of us?" and he was taunted by the question, "Do you think that you can live without them?" (C 8.11.26). In a state of misery and choked with tears, Augustine read a passage from St. Paul and a sense of peace and resolution filled his heart as he yielded to God. Subsequently, he was baptized by St. Ambrose on Easter Sunday in 387. Deciding to devote all his energies to the work of the Church, he abandoned the teaching of rhetoric and returned to his home in Africa in the region now known as Tunisia. In 396 he was made Bishop of Hippo. Augustine died in 430, as the barbarians were taking over the Empire and surging at the gates of Hippo.

Augustine's Task: Understanding the Human Predicament

The content of Augustine's writings slowly evolved as his thought developed in response to the different philosophical and theological issues he faced throughout his life. His early period culminates with his autobiographical *Confessions* (finished around 400). During this period, Augustine tended to be fairly optimistic about the capabilities of reason and mainly addressed topics that can be handled by natural reason alone. His early works include refutations of the Manichaean and skeptical philosophies of his youth. His later writings, which include *City of God* (completed in 426), are more scripturally based and insist more strongly that reason is subordinate to faith. Their explicit theological content reflects both Augustine's developing interests and the threat posed by Christian heresies such as Pelagianism.

In every aspect, Augustine's philosophy draws deeply from the wells of Platonic and Neoplatonic philosophy. He is well aware of this, for he notes that "none of the other philosophers has come so close to us as the Platonists have" (CG 8.5).* Since they "have unlawful possession" of God's truth, we should not shrink from their ideas but can rightfully claim them for ourselves (CD 2.40.60). At the same time that he uses the resources of pagan philosophy, there are few thinkers whose thought was as passionately Christian as Augustine's. "God and the soul, that is what I desire to know. Nothing more? Nothing whatever" (SL 1.7). Augustine never met a purely intellectual problem. All philosophical ideas are either obstacles or vehicles in the journey of the soul to God and eternal life. For this reason, Augustine did not write rigid, systematic treatises, but used the rhetorical style that earned him fame in his first career. His philosophical energies were spent either hammering at the enemies of the faith or paving the road that would lead his audience to God.

Augustine's philosophy emphasized (particularly in his later works) that no aspect of our world can be understood apart from a religious perspective. He refuses to make the distinctions that would be important to Thomas Aquinas centuries later: natural reason versus supernatural revelation, philosophy versus theology, humans understood as natural beings versus humans as spiritual beings. Instead, Augustine insists that knowledge, philosophy, the world, and humanity are always to be understood in the light of their religious significance. Where Scripture is silent on some intellectual issue that concerns him, Augustine is content to adopt the answers of Plato found in the *Meno* and the *Timaeus* and Plotinus in the *Enneads*. These occasions are rare, however, for he thinks that the Bible gives us the final perspective on both our moral and intellectual concerns. For the most part, secular philosophies can only add a few flourishes to this.

---

*Augustine later regretted that he had been so uncritical of the Platonists. Although still retaining many of their insights, he found it necessary to modify their position.

Two central issues lie at the heart of Augustine's philosophy. These are (1) the primacy of the will and (2) the fact that love motivates all action, both human and divine. The doctrine of the primacy of the will has two dimensions, for it applies both to his view of God and humanity. First, with respect to God, everything in the universe is a result of his free and sovereign will. Second, with respect to us, everything human is to be explained on the basis of the will. Hence, unlike the Greeks, Augustine did not believe that reason is primary. According to him, the intellect follows the will, not the other way around. But what determines the will? Augustine's answer is that nothing does; the will is completely free. At this point, the theme of love joins the first one. The will is moved in the direction of what it chooses to love. Like a physical object that is pulled by its weight toward the center of the earth, so every one of us is pulled by the affections of our hearts toward that which is the center of our lives. As Augustine says, "My weight is my love. Wherever I am carried, my love is carrying me" (C 8.9).

The problem we face, according to Augustine, is that ever since the disobedience of the first man and woman, Adam and Eve, the human race has fallen into the downward spiral of sin. The result of this original sin, which every one of us inherits and re-enacts in our own lives, is that every area of human life has been infected and corrupted by sin. Our wills are bent away from God, and the weight of our love is pulled in the wrong direction. We tend toward self-love and love of a corrupt and passing world, both of which prevent us from finding true fulfillment. Augustine tries to convince us that this human predicament affects not only our ethical life but our quest for knowledge and the entire course of human history. In fact, because the human moral predicament permeates all of Augustine's thought, I will not devote a separate section to his ethics. The preceding points lead to one of the major tensions in Augustine's philosophy, which is how to reconcile the total power of God and the effects of our sinful nature on the one hand, with his claim that humans have free will.

Theory of Knowledge: The Truth Is Within

Although Augustine says a great deal about the nature of knowledge, he was not interested in it as an end in itself. Neither was he interested in knowledge for the sake of controlling the physical world. For Augustine, epistemology serves a practical, religious purpose. It weeds out false views of knowledge that subvert the soul's journey to God, and it guides us in the search for truth. Not only is having truth a key ingredient to a happy life, but a clarified vision of truth also brings us closer to the Author of all truth.

THE QUEST FOR CERTAINTY

For the sake of these goals, Augustine was concerned with the quest for certainty. To him, nothing less than certain, eternal, and absolute truth could provide an adequate foundation for one's life. In one of his early works, *Against the Academicians*, he addresses himself to the Skeptics of the New Platonic Academy.* They maintained two theses: (1) nothing can be known, and (2) assent should not be given to anything (AA 3.10.22). Many Skeptics believed that people find wisdom and happiness in pursuing the truth rather than in actually attaining it. According to Augustine, however, someone who does not know the truth cannot be wise nor can someone be happy who never obtains what he or she strives to possess. Thus, to be wise and happy, we must find a way out of skepticism.

To defeat total skepticism, Augustine need only find some proposition *P* such that we are certain *P* is true. As a matter of fact, he finds many propositions that we know to be true. First, he points out that even the Skeptic makes truth claims. The Skeptic claims he knows his own position to be true and that it logically follows from

---

*This was the period in the Academy that was dominated by Carneades (c. 213—c. 128 B.C.). Augustine was probably familiar with the Skeptics primarily through the writings of Cicero.

premises that are true (AA 3.9.18). Here is how Augustine argues that skepticism is self-refuting:

(1) The Skeptics claim we cannot know anything to be true.

(2) To deny that we can know the truth requires a definition of truth: (Carneades uses a definition borrowed from Zeno the Stoic.)

(3) This definition is either true or false.

(4) If this definition is true, then the Skeptics know some truths. (The Skeptics refute their own claim.)

(5) If this definition is false, then it is useless in the defense of Skepticism. (The Skeptics' claim is meaningless, since they have no definition of truth.)

Next, Augustine points out that certain logical propositions are known to be true, such as "Either *P* or *Not-P* is true" and "It is false that *P* and *Not-P* are both true." Without the principles of logic, we could not reason or even articulate a position such as skepticism. For example, we know the following claim must be true: "Either the skeptics' definition is true or it is false" (AA 3.10.21). Continuing to hammer away at the Skeptics' claim that we can't have knowledge, Augustine presents mathematical truths such as "3 x 3 = 9" as truths we can know with certainty.

In the next part of his refutation, Augustine discusses the Skeptics' claim that sense experience is unreliable. His response is that what the senses report to us is always true as long as we do not go beyond the data as they are presented to us and draw unwarranted conclusions from them. For example, if I see that the oar in the water appears to be bent, this is not an illusion but is the literal truth. The oar *appears* to be bent. Augustine makes the important point here that reason needs to interpret the data of the senses before we draw any conclusions about what we really have before us (AA 3.11.26).

From his analysis of the senses, Augustine goes on to discuss yet another kind of certitude. We can be certain about the contents of our own minds as presented to us in self-conscious, inner experience. This includes the experiences we are having, our psychological and cognitive processes, and our feelings. Even our doubts create certainties. In a passage in another work that preceded Descartes's similar but more famous argument by more than twelve hundred years, Augustine argues that his own doubts lead to certainty concerning his own existence:

> For, we are, and we know that we are, and we love to be and to know that we are. . . . In the face of these truths, the quibbles of the skeptics lose their force. If they say, "What if you are mistaken?" well, if I am mistaken, I am. For, if one does not exist, he can by no means be mistaken. . . . I am most certainly not mistaken in knowing that I am. Nor, as a consequence, am I mistaken in knowing that I know. For, just as I know that I am, I also know that I know. And when I love both to be and to know, then I add to the things I know a third and equally important knowledge, the fact that I love. (CG 11.26)

It is ironic that Augustine, who laid the foundations of medieval philosophy, also developed the very point with which Descartes laid the foundations of modern philosophy. This notion is that the quest for knowledge begins with the self. To summarize what Augustine has established thus far, since we know with certainty that some propositions are true, skepticism is wrong and it is reasonable to search for further truths.

PLATONIC RATIONALISM

As with so much of his philosophy, Augustine uses typical Platonic terms and arguments to articulate his epistemology. There are some differences, however. Augustine does not devalue the senses quite as much as Plato does. After all, they were created by God along with the sensory world they deliver to us. The senses have their appropriate role to play in our practical life. Nevertheless, he agrees with Plato that the senses cannot give us eternal, perfect truth and, therefore, must be relegated to a lower level of knowledge. Hence, Augustine accepts the Platonic dualism and maintains that there are two distinct kinds of knowable objects, "those things which the mind perceives by the bodily senses; the other, of those which it perceives by itself" (HT 15.12.21). In

Augustine's view, therefore, the senses are but an instrument used by and subject to the inner person (the mind or soul). Sense experience by itself cannot give us knowledge. The mind must examine, interpret, classify, correlate, and judge the sense data. It does so by referring to nonphysical and eternal reasons that reside within.

Therefore, the highest truths are to be found in the intellect and the inner recesses of the soul. Thus Augustine advises, "Do not go outside thyself, but return to within thyself; for truth resides in the inmost part of man" (TR 39.72). In addition to Platonic reasons for this conviction, Augustine is also mindful of the biblical claim that the soul is made in the image of the God of all truth.

We now need to ask two questions: (1) What is the nature of these inward truths? and (2) How does the mind come to be aware of them? With respect to the first question, Augustine sticks very closely to Plato's theory of the Forms. For example, he refers approvingly to Plato's notion that we can recognize and judge the beauty of physical things only if the nonphysical Form of Beauty resides in the mind:

> If there is any loveliness discerned in the lineaments of the body, or beauty in the movement of music and song, it is the mind that makes this judgment. This means that there must be within the mind a superior form, one that is immaterial and independent of sound and space and time. (CG 8.6)

Similarly, in a series of arguments that would have made Plato proud, Augustine uses mathematics to argue for the existence of a higher reality that transcends the senses and the physical world. Briefly, he argues that physical realities are particular, temporal, changing, and discovered through experience. In contrast, mathematical laws and numbers are universal, eternal, unchanging, and discovered only through the intellect. Therefore, he concludes, there must be two kinds of reality (FCW 2.8).

Not surprisingly, Augustine also includes ethical norms among the higher truths that we know through a kind of "intellectual sight": "we should live justly," "the worse should be subordinate to the better," "equals should be compared with equals," and "to each should be given his own"

(FCW 2.10.113). He argues that since we all share these "true and immutable rules of wisdom," they are not human creations but are objective truths that we discover.

DIVINE ILLUMINATION

How does the mind come to know these eternal truths? Augustine answers this question with his theory of illumination. Although reason operates in a different realm from the senses, Augustine frequently uses the Platonic analogy between physical perception of the external world and our interior, mental vision. He tends to follow Plato very closely, but on some points he departs from the Platonic theory. For example, Plato believed that the mind retains knowledge from a previous existence before this life. Augustine may have originally found this view attractive, but its theological difficulties required him to reject it. Neither does he hold that these truths are simply "programmed" into us and capable of being known by our own, natural reason. Instead, he claims we discover these intelligible realities, eternal truths, forms, divine ideas (Augustine uses all these terms) through the illumination of the divine light. He did not clarify the details of this process, and scholars differ on exactly what Augustine meant to say. Nevertheless, he clearly believed that the divine light is to the mind what the sun is to the eyes (a metaphor that he borrowed from Plato). Thus, every human mind depends on God's light to see the truth.* This does not occur through a mystical, religious experience, for even the minds of the atheists are illumined, although they do not recognize the source of their light.

Even though he rejects Plato's notion of the pre-existence of the soul, Augustine still retains the metaphor of "remembering" to describe the discovery of truth. In fact, as he points out, our word *cognition* comes from the Latin *cogito*, which can mean "I recollect." Thus, the divine light can

---

*To emphasize the universality of divine illumination, Augustine refers to the prologue of the Gospel of John, which says that the true light is that which "enlightens every man who comes into the world" (CG 10.2).

illumine the truth within us, but we may fail to notice it, just as we can look at a physical object and yet not really see it. The process of apprehending the truth is like taking an algebra test and thinking that a certain type of problem is impossible, but suddenly remembering that we do know how to work it after all. In all thinking, the mind is becoming aware of, collecting, and assembling knowledge that was scattered, concealed, and neglected in remote corners of the mind (C 10.11.18).

He refers to the nonsensory contents of the mind as *memoria* (C 10.8.15). Although this includes literal memories, it also includes everything present to the mind, even if only dimly or tacitly known. This would include knowledge of the self, the truths of reason, ethical truths, values, and God himself. When I look inward I get a glimpse of an infinite realm of truths, leading to the paradox that "I myself cannot grasp the totality of what I am" (C 10.8.15). When I explore the depths of my mind, I am astonished to find a transcendent realm revealed to me. Thus, going inward leads me to an upward journey, beyond the physical world, beyond the self, where I will find what is eternal, and finally be led to God.

FAITH AND REASON

Thus far, most of Augustine's epistemology sounds very similar to Plato's. However, a crucial difference is Augustine's claim that reason cannot function properly apart from faith. For Augustine, faith and reason are not two independent and alternative routes to the truth. First, this would eliminate the need for faith. Second, this assumes the total self-sufficiency of human reason, something Augustine refuses to grant. Third, this assumes the intellect is a purely neutral instrument that takes in data and processes it. However, far from being morally neutral, Augustine believes reason is a function of the whole person and is affected by the orientation of our hearts, our passions, and our faith. As he puts it, "Faith seeks, understanding finds; whence the prophet says, 'Unless ye believe, ye shall not understand' " (HT 15.2.2).

If Augustine is correct, reason is not a neutral calculating machine, because it cannot function independently from the rest of life. My cognitive activities and my moral nature affect one another. To put Augustine's point very bluntly, if I am cheating on my income tax, having an affair with my neighbor's spouse, and am smug and complacent about my own moral autonomy, it is unlikely I would be moved by a philosophical proof for the existence of God. To acknowledge a divine lawgiver would require submission of my will and a change in my life that I am not inclined to desire. Even though the divine light illumines every mind, how much of the divine illumination we can see depends on the condition of our heart (CD 1.9.9). If you try to point something out to me on the horizon, I see it only if my eyes are open and turned in the correct direction. Similarly, reason leads me to divine truth only if the will and the desires are properly oriented. Socrates thought that having knowledge of the good leads us to pursue it. But Augustine's own moral struggles convinced him that knowledge does not produce goodness. In fact, the reverse is true. Philosophical reason only finds the light of truth if led by a heart that cherishes the light. According to Augustine, "Faith goes before; understanding follows after" (SR 118.1).

Metaphysics: God, Creation, Freedom, and Evil

THE EXISTENCE OF GOD

Many theistic philosophers in the modern period (such as Descartes and Locke) develop their epistemology independently of theological considerations. Only then do they go on, in good logical order, to provide proofs for the existence of God. Obviously, this was not the case with Augustine, for the light of faith illumines all his philosophical discussions. Nevertheless, he does offer what we may view as arguments for the existence of God. One does not get the impression he intends them to be conclusive proofs that will cause hard-boiled atheists to fall to their knees. They are more like clues or reminders that help people with open hearts find what they seek.

Although he does not believe the finite can ever prove the infinite, Augustine does believe creation gives us evidence of its Creator:

> The very order, changes, and movements in the universe, the very beauty of form in all that is visible, proclaim, however silently, both that the world was created and also that its Creator could be none other than God. (CG 11.4)

Such passages are as much of an argument for God's existence from nature as can be found in Augustine. He thought, no doubt, that sense experience is too uncertain and the physical world it represents is too changeable and unlike the Creator to be an effective basis for belief.

Augustine expends much more ink arguing from the nature of the person to God's existence. He believes God is actually closer to us than the world he has made. The spiritual, inner person, made in the image of God, brings us much closer to what we are seeking than does the physical world. The quest for God leads "from the exterior to the interior, and from the interior to the superior."[2] Augustine's typical approach can be found in *On Free Choice of the Will*, where, as mentioned, he argues for the objective and universal nature of the eternal truths of reason such as found in mathematical and ethical judgments. Briefly, he argues that if there is eternal and necessary truth that is higher than the mind and independent of it, then this must be God, for these are attributes of God himself. Throughout his works, Augustine tends to uncritically identify Plato's Good with God. However, he ignores the fact that Plato's Good and the eternal truths were impersonal and a far cry from the full-blown Judeo-Christian God Augustine slips in at the end of his arguments.

CREATION

The familiar first line of the Bible begins by declaring, "In the beginning God created the heavens and the earth." Augustine, of course, believed this on faith, but he also thought that reason supported this claim. In discussing creation, Augustine makes five important points: (1) God created out of nothing, (2) creation was an act of divine freedom, (3) the world is composed of form and matter, (4) biological species emerge from seminal forms, and (5) God created time itself. As much as he respected and borrowed from Platonic and Neoplatonic thought, Augustine is at pains on this topic to distinguish the Judeo-Christian picture of God's relation to the world from that of the Greeks.

First, he asserts that the world was brought into being out of nothing (*ex nihilo*). Here, he is rejecting all the options favored by the Greeks. The Greeks tended to believe that the world was either eternal or created out of some sort of pre-existing matter separate from God. But the Bible says God created the world without depending on any prior materials, and Augustine thinks reason confirms this. He imagines that the heavens and the earth cry out, "We did not make ourselves, we were made by him who abides for eternity" (C 9.10.25). The reason why they must have been created is because they exhibit change and variation (C 11.4.6). His assumption here is that anything changing is created and anything unchanging (such as the laws of mathematics and God) is eternal. Hence, the world is not eternal, and not a portion of God, either, for that would drag a part of God's being down into the domain where things change and are destroyed. With Plato, Augustine believes that a perfect being could not change, for the only thing he could change into would be a lesser form of being.

Second, Augustine insists that creation was a free act. Since God is sovereign, the world did not flow from him by necessity as Plotinus thought. He created because he wanted to share his goodness with creatures (TR 18.35–36). Third, the world of particulars is based on the eternal forms. In understanding the physical world, Augustine borrows liberally from Plato. Augustine spends an entire chapter of his *Confessions* interpreting the creation story in Genesis to fit his Platonism (C 12). Every part of creation is brought into existence as a combination of form and matter. However, in at least two ways Augustine deviates from Plato's account. One difference is that, for Augustine, the eternal forms, which are the archetypes or exemplars of physical objects, do not autonomously exist on their own, but reside within God's mind. Augustine says that "no determining form by which any mutable being is what it is . . . could have any existence apart from Him who truly exists because His existence is immutable" (CG 8.6).* The other difference is that he rejects Plato's view that the creator of the world (the Demiurge) functions like an architect who imposes the Forms on pre-existing matter. Augustine argues that such formless matter would have needed a creator to cause it to exist (C 11.5.7).

Augustine's fourth thesis about creation is that God has placed rational seeds or seminal reasons (*rationes seminales*) in the world, from which future created beings will emerge.[†] He introduces this thesis to resolve an apparent contradiction in Scripture. On the one hand, it speaks of God as having "created all things together."[3] On the other hand, in Genesis it appears that different kinds of creatures were created on different days.[‡] Augustine's answer is that God did create everything simultaneously but some things were created fully developed and some as undeveloped "seeds." The immense variety of biological organisms that continue to emerge over time has developed from these rational seeds or forces planted in the world. In proposing this account, Augustine is trying to ensure that nothing is left to purely natural forces or the agency of creatures, for God is the cause of everything. Thus, even when new forms of life emerge, it is all part of God's original creation. Although it may seem that Augustine is proposing a version of theistic evolution, his account differs from the biological theory of evolution because there is no emergence of random novelties nor the transformation of one species into another, because the whole developmental scheme is there in the beginning.

Finally, Augustine considers the nature of time by pondering what the book of Genesis means when it says, "In the beginning God created. . . ." According to the Manichaeans, if the world had a beginning, then we are naturally led to ask, "What was God doing before he made heaven and earth?" Augustine rebukes those who give the following frivolous answer to this question: "He was preparing hell for those who pry into mysteries" (C 11.12). His own, more serious answer is that the question is based on the debatable assumption that time was ticking away before creation. If this were so, then why did God create at one particular time rather than sooner or later? The Manichaeans were right—if God was waiting around for eons and then, at a certain time, decided to create the world, this would imply change in God. Augustine's answer to all this is that God did not create the world *in* time, but created the world *and* time together. Since time is change, it, too, is creaturely and must have had a beginning, along with the stars, the planets, the earth, and biological species. As Augustine says, "the changes of things make time" (C 12.8.8). Time is a relational entity. Without creation, nothing would move or change and time would not pass. For God there is neither before nor after he simply is, for his existence is timeless and eternal.

FOREKNOWLEDGE, PROVIDENCE, AND FREE WILL

The previous section concluded with Augustine's view that God created time but does not exist in it, for he exists in eternity. Time is merely the way *we* experience the world. To understand God's relation to time, Augustine looks to an analogy in human experience. He notices he can hold in his mind, all at once, a particular psalm that he knows well. As he repeats it, some of the words recited become past and some are there in memory, waiting to be spoken. Thus, he can anticipate the future words to come (C 11.28.38). So it is with God. All the moments within time are known to God as one eternal present moment. Similarly, Mozart claimed that when the inspiration for a musical piece originally came to him, he did not hear

---

*Although this view can be found in the Neoplatonists, Augustine wrongly assumes that Plato also held it. The problem is that he naively assumes that Plato's Good can be equated with the biblical God.

[†]Augustine's notion of the rational seeds probably came to him from Plotinus but originated with the Stoics.

[‡]Augustine correctly realizes that the word "day" here does not necessarily mean a twenty-four-hour period, but can mean an indefinite period of time.

the notes in his mind successively, as we do when the piece is played. Instead, he could hear the whole composition in his imagination *all at once*, much as we can survey all parts of a painting in one simultaneous experience.[4] Although Mozart's instantaneous experience of a lengthy musical piece is remarkable for a human being, this is the way that God knows every temporal event.

God's foreknowledge seems to raise a problem for human freedom. If God sees ahead of time every action you will perform, then how can your actions be free? You may be wrestling with the decision of whether to go to law school after graduation or to join a business. You may have to decide whether to marry the person you are dating or to become free and unattached again. From your perspective, the outcome of these decisions are not yet decided, but Augustine says God knows what you will do. Your future life is as familiar to him as the events in a movie that you have seen many times. Since God's foreknowledge is infallible, it would seem you are suffering from the illusion of freedom. The script of your life is already contained in the mind of God. Are we forced to choose between God's foreknowledge and human freedom? Augustine doesn't think so. As he says, "God knows all things before they happen; yet, we act by choice in all those things where we feel and know that we cannot act otherwise than willingly" (CG 5.9). According to Augustine's theory, when you freely make the decision to go to law school, you were equally free not to go to law school. However, God knew beforehand that you would *freely* make the choice that you did.

Although problems enough riddle this position, Augustine aggravates them by suggesting that God not only for*eknows* what people will do, he also fore*ordains* their actions. Since God's power is supreme, Augustine thinks that human choices cannot frustrate God's will. "For He is not truly called Almighty if He cannot do whatsoever He pleases, or if the power of His almighty will is hindered by the will of any creature whatsoever" (E 96).

God's intervention in every detail of human history is dramatically illustrated by Augustine's own account of his life. He decided to leave Carthage and go to Rome to seek out better students. Or at least Augustine *thought* that was why he went to Rome. Actually, he says, God made that decision so that Augustine would be led to salvation. As he expresses this in a prayer to God, "You were using my ambitious desires as a means towards putting an end to those desires" (C 5.8). We might try to soften the conflict between human freedom and divine providence by saying that God is a superpsychologist who carries out his plans by using his knowledge of our inner motives, yet without violating our freedom. However, this does not detract from the fact that Augustine thinks that God orchestrates not only external events, but also people's actions. In Augustine's life, God made the students in Carthage incorrigible and the teaching in Rome more attractive.

Augustine does not compromise when he talks about God's power. He says that "God works in the hearts of men to incline their wills whithersoever He wills, whether to good deeds according to His mercy, or to evil after their own deserts" (GFW 43). Although some argue that so much divine sovereignty negates human freedom, Augustine simply replies that the two are compatible. For example, he says faith and works are commanded, but they are also a gift of God so that "we may understand *both* that *we do them*, *and* that *God makes us* to do them" (PS 22, emphasis added). People continue to debate the plausibility of this sort of "both-and" position in this century.

THE PROBLEM OF EVIL

In repeatedly asserting God's omnipotence, Augustine raises the problem of evil. If God is all powerful and good, how can so much suffering and evil infect the world? Before he became a Christian, Augustine thought that the Manichaeans' dualism was the only way to absolve God of blame. If the God of Light is limited in power and is caught in an eternal struggle with the competing power of darkness, then no one can suppose God is responsible for the evil in creation. Of course, the notion of God having a more or less equal adversary is not acceptable to Augustine's Christian theology. Augustine's starting point on this issue is the claim that since God created the world, anything that exists is good (C 7.12.18). Therefore, evil must always be understood as a defect, a corruption, or a perversion of what was created good. Although Augustine derived his solution to the problem of evil from the Neoplatonic tradition, he rejected their tendency to view material reality as essentially evil and in necessary tension with the rational and the spiritual. With the goodness of creation as his initial premise, Augustine offers several ways of understanding the presence of evil.

First, while some things may seem evil to us, they are actually instrumental ways of achieving the good. To use a contemporary example, no one likes to see a baby cry when she receives a vaccination shot. But this actually enables her to achieve something good, namely health. Similarly, Augustine says the calamities of this life encourage us to yearn for the life to come, and not to covet material goods, thus achieving spiritual health (CG 1.8, 22.22). Like the baby, we tend to notice only the immediate problem and miss God's benevolent purpose.

Augustine's second answer is that evil is not an independent reality but is really a type of privation, a lack of something (CG 11.22). Just as a shadow is not substantial in itself but represents the absence of light, so evil is not part of the inventory of the universe but is simply the absence of perfect goodness. But nothing in creation can match the perfect goodness of God, so everything is inevitably imperfect to some degree. If God eliminated all imperfection from the world, then everything except himself would disappear. On the whole, the world is the "masterpiece of our Creator."

> If the beauty of this order fails to delight us, it is because we ourselves, by reason of our mortality, are so enmeshed in this corner of the cosmos that we fail to perceive the beauty of a total pattern in which the particular parts, which seem ugly to us, blend in so harmonious and beautiful a way. (CG 12.4)

However, Augustine acknowledges that it may take an act of faith to believe, contrary to appearances, that all things contribute to the "beauty of a total pattern."

Augustine's third answer to the problem of evil is to shift the blame to human perversity. All natural evils (such as pain, earthquakes) are only apparently evil; the only thing that approaches genuine evil is moral evil. Moral evil is the product of the human will. It too is a privation, in that it is the result of a defective will turning away from God. According to Augustine, Adam, the first man, was the only one who had the freedom not to sin. However, after Adam freely chose to disobey God, the human race lost its freedom and became a slave to sin. Thus, it is impossible for us to not sin. We achieve true moral freedom only when God gives us the gift of grace. Augustine does not believe that the will first turns to God and then receives grace. Instead, we first receive grace, which enables our will to turn to God. For his own purposes, God grants his grace to some but not to others, but this distribution is not based on merit, for then grace would be something God owed us and would be a source of pride (the root origin of all sin), not a gift that God freely bestows. But isn't it unjust for God to give grace to some and not to others? Augustine does not think so. His point can be made as follows: If ten people have borrowed money from me, they all owe me a debt. If I cancel the debt of two of them, the rest can't complain about this because it does not change the original fact that they owe me money. Canceling the debt of some is a gift I freely give, not something any debtor can claim he or she deserves.

Augustine's view of human nature raises again the question of how we can be determined yet free. If our sinful nature makes it impossible not to sin, then it seems we are not free. Yet, since the source of our actions comes within and is rooted in our character, Augustine believes this is sufficient for free will. Are we free to do otherwise than sin? In one sense we are. There are no physical restraints on us, and no logical necessity constrains us. In everything we do, we are following what we love. Who could ask for more freedom? It is just a fact of our condition, according to Augustine, that apart from God's grace our love is distorted.

Philosophy of History and the State

THE RISE OF A CHRISTIAN PHILOSOPHY OF HISTORY

Significantly, until this point we have not discussed the philosophy of history in reference to any previous philosophers. Augustine offers us the first speculative philosophy of history that claims to uncover the purpose and pattern of history. Many Greeks, such as Plato, were concerned only with eternal, unchanging truths, and thus the fleeting, particular events of history held little interest for them. And those who defended a materialist metaphysics thought everything was governed by blind, random forces. No matter what the details of their metaphysics, the typical Greek thought human history follows the same sort of cyclical pattern we find in the seasons. Nations come into being, rise to power, and then fade away, and this cycle is repeated endlessly. There is little more to be said, for there is no overarching purpose to it all. According to Augustine, however, this view implies that the human soul is trapped on an endless, cosmic "merry-go-round" (CG-B 12.14).

In contrast to the Greek view, the Old and the New Testaments of the Bible said that history has meaning and a linear direction. Like a carefully crafted drama, history has a beginning, a middle, and an end. Although God is the author, both he and the human actors have their respective roles to play on the stage of history. Thus, it is not by accident that the first philosopher of history was a Christian.

A concern for the pattern of history fits in with Augustine's Christian vision of the world, but his writings on this topic were provoked by a startling event. The once invincible city of Rome was attacked and ravished for three days by the Goths in 410. They depleted its riches and left corpses and ruins in their wake. Our reaction would be similar to that of the Romans if Washington, DC, were captured and looted by an invading army. This event was met with a great deal of despair throughout the Empire as people

asked, "How could the great city of Rome have fallen?" It did not take long for the answers to come. The Romans who were still pagans blamed Christianity. Rome fell to the barbarians, they said, because she turned away from the gods that had supported her throughout her days of glory. In 382 Christians had removed the Goddess of Victory from the Senate House in Rome, over the protests of the pagans. Furthermore, the Christian emperor Theodosius I had decreed that the worship of Jupiter (the chief Roman god) and Mars (the god of war) and the rest of the pagan gods was a crime punishable by death. It seemed clear to many that the Christians had robbed Rome of its divine protectors and the secret of its success. Augustine defended Christianity with *City of God*, the monumental work he considered his masterpiece. It occupied the last years of his life, for he started it at the age of fifty-nine, in the year 413, and finished at age seventy-two, in 426. It is an encyclopedic work, consisting of twenty-two books and over a thousand pages. In it, he argues that Rome's strength resulted from its civic virtues, for God honored these ideals by granting Rome temporal success. In fact, her highest moral ideals were the same virtues as those taught in Christianity. However, the Romans turned against their better side and fell into decadence and rampant vice. In short, the problem was not that Rome turned to Christianity but that it did not turn soon enough. Accordingly, Augustine spends the first half of this very large volume recounting the sins of Rome's polytheism, sexual depravity, social injustice, and obscene theater shows.* The second half of the book speaks more generally about the drama of human history. The picture he presents is one in which history is seen neither as a product of economic forces, nor political struggles, nor material resources, nor blind chance, but as a moral drama in which the purposes of God and the moral decisions of human creatures are the significant elements.

---

*Augustine's passages have given us a wealth of information about ancient societies and polytheism, because the sources that informed his research are now lost.

THE TWO CITIES

Augustine tells the story of history by means of his famous hypothesis that human history is an ongoing conflict between two kingdoms: the City of the World and the City of God. These two kingdoms are not actual political states. Instead, they represent diametrically opposed spiritual systems that have existed since the human race turned against God and fell from grace. However, every particular political state serves the interests of one or the other spiritual kingdom. Thus, Augustine assumes with Plato that society has the same moral structure as the individual. We are to understand societies as well as individual people in terms of their basic loves or commitments. Each of us is a citizen of one or the other of these "cities," depending on whether we love God or the world. Augustine describes the two cities:

> What we see, then, is that two societies have issued from two kinds of love. Worldly society has flowered from a selfish love which dared to despise even God, whereas the communion of saints is rooted in a love of God that is ready to trample on self. In a word, this latter relies on the Lord, whereas the other boasts that it can get along by itself. (CG 14.28)

Augustine's political philosophy is in sharp opposition to that of the Greeks, who supposed that active participation in the state was a source of fulfillment. For Augustine, the state is a necessary evil, a result of the fall. It was instituted to reign in sinful human nature, which naturally tends toward lawlessness (CG 22.22). Contrary to the vain attempts of all secular utopias, the only truly good society is the community of faithful believers that God has founded and that will reign throughout all eternity. In the meantime, God's people live out their earthly existence in the ambiguity of being part of two kingdoms. Since we live in a particular state, we owe allegiance to it insofar as it does not prevent the worship of the true God. Civil society has the virtue that it provides peace, even if a temporal and imperfect peace. Hence, the citizens of the heavenly kingdom can use the benefits of society. However, we must always realize that in this present life we are mere travelers in a foreign land, for our true home is in heaven, and only there can we find true peace (CG 19.17). Because the earthly state inevitably reflects the corruption of human nature, we must direct our lives according to the laws of the higher kingdom and seek to influence the civil society with the principles of God's kingdom. Augustine makes it clear that the Church is superior to the state because only the Church is the source of the true principles of human conduct. This view on Church–state relations was very influential in the Middle Ages. In the latter part of this age, it caused a great deal of tension as the Church and political kingdoms wrestled for dominance.

THE MEANING OF HISTORY

Augustine's view of history can be summed up in the following passage:

> It is therefore this God, the author and giver of felicity, who, being the one true God, gives earthly dominion both to good men and to evil. And he does this not at random or, as one may say, fortuitously, because he is God, not Fortune. Rather he gives in accordance with the order of events in history, an order completely hidden from us, but perfectly known to God himself. Yet God is not bound in subjection to this order of events; he is himself in control, as the master of events, and arranges the order of things as a governor. (CG-B 4.33)

Several important points lie latent within this passage. First, Augustine is uncompromising when he ascribes to God total, providential control over history. For example, he claims God established Rome:

> It was God's good pleasure, by means of this city, to subdue the whole world, to bring it into a single society of a republic under law, and to bestow upon it a widespread and enduring peace. (CG 18.22)

But this is true not only for Rome, but for all political kingdoms: "We must ascribe to the true God alone the power to grant kingdoms and empires" (CG 5.21). Augustine lists by name good kingdoms as well as evil kingdoms, just and righteous rulers along with cruel tyrants, and says they all receive their power from God (CG 5.21). He controls even the progress and outcome of wars:

The same may be said of the duration of wars. It rests with the decision of God in his just judgment and mercy either to afflict or console mankind, so that some wars come to an end more speedily, others more slowly. (CG 5.22)

Second, Augustine gives a moral interpretation of history. History is not to be understood in terms of economics or politics. Instead, these are simply the end result of the moral forces at work. For example, the Israelites prospered when they worshiped the one true God, but they suffered when they worshiped idols. When Rome prospered, it did so either because it was led by Christian emperors or by rulers who at least tried to follow justice and virtue. Rome eventually declined when its people and rulers turned to immorality. However, Augustine does not think any simple formula can make history's pattern completely transparent. It is an "order completely hidden from us." We must not think that God is not in control whenever the wicked prosper and the good suffer. Even here there is a purpose to it all, for just as fire purifies gold but consumes chaff, so the suffering of good persons serves the end of testing and purifying them, and keeps the faithful from being too attached to their physical well-being and material gain. Although the distribution of rewards and suffering may seem unjust, "in general, bad men come to a bad end, and good men enjoy eventual success" (CG 20.2).

THE PROBLEM OF PROVIDENCE AND FREE WILL IN HISTORY

Once again we face a tension that is persistent throughout Augustine's writings, this time projected from the individual person's level onto the face of history itself. If God is all powerful, is any room left for human decisions? We have been told God orchestrates the events of history to achieve his purposes for individuals and nations. Wars, brutalities, tyrants, and natural calamities, as well as economic and political prosperity and the beauty and bounty of nature, have all been provided by God to punish humanity or to bless it as he sees fit (CG 22.22,24). Once again, Augustine insists both that God is in control and that humans

are responsible. For example, he says that in ancient times God stirred up the enemies of his people to devastate them when they deserved chastisement. This raises the question: Did the invading armies do this on their own, or did God cause them to do it? Augustine's answer is "Both statements to be sure are true, because they both came by their own will, and yet the Lord stirred up their spirit" (GFW 42). However, in the final analysis it seems God is in control. "For the Almighty sets in motion even in the innermost hearts of men the movement of their will" (GFW 42).

THE IMPLICATIONS OF AUGUSTINE'S THEORY OF HISTORY

Some readers of Augustine find his view very encouraging, and others find it troubling. On the one hand, his view leads to optimism because it presents a teleological (purposeful) view of history. When faced with injustice and tremendous social upheavals, many people in Augustine's day and in our own time find it comforting to believe that history is not a collection of random events, but is an ordered series of events fulfilling a purpose.

On the other hand, along with these comforts comes the unsettling conclusion that the outcome of every human decision is already decided. Apparently, we don't make much of a difference at all, if we are merely playing a role in a play that is already written. Furthermore, if we accept Augustine's account of divine providence (things are the way they were meant to be), then we must be very cautious in trying to change the course of events. This leads to a very conservative outlook that encourages acceptance of the status quo. Accordingly, preserving peace and social order, even if it is an evil social order, are priorities for Augustine. For example, he says slavery is not part of the natural order but is the result of sin (CG 19.15). But he apparently thinks it is less serious than sexual sins: "It is better to be the slave of a man than the slave of passion." By living a life of virtue and obedience, the slave is strengthened in character, while the master is harmed by his ruthlessness. Hence, there is little room in Augustine's political theory for the American Revolution or any of the confrontational methods for achieving social change and civil rights that have brought justice to so many societies throughout history.

Evaluation and Significance

WAS AUGUSTINE A PHILOSOPHER?

Anyone who attempts to analyze Augustine's philosophical views must deal with the question of whether he can properly be said to be a philosopher at all. Many would say "No!" for he makes use of biblical authority, and too many of his discussions are replete with theological assumptions. Augustine, however, would probably agree with Simmias in Plato's dialogue *Phaedo*. In this story, Socrates and his friends are speculating about the possibility of life after death. In despair, Simmias says it is almost impossible to achieve certainty in this life about these questions. Perhaps the best we can do, he says, is "to select the best and most dependable theory which human intelligence can supply, and use it as a raft to ride the seas of life— that is, *assuming that we cannot make our journey with greater confidence and security by the surer means of divine revelation*" (emphasis added).[5] Augustine, of course, believes we do have this more sure means of arriving at our destination and need not endure the risks and uncertainties of the tenuous raft of human reason.

Despite his use of supernatural revelation, however, a case could be made that in many passages Augustine is indeed writing as a philosopher. He addressed philosophical themes such as the nature of the self, knowledge, and time, as well as the status of universal truths, the existence of God, and human immortality and provided philosophical arguments to underscore the biblical answers. Whether we think these arguments are good or not is not the issue. Since many of his arguments are clever modifications of Platonic arguments, if Augustine is not a philosopher then neither is Plato. Augustine, no doubt, would not have cared whether the final verdict was that he was only a theologian and not a philosopher. He was simply concerned to pursue the truth and to persuade others of it, using any resources available. He was writing for both a non-Christian and a Christian audience. With respect to the first audience, he realized that intellectual arguments alone would not convert the atheist any more than they had converted him. Nevertheless, the philosophical reasonings of the Neoplatonists did remove some obstacles from the threshold of faith for Augustine and started him on his journey toward God. This is what he hoped his works could do for others. For the Christian audience, he hoped to work out a Christian worldview that would show the implications and relevance of the biblical faith for all the traditional issues of philosophical and cultural concern.

AUGUSTINE'S INFLUENCE

Whether or not you agree with his conclusions, the importance of Augustine's thought is hard to overestimate. Christian thinkers preceding him tried to integrate Christian revelation and Greek philosophy, but Augustine is a pioneer in terms of the comprehensive scope of his topics. Consequently, he has served as a model of Christian scholarship throughout the Middle Ages and up to our own day. Augustine not only influenced the Roman Catholic tradition, however, for he has had a considerable impact on traditional Protestant theology as well. The Protestant Reformers thought they were doing nothing more than returning to the purity of Augustine's theology. John Calvin, the sixteenth-century Reformer, said that he could write the whole of his theology out of Augustine.

In his *City of God*, Augustine raised written history from a mere chronicle of events to the telling of a story, that seeks to reveal the meaning behind the events. Even today, some newspaper editorials and political speeches attribute the rise and fall of nations and leaders to their moral qualities. These examples show how much Augustine has influenced our ways of thinking about world events. Finally, he gave birth to many of the themes of modern philosophy and was, thereby, twelve centuries ahead of his time. His use of an introspective examination of the self as a philosophical starting point is a technique that we will not see again until the Renaissance.

Questions for Understanding

1. Why does Augustine place so much importance on the will?

2. What were Augustine's arguments against skepticism?

3. In what ways did Augustine agree and disagree with Plato?

4. Why does Augustine believe that reason can never be religiously neutral?

5. In what ways does Augustine bring in philosophical considerations in his account of creation?

6. How does Augustine view the relationship between God's foreknowledge and human freedom?

7. What is the problem of evil? In what ways does Augustine attempt to solve it?

8. According to Augustine, what is the nature of human history?

9. What are the two cities? What role do they play in Augustine's account of history?

Questions for Reflection

1. Socrates believed that people do what is wrong out of ignorance of what is really good. What would Augustine say?

2. Think about a time in your life when you made an ethical decision. Would you agree with Augustine that what we love is what determines our will and our intellect? Are there ever times when your intellect determines your will?

3. Do you agree with Augustine that if there were a God who foreknows and controls all events, that this could be consistent with your ability to make free choices? Why?

4. What do you think of Augustine's view that history is not random, but follows a pattern? Do you agree with his emphasis on history as a moral struggle between good and evil?

5. If Augustine had written a book on your country's history, what sorts of facts, events, and patterns would he emphasize?

6. Is Augustine's view of history an optimistic or pessimistic one?

Notes

1. References to the works of Augustine are abbreviated as follows:

AA *Against the Academicians*, trans. Sister Mary Patricia Garvey (Milwaukee: Marquette University Press, 1957).

C   *Confessions*, trans. Henry Chadwick (Oxford, England: Oxford University Press, 1991).

CD *On Christian Doctrine*, trans. J. F. Shaw in *A Select Library of the Nicene and Post-Nicene Fathers of the Christian Church*, vol. 2, ed. Philip Schaff (Buffalo, NY: The Christian Literature Company, 1887).

CG *The City of God*, trans. Gerald G. Walsh, Demetrius B. Zema, Grace Monahan, and Daniel J. Honan (New York: Doubleday Image, 1958).

CG-B *The City of God*, trans. Henry Bettenson (Harmondsworth, Middlesex, England: Penguin Books, 1972).

E   *Enchiridion*, trans. J. F. Shaw in *A Select Library of the Nicene and Post-Nicene Fathers of the Christian Church*, vol. 3, ed. Philip Schaff (Buffalo, NY: The Christian Literature Company, 1887).

CF *Concerning Faith of Things Not Seen*, trans. C. L. Cornish, in *A Select Library of the Nicene and Post-Nicene Fathers of the Christian Church*, vol. 3, ed. Philip Schaff (Buffalo, NY: The Christian Literature Company, 1887).

FCW *On Free Choice of the Will*, trans. Anna S. Benjamin and L. H. Hackstaff (New York: Macmillan, Library of Liberal Arts, 1964).

GFW *On Grace and Free Will*, trans. Peter Holmes, Robert E. Wallis, and Benjamin B. Warfield in *A Select Library of the Nicene and Post-Nicene Fathers of the Christian Church*, vol. 5, ed. Philip Schaff (New York: The Christian Literature Company, 1887).

HT *On the Holy Trinity*, trans. Arthur W. Haddan and W. G. T. Shedd in *A Select Library of the Nicene and Post-Nicene Fathers of the Christian Church*, vol. 3, ed. Philip Schaff (Buffalo, NY: The Christian Literature Company, 1887).

PS *On the Predestination of the Saints*, trans. Peter Holmes, Robert E. Wallis, and Benjamin B. Warfield in *A Select Library of the Nicene and Post-Nicene Fathers of the Christian Church*, vol.

5, ed. Philip Schaff (New York: The Christian Literature Company, 1887).

SL   *Soliloquies*, trans. C. C. Starbuck in *A Select Library of the Nicene and Post-Nicene Fathers of the Christian Church*, vol. 7, ed. Philip Schaff (New York: The Christian Literature Company, 1888).

SR   *Sermons on Selected Lessons of the New Testament*, trans. R. G. MacMullen in *A Select Library of the Nicene and Post-Nicene Fathers of the Christian Church*, vol. 6, ed. Philip Schaff (New York: Scribner's, 1903).

TR   *Of True Religion*, trans. J. H. S. Burleigh (Chicago: Regnery, 1968).

2. Quoted in Armand A. Maurer, *Medieval Philosophy* (New York: Random House, 1962), 8.

3. Ecclesiasticus 18.1. This book is found in the deutero-canonical section of the Catholic Bible. The problem only occurs in the particular translation that Augustine used.

4. Wolfgang Amadeus Mozart, "A Letter" in *The Creative Process*, ed. Brewster Ghiselin (New York: New American Library, Mentor, 1963), 45.

5. Plato, *Phaedo* 85d, trans. Hugh Tredennick in *The Collected Dialogues of Plato*, ed. Edith Hamilton and Huntington Cairns (New York: Random House, Pantheon, 1961).

9

Early Medieval Philosophy

From the Roman World to the Middle Ages

Soon after Augustine's death, the philosophical stream became muddy, and many obstacles arose to dissipate its energy and confuse its direction. The rise of Christianity had brought with it a new conception of the world and a distinct philosophical agenda that forged new channels for the waters of ancient philosophy. But in the early centuries following Augustine these waters stagnated and only a few trickles of fresh philosophical thought appeared. Eventually, however, a number of intellectual, political, and cultural forces came together to form the great tributary of the Middle Ages, and the philosophical stream broke through again with new vigor. The term "Middle Ages" refers to the one thousand-year period in western Europe that falls between the classical period and the modern age. It is also known as the *medieval* period from the Latin words *medium* (middle) and *aevum* (age). This period runs roughly from the fall of Rome in the fifth century to the dramatic changes in politics, religion, philosophy, and the arts in the 1500s. Philosophically,

it can be designated as running from the time of Augustine to the Renaissance. The term "Middle Ages" was originally derogatory. It was coined by the Renaissance thinkers who saw this period as an unfortunate interval of intellectual darkness that interrupted an otherwise continuous stream of progress from the classical period to their own time. This picture eventually changed as later historians came to recognize the importance of the medieval thinkers' accomplishments.

A Survey of the Early Middle Ages

To tell the story of philosophy after Augustine, we must begin with the fall of the Roman Empire. Its collapse resulted from both internal and external problems. Internally, it could not manage its vast size and extent. The empire's ponderous bureaucracy weighed it down and required the distribution of more and more power to the local provinces. As part of the decentralization program, the empire was divided into two regions. The western empire was originally ruled from Rome, but in the early fifth century the center of power was shifted to the better-fortified Ravenna.

The eastern empire was run from Constantinople. The division started out as an administrative convenience, but became permanent, and the empire never achieved unity again.

In the west, external problems accelerated the collapse of the Roman Empire. For many centuries, Germanic tribes from northern Europe had occupied the boundaries of the Roman territories. To maintain its overextended empire the Romans resorted to recruiting non-Romans (whom they called the "barbarians") into its army. Eventually whole alien tribes began to settle within the frontiers and began to dominate the territories. In the late fourth and fifth centuries, the Germanic tribes from the north (the Vandals, Visigoths, and Ostrogoths) moved into the heart of the empire. In 410 the Goths sacked Rome, and in 455 the small but aggressive tribe known as the Vandals raided the city. Their reputation made a mark on our language, for we still refer to looters and destroyers as "vandals." Finally, in 476, the Roman Empire fell, and by the end of the fifth century the western empire was a fragmented collection of tribal kingdoms. The Vandals held North Africa, and the Goths occupied Italy and Spain. Only two of the tribes succeeded in building permanent states. The first was the Franks, who took over Gaul and the Rhineland and gave modern France its name. The second long-lived state was produced by the Angles and the Saxons, who sailed across the North Sea to conquer Britain. Later, in the tenth century, their separate states merged into the single kingdom known as England ("Angle-land"). During the six hundred years from A.D. 400 to 1000 the story of western Europe was dominated by wars and invasions. Violence and anarchy do not provide fertile grounds in which philosophy may flourish. Hence, the political instability of this time prevented any coherent culture from taking root.

THE CHURCH

In the midst of all this change and turmoil, the one institution that managed to survive was the Catholic Church. While the secular empire crumbled around it, the Church retained its cohesion and preserved its character as a central organization and universal institution. Facilitating this was the fact that by the fifth century, the Western Church took on the organizational structure of a monarchy by declaring the bishop of Rome to be the "Father of the Church" or the "Pope" (from the Latin word *papa*). In the face of the cultural vacuum left by the fallen empire, the Church gained strength as the only institution strong enough to endure the changes. Thus, on its shoulders fell the responsibility of preserving the past and shaping the future. It took over many functions that the crumbling civil government could not handle. The Church collected taxes, looked after the food supply, repaired the city walls, maintained courts of criminal law, and used its buildings for hospitals and inns. Most importantly, the Church became the center of education, even though limited to the clergy and the monks.

PERIODS OF DARKNESS AND LIGHT

Despite the remnants of cultural unity preserved by the Church, the early Middle Ages was a time when the stream of culture and philosophy was at its lowest ebb. The period running from the fall of Rome and the death of Augustine to the year 1000 is commonly called the "Dark Ages." This grim picture may result from our limited historical resources, yet the educational and cultural activities of these centuries do seem limited compared with earlier ages. A brief moment of light during these centuries was produced by Charlemagne (Charles the Great), who ruled from A.D. 768 until his death in 814. He started out as the ruler of the Frankish kingdom but ended up uniting all western Europe. He engineered a rare period known as the Carolingian Renaissance, in which education and the arts were promoted. Charlemagne started schools within the cathedrals and monasteries, which attracted scholars from all over Europe. These schools preserved the classical Christian culture of the past, both through instruction and the copying of important texts. Throughout the dark and turbulent period following his death, these schools kept the light of knowledge lit until the eleventh and twelfth centuries, when philosophy blazed brightly again. In the later Middle Ages, most of the great universities of Europe rose from the institutions that Charlemagne had founded.

The Byzantine and Islamic Empires

The eastern division of the Roman Empire came to be known as the Byzantine Empire. Unlike its factious western counterpart, it maintained a reasonable degree of cultural and political unity throughout the Middle Ages. Among the resources it inherited were the two great centers of learning: Athens and Alexandria. When the Christians had been in the minority in the old Roman Empire, they had pleaded for tolerance from the pagans. However, when the Church gained dominance, it did not follow its own moral advice. Consequently, the pagans and the Jews often suffered persecution within Christian lands. In Alexandria, a Neoplatonic school flourished, run by an accomplished female philosopher named Hypatia. In 415 she was brutally murdered by a fanatical Christian mob, who were encouraged by the repressive policies of Cyril, the local bishop. In Athens, the successor to Plato's Academy and other pagan schools continued to prosper. However, the Emperor Justinian the Great closed these schools in 529. Despite this hostility, scholars kept alive the study of Plato, Neoplatonism, and Aristotle and kept their texts from being lost for all time. However, apart from their notable achievements in art and architecture, the Byzantines' preoccupation with theological and political disputes prevented them from making any important contributions to philosophy, science, or literature.

By the eighth century, the new religion of Islam had made its mark as a cultural and political force. The Muslims took control of the eastern, southern, and western shores of the Mediterranean, including Persia, Syria, Egypt, Africa, and Spain. Thus, the heirs of the later Roman Empire were the three great civilizations of the Mediterranean world: the European, the Byzantine, and the Islamic. Of these three, the European world was the most culturally primitive until the eleventh century. The Muslims would come to play an important role in the development of philosophy, for they inherited Aristotle's texts and eventually passed the ancient texts and a rich philosophical tradition on to Western Christianity.

An Overview of Medieval Philosophy

Before we begin to look at the philosophy of this period, it will be useful to set out a map of the terrain. Western philosophy from the beginning of the Christian era up to the close of the Middle Ages can be divided into five periods. The early period of Christian philosophy, which we examined in the last two chapters, is known as the *Patristic period*, which began in the first century A.D. and reached its apex in the philosophical and theological system of St. Augustine.* His was the last example of Christian thought born within the context of classical civilization. However, Augustine's writings were more than an epilogue to the Patristic era—they were also the prologue to the next chapter in philosophy's story. Augustine's Platonic Christianity would prove to be a dominant influence throughout the Middle Ages until the thirteenth century, when his system had to compete with alternative systems of thought based on Aristotle. This new approach would be most fully worked out by St. Thomas Aquinas, the thirteenth-century thinker who represents the culmination of medieval philosophy.

Between St. Augustine and the end of the Middle Ages lay a period of about ten centuries, an expanse of time longer than the whole classical period. This era can be divided into four periods, each of which is covered in a separate chapter. The early part of the Middle Ages (from the fifth to the end of the tenth centuries) was troubled by cultural and political upheavals, including a lot of bloodshed, as western Europe experienced the violent labor pains attending the birth of a new civilization. This period is commonly known as the *Dark Ages*. Despite the predominance of cultural darkness, there were a few bright lights during this

---

*"Patristic" comes from *pater*, the Latin for "father," and refers to the writings of the early Christian thinkers, who are called the "Fathers of the Church."

time. The philosophers Boethius in the early sixth century and John Scotus Erigena in the ninth century stand out as courageous voices in a time when philosophy was neglected. Charlemagne's support of education and the arts also kept alive the philosophical flame—but only barely. Nevertheless, by the ninth century Europe fell behind the classical world by every measure of civilization. The Dark Ages finally ended around the year 1000, when there was a sudden flowering, a fresh awakening of cultural life. The rediscovery of the texts of classical writers fueled the philosophical revival. As a result, we reach the *formative period* of the Middle Ages in the eleventh and twelfth centuries, which are covered in the next chapter. Here, philosophy springs to life once again, with such figures as St. Anselm, Peter Abelard, and a number of Islamic and Jewish scholars. Chapter 11 discusses the *culmination of medieval philosophy* in the thirteenth century, when the rediscovery of Aristotle's philosophy inspired the monumental work of Thomas Aquinas. Finally, Chapter 12 covers the period of the *decline of medieval thought* in the fourteenth century, which began with John Duns Scotus and William of Ockham. The decline of the Middle Ages then sets the stage for the great movements of the Renaissance and Reformation and for the rise of modern science.

Early Medieval Philosophy

Given our knowledge of the intellectual riches of the Greek philosophical tradition, it is startling to realize how few of their works were available throughout most of the medieval period. During the Roman period, Greek books were rarely translated into Latin because scholars who were interested in them could still read the originals. However, after St. Jerome translated most of the Bible into Latin (completed about A.D. 410), knowledge of Greek seemed superfluous and interest in the language declined. Furthermore, classical studies did not survive the social and political turmoil surrounding the fall of the empire. What is worse, basic skills of reading and writing were on the decline.

Because of the scarcity of Latin translations of Greek writings, the early medieval philosophers were familiar with only a few works from the classical period. Their knowledge of Plato was limited to his *Timaeus*, a work they thought pointed to the Christian view of the cosmos. The problem was, this work was a mythological cosmology that did not communicate many of the important ideas Plato's other works contained. The knowledge of Aristotle available at this time was confined to parts of his works on logic. In addition, they had an introduction to Aristotle's *Categories* written by the Neoplatonist Porphyry, a few dialogues of Cicero, and the essays of Seneca. Lucretius's poetic exposition of Epicurean atomism was available, but was not considered important, as indicated by the fact that only a single manuscript copy of his poem survived this time. Thus, until the latter part of the twelfth century, when the classics of Greek philosophy began to find their way into Europe, the early medieval scholars were limited to fragments of the Greek heritage. Although they benefited from this heritage, they were like people trying to get guidance from a jigsaw puzzle picture, but not realizing that many of the crucial pieces were missing. In addition to the poverty of philosophical resources, the times were brutal both in terms of the political violence and the physical conditions people faced. The philosophical stream had narrowed to a trickle, and the intellectual soil did not nourish philosophical fruit. As far as we can tell, there was a dearth of philosophical thinkers between the time of Augustine in the fifth century and the middle of the eleventh century. The two notable exceptions to this were the courageous and innovative figures of Boethius and John Scotus Erigena, both of whom had the rare advantage of knowing the Greek language.

BOETHIUS

Boethius (about A.D. 480–524 or 525) is commonly referred to as "the last of the Romans and the first of the medieval scholastics." His writings were an important channel through which the philosophy of the ancient world flowed into the Middle Ages. He was raised as a Christian in the home of a politically prominent Roman family. While in Athens, where he had been sent for his education, he mastered the Greek language (a rare accomplishment by the sixth century) and was exposed to the leading Greek philosophical traditions. He made it his life's goal to translate the whole of Plato's and Aristotle's works into Latin and to write commentaries on them. In addition, he thought he could harmonize their teachings. However, he did not get as far as he had hoped. If he had finished his task, the complete works of Plato and Aristotle would have been made available in Latin, and medieval philosophy would have developed quite differently from the way it did. We do know Boethius translated Aristotle's writings on logic into Latin and wrote commentaries on them. He also translated and provided several commentaries on the *Introduction to Aristotle's Categories* written by the Neoplatonist Porphyry. Furthermore, he wrote several original treatises on logic of his own, as well as five theological works. Through his scholarship, the medieval scholars learned to reason after the fashion of Aristotelian logic. In addition to his scholarly work, he held a high political office. Although he had received numerous honors, he fell out of favor and was executed on charges of high treason.

During the year he spent in prison awaiting his execution, he wrote *The Consolation of Philosophy*. This was widely read in the Middle Ages and influenced a number of writers. The theme of this work was one he had learned from the Stoics: The contemplation of abstract philosophy brings personal peace. Written in both poetry and prose, the book is a dialogue between the author and Philosophy, who is personified as a majestic but nurturing woman. Their conversation deals with a problem that was very real to Boethius: why a just man can suffer unjustly, while the wicked prosper. The answer he finds draws deeply from the wells of Plato, Aristotle, the Stoics, Plotinus, and Augustine, among others. The gist is that happiness cannot come through external fortune. Since the wicked foolishly pursue the false goods of honor, fame, riches, and bodily pleasure, they will not find happiness. Happiness is to be found beyond this world and is available to the virtuous alone.

In the course of the discussion, he addresses the themes of human freedom and divine providence. He strives to resolve the apparent contradiction between these two propositions: (1) human action is free, and (2) God foreknows everything we will do. Boethius provides what became a classic solution to the problem. For us, he says, there cannot be any infallible foreknowledge of free actions because they have not yet been decided. However, God's relationship to time is different from ours. He does not exist in time, but experiences our past, present, and future as simultaneous moments in his eternal present. Thus, the actions you will perform in the future are already present to him, and they are known by him as your free actions. Just as your knowledge that the sun is currently rising does not determine it to rise, so God's timeless foreknowledge of your free acts does not make them determined.

Throughout this book, Boethius's tone is religious but not explicitly Christian. It was the favorite reading of such literary figures as Dante, Boccaccio, and Chaucer. It contributed to the discussion of faith and reason by working out a natural philosophy based on unaided human reason. Although his works were neglected in the centuries immediately following his death, they guided eleventh-century thinkers when philosophical thought finally revived. The singular significance of Boethius's writings and translations was that they transmitted to the Middle Ages a great deal of the available knowledge concerning Aristotle, and they showed how philosophical categories could be applied to theology. Boethius provided the basic philosophical terms, definitions, and distinctions so important to later writers. Although he suffered in his own time, later generations of medieval scholars considered his works classics and authoritative philosophical resources.

JOHN SCOTUS ERIGENA

We have very few historical records of original philosophical work occurring in the six centuries between Boethius and St. Anselm in the eleventh century. John Scotus Erigena, who lived and died from around 810 to 877, was one of the few philosophers whose work survives. He was born in Ireland and received his education at an Irish monastery.* Ireland had the happy fate of being remote and thus distant from most of the turmoil of the sixth, seventh, and eighth centuries that swept across Europe. The Irish monasteries were centers of learning where a knowledge of Greek was still valued even as it became virtually unknown in the rest of the world. Erigena is universally recognized as having written the first great complete system of philosophy of the Middle Ages, a particularly remarkable accomplishment given the poverty of philosophical works he had available to him. A decisive factor in his originality, no doubt, as well as an important influence on his outlook was the fact that he was unique among his European contemporaries in being able to use what Greek sources were available as an intellectual resource.

Erigena served for years in the court of King Charles the Bald (Charlemagne's grandson), where he was appointed head of the Palace School in France. Erigena appeared to have not only a keen intellect but a sharp wit. After Erigena and King Charles had enjoyed several rounds of strong drink, the king attempted to make fun of the Irish fondness for drink by asking his companion whether anything separated a Scot from a sot. "Only this dinner table," was Erigena's sharp reply. Because of his respect for Erigena's scholarship, Charles commissioned him to translate into Latin the writings of some of the Greek Fathers of the Church. Included among these were a number of writings attributed to Dionysius the Areopagite, who was one of St. Paul's converts, mentioned in Acts 17:34. In these manuscripts, the author gives a decidedly Neoplatonic interpretation of Christianity. Because of their alleged authorship, these writings were accepted by medieval scholars as having almost apostolic authority and were very

well read throughout the medieval period. Much later, however, around the seventeenth century, they were discovered to be forgeries, now attributed to an unknown sixth-century Syrian Neoplatonist whom we now call "Pseudo-Dionysius." Nevertheless, their influence helped impose a Neoplatonic and mystical outlook on the philosophy and theology of the next six centuries. Furthermore, the ideas of Pseudo-Dionysius set the framework for all of Erigena's constructive philosophy.

For Erigena, the goal of philosophy was simply to provide a rational interpretation of revelation. The later medieval understanding of the differing tasks of philosophy and theology would not have occurred to him. Accordingly, he quotes Augustine to support his thesis that "true philosophy is true religion, and conversely, true religion is true philosophy."[1] True to the Christian tradition, Erigena affirms that Sacred Scripture should be followed in all things, but he recognizes it requires interpretation if we are to understand what it says. For Erigena, there are two sources for interpreting Scripture: reason and the Church Fathers. But he emphasizes the priority of reason, for he says that

> Authority indeed proceeds from true reason, reason never proceeds from authority. For all authority which true reason does not endorse is seen to be weak. True reason, however, being ratified and rendered immutable by virtue of itself, needs no additional assent from authority to strengthen it. (DN 1.69)[2]

In saying this, however, he was not brushing aside the authority of the Church Fathers in the name of sovereign, secular reason. Instead, he had faith that true authority and true reason would not conflict on the main issues since they "both spring from a common source, namely, divine wisdom" (DN 1.66).[3] If reason and authority seem to conflict, then one or the other is not genuine. Nevertheless, this methodological stance freed him to interpret both revelation and the doctrinal tradition in the directions his philosophical reason led him.

This approach is evident in his greatest work, *On the Division of Nature*, which was published about 867. The "Nature" referred to in the title embraces the whole of reality, including God and

*Although he was Irish, his name means "John the Scot," for during the early Middle Ages Ireland was known as Scotia. "Erigena," the latter part of his name, meant "of the people of Erin."

his creation. He says Nature has four aspects, which collectively exhaust all the logical possibilities: (1) What creates and is not created (God as the cause of things but who is himself without cause); (2) what creates and is created: the ideas in the Divine Logos, which form the blueprints and primordial causes of all created beings (Erigena's version of the Platonic Forms); (3) what is created but does not create: the created universe itself; and (4) what neither creates nor is created: this is God again, but now viewed as the final end of the creative process. Erigena believed all things would return to their source and be reunited in the being of God. There seems to be little doubt that Erigena's intentions were always to be an orthodox theologian. But he persistently tended to blur the distinction between (1) pantheism (which emphasizes the immanence of God to the point of identifying God and the world) and, in contrast, (2) biblical theism (which protects the transcendence of God and the creator creation distinction). How he saw these two elements as cohering is one of the main problems in understanding him.

Numerous recurring passages in Erigena have all the trademarks of pantheism. Given his Neoplatonic assumptions, it would have been virtually impossible for Erigena to have stuck with the orthodox doctrine that God is absolutely separate from creation. For example, the Neoplatonism he absorbed from Pseudo-Dionysius dictated that the only way one could conceive of the world as depending on God was to suppose the world *participates* in the being of God or *flows* from it. Quoting the authority of the author he thought was Dionysius, he says God "is called the One because He is all things universally; for there is nothing in existence which does not participate in the One" (DN 3.8).[4] Going even further, Erigena asserts that the One "extends Itself into everything and the extension itself is everything" (DN 3.9).[5] There could not be a clearer expression of the identity of God and the world. Erigena argues that there can be no accidents in God, meaning that every aspect of God's nature and all that proceeds from it are necessary. Thus, the universe is a necessary fulfillment of the divine creativity, just as the infinite number series is a rationally neces-

sary procession from its source in the number 1. Without the universe, God would only be a potential creator and thus unfulfilled and defective. If the universe does not flow necessarily from the nature of God, then creation is just an arbitrary and capricious whim on his part. The rational necessity of creation and its comparison to the unfolding of the number series looks back to the Neoplatonist Plotinus and looks forward to the great seventeenth-century metaphysician Spinoza, both of whom are sometimes interpreted as pantheists. Similarly, Erigena frequently uses the Neoplatonic metaphor that God's being is like a river that flows into everything, while the waters remain the same (DN 3.4).[6]

This view of God raises the problem of evil. If the universe is an outflowing of God's being, then why is evil in the world? With Augustine, Erigena believed that just as darkness is not a positive entity in itself but the absence of light, so evil is the absence of good. He also borrows from Augustine the explanation that our experience of evil is due to our limited view of the universe. He quotes Augustine's point that what appears to be evil is like the shadows in a painting. Seen by themselves, they are ugly, but in the context of the whole, they help create the beauty of the painting.

In his account of the fourth division or the final phase of nature's cycle, Erigena speculates that all distinctions and fragmentation will eventually be overcome, for these are the result of a lapse from the unity of God's being. Just as all things originally flow from God's being without diminishing it, so all things will eventually return to the same unity without enriching it. All the longings we feel in our earthly existence are really expressions of the desire to be unified with God again. This account reflects the Greek tendency to absorb all things into eternity. However, it diminishes the significance of time and creation, which are essential features of a Christian perspective. Even one of Erigena's most sympathetic commentators complains about this theory that

It seems to be impossible to retain the reality of the temporal universe in any satisfying sense. For when all has been reabsorbed into the Absolute, what has

the cosmic process accomplished? What is different because anything did ever exist? What has been achieved by the immense structure of the creation, by all the labour and experience and suffering of humanity?[7]

A further difficulty with the notion that all things are absorbed into the unity of God is that it raises problems for the Christian doctrine of immortality. Although Erigena tries very hard to preserve individual immortality, his Neoplatonism always seems to dilute it. For example, he says that at the end of time, "every creature will be cast into the shade, i.e. changed into God, as the stars at the rising of the sun" (DN 3.23).[8]

One of the most interesting issues raised by Erigena is in a passage inspired by Pseudo-Dionysius where Erigena argues that God is above and beyond all categories of being and thought, for to describe him would be to limit him (DN 1.10-14).[9] In this passage Erigena raises the problem of religious language, a problem philosophers of religion wrestled with from this time on into the twentieth century. The problem is, how can we use words and concepts drawn from our finite, earthbound experience to describe an infinite and transcendent being? Borrowing from Pseudo-Dionysius, Erigena's solution is to use both affirmative theology and negative theology. When we affirm that "God is good," we must keep in mind that our human notion of goodness is not adequate to God, so we must immediately add, "God is not good" (for it would be unseemly to suppose that God shares anything in common with finite, human goodness). All our affirmative statements about God are necessarily metaphorical, for human concepts do not do him justice. However, when we are saying what God is *not*, this negative theology may be taken literally. Erigena's (and Pseudo-Dionysius's) final solution is to speak of God only by means of superlative theology. We can say that God is Supertruth, God is Superwisdom, God is Supergood, and so on, thus avoiding the suggestion that his properties bear any similarity to their earthly counterparts. Although we can use these phrases, we cannot have a conceptual understanding of what Supergoodness is other than to know it is superior to ordinary, human concepts and exam-

ples of goodness. The situation is like trying to describe a three-dimensional sphere using only the terminology of plane geometry. We could say the sphere is circular but it is not a circle. It contains an infinite number of circles, yet is more than just a two-dimensional collection of many circles. Since such a God cannot be apprehended intellectually, mystical experience seems the only way to approach him. Thus, even Erigena's attempt to emphasize the transcendence of God forces him to fall back on a Neoplatonic merging with God in mystical experience. Because of the powerful way in which he presents his vision of God, John Scotus Erigena became an important source of inspiration to the later tradition of Christian mysticism as well as to some of the heretical sects in the twelfth and thirteenth centuries.

Despite the abundance of Neoplatonic elements in his thinking (many of which are at odds with traditional Christian theology), Erigena did not see himself as anything but an orthodox theologian. He tries very hard to reconcile his position with Scripture and continually quotes the Church Fathers, especially Augustine. Furthermore, he frequently reminds us that all his language about God is necessarily metaphorical. To be fair to him, his more pantheistic statements must be balanced with those in which he affirms a radical distinction between God and creation. Nevertheless, Erigena's opinion on his own orthodoxy was not shared by the ecclesiastical authorities. Eventually his book was condemned as pantheistic heresy and all copies ordered to be burned in 1225 by Pope Honorious III, who described it as "swarming with worms of heretical perversity." Earlier, another of his works was condemned by the Council of Valence (855) as "Irish porridge" and "the devil's invention."

Even though in his heart Erigena aimed at orthodoxy, his Neoplatonic ideas veered in directions he did not intend. This created problems not only for him but for the whole medieval Church. On the one hand, the writings of Pseudo-Dionysius were thought to be authentic and authoritative. On the other hand, Neoplatonism and Christian orthodoxy pull in different directions on many issues. The Church saw that Erigena's conclusions were heretical, but it was not clear how to avoid them because Neoplatonism was the only philosophical resource available at that time for Christian thinkers. Consequently, in the next couple of centuries after John Scotus Erigena, no one attempted to take up his task of constructing a comprehensive metaphysical system. Instead, Christian philosophers focused their attention on more isolated and manageable philosophical problems. What was lacking was a different model to guide philosophical thought. Philosophers needed a system that would preserve the otherworldly, eternal, and universal elements that were important to Christian theology, while doing justice to this world, the reality of time, and the existence of particulars. Accordingly, when Aristotle's metaphysical manuscripts became available in Europe in the twelfth century, it was possible to begin a new approach to systematic philosophy. Until then, we find philosophers sticking with piecemeal analyses of technical problems.

The Return to Darkness

Despite his courageous and innovative philosophical speculations, the lone voice of John Scotus Erigena did not have much of an impact. Furthermore, the intellectual and cultural momentum created by Charlemagne slowed to a halt after his death in 814. Once again, tribal monarchies arose to fill the political vacuum and a fragmented Europe lay helpless as the invasions began again with a new vigor. The Vikings with their military savagery and enormous sea power raided Europe and wrecked havoc in Hamburg, Paris, and Bordeaux, while the Muslim Saracens invaded Italy. Furthermore, it was a degrading time for the Church, because corruption and control by local political factions dictated the character of the Church at this time. From the years 800 to 1000, the age seemed committed to political instability, corruption, invasions, and violence. While Muslim culture continued to flourish, the rest of western Europe sank to the lowest depths it had ever experienced. Physical conditions were severe as war, disease, and famine set the agenda for people's daily lives. The average person lived only thirty years and fewer than 20 percent of the people

traveled more than 10 miles from their birthplace. During the roughly 150 years from the death of Erigena to the birth of Anselm, there is no record of any significant philosophical voice. Thus began the second Dark Ages in Europe, the darkest of its kind.

Questions for Understanding

1. What are the five periods of Western philosophy in the time frame ranging from the beginning of the Christian era to the close of the Middle Ages?

2. What works of Greek philosophy were available to the early medieval philosophers? What were the effects of this limited knowledge of previous philosophies?

3. What philosophical issues concerned Boethius?

4. How did John Scotus Erigena view the relationship of faith and reason?

5. In what ways did Neoplatonic philosophy influence Erigena's metaphysics?

6. What is the problem of religious language and how did Erigena attempt to solve it?

7. Why did Erigena's contemporaries reject his philosophy?

8. What factors led to the decline of philosophy in the 150 years following the death of Erigena?

Questions for Reflection

1. What are the strengths and weaknesses of Boethius's solution to the problem of divine foreknowledge versus human freedom?

2. How did Erigena's Neoplatonism lead him to pantheism?

3. What are the strengths and weaknesses of Erigena's solution to the problem of religious language?

Notes

1. On Predestination, chap. 1, trans. Allan B. Wolter, in *Medieval Philosophy: From St. Augustine to Nicholas of Cusa*, ed. John F. Wipple and Allan B. Wolter (New York: Macmillan, Free Press, 1969), 111.

2. John Scotus Erigena, *On the Division of Nature*, trans. A. B. Wolter, in Wipple and Wolter, 113–114. All references

to Erigena's book are symbolized in the text as "DN," followed by the chapter and section numbers of the original text.

3. Wipple and Wolter, 114.

4. *Periphyseon: On the Division of Nature*, trans. Myra L. Uhlfelder (Indianapolis: Bobbs-Merrill, Library of Liberal Arts, 1976), 149.

5. Ibid., 152.

6. Ibid., 139.

7. Henry Bett, *Johannes Scotus Erigena: A Study in Medieval Philosophy* (New York: Russell & Russell, 1964), 143.

8. Quoted in Frederick Copleston, *A History of Philosophy* vol. 2, pt. 1 (Garden City, NY: Doubleday, Image Books, 1962), 148.

9. Wipple and Wolter, 122–131.

CHAPTER

10

Philosophy and Theology
in the Eleventh and Twelfth Centuries

The Flowering of the Middle Ages

By the year 1000 the near anarchy and succession of barbarian invasions that had characterized the early Middle Ages had all but passed. During the following centuries, the political, social, and economic institutions of western Europe achieved a stability and coherence that lasted for some five hundred years. The institutions, art, architecture, music, literature, and customs that developed during these centuries form the collection of images most people associate with the Middle Ages. During the period from about 1000 to the late 1200s, medieval civilization reached its highest point of achievement. For this reason, this era is commonly called "the high Middle Ages."

The fresh spirit of this age is symbolized by the rise of the Gothic cathedral. Earlier methods of church architecture had produced squat, massive, earthbound structures that suggested stone fortresses designed to protect the sacred interior from the secular world outside. In contrast, new engineering techniques enabled the roofs to soar to unheard-of heights and replaced large areas of the stone walls with radiant sheets of stained glass. The

slender, skeletal structure of the rib vaulting replaced interior columns and heavy walls. This produced the illusion that the building was almost weightless and supported by the heavens themselves, giving the cathedrals a magical, mystical quality. The central device of the pointed arch not only made the vertical lines more graceful, but almost resembled a pair of hands touching in prayer.

The Gothic cathedral can serve as a symbol of the philosophical endeavors of this time. The fundamental structure of each building was based on the unyielding and universal laws of geometry and physics. But within these boundaries there was a freedom to explore a multitude of designs. The sacred worship within the buildings was illuminated by the light flowing in from the outside as it filtered through the brilliant colors and intricate designs produced by the stained-glass artisan. Similarly, medieval thought was carried on within the firm structure of Christian revelation, while the light of human reason flowed into Christian thought filtered through the patterns of Platonic and Aristotelian philosophy.

The magnificent, soaring designs of the Gothic cathedrals were achieved by orchestrating and

149

AKG London

The interior of Chartres Cathedral, completed in 1220. The architects of medieval cathedrals used stone and stained glass to create a sense of transcendence, lifting the eyes and the heart toward the realm of the spirit. Similarly, medieval philosophers created magnificent conceptual structures out of the building blocks of ideas to point the intellect to God.

resolving opposing tensions within the arches. The earthly materials of stone and the sensuous appeal of beauty pointed beyond themselves and led the eyes and hearts of the people toward heaven. Likewise, the philosophies of the time used the tools of logic to resolve the tensions between faith and reason. This was accomplished by fitting them into their proper places within awe-inspiring conceptual structures that pointed the intellect to God.

A major cause of the burst of new intellectual energy in the high Middle Ages was the rise of universities. During the chaotic centuries following the fall of Rome, there had been a real danger that learning and scholarship would vanish from Europe. It was the monasteries that preserved intellectual culture in the West. They were repositories of precious manuscripts and provided education

to the clergy—the only people thought to need it. In the 800s Charlemagne revived interest in scholarship and the arts. As a result, cathedral schools began to develop in the towns to meet the growing interest in education. The medieval universities grew from these schools as well as from the Italian municipal schools. In the thirteenth century, universities flourished at Paris, Bologna, Naples, Montpellier, Oxford, and Cambridge, to name just a few. By the year 1500 the number of universities exceeded eighty, and many of them still exist today. We still retain many academic traditions that originated with the medieval universities, such as wearing academic robes, granting various academic degrees, and defending written theses.

The importance of the university movement for medieval philosophy is that the universities brought together groups of scholars who preserved the great ideas of the past and advanced knowledge by analyzing the arguments of important texts and debating the significant intellectual issues of the day. As a part of their education, the students were expected to take positions on different issues and defend them against the questioning of their peers and professor. The faculty were under similar pressures, for a teacher who shirked answering a difficult question could be fined or lose his students to a rival. Tradition and orthodoxy still reigned supreme, but this emphasis on questioning, controversy, argument, and debate helped produce a sense of intellectual rigor and a greater openness to new alternatives than existed previously.

Although famine, disease, violence, and ignorance remained inescapable realities in medieval life, these centuries did not lack emotional and intellectual compensations. Life had coherence, purpose, and order. The medieval people had one true faith and one Church with one supreme head, the pope. There was one political system (feudalism) and a dominant economic system (manorial agriculture). There was an established social structure made up of commoners, clergy, and nobility, each fulfilling his or her proper functions. With the earth at the center of the universe and covered by the canopy of the heavens, people had a sense of belonging to a comfortable scheme of things. Although philosophers felt free to explore uncharted intellectual waters, they were not like sailors set adrift on a starless night with no sense of direction, for they had the beacon lights of revelation and tradition to guide their intellectual journeys. Every event in life was divinely ordained, and every person, no matter how humble in social status or intellect, could aspire to a heavenly reward. Thus, the Church offered a unified and comprehensive vision of the cosmos and each person's place within it.

The Rise of Scholasticism

THE NATURE OF SCHOLASTICISM

Scholasticism is the name given to the significant intellectual movement that arose in Europe at this time. Its proponents were called *Schoolmen* or *Scholastics*. Originally the term *Scholastic* applied to anyone who learned or taught in the schools Charlemagne first established back in the eighth century. Eventually *Scholasticism* came to refer to the intellectual project of integrating faith and reason. Although a few theologians were suspicious of philosophical reason, the Scholastics' optimistic rationalism dominated the thought of the Middle Ages.

The unifying purpose of all the Scholastics was to harmonize Church doctrines and the fruits of philosophical speculation. Their philosophies were guided by their faith and their faith was interpreted in terms of their philosophies. To the Scholastics, as Peter Damian (1007–1072) expressed it, theology was the "Queen of the Sciences" and philosophy was her handmaiden. In Scholastic thought, faith guided reason, set its agendas, and gave it the main outlines and landmark truths around which philosophers could build their systems. In turn, Greek philosophy equipped them with tools for elucidating, explaining, and providing rational support for the truths of Scripture. In the early centuries of Christianity, the Patristics had their hands full trying to formulate and systematize the articles of faith. By the time Scholasticism arose, however, there was a fixed body of established doctrine and an organized Church hierarchy to protect the established doctrines. Thus, the teachings of the Church provided the unquestioned framework within which all philosophy had to find its place. Nevertheless, within these bounds the scholar's mind was free to roam and to work out alternative explanations and implications of the revealed truth. The fact that competing philosophical positions arose within the Scholastic movement showed that theology did not dictate all the answers to philosophers.

The method of Scholasticism was the dialectic, a form of argument adapted from Aristotle's works. It was a form of disputation and discussion in which first a problem was framed in the form of a question, such as "Is the existence of God self-evident?" Next, the arguments for and against the different answers were set out. Finally, some resolution was arrived at that either found a balance between the competing positions or defended the truth of one position while refuting the others.

The Scholastics had complete confidence in the power of reason to reach truth, but always balanced this with a reliance on the accepted authorities. These authorities were the Sacred Scriptures, the Church Fathers (especially Augustine), and Boethius's logical commentaries. In later centuries the discovery of Aristotle's complete works and those of his Arab commentators provided additional resources for thought. The way in which the medieval thinkers' philosophizing revolved around authoritative texts is dramatically illustrated by Peter Abelard's treatment of the problem of universals. He discusses the issue in his *Glosses on Porphyry*, which is actually his commentary on Boethius's commentary on Porphyry's commentary on Aristotle's writings on logic!

Although the Scholastics were united in seeking to work out the philosophical implications of their faith, the details of working out this vision provoked controversies that raged throughout the monasteries and universities. Three issues particularly concerned them: (1) the problem of universals, (2) the relation between faith and reason, and (3) the relation of the will to the intellect.

THE CONTROVERSY OVER UNIVERSALS

A leading philosophical controversy during the Middle Ages was the problem of universals. This problem, of course, arose within Greek philosophy with the contrasting positions of Plato and Aristotle, among others. However, the medieval thinkers saw the issue as loaded with theological implications. A universal is something that can be common to many particular things. As such, universals are important elements within our speech and thought about the world. However, a problem arises when we try to get clear about the metaphysical status of universals, for the question may be asked, What relationship do universals have to reality? For the medievals, the problem was provoked by Boethius's translation of Porphyry's *Introduction to Aristotle's Categories*. Porphyry asks three questions about universals:

1. Whether universals
   a. exist in reality independently
      or
   b. exist in the understanding alone
2. If they exist in reality, whether they are
   a. immaterial
      or
   b. material
3. Whether they
   a. are separate from sensible objects
      or
   b. are not separate from sensible objects

Concerning his own position on these questions, Porphyry replied, "I shall refuse to say. . . . Questions of this sort are most exalted business and require very great diligence of inquiry."[1] However, his warning about the difficulty of the problem did not deter the medieval scholars at all, for they believed a number of important theological issues hung on the answer.

To understand the issue facing the medieval thinkers, consider the statement "Socrates is a human." It is clear enough to what I am referring when I use the name "Socrates," but to what am I referring when I use the universal term "human"? I could be referring to the Form or Essence of Humanity (as Plato thought), or I could be merely making a sound that refers to a collection of individuals. Then again, I could be referring to an idea or concept in my mind that is applicable to Socrates. In the first case the universal would have a reality apart from the minds that think it, in the second case it would have merely verbal existence as a sound in our language, and for the third theory it would exist as a mental construction in the mind.

Extreme realism was the position taken by many of the early medieval thinkers. The term "realism" follows from the fact that they believed universals are real things that exist in the world. Hence, from the alternatives listed by Porphyry, they affirmed that (1a) universals exist in reality, and (2a) they are immaterial. The most extensive version went on to affirm the Platonic thesis (3a) that universals are separate from the particular individuals that manifest them. John Scotus Erigena, for example, accepted the Neoplatonic story that the forms exist as intermediaries between God and the physical world. Likewise, St. Anselm in the eleventh century adhered fairly closely to the Platonic view, although he was much more theologically orthodox than Erigena. Most, like William of Champeaux (1070–1121), did not think it necessary to postulate that universals exist independently of individual things. Nevertheless, he believed that the same universal existed within each individual of a species. For example, Bob, Desmond, Sabrina, and Kathy all contain the full essence of humanity. The differences between individuals (hair color, height, and so on) are minor modifications of their essential humanity.

A number of factors led the realists to their position. First, there was an epistemological motivation. Since the eleventh-century thinkers based all their reasoning on Aristotle's logic, they assumed that reasoning proceeded by setting out the logical relationships between universals. Accordingly, if universals do not name real things, then we are reasoning about fictions and we have no knowledge. They were convinced that there must be a one-to-one correspondence between reason and reality. However, theological issues were also at stake. Realism helped make the doctrine of original sin intelligible.* According to the theologian Odo of Tournai (died 1113), who was an extreme realist, humanity consists of a singular nature or universal essence in which we all participate. When the first man and woman sinned, this essence became infected. Since we all participate in this same essence, the infection is passed on to all generations. A further consideration was that the doctrine of the Trinity seemed to require realism. How can the Father, Son, and Holy Spirit be three persons, but one God? The answer is that the divine essence is a single, universal substance, manifested in three particular persons.

Despite these theological considerations, there was a problem with realism. It claimed that indi-

vidual persons participate in the universal of Humanity, but this means that Humanity is included in the universal of Mammal, which is a part of the universal of Animal. Finally (to follow out the logic of this position), everything is subsumed within the reality of the most comprehensive universal, which would be Being itself, the one substance common to all things. But if Being is identical to God, then all things are a part of God and the distinction between God and the world collapses. This sort of pantheism was explicit in John Scotus Erigena. However, most thinkers at this time seemed unaware of this radical implication of their position. Unfortunately, these early thinkers did not have any of Plato's writings except for the *Timaeus*, and until the thirteenth century they had none of Aristotle's criticisms of Platonism. Hence, they were oblivious to many pitfalls of their position that had been identified some fourteen centuries before this current debate.

Nominalism was the other extreme position adopted on this controversy. According to nominalism (from *nomina*, the Latin for "names"), universals are merely names and only individuals are real. To the nominalist, no such thing as "redness" exists apart from particular things such as a red apple, a red sunset, or a red rose. The most extreme version of this view was probably articulated by Roscelin (about 1050–1120), a teacher of logic in France. He was condemned by the Church as a heretic, so we don't know much about him or his views. (The writings of heretics are rarely allowed to survive to tell their own story to history.) Apparently he taught that nothing exists outside of the mind except particulars and that universals do not refer to any independent realities, but are merely names or "vocal winds" (*flatus vocis*) we use to designate groups of particular things. Roscelin would, no doubt, note the absurdity of the statement "I love humanity, it's just people I can't stand." To the nominalist, there is no such thing as "humanity." It is just a shorthand verbal sign we use to stand for Malcolm, Karen, Andrea, George, . . . and the rest of the list of existing human beings. A philosophical problem with this theory was that it seemed to make universals arbitrary and subjective. On what grounds do we give the name "human" to a

---

*This doctrine states that when the first human beings (Adam and Eve) disobeyed God, sin and its consequences became an intrinsic part of the human condition.

collection of particulars if nothing makes these individuals members of the same category except for our assigning them the same label? In addition to this commonsense objection that things in the world seem divided into natural kinds, most medieval thinkers believed that their theology implied an objective order to reality, an order the nominalists seemed to deny. Furthermore, nominalism seemed to undermine the notion of original sin. If each person is unique and separate from Adam, how could his moral transgressions affect us? As for the Trinity, Roscelin consistently concluded that if there is no common essence of divinity, then the Father, Son, and Holy Spirit must be three Gods. The term "Trinity" is merely a sound referring to this collection of individuals. His tri-theism resulted in his being condemned by the Council of Soissons in 1092. Faced with possible excommunication, Roscelin abandoned his position.

Conceptualism was a position that sought a compromise between the first two extremes. This position was introduced by Peter Abelard (1079–1142). Abelard studied under Roscelin as well as William of Champeaux and found weaknesses in both of their extreme positions. Abelard argued that realism implies that universals can have mutually inconsistent qualities. For example, since the universal *animal* is present both in Socrates and a donkey, the substance *animal* is at the same time both rational and irrational. Furthermore, how can two individual men, such as Socrates standing in one place and Plato standing in another place, really be one and the same substance of humanity, as extreme realism seemed to require? Abelard also exposed the pantheism implicit within extreme realism. In response to these criticisms from his student, William modified his position, but not enough to satisfy Abelard. Abelard also attacked nominalism. Accepting Aristotle's definition that a universal is what can be predicated of many things, he argued that universals cannot be simply words, since words are physical sounds and one physical thing cannot be predicated of another thing.

To avoid these problems, Abelard explained that a universal word in itself is just a sound, but it gets its power from the fact that it points to a universal concept. The concept is the word's logical content, significance, or meaning. He says that by means of universal ideas the mind "conceives a common and confused image of many things. . . . When I hear *man* a certain figure arises in my mind which is so related to individual men that it is common to all and proper to none."[2] By suggesting that universals are indistinct and confused images, he makes them similar to the abstract visual image you get when you squint your eyes so that all you can tell is that there is a man before you, but you cannot identify him because of a lack of distinguishing features.

If we take Abelard to be saying that universals are nothing more than general concepts in the mind, then they are simply mental constructions and have no place in reality. Some commentators therefore assign the label of *moderate nominalism* to his position. However, he goes on to say that a universal conception is obtained by abstracting features that are common among several individuals. Hence, universals refer to objective features of things, but are not independent realities apart from things. For example, Socrates and Plato are the same insofar as they are both human, and this identity is found, not in some singular reality outside the mind (as the extreme realists thought), nor in the same sound we apply to each (as the nominalists thought), but in the fact that the same mental concept can be applied to each based on the similar properties they have.

Universals can be *considered separately* from individuals, but they are not genuinely *separate*. Thus Socrates' humanity is one thing and Plato's humanity is another thing, but their objective likeness is the basis of the universal concept of "human." Abelard's position undermined the appeal of extreme realism by showing that someone could deny there is one, identical essence in all members of a species, without denying objectivity to universals. The aspect of his thought that emphasizes the abstraction of objective similarities points in the direction of a moderate realism, a position more fully developed by later thinkers.

Moderate realism became the most favored resolution of the problem of universals for the late medievals.* Abelard was groping his way toward it, but the position became more clearly articulated by thinkers such as Aquinas once Aristotle's complete works were reintroduced to Western thought. Basically, this position claimed that universal ideas are formed by the mind, but are based on the objective features of extramental reality. It was the paradigm of the Scholastic project of finding a synthesis of opposing positions. With the extreme realists, the moderate realists taught that universals are before things (*ante rem*) as patterns in God's mind. With Aristotle, they said that universals exist in things (*in rem*) as properties that make individual things alike. With Aristotle and the conceptualists, they taught that universals are after things (*post rem*) as concepts within the mind formed by abstracting from individual similarities. Finally, with the nominalists they shared the disposition of seeing the individual as the ultimate unit of reality.

THE CONTROVERSY OVER FAITH AND REASON

The second problem dividing the medieval thinkers was one that had haunted the Church Fathers: How do we understand the relationship between the two sources of knowledge—faith and reason? At least five approaches to the question emerged during the Middle Ages. First, some people had complete confidence in reason and let their intellect lead their faith. Among the early thinkers who took this approach were John Scotus Erigena, Roscelin, and Abelard. The last two got into trouble because of their position, and all had their theological works condemned. Second, others tried to swing the pendulum away from reason by giving priority to faith. With the reforms of monastic life introduced around the year 1000, a resurgence of piety led some to see reason as a threat. Peter Damian (1007–1072) was one of the strongest

*The discussion of universals is complicated by the fact that not all scholars draw the boundaries between positions in the same way, nor do they use the terminology in the same way. Further confusion is caused by the fact that it is sometimes not clear what a particular philosopher's position is. This explains why different commentators call Abelard a *moderate nominalist*, a *conceptualist*, or a *moderate realist*.

voices in this movement. He warned of the "blind foolhardiness of these pseudointellectuals who investigate nonproblems" and who presume to diminish the power of God with their trust in puny logic and "arguments based on the meaning of words."[3] Similarly, for St. Bernard of Clairvaux (1091–1153), a mystic and moral reformer, philosophy was useless and a danger to the unwary. Consequently, he was the prosecutor at Abelard's heresy trial. Contrary to attempts to make the faith conform to reason, Bernard said, "I believe though I do not comprehend, and I hold by faith what I cannot grasp with the mind."[4] Third, some, such as St. Anselm, were more moderate and sought for a compromise. Anselm believed that reason could not be autonomous, for faith must lead and reason must follow. At the same time, his confidence in reason went further than that of any other Christian philosopher, for he actually thought he could deductively prove all the major Christian doctrines that he first believed on faith. Although he had a great deal of confidence in reason, he made clear that it must always operate within the bounds of orthodoxy:

> No Christian ought in any way to dispute the truth of what the Catholic Church believes in its heart and confesses with its mouth. But always holding the same faith unquestioningly, loving it and living by it, he ought . . . so far as he is able to seek the reasons for it.[5]

Fourth, St. Thomas Aquinas in the thirteenth century sought a synthesis of faith and reason. He very firmly distinguished between the spheres of theology and philosophy. Thomas believed that our limited minds could not perceive the rationality of some theological doctrines. Thus, many of the doctrines Anselm tried to prove Thomas considered mysteries that can only be known through revelation and accepted on faith. However, Thomas claimed reason is fully competent within its own boundaries and considerations of faith do not need to enter into philosophical arguments. Finally, Thomas believed that the two spheres overlapped somewhat and that some doctrines the humble believer holds on faith (for example, the existence of God) could be proven by the natural light of reason.

Fifth, after Thomas, there was less confidence in the ability of reason to supplement faith. A succession of philosophers progressively narrowed the scope of reason, more and more distancing its relationship to theology. Siger of Brabant, a contemporary of Aquinas, held the doctrine of double truth, which claimed that philosophy could give one answer to a question and theology a different answer. However, Siger made very few attempts to resolve the differences between philosophy and theology. In contrast, Duns Scotus (around 1266–1308) retained the harmony of faith and reason, but allowed for very little overlap between the two. William of Ockham in the fourteenth century was much more extreme. He separated theology and philosophy to protect the truths of faith from the scrutiny of human reason. Claiming that our knowledge of the world yields only probability, he did not think the existence of the biblical God could be proven with any certainty. Furthermore, Ockham separated logic from reality by claiming that it could not tell us about reality but only about the forms of propositions we assert about reality. Finally, the separation of faith and reason was fueled by a vigorous resurgence of mysticism in the fourteenth century that allocated knowledge of God to religious experience and placed it beyond the pale of rational, propositional knowledge.

THE RELATION OF
WILL AND INTELLECT

Another Scholastic controversy concerned the relation of the will and intellect. Everyone agreed that certain categories of human actions are good and others are not. The question was, What is the basis of the goodness of these things? One position claimed that God's intellect precedes his will in making decisions. These philosophers believed that the Platonic universals reside in God's mind. By knowing his own mind, God's intellect is aware of those qualities that are objectively good and his will follows this ideal in creating the world. Similarly, those actions that God's intellect discerns are good are what his will commands us to perform. This position followed the assumptions of either extreme or moderate realism, since it said the good is an objective entity. For obvious reasons,

the position is sometimes called **intellectualism**. One practical implication of this view was that since God's intellect recognizes the good, our minds (miniature versions of his intellect) can likewise recognize what is good, and an ethics based on reason is possible. This led to the medieval revival of the Stoic **natural law theory**, which claims that people can discover moral principles by examining human nature.

The second position was known as **voluntarism**. Its advocates claimed that the divine will had priority over the intellect. In this account, it is God's sovereign will that freely chooses what is to be considered good or evil. The voluntarists objected that the intellectualists' position impinges on God's freedom and power, since it implies his will is bound by the prescribed patterns. The extreme voluntarists consistently followed out the logic of this position and claimed that lying or adultery could have been morally good actions had God willed them to be such. It is no more necessary that promise keeping is morally required than it was necessary that God create crocodiles. However, in the world he chose to create, God did make crocodiles and he did will that promises should be kept. Obviously, in this theory the unaided human reason cannot discern what is morally good, since this is a result of God's free and sovereign decision. Ethics necessarily must be based on some sort of revelation of God's moral choices. This is sometimes called the "divine command" ethical theory. The voluntarists tended to be nominalists because they believed that moral goodness is not an eternal universal, but is a "name" that God freely bestows on certain actions. Since our reason cannot discern what is morally good, our wills must simply obey the created moral order revealed in God's commands.

These conflicting positions on the will and intellect also applied to how the Scholastics understood the creation of the world. The intellectualists claimed that creation was preceded by the eternal forms in God's intellect. Although not all subscribed to a strict, logical determinism, they did believe that the outlines of the world were determined by its fittingness to reason. Hence our reason is the best instrument for discovering the world's order. But for voluntarists such as Duns Scotus and Ockham, the world is radically contingent. If God had wanted to, he could have made an entirely different world from the present one, for his will is primary over his intellect. In proposing this view, their motives were primarily religious ones. They wanted to protect the sovereignty and freedom of God and to make necessary a greater reliance on revelation, while giving less authority to reason. But by stressing the contingency of the world, they made observation more important than speculative reasoning in our attempts to understand the world. Eventually, this shift of emphasis was important in nurturing the rise of modern science.

With these key issues as a background, the remainder of the chapter surveys the thought of St. Anselm and Abelard as well as key figures among the medieval Islamic and Jewish philosophers. Anselm illustrates the application of Platonic rationalism and realism to proofs for God's existence. Abelard illustrates the struggle to balance faith and reason and introduces an early version of moral voluntarism. Next, using representative Islamic and Jewish philosophers, the issue of faith and reason is examined again as it applies to the impact of Aristotle's philosophy on their traditional faiths. The European rediscovery of Aristotle is the final topic of this chapter.

St. Anselm

Anselm (1033–1109) was born into Italian nobility. Against his father's wishes, he decided to become a monk at the Benedictine monastery in the Norman town of Bec. Eventually he became the abbot of the monastery. Although he did not think of himself as gifted at administration, others did not share his opinion, and he was summoned to be the Archbishop of Canterbury. He longed to return to the tranquillity of the cloister, but he reluctantly but faithfully served in this position until his death. His sixteen years in this position were filled with controversy because of political tensions between England and Rome. Against two successive kings, he argued the authority of the pope over that of the crown. Anselm died in 1109 at the age of seventy-six and was canonized in 1494.

His philosophical goal was to provide conclusive arguments to rationally demonstrate the Christian teachings he had accepted on faith. With Augustine, he believed that faith necessarily preceded understanding. "I do not seek to understand that I may believe, but I believe in order to understand," Anselm said in the first chapter of his *Proslogium*.[6] Although he was deeply pious, he was also a confident rationalist. Accordingly, he was convinced that all reasoning should follow the deductive method and that this method would lead to all fundamental truths. During Anselm's time, the boundaries between what could be known by reason versus what required revelation had not yet been made clear. Other philosophers had tried to prove such doctrines as the existence of God. However, Anselm's enthusiasm for rationalism led him to believe he could also provide "necessary reasons" for the truth of such doctrines as the Trinity and Incarnation. Later theologians came to recognize that such matters were beyond the competence of reason and had to be established by faith and revelation.

His most famous argument—and the one that ensured him a place in the history of philosophy forever—is the ontological argument for God's existence found in his *Proslogium*.* After many attempts to reason to God's existence, Anselm said the argument "offered itself" to him in a burst of insight that he considered an answer to prayer. The proof depends on the notion that God is a being greater than any that can be conceived. He directs the argument to the "fool" of Psalm 14 who "hath said in his heart, there is no God." Anselm points out that the fool can understand the definition of God, for to deny God requires that you understand what you are denying. Therefore, God exists at least as an idea in the mind or the understanding. The question is, does God exist outside the mind as well? Anselm's argument attempts to show that

---

*The word *ontological* is derived from the Greek and literally means "having to do with the science of being." Thus, this argument attempts to prove God's existence from the concept of his being. The argument was first given this label by the eighteenth-century German philosopher Immanuel Kant.

it is unintelligible to deny this. His argument may be formulated as follows:

(1) I have, within my understanding, an idea of God.

(2) This idea of God is the idea of a being that is the greatest that can be conceived.

(3) A being is greater if it exists in reality than if it exists only in the understanding.

(4) If God (the greatest conceivable being) exists in the understanding alone, then a greater being can be conceived, namely one that also exists in reality.

(5) But premise (4) is a contradiction, for it says I can conceive of a greater being than the greatest conceivable being.

(6) So if I have an idea of the greatest conceivable being, such a being must exist both in my understanding and in reality.

(7) Therefore, God exists in reality.

This argument is based on Plato's conception of reality as described in his account of the Divided Line. In other words, the proof assumes that the greater the perfection of something, the more reality it has. If we can think of the most perfect sort of being, we will, necessarily, be thinking of the being with the greatest degree of reality. Critics of Anselm, both among his contemporaries and in the modern age, have insisted that existence is not a property on the same order as properties such as knowledge, power, or goodness. We can think of a being perfect in every way, but whether that being exists or not is not part of our conception of its perfection.

Anselm provides another version of the argument in *Proslogium*, chapter III. It was not clear to him that this was a completely different argument, for he saw it as merely an elaboration of the first version. However, most philosophers today think that he stumbled on a completely different, and perhaps stronger, line of reasoning. This argument starts out with the same first two premises as the preceding argument, but then takes a different tack. Instead of talking about existence as such, it focuses on the property of necessary existence. A

being whose nonexistence is impossible is one whose existence is necessary. However, a being whose nonexistence is a rationally conceivable possibility is not a necessary being. This version of the proof argues that necessary existence must be attributed to any being that is perfect to the maximum degree. Here is a formulation of Anselm's second argument:

(1) I have an idea of God.

(2) This idea of God is the idea of a being, which is the greatest that can be conceived.

(3) A being whose nonexistence is impossible is greater than a being whose nonexistence is possible.

(4) Thus, if the greatest possible being's nonexistence is rationally conceivable, then he is not the greatest possible being.

(5) But premise (4) is a contradiction.

(6) So the nonexistence of the greatest possible being cannot be rationally conceivable.

(7) Therefore, God necessarily exists.

Premise (3) is based on the principle that the greatest possible being cannot begin to exist and cannot cease to exist, for in either case something else greater than it must cause it to pass into or out of existence. For example, the Empire State Building *happens* to exist, but it could just as easily not have existed. Possibly there is life in outer space, but then again, perhaps not—it all depends on whether or not there are conditions that produced it. So the greatest possible being is one whose existence does not depend on anything else, and this means it must be a being who does not just happen to exist but who exists necessarily. It follows that *if* God exists, he exists necessarily. But Anselm's point is that the word "if" cannot apply to God's existence, for as soon as we say, "*If* God exists . . ." we are implying that he (like the Empire State Building) conceivably might have not existed. We are stating a contradiction: God is a being whose nonexistence is *possible*, but (by definition) God is a being whose nonexistence is *impossible*. The argument attempts to force us to choose between two alternatives: (1) God exists (and his nonexistence is impossible), or (2) the concept of God is completely meaningless. Thus we must either accept the conclusion or reject the first premise. Certain philosophers in the twentieth century (called *logical positivists*) do maintain that the concept of God is as unintelligible as the concept of a "round square."* However, it seemed clear to Anselm that both theists and atheists are perfectly capable of conceiving of a perfect being such as God. Since we can think of such a being, we cannot suppose his existence is an open question similar to the possibility of life in outer space.

A certain monk named Gaunilo, a contemporary of Anselm, raised a number of objections to the ontological argument in a piece with the witty title "On Behalf of the Fool." He questioned the move from the existence of the greatest conceivable being in the imagination to the existence of such a being in reality. "Isn't it just as easy to imagine the greatest possible island?," Gaunilo asked. If so, must we then conclude, using Anselm's logic, that such an island really exists? The point of this criticism is that Anselm's reasoning would let us rationally prove the actual existence of a wide variety of things (the perfect painting, the perfect steak, the perfect knight), as long as we can imagine that they are the greatest possible member of their species. To summarize Anselm's reply, an island greater than any possible island still would not be a "being than which a greater cannot be conceived." For even the most excellent island is something that, by its nature, is a limited being that has a physical location. Hence, if it exists at location A, it doesn't exist at B. Since we can conceive of it as not existing at B, we can also conceive of it as not existing at all. Thus, he suggests that perfection and necessary existence are qualities that could only be attributed to God.

Gaunilo also attacked premises (1) and (2) of both arguments. Are we really able to fully conceive of a being greater than which none can be conceived? Things we understand, we can understand because we have experiences of them or of things similar to them. However, if the greatest

possible being is singularly unique, then the understanding can only vaguely grope for the significance of these words. Anselm replies that we can compare two things in terms of their different degrees of excellence. From this we can project our notion of a relatively good being to the nth degree and conceive of an absolutely good being. To use a contemporary example, we can see that the social reformer Gandhi is morally superior to the Roman tyrant Nero. However, we can imagine someone who has all Gandhi's virtues but none of his human defects. By this same process, the mind can continue on until we conceive of a being who has all possible virtues to the maximum degree with no defects at all. Thus, our human intellects can form the conception of the greatest possible being.

After Anselm, the ontological argument continued to have admirers and critics throughout the history of philosophy. In the modern period, the rationalists Descartes, Spinoza, and Leibniz defended their own versions of the argument. Philosophers who were more oriented toward experience, such as Aquinas and Ockham, among the medieval thinkers, and Kant in the eighteenth century, harshly criticized the argument even though they took the side of theism. Although many do not think it is cogent, philosophers have not been able to lay the argument to rest. As a testimony to the great genius of this eleventh-century monk, his argument is still alive today and is debated using the sophisticated techniques of twentieth-century logic.

Peter Abelard

Peter Abelard (1079–1142) was born near Nantes, France, into a noble Parisian family. He studied at the new schools of philosophy and theology that had grown up at Chartres and Paris. Although admired as an exceptionally brilliant student, he had a reputation for being a disagreeable and arrogant scholar. After completing a course, he often went on to teach the subject himself in competition with his former teacher. This practice tells a lot about his personality, which was not one most people found endearing. He must not have been without some personal charm, however, for when he was thirty-five he fell into a passionate love affair with Héloïse,

*See Chapter 32 on the logical positivists.

the young niece of an official of Notre Dame Cathedral. She became pregnant, and they arranged a secret marriage. For these reasons her uncle was furious at her lover, and in Abelard's own words, her family punished him by "cutting off those parts of my body with which I had done that which was the cause of their sorrow." He retired to the abbey of St. Denis outside of Paris, where he made his profession as a monk, and Héloïse went to a convent to become a nun. His life continued to be haunted by controversy, as his book *On the Divine Unity and the Trinity* was condemned and burned at an ecclesiastical council at Soissons in 1121. Twenty years later, around 1141, he was summoned to a council at Sens and was prosecuted for heresy because of his *Introduction to Theology*. Abelard died in 1142, and when Héloïse died twenty-two years later she was buried at his side.

Abelard is considered a pioneer in using the Aristotelian dialectic to clarify theological propositions. This form of debate came to be the characteristic style of Scholastic discussions. This technique was exhibited in his most famous book, written in 1121–1122, which was titled *Sic et Non* ("*Yes and No*"). In this work he sets out over 150 theological questions on which the Church Fathers gave conflicting opinions. Contrary to his critics, its purpose was not to produce doubts, but to challenge the minds of students to exercise their intellects by trying to resolve these contradictions. In the Prologue he states, "By doubting we come to questioning, and by questioning we perceive the truth." Abelard's dialectical form of argument was later used by Aquinas with the modification that Aquinas always concluded with his own resolution of the opposing positions. Abelard offended traditionalists because he viewed theology as an opportunity for vigorous debate and questioning rather than for pious meditation and acceptance. Although his theological daring often makes him seem rebellious, he wrote to Héloïse after the condemnation of 1141: "I do not want to be a philosopher if it is necessary to deny Paul. I do not want to be Aristotle if it is necessary to be separated from Christ."[7]

In his discussion of moral problems, Abelard had an important influence on the direction of Scholastic moral theology. He reacted against the legalistic tendencies of his age in which moral goodness was seen simply as an external conformity of an act to the law of God and sin was defined as a factual transgression of law, independent of whether or not the agent knew his action was wrong. Instead, Abelard emphasizes the importance of the intentions and the will of the agent. "God considers not what is done, but in what spirit it is done; and the merit or praise of the agent lies not in the deed, but in the intention." Hence, sin is a contempt for God manifested in our willing what we know to be wrong. But if we act with a sincere conscience and do what we believe is right, we may err, but we do not sin. As theological support for his position, he cites the words of Jesus about his persecutors, "Father, forgive them, for they know not what they do." Abelard's purpose was not to condone simple-minded and ignorant sincerity concerning morality, but to emphasize that the morally good person is one of goodwill who makes a determined effort to know what is good and to act by the best light he or she can find. The fully virtuous act, of course, not only proceeds from the intention to do what is right but also is an act that *is* objectively right, either because it conforms to the natural moral law or to God's specific commands.

Anticipating the position of the fourteenth-century voluntarists, Abelard suggests that there is no necessity to God's moral commands. For this reason, God prescribes different moralities at different times in biblical history. Free choice is basic to God as a lawgiver just as free choice is essential for people to be law followers. But no matter what the material content of the divine law may be, people always have the same formal obligation to obey it.

Abelard was not followed by any distinguishable school of philosophy, but he had a great impact on his time. As we have mentioned previously, his most significant contribution was in his resolution of the controversy over universals. In this, he contributed to the study of how mental concepts are formed and how language functions. Even though most of Aristotle's major works did not become available until later, Abelard anticipated later refinements in philosophy based on these texts. Consequently, he is considered an important contributor to the development of Scholasticism.

Islamic Philosophers

PRESERVING ARISTOTLE'S LEGACY

At a time when the Christian West had but fragments of the works of Plato and Aristotle, Islamic and Jewish philosophers were enjoying the treasures of Greek thought and using them to enrich their speculations. Because of this, Arabian philosophy became one of the main vehicles that carried Aristotle's complete works and later those of Plato to the West. The later Christian medieval scholars were influenced by these Muslim philosophers either by adopting their interpretation of Aristotle or by reacting against their alleged heresies. Similarly, Jewish thinkers of the twelfth century passed on to the West the fruits of their study of Aristotle. Thus, the story of medieval philosophy cannot be told without mentioning the Islamic and Jewish philosophers of this time.

THE RISE OF THE ISLAMIC RELIGION

Islam, which means "submission" (to God's will), is one of the most widespread and powerful monotheistic religions in the world. It is based on the revelations that the prophet Mohammed received over the course of several years. Although he thought his revelations were consistent with those of the Old and New Testaments, he also thought his teachings superseded theirs. His revelations were recorded in the Koran, the holy book of the Islamic religion, and his followers were called Muslims, which means "true believers." The influence of his teachings was so commanding that within a century of Mohammed's death in A.D. 632, his followers had spread Islam to virtually all the inhabited lands from India through North Africa to Spain.

Centuries before the rise of Islam, Christian schools as well as heretical sects in Mesopotamia, Persia, and Syria had kept alive the study of Greek

philosophy and science and preserved and translated the ancient texts of Greece. The Islamic religion gave birth to the Islamic philosophical tradition around 800, when Muslim scholars began to translate these Greek works into Arabic and write commentaries on them. The Arab philosophers had an agenda similar to that of the Christian Scholastics, but in this part of the world the task was to reconcile the teachings of Aristotle with the Koran. The history of Islamic philosophy followed the same pattern as the development of Christian philosophy. In both cases a well-established orthodox tradition developed that was based on revealed scriptures (the Koran or the Bible). In both traditions, some philosophers enthusiastically embraced the Greek philosophies and liberally interpreted their scriptures in order to make their faith conform to reason. However, in both cases defenders of a rigid orthodoxy were suspicious of the impact of philosophy on traditional understandings of the faith. Just as the Christian medieval scholars were influenced by Neoplatonism, partly due to the mistaken identity of the Pseudo-Dionysian text, the same sort of confusion occurred in the Arab world. For example, some of the *Enneads* of Plotinus were translated under the title "Aristotle's Theology." Similarly, the *Book of Causes*, taken from the works of the Athenian Neoplatonist Proclus, were attributed to Aristotle. These textual mistakes helped to promote a Neoplatonic interpretation of Aristotle among Islamic philosophers. The Islamic philosophers fell into two groups, an earlier, eastern group in Baghdad, and a later, western group centered in Spain.

AVICENNA

Avicenna (the Latinized name for Ibn Sīnā; 980–1037) was one of the more important Islamic philosophers. Born in Persia, he was a child prodigy, and learned all the disciplines and great works of literature as a young boy. At age sixteen he knew enough to become a physician. Avicenna spent a busy life practicing medicine and serving as a high government official, while still finding time to pursue his scholarship. Even while traveling a great deal, he wrote 160 books, covering a wide range of topics.

Avicenna tells us he memorized Aristotle's *Metaphysics* by reading it forty times but did not understand it until he read Al-Farabi (died 950), a founder of the Aristotelian tradition among the Muslims. His system was based on Al-Farabi's ideas and a Neoplatonic reading of Aristotle. In developing his metaphysics, Avicenna (like Anselm) argues that God's essence necessarily implies his existence. For every other creature in the world, however, their essence and their existence are two different things. For example, the essence of a unicorn is to be a one-horned, horselike mammal. However, from a description of its properties, we cannot determine whether or not a unicorn exists. Yet if all creatures in themselves are merely possible beings, how do some become actual? Obviously, their existence had to be caused by some other existing being. But this series of causes, which are themselves dependent beings, cannot go on indefinitely. Some necessary being must have originally caused mere possibilities to become actualities. This necessary being, of course, is God. This way of reasoning about necessity and possibility influenced both Jewish and Christian thinkers alike, particularly Maimonides and St. Thomas.

From this rather orthodox starting point, however, Avicenna reasons to a very controversial conclusion. Since God is necessary and without a beginning, Avicenna supposed that this implies that all God's attributes are necessary and without a beginning as well, including God's status as the creator of the world. Revealing his Neoplatonic influences, Avicenna develops the theory that the world and everything in it emanates from God out of rational necessity. Thus God was not free in creating the world, for the divine creativity is a necessary feature of his being. Furthermore, if God and all his attributes are eternal, then his creation of the world must have occurred from all eternity. Hence, the world is eternal, although from all eternity it has depended on and emanated from God. Even though no creature exists necessarily in itself, every creature is a necessary feature of a world system that could not be otherwise than it is. Thus, everything is a part of a logically determined chain of causes. Parts of Avicenna's writings were translated into Latin in the twelfth century, and many Christian thinkers were impressed by the logically rigorous system they provided.

AL-GHAZALI

Al-Ghazali (1058–1111) was a Persian philosopher who could be considered the Islamic counterpart of those voices in Christendom that feared Greek philosophy would corrupt the purity of their faith. In his autobiography, called *Deliverance from Error,* he complained that the problem of philosophical movements is that "the defect of unbelief affects them all." His most influential book was *The Destruction of the Philosophers.** In it, he presents his case against Avicenna and others like him with the passion of a religious fundamentalist along with the intellectual rigor of an accomplished logician. He claimed that the philosophers contradict the Koran, each other, as well as themselves. He considered logic a useful tool as long as it does not make us arrogant. However, logic cannot prove anything in metaphysics and attempting to do so causes unbelief to flourish. He believed philosophical writings should be kept out of the hands of the public, for "just as the poor swimmer must be kept from the slippery banks, so must mankind be kept from reading these books."[8]

The most interesting part of Al-Ghazali's philosophy concerns his analysis of causality. He was disturbed by Avicenna's thesis that the chain of causes and effects flow from God's nature by rational necessity. One consequence of Avicenna's view is that miracles are impossible. A miracle occurs when God causes something to happen that deviates from the normal course of events. But if the system of causes and effects is a rationally necessary whole, then, according to Avicenna's logic, even God could not cause this inevitable pattern

---

*This is sometimes translated as *The Incoherence of the Philosophers.*

to change. Since orthodox Muslim theology teaches the existence of miracles, Al-Ghazali had to undermine the notion of causality that led to this denial of miracles.

Briefly, he argues that neither logic nor experience can establish any necessary connection between so-called causes and their effects. He uses the example of (X) touching a flame to a piece of cotton and (Y) the combustion of the cotton. True, it would violate our expectations to say the flame touched the cotton but the cotton did not burn. However, although conflicting with our past experience, the occurrence of X but not Y would not contradict the laws of logic. Furthermore, a thousand observations of the flame touching the cotton being followed by the combustion of the cotton could only tell us these two events happened simultaneously in the past. These observations could not show us it is logically necessary that the two events will occur together next time. According to Al-Ghazali, there is no other cause but God. Therefore, the "laws of nature" are not causes but simply describe the way God usually makes things happen. However, God can cause any event to be followed by any other event he wills. It follows that a miraculous deviation from the normal sequence of events is logically possible for God.

Al-Ghazali's arguments concerning causality are similar to those of Nicolas Malebranche (1638–1715) and David Hume (1711–1776). Malebranche, like Al-Ghazali, used this sort of argument to support his theism. Hume, however, was not interested in divine causality. Instead, he used a similar analysis of causality to support the skeptical conclusion that causal judgments do not have a logical foundation.

AVERROES

Averroës (Ibn Rushd; 1126–1198) of Cordova was the most outstanding Muslim philosopher in Spain. He came from a family of prominent judges and served for many years as a judge himself. He also achieved prominence as a physician, astronomer, and philosopher. He is best known for his three sets of commentaries on Aristotle. The influ-

ence of these works were so great that the medieval Christian scholars referred to him simply as "the Commentator."

He responded to Al-Ghazali's *Destruction of the Philosophers* by writing a point-by-point refutation of it in a work titled *The Destruction of the Destruction*. In other works he defended the thesis that Aristotle represents the culmination of the human intellect and argued that his philosophy did not conflict with the Koran. He points out that the Koran presents the world as God's handiwork and concludes that this lets us demonstrate God's existence and nature by studying the world. Aristotle's logic, physics, and metaphysics provide us with the tools for such a demonstration, and Averroës cites Aristotle's argument for an Unmoved Mover as an example.

His most famous device for reconciling theology and philosophy is his so-called double-truth theory. He theorizes that the Koran was written for the masses, who do not have great powers of the intellect. For this reason, it was written in an allegorical style to appeal to the emotions and the imagination of the uneducated. Consequently, the philosopher must strip away the surface meaning to uncover the true or "inner meaning." Although the conclusions of philosophical reasoning may seem to conflict with religious tradition, this is only a conflict with the apparent meaning of the scriptures. In the final analysis, truth cannot conflict with truth, so the best of philosophy is consistent with the hidden meaning of the Koran.

Averroës' position was badly misinterpreted by thirteenth-century Christians who opposed him as well as by those who admired him. They mistakenly thought Averroës was saying that some proposition X could be literally true in philosophy while its contradictory, *Not-X*, could be literally true in religion. The faculty at the newly founded University of Paris seemed to enthusiastically endorse this mistaken interpretation in their attempts to adopt Averroës' explication of Aristotle. This group, known as the "Latin Averroists" was headed by Siger of Brabant (about 1240–1284). To embrace many Aristotelian doctrines that were contrary to Church teachings, they tended to shuffle philosophy and theology into separate compartments without any attempt to relate the two. As opposed to this extreme double-truth theory, Averroës was actually saying the truth could be expressed at different levels and in different ways, figuratively in religion and literally in philosophy. Apart from the misinterpretations imposed on him, what is revolutionary about Averroës is that this method of interpretation implies that theology yields its authority to philosophy: the philosopher decides how revelation should be interpreted to make it consistent with philosophical reason.

Averroës' quarrel with the traditionalists led to his disfavor, and his books were burned in Islamic Spain. To prevent any further outbreaks of heresy, a general suppression of Greek philosophy was instituted. Fourteen years after the death of Averroës, the Muslim culture in Spain suffered its own downfall. In 1212, Christian forces defeated a Muslim army at Las Navas de Tolsa, breaking the Muslim hold over Spain. By the close of this century, the Christian reconquest of Spain was complete, except for the region of Grenada, which remained Muslim until 1492. As Western Christendom expanded into Muslim Spain, the works of Averroës found their way into the European universities. By 1250 Latin translations of his Aristotelian commentaries began to make a sensation in Christendom. The effect of Averroës on Christian thought was twofold. On the one hand, his interpretation of Aristotle purged some of the Neoplatonic distortions added by earlier commentaries. His insights on Aristotle's texts were so respected by Christian scholars that, as noted, he was called "the Commentator" by late medieval philosophers. On the other hand, the heretical elements in his philosophy—such as his determinism, the claim that the world is eternal, and his apparent rejection of personal immortality—cast suspicions on any attempts to merge Aristotle with Christian thought. Although Thomas Aquinas seemed to have learned much from his Islamic predecessor, he also labored long and hard to show that Aristotle's thought did not lead to Averroës' heresies. Nevertheless, because of their common link to Aristotle, Aquinas became tainted with Averroism in the minds of many of his critics.

Jewish Philosophers

Like the Islamic thinkers, the Jewish philosophers were concerned to reconcile their conclusions with an orthodox interpretation of their faith. For the Jewish thinkers, this meant developing a philosophical system based on the Old Testament and the Talmud, an enormous commentary on the first five books of the Bible. The greatest medieval Jewish philosopher was Moses Maimonides (1135–1204), who was born at Cordova, in Spain. He was confident of the harmony between faith and reason. He said his *Guide for the Perplexed* was written for those who have studied philosophy and are confused as to how to harmonize it with the faith. If there is an apparent conflict between an airtight philosophical demonstration and the statements in the Old Testament, Maimonides taught that we should interpret the Scriptures allegorically. Although he believed Aristotle had attained the highest in human knowledge, he recognized a genuine conflict between Aristotle's belief in the eternity of the world on the one hand, and revelation on the other, for Scripture makes it clear that the world had a beginning. Maimonides' solution was to show that Aristotle's arguments are not conclusive and need not be accepted. However, despite his attempts to remain faithful to the Talmud in appropriating Aristotle's insights, conservative Jewish scholars branded him a heretic. His purely theological writings were accepted as authoritative, but his philosophical works were condemned and neglected by Jewish scholars until the nineteenth century.

Because of persecution, the European Jewish community became more isolated from the mainstream of society. This benefited their conservative religious leaders, who wished to purge the community of scientific and secular influences. For many centuries, both Judaism and Islam allowed only mysticism to remain as a supplementary source of knowledge to revelation. Thus, after 1200, only the Christian West could take advantage of Aristotle's insights in developing a comprehensive intellectual system. Because of his groundbreaking work in constructing a biblical Aristotelian philosophy, however, Maimonides greatly influenced Christian scholars, especially Aquinas.

The Rediscovery of Aristotle in Europe

In the latter part of the twelfth century, a new world opened up for European thinkers. Greek works on mathematics, astronomy, medicine, and, most importantly, the complete works of Aristotle became available for the first time. Furthermore, some of the latter's Greek commentators as well as the Arabic and Jewish philosophers were being translated into Latin and becoming known. Between 1210 and 1225 nearly all the works of Aristotle had been translated from the Arabic and were beginning to make waves in Western Christendom. The Church met Aristotle's philosophy with a great deal of suspicion, mainly because of the pantheistic accretions that the Arabs had added to it. The necessity and eternity of the world as well as the blurring of the distinction between the creator and creation were doctrines unacceptable to the Christian West. In 1215, the statutes of the University of Paris announced that the study of Aristotle's *Physics* and *Metaphysics* was forbidden. However, this proved ineffective, for scholars continued to study these works and write commentaries on them. Later in the century, scholars in the West began to translate the major works from the original Greek. In consequence, a picture of the authentic Aristotle began to emerge, freed of any pantheistic distortions. By 1254 the *Physics* and the *Metaphysics* were considered so important that they entered the curriculum of the University of Paris. Scholars began to frame their questions in philosophical terms such as the distinction between essence and existence, the difference between necessary and contingent being, and Aristotle's theory of abstraction. With the influx of new philosophical models, the question now had to be asked, can these non-Christian philosophical systems, which came from pagan Greece, Islam, and Judaism, be converted to Christian thought, or should the Christian world avoid them? This question set the agenda for the thirteenth century, when Thomas Aquinas would provide a history-making answer.

Questions for Understanding

1. What factors were responsible for the return to philosophy in the eleventh and twelfth centuries?

2. What was the goal of Scholasticism?

3. What is the problem of universals in the medieval period? In what ways did theological considerations enter into this controversy?

4. What were the various positions taken on the problem of universals, and who were some proponents of each position?

5. What were the various positions taken on the problem of faith and reason during this period, and what were the names of some figures associated with each position?

6. What was the problem of the relationship between the will and the intellect during this period? What were the two major positions in this debate?

7. What was Anselm's ontological argument? In what ways do the two versions of it differ?

8. How did Gaunilo attempt to refute Anselm's argument?

9. What were the key features of Abelard's philosophy?

10. In what ways were the debates within medieval Islamic philosophy similar to those of their Christian counterparts?

11. How did Avicenna attempt to argue for the existence of God?

12. Why does Avicenna believe that the way that the world was created was rationally necessary?

13. What was Al-Ghazali's view of philosophy?

14. How does Al-Ghazali's analysis of causality provide an argument for the possibility of miracles?

15. According to Averroës, what is the relation-ship between Aristotle's philosophy and the Islamic faith?

16. How does Averroës use his double-truth the-ory to reconcile faith and reason?

17. Who was the greatest medieval Jewish phi-losopher? How does he attempt to reconcile faith and reason?

18. In the latter part of the twelfth century, Aris-totle's philosophy was rediscovered in Chris-tian Europe. What were some of the effects of this development?

Questions for Reflection

1. Concerning the relationship between faith and reason, Peter Damian and St. Bernard of Clair-vaux thought that faith and reason were op-posed, whereas Thomas Aquinas thought that reason could supplement faith. Pretend that you are a medieval Christian thinker and con-struct a defense of one or the other position.

2. In the Middle Ages, the two positions on the will and the intellect were intellectualism and voluntarism. Given the theological assump-tions of these thinkers, what arguments did defenders of each view give for their position? What difficulties could opponents point to in each position?

3. Do you think that Anselm's ontological argu-ment is sound? Which premise do you think is the most controversial? Write a short essay either defending or criticizing this premise.

4. What do you think of Al-Ghazali's analysis of causality? Write a brief defense or critique of his view.

Notes

1. Boethius, *Commentary on Porphyry's Introduction*, trans. Richard McKeon, in *Selections from Medieval Philosophers*, vol. 1, ed. Richard McKeon (New York: Scribner's, 1929), 91.

2. *The Glosses of Peter Abelard on Porphyry*, in *Selections from Medieval Philosophers*, vol. 1, ed. Richard McKeon (New York: Scribner's, 1929), 240.

3. *On Divine Omnipotence* (Epist. 2.17), trans. Owen J. Blum in *Medieval Philosophy: From St. Augustine to Nicholas of Cusa*, ed. John F. Wippel and Allan B. Wolter (New York: Macmillan, Free Press, 1969), 150–151.

4. Sermon 76, quoted in A. C. McGiffert, *A History of Christian Thought*, vol. 2 (New York: Scribner's, 1933), 226.

5. *De Fide Trinitatis*, quoted in McGiffert, 186.

6. *Proslogium*, chap. 1, in *Saint Anselm: Basic Writings*, trans. S. N. Deane (La Salle, IL: Open Court, 1962).

7. *Epistola* 17, quoted in Armand A. Maurer, *Medieval Philosophy* (New York: Random House, 1962), 59–60.

8. *Deliverance from Error*, 3.2, quoted in James N. Jordan, *Western Philosophy: From Antiquity to the Middle Ages* (New York: Macmillan, 1987), 350.

11

St. Thomas Aquinas: Aristotle's Philosophy and Christian Thought

The Ox That Roared

Thomas Aquinas was born in 1225 (some say 1224) into a noble Italian family who lived in southern Italy about halfway between Rome and Naples. His father was the Count of Aquino, a man prominent in politics. Thomas was groomed by his family for a career of service in the Church. However, his parents' motives were not as pious as they may seem. They had always dreamed that Thomas would rise to a position of ecclesiastical authority where he would be politically influential and even wealthy. Around age fourteen he was sent to the University of Naples. It was an exciting place to be, abounding in new ideas, partly because the recently discovered Aristotelian texts and their Arabian commentaries had become a prominent part of the curriculum. Thomas came under the influence of the newly formed Dominican Order, which he joined sometime around 1244.

So it might seem that his parents' plans were proceeding nicely. They were not pleased, however, for the Dominicans did not aspire to be influential administrators but were humble and impoverished preachers and scholars. To bring Thomas to his senses, while he was en route to Paris his brothers kidnaped him and locked him in a tower for over a year. Eventually, his family realized the seriousness of his commitment and let him go on to his life's mission.

He picked up his life where it had been interrupted and went to Paris to study philosophy and theology, where he came under the influence of the Dominican theologian Albert the Great.* Aquinas was a very large, rotund person, whose imposing frame was contrasted with his gentle personality. In his classes he quietly absorbed the material without entering into the vigorous discussions of his classmates, who consequently ridiculed him as "the dumb ox." Albert, with keen insight into Thomas's intellectual potential, scolded them saying, "I tell you, the bellows of this 'dumb ox' will awaken all of Christendom." There is a story about Thomas that, although

---

*This name was not a reference to either his fame or his bulk, but was a translation of his German name of Albrecht Gross.

historically questionable, rings true to what we know of his sincere personality. One day, the brothers in the monastery conspired to play a practical joke on poor Brother Thomas. When he came into the room, one of them exclaimed that there was a cow flying in the sky. Thomas slowly ambled over to the window to see it, whereon the monks roared with laughter, asking, "Brother Thomas, did you really think that a cow could fly?" Thomas quietly replied, "I would much rather believe that a cow could fly, than that a brother monk would lie to me."

After earning the highest degree in theology, Aquinas spent the remainder of his life lecturing and writing while alternately residing in Paris and Italy, as well as making frequent journeys to conduct the business of his order and the Church. He was appointed by the Pope to be a theological adviser in conversations with leaders of the Eastern Orthodox Church. Aquinas died at age forty-nine, in 1274, on his way to attend the Council of Lyons to carry out this diplomatic mission.

Aquinas was an astoundingly prolific writer—his works fill some twenty-five volumes. He is said to have kept four secretaries busy at once, dictating different manuscripts in progress to them, which they would then transcribe. His works run the gamut from devotional works, sermons, lectures, technical works in philosophy and theology, as well as commentaries on Aristotle, Boethius, and Pseudo-Dionysius. The *Summa Theologica*, his major work, is longer than the entire collected works of Aristotle. All this was accomplished in the last twenty years of his life while teaching and consulting. While celebrating Mass a few months before he died, he had a mystical experience. "I can write no more," he later said to a friend, "I have seen things which make all my writings like straw." Without any further explanation, he gave up writing. In 1323, within a half-century of his death, he was canonized by the Church, which means he was officially declared a saint. In 1879 Pope Leo XIII recommended the philosophy of Thomas Aquinas as a model for Catholic thought.

Aquinas's Task: Integrating Philosophy and Faith

THE IMPACT OF ARISTOTLE

A dramatic shift in European medieval philosophy began to occur in the twelfth and thirteenth centuries as Aristotle's complete works began to be made widely available. Aristotle was very attractive to anyone who read him seriously, for he offered the most powerful and comprehensive system the medieval world had ever seen. However, his newly discovered works brought with them not only new perspectives, but new problems as well. The main difficulty was that while many found Aristotle's arguments persuasive, a number of his teachings seemed to contradict Christian doctrine. For example, Aristotle taught that the world was eternal and uncreated, and he seemed to deny personal immortality. The Christians who followed Averroës' interpretation of Aristotle tended to modify traditional theology to fit the outlines of their rational systems. Obviously, this caused the Church authorities to be suspicious of Christian philosophers who attempted to make use of the pagan Greek philosophy of Aristotle.* In addition to the problems in Aristotle's teachings, Neoplatonic philosophy had held the minds of Christian thinkers for so long that the empirical and naturalistic perspective of Aristotle seemed alien and dangerous.

Contrary to the fears of the Church authorities, Aquinas believed that adopting Aristotelianism did not necessarily lead to heretical conclusions. He

---

*Aristotle's works on natural philosophy were banned by the Council of Paris in 1210. Various ecclesiastical authorities issued other bans in 1215, 1245, and 1263. The most important condemnation was pronounced by Etienne Tempier, Bishop of Paris, in 1277, a few years after Aquinas's death. The bishop condemned 219 propositions, threatening excommunication to anyone who embraced them. Most of the banned doctrines were those of the Averroists, but some of them were held by Aquinas. A similar condemnation was issued in Oxford eleven days later and again in 1284 and 1286. Eventually, however, largely because of Aquinas's work, the consensus shifted, and Aristotelian Christianity became accepted.

was convinced that Aristotle could be Christianized and could serve as a rich resource for philosophical and theological speculation faithful to the Christian tradition. Although his teacher, Albert the Great, had made some attempts to use Aristotle in a Christian framework, it was Aquinas who became the chief architect of the new philosophical-theological edifice based on this new foundation.

Platonic Christianity had served the needs of the culture for a time. However, the Platonic emphasis on the eternal and its otherworldly notion of the spiritual realm could not keep pace with the changes occurring in the thirteenth century. Increased travel and the flowering of art, architecture, science, and medicine, as well as the rise of the universities, called for a new look at the relationship between Christianity and culture. What was needed was an understanding of how Christianity could hold onto its concern for a transcendent God, as well as its emphasis on the spiritual realm and the afterlife and yet, at the same time, still speak to our here-and-now earthly concerns. By merging Aristotle with Christian theology, Aquinas thought he could gain a perspective on our human involvement in culture, science, politics, and bodily existence that would be philosophically rigorous and theologically adequate.

Aquinas's deep respect for Aristotle is shown by the fact that he frequently refers to him simply as "the Philosopher." However, Aquinas cannot be accused of a slavish duplication of Aristotle's ideas. Aquinas certainly felt free to criticize his Greek model and to dismiss Aristotle's ideas when they did not seem to conform to reason. Aquinas believed that Aristotle's philosophy was superb as far as it goes. But with respect to the distinctive features of the Christian faith, Aristotle was in the dark, and—like any other pagan Greek—in need of divine revelation.

THE SPHERES OF FAITH AND REASON

As discussed in the previous chapter, a major issue during the Middle Ages was the relationship of faith and reason. Accordingly, one of Aquinas's primary tasks was to show how these two sources of knowledge fit together. Those in the Augustinian tradition (which would include the Protestant Reformers in the centuries to come) emphasized the damage sin has done to our rational powers. They believed that the mind must be renewed by grace before reason can function correctly. For this reason, they claimed that religious faith was a necessary prerequisite for philosophical understanding and that philosophy must keep its place as the humble servant of theology. Aquinas, however, believed that sin did not decisively affect our rational powers. Sin affects our moral life but not our rational life. Hence, Aquinas believed that reason can stand on its own two feet as an independent and autonomous source of knowledge apart from faith. For Aquinas, the only faith necessary in pursuing philosophical truth is faith in the power of the human intellect and the intelligibility of the universe. Of course, he shared this commitment with most philosophers in the Western tradition, both Christian and non-Christian.

Thomas Aquinas achieved a great compromise between Christian teaching and philosophy by giving each its due and seeking to show that they could coexist peacefully. Unlike most previous medievals, Aquinas clearly separates theology from philosophy. Theology gives us knowledge through faith and revelation, and philosophy gives us knowledge through the natural powers of human cognition available to all. They differ in their methods, and each is self-contained and independent of the other. Thus, for Aquinas, the realm of human knowledge can be divided into two areas: (1) truths given to us in revelation and known by faith and (2) truths revealed in nature and known by reasoning from experience. We can diagram Aquinas's view of the relationship between faith and reason as shown in Figure 11-1. The two approaches to knowledge are complementary because theology starts from God and moves to knowledge of the world, whereas philosophy moves from empirical facts about nature and reasons to God. Line A–B represents Christian teachings that are matters of faith, known only through revelation. They are beyond the scope of reason, yet they are not contrary to reason. Although we can disprove objections to them and dismiss alleged contradictions or difficulties, they can neither be proven nor disproven. For Aquinas, examples of truths that cannot be demonstrated by natural reason are the Trinity, the Incarnation, original sin, the creation of the world in time, the sacraments, and the last judgment.*

Line C–D represents knowledge based on sensory experience and the self-evident rational principles of philosophy (such as Aristotle's laws of logic). These scientific and philosophical truths cannot be known through revelation. To give an example of Aquinas's point, to understand the biological functions of the heart we must do empirical research on that organ and cannot simply study the word "heart" as it is used in the Bible.

Finally, line B–C is where revelation overlaps with philosophical knowledge. We can approach these truths either from the side of faith or from the side of reason. The existence of God, his essential attributes, the existence of the soul, immortality, and the details of the natural moral law are examples of truths that can be grounded either in faith or proven by reason.

Thus for Aquinas there are two kinds of theology: (1) revealed or supernatural theology (represented by line A–C on the diagram on p. 171) and (2) **natural theology** or theology not based on revelation (line B–C). Natural theology is that discipline within philosophy that seeks to prove conclusions about God based on our natural reason and experience. Where they overlap, theology and philosophy cannot conflict because both reveal truths that have their origin in the Author of all truth. What can conflict are human interpretations or judgments of either. True theology

is only contradicted by false philosophy, and true philosophy conflicts only with false theology.

METHOD

Thomas Aquinas's best-known work is his *Summa Theologica*, a formidable example of natural theology. In this work and others, Aquinas's method of argument is a paradigm of intellectual rigor and follows the technique of dialectic that was refined by Abelard. Aquinas's discussion of each individual issue systematically proceeds through five steps. First, he states the question at issue. Second, he lists numerous "objections." These are standard answers to the question that he considers incorrect but for which some authority can be cited. In doing this, he tries to state his opponents' positions as strongly and fairly as possible. The third section begins with the words "On the contrary. . . ." Here, he provides an answer to the question that contradicts the previous ones but that supports his own views and for which a counterauthority can be cited, such as Scripture or a noted theologian. The fourth and main section begins with "I answer that . . . ," and he goes on to develop his own view and arguments in its defense. Finally, in the fifth section, he details a series of separate replies to each of the objections originally offered against his position. He proceeds in this way, issue after issue, in his attempt to give an exhaustive and definitive treatment of every major question. In doing this he shows that he is conversant with the history of philosophy from the pre-Socratics to the end of Greek philosophy, as well as the Church Fathers and theologians and the leading Arab and Jewish thinkers. No one fails to get his attention as he shows where his predecessors were illuminating and where their reasoning went astray. The structure of each individual issue in the *Summa Theologica* is matched by the tightly crafted structure of the whole work. Some have said that Thomas Aquinas succeeded in constructing a cathedral of reason that rivaled the great feats of architecture of his time. Using Aristotelian logic, his arguments build on one another and produce a philosophical edifice that leads the

---

*Aquinas differs on these points from many of his predecessors and contemporaries. To various degrees, Augustine, Anselm, and Abelard thought that natural reason pointed to the doctrine of the Trinity. Bonaventure (1221–1274) thought that the creation of the world in time was philosophically provable. Finally, Anselm believed that the Incarnation could be shown to be philosophically necessary.

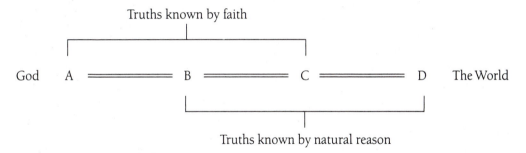

FIGURE 11-1 Thomas Aquinas's view of faith and reason

The Nature of Knowledge: *Reason Processing Experience*

intellect to its Maker. Thus, the architecture of both the medieval cathedral and Aquinas's philosophical system were intended to reflect the tightly woven, purposeful hierarchical structure of the universe itself.

Thomas Aquinas's epistemology reflects the empirical emphasis of Aristotle. Quoting Aristotle, he says that prior to experience the mind is like a blank tablet (ST 1.79.2).[1] Hence, unlike the Platonist theologians, Aquinas does not believe there is any innate knowledge. Even the idea of God is not written on the mind. However, even though the senses provide the intellect with its content, sensory cognition is not enough to explain our knowledge. "Although the operation of the intellect has its origin in the senses, yet, in the thing apprehended through the senses, the intellect knows many things which the senses cannot perceive" (ST 1.78.4).

The intellect is both passive and active. As passive, it receives its raw materials from sense experience. However, in sense experience we are not bombarded with a meaningless, random confusion of isolated sense data. Because the objects of experience are created entities, they are intelligible and contain forms or universals. However, the active part of the intellect must process sense ex-

perience in order to recognize the universals within particular objects. For example, the eyes can show us red things, but reason can isolate the universal of redness. The active intellect, then, functions by abstracting the universals from particulars. Even though the human mind is originally contentless, its nature is such that it has the potential to receive the forms (unlike animals). It is important to note that for Aquinas (unlike Augustine) this is a self-sufficient, natural process that does not need special divine illumination to obtain universal knowledge.

Aquinas could be characterized as a moderate realist. Unlike the extreme realists, he did not believe universals were completely independent realities. The only realities in the world are concrete particulars, and universals exist within particulars. Yet, unlike the nominalists, he did not believe universals are only mental creations. When the mind abstracts universals from objects, it is dealing with real features of the world and not arbitrary categories. For Aquinas, universals first existed from all eternity as ideas within the divine mind. With creation, universals came to exist extramentally in individual substances as their form. Finally, universals exist in the minds of rational creatures when they come to have rational knowledge of particulars through intellectual abstraction.

Given his empiricist starting point, Aquinas has set himself quite a challenge, for he must show that all the intellectual concepts of philosophy and knowledge of spiritual realities such as

God and values somehow derive from the materials of the senses. A further implication of his epistemology, which will become clear in later sections, is that all our knowledge about the world, whether of God, universals, or values, is inferential and indirect.

Metaphysics: From the World to God

THE PHYSICAL WORLD

If we were to follow Aquinas's order of exposition in the *Summa Theologica*, we would begin with his proofs for the existence of God and then go on to consider the created world. However, a number of features of his discussion of God rely on certain principles about the nature of reality that seemed more obvious to his contemporaries than they may to the modern reader. Hence, it will be worthwhile to begin with an overview of his general metaphysical scheme and then see how his conclusions about God fit into this.

Following Aristotle, Aquinas believes that the natural world consists of a collection of concrete individual substances (Lassie the Dog, Socrates the philosopher, the oak tree outside my office, the Hope diamond). Every material substance must be understood in terms of two principles. The first is the substantial form. The form is the universal aspect of the thing, that which all members of a species have in common. The substantial form of humanity, for example, is what gives humans those attributes (physical and mental) that differentiate them from plants and animals, and it is this form that causes them to act in characteristically human ways.

The other aspect of a substance is its matter. We might be inclined to think that the matter of a tree is the woody, fibrous material we associate with the interior of the tree. However, this matter is already the product of the substantial form, and thus it does not exist apart from the substance of the tree. Aquinas's theory of matter attempts to solve two problems that arise from our commonsense understanding of experience. The first one is the problem of continuity. Since one kind of substance can change into another substance (the tree can be burned and reduced to ashes), what accounts for our experience of continuity? The second problem is that of individuation. How can two substances have *identical* qualities (such as two identical vases) and still be two *different* substances?

To solve the first problem, Aquinas says that if there is continuity, there must be a more fundamental kind of matter that persists through any sort of substantial change. If the tree turns into ashes, then there must be something that had the potential to be the wood of the tree *as well as* the matter of the ashes. This is what Aquinas calls *prime matter*. It is pure matter, without any form whatsoever, and thus it does not have any distinctive characteristics of its own, but has the potential to take on any possible form. It may be described as "pure potentiality." Postulating prime matter also solves the problem of individuation. Two substances with the same qualities are different because their matter is different. However, when we look about the world, we will not find any examples of prime matter. This is because all matter we encounter is already formed matter and is found only in this or that particular substance, whether it is a rock, a plant, or an animal. Of course, in Aquinas's Aristotelian universe there are no pure, independently existing forms either, for all forms are only found embodied in substances.

A HIERARCHICAL UNIVERSE

The distinction between form and matter in physical substances is one example of a more general distinction between *actuality* and *potentiality*. We have said that prime matter is pure potentiality. It is the capacity to take on different substantial forms. Forms are on the side of actuality, for they create a particular tree, tiger, or person. Because God is perfect, he alone is fully actualized, for to be imperfect means to have potentialities that are not actualized. Hence, God cannot change. However, the rest of the universe is dynamic. Every created being is somewhere between pure potentiality and complete actualization and has a natural tendency toward further self-development. In trying to fulfill our potential and be all that we can be, we are imitating or coming closer (within the bounds of our finiteness) to the fullness of the divine actuality and perfection.

Aquinas's picture of the universe is of a continuous hierarchy that some have called the "great chain of being." It ranges from inorganic substances at the bottom all the way up to God at the pinnacle. There is such an enormous variety of substances because God's own creation was made to express his fullness. Aquinas even uses this notion to prove the existence of angels. They are like God in that they are purely spiritual beings, yet they are like humans in that they have potentiality. Thus they fill a unique niche in the chain of being. Although Aquinas did not wrestle with issues of ecology, it is clear that on his view, the disappearance of a species would be unfortunate, for it would leave a gap in nature.

Whether or not we accept Aquinas's Aristotelian view of the world, such a metaphysic offers a great deal of intellectual satisfaction because it assures us that the world is not a meaningless and random hodgepodge of blind processes. Since each species has a form, the world is orderly and intelligible and our minds can know it. Furthermore, the world is purposeful, for each sort of thing is in the process of fulfilling its divinely ordained essence. Also, objective value judgments (such as "better" or "worse") are possible because the excellence of any natural creature can be graded in terms of how fully it realizes the potential inherent in its essence. Finally, creatures can be ranked as higher or lower depending on how close they are to God on the scale of being. Because there is this objective hierarchy, we would save the life of a human being before that of a snail. This is because humans are higher than the animals and just a little lower than the angels. All of physical nature reflects the divine nature and is important, but humans more fully exhibit the image of God and, thereby, have more dignity and worth.

ESSENCE AND EXISTENCE

The potentiality–actuality distinction is exhibited in another distinction, the relation between *essence* and *existence*. **Essence** accounts for what a thing is. It is what is described in dictionary definitions. However, (1) the nature or essence of something differs from (2) the fact that it exists. We could describe to a child the respective properties of kangaroos and unicorns. She would then understand the essence of each kind of creature, but this knowledge alone would not tell her that one of these creatures exists and the other doesn't. So, with respect to all finite beings, their essence is something independent of their existence. But this distinction is not present in God, for God's essence implies his existence. God is a being so great nothing greater can be thought. Such a being could not pass out of existence, as did the dinosaurs, nor could he just happen to exist, as do kangaroos. Hence, if there is a God, his nature is such that he would exist *necessarily*.

This sounds very much like Anselm's ontological argument. However, Aquinas rejects this argument because even though we can understand the term "God" we do not have a direct apprehension of the divine essence. If we did, we would see that his essence is identical to his existence. However, lacking this complete knowledge of the divine essence, we cannot argue from it to God's actual existence as Anselm tries to do. This is consistent with Aquinas's epistemology, for he continually insists that reason must work from the materials given to it by sense experience. Hence, as we will see in the next section, any arguments for God's existence must, necessarily, begin with human experience of the world.

THE EXISTENCE OF GOD

Aquinas presents us with five arguments for the existence of God (using his own words, these are commonly referred to as "the five ways") (ST 1.2.3). He claims no originality for these proofs, since he draws on arguments proposed by Aristotle and some of the latter's Arab and Jewish commentators. However, Aquinas articulates and packages these arguments so artfully that they have become the model for theistic proofs throughout the centuries. Every one of the five ways has this general outline:

(1) If the world has feature X, then there is a God.

(2) The world has feature X.

(3) Therefore, there is a God.

In each of the arguments, he claims that the feature of the world being focused on is one that cannot be explained on the basis of the finite, natural world alone. Hence, Aquinas is drawing our attention to five facts about the world that he believes point to the existence of God. The first three arguments are similar, in that they depend on the principle that an infinite regress of causes is inconceivable. These three "ways" to God are various forms of what is known in modern times as the **cosmological argument**.

The first proof starts from the fact that motion occurs in the world. "Motion" here is understood in the broad Aristotelian sense of any change from a potential state to an actual state. This not only includes changes in location but also refers to, say, a change in temperature or color. He argues that any change presupposes some agent that brings it about. But if the agent is itself a changing being, it too can be moved only by the action of some other agent. However, such a series of agents cannot be infinite. The whole process of things actualizing the potential in other things needs some ultimate ground. Hence, there must be a first Unmoved Mover—a being that is not itself changing but is the ultimate source of the series of changes we observe in the world. To illustrate this point, we can imagine a set of pool balls sitting on a table, racked up in a triangular formation. Although those balls have the potential to move, they will sit there motionless, for all eternity, unless some agent intervenes within the system to set them in motion. If we walked into a room where they *were* in motion and saw the cue ball hitting the number 3 ball, which in turn set the number 10 ball in motion, and even if no one was currently visible, we would still know that *someone or something* had been there to introduce motion into the system. Once the cue ball is in motion, it can impart its motion to others, but the system by itself cannot actualize its own potential for motion. Even if the balls had been in motion continuously from all eternity, they would still need a cause of their eternal motion.

How can something cause motion without itself moving? Here, Aquinas is relying on Aristotle's notion that it is possible for one thing to move another without the cause itself being in motion. For example, you can be madly in love with someone and that love can affect your behavior, but (unfortunately) the object of your love may be unmoved by you in turn (ST 1.105.2). Consequently, the person that causes a response in you is an "unmoved mover."

The second way is an argument from efficient causation. In nature we see that one event is caused by another event that was itself caused by yet another event. There cannot be an infinite series of such causes, because unless there is a first cause that is sufficient unto itself, the whole series of dependent causes and effects is unaccounted for. To illustrate, imagine a long chain hanging in the air. There is no problem in explaining the cause of link 1 being suspended, because we can see that it is supported by link 2, and this one, in turn, is supported by link 3, and so on. However, at some point the entire series of links must be supported by something that does not depend for its support on something else. Without a self-supporting point on which the whole chain depends, the entire chain will never be supported. This First Cause for all the intermediate causes in the world is God.

The third way shifts the emphasis a little and proceeds from the notions of possibility and necessity. This argument takes the following form:

(1) In nature we find things that come into existence and pass out of existence. (Their existence and non-existence are both possible.)

(2) That which does not exist can only begin to exist through something that already has existence.

(3) There cannot be an infinity of merely possible beings who depend for their existence on something else.

(4) Therefore, there must be some being who exists by its own necessity and is not dependent on anything but who can impart existence to everything else.

(5) This necessary being is what all people speak of as God.

To illustrate Aquinas's point, imagine a series of mirrors in a dark room. It is possible for the mirrors to reflect light, but this possibility must be actualized. Now let us suppose that mirror 1 is reflecting light. Where did it come from? Let's say it is receiving light that is being reflected off the surface of mirror 2. But what is the cause of its light? It has received light that was being reflected off of mirror 3, and so on. In the case of any particular mirror, we may be able to account for its light by finding its source in some other mirror. However, this process cannot go on forever. Since mirrors cannot generate their own light, the fact that any one of them is reflecting light must mean that light entered the system from some source outside the system that did not need to receive its light from another (such as a flashlight). Even if we postulate an infinite number of mirrors, each reflecting another's light, this will not solve the problem if none of these mirrors produce their own light. Furthermore, there must be more than just an original source of light at the beginning. Unless some *continuous* source of light sustains the activity of the mirrors' reflection of light, the whole system will lapse back into darkness. Just as the flashlight accounts for its own light and can in turn provide it to others, so there must be a necessary being whose essence it is to exist and who can provide existence to others.

Notice that this argument is similar to Anselm's ontological argument in that they both conclude that a necessary being exists, which is God. However, they differ in that Aquinas arrived at this conclusion through experience and not from the concept of God alone. Notice also that in each of these first three arguments, one particular event (whether a case of motion or change, a given effect, or the bringing of a possible being into existence) can be explained by another neighboring event within the system. However, if we want an ultimate explanation of how the entire series of events could exist at all, we must go outside the system to an entirely different type of reality. So far, these first three arguments establish the existence of an ultimate cause. However, Aristotle used similar arguments to defend the existence of his impersonal divinity. Thus, Aquinas's final two proofs

help round out the picture of the Unmoved Mover by introducing elements that do more to suggest the presence of personality.

The fourth way focuses on degrees of perfection. It starts from the existence of degrees of value or perfection and claims that they imply the existence of a supremely perfect being as their source. When we see the cool, soft light of the moon, we realize that it is caused by, and is a diminished reflection of, the brilliant, blazing light of the sun. Similarly, if things are more or less true, good, or noble, it must be that they reflect or participate to various degrees in that which is the fullest manifestation of these qualities. In arguing thus, Aquinas assumes, with the Platonists, that the most degree of value is necessarily associated with the most degree of reality. So he concludes that since degrees of value imply an ultimate source of value, there is a supreme being in which all perfections are realized.

The fifth way argues from the evidence of design in the world. Aquinas notes that most of nature is blind and unintelligent, yet it seems to be orderly and to achieve purposeful ends. To use philosophical terminology, Aquinas believes the world is a **teleological** system. However, an end that does not yet exist cannot direct its own realization. Only if the final goal is contained in the mind of an intelligent architect who guides the process can we account for the existence of a well-designed system. So, Aquinas concludes that "some intelligent being exists by whom all natural things are directed to their end."

A few points need to be clarified concerning these arguments. Contrary to what some of his critics assume, Aquinas never uses the principle that "everything must have a cause" in his argument, because this would lead to the absurd question of "What caused God?" This formulation of the causal principle would be as false as saying that "everything that emits light must have received its light from something else," which would mean that the light of the flashlight must get its light from another light source. Instead, Aquinas is actually claiming that "everything which is merely potential (and thus is dependent and not self-sufficient) must be caused by some other actuality." This principle shows why everything in nature requires an ultimate first cause, but it does not include God in its scope.

Another confusion is that some critics assume that Aquinas's arguments are seeking to prove that the world had a beginning in time. These critics suppose that if we can show it is possible that the world always existed, this will undermine the necessity for a first cause of the world. On the contrary, Aristotle both believed that the world was eternal *and* that it required an Unmoved Mover. Although Aquinas does not believe the arguments given for the eternity of the world are conclusive, he does think this is logically possible. Why then would an always existing universe require a first cause? To illustrate the type of answer Aquinas gives, try to imagine an oil lamp with a flame that existed from all eternity. The flame would have existed for an infinite amount of time in the past. Nevertheless, from all eternity, the flame's existence would have depended on the oil that sustains it. If the oil had not existed, neither would the flame. Thus, even though the flame was eternal, it would have been an eternally dependent entity. Similarly, even if the world had been eternal, it still would have needed an ultimate cause to sustain it.

This means that when Aquinas says God is the first cause, he does not mean that God is necessarily a *temporally* first cause. He is not talking about a horizontal causal series stretching through time, but about a vertical causal series, operating right here and now with God at the apex. In other words, Aquinas's picture of God's causal relationship to the world is really not like that of the colliding pool balls, where we are talking about a linear, temporal series of causes and effects. Instead, his vision of the universe is better illustrated by our example of the hanging chain, where the series of dependent causes and effects are contemporary with one another and where, at each moment of their existence, they continuously depend on some self-sufficient cause to support them. For this reason, God is primarily a continuously sustaining cause and not necessarily an initiating cause.

Although Aquinas thinks the eternity of the world is consistent with his theistic arguments, he does not think we can prove the world always existed. Can we then prove the world must have had a beginning in time? Some medieval philosophers such as St. Bonaventure thought that we could logically prove just that. However, Aquinas does not find such arguments persuasive either (ST 1.46.1,2). Hence, this issue is not something reason can resolve. As a matter of fact, Aquinas does believe the world had a beginning, but says the only way we can know this is that the book of Genesis in the Bible tells us so. It is an issue to be resolved by revelation, not by philosophy as Aristotle and Bonaventure thought.

Aquinas claims his five proofs have established the existence of a supreme being who is an unchanging, uncaused, intrinsically necessary being, and who is an absolutely perfect, purposeful cause. At least two general criticisms have been raised against the proofs as a whole. First, why couldn't we conclude that each of the preceding five properties apply to different beings? If there are five different proofs, maybe there are five different gods. His answer is that different beings are distinguished by the fact that they have different properties. All the proofs point to a being who is absolutely perfect and unlimited. If two beings were perfect in every respect, they would have identical properties and would really be the same. Furthermore, there cannot be two unlimited beings, for then they would limit each other and would no longer be unlimited. Hence, there is only one God.

The second criticism concerns the fact that Aquinas ends each argument with different variations on the phrase "And this everyone understands to be God." Both religious and non-religious critics say that the abstract metaphysical cause talked of by these arguments is a far cry from the personal, loving God of the Bible. Aquinas does not claim the proofs give us a complete picture of God. This is why he believes revelation must supplement reason. But he would insist that they do give us some of the more important qualities of God. For example, the fourth proof shows that God is ultimate perfection. Since, by his definition, a perfect being must be perfect in goodness and love, this suggests that the ultimate being is a personal being.

Because of these five arguments, Thomas Aquinas has an established place in history as one of the most forceful proponents of natural theology. However, not everyone was convinced that he had successfully provided a rational proof of God's existence. When we get to David Hume and Immanuel Kant in the eighteenth century, these arguments come under some fresh criticism.

THE PROBLEM OF RELIGIOUS LANGUAGE

A problem that lurks in all discussions of God is the problem of religious language. How can we speak about an infinite and perfect being if the language we speak is drawn from the world of finite and imperfect creatures? For example, we may use the word *good* to talk about a friend. However, if we then say, "God is good," it seems we are saying God is good in the same sense our friend is good. But surely this will not do, for God's goodness cannot be equated with human goodness. Therefore, the positive terms we use to talk about humans cannot be used univocally (with the same meaning) to talk about God. Must we then use a word such as *good* equivocally (with different meanings) when we talk about humans and about God? For example, when we say that a trumpet's pitch, a bottle of soda, and a pancake are all "flat," the word has a completely different meaning in each case. However, this explanation doesn't work either. First, if all our knowledge begins with experience, as Aquinas believes, then the meaning of our terms, even those that apply to God, must have some origin in the realm of human experience. We cannot use terms that apply to God uniquely, since we lack the direct experience of God's essence that would be necessary to give these terms their special meaning. Second, Aquinas *does* want to say there is *some* similarity between human and divine goodness, even if they are not exactly the same, for humans are created in the image of God.

Aquinas's first solution is the negative way. This approach was common among the earlier medieval thinkers and is the favorite solution of the mystics. The negative way claims we can speak of God's properties by negating the proper-

ties common to finite creatures. For example, we may say God is immutable (without change), eternal (not bound by time), or incorporeal (lacking a physical body). However, it is never sufficient to define something in terms of what that thing is *not*. We must be capable of asserting something positive about God.

The second approach, therefore, is the way of analogy. This method lets us start from an object *A* that is directly known and then to go on to infer information about an object *B* that is not directly known. For example, I do not know what it is like to have the responsibilities of the nation's President. However, I have been a president of a local organization and do know what it is like to have minor responsibilities. Since I know that the position of U.S. President is of overwhelming importance compared to that of the president of a small organization, I can know by analogy that the responsibilities of national leadership are proportionally greater than the responsibilities of local leadership. Hence, if we know what it is like for a friend to be good, wise, and intelligent within the limitations of human nature, and if such human properties are diminished approximations of God's attributes, then we can have some knowledge of what goodness, wisdom, and intelligence would mean when attributed to an infinite being.

Moral Philosophy: Human Nature and Divine Law

TELEOLOGICAL ETHICS

As one would expect, Thomas Aquinas's moral theory is a Christian adaptation of Aristotle's *Nicomachean Ethics*. Following in Aristotle's footsteps, Aquinas's ethics is rooted in his teleological metaphysics. Every event in the universe, he says, whether it is the falling of a stone or the blossoming of a fruit tree, occurs because there is some end toward which it is directed. As with the rest of nature, humans have their own natural ends and inclinations. However, we are the only earthly creatures that can consciously choose if and how we will fulfill a given end. Ethics, then, concerns what ends are worthy for humans to pursue. Hence, the moral good is not something alien to us, but is the fulfillment of our natural end. Conversely, evil is a kind of deficiency or privation. It prevents us from achieving fulfillment.

Aquinas says that all genuine actions are either good or bad, none are morally indifferent (ST 1-2.18.9). This is because deliberately chosen actions always seek to achieve some end that will be good or bad. Aquinas makes a distinction between human actions and the acts of humans (ST 1-2.1.1). The former are voluntary, consciously willed actions chosen because the person's reason seeks some end. The latter are simply unconscious or involuntary behaviors, such as absentmindedly scratching one's head or a sneeze. These latter behaviors are neither morally good nor bad. Only voluntary, deliberative actions have moral qualities. Aquinas definitely makes the intellect primary in ethics. Although the will naturally desires what is good, it needs reason to tell it what genuinely is good and the appropriate means for achieving the good.

Aquinas gives three factors that determine whether or not an action is morally good or evil. These are (1) the *object* of the action, (2) the *circumstances*, and (3) the *end* that is sought. To use Aquinas's example, giving alms to the poor is an action that has as its object the transfer of money to a needy person. Taken in isolation, this object is good. However, the circumstances play some role in the moral evaluation of the action. If the money I gave was stolen, then the goodness of the object is tarnished by the evil of the circumstances. Or if the person's needs are trivial, but the financial burdens of my family are urgent, the circumstances would again affect the moral quality of the action. Finally, even if the object and the circumstances were morally good, if the end I was trying to achieve was merely public praise, then the end or motive would not be morally worthy. Since these three factors may differ in their goodness or badness, Aquinas says that an action is not *absolutely* good unless the object, circumstances, and end are all good.

Thus far, Aquinas's moral theory is fairly consistent with the Aristotelian model. However, there is a problem. Aristotle has a purely naturalistic ethics. He treats humans as though they were simply one species among many in nature. Although Aristotle believes humans are unique in that they are rational, he has no sense that we have a spiritual nature and a special relationship to God. For example, his ethics contains no notion of obedience to divine commands. For humans as natural creatures, the final end of our life is the happiness and self-fulfillment found in the appropriate development of all categories of human excellence, particularly that of intellectual virtue. Aquinas believed that Aristotle gave us a vision of the imperfect and temporal happiness humans can achieve in this life through our natural resources. It is as good an ethics as we will ever find, *as far as it goes*. However, for Aquinas's Christian understanding of human life, the naturalistic ethics of Aristotle did not go far enough. We yearn for the good in its fullest form. But any good found in the natural realm can only be a particular and imperfect, finite good. Nature does not provide the means to fulfill our spiritual nature, but points beyond itself to what does fulfill us. If the purpose of our life is possession of the supreme good, this can only be found in God himself. This is not found in mere knowledge about God, but through acquaintance with God, achieved in the vision of the divine essence. Since knowledge of God attainable in this life is always imperfect, our natural desire for ultimate fulfillment points to the necessity of an afterlife.

THE NATURAL LAW

Because we were created by God to live a certain way, we can reflect on human nature and discover certain natural guidelines that will help us actualize our human potentialities. This is what Aquinas calls the **natural law** in morality.* Since human nature stays basically the same from culture to culture and century to century, the precepts of the

---

*The notion of the natural law in morality was introduced by the Greeks and developed by the Stoics. It was also a central feature of Augustine's early moral philosophy in *On Free Choice of the Will*.

natural law are universal and self-evident to reason. Previously, we had said that an action is absolutely good if the object, circumstances, and end are good. But how do we determine when these are good? The answer is that the good is what is in accordance with reason, and this is defined as being in conformity to the natural law of morality. Following his hierarchy from the lowest forms of life on through the higher animals and up to human life, Aquinas seeks to show that by reflecting on what is in accord with nature and our natural inclinations, we can derive moral principles. First of all, there is a natural tendency among all creatures to preserve their own life. The principle "Life is to be preserved" comes from this. Specifically, for Aquinas this means that not only murder but also suicide would violate natural law. Second, all animals seek to preserve their species and care for their offspring. For humans, this requires not only obvious biological and emotional nurturing of our young, but also educating our children and helping them achieve all their potential. Third, since we are higher than the beasts, we have an inclination to fully realize all our rational, human capacities. This leads to the obligation to pursue truth (including the knowledge of God) and to follow all the precepts necessary to live harmoniously in society.

If the natural law is universal and available to every rational creature, why don't all people agree on it? The answer is that they are blinded by passion, bad habits, and ignorance (ST 1-2.94.6). Thus, the person who is unaware of the natural law is like a color-blind person. In both cases, the person has limited capacities and cannot perceive reality normally. Some people think that something like the natural moral law is programed within our conscience. However, for Aquinas, the conscience is not a source of knowledge as much as it is the rational activity of applying moral knowledge to particular cases (ST 1.79.13). But what if reason errs in making such moral judgments? For example, suppose our reason tells us that something evil is good or that what is really good is forbidden? Ignorance can cause us to have a clear conscience while doing wrong and a guilty conscience for

doing something that is right. Aquinas answers that "every will at variance with reason, whether right or erring, is always evil" (ST 1-2.19.5). In other words, the most that can be asked of people is that they follow their informed conscience to the best of their ability. If our conscience is objectively mistaken, we are still judged by how we followed the moral light as we perceived it.

THE FOUR LAWS

For Aquinas it is important to show the link between morality and metaphysics. Hence, he explains that the moral law written into our nature is an expression of God's eternal law. Contrary to the voluntarists, Aquinas believes that the moral law is not based on the arbitrary decision of God's will but is an expression of the divine reason, which is rooted in God's nature. Since God's nature is not arbitrary, neither is the moral law.

Aquinas believes that there are actually four kinds of laws or, more accurately, four ways in which God's law is manifested. In each case, the law is rooted in the rational order that God created. First of all, there is the *eternal law*, the rational order that the ruler of the universe established for his creation. All things are subject to the eternal law. The apples falling to the earth and flames rising to the sky all manifest the order created by the eternal law. Thus, for Aquinas, the phrase "the laws of nature" is more than a metaphor. Although all of nature follows the eternal law blindly, only humans can reflect on the moral dimensions of God's law and we alone have the capacity to obey it or disobey it. Second, the *natural law* (which has already been discussed) is the law available to reason that governs human moral behavior. The natural law guides us insofar as we are natural and social creatures. It leads us to fulfill the Aristotelian model of moral character by developing the classical Greek virtues of temperance, courage, justice, and wisdom. Third, there is the *divine law*, which is given to us in revelation. The divine law goes beyond natural law and guides us in achieving eternal happiness. In following this law, the natural virtues are surpassed by the theological virtues of faith, hope, and love. Unlike the natural virtues, however, these can only be attained through the workings of God's grace (ST 1-2.62.1). The fourth kind of law is the *human law* instituted by governments. However, if such law is legitimate, it too is rooted in God's eternal law. Hence in obeying a legitimate law, we are obeying God. Quoting Augustine, Aquinas says, "in temporal law there is nothing just and lawful but what man has drawn from the eternal law" (ST 1-2.93.3). In his discussion of the human or temporal law, Aquinas's political philosophy emerges.

Political Philosophy

In the eight hundred years from Augustine to Aquinas one finds few significant discussions of the nature of the political state in medieval philosophy. The dominance of Neoplatonism in this period led philosophers to be concerned mainly with eternal realities and the questions of metaphysics and logic. However, as Aristotle's complete works became available, philosophers once again began to address questions of political theory. Also, as society became more stable and civilization flourished, philosophical questions concerning the nature of the state, the law, and political obligation became more of a concern.

Aquinas's political philosophy focuses on the nature of political laws. He defines law as "an ordinance of reason for the common good, promulgated by him who has care of the community" (ST 1-2.90.4). Some laws are concerned with elaborating and enforcing the natural law (such as laws against murder and theft). These sorts of laws should be the same everywhere. However, other laws set out details left open by the natural law and are instituted for the sake of uniformity in a particular society. For example, laws stating what penalties should be imposed for particular crimes are not detailed in the natural law. In our own day, the law in the United States dictates that cars should drive on the right side of the road, whereas other countries may specify the left side of the road. Although the details are arbitrary, such laws ensure human safety and follow from the universal prin-

ciple that life should be preserved. However, whether directly or indirectly, all civil laws receive their validity from the principles of the natural law. Any human law that violates natural law is not a genuine law at all and does not require our obedience. In some cases, it is the lesser evil to obey laws, to keep the peace, while in other cases civil disobedience in the name of the higher law may be necessary (ST 1-2.96.4).

What should be the extent of law? Thomas says that a human attempt to illegalize all forms of immoral behavior would be self-defeating, because human nature would make such a goal impossible to realize. If every form of wrong behavior were illegal, we would all be in jail! Generally, law should be concerned only with major evils, namely, those that harm others and undermine an ordered human society. In other words, human law is restricted to the sphere of people in their mutual relations (ST 1-2.100.2). Hence, political legislation is to concern itself only with justice, and should refrain from issues that concern the spiritual community and private, individual morality.

According to Aquinas, civil society is natural and requires no justification. His position agrees with that of the Greeks. However, it contrasts with that of Augustine, who thought government was a necessary evil brought into being in response to human perversity. It also disagrees with the Enlightenment philosophers, who tended to see society as an artificially created order. For this reason, they felt the need to develop theories explaining why government was justified. But Aquinas says that even "in the state of innocence [humans] would have led a social life" (ST 1.96.4). He goes on to argue that any society always requires some system of governance and someone to look after the common good, so human nature necessitates the institution of government. Although government as such does not need to be justified, he does say that any particular form of government or the authority of any particular leader does need some warrant. For Aquinas, the ideal state combines different elements. It has one ruler, whose power is balanced by other governing bodies, all of whom are selected by the will of the people (ST 1-2.105.1).

Evaluation and Significance

THE REJECTION OF
PLATONIC DUALISM

Aquinas presents nature as a unified and continuous spectrum of beings from the rocks and plants, up to the lowliest larvae, and then to the higher animals, until we reach the apex with those creatures capable of reason, free choice, moral decisions, and spiritual life, namely, humans and angels. This picture was influenced by the Neoplatonists and Augustine, yet Aquinas rejects the Platonic assumption that the physical world is a shadow world that is not fully real. This dualistic theme in Plato unfortunately suggested a tension between the spiritual realm and the natural, physical world. For Aquinas, however, physical nature is not alien to the spiritual dimension, for this entire "chain of being" pointed to and found its final end in God. This metaphysical vision enabled Aquinas to give more weight to the biblical doctrine of the goodness of creation. In contrast to Platonic Christianity, Aquinas did not view the body as an unfortunate prison in which the soul resides. Instead, the body is important for knowledge, and it is what makes us the unique individuals we are. In this way, he enabled his contemporaries to rediscover their humanity. Not only are we spiritual beings with an eternal destiny, but we are a part of nature as well. By giving more importance to the physical world and our here-and-now, earthly existence, Thomas Aquinas provided a better foundation for the works of human culture such as science, politics, law, and the arts than was possible in an Augustinian picture of the world.

SCIENCE AND THEOLOGY

Aquinas's focus on the physical world and the value of natural explanations raised the question of the relationship between science and theology. This would prove an important question that would be continuously debated all the way into our century. It is useful, therefore, to examine the insights and problems of Aquinas's position on this issue. The problem he faced was that on the one hand, science explains events in terms of physical causes. On the other hand, he viewed nature as governed by divine providence. His teleological argument for God, found in the fifth way, emphasizes that events in nature can only be explained if we see them as fulfilling God's purposes. We have, then, two kinds of explanations. Is the life-giving rain caused by the moisture-saturated clouds, or is it provided by God's benevolence? Is a newborn baby a result of biological causes, or is it a gift from God? To answer these questions, Aquinas develops a theory of dual causality, drawing on Aristotle's theory that different sorts of causes explain a particular event:

> It is . . . clear that the same effect is ascribed to a natural cause and to God, not as though part were effected by God and part by the natural agent; but the whole effect proceeds from each, yet in different ways, just as the whole of one and the same effect is ascribed to the instrument, again the whole is ascribed to the principal agent.[2]

To illustrate Aquinas's point, when someone comes into my kitchen and asks, "Why is the water boiling?" two completely different answers could be given, both equally correct. I could give a *scientific* answer in terms of the immediate *efficient and material causes* and say, "The water is boiling *because* the fire is heating the bottom of the pot, which is transferring its heat to the water, which is causing air bubbles to rise to the surface." On the other hand, I could provide a *teleological* answer in terms of the *final cause* and simply say, "The water is boiling *because* I am going to cook some potatoes." The two answers appeal to different principles and serve different purposes, but they are completely complementary. In the same way, Aquinas believes we can explain natural events in terms of natural causes, without having to abandon our belief in God's providence and governance of the world. Although the physical properties, laws, and materials of creation are what immediately cause natural events to occur, it is God who has orchestrated this order of nature to carry out his will. Thus, Aquinas might say it is appropriate to think about both the physical properties of clouds *and* God's benevolence when trying to explain the fact that the rain falls and nourishes our crops. This way of reconciling the scientific and religious views of the world would be important to many of the thinkers in the modern period who were both scientists and Christians.

It is significant that Aquinas was seeking a way to reconcile the science of his day with a theistic vision of the universe. In doing so, he certainly provided a richer basis for pursuing a scientific knowledge of the world than the otherworldly approach of some medievals. Nevertheless, as we shall see when we get to the Renaissance, a major shortcoming of Aquinas's project lies—in the phrase just used—in "the science of his day." Because the science available to people at this time was Aristotelian science, not only did their theological explanations of natural events use teleology, but their scientific explanations were infected with it too. They thought every part of nature was trying to fulfill its divinely appointed end. The stone falls because its natural end is to be reunited with the earth. The acorn grows into an oak tree because this is its natural purpose. As you can see, explaining natural events in terms of the purposes they are meant to fulfill provides only a rather thin and inadequate explanation of things. The Aristotelian emphasis on essences meant that nature was mainly understood in terms of eternal and logical relationships rather than temporal and causal ones. Thus, even though Aquinas gave more importance to physical processes than Christian theologians ever had before, only when people abandoned the Aristotelian model of providing teleological explanations of events could science mature. Instead of speculating how the purposes and ends of natural things fit into God's plan, scientists eventually learned to pay more attention to the details and regularities of the material and efficient causes themselves.

With Aquinas, we reach the culmination of medieval philosophy. In the following chapter, we survey the intellectual causes that played a role in unraveling the fabric of Scholasticism.

Questions for Understanding

1. How did Aquinas attempt to reconcile the spheres of faith and reason?

2. What is the meaning of "natural theology"? How does Aquinas illustrate this concept?

3. According to Aquinas, how do reason and experience both contribute to knowledge? Why do we need both?

4. Using Aquinas's Aristotelian metaphysics, explain what happens when the wood in a tree is transformed into a bookcase.

5. What does Aquinas mean by "essence"? How is the relationship between essence and existence different for God than it is for any other creature?

6. Why does Aquinas reject Anselm's ontological argument?

7. Briefly describe the five kinds of arguments Aquinas uses to prove God's existence.

8. State in your own words what it means to say that Aquinas believes the world is a "teleological system"?

9. Since Aquinas believed that the world needs a cause, why does he also believe that it is logically possible that the world had always existed? What does he mean by "cause" here?

10. What is the problem of religious language? What are several ways that Aquinas attempts to solve it?

11. In Aquinas's ethics, what three factors determine the rightness or wrongness of an action?

12. What does the term "natural law" mean in the context of ethics? How does Aquinas use this notion in developing his ethical theory?

13. Why does Aquinas believe that there are four different kinds of laws? What is their relationship?

14. According to Aquinas, what is the basis of our civil laws? What sorts of activities should be regulated by law?

15. How does Aquinas attempt to harmonize scientific explanations with theological explanations of the world?

Questions for Reflection

1. In what ways is Aquinas's philosophy more like Aristotle's than Plato's? What were some of the consequences of Aquinas's rejection of Platonic dualism?

2. Basing your answer on Aquinas's philosophy, give an example of something that can only be known by reason but not by faith. What is something that can only be known by faith? What is an example of a truth that can be known both by faith (revelation) and reason?

3. Imagine that you are Aquinas. A very pious critic (such as Tertullian in chapter 7) says that Christian philosophers should not be borrowing from non-Christian thought such as Aristotle's philosophy. How would Aquinas reply to this objection?

4. Which one of Aquinas's arguments for God do you think is the strongest? Why? Which one do you think is the weakest? Why?

5. Using Aquinas's three criteria for determining the moral worth of an action, evaluate the morality of each of the following actions: (a) sticking a knife in a person to cause him pain, (b) a surgeon sticking a knife into a patient on the operating table to remove a tumor, (c) saving the life of a person by giving her medicine, (d) accidentally saving the life of a person by giving her medicine when you mistakenly thought it was poison, (e) stealing money to give to a charity, (f) giving your own money to a charity because of the good publicity it will bring to your political campaign.

6. Think of examples from human behavior that would support Aquinas's notion that there is a universal moral law. Think of some examples that would count against this view.

7. For the purposes of this exercise, assume that you agree with Aquinas's view of natural law and political philosophy. In the light of his philosophy, develop arguments to show that the law should either permit or forbid each of the following activities: (a) slavery, (b) pornography, (c) abortion, (d) (an issue of your choice).

8. Suppose someone says that modern science has eliminated the need for God in explaining the world. How might Aquinas respond?

Notes

1. This and other references to *Summa Theologica* are symbolized as ST. Quotations are taken from *Basic Writings of Saint Thomas Aquinas*, 2 vols., ed. Anton C. Pegis (New York: Random House, 1945). The three numbers in the references refer to the numbers of the part, question, and article.

2. *Summa Contra Gentiles* 3.70, in *Basic Writings of Saint Thomas Aquinas*, vol. 2.

12

The Unraveling of
the Medieval Synthesis

IN THE PERIOD FROM 1300 TO 1500, THE MIGHTY stream of medieval thought developed a rapid succession of shifting currents, breaking it into a number of separate rivulets, each seeking its own, new direction. The philosophical changes are what concern us here; these did not occur in isolation from the social, economic, and political changes that affected every area of European life at this time. By the thirteenth century, the spiritual prestige and political power of the papacy had declined. Many in the fold were scandalized by the series of worldly popes and cardinals that tarnished the ideals of the Church. The excessive wealth and privilege of the Church produced calls for reform among some and a retreat from the institutional Church into personal piety among others. The criticisms of the Church by John Wyclif in England and John Huss in Bohemia provided early forewarnings of the Reformation. Furthermore, the confusion of spiritual authority with political allegiances produced the Great Schism from 1378 to 1415, when there were two rival popes, a French pope in Avignon and an Italian pope in Rome.

The Church had to deal not only with a crisis of authority and spiritual disillusionment, but with shifting political currents as well. For centuries, the Church had been a powerful international organization that prospered in the context of weak secular states. However, the dissension within the Church played into the hands of the rising powers among the political states. As Europe grew richer, the secular kingdoms became more autonomous from Rome. The rediscovery of Aristotle's *Politics* promoted the viewpoint that the state was a natural entity, which was justified on moral and rational grounds, rather than an institution that received its authority from God and the Church. However, the secular kingdoms did not lack turmoil. The Hundred Years War between England and France fueled the spirit of nationalism. Furthermore, the times were characterized by economic and social unrest, and peasants' revolts broke out in France and England. Despite these problems, however, by the last half of the fifteenth century the emerging emphasis on royal sovereignty culminated in strong monarchies in England, France, and Spain, which would be major players in western European life for centuries to come. These states did not sever their relationship with the Church, but their reliance on it severely diminished. These and other factors threatened the rigid stability of the medieval scheme of things. The taken-for-granted triad of hierarchy, authority, and unity were ideals that had dominated people's spiritual, intellectual, and political lives for centuries. However, these three pillars of the Middle Ages were now beginning to crumble.

While these controversies and changes were occurring in the larger society, a number of the influential philosophers of the fourteenth century began to move away from some of the essential principles of Scholasticism. This marked the beginning of the decline of medieval philosophy. Although they chipped away at the intellectual foundations of the Scholastic systems, these thinkers did so from the standpoint of a sincere Christian faith. They were convinced that faith was best served by freeing it from entanglements with philosophy. The driving force of their thought was a strong emphasis on the omnipotence of God. Their religious creed dictated that God's actions are totally free and beyond the ability of reason to analyze or explain.

To preview this chapter, the focus on the absolute power of God led to a number of radical conclusions. The first was *antirationalism*. Aquinas believed an all-powerful God can do whatever is logically possible. However, the critics who followed claimed that the realm of the possible is larger than Aquinas ever imagined. Hence, reason is not competent to determine the way the world is or must be. The desire to limit reason took the form of empiricism in some thinkers and of mysticism in others. The second feature of this period was *nominalism*. Universals were held in suspicion,

and the concrete reality of individuals was upheld. Third, *confidence in natural theology declined*. Philosophers argued that doctrines such as the existence of God and the immortality of the human soul could not be definitively proven by reason, as Aquinas had thought. They claimed these doctrines can only be known and affirmed on the basis of revelation and faith. Fourth, *voluntarism* became the central theme in ethics. This position claims that the will has priority over the intellect. If God's intellect does not impose limits on his will, then he is completely free in choosing what is morally good. This means that human reason cannot determine what is morally good. Thus, moral obligation is not a matter of following reason's directions but in obeying God's sovereign commands. Fifth, the ideas of this century provided *a new approach to natural science*. If no rational forms guided God's free creation of the world, then the world is completely contingent. Human reason employed in metaphysical speculation cannot tell us what the world is like. Only observation will tell us what sort of world God made. As Etienne Gilson described this stage of philosophy,

> After a brief honeymoon [one might almost have said, before the wedding breakfast was over], theology and philosophy think they see that their marriage was a mistake. While waiting for the decree of divorce, which is not long in coming, they proceed to divide their effects. Each resumes possession of its own problems, and warns the other against interference.[1]

The grounds for this divorce were laid by such thinkers as John Duns Scotus, William of Ockham, and the mystic Meister Eckhart.

JOHN DUNS SCOTUS

|||

The Subtle Scottish Professor

Little is known for sure about John Duns Scotus's life. He was born somewhere around 1266 in Scotland.* As a young man, he entered the Franciscan order and went on to study at Oxford and Paris, exhibiting a sharp mind and an aptitude for mathematics. He spent his life lecturing and writing at Oxford, Paris, and Cologne. After working in the latter city for only a year, he died in 1308, in his early forties. The authenticity of Scotus's works is very much disputed. Some works are clearly authentic, while others once attributed to him are now known to be unauthentic, and scholars disagree about yet other manuscripts. Duns Scotus is difficult to read, because he is not a clear writer. Nevertheless, most agree that the difficulty of his writings stems as much from his intellectually challenging and subtle arguments as from his lack of writing skills. In fact, his contemporaries called him Doctor Subtilis ("The Subtle Doctor"). He had many followers, who were known as "Dunsmen" or "dunces." They were the prime objects of vilification by the Renaissance humanists, who viewed them and their Scholastic philosophy as barriers to enlightenment and intellectual progress. As a result, the name *dunce* came to mean a dull, ignorant person.

Theory of Knowledge: Restricting Reason

In this brief summary, we will ignore the overly complicated details of Scotus's epistemology and simply note his differences with Thomas Aquinas on the issue of faith and reason. Scotus agrees with Aquinas that there can be no conflict between truths of faith and truths of reason, and he uses philosophical reasoning to defend his theories. But Duns Scotus restricts the sphere of reason much more than Aquinas did. Scotus's studies in mathematics gave him a model of what real demonstration was, and by comparison a great deal of Aquinas's arguments in natural theology fell short. Although he agreed with Aquinas that the Trinity cannot be proven by reason, Scotus also excluded from rational discussion or proof such topics as a number of the aspects of God's nature, as well as divine providence and the immortality of soul. Only faith can give us certainty in these matters, he claimed. Contrary to the Thomistic position,† philosophy and theology are completely different types of inquiry for Scotus. Whereas philosophy is a theoretical discipline, the knowledge sought for in theology, he says, "should be described as practical."[2] Scotus's attempt to impose limits on the sphere of reason was the first step in the unraveling of the Scholastic synthesis of faith and reason. Later thinkers would be much more radical in limiting reason.

Metaphysics: Moving Away from Scholasticism

UNIVERSALS AND INDIVIDUALITY

On the issue of universals, Scotus avoids all the traditional answers. Contrary to the realists, he claims that only individuals are real, but in opposition to the nominalists he believed that universals do have some objective reality. Although this would seem to place him in agreement with Aquinas, they differ on what distinguishes one individual of a species from another. Aquinas thought that it had to be their individual matter that distinguished Socrates from Plato, because they both exemplify the same form of humanity. However, Scotus argues that

---

*"Scotus" means "the Scot." In Scotus's time, unlike that of John Scotus Erigena four centuries earlier, only inhabitants of Scotland, and not the Irish, were called Scots.

†The adjective *Thomistic* is derived from the name "Thomas of Aquinas."

since matter is an indefinite bundle of potentialities, it cannot define the concrete individuality of a Socrates. Nor can something so indefinite be the object of knowledge. If the Thomistic answer fails, how does Scotus think we can have knowledge of individuals? Since Scotus retained the Aristotelian assumption that we can only know forms, if we can know concrete individuals at all, a form must constitute each individual thing. Inherent in the universal nature (the essence or *whatness* of any particular) is the individual nature (its *thisness*). The Latin term for this individuating difference is *haecceitas*. Just as there is a form of humanity, so there is a form unique to Socrates and one unique to Plato that are the unique but fully knowable features of each person. The form of "human" does not exist separately from "Platoneity" (as we may call Plato's unique form), but it may be distinguished in a formal way. Although this attempt to combine a Greek notion of universals with a greater focus on individuality is somewhat complicated, Duns Scotus's emphasis on the reality of individuals took a beginning step away from the worldview of the medieval thinkers.

NATURAL THEOLOGY

Concerning arguments for the existence of God, Scotus seems to agree with Aquinas that such demonstrations must be based on our experience of the world. However, he questions the absolute certainty of most of the Thomistic proofs. For example, he says the argument from motion shows there must be a first mover. However, any proof taken from the physical world cannot go beyond the physical world. Hence, this argument limits us to the world of motion and does not give us a necessary divine being that is the cause of all other beings. However, Scotus does find some value in reconstructed versions of the arguments from efficient causality and contingency. Finally, unlike Thomas, he does find value in Anselm's ontological argument but thinks it needs to be "touched up" with a premise stating that a necessary being is possible. However, he thinks the only evidence we can give for the possibility of such a being is some "persuasive considerations." In doing so, he

changes it into an empirical and probabilistic argument. In summary, Duns Scotus believed the theistic arguments were considerably weaker than Aquinas supposed, for they tend to be probability arguments only and not rigorous demonstrations.

Duns Scotus similarly differs with Aquinas on the issue of immortality. Thomas Aquinas believed the human soul necessarily survived the death of the body. Once again, Scotus says this is a matter of probability only. After all, God could have created the soul in such a way that it would perish with the body. Although it is reasonable to suppose the soul is immortal, this cannot be demonstrated. Our certainty that the soul was, in fact, given an immortal nature by God is based on faith alone. This is a good example of the way in which these late medieval writers tended to give faith sovereignty over much of the domain that Thomas Aquinas thought should be shared with reason.

Moral Philosophy and the Primacy of the Will

An important issue in both the psychology and the ethics of medieval philosophy was the relationship between the will and the intellect.* For Aquinas, the intellect was the higher, nobler, and more worthy faculty of the soul. For Duns Scotus, however, the will is superior to the intellect, a claim that aligns him with voluntarism and Augustine's later thought. Scotus's arguments are that, first, knowledge is simply an instrument of the will. The intellect provides the will with information and alternatives, but it is the will that decides between the alternatives. Second, the will can move the intellect in the sense that we can choose what we will think about. Third, the will is completely free and cannot be determined by anything, including the intellect. Thomas Aquinas agreed with the Greeks that we necessarily will what we think to be the highest good. However, Scotus asserts that the will is not determined by a knowledge of the good, but only chooses the good

---

*See Chapter 10 for the initial discussion of this issue.

if it freely decides to do so. Whereas the intellect is determined by the object known, the will can accept or reject what is brought before it. Hence, "the total cause of willing in the will is the will."[3] Whereas Aquinas's intellectualism dictated that we find eternal blessedness in contemplating God, Scotus's voluntarism led him to say that we find blessedness in the love of God, an act of the will that unites us with him. Hence, Scotus does not agree with Aquinas that morality is based on the natural tendency to pursue happiness. Instead, morality may require an act of justice that interferes with our own advantage and happiness. The obligations of morality depend solely on what God commands, independent of considerations of personal happiness. Aquinas thought we can discern the moral law by studying human nature, but Duns Scotus thought there is no way to learn ethical truths by natural means.

This voluntarism also applies to God. His actions are not determined by his reason. Duns Scotus thought this must be the case if God is completely free and fully omnipotent. Consequently, our reason cannot know his purposes or deduce his actions from *a priori* principles. Since all things are contingent on the free will of God, there is no rational necessity to things and the universe could have been otherwise than it is. If God's choices were logically necessary, we could reason out the details of the world like a system of Euclidean geometry. Since we cannot do so, it is clear God was free in creating the world and, hence, the features of creation are all contingent.

The command to love God is the only moral law concerned with what is good in itself. All other actions are good simply because they are commanded by God and not because of the ends they achieve. However, Scotus qualifies this point by saying that the first set of commands in the Ten Commandments are rationally necessary moral truths. These are the commands that say you should have no other gods but the one true God, you should not make any idols, you should not take the name of the Lord your God in vain, and you should remember the Sabbath day to keep it holy. Scotus argues that these commands follow from God's love of himself, and it would be self-contradictory for him to command otherwise. Hence, if there is any natural law, it is to be found here. However, the rest of the divine commandments are products of God's sovereign will, and therefore they are not rationally necessary. Their only claim on our conscience is that God commanded them. Presumably, God could have just as easily decreed that murder, adultery, and stealing were not wrong.

In summary, although John Duns Scotus differed from the thinkers of the thirteenth century on a number of points, in many ways he was continuous with them. He serves as a transitional figure to the later theologians (such as William of Ockham) who took what were mere tendencies in Scotus and carried them to their furthest extreme.

WILLIAM OF OCKHAM

Ockham's Controversial Life

William of Ockham was born sometime between 1280 and 1290 in the village of Ockham, near London. He entered the Franciscan order at an early age and studied theology at Oxford. Although he had completed his courses and had begun lecturing and writing, he never achieved his master's degree because some suspected that he had embraced dangerous and heretical doctrines. The end result was that in 1324 he was summoned to the papal court in Avignon, France, and was forced to remain there for four years while a commission of theologians investigated the charges of heresy. He filled these years of waiting by writing on theology, philosophy, and physics. In 1327, while still at Avignon, he became involved in a controversy over how literally St. Francis's vow of poverty should be interpreted. Ockham sided with the head of the Franciscan order in condemning the materialism and excesses of the papacy and in attempting to return the Church back to Francis's ideal of a simple lifestyle. In 1328 it became clear that Pope John XXII was about to issue an official condemnation of their position. Consequently, Ockham and his superior fled and sought the protection of Emperor Louis of Bavaria. On his arrival, Ockham supposedly said to the Emperor, "Protect me with your sword, and I will defend you with my pen." Ockham and the others involved in the revolt were excommunicated by the Pope. Ockham then took up residence in Munich and continued to write. At this point in his life, he moved into more extreme political positions and wrote tracts opposing the Pope's claim to temporal power. His writings developed a political theory that pointed in the direction of the secularization of politics. After Louis's death in 1347, it appears that Ockham may have sought to be reconciled with Pope Clement VI, but it is not clear whether or not this took place. While the facts of his death are not certain, Ockham is believed to have died in 1349 of the Black Plague that devastated northern Europe at this time.

Ockham's Two Tasks

Ockham's philosophy was guided by two fundamental themes. The first was a very rigorous conception of God's omnipotence. He takes this to be the supreme principle that must inform all our thinking about the world. As he expresses it, "I believe in God, father almighty; which I understand thus, that everything which does not involve a manifest contradiction is to be attributed to the divine power."[4] On the face of it, this sounds like a very pious affirmation of faith. Indeed, for Ockham, it was just that. However, as we will see, from this central conviction he draws some very radical conclusions in the areas of epistemology, metaphysics, and ethics. Basically, he argues that if God is all-powerful, then his creation of the world was not guided by any rational necessities. Everything

in the world is **contingent**.* Since this is the case, then only experience can tell us about the existence of things in the world and their properties.

Ockham's second guiding theme was a rigorous empiricism that condemned any tendencies to go beyond experience by appealing to unnecessary hypothetical or speculative explanations. This was a methodological principle that later writers called **"Ockham's razor"** and that modern scientists now call the "principle of parsimony" or the "principle of economy." One of the ways Ockham expressed it was to say, "What can be explained on fewer principles is explained needlessly by more."[5] This principle works like a razor because it "shaves" off all unnecessary entities in our explanations. Ockham particularly used this principle in his attempts to show that reality can be explained without appeal to the realm of universals. Although this principle was not original to him (it can be found in Aristotle), it followed from Ockham's very austere view of what was really necessary to account for the world. This principle turned out to be very influential in the replacement of Aristotelian science by the much more economical theories of modern science.

Theory of Knowledge: Denying Universals

KNOWLEDGE BEGINS IN EXPERIENCE

Ockham began his epistemology with a strong statement of empiricism. He says all knowledge about the world is grounded in *intuitive knowledge*.† As he expresses it, "Nothing can be naturally known in itself, unless it is known intuitively."[6] Intuitive knowledge includes our perception of external things as well as our immediate awareness of our own inner states such as acts of will, joy, and

---

*The existence of something is contingent if there is no logical contradiction in either supposing that it exists or does not exist. For example, kangaroos exist in our world, but we can imagine a world without them. Hence, kangaroos are contingent beings.
†"Intuition" here does not mean some sort of inner feeling or insight, but refers to whatever is directly evident to the mind.

sorrow. He sometimes refers to intuitive knowledge as "experimental knowledge." Since, under normal conditions, intuitive knowledge is directly related to its object, it can tell us about what does or does not exist.

Any knowledge not related to an object of immediate experience is a derivative form of knowledge called *abstractive knowledge*. This knowledge is a pale residue left in the mind by our original experiences. The objects of these experiences are retained in the mind as concepts or mental signs. Concepts cannot provide evidence of what exists, as does intuitive knowledge, since the object that once produced them may no longer exist. However, they do serve as the vehicles of the understanding. Abstractive knowledge includes the image or memory of a specific thing minus the concrete details of its existence. Abstractive knowledge also includes what we usually call "abstract ideas" or ideas that refer to an entire category of individuals such as "animal," "tree," and "book." These ideas appear to be universals, because they are vague and indistinct representations that gloss over the details of the many particular individuals that were the cause of these ideas. However, they are not true universals, because they lack any sort of metaphysical status of their own.

Ockham's Nominalism

The most important parts of Ockham's epistemology revolve around his theory of signs. A sign is something that stands for or represents something else. There are two kinds of signs: natural and conventional. Natural signs occur whenever an object signifies its cause. For example, smoke is a sign of fire. However, another kind of natural sign is produced by perception when a particular object creates an image or mental picture within us. For example, when we see a red rose it causes a red rose image to be retained in our mind. This kind of sign has some degree of universality because the image will be the same for all people with similar experiences. The mental image or concept is a natural sign of its cause and is able to signify the rose. Conventional signs, in contrast,

are produced when each culture invents words to refer to these mental images.

Some terms are signs of specific individuals, such as "Plato." Other terms are signs of many individuals, such as "human." Whereas Aquinas thought that the common features of humanity shared by Socrates and Plato were real features of the world, Ockham insisted that universal statements are really a summary of the particular judgments we make about individuals. Saying, "All dogs are furry," is a shorthand way of saying, "Lassie the dog is furry, and Spot the dog is furry, and Rover the dog is furry, and so on." There is not some additional reality, in addition to the individual dogs, the form of "Furriness," in which all these dogs participate. Instead, the verbal sign "furry" signifies the mental sign that was formed by numerous experiences with creatures with similar properties. These mental images and the terms attached to them are all we need to explain human thinking. Thus we can do without all the excess baggage of the theory of universals. Hence, there are no universals in things themselves, and neither do any exist in our minds. Instead, there are only mental signs that refer to individuals or groups of individuals and that serve as the tools of thought. We think *about* particulars, but we think *with* mental signs.

In the final analysis, Ockham has reduced the metaphysical problem of universals to simply this question of logic: How can we use general terms and proper names in propositions to refer to individuals? Ockham's nominalism should be distinguished from the extreme nominalism of Roscelin and his school. They recognized only conventional signs in human thought, whereas Ockham recognizes that concepts function as natural signs. Thus, some prefer to call him a "conceptualist" or "terminist."

Since universals do not really exist, God cannot conceive of them either. God can have an idea of what he is going to create, but this is always an idea of a particular individual. If we say God created the human species, God did not have in mind the form of "Humanity." Instead, he had in mind the multitude of distinct individual people, all of whom somewhat resemble each other. That is all there is to the notion of species.

Metaphysics and the Limits of Reason

THE PRIMACY OF THE INDIVIDUAL

The key to Ockham's view of reality is his conviction that the concrete individual is the only true and genuine reality, the only object of scientific study. The world is a world of individuals that have the qualities they have because this is how God chose to create them. If there were eternal essences, these would limit God's power to freely create as he wished. The fact that God created the world gives us no knowledge of what is there or what it is like. Likewise, examining the world does not give us rational knowledge that there is a God. If everything in the world is contingent, then there are no necessary connections that allow us to draw inferences from one thing to the nature or existence of another thing.

CAUSALITY

Ockham's empiricism and his emphasis on the contingency of all features of the world, led him to take a very radical position on the nature of causality. He believed we could know that every event had some cause or other. However, he realized that experience can only give us probability judgments about the relationship between one specific type of cause and a specific effect. Ordinarily, when we say that "X causes Y" we are saying that whenever X occurs it is followed by Y and that some power in X makes it necessary that Y will occur. However, Ockham argues that all that we really experience is a regularity within experience such that when X is present Y is present, and when X is absent Y is absent. We never experience the hypothesized causal power in X nor the alleged necessity of its effect. There may be a causal relation between X and Y as a matter of fact, but it cannot be known with certainty. For example, we observe that when fire is present (X), things become hot (Y). However, apart from experiencing this sequence, the knowledge of fire alone could not tell us its effect. If he had wanted to, God could have arranged it that the presence of fire would be correlated with things becoming cold. Only experience can tell us what to expect from a given cause, and this knowledge is always probable. If there is no logically necessary relationship between X and Y, then God can, on occasion, produce Y without it being preceded by X, as is normally the case. Hence, Ockham's empiricism provides support for his belief in the possibility of miracles. Normally, God maintains the uniformity of nature, and it is the normal, regular sequences that science studies. But if everything is contingent, there is no contradiction in supposing that God could change the normal sequence of events. The contingency of creation casts doubt on our ability to "capture" the structure of reality in our theories—an assumption central to most of the preceding Western philosophical tradition.

THE DECLINE OF METAPHYSICS

The outcome of Ockham's position is that the importance of metaphysics severely diminishes. Logic simply tells us about the relationship between our mental signs and propositions. It cannot give us factual information about the world, because this can only be provided by experience. Ockham's razor dictated that we should not try to explain something *in* the world by speculating about what is *behind* and *beyond* it. He dismissed any explanation in terms of final causes, saying that they are mere metaphors. Applying his standards of evidence, he showed that many of Aristotle's principles in physics and astronomy were not necessary and self-evident and suggested that any given phenomenon could be explained by many different speculative theories. Furthermore, his view of causality had an enormous impact on the rise of modern science. Instead of trying to find the logical relations between things (for there are no logical necessities in the world), the scientist should instead faithfully observe and catalogue only the empirical facts and their regular sequences. This approach had both good and bad consequences for science. It was a helpful corrective to the medieval-Aristotelian tendency to reason about what *must* be the case instead of observing what actually *is* the case. Under the new approach, empirical discoveries were made that would have been overlooked by the older methods. However, cataloguing observations alone would not have given us the powerful laws and theories of modern physics, for (contrary to Ockham) science cannot do without speculation and theorizing. We now know that what we see (the readings of our instruments and medium-sized objects) can be understood only in terms of entities that we cannot observe directly (subatomic particles). Science cannot avoid theorizing about what is behind and beyond the observable facts. Furthermore, in their attempts to mathematically comprehend the world, modern scientists assume (contrary to Ockham) that there are logically necessary relationships in nature.

REJECTION OF NATURAL THEOLOGY

What Ockham has said thus far allows no foothold for natural theology. Since all knowledge of what exists arises from experience (intuitive knowledge), and since we do not have direct experience of God in this life, we cannot prove his existence or attributes. Only faith and revelation can tell us about these matters. Furthermore, his view on causality undermines the Thomistic arguments. If we only know an effect, we can know that it has *a* cause, but apart from past experience of the causes of similar effects, we cannot reason to the nature of an unknown cause. Hence, we cannot reason from our knowledge of the world to the nature of its cause. To make this point, Ockham critically examines the traditional arguments for the existence of God. The only argument he admits might have some value is Aquinas's argument from efficient causality. Although he believes it can be proven that the world requires some conserving cause, he does not think that reason can show that there is only one such cause nor that this cause has the attrib-

utes of the biblical God. Thus, when we rely on natural reason, probability has replaced Aquinas's certainty about metaphysical issues.

Ockham's razor also affected other issues in natural theology besides the existence of God. Whereas philosophers from Plato to Aquinas thought they could prove that humans had a spiritual nature and were immortal, Ockham says we can only know this on the basis of revelation. All we experience are our internal activities and states such as thinking, willing, joy, and sorrow. We have no experience of the spiritual substance that underlies these psychological activities. Thus, we cannot prove that there is a soul, much less that it is immortal.

Moral Philosophy: Radical Voluntarism

With Duns Scotus, Ockham's moral philosophy revolves around the notion of freedom of the will, both human and divine. It is our free will that makes us moral agents. If an action is determined by natural causes, the person is not responsible and can neither be praised nor blamed. Furthermore, it is the will that makes an action morally good or bad. An otherwise good action done from an evil intention is not a morally good act.

Ockham's very strong view of God's omnipotence makes his moral theory extremely radical. If God is all-powerful, then the whole created order is contingent and a product of divine free choice. However, Ockham includes the moral law within the contingent order of the world. Since there is no universal essence of human nature in the divine mind, no unchangeable natural law follows from this essence. Not only could God have created humans any way he chose, but after creating them he could also have created any moral laws for them he chose. Thus, Ockham pushes the tendencies in Scotus's moral philosophy to their furthest extreme. For Ockham, God is not bound by any law or principles. He is free in thought, will, and action, and therefore anything is possible that is not a contradiction. Hence, actions now considered sins, such as murder and adultery, could have been ethically good, and their performance meritorious, if God had willed them so. However, as a matter of contingent fact, such acts are wrong in the current moral order, simply because this is what God has decided. From these examples, there is clearly no way we can reason to the rightness or wrongness of an action by appealing to natural law. We are totally dependent on revelation for ethical conclusions, because this is the only way we can know what God willed.

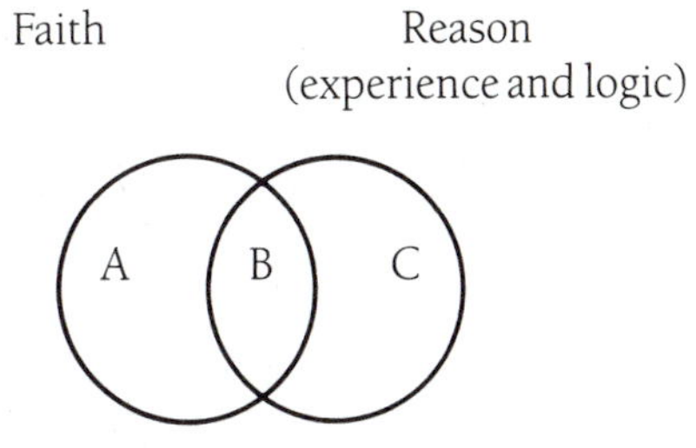

FIGURE 12-1 Thomas Aquinas's model

Summary and Evaluation of Ockham

The ideas Ockham set in motion led to bitter disputes between the realists and nominalists. In 1339 the University of Paris prohibited the use of Ockham's books and in 1340 officially rejected nominalism. More than a century later in 1473, all the teachers in the university were bound by oath to teach realism. However, other universities founded at this time embraced much more freedom of thought and permitted nominalism: Prague in 1348, Vienna in 1365, Heidelberg in 1386, Cologne in 1388.

Ockham's views on the relationship between the various kinds of reality and spheres of knowledge both unraveled the Scholastic synthesis of faith and reason as well as opened the door to the autonomy of science. The difference between Thomas Aquinas and William of Ockham can be illustrated by the circles in Figure 12-1. For Thomas, the spheres of faith and reason were intertwined. The propositions of faith are known through biblical revelation and Church authority. Reason includes all the information that can be gained from our natural cognitive capacities through the combination of experience and logic. Although some truths could only be known on the basis of faith and revelation (A), some of the truths about supernatural things (B) also fall within the domain of philosophy and can be proven by reason. Likewise, truths about the natural world (C) can be arrived at by reasoning about experience.

Whereas Aquinas had announced a marriage between revelation and natural knowledge, Ock-ham initiated divorce proceedings between them (see Figure 12-2). For Ockham, the truths of theology are completely separate from what we can know through experience or logic. The supernatural and the natural operate in different spheres with different concerns. By means of revelation, faith (A) can give us knowledge about God and spiritual realities. However, it cannot give us knowledge about the world, for given the freedom of God, theology cannot tell us the way that the world is or must be. It is experience (B) that tells us what the created world is like. But from our knowledge of the world, we cannot reason back to God or his attributes because an effect by itself cannot tell us about its cause. Logic (C) is isolated in a sphere by itself and can neither tell us about divine things nor about the world. Logic only tells us about the relationship between propositions. Since reason cannot give us any substantive knowledge about reality (divine or natural), philosophy is almost left without a mission. Ockham's philosophical conclusions attempt to establish the appropriate boundaries between the different spheres of knowledge, but once these are clarified, philosophy can make few (if any) contributions to our knowledge.

In thus drawing the boundaries of knowledge, Ockham's goal was to protect faith from the encroachments of philosophy and science. Faith was in a hermetically sealed sphere unto itself. No argument of the philosophers or new discovery in science could count for or against what the Christian believes. However, in putting theology beyond the reach of reason, Ockham unintentionally freed both philosophy and science to independently pursue their own concerns without the burden of

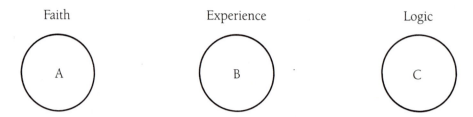

FIGURE 12-2 William of Ockham's model

making their results consistent with theological traditions. Since reason was forbidden to concern itself with matters of faith, it could now concentrate on natural phenomena. In William of Ockham, philosophy was no longer the handmaiden of theology, but took on the new role of being an independent entrepreneur. Although many accused him of being skeptical and of attacking the intellectual foundations of religion, Ockham appeared to have a firm, personal commitment to the Christian faith. However, though his intentions were thoroughly pious, Ockham actually encouraged the secularization of philosophy and science. His emphasis on faith and revelation also influenced the Reformation, as Protestant theologians sought to rediscover the simple doctrines of the Bible, freed from the baggage of theological traditions. One historian says that "for sheer destructive capacity" Ockham was unequaled in this period of time.[7]

CHANGES IN THE METHODS OF SCIENCE

William of Ockham's philosophy set in motion a number of changes in how scientists perceived their task. First, his empiricism emphasized that experience is the key to understanding the world. Second, his methodological "razor" recommended that scientists stick to the facts and do away with all metaphysical speculation. Although this was a helpful corrective to the tendency of medieval scientists to force their observations into the confines of their Aristotelian assumptions, this fear of speculation would eventually need to be moderated to make room for the role of theory in science. Third, Ockham's emphasis on the freedom of God and the contingency of the world actually favored science, even though his position was motivated sheerly by theological concerns. If we can't reason about how the world necessarily *must* be, we can only look and see how God happened to make it.

Ockham's ideas generated a new interest in mathematics, astronomy, and physics by freeing scientists of the burden of making their conclusions consistent with theological and philosophical traditions.

One example must suffice to show how the revolution in science began to take place within the fourteenth century. Medieval scientists had taken for granted (following Aristotle) that the earth was the natural resting place of all terrestrial objects. Thus, they considered it the essence of material bodies to "desire" their natural place. This example shows the tendency of medieval scientists to explain the world in terms of final causes, or the end sought by objects. They knew that bodies accelerate as they fall, but they theorized that as a falling body gets closer to its goal, its natural appetite is increased and it speeds up its journey home. John Buridan (around 1320–1382), a student of Ockham, rejected this answer on an experimental basis. If velocity was merely a function of proximity to earth, then a stone dropped from a tower ought to have the same velocity when it reaches a point 1 foot from the earth as a similar stone at that position that had been dropped from a height of only 4 feet. But obviously, a stone whose starting point was a great height will be moving much faster. A stone dropped from a tower can kill a bystander, but the same stone dropped from a few feet cannot. Accordingly, Buridan developed a new account of the physics of acceleration. Using Ockham's razor, he gave a simpler account of the phenomenon without appealing to final causes or natural ends.

MYSTICISM

Ockham's nominalism and radical empiricism helped support the growing movement of mysticism. If logic cannot tell us about God and we can only know what we directly experience, then instead of trying to *understand* God conceptually, we should strive to *experience* him. Religious mysticism emphasizes that God can only be known through a special kind of religious experience. The typical mystic claims that language and reason are too limited and abstract to adequately comprehend an infinite and transcendent God. Therefore, the mystic seeks to rise above our normal modes of cognition and encounter God in an overwhelming, religious experience. This experience is characterized by an immediate feeling of the absolute oneness of the self with the divine and a sense of peace and bliss. The mystics' claim that they could directly encounter the object of knowledge (God) was the religious version of what Ockham called "intuitive knowledge." Mysticism was a persistent movement throughout most of the medieval period. However, it became much more prevalent toward the end of the thirteenth century. By downplaying the importance of reason and propositional knowledge, it became another force that undermined Scholastic rationalism.

The greatest mystic of this time was Meister Eckhart (1260–1327), a German Dominican. Even though he was very influential, his writings were condemned in 1329, two years after his death. Although he worked from within a Thomistic framework, his metaphysical inquiries were always directed toward the goal of charting the soul's journey toward oneness with the divine. Influenced by the Neoplatonic tradition, Eckhart viewed God as the One, an absolutely transcendent unity.* Since we use definitions and concepts to limit and grasp what we are trying to understand, they are inadequate instruments for apprehending God. God cannot be captured in the snare of reason. The consequences of this conviction may be the reason some labeled Eckhart a heretic. He frequently put forth a thesis and defended it and then turned around and defended its antithesis. Although this gives the impression that he was contradicting himself, he may have been trying to show the impossibility of pouring the divine nature into our limited intellectual categories. To use an analogy, suppose the only color words we had were *red* and *blue*. How would we describe a purple object? We might first say it is red. But this does not quite fit, so then we would describe it as blue. But this is not accurate either. Purple is both red and blue, and it is neither red nor blue. Just as these limited color categories are inadequate to describe the color purple, so Eckhart thought our theological categories were necessarily inadequate to describe God.

When the Church authorities looked at some of Eckhart's bold and exaggerated statements in isolation, they thought he was teaching heresies.

---

*Notice the similarities of these terms to those of Pseudo-Dionysius and John Scotus Erigena in Chapter 9.

For example, following the Neoplatonists, he says that God is above being or existence, since he is the source of being. Yet in other passages he says God is existence itself. Furthermore, he claims God is not like a craftsman whose product exists outside himself, implying that creation exists as a part of the being of God. When his critics focused narrowly on such passages apart from his other statements, they understandably assumed he was guilty of the heresy of pantheism. However, in other passages he balances out the picture by saying that God and his creation are distinct and that God is above it.

As with any mystic, the goal of Eckhart's theology was not to proliferate ideas about God but to lead the soul to union with God. Below the level of the intellect, in the innermost recesses of the soul, is the human essence, the "spark" that contains the divine image. This is the part of us capable of joining with God in a mystical union.

"God and I, we are one," Eckhart says.[8] Just as fire changes wood into itself, "so are we changed into God."[9] To achieve this unity, we must negate our individuality. We must empty our souls of everything until we know nothing, desire nothing, and have nothing. Just as I cannot give you anything if your hand is closed and grasping something else, so the soul must be open and empty, purged of even the desire for God and eternity, before God can fill it with himself.

Despite his call to rise above the limits of reason, Meister Eckhart always maintained an interest in metaphysical speculation. His followers, however, tended to leave this focus behind and emphasized the more religiously practical and experiential side of his thought. The influence of his religious mysticism has lasted through the centuries. The great Protestant Reformer Martin Luther was so inspired by his writings that he published one of them under the title of *A German Theology*.

THE DECLINE OF MEDIEVAL PHILOSOPHY

We began our discussion of the high Middle Ages in Chapter 10 with a comparison between the soaring structures of the Gothic cathedrals and the intellectual systems of the Scholastics. Once again, the architecture of the times may serve as a metaphor for the developments in philosophy. The Beauvais Cathedral in France was begun in 1247, about the time that Aquinas began his theological studies. With a ceiling that rose to a height of 157 feet, it was to be the ultimate realization of the architects' obsession to thrust their buildings into the skies. However, ten years after Aquinas died (in 1284), the main structural arches of Beauvais collapsed, unable to bear the weight that had been imposed on them. From then on, the grandiose attempts to push church architecture beyond all previous limits were abandoned. Architects became more conservative

and the size of their cathedrals became more modest, as they recognized the limits of our human abilities to penetrate the heavens with our earthbound structures.

Similarly, the influential thinkers in the fourteenth century became convinced of the limits of human reason and their philosophies were correspondingly modest in their aspirations. Nominalism, voluntarism, the separation of faith and reason, Ockham's empiricism, and the rise of mysticism all contributed to the collapse of the "cathedrals of reason" that thinkers such as Aquinas had labored to build. From Ockham's insistence that theology be based on revelation and not on philosophy, it was a short step to reducing revelation to the words of Scripture alone. This was a step taken by John Wyclif and the later Protestant Reformers. In fact, Martin Luther, the great sixteenth-century

Reformer, was deeply influenced by his reading of Ockham. Those who followed after Ockham credited him with replacing the old ways of thinking with the "new way" (via moderna). However, from the enthusiasm of the Ockhamites it would be incorrect to suppose that the achievements of the Scholastics were abandoned on the trash heap of history. An updated Thomism continues on in the twentieth century as a live philosophical movement. Even the philosophers in the seventeenth century, who so desperately wanted to separate themselves from the Middle Ages, still depended on the terminology and conceptions of the age they disdained. For example, Descartes, Spinoza, Leibniz, and Locke were indebted to their medieval predecessors for their arguments for the existence of God as well as their discussions of substance and causality.[10]

For us in the twentieth century, products of five centuries of modern thought, much in medieval thought appears dusty, antiquarian, outmoded, and abstract. Thus, it may be helpful to leave this chapter with some sense of what made the medieval outlook so satisfying for a thousand years. The historian of philosophy W. T. Jones has expressed it nicely:

> Perhaps the principal element of this world view was its sacramental outlook. What made Augustine, Aquinas, and the other medieval thinkers so fundamentally alike was this outlook they shared. What distinguishes the modern mind so sharply from the medieval mind is that modern men have largely lost that outlook and now share the basically secular point of view of the Greeks. To say that medieval men looked on this world as a sacrament means, first, that they conceived this world to be but the visible sign of an invisible reality, a world thoroughly impregnated with the energy, purpose, and love of its Creator, who dwells in it as He dwells in the bread and wine on the altar. Second, it means that medieval men conceived of this world as a sacrifice to be freely and gratefully dedicated to the all-good, all-true Giver. Thus, whereas for us (and for the Greeks) the world by and large means just what it seems to be, for men of the Middle Ages it meant something beyond itself and immeasurably better. Whereas for us

> (and for the Greeks) life on earth is its own end, for medieval men life's true end was beyond this world. It can hardly be denied that this sacramental point of view was a block to progress—progress in knowledge of how to control the environment and utilize it for this-worldly purposes. To many it seems equally obvious, now that this viewpoint has disappeared, that men have rid themselves of much that was a liability—ignorance, superstition, intolerance. What is not so obvious is that the modern world has also lost something of value. If the sacramental outlook of the Middle Ages manifested itself here and there in what a modern clinician would describe as acute psychopathology, it also manifested itself in serenity and confidence, in a sense of purpose, meaningfulness, and fulfillment—qualities that the modern clinician looks for in vain among his contemporaries.[11]

Questions for Understanding

1. What changes occurred in the period from 1300 to 1500 that either caused or signaled the decline of Scholasticism?

2. List some of the ways in which Duns Scotus's philosophy differed from Aquinas's.

3. What does Ockham mean when he says everything in the world is contingent? What are the implications of this for the project of a metaphysics based on reason?

4. What is "Ockham's razor"?

5. In what ways did Ockham's view undermine Aquinas's natural theology?

6. What are the implications of Okham's voluntarism for ethics? How does it differ from Aquinas's approach?

7. How do Aquinas and Ockham differ on the relationship between faith and reason?

8. How do the outlooks of Aquinas and Meister Eckhart differ?

Questions for Reflection

1. What are some reasons for either accepting or rejecting Ockham's voluntarism?

2. Ockham's philosophy was largely motivated by theological concerns. Nevertheless, briefly

set out some of the reasons his philosophy contributed to the rise of modern science.

3. Reread the quote by W. T. Jones at the end of the chapter. Construct an argument to support the view that the medieval worldview was a more satisfying one than ours. Construct an argument for the opposite conclusion. Which argument do you think is the stronger one?

Notes

1. Quoted in David Knowles, *The Evolution of Medieval Thought* (Baltimore: Helicon Press, 1962), 300.

2. Quoted in Gordon Leff, *Medieval Thought: St. Augustine to Ockham* (Chicago: Quadrangle Books, 1959), 164.

3. Quoted in Leff, 270.

4. Quodlibet 6, Question 6, in *Selections from Medieval Philosophers*, vol. 2, ed. Richard McKeon (New York: Scribner's, 1958), 373.

5. Quoted in E. A. Moody, *The Logic of William of Ockham* (New York: Russell & Russell, 1965), 49.

6. 1 Sent. 3.2, F, quoted in Frederick Copleston, *A History of Philosophy* vol. 3, part 1 (Garden City, NY: Doubleday Image, 1963), 74.

7. Leff, 279.

8. Sermon 6 of the German sermons, trans. Edmund Colledge in *Meister Eckhart: The Essential Sermons, Commentaries, Treatises, and Defense*, ed. Edmund Colledge and Bernard McGinn, *The Classics of Western Spirituality* (New York: Paulist Press, 1981), 188.

9. Ibid., 189.

10. These points are made by Julius R. Weinberg in *A Short History of Medieval Philosophy* (Princeton, NJ: Princeton University Press, 1967), 291.

11. W. T. Jones, *A History of Western Philosophy*, 2d ed., vol. 2, *The Medieval Mind* (New York: Harcourt, Brace & World, 1969), xix.

III

THE MODERN PERIOD

Cultural Context: Renaissance, Reformation, and the Rise of Modern Science

WITH THE DEATH OF WILLIAM OF OCKHAM sometime around the year 1349, Scholastic philosophy lost its last significant writer, an indication that medieval philosophy had run its course. There would not be another philosopher of importance until Francis Bacon first began publishing in the early 1600s. In the meantime, while philosophy was retooling and changing its gears, the period of history known as the Renaissance was coming into focus. The term *Renaissance* means "rebirth" and roughly designates the period from 1350 to 1650. Obviously, people did not stop thinking in medieval ways on January 1, 1350. But somewhere around this time, a new spirit began to stir within the culture. This age considered itself a reawakening of the *human* spirit that had lain dormant for the long interval of the medieval period. The term *Middle Ages*, coined around 1450, refers to the thousand-year period running roughly from Augustine to Ockham. The people of the Renaissance considered the medieval period a lapse, an unfortunate detour from the intellectual and cultural progress that began in classical Greece.

During the Renaissance Christopher Columbus sought a shorter route to India and ended up sailing into the Western Hemisphere. For our purposes, his voyage of discovery can serve as a metaphor of the changes occurring at this time. The "New World" expanded European people's geographical horizons, requiring that all the previous maps be revised. In the same way, the Renaissance thinkers were revising all their conceptual maps as they expanded the horizons of literature, religion, economics, science, and philosophy.

Five significant forces interacted together to shape the Renaissance period and its aftermath. First, the rise of Renaissance humanism was a movement within art and literature prompted by the rediscovery of Greek and Roman classics. Second, the Protestant Reformation led to a radical rethinking of existing religious institutions and authority. Third, large-scale social, economic, and political changes affected every area of life. Fourth, the rise of modern science dramatically affected how people viewed their world. Fifth, philosophers proposed new methods for seeking knowledge as they tried to sweep away the past and rebuild the edifice of human knowledge on a new foundation.

Renaissance Humanism

As a cultural movement, the Renaissance began in Italy during the fourteenth century and rapidly spread throughout the rest of Europe. "Humanism" is the word most frequently used to summarize the dominant interests of this age. Hence, it is important to understand what this word means in this context. Since the latter part of the twentieth century, the word *humanism* has been used almost exclusively as a contraction of "secular humanism." However, in the fourteenth and fifteenth centuries, it was a banner carried by thinkers who were predominantly Christian in their outlook. They sought for a new way of understanding the relationship between God, the world, and humanity. The celebration of the richness of the human spirit, the fruits of culture, and the beauty of creation was no longer seen as a turning away from God and spiritual things, but as a way of bringing them down to earth. The artists and writers of this age reveled in the goodness of creation because it was made by a wonderful God. They revered the works of human culture because humanity reflects the divine spirit. In a 1390 letter, a Florentine humanist wrote to a follower of Ockham,

> Do not believe, my friend, that to flee the crowd, to avoid the sight of beautiful things, to shut oneself up in a cloister, is the way to perfection. In fleeing from the world you may topple down from heaven to earth, whereas I, remaining among earthly things, shall be able to lift my heart securely up to heaven. In striving and working, in caring for your family, your friends, your city which comprises all, you cannot but follow the right way to please God.[1]

The most important intellectual event of this time was the rebirth of interest in Greek and Roman literature. Toward the end of the fourteenth century, Greek manuscripts became more widely available in the West. This process was accelerated by the fall of Constantinople in 1453 to the Turks. Constantinople had been a repository of a great mass of ancient Greek manuscripts. As Greek refugees fled the Turks, they brought their language and their manuscripts with them to Europe. Scholars also rediscovered ancient manuscripts that had long lain neglected in monastery libraries and storerooms.

Although the West was familiar with some of Plato's thought and had rediscovered Aristotle in the twelfth century, large portions of their writings had been unavailable. As Latin translations made the complete dialogues of Plato accessible, they sparked an anti-Aristotelian reaction. Aristotle was identified with what many considered to be the logic-chopping, arid, intellectual disputes of the Scholastics. From this perspective, Plato seemed to offer a breath of fresh air, a way for scholars to free their thought from their medieval chains. What was important was the fresh examination of the original texts that ensued. Although scholars needed time to free themselves from their medieval assumptions, at least they could read Plato and Aristotle directly, without having to trust their predecessors' commentaries. Finally, they could enjoy philosophy as an intellectual adventure, rather than merely as a means for defending orthodoxy.

Technology played a role in this rebirth of culture. The invention of the printing press in 1447 had an enormous impact on the culture. Before this, the works of great authors had been available only to nobles or wealthy scholars in the form of handwritten manuscripts. Now intellectual pursuits were given a broader social base. The dramatic change from hand-copied books to mass-produced works is illustrated by the following numbers:

> Forty-five copyists working for two years under Cosimo de Medici produced only two hundred volumes; by 1500 there were in Europe at least nine million books, of thirty thousand titles, and over a thousand printers.[2]

As a result, Plato, Homer, and Cicero became popular best-sellers among the well educated.

The most important outcome of this development was that learning was no longer confined to the clergy, which meant that intellectuals were no longer exclusively theologians. Significantly, from the remaining centuries none of the philosophers whom we will study were clergymen or professional theologians, with the exception of George Berkeley (an Anglican Bishop) in the eighteenth century and Søren Kierkegaard (who never served as a cleric) in the nineteenth century. Furthermore, until we get to Immanuel Kant, none of the philosophers held academic positions.

The world of scholarship and daily life moved closer together as the common tongues such as English and French began to replace Latin in scholarly literature. Rejecting medieval Scholasticism as sterile, abstract intellectualism, many thinkers turned to literature and the arts as a remedy. Renaissance writers commonly believed the classics were the perfection of style, the most ennobling and unsurpassable works humanity had produced. Consequently, they practically idolized and worshiped the classical tradition. This generated an interest in literary studies, and writers tried to copy the elegant style of the classical writers. As the classical style of writing became popular, it brought with it the classical point of view. This outlook gave priority to the autonomy and independence of the individual thinker and exalted the value and dignity of the human personality. People enjoyed a freedom of thought unknown since the time of Alexander the Great.

Desiderius Erasmus (1466–1536) is one of the clearest examples of the spirit of Renaissance humanism. In addition to being one of the greatest classical scholars of his time, Erasmus was known as a popular and entertaining writer. His writings provided a new model for literary expression, and his enthusiasm for classical literature influenced the educational ideals of the age.

Although he was a humanist who exalted the works of the human spirit, he was also a sincere Christian who adopted the "philosophy of Christ" as his model. Finding no tension between pagan classical works and his faith, Erasmus believed the classics held resources that could enhance a thoroughly Christian outlook on life. In a 1522 dialogue called "The Godly Feast," one of his characters says,

> . . . *whatever is devout and contributes to good morals should not be called profane. Sacred Scripture is of course the basic authority in everything; yet I sometimes run across ancient sayings or pagan writings—even the poets—so purely and reverently and admirably expressed that I can't help believing their authors' hearts were moved by some divine power. And perhaps the spirit of Christ is more widespread than we understand, and the company of saints includes many not in our calendar.* [3]

As the conversation continues, another person reflects on Socrates' calmness in the face of death and remarks, "I can hardly help exclaiming, 'Saint Socrates, pray for us!'" [4] Such passages clearly show the admiration Renaissance writers felt for the classical mind as well as the boldness of these sixteenth-century writers.

One of Erasmus's best-known works was *The Praise of Folly* (1509), a witty, ironical, satirical masterpiece in which the personified character of Folly presents all the virtues and foibles of human nature and society. Erasmus attacked the ignorance, hypocrisy, and cruelty of his society in this work; his harshest words were reserved for the Church, including its stuffy theologians, its corrupt and ignorant monks, and its power-loving officials. Naturally, his yearnings for the simple faith of the early Church and his attacks on the contemporary one inspired the Protestant reformers. But Erasmus was interested only in healing the Church, not dividing it. The gentle humanism of Erasmus and his refusal to break with the Church led to his bitter feud with Martin Luther and other Protestant reformers. At the same time, his liberal views provoked the abuse of the conservatives.

It may seem ironic that an age seeking a fresh start seemed only capable of resurrecting the ancient past. However, it is extraordinarily hard to think brand-new ideas and create novel forms of expression. Sometimes we are only able to break from the encrusted patterns of our immediate past by reviving an older model. The Renaissance thinker had all the excitement, fascination, and nostalgia of a middle-aged person going through her possessions in an attic and discovering her own diaries, letters, poetry, and other treasures that had been long packed away and forgotten. By getting in touch with her youthful years and the hopes and dreams that she had laid aside, she can, perhaps, recapture the spirit of her younger, fresher self and allow it to revive her present. Much in the same way, Renaissance thinkers sought to renew their culture by recovering the classical expressions of the human spirit.

The spirit of the times can be seen in the changes occurring in art. Medieval art was highly symbolic. Its purpose was not to portray what was human and earthly, but to use the form of visual representation to turn people's minds heavenward. Where medieval paintings tended to have gilt backgrounds symbolizing heaven, Renaissance paintings showed lush landscapes. Previously, the traditional subjects of art were biblical stories and medieval legends of the saints. These now gave way to classical themes and contemporary subjects. Whether the subject of the painting was the Christian Madonna or the Greek goddess Venus did not seem to matter, for it was the human form of these personages that was the focus. Often one finds curious mixtures of the old and the new in Renaissance art. A painter might paint a landscape with rolling hills and luxuriant foliage, showing that he was reveling in the beauty of nature, but then he would stick a nativity scene in the corner as though this was necessary to justify his art. Sometimes pagan and Christian symbols mix in the same painting. Artists began studying human physiology and tried to create lifelike figures showing real emotions. As the scientists began to conceive the world mathematically, so the artists began to introduce the mathematical principles of linear perspective into their paintings to show space and depth on a flat surface.

This period produced some of history's greatest artists, a list too long to enumerate, but in the fifteenth century alone it includes Van Eyck, Botticelli, Dürer, Michelangelo, Raphael, Titian, and Holbein. Leonardo da Vinci particularly stands out as the person who fulfilled the Renaissance ideal of the "universal genius." With an insatiable curiosity and an experimental mind, he opened new doorways not only in art, but in physiology, engineering, and science. Renaissance artists, as well as musicians, writers, and scientists, were energized by the classical ideals, passion for beauty, experimental spirit, and fascination with nature that gave this age its distinct identity.

The Protestant Reformation

During the thirteenth century, the medieval Church had reached the pinnacle of its influence and power. Great cathedrals were built, new monastic orders were founded, and Scholastic philosophy had its greatest hour. But in the fourteenth and fifteenth centuries, the Church declined politically and spiritually. Political battles brought about the Great Schism, which lasted from 1378 to 1417. During this time, the Church was divided into two opposing factions, each with its own pope and college of cardinals. Secular rulers jumped into the battle and supported whichever side would serve their interests. Scandals were created by many of the clergy, who fell into worldly self-indulgence and used their position to fulfill their lust and greed, eliciting the rebuke of writers such as Erasmus. But attempts at reform were continuously ignored or suppressed, making the time ripe for a major religious revolt.

In Germany, an idealistic, young Augustinian monk named Martin Luther (1483–1546) brought concerns over the condition of the Church to a crisis point. He originally had no desire to confront the authority of the Church, much less cause it to split. The immediate focus of his concern was the sale of papal indulgences by a Dominican friar named Tetzel. This man claimed that for a fee, a person could buy relief from both the guilt and penalties for one's sins. Convinced that the practice was theologically suspect, Luther nailed his criticisms, the famous "Ninety-Five Theses," to the door of the Wittenberg Castle church in 1517. Eventually, this local controversy made such a clatter that it reached Rome. By this time, the issue of indulgences had broadened out to encompass fundamental issues on theology and Church authority. When both the Church and Luther refused to back down from their position,

Pope Leo X found it necessary to excommunicate Luther in 1520. Thus started the Protestant Reformation and the widespread religious, intellectual, cultural, and political changes that it brought in its wake. Much of northern Europe joined Luther's revolt before long. Several other religious rebellions broke out at this time. In 1530 England broke away from Rome over the issue of Henry VIII's dispute with the Pope over his divorce. In Geneva, Switzerland, John Calvin (1509–1564) developed a reformed theology that attracted followers in France, Holland, Scotland, and England. Among the major Protestant movements, Calvinism deviated the most radically from Catholicism in doctrine and practice.

Luther was by no means a radical theologian. He still retained what he considered of value in medieval theology. Following Augustine, Luther taught the authority of Sacred Scripture, the depravity of human nature, God's punishment for sin, and the need for salvation through the sacrifice of Christ. Furthermore, he tended to be suspicious of the humanists and the new science. Nevertheless, in spite of himself, his religious revolt had a sweeping impact on the larger culture. The Reformation was not simply the replacement of one set of religious doctrines with another set. It brought with it a whole new outlook, which had widespread cultural implications. Luther was influenced philosophically by William of Ockham. Ockham's empirical approach and his skeptical attitude toward the rational metaphysics of Thomas Aquinas had chipped away at the foundations of the tightly organized system of medieval theology and philosophy. Luther himself rejected Scholastic theology as nothing but arid intellectualism, and emphasized a religious faith that sprang from one's inner, emotional life. Furthermore, he stressed the "priesthood of believers." This meant that each individual has direct access to God and does not need to go through a priest or the institutional Church. Luther was optimistic concerning the power of revealed truth to manifest itself and taught that people could follow their own interpretation of the Bible and individual conscience. In undermining the religious authority of the Catholic Church, downplaying subservience to tradition, and giving the individual a new importance, the Reformation had the side effect of eliciting a general reaction against all intellectual authorities and traditions. This fed into the new spirit of freedom and individualism that was sweeping through literature and philosophy. Hence, Luther's pastoral advice to believers became translated into a new philosophical creed: Listen to your own spirit, follow your own personal reflections.

Social and Political Changes

In the political realm, the growing spirit of nationalism was partially fueled by the Protestant Reformation. Indeed, as kings turned away from Rome it was questionable whether their motives were theological or political. This destroyed the religious unity of Europe and inevitably led to outbreaks of religious-political wars. Ultimately, however, this resulted in a spirit of skepticism and tolerance in reaction to the counterproductive strife and confusion produced by theological fanaticism. As the essayist Michel de Montaigne (1533–1592) declared, "It is rating one's conjectures at a very high price to roast a man on the strength of them." As people grew weary of theological battles, they turned to secular learning, especially mathematics and science.

The world of commerce was undergoing a rapid expansion. A money economy replaced the crude barter and exchange economy of the early Middle Ages. The rise of banking and emerging capitalism created a need for firm and stable governments. Taking advantage of the vacuum of authority, the middle-class commercial interests became the dominant political and social power. All this caused, of course, an increased interest in life on earth. However, it was not yet time for culture to become fully secularized. Instead, the culture united the life of the flesh and the spirit, abandoning the medieval dualism of heaven and earth. The forces at work in this era did not operate in separate compartments. For example, Luther's theology also had the effect of giving a new dignity and worth to the everyday life of the average person. As he says in one of his writings,

What you do in your house is worth as much as if you did it up in heaven for our Lord God. . . . It looks like a great thing when a monk renounces everything and goes into a cloister, carries on a life of asceticism, fast, watches, and prays. . . . On the other hand, it looks like a small thing when a maid cooks and cleans and does other housework. But because God's command is there, even such a small work must be praised as a service of God far surpassing the holiness and asceticism of all the monks and nuns.[5]

This means that ordinary economic activities are good and can serve an elevating, spiritual purpose. This theme was also emphasized and expanded by the followers of John Calvin. The eventual impact of this idea on cultural and economic life would be enormous. Later sociologists would call this the "Protestant ethic." It meant that hard work, thrift, and fulfilling one's vocational calling were religiously virtuous. And these were exactly the values needed for the new commercial undertakings.

The Rise of Modern Science

A prevalent myth about the Renaissance says that when medieval thought was abandoned, science immediately flourished. However, in the early Renaissance period there was not much we would recognize as scientific thought. We must remember that initially the Renaissance was a rebirth of ancient thought more than it was a moving forward into new ways of thinking. Belief in astrology, magic, alchemy, and witchcraft was alive and well in the Renaissance view of the world. Long overdue, the scientific revolution began toward the end of the sixteenth century, with a group of thinkers who had different interests from the humanists.

We have to understand the discoveries of the early scientists of this era in terms of the background of accepted ideas they challenged. In the second century A.D., Ptolemy of Alexandria developed the orthodox view. With Aristotle and the ancients, he held to the geocentric theory that the earth was the center of the universe and the sun and the planets circled around it. But to fit his observations of the planetary motions into this scheme, he had to suppose that each planet not only revolved around the earth, but also made pe-

riodic little loops, called *epicycles*, within its main orbit. Eventually, as astronomical observations became more accurate, scientists had to postulate epicycles within epicycles. Quite frankly, the picture was messy and the planets looked as if they had hiccups as they made loops within loops while circling the earth.

Despite the awkwardness of this picture, all known astronomical data fit within it. Furthermore, the scheme supported the theological belief that since the earth was the center of God's concern, it should also be the center of the universe. Finally, Scripture clearly taught in many passages that "the world is firmly established, it will not be moved" (Ps. 93:1). As a result, Ptolemy's theory had no serious challengers for fourteen centuries. If this were a history of science, we would need to mention many names to trace how Aristotelian science and the Ptolemaic theory were laid to rest. For our purposes, however, the two most significant figures are Copernicus and Galileo.

THE COPERNICAN REVOLUTION

Nicolaus Copernicus (1473–1543) was a Catholic, Polish clergyman, and scientist of unimpeachable theological orthodoxy. However, for reasons that will be set out shortly, his 1543 book *The Revolutions of the Heavenly Bodies* challenged the prevailing orthodoxy in astronomy. Using both observations and mathematics, he revolutionized astronomy with his heliocentric theory. This theory placed the sun at the center of things and supposed that the earth, like the other planets, revolves on its own axis while also revolving around the sun. Copernicus's theory was not based on any new factual discovery as much as it was rooted in his Neoplatonism, which dictated that perfect motion is a uniform circular motion around a center. (In fact, Platonists had earlier debated the Aristotelians on this issue.) By placing the sun at the center of the earth's and planets' orbits, he radically reduced, by more than one-half, the number of epicycles required to picture the solar system. In this way, he replaced most of the messy, bumpy orbits with aesthetically and intellectually pleasing circular motions. Even though his motives were based on Neoplatonic superstitions about the virtues of circularity, Copernicus was scientifically correct in preferring a simpler and more elegant explanation to a complicated and awkward one.

The rancorous controversy that developed between the new astronomy and the Church is well-known, but it is important to understand that the scientific objections were just as formidable as any theological problems. If the earth is whirling around on its axis, an object dropped from a tower should fall a good distance to the west instead of at the base of the tower, as actually happens. In terms of the physics of the time, there was no way to explain this discrepancy.* This scientific problem and others did not leave many reasons to believe the overwhelmingly counterintuitive theory. Besides, there were no facts that Copernicus could explain or predict that could not be handled by the old theory.

Fearing controversy, Copernicus withheld publication of his book, but it was finally published a few days before his death in 1543. Initially, it did not create much of a stir and it escaped official Catholic condemnation until the time of Galileo. This was partly due to the fact that the book was dedicated to the Pope. Furthermore, a friend, who was a Lutheran clergyman, had added a preface saying that the theory is only a hypothesis intended to ease the calculation of the planetary motions, but does not pretend to actually describe the heavens.

A student room at the University of Ferrara where Nicolaus Copernicus was made a doctor of canon law in 1503. Copernicus developed a history-changing theory that demoted the earth from the center of the universe to its status as simply another planet revolving around the sun.

THE GALILEO INCIDENT

Galileo Galilei (1564–1642) was born almost on the day Michelangelo died and died in the year Newton was born. Galileo developed a telescope capable of magnifying its objects one thousand times. Through its lenses, he observed the satellites of Jupiter, Saturn's rings, sun spots, the phases of Venus, and the moon's craters. These findings disturbed the Aristotelian picture of the heavenly bodies. Jupiter's moons provided a model of our solar system, giving plausibility to the Copernican account. Furthermore, the other observations refuted the Aristotelian theory that the earth is changing and imperfect, while the heavens are unchanging and perfect. Galileo was a devout Catholic and sought to reconcile the new science with the old religion by suggesting that science and religion do not compete but have two different purposes. As he put it, the Bible has been given to us "to teach us how to go to heaven, not how the heavens go." Although he had already been questioned by the authorities on his views, he thought the time was right to publish *Dialogue Concerning*

*This problem was solved only after Galileo formulated the law of inertia.

the *Two Chief Systems of the World* in 1632. However, he came under extreme attack because he was not content to accept the Copernican theory as simply a hypothesis to make our calculations easier. Instead, he boldly insisted that the theory correctly described the heavens. As a result, he was summoned before the Inquisition, his book was condemned, and he was forced to deny his theory on his knees. Furthermore, he was placed under house arrest in Florence, where he remained until his death. This was the end of Galileo's career, but the forceful prose of his writing and the drama of his clash with the Church stirred people's imaginations throughout Europe. It was too late to turn the clock back, for the old ideas had been fatally wounded.

THE IMPLICATIONS OF THE NEW SCIENCE

The new science did not simply replace one set of facts with another set. It brought with it a whole new outlook on the world that had philosophical implications. First, Galileo combined the materialistic atomism of the Greek philosopher Democritus with the mathematical ideals of the Pythagoreans and Plato to form a new, mathematical, and mechanical conception of the world. According to Galileo, we experience two kinds of qualities. The **primary qualities** are those that can be quantified, such as size, shape, motion, mass, and number. **Secondary qualities** are subjective qualities such as color, odor, and the experience of sound. The radical conclusion he drew from this was that nature in itself is made up of only the mathematical, primary qualities. The rest, those qualities we encounter in everyday experience, merely present nature as we subjectively experience it. Galileo was quite forthright about the fact that his scientific outlook did violence to the world of our ordinary senses. What this amounts to is that the real world is a world of particles in motion that has very little in the way of human qualities about it. As E. A. Burtt describes the outcome of this view,

> The world that people had thought themselves living in—a world rich with colour and sound, redolent with fragrance, filled with gladness, love and beauty, speaking everywhere of purposive harmony and creative ideals—was crowded now into minute corners in the brains of scattered organic beings. The really important world outside was a world hard, cold, colourless, silent, and dead; a world of quantity, a world of mathematically computable motions in mechanical regularity.[6]

This distinction between primary and secondary qualities became very important to the philosophers of the seventeenth and eighteenth centuries as they wrestled with the question of how we can be sure that our experience tells us about the world if its contents differ so radically from it.

Another important change that modern science introduced was that it replaced teleological explanations with descriptive, mechanical explanations. A **teleological explanation** explains events in terms of their purpose. When the Aristotelian asked, "Why do stones fall?" the answer was, "Stones fall *in order to* achieve their natural state, which is to be at rest on the earth." Likewise, when the medievals asked, "Why does it rain?" the answer was, "God has provided the rain *in order to* nourish our crops." In Aristotle's terms, these explanations were providing the *final cause* of an event. However, Galileo did not ask *why* objects fall but *how* they fall. He sought a description of the outward, observable behavior of things and not their inner meaning or divine purpose. Likewise, scientists would eventually explain rain in terms of meteorological conditions, leaving unmentioned its role in human life. Hence, the difference made by the new science was not simply that it gave new answers, but that it asked new questions. The new questions revolved around mathematical relationships, physical conditions, and mechanistic processes.

As scientists began to eliminate final causes from their explanations, God was no longer viewed as the Supreme Good that drew all things toward their final end. Furthermore, when they found that mathematical, physical laws were sufficient explanations for natural events, the need to postulate God's active intervention in the world diminished. Instead, God became the First Cause that set matter in motion, after which it operated autonomously in terms of its own causal laws.

Obviously, this shuffled the world of science and nature into one compartment and the world of religion and the supernatural into another. However, since most of the early scientists and philosophers were theists, this left them with the question of how the two compartments fit together to form one reality.

The new astronomy forced people to renegotiate their relationship with the cosmos. No longer was the night sky a comfortable dome, nestled close to the earth, lit up by thousands of tiny, sparkling lights, and with heaven and the choirs of angels just beyond what we can see. Instead, people now realized that the earth was just a speck in the dark, loneliness of infinite space. The Oxford mathematician Thomas Digges lamented that if the throne of God really was beyond the fixed stars, it was a fearfully great distance away. In the seventeenth century, the scientist and religious writer Blaise Pascal confessed that "the eternal silence of these infinite spaces terrifies me."

Philosophy in a New Key

It took centuries to appreciate the effects of the vast social and intellectual changes the Renaissance thinkers produced. Nevertheless, once these forces were set into motion, they built up a momentum that prevented any return to the spirit and framework of the Middle Ages. It was only a matter of time, therefore, before philosophy was swept up in this stream and became a cultural force again.

The agenda of the early modern philosophers was twofold. First, they wanted to sweep away the past. Aristotelian science, which had once seemed so obvious, had prevailed for well over a thousand years, but it had been mistaken in its most fundamental conceptions. With the fall of Aristotle's science his philosophy declined as well. Since questionable scientific, theological, and philosophical beliefs had been carried through the ages on the back of tradition and authority, these, too, were now held in suspicion. Modern philosophers were determined not to accept any belief unless they could convince themselves of it on their own.

In the Middle Ages, even an innovative thinker such as Thomas Aquinas never started on a topic without first quoting the authorities, namely, Aristotle and the Church Fathers. In essays of the modern period, however, we find phrases that would have been thought to be presumptuous in earlier times: "It seems to me that . . ." or "Contrary to accepted opinion, I have found that. . . ."

The second main theme of the modern period was the search for the perfect, philosophical method. It does no good to reject the theories of the past, unless we are sure we have something better to put in their place. But how will we know it is better, unless we have some method that guarantees its truth? Hence, the modern period in philosophy begins with an obsessive concern with the method for finding knowledge. Thus epistemology (theory of knowledge) and philosophy of mind are key issues in this period. Unfortunately, philosophers eventually came to the disillusioning realization that no method seemed to yield indubitable truths and a consensus of opinion. Hence, the search for a method is a theme that we will follow all the way into the twentieth century.

The two philosophical methods that dominated the modern period up until Immanuel Kant were rationalism and empiricism. The basic issue dividing the two positions is the origin of our knowledge. Rationalists believe some knowledge is *a priori*. **A priori** knowledge is knowledge obtained through reason, prior to or independently of experience. For example, rationalists claim that logical and mathematical truths are known by the mind apart from experience. Some rationalists claim that truths about God, metaphysics, and ethics are also known *a priori*. In contrast, the empiricists claim that all knowledge about the world is *a posteriori* or empirical. **A posteriori** (or **empirical**) knowledge is derived from experience. For example, the statement "Sugar is sweet" could only be known from experience. The empiricists believe that all our knowledge is of this sort. Figure 13-1 serves as a rough overview of the main differences between rationalism and empiricism in the seventeenth and eighteenth centuries.

Although this overview can help you understand the next eight philosophers we discuss, a few

Continental Rationalism	British Empiricism
1. Philosophers: Descartes, Spinoza, Leibniz.	1. Philosophers: Bacon, Hobbes, Locke, Berkeley, Hume.
2. Centered in France, Holland, Germany.	2. Centered in England, Ireland, Scotland.
3. Genuine knowledge has its foundation in thought or reason.	3. Genuine knowledge has its foundation in experience.
4. The mind is full of rational content. It contains (a) inborn ideas, or (b) innate principles, or (c) a rational structure complete with logical categories.	4. The mind is a "blank tablet." It has no content except what experience provides.
5. Foundational knowledge is self-evident, certain, and known independently of experience.	5. All knowledge about the world is probable, contingent, and based on experience.
6. Foundational truths are universal because they are part of the content of every mind and are necessary features of the world.	6. Some ideas seem to be universal because some features of human experience and the world are universal.

FIGURE 13-1

oversimplifications need correcting. First, while the rationalists give special priority to the role of reason, even the empiricists stress the importance of reason in the sense of being "reasonable." For all these philosophers, this means having a mind free from all passions, prejudices, traditions, and dogmas. It also means accepting no conclusion unless its truth can be supported by good reasons. Second, the thinkers in each tradition do not always fall neatly into their stereotypical category. For example, René Descartes is not always consistent in his rationalism. Benedict Spinoza and Gottfried Leibniz are much more consistent, but at the expense of being much more radical. Similarly, John Locke is not always a consistent empiricist, while George Berkeley and David Hume are more consistent but extreme. Third, sometimes two thinkers differ on their theory of knowledge and yet lie closer together on other issues than with members of their own tradition. For example, although Descartes and Locke held differing epistemologies, they were both metaphysical dualists, in that they believed that the mind and body were different substances. Similarly, Leibniz and Berkeley differ on their epistemology, but they are both metaphysical idealists, denying that physical substances are different from mental substances.

Questions for Understanding

1. What does the word "Renaissance" mean literally? Why is this an appropriate label for this age?

2. Why should Renaissance humanism not be considered an anti-religious movement?

3. List significant developments in the following fields that contributed to the birth of this new age: (a) philosophy, (b) technology, (c) education, (d) art, (e) religion, (f) politics, (h) economics, (i) science.

4. What were some key issues in Martin Luther's reform movement in religion?

5. What were some side effects of Luther's religious impact on philosophy and literature?

6. What was the Copernican revolution?

7. What contributions did Galileo make? How were they received by his contemporaries?

8. What is the distinction between primary qualities and secondary qualities? What were the implications of this distinction?

9. What does it mean to say "mechanistic explanations replaced teleological explanations"? Give some examples.

10. What changes began taking place in philosophy at this time?

11. What are the differences between the rationalism and empiricism that emerged at this time?

12. What is the distinction between *a priori* knowledge and *a posteriori* knowledge?

Questions for Reflection

1. Find examples of medieval and Renaissance art. How do the styles of painting differ? What differences are there in the content? In what ways do the paintings of each period reflect the philosophies of each period?

2. Although Galileo ran into conflict with his church, he did not believe that his science was opposed to religion. If you were Galileo, how would you convince the religious authorities of the time that your science was not a danger to religious faith?

3. Reread the section on "The Implications of the New Science." Galileo began to understand the world mathematically as opposed to the view of the world given to us in our everyday sense experience. What are the advantages of viewing the world as he did? Do you agree with E. A. Burtt that the mathematical approach leaves something out? Is there more than one way to understand the world. Is there a place for both physics and poetry?

Notes

1. Coluccio Salutati, quoted in *The Age of Adventure: The Renaissance Philosophers*, ed. Giorgio De Santillana (New York: Mentor, New American Library, 1956), 12.

2. John Herman Randall, Jr., *The Making of the Modern Mind* (Boston: Houghton Mifflin, 1940), 119.

3. Erasmus, "The Godly Feast," in *The Colloquies of Erasmus*, trans. Craig R. Thompson (Chicago and London: University of Chicago Press, 1965), 65.

4. Ibid., 68.

5. Martin Luther, *Christian Liberty*, quoted in Randall, *The Making of the Modern Mind*, 140.

6. Edwin A. Burtt, *The Metaphysical Foundations of Modern Physical Science*, rev. ed. (Garden City, NY: Doubleday Anchor Books, 1932), 238–239.

CHAPTER

14

Early Empiricists:
Francis Bacon and Thomas Hobbes

WITH THE OPENING OF NEW HORIZONS BY THE Renaissance, it became time for philosophers to reassess where they were and where they needed to be going. Two early philosophical pioneers in the modern era were Francis Bacon and Thomas Hobbes. They looked to science and, consequently, to experience for the directions they were to take in philosophy. As with any explorer trekking through new terrain, they were naively optimistic and not always aware of the problems that lay ahead. However, they had seen how nature had rewarded the dreams of scientists and explorers, and they dared to look for similar results in philosophy. Bacon's own dreams were inspired by the discovery of America. Comparing himself to Columbus, he spoke of "the breath of hope which blows on us from that new continent" (NO 1:92, 114).[1]

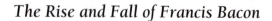

FRANCIS BACON

The Rise and Fall of Francis Bacon

Francis Bacon (1561–1626) was born in London to a powerful family close to the court of Elizabeth. His father was a prominent statesman and his uncle, Lord Burghley, was the most powerful man in Britain. Bacon's mother was a well-educated and pious Puritan. Both her respect for education and her Puritanism had a profound effect on Bacon.

At the age of twelve, Bacon went to Trinity College at Cambridge, where he studied law. By the time he was sixteen, he was on the staff of the English ambassador to France. Bacon was ambitious, and given his family connections and education, he looked forward to a distinguished career in public service. However, when he was eighteen his father died and left little in the way of financial support for him. The rest of his life

212

he was seldom out of debt and was always engaged in a frantic search for opportunities. Nevertheless, initially things seemed to be going his way, despite this setback. In 1584, when he was twenty-three, Bacon entered Parliament and his career advanced steadily. In 1618 he became Lord Chancellor, the highest appointed office in the land. Just when it had seemed as though Bacon had fulfilled his ambitions, in 1621 he was accused of accepting bribes as a judge. Bacon admitted he had accepted gifts from litigants, but insisted this had not influenced his judicial decisions. Pleading guilty and offering no defense, he was removed from office, but was given a reduced fine and had to spend only a few days imprisoned in the Tower of London. Both during and after the time he was in public service, Bacon managed to write several philosophical treatises. Bacon's life came to an abrupt and absurd end when the quest for scientific knowledge caused him to die of bronchitis on April 9, 1626. He had become sick after standing out in frigid weather stuffing a chicken with snow to study techniques of refrigeration.

Bacon's Task: The Reconstruction of All Knowledge

Bacon tells us his goal was to accomplish a "total reconstruction of sciences, arts, and all human knowledge, raised upon the proper foundations" (GI 2). This statement expressed the two themes that were typical of his age: (1) *a radical criticism of the past*—we must sweep away the cobwebs of medieval thought and the rubble of tradition before we do anything else, and (2) *heady optimism concerning the future*—the right method will lead us into an intellectual and social utopia. In addition to his shorter works and essays, Bacon had planned a major writing project, but never completed it. What he did accomplish was the outline of his plan, called *The Great Instauration*. The word *instauration* connotes a restoration or renewal after decay. He also completed large sec-

tions of his *Novum Organum* ("New Instrument or Method"). The titles of these works capture the spirit of the time. Philosophers and scientists such as Bacon had a sense that they were standing on the threshold of something new with a methodological key (scientific philosophy) that would unlock any mystery.

Like William of Ockham before him, Bacon tried to maintain a hard and fast division between philosophy (including natural philosophy or science) on the one hand and theology on the other. Although he firmly believed in revelation, he thought it should play no part in our attempts to understand nature. His theological views sometimes color his outlook, but he avoided drawing philosophical conclusions from them. Hence, he had no problems with a thoroughgoing materialistic and mechanistic account of nature, for he did not think this would detract from what theology tells us about immaterial reality. Concerning teleological explanations or the attempt to explain natural phenomena in terms of their purpose, he says, "Inquiry into final causes is sterile and, like a virgin consecrated to God, produces nothing."[2] In his promotion of mechanism, it is clear how far even pious philosophers such as Bacon had moved away from the medieval worldview by this time.

Bacon's mind was very practical, and he was the one who originated the slogan "Knowledge is power" (NO 1:3). It seemed to him that all the vast, complicated systems of the medieval thinkers had provided nothing that could be used to conquer nature. This was because their thought had no ties to observable facts. Hence, he believed that the "true and lawful goal of the sciences is . . . that human life be endowed with new discoveries and powers" (NO 1:81). Again, the difference between the medieval spirit and that of the Renaissance is suggested by the fact that the personal piety of someone like Bacon could be wedded with an unbounded humanism whose goal was to extend "the power and greatness of man" and who proclaimed that through the arts and sciences it was now possible to say that "man is a god to man" (NO 1:116, 129).

The Route to Knowledge: From Idols to Induction

THE CORRUPTION OF THE MIND

Epistemology or the theory of knowledge was Bacon's major area of concern. Throughout his discussions his Puritan background reveals itself in the theological coloring he gives to the theory of knowledge. For example, he suggests that the relationship between the mind and nature was meant to be natural and unimpeded, much like the relationship between the first humans and God in the Garden of Eden. However, the epistemological analogue of sin is our temptation to engage in speculation and the construction of abstruse metaphysical systems. This has interfered with our perfect relationship to nature, and we have fallen into epistemological corruption, Bacon says, just as Adam and Eve were thrust out of their paradise:

> For man by the fall fell at the same time from his state of innocency and from his dominion over creation. Both of these losses, however, can even in this life be in some part repaired; the former by religion and faith, the latter by arts and sciences. (NO 2.52)

In our original state of innocence, the mind was so harmonious with nature that it functioned like a mirror that clearly reflected the genuine light of nature. However, the surface of our cognitive mirror has become dirty, rough, and uneven from the effects of the passions as well as the errors of tradition. Consequently, it distorts the image of nature and mixes its own notions with the data that come to us from experience. Once we clean and smooth its surface again, the acquisition of knowledge will be almost effortless (GI 24-25).

RESTORATION OF THE MIND'S ORIGINAL CONDITION

To restore the mind to its original state of purity, we must remove the "idols" that corrupt its natural powers (notice again the religious metaphor). Bacon lists four idols that distract the mind from its proper task (NO 1:38-68).

1. *The Idols of the Tribe* are those that inhere within human nature itself. These idols are the many ways we read human desires into nature by supposing there is more order and regularity in the world than is really there. We have a tendency to make the facts fit our own, favorite conclusions. For example, he cites the belief that the planets move in perfect circles, an assumption based on the belief that circles are perfect figures and aesthetically pleasing. The appeal of teleological explanations that impute purposes into natural events is another example of this idol.

2. *The Idols of the Cave* is a metaphor derived from Plato's famous allegory. These idols are unique to each individual. Each of us dwells in our own, little "cave" in that our vision is limited by our dispositions, education, reading, and the authorities we admire. Our experience is filtered through our biases and idiosyncracies, so that our philosophy follows the pattern of our biography more than that of reality. To the pessimist the cup is half empty, while the optimist sees the same cup as half full. To neutralize our natural prejudices, Bacon offers the following advice:

> Let every student of nature take this as a rule,— that whatever his mind seizes and dwells upon with peculiar satisfaction is to be held in suspicion, and that so much the more care is to be taken in dealing with such questions to keep the understanding even and clear. (NO 1:58)

3. *The Idols of the Marketplace* are the problems of language that interfere with the pursuit of truth. (The marketplace is filled with the cacophony of voices of people doing commerce together.) Language can cause two sorts of error. First, we have names for things that do not exist, but the existence of their labels can make us believe otherwise. For example, people attribute events to "Good Fortune" or "Bad Luck" as though these phrases refer to actual events that have explanatory power. Second, we get sloppy when we use abstract terms and fail to realize they are full of vagueness and ambiguity. For example, a "heavy" baby weighs less than a "light" cow. Similarly, it is easy to forget the same word can have different meanings, as when

we speak of heavy cream, heavy sorrow, and a heavy courseload.

4. *The Idols of the Theater* are the result of the various dogmatic systems of philosophy. As Bacon explains his own metaphor, "All the received systems are but so many stage-plays, representing worlds of their own creation after an unreal and scenic fashion" (NO 1:44). He criticizes previous philosophers such as Plato and Aristotle for creating large-scale coherent systems in which they define one concept in terms of another concept, but like the world of a fictional plot there is no connection to the real world of established facts.

BACON'S INDUCTIVE METHOD

Once we have cleared away the obstructions to knowledge, we need a method that will help us read the book of nature. However, Bacon despises the deductive logic of Aristotle and the medieval scholars. The deductive syllogism starts with given premises, which consist of words, which are symbols of concepts. However, if our original concepts are confused and not adequately grounded in the facts, then the whole structure of reasoning will simply "fix and give stability to" the original errors. "Our only hope therefore lies in a true induction" (NO 1:11-14).

The method of induction proceeds from particular facts given in observation and then rises cautiously to the level of generalizations. However, Bacon says that previous notions of the inductive method consisted of collecting a multitude of observations and then immediately leaping to generalizations. This does not provide us with scientific knowledge, for it results in hasty and inaccurate generalizations. Hence, we must look for a law or a form within the data. These are interchangeable terms, for the "form of heat" is nothing more than the "law of heat." However, when Bacon describes what a form is, it comes close to the notion of a medieval essence. In fact, when he describes his scientific procedures, the term *essence* appears. Thus, in using the term *form* to describe the product of scientific inquiry, a term that no scientist would use today, Bacon was not as free from medieval thought categories as he had supposed.

To discover the forms in nature, Bacon proposes a systematic procedure that he called the "tables of inquiry." To discover the form of heat, for example, we must list all the cases where heat is present, such as the rays of the sun, sparks struck from flint, interiors of animals, the taste of strong spices, and so on. Bacon calls this the "Table of Essence and Presence." Second, we should make a list of cases that are similar to the first list, but where the particular effect is missing. If we are studying heat, for example, we would note that the light from the moon is cool and, compared to animals, the bodies of fishes lack warmth. This list will be called the "Table of Deviation or Absence in Proximity." Third, we construct the "Table of Degrees" or "Table of Comparison." This is a list of cases in which the nature whose form we are studying is present in various degrees. For example, animals become more heated when exercising or suffering from a fever.

Having systematically collected our data, the real process of induction begins. We examine the tables to find "such a nature as is always present or absent with the given nature, and always increases and decreases with it" (NO 2:15). In the case of heat, he finds that it is an expanding and restrained motion that makes its way through the smaller parts of bodies. In the rest of his text he goes on to delineate the further steps that are necessary to isolate and verify the form of the phenomenon being studied.

Bacon's Scientific Humanism

Francis Bacon offers us an insight into the tremendous excitement and optimism that reverberated throughout the Renaissance and accompanied the rise of modern science. He believed that if committees of scientists went to work and followed his detailed program, after a few years there would be no more scientific discoveries to be made. The reason for this extraordinary optimism was that he thought that the scientific method was like a machine into which we pour the data of nature and receive scientific laws out the other end. After completing one of his works, he wrote a dedicatory letter to King James I in which he said, "I have provided the machine, but the stuff must be gathered from the facts of nature" (GI 6).

Bacon's epistemology has been compared to the outlook of the Protestant Reformation. Luther had preached that every believer has direct access to the throne of God. What is required is that we simply open ourselves to his grace. Similarly, Bacon thought that the ability to receive truth from nature is our natural state. It is available to each person, no matter what their intellectual qualifications, if we are simply open to it and employ the right methodology. As he describes it, "the course I propose for the discovery of sciences is such as leaves but little to the acuteness and strength of wits, but places all wits and understandings on a level" (NO 1:61). In this same passage he repeats the machine metaphor, stating that the freehand drawing of a straight line or perfect circle takes some talent, but anyone can do it effortlessly with the proper instrument such as a ruler or compass.

Bacon revealed his vision of the practical applications of science in an unfinished, futuristic fable called *New Atlantis*. This scientifically transformed society spun from Bacon's imagination had what we would now call airplanes, submarines, genetic engineering, robots, and climate-controlled environments. This fictional world concretely illustrated what Bacon had envisioned in the *Novum Organum* when he proclaimed "the empire of man over things" and "the power and dominion of the human race itself over the universe" (NO 1:129). One cannot help but wonder if Bacon's enthusiasm would have been diminished if he could have peeked into our age where the fruits of technology have also produced the poisonous seeds of nuclear destruction and environmental disasters.

Evaluation and Significance of Bacon

For all his celebration and formalizing of the scientific method, Francis Bacon never made any

important scientific discoveries himself. His most important contribution was as a cheerleader for scientific inquiry. In this role, he did give a vision to his contemporaries. Bacon was quoted more in seventeenth-century England than any other philosophical writer and achieved international fame. He has been called the "secretary of nature" and "the trumpeter of his time."

Although Bacon was very influential, most historians of philosophy do not consider him a very profound philosopher. Bacon did not understand the role of hypothesis, theory, imagination, and speculation in the pursuit of scientific knowledge. He thought that once we had collected and carefully catalogued a series of facts, the scientific laws would be staring us in the face. His comparison of the scientific method to a machine ignores the role of genius, imagination, and even happenstance in making scientific discoveries. Bacon reacted so strongly to the unfounded theories of the medieval thinkers that he thought science could only advance if it avoided theories altogether. He says, for example, to abolish the Idols of the Marketplace caused by idle theories "it is only necessary that all theories should be steadily rejected and dismissed as obsolete" (NO 1:60).

Because Bacon did not recognize the role of powerful theories in legitimate science, his discussion of the great scientists failed to mention Kepler, and in his review of mechanics he did not mention Galileo. He rejected Copernicus's theory and did not understand William Harvey's work on the blood. Finally, Bacon failed to appreciate the importance of mathematics, seeing it only as a "handmaiden" to inductive science. The consensus of later opinion is that Bacon's view of the scientific method was too naive to ever produce great science.

In spite of his shortcomings, Bacon's contribution to the history of philosophy is threefold: (1) he was an early leader in the empiricist movement, (2) he was a pioneer in the attempt to systematize the scientific method, and (3) he was the founder of modern inductive logic.

THOMAS HOBBES

|||

Hobbes's Life: Controversy and Innovation

Thomas Hobbes (1588–1679) was born in England to an uneducated vicar. He attended Oxford University where he was subjected to a Scholasticist education consisting mainly of logic and the philosophy of Aristotle. Dissatisfied with the stultifying ideas he had to memorize, Hobbes continually criticized the universities of his day in his later writings. After completing his education, he spent most of his life working as a tutor and companion to the prominent Cavendish family. His employment with this wealthy family through successive generations had the fortunate result of giving him the opportunity to travel and meet the leading figures of the day. Hobbes knew Francis Bacon and assisted him in translating several essays into Latin. In Italy he met Galileo and in Paris Hobbes met with Descartes's colleagues and may even have met Descartes himself. Hobbes wrote carefully reasoned objections to Descartes's *Meditations* and Descartes published the criticisms along with his own responses.

There were three important influences on Hobbes's thought. First, there was his discovery of Galileo's writings. As will soon be obvious, Galileo's physics provided the model for Hobbes's philosophy. Second, there was his discovery of Euclidean geometry at age forty. Hobbes was impressed with the axiomatic method of demonstration, and, although he was an empiricist, he sought to emulate Euclid's rigorous procedures in some of his writings.

The third important influence on Hobbes was the Civil War in England, which began in 1642, following a long period of tension.* When it was clear

*The tensions began with King James I and were inherited by his son Charles I. The monarchs insisted on absolute power based on the doctrine of the divine right of kings. Parliament wanted less royal authority. The Crown was supported by the nobles and the Anglican and Roman Catholic Churches. Parliament was supported by the middle-class townsmen and the Puritan Dissenters.

that civil war was imminent, Hobbes fled to France in 1640. He remained there for eleven years and enjoyed the intellectual company of important philosophers and scientists in Paris. In 1649, King Charles I was executed and Oliver Cromwell took over the government. While in Paris, Hobbes served as a tutor to the Prince of Wales, who was in exile there and would later become Charles II. However, the publication of his *Leviathan* in 1651 brought this to an end. He was called the "father of atheists" and unsuitable to teach the young prince. Furthermore, Catholic France did not appreciate his attacks on established religion. Consequently, Hobbes returned home and worked out an understanding with Cromwell. In 1660 the monarchy was restored under Charles II. Charles fondly remembered his former tutor and treated him well.

Hobbes's Task: Making Physics Sovereign in Philosophy

Hobbes had one, single-minded goal, which was to recast the study of physical nature, human nature, and human society. His new approach to the old questions used a single, scientific method throughout all the various fields. Hobbes recognized that economy of thought was central to science. The goal is always to reduce the multiplicity of phenomena to the simplest possible laws and basic elements. Hence, since Galileo had successfully explained nature in terms of matter in motion, this seemed the appropriate model for philosophy as well.

Two pillars supported Hobbes's thought. The first was the epistemological position of empiricism, the claim that all our knowledge comes through the senses. The second pillar was metaphysical materialism, the claim that reality is nothing but matter in motion. Hence, the only science we need, according to Hobbes, is physics. Although it may seem that this would make Hobbes an atheist, he backpedals away from this conclusion. He admits that nature suggests there is an ultimate cause, such as a God. However, he says the notion of a nonphysical substance is meaningless. Therefore, the only meaning we can give to "spirit" would be to conceive of it as a very fine and transparent physical substance. In the final analysis, we may be able to affirm *that* God exists, but we cannot understand *what* God is, for we can only know what makes an impact on the senses. Hence, the nature of God is of no interest to philosophy or science. In this way, Hobbes deftly left the problem of God to the theologians and relieved his philosophy of any further concern with this notion.

According to Hobbes's analysis, reality can be divided into two kinds of bodies: (1) natural bodies (such as stones, planets, living organisms) and (2) political bodies (which are artificial bodies). Philosophy searches for the causal laws and characteristics of each kind of body. It is nothing more than a more general application of the principles of science. For Hobbes, there are specific approaches to be taken to the study of each kind of body. The most general discipline is "first philosophy," which replaces traditional metaphysics. It is an examination of those properties common to all bodies in general and studies "motion and magnitude in the abstract." Among his conclusions here is the thesis that every event in the universe, including the entire scope of the future, is necessarily determined by previous causes. The second approach is practiced in the special sciences, such as astronomy and physics, that study the motions of particular bodies moving at determinate velocities.

Third, there is the science of human bodies. A living body, such as ours, is a more complex sort of body, for it has many kinds of internal motions. A physicist can study the motion of a planet only because its motion is causing motions within his body. What we need, therefore, is a scientific explanation of human bodies on the same terms that we study the rest of the universe. To make his point, he gives an engineer's description of a living organism: "For what is the heart, but a spring; and the nerves, but so many strings, and the joints, but so many wheels, giving a motion to the whole body, such as was intended by the artificer?" (L, intro.).[3]

Note that Hobbes's theoretical program was extraordinarily controversial in his time. Most of his contemporaries thought human beings were the crown of creation, with a dignity and spiritual nature that far transcended anything else in the world. However, Hobbes thought it was irrational to suppose that human nature is any different from the rest of nature. Therefore, the methods of the physical sciences are appropriate for studying human beings and their activities.

Fourth, generalizing from his goals for a science of human nature, Hobbes believed he could apply the precise methods of physics to society as a whole. If individual humans are nothing but bodies in motion, then we can formulate the laws that govern their interactions. By understanding these laws, we can bring about peace and order within society just as a physician adjusts the balance of chemicals in one's body to produce health. Hence, Hobbes attempts to transform political philosophy into political *science*.

The Physics of Knowledge

PSYCHOLOGICAL MOTIONS

Hobbes bases his epistemology on a mechanistic psychology. Since he assumes that everything that happens in the universe is a type of motion, mental events are identical to motions within our body. Our thoughts are particular sorts of motions that serve as representations or appearances of objects outside the body. Thoughts are first introduced through the senses:

> The original of them all [i.e., thoughts] is that which we call sense, for there is no conception in a man's mind which hath not first, totally or by parts, been begotten upon the organs of sense. The rest are derived from that original. (L 131)

As physical motions from the objects in the external world impinge on our sense organs, they produce sensations or what Hobbes variously calls *images*, *phantasms*, or *fancy*. We experience such things as colors, musical tones, savory tastes, fragrances, and softness. However, these "phenomenal qualities," as we call them today, are not present (strictly speaking) either in the external objects themselves or in the motions within our bodies. The just-mentioned qualitative terms are not quantitative terms that describe motions. Instead, they describe "appearances" or "phantasms" produced by motions. For example, when we see the rich, red hues of a sunset, we are really experiencing the motions of light rays. When we look at the moon, this phantasm has the appearance of a bright, luminous disk that is about the same size as a half-dollar. For these reasons, it seemed obvious to Hobbes that the object itself and what we directly experience are two different things.

From the original motion of perception, Hobbes says, all the rest of the brain's motions arise. Imagination and memory are nothing more than "decaying sense." They are like the ripples in a pool of water that continue long after the impact of the pebble tossed into it. Hence, Hobbes explains psychological phenomena such as afterimages using the physicists' principle of inertia. Once something is set in motion, it tends to continue in motion. The imagination can add or subtract the images it contains to create fictional notions of things like unicorns. However, the elements of what we imagine had to first be present in sensation. Similarly, the memories of your first-grade teacher are the faint motions remaining from your original sensations. The images in imagination and memory are not as vivid as perception because new motions gradually obscure the original motions.

Another psychological law Hobbes formulates is that those images that succeed one another in experience tend to be associated in the imagination. When we see lightning, for example, we have come to expect thunder. Some of these associations are more subjective than others. If you fell in love one April, for example, the smell of springtime flowers in the future will bring forth the memory of that happy experience. In this way, we can explain the activity of thinking by the fact that ideas tend to follow each other in thought when they followed each other in sensation. Something similar to a "chemical bond" between ideas causes some to cohere together but not others. Hobbes's attempt to formulate the "laws of motion" governing human cognition laid the foundations for what

would later become the science of associationistic psychology.

VERBAL MOTIONS

So far, Hobbes's account of experience applies equally well to the cognitive behavior of the psychologist's laboratory rat and to the psychology of a philosopher. What, then, distinguishes humans from animals? The differentiating factor is not a soul nor some non-physical faculty of reason. Instead, our uniqueness is bound up with language. Humans can give names "or other voluntary signs" to sensations. Both a human and a cat associate the sound of a bird with the image of the bird itself. For humans, however, the visual symbols B-I-R-D make the same association.

Hobbes's theory of language is a form of **nominalism**. This means there are no real universals as Plato and Aristotle thought, only universal names that stand for a collection of similar, individual things. Words are marks that stand for sensations such that the relations between words correspond to the relations between events. For this reason, when you read the word *lightning*, you are likely to think of the word *thunder*. By introducing our ability to manipulate signs, Hobbes can account for our ability to reason. Reasoning is "nothing but *reckoning*, that is adding and subtracting, of the consequences of general names agreed upon for the marking and signifying of our thoughts" (L 1:5).*

The sort of knowledge that results from this activity is science. Reason does not tell us about the world but only gives us the consequences of our definitions. Hence, reason always gives us conditional knowledge:

> And for the knowledge of consequence, which I have said before is called science, it is not absolute but conditional. No man can know by discourse that this or that is, has been, or will be; which is to know absolutely: but only, that if this be, that is; if this has

---

*This "computational model of the mind" has been the basis of most of the artificial intelligence research in the twentieth century.

been, that has been; if this shall be, that shall be: which is to know conditionally. (L 1:7)

What this theory implies is that reason is divorced from reality. It can give us no knowledge apart from simply disclosing to us the relationships that exist between ideas that are already located in the mind, ideas that have come from sensation. Therefore, the rationalists' attempt to use reason alone to tell us about the ultimate nature of reality is in vain. This conclusion would be the foundation of empiricism all the way into the twentieth century.

Metaphysics: All Motion Is Determined

As should be clear, Hobbes's theory of knowledge is simply the attempt to work out the implications of his metaphysical materialism. However, there are other implications to be drawn from his metaphysics. If seventeenth-century physics gives us the final word on the nature of the world, then this implies that every event in the world is determined. We may think that future events are contingent and the products of chance, but this is simply because we are ignorant of their causes. Hence, uncertainty or unpredictability is a feature of our knowledge, not of the events themselves.

Since the same sorts of laws that govern falling stones also govern human activity, it follows that our behavior is absolutely determined. Furthermore, the more we understand the laws that govern the complicated system of human motions, the more our behavior will be as predictable as any astronomical event. But how can Hobbes account for our seemly purposeful, intentional actions on this deterministic model? He begins by making a distinction between *vital* and *voluntary* motions. Vital motions are such automatic activities as the circulation of the blood, breathing, digestion, and so on. Since, for the most part, these are not consciously chosen motions, we have no problems seeing these activities as determined by our nervous system and bodily state. The problem is with the so-called voluntary motions, which would include conversing, buying a book, or choosing a friend. Here, we want to insist that we have free

will. Hobbes says that all voluntary motions begin with a type of motion he calls *endeavor*. Endeavor manifests itself as either (1) desire, which is motion toward something, or as (2) aversion, which is motion away from something. For each individual, these are correlated with what is experienced as pleasurable or painful. In this way, Hobbes derives our psychological activities from our physiological responses.

An objection quite naturally arises at this point. If our behavior is so neatly determined and predictable, how does Hobbes account for the activity of deliberation when we have to make a decision? For example, we may feel inclined to make some sort of commitment (to a person, to a job) at the same time we have reservations about this course of action. Hobbes explains this by saying we are experiencing either (1) an alternating succession of the feelings of desire and aversion, or (2) the motion between two competing desires, or (3) two conflicting aversions. When we deliberate, we are like a yo-yo that is responding to the downward pull of gravity at the same time it is being pulled upward by the tension of the string. With people, as with yo-yos, one force will be stronger at any given time and will ultimately prevail. Hence, the end result is the mechanical outcome of all the forces, in which the strongest inclination wins out within us. We call this last motion "an act of the will." But it is a will that has been mechanically determined by all the forces acting on it. In the final analysis, our behavior is no more free than that of the planets.

Ethical Motions

If matter in motion is all that there is, how can Hobbes explain the phenomenon of human morality? He explains it in the same way the Epicurean materialists did in ancient Greece and the same way that metaphysical materialists will always explain it. The answer lies in the laws of human psychology. The object of a desire is something we call *good*, and the object of aversion we call *evil*. Hence, "good" and "evil" are terms derived from pleasure and pain. Since different people find different things pleasurable or painful, good and evil are inescapably subjective notions. Psychologically, we are all egoistic hedonists, inevitably guided by our own pursuit of pleasure. Hence, Hobbes is a psychological hedonist (claiming we always seek pleasure and the avoidance of pain) as well as a psychological egoist (claiming we always seek our own pleasure). If these factual claims about human psychology are correct, then there is little more to be said about ethical theory. Good is simply what makes me feel good, and that is what I will pursue. To ask whether I ought or ought not to act this way is an irrelevant question.

One final question remains, however. If we are all egoists, seeking after our own good, how can we ever live together harmoniously in a community? This question takes us to the last, and most important part of Hobbes's philosophy—his political theory.

The Physics of Political Bodies

A PERSONAL AGENDA AND A THEORETICAL PROGRAM

Hobbes lived in an unsettled period in English history. He was caught in a civil war between the defenders of the throne and the anti-royalists. He switched allegiances several times, but his timing was always off. When he sought to appease the side in power, he only ended up putting his life in jeopardy with the other side. From this experience, he drew three lessons:

1. Where there is not a stable government, there is chaos.
2. Chaos is to be avoided at all costs.
3. Chaos is prevented only if the government is strong.

These three conclusions stand in the background of all Hobbes's political thought. Because of these concerns, Hobbes attempts to consistently apply his methodological principles to solving the problems of political theory. The culmination of his program is to analyze the structure and nature of the political state in terms of moving bodies.

Hobbes provides a logical analysis that seeks to explain the phenomenon of society. Following the method of geometry, which he admired, he begins with a set of axioms about human nature he considers indubitable and then deduces a series of theorems from them. It is important to understand that he does not claim this is a historical account of how society actually emerged. Instead, he tries to show why government is justified in terms of the laws of human nature and what form it must take if it is to be rational. To use an analogy, the laws of physics cannot tell us where a particular baseball came from. However, a physicist can provide a rational explanation of why a baseball behaves the way it does, say, when a pitcher throws a curve and what conditions must be present for the ball to function optimally.

THE STATE OF NATURE

Hobbes begins with a thought experiment. What would our situation be like if there were no government? He calls this the "state of nature." In the state of nature, we are all "equal" and have the "right" to anything necessary for survival. Obviously, he does not mean we are all physically equal. What he means is that without society, no one has any special rights, privileges, restrictions, rank, or status. Furthermore, if the world consists of only physical facts (including psychological facts), then there is no objective moral order to which we are subject. The term *right* as it functions in the state of nature means "freedom based on power." As Hobbes says, "every man has a right to every thing; even to one another's body."

Given the fact that Hobbes says that we are all egoists, looking out for "number 1," the state of nature is obviously not going to be very hospitable. According to Aristotle, humans are naturally social animals. However, Hobbes would say that without social conditioning, we have no built-in affinity or sympathy for the others of our species. Altruism is not a natural emotion. The state of nature, then, is a state of fear. Like billiard balls moving about and colliding, we are bodies in motion driven only by our individual desire to survive and with nothing that would guarantee any sort of harmony between our motions:

In such condition, there is no place for industry, because the fruit thereof is uncertain: and consequently no culture of the earth; no navigation, nor use of the commodities that may be imported by sea; no commodious building; no instruments of moving, and removing, such things as require much force; no knowledge of the face of the earth; no account of time; no arts; no letters; no society; and which is worst of all, continual fear, and danger of violent death; and the life of man, solitary, poor, nasty, brutish, short. (L 1:13)

This illustration from the title page of Thomas Hobbes's Leviathan *(1651) shows an all-powerful sovereign looming large and reigning over the land. A close examination shows that the ruler's body is composed of hundreds of individuals. To secure peace, according to Hobbes, people must "confer all their power and strength upon one man, or upon one assembly of men that may reduce all their wills by plurality of voices, unto one will."*

THE NATURAL LAWS

The only thing that prevents total chaos is the presence of certain "natural laws." When Hobbes uses this term, it has no relation to the notion of natural law developed by the Stoic or medieval philosophers. When they spoke of the natural law, they were referring to an absolute moral order. For Hobbes, however, these laws are general rules that we discover, based on our understanding of physical reality. We all start from a basic premise: *I want to survive.* From this we can deduce the following natural law: *one ought to seek peace and follow it or, failing that, be prepared to defend oneself by any means necessary.* We must give priority to the first half of this principle, for no individual is ever powerful enough to ensure his or her own survival. Even the biggest bully can have others gang up on him.

From the law of nature that we ought to seek peace, we can derive a further law: *one ought to give up all individual rights, provided that everyone else does so as well, in order to preserve peace.* This is sort of a "selfish golden rule," for we are inclined to follow it not because of any desire to be virtuous, but because each person is looking out for his or her own best interests. However, since we are all egoists, what will ensure that we will all keep our promises? To guarantee that we will all abide by this mutual agreement to restrict our power over one another, "there must be some coercive power, to compel men equally to the performance of their covenants" (L 1:15). We accomplish this by creating a government:

> *The only way [for people] to erect such a common power . . . is, to confer all their power and strength upon one man, or upon one assembly of men, that may reduce all their wills, by plurality of voices, unto one will. (L 2:17)*

Hobbes refers to this body of government as "an artificial man" and the "great LEVIATHAN" (meaning a huge being). He even calls it "that *mortal* god" (a phrase that terrifies everyone who is not as optimistic as Hobbes is about the benefits of an absolute sovereign). This is the beginning of what has come to be known as the **social contract the-**

ory of government. Governments are not instituted by God, but are human creations that we bring about to secure our own egoistic goals.

THE SOCIAL CONTRACT

To survive peacefully, we must all give up our rights to one ruler or assembly. Hobbes says it is as though every individual signs this agreement:

> I authorize and give up my right of governing myself, to this man, or to this assembly of men, on this condition, that thou give up thy right to him, and authorize all his actions in like manner. (L 2:17)

Unlike the later contract theories of John Locke and Jean Jacques Rousseau, the contract is among individuals and not between the citizens and the sovereign. Once we agree to bring the sovereign into power, we no longer have any rights over it. The theory does not require any particular form of government (Hobbes preferred a single ruler but acknowledged the possibility of an assembly). Furthermore, there is no notion of a division of power. This is because Hobbes says the English Civil War resulted from the division of power among the king, lords, and the House of Commons.

From his own experience of political chaos, Hobbes concluded that the worst tyrant is better than no government at all or a weak, ineffective government. Hence, his sovereign has absolute power. Since we give up all our rights to the sovereign, the only rights we have are those the government finds it expedient to grant. It is logically impossible for the sovereign to act justly or unjustly, since all law and justice stem from the governmental authority. If the people were allowed to decide which laws were just, this would lead to anarchy. Hobbes details some features of such a society, but the way he derives a political theory from his beginning premises is all that is important for our purposes.

Hobbes always sought for peace so that he could pursue his intellectual projects unhindered. Ironically, his book brought him anything but peace and quiet. On the one hand, the royalists were not happy with his dismissal of the divine right of kings as the foundation of governmental authority. They wanted something more substantial, eternal, and dignified than a sovereign created out of desperation by the contract of the people. On the other hand, Hobbes upset the champions of a people's democracy by the absolute authority his theory gave to the sovereign. Consequently, Hobbes's innovative theory was caught in the cross fire of the more traditional approaches.

Evaluation and Significance of Hobbes

Hobbes's theory of perception and his psychological laws provided later thinkers with a model of scientific epistemology. However, Hobbes's account of perception contains at least two difficulties that he never recognized. First of all, his theory of experience divides the world into two realms. The first is the outer world of real bodies in motion. The second is the inner world of the mind, where we encounter the phantasms and their associated products that perception originally produced in us. However, how can we be sure we can accurately know what is going on in the external world if all we have are appearances and illusions? Obviously, we can never jump outside sense experience to compare it with its alleged object. Second, if there are "appearances," there is something that appears, and something that is appeared to. The spectator of appearances is consciousness. But where and how in this busy world of matter in motion does consciousness arise? If consciousness is a motion, it is a strange sort of motion that is capable of observing and being appeared to by all other motions. Hobbes never addressed these problems, and it was left to other philosophers to lose sleep over them.

Thomas Hobbes was a very important and innovative figure for his time. He made the first attempt to develop a total, materialistic monism in the modern period. His research program of using natural science as a model for the human sciences of psychology, sociology, and political theory was like a torch passed on by its advocates through the various periods of history into the twentieth century.

It was the last part of Hobbes's project, his political theory, that has brought him the most fame. In fact, many consider him the founder of modern political science. Karl Marx, the well-known nineteenth-century political theorist, once said, "Hobbes is the father of us all." His political theory turned an important corner in the history of thought. His great innovation was in seeing the state as a human, artificial creation. It is not based on eternal principles (as in Plato), nor is it intrinsic to human nature (as in Aristotle), nor is it a divinely ordained institution (as in medieval thought). Furthermore, by describing the state of nature as a collection of separate individuals, he fueled the spirit of individualism that has been both a blessing and a curse in the modern age. Hobbes's notions of the state of nature and the social contract would become important models for philosophies of human nature and politics in the centuries to come.

Hobbes's theory was also an important step toward the secularization of culture. By giving lip service to theology, while carrying on his science and philosophy independently of it, he strengthened this significant movement in modern thought. Specifically, he divorced civil life from theology and, thereby, made government an object of rational analysis rather than a divine institution that descended from above.

The unfinished details and problems of the Hobbesian system left plenty of work to keep future philosophers busy: (1) How do we know that our experiences correctly represent the outer world? (2) Can materialism explain consciousness and the knowing subject that is present in all experiencing? (3) Is it possible to take seriously the methods and results of the physical sciences and yet preserve traditional notions of purpose, human freedom, and values? The next chapter describes René Descartes's attempt to answer these questions by offering an alternative model.

Questions for Understanding

1. What were Bacon's four idols of the mind? Provide your own examples of each one. What was Bacon's purpose in identifying them?

2. What was Bacon's inductive method? How do his tables of inquiry illustrate his method?

3. Why was Bacon so optimistic about the role that science would play in human affairs?

4. What were the main contributions that Bacon made to science and philosophy?

5. What is Hobbes's theory of the following: perception, imagination, memory, thought?

6. Why does Hobbes believe that all human actions are determined?

7. How does Hobbes explain the fact that we sometimes seem undecided and unable to make up our minds?

8. How does Hobbes apply his view that everything is matter in motion to ethics?

9. What does Hobbes mean by the state of nature?

10. If there is no government, what sort of laws govern us, according to Hobbes?

11. Why does Hobbes believe that people will be compelled to create a government?

12. What is the social contract?

Questions for Reflection

1. Do you agree or disagree with Bacon, that it is possible to break free totally from all past thought? Why?

2. To what degree do we follow the methods of Bacon's tables of inquiry in science today? In what ways might they be limited?

3. In what ways has Bacon's scientific optimism been fulfilled? What consequences of modern science and technology in our day might dismay Bacon?

4. To what extent do you agree or disagree with Hobbes's notion that human psychological processes can be understood in terms of matter in motion? Why do you take this position?

5. Does Hobbes's social contract theory give us a good basis for understanding the basis of government? Would you want to live in a government run on Hobbesian principles? Why? If

not, what changes would you make to his political theory?

6. In what ways was Hobbes's philosophy innovative in his time?

7. Why are both Bacon and Hobbes considered early examples of modern empiricism?

Notes

1. The works of Francis Bacon are referenced using the following abbreviations:

GI   *The Great Instauration* in *The Great Instauration and New Atlantis*, ed. J. Weinberger (Arlington Heights, IL: AHM Publishing, 1980). All references to this work are to the page number of this edition.

NO   *Novum Organum* in *The English Philosophers from Bacon to Mill*, ed. Edwin A. Burtt (New York: Modern Library, Random House, 1939). Quotations from this work are referenced by referring either to book 1 or 2 and then to the number of the aphorism.

2. Quoted in Frederick Copleston, *A History of Philosophy*, vol. 3, pt. 2 (Garden City, NY: Image Books, Doubleday, 1953), 108.

3. Quotations from Thomas Hobbes's work are from *Leviathan: or the Matter, Form, and Power of a Commonwealth Ecclesiastical and Civil*, in *The English Philosophers from Bacon to Mill*, ed. Edwin A. Burtt (New York: Modern Library, Random House, 1939). References are to the part number, followed by the chapter number of Hobbes's work. It is cited in the text using the abbreviation L.

15

René Descartes:
Founder of Modern Philosophy

Descartes's Life: World Traveler and Intellectual Explorer

Descartes was born on March 31, 1596, in the small town of La Haye, France. The house in which he was born is still there, and the town has been renamed "Descartes" in his honor. He lived in a pivotal time. He was born some one hundred years after Columbus sailed to the Americas and some fifty years after Copernicus published his controversial work. Shakespeare was in his prime at this time. Descartes died in 1650, and almost forty years later Newton published his ground-breaking work in physics.

As a young man, Descartes received a good Scholastic education at the Jesuit college of La Flèche, one of the most famous schools in Europe. From there he went on to obtain a law degree. Feeling restless, and with a family fortune to support him, he began a series of travels. He joined several armies to see the world and continue his education. On November 10, 1619, when he was twenty-three, he was shut in by the harsh winter and spent the day in intense philo-

sophical reflection. That evening, the intellectual excitement of the day culminated in three vivid dreams. The dreams gave him a vision of his mission in life: to find the key to the mysteries of nature in a new philosophy based on mathematical reason. In gratitude for what he considered a divine vision, he took a vow to make a pilgrimage to the shrine of Our Lady of Loretto in Italy, which he later fulfilled.

By the end of the 1620s Descartes had completed *Rules for the Direction of the Mind*, his first major work. However, it was not published until after his death. In 1633 he had finished *Le Monde* ("The World"), a book on physics that presented the world as essentially matter in motion. He was all set to publish it when, in June of that year, the Inquisition in Rome formally condemned Galileo. Galileo's heresy was that he attacked the Aristotelian (and the Church's) view of the world. Since *Le Monde* agreed with Galileo's position, Descartes prudently sent his treatise away to a friend, to avoid the temptation to publish it. (It was eventually published in 1664, after his death.) Some argue that Descartes's references to God in his works were insincere and were only an attempt to appease the Church. However, despite some of his disagreements with the Church, his piety seemed genuine. This is made clear by his pilgrimage to the shrine in Italy as well as by his hopes that his philosophy would be of service to theology. Furthermore, the existence of God in his system plays too central a role to be a mere public relations gambit.

Eventually, he overcame his fear of public attention and began to publish some of his work. In 1637 he brought out *Discourse on the Method of Rightly Conducting One's Reason and Seeking the Truth in the Sciences*. Descartes originally wrote it in French instead of the traditional language of scholarship, Latin. In doing so, he hoped to appeal to the educated public instead of the academic clerics, who were likely to reject it. In August 1641 he brought out his masterpiece, *Meditations on First Philosophy*, one of the most engaging collections of arguments in the history of philosophy. Then, in 1644, he published *Principles of Philosophy*. He had hoped this book would be used as a university textbook in place of the current texts based on Aristotelian philosophy. At the end of the book he immodestly concludes that once people understand his method, they will see that the universe "can hardly be intelligibly explained except in the way I have suggested" (PP 4.206, 291).[1]

The last work published in his lifetime was *Passions of the Soul* in 1649. That same year, Queen Christina of Sweden, who had read the *Principles* and a draft of the *Passions*, invited Descartes to come be her personal tutor. He was reluctant to go, writing to a friend that Sweden was the land of "bears, rocks and ice." Nevertheless, he did go and was saddled with the unpleasant schedule of meeting with her three times a week at 5 o'clock in the morning. Descartes had always been a late riser because of his frail health, and his constitution could not take the frigid cold and the early hours. The climate and schedule wore him down until he caught pneumonia and died on February 11, 1650.

Descartes's Philosophical Agenda

Descartes was driven to his philosophical explorations by his keen dissatisfaction with the state of philosophy and science in his day. Concerning the traditional philosophy he had learned he says, "it has been cultivated for many centuries by the most excellent minds and yet there is still no point in it which is not disputed and hence doubtful" (D 1.8, 114-115). Since the other sciences began with philosophical presuppositions, Descartes concludes that "nothing solid could have been built upon such shaky foundations" (D 1.9, 115). He took these problems very personally, thinking he had wasted many years in formal education that had left him with ashes instead of a secure intellectual foundation for life:

> From my childhood I have been nourished upon letters, and because I was persuaded that by their means one could acquire a clear and certain knowledge of all that is useful in life, I was extremely eager to learn them. But as soon as I had completed the course of study at the end of which one is normally admitted to the ranks of the learned, I completely changed my opinion. For I found myself beset by so many doubts and errors that I came to think I had gained nothing from my attempts to become educated but increasing recognition of my ignorance. (D 1.4, 112-113)

Weary of textbooks and schools that merely repeated the tired, old ideas of Aristotle and the dogmas of Scholasticism, Descartes left his teachers behind and began to travel. His travels were not for the purpose of sightseeing but served as an intellectual journey in which he attempted to study "the great book of the world." However, this pursuit only led to further confusion, doubt, and despair as he encountered the diversity of opinions throughout the world. Finally, he says, "I resolved one day to undertake studies within myself too and to use all the powers of my mind in choosing the paths I should follow" (D 1.10, 116).

Descartes's decision to make himself the object of study and to look inward to find the truth, reminds one of Augustine's advice: "Return within yourself. In the inward man dwells truth."[2] Nevertheless, while Augustine's goal was to find the truth that would lead to a knowledge of God and salvation of the soul, Descartes's hope was to find a solid foundation for scientific knowledge. This autobiographical, individualistic approach to philosophy earned Descartes the title "Father of Modern Philosophy." Medieval philosophers used philosophical proofs to establish their conclusions, but it was also quite common to lend authority to one's ideas by quoting the Bible, the Church Fathers, or Aristotle. Sharply deviating from tradition, Descartes very rarely quotes anyone. Instead, we have the image of a solitary thinker, hammering out for himself the truths by which he would live. Hence, Descartes continually says, "it seems to *me* . . . ," or "*I* am convinced . . . ," or "*I* have found that. . . ." The personal pronoun asserts itself with a frequency that earlier ages might have thought impious. Descartes was convinced that individuals had the necessary intellectual equipment to discover truth on their own. However, although each person had to personally discover the truth, he believed (as did Socrates) that our separate intellectual journeys would take us to the same destination.

Descartes's work as a philosopher revolved around three goals. The first goal was to find certainty. This concern was an obsession that dominated all his philosophical thought. For Descartes, doubts about what to believe and the conflicting opinions he found everywhere he looked were not only psychologically disturbing, but weakened the foundations of all the sciences. Descartes's second goal was to fulfill the dream of a universal science. This goal required him to find a unified set of principles from which he could deduce all the answers to scientific questions.

Descartes discussed the first two goals in his theory of knowledge and addressed the third goal in his metaphysics. This last goal was that of reconciling the mechanistic view of the world found in science with human freedom and his own religious perspective. The picture of the world as a giant, deterministic physical machine threatened the uniqueness and freedom of the human soul and seemed to leave little room for God. Although Hobbes was comfortable in viewing people as simply physical mechanisms, Descartes wanted to give science its due respect while preserving spiritual realities and human freedom.

The Discovery of a Method

Descartes addressed his first two concerns (the search for certainty and the dream of a universal science) by turning to mathematics. In his student days he had fallen in love with the discipline. In contrast with the confusion he found in all other subjects, mathematics delighted him with "the certainty and self-evidence of its reasonings" (D 1.7, 114). This delight turned to conviction in the winter of 1619, when he became convinced there was a universal method contained within mathematical research that could be applied to all questions. He expressed this insight in the *Discourse*:

> Those long chains composed of very simple and easy reasonings, which geometers customarily use to arrive at their most difficult demonstrations, had given me occasion to suppose that all the things which can fall under human knowledge are interconnected in the same way. And I thought that, provided we refrain from accepting anything as true which is not, and always keep to the order required for deducing one thing from another, there can be nothing too remote to be reached in the end or too well hidden to be discovered. (D 2.19, 120)

Descartes argued that the method of mathematics consists of two mental operations. The first operation is that of *intuition*. By this he does not mean some sort of nonrational, subjective conviction or hunch. Instead, he means the recognition of self-evident truths. Examples of self-evident truths would be the axioms of geometry (for example, things equal to the same thing are equal to each other) or the simple truths of arithmetic ($2 + 3 = 5$) or the basic principles of logic. If we are thinking clearly when we inspect a self-evident truth, we will simply see it is true. We do not need to derive it from any other truth, for it carries its own credentials. Descartes believed such ideas are inborn or innate. (He concluded later that God implants them within us.) This does not mean that we are always aware of these ideas, however. It merely means we could not derive them from sense experience; we discover them through a kind of intellectual "vision."*

The second operation of reason is *deduction*. Descartes describes this as a necessary inference from other propositions that are known with certainty. Just as Euclid started with ten axioms and deduced some five hundred theorems from them, so we can proceed from any self-evident truth by a series of carefully constructed logical steps to a conclusion that is just as certain as our starting point. Descartes was so confident of the philosophical method he had borrowed from mathematics that he actually thought the search for *all* truth could be completed by carefully applying his rules.

He seemed to have been led to this optimistic hope by the success of his own mathematical discoveries. Even if he had never been a great philosopher, his place in history would have been assured by virtue of the fact that he was the first to publish (if not to discover) the principles of analytic geometry (in 1637). With his equations, the figures of plane geometry could be represented as algebraic formulas. Hence, we have spatial figures (such as we encounter in the physical world) yielding to an analysis in terms of numbers and variables. With brilliant insight, he showed that the physical world could be translated into mathematical forms. In so doing, he fulfilled the ancient dream of such mathematically inspired philosophers as Pythagoras and Plato. Descartes was convinced that the method of reasoning used in mathematics could bring order to our knowledge, regardless of the subject:

> I came to see that the exclusive concern of mathematics is with questions of order or measure and that it is irrelevant whether the measure in question involves numbers, shapes, stars, sounds, or any other object whatever. (R 4.377-378, 19)

Finding the Foundations of Knowledge

The most definitive and eloquent statement of Descartes's philosophy appears in his *Meditations on First Philosophy*. Although he wrote the six meditations as though he had made his discoveries during six days of sustained thought, he had actually been working on these issues for ten years. Descartes, perhaps, chose a literary form he had learned from his Jesuit college. It was common for the faithful to spend the six days of Holy Week focusing inwardly and studying the spiritual meditations of Ignatius Loyola, the founder of the Jesuit order. In a similar fashion, but with a more philosophical purpose, Descartes provides us with a series of mental exercises and invites us to meditate along with him, that each of us might find the truth within.

METHOD OF DOUBT

Descartes begins the *Meditations* with the innocuous remark that "some years ago I was struck by the large number of falsehoods that I had accepted as true in my childhood" (M 1.17, 12). Although every one of us has had this unsettling realization, Descartes is especially noted for the seriousness with which he viewed this problem and the radical solution he proposes for it:

> I realized that it was necessary, once in the course of my life, to demolish everything completely and start again right from the foundations. (M 1.17, 12)

Thus begins what is known as Descartes's "method of doubt." In a letter to one of his critics, Descartes describes his project with a very apt metaphor (OR 7:481, 63). Suppose we have a basket of apples, he says, and we suspect some are rotten. If we remove only the bad ones that happen to catch our eye, we risk missing some, which may infect the rest. The only safe procedure, therefore,

---

*The claim that we can obtain knowledge through a nonsensory intellectual vision is an essential doctrine of rationalism. Plato makes use of this notion in discussing our knowledge of the Forms as does Augustine in explaining how divine illumination enables us to "see" eternal truths.

is to empty the whole basket, carefully inspect the apples one by one, and return to the basket only those that are sound. The apples, of course, are Descartes's beliefs. The rotten ones are false beliefs, and the good apples are true beliefs. The basket is the mind, and the dumping of the apples is Descartes's method of doubt. To use another metaphor, Descartes submerges his entire belief system in an acid bath of doubt. Many beliefs will not endure this process. But if any beliefs come through unscathed, he will know these beliefs have a certainty beyond any possible doubt.

In the *Second Meditation*, by means of yet another metaphor, Descartes compares himself to Archimedes. Archimedes, you will recall, was the Greek who discovered the principle of the lever. He claimed that if he had a fixed and unmovable fulcrum, he could lift the earth. Descartes indicates that he is searching for a philosophical "Archimedean point," a truth so certain and indubitable that the entire structure of knowledge may be supported on its base.

Is it really possible to doubt *everything* that I believe? I can certainly doubt some of my beliefs. For example, I may think I remember unplugging the iron when I left the house and yet have nagging doubts about whether I really did or not. But can I doubt that this is a book that I am reading? And surely only a lunatic would doubt that 2 + 2 = 4. However, in doubting these sorts of beliefs, Descartes is not asserting skepticism (despite what some of his contemporaries thought). His position is more properly labeled "methodological skepticism." He is using the skeptical stance as a tool or method for testing his beliefs. But why is it necessary to doubt beliefs that are obviously true? The problem is that these taken-for-granted beliefs may be some of the most dangerous ones we have. To previous ages, nothing was more certain than that the sun revolved around the earth. That, too, was thought something only a lunatic would doubt. Once Descartes decides to screen and test his beliefs, he cannot let up his guard for one minute, lest some false belief sneaks in, leaving him back where he started.

Since his beliefs are so numerous, how can he possibly examine every one of them? Fortunately,

this tedious process is not necessary, for he finds that he can group his beliefs into a small number of categories and examine each general category in turn. Descartes's *First Meditation* takes the form of a challenging philosophical game. At each turn he produces a belief about which he is certain. Then he uses his creative imagination to see if there is any way to imagine he could be mistaken. Once he has found any possibility of doubting the belief, then he must suspend believing it and see if there is another belief that will fare better. Although it has some of the elements of a mental game, this process is actually very serious, for Descartes is trying to find the foundations on which to live his life.

The first group of beliefs he examines are those based on sense perception. This set of beliefs constitutes a considerably large number of our beliefs. It is not difficult to manufacture doubts here, for our senses often deceive us. Optical illusions (such as the "water" on a hot road in the summer), magicians' tricks, thinking I see a friend across campus when it is really a stranger, and many other everyday examples furnish us with evidence of Descartes's point. The moral he draws here is that "it is prudent never to trust completely those who have deceived us even once."

But some sense experiences seem so real that one would think only a lunatic would doubt them. For example, it would be hard to doubt your belief that you are now reading a philosophy book. But even here, Descartes can generate some doubts. He says we must remember we often find dreams extraordinarily real. Sharing his own experiences, he says, "How many times has it occurred that the quiet of the night made me dream of my usual habits: that I was here, clothed in a dressing gown, and sitting by the fire, although I was in fact lying undressed in bed!" If you suspect this is happening, you can pinch yourself to see if you're awake. But alas, you may only be dreaming that you are pinching yourself. The only way you find out that you *were* dreaming (past tense) is to wake up. But suppose your experiences right now are a dream that has not yet been interrupted? The point is that the most vivid sense experience does not give us the foundational belief we need because we have no effective way to distinguish it from a dream.

At this point, Descartes comes up with a difficult challenge for his methodological doubt. The simple truths of arithmetic and geometry seem to be beyond doubt. "For whether I am awake or asleep, two and three added together are five, and a square has no more than four sides. It seems impossible that such transparent truths should incur any suspicion of being false" (M 1.20, 14). Nevertheless, Descartes says he can imagine there is a very powerful God that injects false beliefs in his mind. In other words, the truth may be that 2 + 3 = 7 1/2 but God makes us believe the answer is 5. If such deception seems contrary to the notion of God, Descartes says we can adjust the premise and imagine that some very powerful evil spirit is giving us physical and mathematical illusions. This supposition may seem very bizarre. Nevertheless, it is at least logically possible that our entire world is a vast illusion and our most fundamental beliefs are all false. If this is at least possible, then we do not have the sort of certainty Descartes thinks we so desperately need.

THE FOUNDATION OF CERTAINTY

As Descartes ends the *First Meditation*, he seems in worse shape than when he began. When he started this intellectual experiment, he had doubts about some of the beliefs he had acquired in his education. Now, however, he is left with the tragic conviction "There is not one of my former beliefs about which a doubt may not properly be raised" (M 1.21, 14-15). But wait! Here is the Archimedean point he is seeking. If he is sure of nothing else, he is at least certain he is doubting. What would happen if he applied his method of doubt to this belief? When he tries to doubt the proposition "I am in doubt," he actually ends up proving it! Furthermore, if he doubts, then he must exist. It is clear, then, that he exists as a doubter. Even if an evil demon is deceiving him about the existence of "the sky, the air, the earth, colors, shapes, sounds" as well as all his mathematical knowledge, the demon could not deceive him if Descartes did not exist as a conscious being. To be a deceiver, the great deceiver needs a victim.

An engraving of Descartes deep in thought while walking the streets of Amsterdam. Consumed by the need for certainty, Descartes wrote, "I realized that it was necessary, once in the course of my life, to demolish everything completely and start again right from the foundations."

The rock-solid foundation Descartes has been looking for is thus found in the proposition "I am, I exist." In the *Discourse*, he states his discovery as "I think, therefore I am."* He is directly acquainted with his own acts of thinking. Whether this thinking takes the form of doubting or some other cognitive activity, it is impossible to deny this is occurring. Accordingly, every time he asserts, "I am thinking," he must assert the *I*. In other words, he

*Commentators often express the phrase "I think, therefore I am" in its Latin form, which is *"Cogito ergo sum."* This was how Descartes stated it in *Principles of Philosophy*, which he wrote in Latin.

necessarily must assert the existence of the self who is doing the thinking.

THE NATURE OF THE SELF

Having established the certainty of his own existence, it now occurs to Descartes that he must carefully define what kind of being he is. In what way does he identify himself? For a moment, Descartes is tempted to identify himself with his body. After all, he is accustomed to saying, "I am eating" or "I am walking." But this will not do, because his entire knowledge of his body comes through his sense experience, such as the physical sensations he has when he is eating or walking. The problem is that despite his recent triumph over *total* skepticism, he still has no reason to trust his senses, including the sensing of his own body. Since it was his own thinking that made him certain he exists, Descartes affirms, "I am, then . . . only a thing that thinks; that is, I am a mind" (M 2.27, 18). Thus, when Descartes says, "I exist," what he means is that he knows that his mind exists, but he does not yet know that his body exists.

It may seem absurd to suppose that one can exist as a conscious mind divorced from a body. Nevertheless, this notion is found in many traditional teachings concerning personal immortality. Furthermore, we can consider the medical phenomenon of the "phantom limb." (Descartes was familiar with this medical curiosity.) Someone who has had an arm amputated often feels itching in the missing fingers. The frustration is that the itch cannot be scratched because the apparent source of the sensation, the fingers of the amputated arm, no longer exist. The severed nerves in the stump send messages to the brain, which it mistakenly interprets as coming from the missing hand. Such patients think they are having feelings in a bodily part that is no longer there. Descartes has no way to be sure that all his bodily sensations are not of this nature.

Even though Descartes is directly aware that his thoughts exist, how can he be sure that behind these passing thoughts he exists as a thinking being or an enduring mental substance? It may seem to be perfectly obvious that thoughts do not roam around on their own but are related to a mind that thinks them. Nevertheless, Descartes's rigorous method prevented him from accepting anything he could not prove. Therefore, critics think he should have said, "Thinking is going on" rather than "I am a thinking being."

THE CRITERIA OF TRUTH

At this point, Descartes's hard-fought victory over skepticism seems empty. True, he knows for sure that he exists as a mind that thinks, doubts, loves, hates, wills, imagines, and has experiences. But that is all he knows. If he can go no further than this, he is stuck in a position known as solipsism. **Solipsism** is the view that there is no reality outside of one's mind. Everything that exists is but an idea or experience within one's mind. This meager amount of certainty is not what Descartes was hoping for. Making the best of it, he begins to explore the only reality he has available: his mind and its contents. What made him certain of his own existence? He discovers that what convinced him of this truth was that it was *clear* and *distinct*. Hence, the general principle that he derives from this discovery is that "whatever I perceive very clearly and distinctly is true" (M 3.35, 24). Perhaps this principle can be used as a bridge to obtain knowledge about the physical world.

Nevertheless, one nagging problem still needs to be resolved. It is still possible (though not plausible) to imagine that God leads me to be mistaken about things that seem obvious. Hence, Descartes says, "As soon as the opportunity arises I must examine whether there is a God, and, if there is, whether he can be a deceiver. For if I do not know this, it seems that I can never be quite certain about anything else" (M 3.36, 25). The next step in Descartes's intellectual journey, therefore, is to prove the existence of a nondeceiving God.

Metaphysics: God, World, Minds, and Bodies

Throughout the *Meditations*, Descartes's primary concern is epistemology, so he never stops tinkering with his theory of knowledge. Nevertheless, in the final three meditations he moves from the epistemological problem of certainty to metaphysical questions about reality. These include the existence of God, the existence of the physical world, and the mind–body relationship. The first item on his agenda is to prove the existence of a good God.

THE CAUSAL ARGUMENT FOR GOD'S EXISTENCE

Notice what limited materials Descartes has at his disposal for proving God's existence. Because Thomas Aquinas did not doubt the existence of the world, he could use facts about the world in his proofs. However, Descartes does not yet know if there is an external world. Somehow, Descartes must reason to God using only the contents of his own mind. I will set out Descartes's argument in outline form and then go on to discuss it in more detail:

(1) Something cannot be derived from nothing. In other words, all effects (including ideas) are caused by something.

(2) There must be at least as much reality in the cause as there is in the effect.

(3) I have an idea of God (as an infinite and perfect being).

(4) The idea of God in my mind is an effect that was caused by something.

(5) I am finite and imperfect, and thus I could not be the cause of the idea of an infinite and perfect God.

(6) Only an infinite and perfect being could be the cause of such an idea.

(7) Therefore, God (an infinite and perfect being) exists.

The first step of the argument is a familiar one. It is a commonly held (but not uncontroversial) belief that has long been a premise in arguments for God's existence. In his discussion of the second step, Descartes's actual argument becomes somewhat complex, but its main thrust can be summarized very simply. He says that a cold object (such as a pot of water) cannot become hot unless something else causes that heat. But the cause must have at least as high a degree of heat as the effect. Not only is it impossible for something to come from nothing, it is likewise impossible for one level of reality (the boiling of a pot of water) to be produced by a cause that is less than the effect (a cold stove).

Just as the heated water is an effect that requires a cause, so Descartes's idea of an infinite and perfect being is an effect or a phenomenon that requires some explanation. One possibility is simply that he could have produced the idea himself. Although he thinks it possible that a finite person can manufacture the idea of another finite object (the mental fiction of a mermaid for example), he does not think this is plausible with respect to the idea of God. As Descartes puts it, "My perception of the infinite, that is God, is in some way prior to my perception of the finite, that is myself" (M 3.45, 31). Since "finite" means "that which is limited," I can understand my own finitude only if I see my finite being as a deficient version of a greater being. An imperfect mind producing the idea of perfection would be like a cold stove producing heated water. "For how could I understand that . . . I lacked something—and that I was not wholly perfect, unless there were in me some idea of a more perfect being which enabled me to recognize my own defects by comparison?" (M 3.46, 31). Ordinarily, the ideas in my mind do not tell me if there is an external reality. However, the idea of perfection is unique. If I could not have produced it myself, then "it will necessarily follow that I am not alone in the world, but that some other thing which is the cause of this idea also exists" (M 3.42, 29).

CRITICISMS OF DESCARTES'S CAUSAL ARGUMENT FOR GOD

Since Descartes has started us on the program of being rigorously skeptical of all our beliefs, we must ask him why he is so certain that every effect must have a cause and that a cause must have as great a degree of reality or perfection as is found in the effect. His answer is that the "light of nature" teaches us that this is so. Many Renaissance writers thought the light of nature was a natural mental faculty that enabled us to immediately apprehend self-evident truths. That this piece of psychological theory seems so strange to many modern ears suggests it is not as obvious and indubitable as Descartes thought. Furthermore, he wants to make a distinction between *natural impulses* that cause us to believe certain things (but which can lead us to false beliefs) and the revelations of the *light of nature* (which always lead us to the truth) (M 38-39, 26-27). The problem Descartes never resolves is how we can know when the infallible light of nature is guiding us, as opposed to when our unreliable natural impulses are leading us. In both cases, what we are inclined to believe *seems* to be true. Without any further criteria to distinguish the two sources of belief, we can have little confidence that it is the light of nature at work within us.

Furthermore, it seems strange that Descartes finds it possible to doubt that 2 + 3 = 5, but cannot doubt the more complex and loaded metaphysical principle that "there must be at least as much reality in the total efficient cause as in its effect." Without extensive qualification, Descartes's principle could not account for the production of emergent properties such as when two cold substances chemically react and produce heat or light. In one of his many replies to the objections of his critics, he tries to put his arguments in the form of a geometrical proof. Here, he lists the principle as an "axiom or common notion," indicating that it is so obvious that it can be accepted without further discussion. But it was just such taken-for-granted beliefs that Descartes said were subject to doubt no matter how obvious they appeared. At this point in the argument, it is clear he has cheated on the rigorous rules of method he set down initially.

Several theologians of Descartes's time (who were more empiricist than Descartes) questioned the claim that infinity and perfection must precede all thoughts of finitude and imperfection. As one of them put it, "I can surely take a given degree of being, which I perceive within myself, and add on

a further degree, and thus construct the idea of a perfect being from all the degrees which are capable of being added on" (OR 2.123, 82). For example, think about your own modest amount of knowledge. Next think about someone having twice this amount of knowledge. Then imagine that this quantity is repeatedly doubled as many times as there are whole numbers. You will have imaginatively constructed the notion of an infinite amount of knowledge. If finite minds can construct the idea of infinity or perfection in this way, we do not need to look outside of ourselves for the origin of this idea.

It is worth noting that the theologians who used this argument as well as the empiricist John Locke, who would make use of it fifty years later, did not disagree with the conclusion "God exists." They simply did not think Descartes had provided good arguments for this belief. Hence, a theist who is a rationalist and another who is an empiricist differ radically in their epistemological starting points, but end up with the same conclusion. Similarly, two atheists could arrive at their respective beliefs, using two different and conflicting theories of knowledge. This illustrates the important point that philosophy is not simply concerned with the beliefs we hold, but with the way in which we arrive at those beliefs.

FURTHER ARGUMENTS FOR GOD'S EXISTENCE

In the *Meditations*, Descartes provides two other arguments for the existence of God. The second argument is another causal argument that seeks to show that his own sustained existence requires an adequate cause. Using a variation of his first proof, he argues that a being such as himself who contains the idea of perfection could not come from an imperfect cause. In the course of searching for an explanation of his own, sustained existence, he introduces the principle that there cannot be an infinite regress of causes. Therefore, these causes must culminate in an ultimate cause.

For Descartes's third proof of God, we must jump ahead to the *Fifth Meditation*. Here he employs a version of the ontological argument developed by St. Anselm in the eleventh century. The main outline of Descartes's argument is as follows:

(1) I have the idea of a God that possesses all perfections.

(2) Existence is a kind of perfection.

(3) If the God I am thinking of lacked existence, then he would not be perfect.

(4) Hence, if I can have the idea of a perfect God, I must conclude that existence is one of his essential properties.

(5) If existence is one of God's essential properties, he must exist.

(6) Therefore, God exists.

Descartes's argument is based on the notion that when I clearly understand the idea of something, I will be led to conceive of all the essential properties of that object. For example, he says that if I have a clear and distinct idea of a triangle, I will see that one of its essential properties is that the sum of its angles is 180 degrees. If I am thinking of something that does not have this property, then whatever I am thinking of is not a triangle. Similarly, it is impossible to think of a mountain without conceiving of its corresponding valley.

　　Now the idea of God is normally thought to be the idea of a perfect being. One does not have to be a believer to affirm this. Even the atheist who denies there is a God must have some idea of the being he is denying. Since the idea of God is the idea of a perfect being, such a being cannot lack any perfections, including existence. No other being besides God has existence as a part of its essence. For example, having a valley is part of the essence of a mountain, while existence is not one of its essential properties. Therefore, we can think about mountains that do not exist. But with God, Descartes claims, it is different. It would be contradictory to say, "I can think of a perfect being who necessarily has the property of existence but who does not exist."

GOD AND THE VALIDITY OF REASON

Having satisfied himself that a perfect God exists, he also knows that this God would not deceive us, for this would make him morally imperfect. In the *Fourth Meditation* Descartes considers what progress this offers him in the area of epistemology. Since God has created our cognitive faculties and is not malicious or deceptive, Descartes is confident that when he uses his reason properly, it cannot fail to lead him to truth. In other words, he now knows that anything that appears clearly and distinctly to his reason must be true. However, many have found a problem here. This difficulty has been called "the Cartesian circle."* Descartes originally said it was necessary to prove the existence of a nondeceptive God to be sure that ideas that seem clear and distinct are not just illusions, but really are true. If he is correct in saying this, then he surely cannot use the criteria of clarity and distinctness in his proof of God. This criticism was effectively stated by Descartes's contemporary, Antoine Arnauld:

> I have one further worry, namely how the author avoids reasoning in a circle when he says that we are sure that what we clearly and distinctly perceive is true only because God exists.
>
> But we can be sure that God exists only because we clearly and distinctly perceive this. Hence, before we can be sure that God exists, we ought to be able to be sure that whatever we perceive clearly and evidently is true. (OR 4.214, 106)

The lesson to be learned here is that although it is important to be critical of our taken-for-granted beliefs, we cannot begin philosophizing in a total cognitive void. We can doubt our beliefs piecemeal, but not all of them at the same time. If we doubt everything, we have no toehold to climb out of the abyss. Even if we grant Descartes the first step of his own existence, he still needs to trust logic and his clear and distinct intuitions in order to move to any other conclusions. However, his method of doubt does not allow him this luxury.

---

*"Cartesian" is an adjective derived from Descartes's name.

Descartes started out wondering if he could ever be sure of the truth of his beliefs. However, now that God guarantees the reliability of our reasoning processes, Descartes is faced with the opposite problem. How is it possible for us ever to be in error? His answer is very simple:

> So what then is the source of my mistakes? It must be simply this: the scope of the will is wider than that of the intellect; but instead of restricting it within the same limits, I extend its use to matters which I do not understand. Since the will is indifferent in such cases, it easily turns aside from what is true and good, and this is the source of my error and sin. (M 4.58, 40-41)

In other words, while my understanding is limited, my will races ahead and embraces beliefs that have not been carefully checked out. It takes discipline, therefore, to restrain my will and to affirm only those propositions I have a right to believe. In a classic statement of rationalistic optimism, Descartes claims that when reasoning carefully, "it is quite impossible for me to go wrong" (M 4.62, 43). His discussion here is very shrewd, for it accomplishes two things. On the one hand, he accounts for human error by giving lip service to human finiteness, fallibility, and even sin. In doing this he has stayed within the bounds of traditional theology and avoided the charge of arrogant pride. On the other hand, he has said that when the correct philosophical method (his own) is carefully applied, human reason cannot fail in its pursuit of truth. This second thesis is clearly the one Descartes is most enthusiastic about, for it is the doorway to the new age of reason and science.

Thus far, Descartes's rationalistic method has led him out of the dark cavern of skepticism. He is now absolutely certain of the following facts: (1) he exists as a thinking being, and (2) God exists. The second belief is particularly important, for it released him from the prison of his own mind. He now knows something exists besides his own mind and its ideas. But much is still lacking. He still does not know for sure that the physical world is real, and these doubts still extend to his knowledge of his own body. This is not only personally disconcerting but also intellectually problematic. After all, unless we can be certain of our knowledge of the physical world, all the marvelous discoveries of recent science are left hanging without any adequate foundation. How can he use his certainty of God's existence as a bridge to the external world?

THE EXISTENCE OF THE PHYSICAL WORLD

Descartes's argument for the existence of the world is very simple. Starting again with his own ideas, he notices that he has ideas of physical objects. He has experiences, for example, of coins, chairs, trees, dogs, wine, and cheese. The question is whether or not anything in the external world corresponds to these ideas. After all, he conjectured in the *First Meditation* that the whole of his experience could be a dream. Descartes asks the same question about these ideas that he asked about the idea of God. What caused these ideas? One possibility is that I am the cause of these ideas. But this is obviously false, because I seem to be completely passive in perception. The chilly, cold winds of winter are thrust on me. I don't choose this experience. A more plausible theory is that God produces the ideas of a physical world within me. But this theory has one major flaw. If there is no physical world and God gives me the illusion that there is one, then he is a deceiver. But we saw earlier that God must be perfect and, therefore, cannot be a deceiver. There is only one final possibility, that the world more or less conforms to the way I experience it. If I experience wet, cool water on a hot summer day, it is because the water is really there and the sun is really there, giving me these experiences.

All his life he had naively believed that there is a physical world without considering the possibility that this could be an illusion. Now, however, he is confident he has rigorous, philosophical reasons for this belief. He acknowledges that physical objects are not always exactly the way they appear to the senses. However, he points out that sensory illusions can be overcome through rational understanding. For example, if we see a stick in the water, we may jump to the conclusion that the stick is really bent. In doing so, however, we are relying on the confused perceptions of the senses instead of allowing reason to guide us. What we are actually seeing, by means of light rays that are being bent as they pass through the water, is a straight stick. Once our minds understand the scientific laws of refraction, we will not be the victims of an optical illusion but will understand the stick as it really is.

Despite the confusions of sense perception, Descartes affirms that physical things "possess all the properties which I clearly and distinctly understand, that is, all those which, viewed in general terms, are comprised within the subject-matter of pure mathematics" (M 6.80, 55). In these few words he is making a very important point that will have a long-term ripple effect on later philosophers and even on how we view the world today. In this passage, Descartes is giving momentum to Galileo's view that the real nature of the physical universe is mathematical. In other words, the objective properties of an object consist only of its spatial extension (its size, shape, and motion). But what about the colors, tastes, sounds, and all those qualities in our experience that make the world so rich and enjoyable? We can imagine Descartes replying,

You've said it correctly. Those are only qualities in our experience. They are not properties of the objects themselves. These qualities are the subjective effects on our sense organs that are caused by the objective qualities in the world.

Let the poets wax eloquent about the smell of the rose, let the artists dazzle us with their colors, let us still enjoy the wispy sounds of the flute. These perceived objects delight our senses. But let's be clear about one thing, Descartes says: these sensory experiences give us only the world of appearances. Through scientific reason we will find the formulas that accurately describe the physical world.

Descartes has now fully recovered from the sea of doubt that engulfed him at the beginning of his journey. With the proof of the physical world in hand, scientists can now pick up where they left off, secure and confident of the intellectual foundations of their enterprise. Descartes had hoped people would be grateful for his efforts, but many were not. For some, it seemed impious that God

was not the center and focus of Descartes's system. Descartes began with himself and ended with the physical world. It seemed as though God was simply a stepping-stone to get from one to the other. At least, this is what the French philosopher and mathematician, Blaise Pascal (1623–1662) claimed. A very devout Catholic, he wrote the following note some fifteen years after the first appearance of the Meditations:

I cannot forgive Descartes. In all his philosophy he would have been quite willing to dispense with God. But he could not help granting him a flick of the forefinger to start the world in motion; beyond this, he has no further need of God.[3]

THE MIND–BODY RELATION

Now that Descartes has rescued himself from skepticism and has recovered the reality of the world, we need to see exactly what sort of reality has been recovered. To get clear on this, Descartes uncritically dredges up the Greek and medieval notion of substance. He defines substance as "a thing which exists in such a way as to depend on no other thing for its existence" (PP 1.51, 210). Obviously, only God would fully fit this description, since everything else depends on him. Nevertheless, in a limited and analogical sense, created things can be called substances. According to Descartes there are two main categories of substances: mental substances and physical substances. This implies that the mind and body are two completely different entities. You will recall that Descartes started out by being sure of his own mental existence but in doubt as to whether or not his body existed. This led him to conclude that the mind is a separate substance from the body because it does not need the body in order to exist or to be understood. Furthermore, the mind and the body are separate substances because they have completely different attributes. Minds are capable of conscious acts such as thinking, doubting, and willing. Bodies are not conscious and are simply moved by mechanical forces acting on them. Minds are not extended and so do not take up space. They are a kind of nonphysical or spiritual reality. Because they are not extended, they are not made up of parts and cannot be divided. Bodies, of course, are extended, occupy space, and can be divided into more elementary particles.

The picture that emerges is that human beings are made up of two different kinds of reality somehow linked together. On the one hand, we have bodies and are a part of the physical world. The body is a machine made out of flesh and bone. Your joints and tendons act like pivots, pulleys, and ropes. Your heart is a pump, and your lungs are bellows. In this way we are just like animals. But to Descartes, all animals except for humans were nothing but machines. Hence, to the Cartesian it is impossible to be cruel to animals, because without minds, they cannot feel anything. When an animal cries, it is merely a sound the mechanism makes, just as your car squeals when it needs lubrication. Humans, however, are unique in that they also possess minds. According to Descartes, your mind (which is identical to your soul) is the "real" you. If you lose an arm or a leg, your bodily mechanism is impaired but you are still as complete a person as before.

Descartes's position here is a kind of dualism. **Dualism** is the name for any theory that postulates two kinds of ultimate and irreducible principles or elements. More specifically, what we have here is a metaphysical dualism. **Metaphysical dualism** refers to any theory that claims that there are two ultimate and irreducible kinds of reality. To be even more specific, because Descartes's theory concerns the relationship between the mind and the body, it can be called *mind–body dualism* or *psychophysical dualism*. Since Descartes has given the classic statement of this position, it is also commonly referred to as *Cartesian dualism* in his honor.

DESCARTES'S COMPROMISE

This dualistic scheme has sometimes been called the "Cartesian compromise." Descartes was an enthusiastic champion of the new, mechanistic science. He was also a sincere Catholic. One of his concerns, therefore, was to reconcile the scientific and religious views of the world. By dividing reality up into completely separate territories, he was able to accomplish this goal. One part of reality is made up of physical substances. These can be studied by science and explained by mechanistic principles. This part of the universe is a giant, clocklike mechanism. All events in this realm are determined by the laws that physicists discover. Hence, we make observations, formulate physical laws, and make accurate predictions about physical events. Insofar as we are bodies, science can explain our physical motions. Another part of reality is made up of mental or spiritual substances. Our minds are free to think and will as we wish, because mental substances are not governed by mechanical laws. In this way, people (unlike their bodies) have genuine free will. If you jump into a swimming pool, for example, the falling of your body is governed by the laws of nature. Your decision to make that jump, however, is freely chosen and cannot be explained by physics.

In the physical realm, science is the dominant authority and gives us the truth. We do not consult the Church or the Bible to see how fast the heart pumps its blood. Science informs us about that. But according to the Cartesian compromise, science cannot tell us about the eternal destiny of our souls, because it can tell us only about our bodies. Hence, in the spiritual realm, says Descartes, religion still retains its authority and truth.

INTERACTIONISM

At first glance, Descartes's strategy of assigning minds and bodies to two separate domains of reality may seem like a plausible compromise. However, there are difficult, nagging problems with this solution. Since we are made up of both a mind *and* a body, how do the two of them coexist? One theory might be that the mind is like a pilot that directs the ship, which is the body. However, Descartes recognizes that this model is not correct. He says that if this picture were correct, when our bodies were wounded we should no more feel pain than a pilot does when his ship is damaged. The problem is that our minds are much more intimately related to our bodies than this. The two seem to mutually influence one another. If I go without sleep, or take cold medicine, or am physically uncomfortable, my mind doesn't work very effectively. But if I am worried or mentally distressed, my stomach tenses up. Furthermore, if I mentally decide I want that slice of pizza before me, my hand reaches out to grab it. My mind is capable of putting my body into motion and vice versa. I can understand how one thought can lead to another thought. Similarly, I can understand how one physical object can move another physical object. But how does my mind move my body, and how can my body affect my mind? In other words, how is it possible for a spiritual substance and a physical substance to interact? The mind has no gears or muscles or chemicals by which to move other things or to be moved. Descartes has created quite a problem for his metaphysics. He has so radically separated the mind and body that it is not clear how they work together as effectively as they do.

Unfortunately, Descartes's solution to this problem is not very helpful. He was aware that there was a small gland located at the base of the brain (the pineal gland), which seemed to be very important, but there was no consensus at the time as to what it did. So he had an organ that needed a function to explain its purpose. He also had a function (mind–body interaction) that needed a location. The two problems seemed to fit together like the pieces of a jigsaw puzzle. Given what he knew, it made sense to see in this a common solution to his two problems. Hence, he thought the pineal gland was affected by "vital spirits", and through this intermediary, the soul could alter the motions in the brain, which then could affect the body and vice versa (PS 1.31, 340). It seems obvious, however, that making the pineal gland the location of the mind–body interaction still fails to explain how physical matter influences and is influenced by a spiritual substance.

At this point the Cartesian compromise seems to break down. By separating mental substances and physical substances, he neatly placed religion, the human person, and freedom in one compartment, and science, mechanism, and determinism in another compartment, where they would not interfere with one another's domain. Thus, while science can explain the process of digestion in my

body, it cannot explain mental events such as my decision to join a church, for example. The latter is not a chemical or physical event but a free decision originating in my mind and based on my spiritual values. However, because the interplay of the mind and body is so obvious to our ordinary experience, Descartes had to introduce his theory of interactionism.

The problem is, however, if our minds can influence the physical world through our bodies, then much in the physical world cannot be explained by mechanistic science. The universe is not a self-sufficient clocklike mechanism after all. Yet if the physical forces affecting the body can cause mental events, then our mental life and behavior are, to a large degree, products of the physical environment. In the first case, science is stymied because it could never sort out all spiritual and physical causes of an event. In the second case, our mental life is sucked into the clocklike physical universe, where *everything* can be explained deterministically in terms of particles in motion, as Hobbes believed. In this picture, Descartes's revolutionary ideas could well be just the inevitable outcome of the purposeless, neurochemical events in his brain.

Because interactionism carries with it so many problems, many Cartesians found it necessary to deny it. Arnold Geulincx (1624–1669) claimed that mental events and physical events are causally independent processes that only seem to influence one another. In one of his discussions, Geulincx said God arranges the two parallel series of mental and physical events to work together like two clocks that are set to strike the hour at the same time. Since God has foreseen that I am now willing my pen to write on this paper, he has arranged the physical world so that my hand and the pen move simultaneously with my mental willing. This position is sometimes known as **parallelism**.* Similarly, Nicolas Malebranche (1638–1715) claimed that mental events do not cause physical events nor

---

*Gottfried Leibniz's doctrine of the pre-established harmony, discussed in Chapter 17, borrowed the two clocks analogy of the parallelists.

vice versa. Instead, each type of event is the occasion on which God produces correlated events in the other realm. For this reason, Malebranche's position is sometimes called **occasionalism**.

Evaluation and Significance

As with so many philosophers, Descartes's legacy to history is not so much his answers as it is the questions he raised. These were of such lasting importance that philosophers and scientists today are still trying to come to terms with the Cartesian agenda.

We can survey Descartes's impact by evaluating the success of each of the three goals of his philosophy. First, there was his ideal of certainty. This set a level of expectations that has haunted all Western thought down through the centuries. Do we need Cartesian certainty? What if we can't have it? Then what? Should we despair or settle for less? If reason does not fulfill its Cartesian promises, is there another route to knowledge? There were several different responses to these questions. On the one hand, the Continental rationalists took up the Cartesian torch and steadfastly continued down the road of reason in search of certainty. On the other hand, the ideal of certainty led to skepticism on the part of those who claimed we need the ideal but despaired of ever finding it. The empiricist David Hume, for example, accepted Descartes's postulate that knowledge equals certainty. However, because he believed that Descartes's rational system was built on sand, Hume claimed that we can't have much in the way of knowledge. Other empiricists such as John Locke were willing to accept mere probability in our knowledge of the external world, claiming that was all we needed to make it through life.

Descartes's second goal of achieving a universal science remained alive in the rationalistic tradition and spilled over into large segments of the empiricist movement as well. Although many disagreed with him concerning the exact method to be used, the dream of a single explanatory scheme that could subdue every fact in the universe and bring them all within its domain has tantalized philosophers all the way up into our century.

For many philosophers, however, Descartes's failure to achieve his third goal of reconciling science and religion turned this dream into a nightmare of problems. By Descartes's time, science had become too powerful an instrument of knowledge for there to be any possibility of abandoning it and turning back the clock to the Middle Ages. At the same time, religion continued to be an important influence in the centuries following Descartes. For many thinkers, the personal and philosophical attractions of theism were too strong to give it up lightly. Consequently, most of the great scientists in this early modern period were also people of great faith. Therefore, a great deal of intellectual energy was employed trying to weave the new science into the fabric of traditional religion.

Even in our century, the Cartesian tensions are still alive. To be sure, many have opted to settle the issue once and for all by abandoning the walls Descartes established to keep science within its bounds, thus allowing scientific explanations to expand into all the territories of human experience. Nevertheless, even among some who are not particularly religious, there is still a desire to retain the uniqueness, dignity, and freedom of persons and to keep our species from being swallowed up by the mechanistic conception of nature.

In the fields of cognitive science and artificial intelligence, the discussion has taken a particularly lively turn as scientists have tried to make computers simulate mental processes. Some, like Descartes, believe that machines can mimic our behavior but cannot think in the fullest sense of the word. Others, of a more Hobbesian persuasion, believe that computers are actually Cartesian thinkers made out of microchips (or that humans are, more or less, computers made out of meat). Only time (and further research and debate) will tell who is correct.

Questions for Understanding

1. Why is Descartes called the "Father of Modern Philosophy?" Why was his decision to begin philosophy with himself considered to be radical in his time?

2. What were Descartes's three goals?

3. What are the two operations of mathematical reasoning that Descartes thought would be the key to philosophical discoveries?

4. What is Descartes's method of doubt? Why does he begin his philosophical explorations with doubt?

5. What reasons does Descartes find for doubting each of the following: general beliefs based on sense perception, vivid sensory experiences, the truth of mathematics.

6. What is Descartes's first bedrock of certainty?

7. When Descartes says "I exist?" what does he mean?

8. What is the phenomenon of the "phantom limb" and how did it support Descartes's doubts about his own body?

9. How does Descartes prove the existence of God, since he is unsure of the existence of the world? Set out the steps of his causal argument.

10. Set out the steps of Descartes's version of the ontological argument.

11. How does the existence of God give Descartes confidence in his reason. What is the Cartesian circle objection to this?

12. How does Descartes regain his confidence in the existence of the external world?

13. According to Descartes, what is the relationship between the mind and the body?

14. How does Descartes reconcile mechanistic science with religion and human free will?

15. What is the problem with Descartes's interactionism? How does he attempt to solve it?

Questions for Reflection

1. Evaluate Descartes's program of doubting everything he formerly believed. Is it possible to do this? Is it desirable? Why?

2. List five propositions you are certain are true. What basis might Descartes find for doubting them? Do you agree with him that these beliefs can be doubted? Why or why not?

3. In his first argument for God, Descartes maintains that the ideas of "perfection" and "infinity" could not be derived from experience. Do you agree with this thesis?

4. Consider one of Descartes's arguments for God. What are some objections that have been made or could be made to the argument? Which premise is the weakest? How would you defend or refute the argument?

5. Do you agree or disagree with Descartes that, apart from our own existence, the certainty of our beliefs about the world depend upon God? What would be an alternative view that does not depend upon God?

6. Develop an argument that either supports or critiques Descartes's thesis that the mind and body are separate substances.

7. How might Descartes respond to a contemporary brain scientist who claims that all our cognitive processes can be explained by the brain without our postulating a nonphysical mind?

8. Do you think that the "Cartesian compromise" is plausible? In other words, has Descartes found an effective way to reconcile science, mechanism, and determinism with religion and human freedom?

Notes

1. Quotations from the works of René Descartes are referenced in the text using the following abbreviations.

D   *Discourse on the Method*, in *The Philosophical Writings of Descartes*, vol. 1, trans. John Cottingham, Robert Stoothoff, and Dugald Murdoch (Cambridge, England: Cambridge University Press, 1985). The references are to the part number and page number in the classic French edition, followed by the page number in this edition.

M   *Meditations on First Philosophy*, trans. John Cottingham (Cambridge, England: Cambridge University Press, 1986). The references are to the meditation number and page number in the classic French edition, followed by the page number in this edition.

OR   *Objections and Replies*, in *Meditations on First Philosophy*. The references are to the number of the set of objections and the page number in the classic French edition, followed by the page number in this edition.

PP   *Principles of Philosophy*, in *The Philosophical Writings of Descartes*. The references are to the part number and paragraph number in Descartes's work, followed by the page number in this edition.

PS   *Passions of the Soul*, in *The Philosophical Writings of Descartes*. The references are to the part number and the paragraph number in Descartes's work, followed by the page number in this edition.

R   *Rules for the Direction of the Mind*, in *The Philosophical Writings of Descartes*. The references are to the rule number and the page number in the classic French edition, followed by the page number in this edition.

2. St. Augustine, *Of True Religion*, §72, trans. J. H. S. Burleigh (Chicago: Regnery, 1953), 69.

3. Blaise Pascal, *Pensées: Thoughts on Religion and Other Subjects*, trans. William Finlayson Trotter (New York: Washington Square Press, 1965), §77.

16

Benedict (Baruch) Spinoza: Rationalist and Mystic

Spinoza's Life: Heresy, Lens Grinding, and Philosophy

Baruch Spinoza (or Espinosa) was born in Amsterdam in 1632. It was a time of significant scientific progress, particularly in astronomy. Galileo published his important work *Dialogues* in this year, and Johannes Kepler had died only two years before. In ten years Isaac Newton would be born. Spinoza's Portuguese parents were part of a community of Jews who had fled Spain and Portugal, where the laws required them to adopt the Christian religion. Holland was well known as a sanctuary of tolerance for refugees from political and religious persecution. As a child, Spinoza showed great promise and was trained to be a rabbi. From his family's community he learned Portuguese and Spanish, from his native land he learned Dutch, and in school he learned Hebrew and eventually Latin. At age twenty he began a serious study of philosophy from a Gentile teacher who was well versed in Scholasticism as well as Descartes's "new" philosophy.

To the dismay of his Jewish elders, Spinoza's intellectual vision began to range beyond the boundaries of orthodox Jewish teachings. At age twenty-two, Baruch expressed his independence by changing his name to Benedictus ("Blessed"), which is the Latin or Christian equivalent of his former name. Still in his early twenties, Spinoza began to express doubts about the immortality of the soul and the existence of angels, and the people of the Jewish community began to murmur the words "heresy" and "independent thinking" behind his back. They were afraid such ideas would offend their Christian hosts and were concerned to protect the integrity of the faith for which they had been persecuted.

When persuasion and even bribery would not silence him, the Jewish community pronounced a formal sentence of excommunication on July 27, 1656, when Spinoza was nearly twenty-four. Failing to turn him from his "evil opinions and doings," the heads of the Ecclesiastical Council announced that Baruch Spinoza was officially sentenced to damnation, with the following curse:

Cursed be he by day, and cursed be he by night; cursed be he when he lieth down, and cursed be he when he riseth up; cursed be he when he goeth out and cursed be he when he cometh in; the Lord will not pardon him; the wrath and fury of the Lord will be kindled against this man, and bring down upon him all the curses which are written in the Book of the Law; and the Lord will destroy his name from under the heavens; and, to his undoing, the Lord will cut him off from all the tribes of Israel, with all the curses of the firmament which are written in the Book of the Law; but ye that cleave unto the Lord God live all of you this day!

We ordain that no one may communicate with him verbally or in writing, nor show him any favour, nor stay under the same roof with him, nor be within four cubits of him, nor read anything composed or written by him.[1]

As if this were not enough, not too long after the condemnation an attempt was made on his life.

Leaving these painful experiences behind, Spinoza spent the remainder of his life seeking a peaceful existence in working and writing. He had learned the trade of grinding and polishing telescope and microscope lenses. His chosen profession of making optical lenses symbolizes the rise of a scientific culture in seventeenth-century Europe as well his aptitude for careful, exacting work that carried over to his philosophical writings. His work gave him a modest income and still left time to write and discuss philosophy with friends.

Eventually, Spinoza's reputation grew and he carried on correspondence with leading philosophers and scientists of the time. He was offered the chair of philosophy at Heidelberg University in 1673 but refused it, thinking it would compromise his desire for peace and the freedom to speak on controversial issues. He died quietly in 1677 after many years of battling tuberculosis, which may have been aggravated by his continuous exposure to glass dust. Everyone who knew him spoke of him with affection and remembered him as an intellectual who sincerely lived his philosophy.

Spinoza wrote a number of works that he never published in his lifetime. He saw only two of his books go to press: *Principles of Cartesian Philosophy* (1663) and the anonymous *Theologico-Political Treatise* (1670). The latter work went through five editions before the government banned it. As the title suggests, it covered both religious and political topics, this combination being necessary in an age when controversies raged over the relationship of church and state. In addition to its eloquent defense of individual liberty, it was one of the first works in biblical criticism, which is the attempt to analyze the Bible using secular techniques of historical scholarship. Spinoza refrained from publishing what would become his most famous work, *Ethics Demonstrated in Geometrical Order*, because he was afraid it would be misunderstood and vilified by theologians. A friend published it after Spinoza's death.

Task: To Achieve Freedom from Bondage

Spinoza's works are full of abstract epistemological and metaphysical discussions. It is easy to get lost in the details and lose sight of the fact that the whole purpose of his theoretical conclusions is to lay the foundation for ethics. Ethics for Spinoza is not a list of dos and don'ts. Instead, it is a way of thinking that leads to a way of looking at the world, which leads to a way of acting, which will lead to freedom from human bondage. He sees us as enslaved by our affections, so bound up with the things we love and want that they rule our lives. When we stake our happiness on our care for life, health, riches, esteem, pleasure, or friends, we tie ourselves to those things that are always precarious. The painful experiences he had suffered showed Spinoza the futility of seeking lasting satisfaction in the love of anything perishable:

After experience had taught me that all the usual surroundings of social life are vain and futile; seeing that none of the objects of my fears contained in themselves anything either good or bad, except in so far as the mind is affected by them, I finally resolved to inquire whether there might be some real good having power to communicate itself, which would affect the mind singly, to the exclusion of all else: whether, in fact, there might be anything of which the discovery and attainment would enable me to enjoy continuous, supreme, and unending happiness.[2]

In the midst of our fear and anxiety, Spinoza suggests, there is a way to emancipation. The answer is to have an intellectual love for what is eternal and infinite, for what is changeless and complete. The object of such a love can only be the whole logically necessary system of nature, which Spinoza identifies with God or substance. Only by attaining this sort of love will we find a safe harbor from the vicissitudes of fleeting experiences and fortune.

Spinoza's Geometrical Method

Spinoza agrees with Galileo and Descartes that mathematics is the key to the structure of the universe. Consequently, he also agrees with Descartes that the method used in philosophy should imitate the method used in mathematics. But Descartes never carried through on his mathematical ideal, for the writing form he used was the essay. Spinoza, however, actually carries his methodological assumptions into the style of his presentation. This is illustrated in his major work, *Ethics*. As he says in the subtitle, ethics will be "demonstrated in geometrical order."[3] The book is an elegant and carefully orchestrated work in which each proposition fits neatly into its appointed place. Generally, each of its five main parts begins with a series of numbered definitions, then a list of axioms, and finally a series of numbered propositions, which are derived from the preceding definitions and axioms in good Euclidean fashion. The work contains a total of 259 demonstrated propositions. Continuing to follow Euclid's style, Spinoza ends each proof with the letters *Q.E.D.*, which stand for *quod erat demonstrandum* or "which was to be demonstrated."

There is some debate over how inescapably self-evident Spinoza thought his axioms to be. Clearly, he thought philosophy should be done in an architectural manner, starting with simple, foundational truths, and from this foundation carefully building up the edifice of human knowledge, brick by brick, using the mortar of rigorous deductive logic. Looked at as a totality, Spinoza's *Ethics* has an austere but serene beauty, evoking the same feelings one gets when looking at the Egyptian pyramids. Its base is Part One, which begins with a series of definitions and propositions concerning the nature of God. From there it rises to the pinnacle of Proposition 42 in Part Five, where he demonstrates that the supreme blessedness is achieved when the mind delights in divine love.

Several interrelated assumptions lie at the base of all Spinoza's arguments. Spinoza believes that to have a conception of anything is to explain it. To explain something requires one to give an account of its cause. The cause of something is what brings it into existence and what makes it the sort of being it is. Finally, Spinoza asserts that "from a given determinate cause an effect necessarily follows" and "the knowledge of an effect depends upon and involves the knowledge of the cause" (E 1, ax. 3 and 4). Later, he argues that "the order and connection of ideas is the same as the order and connection of things" (E 2.7).* The effect of these three statements is to collapse causal connections and logical connections. Thus, when he says that "A causes B," he means that "the concept of A contains the concept of B," and "B cannot be thought of apart from A." As we will see, these assumptions lead Spinoza to claim that nothing can be understood in isolation. Every event in the world is not only *causally* connected to the whole, but it is also *logically* connected to the whole, just like the theorems in a mathematical system.

Theory of Knowledge: Necessity Rules

THE NATURE OF TRUTH

It is impossible to fully understand Spinoza's epistemology apart from his metaphysics. Nevertheless, a couple of points are worth noting at the outset. First, his conception of philosophical method makes it clear that he was as thoroughgoing a

---

*Spinoza offers a proof for this proposition in Part Two of this work, but this claim has been an underlying assumption in everything that has preceded it.

rationalist as we will find in the modern period. For Spinoza, the rational is the real and the real is the rational. Second, from his methodological assumptions it follows that the fabric of the universe is woven from the warp and woof of logical necessity. "In Nature there is nothing contingent, but all things are determined from the necessity of the divine nature to exist and act in a certain manner" (E 1.29).

Most thinkers have no problem with the notion that the properties of a triangle follow necessarily from an understanding of its essence. However, it is hard to swallow the notion that the proposition "an apple just fell from the tree outside my window" is also an example of such necessity. It is even harder to suppose that what I choose for dinner tonight is logically determined. Yet Spinoza seems to think if we understand all the prior causes of an event in perfect detail, including the mathematical and physical laws governing it and the way in which it fits into the total scheme of things, we would understand its necessity.

Why, then, do some events *seem* contingent to us? Spinoza replies that "a thing cannot be called contingent unless with reference to a deficiency in our knowledge." When we fail to see that everything is necessary, it is "because the order of causes is concealed from us" (E 1.33, n. 1). Hence, while we can deduce *some* truths a priori, only someone with the exhaustive knowledge of the divine mind could deduce the existence and behavior of any particular thing. The important point is that all truths are capable of demonstration, though not for the human intellect.

THE THREE LEVELS OF COGNITION

This discussion leads into Spinoza's three grades of cognition. All human ideas fall into three categories, which range from the most inadequate and confused to the highest possible level of human knowledge. The first level of cognition is *opinion or imagination*. This is the source of inadequate ideas and false beliefs. The most inadequate form of information is mere secondhand opinion (for exam-

ple, my belief that I was born on such and such a day). It also includes perception arising from signs, such as the ideas and images I get from hearing or reading certain words. The most common form of this low-grade cognition is what I receive from vague experience. Through repeated experiences (say, of a horse) we form a universal *image* of that category. However, since these general ideas are based on mechanical, physiological processes of association, they do not reflect the true, underlying logical connection between things. Hence, sense experience represents things to us "in a mutilated and confused manner and without order to the intellect" (E 2.40, n. 2).

In contrast to the random products of sense experience, the next two levels of cognition give us adequate knowledge and necessary truths. The second level is *reason*. Reason goes beyond fleeting sense experience and searches out the underlying chain of reasons or causes that make something what it is:

> It is in the nature of reason to perceive things truly, that is to say, as they are in themselves, that is to say, not as contingent but as necessary. (E 2.44, demo.)

In a celebrated phrase, Spinoza says that "it is of the nature of reason to perceive things under a certain form of eternity" (E 2.44, corol.). Included under rational knowledge are clear and distinct intuitions into the universal characteristics of things and deductions from self-evident axioms.

The third and highest level of knowledge is *intuition*. Spinoza is not as clear about this as we would like, for he describes its beneficial effects more than he does its nature. It is best seen as an integrated vision of the whole that arises out of the level of reason. Perhaps it is like a mathematician's sense of and admiration for the logical coherence of a very long proof that comes in a flash, even before she has worked out the details. A completely adequate understanding of the logical necessity of the whole scheme of things is possible only for God, although we are able to grasp minor versions of it. As Spinoza confesses, "the things which I have been able to know by this kind of knowledge are as yet very few."[4]

Metaphysics: God Is the Only Reality

SUBSTANCE AND GOD

We now come to the heart of Spinoza's system, which is his discussion of the concept of substance or God. His definition of substance is the fountainhead from which the rest of his system flows in good logical order. Definition 3 in Part One states,

> By substance I understand that which is in itself and is conceived through itself; in other words, that the conception of which does not need the conception of another thing from which it must be formed.

We can understand his concept of substance by contrasting it with other notions. If we think of a child, for example, we would be likely to think about her parents. Similarly, the thought of smoke leads to the thought of fire or some cause that produced the smoke. However, if the thought of some entity does not require any other concept to make it intelligible, then it does not depend on a cause outside of itself. Such a being would be a substance, for it would be completely self-contained both in thought and in existence. Spinoza goes on to argue that substance is necessarily infinite. If it were finite, then we would have to conceive of something external to it that constitutes its limits. But then it would not be self-sufficient and logically independent.

Even though the concept of substance has played a major role in philosophy ever since Aristotle, Spinoza gives us a much more rigorous definition. For Aristotle, a particular thing (such as Socrates) is a substance because it can exist on its own, in a way that its properties, such as baldness, cannot. Similarly, Descartes begins with a definition of substance similar to Spinoza's but then goes on to apply the term to finite, created substances such as human minds and bodies. For Spinoza, however, Aristotle's and Descartes's theories dilute the original meaning of substance. If substance is something entirely self-sufficient and logically independent of anything else, then finite minds and bodies would not fit this description.

At the very beginning of the *Ethics*, Spinoza provides a rather traditional definition of God using the terminology of his age:

> By God I understand Being absolutely infinite, that is to say, substance consisting of infinite attributes, each of which expresses eternal and infinite essence. (def. 6)

Spinoza combines this definition with his axioms and previously demonstrated propositions to prove that any substance, including God, necessarily exists. Here, Spinoza's radically consistent rationalism clearly reveals itself. Many philosophers, such as Aquinas, started with the world of sense experience and worked from there to prove God's existence. Although Descartes eventually made use of an ontological argument, he first began with his own existence. For Spinoza, however, the order of thought must follow the order of reality. Since "everyone must admit that without God nothing can be nor can be conceived," Spinoza says, it follows that "the divine nature ought to be studied first, because it is first in the order of knowledge and in the order of things" (E 2.10, n.).

Accordingly, without appealing to any facts about the world, Spinoza provides an ontological argument to show that the concept of substance (and this includes the divine substance) implies that any substance necessarily exists:

(1) The concept of a substance is the concept of that which is completely self-contained, for it does not need the concept of anything else to make it intelligible (def. 3).

(2) If (a) a substance had a cause, then (b) to understand that substance we would have to have knowledge of its cause (ax. 4).

(3) But 2b contradicts the definition in premise 1.

(4) Hence, a substance cannot have a cause.

(5) According to definition 6, God is a substance.

(6) It follows that God does not have a cause and, therefore, must necessarily exist.

As with any version of the ontological argument, this one assumes that the notions of God and substance given in the definitions are conceivable. However, Spinoza would argue that no one could find a contradiction or lack of coherence in these definitions. So far, we have a complicated but seemingly orthodox presentation of the ontological argument.* On the surface, it does not seem to raise any problems for traditional Judeo-Christian theology. However, some very novel and radical conclusions lie latent within Spinoza's definitions and arguments. Spinoza not only argues that anything that is truly a substance necessarily exists, but he thinks he can demonstrate the surprising conclusion that only *one* substance exists. In other words, nothing besides God exists unless it is simply a mode of his being. The argument goes like this:

(1) A second substance would either have the same nature as God or a different one.

(2) It could not have exactly the same nature as God, for then the two of them would be indistinguishable and, hence, would be the same being (E 1.5).

(3) If another substance had a nature similar to God's while remaining numerically distinct from him, there would have to be some reason outside of their nature why there exists only two of them instead of three or more such beings. But there cannot be any reason external to a substance why it exists. So, there cannot be a substance similar to God but numerically distinct from him (E 1.8, n. 2).

(4) Since God is infinite in his attributes, if a substance is different in nature from God, it can only differ by lacking one of his infinite perfections.

(5) From premise 4 it follows that a substance different from God would be a limited being that, nevertheless, existed independently of

him. But this is absurd, for such a being would be a limitation of God's nature.

(6) Therefore, God is the only substance that exists, and everything else is a mode of his being (E 1.14).

Spinoza follows this conclusion with the proposition "Whatever is, is in God, and nothing can either be or be conceived without God" (E 1.15). In other words, God is the totality. He is immanent in the world and not transcendent to it. Hence, God is all inclusive in the fullest sense of the word. This sort of position is commonly called **pantheism**.

Throughout the Middle Ages, philosophical theologians always found it important to give an account of the relationship between God *and* nature. We find no such account in Spinoza, for there is no separation between the two. For him the fundamental reality is "that eternal and infinite Being whom we call God or Nature" (E 4, preface). Notice that he refers to God *or* Nature as though the two labels refer to the same entity. Thus, when he says that all things are "in" God he does not mean this in the weak sense that all things are dependent on God, as the traditional theistic philosophers affirmed. Instead, he claims all individual beings are merely modifications or modes of God's attributes (E 1.25, corol.). In other words, the relationship of individual things (including you) to God, is similar to the relationship of water, ice, or steam, to H_2O. Like the various modes of H_2O, everything in nature is simply an aspect or mode of God's being.

Besides identifying God and nature, Spinoza deprives God of any qualities of personhood. Traditional Western theism described God as one who thinks, initiates plans, makes choices, attends to the needs of his creation, and so on. However, Spinoza says that "neither intellect nor will pertains to the nature of God," at least not in the sense these terms are ordinarily used (E 1.17, n.). He explains to one of his critics that attributing such activities to God is merely fulfilling a psychological need to create God in our own image:

I believe that a triangle, if it could speak, would likewise say that God is eminently triangular, and a

---

*Spinoza actually gives at least four arguments for God's existence, with one of them being an *a posteriori* argument. His exposition of these are not always clear, so different commentators have arrived at slightly different formulations of his various arguments.

circle that God's nature is eminently circular. In this way each would ascribe to God its own attributes, assuming itself to be like God, and regarding all else as ill-formed.[5]

ATHEIST OR RELIGIOUS MYSTIC?

Although Western sensibilities may be offended by this collapse of the distinction between God and nature, it does offer some intellectual and practical rewards to our modern society. For example, Spinoza makes intellectual inquiry a spiritual activity. The more we know the world around us, the more we know God (E 5.24). For Spinoza there is no divorce between our intellectual life and the love of God. In this view, religious anti-intellectualism would be a contradiction in terms. Furthermore, if we shared Spinoza's opinion that nature and the being of God are united, this would promote a healthy environmental awareness and reverence for nature. Finally, this would encourage social harmony, for loving others would be literally loving an aspect of God's very being.

Because of his eloquent expression of his intellectual love of God, the nineteenth-century romantics referred to Spinoza as "the God-intoxicated man." But in his day many labeled him an "atheist." Indeed, some have claimed that if God is identified with everything, then the concept is empty. Perhaps all Spinoza has done is to give a strange three-letter label ("God") to what most people simply call "nature." After all, many an atheist has felt a certain amount of awe when contemplating nature without baptizing this feeling with any religious connotations.

Despite these different assessments of Spinoza, one thing is clear: Most of his predecessors and contemporaries thought that there were only two alternatives. One could (1) believe in the God of traditional theism or (2) embrace atheism. However, Spinoza realized this constituted a false dilemma. Rejecting both positions, Spinoza creatively sought a new conception of God more consistent with the very same philosophical principles held by his more orthodox contemporaries and critics.

FREEDOM AND NECESSITY

Spinoza seems to contradict himself when he asserts both that "God alone is a free cause" and that "God does not act from freedom of the will" (E 1.17, corol. 2; 1.32, corol. 1). However, Spinoza's point is that God is a "free cause" because his actions are not compelled or determined by anything external to him, but God does not act from "freedom of the will," because his actions are determined by the laws of his own nature (E 1, def. 7). However, not even God chooses his own nature, for it is what it is and what it must be. Therefore, God is *free* from external compulsion but internally *determined*. This is very different from the popular conception of God as the master artist who creatively and freely chooses what he will create. In contrast, Spinoza states that "things could have been produced by God in no other manner and in no other order than that in which they have been produced" (E 1.33). Since Spinoza has already argued that all things necessarily follow from God's given nature, to imagine that the world could have been other than it is would mean that God's nature could have been other than it is, which would be absurd. This is why Spinoza claims there is no contingency in nature.

Spinoza's view of God implies there are only two ways to categorize events. First, some are necessary and constitute the whole of our actual world. Second, some events are impossible and are excluded from reality by the nature of the divine order. There is no middle category of contingent events that merely happen to be the case or merely happen not to be the case. Try to imagine a computer program that does not take any input from the outside. Everything the computer does is a logical outcome of the program. The program may be too massive for any one person to predict exactly what it will do. Hence, the computer's output may seem unpredictable and come as a surprise. This fact might even cause one to naively suppose the computer is making free and spontaneous decisions. However, everything that occurs as the program is running was built into it from the beginning. Similarly, for Spinoza, "all things follow from the eternal decree of God, according to that same necessity by which it follows from the essence of a triangle that its three angles are equal to two right angles" (E 2.49, n.). When he speaks of "the eternal decree of God," we must not suppose this represents a decision on God's part. God no more chooses to create the world in a certain way than he chooses to make 7 a prime number. We tend to view nature in terms of final causes, thinking that events in nature are fulfilling some purpose. However, if everything follows from strict logical necessity, the notion of purpose in nature or God is an anthropological fiction. God cannot work to accomplish some end, for this supposes he seeks something he lacks. If we fully understood the divine nature, we would see that everything that happens, whether we experience it as tragic or joyous, is completely inevitable.

The implications for freedom of the will are clear. Free will, like contingency, is an illusion based on inadequate knowledge of the divine nature and of how the whole scheme of things logically proceeds from that nature. Spinoza suggests that if a stone traveling through the air were conscious, it would feel as though it were free and were choosing to move and land where it does.[6] Similarly, humans

> are deceived because they think themselves free, and the sole reason for thinking so is that they are conscious of their own actions, and ignorant of the causes by which those actions are determined. (E 2.35, n.)

For example, let's say you have always wanted to play the guitar. One day you finally sign up for guitar lessons. You have the feeling this action is the result of a spontaneous and undetermined choice on your part. However, Spinoza would say that you, like the stone, hold this mistaken belief because you are ignorant of the causes that originally produced that desire within you.

THE MIND-BODY PROBLEM

Spinoza's solution to the mind-body problem begins with his discussion of God's attributes. He defines an attribute as "that which the intellect perceives of substance as constituting its essence"

(E 1, def. 4). Not surprisingly, when he describes God's attributes, he asserts, "Thought is an attribute of God, or God is a thinking thing" (E 2.1). That statement, in itself, would not have been problematic to Spinoza's Jewish and Christian contemporaries. However, Spinoza reveals the radical nature of his system when he goes on to also claim, "Extension is an attribute of God, or God is an extended thing" (E 2.2). Although this presents a very nontraditional conception of God, this claim is consistent with Spinoza's view that everything in nature is a mode of God's being. Although God has an infinite number of attributes, the only ones our limited minds can know are thought and extension. Hence, our understanding of the world, including human nature, will necessarily be in terms of these two dimensions.

Ever since the rise of modern science, one of the most persistent questions has been, How do thought and extension or the mind and the body relate? For Thomas Hobbes, matter alone was fundamental and what we call the mind is merely a set of motions in the body. Descartes, however, claimed matter and mind are two independent kinds of reality that interact. However, Spinoza thinks neither of these views is correct. Contrary to Hobbes's attempt to reduce everything to matter in motion, Spinoza argues that thought cannot be understood in purely physical terms. Contrary to Descartes's dualism, Spinoza replies that "the mind and the body are one and the same thing, conceived at one time under the attribute of thought, and at another under that of extension" (E 3.2, n.).

There is only one kind of reality, but everything can be talked about or experienced in two ways. To resort to an analogy, think of the typical optical lens that Spinoza ground when he was not doing philosophy. From one point of view, the lens is concave—it curves inward. From the other side, it is convex—it curves outward. The same reality has two different aspects. Similarly, Spinoza would say that thought and extension represent two ways of looking at the same reality. For example, a circle can be represented as an extended shape (see Figure 16-1). However, a circle can also be represented in thought by an algebraic formula:

FIGURE 16-1

$$(x - h)^2 + (y - k)^2 = r^2$$

To use another example, when you are thinking about philosophy, you experience this process from the inside as a succession of ideas. However, the physiologist can study your thought processes from the outside as a causal series of electrical events in the brain. Descartes would describe any such correlation between physical events and mental events as evidence that the two distinct substances were causally interacting. However, Spinoza would say the physical events *are* the mental events and vice versa. This position has been revived by some thinkers in our day and is referred to as the "dual-aspect theory."

Think of a rose you see in the garden. Spinoza would say you are seeing a certain mode of God–Nature in terms of the attribute of extension. However, the rose can also be viewed in terms of the attribute of thought, insofar as it is an idea in the divine mind. But if God is omniscient, there is nothing in the reality of the rose that you see and smell that is not also included in God's idea of it. So the object and the idea are actually identical, for the one does not have any properties not included in the other.

Although thought and extension are two sides of the same coin, so to speak, each dimension is self-contained and can be understood without reference to the other. Furthermore, the language of thought cannot be reduced to the language of physics nor vice versa. Whereas Descartes divided reality in half, one part being mental and the other part being physical, Spinoza says either category is equally suitable for describing the *whole* of reality. As he expresses it,

> When things are considered as modes of thought we must explain the order of the whole of Nature or the connection of causes by the attribute of thought alone, and when things are considered as modes of extension, the order of the whole of Nature must be explained through the attribute of extension alone. (E 2.7, n.)

Imagine, for example, a music critic describing a symphony's performance in terms of the tempo, the harmonies, the musical mood, and so forth. At the same time, a physicist could describe the music in terms of the physics of sound waves. Each is giving a complete account of the same reality, but the critic does not bring in the concepts of physics in his account, and the scientist does not resort to the concepts of musical aesthetics in her account. The two descriptions are compatible and complementary, but incommensurable.

Ethics: How to Be Free from Bondage

Spinoza applies his metaphysics to the questions of human conduct in the last three parts of his *Ethics*. Part Three deals with the nature of the emotions, while Part Four, titled "Of Human Bondage," shows how all our problems stem from the fact that we are slaves to our own passions. Finally, Part Five demonstrates the power of the intellect to overcome this bondage. He begins his discussion of the emotions with the complaint that most people who have written about the emotions and human conduct have supposed that people are somehow outside the laws of nature. However, since everything is governed by necessity, the geometrical method applies to humans as well as triangles. Thus, he proposes to "treat by a geometrical method the vices and follies of men" and announces, "I shall consider human actions and appetites just as if I were considering lines, planes, or bodies" (E 3, preface). Accordingly, Spinoza gives a detailed classification of the emotions and deduces their effects, following his geometric method of analysis. Since he assumes that the emotions follow a logical order and that their effects are as predictable as a physics experiment, he believes that a careful scientific analysis will give us the means to have control over them.

Spinoza begins his scientific approach to ethics with the claim that the drive for self-preservation is the basic law of nature. This inner force is called *conatus*, which means "striving" or "endeavor." "Each thing, in so far as it is in itself, endeavors to persevere in its being" (E 3.6). Spinoza identifies the essence of a thing with the particular kind of active force working within it. Hence, for something to "persevere in its being" means more than simply existing. It means striving to fulfill its nature. *Conatus* is not limited to humans alone, but is found in all nature. For nonliving things, this striving may be manifested only as inertia, the tendency of things to remain in the same state. In a plant, *conatus* is exhibited in its continual striving to send its roots deep into the soil or to turn toward the sun. In human beings this endeavor is called *will* when it has reference to the mind alone, *appetite* when it is related to both the mind and body, and *desire* when we are conscious of this striving.

People, unlike rocks or plants, have self-awareness. Because of this, we can be self-determining beings. I will be a fulfilled person to the degree I realize my own, inner nature. However, I will not be a self-determined person if I strive toward illusory goals such as fame, riches, and sensual pleasure. This is because my ability to achieve these goals depends on circumstances I cannot control. Thus, the key to happiness is to be an inner-directed person, not one buffeted about by outside causes. Only by rationally understanding the events around me can I be in charge of my life in this way.

According to Spinoza, our mind both acts and is acted on: insofar as it has adequate ideas, it is initiating activity; but insofar as it has inadequate ideas, it is acted on (E 3.1). Having inadequate ideas causes us to be acted on because we become victimized by our own emotions. After all, the word *passion* is related to *passive*. In other words, the passions are not something we do, but something that happens to us. When we are in the grip of our passions, we are "like the waves of the sea agitated by contrary winds, we fluctuate in our ignorance of our future and destiny" (E 3.59, n.). However, reason gives us adequate ideas that free us from the grip of the emotions. Spinoza points out that "a passion ceases to be a passion as soon as we form a clear and distinct idea of it" (E 5.3). Although he may be too optimistic about the power of the intellect, it is true that intellectualizing an emotional state increases our power over it. For example, anger is the sort of emotion that takes over us. However, when we observe our emotional reaction from the standpoint of a detached spectator and begin analyzing what caused us to become so upset, we regain control and the power of the anger is dissipated.

Spinoza, however, is interested in more than just a moment-by-moment response to the passions. What is needed is a comprehensive understanding of their causes. He says all the emotions are responses to objects in the past, present, or future. What is common to them is that they are based on the illusion that events in the past or present could have gone differently from the way they did or that the future is not yet determined. We will achieve emotional liberation only when we realize that necessity reigns supreme and everything is as it must be. Thus, if everything is necessary, to feel remorse over something that happened makes no more sense than feeling bad that the angles of a triangle add up to 180 degrees instead of 200 degrees. Similarly, to either hope or fear that some future event X will occur instead of Y is as foolish as hoping that tomorrow, fire will be cold.

When we are relieved of the illusion of contingency, we will no longer feel absolutely dependent on our circumstances and will be in control of our lives. We can never have total freedom, but reason can work within the limitations of our nature to give us some measure of power over our lives. "In so far as the mind understands all things as necessary, so far has it greater power over the emotions, or suffers less from them" (E 5.6). This sort of understanding gives us serenity, an essential ingredient in happiness. In summary, the way to serenity and emotional liberation is twofold: (1) recognize that everything that happens is necessary and (2) embrace this with resignation and acceptance. Paradoxically, freedom from the bondage of the passions is not release from necessity but the recognition and acceptance of necessity.

If everything is determined and could not be other than it is, then "good" and "evil" are not terms that could apply to nature. Since nothing is good or evil in itself, these terms refer to our subjective evaluations of how something affects our interests and concerns. Spinoza says that "we neither strive for, wish, seek, nor desire anything because we think it to be good, but, on the contrary, we adjudge a thing to be good because we strive for, wish, seek, or desire it" (E 3.9). Similarly, when we feel adverse to something we call it "evil." This position is called **moral relativism** because it claims there is no absolute standard for moral judgments. They are relative to each individual's perceptions:

> For one and the same thing may at the same time be both good and evil or indifferent. Music, for example, is good to a melancholy person, bad to one mourning, while to a deaf man it is neither good nor bad. (E 4, preface)

For Spinoza, the life of virtue achieves the sort of power and independence consistent with our inner drive for self-preservation:

> Since reason demands nothing which is opposed to nature, it demands, therefore, that every person should love himself, should seek his own profit . . . and absolutely that every one should endeavor, as far as in him lies, to preserve his own being. (E 4.18, n.)

Initially, this sounds like a form of egoism, where the goal in life is simply to serve one's own, individual interests. However, throughout Spinoza's whole book on ethics, what is strangely lacking is any notion of the individual self that was so prominent in Descartes's philosophy. This is because the notion that we are each isolated, unique selves with our own private interests is an illusion. Contrary to this, the path to serenity is to see things under the aspect of eternity (*sub specie aeternitatis*). When I rise from the level of confused thought and see myself as a mode of an all-inclusive rational order, I will see how my striving to preserve my own being merges with others' interests:

> Men can desire, I say, nothing more excellent for the preservation of their being than that all should so agree at every point that the minds and bodies of all should form, as it were, one mind and one body . . . and that all should together seek the common good of all. (E 4.18, n.)

When I see things as part of an eternal, logically connected system with God as its cause, I have arrived at the highest form of knowledge. From this arises what Spinoza calls "the intellectual love of God," which he identifies with "our salvation, or blessedness, or freedom" (E 5.33, 5.36 corol.). However, we should not mistake this for the love of traditional religious piety. Since God does not have personal characteristics, "he who loves God cannot strive that God should love him in return" (E 5.19). Since God is totally self-determined, he is free of all passion and is neither gripped by joy, sorrow, love, nor hate (E 5.17). However, since we are all modes of his being, "God, in so far as He loves Himself, loves men" (E 5.36, corol.). Thus, our love for God is purely intellectual, but it gives us an inspiring, integrating vision of life. It is like the mental satisfaction scientists or mathematicians experience when they sense the magnificence of the logically ordered cosmos.

Consistent with what he has said thus far, Spinoza does not allow for any conscious, individual immortality beyond death. Nevertheless, he does say that "the human mind cannot be absolutely destroyed with the body, but something of it remains which is eternal" (E 5.23). This seems to mean that each of us has our necessary place within the whole eternal order of things. If our minds rise above the illusion of particularity and become united with what is universal, the passing flow of temporal events can never deny us this hold on eternity.

Spinoza ends his *Ethics* with the following eloquent summary:

> I have finished everything I wished to explain concerning the power of the mind over the emotions and concerning its freedom. From what has been said we see what is the strength of the wise man, and how much he surpasses the ignorant who is driven forward by lust alone. . . . The wise man, in so far as he is considered as such, is scarcely ever moved in his mind, but, being conscious by a certain eternal necessity of himself, of God, and of things, never

ceases to be, and always enjoys true peace of soul. If the way which, as I have shown, leads hither seem very difficult, it can nevertheless be found. It must indeed be difficult since it is so seldom discovered, for if salvation lay ready to hand and could be discovered without great labor, how could it be possible that it should be neglected almost by everybody? But all noble things are as difficult as they are rare. (E 5.42, n.)

Evaluation and Significance

The same two critical questions asked earlier about Stoicism can also be addressed to Spinoza. First, we can ask, Does Spinoza's account provide a desirable picture of what human life should be about? Although the recognition that all is governed by necessity can lead to serenity, isn't it a serenity based on passivity? The sort of detachment and apathy that could make us carefree would also hinder meaningful human relations. Spinoza's critics complain that his ethical theory is suited for a reclusive, celibate lens grinder, but not for people who have commitments to families, friends, and social responsibilities. Will we be motivated to struggle against injustice and to actively try to change the world for the better if we think everything was already determined to be the way it is?*

Secondly, we can ask, Is Spinoza's philosophy coherent? How can we readjust our moral attitude if everything is necessary? We are advised to rise above inadequate ideas, yet he says that inadequate and confused ideas follow by necessity (E 2.36). In the Preface to Part Three, he criticizes those (such as Descartes) who think that people are free of the necessary order of nature. If our emotional reac-

tions are not the inevitable effect of causes operating on us, but can be controlled by reason, then it does seem that Spinoza agrees with Descartes that there is a necessity-free zone within reality that is occupied by the human mind.

Even if it is hard to make his discussion of the meaning of human life (in the last three parts of *Ethics*) coherent with the first two parts on metaphysics, much in Spinoza's vision of human life is valuable. Spinoza will always be admired for his attempt to gain a rationally coherent view of the whole of things and to apply this vision to the pressing questions of human existence. Nevertheless, in the period immediately following his death Spinoza's thought was soon eclipsed by other competing philosophies. Even those who had Spinoza's taste for rationalistic, speculative metaphysics, turned to the alternative system Leibniz was developing in Germany. Those who sought a more straightforward and commonsense philosophy chose the path set out by Locke's empiricism in England.

Spinoza's popularity was rekindled when his ideas were embraced by the late-eighteenth-century romantics such as the poet Novalis, who labeled him the "god-intoxicated philosopher," as well as Goethe, Schelling, Coleridge, Wordsworth, and the theologian Schleiermacher. They found in his happy unity of God, persons, and nature a vision that reverberated with their own. Furthermore, his importance to the nineteenth-century metaphysicians is illustrated by Hegel's recommendation that "when one begins to philosophize one must be first a Spinozist."[7] Interestingly, but misguidedly, the Marxists saw Spinoza's theory of mind as a forerunner of their own dialectical materialism and favorably compared his epistemology with the Marxist theory of ideology.[8]

To our twentieth-century minds, with our preference for the secure world of hard, empirical facts, Spinoza's philosophy seems to get lost in a cloudy system of philosophical abstractions. However, many in our century have found it an effective way to humanize the scientific account of the world. For example, some philosophers find Spinoza's solution to the mind–body problem attractive for the way in which it allows our

---

*This criticism is not meant to imply that Spinoza was calloused and uncaring toward people. In fact, just the opposite is true, for he had a number of close friends and was concerned about the political life of his nation. In 1672, the De Witt brothers, liberal leaders in the Dutch government, were blamed for the country's problems and were hanged by an angry mob. Spinoza knew them personally and had deep respect for them. Enraged by the injustice, Spinoza abandoned his usual quiet demeanor and tried to rush out into the streets to denounce the murders. His life was saved by friends who locked him in his room.

traditional mental vocabulary to coexist with our scientific language about the brain, without resorting to Descartes's dualism. Those who have embraced Spinoza's philosophy have been moved by either its emotional appeal or its intellectual charms. Emotionally, it promises serenity to those who view the passing events of life in the light of eternity. Intellectually, it provides a vision of the rational unity of the whole scheme of things.

A contemporary example of one who found Spinoza appealing for both reasons is Albert Einstein, the great twentieth-century physicist. Einstein once said, "I believe in Spinoza's God who reveals himself in the orderly harmony of what exists."[9] With Spinoza, he believed that religion and science flow from the same spirit: "The cosmic religious experience is the strongest and noblest driving force behind scientific research."[10] Finally, Einstein agreed with his seventeenth-century model that the world is a logically determined order best known through reason and not through loose, empirical probabilities. As Einstein said several times, "God does not play dice with the world."[11] This conviction inspired him throughout his life to find the exact mathematical formulas to correctly describe the order of the world. This combination of Spinoza's seventeenth-century metaphysics and twentieth-century physics shows once again how philosophical ideas can lead robust lives that continue far beyond their author's time.

Questions for Understanding

1. What was the main goal of Spinoza's philosophy?
2. How does Spinoza use mathematics as his model in doing philosophy?
3. What is Spinoza's notion of "cause"? What do you think of this definition? What are some implications of defining "cause" in this way?
4. According to Spinoza, what are the three levels of cognition?
5. What does Spinoza mean by "substance"? How does his view differ from Aristotle's and Descartes's? Why does he think that God is

the only substance that exists? What are the implications of this view?
6. Why does Spinoza treat God and nature as one and the same? What is the label that is given to this sort of position? What are the implications of this position?
7. Why does Spinoza conclude that the nature of God makes everything logically necessary and free will an illusion?
8. How would Spinoza respond to Descartes's view that the mind and body are completely separate?
9. According to Spinoza, what should our attitude be toward our emotions?
10. Why does it follow from Spinoza's position that God cannot feel love, joy, or sorrow?
11. What advice does Spinoza give us in our quest to be free from bondage and be fulfilled persons?

Questions for Reflection

1. Consider Spinoza's argument for the conclusion "God is the only substance that exists and everything else is a mode of his being." Do you think this view is plausible? Is every believer in God forced, by Spinoza's logic, to accept this conclusion? If not, how might a theist argue against this conclusion?
2. Given Spinoza's identification of God and nature, do you agree with his persecutors that Spinoza's philosophy is a thinly disguised atheism? Or do you agree with the romantics that he was a deeply religious mystic?
3. Evaluate Spinoza's view that everything flows with logical necessity from God's nature. Do you agree with him that everything is as it must be? If one starts with God, as Spinoza does, is there any other alternative? How so? What would be the practical implications of accepting this conclusion?
4. Consider your own inner, conscious experience, including your thoughts, your feelings, your sensations. Now consider how a brain scientist might explain these same experiences

as various brain states. In what way is Spinoza's position on the mind-body problem an attempt to reconcile both points of view? Do you think he is successful in this attempt?

5. Think of a time when you experienced a deep disappointment. If you had accepted Spinoza's philosophy of life, how would this have affected your attitude toward this experience? Throughout this day and the next, consider how viewing the world through Spinoza's philosophy would affect how you lived. Do you think his approach would lead to a more serene and peaceful approach to life?

6. What do you think is the most insightful feature of Spinoza's philosophy? What do you like the least or find the least plausible?

Notes

1. Quoted in Roger Scruton, *Spinoza* (Oxford, England: Oxford University Press, 1986), 8–9.

2. "On the Improvement of the Understanding," trans. R. H. M. Elwes, in *Ethics, Preceded by "On the Improvement of the Understanding,"* ed. James Gutmann (New York: Hafner, 1966), 3.

3. References to *Ethics* are indicated by the abbreviation "E." The number following it refers to one of the five parts of the book and the number following the decimal point indicates the proposition number. The abbreviations ax., def., demo., n., and corol. will stand for axiom, definition, demonstration, note, and corollary, respectively. All quotations to this work are from *Ethics*, ed. James Gutmann, trans. William Hale White and Amelia Hutchinson Stirling (New York: Hafner, 1966).

4. "On the Improvement of the Understanding," 9.

5. Letter 56 (to Hugh Boxel) in Baruch Spinoza, *The Ethics and Selected Letters*, ed. Seymour Feldman, trans. Samuel Shirley (Indianapolis: Hackett, 1982), 247.

6. Letter 58 (to G. H. Schuller) in Spinoza, *The Ethics and Selected Letters*, ed. Seymour Feldman, 250.

7. Quoted in Frederick C. Beiser, "Introduction: Hegel and the Problem of Metaphysics" in *The Cambridge Companion to Hegel*, ed. Frederick C. Beiser (Cambridge, England: Cambridge University Press, 1993), 5.

8. Scruton, 113.

9. *New York Times*, April 25, 1929, p. 60.

10. Ronald W. Clark, *Einstein: The Life and Times* (New York: World Publishing, 1971), 425.

11. Clark, 340.

17

Gottfried Leibniz:
The Optimistic Rationalist

WHILE THE RENAISSANCE PRODUCED ENORMOUS changes throughout England and most of Europe, German culture remained stagnant prior to the eighteenth century. In the period that produced such great writers and thinkers as Shakespeare, Bacon, Milton, and Locke in England, or Montaigne, Racine, Molière, Pascal, and Descartes in France, no comparable list of German thinkers can be compiled. Even the German language reflected this state of affairs. The ordinary person used it in the marketplace, but the upper classes spoke French while German scholars still wrote in Latin. The divisive theological controversies following the Reformation and the Thirty Years' War (1618–1648) did not provide fertile soil for science and philosophy to flourish.[1]

It is significant that Leibniz, one of Germany's greatest geniuses, appeared in this intellectually barren environment. It is also remarkable that he was able to master and weave into a comprehensive system all the major academic disciplines of his day. Leibniz distinguished himself as a lawyer, diplomat, scientist, inventor, poet, philologist, logician, mathematician, moralist, theologian, historian, and philosopher. Because of his breadth of knowledge, he was able to produce one of history's most ambitious schemes for integrating the findings of modern science and philosophy with the centuries-old Christian worldview.

Leibniz's Life: Diplomat, Scientist, and Philosopher

Gottfried Wilhelm Leibniz was born in 1646 in Leipzig, Germany. His father was a professor of moral philosophy at the University of Leipzig. Leibniz's genius was apparent from the beginning. As a young boy, he learned to read the Greek and Latin classics in their original languages. He once bragged that when he was about thirteen, he could read Scholastic philosophers with the same ease that most people read romance novels. Leibniz entered the University of Leipzig at age fifteen and graduated at age seventeen. After a brief stint at Jena, where he studied mathematics, he returned to Leipzig to work on a degree in law. However, academic politics intervened and a committee of faculty and students voted against giving him a doctorate (possibly because of his young age). This painful experience drove him to the University of Altdorf, near Nuremberg, where he was readily accepted. After completing his dissertation there, he not only received his doctoral degree in law at twenty-one years of age, but was also offered a professorship. However, he decided against an academic life in order to pursue the more active and lucrative career of a diplomat and government administrator.

As it turned out, this career decision actually helped his intellectual life, for his diplomatic travels throughout Europe led him to personal contact and correspondence with the leading intellectuals in England and Europe. In Paris he met the great Cartesian Nicolas Malebranche and began to study Descartes. While in London he met Robert Boyle, the famous chemist, and Henry Oldenburg, secretary of the Royal Society, one of the leading scientific institutions in the modern period. On demonstrating his state-of-the-art calculating machine (besides adding and subtracting, it extracted roots, multiplied, and divided), Leibniz was made a member of the Royal Society. In Holland, he visited with Spinoza and studied his manuscripts. However, although Leibniz's travels and multiple interests stimulated his intellect, they also prevented him from producing a unified, systematic work consistent with his large-scale vision. Instead, we find his philosophy scattered throughout letters, articles, pamphlets, and short essays as well as in a vast wealth of unpublished manuscripts.

Leibniz's diplomatic skills and incessant quest for unity and harmony led him to attempt to reconcile the Catholic and Protestant churches. He theorized that there should be a number of essential propositions in theology that both churches could agree on. He also hoped to unify all the European states. Obviously, he was not successful in carrying out these projects. In his later years, Leibniz was involved in an acrimonious debate with Newton as to who was the true author of the infinitesimal calculus. Each accused the other of stealing the idea. Clearly they both deserve the credit, for they were both working on it independently at the same time. This tells us something about the history of ideas: the intellectual soil was ready for this next great advance in mathematics

and there happened to be not one, but two geniuses capable of bringing it to fruition. As it turned out, Leibniz's notation was more convenient than Newton's, and thus Leibniz's approach is still used today. Although Leibniz had enjoyed a life in the public limelight, his popularity declined at the end of his life. He died in obscurity in 1716, and only his secretary attended the funeral.

Task: The Search for Unity and Harmony

Leibniz's philosophical task can be best understood in the light of his career as a diplomat. The diplomat must reconcile divergent points of view and merge them into a harmonious, unified compact. Similarly, in his philosophy Leibniz attempts to use the principles of mathematics and theology to work out his vision of a universal, cosmic harmony. In doing so, he hopes to reconcile science and religion, mechanism and teleology, modern and ancient philosophy. He does not think this has yet been accomplished, for he complains that "our human knowledge of nature seems to me at present like a shop well provided with all kinds of wares without any order or inventory" (L 357).[2]

Method: Logic Is the Key

With his rationalistic predecessors, Leibniz thinks the principles of logic and the methods found in mathematics can provide us with the method for finding the truth about reality. This conviction follows partly from his great confidence in logic and partly from his theology, for, like Galileo before him, Leibniz believes the universe is a harmonious system written in a mathematical language by God. Descartes and Spinoza shared this same methodological ideal, but Leibniz is not satisfied with their systems. He suspects that Descartes's thought leads to Spinoza's position, which leads to atheism.

Leibniz's lifelong search for a universal, logically perfect language (what he called "a universal characteristic") gives us a fascinating insight into his methodological ideal. He starts with the discovery that complex concepts in arithmetic can be reduced to combinations of more elementary concepts. In pursuing this, he eventually developed the system of binary mathematics (now used in computer science) in which all the numbers may be expressed as combinations of 1's and 0's. However, he believes this principle can be extended beyond mathematics and applied to all the areas of knowledge such as physics, metaphysics, theology, ethics, and jurisprudence (the philosophy of law).

The first step of his project is to reduce all concepts into their elementary units. "The elements are simples; in geometry figures, a triangle, circle, etc.; in jurisprudence an action, a promise, a sale, etc." (L 133). Next he represents them by mathematical symbols, which then form an alphabet of human thought. Just as all the writings of the philosophers can be represented as a combination of the twenty-six letters of the alphabet, so everything that can be thought could be represented by combinations of Leibniz's mathematical symbols. The final step would be to formulate the correct rules for combining these symbols. The goal would be to make the grammar of this symbolic language correspond to the logical structure of the world. Thus, true propositions would be those that followed this logical syntax, and false propositions would show up as ungrammatical combinations.

The application of this method would be threefold. First it would allow philosophers and scientists of different nationalities to converse in a universal logical language. Second, it would allow new truths to be discovered by finding which combinations of symbolized thoughts follow the logical rules. Third, it would provide an objective means of resolving philosophical controversies. When philosophical controversies arose, the philosophers would take up their pencils like two accountants and say, "Let us calculate."[3] In this way, the mathematical method would resolve all the disputes that have raged throughout human history.

This project assumes, of course, that it is possible to distill all the complexity of human thought into a select list of elementary and independent concepts. Furthermore, Leibniz naively assumes the task would yield to machinelike persistence:

I think that a few selected men could finish the matter in five years. It would take them only two, however, to work out, by an infallible calculus, the doctrines most useful for life, that is, those of morality and metaphysics. (L 344)

Although Leibniz never finished this enormous (and, perhaps impossible) task, his vision does give us an insight into his passion for making the world logically coherent. As we will see next, this vision leads him to search for the rationally necessary features of human knowledge.

Theory of Knowledge: Unpacking the Truths of Reason

INNATE IDEAS

With Plato and Descartes, Leibniz believes that some ideas (such as those we find in logic and mathematics) could not be derived from the senses. He argues that sense experience can never give us truths that are certain and necessary, so if some items of our knowledge have these qualities, they must be innate ideas that the mind discovers within itself. Leibniz presents his defense of innate ideas in his *New Essays on the Human Understanding*. This is his counterattack on the *Essay Concerning Human Understanding* (1689) in which the British empiricist John Locke vigorously criticized the theory of innate ideas. In this work, Locke claimed that there is nothing in the intellect that was not first in the senses. Leibniz suggests this claim should be rewritten to read, "There is nothing in the intellect that was not first in the senses, *except for the intellect itself*." His point is that we could never have the knowledge we have if Locke were correct in stating that the mind is a "blank tablet."

The mind must have some structure that predisposes it to discover universal and necessary truths. Leibniz compares the mind to a block of marble structured by the veins running through it. The structure of the marble determines what sort of shape the sculptor can extract from the block. In this sense we could say the statue of, say, Hercules was innate in the block of marble from the beginning (W 372-373). However, it takes the blows of the sculptor to reveal the inner structure of the marble. In the same way, even though experience is not the source of necessary truth, the impact of experience can reveal the truths latent in the mind (W 372-373).

Locke and the other empiricists argued that if innate ideas existed in the mind, we would always have been aware of them. However, Leibniz replies that this assumes that the mind is completely transparent and assumes that all the contents of the mind exist at the level of explicit, conscious awareness. Leibniz cautions,

> We must not imagine that these eternal laws of the reason can be read in the soul as in an open book, . . . but it is enough that they can be discovered in us by force of attention, for which occasions are furnished by the senses. (W 370)

For example, before the child studies geometry she is not aware of its truths. But her mind has a certain innate receptivity or disposition to discover and recognize the truths of geometry under the right conditions. Thus, innate truths are not originally present as explicit, fully formed knowledge, but exist in us as "inclinations, dispositions, habits, or natural capacities" to think in certain ways (W 373). Although Leibniz is a rationalist, he recognizes that experience can help transform latent or dispositional knowledge into explicit knowledge.

In pointing out that innate ideas can be implicit in the mind without our being aware of them, Leibniz has outlined a fairly sophisticated account of experience. Both Descartes and Locke tended to view the mind as a transparent box such that we are able to immediately "see" all of its contents when we introspect. However, Leibniz points out that we can experience something without being consciously aware of it. The example he uses is that of people who do not take notice of the roar of a waterfall because they have lived near it for a long time. They are still experiencing the sounds, but these perceptions no longer reside at the top level of awareness (W 375).

According to Leibniz's model of the mind, the mind has "depth," enabling its contents to range from those which are clearly perceived, to those

we experience in a confused or indistinct sort of way, all the way down to those that are unconscious and deeply latent. This account puts Leibniz's theory much closer to twentieth-century psychology than the naive models of the mind embraced by both the rationalists and the empiricists of his time.

NECESSITY AND CONTINGENCY

Leibniz's insistence that some knowledge is innate, points to one of the most important distinctions in his philosophy: the distinction between truths of reason and truths of fact. As he states it, "truths of reasoning are necessary, and their opposite is impossible; those of *fact* are contingent, and their opposite is possible" (M 33). Truths of reason rest on the principle of contradiction or what he sometimes calls the "principle of identity." The principle of contradiction states that if a proposition (call it *P*) is self-contradictory, then its opposite, *Not-P*, must be true. The principle of identity simply states that "*P* is *P*" or "each thing is what it is." The statement, "the equilateral rectangle is a rectangle," is clearly a truth of reason, for to deny it is to state a contradiction. This sort of proposition is what Leibniz calls an "identical proposition" and what logicians today call a "tautology," for it repeats the same thing without giving us any additional information. According to Leibniz, all truths of reason are identical propositions or can be logically reduced to one.

Truths of fact are the opposite of truths of reason. Truths of facts are any statements that cannot be reduced to identical propositions, for we *can* deny them without asserting a logical contradiction. For example, we cannot deny that "a bachelor is an unmarried, adult male," for this is a logically necessary statement or a truth of reason. However, even though it is factually true that "Socrates was married" we can deny it and assert that "Socrates was unmarried" without stating a logical contradiction. The second statement about Socrates is factually false, but the principle of contradiction could not tell us this was so, and we would have to consult the facts to know it was untrue.

Truths of fact rest on the principle of sufficient reason, which states that "no fact can be real or existent, no statement true, unless there be a sufficient reason why it is so and not otherwise" (M 32). However, Leibniz adds that "most often these reasons cannot be known to us." This is because we can know something is the case without exhaustively understanding all the sufficient reasons that make it the way it is. Only God's infinite mind is capable of this.

Since truths of reason (such as the theorems of geometry) are based on the laws of logic, they necessarily must be the way they are. However, truths of fact are contingent—they are true because the world happens to be the way it is. It happens to be true that grass is green, but we can imagine that the world had been created such that grass turned out red. Truths of reason deal with what is possible or not possible. Truths of fact deal with what exists and doesn't exist.* As was discussed in the previous chapter, Spinoza questioned this distinction between necessary truths and contingent truths. He claimed that our belief in contingency was merely the result of the limitations of our understanding. If we saw things from God's perspective, Spinoza argued, we would see that every detail in the world was as necessary and unchangeable as the theorems of geometry. Leibniz tries very hard to avoid this conclusion. By insisting that the details of the world are contingent, he preserves the traditional belief that God was free to create the world in any way he chose. But many commentators think that Leibniz is not successful in this and suspect that his system collapses into Spinoza's logically determined system.

Leibniz teeters on the brink of Spinoza's system when he claims that

> Always, in every true affirmative proposition, whether necessary or contingent, universal or particular, the notion of the predicate is in some way included in that of the subject. . . . Otherwise I know not what truth is. (L 517)[4]

This claim raises no problems for truths of reason, for when I say, "A triangle is a three-sided figure,"

the predicate ("three-sided figure") is part of the meaning of "triangle" and thus is "contained" in the concept of triangularity. The difficulty arises when we apply Leibniz's statement to contingent truths. It surely does not seem the idea of Socrates necessarily includes the idea of being married, in the way the concept of a triangle includes the property of being three-sided. Similarly, you do not think that everything you are, all the things you do, all the choices you have made, in short, everything that is true or *will be* true about you, are all necessary to being the person you are. However, Leibniz says you are mistaken about this.

Here is what he seems to have in mind. We know that Socrates was a short, stout, fifth-century, male, Greek philosopher. If one of his properties had been different (let's say he had been tall instead of short), this would not seem to significantly change his identity. Now, one by one, change each one of his remaining five properties into the following properties: slender, twentieth-century, female, Swedish track star. Even though we can imagine that the resulting person was still named "Socrates," we clearly no longer have the same person, but we have imagined a completely different individual with the same name. But which properties of Socrates are essential to his identity? At what point does our conception cease to be of Socrates? There seems to be no nonarbitrary cutoff point. For Leibniz, if any details in Socrates' properties change, we end up with a different person. Socrates is identical to all his predicates and this includes all his choices, all the events in his life, and all his relationships.

Having said all this, Leibniz still insists that the necessity of Socrates being a philosopher is not an absolute necessity of the same type as the properties of a triangle. If we deny the statement "Socrates was a philosopher," we do not assert a logical contradiction. Yet, given the contingent fact that the person known as Socrates existed, the events that unfolded from his character were necessary. In themselves, these events are contingent, since they can be denied without violating the rules of logic. They do have, however, a relative necessity with respect to the character and existence of Socrates.

---

*God is the one exception to this distinction, for Leibniz uses the ontological argument in an attempt to prove that God's existence is a necessary truth of reason.

Even though the concept of Socrates contains all his properties, we clearly cannot analyze our idea of Socrates and deduce his properties the way we can a triangle. Leibniz accounts for this difference by appealing to the difference between a finite analysis and an infinite analysis:

> In the case of a contingent truth, even though the predicate is really in the subject, yet one never arrives at a demonstration of an identity, even though the resolution of each term is continued indefinitely. In such cases it is only God, who comprehends the infinite at once, who can see how the one is in the other, and can understand a priori the perfect reason for the truth. In created things this is supplied a posteriori, by experience.[5]

Leibniz says, for example, that God knew *a priori* of Alexander the Great whether he would die a natural death or by poison. The unique identity of anything consists of all its properties. Thus, the fact that we cannot deduce all Socrates' or Alexander's properties is because our ideas of them are incomplete and vague. However, we can deduce the properties of a triangle because we do have a clear idea of its nature and can analyze it in a finite number of steps. This position may still seem puzzling but will become clearer in the next section when we discuss Leibniz's view of the creation of the world.

Metaphysics: God as the Divine Programmer

DOES GOD EXIST?

Leibniz gives a number of arguments for the existence of God. These include a version of the ontological argument (previously developed by St. Anselm in the eleventh century and Descartes in the seventeenth century) and the argument from eternal and necessary truths (St. Augustine's favorite argument). He also presented the argument from design (commonly called the "teleological argument"). Leibniz's version of this is unique, for he does not simply argue from the beauty and harmony of nature but argues from the pre-established harmony of all substances (a notion that will be

discussed later). Finally, he formulates a version of the cosmological argument, using his principle of sufficient reason. Although he does add his own twists to these age-old arguments, we will not discuss them here, because they are too similar to the previous versions.

IS THIS THE BEST OF ALL POSSIBLE WORLDS?

One of the most interesting features of Leibniz's metaphysics is his famous (and astonishing) claim that this is "the best of all possible worlds." What could he possibly mean? At first glance, this claim seems implausible. However, Leibniz was not claiming that every single event taken in isolation (such as an earthquake) is the best thing imaginable. Instead, he is asserting that the world taken as a whole, the sum of world history from beginning to end, is a better story than any other that could be told. Before creation, God was like a screenwriter trying to choose from among all the possible plots, characters, props, set designs, and camera angles of the movie he was about to produce. For example, among all the possible worlds arrayed before the infinite mind of God there is a world just like ours, except without giraffes. There is another imaginable world just like ours in which rain tastes like lemonade. There are also worlds that differ radically from ours. Of course, God does not consider worlds that contain round squares, for such worlds would not be logically possible.

Out of all the infinite possibilities, how does God choose which one to create? Leibniz gives us the answer in the following argument:

(1) God is a morally perfect, all-knowing, and all-powerful being.

(2) A morally perfect, all-knowing, all-powerful being always chooses the best of all possible alternatives.

(3) God chose to create *this* world.

(4) Therefore, this is the best of all possible worlds.

A number of points need to be clarified about this argument. First, since only God is perfect and everything created will be finite and limited, no world will ever be perfect. Thus, any world God chose to create would have pluses and minuses. For example, a world without any living creatures would be a world without any suffering and moral evil. But this benefit would be eclipsed by the enormous minus that an empty, lifeless world would be very sterile and dull. The best world contains the optimal balance of all possible values. Leibniz summarizes these values under two headings: "As great a variety as possible, but with the greatest possible order" (M 58).

Second, the argument assumes there can only be *one* optimal world. However, Leibniz never makes clear why there could not be other worlds different from ours that would be equal in variety and order. Third, if (1) there is only one best world and (2) God's goodness dictated that he could not have chosen any world but the best, then it seems the other worlds really were not live options after all. In other words, statements 1 and 2 imply it was necessary for God to create this particular world. If this reasoning is correct, then Leibniz's position really does lead to Spinoza's claim that "things could have been produced by God in no other manner and in no other order than that in which they have been produced."[6]

An astonishing conclusion that follows from Leibniz's premises is that *you*, the person reading this book right now, *had* to exist. This does not mean your existence is logically necessary, because we can conceive of worlds in which you don't exist without running into a contradiction. However, a Leibnizian metaphysical argument can be constructed to demonstrate that your existence in this world is *morally* necessary. It goes as follows:

(1) We can conceive of two types of worlds:

    (a) A world (like the present one) in which you exist

    (b) Another world that differs from this one only in the respect that your existence and all of its consequences are absent

(2) As demonstrated previously, God chose to create world (a), the one in which you exist, because this one is the best of all possible worlds.

(3) Hence, the fact you exist makes this a better world than any other possible world.

(4) Therefore, it was necessary for you to exist in order for God to make this the best of all possible worlds.

It is, no doubt, comforting to consider that your contribution to the world's richness is irreplaceable. However, there is a catch. Apparently, in God's infinite wisdom, a world with Hitler is also better than a world without him. Our finite minds might not be able to figure this one out, but Leibniz's premises lead to that conclusion. This requires Leibniz to say something about the problem of evil.

WHY IS THERE EVIL IN THE BEST OF ALL POSSIBLE WORLDS?

Leibniz addresses the problem of evil in his *Theodicy*, a term that means "the justification of the ways of God." According to Leibniz, there are three categories of evil. "Evil may be taken metaphysically, physically and morally. *Metaphysical evil* consists in mere imperfection, *physical evil* in suffering, and *moral evil* in sin."[7]

First, Leibniz addresses the problem of metaphysical evil. Metaphysical evil is imperfection, the unavoidable imperfection present in any being that is finite. Since Leibniz thinks it obvious that existence is better than nonexistence, it follows that an imperfect world is better than no world at all. Since evil is a privation or the negative quality of lacking perfection, it cannot be said that evil is a positive reality God created.

A critic might reply that it seems possible even an imperfect world could be free of suffering, or what Leibniz calls "physical evil." Leibniz handles the problem of physical evil with an *a priori* argument. Since he has argued this must be the best world, then even the sufferings of its creatures must somehow contribute to the overall good of the total system. For example, suffering can build character and draw out the best in us. To this Leibniz adds the empirical observation that there is more physical good in the world than physical evil. However, some critics say that although suffering may sometimes serve a greater good, much suffering in the world is gratuitous and demoralizing and does not seem justified. Furthermore, they insist Leibniz must show that the extreme amount of suffering in the world is better than a lesser amount of beneficial suffering would be.

Finally, Leibniz explains why moral evil exists. Moral evil is caused by the free choices of people who lack a rightly ordered will. Thus, God cannot be blamed for the existence of moral evil. However, whether or not Leibniz can reconcile human moral freedom with his doctrine that God determines every event in the world is an important issue we will take up later.

THE PROBLEMS DESCARTES COULD NEVER SOLVE

Leibniz's primary goal is to develop a metaphysical theory that will make his theology coherent with the science of his day. To do this, he must answer the question "What are the fundamental constituents of reality?" or, in the terminology of his day, "What are the ultimate substances?" Descartes believed the world contains two kinds of substances: minds and matter. However, Leibniz has problems with Descartes's view that the substances studied by physicists are nothing but extended bits of matter. He raises several problems with Descartes's position, of which we will mention three. First, the dynamic, energetic nature of physical things indicates that substances cannot be inert chunks of matter, but must be internally active centers of *force*. The second reason why matter cannot be a fundamental substance is that it is infinitely divisible. Starting with extended matter, we can never get down to any fundamental units. If the substances studied by science are truly fundamental, they must be indivisible.

The third problem facing Descartes, which he never solved satisfactorily, was how to relate minds to the world of matter, once he has defined them as separate types of reality. On all these issues, Spinoza's position is no better. He claimed there was only one substance in the whole of reality. However, Leibniz finds this monistic view implausible, because the existence of plurality in the world seems too evident. When Spinoza says the one substance is made up of the two attributes of thought and extension, each with their own set of principles, he leaves our world as hopelessly divided as Descartes did.

If Cartesian dualism is too problematic, then there are only two other possibilities. One is that reality is nothing but matter. However, Leibniz says this view cannot account for the existence of consciousness. To paraphrase one of his arguments, he says that if he could be miniaturized and if he roamed about in your brain, he would encounter all the machinery of the brain, but he would never encounter your pains, feelings, and sensations (M 17). Consciousness is distinct from extended matter. The only other alternative—and the one he supports—is that reality is basically mental and matter "is a phenomenon like a rainbow."[8] In other words, it is not something substantial in itself but is the product of something more fundamental.

Leibniz's criticism of Descartes is based on the insight that the ultimate units of the world of science are centers of force and not particles of matter in motion. He says that these centers of force are *real* indivisible points, which he calls *metaphysical points*. Unlike physical points, they have no extension, and unlike mathematical points, they are not theoretical abstractions or fictions, but objective realities. This relates to his infinitesimal calculus, which was the attempt to deal with motion as a continuum made up of an infinite number of infinitesimal points as opposed to a series of discrete leaps. Furthermore, his notion that reality is a mathematically ordered continuum of forces foreshadowed the discovery of modern physics that matter and energy are interchangeable. Although he was centuries ahead of the science of his time in proposing this idea, its details were too speculative to be of much use to the physics of his day. Fortunately, we do not need to delve into the intricacies of Leibniz's calculus or physics to understand his metaphysics. As we shall see in the next section, all we need to know in order to understand reality is to look into our own experience.

ARE YOU A MONAD?

The fundamental units of reality are what Leibniz calls *monads*. The term is derived from *monas*, a Greek word meaning "unity" or "that which is one." According to Leibniz, the universe consists of an infinity of simple, nonmaterial substances or monads. The best way to understand a monad is to realize that your own mind is one. According to Leibniz's view, minds cannot be extended because it makes no sense to say that your mind is rectangular or two feet long. Furthermore, non-physical monads (or minds) are the only things in the universe that could be indivisible, unified atoms. True, your mind contains a spectrum of thoughts, perceptions, feelings, desires. But none of these can exist on its own. Hence, all these diverse components merge together to form one, unified mental experience.

The chief activity of monads is perception. High-level monads, such as God's mind and ours, are consciously aware of what they perceive. When perception is conscious, it is called *apperception*. Since monads make up the whole of reality, perception, whether conscious or not, is an activity that occurs in every portion of reality. For example, consider the experience of a human being. The person feels, experiences, or perceives the world around her. But she is not simply passive in this, for a person is an internal source of activity. In perceiving the world, she also responds to it in various ways. We could apply this analysis all the way down the hierarchy of nature. Although conscious awareness only applies to high-level minds, we never reach a point where there is no longer some sort of low-level and vague perceiving, experiencing, feeling, and responding. For example, the lowly white blood corpuscle has an inner vitality and unconsciously seeks out an infection and "feels" the presence of a germ. If Leibniz were writing today, he would say the activity of electrons also illustrates his thesis.

The point is that nature is a continuum. Nowhere do we discover the dead, inert, lifeless, hunks of matter that seventeenth-century physicists thought were the building blocks of the phys-ical world. Leibniz was familiar with observations made with a new type of microscope that displayed a vast world of tiny living things in what had formerly been considered inanimate matter. Leibniz's position is sometimes called **idealism**, which is the claim that reality is fundamentally mental in nature. It has also been called **panpsychism**—the claim that everything is made up of minds or souls.

Employing the notion of the continuum he used in mathematics, Leibniz says the world follows the law of continuity or the principle that nature never makes leaps (W 378). Hence, nature is filled by monads exhibiting every conceivable level of awareness and variety of perspectives, all the way from God's mind down to the most minimal level possible. Leibniz coins the term "the identity of indiscernibles" when he argues that two absolutely identical monads could not be distinguished and therefore could not really be two different things. Just as there cannot be two number 7s in the number series, so there cannot be two monads with the same point of view. Hence, each monad in the continuous hierarchy of nature must be absolutely unique.

MONADS ARE WINDOWLESS

If Leibniz has convinced you that perception is found all throughout nature, the next question is, How do monads interact? His surprising answer is, they *don't*. Each monad is a self-enclosed and self-sufficient unit, complete unto itself. Leibniz expresses this memorably: "the monads have no windows through which anything can enter or depart" (M 7). Look about you. You are experiencing the world. Or, to put it another way, the world is represented within you. You are not only experiencing the room you are in, but physicists tell us you are influenced by the gravitational pull of the farthest star in the universe (but at a level too low to notice). Thus, your experience (in the broadest sense) includes what you are consciously aware of as well as what is felt only subliminally. In this way, the *whole* world is represented within your experience, although the various items within it are perceived with differing degrees of clarity. In Leibniz's picture, there is no dichotomy between the world within your experience and some unknown world outside it. This allows Leibniz to avoid Descartes's problem of how something outside your experience can get into your experience and the question of whether or not your experience corresponds to what is outside of it.

Of course, other people have an internally represented world also. Since you can never leap inside my consciousness, our worlds of experience are absolutely separate and impenetrable (they are windowless). Although our experiences are never identical (for we each experience the world from a different point of view), their contents correspond to one another. To use an analogy to make this clear, try to imagine that our individual fields of experience are like different TV screens showing similar videotapes. When you see a car chase on your screen, I'll see a similar car chase on mine. Furthermore, imagine our respective pictures of the same scene are shot from different camera angles, from different distances, and with different levels of focus. Just like our individual videoscreens, each monad "mirrors" the entire world in its unique way. For example, the way you experience the garden is different from how a worm experiences it. To use a phrase unfamiliar to Leibniz, each of us lives in our own "virtual reality," except that there is no additional reality outside of the sum total of ours and God's experiences.

THE PRE-ESTABLISHED HARMONY OF THE WORLD

If there is no external world apart from our experiences, what causes them? The answer is that God has "programmed" them into us from the beginning. Remember the analogy of God as a screenwriter. When he created the world, he wrote you into the "script." The "you" here includes all of your life's experiences. To continue the analogy, your life as you are experiencing it now is the playing of the videotape that God produced. Likewise, for every other monad "the present is big with the future and laden with the past" as it con-tinuously unfolds its own story and perspective on the universe (W 376). Leibniz says that

> Each body feels all that happens in the universe, so that he who sees all could read in each what happens everywhere, and even what has been or shall be. (M 61)

If nothing can be affected by what is outside its experience, then each monad must contain within itself the principle of its own activity. This inner drive toward self-development is what Leibniz calls *appetition*. When appetition is conscious, it manifests itself as purpose or will. Nevertheless, every part of nature is driven by its own internal desires, whether this is conscious or not. For example, you have desires you strive to fulfill, and so does the sunflower. The sunflower turns toward the sun and strives to fulfill all its potentiality for maximum growth. Iron filings fulfill their nature when they are drawn to the magnet.

This account of the plurality of monads raises the question, In what sense is there one world? Maybe we are each experiencing radically different universes. Leibniz addresses this problem with his notion of the **pre-established harmony**. When he created the world, God designed the internal nature of each monad so that the experience of any given monad corresponds, with varying degrees of clarity, to the experience of any other monad. Imagine a whole orchestra in which each individual musician is locked in a separate room. They have before them the same score and similarly calibrated metronomes. Each musician plays his or her part, without interacting with the other musicians. Collectively, they produce the totality of the symphony.[9] Leibniz also uses the example of two clocks synchronized so that they move their hands in unison, even though there is no causal interaction between them (W 118).

EXTENSION, SPACE, AND TIME

Even if Leibniz has convinced us that every part of nature is permeated by active, responsive, units of mental life, a problem still needs to be addressed. Since these minds or monads are unextended and indivisible, how do we account for our experience of extended things? Let us return to Leibniz's example of the rainbow. When we look at a rainbow, it looks like a broad, multicolored band stretched across the sky. However, we know it is really not a unified object, but an appearance created by a multiplicity of water droplets. Similarly, extension is not a property of things themselves, but is the way things appear to us. When we experience a repetition of monads similar to one another, we appear to see an extended object. In the same way, a painter can juxtapose dabs of paint on a canvas to create the illusion of depth and the appearance of spatial extension that isn't really there. Of course, like all analogies these examples eventually break down. The drops of water making the rainbow and the drops of paint creating the appearance of depth present themselves to us as small, extended particles. In reality, however, they themselves are also appearances created from innumerable, unextended monads.

One implication that follows from this is that space and time do not exist apart from our spatially and temporally organized experiences. We tend to think in terms of Newton's commonsense view that space is like a vast container. According to Newton, if you removed all the physical bodies from the universe, something would still remain: empty space. Hence, for Newton space is an absolute, self-subsisting entity. But according to Leibniz, space is not a thing that exists all by itself. Instead, it is a system of relations between the elements of our experience. Similarly, time is not like a stream in which we float. It does not exist by itself. Time is simply a measure of the successive relationship between the events we experience. On Leibniz's view, space and time are relative—the pivotal thesis in Albert Einstein's twentieth-century revolution of physics.

THE MIND–BODY PROBLEM REVISITED

Leibniz thinks his metaphysical system solves the problem of how our minds relate to our bodies. He has argued that what we call physical bodies are actually collections of infinitely small monads.

However, some bodies, such as a pile of sand, are mere aggregates, because they do not contain any unifying principle. However, organic bodies are communities of monads whose activities are harmonized with those of a dominant monad, which is the mind or soul of the creature. You experience all the monads in the universe to various degrees, but the monads in your body are the ones you experience the most clearly and directly. Of course, there cannot be any direct interaction between the mind and body, for all monads are windowless. Instead, God has correlated the changes in your mind and body to work in perfect harmony. When the monads in your stomach are experiencing discomfort, a corresponding feeling occurs in your mind. When you want to pick up a pencil, the monads comprising your hand respond appropriately. This paints quite a fantastic picture, yet it does solve the problems Descartes had with mind–body interaction.

TELEOLOGY AND MECHANISM RECONCILED

The pre-established harmony of our mind monad with the collections of monads we think of as material things enables Leibniz to reconcile teleological explanations (in terms of purposes and final ends) and mechanical explanations. Since bodies follow fixed laws, it does no harm, and it serves the purposes of ordinary life if we speak of bodies as acting on one another according to mechanical principles. However, the most refined level of explanation would refer to the actions of bodies as the unfolding of their inner natures in the direction of their God-ordained final ends. As Leibniz states it,

> Souls act according to the laws of final causes, by appetitions [desires], ends and means. Bodies act in accordance with the laws of efficient causes or of motion. And the two realms, that of efficient causes and that of final causes, are in harmony with each other. (M 79)

The difference between these two realms is the difference between looking at events from the outside or from the inside. An outside observer such as a physiologist could explain your behavior as the result of mechanical events occurring in your brain. But from the inside, you see your own choices as resulting from your desires, your will, and your nature. Normally, we view the behavior of the billiard ball from the standpoint of physics. However, if we could understand the unconscious perceptions and appetition of the monads within it, we would also see its behavior as the unfolding of its inner nature. However, while this notion of two orders serves the purposes of science, in the final analysis we must see the material kingdom as forming part of a purposive system ordained by God. Thus, physics needs to be supplemented by metaphysics and theology.

IS FREEDOM COMPATIBLE WITH DETERMINISM?

Many find Leibniz's vision of the universe unattractive because it seems to deny human freedom. After all, if everything you will do or that will happen to you is already packed into the person you are, it seems everything is determined. It is worth noting this is not a problem unique to Leibniz, for many traditional views of God claim he knows and plans the future. If this is true, then all your actions are the unfolding of a scenario God created.

Leibniz, however, insists this does not mean that you are not free. For him, freedom is identical to unimpeded self-development and not to arbitrary, unpredictable, spontaneous actions. You would lack freedom only if your actions were controlled from without. But Leibniz does not believe God is a puppetmaster who is pulling your strings and making you act in ways you do not choose or do not control. Given who you are, your actions are the result of your values and your character. They flow from your inner essence. Whether you decide to play some rock music or a classical piece at any given time is your free decision. Still, this choice follows from your preferences, tastes, and inclinations. If I knew these perfectly, I would be able to predict what you would choose. Generally, the better we know a person, the more their behavior is predictable.

Leibniz's position is a version of **compatibilism**. This is the claim that (1) Everything a person does that is not the result of external coercion is determined by his or her own internal character, and (2) If our choices are determined by our own character, this is all that could be reasonably meant by human freedom. Thus, the compatibilist (such as Leibniz) claims it is coherent to say we are both determined *and* free. At last it is clear why Leibniz says the subject contains all of its predicates. When God chose to create this world, he chose to create you. But who you are is your personality, your desires, and every event that will occur within your experience. God could have created a world in which you would not now be reading this book. But this would be a different world, and you would be a different person. Hence, if someone had the total conception of you God had when he created this world, she would know your entire life the way Shakespeare knew Hamlet's.

For many people, whether their actions are the result of external forces determining them or the result of some sort of inner, psychological programming, does not, in the final analysis, make a whole lot of difference. We like to think our choices (whom to date, what career to pursue, our ethical decisions, and so on) are not "written" into our personality but result from spontaneous decisions on our part. In other words, we like to think that given our personality and all the antecedent events leading up to a decision, the outcome is not already prescribed. If you are a theist, but reject Leibniz's limited view of freedom, then you must work out a way of reconciling spontaneous human freedom with God's knowledge of his own creation. If you are not a theist, and also reject Leibniz's limited view of freedom, then you must find a way to include spontaneous human freedom within the causally determined order of nature. Either way, Leibniz has given us some hard philosophical work to do.

Evaluation and Significance

Despite Leibniz's rigorously formulated arguments, there have been a number of criticisms of his position. For example, Leibniz's announcement that "this is the best of possible worlds" provoked ridicule in many quarters. In 1755, a generation after Leibniz wrote these memorable words, a devastating earthquake in Lisbon shocked the cosmic optimism of the eighteenth century. Four years later, Voltaire, the French essayist, responded to this tragedy with *Candide*, a bitter satire of Leibniz's happy vision of the world. The story is crammed with all the brutality human beings and nature can inflict. A central character is the optimistic philosopher Pangloss, who goes about cheerfully proclaiming that there is a "sufficient reason" for all the overwhelming human suffering lying about him. After experiencing the carnage created by numerous instances of human brutality and natural disasters (including the Lisbon earthquake), Candide (Pangloss's young pupil) exclaims, "If this is the best of all possible worlds, what are the others like?"[10]

Others find problems with Leibniz's view that people are free but their natures are determined by God's plan. The problem is illustrated by the characters in W. Somerset Maugham's *Of Human Bondage*, where Philip says,

> *"Before I do anything I feel that I have a choice, and that influences what I do; but afterwards, when the thing is done, I believe that it was inevitable from all eternity."— "What do you deduce from that?" asked Hayward.—"Why merely the futility of regret. It's no good crying over spilt milk, because all the forces of the universe were bent on spilling it."*[11]

Of course, the problems of evil and of human freedom cannot be adequately solved through novelistic treatments. Nevertheless, the sentiments illustrated in these novels have given rise to a number of philosophical critiques of Leibniz.

A criticism that Leibniz himself would have found devastating, if it were made to stick, is the charge that his position collapses into Spinoza's. Leibniz continually tried to drive a wedge between his ideas and Spinoza's position, because he found both its metaphysical and theological conclusions to be intolerable. But many suspect he was not successful. For example, Leibniz's notion that God is the supreme monad whose experience includes the infinite experiences of all the other monads comes very close to Spinoza's view that we are all modes of the one divine substance. Furthermore, when Leibniz says that God's nature required that he create *this* exact world, and that the world is a rational system such that its details can be derived from the concept of anything in it, he ends up reintroducing a Spinoza-like necessity into the foundation of the whole scheme.

Despite the criticisms of some contemporaries, Leibniz's system had enormous appeal. It dominated German thought for over a century and was instrumental in bringing the Enlightenment to his homeland. In the eighteenth century, Leibniz's system was the paradigm of rationalistic metaphysics. Thus, it served both as a model for metaphysicians and as a target for those, such as Kant, who thought the rationalists had pushed reason beyond its built-in limitations.

Most of Leibniz's works were not published, but lay hidden for centuries in the Royal Library at Hanover and were not discovered until the twentieth century. Because his far-reaching work in symbolic logic was not available, scholars had to rediscover ideas that had already been worked out long ago by Leibniz. In the early part of the twentieth century, logicians and analytic philosophers marveled at the richness of his work in logic, while dismissing his theology and monadology as antiquated nonsense. His dream of constructing a universal, logically perfect language inspired the efforts of such logicians as Bertrand Russell. Furthermore, Leibniz's vision of reducing all human thought to mathematical symbols has knowingly or unknowingly been appropriated by artificial intelligence researchers. In the latter half of the twentieth century, metaphysics and philosophical theology experienced a revival, and a new appreciation for Leibniz's efforts in these areas resulted.

Questions for Understanding

1. Why did Leibniz attempt to construct a universal, logical language?

2. What was Leibniz's theory of innate ideas? How did he respond to Locke's criticism of this notion?

3. What is Leibniz's distinction between truths of fact and truths of reason?

4. Why would Leibniz say that all of your properties and the facts about you are absolutely necessary to your identity?

5. Why does Leibniz believe that this is the best of all possible worlds? What does he mean by this?

6. How does Leibniz explain the fact that there is so much suffering and evil if this is the best of all possible worlds?

7. What are Leibniz's criticisms of Descartes's metaphysics? How does he avoid both Cartesian dualism and materialism?

8. What are monads, according to Leibniz? What is their chief activity? What does it mean to say that they are "windowless"? Why does Leibniz think that this notion makes sense out of our experience?

9. What does "idealism" mean?

10. What does Leibniz mean by "pre-established harmony"? What problems is he trying to solve with this notion?

11. What is Leibniz's concept of extension, space, and time? In what ways is his view an attack upon Newton's physics?

12. How does Leibniz attempt to solve the mind–body problem?

13. How does Leibniz reconcile teleological explanations with mechanistic explanations? In what way does he think this will reconcile religion and science?

14. How does Leibniz argue that we are both free and determined? Why could his position be called "compatibilism"?

Questions for Reflection

1. Do you think that Leibniz is correct in arguing that we could not reason or have knowledge if the mind is a "blank tablet"? If he is correct on this, what sort of content or capacities must the mind have prior to experience? What do you think of his view that we can know something without being explicitly aware of this knowledge?

2. Do you agree with Leibniz that every detail in the world, including those that make up your identity are necessary? In other words, suppose that you were to agree with Leibniz that God created the world and that in doing so he knew that you would be a part of it. Would this imply, as Leibniz thinks it does, that every fact about you is a necessary feature of the world as God created it? What would be the implications of this position?

3. What do you think of Leibniz's argument that this is the best of all possible worlds? Is it possible to be a theist and not accept this conclusion? How so? What are the implications of accepting this position? To what extent does the existence of unmerited suffering count against this view? To what degree is Leibniz successful in handling the problem of evil and suffering?

4. Try to view the world through Leibniz's eyes. For example, imagine that your mind is a monad and that your experiences constitute your world. Your world of experiences is similar to but different than your friends' worlds as well as the world of any other creature. Furthermore, imagine that this is all that reality consists of: your experiences, others' experiences, and God's total experience. What problems (if any) do you have with this view? What sorts of phenomena does it explain and what doesn't it explain?

5. If everything you do flows from your choices, which are a product of your personality, is this enough to consider yourself free? Where did your personality come from? Did you choose it or is this simply who you happen to be? If your personality was not chosen by you, but actions based on your personality are free, does this mean that we are both determined and free, as Leibniz claims? If not, what is the flaw in Leibniz's argument? In other words, do you agree or disagree with his notion of "freedom"?

6. How might it be argued that Leibniz's position is closer to Spinoza's than the former would have liked to believe?

Notes

1. Many of these points are discussed in Frank Thilly, *A History of Philosophy*, revised by Ledger Wood (New York: Holt, Rinehart and Winston, 1957), 385.

2. References to collections of Leibniz's works are abbreviated as follows:

   L   *Gottfried Wilhelm Leibniz. Philosophical Papers and Letters*, trans. and ed. L. E. Loemker, 2 vols. (Chicago: University of Chicago Press, 1956).

   M   *Monadology*, trans. George Martin Duncan, in *The European Philosophers from Descartes to Nietzsche*, ed. Monroe C. Beardsley (New York: Random House, 1960). References are made in terms of the paragraph numbers of Leibniz's work.

   W   *Leibniz Selections*, ed. Philip P. Wiener (New York: Scribner's, 1951).

3. Quoted in Bertrand Russell, *A Critical Exposition of the Philosophy of Leibniz* (London: Allen & Unwin, 1937), 170.

4. Correspondence with Arnauld, July 14, 1686.

5. Quoted in John Cottingham, *The Rationalists*, A History of Western Philosophy: 4 (Oxford, England: Oxford University Press, 1988), 68.

6. Spinoza, *Ethics*, pt. 1, prop. 33.

7. *Theodicy, Essays on the Goodness of God, the Freedom of Man and the Origin of Evil*, ed. Austin Farrer, trans. E. M. Huggard (New Haven, CT: Yale University Press, 1952), §21.

8. Quoted in Stuart Brown, *Leibniz*, Philosophers in Context (Minneapolis: University of Minnesota Press, 1984), 43.

9. Letter to Arnauld, April 30, 1687, in *Leibniz: Basic Writings*, trans. George R. Montgomery (La Salle, IL: Open Court, 1968), 188.

10. *Candide*, chap. 6.

11. *Of Human Bondage*, chap. 67.

18

Cultural Context: The Enlightenment and the Age of Newton

THE HISTORIAN OF THE EIGHTEENTH CENTURY does not have to search very far for an appropriate title for this period. The thinkers of this age presided at their own christening. The eighteenth-century writers spoke of their own time as the Age of Enlightenment. Their time was special, they thought, for reason had now made good on its promise. It had showed the way to progress in science, philosophy, religion, politics, and the arts. The pure, brilliant light of reason would vanquish once and for all the darkness in which humanity had previously labored and lived. What was this darkness? It was passion, prejudice, authority, and dogma. The pride shining through the self-proclaimed title of "Enlightenment" reveals the mood of the times. In any account you will read of this period, the words "hope," "optimism," "confidence," and "happiness" abound. As one writer aptly put it, "the eighteenth century is perhaps the last period in the history of Western Europe when human omniscience was thought to be an attainable goal."[1]

The Enlightenment did not, of course, suddenly spring into being. It was the culmination of many of the cultural and intellectual trends we have discussed in previous chapters. However, for our purposes, the overture began with the publishing of Sir Isaac Newton's great scientific work *Principia Mathematica* in 1687.* The opening act was John Locke's *An Essay Concerning Human Understanding* (1690) and the beginning of the final scene was Immanuel Kant's *Critique of Pure Reason*, first published in 1781. By the time Kant published his 1784 essay "What Is Enlightenment?" answering such a question was superfluous. No one had to be told by Kant that "Enlightenment is man's leaving his self-caused immaturity."

The Impact of Newton's Science

It is impossible to appreciate the philosophy of the eighteenth-century philosophers without taking note of the enormous influence Newtonian science had on this period. It is interesting that

---

*The full title is *Philosophiae Naturalis Principia Mathematica*, which means "Mathematical Principles of Natural Philosophy."

Newton was born in the year 1642, the same year that Galileo died. It is almost as though the earlier scientist passed on the torch of scientific inquiry to his successor as he left this world. This poetic coincidence would not have escaped Newton, for he was well aware of his debt to his predecessors. As he says in a letter, "If I have seen farther [than other scientists], it is because I have stood upon the shoulders of Giants."[2]

There is much we can learn from the case of Newton concerning the process of intellectual history. History is often made by the fortuitous combination of the right circumstances and the gifted genius. The work of Isaac Newton is a clear case of fertile intellectual soil accumulating for centuries, while being cultivated and seeded by previous thinkers, until it was finally brought to harvest by a great intellect. This was strikingly demonstrated by the fact that Newton and Leibniz both, independently, discovered infinitesimal calculus. Newton's achievement in physics consisted in developing a single, comprehensive theory from which he could derive both Galileo's laws describing the motion of falling bodies and Kepler's laws of the planetary motions. It was as though previous scientists had each been working on parts of a jigsaw puzzle, one piecing together a field of wildflowers, the other piecing together some clouds, all with the hope that somehow they were working on the same picture. Along came Newton who showed that the contributions of previous scientists could indeed be integrated into a single coherent and beautiful picture of nature. Imagine yourself in the seventeenth century, standing on the beach under a moonlit sky, tossing pebbles into the waves as the tide rolls in. Would you have thought that the motion of the moon and the planets up there in the sky, the trajectory made by your pebbles as they fell back to earth, and the movement of the approaching tide could all be explained by the same fundamental laws? So stupendous was Newton's achievement that it provided the framework for science for over two hundred years, until Albert Einstein provided a new model of the cosmos in the twentieth century.

AKG London

Sir Isaac Newton investigating sunlight with a prism, showing how rainbows are produced. Such experiments destroyed the mystical significance that was attached to light. The romantic poet John Keats would later complain that scientific philosophy attempts to "unweave a rainbow." Even though Newton's science distressed traditionalists, it had an extraordinary impact on philosophers.

Newton's discoveries dealt the final blow to any lingering remnants of the Aristotelian science of the Middle Ages. Aristotle thought that there was a major gulf between earthly matters and celestial affairs. These two spheres operated according to completely different laws. For the medievals, this was reinforced by their theological distinction between heaven and earth. But after Newton it was absolutely clear there are no special, sacred spaces in the physical realm. The heavens and the earth are made of the same materials and follow the same laws. The universe became increasingly less mysterious and more open to human understanding, prediction, and even control. Earlier, Robert Boyle, the great chemist, had mused that the universe was like a great clock. Now Newton had given mathematical substance to this image.

By the time Newton published his *Principia*, it became clear that mathematical, experimental science was no longer the new kid on the block—it was now the "king of the mountain." All philosophy (and religion) hereafter had to come to terms with it in some way or another. To the Enlightenment, Newton was more than a great physicist, he was a cultural hero. Alexander Pope voiced the spirit of the age when he said,

> Nature and Nature's laws lay hid in night:
> God said, Let Newton be! and all was Light.

In his book on the rise of modern science, E. A. Burtt makes the ironic observation that "Newton enjoys the remarkable distinction of having become an authority paralleled only by Aristotle to an age characterized through and through by rebellion against authority."[3] Both the rationalists and the empiricists claimed Newton as their own. Indeed, the great synthesizing mind of Newton recognized the importance of both the deductive, mathematical approach favored by scientists and philosophers such as Galileo Galilei and René Descartes, as well as the inductive, experimental approach favored by those such as Francis Bacon and Robert Boyle. Nevertheless, the net effect of Newton's method was to tilt the scales more in the direction of the empiricists. Even though his remarks were not completely consistent with his practice, Newton ended the *Principia* by denouncing any speculative theories (which he called "hypotheses") that are not firmly rooted in the empirical data. As we will see in the next three chapters, this concern to trace the genealogy of all our affirmations back to the bedrock of experience played an important role in the epistemology of the British philosophers.

Newton, therefore, wanted to put science on a severe cognitive diet. This means that we must avoid the fatty and rich fare of speculative metaphysics and stick to the lean and unadulterated data of experience. For example, his law of gravitation states that the force of attraction (F) between any two bodies (M_1 and M_2) separated by distance R, where G is a universal constant, is as follows:

$$F = \frac{G\,M_1 M_2}{R^2}$$

This law of gravitation describes the observable behavior of bodies and enables us to calculate future observations. However, it does not attempt to explain what gravity *is* or what *causes* the attraction between bodies. As Newton expressed it,

> *Hitherto I have not been able to discover the cause of those properties of gravity from phenomena, and I frame no hypotheses; for whatever is not deduced from the phenomena is to be called an hypothesis; and hypotheses, whether metaphysical or physical, whether of occult qualities or mechanical, have no place in experimental science.*[4]

This represents a significant turning point in the history of thought, for Newton was telling scientists to give up all attempts to deal with essences and the underlying reality of things. Henceforth, science is to only describe the patterns of phenomena. The reality that lies behind, underneath, or beyond the phenomena cannot be scientifically comprehended. The implications of this methodological principle will become clearer step-by-step as we move in the next four chapters through the thought of John Locke, George Berkeley, David Hume, and finally Immanuel Kant. Philosophy began with the early Greeks' attempts to distinguish appearance and reality. After Newton, however, it gradually became apparent that the more science and experience were considered the sole basis of knowledge, the less we could know about reality in itself apart from the way it appears to us.

Philosophizing in a Newtonian Style

The philosophers of the time thought that just as Newton had resolved all mysteries concerning physical bodies, so now the task was to apply the same methods of experimental observation to the mysteries concerning human existence. The operations of the human mind, ethics, and politics were thought to be a collection of phenomena that could be explained in terms of descriptive laws. Hence, the philosophers of this time all aspired to be the "Newton" of the human sciences. The titles of the leading works of this period seemed to be permutations of the same set of interchangeable words concerned with epistemology. There was, for example, Locke's *An Essay Concerning Human Understanding*, Berkeley's *A Treatise Concerning the Principles of Human Knowledge*, and Hume's *An Enquiry Concerning Human Understanding*, as well as his *A Treatise of Human Nature*. The most extreme expression of this scientific approach to human nature was found in the works of Julien La Mettrie (1709–1751). Among his many controversial books was *Man the Machine* (1747). La Mettrie said that the true philosopher is an engineer who analyzes the apparatus of the human mind. Although his theory was crude, it was way ahead of its time, for it pointed toward the twentieth-century theory that the brain is like an organic computer. However, unlike La Mettrie, most philosophers at this time did not fully understand the reductionistic and deterministic implications of their own scientific and mechanistic approach to the human sciences. Instead (to exaggerate a bit), it almost seemed as though they saw scientific epistemology as a more efficient method for doing what the poets had always tried to do—provide us with an enriched self-understanding.

The model of Newtonian physics haunted the epistemology of this era. Corresponding to the physical particles whose laws of motion Newton unveiled, ideas were thought to be mental particles that could be analyzed down into fundamental, atomic units. Hence, all the ideas contained within the dialogues of Plato, the works of Shakespeare, and even the formulas of Newton, if they had any meaning at all, were considered to be complexes made up of simple ideas derived from experience. Corresponding to the outer space of the astronomer was the "inner space" of the mind, a container within which ideas floated and connected together according to psychological laws. Although this model of the mind assured philosophers that epistemology could duplicate the successes of physics, we have already seen in Descartes and will later see with Hume that this dichotomy between the inner, mental world and the outer, physical world created problems. If all mental awareness takes place within the container of the mind, how do we know that what appears on the inside represents what is going on in the outside world? As we have seen, Leibniz's idealism tried to get around that problem by rejecting the mental physical dualism on which it rested. Berkeley, likewise, developed a metaphysical idealism to overcome the problem. In wrestling with epistemological and metaphysical puzzles created by the philosophies of their time, Leibniz and Berkeley were among the first thinkers to question the Newtonian model. The alternative viewpoints they launched would come to fruition in the twentieth century with the physics of Albert Einstein and the process philosophy of Alfred North Whitehead.

The Consequences for Religion

In addition to its impact on philosophy, Newtonian science made waves within the religious sensibilities of the age as well. At first, people feared that the new physics would undermine religion. After all, Newton provided natural explanations for a great deal of celestial phenomena once thought to result from the direct providence of God. The notion that the universe was a clockwork mechanism did not mesh well with the theology of the day, which still clung to many medieval assumptions. As one critic of the new science complained, if the universe is ruled by geometry and mechanical laws, "I cannot any way comprehend how God can do any miracles."[5] Many feared that materialism and atheism would ride in on the coattails of mechanistic science and take over the culture. Nevertheless, Newton himself was a deeply pious Christian and even wrote works on theology and biblical exposition. For him, science revealed a universe that was majestic and marvelous in its design, pointing to the greatness of its creator. Newton expressed his scientific piety in a letter to a friend:

> When I wrote my treatise about our system, I had an eye upon such principles as might work with considering men for the belief of a deity; and nothing can rejoice me more than to find it useful for that purpose.[6]

Newton's argument for God was based not only on the evidence of design, but also on the problems within his own physics. First, Newton could not explain why the gravitational attraction of the stars does not cause them to collapse together. Second, he observed what seemed to be irregularities in the universe that would eventually cause it to run down. Because he could not solve these problems scientifically, he assumed that God actively intervened to keep the world machine going. However, this created what is known as a "God-of-the-gaps." It is risky to use gaps within our scientific knowledge as evidence for the necessity of God. When these gaps are eventually filled as scientific knowledge expands, there seems to be less need to believe in God. This is exactly what happened in Newton's case. Eighteenth-century scientists showed that further developments of Newton's physics could explain all the problematic phenomena and that the planetary orbits were not as irregular as Newton had supposed. Accordingly, the story is told that when the French astronomer Laplace presented his 1796 work to Napoleon, the general asked about God's role in explaining planetary motion. Laplace is said to have replied, "Sire, I have no need of that hypothesis."

From the beginning of modern science all the way up to and through the twentieth century, many, if not the majority, of the leading scientists and philosophers have been theists of some sort. Nevertheless, the ability to explain physical events on the basis of natural causes made a secular view of the world more viable than at any previous stage in history. Historically, the emergence of unbelief went through several overlapping stages in the modern period. (1) Initially, most scientists and philosophers, such as Newton, saw religion and science as co-equal partners in the search for truth. Among the philosophers in this period, George Berkeley stands out as one who taught the perfect

convergence of religion and science when both are properly understood. (2) Gradually the viewpoint emerged that the claims of revealed religion should be accepted, but only after they have been trimmed down to conform to the scientific outlook. Although John Locke could be identified with the previous position, he also fits in here, for he introduced the notion that the credentials of revelation must be approved by reason before we can believe it. (3) As science gained greater authority, the position of deism emerged. The deists claimed that the world machine is a perfectly ordered mechanism, understandable on its own terms. Hence, while they believed that God created the world, they thought it unreasonable to suppose that he needs to intervene in the processes of nature. Furthermore, they believed that autonomous human reason is self-sufficient to discover all truths about nature, religion, and morality without relying on revelation. Many of the key figures in the American Revolution such as Thomas Paine, Thomas Jefferson, and Benjamin Franklin were deists. (4) Agnosticism or religious skepticism began to appear in the works of such thinkers as David Hume. The agnostics urged that we must suspend judgment concerning God's existence, for reason does not give us any grounds for believing in a deity, although it cannot prove that one does not exist. Immanuel Kant agreed with Hume that we cannot have *knowledge* of God, because knowledge about what exists is to be found only in the sciences. However, he tempered this theoretical agnosticism with the notion that we still find it compelling to postulate a deity. (5) Finally, full-blown naturalism or atheism appeared. However, in terms of the major figures in philosophy, it would not have a strong voice until the nineteenth century. Its proponents claimed that the philosophical and scientific evidence is stacked against the God hypothesis. Therefore, the rational person will reject it, just as we have the flat-earth theory and the theory that diseases have supernatural causes.

The French Enlightenment

It did not take long for the spirit of the Enlightenment to find its way to France. This spirit was embodied in a group of eighteenth-century French writers known as the *philosophes* (from the French term for philosopher). In spite of their name, they were primarily literary intellectuals rather than technical philosophers. Nevertheless, they used their considerable skill with words to popularize the Enlightenment among the educated public. Representing a wide range of talents, they used novels, poems, essays, historical studies, political writings, scientific treatises, dictionaries, and an encyclopedia to disseminate their philosophical and political ideas. They were popular guests at the French *salons*, the equivalent of elite cocktail parties where fashionable intellectuals mingled with European aristocracy to discuss the current (and often scandalous) ideas of the day. Leading *philosophes* were Montesquieu, Voltaire, La Mettrie, Rousseau, Diderot, Condillac, Helvétius, d'Alembert, Holbach, and Condorcet, among others. Their works were replete with social criticism that attacked bigotry, ignorance, the hypocrisy of organized religion, and oppressive political institutions. More positively, the *philosophes* believed in the power of reason, the ideal of progress, and the perfectibility of humanity. Although they continually clashed with established religion, many *philosophes*, such as Voltaire, were deists who held that belief in God supported morality and social order. However, their company also included materialists and atheists. Diderot, for example, said that a deist was a man who had not lived long enough—or wisely enough—to become an atheist.

The initial influx of fresh ideas were imported to France from across the English Channel. Montesquieu (1689–1755) and Voltaire (1694–1778) were enamored of English culture and thought. Newton and Locke were their heroes, and the English system, with its ideals of freedom and tolerance, was their political ideal. Montesquieu's influential works included his early satirical attack on French culture and religion in the *Persian Letters* (1721) as well as his work on political science, *The Spirit of Laws* (1748). Voltaire's influential works ranged in style from a celebration of English philosophy and culture in *Lettres philosophiques* (1734) to his famous satirical novel *Candide* (1759).

One of the notable accomplishments of the *philosophes* was the French *Encyclopédie*. Many writers contributed to it; however, the burden of editing it eventually fell on Diderot, who received some assistance from d'Alembert. In addition to scientific, mathematical, and technological subjects, it also included thinly veiled attacks on orthodox religion and prevailing social institutions. More than just a reference work, it was a manifesto of the Enlightenment. In a pithy statement of secular faith, one of its articles proclaimed, "Reason is to the *philosophe* what grace is to the Christian." Although there were many quarrels among the editors and continual battles with censorship, over three decades the work grew to thirty-five volumes. Recognizing its influence, alarmed conservatives attacked it for promoting deism, materialism, and irreligion. Indeed, compared with the attempts of present-day reference works to be objective and impersonal, the *Encyclopédie* had all the subjective style and polemical tone of a newspaper opinion page. Diderot bluntly acknowledges that the purpose of the project was not simply to impart information but "to change the general way of thinking." Despite attempts to suppress it, the work proved to be enormously popular and succeeded in disseminating the ideals of the Enlightenment among the reading public.

Summary of the Enlightenment

Although eighteenth-century philosophers differed on the details, the four pillars of Enlightenment thought were nature, reason, experience, and progress. Nature was viewed as orderly, governed by laws, and basically benevolent. Human nature was likewise seen as orderly, governed by laws, and basically benevolent, or at least it will be once we remove the distractions of passion and dogma and let reason prevail. Whether reason was understood as a source of *a priori* knowledge as the rationalists thought or simply as an instrument to organize experience as the empiricists claimed, it was thought to be the great equalizer among people. Everyone has the basic capacity to be reasonable, and by learning from experience and with the help of education our rational powers will be released. Hence all problems, theoretical or social, can be solved through science and concerted, rational effort. The Enlightenment's optimism and faith in progress was summarized in the words of Kant:

Do we live at present in an enlightened age? The answer is: No, but in an age of enlightenment.

Already, Kant claimed, conditions were developing that would enable people to

work freely and reduce gradually the hindrances preventing a general enlightenment and an escape from self-caused immaturity. In this sense, this age is the age of enlightenment.[7]

Questions for Understanding

1. How did Issac Newton's physics deal a blow to Aristotelian and medieval science?

2. In what ways did Newton's methods influence both rationalists and empiricists?

3. How was Newton's physics used as a model for epistemology and philosophy of mind?

4. Why did some see Newton's physics as the enemy of religion? Why did Newton believe his science was supportive of religious views?

5. Why did Newton feel the need to resort to a "God-of-the-gaps" explanation in his science?

6. What is deism and how was it influenced by developments in science?

7. Who were the *philosophes*?

8. What were the four pillars of Enlightenment thought?

Questions for Reflection

1. The Enlightenment thinkers were in awe of science and had great hopes for it. Do you think our age is more optimistic about science or less than theirs?

2. Which one of the fundamental assumptions of the Enlightenment do you most agree with? Which one do you think is the most problematic?

Notes

1. Isaiah Berlin, ed., *The Age of Enlightenment* (New York: Mentor, The New American Library, 1956), 14.

2. In a letter to Robert Hooke, February 5, 1675/6, in *The Correspondence of Isaac Newton*, vol. 1, ed. H. W. Turnbull (Cambridge, England: Cambridge University Press, 1959), 416.

3. Edwin A. Burtt, *The Metaphysical Foundations of Modern Physical Science*, rev. ed. (Garden City, NY: Doubleday, 1932), 207.

4. *Newton's Principia*, vol. 2, *The System of the World*, trans. Andrew Motte, rev. Florian Cajori (Berkeley: University of California Press, 1962), 547.

5. Henry Stubbe, quoted in Richard S. Westfall, *Science and Religion in Seventeenth-Century England* (New Haven, CT: Yale University Press, 1958), 24.

6. Quoted in Richard Westfall, 193.

7. Immanuel Kant, "What Is Enlightenment?" trans. Carl J. Friedrich, in *The Philosophy of Kant: Immanuel Kant's Moral and Political Writings*, ed. Carl J. Friedrich (New York: The Modern Library, 1949), 138.

19

John Locke:
The Rise of Modern Empiricism

Physician, Political Adviser, and Philosopher

John Locke was born in 1632 into a Puritan home. His father was a lawyer of somewhat meager means. At Oxford University Locke studied theology, natural science, philosophy, and medicine. A contemporary of his said that as an undergraduate Locke was "a man of turbulent spirit, clamorous and never contented." Part of the problem was that Locke found the stodgy Scholasticism that still pervaded the Oxford of his day to be "perplexed with obscure terms and useless questions." While the lectures of his teachers repelled him, his private reading of Descartes attracted him to philosophy. Locke, no doubt, found a kindred spirit in Descartes, for they were both disillusioned with their education.

Locke stayed at Oxford for a while to lecture in Greek and rhetoric. However, it was public life and not academics that would occupy the majority of his life. During the years 1667 to 1683 he was the personal physician and adviser to Lord Ashley (later to become the Earl of Shaftesbury). Before doing any work in political philosophy,

Locke acquired a good deal of practical, political experience through his association with Shaftesbury. In addition to holding a number of political positions, Locke helped draft a constitution for the American Carolinas in 1669.

For decades, England had been embroiled in a power struggle between Parliament and the throne. Locke supported the growing demand for parliamentary rights against the supremacy of the king. However, when James II gained the throne the political tide turned against Locke, forcing him to flee to Holland in 1683. Holland was still a land of toleration and refuge for displaced intellectuals, just as it had been in Spinoza's day. However, after the 1688 bloodless overthrow of James II in the "Glorious Revolution," Locke was able to return to England in 1689 under the reign of William of Orange. Once again he held several important public offices. More importantly, he released a flood of writings composed during his year in exile. His two most important works were *Two Treatises on Government* and *An Essay Concerning Human Understanding*, both published in 1690. *Letters Concerning Toleration* came out during the years 1689–1692. Other works of interest were

Some Thoughts Concerning Education (1693) and *The Reasonableness of Christianity* (1695). In 1691 recurring ill health sent him into partial retirement. He moved to the country, twenty miles out of London, to seek more tranquil surroundings. The last years of his life were spent enjoying the quiet companionship of close friends and studying the Scriptures. There, in the home of friends, he died quietly in 1704.

Locke's Task: Discovering What We Can Know

It is commonly held that the Age of Enlightenment was ushered in with the publication of Locke's seminal work *An Essay Concerning Human Understanding* in 1690. With the possible exception of the Bible, no book was more influential in the eighteenth century than Locke's *Essay*. He confides that the idea for the work began some twenty years earlier, when

> *Five or six friends meeting at my chamber, and discoursing on a subject very remote from this, found themselves quickly at a stand, by the difficulties that rose on every side. After we had awhile puzzled ourselves without coming any nearer a resolution of those doubts which perplexed us, it came into my thoughts that we took a wrong course; and that before we set ourselves upon inquiries of that nature, it was necessary to examine our own abilities, and see what* objects *our understandings were, or were not, fitted to deal with.*[1]

From what we can tell, the discussion apparently concerned morality and religion. It became clear to Locke that he and his friends were attempting to construct the top floor of the edifice of knowledge without first attending to the foundations. He realized that first one had to examine the groundwork of human understanding and then see if it could support inquiry at the higher levels of human concern (such as God and ethics). So he made it his task to "inquire into the original [sources], certainty, and extent of *human knowledge*, together with the grounds and degrees of *belief*, *opinion*, and *assent*."[2] Locke was prepared to accept the conclusion that every question does not

have a humanly available answer. Although this may be disappointing, it is useful information, for it will prevent our understanding from vainly trying to reach beyond our grasp. As he put it, "If we can find out how far the understanding can extend its view; how far it has faculties to attain certainty; and in what cases it can only judge and guess, we may learn to content ourselves with what is attainable by us in this state."[3]

Locke's description of his project shows he shared Descartes's thirst for certainty. However, Locke tempered it with a new humbleness and lowering of expectations that would become a trademark of the empiricist tradition. Locke finds security in the practical and the mundane and refuses to indulge in any speculative flights of fancy. As he metaphorically puts it, we may desire the full light of the sun in which to do our work, but we will have to be satisfied with the more limited candlelight of the human intellect: "The candle that is set up in us shines bright enough for all our purposes. The discoveries we can make with this ought to satisfy us."[4]

Locke's Method for Analyzing Ideas

The focus of Locke's *Essay* is "ideas." These are not the objects of knowledge so much as its building blocks. It is important to understand the unique meaning Locke gives this term because it differs from the meaning it has for us today. He says that an idea is anything that is "the immediate object of perception, thought, or understanding" (E 2.8.8).[5] He offers us a random collection of examples to illustrate what he means by ideas. They are the sorts of things expressed by the words "whiteness, hardness, sweetness, thinking, motion, man, elephant, army, drunkenness and others" (E 2.1.1). Notice that by "idea" Locke and the empiricists do not mean only concepts or abstract notions such as "justice" or "infinity." Ideas can also be the very specific and concrete qualities found in sensation, such as colors, tastes, and sounds.

The method Locke proposes for examining ideas is the "historical plain method." The term *historical* here refers to his conviction that the genealogy of our ideas must be traced back until we get to their original sources. This process is not one of logical analysis, but is a concrete approach concerned with how ideas arise in our personal histories. The word *plain*, no doubt, was intended to communicate the fact that the method employs down-to-earth common sense and avoids all speculative, theoretical fluff. Because Locke is an empiricist, he argues that all knowledge arises out of experience. In the sections that follow, notice how Locke tries to clarify and validate our ideas by seeing if they can or cannot be derived from experience. To prepare for George Berkeley's and David Hume's discussions of Locke in the following chapters, try assessing for yourself how consistently Locke's results adhere to the requirements of his method.

Locke's Empirical Theory of Knowledge

CRITIQUE OF INNATE IDEAS

As with Bacon and Descartes before him, Locke's mission can be viewed as a kind of epistemological urban renewal project. His first project was to clear away the debris of unintelligible terms and useless systems of thought. Only then could he make a fresh start on more modern construction. Locke thought that the "master builders" in this intellectual project were the great scientists of his time, especially the "incomparable Mr. Newton." Locke's modest goal, as a philosopher, was to be "employed as an under-labourer in clearing the ground a little, and removing some of the rubbish that lies in the way to knowledge."[6] The "rubbish" he most wanted to sweep away was the doctrine of **innate ideas**. This theory claims that some kinds of ideas, principles, or knowledge are not acquired through experience, but are built into the mind itself. This doctrine was a standard thesis in the rationalistic tradition from Plato to Leibniz, but Locke raises a number of fundamental objections to it.

Typical examples of innate knowledge are logical principles such as "Whatever is, is" (the law

of identity) or "It is impossible for the same thing to be and not to be" (the law of noncontradiction) or mathematical principles such as "The whole is greater than a part." Furthermore, both within philosophical tradition and among many of Locke's contemporaries the claim was made that moral principles as well as the concept of God were innate.

A favorite argument for innate knowledge is based on the claim that there is universal agreement concerning certain principles. First, Locke argues that even if this were true, it would not prove that the principles were innate. There could be some other reason why people come to have some ideas in common. For example, all cultures have ideas corresponding to fire, sun, heat, and numbers, but these ideas are universal because human experience is uniform, not because they are innate. Second, Locke points out that not all people know the preceding logical principles. Many children, mentally deficient people, and people in prescientific cultures do not exhibit knowledge of these truths. But if these principles really were "naturally imprinted" on the mind, everyone would know them. To say that we have these ideas but are not aware of them is absurd: "No proposition can be said to be in the mind which it never yet knew, which it was never yet conscious of" (E 1.1.5).

The claim that some moral principles are innate fares even worse in Locke's analysis. Locke gives a brief survey of the wide range of moral practices in cultures other than our own to illustrate the lack of consensus in ethical beliefs. It is important to note that he does not reject the existence of universal moral principles, but he merely rejects the claim that they are innate.

SIMPLE IDEAS

If knowledge does not originate in the mind, how then does it end up there? The answer, according to Locke, is "through experience." He asks us to suppose that the mind is like a blank sheet of white paper on which experience makes its marks. We come naked into this world both physically and mentally. Whatever ideas are found in the mind must have been deposited there by some experience. In another passage he compares the mind to a dark closet (E 2.11.17). We may update his simile by saying that the mind, for Locke, is like the interior of a camera. Through the opening of the lens (representing the various senses), the external world is able to deposit images within the camera.

Notice the spatial metaphor shaping Locke's thought here. The mind is a kind of empty container that holds the atoms of thought. In this way, Locke and his fellow empiricists were attempting to emulate Newton's science of physical particles by discovering the laws that govern the motion of mental particles. For Locke, there is a direct relationship between his own "physics" of the mind and Newtonian physics. The world is made up of particles in motion, some of which bombard the senses. For example, particles of odor hit the nose and sound waves strike the eardrum. Part of their effect is that they leave traces of themselves in the form of ideas in the mind. The most fundamental and original mental particles are *simple ideas*. These are atoms of thought that cannot be analyzed into anything simpler. For example, a dictionary will define "yellow" as the color of a ripe lemon. It can refer you only to the elements of your experience to make the idea clear. The mind cannot invent a brand-new simple idea or know one it has not experienced. It can only passively receive such ideas from experience, just as the camera film receives the light through the lens. Once it has acquired a collection of simple ideas, however, it can process them by repeating them, comparing them, or uniting them into various combinations.

Simple ideas come in two varieties. The first consists of all the ideas that come from sensation. These are the ideas we have of such qualities as yellow, white, heat, cold, soft, hard, bitter, and sweet (E 2.1.3). Notice that this list does not consist of objects such as books or elephants. Such objects are excluded because the fundamental elements of our knowledge of the external world consist only of the minute data of sensation. The second category of simple ideas are the ideas of reflection. These are gained from our experience of our own mental operations. Today we would

call this "knowledge from introspection." Hence, we have ideas of perception, thinking, doubting, believing, reasoning, knowing, willing, as well as of the emotions and other psychological states. It is because we can observe the mind at work that we can think about thinking (or any other psychological activity or state).

Locke makes clear that all the ideas we have flow from these two fountains of experience:

> The understanding seems to me not to have the least glimmering of any ideas which it doth not receive from one of these two. External objects furnish the mind with the ideas of sensible qualities, which are all those different perceptions they produce in us; and the mind furnishes the understanding with ideas of its own operations. (E 2.1.5)

Locke then challenges us to refute his thesis:

> Let any one examine his own thoughts, and thoroughly search into his understanding; and then let him tell me, whether all the original ideas he has there, are any other than of the objects of his senses, or of the operations of his mind. . . . And how great a mass of knowledge soever he imagines to be lodged there, he will, upon taking a strict view, see that he has not any idea in his mind but what one of these two have imprinted. (E 2.1.5)

In other words, a man who was blind from birth cannot have the idea of redness, nor can a deaf woman have any idea of the sound of a flute, nor can you have an idea of the taste of rattlesnake meat unless you have at some time experienced it.

COMPLEX IDEAS

Like the camera film that receives and records the light that enters through its lens, so the human mind passively receives simple ideas through experience. However, these ideas are single sounds, colors, and other pings of sensation. Where do we get the ideas of unified objects such as books and elephants? For Locke, although the mind cannot originate ideas, it can process them into more *complex ideas*. These are combinations of simple ideas that can be treated as unities and given their own names, such as "beauty, gratitude, a man, an army, the universe" (E 2.12.1). In the fourth edition of his *Essay*, Locke classifies complex ideas according to the three activities of the mind that produce them: compounding, relating, and abstracting. The first sort of complex ideas are formed by compounding or uniting together two or more simple ideas. We can combine several ideas of the same type. For example, several observations of space can be combined together in our minds to form the idea of immense space. Hence, from our limited experience of space, we can conceive of the enormous quantities spoken of by astronomers. The idea we have of an apple is the combination of the simpler ideas of red, round, sweet, and so on.

The second activity of the mind produces ideas of relation. These are produced by comparing one idea with another. For example, the idea of "taller" could only come about by relating our ideas of two other things. Husband and wife, father and son, bigger and smaller, cause and effect are examples of ideas that are not experienced alone but are derived from observing relations.

Finally, the process of abstraction gives us a very important set of ideas called *abstract* or *general ideas*. From what Locke has said thus far, it is easy to see how I can form the idea of a particular book. A given book is the combination of the ideas of its particular color, weight, size, rectangularity, and so on. But what if I want to think about books in general and not just one particular book? Locke says we can form the general idea of "book" by abstracting all the qualities they have in common and ignoring their individual distinctions. For example, individual books come in all colors and sizes, but all books-in-general are rectangular objects containing pages with writing or pictures on them.

Even something as abstract and seemingly remote from experience as the notion of "infinity" can be built up from experience. Locke says that the idea of "infinity" comes from "the power we observe in ourselves of repeating without end, our own ideas" (E 2.17.6). Thus, we can take our own experiences of time and space and extrapolate them imaginatively to get the concepts of eternity and the great distances that astronomers discuss. However, Locke cautions that while this method will give us a vague understanding of the infinity of space, we cannot hold in our minds the posi-

tive and definite idea of "space infinite" (E 2.17.7). The latter would require us to think of the unending series of repeated ideas as a completed series. Only an infinite mind could contain such an enormous idea.

PRIMARY AND SECONDARY QUALITIES

Unlike Descartes, Locke never doubted that there was an external world and that we could know it. His position, however, raises an important question: If our ideas constitute the sum of our knowledge, and our ideas are in the mind, then how can our knowledge relate to the external world? To answer this question, Locke makes a crucial (but problematic) distinction concerning the simple ideas we encounter in sensation. He introduces the term *quality* to refer to a power in matter to produce ideas in our mind. If we experience a snowball as white, cold, and round, that must mean that snowballs have the power to produce such ideas. Some qualities actually inhere in the external object itself. They are the genuine and objective properties of that object. These are what he calls the *primary qualities* of a body. Examples of primary qualities would be solidity, extension, shape, motion or rest, and number. Even if no one is observing the snowball as it lies on the ground, it takes up a definite amount of space, is round, at rest, and is singular and not plural. The ideas corresponding to these qualities are a faithful representation of how things really are in the external world.

There is a second set of qualities, however. These *secondary qualities* indicate that bodies have the power to produce subjective experiences in us. These sorts of qualities we experience are not in the objects themselves. Examples would be the sensations of colors, sound, tastes, odors, warmth or coldness, and so forth. Why does Locke make this distinction? He makes it because he thinks a clear-headed reflection on common experience demands it. For example, we may have different opinions about the height of a particular object, but we can check our opinions against the objective properties of the object itself. However, when I say the tea is too bitter and you experience it as sweet, we realize the same tea can affect our palates in different ways. Similarly, an orange is always spherical and not cubic no matter what the viewing conditions may be. However, as any artist knows, the color of the orange will change when viewed in sunlight or shadow, with an incandescent or fluorescent lamp. The shape remains stable and the color changes because shape is a primary quality and color is a secondary quality. The motion of the violin string (a primary quality) produces motion in the air, which produces the sensation of sound in our ears (a secondary quality). The vibrating string is not melodious or haunting; it is just a physical object in motion. But we may experience the effects of this motion as melodious or haunting music. The same fire can cause the sensation of warmth or pain in us. Just as we would say the pain is in us and not in the fire, so we should understand that the warmth is a sensation in us produced by the primary qualities in the fire. (This distinction seems simple enough, but later George Berkeley argued that there are enormous problems with it.)

Significantly, Locke's primary qualities are the ones that can be quantified and studied in physics. Here he is following Galileo and Descartes in his attempt to mathematize nature. He proposes that the real properties of the world are only those that can be examined scientifically. All other qualities are merely by-products of these. This implies that the world of the poet, the artist, and naive experience is a world of appearances. The world of Newtonian science, which lacks colors, odors, or sounds, is the real world. In this way, Locke's theory further widened the gap between the world as we experience it and the world as presented by science.*

REPRESENTATIVE REALISM

Locke's epistemology is commonly called representative realism in today's terminology. **Representative realism** claims that the mind is directly

---

*Later writers rebelled against the claim that only science presents us with the real world. These include Kant (Chapter 22), the romantics (Chapter 23), the phenomenologists (Husserl, Chapter 33), and the existentialists, including Kierkegaard (Chapter 26), Nietzsche (Chapter 27), and Heidegger (Chapter 33).

acquainted only with its own ideas, but that these ideas are caused by and represent objects external to the mind. Using the tenets of representative realism, we can make sense of a number of experiences. For example, if you look at a coin as you turn it around in your fingers, the actual shape of the silver patch in your visual field will change from circular to elliptical. As it reflects the light from different angles, its color will change also. You realize, of course, that the coin itself is not changing but merely the ideas (in the Lockean sense) that represent that coin to you. Thus, while your ideas are caused by the object in the external world, and give you objective information about it, you cannot directly examine the object as it is in itself.

DEGREES OF KNOWLEDGE

In the last book of the *Essay*, Locke presents the degrees of knowledge that are available to us. Thus far he has developed a theory of ideas, the materials of our knowledge. Now he shows how knowledge is constructed out of these elements. Locke defines knowledge as "the perception of the connection and agreement, or disagreement and repugnancy of any of our ideas" (E 4.1.2). In other words, in obtaining knowledge we are observing how our ideas fit or do not fit together. A true proposition is one in which the ideas are properly related. Three degrees or varieties of knowledge are available to the human mind (E 4.2.1-15). First, there is what Locke calls "intuitive knowledge." This occurs when the connection between ideas is seen immediately. Thus, we know that "white is not black, that a circle is not a triangle, that three are more than two, and equal to one and two" by merely examining these ideas. This sort of knowledge is like bright sunshine; it "leaves no room for hesitation, doubt, or examination, but the mind is presently filled with the clear light of it." This knowledge is absolutely certain and provides the foundation for all other knowledge. The only sort of knowledge of existence available to us here is knowledge of our own existence.

Second, there is "demonstrative knowledge." Here, the connection between ideas is not immediate but is established by forming a chain of logical steps as in a mathematical proof. Thus, we have demonstrative knowledge that the angles of a triangle add up to 180 degrees. Furthermore, we can have demonstrative knowledge of God's existence. Demonstrative knowledge also gives us certainty, if we are careful in forming each link in the logical chain. However, since it is always possible to make a mistake in our reasoning process, this form of knowledge is not quite so "clear and bright, nor the assent so ready, as in intuitive knowledge." Thus far, Locke's indebtedness to Descartes is clear, for this discussion conforms almost exactly to the Cartesian epistemology. For the same reason, it is clear that Locke could hardly be called a "pure empiricist."

The third degree of knowledge is "sensitive knowledge." Apart from our own existence and God's, all judgments concerning the existence and nature of objects in the external world falls into this category. The Cartesian side of Locke says that this knowledge falls short of the kind of certainty we can have with the first two varieties. Nevertheless, the empiricist side of Locke reassures us that the evidence of objects outside of us is so highly probable that it "puts us past doubting." Attaining absolute certainty about every issue in daily life is impossible. Nevertheless, Locke says we do not need certainty to live successfully.

Although he is unrelenting in maintaining that experience is the source of all our ideas, Locke is modest and even pessimistic on the question of how much certainty we can hope to find in experimental science. Experience can show us that gold has always had a particular color, weight, and degree of malleability. However, since we cannot discern any necessary connections between these ideas, as we can with the properties of triangles, we can never be certain that when some of these properties are present, others will be also. At times, however, he indicates that this lack of certain and universal knowledge about the workings of the physical world is not a permanent condition but may be the result of temporary ignorance. With improved instruments and experimental techniques, the situation can be remedied. Thus he says if we could ever have knowledge of the "minute constituent parts of any two bodies" (what

we would call nuclear physics today), we would be able to determine their effects on each other "as we do now the properties of a square or triangle" (E 4.3.25).

Metaphysics: The Reality Behind the Appearances

Locke did not write a separate work on metaphysics. He wove everything on this topic in and out of his theory of knowledge. Nevertheless, in addition to discussing how we know, he is interested in the reality of what we know. Thus far, he has given us a theory of how we arrive at all the ideas we have. When we experience the ideas of redness, roundness, crunchiness, and sweetness together, we apply to this collection of experiences the label "apple." But something here needs to be explained. Why do these sorts of experiences always occur to us in clusters? If they are distinct sensations, why are they never separate and free-floating? We don't perceive sweetness standing alone by itself. We always experience a sweet *something*, whether it be an apple, a lump of sugar, or a candy bar. Locke says we need the idea of substance. **Substance** literally means "that which stands under." The substance of the apple, then, is a kind of substrate in which the qualities that produce our experiences of redness, roundness, and crunchiness inhere. The problem is that we cannot have knowledge of substances in themselves, for we have direct experience only of the ideas they support.

Locke is too committed to common sense to deny that something out there underlies our ideas. However, the notion of substance is clearly a problem for his position and undermines the rigor of his empiricism. Since we do not experience substances, what are they like and how can we be sure they are there? Locke replies that if someone were asked these questions, he could only say that substance was "something, he knew not what" and that it was "the supposed, but unknown, support of those qualities we find existing" (E 2.23.2).

Locke uses our limited knowledge of material substances in a subtle and unusual way to support his religious outlook. Typically, the religious skeptic says we can be certain matter exists but we have no evidence for any spiritual realities. Actually, Locke says, our idea of spiritual substance is just as clear and well founded as our idea of physical substance (E 2.23.5). After all, we never encounter material substances themselves, only the qualities that inhere within them. In the same way, through reflection, I encounter my mental activities, which I must suppose inhere within some spiritual substance just as I suppose there is material substance underlying what I perceive. Thus, "we have as many and as clear ideas belonging to spirit as we have belonging to body, the substance of each being equally unknown to us" (E 2.23.28). For Locke, the commonsense philosopher, just as it is reasonable to assume there is matter, so it is reasonable to assume there are spiritual substances. However, the skeptical David Hume later uses this same argument to show that both material and spiritual substances are suspect.

Looked at broadly, Locke's metaphysics was similar to Descartes's. Since Locke believes in both physical and spiritual substances, he is a dualist. Furthermore, similar to Descartes, he holds to an interactionist theory of the mind–body relationship. His discussion of the divine substance will be taken up in a later section on religion.

What Is the Source of Moral Knowledge?

Locke originally began his long discourse on the nature of human understanding because he thought the waters of moral theory were so muddy. Having first clarified epistemological issues, he can now address the more difficult questions of morality. His theory of knowledge revealed there is only a rather modest fund of things we can genuinely know. However, Locke did not find this too troubling because the amount of knowledge available is enough for practical living. What, then, can the Lockean theory tell us about how to find the moral principles that will guide our lives?

Locke has already argued that there are no innate moral principles "written on the heart." If the

mind begins as a blank slate, therefore, all our moral knowledge must come from experience. Since we have no direct sensations corresponding to "good" and "evil," we must find some other sensations from which these notions may be derived. As is typical of empiricist moral theory, Locke begins with our experiences of pain and pleasure. He says we call "good" whatever tends to cause pleasure in us and "evil," anything that tends to produce pain. This suggests that morality can be based on empirical generalizations.

Thus far, his position sounds like the sort of hedonism we encountered earlier in our studies of the Epicureans and Hobbes. While holding to this position, however, Locke goes on to say that moral good and evil are to be identified with the conformity or disagreement of our actions to some law (E 2.28.5). There are three kinds of law: (1) the divine law, (2) the civil law, and (3) the law of opinion or reputation. Because the last two laws are of human origin, we should not be surprised that their details differ from society to society and that they sometimes deviate from the divine law. However, since conformity to God's law tends to advance the general good of humankind, we should not be surprised that there is also a central core of agreement among these three sources of moral guidance. In fact, Locke says that God's law may be discovered either through "the light of nature" or "the voice of revelation" (E 2.28.8). Hence, we are not dependent on revelation to know moral truths, for it is possible to discover them using our reason and experience.

The rationalist side of Locke asserts itself when he says that "morality is capable of demonstration as well as mathematics" (E 4.12.8). Locke provides us with some unconvincing examples of rationally demonstrated moral principles, among which is "Where there is no property, there is no injustice" (E 4.3.18). He claims this truth is as certain as any demonstration in Euclidean geometry. Locke goes on to explain that property is the right to anything and injustice is the violation of that right. But if we substitute one equivalent term for another, the original phrase becomes "Where there is no right to anything there can be no violations of that right." Explained in this way, this "moral principle" turns out to be an uninteresting tautology or logical truth similar to "A = A." Similarly, Locke claims that "No government allows absolute liberty" is a rational truth. But once again, to be a government means to have laws and thus a restriction of liberty is trivially involved in the concept of government. In both these truisms, all the really interesting questions are avoided, such as "What is public property, and what is private property?" and "What are legitimate governmental restrictions on individual liberty?" As Berkeley expressed it, "Locke's instances of demonstration in morality are . . . trifling propositions."[7]

In contrast to his rationalistic account of ethics, Locke also provides an empirical account. Locke points out that though the moral codes of various cultures differ, they also have a high degree of uniformity. How do we account for this? Locke's answer is that experience can teach us which forms of behavior are most satisfying and which are not. The law of opinion or reputation, based on the traditions of society, tends to reflect the wisdom of collective experience. Thus a society based on treachery and deceit will not be a very pleasant place in which to live, nor is it likely to survive very long. Hence, a society that applies empirical reasoning to moral conduct will conform (knowingly or unknowingly) to God's law.

Locke's moral theory is full of tensions and ambiguities. At times it looks backward to medieval thought, and at other moments it looks forward to modern secular thought. On the one hand, Locke believes the moral law is given to us in revelation. On the other hand, he believes that unaided human reason and experience can determine what is right or wrong. The former belief stresses divine authority and the latter stresses human autonomy to a degree that would make revelation superfluous. The traditional side of Locke stresses God-ordained, rational moral principles. However, his empiricism opens the door to the possibility that morality could change if the empirical consequences of our behavior change. Finally, at times Locke reads as though duty or conformity to law were the prime motive of ethics and pleasure were merely its accompaniment. At other times it sounds as though pleasure and rational self-interest were at the base

of ethics and moral virtue were merely a way to achieve those ends.

An Empirical Philosophy of Religion

EMPIRICAL ORIGINS OF THE IDEA OF GOD

Along with morality, religion was one of the topics Locke's *Essay* was to clarify. However, given his view that all our thoughts are more or less limited to what we can experience, it is not surprising that we do not find him developing a full-fledged philosophical theology. Nevertheless, he does think we can at least derive the idea of God and, furthermore, we can have demonstrative knowledge of his existence. It should be clear that Locke cannot begin where Descartes began—that is, with a full-blown, innate idea of God as part of the resident contents of the human mind. Instead, he must show we can construct the idea of an infinite God from the finite materials of experience. Thus, starting from reflective knowledge of our own minds and our finite experiences of human existence, duration, knowledge, power, wisdom, and all other positive qualities, "we enlarge every one of these with our idea of infinity; and so putting them together, make our complex idea of God" (E 2.23.33).

Notice how radically Locke differs from the rationalists such as Plato and Descartes. For them, the idea of perfection is primary and our idea of imperfection is derived from the supreme archetype. Locke reverses this picture and constructs the idea of God by extrapolating from our finitude. The process is much like that of a scientist who plots the points of the experimental data on a graph and then imagines what the curve connecting the points would look like if it were extended beyond the borders of the graph. Obviously, Descartes's proof for God from the idea of perfection will not work for Locke since Locke believes it is simply a complex idea we manufacture. In fact, he suggests that the argument from the idea of perfection is "an ill way of establishing this truth and silencing atheists"

(E 4.10.7). His reasons are that some people have no idea of God and those who do have so many conflicting interpretations of the idea.

DEMONSTRATING GOD'S EXISTENCE

Even though we arrive at the *concept* of God from the materials of our finite experience, Locke thinks we can prove the *existence* of God with as much certainty as we prove theorems in geometry. Accordingly, he provides an argument for God that is a combination of the causal argument and the argument from design (E 4.10.2-11). In his premises, he uses the following empirical facts: the existence of the world; the existence of thinking, knowing, conscious beings such as ourselves; and the order, harmony, and beauty of nature. To these he adds the same two rational intuitions Descartes used: (1) Something cannot come from nothing, and (2) The cause of anything must have all the perfections that it imparts to its effect. From these he deduces the existence of an eternal, powerful, and intelligent cause.

LOCKE'S INFLUENCE ON DEISM

Thus far, Locke's philosophy of religion is standard and traditional. Nevertheless, his further thoughts on religion influenced some of the religious controversies of the time. Although Locke himself subscribed to a more or less traditional Christianity, both his *Essay* and his book on *The Reasonableness of Christianity* (1695) contributed to the rising tide of deism. **Deism** is a system of thought, based on reason, which acknowledges the existence of God and his creation of the world, but denies that God intervenes in the world either in the form of miracles or revelation. Their break with orthodox Christianity lay in their rejection of any sort of divine involvement with the world or human affairs. The world is a self-sufficient, rational system that runs according to divinely created natural laws, the deists said. Therefore, there is no need for further divine activity within it. Furthermore, since human beings have been given reason and experience, they have all that is necessary to discover truth in the realms of science, morality,

and religion. Hence, supernatural revelation is unnecessary.

Here again, we find a tension in Locke's position, which is clothed in the terminology of traditional views while pointing forward to more radical positions. Locke sincerely believed that divinely revealed truths are absolutely certain. However, he asserted that if any alleged revelation is contrary to reason, it must be rejected. Locke did, however, allow that some propositions in revelation are "above reason," in the sense that reason cannot judge them to be either true or false. In these cases, it is permissible to believe something on faith (E 4.18.9). Unfortunately, Locke did not make clear how we are to discern the difference between propositions that are contrary to reason and those that are merely above reason. Although Locke leaned toward more traditional Christianity, he set the stage for deism by insisting that human reason is more clear and certain than any revelation and that it is the final judge of what is revelation and what is not. The result was that traditional religious thought was pruned of any doctrines that could not be justified at the bar of reason and common sense. The spirit of the age (which Locke helped to shape) was infused with the sentiment that rationality and tolerance could best be served if people keep their theological baggage to a minimum. There was a great deal of discussion in the eighteenth century of "natural religion" that is, religion based on our natural, rational faculties alone. Many thinkers shifted from the view that reason confirmed or supplemented faith to the view that reason could now replace it entirely. The deists rejected Locke's supposition that there could be religious truths that were above reason.

A Political Theory for the Enlightenment

One of Locke's most important contributions was in the area of political philosophy. The England of Locke's day was caught in a stormy political upheaval. Those in favor of a more democratic and popular government with a Protestant throne were trying to overthrow the bonds of a Catholic absolute monarchy. Locke's theories on politics, which had many far-reaching effects, were actually a brilliant summary and elaboration of many of the prevailing political sentiments of his time. Locke's reflections on politics are presented in his *Two Treatises on Government*, published anonymously in 1690, the same year as his *Essay*. In the preface, he states that he wants to justify the revolution of 1688. Actually, although the timing of the *Treatises* was opportune, he had been working on them several years before the political reversal occurred.

THE STATE OF NATURE

As with Hobbes before him, Locke begins his theory of society by discussing the state of nature. The state of nature was a situation before the invention of civil government in which people were independent and free, a state of total equality in the sense that no one had any jurisdiction over any other. It is not crucial to Locke's argument that he demonstrate that the state of nature actually existed at the beginning of human history. Instead, he is trying to make the logical point that the status of the individual is more fundamental than that of the government. Nevertheless, he believes the American wilderness of his time serves as an example of such a condition, as do the relationships between sovereign nations, or the relationship between two individuals on a desert island. Locke, a product of his times, began with many of the unquestioned assumptions that were floating around the seventeenth century. Prominent among these was the notion that people are independent, atomic individuals and that society is simply a complex collection of individuals. Thus, the relationship between simple and complex ideas has been mirrored in social philosophy. It is significant that *Robinson Crusoe* was published in this century by Locke's contemporary, Daniel Defoe. This story of one solitary person, facing nature with only his God and his goat as companions, was a literary version of the individualistic starting point we find in Enlightenment social theory.

Although Locke's method of weaving political philosophy from the state of nature is similar to Hobbes's, Locke gives us a completely different description of what it would be like. For Hobbes it was a state of war. Locke has a much more optimistic view of human nature, however. He describes life without government as one of peace, goodwill, and mutual assistance. Of course, there will be a few troublemakers, but on the whole people will get along quite well. Without government, people would be bound only by the law of nature or reason, which is "intelligible and plain" to everyone. Although each individual in the state of nature is completely free and independent, Locke thinks there would be natural and informal social relationships in such a state. Thus, he is not quite the extreme individualist that Hobbes was.

NATURAL LAW AND HUMAN RIGHTS

Locke is an example of a natural law theorist. He believes that certain moral laws are as much a part of nature as those physics describes. For example, he does not believe our fundamental human rights are bestowed on us by the government. Even without civil laws, he claims, everyone has natural, God-given rights. The notion of natural rights is a crucial one in his theory. Since we did not receive these rights from the government but had them before it came into existence, the government cannot legitimately take them away. This concept was very important to the founders of the American government and is echoed in the Declaration of Independence and embodied in the Bill of Rights.

A primary law of nature is that no one ought to harm another in life, liberty, or possessions. Natural resources (air, water, soil, and trees) are common property, free to all to use as they need. However, if I mix my labor with a part of nature, then it becomes my property. For example, the soil is freely available to everyone, but if I clear the land and till the ground and plant seeds, then both the land and its harvest belong to me. This account is called Locke's "labor theory of property." Locke differs here from Hobbes, who thought that without government there could not be any way to define property within an unbounded nature.

THE SOCIAL CONTRACT

If the state of nature is basically one of peace and goodwill and one in which we have basic rights, then why would we ever need government? Locke's reply is that the state of nature is tolerable but not convenient. Even though we could survive without society, humans are naturally inclined toward it. Furthermore, there are a number of reasons why government and laws would make life better. First, even though there is the natural law, we need a written and agreed-on law to resolve controversies among individuals. In this way, human bias will not enter into judgments concerning individual cases. Second, even though each individual in nature may punish wrongdoing, an officially appointed, indifferent judge could apply the laws in a manner more equitable than a person whose personal interests were at stake. Third, we need a government to enforce the laws on behalf of the powerless.

At this point, Locke introduces the fiction of the social contract used by Hobbes before him. By now, it had become a common device to explain the origin and justification of government. According to this account, people unite together for their mutual benefit and transfer some of their individual power to a political body. There is an initial contract to form a government, based on unanimous consent. This is then followed by a formal agreement in the form of a constitution that is decided on by a majority vote. Locke does not specify what form the government should take. His ideas could be applied to a constitutional monarchy as well as to a democracy as long as power ultimately lies with the people. For those of us who did not actually sign the contract, Locke says we have given tacit consent to it by virtue of the fact that we have lived in our society and received its benefits.

THE LIMITS OF GOVERNMENT

Locke's vision of government was one of the early formulations of classical liberalism. He stated that the power of government may not extend beyond that required by the common good. His view of government differed radically from that of Hobbes.

For the latter, the people were desperate for law and order and so would be willing to surrender all their power to the government. For Locke, government is a convenience, not a necessity; hence, we can dictate the terms of the bargain. Instead of *surrendering* our power to the government, we *delegate* it for the mutual preservation of our lives, estates, and liberties. The government is our creation; therefore, it is our servant. The final feature of the social contract is the method of majority rule. Locke was a firm believer in *common* sense; hence, he believed that the community of common citizens should have the ultimate sovereignty.

In contrast to Hobbes once again, Locke states that the government must rule by laws and not simply by force or an arbitrary will. Here, his strange mixture of rationalism and empiricism arises again. In his rationalistic mode, he stresses that the government does not invent the laws but seeks to discover what the natural laws are and makes its civil laws conform to these eternal laws. In a more empirical mode, he emphasizes the need for empirical research (or what we would now call *sociology* or *political science*) to determine what laws and social structures create the best society. In one of his journals, he suggests that public policy should be conducted like medicine. In both cases, whether or not a remedy will work cannot be determined *a priori* but is a matter of probability and experience.

With brilliant insight, Locke suggested that the government should be divided into separate branches, each serving as a limit on the power of the other units. He called these the *executive*, *legislative*, and *federative branches*. The latter would supervise the relations between the government and foreign nations. He also mentions the judiciary, but it was Montesquieu (1689–1755), writing under the influence of Locke, who made the judiciary the third branch of government. When the founding fathers of the American republic divided their government into the executive, legislative, and judicial branches, they were drawing on the ideas of both Locke and Montesquieu.

One of the most influential features of Locke's thought concerned his ideas on revolution. For Hobbes, the danger of anarchy was worse than that of tyranny. Hence, he did not provide much in the way of legitimate grounds for overthrowing an oppressive government. For Locke, tyranny is more likely than anarchy. Furthermore, he insists that the right to rebellion is not the same as anarchy. Thus, Locke provides the grounds for a right to revolution. If a government should exceed its legitimate authority, the social contract is broken, and the citizens may replace it. But who shall decide when the government is out of bounds? Locke succinctly answers, "The people shall be judge."[8] But, as always, Locke's view is very balanced, for he cautions there should not be a call for revolution "upon every little mismanagement in public affairs."[9]

LOCKE'S EIGHTEENTH-CENTURY ASSUMPTIONS

Despite Locke's eloquent discussions of freedom and human rights, we should not think that these terms had the same meaning for him as they have come to have for us today. For example, he believed that captives taken in a just war are "by the right of nature" the slaves of their captors.[10] Furthermore, in his famous *Letter Concerning Toleration* he concluded that the principle of toleration did not apply to Roman Catholics, because they owed their allegiance to the Pope and not the state. Neither, he claimed, should toleration be extended to atheists. Furthermore, when he defended liberty he was thinking mostly of the liberty of the aristocratic establishment, of which he was a part. Finally, as John Stuart Mill would point out a century and a half later, Locke's emphasis on majority rule did not take into account the possibility that the majority could itself become a tyranny just as dangerous as that of a despotic monarch.

Although a product of his time, and an apologist for the political sentiments of his contemporaries, Locke was also a maker of his time. The notions of the state of nature, the natural moral law, natural rights, the social contract, and the right of revolution were the intellectual currency of eighteenth-century political thought. For example, when writing the American Declaration of Independence, Thomas Jefferson said that his ideas were not new but followed the thought of writers such as Locke. When the colonists shouted, "No taxation without representation!" they were virtually quoting Locke. Through Montesquieu and others, Locke also influenced French thought. Locke might not have sanctioned the American and French revolutions (being too much of a moderate), but it is certain these movements grew from seeds he had planted.

Evaluation and Significance

Despite Locke's enormous influence on the Enlightenment, the classic criticisms of his theories were made by his contemporaries and immediate successors. Two of these criticisms are worth mentioning. The first concerns his attack on innate ideas, and the second is directed against his representative realism.

DEFENDING INNATE KNOWLEDGE

Although the empiricists thought Locke's attack on innate ideas was the last word on the subject, others were of a different opinion. Some commentators have claimed that Locke attacks a version of the doctrine that no one ever held. His contemporary, Leibniz, pointed out that there is a difference between having certain rational principles and being aware of them. Locke assumes an idea is in the mind, in the same way a ball is in a box. Ideas, for him, are always indubitably present to the mind, if they are present at all. Leibniz, by contrast, was much more sensitive to what we now call *tacit knowledge*. He argued that we are not always explicitly aware of all that we know. Young children, for example, use the law of noncontradiction without knowing that they are doing so.

Furthermore, when Locke says in his essay that "there is nothing in the intellect which was not first in the senses," Leibniz added "except the intellect itself." In other words, if the mind has no content whatsoever, how can it ever make sense out of the booming, buzzing confusion of experience? It would be like a computer without any logic circuits. In both cases, there would be no principle by means of which either the mind or the computer could organize its data. Later, in the eighteenth century, Immanuel Kant would expand this point into an entire epistemology. Most philosophers today agree that we are not born with any *ideas*, yet many of these still cling to the theory that our minds have innate *capacities* or *structures*. Despite Locke's arguments, the thesis of innate knowledge was revived in the twentieth century in the field of linguistics by Noam Chomsky and his followers.*

CRITICS OF
REPRESENTATIVE REALISM

Locke believed we do not know the external world directly, but it is represented to us by our ideas. There is, however, a major problem with Locke's theory. He himself expressed the difficulty well:

> It is evident the mind knows not things immediately, but only by the intervention of the ideas it has of them. Our knowledge therefore is real only so far as there is a conformity between our ideas and the reality of things. But what shall be here the criterion? How shall the mind, when it perceives nothing but its own ideas, know that they agree with things themselves? (E 4.4.3)

We could call this the "inner–outer" problem. If we know only the interior contents of the mind, how can we know their relationship to the outer world? Locke answers his own question by arguing that we do not invent simple ideas (that is, we do not manufacture our own experience), therefore they must be causal effects of external objects. Furthermore, he says, our ideas will conform to their objects to the extent intended by "the wisdom and will of our Maker." The theological reference here contains an echo of Descartes's argument for the validity of our perceptual knowledge. The problem still remains, however, in determining which ideas accurately represent their

objects *and* which are merely secondary qualities that do not resemble them. For example, if you vigorously rub your eyes, you will experience flashes of light even though the lights are not flashing in the room. How do you know for sure when your perceptual organs are or are not producing ideas on their own in this way?

According to Locke, we are each like a person confined to a windowless room who only has photographs of what is outside. We can compare one photograph with another one, but cannot compare them to the world outside our walls. Who knows what distortions the camera lens has produced? To raise the problem in another way, try the experiment of comparing the similarities and differences between (1) this book and (2) all your sense experiences of this book. The experiment cannot be carried out because you never break out of the walls of your own experience. Critics, such as George Berkeley, later charged that Locke's inner–outer problem opens the door to skepticism, indicating that the Lockean assumptions need to be overhauled.

LOCKE'S SIGNIFICANCE

At the start of his philosophical journey, John Locke took it as his mission to set out the grounds of knowledge, ethics, politics, and religion. In tackling this set of problems, he took on a task of immense proportions that he had inherited from the rationalists. His unflagging philosophical optimism is indicated by the fact that he hoped to accomplish this mission with the modest and humble tools of empiricism. However, the grandeur of the issues he tackled was always tempered by his philosophical motto: "Our business here is not to know all things, but those which concern our conduct"[11] Throughout his life, his work was guided by a sense of balance and a down-to-earth practicality. The philosopher George Santayana was, no doubt, correct when he remarked, "Had Locke's mind been more profound, it might have been less influential."[12] Locke always attempted to steer a path between dogmatism and skepticism. When the demands of philosophical rigor seemed to point to skepticism, Locke always yielded to the wisdom of common

---

*Chomsky argued that children's linguistic experience is too limited to explain the complex linguistic skills they develop. He theorized that children are born with innate grammatical structures that are common to all languages. These innate rules form the necessary framework for acquiring the specific features of their native tongue.

sense. As he expressed it, "If we will disbelieve everything, because we cannot certainly know all things, we shall [act] as wisely as he who would not use his legs, but sit still and perish, because he had no wings to fly."[13] This sort of balanced viewpoint, undergirded by his analytical, empirical arguments, earned Locke the title of the "father of modern empiricism." Despite the defects his critics find in Locke's philosophy, everyone acknowledges that much of modern philosophy and culture bears his imprint.

Questions for Understanding

1. What did Locke take to be his philosophical mission?

2. How does Locke define "idea"?

3. What does Locke mean by the "historical plain method"?

4. What arguments does Locke raise against the doctrine of innate ideas?

5. What are simple ideas? Provide several of your own examples. How was this notion inspired by Newton's physics? What are the two varieties of simple ideas?

6. What are complex ideas and what are the three ways in which they are formed? Provide several examples of ideas originating in each of these three ways.

7. What is the distinction Locke draws between primary qualities and secondary qualities? What would be some examples of each? How does this distinction relate to his scientific view of the world?

8. What is representative realism?

9. What are the three degrees of knowledge, according to Locke?

10. What does Locke mean by "substance"? Why does he believe that there must be substances underlying everything we experience? In what ways is his metaphysics similar to that of Descartes?

11. How does Locke try to build a moral theory on his empiricism? What are some of the tensions in his moral theory?

12. How does Locke differ from Descartes in explaining how we arrive at the idea of God?

13. In what ways did Locke influence deism?

14. What does Locke mean by the "state of nature"? How does his notion differ from Hobbes's?

15. Why does Locke believe that people have natural rights that are not given to them by the government? What are the implications of this view for political theory?

16. According to Locke, why do people form governments? What role does the social contract play in the formation and justification of government?

17. What is Locke's view on the role of government and the limits of its power?

18. What are some problems that have been raised with Locke's view that prior to experience the mind is a "blank tablet"?

19. What are some problems that have been raised with Locke's representative realism?

Questions for Reflection

1. What was Locke's challenge concerning the origin of ideas? See if you can come up with some counterexamples of ideas that did not originate in one of the two ways Locke lists.

2. Descartes believed that he had to have absolute certainty to have knowledge. How would Locke respond to this view?

3. Consider the different accounts Descartes and Locke give concerning how it is possible for our limited minds to have the ideas of "God," "perfection," and "infinity." Whose account do you think is most plausible? What are the problems with the opposing theory?

4. List the properties of an object in your room. For each property, classify it as either a primary quality or a secondary quality according to Locke's theory.

5. According to their views of the state of nature, Hobbes was pessimistic about human nature and Locke was optimistic. Who do you think gives the most realistic account?

6. If Locke were running for the highest elected office in your country, which of his political ideas would be met with favor today? Which of his political ideas might be controversial in today's political climate?

Notes

1. John Locke, "The Epistle to the Reader," in *An Essay Concerning Human Understanding*, vol. 1, ed. Alexander Campbell Fraser (Oxford, England: The Clarendon Press, 1894), 9.

2. John Locke, "Introduction," §2, in *Essay Concerning Human Understanding*.

3. Ibid., §4.

4. Ibid., §5.

5. Hereafter, quotations from the main body of Locke's *Essay Concerning Human Understanding* are referenced in the text using the abbreviation "E." The three numbers in the reference, separated by periods, refer to the book, chapter, and paragraph numbers, respectively.

6. Locke, "Epistle to the Reader," 14.

7. George Berkeley, *Philosophical Commentaries*, in *The Works of George Berkeley: Bishop of Cloyne*, ed. A. A. Luce and T. E. Jessop (London: Nelson, 1948), 1.84.

8. John Locke, *An Essay Concerning the True Original, Extent and End of Civil Government*, in *Two Treatises of Government*, §240.

9. Ibid., §224.

10. Ibid., §85.

11. Locke, "Introduction," §6.

12. George Santayana, *Some Turns of Thought in Modern Philosophy* (New York: Scribner's, 1933), 3.

13. Locke, "Introduction," §5.

CHAPTER

20

George Berkeley:
Following the Road
of Empiricism

Philosopher, Educator, and Bishop

George Berkeley, Ireland's most eminent philosopher, was born near the city of Kilkenny on March 12, 1685, into a family of English descent. At age 15, he entered Trinity College in Dublin, where he was exposed to the philosophies of Descartes, Malebranche, and Locke, as well as the work of Newton and other leading scientists. In 1710 he was ordained as a priest in the Anglican Church. Berkeley's travels convinced him that the culture of Europe was in a state of decay, but that a fresh new spirit was alive in America. Inspired by this new land, he wrote a poem of which the last stanza was

Westward the Course of Empire takes its Way;
The four first Acts already past,
A fifth shall close the Drama with the Day;
Time's noblest Offspring is the last.

Accordingly, Berkeley had a vision of founding a college on the island of Bermuda where he would educate the sons of the English planters and the native Americans (or Indians). He received approval from Parliament and the promise of both public and private funds. In 1728 he married and

set sail for America with some companions and his new wife. He changed his original plans, however, and moved the project to Newport, Rhode Island. Unfortunately, the funding never came through, and after three years he returned to London. In 1734 he was appointed Bishop of Cloyne. He spent the last few years of his life promoting the medicinal properties of tar water, a remedy he learned from the American Indians. On January 14, 1753, he died peacefully in Oxford and was buried in the Chapel of Christ Church.

Despite the failure of his educational project, Berkeley had an influence on American education. Because of his poem foretelling the westward expansion of the newly emerging nation, the state of California established its university in a city named after Berkeley. Likewise, the Berkeley Divinity School in New Haven, Connecticut, is a tribute to his work in America. The first president of King's College (later to become Columbia University) followed Berkeley's personal advice in establishing the new school. Berkeley provided Yale University (then a small struggling college for the training of ministers and teachers) with the finest library in America at that time. He also endowed the school with a scholarship fund. Harvard University also benefited from a gift of books.

Berkeley's Task: Battling Skepticism and Unbelief

The project Berkeley set for himself is clear from the rather descriptive title of one of his major works published in 1710: *A Treatise concerning the Principles of Human Knowledge wherein the chief causes of error and difficulty in the Sciences, with the grounds of Scepticism, Atheism and Irreligion, are inquired into.* In this work, he says that the causes of error in the sciences are the metaphysical assumptions of Newtonian physics. The grounds of skepticism, he says, lie in Locke's epistemology. The errors he saw within these two systems of thought, then, are the prime targets of Berkeley's philosophy.

Berkeley was well aware that many scientists, including Newton himself, were people of great faith who saw the new science as pointing to the majesty of God. However, Berkeley saw sinister implications lurking in the science celebrated in his day. It seemed that as the Newtonian view of the world advanced, God was getting pushed out of the scheme of things. After all, in prescientific times God was thought to be responsible for all events in the world: the rising and setting of the sun, the glories of the rainbow, the bursting forth of life from the soil. But now these events were explained by means of the impersonal, mechanical principles governing matter in motion. Berkeley had no quarrel with genuine science if it meant simply the description of regularities in experience. But in his mind, the science practiced in his day went beyond this solid ground of experience, into murky metaphysical waters. His problem, then, was to find a way to retain the validity of science while preserving the necessary role of God in world events.

The chief culprit here, according to Berkeley, is the belief in matter. Matter was thought to be an independently existing substance that was intelligible on its own terms, without reference to God. From the belief in such a material world, it is a short jump to the conclusion that God is un-

necessary. In order to dispense with the need for theological explanations, atheism and deism required an orderly, self-sufficient material world. If Berkeley could show that the idea of matter is unintelligible or even that matter does not exist, then he could pull the rug out from under atheism. We would then be thrust back to the view that a spiritual reality is necessary to explain the world and experience.

Berkeley's position is commonly referred to as a form of idealism. However, he himself called it "immaterialism." This position claims that only two kinds of things exist in reality: (1) minds (or spirits), and (2) the ideas they perceive. Concerning the objects of our everyday experience, Berkeley's famous formula is "*Esse est percipi*" or "To be is to be perceived." Thus, the central thesis of his position is that

> . . . all the choir of heaven and furniture of the earth, in a word, all those bodies which compose the mighty frame of the world, have not any subsistence without a mind—that their being is to be perceived or known. (P §6)[1]

Berkeley's motivation was religious, but his arguments were thoroughly philosophical and cannot be dismissed as simply the rantings of an overly pious clergyman. In his own words, "As it was my intention to convince skeptics and infidels by reason, so it has been my endeavor strictly to observe the most rigid laws of reasoning" (D 6-7). In addition to the theological goals of his philosophy, there were also a number of philosophical payoffs. Prime among these was his claim to have headed off the devastating skepticism that he believed flowed from Locke's epistemology. According to Locke, all we know are the ideas in our minds. But if this is true, then our knowledge is never of reality, since we cannot get behind the veil of our ideas. Even though Locke claimed that some of our ideas are copies of the elements of the real world (primary qualities), we can never compare them with the real world to know that this is so. Hence, we can never know if our so-called knowledge bears any relationship whatsoever to what is real. In this way, claimed Berkeley, Locke had led philosophy into the quagmire of skepticism.

In response to the philosophers of his day, Berkeley took his mission to be that of "eternally banishing metaphysics" and "recalling men to common sense" (PC §751). Despite all the complications and oddities of his position, Berkeley claimed that his views were identical with those of the person in the street who has not been seduced by philosophy. Common sense tells us that what we experience is real, and reality is exactly as we experience it to be.

Berkeley's Reform of Empiricism

Berkeley begins where Locke began. Berkeley had the utmost respect for his predecessor, calling him "as clear a writer as I have met with." Nevertheless, the good Bishop engaged in a systematic criticism of Locke's philosophy as the result of taking to heart the latter's advice "to use my own judgment, see with my own eyes and not with another's" (PC §688). If we employ Locke's plain historical method, Berkeley claimed, it will lead us to conclusions Locke never entertained. Thus, Berkeley's goal was to be a ruthlessly consistent empiricist (a goal that Locke's commitment to common sense kept him from achieving). We can imagine Berkeley saying to Locke and the Newtonian scientists, "So, you believe that all our knowledge comes from ideas that originate in experience? So do I! But let's see where this belief takes us. You have not been consistent enough in your empiricism because you believe that one can know a material world that lies outside the scope of our experience."

BERKELEY'S THEORY OF IDEAS

To understand Berkeley's philosophy and how it differs from Locke's, we must get clear on Berkeley's notion of "ideas." The term "idea" in his philosophy somewhat resembles what it means in early passages of Locke's work. Ideas are such things as the colors of a rainbow, the wetness of water, the fragrance of a rose, the taste of lemons, or the sound of a bell. Consistent with Locke, "ideas" can also refer to the operations and states of the mind that we experience, such as willing, doubting, and loving. Thus, ideas are images or sensory data that are directly present to the mind either in vivid sense experience or in the less vivid presentations of either memory or imagination. Hence, when Berkeley says that we have the idea of fire, he does not mean that we simply have the concept of fire or a linguistic description of fire. Instead, he means we have the experience or the memory of searing heat and bright, yellow-red light. In reading Berkeley, therefore, it is better to associate the term "idea" with the words *experience* and *sensation* rather than the words *concept* and *description*.

CRITIQUE OF ABSTRACT IDEAS

Berkeley initially agrees with Locke on these points, but he radically departs from Locke in the introduction to the *Principles*. Specifically, he attempts to refute Locke's theory of abstract ideas. According to Locke's view, we can take our experiences of many particular dogs and abstract from them all their common properties. In this way, we can arrive at the abstract idea of "dog." It is a generic concept that refers to poodles and St. Bernards, tan dogs and white dogs, fluffy-coated dogs and sleek, short-haired dogs. For Berkeley, however, an idea is always a *particular* image. Hence, we cannot have the picture of a dog in our mind that is neither big nor little, dark nor light, young nor old. Even less can we entertain the abstract idea of "animal" in which we are not thinking of any particular bird, beast, or fish. We can think of, speak about, and imagine only particular things.

Berkeley does believe, however, that we can have "general ideas." We have a general idea when we use one particular idea to stand for all other similar particular things. Thus, the word *dog* is a shorthand way of referring to Spot, Fido, Lassie, and all other particular dogs. It does not, however, stand for an abstract idea or the universal form of "dogness" as Plato and some of the medieval philosophers thought. Thus, Berkeley's position here is a version of nominalism, the view that universals are not real, but merely words.

Berkeley's attack on abstract ideas is an attack on an epistemology that would allow us to depart from the rock-solid foundation of experience.

Since I don't experience "dogs in general" nor the essence of dogness, such notions should be excluded from any pure empiricism. If we aren't careful, Berkeley cautions, language can become a veil that separates us from a clear view of our own "naked, undisguised ideas" (P, intro., §25). We tend to become trapped in a world of empty words and fail to question whether there are any concrete experiences to which they can be linked. The central goal of Berkeley's philosophy is to convince us that no abstract idea is more seductive than that of "matter." He finds it simply an empty word that refers to nothing we can find in experience.

ARGUMENT FROM THE MENTAL DEPENDENCY OF IDEAS

To get the flavor of Berkeley's approach, we will look at one of his central arguments in which he analyzes the nature of "sensible objects" (P §4). By this term he means simply any objects that can be perceived by the senses, such as houses, mountains, rivers, or apples. These are what we would ordinarily call "physical objects." However, this term prejudices the issue because it assumes the materiality of these objects, and this is exactly what Berkeley wants to question. We will call this argument "the argument from the mental dependency of ideas." It has this general outline:

(1) Sensible objects (houses, mountains, and so on) are things present to us in sense experience.

(2) What is presented to us in sense experience consists solely of our ideas.

(3) Ideas exist solely in our minds.

(4) Therefore, sensible objects exist solely in our minds.

The steps of this argument can be made a little bit more concrete by looking at an example of a sensible object such as an apple. What do you mean by the word *apple*? If you describe an apple, you might say it is round, red, hard, crunchy, and sweet. But all these qualities refer to kinds of experiences or sensations (step 1). It now seems as though your entire conception of an apple consists of a collection of ideas that are experienced and, hence, that exist in your mind (steps 2 and 3). Notice that in describing an apple you mentioned all the qualities of the apple found in your experience, but you did not mention its matter. Of course, if by "matter" you simply mean its hardness, then you are referring to an experience or "idea" you have. However, if by matter you mean (as Locke did) some sort of substratum, a something-I-know-not-what, which supports all the qualities in experience, but is not itself experienced, then you have violated the empiricist starting point. It follows, then, that the only apple we know of is the apple that exists as a collection of ideas in the mind (step 4).

Strip away the perceived qualities of the apple, and what you have left is something without shape, color, odor, taste, or texture—a kind of nothingness. Furthermore, since you cannot describe its matter (you can describe only ideas presented in experience), why do you even believe this matter exists in addition to the experiences you have? According to Berkeley, our apple experiences are not caused by the "real" apple. Instead, our apple experiences *are* the real apple.

Probably you will find Berkeley's position quaint, odd, zany, or (at worst) insane. You are not alone. Many of his contemporaries had the same reaction when the *Principles* was first published. Among his contemporaries, a physician declared that Berkeley was mad, and a bishop deplored his vain thirst for novelty. Nevertheless, Berkeley's arguments have persistently haunted philosophy down through the centuries and are still the subject of discussion among contemporary philosophers today.

Because his *Principles* received such a devastatingly poor reception, Berkeley tried again, with a more popular work titled *Three Dialogues Between Hylas and Philonous*, published in 1713. In writing this work, he employed his literary skills to their fullest extent. His arguments are manifold as well as complex, subtle, and seductive, and we can examine only some of the highlights here. The two people in this fictional conversation are two British college students meeting on campus to share their thoughts. The first is Hylas, whose name is similar to a Greek term for matter. Appropriately, he is a materialist and very close in spirit to John Locke's philosophy. The second student is Philonous, whose name literally means "mind lover." Philonous delivers Berkeley's punchlines while Hylas is the setup man.

After some initial verbal sparring, the disagreement between the two crystallizes with Philonous suggesting that "the reality of sensible things consists in being perceived" and Hylas insisting that "to exist is one thing, and to be perceived is another" (D 14). Hylas begins by defending a position that is now called **naive realism**. It can be defined as the belief that the properties we perceive objects to have are the properties that they really do have in the external world. Berkeley has no problem with the first part of that formula; the latter part, which assumes an external material world corresponding to our ideas, is the focus of his arguments for immaterialism.

ARGUMENT FROM
PAIN AND PLEASURE

To defend immaterialism, Berkeley has Philonous employ a strategy that could be called "the argument from pain and pleasure." This argument was mentioned in passing by both Locke and Hume, but Berkeley uses it as a major weapon in his arsenal. The argument goes something like this:

(1) Some quality q (a temperature, a taste, an odor) is experienced as either a pain or a pleasure.

(2) Pain and pleasure are not the properties of external objects but exist only when they are perceived.

(3) Therefore, quality q is not the property of an external object but exists only when it is perceived.

Philonous takes heat as the first example, since most people believe that it exists in objects external to us. However, he observes that when we experience extreme heat (as when touching a flame), what we actually encounter is intense pain (step 1). But no one would want to say that pain is out there in the external world, residing in the fireplace. Obviously, pain is a kind of sensation and exists only when a mind perceives it (step 2).

Hylas tries to escape the force of the argument by insisting that the heat is in the external object, while pain is merely a consequence of it. Philonous, however, argues that we cannot separate them in this way, because we have only one, distinct sensation when experiencing the flame. Thus, our experience of intense heat is the same as the feeling of pain, which is internal to the perceiving mind (step 3). The same argument applies to all the other ranges of heat because we experience them as either painful or pleasant sensations. We can obviously make the same point with coldness.

ARGUMENT FROM
PERCEIVER RELATIVITY

At this point, Philonous introduces another typical Berkeleian argument. This is often called "the argument from perceiver relativity." Philonous applies this argument by means of a simple experiment. Imagine that one of your hands has been heated in hot water, and you now place it in a bucket of lukewarm water. By contrast, this water will feel cold. But if your hand is cold and is placed in the same lukewarm water, this water will now seem warm. Can the same water be both cold and warm at the same time? To avoid this contradiction, Hylas concedes that "heat and cold are only sensations existing in our minds."

The specifics of this experiment can be generalized into an argument of the following form:

(1) Quality q_1 (coldness), is perceived when experiencing object o (water) under condition c_1 (a warm hand).

(2) Quality q_2 (heat) is perceived when experiencing object o under condition c_2 (a cold hand).

(3) Conditions c_1 and c_2 are different conditions of the perceiver that do not change object o.

(4) Qualities q_1 and q_2 are such that it is contradictory to suppose that object o could be both of these at the same time.

(5) Therefore, qualities q_1 and q_2 exist in the perceiver and not in object o

With Hylas's concession (step 5) under his belt, Philonous applies the same set of arguments to many other sensory qualities. We experience the sweetness of sugar or the bitterness of a herb as particular kinds of pleasure and pain respectively. Since material objects cannot contain pleasure or pain, these qualities experienced through taste must reside in the mind. The same sort of reasoning would also apply to odors. What about sounds? Do sounds exist only when they are perceived? Berkeley uses the argument from the mental dependency of ideas here. If "sound" means exactly what we experience when, say, a bell rings, then of course sound cannot exist if no one is having the experience. Without a perceiver, the ringing bell may be a sort of motion, but motions cannot be loud, sweet, dissonant, or melodious, as can sounds. Motions can only be seen or felt, but not heard, so they are not sounds. The famous riddle "If a tree falls in the forest and no one hears it, does it make a sound?" is derived from Berkeley's arguments.

Colors are handled with the relativity argument. The color of an object will vary depending on the lighting, the condition of our eyes, and the instruments through which we view it. The clouds in a sunset appear red and purple, but we know that water vapor has no such color. Objects seen through a microscope have colors that are not revealed to the naked eye. How, then, can we speak of the "real" colors of things? This sort of variability shows that color is a mode of our perception and not a property of objects themselves.

INSEPARABILITY OF PRIMARY AND SECONDARY QUALITIES

Thus far, John Locke would have little to quarrel with in Berkeley's position. In fact, many of the arguments Philonous uses are similar to those Locke used to show that the secondary qualities we experience are not in the objects themselves. With his naive realism in disarray, Hylas introduces Locke's distinction between primary qualities and secondary qualities to avoid being swept into Philonous's whirlpool of immaterialism.

Hylas concedes that the secondary qualities such as temperatures, tastes, smells, sounds, and colors cannot exist apart from the mind. But he stands firm on the primary qualities of extension, figure, solidity, quantity, motion, and rest, claiming that these certainly exist in external, material objects. Philonous responds by showing, in effect, that the same arguments that he and Locke used to demonstrate the mind dependence of secondary qualities can be used just as easily against primary qualities.

To make this point he employs the "inseparability argument." This argument is as follows:

(1) So-called primary and secondary qualities cannot be separated in the mind, because they always appear together and are perceived in the same way.

(2) Thus, if one quality is mind dependent, the other will be also.

(3) We have shown that secondary qualities are mind dependent.

(4) Therefore, primary qualities are mind dependent.

For example, you never experience redness all by itself. You experience a red tomato, a red crayon, red tulip, or a red something. The color, smell, and taste of objects are all part of the same experience in which you perceive their extension. So how can you say that one part of your experience (the color) is subjective, but another feature of your experience (the shape and extension) is objective? How do you know tomatoes are round? You know this because you see round patches of redness when you look at them. Hence, the experience of extension is always mediated, in one way or another, through your experience of so-called secondary qualities. If secondary qualities exist only for the mind that perceives them, then the primary qualities must have the same status.

Philonous uses the relativity argument in his discussion of specific primary qualities. For example, he says that an object that appears minutely small to us would be enormously large to a mite. Hence, the sense of size is relative to the perceiver. How about motion? Surely that occurs in the external world. Nevertheless, what is motion but the succession of ideas in one's mind? To see this point clearly, suppose you are on a fast-moving train. The images of the countryside will pass by very quickly. At the same time, a train moving at the exact same speed and direction as yours on an adjoining track will appear immobile. "Motion," then, is just a name we give to the speed and changing relation of ideas as they succeed one another in a perceiving mind.

Later in the discussion Hylas and Philonous discuss distance. Since the perception of distance is one way in which we identify extension, it is an interesting test case for determining whether or not the primary qualities are mind dependent. Philonous first points out that in dreams we have the appearance of objects being distant. However, it is obvious that the distance we perceive is merely an appearance to the mind and does not indicate any real extension. This lends plausibility to the thesis that even our waking experience is like this. (The same argument, of course, could be used for any of the primary qualities.) Furthermore, when a house appears to be far away, do we actually experience something called "spatial distance"? No, it seems not. What we actually experience is a house that looks very small. As we move toward it, we will experience successive ideas of the house, in which it will appear increasingly larger. But all we have are various experiences of smaller and larger house images. Thus it seems that when we experience a familiar object as being relatively small, we associate this experience with the concept of "distance." However, since the appearance of size is relative to the perceiver, so is distance. Philonous asks Hylas to consider a man born blind who is suddenly enabled to see. At first, his untrained eyes would not be able to interpret the visual images as presenting the quality of distance to his sight. He would have to learn how to correlate these visual clues with the notion of distance.

ARGUMENT FROM THE IMAGINATION

Even though Hylas is befuddled by these arguments, he still is not convinced. So, in the midst of discussing the primary qualities, Philonous offers yet another argument to support the claim that "to be is to be perceived." This could be called "the argument from the imagination." It comes in the form of a challenge. He promises Hylas that if the latter can conceive of any sensible object existing apart from the mind, he will readily abandon his immaterialism. Hylas takes the bait and asserts that nothing is easier than "to conceive a tree or house existing by itself, independent of and unperceived by, any mind" (D 41). We can imagine, for example, a tree located in some distant forest where no human being has ever set foot. It is seemingly sitting there alone without being present to anyone's mind. But Philonous points out that one item in this thought experiment has been neglected. In conceiving of such a tree, it is present to Hylas's mind. Conceiving is an operation of the mind. Hence, the object of conception (the tree) is an idea that, by definition, must be in the mind. Hylas has failed to carry out the conditions of the test. He cannot claim that the conception of a tree is *present in his mind* at the same time that it is *not present in a mind* without contradicting himself.

CRITIQUE OF THE REPRESENTATIVE THEORY OF PERCEPTION

At the end of the *First Dialogue*, Philonous delivers the final blow to Lockean epistemology by attacking the representative or copy theory of perception. Although he concedes ideas are in the mind, Hylas offers the Lockean claim that some of them may be copies or pictures of objects external to us. In this way, we can indirectly perceive the external object. To use an example from art, a picture of someone (the copy) allows us to perceive the real person in an indirect fashion.

But Philonous objects. All we see in the picture is a series of colors and figures. If these suggest to us the idea of the genuine person, it is because we have had some previous experience that associated the two. Similarly, I can be said to hear a coach, says Philonous, but all I really hear is just sound. If I associate these sounds with the coach, it is because in a previous experience I have heard the same sound when I have seen the coach. All we have, then, is the correlation of one idea (or kind of experience) with another one. We never get beyond the circle of ideas. Hence, we can never say that an idea is a copy of an external, "real" object because if all we know are ideas, we can never experience the connection. Besides, if both primary and secondary qualities are present to me as ideas, what would "real" objects be like if they were devoid of any sensible qualities? They certainly would not be like any of our ideas. "Can a real thing, in itself *invisible*, be like a *color*, or a real thing which is not *audible*, be like a *sound*? In a word, can anything be like a sensation or idea, but another sensation or idea?" (D 48).

Metaphysics: Reality as Mind and Ideas

As with all the classical empiricists, no clear-cut distinction can be made between Berkeley's epistemology and his metaphysics. His account of how we obtain knowledge is interspersed with his account of what sort of reality there is to know. Already it is clear that the only things that can exist in Berkeley's world are ideas and the minds that know them. Nevertheless, under the heading of *metaphysics* we will examine, in turn, Berkeley's views on the existence of our world, the being of God, and then the laws of nature.

THE EXISTENCE OF THE WORLD

A common mistake people make in first attempting to understand Berkeley is to assume that he denies the existence of our world and the things in it. At one point Hylas asks, "What difference is there between real things and chimeras formed by the imagination or the visions of a dream, since they are all equally in the mind?" (D 82). Philonous answers that the visions of a dream are "dim, irregular, and confused" whereas our ideas of real things are "more vivid and clear." We distinguish dreams and hallucinations from clearheaded, waking experience by comparing one experience with another. It is a distinction we

make between two kinds of experiences not between experience and some independent reality outside of experience. We can do the same in Berkeley's system. As he expresses it, "by the principles premised, we are not deprived of any one thing in Nature. Whatever we see, feel, hear, or anywise conceive or understand, remains as secure as ever, and is as real as ever" (P §34).

In other words, Berkeley has no intentions of denying the existence of any part of our world. He is merely analyzing what the term "existence" means. How do we know some object exists? We say that something exists when we (or somebody else) can perceive the object. "The table I write on, I say exists, that is, I see and feel it; and if I were out of my study I should say it existed—meaning thereby that if I was in my study I might perceive it, or that some other spirit actually does perceive it" (P §3).

Samuel Johnson, a famous English writer and contemporary of Berkeley, fell prey to a typical misunderstanding of the Bishop's arguments. After disparaging Berkeley's system, Johnson kicked a stone, sending it flying into the air, saying, "I refute him thus." But Johnson's "refutation" misses the point. What does kicking the stone prove? He experiences the solidity of the stone and has the visual experience of seeing it fly through his field of vision. What he has encountered is a series of ideas. This is perfectly consistent with Berkeley's position. Kicking a stone is nothing but the series of sensations just described, and we can have these without postulating any material body.

Berkeley is sensitive to the apparent absurdities that seem to arise from his view of existence. If "apple" is just a name we apply to the combined ideas we experience of redness, roundness, moistness, crunchiness, and sweetness, then when we eat an apple, are we just eating *ideas*? Berkeley agrees that this way of phrasing it seems "very harsh" (P §38). But he claims this is only because we customarily do not use the word *ideas* to refer to the collections of sensible qualities that we ordinarily call "things." However, he concedes that once we understand that items such as apples consist entirely of sensory qualities, he has no objection to our referring to them as things. His advice on these issues is to "think with the learned and speak with the vulgar" (P §51). Just as we still say that "the sun rises" or "the sun sets," even though we subscribe to the Copernican system, so we can allow a certain looseness in our speech about objects as long as our philosophical understanding is more sophisticated than our speech indicates.

GOD'S EXISTENCE

One of the major goals of Bishop Berkeley's intricate epistemological arguments was to restore the place of religious belief in an age that was drifting toward skepticism and unbelief. Hence, it is not surprising that he tries to apply his conclusions about ideas to the issue of God's existence.

Berkeley believes that if we follow his arguments concerning the intellectual bankruptcy of materialism, we will be driven to assert the existence of God by a process of elimination. After his extended discussion of ideas, the question naturally arises, What causes our ideas? Berkeley considers all the possible causes (P §25). First, we could suppose that one idea causes another. However, ideas are passive and inert. They do not seem to have any power or activity. For example, the yellowness of a lemon does not produce the sensation of its tartness. Second, we could hypothesize that the material substance of the lemon produces both the idea of yellow and tartness within our minds. But this is the Lockean position that Berkeley believes has been decisively refuted. The only alternative left, then, in answering this question is to say that "the cause of ideas is an incorporeal, active substance or spirit" (P §26). Although there are some complications here, when Berkeley uses the term "spiritual substance" he means it to be identical with such terms as "will," "soul," "spirit," "mind," or "self." In Berkeley's system, the only causal agents in the world are spiritual substances.

But does your mind or spirit explain the existence of your ideas? Obviously, the images produced in your imagination are caused by you. However, the ideas found in the world of sensory experience impinge on you and are not under your control. When you bite into a lemon, the idea or sensation of its tartness immediately occurs in your conscious experience. If you and I cannot produce the world of our ideas through an act of will, then some other will or spirit must be responsible for the existence of these ideas. We have, then, a species of the causal argument for God. We cannot argue from the existence of the material world to God as Thomas Aquinas tried to do, for "matter" is only an empty noise signifying nothing. But we are forced, thinks Berkeley, to postulate the being of God to explain our own sensory ideas. It is God who provides us with the rich set of ideas of rainbows, hills, butterflies, oceans, and all the wonders of our world. God gives these ideas directly to our minds without requiring the superfluous "middleman" of matter.

Berkeley's view of the nature of perception and reality can be illustrated by using diagrams to contrast his position with that of Descartes and Locke (see Figures 20-1 and 20-2). As Figure 20-1 illustrates, Descartes and Locke believed that (A) *God* (a spiritual substance) (1) *created* (B) *the material world* (represented by an apple), which (2) *influences* (C) *my physical body*, which (3) *produces*, within (D) *my mind* (a spiritual substance), (E) *ideas of the world* (the image of the apple). According to Berkeley's much simpler picture in Figure 20-2, (A) *God* (a spiritual substance) (1) *creates*, within (B) *my mind* (a spiritual substance), (C) *a world of ideas*. Notice that for Descartes and Locke, the mind contains *ideas of the world*, since they represent an external reality. For Berkeley, the mind contains *a world of ideas*, since that is the only world God has created.

How does Berkeley leap from the conclusion that some spirit other than our own produces our ideas to the claim that this spirit is identical to the traditional concept of God? He seems to believe, along with most of the theists of his day, that the orderliness and magnitude of nature is so great that nothing short of an infinite being could meet the job description of such a creator.

Even though Berkeley refers to his argument as a "demonstration," it clearly provides only some partial evidence for God's existence. The argument

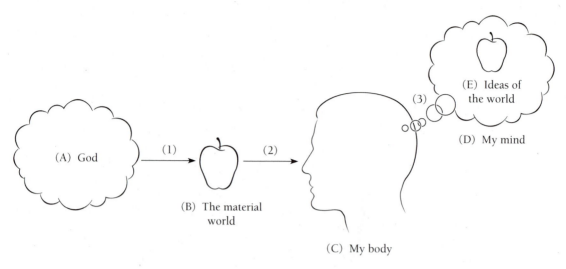

(A) God

(1)

(B) The material world

(2)

(C) My body

(3)

(D) My mind

(E) Ideas of the world

FIGURE 20-1 Descartes's and Locke's view of perception

is suggestive and probabilistic, but not conclusive. Contrary to Berkeley, David Hume later argued that if the world is finite, it requires, at best, only a very great but finite cause. Furthermore, to say that each idea has some spiritual cause apart from us does not establish that only *one* spirit is at work causing our ideas. It is theoretically possible that many different spirits are causing the various ideas in our minds. Certainly, Berkeley's causal argument, by itself, has not shown us that the cause of our ideas must be eternal and perfect and have all the other properties that Berkeley so quickly sneaks into his conclusion.

The being of God handily answers a nagging question in Berkeley's philosophy. If the room you are sitting in exists because you are perceiving it, will it disappear if you close your eyes? Do objects stutter in and out of existence whenever you go in or out of your room? Berkeley says no. Our commonsense belief that objects continue in existence in such circumstances is correct. God both creates the idea of the room in your mind and perceives it in his own mind. Thus, when you close your eyes and no longer perceive the room, it still exists because God perceives it. Questions still might arise here. Nevertheless, throughout all his works, Berkeley is diligent in presenting

every objection to his philosophy that he can imagine and seeking to provide an answer from within his system.

Having established the relationship between God and the world in this way, Berkeley believes that he has accomplished some of the religious goals of his philosophy, thus providing his age with a remedy for the corrosive effects of deism and unbelief. He feared that the mechanistic, Newtonian view of the universe left his culture with a distant, sterile deity, unable to inspire piety and morality. In one of his works, *Alciphron*, he says of the deist position,

> Some philosophers, being convinced of the wisdom and power of the Creator, from the make and contrivance of organized bodies and orderly system of the world, did nevertheless imagine that he left this system with all its parts and contents well adjusted and put in motion, as an artist leaves a clock, to go thenceforward of itself for a certain period.[2]

He refutes the deist position, however, saying that his own proof established God as

> not a Creator merely, but a provident Governor, actually and intimately present, and attentive to all our interests and motions, who watches over our conduct, and takes care of our minutest actions and

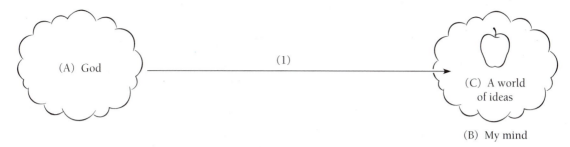

FIGURE 20-2 Berkeley's view of perception

designs throughout the whole course of our lives, informing, admonishing, and directing incessantly, in a most evident and sensible manner.[3]

SCIENCE AND THE LAWS OF NATURE

These theological remarks might make it appear that Berkeley's position was in competition with a scientific understanding of the world. However, this is not the case. Berkeley did not want to discard the genuine fruits of the science of his day. He merely wanted to free it from problematic metaphysical assumptions. How then do we do science without a material world to study? Berkeley wants us to understand that his system in no way eliminates the laws of nature or the scientific formulas that describe those laws. He assures us that "there is not any one phenomenon explained on that supposition [that matter exists] which may not as well be explained without it" (P §50). Thus, for his own purpose he employs Ockham's razor, one of the principles that gave rise to the scientific enterprise (see Chapter 12). This is the strategy of looking for the simplest, most economical explanation, while discarding superfluous entities and principles.

What are laws of nature? According to Berkeley, they are simply descriptions of the predictable ways in which some ideas regularly follow other ideas. He points out, however, that there are no necessary connections between the ideas of experience. It is not logically necessary that water freezes when the thermometer registers 32° F. It

would not be a contradiction to imagine it freezing at 51° F. Hence, the empirical method of learning from experience must be employed here.

What about causality? When we touch a flame we feel pain. But since there is no physical fire to contact a material body, does the fire *cause* the pain? Consistent with his own position, Berkeley says no. What we refer to as a "cause" is really only a sign. "Effects" are simply what is signified by the sign. Thus, when we sense the presence of fire, this warns us that we will feel pain; it does not cause the pain. To use an analogy, when my alarm clock goes off at 6:30 A.M., that is a sign that it is morning. However, the ringing of the alarm does not cause the sun to rise, nor vice versa. Berkeley's point is that scientists will avoid error if they merely record the uniform order of ideas in experience and do not suppose they are studying physical substances. Berkeley's view that the laws of nature are merely descriptions of regularities in experience is very modern. Similar views have been held by some philosophers of science in the twentieth century who sought to avoid all metaphysical assumptions—including those of Berkeley.*

For Berkeley, the regularities discovered by science result from the fact that each moment of our experience is directly produced by God. If you experience a lemon, you will (not surprisingly)

---

*Examples of such philosophers of science would be the pragmatists, discussed in Chapter 30, and the logical positivists, discussed in Chapter 32.

find it to have a yellow, textured surface and a tart taste. These phenomena occur because God creates within your mind the experiences of yellowness, texture, and tartness. God could, if he chose to do so, provide you with the sight and texture of a lemon, but give you the taste sensation of bubble gum. He doesn't play such tricks, of course. Nature is orderly. We can count on it. We can expect bread to be nourishing, rain to be wet, and cyanide to be deadly. This orderliness and consistency is a testimony to the consistency and goodness of God. In Berkeley's account, science does not eliminate religion; instead, science actually requires God to guarantee the uniformity of natural events. Since *all* natural events are the result of direct acts of God, the miracles recorded in the Bible are not at all problematic. For certain purposes, God may deviate from the normal schedule of events. He may make a liquid look and taste like water one minute and look and taste like wine the next minute. But such a miracle is no more and no less a supernatural event than the falling of an apple to the earth.

At one point, Hylas brings in the biblical account of creation to refute Philonous. The Scriptures say God created the heavens and the earth as well as the sea, plants, and animals. It does not say he created ideas, Hylas insists. But Philonous points out that neither do the Scriptures say God created matter. He *did* create the sea. But what is the sea he created? He created the ideas of wetness, the smell of saltwater, the sight of a deep blue expanse topped with frothy whiteness, and the rolling images of waves. He created everything we experience, just as we experience it, but he did not create matter.

In his philosophy of nature, Berkeley bravely challenged some of the leading concepts in the Newtonian physics of his day. Newton held that absolute space and absolute time existed as part of the furniture of the universe and that motion was absolute. Berkeley argues that these are untenable abstractions and that these terms do not refer to things that exist on their own, but only to relations between experiences. The term "space," for example, refers to our experience of movement and the relations between our ideas of bod-

ies. We cannot form an idea of pure space devoid of bodies and movement (P §116). Time is simply our experience of the succession of ideas in our minds (P §§97, 98). Concerning motion, Berkeley says that "it does not appear to me that there can be any motion other than *relative*; so that to conceive motion there must be at least conceived two bodies, whereof the distance or position in regard to each other is varied" (P §112). These remarks make Berkeley's system a forerunner of the theories of Albert Einstein, the twentieth-century physicist, who revolutionized science by theorizing that space, time, and motion are relative and not absolute. Berkeley made similar remarks about gravity and force, claiming that they were not metaphysical entities or causes, but merely mathematical expressions of the predictable relationships between events. Although Berkeley's philosophy was out of step with his own times, many of his discussions of scientific topics are astonishingly modern.

PROBLEMS WITH SPIRITUAL SUBSTANCES

In the *Dialogues*, Philonous presents a major problem for Berkeley's view of God. It is clear that God is not a sensory quality. He is not round, blue, or sweet. According to Berkeley, however, we can have ideas only of sensory qualities. Hence, it seems to follow that we cannot have an idea of God. Hylas justifiably complains,

> Since, therefore, you have no idea of the mind of God, how can you conceive it possible that things should exist in His mind? Or, if you can conceive the mind of God without having an idea of it, why may not I be allowed to conceive the existence of matter, notwithstanding I have no idea of it? (D 77-78)

John Locke had also pointed to such a parity between material substance and spiritual substance. In fact, he argued that since matter obviously exists, then spirit must also. Hylas uses the parity argument in reverse to show that since Philonous admits unperceived spiritual substance, he must be consistent and admit the possibility of unperceived matter.

Berkeley patches over the problem by having Philonous introduce a distinction between "ideas" and "notions." I cannot have an *idea* of my mind the way I can the sweetness of sugar. Nevertheless, because I am directly aware of my own mental operations (such as thinking, willing, and loving) I can form a *notion* of my mind through reflection. Thus, I can know my mind, even though this notion is not an idea in the sense of perceiving something such as a color, sound, or taste. My acquaintance with my own mind allows me to use an analogical and probabilistic argument that suggests the existence of other finite minds. Similarly, I can extend and amplify this notion of my own mind to come up with the notion of a Perfect Mind. The causal argument, discussed earlier, gives one a basis for concluding that this notion has reality.

This whole line of reasoning begins with a premise borrowed from Descartes that claims I have direct acquaintance with my own mind or self. Problems arise with this premise, however. In passing, Hylas complains, "Notwithstanding all you have said, to me it seems that according to your own way of thinking, and in consequence of your own principles, it should follow that you are only a system of floating ideas without any substance to support them" (D 80). In other words, I may be acquainted with my own acts of loving, willing, thinking, and so on. But these are transitory psychological states and operations. They are only "floating ideas" and are not identical with an enduring, spiritual substance that stays essentially the same throughout the flow of my stream of consciousness. Do I then really have any direct acquaintance with my own spiritual substance? Even though Hylas drops this line of attack much too quickly, David Hume later takes this problem and runs with it. But the difficulty of this problem did not seem to make a sufficient impact on Berkeley.

Evaluation and Significance

Critics have found several problems in Berkeley's main thesis. Some have claimed that Berkeley's system teeters precariously on the edge of three unacceptable positions. The first is solipsism. **Solipsism** is the claim that there is no reality out-

side of my own mind and its contents. Although few philosophers have seriously defended such a position, it has served as a warning signal that the premises that lead to it are flawed. If Berkeley means to claim that the only reality I can know or even think about consists of those objects I perceive, then reality as I understand it is reduced to the subjective contents of my mind. Berkeley, of course, would reject this position by claiming that God also perceives these objects. Thus, they have some objective existence apart from me.

Here, however, a second problem arises. Are my ideas merely representations or copies of God's ideas of an object? Some of Berkeley's remarks suggest that our ideas are merely specific versions of the divine archetypes. In other words, reality as it exists for God is not identical with what human beings directly know. If this interpretation is correct, then he comes close to lapsing into a version of the representative realism he found so problematic in Locke. In this case, our experience of reality would not be direct and unmediated, which was one of the selling points of Berkeley's philosophy.

Third, if we seek to avoid the first two alternatives by claiming that our ideas are not distinct from God's ideas, then it would seem our minds overlap or participate in the divine mind. Berkeley would find this conclusion theologically unacceptable. Thus, Berkeley seems to be caught between solipsism, representative realism, or some form of pantheistic overlap between our minds and God's mind.

There are problems with Berkeley's claim that we cannot conceive of an object that exists unperceived. True, *while* I am conceiving something it is necessarily related to my mind. Nevertheless, this does not mean the statement "There are some objects unthought of or unperceived" makes no sense. Part of Berkeley's problem is that he tends to collapse the distinction between perceiving and conceiving, because he believes we think only in images. Thus, seeing a house and thinking of a house are similar because in both cases we have an image before our minds. But Berkeley's view is incorrect. As Descartes pointed out, we can think of a chiliogon (a thousand-sided figure), but we cannot form the image of it in our minds.[4] Thus, we can refer to objects in language and in thought and have a clear understanding of their properties without either perceiving them or imagining them.

As noted before, Berkeley's awkward concept of "notion" raises further problems. One becomes suspicious that the concept of "notion" is an artificial category he conjured up in order to have an epistemological pigeonhole in which to place the nonsensory concepts of God and the self. Indeed, Berkeley did not add the doctrine of notions until he revised later editions of the *Principles* and wrote the *Dialogues*. The difficulty did not seem to occur to him when he first wrote the *Principles*. However, once Berkeley allows us to think about and discuss unperceived entities such as other human minds and God, he creates a sizable crack in his system that threatens its structural integrity.

Finally, most people would have a hard time agreeing with Berkeley's claim that he is on the side of common sense and that he repudiates all the "uncouth paradoxes, difficulties, and inconsistencies" of the philosophers (P, intro., §1). If Berkeley's arguments are not as airtight as he thought, then it would seem that the thesis that objects exist independent of our experience of them is a simpler and more plausible explanation. Even within his own theological context, it seems more coherent to believe the baby is in pain because a physical diaper pin is sticking him, rather than that a supposedly benevolent God is at that moment directly inflicting the baby with pain sensations.

The verdict of history has agreed with David Hume's assessment of the bishop's arguments: "They admit of no answer and produce no conviction. Their only effect is to cause . . . momentary amazement and irresolution and confusion."[5] Berkeley's arguments against matter and his immaterialist alternative have not achieved any real and lasting success. Even theists have not found Berkeley's system to be helpful in undermining "all the monstrous systems of the atheists."

Nevertheless, Berkeley did contribute to the progress of philosophical discussion in several ways. First, he raised some helpful questions concerning the metaphysical assumptions of both his rationalistic and empiricist predecessors. Second,

for better or for worse, his uncomfortable conclusions showed where a thoroughgoing, narrow empiricism can lead. In response, some philosophers concluded that empiricism must be abandoned or, at best, modified. Others, who adhere to a position known as **phenomenalism**, "bite the bullet" and hold that all we can know are ideas or sense data. Accordingly, they do away with all metaphysics, including the ideas of self and God that Berkeley tried to retain. Third, his approach to philosophical analysis and the issues he dealt with, especially his theories of language and perception, have had a significant influence on the tradition of British empiricism. Finally, as was mentioned earlier, his anti-Newtonian philosophy of science was reinvented in the twentieth century. If nothing else, this part of his thought shows the originality of his philosophical mind and his ability to rise above the widespread assumptions of his time. These are two essential requirements for significant, philosophical work.

Questions for Understanding

1. Why does Berkeley claim that the belief in an external, material world leads to deism and atheism?

2. Why does Berkeley claim that Locke's epistemology leads to skepticism?

3. What does Berkeley mean when he says "to be is to be perceived"?

4. What does Berkeley mean by "idea"?

5. Why does Berkeley claim there is no such thing as an abstract idea?

6. Formulate the following arguments of Berkeley: (a) the argument from the mental dependency of ideas, (b) the argument from pain and pleasure, (c) the argument from perceiver relativity, (d) the argument from the imagination.

7. How and why does Berkeley disagree with Locke on primary and secondary qualities?

8. Why does Berkeley reject Locke's representative realism?

9. Since Berkeley believes that a material, external world does not exist, how does he distinguish between dreams and reality?

10. What is Berkeley's argument for the existence of God?

11. If matter does not exist, why does Berkeley believe that science is possible?

12. How does Berkeley's view of space and time differ from that of Newton?

13. If all we can know are our sensations, how does Berkeley allow us to talk about nonsensory entities such as God and minds?

Questions for Reflection

1. How is Berkeley's philosophy similar to Locke's? Where do they disagree?

2. Which one of Berkeley's arguments do you think is the weakest? Why?

3. From within Berkeley's philosophy, what does it mean to say "There is a book on my table"?

4. If we accept Berkeley's philosophy, how does this provide an answer to skepticism? In what ways does his philosophy undermine atheism?

5. How is this statement a misunderstanding of Berkeley's philosophy? "According to Berkeley, the chair on which I am sitting does not exist, but is only an illusion."

Notes

1. Quotations from George Berkeley's works are referenced in the text using the following abbreviations.

D   *Three Dialogues Between Hylas and Philonous*, ed. Colin M. Turbayne (Indianapolis: Library of Liberal Arts, Bobbs-Merrill, 1954). References to this work are made in terms of the page numbers of this edition.

P   *A Treatise Concerning the Principles of Human Knowledge*, ed. Colin M. Turbayne (Indianapolis: Library of Liberal Arts, Bobbs-Merrill, 1957). References to this work are made in terms of Berkeley's numbers.

PC   *Philosophical Commentaries*, in *The Works of George Berkeley, Bishop of Cloyne*, vol. 1, ed. A. A. Luce and T. E. Jessop (London: Nelson, 1948). References to this work are made in terms of section numbers.

2. George Berkeley, *Alciphron*, dialogue 4, §14, in *The Works of George Berkeley: Bishop of Cloyne*, ed. A. A. Luce and T. E. Jessop (London: Nelson, 1950), 3.160.

3. Ibid.

4. René Descartes, *Meditations on First Philosophy*, trans. John Cottingham (Cambridge, England: Cambridge University Press, 1986), 50. This may be found in Meditation 6, p. 72 of the classic French edition.

5. David Hume, *An Enquiry Concerning Human Understanding*, sec. 12, pt.1, in *The English Philosophers from Bacon to Mill*, ed. Edwin A. Burtt (New York: The Modern Library, 1939), 682.

21

David Hume:
The Scottish Skeptic

Hume's Life: A Passion for Literary Fame

David Hume was born in 1711 in Edinburgh, Scotland, into a Calvinist family of modest means. He attended Edinburgh University, where he studied the standard subjects of classics, mathematics, science, and philosophy. After he left the university, his family assumed he would pursue a career in law, as had many in his family. However, while they thought he was reading law, he was actually pouring himself into literature and philosophy. In his early twenties, Hume went to France for three years, where he wrote *A Treatise of Human Nature*. Hume once confessed that the hope of achieving literary fame was his "ruling passion."[1] He thought his first work would not only give him the reputation he sought, but would also produce a revolution in philosophy. Although it is now considered a philosophical classic, Hume's contemporaries received it with resounding indifference. As Hume said, it "fell dead-born from the press." In 1745 he had another career setback when he failed to obtain a position in ethics at Edinburgh University. His skeptical and religious opinions were appar-

ently too controversial for the people of that time. (To rectify their oversight, the philosophy department there is now housed in a building named after him.)

In an attempt to salvage the *Treatise*, Hume wrote a more popular and lively version of the first two parts of that work and published it in 1748. This was eventually known as *An Enquiry Concerning Human Understanding*. In 1751, a revised version of the third part of the *Treatise* was published as *An Enquiry Concerning the Principles of Morals*. As Hume's fame increased, so did the attacks on his unorthodox ideas. This resulted in another disappointment in 1752 when he failed to land an academic position at the University of Glasgow. His scandalous reputation was further enhanced by his *Natural History of Religion*, released in 1757. It was a less-than-sympathetic account of the origins of the religious impulse in human experience. Learning from this experience and having a desire "to live quietly and keep remote from all clamour," Hume withheld publication of *Dialogues Concerning Natural Religion* until after his death. It has since become a classic in the philosophy of religion.

His six-volume *History of England*, which appeared during the years 1754 to 1762, finally brought him the recognition he so deeply desired. By his own account, his writings at this point had made him "not only independent but opulent." In 1763 he went to Paris to serve as an assistant to the English ambassador. His reputation as a historian and man of letters preceded him, and his three years in France were spent living the life of a celebrity and being the idol of all the leading social circles. He lived out the last years of his life in his hometown of Edinburgh where he was the leading light in Scottish intellectual and literary circles. In 1776 he died after suffering from either cancer or ulcerative colitis.

Although his philosophy was filled with the hard edges of skepticism and his pointed criticisms of traditional thought, Hume was actually a kind and gentle soul in his personal relationships. Although he never married, there were several women within the circle of his closest friends. He described himself in his autobiography as follows:

> I was . . . a man of mild dispositions, of command of temper, of an open, social, and cheerful humour, capable of attachment, but little susceptible of enmity, and of great moderation in all my passions. Even my love of literary fame, my ruling passion, never soured my humour, notwithstanding my frequent disappointments.

The testimony of his companions indicates that this self-assessment is accurate. His friends loved to call him "St. David." As a result, the street on which he lived is still called St. David Street today.

Task: Unlocking the Secrets of Human Nature

Even though the science of his century had made remarkable strides in rebuilding the structures of knowledge anew, Hume was distressed by the wobbling and looseness he detected in these structures. To him this was a sure indication that all was not well with its foundations. As he put it, "There is nothing which is not the subject of debate, and in which men of learning are not of contrary opinions. . . . Disputes are multiplied, as if every thing was uncertain" (T, intro.).[2] The problem is that human nature, the source of all our cognitive powers, is inadequately understood. Therefore, the most direct route to knowledge is

> instead of taking now and then a castle or village on the frontier, to march up directly to the capital or center of these sciences, to human nature itself; which being once masters of, we may every where else hope for an easy victory. (T, intro.)

Hence, without any charade of false modesty, Hume declared his goal to be that of setting out the foundations for all the other sciences. It will be interesting to keep this claim in mind as we study the development of Hume's philosophy, for there is a certain irony here. He presents himself as a stonemason, setting out the foundations of the sciences, but his actual results will make him appear more like a demolition expert, destroying any hopes of scientific knowledge.

Theory of Knowledge: The Gulf Between Reason and the World

THE ORIGINS OF OUR IDEAS

Hume begins his philosophy with an analysis of our *perceptions*. These are simply the contents of consciousness (what Descartes and Locke called *ideas*). But introspection shows us that perceptions fall into two classes. For example, there is the experience of warmth we have when lying on the beach in the summer. But when we are enduring the chilling blasts of a winter wind, that previous experience of warmth is only a dim memory. The warmth as remembered or imagined is a copy of the original experience, but differs from it in the degree of force or liveliness.

Hume refers to our original experiences as *impressions*. Impressions may be either sensations or the immediate and original contents of our own psychological states. In Hume's words, impressions are "our more lively perceptions, when we hear, or see, or feel, or love, or hate, or desire, or will" (EHU 2). The less forceful copies or faint images of our impressions are called *ideas*. (Notice that his use of the term "idea" is more restricted than that of Descartes or Locke, who used it to refer to both kinds of Hume's perceptions.) It is an impression when we experience the taste of oysters and an idea when we recall it months later. The experience of anger is an impression, but the thought of yesterday's fit of anger is an idea.

Hume claims there is a one-to-one correspondence between impressions and ideas. We have no ideas except those that are parasitic, in one form or another, on impressions. Here, he issues one of his many challenges:

> Those who would assert that this position is not universally true, nor without exception, have only one, and that an easy, method of refuting it by producing that idea which, in their opinion, is not derived from this source. (EHU 2)

It may appear that the imagination has the ability to fly far beyond the bounds of experience. A storyteller such as Lewis Carroll, for example, has given us the fantastic world of Alice's Wonderland. However, Carroll formed every creature and event in that zany, fictional world by creatively combining elements of his previous experiences. Take a conversation with an acquaintance, add to that your visual impression of flowers, throw in the personality of some pompous, disagreeable person you know, and you will have fabricated the idea of the talking flowers Alice encountered.

According to Hume's theory, the "creative power of the mind amounts to no more than the faculty of compounding, transposing, augmenting, or diminishing the materials afforded us by the senses and experience" (EHU 2). Without the original impressions, the mind can have no real content. A blind man can have no idea what "red" means, and a deaf man has no notion of what a sound is like.

THE ASSOCIATION OF IDEAS

Hume carries his science of the mind further by setting out the laws of association. Recall that the empiricists of the eighteenth century saw experience as composed of atomistic units, corresponding to the physicists' particles in motion. Just as Newton had set out the laws governing physical particles, so the task of philosophy was to set out the laws controlling mental particles. Thus, Hume is looking for "some bond of union" or a "gentle force" that attracts one idea to another by a kind of mental gravity (T 1.1.4). The idea of a burnt finger normally is associated with the idea of pain and not with the idea of sweetness. A photograph of someone's eyes might lead us to guess whose face they belong to. These sorts of experiences make it evident that

> there is a principle of connection between the different thoughts or ideas of the mind, and that, in their appearance to the memory or imagination, they introduce each other with a certain degree of method and regularity. (EHU 3)

The question now arises, "How do ideas become connected together in the mind?" In answering this question, Hume discovers his three principles of the association of ideas. The first principle is called *resemblance*. Consider, for example, how a political cartoon of the President naturally leads you to think of the real-life President it represents. Ideas that are similar tend to be associated together. Second, the thought of one apartment in a building leads to thoughts of the adjoining apartments and to the building as a whole. Thus, ideas that appear together in space and time tend to be linked together in thought. This is the principle of *contiguity*. Finally, the experience of striking one's thumb with a hammer while driving a nail is associated with pain. This is the principle of *cause and effect* at work. When one event regularly succeeds another, we tend to associate them.

TWO KINDS OF REASONING

Before we leave this discussion of Hume's theory of knowledge, we need to look at an important distinction he makes between two kinds of reasoning and the kinds of knowledge they produce. This distinction is important not only because it looms large in Hume's discussion of metaphysical topics, but also because it has been taken for granted as the foundation stone of twentieth-century empiricism. Hume introduces this distinction by asserting that

> All the objects of human reason or inquiry may naturally be divided into two kinds, to wit, Relations of Ideas, and Matters of Fact. *Of the first kind are the sciences of Geometry, Algebra, and Arithmetic; and in short, every affirmation which is either intuitively or demonstratively certain. . . . Matters of fact, which are the second objects of human reason, are not ascertained in the same manner; nor is our evidence of their truth, however great, of a like nature with the foregoing.* (EHU 4.1)

The distinctive feature of propositions that express relations of ideas is that they are necessary truths. In other words, to deny them would be to assert a contradiction. We know that 2 + 2 = 4 not by observation or experimentation but by analyzing the relationships between these symbols as we have defined them. Our knowledge of the external world is irrelevant to the truth of these kinds of propositions because we do not base their certainty on any external facts. Hume says that "though there never were a circle or triangle in nature, the truths demonstrated by Euclid would forever retain their certainty and evidence" (EHU 4.1).

Matters of fact are quite different. Hume suggests that you may find it highly probable that the sun will rise tomorrow. However, you would not be expressing a logical contradiction if you asserted that "the sun will *not* rise tomorrow." For example, we could imagine some cosmic catastrophe that would make that true. Thus, even if "the sun *will* rise tomorrow" is a true statement, its truth is neither logically necessary nor certain. Reason alone cannot decide whether a factual statement is true or false.

Since reason cannot tell us about matters of fact, they have to be discovered through experience. To make this point, Hume asks us to imagine the situation described in the ancient story of the first human, Adam, who was facing the world for the first time, without any background of experience:

> *Adam, though his rational faculties be supposed, at the very first, entirely perfect, could not have inferred from the fluidity and transparency of water that it would suffocate him, or from the light and warmth of fire that it would consume him. No object ever discovers, by the qualities which appear to the senses, either the causes which produced it or the effects which will arise from it; nor can our reason, unassisted by experience, ever draw any inference concerning real existence and matter of fact.* (EHU 4.1)

In this discussion, Hume digs an impassable trench between these two kinds of knowledge that completely undermines the bridge between reason and the world that had been essential to the metaphysical conclusions of the rationalists. On the one side of the gulf, where reason is king, we have relations of ideas. These truths are necessary and, therefore, are absolutely certain. The cruel catch is that for all their certainty, they tell us nothing about the real world that lies across the chasm.

One may object that the Pythagorean theorem surely can guide us in laying out a triangular flower bed. However, Hume would say that though this theorem does follow from the ideas expressed in Euclidean axioms and definitions, whether or not it applies to our flower bed is a matter of observation. For example, in the nineteenth century mathematicians developed non-Euclidean systems of geometry that turned out to be useful in making special kinds of calculations in astronomy. Hume, of course, would not have known of this example. Nevertheless, it makes his point very forcefully. Given Euclid's starting point, you can reason to Euclid's theorems. However, whether or not these theorems apply to this or that problem in astronomy is a factual issue.

On the other side of the gulf, where experience is king, we reason about matters of fact. These do give us information about the world. The cruel catch in this realm, however, is that empirical judgments do not have the certainty nor necessity that logical truths enjoy. At best, matters of fact are based on various degrees of probability. As we will see shortly, Hume tries to show that our basis for confidence in matters of fact may be even more tenuous than suggested here.

IMPLICATIONS OF THE THEORY OF KNOWLEDGE

Thus far, we have a number of interesting observations about how our understanding works, but where is Hume going with these remarks? He leaves no doubts about their impact. His empiricism dictates that impressions have priority in the order of knowledge. Impressions are the strong and vivid originals of experience. They force themselves on us in such a way that our consciousness can only passively receive them. Ideas, in contrast, are feeble and derivative copies. If we can trace an idea back to its corresponding impression, then its credentials are validated. However, any philosophical term not tied to original impressions in this way is empty and useless. It does not have even the faint content of a legitimate idea.

Hume's science of the mind, therefore, has yielded a simple test that will clarify all philosophical discussions.

> When we entertain, therefore, any suspicion that a philosophical term is employed without any meaning or idea (as is but too frequent), we need but enquire, from what impression is that supposed idea derived? And if it be impossible to assign any, this will serve to confirm our suspicion. (EHU 2)

In this way, he hoped to "banish all that jargon which has so long taken possession of metaphysical reasonings and drawn disgrace upon them" (EHU 2).

Furthermore, in the last paragraph of his first *Enquiry*, in a passage that is breathtaking because of its intellectual brutality, Hume claims that his discussion of the two kinds of reasoning provides us with a simple but effective instrument for separating the wheat from the chaff in any discussion that we may encounter:

> When we run over libraries, persuaded of these principles, what havoc must we make? If we take in our hand any volume—of divinity or school metaphysics, for instance—let us ask, Does it contain any abstract reasoning concerning quantity or number? *No.* Does it contain any experimental reasoning concerning matter of fact and existence? *No.*

> Commit it then to the flames: for it can contain nothing but sophistry and illusion. (EHU 12.3)

Metaphysics: Skeptical Doubts About Reality

SUBSTANCE: AN EMPTY IDEA

With the groundwork laid in the theory of knowledge, Hume goes on to apply the empirical criterion of meaning to the areas of philosophy that had been the center of so much controversy and confusion. He takes as his first target the venerable idea of substance. At this point we see his first radical break from the traditions of the past, including that of his own British empiricism. Although Locke and Berkeley were card-carrying empiricists and sought to subject all knowledge claims to the bar of experience, they agreed with Descartes that the idea of substance was indispensable. Locke (but not Berkeley) believed the external world was populated with material substances. For example, we associate a number of experiences with the idea of an apple (redness, roundness, sweetness). Locke thought it incomprehensible that there was no entity or substance in which the apple's qualities inhered. However, Hume challenges us to find the idea of substance in our fleeting experiences of colors, sounds, or tastes (T 1.1.6).

Not only is the philosophers' notion of substance eliminated in Hume's radical empiricism, but even our commonsense notion of an independently, existing, external world comes into question. All we can know is the flow of impressions. Obviously, however, we have no impression of the connection between the world of experience and something outside of experience. Hume is not denying that there is an external world, he is just saying we cannot produce any evidence to justify this belief.

SELF: THE STREAM OF CONSCIOUSNESS

Concerning the existence of material substances, Hume agrees with Berkeley that Locke's idea of a material substance, a "something-I-know-not-what" that is never experienced, was not justified by his empirical method. But Berkeley's alternative view did not fare any better when subjected to the same empirical criteria. Hume claims that the idea of a mental substance (or of a mind or self) cannot be traced to experience either. Now this would seem very startling to Descartes, for it was the knowledge of his own self that Descartes thought to be the paradigm of certainty. Notice that a common expression in popular psychology is "I am trying to find myself." But can the self ever be found? What would it look like if we found it?

Hume maintains that when we introspect we only find some particular perception of one sort or another. If you focus on your experience right now, you may find puzzlement, tiredness, heat, light, anger, pleasure, or similar such perceptions. What you do not find is a self, Hume says. We experience a passing flow of psychological states, and that's it.* Since the self is supposed to be something that endures throughout your changing moods and states, this passing flow of momentary states cannot be the real you. Hume states his position very forthrightly. He says that a person is

> nothing but a bundle or collection of different perceptions, which succeed each other with an inconceivable rapidity, and are in a perpetual flux and movement. . . . The mind is a kind of theatre, where several perceptions successively make their appearance; pass, re-pass, glide away, and mingle in an infinite variety of postures and situations. There is properly no simplicity in it at one time, nor identity in different; whatever natural propension we may have to imagine that simplicity and identity. The comparison of the theatre must not mislead us. They are the successive perceptions only, that constitute the mind; nor have we the most distant notion of the place, where these scenes are represented, or of the materials, of which it is compos'd. (T 1.4.6)

*With this notion of the self, Hume would have appreciated modern novels such as James Joyce's *Ulysses*, where the narrator does not present a unified point of view but merely a stream of consciousness.

CAUSALITY: WILL THE SUN RISE TOMORROW?

We come now to what is the most famous and puzzling problem Hume left to the modern age. This is his conclusion concerning the notion of causality. It is important to recall that Newton's laws of physical motion had launched many of the ideas of the eighteenth century. Both scientists and philosophers tried to model their research after Newton's successful methods. The search for causes was the driving force behind the rise of science. Newton had shown the unifying and explanatory power of science by discovering one set of causal laws that could explain the motions of comets, tides, planets, falling apples, pendulums, and cannonballs. To undermine the notion that "every effect has a cause" would shatter the foundations of science. Even such an ordinary belief as "the sun will rise tomorrow" is built on this causal assumption, along with the conviction that the causal relationships of the past will remain constant. Yet Hume attacks these assumptions with arguments that are the philosophical equivalent of a wrecking ball.

By now you may have anticipated that Hume will ask for the impression from which we derive the concept of causality. Let's see how we use the notion of causality in everyday life. You see a flame touch your skin, and then you feel a painful sensation. You naturally conclude that the flame caused the pain. It is a lesson every child learns early in life. But according to Hume, all you have actually experienced are two impressions, the visual appearance of the flame and the feeling of pain. Where is the impression of causality?

The experience just mentioned can be broken down a little bit further, following Hume's analysis. What you actually experienced are three phenomena:

1. First, there is the relation of *contiguity*. The cause must make contact with its effect in some way. In our example, the flame touched the finger and then you felt pain. If someone struck a match 100 yards away and then your finger hurt, you would be unlikely to suppose

there was a causal relation between the two. If two events are a great distance apart, causality is assumed only if we suppose there is some series of connections that relate the two. Thus, you can flip a switch and lights can go on yards away when there are wires connecting the two.

2. There is also the relation of *priority in time*. Your finger hurt immediately *after* the flame touched it. If the two events were separated by two years or if your finger began hurting *before* the flame was lit, you would not suppose the two to be causally related.

3. But these elements alone are not enough to account for our idea of causality. To these we must add the notion of *constant conjunction*. If you scratched your head and thunder rolled, you would not take the two events to be significantly related. After all, you have observed thunder to occur when you did not scratch your head, and, furthermore, scratching does not usually produce thunder. You would consider the juxtaposition of the two events a coincidence, if you related them at all. With fire and pain, however, it is different. The two events are constantly joined. That is, we observe that pain consistently follows the touching of a flame.

So far, these three elements (contiguity, priority, and constant conjunction) are all grounded in observation. But to these kinds of observations, Hume says, we add the further idea of a *necessary connection*. This is exactly what we mean by causality. We do not consider there to be a necessary connection between scratching and thunder as we do between touching fire and pain. The idea of necessary connection is what is being assumed when we say that touching fire causes pain.

What is this element we call a "necessary connection"? It certainly is different from the necessary connection we find between the definition of a triangle and the sum of its angles being 180 degrees. The connection in the case of fire really is not "necessary" at all. Unlike the necessary relations between mathematical ideas, we could imagine (without contradiction) a world in which the

relationships between physical events were quite different. For example, it could be possible that fire produced a soothing coolness to the touch. If we had never experienced fire before, we would not know its effects. That is why scientists must have laboratories, but mathematicians do not.

Furthermore, Hume asks, is there an impression from which we can derive the idea of necessary connection? It appears not. "All events seem entirely loose and separate. One event follows another; but we never can observe any tie between them. They seem *conjoined*, but never *connected*" (EHU 7.2). Therefore, causality is merely an idea we add to our experience of events related by contiguity, priority, and constant conjunction.

We may try to shore up the crumbling foundations of our concept of causality by putting a distance between two kinds of cases that we have considered. On the one hand, we have "genuine" causal connections, such as the touching of fire followed by pain. On the other hand, we have pseudo-causal relationships, such as scratching followed by thunder. We might be inclined to say something like "Sure, sometimes people make false causal inferences. But in cases such as fire and pain, the experiences of millions of people assure us that there is a regular, inviolable pattern here."

However, as Hume would be quick to point out, you are making these judgments about the real causal relationships based on what has been true in the past. It has *always* been true that normal people get burned when they touch fire. But how do we know this will be true in the future? The argument you are using may be set out thus:

(1) In the past, every time people touched fire, they experienced pain.

(2) The laws of nature will continue to operate in the future just as they have in the past.

(3) Therefore, if I touch the fire now, I will experience pain.

Let us assume that the first premise is acceptable. Then the only question that remains before we accept statement 3 is the truth of the second premise. Do we know statement 2 to be true? This statement is called the "principle of induction" or the "principle of the uniformity of nature."* It is a statement whose truth we assume in every moment of our waking life. Its truth does not seem to be based on reason, for there is no logical contradiction in imagining that fire could change its properties and produce a cooling effect or that any other causal relationship could be different from the way it is. It seems, then, that the principle of induction would have to be a matter-of-fact claim based on experience. So maybe we could justify it with the following argument:

(1) In the past I have observed numerous cases where two events have been consistently conjoined together.

(2) It has always been the case at a future time that these same pairs of events continued to be conjoined.

(3) Therefore, the laws of nature will continue to operate in the future just as they have in the past.

However, this argument assumes what it is trying to prove. Statements 1 and 2 simply tell us that in the past, we have always found that the future was like the past. But this past experience cannot guarantee that this will always be true in the future, unless we once again simply assume the principle of induction.*

What Hume has shown is that we base all our ordinary judgments and scientific knowledge on a fundamental principle that is totally without rational foundation. It is important to note that Hume has not shown and does not claim to have shown that there *are* no cause–effect relations in the world. He merely claims that we cannot rationally *support* such a belief. In a letter to a correspondent he writes,

> I never asserted so absurd a Proposition as that any thing might arise without a Cause: I only maintain'd, that our Certainty of the Falsehood of that Proposition proceeded neither from Intuition nor Demonstration; but from another Source.[3]

*Induction is the form of reasoning we use when we argue from what is true of one set of facts, to what is true of further facts of the same kind.

If neither experience nor reason are the source of our belief in causality, where does this belief come from? Hume's answer is simple: custom or habit. In other words, it is a feature of our psychological makeup that we believe some things for which there is no evidence. In Pavlov's famous experiments with behavioral conditioning, the Russian physiologist rang a bell just before he fed his dogs. The two events were so constantly conjoined that the dogs began to salivate in anticipation when the bell was rung. Obviously, the sound of a bell has no necessary connection to the delivery of food. Nevertheless, the two were constantly conjoined in the dogs' experience. But can we say that the most constantly conjoined events in *our* experience are any different from that experiment? "Fire always produces pain," we say. "The sound of a bell always causes food to appear," the dogs reasoned.

There is a great deal of irony in Hume's conclusion that "custom, then, is the great guide of human life" (EHU 5.1). Philosophy began when critical thinkers began questioning the customary beliefs of their time and culture and tried to find rational foundations for their knowledge of the world. However, Hume says that with respect to causality, such rational foundations cannot be found and we are thrust back on our pre-philosophical customs and beliefs.

Ethics: The Rule of the Passions— The Slavery of Reason

Hume's most important contribution to philosophy was his theory of knowledge. Nevertheless, he also commands an important position in the history of ethics. In fact, he declared that the moral philosophy expressed in his *Enquiry Concerning the Principles of Morals* was "his best work."

When Hume approaches the topic of ethics, he finds that it also is a subject that has been handled badly. As he sees it, "moral philosophy seems hitherto to have received less improvement than either geometry or physics" (EHU 7.1). However, he is not using the reference to science here as simply a colorful metaphor for the need for progress in moral theory. Instead, he follows in the mainstream of Enlightenment thought, which tried to make the scientific method the universal key that would unlock the answers to all our problems. Indeed, Hume's *Treatise of Human Nature* bore the subtitle *An Attempt to Introduce the Experimental Method of Reasoning into Moral Subjects.*

As a result of his scientific pretensions, Hume's project tends to be descriptive rather than prescriptive. He attempts to describe how moral principles arise and function in human life rather than to moralize about what we ought to do. Hence, he speaks more like an anthropologist or psychologist than a moral reformer or an advocate. Rather than deriving our ethical terms from some transcendent code, he ties them to psychological observations. Because morality is natural to our species, he assumes that, generally, people share the same moral impulses. Much of the time, therefore, he makes his case by simply referring you to your own moral feelings.

Hume's theory of ethics follows consistently from all he has said about knowledge. Just as he showed that reason cannot provide us with knowledge about the world, so he argues that reason plays a very limited role in our moral life. Recall that he claims that all genuine objects of inquiry concern either the relations of ideas or matters of fact. But when we make a moral judgment such as "Lying is wrong," how are we to analyze it? Hume explores these two ways in which reason could be the source of morality.

One possibility is that moral judgments express the relations of ideas. If this is the case, then ethical truths would be as eternally true as mathematics and the mind could discover them apart from any experience. Hume describes those who hold this position as claiming that

> There are eternal fitnesses and unfitnesses of things, which are the same to every rational being that considers them; that the immutable measures of right and wrong impose an obligation, not only on human creatures, but also on the Deity himself: All these systems concur in the opinion, that morality, like truth, is discern'd merely by ideas, and by their juxta-position and comparison. (T 3.1.1)

But can reason do the job of moral decision making for us? Hume thinks not, for the purpose of morality is to influence and guide our actions. Reason, under Hume's analysis, is impotent to do so. Reason, he says, is used to discover truth or falsehood. It tells us what is logically necessary and what is contradictory. But when I face a moral dilemma, I am not concerned simply with what is *true*, but with what I *ought* to do. A dishonest accountant can add just as well as an honest one. Reason only guides her to the correct mathematical sums; it does not lead her to honestly report those figures. Without some sort of desire to be honest, she is not led to tell the truth. Hume concludes, then, that "reason is wholly inactive, and can never be the source of so active a principle as conscience, or a sense of morals" (T 3.1.1).

What about the second sort of inference that reason can make? Does reason produce moral principles by deriving them from matters of fact? Hume quickly disposes of this suggestion. He asks us to consider any action that we consider to be morally reprehensible, such as a willful murder. "Examine it in all lights, and see if you can find that matter of fact, or real existence, which you call *vice*" (T 3.1.1). In other words, we may find the coldness of the corpse, the redness of his blood, the smoking gun, and the eyewitness accounts of the assailant's actions. Our knowledge of these facts is based on sensory impressions. However, even if Sherlock Holmes examined the murder scene, he would never see, touch, taste, feel, or hear some quality called "moral wrongness."

Hume says that the sense of wrongness will elude us as long as we attend to the facts in the external scene, because vice or moral evil is not a matter-of-fact issue at all. "You never can find it, till you turn your reflection into your own breast, and find a sentiment of disapprobation [disapproval], which arises in you, towards this action" (T 3.1.1). Here, then, is the source of morality. It is not derived from either deductive or inductive operations of our reason. Instead, morality arises from sentiment, feelings, or the passions.

Feelings cannot be correct or incorrect in the sense that a mathematical sum can. We simply have feelings and they do not pretend to represent anything. Hence, they can neither conform to reason nor be contrary to it. Hume states this dramatically by saying, "'Tis not contrary to reason to prefer the destruction of the whole world to the scratching of my finger" (T 2.3.3). We may be appalled at someone who has such a preference, but that illustrates Hume's point. We are reacting with a moral sentiment of disgust at this person's priorities. "When you pronounce any action or character to be vicious, you mean nothing but that from the constitution of your nature you have a feeling or sentiment of blame from the contemplation of it" (T 3.1.1).

For some of Hume's contemporaries, God planted this moral sense within us to point us in the direction of moral purity and universal happiness. Hume, however, treats our moral sentiments as simply natural, psychological givens. The human community can survive because most of us seem to have the same kinds of moral feelings and these feelings tend to lead us to work for the good of the community.

Hume radically disagrees with many of the great traditions of ethics on this point. For example, Plato presented the passions as raging beasts that will devour us unless reason becomes their master. But Hume turns this around and says that the "beasts" should be the keepers of the zoo.

> Reason is, and ought only to be, the slave of the passions, and can never pretend to any other office than to serve and obey them. (T 2.3.3)

> Morality, therefore, is more properly felt than judg'd of. (T 3.1.2)

Even his own empiricist predecessor, John Locke, thought we could reason from experience to what we ought to do. On the contrary, says Hume, experience can only give us impressions. But impressions of colors, odors, or sounds are not moral values and do not produce a sense of oughtness. Therefore, our sense of moral approval or disapproval can only arise out of our feelings.

Once he has established feelings as the bedrock of morality, Hume must show how moral rules arise from this foundation. He argues that moral rules have two sources: social utility and sympathy. First, Hume observes that some moral rules do not seem to follow our natural inclinations. For example, Hume discusses such principles as justice, the obligation to keep promises, allegiance to one's government, and chastity. What is the basis of these moral principles? In each case, Hume shows that in the long run social utility or practical convenience motivates us to follow these rules. These moral concerns are *artificial virtues*. My immediate impulses alone could lead me to act unjustly, break my promises, disobey the law, or be wildly promiscuous when it was convenient to do so. Therefore, the principles that restrain me from these acts do not result from natural impulses but are artificial, human inventions that serve everyone's long-term interests. Generally, I am better off, for example, if everyone keeps promises and obeys the law.

In this way, my calculating self-interest leads me to follow rules that benefit society as a whole. However, Hume thinks there is a second source of morality besides social utility. He points out that even when "injustice is so distant from us, as no way to affect our interest, it still displeases us" (T 3.2.2). Why is this? His answer is that we experience the feeling of *sympathy* in such cases. "Thus self-interest is the original motive to the establishment of justice: but a sympathy with public interest is the source of the moral approbation [approval], which attends that virtue" (T 3.2.2). Hume points out that we will feel more sympathy with those who are close to us than with those who are very distant. Nevertheless, we generalize from such immediate feelings and approve or disapprove of actions that are remote from us in distance or time, even though their emotional impact on us is not very strong (T 3.3.1). Thus I can be disgusted by the actions of the depraved Emperor Nero who lived over a thousand years ago, even though I do not know him or his victims.

The emotion of sympathy can take the form of a general benevolence for all humanity. Hume says that "this sentiment can be no other than a feeling for the happiness of mankind, and a resentment of their misery; since these are the different ends which virtue and vice have a tendency to provide" (EPM, app. 1). For this reason, Hume is disenchanted with the thought of Epicurus, Hobbes, and even Locke. He claims they all imply that benevolence, no matter how sincere, is always an unconscious modification of self-love (EPM, app. 2). Hume the empiricist complains that human experience refutes any such psychological egoism. "To the most careless observer there appear to be such dispositions as benevolence and generosity; such affections as love, friendship, compassion, gratitude" (EPM, app. 2). Sympathetic benevolence is natural to our species. It is a principle that cannot be reduced to or explained by any other principle or motive; it is our moral bedrock. For this reason, Hume says that

> It is needless to push our researches so far as to ask, why we have humanity or a fellow-feeling with others. It is sufficient, that this is experienced to be a principle in human nature. We must stop somewhere in our examination of causes. (EPM 5.2)

Philosophy of Religion: Searching for What We Cannot Find

GOD'S EXISTENCE CANNOT BE PROVEN

Having found Hume to be skeptical about our belief in the external world, the self, and causality, it should not come as a surprise that he is also skeptical about religious beliefs. Hume argues that all attempts fail that base religious belief on either *a priori* or empirical arguments. His fullest treatment of the theistic proofs is in his *Dialogues Concerning Natural Religion*. This takes the form of a conversation between three people. Cleanthes is a theist who uses empirical arguments for God. Demea is a pious and orthodox believer who alternates between faith and rationalistic arguments to justify his beliefs. Finally, there is Philo the skeptic. Through the voice of Philo, Hume attacks traditional religious philosophy on two fronts. First, he tries to show that all the standard arguments for the existence of God fail. Second, he

maintains that even if such arguments point to the existence of a first cause, the nature of such a being will be a far cry from the God of traditional theism.*

We first consider Hume's refutations of the theistic proofs. In Part IX of the *Dialogues*, Philo argues that reason alone cannot establish anything concerning matters of fact. Since all existence claims are factual matters, *a priori* reasoning cannot help us here. Anything we can conceive of as existing (even God), we can also conceive of as not existing. "Consequently there is no being whose existence is demonstrable" (D 233). Or, to put it another way, "necessary existence" has no meaning. Necessity applies only to the relations between ideas. However, if we do insist on talking about a necessary being, why not suppose that the universe itself is necessary and eliminate the need for God?

In another passage, Hume quickly disposes of all empirical arguments that rest on the premise that "every event must have a cause." In his earlier books, Hume argued that causality is just a habit of mind based on the constant conjunction of particular events in our experience. In the present work, Philo points out that it is reasonable to suppose that a particular house had a builder because we have seen a constant conjunction between the existence of houses and builders creating them. However, since we know only one universe, it is difficult to reason about how universes do or do not come into existence (D 187). There is not a constant conjunction of many universes and their causes in our experience.

In his second line of attack, Philo goes along with the premise that "like effects prove like causes" and the conclusion that "there is a cause of the universe." However, he shows that this sort of theistic proof leads to five difficulties for the traditional theist. First, Hume points out that from a finite effect you cannot conclude an infinite cause (D 329). To use an illustration from the first *En-*

---

*Although there has been some debate over which character represents Hume's opinion, there are no good reasons to suppose it is anyone other than Philo.

quiry, if we have a scale in which 10 ounces is being lifted on one side by an unknown quantity on the other side, all we know is that the unknown weight is at least greater than 10 ounces. But it would go far beyond the evidence to conclude that it weighs 100 ounces (much less an infinite number of ounces) (EHU 11). Therefore, we cannot conclude that the cause of the finite world is unlimited, for it only needs to be as great as its effect.

Second, we cannot assume that the cause of the world is perfect. After all, we have no reason to suppose the effect (creation) is perfect. We could imagine many improvements we might make in the world (the absence of cancer cells and tornados, for example). Furthermore, with no other universe to compare it to, we have no standard by which to evaluate the goodness of ours.

Third, even if we suppose the world is as good as could be, this still does not provide evidence for the excellence of its designer. After all (to use a contemporary example), the invention of our sleek, modern jets was preceded by many stupid attempts of inventors tying boards to their arms and trying to fly. As Hume puts it,

> Many worlds might have been botched and bungled, throughout an eternity, ere this system was struck out: Much labour lost: Many fruitless trials made: And a slow, but continued improvement carried on during infinite ages in the art of world-making. (D 207)

Fourth, what evidence do we have that there is only one God? It takes many workers to construct a ship. If we are going to use the analogy of human contrivances, polytheism might be the best explanation for something as great as the universe. Fifth, if we are using an anthropomorphic analogy from human craftsmen to the divine artisan, why not go all the way and suppose that the architect of the physical world is also physical?

In further passages, Philo questions the whole mechanistic metaphor that had been popular since the beginning of Newtonian science. Philo points out that "The world plainly resembles more an animal or a vegetable, than it does a watch or a knitting-loom" (D 218). Thus, it might have emerged through some sort of organic, evolutionary process. In a prophetic passage that looked forward to Darwin's theory of natural selection, Philo dismisses the appeal to design in nature. Quite simply, he says that if an animal were not adjusted to its environment it would not survive. Thus, we should not be surprised that those animals that have survived are so marvelously adopted to their environment.

HUME'S ATTITUDE TOWARD RELIGION

Hume was raised in the Calvinist tradition, but he abandoned personal religion at an early age. Consequently, Hume approached religion as simply a human phenomenon that he studied from the viewpoint of an outsider. A few weeks before Hume's death, when he was visibly ill, a gentleman by the name of James Boswell visited him. Boswell would later be known for his biography of the famous literary figure, Samuel Johnson. As Hume lay on his deathbed, Boswell asked him if he believed in life after death. According to Boswell, Hume replied that "it was possible that a piece of coal put upon the fire would not burn."[4] In other words, Hume was pointing out that it is logically possible for a piece of coal not to burn, but there is no basis for expecting this to happen. Comparing this possible but unbelievable event to immortality, Hume went on to say that "it was a most unreasonable fancy that we should exist for ever."

In his attack on our belief in causality, Hume stated that we live in a world in which "all events seem entirely loose and separate." If this is the case, then anything is possible. It is possible that atheism is correct and nothing out there in the universe is either intelligent or benevolent. However, it is also possible that the most crude and superstitious belief in God is true. Neither reason nor experience can definitively rule out either possibility. Thus, it is important to understand that Hume is not an atheist. He has attacked the soundness of the typical arguments used to establish God's existence. However, showing that an argument fails to support its conclusion does not prove the conclusion is false. Thus, Hume does not claim to have established the conclusion that God does not exist.

The proper label for Hume's position on religion is **agnosticism**. The agnostic denies that we have adequate evidence either for or against God's existence. The most rational approach, the agnostic claims, is to suspend judgment on the issue of God while keeping your mind open. However, as his conversation with Boswell indicated, just because something is possible does not give us total license to believe what we wish. In his famous essay against belief in miracles, Hume states that "a wise man . . . proportions his belief to the evidence" (EHU 10.1). In matters of religion, therefore, Hume seems to suggest that the burden of proof rests on the believer, because theism is making an extraordinary claim that goes far beyond what we find in experience.

Even though Hume's criticisms undermine the attempts to rationally demonstrate the God of traditional religion, he does think we can establish one conclusion on the basis of philosophical theology: "That the cause or causes of order in the universe probably bear some remote analogy to human intelligence" (D 281). However, this conclusion is too ambiguous and obscure to make the case for either theism or atheism. Hume finds it provokes a sense of melancholy because it shows that our best reasoning only provides a dim light on life's important questions.

We cannot leave Hume's philosophy of religion without quoting a passage that never ceases to be a source of puzzlement to commentators. At the end of his book, Hume says,

> A person, seasoned with a just sense of the imperfections of natural reason, will fly to revealed truth with the greatest of avidity: While the haughty dogmatist, persuaded that he can erect a complete system of theology by the mere help of philosophy, disdains any further aid and rejects this adventitious instructor. To be a philosophical Sceptic is, in a man of letters, the first and most essential step towards being a sound, believing Christian. (D 282)

There are at least two ways of interpreting this passage. First, Hume could be saying that, although he personally was not a man of faith, his skepticism actually made room for faith by showing the limited powers of reason. Or Hume could be speaking ironically and cynically, and saying that if you want to be a Christian then you had better be a skeptic because knowledge will make it impossible to believe what your faith requires you to believe.

Evaluation and Significance

After surveying the wreckage of our philosophical certitudes and commonsense beliefs with the treadmarks of Hume's philosophical bulldozer on them, it is ironic to recall his original task. This was to "propose a complete system of the sciences, built on a foundation almost entirely new, and the only one upon which they can stand with any security" (T, intro.). Even Hume himself was overwhelmed by what he had done:

> The intense view of these manifold contradictions and imperfections in human reason has so wrought upon me, and heated my brain, that I am ready to reject all belief and reasoning, and can look upon no opinion even as more probable or likely than another. Where am I, or what? From what causes do I turn? . . . I am confounded with all these questions, and begin to fancy myself in the most deplorable condition imaginable, inviron'd with the deepest darkness, and utterly depriv'd of the use of every member and faculty. (T 1.4.7)

If Hume believes that he has demolished all the foundations of our knowledge claims, how does he go on living? For Hume, the answer is simple and can be distilled into two propositions:

1. Reason cannot demonstrate even our most fundamental beliefs.

2. *But* there is no need to rationally demonstrate our fundamental beliefs for them to be practically useful.

By itself, reason leaves us with nothing but abstractions and convinces us it is no more rational to believe fire will feel hot than to believe it will feel cold. However, what saves us from skepticism, and returns us to life is the combination of nature itself, our gut-level instincts, the powerful demands of practical necessity, and even the distractions of our nonphilosophical life:

Most fortunately it happens, that since reason is incapable of dispelling these clouds, nature herself suffices to that purpose, and cures me of this philosophical melancholy and delirium. . . . I dine, I play a game of backgammon, I converse, and am merry with my friends; and when after three or four hours' amusement, I wou'd return to these speculations, they appear so cold, and strain'd, and ridiculous, that I cannot find in my heart to enter into them any farther. (T 1.4.7)

When reason leaves us paralyzed with doubt, nature takes over and allows us to go on with life. "Nature will always maintain her rights, and prevail in the end over any abstract reasoning whatsoever" (EHU 5.1). Reason may doubt the existence of the external world, but Hume will still stoke his stove when he is cold. Reason may doubt that there are causes and effects, but Hume will avoid touching the fire and will drink water when he is thirsty.

Hume, therefore, says that a total skepticism is impossible. In its place, he recommends a "mitigated scepticism." This does not affect how we live our daily lives, but it will affect our philosophical speculations, for it will serve as a therapeutic antidote to the pretensions of human reason. For the philosophical dogmatists, it "would naturally inspire them with more modesty and reserve, and diminish their fond opinion of themselves and their prejudice against antagonists" (EHU 12.3). In the final analysis, Hume is skeptical even of his skepticism. "A true sceptic will be diffident [uncertain] of his philosophical doubts, as well as of his philosophical conviction" (T 1.4.7).

As is typical in the history of thought, a giant pendulum swing has taken place in the period from Descartes to Hume. The first movement came when Descartes claimed that knowledge requires total certainty and that he had attained it. Although Locke lowered the goals of epistemology, he still thought that sense experience could give us as much certainty as is practically necessary. This age had an unwavering confidence in the power of reason and experience to build a firm foundation for scientific, ethical, and religious knowledge. However, Hume's critical questioning made the foundation look more like shifting sand than solid rock. Hume began by assuming Descartes's all-or-nothing attitude toward knowledge. However, once he showed that reason cannot give us total certainty about anything in the world, Hume concluded that we have no knowledge at all.

With Hume, the philosophical pendulum swung from rational certainty to skepticism.* However, skepticism never remains unchallenged for long. If we can learn anything from the past (a premise that Hume challenged), then in the next chapter we should expect another pendulum swing that will move philosophy back toward claims of greater certainty and knowledge.

Questions for Understanding

1. What task did Hume hope to accomplish?

2. What is the distinction Hume makes between impressions and ideas?

3. What are the three ways in which one idea becomes associated with another idea?

4. What are the two kinds of reasoning and how do they differ? Provide several examples of your own to illustrate each kind of reasoning.

5. Why is Hume skeptical about the notions of substance, self, and causality?

6. What are the four elements that go into our causal judgments? Which one is not based on experience? How does this affect our certainty concerning causal judgments?

7. What does Hume mean when he says reason is the slave of the passions?

8. What is the basis of our moral rules, according to Hume?

9. Why does Hume think that reason alone cannot prove God's existence?

10. What are the various arguments Hume uses to refute those who claim that God must exist because the world must have had a cause?

*Think back over the history of philosophy to other periods where skeptical philosophies arose. To what degree were they reactions to their predecessor's claims to have achieved certainty? Notice also, that skepticism always motivates new directions in epistemology in the attempt to reclaim confidence in human knowledge again.

11. Why is Hume considered to be an agnostic rather than an atheist?

12. How would Hume respond to the following criticism? "Since you believe that there is practically nothing we can believe with certainty, on what basis do you go on living?"

Questions for Reflection

1. Do you agree with Hume that all of our ideas can be traced back to sensory impressions?

2. Is Hume correct in maintaining that all reasoning concerns either relations of ideas or matters of fact? What does he think are the limitations of each type of reasoning? What are the implications of Hume's position for philosophy?

3. Imagine that Descartes engaged Hume in a philosophical debate. How might Descartes try to refute Hume's position and how would Hume respond?

4. Both Locke and Hume begin with empiricism, but Hume's conclusions are much more skeptical and radical than Locke's. At what points do their empiricist philosophies diverge?

5. Which of the following two statements do you think is more correct? (a) Locke's empiricism is more convincing because it is rooted in common sense. (b) Hume's empiricism is more convincing because it is more consistent and rigorous.

6. Hume believes that when we introspect we never experience such a thing as the "self." Instead, we find merely a passing flow of psychological states. Do you agree with this? What would Descartes say? If you accepted Hume's skeptical view of the self, what practical difference would it make to your life?

Notes

1. Hume's own comments about his life may be found in *My Own Life* reprinted in Ernest C. Mossner, *The Life of David Hume*, 2d ed. (Oxford, England: Oxford University Press, 1980), 611–615.

2. References to Hume's works are as follows:

   D   *Hume's Dialogues Concerning Natural Religion*, ed. Norman Kemp Smith (Oxford, England: Clarendon Press, 1935). The numbers in the reference refer to the pages of this edition.

   EHU *Enquiry Concerning the Human Understanding.* The numbers in the reference refer to the section and part.

   EPM *Enquiry Concerning the Principles of Morals.* The reference numbers follow the same format as those for EHU.

   T   *A Treatise of Human Nature.* The numbers in the reference refer to the book, part, and section numbers, respectively.

3. David Hume, *The Letters of David Hume*, vol. 1, ed. J. Y. T. Greig (Oxford, England: Clarendon Press, 1932), 187.

4. From "An Account of My Last Interview with David Hume, Esq." in *Private Papers of James Boswell*, vol. 12, ed. Geoffrey Scott and Frederick A. Pottle, reprinted in *Hume's Dialogues Concerning Natural Religion*, ed. Norman Kemp Smith, 98.

22

Immanuel Kant: Finding the Powers and the Limits of the Mind

Kant's Life: A Methodical Man with Revolutionary Thoughts

Immanuel Kant was born in Königsberg, East Prussia, on April 22, 1724. His parents were Pietists, a sect of Protestants who lived severe, puritanical lives and emphasized faith and religious feelings over reason and theological doctrines. Although Kant's later religious thought was hardly orthodox, he was always sensitive to the longings of the heart that cannot be met by the cold dictates of theoretical reason. He went to school at the University of Königsberg and later ended up becoming a professor there himself. Virtually no area of knowledge remained untouched by Kant, for he lectured on metaphysics, logic, ethics, aesthetics, and philosophical theology, as well as mathematics, physics, geography, and anthropology. In addition to his groundbreaking work in philosophy, he also made significant contributions in some of the sciences. Despite the fact that Kant was very rigid and strict in his personal lifestyle, his contemporaries describe his lectures as humorous, entertaining, and even playful.

Although his intellectual stature was imposing, his physical size was diminutive. Kant stood little more than five feet in height and had trouble making clothes fit his frail, thin frame and sunken chest. Nevertheless, he enjoyed the company of women and considered proposing several times, but his concern over finances prevented him from ever making a commitment. By most people's standards, he lived a very limited existence. He was well acquainted with geography and current events, yet he never traveled more than sixty miles from the place of his birth. Although he helped out his family members financially, he never felt very close to his sisters and brother. He did have a close circle of friends, but Kant gradually became more of a recluse as he grew older. In 1797 he retired from public lecturing and, after a period of illness, died on February 12, 1804.

Kant's life was rather uneventful, but the same could not be said of his ideas. The term "revolution" is frequently used in reference to Immanuel Kant's philosophy. However, this is not because of any effect he had on the prevailing political system, but because of the radical upheaval he caused within the established intellectual tradition. From this little, methodical man flowed enormous and powerful ideas. The impact of the Kantian revolution was so significant that after his death the history of modern philosophy would be forevermore divided into the "pre-Kantian" and the "post-Kantian" periods. His orderly and disciplined life is described for us in a charming portrait by the poet Heinrich Heine:

> The history of the life of Immanuel Kant is hard to write, inasmuch as he had neither life nor history, for he lived a mechanically ordered and abstract old bachelor life in a quiet retired street in Königsberg, an old town on the northeast border of Germany. I do not believe that the great clock of the cathedral there did its daily work more dispassionately and regularly than its compatriot Immanuel Kant. Rising, coffee drinking, writing, reading college lectures, eating, walking, all had their fixed time, and the neighbors knew that it was exactly half past three when Immanuel Kant in his grey coat, with his bamboo cane in his hand, left his house door and went to the Lime tree avenue, which is still called, in memory of him, the Philosopher's Walk. . . . Strange contrast between the external life of the man and his destroying, world-crushing thought! In very truth, if the citizens of Königsberg had dreamed of the real meaning of his thought, they would have experienced at his sight a greater horror than they would on beholding an executioner who only kills men. But the good people saw nothing in him but a professor of philosophy, and when he at the regular hour passed by, they greeted him as a friend, and regulated their watches by him.[1]

Task: Avoiding Dogmatism and Skepticism

As a student, Kant was raised in the tradition of Leibnizian rationalism. Its chief spokesman was Christian Wolff (1679–1754), a somewhat mediocre systematizer of Leibniz's thought. The spirit of this German rationalism is captured in the smug and extravagant title of one of Wolff's works, *Reasonable Thoughts on God, the World, the Soul of Man, and All Things in General*. Although Kant was immersed in this system of philosophy,

when he was in the middle of his career he read David Hume's empiricist arguments. This revelatory experience, in Kant's own words, awakened him from his "dogmatic slumber."[2] He became disillusioned with the philosophy of his youth and referred to it as "dogmatic rationalism" because its proponents failed to critically assess the powers of human reason before they launched into their grandiose speculations. Thereafter, his lifelong work was an attempt to resolve the tensions between the rationalism of his youth and the insights of the empiricists.

The key assumption that provided the starting point for all of Kant's thought was the unwavering conviction that we *do* have knowledge, which is to be found in mathematics and Newtonian physics. Kant never doubted that the fundamental propositions of this knowledge were universal and necessary and that no future discoveries would ever shake our conviction of their truth.

Three tasks emerged from this initial conviction. First, there was a need to get clear on the foundations of scientific knowledge. Kant agreed with the rationalists that anything that deserves to be called *knowledge* must be universal, necessary, and certain. The rationalists, however, had very little use for perception, which Kant knew was essential to the doing of science. Kant agreed with Hume that logical propositions alone do not give us knowledge of the world of experience but only of the relations of our own ideas. Accordingly, the rationalists' account could not be the whole story. Consequently, he agreed with the empiricists that all knowledge begins with experience.

But empiricism, too, had its drawbacks. As Hume had pointed out, experience alone cannot give us the universal, necessary, and certain knowledge Kant required. This led Hume to conclude that the connections between the items of experience are based on nothing more than psychological habits. Thus, since we are confined within the world of our own, subjective experience, Hume could find no grounds for supposing that the contents of our minds conform to the external world.

Although Kant had learned from Hume, he was repelled by Humean skepticism. A theory of knowledge, such as Hume's empiricism, that undermined the validity of scientific knowledge must be deeply flawed. Consequently, Kant's first task was to develop a new understanding of knowledge that would undergird science and steer between the dogmatism of the rationalists and the skepticism of the empiricists while retaining the insights of each.

Kant's second task was to resolve the tensions between mechanistic science on the one hand, and religion, morality, and human freedom on the other. Where in the world of particles in motion is there a place for God? If scientific knowledge only gives us information about physical facts, how do we arrive at values and moral norms? If the world presented by science is thoroughly mechanistic and deterministic, will we have to abandon our view of persons as free, responsible moral agents? To find a satisfactory answer to these questions Kant said that he had to "deny knowledge, in order to make room for faith" (CPR Bxxx).[3] By this he meant that the domain of scientific knowledge was limited and that our deepest human concerns must be based on something other than empirical data.

His third task was to address the crisis of metaphysics. Traditional metaphysics and its sister, theology, had proceeded on the assumption that reason could tell us about realities that transcend experience. But the results of metaphysical speculation had been disappointing to Kant. There was no agreement or progress in metaphysics such as there was in the sciences. Metaphysics, according to Kant, was "a dark ocean without coasts and without lighthouses."[4] After reading Hume, Kant knew that he could not return to the dogmatic metaphysics of Leibniz and Wolff. However, while Hume wanted to burn all books on metaphysics, Kant thought that metaphysical concerns were unavoidable and expressed something deep and significant in the human spirit. According to Kant, it is no more possible to give up metaphysics just because some of it is nonsense than it would be to stop breathing just because some air is impure.[5] His third task, therefore, was to explain why traditional metaphysics had failed and then to develop a more humble and chastened version of it.

We could take as the motto of Kant's philosophy his statement that "two things fill the mind with ever new and increasing admiration and awe . . . *the starry heavens above me and the moral law within me.*"[6] The study of the starry heavens is the province of mathematics and Newtonian physics, which Kant accepted without question. But equally without question is the fact that we feel not only the force of physical laws but also that of the moral law. How to reconcile these two dimensions of human experience within a revised understanding of metaphysics was one of Kant's major concerns.

Theory of Knowledge: The Mind Makes Experience Possible

CRITICAL PHILOSOPHY

In opposition to the "dogmatic philosophy" that preceded him, Kant referred to his own thought as "critical philosophy." Accordingly, his major work took the form of three critiques. His most important work, dealing with epistemology and metaphysics, was the *Critique of Pure Reason*. By calling his approach a "critical philosophy," Kant was not calling for a mean-spirited, negative attitude in philosophy that rejects everything. On the contrary, the word *critique* comes from a Greek word that means "to sort" or "to sift out." Thus, Kant's goal was to set out the legitimate claims of reason and filter out all groundless claims.

KANT'S COPERNICAN REVOLUTION

In the first line of the *Critique of Pure Reason*, Kant states, "There can be no doubt that all our knowledge begins with experience." On this issue there is no question that Kant casts his lot with the empiricists. But he was well aware that lurking in the empiricists' rich world of colors, sights, and sounds was the specter of Humean skepticism. To avoid this he adds, "But though all our knowledge begins with experience, it does not follow that it all arises out of experience," thus indicating that there was still a need for some of the rationalists' assumptions.

Kant received a clue to the nature of knowledge from the example of Copernicus's great insight. Copernicus rejected the theory that the sun revolves around the earth because it did not adequately account for the data. Accordingly, he proposed that we switch the center of focus and see if it would make more sense to suppose that the earth revolves around the sun. Similarly, Kant proposes a "Copernican revolution" in epistemology. The empiricists thought that the mind is passive when confronting the world and simply records impressions. In this picture, *knowledge conforms to its objects*. But can we know that it does? Hume pointed out that we can never get outside the world of our experience to compare its contents with the outside world. To avoid Hume's skepticism, Kant (like Copernicus) reverses this commonsense picture. He asks us to consider the possibility that *objects conform to our knowledge* (CPR Bxvi). In other words, for sense data to be experienced as objects by us, the mind must impose a certain rational structure on them.

It is important to get clear on what Kant is and is not saying here. He is not saying that the mind brings reality into existence out of nothing. But he is saying that the way in which reality *appears* to us (the only reality that we can know) depends on the contribution of both the senses and the intellect, or mind. The mind imposes its own form on the material of experience, and through this activity we have objects to be known. To use an analogy, we can imagine a person with extremely bad eyesight, for whom the whole world appears to be a blur of indistinguishable shapes and colors. There are no identifiable objects in his visual field. When he puts on his glasses, however, everything comes into focus, and he now sees a world of objects. In this example, the person's visual experience is a product of both the sensory data and the way in which the lenses process this input.

Although we may distinguish two elements in this experience (receiving the data and the work of the lenses), it is not really a two-step process. The person opens his eyes, peers through the glasses, and instantly sees objects before him. According to Kant, a similar event occurs in all experience.

When we become aware of objects, the mind (like the glasses) has already done its work, and what we experience is sensory input that has been processed by the mind. Hence, it is not a conscious process that we voluntarily control. Nevertheless, it is an activity the mind is performing all the time.

The analogy of the glasses has some shortcomings. The objects that the eyeglasses present to us already have their own, independent structure in the external world. The glasses merely enable us to see these objects. According to Kant, however, the fact that collections of sense data are designated as "objects" is *entirely* a result of the order that the mind imposes on sensation.

To use another analogy to get at Kant's notion of how the mind forms the content of experience, think of the mind as similar to a cookie press. Into the tube of the cookie press goes some dough, which is pressed through a certain form (such as a star). This process gives the resulting cookies the starlike form they have. Without content, the cookie press would be useless, but without some form being imposed on the clump of dough, we would not have cookies, but an unstructured blob. If we are ignorant of what kind of dough goes into the press, then we cannot predict the color, the taste, or the texture of the cookies that come out. Nevertheless, we can know that the cookies will have whatever form is used to create them.

The point of these analogies is that Kant believes our experience is a product of both what comes from the external world (the mind does not create this) and the particular structure that the mind imposes on it. We can't jump outside of our experience to compare reality as it appears to us with reality as it exists in itself before the mind processes it. However, if all human minds are structured in the same way, then within the bounds of human experience, it is possible to have knowledge that is universal and objective.

THE VARIETIES OF JUDGMENTS

Knowledge always appears in the form of judgments in which something is affirmed or denied. Therefore, to get clear about knowledge, we must

Giraudon/Art Resource, NY

Paul Signac, The Dining Room. *The nineteenth-century French neo-impressionist Paul Signac created paintings with dabs of paint in a style called pointillism. When examined in detail, the dining room scene is revealed to be a collection of different colored dots. Our mind organizes the dots into meaningful patterns of forms and objects and interprets the two-dimensional canvas as three-dimensional space. According to Kant, all experience is a matter of the mind imposing its structure on the world by organizing bare sense data into meaninful objects within a temporal and spatial matrix.*

examine the kinds of judgments that we make. Kant begins this project by presenting the two categories of judgments: analytic and synthetic. **Analytic judgments** are based on the principle of contradiction. For example, "all bachelors are unmarried" is a true analytic judgment because the contradiction of this statement is necessarily false. We can confirm the truth of this judgment not by going out and gathering facts but merely by *analyzing* the meaning of the terms. The predicate "unmarried" is already contained within the subject "bachelors." Furthermore, because the truth of this judgment is independent of any particular facts, it does not give us any new knowledge about the world. **Synthetic judgments**, however, do

give us new information about the world. For example, "All the bachelors in this class are six feet tall" is a synthetic judgment. Judgments of this sort *synthesize* or bring together the subject ("bachelors in this class") with the predicate ("six feet tall"). It would not be a logical contradiction to deny this statement about bachelors.

In addition to these two kinds of judgments, there are two kinds of knowledge: *a priori* and *a posteriori*. **A priori** knowledge is knowledge that can be obtained independently of experience. Clearly, all analytic judgments are cases of *a priori* knowledge. To know "all bachelors are unmarried" I do not need any empirical data. **A posteriori knowledge**, in contrast, is knowledge obtained from experience. "All the bachelors in this class are six feet tall" cannot be known to be true apart from experience. Hence, it is an example of *a posteriori* knowledge.

These classifications give us four kinds of judgments. It is helpful to list each of them, along with its basis and some examples.

1. **Analytic *a priori*.** *Basis:* the principle of contradiction. *Examples:* "All bodies are extended," "Every parent has a child." By analyzing the terms "body" or "parent," we can know the truth of these judgments.

2. **Analytic *a posteriori*.** There are no such judgments. If a judgment were analytic, it would not be one that was based on experience.

3. **Synthetic *a posteriori*.** *Basis:* experience. *Examples:* most of our judgments from the particular observations of ordinary experience to the general laws of science would fall here, such as "This ball is falling" and "All falling objects accelerate at a rate of thirty-two feet per second squared."

Thus far, Hume would agree with Kant's conclusions. However, the controversy arises with the last (fourth) category:

4. **Synthetic *a priori*** judgments.

Are any such judgments possible? In other words, can we find some judgments that are synthetic (give us knowledge about the world) and at the same time *a priori* (do not require experience to confirm them)? Kant claims there *are* such judgments. For example, we are confident that "all events have a cause." Notice that we don't say that *most* events or *many* events, but that *all* events have this property. However, on the basis of a collection of particular experiences we could not arrive at the absolute conviction that this must be true of *all* events. We bring this information to our experience of the world rather than deriving it from experience. For this reason it is *a priori* knowledge. Unlike analytic judgments, however, it does give us information about the world. Hence, Kant maintains that the notion of "cause" is not packed into the notion of "event," as is the case with "un-

married" and "bachelor." For this reason the statement of universal causality is an example of synthetic knowledge.*

If Kant is correct about synthetic *a priori* judgments, then there is a kind of knowledge that gives us more than we get from analyzing concepts and more than we get from collecting sense impressions. Given the fact that we do make such judgments, the question Kant is concerned with is, How are these unique sorts of judgments possible? How are synthetic *a priori* judgments possible in mathematics? How are synthetic *a priori* judgments possible in physics? Are synthetic *a priori* judgments possible in metaphysics and morality at all?

THE TRANSCENDENTAL METHOD

Since Kant is looking for the grounds of our universal and necessary knowledge about the world, the method of the empiricists will be of no use. They tried to argue from particular facts to generalizations based on those facts. However, because our experience is always limited, empirical information will always be inconclusive. Any future experience can always contradict our most cherished beliefs. To carry out his project, Kant uses what he calls the **transcendental method**. This method proceeds from the nature of experience in general to the necessary conditions of its possibility. Hence, the transcendental structures of experience are those formal features that are not limited to any particular experience but are the universal and necessary features of all experi-

---

*Kant also uses mathematical judgments as examples of synthetic *a priori* knowledge. I can know prior to experience that "7 + 5 = 12" is a universal and necessary truth. Yet, Kant claims, by analyzing the concept of "7" and the concept of "5" and the concept of their union, I do not find that they explicitly contain the concept of "12." Hence, in addition to being *a priori* knowledge it is also a synthetic judgment. Similarly, the propositions of pure geometry such as "a straight line is the shortest distance between two points" qualify as synthetic *a priori* knowledge. The concept of "straight" in itself refers only to the quality of the line and does not contain quantitative notions such as "shortest." Yet we know without experimenting that this statement will necessarily always be true.

ence.* If it is impossible to imagine an experience without a certain structural feature, then that is evidence that the feature is a necessary condition of the experience. To preview the following sections, Kant argues that if we can make spatial judgments about our experience, then a transcendental condition of this is that we have minds that structure experience spatially. Similarly, if we can make causal judgments, it must be because we have minds capable of organizing experience in terms of a causal order.

SPACE AND TIME: THE FORMS OF SENSE PERCEPTION

Scientific knowledge deals with objects that are in space and time. Therefore, to understand how we are able to know the world it is important to understand how we are able to experience things spatially and temporally. Kant's thesis is that space and time are not mysterious sorts of "things" within experience but are fundamental frames of reference in terms of which objects appear to us. Kant calls them the "forms of intuition."†

To understand what Kant is getting at, try this thought experiment. One by one, imaginatively subtract all the objects from the world until nothing is left but empty space without objects. This seems to be conceivable. Now try to imagine a world in which there are objects but no space. For example, think what it would be like to experience a box that didn't have three dimensions. It can't be done. Why not? The reason is that spatial qualities are different from the qualities and objects of sensation. This is because space is one of the mind's forms of arranging sensations but it is not itself a sensation. We don't experience

space, but we experience objects that are spatially structured in a particular way. Kant calls space the form of outer sense because it structures the experience of objects external to us.

A similar analysis is carried out with respect to time. Time, like space, is not a thing existing in itself out there in the world. Instead, it is a form in which objects appear to us. Kant calls time the "form of inner sense" because mental states necessarily occur to us in a temporal succession. Kant points out that traditional notions of God (such as we find in Augustine or Aquinas) assert that God is above time. If this is the case, then the temporal sequence of past, present, and future events that appear to us are simultaneously experienced by God in one, unified vision. This classical tradition in theology underscores Kant's point that time cannot be a feature of reality itself (since God doesn't experience it) but is merely a condition of the human experience of reality.

Kant's theory of space and time was proposed in order to explain how mathematics could give us synthetic *a priori* knowledge. Geometry, for example, is the science of the properties of space. Less plausibly, Kant says arithmetic is a way of processing numbers, hence it involves temporality. By tying mathematics to space and time *and* by showing that the latter are the universal and necessary structures of the way in which we experience nature, Kant could preserve the *a priori* nature of mathematics while showing that it does give us information about the world of experience that science studies.

THE CATEGORIES OF THE UNDERSTANDING

For a complete account of knowledge, Kant says we must realize that

> There are two stems of human knowledge, namely, sensibility *and* understanding, *which perhaps spring from a common, but to us unknown, root. Through the former, objects are given to us, through the latter, they are thought.* (CPR A15, B29)

Thus far he has explained the aspect of human knowledge that he calls "sensibility" in his explanation of how sense perception is structured by the

---

*The term "transcendental" should not be confused with "transcendent." The transcendent is that which is beyond all possible experience (which, in Kant's view, would make it something we could never know).

†"Intuition" here is not to be confused with our use of the term to refer to a special gift of insight. Instead, **intuition** means "the object of the mind's direct awareness." For example, to experience the redness of a rose is to have a sensation or a sensory intuition. According to Kant, all human intuition is limited to sensory awareness.

forms of intuition of space and time. Sensations and the forms of intuition alone, however, do not explain how we are able to know the objects of ordinary experience such as dogs, chairs, and bananas. If the mechanism of perception constituted the whole of our cognitive apparatus, we would have only spatially and temporally located sensations (bits of colors, sounds, smells, tastes, textures) but not knowledge. To have full-blown knowledge, there needs to be a further set of organizing principles. These principles are found in the faculty of the understanding. Just as the cookie is the product of a certain content (the dough) being processed by a form (the cookie press), so knowledge is the product of sensibility and understanding working together:

> To neither of these powers may a preference be given over the other. Without sensibility no object would be given to us, without understanding no object would be thought. Thoughts without content are empty, intuitions without concepts are blind. . . . The understanding can intuit nothing, the senses can think nothing. Only through their union can knowledge arise. (CPR A51, B75)

Knowledge is more than sense data—it takes the form of judgments that can be expressed in propositions. For example, perceiving someone striking a gong followed by the experience of a sound is not the same as knowing that "striking the gong caused the sound." The two experiences must be connected in thought in a certain way. The understanding actively organizes experience by means of pure concepts or categories of the understanding. They are called *pure* concepts because they are *a priori* and are not derived from experience.

To uncover the categories that the mind uses, Kant first catalogues the kinds of judgments we make. In doing this, he takes his cue from Aristotelian logic, which he thought was the final word in logic. Skipping over the details, Kant finds that there are twelve kinds of judgments. From the different types of judgments that we make about experience, Kant thinks we can deduce the concepts or categories necessary to make those judgments. Hence, there are twelve *a priori*

concepts or categories that constitute the general nature of any possible object but that are not derived from experience. In other words, they represent the way the mind structures experience. The twelve categories are broken down into groups of three, which fall under four headings: (1) *quantity* (unity, plurality, totality), (2) *quality* (reality, negation, limitation), (3) *relation* (substance, causality, community or reciprocity), and (4) *modality* (possibility–impossibility, existence–nonexistence, necessity–contingency). It would be too lengthy to discuss all these, so we will focus on the categories of substance and causality, because these are the ones that are crucial to Hume's skepticism.

ANSWERING HUME'S SKEPTICISM

According to Hume, we can never have *a priori* knowledge of the world of experience because we can never know that it is anything more than a flow of unconnected impressions in which anything is possible and nothing is logically necessary. As a matter of fact, experience does appear this way in dreams where it is possible for clocks to melt and change into flowers that then explode in a burst of color. In dreams anything can happen, and any experience can be followed by any other experience. However, we label these experiences as "subjective" because we can contrast them with the realm of objective experiences. For example, the successive appearances of the clock that we see on our dresser are the same from moment to moment. For this reason we say, "There is a clock," and not simply "I am experiencing sensory images that have the appearance of a clock." According to Kant, when sensations appear together in more or less consistent and permanent groups and when they are similar to what is experienced by others, we experience these collections of sensations as *objects* within the objective world.

We are able to form empirical concepts such as "frog," "star," or "apple" by means of the category of *substance*. By means of this category, for example, we organize the sensations of redness, roundness, sweetness, and crunchiness into the unity we call "apple." Kant agrees with Hume that substance is not an empirical category acquired through sensation. At the same time, it is not some metaphysical reality beneath the appearances as Descartes and Locke thought. Instead, substance is a logical category by means of which the mind picks out various groups of sensations from the flow of experience and unifies them into meaningful units that we identify as objects. We can sometimes be mistaken in identifying particular complexes of sensations, but we will always organize experience in terms of substances.

Kant applies a similar analysis to the category of *causality*. Hume believed that the notion of causality was purely a subjective addition to what is experienced. For him, all experience consists of a succession of unrelated impressions. Once again, this *does* describe certain types of experience. For example, imagine that you coughed and a second later lightning flashed in the sky. You would characterize this as simply an accidental succession of one event after another. In contrast, we do find instances of a rule-ordered succession of events. You often see lightning and then hear a thunderclap or get static on your radio. Although you do not connect the cough and the lightning, you do find that the sequence of lightning–thunder follows an objective pattern.

Contrary to Hume, we do distinguish between the statements "Every lemon has a sour taste" and "Every event has a cause." Although the first statement has been confirmed by all our experience, we could imagine a world in which this was not true. However, we could not imagine a possible world in which there were no causal order at all. The difference is that the statement about lemons is a contingent *a posteriori* truth and the statement about events is a synthetic *a priori* truth that describes the sort of structure the mind gives to experience. Apart from experience, we cannot determine what specific cause–effect relationships there are. Likewise, we sometimes mistake an accidental order of events for a rule-ordered pattern. Nevertheless, we will always expect to find a causal order of some sort because the mind will always organize experience in this way. As was the case with substance, causality is not a metaphysical category that gives us knowledge about the reality outside of our experience. However, it does tell us we will inevitably find experience organized into causal patterns.

To summarize, Hume's theory of experience seems to collapse the distinction we make between a subjective assemblage of sensations (such as we find in dreams) and objective collections of sensations (enduring objects) that fall under the category of *substance*. Likewise, his theory eliminates the distinction between accidental conjunctions of events and objective, rule-ordered patterns that fall under the category of *causality*. For Kant, however, these distinctions are genuine ones within the world of experience. Notice that he is claiming these distinctions are distinctions *within* experience and not between the world of experience and some independent reality. Hence, the difference between the subjective and the objective is the difference between experiences in which there is no consistent pattern and experiences in which we do find a consistent, rule-ordered, interpersonal pattern. Only if the world was fundamentally structured in this way could it be experienced, thought about, talked about, and shared with others. Other beings such as God or horseflies may experience the world quite differently. But the categories of the understanding govern the way in which humans necessarily experience reality.

KANT'S THEORY OF EXPERIENCE

Let's examine the sort of work the mind performs on intuitions. Kant says we are confronted with a plurality of various sense impressions that he calls the "manifold of experience." He agrees with Hume that by themselves these sensations would be discrete and unconnected. Yet our experience is not a humble-jumble of impressions, but is unified. What is the source of this unity? The impressions themselves do not contain their own unity, nor is the unity one further item in experience. Hence, it is clear to Kant that the unity results from the synthesizing activity of the mind.

To make clear how this works, let's consider how you experience a melody. Let's suppose you are driving down the road listening to your car radio. You suddenly are aware you are listening to the opening bars of Beethoven's Fifth Symphony. The first four musical notes you hear are the familiar *G, G, G, C,* that sound like "Ta—Ta—Ta———Dummmm." To experience this series *as* a melody, you must first separate these four sounds out from other sounds (the roar of the engine, the static of the radio, the honking of nearby cars) and hold them together in one experience. Kant refers to this as the *synthesis of apprehension in intuition.*

However, if you had instant amnesia after hearing each note, you would experience four solitary sounds but would not experience the successive notes as moments in a unified melody. Hence, to identify something as "the second note," the first one must be reproduced or remembered in your imagination and so on for the remaining notes. Kant calls this the *synthesis of reproduction in imagination.* Finally, simply remembering the sequence of notes is not enough. You must view them as parts of a unified whole and understand them by means of a concept ("melody") in one act of consciousness. Kant calls this the *synthesis of recognition in a concept.*

Obviously, the concepts that play a role in this experience ("Beethoven," "musical notes," "cello") are empirical concepts that are learned from experience. But you could not have these concepts without the operation of *a priori* concepts such as "plurality," "totality," "substance," "causality," and so on. Try applying this analysis to other experiences. Look about the room you are currently in. You are not bombarded with a confusing flow of sensory impressions, but you see an organized array of spatial-temporal objects, conceptualized into meaningful units and relationships within your experience. These examples illustrate a shortcoming of the previous analogies between our mental categories and the optical lenses or the cookie press. Unlike these mechanisms, the categories are not static forms through which sensations are filtered. Instead, they represent ways in which the mind *actively* synthesizes the elements of experience into a unity.

These examples also illustrate what Kant means when he says that "objects conform to the mind." Without the synthesizing activity of the mind and its categories, there would be no objects in our experience that we could designate with words such as "melody" or "book." Instead, there would only be a fragmented, unintelligible flow of sensations. In fact, even the latter description makes use of empirical concepts ("fragmented" and "flow") that require the logical category of "plurality" as well as the forms of space and time for their application. Hence, without the mind's categories, we could not even know this much about our experience. Finding that experience will always have a universal and necessary structure, Kant thought that he had provided all the foundation that the enterprise of science requires.

Metaphysics: Bumping Against the Limits of Reason

PHENOMENA AND NOUMENA

Kant has argued that synthetic *a priori* judgments are possible in mathematics and physics and that they serve the purpose of making sense of our experience. But are they possible in metaphysics? The discussion of his epistemology should have made clear that Kant is pessimistic about the ability of the human mind to acquire theoretical knowledge of any reality lying beyond the boundaries of human experience. All our knowledge about the world is limited to what can be perceived in space and time and known through the categories of the understanding. Because we are burdened by our own finitude, to seek a knowledge of reality that transcends these human forms is like trying to lift ourselves up by our own bootstraps or like attempting to jump out of our own skin. For this reason Kant called traditional metaphysics "transcendent illusions" (CPR A295/B352).

The philosophical traditions begun by both Descartes and Locke had assumed there was a dichotomy between our ideas and the real world. The problem then arose of how we can know our ideas correspond to the real world. For Kant, however, the only world that can ever make any sense to us is the world of objects that appear within experience. He refers to these things-as-they-appear-to-us as the **phenomena**. In a practical sense, the phenomenal world *is* the real world and the notion of such a world corresponding to anything "outside" of it is unintelligible. However, we cannot help talking about what is on the other side of the boundaries of sense and intelligibility. These things-in-themselves that are not structured by the mind's categories are what Kant calls the **noumena**. We cannot assign any positive content to the concept of the noumena. The concept is merely a limiting concept or a way of pointing to what lies beyond any possible experience.

It might seem as though it would be improper to even talk about the noumena at all if they are essentially unknowable. However, Kant could not let go of the notion of some sort of reality out there that was independent of what appears within experience. After all, we do not manufacture the contents of our knowledge; we only provide them with a particular form. It would seem to follow, then, that the contents of sensation must be the product of something out there that causes them. Indeed, when Kant refers to the phenomena as "appearances," he suggests they are related to the noumena in some way. But Kant has been criticized here for applying the concept of "cause" to that which lies outside of experience. Remember that for Kant "causality" is one of the twelve categories by means of which our minds structure experience. At the same time, he denies that we can employ the concept of causality to make metaphysical judgments about reality-in-itself (the noumenon). Causal judgments can apply only to what appears within experience. This leaves us with a dilemma in interpreting Kant. If Kant suggests that the phenomena are appearances caused by an external reality, he has violated his own epistemology. In contrast, if he denies that things-in-themselves *cause* the phenomena, then how does he think they are related? Kant scholars have had a difficult time understanding his position on this issue.

THE TRANSCENDENT ILLUSIONS OF METAPHYSICS

Thus far, we have discussed the two faculties of sensation and understanding. In addition to these, Kant says *reason* constitutes a third faculty of the mind. In logic, reason is employed to order and unify the products of the understanding. However, pure reason also produces its own concepts, which (unlike the concepts of the understanding) refer to what transcends any possible experience. The three transcendental ideas of pure reason are *self*, *the cosmos*, and *God*. As we will see later, the ideas of pure reason have their appropriate function. The problem is that reason falls into the trap of applying the categories of the understanding beyond the sphere of their legitimate employment within experience (the realm of phenomena). Since theoretical knowledge is limited to the domain of experience, the pretension of pure reason to fly beyond experience and draw conclusions about the noumena leads to a tangle of paradoxes and illusions. Accordingly, Kant discusses three main areas in traditional metaphysics (self, cosmos, and God) that have resulted in "transcendent illusions."

THE ELUSIVE SELF

We have the notion that behind the passing flow of our individual psychological states there is the self, a soul, or some sort of enduring but nonphysical substance. Thoughts and experiences do not float around unaccompanied. They are always the thoughts or experiences of some subject. Thus, the judgment "Roses are fragrant" is always a judgment made by someone and, for this reason, every thought is explicitly or implicitly preceded by "I think." Furthermore, as we have seen, without the synthesizing activity of the self, we could not have the unified experiences that we have. Kant agrees with Hume that we never have an impression of this self. We can have experiences of dogs, cabbages, and watches, or of doubts, hopes, and fears, but we can never apprehend the self that is having these experiences. However, contrary to Hume, while the self is not a content of experience, Kant says it is one of the necessary conditions for experience to exist at all.

Although Descartes might agree with the discussion up to this point, Kant believes Descartes made a terrible error by supposing he could know the self as a substance. Since Kant insists that substance can only be used as a category for unifying elements *within* experience, it cannot be applied to what stands behind experience. The self Descartes discovered was the *empirical self*. To distinguish the empirical self that we can know through introspection from the trans-empirical self, Kant refers to the latter as the "transcendental ego" or the "transcendental unity of apperception." Although we must think of our experiences as if they are related to a unifying principle, this source of unity can neither appear within space and time nor be conceptualized through the categories of the understanding. This self is the ultimate subject that underlies all experience and can never be known as an object of introspection or scientific knowledge. Hence, it is a part of the unknowable noumena, and Kant refers to it as *X*, an undefinable variable.

Saying that the essential self is unknowable does not mean psychologists must clean out their desks and quit work. We can introspect and find a parade of psychological states such as doubt and belief or personality traits such as introversion and optimism that constitute the empirical self. However, the self that may serve as an object of scientific study is not the same as the transcendental ego. Hence, psychologists can study different personalities and determine the lawlike regularities that govern their behavior. However, what they are studying is a set of appearances or phenomena and not the essential self behind the appearances. In this way, Kant attempted to give science its due, while protecting the human person from merely being a determined scientific object like a pendulum.

THE UNTHINKABLE COSMOS

The second metaphysical illusion is the assumption that we can reason about the cosmos (or the world-as-a-totality). Once again, all that we know

are bits and pieces of world experience, but the totality is never experienced. With John Locke, we may think that we can imaginatively add together our finite experiences of the world and extrapolate to the idea of the totality. However, to think of the world as a whole, we would have to take a God-like perspective outside space and time. According to Kant, this would require jumping outside the bounds of our human ways of conceptualizing experience.

Kant attempts to show that reason falls into a tangle of inconsistencies when it goes beyond its proper limits. To demonstrate this, he produces four pairs of opposing viewpoints that he calls "the antinomies of reason." An **antinomy** is a pair of seemingly reasonable conclusions that flatly conflict with each other and, hence, cannot both be true. Kant gives rational arguments for each opposing side of four key metaphysical issues. The problem is that the opposing arguments seem equally cogent. Leaving out the details of his arguments, the four antinomies he lists are

1a. The world had a beginning in time and is limited in space.

1b. The world had no beginning and is infinite in time and space.

2a. Everything can be analyzed into basic elements.

2b. Nothing can be analyzed into basic elements.

3a. Some events are free and undetermined.

3b. There is no freedom, for all events are determined by previous causes.

4a. There is a necessary being in the universe.

4b. There is not a necessary being in the universe.

By providing rational arguments for each side of these dichotomies, Kant tries to show that reasoning about these topics leads us to nonsense. This is a sure sign that reason has gone beyond its proper bounds.

Kant says that the first statement in each pair (the thesis) characterizes the stance of dogmatic rationalism. The second statement (the antithesis) characterizes the position of an equally dogmatic empiricism. Kant is sympathetic with the metaphysical yearnings of the rationalist, for he believes that the stance of pure empiricism is unlivable:

> If there is no primordial being distinct from the world, if the world is without beginning and therefore without an Author, if our will is not free, if the soul is divisible and perishable like matter, moral ideas and principles lose all validity. (CPR A468/B496)*

At the same time, Kant agrees with the empiricist's charge that metaphysical claims are dogmatic pretensions that cannot be proven. The problem is that both the rationalist and the empiricist presuppose what we cannot know. The dogmatic rationalist makes claims about the noumena, or what transcends our finite experience. In contrast, the dogmatic empiricist limits reality to the phenomena and assumes that sensory appearances are the same as things-in-themselves.

Kant resolves the first two antinomies by saying that the opposing positions are all false, because they are based on the unacceptable assumption that we can think of the world itself as a totality. With respect to the last two antinomies, he says that the second statement in each pair is true for the world *insofar as* it appears within experience (as phenomena). At the same time, this leaves open the possibility that the first statement of each pair could be true of the noumenon that transcends experience, even though this reality-in-itself is unknowable. Although statements about the noumenon can never constitute theoretical knowledge, they could be the product of "intellectual *presuppositions* and *faith*" (CPR A470/B498). For example, this approach allows Kant to say that human actions are determined by the laws of nature when viewed *as* scientific phenomena. At the same time, when he discusses morality Kant postulates there is more to us than what appears to scientific observation. From the standpoint of morality, we must understand ourselves as noumenal selves who are free and undetermined agents.

GOD: NEITHER PROVABLE NOR DISPROVABLE

Finally, any rational metaphysics that seeks to prove the existence of God runs against the boundaries of reason. Kant believes there are three ways one may try to prove the existence of God through speculative reason. For each of these arguments, he gives detailed refutations to show that the proof fails.

The first argument is the ontological argument as used by Anselm, Descartes, and Leibniz. Recall that this is an *a priori* argument that begins with the concept of a perfect being. The version of the argument Kant refutes could be formulated as follows:*

(1) I can conceive of a perfect being.

(2) If I can conceive of something, it is possible for it to exist.

(3) So it is possible for there to be a perfect being.

(4) If there is a perfect being, it cannot lack any perfections.

(5) Existence is a perfection.

(6) So, if there is a perfect being, it necessarily must have the property of existence.

(7) Hence, it is possible there is a perfect being that necessarily exists (its nonexistence is impossible).

(8) But it makes no sense to say that there could be something whose nonexistence is impossible at the same time that its nonexistence is possible.

(9) Therefore, a perfect being must necessarily exist.

Kant attacks this argument at two points. First, he focuses on premise 6. He agrees with the statement that the concept of God includes the concept of an absolutely necessary being. However, he compares this with the essence of a triangle. If something is a triangle, then it must have

---

*This may not be the strongest version of the ontological argument. Nevertheless, it seems to be the one Kant is refuting.

three angles. The problem is, this does not tell us whether or not triangles actually exist. If I deny there are triangles, then I do not need to affirm that there are three-angled figures. Similarly, we may state, "If there is a God, then there is a being that necessarily exists." However, if I deny there is a God, then I may also reject the claim that there is a necessary being. In this way, Kant seeks to block the move from concepts to existence.

His second attack is directed against premise 5. According to Kant, "Existence is not a predicate." In other words, existence is not a property that may be added to the concept of something and that would enrich the concept. Try this thought experiment. Think of a white cat sitting on your desk. Now add to the concept of "a white cat on my desk" the property of existence. Adding the property of existence does not change the original picture at all. Hence the concept of "a white cat sitting on my desk" is indistinguishable from the concept of "an *existing* white cat sitting on my desk." Since Kant believes that existence is not a property, it cannot be an essential part of our concept of God. In other words, denying that God exists is not like denying that a husband is married. Kant says that arguing from our concept of God to his existence in the world is like a merchant adding zeros to his checkbook balance and supposing that he is increasing his wealth.

Next, Kant takes on the cosmological argument. This proof argues from the existence of things that need a cause to the existence of an ultimate cause whose existence is necessary. The problem is that it rests on the principle that "every event has a cause." But as Kant has previously explained, this principle only applies to things within the world of experience. We cannot apply it to the cosmos as a whole that is beyond experience. Furthermore, because the cosmological argument uses the notion of a "necessary being" it rests on the ontological argument, which Kant has already dismissed.

Finally, Kant attacks the teleological argument or the argument from design.* This argument

moves from the evidence of purposeful order in the world to the conclusion that the world was caused by an intelligent designer. Kant has a great deal of respect for this argument, for he says, "it is the oldest, the clearest, and the most accordant with the common reason of mankind" (CPR A623/B651). He goes on to suggest that it provides a motive for scientists to look for the connections within nature and that the proof is strengthened by each new scientific discovery of order.

However, in the final analysis he thinks this argument also fails. At best, the argument could only prove that the form of the world had an architect who imposed order on matter that already existed. If we want to prove that a creator brought everything into being, we must supplement the design argument with the cosmological argument. Since the latter has been shown to be invalid, it cannot fill in the gaps in the current argument.

Kant's conclusion, then, is that attempts to demonstrate God's existence are "altogether fruitless and by their nature null and void" (CPR A636/B664). There is a corollary to this, however. His arguments against rationalistic theology also imply that the nonexistence of God cannot be demonstrated either. Hence both the believer and the atheist who claim to *know* (in the strongest sense of the word) the truth about God's existence, are equally dogmatic and mistaken. Although the failure of speculative reason leaves us without knowledge in this area, it at least allows for the possibility that the religious vision of the world can be based on a practical or moral faith. As he says in the Preface to his first *Critique*, he sought to "deny *knowledge*, in order to make room for *faith*" (CPR Bxxx).

REGULATIVE USE OF THE CONCEPTS OF PURE REASON

Even though Kant was very critical of dogmatic metaphysics, he did not agree with Hume that we should burn all books on theology or metaphysics. Although metaphysics may consist of transcendental illusions, he says these are "irresistible illusions" (CPR A642/B670, A297 98/B353 54). The human mind is burdened "by questions

---

*Kant calls this argument "the physico-theological proof."

which, as prescribed by the very nature of reason itself, it is not able to ignore, but which, as transcending all its powers, it is also not able to answer" (CPR Avii). But the notions of self, cosmos, and God are more than just compulsive ways of thinking, for they play a positive role in our thinking. Even though we cannot know them as objects of experience, these regulative ideas help us to think about our experience.

What, then, is their legitimate employment? They are useful in helping us to regulate our thought. To use an analogy, the regulative ideas function like the converging lines in a painting that lead to an infinite point beyond the horizon. The perspective lines regulate our perception within a two-dimensional painting and help us visualize it as containing three-dimensional objects located in a landscape that continues beyond the horizon. In doing this, they provide a meaningful frame of reference for the elements that actually occur within the picture.

Moreover, even though we can't have rational knowledge of the self, the cosmos, and God, it is useful in thinking about experience to act *as if* we had this knowledge. They are the goals or ideals of reason, though not its objects. For example, empirical psychology strives to bring together mental phenomena such as desires, emotions, thoughts, and images into a unified scheme *as if* there were a permanent, substantial subject behind it all.

With respect to the world, all we know is the finite collection of objects we have actually experienced. However, it is helpful to think of the world *as if* it were composed of a totality of objects, including those we have not yet discovered. The notion of the world-as-a-totality stands for what we would know if science could answer all the possible questions about the universe. Thus, it leads the scientist to keep asking questions in order to move closer to this unattainable ideal.

Finally, the notion of God enables us to think of the world *as if* it were a systematic unity with a single, intelligent, and purposeful cause. This will motivate reason to continually try to make our picture of the world coherent. In summary, the three concepts of self, cosmos, and God are not the basis of metaphysical knowledge. Instead,

they are regulative concepts that provide points of reference beyond all possible experience that help us to order and make sense out of what occurs within experience.

Because of the ambiguities in Kant's account, later philosophers differed concerning the implications of Kant's philosophy. Some post-Kantian philosophers claimed that while the self, the world, and God cannot be objects of knowledge, they are realities that must exist beyond the reach of reason because thought could not function without them. Others said these three concepts are nothing more than useful fictions like "the perfect society" or "frictionless surfaces" or "the sum of all numbers" that we project for theoretical purposes.

Ethics as a Rational Discipline

THE NATURE OF ETHICS

In the *Critique of Pure Reason* Kant uncovered the principles of reason that give us knowledge of the world of experience. He refers to this study as the investigation of *theoretical reason*. If knowledge of "the starry heavens above" and of physical nature in general was our only concern, Kant could have retired from writing at this point. However, another aspect of reality and another domain of law would have been neglected if he had quit with the first *Critique*. We not only know the world as spectators, but we also act within it. On the one hand, we encounter natural objects (including our own bodies and empirical selves) that are governed by scientific laws. On the other hand, we also encounter persons, the one type of reality we know both from the inside as well as from the outside.

Persons feel the pull of "the moral law within," a governing principle that differs from those that explain the behavior of natural objects. The aspect of reason at work in this second domain is called *practical reason*. However, Kant is quick to point out that even though we can speak about reason in two ways, "in the final analysis there can be but one and the same reason which must be differentiated only in application" (FMM 8).[7] To make his foundational philosophy complete, therefore, Kant came out with several works on ethics a few years after he published his first *Critique*. Of these, the two most important are *The Foundations of the Metaphysics of Morals* (1785) and the *Critique of Practical Reason* (1787). His moral philosophy became one of his most important contributions to the history of thought. Consequently, the Kantian approach to ethics still stands today as one of the leading resources of ethical insight as we face the troubling issues our contemporary culture is encountering in the areas of political, legal, medical, and business ethics.

Kant's moral theory emphasizes duties, motives, the dignity and worth of persons, and a moral law that is absolute and unchanging. In this, he retains some of the elements of his own Christian roots. But when it comes to deciding what the moral law is, no mention is made of God and his commands. He says our ability to identify God with the highest good and to attribute goodness to the great religious figures in history requires that we already have an *a priori* conception of moral perfection.

Similarly, Kant's uncompromising rationalism led him to insist that the principles of morality cannot be derived from any empirical facts about human practices such as we find in anthropology. On this one point, Kant agrees with Hume that we cannot validly move from a description of what *is* the case to any notion of what we *ought* to do. For Kant, the way around this problem is to apply his Copernican revolution to our moral life. If moral principles cannot be derived from experience, then the mind must bring its own, rational principles to experience. Hence, in Kant's analysis, acting morally can be reduced to acting rationally and acting immorally is one species of acting irrationally.

THE GOOD WILL

Kant's moral theory begins with the claim that "Nothing in the world . . . can possibly be conceived which could be called good without qualification except a *good will*" (FMM 9). There are, of course, other things we count as good. Kant lists three categories of such good things: (1) *mental abilities* (such as intelligence, wit, judgment); (2) *qualities of temperament* (such as courage, resoluteness,

perseverance); and (3) *gifts of fortune* (such as power, riches, honor, health, happiness). However, although these things are certainly good, they are not good without qualification. Without a good will, the positive qualities could be misused for evil ends. For a hardened criminal to be intelligent, cool-headed, courageous, powerful, and rich would only enhance the evil he could do rather than contributing to his moral goodness. Unlike any other positive quality, the good will is always good under any circumstances. If a will that is good is at the heart of morality, how do we identify such a will when we are trying to evaluate our own moral character or those of others? Kant first of all makes clear what is *irrelevant* in identifying a moral will. It matters little in assessing the goodness of a person's will what it is she actually accomplishes:

> Even if it should happen that, by a particularly unfortunate fate or by the [stingy] provision of stepmotherly nature, this will should be wholly lacking in power to accomplish its purpose, and if even the greatest effort would not avail it to achieve anything of its end, and if there remained only the good will (not as a mere wish but as the summoning of all the means in our power), it would sparkle like a jewel in its own right, as something that had its full worth in itself. (FMM 10)

For example, Heidi may recognize the call of moral duty and risk her life to save a drowning child. However, even though she did not achieve her goal, the goodness of the will motivating these actions still shines brightly.

If the actual success of one's moral endeavors is not what makes the will good, the examples just mentioned might lead us to suppose that the fact that Heidi *intended* to produce a good consequence (saving the child) is what made her action morally good. Yet Kant does not think this is enough. We can intend to do the right action from many different motives. We can even do the right action for morally tainted reasons. For example, Heidi may be running for mayor and may think the publicity from this sacrificial action will be good for her campaign. Or she might be seeking a reward. This would raise the question of whether or not she would have performed this action anyway if she weren't interested in publicity or the money. Consequently, merely intending the right action cannot be the basic criterion for moral goodness.

To elicit further features of Kant's position, let's try a different variation of the story. Suppose Heidi's motive for saving the child was not so calculating. Imagine she was moved by pity on hearing the cries of the child. In this case she would be acting on the basis of her feelings or what Kant calls inclination. The problem with this, however, is that our feelings come and go but the demands of morality are a constant. Sometimes the moral person must do things she does not really feel like doing. For this reason, Kant insists that morality must be based on rational principles and cannot be driven by any variable conditions such as feelings or inclinations.

We have eliminated actual consequences, intended consequences, and feelings or inclinations as the source of the will's moral goodness. What else is left? To illustrate his answer, Kant asks us to imagine a man who has the power and the moral obligation to help others in distress but is so clouded by his own sorrows that he is emotionally numb to the feelings of others. "And now suppose him to tear himself, unsolicited by inclination, out of this dead insensibility and to perform this action only from duty and without any inclination—then for the first time his action has genuine moral worth" (FMM 14). As a further example of this point, Kant refers to those passages in the Bible that command us to love our neighbor and even our enemy (FMM 15 16). If we were being commanded to feel a certain way, this would be an absurd commandment because we cannot simply will a particular feeling. Instead, Kant says, we are being asked to act lovingly toward others for the sake of *duty*. We now have the answer to the question of what makes a person's will morally good. It is a will that is moved to act on the basis of moral duty. It is concerned to do what is right from the sole motive that it is the morally right action to perform.

At this point it will be useful to introduce an important distinction that Kant makes. He says there is a difference between acting in accordance with duty and acting from duty. If a merchant refuses to cheat his customers because he wants to maintain a good reputation and get repeat business, he is doing what is right. However, though he is *acting in accordance with duty*, his motive is one of self-interest guided by prudence. However, if his motive is one of conforming to the moral law and thus *acting from duty*, then and only then does the action have moral worth, for it proceeds from a good will. The focus on duty makes Kant's theory an example of what is known as **deontological ethics** (from the Greek word *deon*, meaning duty or obligation). It is in contrast to **teleological ethics** or **consequentialism**, which claims that the goal or outcome of an action is what determines its moral value.*

REASON AS THE SOURCE OF THE MORAL LAW

If the morally good will is one that performs actions out of a sense of duty and duty is conformity to the moral law, then how do I determine what is the moral law? Without an answer to this question, the good will would be well intentioned but morally blind. A moral law is a rule for guiding behavior. It is a kind of command or imperative. Kant makes a distinction between two kinds of imperatives. The first sort is a *hypothetical imperative*. It says, "If you want X then do Y." This rule tells me what I "ought" to do, but the ought is contingent on my desiring the goal following the "if." For example, I may be told, "If you want a nice lawn, then you must fertilize your grass." Kant calls this type of hypothetical statement a technical imperative. It tells me what means I must use to achieve an end I may desire.

However, if I couldn't care less whether I have a nice lawn or not, then the command is of no concern to me. Hence, a genuinely moral "ought" cannot be based on what goals I happen to have. A further problem with hypothetical imperatives is that "whether the end is reasonable and good is not in question at all, for the question is only of what

---

*The utilitarianism of Jeremy Bentham and John Stuart Mill discussed in a later chapter shows how consequentialists respond to Kant's deontological approach.

must be done in order to attain it" (FMM 32). For example, I may be told, "If you want to murder a rival colleague, you ought to use a strong poison." This illustrates the point that there are hypothetical imperatives that are useful for obtaining immoral ends.

Some hypothetical imperatives fall under the heading of pragmatic imperatives or counsels of prudence. These offer advice on how to enhance one's own welfare and happiness. When we were children, we were given these sorts of rules by our parents. For example, "If you want people to believe you, then you ought always to tell the truth" and "If you want to be happy, you should seek other people's happiness." Although the goals in these commands may be worthy, these are not moral commands because they depend on subjective conditions that create my own happiness.

A genuinely moral command is not a hypothetical imperative. According to Kant, the moral law is presented to us as a **categorical imperative**. It tells you what you ought, should, or must do, but it does not depend on any prior conditions, or subjective wants and wishes, and it contains no qualifications. It takes the form "Do X!" It is not preceded by an if clause for it tells you what you are morally commanded to do under all conditions and at all times. However, if such a moral law does not come from some external lawgiver such as God, who issues such commands to you? The lawgiver for Kant is reason itself. A rational rule is one that is universal and consistent. It is universal in that it is a rule that applies to all people, at all times, and in all circumstances. It is consistent in that it does not lead to any contradictions.

Before applying this to morality, let's look at how rationality functions in several examples that do not directly involve ethics. In mathematics it is a rule that $2 + 2 = 4$. It does not matter who is doing the calculation, what her circumstances are, and it does not matter whether we like the consequences of applying the rule or not. The rule must be followed if we are to be rational.

However, some rules are, by their very nature, irrational. This is because they could not be consistently followed by everyone or because they undermine the very activity to which the rule applies. Suppose your mother has a dinner rule that says, "Before you serve yourself, make sure everyone else is served first." If *everyone* followed this rule, no one would ever be able to eat (thus defeating the whole purpose of the rule). Similarly, suppose a baseball player signs a contract that sets out all the conditions that bind both the employee and the employer. However, if the last line of the contract reads, "If either of the parties wishes not to abide by the above conditions, he or she does not have to," at that point it ceases to be a contract. If a contractual condition undermines the very meaning of a contract, it is an irrational rule. In the same way, the criterion for the rules we use in ethics is that they must be rationally consistent.

THE CATEGORICAL IMPERATIVE I: CONFORMITY TO A UNIVERSAL LAW

With these examples to build on, we can now set out the categorical imperative that Kant regards as the supreme moral principle. Kant expresses the first version of his moral principle in this way:

> There is, therefore, only one categorical imperative. It is: Act only according to that maxim by which you can at the same time will that it should become a universal law. (FMM 39)

A maxim is a general rule that tells us what we should and should not do. However, notice that Kant has not given us any specific maxims. Instead, he has given us the principle that we use to decide which maxims establish our actual moral obligations and which ones do not.

Let's examine one of the examples Kant uses to illustrate his categorical imperative. Suppose you need to borrow some money but to do so you must promise to repay it even though you know full well that you will not be able to keep the promise. If you apply Kant's principle, you will discover that the maxim on which you are acting is "If I need to make a promise I may do so, even though I do not intend to keep it." But could you rationally will that this would become a universal law that everyone followed? Surely not. If everyone adopted this rule, then promise making would be meaningless and there would be no point in making or accepting promises. Your deceitful promise will be accepted *only* if others have respect for promises. Hence, you can apply your rule concerning promises only if no one else follows it.

Notice that Kant's point is *not* that a society in which people did not keep their promises would be very unpleasant. This would make the empirical consequences of the action the criteria for whether it is right or wrong. Kant's point is more subtle and logical. He is saying that a moral rule governing an activity (promise making) that would eliminate the activity in question would be a self-defeating (and thereby an inconsistent or irrational) rule.

Kant's criteria of universalizing our maxims captures some of our everyday moral intuitions. When you were young, your mother probably censured your behavior at some time or other by saying, "What if everyone behaved the way you do?" Again, the Golden Rule of the Gospels says, "Do unto others as you would have them do unto you." Similarly, we say to people, "Don't make yourself an exception. Don't be a hypocrite." Hence, the professor who flunks students for plagiarizing their papers at the same time that he steals and publishes another person's research is making himself an exception to the rule he expects his students and colleagues to follow.

THE CATEGORICAL IMPERATIVE II: PERSONS AS ENDS IN THEMSELVES

Kant believes that there is only one principle of morality, but that it can be given at least three different formulations. Each one is equivalent to the others, but each one emphasizes a different aspect of the morality of reason. His second version of the categorical imperative is as follows:

> Act so that you treat humanity, whether in your own person or in that of another, always as an end and never as a means only. (FMM 47)

This means that each person has intrinsic worth and dignity and that we should not use people or treat them like things. Kant's argument for this principle could be paraphrased in the following manner. Mere things such as cars, jewels, works of art, or tools have value only if persons endow them with value. In other words, a Rembrandt painting will sell for $1 million only because many people desire it. Accordingly, such things only have *conditional* value because if people stop desiring them, they will be worthless. However, insofar as persons are noumenal selves that transcend their empirical appearances, persons are not things. Since persons are the source of all conditional value, they cannot have conditional value themselves, but must have *absolute* or *intrinsic* value. No one can give you your worth as a person, nor can he or she take it away. An acquaintance may treat you like a thing, the only value of which is to serve his or her ends, but this is being inconsistent. Such a person is acting as though he or she alone has absolute value, while others are mere things to be used. Thus, the person is following the maxim "I will treat others as things" but could not consistently persuade others to follow this rule in return. Thus, the person is making him- or herself an exception.

Sometimes it may seem as though we cannot avoid using people as things to serve our own ends. For example, when you buy stamps from the postal clerk, you are using that person as a source of stamps. However, notice that Kant said we should treat persons "always as an end and never as a means *only*." Hence, even in impersonal transactions where we are mainly interested in a person for the services that he or she can perform for us, we should never act in a rude or manipulative manner, and we should always be mindful of the fact that it is a person with whom we are dealing.

An important feature of this formulation of the moral imperative is that Kant explicitly claims that we should treat ourselves with respect and not merely as a means to some end. Many ethical theorists (the utilitarians, for example) believe that ethics only governs our relations with others. However, one implication that follows from Kantian ethics is that we have moral duties to ourselves and not just to others. For this reason, Kant condemns suicide. If I decide to terminate my life in order to escape my pains and disappointments, I am treating myself as though I were a thing that is determined by external circumstances. Instead, I should respect the dignity and worth of my own personhood and treat it as having a value that transcends every other consideration. In the act of suicide, I am destroying humanity (represented by myself) and treating it as a means to achieve some other end (freedom from burdens). In another application of this principle, Kant says that even if I were stranded alone on a desert island, I would have duties to myself. For example, I should do what I could to improve myself and make use of my talents, instead of lapsing into idleness and self-indulgence.

THE CATEGORICAL IMPERATIVE III: PERSONS AS MORAL LEGISLATORS

Kant's third formulation of the categorical imperative centers on "the idea of the will of every rational being as making universal law" (FMM 49). This is sometimes called the "principle of autonomy." Central to the autonomy of the will is freedom. When my moral principles are based on an external authority or even my own inclinations, my reason is not acting freely but is bound by something alien to it. Hence, the moral law is not something that imposes itself on me from without, but is an expression of my own, rational nature. In morality, each person wears two hats. Insofar as we are truly moral agents, we are bound by the moral law. However, insofar as we are rational persons, we are autonomous legislators of the moral law. If all people obeyed the law of reason, they would constitute a perfect community (a kingdom of ends, Kant calls it), in which everyone would be autonomous, yet everyone would follow the same, universal morality.

THE THREE POSTULATES OF MORALITY

Kant believes that there are three conceptions that cannot be proven and cannot even be objects of knowledge and yet that are conceptions that our minds find irresistible because they undergird all moral endeavor. These are human freedom, immortality, and God.

First, *human freedom* must be postulated if morality is to make any sense. Freedom is not something that can be observed scientifically. From the standpoint of scientific knowledge, every event is determined by natural causes and human behavior is just a set of events that can be analyzed in terms of the laws of psychology and physiology. However, turning from science to our inner moral experience, we find the law of moral duty commands us to obey it unconditionally. Yet if there is something *I ought to do*, this implies it is something *I can do*. Hence, only if I am a free agent can I carry out the demands of morality. Over and above the empirical self, which is subject to causal laws and can be studied by the behavioral sciences, there is the noumenal self, our real self, which is the source of moral action. Although the freedom of the self is not something we can prove, the idea is a practical necessity if the whole of human morality is to make any sense. Since human life would be meaningless without morality, we must think of ourselves as free.

The second postulate of morality is *immortality*. Kant argues that the moral law is not indulgent. It does not say, "Do your best, but if you yield to temptation, that is OK." Instead, we are obligated to bring our will into perfect conformity with the demands of duty. However, no one is capable of fulfilling this demand during his or her lifetime. Therefore, Kant argues, it is a practical necessity for us to have an endless time span in which to make progress toward this perfect ideal. "This infinite progress is possible, however, only under the presupposition of an infinitely enduring existence and personality of the same rational being; this is called the immortality of the soul."[8]

Finally, we are led by a similar kind of rational faith to postulate *the existence of God*. Kant does not think the hope for eternal life can ever be the motive for doing what is right. If this is my motivation, then I am doing the good not because it is my duty, but because I have calculated what is in my own, long-term interests. Nevertheless, Kant says something within us cries out that living a morally good life should be correlated with finding happiness. Obviously, however, we do not find any necessary connection within human experience between virtue and happiness. Therefore, for our moral intuitions to make sense, there must be a cause that transcends nature and that will bring about a just distribution of happiness at some future date. For this reason, "it is morally necessary to assume the existence of God."[9] Of course, Kant has made perfectly clear that morality is rational and autonomous and does not depend on divine commands for its authority. Nevertheless, he thinks the sphere of morality naturally leads to the sphere of religion.

Evaluation and Significance

Little needs to be said about the significance of Kant's ideas at this point since a large part of the philosophical dialogue of the nineteenth and twentieth centuries was an attempt to come to terms with their implications. Some philosophers believed Kant's Copernican revolution in knowledge had established the correct order in philosophy, and they devoted their efforts to applying its principles to every area of human endeavor. Other philosophers considered it a good start, but worried that it had not been radical enough and pushed his revolutionary ideas further than he could have imagined. Still others attempted a counterrevolution to restore the reign of the traditional approaches to epistemology and metaphysics.

   In short, no matter what their assessment of Kant may have been, philosophers could not ignore him. In the remaining chapters we will see that a large number of the philosophical controversies explicitly or implicitly revolve around the Kantian agenda: (1) the objectivity of our knowledge, (2) the relationship of the knower and the known, (3) the powers and limits of science and reason, (4) the nature of the self, and (5) the status of moral judgments and religious knowledge.

Questions for Understanding

1. What was Kant's fundamental conviction about knowledge? What three tasks emerged from this?

2. Explain what Kant meant by calling his approach "critical philosophy."

3. Why does Kant compare his theory of knowledge to the Copernican revolution?

4. What does Kant mean when he says that the objects of experience conform to our knowledge?

5. Explain the meaning of the following terms: analytic judgments, synthetic judgments, *a priori* knowledge, *a posteriori* knowledge.

6. Provide examples of each of the following categories of judgments: analytic *a priori*, synthetic *a posteriori*, synthetic *a priori*.

7. What is the special meaning Kant gives to the term "intuition"?

8. Explain what Kant means when he says space and time are not "things" in experience but are the "forms of intuition."

9. Why does Kant claim that sense data alone could not explain our experience? What contribution do the categories of the understanding make to experience?

10. Explain what Kant means when he says "thoughts without content are empty, intuitions without concepts are blind."

11. In what way does Kant attempt to refute Hume's skepticism? Do you think he is successful?

12. Explain Kant's distinction between the phenomena and the noumena in your own words.

13. Explain Kant's view of each of the following concepts: the self, the cosmos, God. Why does he refer to them as "transcendent illusions"?

14. What is an antinomy? In what circumstances does reason produce antinomies?

15. What are Kant's objections to (a) the ontological argument, (b) the cosmological argument, and (c) the teleological argument? Is Kant's final position antagonistic or sympathetic toward religious belief?

16. Since Kant agrees with Hume that we cannot have knowledge of the self, the cosmos, or God, why does he claim (unlike Hume) that these ideas make an important contribution to our thinking?

17. Why does Kant say that the only thing that can be good without qualification is the good will?

18. What characteristic makes a person's will morally good?

19. What is the difference between acting in accordance with duty and acting from duty?

20. What does it mean for something to be a categorical imperative as opposed to a hypothetical imperative?

21. What are the three versions of the categorical imperative?

22. According to Kant, what are the three postulates of morality? Do you agree with him that these cannot be proven? Do you think Kant is correct in claiming that these three conceptions undergird all morality?

Questions for Reflection

1. Why might it be appropriate to think of Kant as a "rational empiricist" or an "empirical rationalist"? How successful was Kant in combining the insights of both rationalism and empiricism?

2. Look about the room and imagine that you are being bombarded with sensory impressions but that your mind does not have the ability to categorize or organize them into a meaningful collection of experiences. What would this be like? Is Kant correct in maintaining that the mind makes a contribution to experience?

3. Kant has attempted to avoid Humean skepticism by arguing that we can have rationally certain and necessary knowledge as long as we realize that this knowledge is limited to the world as we experience it. The cruel catch is that human knowledge in general (and science in particular) cannot tell us about reality as it really is, but only about reality as it is filtered through our human ways of apprehending it. If Kant is correct, how serious a limitation is this? Is it possible to live with such a limited view of knowledge? Is there any way to avoid the limitations Kant places on our knowledge?

4. If all that we can know is the phenomenal realm, is Kant "cheating" on his own principles in postulating a noumenal world outside of it?

5. Do you agree with Kant that neither consequences nor feelings should play a role in making moral judgments?

6. Think of a practical example of how Kant's categorical imperative (version I) could be used to resolve a moral controversy. Think of another example of how Kant's categorical imperative (version II) could be used to decide what is right or wrong. Can you think of any moral problem where the categorical imperative would not provide a definite solution?

Notes

1. Heinrich Heine, *Germany, Works*, vol. 5, 136 137, quoted in *The Age of Ideology: The 19th Century Philosophers*, ed. Henry D. Aiken (New York: New American Library, 1956), 27–28.

2. Immanuel Kant, *Prolegomena to Any Future Metaphysics*, trans. Paul Carus, revised by James W. Ellington (Indianapolis: Hackett, 1977), 5.

3. CPR will be used to abbreviate references to Kant's *Critique of Pure Reason*, trans. Norman Kemp Smith (New York: St. Martin's Press, 1965). Kant published two editions of this work, the first in 1781 (referred to as A) and the second in 1787 (referred to as B). The quotations from this work are given in terms of the pagination of the original editions, which are indicated in the margins of most English translations.

4. Immanuel Kant, *Der Einzig Mögliche Beweisgrund (The One Possible Basis for a Demonstration of the Existence of God)*, trans. Gordon Treash (New York: Abaris Books, 1979), preface.

5. *Prolegomena to Any Future Metaphysics*, trans. Lewis W. Beck (New York: The Liberal Arts Press, 1951), 116.

6. *Critique of Practical Reason*, trans. Lewis White Beck (Chicago: University of Chicago Press, 1949), pt. 2, conclusion.

7. FMM will be used to refer to Immanuel Kant's *Foundations of the Metaphysics of Morals*, trans. Lewis White Beck (Indianapolis: Bobbs-Merrill, Library of Liberal Arts, 1959).

8. *Critique of Practical Reason*, pt. 1, bk. 2, chap. 2, §4.

9. Ibid., §5.

23

The Nineteenth-Century Cultural Context: Romanticism, Science, and the Sense of History

IT IS NEARLY IMPOSSIBLE TO SUMMARIZE THE thought of the nineteenth century in terms of any single, unified theme. Indeed, the philosophies of this period could be viewed as a number of streams moving in diverging directions. However, if we trace these streams back to their point of origin, we will find that, with two exceptions, they all flow out from the system of Immanuel Kant. The two exceptions are the positivism of Auguste Comte and the utilitarianism of Jeremy Bentham and John Stuart Mill. Yet even in these cases, it is helpful to view their epistemologies in the light of distinctions Kant had established. After Kant, philosophy could never be the same again. His impact was so great that it is common to label philosophical outlooks as "pre-Kantian" or "post-Kantian." Because Kant's system was so comprehensive and complex as well as riddled with numerous conflicting tendencies, it was difficult to embrace it as a whole. Thus, later philosophers were content to make complete philosophies out of selected parts of the Kantian system, while discarding those parts they found incoherent. Even those who most fully inherited Kant's ideas carried them in directions he never anticipated and would not have approved.

The primary nineteenth-century movements and thinkers that followed after Kant were German idealism, romanticism, the positivism of Auguste Comte, the utilitarianism of Bentham and Mill, the historical materialism of Karl Marx, and the existentialism of Søren Kierkegaard and Friedrich Nietzsche. In the remainder of this chapter, we lay the groundwork for the transition from Kant to the philosophy of the nineteenth century. First, we briefly suggest how these various movements dealt with Kant's phenomena–noumena distinction. This is followed by brief discussions of the German idealists and the romantics, since they will not be given a chapter-length treatment later on. Finally, by way of preview, we will discuss how the nineteenth-century movements addressed the topics of history and reason.

Overcoming the Kantian Dualism

The major problem that all these thinkers had with Kant's system was its objectionable dualism. On the one hand, Kant limited rational knowledge to the world of spatial-temporal experience called the *phenomena.* The phenomenal world gives us reality, not naked and unadorned, but as it appears after being structured by the categories of the mind. Nevertheless, it is the only world we know and it is the world science studies. On the other hand, Kant could not free himself from the conviction that beyond the phenomenal world, beyond the world as it appears to us, is reality as it is in itself—the noumenal realm. Kant's critics were quick to point out that it makes no sense for Kant to say we can know *only* what appears in experience at the same time he claims to know there is a reality that transcends experience. Furthermore, although Kant's suggestion that the real world "causes" the world of phenomena has a certain commonsense appeal, it is not consistent with his claim that causality is a category that the mind imposes on experience and cannot be applied outside of what is empirically given.

The post-Kantian movements sought to resolve this problem in a number of ways. The German idealists and the romantics denied that we were cut off from ultimate reality, as Kant had claimed. Although they agreed the world of the empirical sciences is merely a system of appearances, they did not draw the Kantian conclusion that reality-in-itself is a mysterious, unapproachable region. Instead, they claimed, reality is exactly what we encounter in experience when we approach it in the proper way. However, they described the world of experience as broader and richer than Kant ever imagined, for they included moral, aesthetic, and religious experience within its scope.

Both the idealists and the romantics believed the mind has intuitive powers that transcend the limitations of science and reveal the heart of reality to us. Others, such as the positivists and the utilitarians, claimed the world described by science (Kant's phenomenal realm) was the only world worth talking about. Thus, they avoided the sort of problematic dualism found in Kant by dismissing the meaningfulness of talking about a transcendent reality altogether. Since the only reality we experience is sense data, they claimed, science can describe only the regularities that occur within experience, but it cannot speculate about ultimate causes or any other metaphysical entities. Karl

Marx reacted against the idealism and metaphysical speculations of his countrymen and sought to bring philosophy out of the clouds and back to earth. He had no problems with metaphysics but claimed that it had to take the form of a hardheaded scientific materialism.

Finally, the existentialists offered their own alternatives to Kantian philosophy. From its very beginnings in the nineteenth century, this movement came in two versions. First, religious existentialism was set in motion by Søren Kierkegaard. For Kierkegaard, there was a transcendent reality beyond the world of space and time, namely, God. In Kierkegaard's view, Kant was right in saying scientific and philosophical reason could not reveal this reality to us, for God can be known only in an act of personal faith. The second version of existentialism took an atheistic form in the writings of Friedrich Nietzsche. Taking Kant's position to the extreme, Nietzsche said we cannot know any reality beyond the appearances, but added that the appearances are creatively structured by the subjective needs and values of each individual person. Thus, there is nothing absolute and everything is subjective.

German Idealism

The immediate heirs of Kantian philosophy were the German idealists. As we saw with Berkeley and Leibniz, the metaphysical idealist is not necessarily one who has high ideals (although this is usually true of such philosophers). Instead, **idealism** refers to the theory that everything must be understood as intrinsically dependent on some sort of mental or spiritual reality. Although they were influenced by Kant, the idealists who followed after him were impatient with Kant's narrow definition of knowledge and his obsession with the limitations of the mind. According to their outlook, Kant's unnecessarily cautious approach condemned human knowledge to dwell in a sterile, minuscule, and trivial domain with nothing to give it spiritual nourishment.

The idealists had a yearning for infinity (which provoked their critics to label them "fanatics for totality"). Accordingly, the idealists sought to burst

through the epistemological walls Kant had so painstakingly built. In doing so, they hoped to show that reality itself, not just the world of appearances, could be encompassed by the mind. The word "encompassed" may be misleading, for it suggests an independently existing reality to which the mind may or may not be related. However, this is exactly what idealism denied. The idealists charged that Kant had limited the range of experience too severely. (Hegel contemptuously quipped that Kant's view of experience was "a snuff box here, and a candlestick there.")[1] According to the idealists, the real world is not apprehended through a scientific analysis of bits of sense data but by some sort of intellectual intuition provoked by moral or aesthetic experience. Since ultimate reality is spiritual and not material, it can support the highest aspirations of the human spirit as manifested in morals, art, and religion.

FICHTE: REALITY IS KNOWN IN MORAL EXPERIENCE

One of the first to overhaul Kantian philosophy was Johann Gottlieb Fichte (1762–1814). In a 1793 letter, Fichte stated his assessment of Kant:

> My conviction is that Kant has only indicated the truth but neither unfolded nor proved it. This singular man has a power of divining truth, without being himself conscious of the grounds on which he rests.[2]

Although Fichte saw himself as carrying out Kant's ideas, it angered Kant that Fichte considered Kantian philosophy to be incomplete. Accordingly, Kant denied that there was any similarity between his ideas and Fichte's.

How did Fichte propose to "unfold" the insights of Kant? He did it by beginning with the notion of freedom. Whereas Kant had made freedom a postulate of morality, Fichte moved it to the center stage of his philosophy. In his view, freedom is a presupposition not only of action but of human cognition as well. Kant had said that there is only one universal set of categories that structure experience and thus we have no choice as to how we shall view the world. For Fichte there are many different ways to understand the

world. The effect of this modification is to personalize Kant's Copernican revolution. The world is my world. The categories I employ are those necessary to make my world meaningful. Thus philosophy begins with the choice between ultimate principles, and this commitment is made on the basis of temperament and not objective evidence.* In Fichte's own words,

> What sort of philosophy one chooses depends, therefore, on what sort of man one is; for a philosophical system is not a dead piece of furniture that we can reject or accept as we wish; it is rather a thing animated by the soul of the person who holds it.[3]

The question that concerns Fichte is, What is the ground and meaning of experience? Basically, he thinks there are two alternatives. First, what he calls "dogmatism" seeks for the foundation of experience in an independent external reality (the Kantian thing-in-itself). This approach interprets inner experience in terms of the outer world. This is the standpoint of the scientist and is assumed by both the rationalists and empiricists before Kant. In contrast, Fichte favors idealism. According to this outlook, the ground of experience is found in our own, deepest nature—the self. This approach interprets the outer world in terms of our inner experience. If we limit ourselves to scientific knowledge, as the dogmatist does, we will never get beyond the causal order and will see ourselves as passive objects, subject to the deterministic machinery of nature. However, through an intellectual intuition, we can become conscious of the law of morality. As Kant showed, this requires us to think of ourselves as free, self-determining agents, pursuing our moral projects in a world that presents us with meaningful options.

How then shall we think of ourselves and our world? For Fichte, this is not a theoretical question, but an intensely practical one. Like the twentieth-century pragmatists (who were influenced by Fichte), he thought that our beliefs cannot be proven by means of metaphysical arguments. Instead, what makes a belief viable is the way it

---

*This will be a central theme for the existentialists such as Kierkegaard and Nietzsche.

affects our lives and serves our interests. For example, the scientific method is not written in the sky and the "facts" do not shout their own interpretation. If we choose to approach nature scientifically, it is because we believe this method serves our interests and makes our world meaningful. In the final analysis, even science is based on subjective commitments and acts of practical faith. Thus, idealism reigns supreme, for the world I live in is always a world structured by the way I approach it.

Fichte provides further motives for making the self the foundation of experience. First, we know the inner world better than the outer one, so this is where philosophy should begin. Second, if we start with a plurality of matter in motion, we will never be able to derive a unified mind and consciousness from this. But if we begin with our inner experience of being a unified, creative self, we will have the basis for giving meaning to everything else. Thus, the items within your world come and go, but behind all its reality is the constant activity of the self. To illustrate the fact that the self stands behind all manifestations of the world, Fichte once said to his students, "Gentlemen, think the wall." He then said, "Gentlemen, think him who thought the wall."[4] In other words, behind everything that appears is the self that grounds those appearances. Look about you. The world you experience is not a collection of meaningless bits of sense data at which you, like a camera lens, passively glare. Instead, the world of your experience is structured by your interests and values and is an arena in which you make choices and realize your moral ideals. According to Fichte,

> The Nature on which I have to act is not a foreign element, called into existence without reference to me, into which I cannot penetrate. It is molded by my own laws of thought, and must be in harmony with them; it must be thoroughly transparent, knowable, and penetrable to me, even to its inmost recesses. In all its phenomena it expresses nothing but the connections and relations of my own being to myself; and as surely as I may hope to know myself, so surely may I expect to comprehend it.[5]

Thus, the "external world" is not so external after all. True, if you open your eyes, you will encounter a manifold of sensations that are, inescapably, a part of your experience. However, you will not encounter meaningful objects until your mind creatively makes it your world. You may see the world as matter in motion that you manipulate and analyze, or as a world of human drama full of love affairs and tragedy about which you write plays, or as a sphere of duties that you seek to fulfill through your own moral endeavors. However, any way you experience the world, it is always a world you have made in your own image.

In his earlier writings, Fichte makes it sound as if my world were the product of my individual ego. If this were true, then there would be as many worlds as there were human knowers. However, in his later writings he makes it clear that the world is the product of a Cosmic Mind or Absolute Ego. Initially, this Absolute sounds a lot like God, but in Fichte's account the Absolute lacks the anthropomorphic qualities of the traditional Western concept of deity. Instead, it is more like an impersonal but rational moral order that is in the process of evolving. Like our own consciousness, it strives to realize itself in perfect self-awareness. In fact, the human will or consciousness is an expression of the Absolute Spirit. The real world is not a world of dead things, arranged in a spatial-temporal order, but is a dynamic, spiritual process in which we participate. In our moral experience the innermost center of this reality is opened up to us.

SCHELLING: REALITY IS KNOWN IN AESTHETIC EXPERIENCE

Another important German idealist is Friedrich Wilhelm Joseph von Schelling (1775–1854). He was a disciple of Fichte and a colleague of Hegel (who was significantly influenced by Schelling). Schelling placed a greater emphasis than Fichte did on physical nature as the objective form of the Absolute. Furthermore, he saw aesthetic experience (as opposed to moral experience) as the window to reality. The Absolute is described as the indubitable, all-encompassing, self-creating, unifying principle of reality that permeates nature. Thus, we can understand nature because it is made up of the same spirit that is in us. Just as

a baby develops from an instinct-driven, biological organism to a fully conscious, rational adult, so nature as a whole is continually unfolding throughout history to reach higher levels of self-consciousness. Thus, the world-spirit evolves from the unconscious, instinctive, purposive force found in inorganic and organic nature, until it realizes itself in the creativity of the artist and the rational self-consciousness of the philosopher.

For Schelling, artistic creation and aesthetic intuition are the highest moments of knowledge. In aesthetic experience, the two forms of the Absolute, the unconscious and the conscious forces, are fused in a glorious synthesis. Through artistic creations, the infinite manifests itself in finite form. Even nature itself is one, vast work of art, manifested in everything from the intricate structure of crystals to the grand, visual symphony of a sunset. Accordingly, Coleridge and all the romantic poets made Schelling their official philosopher, for he provided a metaphysical basis to art. Much later in his career, as he placed greater emphasis on the intuitions of the artist over those of the philosopher, Schelling objected to Hegel's abstract rationalism. His objection was that concepts are too static and limited to capture the dynamic and infinite qualities of reality. In this way, he laid some of the bricks on the road to existentialism. One founder of existentialism, Søren Kierkegaard, listened to Schelling's lectures in Berlin in the 1840s and later echoed these objections to Hegelian rationalism.

The idealism of Fichte and Schelling is significant because of their impact on the romantic movement and, most importantly, for their influence on the most famous idealist of all time, G. W. F. Hegel. By way of preview, their influence on Hegel can be summarized in four main points. First, Fichte concluded that reason is not static but that its categories are continually evolving because of opposing tendencies in thought and reality (known as the *thesis* and *antithesis*) that are resolved at a higher level (the *synthesis*). This three-step process is known as the *dialectic*. Although Hegel's thought does not conform to this rigid pattern, he did borrow the notion that opposing tendencies cause both our concepts and reality to

evolve. Second, Hegel adopted the notion that reality is fundamentally a continuously unfolding spiritual force that comes to fulfillment in human history. Thus, the cosmos is more like an organism than the clockwork mechanism proposed by the Enlightenment thinkers. Third, while Hegel was much more of a rationalist than his predecessors, he adopted their very broad notion of reason that made it more akin to our moral and aesthetic intuitions than to the calculations of the mathematician. Fourth, what is most significant about these idealists is that they revived metaphysics even though it had seemed to be a terminal patient when Kant was finished with it. The idealists claimed to have broken down the Kantian wall between our knowledge and reality as it is in itself, once again opening up the possibility of grand, visionary, metaphysical speculation.

Romanticism

The philosophical vision of the German idealists had much in common with the broader movement of romanticism. Romanticism was a quasi-philosophical literary and artistic movement that reacted against the Enlightenment picture of the universe as a machine that could best be studied by the analytical techniques of the sciences. For the romantics, the scientific vision of the world was too alienating, for it threatened to turn our moral, aesthetic, and religious longings into isolated aberrations within an otherwise mathematically ordered cosmos. As the romantics looked out on nature, they did not see atomistic particles in motion. Instead, they felt they were in the mystical presence of an organic unity that resonated with the human spirit. Furthermore, they were convinced that logic and telescopes missed what was most important about reality. Rather than reason and science revealing the secrets of this world to us, they fragmented nature and turned it into a catalogue of abstractions. In place of the banquet table of life, full of rich colors, tastes, and textures, science offered us only a cookbook of recipes. To be sure, every savory dish present at the banquet of nature was represented in the scientists' recipes. But to mistake the scientists' calculations for the fullness of reality would lead to spiritual starvation. The physicist could summarize the sunset and rainbow in optical equations, and the physiologist could describe the body of one's lover as a machine made up of organic pumps, tubing, levers, and pulleys. However, in each case the scientific account missed the beauty and the mystery of these realities.

Because its adherents were disdainful of logic and doctrines, romanticism was not a sharply defined movement. It is better understood as a mood or temperament, giving rise to many "romanticisms," rather than a single set of commonly held doctrines. Nevertheless, some themes were common to the romantics, such as intuition as a source of truth, distrust of logic and the sciences, the value of the emotions, love of nature, the view of nature as spiritual, the quest for new experience, and an adoration of classical antiquity. Because of their suspicion of reason, the romantics had a more direct impact on art and literature than on philosophy. Nevertheless, the movement inspired philosophers to expand their vision of the world, and in turn philosophers did influence the romantics. Although romanticism was not a direct offshoot of German idealism, the romantics were influenced by these philosophers' description of nature as spiritual and dynamic. Furthermore, the two movements agreed that through the emotions, intuition, and aesthetic experience we could penetrate to the core of reality and experience a spiritual oneness with the world. With Shakespeare's Hamlet, the romantics proclaimed to the Enlightenment that "there are more things in heaven and earth . . . , than are dreamt of in your philosophy."[6] Whereas Descartes had launched modern philosophy with his proclamation "I think, therefore I am," we could imagine the romantics replying, "I *feel*, therefore I am."

To understand the rise of romanticism, we need to slip back to the eighteenth century to look at a thinker we have bypassed. The forerunner of romanticism is generally considered to be the French writer Jean-Jacques Rousseau (1712–1778). Even though he lived through the Enlightenment, he was out of step with his time and revolted against his contemporaries' obsession with reason and science. Rousseau's thought was full of a number of conflicting tendencies, but for our purposes we will only mention those themes that led to romanticism.

In *Discourse on the Sciences and Arts* (1750), Rousseau asked whether scientific knowledge has value. With some inconsistency he praised Bacon, Descartes, and Newton for the advances they have brought. Nevertheless, his conclusion was that the only knowledge worth having is virtue, for which we do not need science because the principles of virtue are engraved on every heart. Central to Rousseau's thought was a romantic primitivism that argued that humans in their natural state were good, but that society in its present form corrupts us. If civilization is artificial and corrupting, then by returning to nature we would find the innocence we lost.* To this, Voltaire, his contemporary and leading critic, replied contemptuously that Rousseau wished people to go back to a four-legged, animal existence.

Rousseau's literary success reached its high point with two sentimental novels. The first was *The New Héloise* (1761), a story about the seduction and reclaimed virtue of a young maiden who preaches the value of a higher form of love that transcends the physical. It is said to have reduced all Europe to tears. The second novel was *Émile* (1762), which was a fictional treatise on education. In telling the story of the education of a young boy, Rousseau reveals his ideas about the proper education for life. Its message was "All is well when it leaves the hands of the Creator of things; all degenerates in the hands of man." It emphasized that children are naturally innocent and good. During their early years they should be trained in the classroom of nature, keeping them free of the stifling influence of books. Only between the ages of twelve and fifteen should intellectual subjects be introduced.

Rousseau's sense of the divinity and beauty of nature was echoed by the romantic poets of the

---

*This theme became a popular one with writers such as James Fenimore Cooper (1789–1851) and Herman Melville (1819–1891). In their novels they depict the white man as corrupt in contrast to the innocence of their Native American characters.

Casper David Friedrich, Man Looking at Mountains, with Rainbow. *The romantics reveled in the mystical beauty of nature and rebelled against the attempts of scientists to reduce marvels such as a rainbow to a series of mathematical formulas.*

nineteenth century. In William Wordsworth's "Lines Composed a Few Miles above Tintern Abbey" (1798) he captures the romantics' disdain for reason, science, and formal learning, as well as their insistence that nature is the genuine source of moral and spiritual truth.

> *One impulse from a vernal wood*
> *May teach you more of man,*
> *Of moral evil and of good,*
> *Than all the sages can.*
>
> *Sweet is the lore which Nature brings;*
> *Our meddling intellect*
> *Mis-shapes the beauteous forms of things—*
> *We murder to dissect.*

Although they had little interest in the philosophical details, the romantics captured the Kantian insight concerning the creative role of the mind in shaping our experience of reality. This is clearly illustrated in Coleridge's statement that

> *Newton was a mere materialist. Mind, in his system is always passive—a lazy looker-on in an external*

world. . . . Any system built on the passiveness of the mind must be false.[7]

To summarize, the romantics raised questions about the adequacy of reason as an instrument for knowing reality. In turn, they elevated the feelings and human subjectivity as more appropriate means for grasping what was true about life. They had a disdain for the universal and glorified individuality, subjectivity, and creativity. These themes would later be revived in the existentialism of Kierkegaard and Nietzsche. Finally, while Hegel made a number of harsh statements about the romantics, he did not remain immune to their influence. Like the romantic poets, Hegel strongly felt the unity of all things. Furthermore, he agreed with the romantics that every finite aspect of nature and every individual person is but a partial manifestation of a larger spiritual reality in which everything is perfectly harmonized.

The Importance of History

With the exception of Augustine, it is significant that very little has been said so far about the role of history in our understanding of human experience. From the very beginning, most philosophers, particularly the rationalists, were concerned with the search for eternal, timeless truths. Even though Augustine thought historical change was important, its significance to him lay in the way it mirrored eternal principles. Likewise, even though the British empiricists emphasized the changing world of the senses as the primary source of our knowledge, they found within the mind and nature alike, an established pattern impervious to historical changes. Furthermore, the empiricists and the rationalists alike, assumed human nature could be defined in terms of a singular, unchanging essence. Kant exploited these assumptions when he declared that the ground of universal and necessary knowledge lies in the universal and static structure of the human mind.

This outlook changed dramatically in the nineteenth century. To the philosophers of this time, history was all-important to philosophy. Hence, a unique feature of this century was that history was regarded from a philosophical viewpoint, and even more importantly, philosophy was regarded from a historical point of view. That this was a time of enormous historical change helped fuel this outlook. Living in the aftermath of the American and French Revolutions, facing social ferment, feeling the pressures for social reform and more revolutions, watching the rise of the Industrial Revolution, and marveling at the rapid development of the sciences, the thinkers of this century were persuaded that every tradition and idea eventually runs its course and is replaced by new ways of thinking and living. However, the observation that ideas and cultures change and are replaced by new ones was certainly not original to this century. What did uniquely characterize this era were the themes of (1) evolutionary development, (2) historicism, and (3) progress.

THE EVOLUTIONARY MODEL

The idea of evolutionary development was, of course, employed by Charles Darwin in his groundbreaking *On the Origin of Species* (1859) to explain how totally new species emerged from previous biological forms. His theory showed that even the categories of nature were not fixed for all time but were in continual flux. Although Darwin himself had little interest in the philosophical applications of his theory of evolution, it served as a powerful metaphor for philosophers who wanted to understand humanity as moving toward progressively higher stages of intellectual, moral, and social development.

Prior to and independently of Darwin's scientific research, the idea of evolutionary or dialectical development had been applied in Germany by the Hegelians and the Marxists to explain all reality, including the course history had taken in the past and would take in the future. For these philosophers, the new approach to biology seemed to provide scientific confirmation of the dynamic view of reality they had already arrived at in their studies. Common to both the biological and philosophical theories was the notion that a dynamic principle at work in the world caused nature or history to pass through successive stages. Change occurred when existing forms of organization (biological species or historical eras) faced the challenges that beset them by producing radically new forms. Included in these theories was the supposition that every emerging novelty represented some sort of advance over previous stages and, furthermore, that the total process followed a consistent pattern.

THE RISE OF HISTORICISM

The thesis of historicism was built on this view of historical change. **Historicism** claims that everything human is affected by the processes of history, such that any truth claim only has validity in terms of its place and role in this historical development. As Hegel expressed it, "Whatever happens, every individual is a child of his time; so philosophy is its own time apprehended in thoughts."[8] No idea has a single, fixed meaning, and no form of understanding has an eternal, unchanging relationship to the truth. This outlook was based on the Kantian insight that the mind is not passive in its encounter with the world, but is active and creative in structuring how the world appears to us. Consequently, Kant claimed, the world we experience reflects not the structure of reality in itself but rather the form of human understanding. Although apparently introducing human subjectivity into cognition, Kant could still preserve the notion of universal and objective knowledge because he insisted that the categories of the mind are the same for all. However, once we abandon this thesis, we end up with the possibility that the world can be structured and experienced in many ways.

Hegel and Marx illustrate this move to a multiplicity of perspectives. According to them, different historical eras have different conceptual structures and different rational ideals. This is because reason itself undergoes historical evolution as it is continually affected by the changing conditions of individual and social life. Nevertheless, for both of them, the historical emergence of new social and conceptual structures was not accidental but conformed to an identifiable rational pattern.

For the romantics and the existentialists, however, the focus was much more on the evolution of the individual's personal stance toward the world. This process was not the result of an inevitable historical logic, but flowed from free choices as each individual sought personal authenticity and power. For example, while Kierkegaard had no interest in world history, he brought Hegel's notion of dialectical development down to the personal level. The road to personal fulfillment, Kierkegaard claimed, will carry a person through several distinct stages. At each new stage the individual's outlook toward life becomes radically revised, and this process prepares the way for the movement to the next higher stage. Similarly, Nietzsche set forth the "genealogy of morals" in which he claimed that our moral systems are historical residues of individual attempts to express personal power or to inhibit it in others.

THE IDEAL OF PROGRESS

Finally, the nineteenth century's understanding of history was permeated with the notion of progress. A pessimist could look at the restless changes of human history and conclude that the world is a dismal and endless parade of failed cultural experiments. However, the majority opinion

among nineteenth-century philosophers reflected an unrestrained optimism. To them, it was easy for the discerning philosopher to find within the apparent chaos of history a clear linear development that pointed toward some sort of fulfillment. This idea came out most clearly in Hegel's and Marx's philosophies of history. Even though they both thought reason took different forms in different historical periods, they resisted a total relativism that would rob reason of any significance. As each era gives way to its successor, they claimed, it follows a logical pattern that gives intelligibility to the process and moves history closer to its culmination.

Although lacking Hegel's and Marx's sense of historical inevitability, Comte saw his age as the culmination of a long, progressive development of the human intellect. Along with the utilitarians, he called for a new scientific understanding of psychology and social dynamics to direct society's development toward a more rational order. Although cynical about what Western civilization had accomplished thus far, Nietzsche proclaimed that we were at the dawn of a new age, when a new breed of philosophers would rise up to overthrow the stagnant values of the present age. The notion that humanity was establishing a new, earthly paradise was boldly expressed by the French writer, Jules Castagnary:

> Beside the divine garden from which I have been expelled, I will erect a new Eden. . . . At its entrance I will set up Progress . . . and I will give a flaming sword into his hand and he will say to God, "Thou shalt not enter here." And thus it was that men began to build up the human community.[9]

Many, such as Comte, Marx, and Nietzsche, saw progress as humanity coming of age and discarding its mythological divinities; others, such as the conservative Hegelians, saw progress in terms of an immanent God working out his will in human history. Either way, progress was a theme trumpeted throughout the nineteenth century in popular literature, poetry, and the newspapers, as well as in philosophical systems.

This faith in progress did not lack dissenters, however. Kierkegaard, for example, believed his age had sunk to such depths that it was beyond any merely human remedy:

> Each age has its own characteristic depravity. Ours is perhaps not pleasure or indulgence or sensuality, but rather a dissolute pantheistic contempt for the individual man. In the midst of all our exultation over the achievements of the age and the nineteenth century, there sounds a note of poorly conceived contempt for the individual man; in the midst of the self-importance of the contemporary generation there is revealed a sense of despair over being human.[10]

For this melancholy Christian philosopher, it was foolish to search for some sort of social or historical salvation as the remedy for the infirmities of the human condition. Fulfillment could only be achieved on a personal level, within the confines of each individual's personal history, through a radical leap to religious faith.

Fyodor Dostoevsky (1821–1881) was another precursor of existentialism who expressed dissatisfaction with the modern age in his short story *Notes from Underground*. Whereas the Comtean positivists, the utilitarians, and the Marxists embraced the dream of science in their attempts to understand, predict, and control human actions, Dostoevsky was repelled by the encroachments of the scientific outlook on human freedom. As his disillusioned, bitter character expresses it, science tries to convince a person that

> he does not really have either caprice or will of his own and that he has never had it, and that he himself is something like a piano key or an organ stop.[11]

However, if we are nothing but mechanisms, then all human actions will conform to the laws of nature and "everything will be so clearly calculated and designated that there will be no more incidents or adventures in the world." Madness would be preferable to this sort of dehumanizing rationality for "the whole work of man seems really to consist in nothing but proving to himself continually that he is a man and not an organ stop."[12] To those who saw history as the outworking of a grand and glorious rational scheme, Dostoevsky's pessimistic critic complains, "One may say anything about the history of the world—anything that might enter the most disordered imagination. The only thing one cannot say is that it is rational. The very word sticks in one's throat."[13]

Despite the pessimism of a few dissenters, most people in the nineteenth century lived and breathed the unquestioned conviction that theirs was a time of significant historical fruition and that they were experiencing the dawn of a glorious new age. This optimism was eloquently expressed by Hegel in terms of an underlying history-making Spirit breaking forth from the dead weight of the past:

> It is not difficult to see that ours is a birth-time and a period of transition to a new era. . . . Spirit is indeed never at rest but always engaged in moving forward. But just as the first breath drawn by a child after its long, quiet nourishment breaks the gradualness of merely quantitative growth—there is a qualitative leap, and the child is born—so likewise the Spirit in its formation matures slowly and quietly into its new shape, dissolving bit by bit the structure of its previous world, whose tottering state is only hinted at by isolated symptoms. The frivolity and boredom which unsettle the established order, the vague foreboding of something unknown, these are the heralds of approaching change. The gradual crumbling that left unaltered the face of the whole is cut short by a sunburst which, in one flash, illuminates the features of the new world.[14]

Questions About Reason and Subjectivity

Another theme that loomed large in the nineteenth century concerned the limitations and powers of reason. This issue came to the fore in the eighteenth century when Hume argued that reason had very little relevance to our knowledge of the world and to how we live our lives. In all our practical engagements, he claimed, "Reason is and ought to be the slave of the passions." Although Kant agreed that reason has its limitations, he thought it had an *a priori* structure that provided a basis for our scientific and ethical endeavors. The German idealists were not happy with the boundaries of reason marked out by Kant and thought that the route to escape these limits could

The Crystal Palace, London, 1851, designed by Joseph Paxton. Constructed out of iron and glass, the structure covered nineteen acres and displayed an international exhibit of industrial progress. This shrine to science and technology represented the nineteenth century's faith in progress, which was exemplified in the philosophies of positivism and utilitarianism. However, the writer Fyodor Dostoevsky, in his Notes from Underground *(1864), ridiculed his contemporaries' scientific optimism by comparing it to belief in "a palace of crystal that can never be destroyed."*

be found in the self's inner experience. Building on their ideas, but taking a turn back toward rationalism, Hegel argued there was no separation between reason, the self, and reality because our concepts, self-consciousness, and reality were manifestations of one, all-encompassing Spirit that was developing in history.

As was discussed earlier, the romantics were relentless in their attack on the sterility of scientific and philosophical reason. This was eloquently expressed in John Keats's 1820 poem *Lamia*:

> *. . . Do not all charms fly*
> *At the mere touch of cold philosophy?*
> *There was an awful rainbow once in heaven:*
> *We know her woof, her texture; she is given*
> *In the dull catalogue of common things.*

> *Philosophy will clip an Angel's wings,*
> *Conquer all mysterious by rule and line,*
> *Empty the haunted air, and gnomed mine—*
> *Unweave a rainbow. . . . (Lamia, pt. 2)*

The existentialists, like the romantics, disdained the pretensions of philosophical reason. Both Kierkegaard and Nietzsche thought that the truth lay in subjectivity and that objective reason was merely a mask for those that feared self-disclosure.

Against all the philosophers just mentioned who found the world that science presented to us to be too confining, the positivists and utilitarians were quite comfortable within these limits. Being empiricists, they believed reason alone could tell us little about reality, for reason was mainly an instrument for organizing the data of experience.

Accordingly, they avoided any hint of metaphysical speculation and stuck only with what appears in experience.

Although Marx agreed reason could not provide us with the transcendent reality of the idealists and the romantics, he thought nature and history were governed by inescapable rational laws that science could disclose to us. Thus, unlike the positivists and utilitarians, he was not afraid to make metaphysical claims as long as they were grounded in material reality and not in the ethereal cloudland of the idealists. However, he also was suspicious of most philosophers' employment of reason, for reason tends to be a slave of our vested economic and social interests.

Summary of the Nineteenth-Century Agenda

From this brief overview, it is clear how a great deal of nineteenth-century thought could be seen as an attempt to come to terms with Kant. In the remaining chapters on the nineteenth century, the following questions are pivotal for the post-Kantian philosophers:

1. Can reason tell us about the nature of reality?
2. Can we know any reality that transcends phenomenal experience?
3. Can science and its laws adequately explain the human person?
4. Can knowledge be objective, or is it inescapably subjective?
5. Is the self
   a. an all-encompassing Absolute of which individual selves are finite manifestations (Hegel)?
   b. merely a sum of behavior or a bundle of psychological states (Comte, Bentham, Mill)?
   c. a product of the historical process (Hegel, Marx)?
   d. the unique center of my subjectivity from which I freely choose my outlook on life and all my values (Kierkegaard, Nietzsche)?

6. To what extent can we choose our destiny, and to what extent are we governed by our society and the forces of history?

Questions for Understanding

1. What are the various ways in which post-Kantian philosophers tried to avoid Kant's problematic dualism between reality-for-us (the phenomena) and reality-in-itself (the noumena)?
2. As the book defines the term, what does "idealism" mean?
3. In what ways did Fichte modify Kant's theory?
4. According to Schelling, what sort of human experience gives us the best window on reality?
5. How did the romantics critique the rational, scientific view of the world?
6. In what ways did history become the center of concern for nineteenth-century philosophers?

Questions for Reflection

1. Consider either Fichte's or Schelling's idealism. Do you think this perspective is more plausible or less plausible than Kant's philosophy?
2. Find examples in our contemporary age of reactions against science and technology that are similar to the views of the romantics. In what ways is our age becoming more scientific in its outlook on the world? In what ways is our age not completely enamored with science or is even anti-scientific?
3. Obviously, we are experiencing continual technological progress in our age. However, do you also agree with the nineteenth-century optimists that a pattern of continual moral, cultural, and rational progress is revealing itself in history? Or do you agree with the pessimism of Kierkegaard and Dostoevsky that the history of our culture is in a state of decline?

Notes

1. Quoted in Lewis White Beck, "German Philosophy," in *The Encyclopedia of Philosophy*, vol. 3 (New York: Macmillan, 1967), 302.

2. Letter to F. I. Niethammer, quoted in Stanley L. Jaki *The Road of Science and the Ways to God* (Chicago: University of Chicago Press, 1978), 128.

3. *Science of Knowledge*, trans. Peter Heath and John Lachs (Cambridge, England: Cambridge University Press, 1982), 16.

4. Quoted in Frederick Copleston, *A History of Philosophy*, vol. 7, pt. 1, *Fichte to Hegel* (Garden City, NY: Doubleday, Image Books, 1963), 60.

5. *The Vocation of Man*, trans. William Smith, ed. Roderick M. Chisholm (Indianapolis: Bobbs-Merrill, The Library of Liberal Arts, 1956), 93.

6. William Shakespeare, *Hamlet*, act I, sc. 5, ll. 165–166.

7. Quoted in Roland Stromberg, *An Intellectual History of Modern Europe* (New York: Appleton-Century-Crofts, 1966), 218.

8. G. W. F. Hegel, *Hegel's Philosophy of Right*, trans. T. M. Knox (Oxford, England: Oxford University Press, 1964), 11.

9. Jules Castagnary, *Philosophie du Salon de 1857*, quoted in Franklin L. Baumer, *Modern European Thought* (New York: Macmillan, 1977), 335.

10. Søren Kierkegaard, *Concluding Unscientific Postscript*, trans. David F. Swenson and Walter Lowrie (Princeton, NJ: Princeton University Press, 1941), 317.

11. Fyodor Dostoevsky, *Notes from Underground* in *Existentialism*, ed. Robert C. Solomon (New York: The Modern Library, 1974), 36.

12. Ibid., 42.

13. Ibid., 41.

14. G. W. F. Hegel, *Phenomenology of Spirit*, trans. A. V. Miller (Oxford, England: Oxford University Press, 1977), §11.

CHAPTER

24

G. W. F. Hegel:
Biographer of the World Spirit

✦

GEORG WILHELM FRIEDRICH HEGEL WAS A MAN of many contradictions. A brief list of the conflicting images of this man and his thought will give a clue to the difficulties one faces in trying to understand him. (1) His university professors reported he was an average student with only a mediocre grasp of philosophy. Yet most scholars now consider him one of the greatest thinkers of modern philosophy. (2) Hegel was an arch-rationalist who thought that all reality conformed to a rational pattern. Yet he insisted that "nothing great in the world has been accomplished without passion" (RH 29).[1] (3) Some view Hegel as a theist and others as an atheist, and advocates of each interpretation quote Hegel's own words in defense of their position. (4) Hegel saw all history as leading to the realization of human freedom and yet also saw individuals as the pawns of the irresistible force of historical destiny. (5) Finally, Hegel has been both praised and damned as a defender of the political status quo. Yet through his influence on Karl Marx, Hegel's ideas inspired the birth of revolutionary socialism.

The snarl of conflicting interpretations of Hegel may seem a barrier to one who is beginning the task of understanding his philosophy. But ironically, it actually may be the appropriate beginning point for entering his system. Hegel believed that contradictions, tensions, ironies, paradoxes, oppositions, and reversals are at the heart of all thought and even reality itself. He exposed our temptation to latch onto one-sided views and partial truths, in which each perspective claims it is the absolute truth, the stopping point for thought. Instead, he insisted, the truth is multifaceted and each set of oppositions points to a higher, more all-encompassing viewpoint.

Hegel's Life:
From Average Student to
World-Famous Philosopher

G. F. W. Hegel was born in Stuttgart in southern Germany in 1770. In the same year, Beethoven was born and Kant was made a professor at Königsberg. Napoleon had been born one year earlier. Hegel's father was a minor civil servant, and his mother was a well-educated and intelligent woman who taught her young son Latin.

Taking advantage of the opportunity for a state-sponsored education, he entered the Protestant theological seminary at the University of Tübingen in 1788 where he made friends with the poet Hölderlin and with a young, brilliant philosophy student named Friedrich Schelling. Surrounded by stiff intellectual competition, Hegel did not distinguish himself in the eyes of his professors. However, although Schelling went on to become a famous philosopher before anyone even knew of Hegel, Schelling's reputation was later eclipsed by that of his university classmate.

After graduation, Hegel spent several years as a tutor to a succession of wealthy families. During this period, his interest in philosophy blossomed and he began to read and write extensively. In 1801 he became an instructor at the University of Jena, where his friend Schelling had succeeded Fichte as professor of philosophy and was becoming quite well known. Because Hegel did not yet have any reputation, he could only lecture privately to a small handful of students, who paid him modest fees. At Jena, Hegel began to write his first major work, *The Phenomenology of Spirit*. When Napoleon's forces invaded Jena on October 13, 1806, Hegel quickly sent off the only copy of his manuscript, while the battle raged, to meet his publisher's deadline. Fortunately, it survived the confusion intact and was published in 1807.

As a result of the French occupation, the university was closed down. Hegel went on to work for a year as a newspaper editor and then from 1808 to 1816 he was headmaster of a *Gymnasium* (high school) in Nuremberg. In 1811 he married the daughter of an old Nuremberg family, and she gave him two sons, one of whom became a well-known historian. While still at Nuremberg, he published his three-volume *Science of Logic*. Having begun to achieve a reputation in philosophy, he was invited to become professor of philosophy at Heidelberg, where he served from 1816 to 1818 and published his *Encyclopedia of the Philosophical Sciences*. Finally, at the high point of his career, he was appointed to a prestigious chair of philosophy at the University of Berlin, where his lectures

and writings made him a legend in his own time. A devoted following of students kept careful copies of his notes and published his philosophical lectures on history, art, religion, and the history of philosophy after his death. In 1831, Georg W. F. Hegel died in a cholera epidemic.

Task: Fitting the Pieces of History and Reality Together

Hegel's task can be summarized in the following key principles, which he sought to demonstrate throughout all his writings.

1. *The goal of philosophy is to achieve a unified, systematic understanding of the whole of things.* Obviously, our current knowledge falls short of this ideal. We see the world as made up of separate objects and events, and our universities are composed of separate departments, each teaching a collection of courses focusing in on some particular subject matter. But we know we live in a *universe*. We need, then, to overcome all fragmentation, divisions, and dichotomies to get a sense of the unity of it all. This leads to the second major point, which is . . .

2. *Every particular truth and every particular thing can only be understood as a partial aspect of the totality.* In order to completely understand *you*, I would also have to understand the larger context in which you developed: your political, cultural, economic, biological, and geographical environment. To understand these, I would need to know the totality of human and natural history, for everything is related to everything else. The point is that any particular thing (or any particular concept) is a fragment torn from the whole and must be understood in terms of its relationship to the total context in which it has its existence. If everything must be understood as part of a larger context, then . . .

3. *Nothing can be understood apart from its place in history.* Hegel believes that every idea, physical object, culture, or historical era is just a slice of an ongoing historical process. Thus Hegel gave a new importance to history. After Hegel, history was no longer viewed as simply a museum of dusty relics of past events, nor as merely a collection of interesting stories. Instead, Hegel sees the discipline of history as significant because it can reveal profound truths about ourselves and the nature of reality. If reality is ultimately a seamless fabric in which all the threads are woven together in a coherent way, then this suggests that . . .

4. *"What is rational is real and what is real is rational"* (PR, preface).* Hegel is a rationalist and believes there is a harmony between human reason and the world. Because of this conviction, Hegel thinks he can overcome the alleged gap between our concepts and reality. As he puts it, "the ultimate aim and the business of philosophy is to reconcile thought or the Concept with reality."[2]† Although Hegel is a rationalist, he does not believe that with our reason alone we can generate the details of reality while sitting in our armchairs (contrary to some misinterpretations of him). He believes experience plays a role in knowledge. However, this is consistent with his rationalism, because he thinks experience contains within itself a certain logical order.

Theory of Knowledge: Reason Reveals Reality

Hegel's epistemology revolves around his slogan "the rational is the real." This is a nice, optimistic formula, but how can we be sure this is the case? We, like Hegel in his time, have surveyed some twenty-four hundred years of philosophical history, full of conflicting accounts of reality and always bordering on the abyss of skepticism. Therefore, what grounds do we have for supposing that even our most rationally coherent system of thought is any more than a self-enclosed system that is wildly "out of synch" with reality? A good place to start answering this question is with Hegel's notion of how ideas develop through a process called "the dialectic."

DIALECTIC

The word **dialectic** derives from the Greek word for "conversation" and refers to the way our ideas develop through a process of conflict and opposition.† Hegel believes ideas have their own internal laws of change, so that when a partial truth is examined and pushed to its limits, it will reveal its own inadequacies at the same time that it points to its successor. Thus every idea is a roadside inn, only a temporary stopping place on the mind's journey toward completely adequate knowledge.

Many commentators describe Hegel's dialectic as a triadic process starting with an initial idea, called the *thesis*, which is then opposed by another standpoint called the *antithesis*. The tension between these two is then resolved by moving to a higher-order perspective called the *synthesis*. But this third stage now becomes a thesis, which produces its own antithesis, and the process continues. For example, Parmenides says that reality is unchanging and permanent. However, it would seem impossible for us to come to know this, since "coming to know something" involves a change in our understanding. The antithesis to this philosophy was found in Heraclitus, who said reality is constantly changing. However, this idea is inadequate, for if reality is continually changing and I am changing, then there is nothing enduring to know and no enduring person to know it. The synthesis of these two positions is found in Plato, who said that one aspect of reality is permanent (the eternal Forms) and another aspect of reality is changing (the physical world). Thus, two partial truths led to a more comprehensive viewpoint, which historically led to further developments.

---

*In T. M. Knox's translation of this passage from the *Philosophy of Right*, he substitutes the word *actual* for *real*. However, for our purposes the word *real* is more suitable and follows the convention of many commentators.
†The current English translations (produced in Britain) render *"Begriff"* as "Notion." However, in this and all similar quotations, I have changed it to "Concept" for the sake of clarity.

†In Plato's dialogues, Socrates employed a dialectical method in which the confrontation of opposing ideas in the course of a conversation progressively led to more and more refined ideas, thus bringing the participants ever closer to the truth.

As common as it is to view Hegel's philosophy in terms of this triadic pattern, this interpretation is itself only partially true, for it fits only some of the movements of Hegel's thought. The problem is that Hegel rarely uses the terms "thesis," "antithesis," and "synthesis." Instead, this terminology was used by Hegel's predecessor, Fichte. Although Hegel does have a tendency to divide things up in triads, he does not always do so. For example, sometimes an idea is found to contain an absurdity within itself, instead of being contradicted by a second idea. In other cases, an idea is found to be incomplete and is filled out or supplemented by another standpoint. Sometimes, two complementary ideas are found to presuppose a third, more comprehensive notion. The point of Hegel's dialectic is that, short of a perfect knowledge of the totality, our ideas are always one-sided and inadequate and, thus, they have a restless tendency to find their fulfillment in progressively more complete viewpoints.

Another problem of interpretation concerns the type of necessity Hegel attributes to the dialectical process. He certainly does use the term "necessity," causing some readers to fault him when his ideas do not follow one another with a strict, logical rigor. More often than not, however, the way he sees ideas connected together is more like the parts of a novel or a symphony, in which each moment anticipates and leads naturally to the next one without logically entailing it. To understand the implications of Hegel's dialectic, we need to examine how he answers two of the traditional questions in epistemology.

BEGINNING THE SEARCH FOR KNOWLEDGE

Hegel begins his *Phenomenology of Spirit* with a critique of modern epistemology. He takes on the underlying assumptions that motivated modern philosophy as it began with Descartes and Locke and culminated in Kant. To contrast Hegel with his predecessors, we will give the traditional responses to several questions, show the problems Hegel has with their answers, and then indicate his alternative solutions.

1. *How do we find the criterion for knowledge?* The modern philosophers before Hegel believed that before we can begin the quest for knowledge, we need to *know* the correct criterion to justify our beliefs. But this puts us in a vicious circle, for before we can have knowledge, we must first have some knowledge! However, it seems that any criterion for knowledge that we assume at the beginning will be arbitrary and in need of justification itself. Hegel says that philosophers who are obsessed with finding the correct criterion or the correct method are like someone who will not venture into the water until he has learned how to swim. Obviously, we can only become skilled at swimming by jumping into the water, thrashing around, feeling the buoyancy of our own body, trying a few strokes, finding what works and what doesn't, and then refining our technique. Similarly, in philosophy we can do nothing else but begin where we begin. However, in the process we will find that "consciousness provides its own criterion from within itself, so that the investigation becomes a comparison of consciousness with itself" (PS §84).

What he means is that we can start with any proposed approach to knowledge. We then sympathetically enter into it, accepting it on its own terms, and try it out to see if it fulfills its promise. Hegel believes that any inadequate conception of knowledge will eventually fail according to its own standards. Nevertheless, in the midst of this disillusionment or failure, we will find pointers to a new or more adequate approach to knowledge. Thus, the adequate criterion for knowledge arises through a continuously self-correcting process.

2. *How is the mind related to reality?* Epistemologists from Descartes to Kant made a sharp distinction between the contents of the mind and the thing-in-itself. The task then became one of determining whether or not there is any correspondence between the two realms. However, according to Hegel, this approach will inevitably end in skepticism. To understand how Hegel overcomes Kant's dualism, we might ask, "How did we come to distinguish between our beliefs and reality as it is in itself?" To answer this question, Hegel asks us to examine the process by which we modify our beliefs. The distinction between beliefs and their objects arises solely within the mind as we continually move from conceptions that turn out to be simplistic and inadequate, to ones that are more comprehensive and coherent. For example, a teacher may initially seem harsh and critical, even though these characterizations conflict with the fact that she also seems very caring. A more adequate perspective may be that she is unusually critical not because she is mean, but because she respects you so highly that she is unrelenting in demanding the very best from you. But notice that this process of moving from one conceptualized object to another, more comprehensive conceptualization, is something that takes place solely within consciousness. It does not occur by jumping outside our mind to compare its ideas with the "brute facts" lying out in the external world. Thus, the dichotomy between object and idea is a dichotomy that is continually being overcome within the developing stages of our understanding.

THE JOURNEY OF CONSCIOUSNESS

We can get a glimpse of how dialectical reasoning works by examining some of its initial movements in the *Phenomenology of Spirit*, a work that Hegel referred to as his "voyage of discovery." Phenomenology, as Hegel understands it, is the "study of phenomena" or a systematic examination of what appears within experience, in an attempt to understand its necessary structure. Hegel describes it as the "Science of the *experience of consciousness*" (PS §88). It is important to understand that when Hegel talks about "experience," he does not mean isolated "pings" of sensation, as did the British empiricists. No one, including John Locke, experiences the world that way. Instead, "experience" refers to our various ways of being in the world and relating to it. Hegel uses the word in much the same sense as we talk about "the college experience" or "the experience of falling in love."

When Kant analyzed the structure of experience, he found a single set of categories that were the same for all rational minds. Hegel, however, finds a variety of possible forms of experience.

J. Loewenberg describes the subject of the *Phenomenology* as

> *different and recurrent views of life—sensuous and intellectual, emotional and reflective, practical and theoretical, mystic and philistine, sceptical and dogmatic, empirical and speculative, conservative and radical, selfish and social, religious and secular.*[3]

Each claims for itself total reasonableness and mastery of all reality and human experience. Embarking on a dialectical journey, Hegel explores each way of looking at the world until its inadequacies are exposed and a richer, more adequate approach emerges from its failure.

Hegel begins this process with the simplest, most commonsense view of knowledge. (Yet, for all its simplicity, this is the starting point of the classical empiricists.) This is the viewpoint that knowledge is a direct sensory awareness of some object that requires no assistance from the mind. He calls this standpoint *sense certainty*. Hegel asks us to try to adopt this form of consciousness to see if it is possible. Focus in on your experience of an object, your perception of a pencil, for example. Avoid bringing any concepts or thoughts to this experience, allowing your senses and understanding to remain completely passive. At first, this approach to the world appears the most concrete, richest, truest, and indubitable form of knowledge. Since the mind is contributing nothing of its own to the content of the experience, nothing stands between your consciousness and the pure immediacy of the object within your visual field.

What is the content of your experience when it is freed of any conceptual interpretations? You cannot be aware that you are experiencing a "pencil" or even something "yellow, cylindrical, and long," for this involves smuggling concepts into the experience. All you can say about what you are experiencing is "*this*-here-now." But these terms are universals that may apply to any object whatsoever. Tomorrow, in another place, "this here now" will designate a completely different object for you. Hence, sense certainty is the most empty and abstract form of consciousness. Its entire content is simply the awareness that "something is there," which also characterizes the experience of anything and everything. Just when we thought we had the most concrete, particular, and indubitable form of experience, it turned into the most abstract, universal, and useless level of experience. The problem is that without concepts, your experience would be as indistinct and undifferentiated as an oyster's experience.

As a result of this analysis, we see that consciousness must be active. It does not passively receive objects, but interprets them, brings them under universal concepts. This leads to the second stage, which is *perception*. Here you view objects as things possessing universal properties. Once again, Hegel pushes this form of consciousness to its limits and finds that this still does not give a satisfactory account of experience. The problem is that our experience consists of unified, enduring objects, not just bundles of changing and arbitrary properties.

We now find we must move beyond perception as a form of consciousness to the third stage, which is *understanding*. Here, we conceive of objects in terms of lawlike forces that account for the unity of the object, while producing its changing properties. The forces Hegel is referring to here are those described by Newton's laws of physics. Although these supposedly describe the realities beyond the appearances, this aspect of the object is not really the Kantian thing-in-itself, because the mind is capable of knowing it.

Thus far, the stages of sense certainty, perception, and understanding are progressive stages of bare *consciousness*. From here, the dialectic carries us on to the next level of *self-consciousness*. When we were at the level of "understanding," consciousness supposed that the laws it was studying were something entirely external. However, when the mind becomes aware of its own activity, it discovers that these laws are imputed by the understanding itself, since the concepts we employ in this process, such as "gravity" and "force," are not things we directly encounter in experience. Therefore, they are part of the framework our understanding uses to help us grasp what we experience. When scientists give us their deepest understanding of the universe, it is always in terms of theoreti-

cal constructs and mathematical formulas. But these are not discovered in the same sense that a new species of flower is discovered. Instead, the constructs of science are *products of the mind* and of an intellectual framework that has taken centuries to unfold. In a similar fashion, the later chapters of the *Phenomenology* pass through increasing levels of self-awareness and continue to explore the way in which consciousness and its world emerge together.

HISTORICISM

Hegel's *Phenomenology* could be viewed as one, very large "thought experiment" that shows how the mind can move from inadequate conceptions to increasingly more adequate ones. However, he believes something like this actually took place in intellectual history. A crucial feature of Hegel's philosophy is his commitment to historicism. **Historicism** is the claim that ideas are not eternal objects but are products of their time and that the truth of any idea cannot be understood apart from its origin and role in its historical setting. A superficial and cynical look at the history of philosophy may give the impression that it is merely a collection of differing opinions, a comedy of errors. Philosophers just can't seem to get it right.

For Hegel, however, there is logic and purpose to this development. A fruit does not come out of the ground fully formed—it comes from a seed, which goes through a number of stages before the fully formed fruit emerges. The same is true with the history of ideas. No stage can be understood in isolation, for each one is a necessary prelude to the next one. To suppose that Thales in 600 B.C. could have produced Kant's system, if only he had been clever enough, is like supposing that the apple could pop out of the ground fully formed. Each historical idea or stage is incomplete, one-sided, full of tensions, and can only fulfill its own ideals by giving birth to its successor. In this way, the history of philosophy is a dialectical development that will be complete when there are no longer any gaps, contradictions, impossible assumptions, unfulfilled ideals, or further directions to be explored within our ideas.

ABSOLUTE KNOWLEDGE

When Hegel did away with the unknowable Kantian thing-in-itself that lies beyond the limits of knowledge, he did not mean to imply that right now there is perfect coherence between our ideas and reality. Instead, consciousness continually becomes more adequate to its object, and, in this process, the object of our knowledge undergoes a transformation and becomes more rational. The ultimate goal of this process is *absolute knowledge*. Thus, the goal of philosophy "is the point where knowledge no longer needs to go beyond itself, where knowledge finds itself, where Concept corresponds to object and object to Concept" (PS §80). This is not a correspondence between the mind and something external to it. Instead, it is a perfect harmony between (1) the object as it is present to the mind and (2) the way the mind conceptualizes it. Hegel ends up with a **coherence theory of truth**. This is the claim that our ideas will be true when they each find their place within a perfectly coherent system. This view is based on the conviction that reality in itself is rational through and through, and that its rationality is one in which our minds participate. When reason has completed its historical task, no incomprehensible mysteries will remain, for everything can be penetrated by the power of reason.

WHOSE MIND, WHOSE CONSCIOUSNESS ARE WE TALKING ABOUT?

One crucial question has been ignored in talking about the development of consciousness: Whose consciousness is going through this process? There are three equally correct answers to this question. First, the movement from one idea to the next is a logical progression carried out within the mind of the philosopher (Hegel and us). Second, the process from a mute immersion in experience (which the theory of sense certainty describes) all the way up to full, reflective awareness is the journey that each individual takes from infancy to intellectual maturity. Finally, the intellectual development of each individual retraces the journey the human species has made through history (PS §28). For example, when you learn mathematics, you start with arithmetic and then go on to geometry, algebra, calculus, and beyond. But in doing this, your individual mind is starting with the early Greeks and following the intellectual development of "humanity's mind." The notion that beyond individual minds a universal mind or spirit is developing through history leads us very quickly into Hegel's metaphysics.

Metaphysics: Reason Becoming Self-Conscious

HEGEL'S IDEALISM

Hegel's epistemology can be seen as a demonstration of the formula "the rational is the real." In other words, he is a rationalist who believes reason can give us knowledge of reality. His metaphysics can be seen as the other side of this coin. That is, his metaphysics follows from his conviction that "the real is the rational." If reality has a rational structure, then the logic of the dialectic applies not only to our concepts but to reality itself. This implies that in some sense the world itself contains conflicts or oppositions out of which new forms of existence shape themselves. Thus, a half-century before Charles Darwin published his famous work on biological evolution, Hegel was proposing that all reality is evolving. The way this occurs is spelled out in Hegel's version of metaphysical idealism.

Hegel pictures the world as permeated by a dynamic spiritual force that is in the process of unfolding itself and bringing to fruition a rational purpose. Throughout Hegel's writings, he speaks of this animating principle as the *Absolute Idea*.* For this reason, Hegel has been labeled an idealist. Traditionally, **idealism** is the claim that all reality is reducible to or dependent on some sort of mental reality (such as a mind or spirit). However,

---

*Sometimes it is simply referred to as the *Absolute* or the *Idea*. Frequently, he gives this notion a more personal or religious ring by referring to it as *Spirit*. When he is discussing the flow of history, he speaks of the *World Spirit*.

in working out the details of Hegel's idealism numerous controversies have arisen concerning how to characterize his position. At least four key questions must be asked to clarify the confusions about his idealism: (1) Does Hegel believe that objects exist only in the mind? (2) What is the relationship between mind and nature? (3) What is the relationship between the Absolute Spirit and the human spirit? and (4) Does Hegel believe there is a Spirit that transcends the human spirit, in some sense like traditional theism?

DO OBJECTS EXIST ONLY IN THE MIND?

Any careful reading of Hegel answers "no" to the question "Do objects exist only in the mind?" Too often, however, Hegel's idealism is confused with either Berkeley's or Kant's idealism. According to Berkeley, objects are only collections of ideas within the mind. According to Kant, the mind creates the objects encountered in experience by imposing its concepts on the materials of sense experience. However, these "subjective idealisms" (as Hegel calls them) bear no resemblance to his position, for Hegel makes it absolutely clear that natural objects such as rocks and plants existed long before fully conscious minds appeared in the world.[4] To distinguish his own position from theirs, Hegel chose the label *absolute idealism*.

What Hegel means by "absolute idealism" becomes clearer when we understand his notion of the "Absolute." The Absolute should not be understood as a specific thing over and against the rest of the world. The Absolute, as the very term implies, is what is completely self-contained in the sense that it does not need anything else in order to exist or be conceived. To Hegel, the only thing that satisfies this definition is reality-as-a-whole.* However, he insists the Absolute is not

only the ultimate substance, but also is a living subject.† Thus life, mentality, subjectivity, spirit, or consciousness is intrinsic to the nature of reality as a whole. Rather than objects having their existence within individual minds (subjective idealism), Hegel's absolute idealism claims that Mind (in a sense to be explained shortly) is inherent in the objects of the world. Hegel explains there is an intimacy between the mind and reality-in-itself: "To him who looks at the world rationally the world looks rationally back" (RH 13).

WHAT IS THE RELATIONSHIP BETWEEN MIND AND NATURE?

All this sounds very inspiring but lacks credibility. Can it really make good sense to suggest that mind and nature are, in some sense, part of one, joint venture? Most would find Locke's position much more plausible: objects are out there in the world, while concepts are in the mind. However, Locke never satisfactorily answered the question of how we know that these objects and our concepts are harmonious. Berkeley and Kant solved that problem by making both objects and concepts dependent on mind. According to Hegel, however, we will never have knowledge unless concepts are out there, as the primary constituent of reality-in-itself. For this reason he says that "the concept is the genuine first; and things are what they are through the action of the concept, immanent in them, revealing itself in them."[5]

To make this very difficult notion clear, we need to understand that Hegel borrowed from Aristotle the notion of nature as a teleological (purposeful) system.[6] To illustrate the purposeful and rational nature of the world, consider the acorn. It doesn't grow into a cabbage, but will always grow into an oak. This is possible because the acorn contains some sort of "blueprint" for its own self-actualization. To use Hegel's term, we may say that within the acorn is "the Idea" of its final end, the oak.

---

*Hegel was influenced here by similar conceptions in Schelling and Spinoza. As he once said, "When one begins to philosophize one must be first a Spinozist." Quoted by Frederick C. Beiser in *"Introduction: Hegel and the Problem of Metaphysics"* in *The Cambridge Companion to Hegel*, ed. Frederick C. Beiser (Cambridge, England: Cambridge University Press, 1993), 5.

†As he states it, "The living Substance is being which is in truth *Subject*" (PS §18).

For Hegel, reality as a whole may be considered using the analogy of the plant. When he refers to "the Idea," he is speaking of the overall rational scheme for reality. When he says the Idea is what is real, he is not saying there is nothing more than this. What he is saying is that all that exists is directed by the Idea's structure.[7] Thus the totality, the Absolute, is an organic totality, in which each individual, including chemicals, plants, worms, humans, and (as we shall see later) ethical communities, political states, works of art, religions, and philosophical movements have their life.

Obviously, when the plant is following its developmental plan, it is not doing so in a conscious way. In nature, mind is present, but it is "mind asleep" (PR §258A). Following Schelling, Hegel calls nature a petrified or unconscious intelligence. But if nature is an unconscious rationality, when does it wake up? It does so in the rise of human consciousness. With humanity, a part of nature has emerged that is not only conscious, but also self-conscious and able to reflect, understand, choose, and become progressively more rational with each new age of science and philosophy.

As Descartes found, once you separate mind and matter, it becomes hard to get them back again. For this reason, Hegel wants to avoid the problems of any sort of dualism. Hegel's solution is to claim that what we call "mind" and what we call "matter" are simply two poles on the same continuum, with reality starting out favoring the material end but having a tendency to realize itself by moving toward the mental end. On this point, among others, Hegel was influenced by Friedrich Schelling's view that "mind is the most organized and developed form of matter, and matter is the least organized and developed form of mind."[8]

HOW ARE THE ABSOLUTE SPIRIT AND HUMAN SPIRIT RELATED?

Hegel sometimes uses the German word *Geist*, meaning "Spirit," to speak of the subjective aspect of the Absolute. A halo of traditional religious connotations obviously surrounds "spirit," as explored in the next section.* For now, note that Hegel speaks of Spirit in very active, anthropomorphic ways.[†] Despite the ethereal, mystical associations of the word, Hegel largely uses the term "Spirit" in the same down-to-earth sense in which we commonly speak of "school spirit." School spirit lives in and through the individual fans and team members, for without them it would not exist. Yet it is larger than any particular collection of students, for the personality and identity of the school remains even though its students come and go. In this same way, we talk of "the spirit of the age," as when we use such phrases as "the spirit of the Renaissance" to speak of the collective identity of the people in a particular time or nation. In each case, the individual people are participating in a whole that is larger than the sum of its members.[‡]

Prior to nineteenth-century German idealism, the activity of thought was usually considered the product of individual minds. However, the German idealists, particularly Hegel, developed a social theory of the mind. According to Hegel, your thoughts do not spring spontaneously out of the isolated privacy of your mind. Instead, the way in which you think is a product of your culture and of the many minds that preceded yours. When you do geometry, you are participating in Euclid's mental life, and when you think about the physical world, your thoughts are part of the conceptual ripples set in motion by Newton. Thus, even in your most creative moments your mental life is permeated by the spirit of Western civilization that is itself the collective product of many minds.

---

*The Christian term "Holy *Ghost*" (Holy Spirit) is related to the term "*Geist*." Fearing unwanted religious connotations, some translators render Hegel's term as "Mind." However, in spite of possible misunderstandings, "Spirit" is probably the preferred translation.

[†]For example, in speaking of the historical changes in his time, Hegel says, "Spirit has broken with the world it has hitherto inhabited and imagined, and is of a mind to submerge it in the past, and in the labour of its own transformation" (PS §11).

[‡]Robert Solomon makes the interesting observation that the very idea of a "spirit of the times" was a nineteenth-century innovation, for it seemed not to exist in the vocabulary before Hegel's time. Robert C. Solomon, *In the Spirit of Hegel* (Oxford, England: Oxford University Press, 1983), 252.

In Hegel's view, we are not so many isolated, mental threads but are part of a larger, social, mental, and spiritual fabric, known as the Absolute Spirit.

WAS HEGEL A THEIST?

The last question—was Hegel a theist?—is, perhaps, the most controversial of all. Hegel's interpreters tend to answer this question in one of two ways: (1) The Hegelian Spirit is transcendent in a way that would make Hegel a theist or (2) Spirit transcends individual minds simply in the sense of being the collective spirit of humanity.

1. *The Theistic Hegel* Many have interpreted Hegel as a theist. According to them, Hegel presents the material world as a projection of the divine thought, much as the world of *Hamlet* is a product of Shakespeare's thought. Hegel often uses very blunt theistic language that sounds too straightforward to be merely figurative. For example, he says, "God governs the world. The actual working of His government, the carrying out of His plan is the history of the world" (RH 47). However, this represents a very nontraditional view of God, for he is a God in process, a being becoming more enriched as he relates to a changing world and develops with it.

2. *The Secular-Humanist Hegel* Despite these references to God and his activity, it is not obvious that Spirit is a quasi-theistic God. Some interpreters seek to demystify Hegel's references to Spirit by treating them as merely picturesque metaphors used to describe the way individuals can collectively contribute to the pattern of events unfolding around them without being aware of doing so. For example, the following passage seems to suggest that the divine and the human are one:

> The realm of Spirit consists in what is produced by man. One may have all sorts of ideas about the Kingdom of God; but it is always a realm of Spirit to be realized and brought about in man. (RH 20)

Furthermore, Hegel says that the point where "Spirit and Nature unite" is none other than "human nature" (RH 20-21). The poet Heinrich Heine, who was once Hegel's student, supported a humanistic interpretation of his former teacher:

> I was young and proud, and it pleased my vanity when I learned from Hegel that it was not the dear God who lived in heaven that was God, as my grandmother supposed, but I myself here on earth.[9]

From these sorts of remarks, many Hegelians conclude that "God" comes into conscious existence in humanity's awareness of its own divinity. Other secular Hegelians view "God" as merely a Kantian regulative idea, an ideal of perfect knowledge and unity that organizes our cognitive endeavors.

Applying Hegel's dialectical logic to his own position, these two perspectives may be too limited to capture Hegel's thought. Hegel is clearly a transitional figure between the traditional religious worldview and the contemporary secular view. On the one hand, he retains much of the religious vision of the world: nature is spiritual, and there is an overall meaning and purpose at work in history. On the other hand, he is pushing toward a secular-humanist view: nothing transcends nature, and humanity is the sovereign source of all value in the world. Perhaps, in the final analysis, Hegel is Hegel and neither the religious philosophers nor the atheists can rightly claim him as their own.

Ethics and Community Life

As the rationality in nature becomes fully explicit and self-aware through its realization in the human spirit, the human community creates a second world of its own that consists of ethical, political, legal institutions and all our other cultural accomplishments. In these institutions, reason becomes actual and externalizes itself. Look at the world about you. You see trees, mountains, lakes, and animals. However, you also see courts of law, universities, laboratories, banks, stores, art museums, and churches. Nature has become enriched by the development of the cultural and intellectual creations of the human community. However, communities and cultures cannot exist without social values that bind them together into a unity. Hence, the next chapter of Hegel's story deals with the way in which ethical consciousness develops in history.

What is the source of moral principles? Hegel complains that seventeenth- and eighteenth-century writers act as though ethical values can arise in a vacuum. They supposed that each autonomous individual, in the privacy of his or her study, could generate ethical norms on the basis of their own, rational convictions. In contrast, Hegel says we are born into a community and become fully mature persons by being socialized. From the very beginning we define our self-identity and form our concept of the overall scheme of things in terms of our communal life. In both his ethical and political theory, therefore, Hegel consistently applies his basic conviction that the particular can only be understood in terms of the whole.

The German term Hegel uses when he refers to ethics is *Sittlichkeit*, which could be translated as "customary ethics" or "community ethical life." For Hegel, ethics is not just a set of moral commandments but consists of the whole social fabric. The ethical life of a community includes explicit rules as well as implicit attitudes, values, and forms of life. Thus, Hegel's discussion of ethics is very broad and very concrete. Ethical concerns are rooted in a community's total life, including its practices, rituals, social roles, duties, manners, relationships of intimacy, family life, leisure, work, and modes of worship. At this point it would seem as though Hegel has reduced ethics to anthropology. However, although Hegel believes we cannot lift ourselves up by our own bootstraps to escape our concrete moral traditions, he says that a rational ideal unfolding in them is moving toward a universal ethics.

CUSTOM AS THE SOURCE OF ETHICAL VALUES

To understand the development of moral consciousness, Hegel looks back with admiration to ancient Greece. The Greek city-states, such as Athens, represent a model of the ethical community in which people find their identity, happiness, and sense of meaning by participating in the life of the society. Despite his nostalgia for the community life of the ancient Greeks, Hegel believes their approach was limited and destined to be superseded by other forms. In their world, the harmony individuals felt with the laws and customs of their society was based on "immediacy." They were simply immersed in their society without any sense of themselves as reflective, self-conscious individuals. Thus, their values were uncritically accepted and thought to be part of the fabric of the universe.

THE RISE OF INDIVIDUALISTIC MORALITY

The breakdown of the Greek ethical world occurred when increased travel made people aware that other communities had quite different customs. The Sophists exploited this fact and argued that the Greeks were not participating in a universal order founded on nature, but were only adhering to the humanly invented conventions of their particular community. Freed from blind conformity to society's norms, each individual became "his own living truth" (PS §355). This self-consciousness became more rational in Socrates, who sought for a universal order within each individual's understanding. This new level of awareness set the modern age in motion, an age in which "the individual is sent out into the world by his own spirit to seek his happiness" (PS §356). However, while this represented an advance over the uncritical spirit of the early Greeks, it also caused a sense of alienation. Individuals became fragmented as their public and private lives became separated. Hegel examines a number of attempts to develop an individualistic ethics. In each case, he argues that the morality they embrace depends on concepts that can only be made meaningful within the shared practices of an ethical community. We can get a glimpse of his argument by examining his treatment of Kant's theory, which Hegel believes is the highest expression of individual, autonomous morality.

KANT: THE CULMINATION OF INDIVIDUALISTIC ETHICS

Hegel refers to the Kantian approach as "morality," which he considers a one-sided concept that must be completed in terms of Hegel's own concept of "community ethical life" (*Sittlichkeit*). Kant tried to unite individual autonomy with the notion of a universal moral law. However, Hegel finds that Kant leaves us with a set of bloodless, formal principles that have no relationship to the community life from which our ethical concerns get their content. Furthermore, whereas Kant tended to make a rigid dichotomy between moral duty and desire, Hegel agrees with Aristotle that the virtuous person is one who not only does her duty but one who finds her deepest desires and inclinations fulfilled in doing so. According to Kant, the way to decide if a proposed course of action is moral is to ask yourself if the maxim or rule guiding that action could rationally serve as a universal law that everyone followed. To use one of Kant's examples, let us suppose I decide to steal someone else's property. If I try to justify this action, it would have to be on the basis of this rule: "You may take another's property whenever you choose." Kant believed that if this rule were made universal, it would lead to a contradiction, for the whole institution of private property would disappear. However, Hegel replies that he can't find a contradiction here. All that Kant has shown is that one cannot advocate both (1) a rule that justifies stealing and (2) the institution of private property. What Kant has not shown is that the institution of private property is desirable. You could accept (1) if you reject (2). Hegel's conclusion is that the immoral rule justifying stealing or any other such rule will never contradict itself and can consistently be universalized. However, we reject the rule that permits stealing because it contradicts the conditions that are essential for society as we know it to effectively function. Thus, while Kant thought his formal principles could pull morality out of the air, they get their content from those social conditions that are required for human life to flourish.

ETHICAL LIFE

In the final turn of the dialectic, consciousness returns to where it started, to a world of social roles and institutions. However, there is a difference. At this stage the acceptance of cultural institutions and norms is no longer an unreflective and taken-for-granted immersion in the culture. Neither are these norms seen as something alien and imposed on us. Rather, they are seen as the rational expression of one's own, deepest self. The source of moral virtue, along with happiness and fulfillment, is found in being rooted in a particular community:

> If men are to act, they must not only intend the good but must know whether this or that particular course is good. What special course of action is good or not, right or wrong, is determined, for the ordinary circumstances of private life, by the laws and customs of a state. It is not too difficult to know them. . . . Each individual has his position; he knows, on the whole, what a lawful and honorable course of conduct is. (RH 37)

At first glance, this view seems objectionable. Hegel appears to be advocating a social conformism in which every society's practices would be automatically justified. He seems to allow no room for the social reformer, the rebel, or the revolutionary. However, Hegel is not calling for a naive acceptance of society's practices as such (that would be turning the clock back to ancient Greece). Instead, he thinks we can find the guidance for our moral lives from the rationality working itself out within society. The key point is that a society often imperfectly realizes its ethical ideals in its practice. Thus, our society's ideals can stand in judgment on its own current condition. All the great reformers, including the Old Testament prophets, Jesus, Marx, Gandhi, and Martin Luther King, Jr., criticized their society in the name of values that society had nurtured within them. They did not preach values alien to their society, but instituted reform by confronting the contradictions within their society.

In the final analysis, Hegel thinks the distinction between personal ethics and political theory is artificial. For Hegel, to be an ethical person involves fulfilling one's duties in a state that is rationally organized. Hence, from ethics we must turn to political philosophy, for "the state is the actuality of the ethical Idea" (PR §257).

Political Philosophy: The Glorification of the State

Hegel's political philosophy begins with the commonsense assertion that we are all striving for freedom. However, he moves very quickly to the controversial thesis that the individual's freedom can only be realized in the state. This seems to be paradoxical, for we tend to see the state as a coercive institution whose main activity is to limit our freedom. How, then, can the state be the source of our freedom?

To get clear on Hegel's political philosophy, it is necessary to get clear on how Hegel understands freedom. We tend to think of freedom as a negative condition: the unhindered capacity to do as we please without any restrictions. However, Hegel says that this sort of freedom is "abstract" and entirely unsatisfactory. To use an example, a child may feel that if she were completely free she could stay home from school and play video games. However, her parents force her to go to school. Yet, paradoxically, by restricting her immediate choices, her parents are actually maximizing her freedom by giving her the education that will enable her to pursue a career and make meaningful choices in the future. As with the child, we can be self-actualized and concretely free individuals only by rising above our personal impulses and serving universal and community ends embodied in the rational organization of state. For example, being a member of a family or a member of one's profession always involves some sacrifice of immediate pleasures and interests. Furthermore, the law requires parents to support their children and professionals to fulfill their contractual obligations. Yet for most of these people, these are not burdens they feel are imposed on them from without, for they find personal satisfaction in carrying out the duties of parenthood or a career.

When Hegel talks about the state, he sees it as a community fulfilling a positive ethical purpose. True, the government does consist of bureaucracies and agencies that enforce the laws, making the state appear as a coercive authority standing over us. He refers to this aspect of society as "civil society" or the "external state," which

has the negative function of maintaining order (PR §183). However, the political and economic structures of a society are but the skeleton that supports the real life of the state, which is the spiritual activity of the people manifested in their language, law, morality, science, art, music, poetry, architecture, religion, and philosophy:

> For the state is not the abstract confronting the citizens; they are parts of it, like members of an organic body, where no member is end and none is means. It is the realization of Freedom, of the absolute, final purpose, and exists for its own sake. (RH 52)

Hegel thinks a free and rational community of this kind has been realized in the state as it actually exists in the modern age. However, his depiction of the glories of life in the state seems to provoke an obvious objection. If the present-day state is the realization of the ethical ideal, doesn't this imply that the status quo is immune to criticism? Even worse, doesn't this implication lay the groundwork for totalitarianism? On this point, Hegel has both his critics and his defenders.

CRITICISM: HEGEL DEIFIES THE STATUS QUO

Those who criticize Hegel as being a conservative reactionary or a defender of totalitarianism have a number of texts to use as ammunition. Consider, for example, the following three passages:

- "The state is the divine Idea as it exists on earth" (RH 53).
- "The march of God in the world, that is what the state is" (PR §258A).
- "Man must therefore venerate the state as a secular deity" (PR §272A).

The theological tone of these passages echoes the spirit of Browning's 1841 poem:

> God's in his heaven—
> All's right with the world![10]

For Hegel, apparently, not only is everything right with the world, but in particular all's right with his own Prussian state. In his *Philosophy of History*, the highest expression of freedom is found in the German world. He says that "the German Spirit is the Spirit of the new World. Its aim is the realization of absolute Truth as the unlimited self-determination of Freedom" (PH 341). It should come as no surprise that, in his own time, Hegel's philosophy was considered the official philosophy of the Prussian state. Karl Popper, one of Hegel's harshest critics, declared that Hegel had one aim: "to fight against the open society, and thus to serve his employer, [King] Frederick William of Prussia."[11]

DEFENSE: HEGEL DOES NOT DEIFY THE STATUS QUO

A number of replies have been made to the charge that Hegel endorses totalitarianism. First, when Hegel praises the state, he is not talking about just any state. He says that it is the "rational state" that he celebrates, the state that individuals would choose to serve, because their freedom and fulfillment would be maximized by participating in it:

> A state is then well constituted and internally vigorous when the private interest of its citizens is one with the common interest of the state, and the one finds gratification and realization in the other. (RH 30)

He calls this "a most important proposition." Second, Hegel does not think that all the practices of a state are justified, even if it is the highest level of political progress for its time. As he says,

> a particular law may be shown to be wholly grounded in and consistent with the circumstances and with existing legally established institutions, and yet it may be wrong and irrational in its essential character. (PR §3)

Finally, it is not Hegel's intention to deify any particular state (not even the Prussian state of his day), for every state has its share of "caprice, chance, and error, and bad behaviour." Instead, he is revering the *ideal* of the rational state, an ideal that makes human life worthwhile to the degree that it is realized in concrete, historical entities:

> In considering the Idea of the state, we must not have our eyes on particular states or on particular institutions. Instead we must consider the Idea, this actual God, by itself. (PR §258A)

Philosophy of History: Are We Pawns in History's Game?

If we look at the thousands of years of human history, we find an overwhelming succession of births, love affairs, deaths, artistic masterpieces, intellectual achievements, architectural monuments, terrifying wars, hopeful revolutions, great empires, and extinct civilizations. But what is the point of it all? Does history have any meaning? Or are the cynics correct when they say that human history is merely "sound and fury, signifying nothing" or "one damned thing after another"? If Hegel had accomplished nothing else, he would be justly famous for making us aware of the importance of history, a topic most philosophers had neglected.

HISTORY IS PURPOSEFUL

At first glance, much in history leaves us with a sense of "hopeless sadness." History appears to be

> the slaughter-bench at which the happiness of peoples, the wisdom of states, and the virtue of individuals have been sacrificed. (RH 27)

In spite of this gloomy picture, Hegel believes there is a redeeming purpose to it all. If we look below the surface events of history, we will see that

> it has proceeded rationally, that it represents the rationally necessary course of the World Spirit, the Spirit whose nature is indeed always one and the same, but whose one nature unfolds in the course of the world. (RH 12)

What is this nature that is unfolding? It is nothing less than freedom, for "world history is the progress of the consciousness of freedom" (RH 24). However, merely being aware of freedom does not mean it has been fully attained. So the whole sweep of world history is a process of the human spirit becoming aware of and realizing its freedom.

As we saw in Hegel's view of the state, freedom cannot be located within the individual person, but must be made concrete and realized in the context of a national culture. Giving a triadic overview of how the idea of freedom has gradually become realized in history, Hegel says that in ancient Asian societies only *one* person was free (the ruler); in the Greek and Roman worlds, there was progress, for the human spirit realized that *some* of the people were free (the citizens, but not the slaves); finally, in the modern world, it is recognized that *all* are free.

There is a certain amount of humor and irony in Hegel's account of history. While each individual and nation is busily pursuing their own special interests, "they are all the time the unconscious tools and organs of the world mind at work within them" (PR §344). Thus, behind the scenes of history the "cunning of Reason" uses the passions and desires of individuals to accomplish its purposes (RH 44). Unlike the Enlightenment thinkers, Hegel does not think individuals are fundamental in society. Individual people are like the waves on the surface of the ocean. Waves are not something distinct and separate from the ocean, but they arise out of it and return to it and are simply a manifestation of the forces at work in that great body of water. Your relationship to your society is like that. For example, in your personal life you are pursuing your subjective, particular interests in terms of your educational choices, pursuit of a career, choice of clothes, and Friday night recreational activities. On the one hand, in doing these things you are a product of your culture. The choices available to you are made possible by your society. Furthermore, your desires are influenced by the fads, trends, public discourse, and values prevalent in your culture. On the other hand, the life of your nation is shaped by your decisions and those of the rest of its people. The cumulative decisions made by people such as you affect the balance of trade, the life and death of corporations, the job market, the political life of the nation, and its cultural institutions. Our collective behavior is a manifestation of rational laws that economists and social scientists try to formulate.

Although individuals all have their roles to play in the scheme of things, the most effective agents of change are the great leaders, those whom Hegel calls "world-historical individuals." Who are these figures? Hegel cites Alexander the Great, Caesar, and Napoleon as examples. They were men driven by passion to fulfill their own political goals. Nevertheless, they were the unwitting instruments that history used to bring forth the next stage in its development:

> *Such individuals have no consciousness of the Idea as such. They are practical and political men. But at the same time they are thinkers with insight into what is needed and timely. They see the very truth of their age and their world, the next genus, so to speak, which is already formed in the womb of time. It is theirs to know this new universal, the necessary state of their world, to make it their own aim and put all their energy into it. (RH 40)*

In following their historical destiny, the great historical figures may cause suffering: "But so mighty a figure must trample down many an innocent flower, crush to pieces many things in its path" (RH 43). We should not blame them, however, for in every great change in history some people will be hurt. Even the world-historical individuals are subject to this process, for when they have served their role in history

> *they fall off like empty hulls from the kernel. They die early like Alexander, they are murdered like Caesar, transported to Saint Helena like Napoleon. (RH 41)*

World-historical individuals bring about the decisive moments in history, but their significance must be understood in the larger context of the life of nations.

Hegel maintains that, in the final analysis, nations are the true individuals in history. Nations rise and fall according to the rhythms at work in the development of history. At any given stage of history a particular nation will be called into prominence to make its unique contribution to humanity's progress toward self-consciousness and freedom.

> *This nation is dominant in world history during this one epoch, and it is only once that it can make its hour strike. In contrast with this its absolute right of being the vehicle of this present stage in the world*

mind's development, the minds of the other nations are without rights, and they, along with those whose hour has struck already, count no longer in world history. (PR §347)

History shows us great moments of human achievement but also reveals tremendous cruelty and times when the whole world seems insane, leading us to wonder whether it all has any purpose. However, Hegel says each moment of history is at least partially justified because of the role it plays in the total story. Even those times of great suffering and apparently irredeemable evil are like a mother's pains that are necessary to birth her own offspring. We will never understand history if we get lost in the details and fail to comprehend the larger picture:

> *The insight then to which . . . philosophy should lead us is that the actual world is as it ought to be, that the truly good, the universal divine Reason is the power capable of actualizing itself. This good, this Reason, in its most concrete representation, is God. God governs the world. (RH 47)*

Thus Hegel confidently embraces the breathtaking conclusion that the way things have developed is the way things were rationally meant to be.

ART, RELIGION, PHILOSOPHY

In the final stages of Hegel's dialectic, the Absolute Spirit is manifested most fully within the human activities of artistic expression, worship, and philosophical speculation. Art, religion, and philosophy all have the same purpose, for they are different attempts to comprehend the Absolute Idea. Or, more accurately, Hegel believes they are progressively more explicit ways in which the Absolute Idea becomes self-conscious within the human spirit. First, art expresses the Idea in terms of immediacy by appealing to the senses. Instead of speaking the truth about reality, the artist attempts to show it. Hegel's theory of art follows the spirit of German romanticism, for he believes that art has both a spiritual and cognitive function. When the artist paints a landscape, she does not simply duplicate nature. There is a difference be-

tween a work of art and an illustration in a biology textbook. The artist transforms nature to communicate a vision of the world that will reveal its inner meaning and spiritual content.

Art can only point to the spiritual meaning of the whole of things through aesthetic feelings; religion expresses it in a more objective and explicit form through the use of stories and images. As always, Hegel goes through the history of religion to show a progressive refinement of human conceptions of the rational purpose at work in the world. He thinks Christianity is the highest historical expression of the religious impulse because it views reality in terms of an infinite Spirit that becomes united with humanity. However, while religion has more conceptual content than art, it is still not purely rational, for it remains at the level of "pictorial thought." Hence, Hegel does not view such Christian doctrines as the creation of the world or the incarnation of God in a human form as literally true. Instead, they are myths that anticipate the more comprehensive truths of philosophy.

Philosophy is the highest achievement of the human spirit. Although it does not deny the insights of religion, philosophy captures, at a much more sophisticated level of understanding, what was of value in religion. Although history may seem to present an overwhelming multitude of philosophies, Hegel says there has been really only a single philosophy, manifesting itself in various aspects. The last philosophy of an epoch sums up all previous stages of philosophy and is the highest stage that spiritual consciousness has reached at that point in history.

THE END OF HISTORY?

Hegel's philosophy paints the picture of human history as a spiritual–intellectual development in which a rational purpose is unfolding and being realized. This raises the question, Where is history heading and when will we get there? Many believe that Hegel views his system as the culmination of philosophy, in that it has at last reached the absolute knowledge that reason was struggling toward throughout the centuries. This does not mean that Hegel claims he has achieved complete knowledge of every detail in the world. Instead, absolute knowledge consists of a coherent framework of concepts in terms of which the totality of reality can be comprehended, and in which all previous philosophies take their place as merely partial truths.

Many passages suggest that Hegel thought his system was the final one. Yet some lingering questions still remain about how he conceives the role of his philosophy in history. Does he think his philosophy is the Absolute fully revealed in all its glory? Or does he think it is only the *next* stage in the autobiography of the World Spirit, a stage that later philosophical insights eventually will supersede? Some commentators see a tension between Hegel the absolute idealist and Hegel the historical relativist. His relativism comes out in his statements that "every individual is a child of his time" and philosophy is "its own time apprehended in thoughts." Furthermore, he states that "it is just as absurd to fancy that a philosophy can transcend its contemporary world as it is to fancy that an individual can overleap his own age" (PR, preface). If Hegel truly believed these words, then he would have to agree that while his system may have captured the understanding of his own age, it could not be the final fruit of human reason. Instead, it would be destined to become the soil from which further developments in philosophy would spring forth. If this was his meaning, he certainly was correct. However, it remains a controversial issue as to whether the "real" Hegel is the metaphysical system builder who lusted after finality or the historical relativist who was fascinated by the changing kaleidoscope of ideas and events.

Evaluation and Significance

EVALUATION OF HEGEL

Hegel's thought has so many facets that the final verdict on him will be determined by which facet is given prominence. In the final analysis, your assessment of Hegel will depend on whether or not you agree with his most fundamental claim, which is *history is moving toward the fulfillment of a ratio-*

nal ideal. Many do not find themselves capable of this enormous faith that reason and reality are converging toward a single, all-encompassing system that will harmonize all the conflicts and tensions within human thought and life. Although this rational faith is appealing, maybe the universe does not confirm to our intellectual needs and fancies. To this skepticism Hegel could reply that the rationality of the universe is presupposed by all we do, even if we try to deny it verbally. But even if we accept Hegel's faith in the rationality of the whole scheme of things, how do we know the human community is indeed progressing toward it instead of away from it? The questions that need to be asked here are (1) Does Hegel's scheme make sense out of human experience? and (2) Is it consistent with the data of intellectual, economic, political, and cultural history? In the chapters to follow, we will see that these questions were addressed by Hegel's successors.

HEGEL'S INFLUENCE

Many in the nineteenth century eagerly embraced Hegel's system. It was intellectually satisfying, because it provided a coherent way to weave together every area of human experience. Its impact on the discipline of history and on the way scholars understood the historical development of every other discipline is hard to overestimate. Furthermore, it was emotionally satisfying, for in the midst of political and social upheavals it assured people that a rational pattern was unfolding and that historical events had an ultimate purpose. For these reasons, Hegelianism triumphed in academic circles. Despite a tendency for British and American philosophers to resist the grand speculations of the Europeans, by the end of the century the leading philosophers in the Anglo-American world had embraced Hegelian thought.

In addition to his influence on philosophy as such, Hegel also had a significant impact on the social sciences. For example, he provided a helpful corrective to the extreme individualism of many seventeenth- and eighteenth-century thinkers, who tended to see society as simply a collection of many separate and distinct people. Instead, Hegel made us realize that our lives take shape within a particular society and that our social and intellectual environment is as much a part of us as the air we breathe. He drew attention to the fact that society is more than the sum of its individuals, for in each age is a spirit of the time. Furthermore, he made us aware that ideas and cultural forces have a momentum of their own that shapes us as much as we shape them.

Questions for Understanding

1. What are the four key principles of Hegel's philosophy?

2. What is Hegel's notion of dialectic? According to Hegel, how does this notion explain the way our understanding develops? How does Hegel use this notion to explain how history develops?

3. What is historicism? In what ways does it characterize Hegel's account of history?

4. Why does Hegel believe that pure sense experience ("sense certainty") cannot give us knowledge worth having?

5. Explain in what sense Hegel believes there is an intimate relationship between mind and nature.

6. What is the relationship between the Absolute Spirit and the human spirit?

7. Why does Hegel believe that our minds are not isolated, individual units that are separate from the larger cultural and historical fabric?

8. In what ways is Hegel's Absolute similar to and different from the God of traditional religions?

9. Describe the stages of the evolution of ethics according to Hegel's view.

10. In what ways does Hegel disagree with Kant's ethics?

11. In what ways does Hegel's view of the state provide intellectual ammunition for both conservatives and revolutionaries?

12. Why does Hegel believe that history is a force that is larger than the actions of particular individuals?

13. What is meant by "world-historical individuals"? What role do they play in history?

14. How are art, religion, and philosophy similar, according to Hegel? How are they different?

Questions for Reflection

1. Do you agree with Hegel that history is the unfolding of a rational pattern or is it just a collection of events without any overall meaning?

2. Think about the last decade, including its political events, economic developments, cultural developments, its fads, predominant values, and so on. Consider how Hegel might have explained all of this as flowing from the previous stages in history. To what extent does this Hegelian analysis make sense?

3. Do you agree with Hegel that one cannot find true freedom nor fulfillment apart from the life of the community? If you disagree with Hegel here, to what extent are your ideas on this issue a reflection of the spirit of your age?

4. In what ways do you find Hegel's view of history and your place in the grand scheme of things to be an optimistic outlook? In what ways do you find it pessimistic?

Notes

1. References to Hegel's works are as follows:

   PH *The Philosophy of History*, trans. J. Sibree (New York: Dover, 1956). References are given in terms of the page numbers of this edition.

   PR *Hegel's Philosophy of Right*, trans. T. M. Knox (Oxford, England: Oxford University Press, 1964). References are given in terms of Hegel's paragraph numbers.

   PS *Phenomenology of Spirit*, trans. A. V. Miller (Oxford, England: Oxford University Press, 1977). References are given in terms of Hegel's paragraph numbers.

   RH *Reason in History: A General Introduction to the Philosophy of History*, trans. Robert S. Hartman

(Indianapolis: Bobbs-Merrill, Library of Liberal Arts, 1953). References are given in terms of the page numbers of this edition.

2. *Lectures on the History of Philosophy*, vol. 3, trans. E. B. Spiers and J. Burdon Sanderson (New York: Humanities Press, 1962), 545, quoted in Robert C. Solomon, *In the Spirit of Hegel* (Oxford, England: Oxford University Press, 1983), 223.

3. *Hegel: Selections*, ed. J. Loewenberg (New York: Scribner's, 1929), xviii.

4. Hegel, *Philosophy of Nature*, trans. A. V. Miller (Oxford, England: Oxford University Press, 1970), §338 ff.

5. *The Logic of Hegel translated from the Encyclopedia of the Philosophical Sciences*, trans. William Wallace (Oxford, England: Oxford University Press, 1873), 163 Z2, quoted in Thomas E. Wartenberg, "Hegel's Idealism: The Logic of Conceptuality," in *The Cambridge Companion to Hegel*, ed. Frederick C. Beiser (Cambridge, England: Cambridge University Press, 1993), 102.

6. In this section I am indebted to Thomas E. Wartenberg's discussion in "Hegel's Idealism: The Logic of Conceptuality," in *The Cambridge Companion to Hegel*, ed. Frederick C. Beiser (Cambridge, England: Cambridge University Press, 1993), 102–129.

7. Wartenberg, 109.

8. Frederick C. Beiser, "Introduction: Hegel and the Problem of Metaphysics," in Beiser, *Cambridge Companion to Hegel*, 6.

9. Quoted in Walter Kaufmann, *Hegel: A Reinterpretation* (Garden City, NY: Anchor Books, 1966), 367.

10. Robert Browning, *Pippa Passes*, pt. 1.

11. Karl Popper, *The Open Society and Its Enemies*, vol. 2 (London: Routledge & Kegan Paul, 1966), 32.

25

Karl Marx:
A Philosophy for
Changing the World

"A SPECTRE IS HAUNTING EUROPE—THE SPECtre of Communism." These dramatic words open the *Communist Manifesto*, a political tract written by Karl Marx and Friedrich Engels in 1848. Its lyrical style and emotional power were intended to make it a battle hymn for the vast army of angry, oppressed workers at a time when Europe was erupting with riots and revolutions that shook monarchies and governments at their very foundations. The closing words of this document capture the revolutionary spirit of the times. "The proletarians have nothing to lose but their chains. They have a world to win. WORKING MEN OF ALL COUNTRIES, UNITE!" (CM, T 473, 500).[1]

People debate the credibility of Marx's theories, but no one disputes their influence. No philosopher in history can claim to have had an international, organized, and activist following of such proportions. However, there is a startling irony in the difference between this philosopher's aura and his life. Karl Marx's name has practically become the symbol of revolution. However, Marx spent little time in direct political activity in the streets. In-

stead, his life consisted of endless studying and writing in the library of the British Museum, where he worked every day at the same desk from nine in the morning until it closed at seven at night. He followed this day by long hours of work at home, until exhaustion and the need for sleep ended his day. Ironically, although his ideas shaped a large part of the twentieth century, Marx lived a life of relative obscurity and isolation. Had it not been for the company of his family and a small group of intimate friends and political associates, he would hardly have been distinguishable from a medieval monk, cloistered in the world of his books and manuscripts. A further irony is that while frequently discounting the power of words and ideas (he called them "the brain phantoms of philosophers"), he showed what formidable weapons they could be. As a result of his theories, governments have been overthrown, maps have been changed, and his name has become a household word in the twentieth century. The power of Marx can only begin to be understood by tracing the events and the ideas that shaped this extraordinary mind.

Marx's Life: The Making of a Radical

Karl Marx was born on May 5, 1818, in Trier, in the Rhineland of Germany. He descended, on the male side, from a long line of Jewish rabbis. However, his father, who made a comfortable living as a lawyer, converted to Lutheranism when Marx was six. This was politically and economically necessary because of new legislation that excluded Jews from government service. At age seventeen, Karl Marx entered the University of Bonn to study law. After a year, he transferred to the University of Berlin where (to his father's dismay) he joined a radical group known as the Young Hegelians. Although Hegel had been dead for five years, the German universities were charged with his influence and philosophical debates filled the air. Marx became caught up in the excitement and abandoned law for the study of philosophy. Finally, he ended up at the University of Jena in 1841, where he received a doctorate after completing a thesis on the materialistic philosophies of Epicurus and Democritus. Although Marx was destined for a career as a philosophy professor, the conservative Prussian government closed this option when they prohibited the radical Hegelians such as Marx from teaching in the universities. Cut off from any hopes of pursuing an academic career, Marx turned to journalism. From 1842 to 1849 he edited a succession of political journals and worked on his own manuscripts. During these years he was a continual refugee, moving from Cologne to Paris to Brussels and back to Cologne. In each case, his radical journals were officially banned and the government forced him to leave the country. He finally settled in London in the fall of 1849, where he remained the rest of his life.

Amid the continual turmoil of his life, Marx found stability in two important relationships. The first was his wife Jenny, whom he married in 1843. They had six children, but only three reached adulthood. According to the later accounts of his children, he was a wonderful, playful father and a good husband. Jenny not only gave him emotional support but helped with his manuscripts and made frequent visits to the pawnshop with personal belongings to keep the family out of debt.

The other important relationship was with Friedrich Engels, a lifelong friend, collaborator, and frequent source of financial support. Marx and Engels first met in 1842 when they were both involved in journalism. They began to pool their ideas and become active together in various workers' organizations. Engels came from a well-to-do family that owned a textile business in Manchester. Despite his business involvements, Engels's political views were quite radical. Engels is considered the better writer of the two and with this gift, along with his knowledge of the world of business and economics, he made important contributions to Marx's projects.

Marx lived a life plagued by poverty, chronic illness, and the childhood death of three of his six children, resulting from the grim conditions in which they lived. His only source of genuine income was his job as a European correspondent for the *New York Tribune* from 1851 to 1862. The rest of the time he survived on family donations, loans, and the subsidies that Engels gave him. Marx's spirit was broken when Jenny, his wife and faithful co-worker, died in 1881 after a long bout with cancer. After suffering for months from a diseased lung, Marx died on March 14, 1883, while sleeping in his favorite armchair in his study. He was buried next to his wife in Highgate Cemetery near London.

Marx's Background and Influences

When Karl Marx came to the University of Berlin in 1836, the spirit of Hegel dominated the intellectual life throughout Germany. The complexities of Hegel's system as well as its myriad ambiguities and internal tensions caused Hegel's followers to split into two conflicting groups. Many argued for a right-wing, conservative interpretation of Hegel, but they were opposed by the left-wing, radical Young Hegelians. The excitement of this controversy enticed Marx to plunge into philosophy and become one of the leaders of the Young Hegelian movement.

THE RATIONAL SOCIETY: ACTUAL OR POTENTIAL?

One of the tensions in Hegel's thought that produced these two factions is his claim that "the real is the rational and the rational is the real." His conservative followers latched onto the first half of the statement "The real is the rational." From this they concluded that the status quo is justified and beyond question because it is a necessary outcome of the rational process of history's dialectic. The radicals lined up behind the second half of the statement, and proclaimed that "the rational is the real." Because they believed that the present society is not rational, they argued it is still in process and not yet fully real. Thus, the truly rational state is still over the horizon, waiting to be actualized by the next dialectical movement of history. Viewing the current social conditions through the eyes of Hegel's dialectic, the radicals saw their society as an unstable collection of contradictions. At age twenty-five and already a dedicated radical, Marx wrote a letter proclaiming that "The state everywhere presupposes that reason has been realized. But in just this way it everywhere comes into contradiction between its ideal mission and its real preconditions" (T 14).[2] What was needed was for the contradiction to be made manifest through a "ruthless criticism of everything existing," leading to the negation of the present social order by a new one that would resolve all the tensions.

GOD: ABSOLUTE SPIRIT OR HUMANITY?

Another ambiguity in Hegel's thought occurred in his perplexing remarks about God. On the one hand, his words dripped with piety as he wrote about God moving through the events of history. On the other hand, he seemed to identify God and humanity when he claimed that the Absolute Spirit exists only in and through the human spirit.

Emphasizing the theistic side of Hegel, the conservatives translated his thought into the terms of a more or less traditional Christian theology. At the same time, the early left-wing Hegelians promoted a pantheistic interpretation that was incompatible with Christianity. However, the radicals soon went beyond religion altogether and claimed that when Hegel's ideas were stripped of their theological and mythological trappings, we would find a naturalistic humanism and atheism beneath the surface. Abandoning the conservative's belief that the divine reveals itself in the human spirit, the radicals proclaimed that humanity is the only divinity worth believing in.

This latter interpretation was fueled by the 1841 publication of *The Essence of Christianity* by Ludwig Feuerbach, a major figure in Young Hegelian circles. According to Feuerbach, religion is created by humanity through an unconscious process of projection. We have projected all our perfection and unlimited possibilities onto a transcendent, supreme being in the great beyond, Feuerbach said, leaving us alienated from our own humanity. The value of Hegel's thought is not that it describes an Absolute that is over and above humanity, but that it reveals to us our human nature and humanity's achievements.

Marx, along with the other Young Hegelians, enthusiastically embraced Feuerbach's ideas, for the latter had deftly translated Hegelian thought into a naturalistic humanism. In 1842, Marx playfully wrote, "There is no other way for you to *truth* and *freedom*, but through a *stream of fire*."[3] ("Stream of fire" in German is *Feuer Bach*.) Not long after, however, Marx concluded that Feuerbach had not been radical enough in describing the human situation. Religion is the symptom, not the cause of our malaise, Marx claimed. To complete Feuerbach's analysis, we must dig beneath the surface to find the explanation of why people are unable to find happiness and fulfillment in this world and feel the need to create a heavenly world beyond this one. In one of his most famous passages, Marx compares religion to a dose of opium that anesthetizes people, keeping them from realizing the true source of their suffering.

Religion is the sigh of the oppressed creature, the sentiment of a heartless world, and the soul of soulless conditions. It is the opium of the people.

The abolition of religion as the illusory happiness of men, is a demand for their real happiness. The call to abandon their illusions about their condition is a call to abandon a condition which requires illusions. (CHPR, T 54)

Marx conceded that Feuerbach had been right—our problem is a false religious consciousness in which we degrade ourselves by worshiping an idol of our own making. However, Feuerbach had incorrectly identified this idol. According to Marx, our modern commercial world has created a religion in which money is god:

Money is the jealous god of Israel, beside which no other god may exist. Money abases all the gods of mankind and changes them into commodities. Money is the universal and self-sufficient value of all things. It has, therefore, deprived the whole world, both the human world and nature, of their own proper value. Money is the alienated essence of man's work and existence; this essence dominates him and he worships it. (T 50)[4]

This new "religion" has reduced all human relations to "naked self-interest" and "callous cash payment" and has drowned all ideals in "the icy water of egotistical calculation" (CM, T 475).

Task: Achieving an Earthly Salvation

Given this background, Marx takes it as his task to (1) bring the ideals of justice and freedom down to earth to create a rational, humane society, (2) show that the emancipation of the human spirit can be achieved on a secular base, and (3) use the resources of philosophy and science to achieve these goals.

THE STRUGGLE TOWARD A RATIONAL, HUMANE SOCIETY

The Enlightenment philosophers found the world they lived in quite congenial. The spirit of the eighteenth century was captured in the words of J. G. Buhl in 1796: "Of no century can it be said with so much truth as of the eighteenth that it utilized the achievements of its predecessors to bring humanity to a greater physical, intellectual, and moral perfection."[5] However, Marx has quite a different assessment of human history. In the first chapter of the *Communist Manifesto*, he gives a grim picture of human history as a continuous struggle between the haves and the have-nots, the exploiters and the exploited.

The history of all hitherto existing society is the history of class struggles.

Freeman and slave, patrician and plebeian, lord and serf, guild-master and journeyman, in a word, oppressor and oppressed, stood in constant opposition to one another, carried on an uninterrupted, now hidden, now open fight, a fight that each time ended, either in a revolutionary re-constitution of society at large, or in the common ruin of the contending classes. (CM, T 474)

In the modern era, this struggle has been carried on between two classes: the bourgeoisie and the proletariat. The bourgeoisie are the capitalists, or the owners of the means of industrial production and the employers of wage labor, as well as those in the middle class who benefit from the current economic system.* The other half of society is made up of the proletariat or the workers, who own no property and who must survive by selling their labor as a commodity.†

The elements of the capitalist system are private property, the profit motive, wage labor, and economic competition.‡ "Private property" as used

---

*The name "bourgeoisie" originally meant "townsmen" and referred to the new class of merchants, moneylenders, and masters of the crafts guilds that arose at the end of the Middle Ages.
†"Proletarian" comes from a Latin word that means "propertyless."
‡It is hard for us to imagine that the value of competition, the quest for profit, and the accumulation of wealth were not always thought reasonable goals. But these values are unique to the postmedieval age. For an interesting discussion of this, see Robert L. Heilbroner, *The Worldly Philosophers* (New York: Simon & Schuster, 1953), chap. 2.

by Marx does not refer to consumer goods, such as one's own toothbrush and clothes. Rather, it refers to private ownership of the means of production (originally the small manufacturing shops, then the industrialized factories, and today the large international corporations). The capitalist is driven by the profit motive. His goal is to use the means of production he owns to produce commodities to be sold for a profit so that the profits may be invested in more means of production to make more profit to be reinvested, and so on, and so on. The capitalist's creed is "Accumulate, accumulate! That is Moses and the prophets! . . . Accumulation for the sake of accumulation, production for the sake of production" (CI 742). Profits are made by exploiting wage labor. The lower the wages the worker gets paid, the more profit the capitalist makes. Thus, the interests of the capitalist and the laborer inevitably conflict. Finally, the capitalist is not only engaged in a struggle with his workers, he is caught in a competitive struggle with his fellow capitalists. As we will see later, Marx is convinced these internal struggles within the capitalist system will lead it to self-destruction.

In the first volume of his massive work *Capital*, Marx spends almost half of its 750 pages documenting the ways in which the working class are oppressed and exploited by the factory owners. Much of this material is taken from British government documents, and most of these are reports of factory inspectors. Summing up this data, Marx says that the vision of hell in Dante's *Inferno* pales in comparison to the inhuman degradation of industrial England. One official reported this about the lace factories:

> Children of nine or ten years are dragged from their squalid beds at two, three, or four o'clock in the morning and compelled to work for a bare subsistence until ten, eleven, or twelve at night, their limbs wearing away, their frames dwindling, their faces whitening, and their humanity absolutely sinking into a stone-like torpor, utterly horrible to contemplate. (CI, T 367)

Small children, women, and men of the working class daily faced the threat of death and dismemberment from dangerous machines, as well as the physical assaults of overwork, unsanitary working and living conditions, malnutrition, and a host of resulting diseases. In trying to sort out the enormous complexities and crushing details of Marx's philosophical, historical, and economic theories, it is important to remember that underlying them was a concern for the real suffering of men, women, and children in his time.

THE SALVATION OF HUMANITY

Marx saw his complex theories as the way to fulfill what could only be called a spiritual mission. Against the voices of resignation, acquiescence, and hopelessness, he had faith that the grim reality of most people's lives were not the way things were meant to be and that changes could be made. Thus, Marx's philosophy could be viewed as a secular version of Milton's theological, literary masterpieces, *Paradise Lost* and *Paradise Regained*.* In Marx's materialistic theology, the state of original innocence was that of primitive, tribal communism where the community held everything in common. The Fall occurred with the rise of private property and class divisions. From then on, history has been a long struggle to overcome the forces of evil. The proletariat have been destined to be the bearers of world history, for through their suffering they will lead to the redemption of humanity. The communist revolution will bring about the final judgment when the evils of private property and class division will be abolished, and humanity will then settle into a state of unending paradise. Marx is not reluctant to phrase his vision in theological terms. For example, he says that "to have its sins forgiven, mankind has only to declare them to be what they really are" (T 15)[6] and he prophesies that the triumph of the proletariat will lead to "the total redemption of humanity" (CHPR, T 64).

---

*Engels supported this comparison when he said that "both Christianity and the workers' socialism preach forthcoming salvation from bondage and misery; Christianity places this salvation in a life beyond, after death, in heaven; socialism places it in this world, in a transformation of society." Friedrich Engels, "On the History of Early Christianity," in *Marx & Engels: Basic Writings on Politics & Philosophy*, ed. Lewis S. Feuer (Garden City, NY: Anchor Books, 1959), 168.

© Bettmann/CORBIS

Houseless and Hungry (1869), by Luke Fildes.
According to the government documents Marx cited,
the industrial revolution created a mass of downtrodden
workers, including women and small children, who
suffered from poverty, overwork, brutal living
conditions, malnutrition, and disease.

THE REALIZATION OF PHILOSOPHY

To lead the way to this worldly redemption, Marx says, philosophy must plant its feet where the battle is being fought. In the nineteenth century, the Germans' fondness for grandiose, speculative philosophy was ridiculed by saying that England ruled the sea with its mighty navy, France ruled the land with its powerful army, whereas Germany ruled the clouds with its battalion of metaphysicians. Contrary to Hegel's misty picture of history as the unfolding of the World Spirit, it was clear to Marx that the only demonstrable reality was matter. Hence, any philosophy that is humanly meaningful must first begin with real individuals and the concrete economic and social conditions in which they live, not with abstract ideas:

> In direct contrast to German philosophy which descends from heaven to earth, here we ascend from earth to heaven. . . . We set out from real, active men, and on the basis of their real life-process we demonstrate the development of the ideological reflexes and echoes of this life-process. (GI, T 154)

What was needed, Marx thought, was a scientific study of the laws of history. In the preface to the first edition of *Capital*, Marx explains that "it is the ultimate aim of this work to lay bare the economic law of motion of modern society" (CI, T 297). Similarly, at Marx's funeral his colleague Engels proclaimed that "just as Darwin discovered the law of development of organic nature, so Marx discovered the law of development of human history" (T 681).[7] Thus, Marx believed that a scientific understanding of human nature and the physical universe would solve all our social problems (GI, T 166). As he says in a famous quote, "the philosophers have only *interpreted* the world, in various ways; the point is to *change* it" (T 145).[8]

The Early Marx: The Tragedy of Human Alienation

Up until the 1930s both Marx's sympathizers and his critics had viewed his philosophy primarily as a ponderous economic and social theory that purported to give a scientific analysis of the large-scale forces operating in human history. The bulk of what we knew about Marx's system, represented by his monumental work in *Capital*, seemed to have little concern for the individual and ignored any issues of existential significance. In 1932, however, Marx's early, unpublished manuscripts, now known as the *Economic and Philosophic Manuscripts of 1844*, came to light, which necessitated a complete reassessment of Marx's ideas. In this series of essays, written when he was twenty-six, Marx speaks eloquently about the human condition and the sense of alienation that has swept over humanity. Paralleling similar concerns in the existentialists, Marx claimed that the happy optimism of the nineteenth century that resulted from its uncritical faith in science, technology, and human progress, rested on a rotten underside.

WHAT DOES IT MEAN TO BE HUMAN?

Alienation is a state of being separated from one's true self. What concrete conditions make us fulfilled human beings? Marx says we differ from animals because we *produce* the means of our subsistence. Not only do humans engage in work to fulfill their needs, they do so in conscious, creative ways. The bee constructs a honeycomb by blind instinct, but the architect conceives her creation in the imagination before building it. Furthermore, our creativity goes beyond merely meeting our immediate, physical needs. The human species "forms things in accordance with the laws of beauty" (EPM, T 76). In other words, to be human is to engage in productive work and, by doing so, experiencing the fulfillment that comes from free, spontaneous, and creative activity.

In earlier times, a person would toil long, hard hours to cultivate the soil, construct a home, or build his fishing craft. He did not live a life of luxury, but he had the experience of meaningful labor. He owned his tools and materials, and he owned the product of his labor. It was the external embodiment of his individual, creative powers. But as capitalism developed, the workers'

relation to their labor changed. The means of production gradually fell into the hands of a few people. The majority, who were propertyless, had only one way to survive, and that was to sell their labor as a commodity. This poses as a free exchange between the employer and the employee. However, the worker's lack of economic power turns it into a form of servitude. The problem is that if meaningful work is the fundamental defining quality of human life, and if our work is alienating, then we are alienated from ourselves. The laborer is alienated in four ways:

First, *workers are alienated from the products of their labor*. The laborers' creations are appropriated by strangers as their private property to be turned into their profits:

> It is true that labour produces for the rich wonderful things—but for the worker it produces privation. It produces palaces—but for the worker, hovels. It produces beauty— but for the worker, deformity. It replaces labour by machines—but some of the workers it throws back to a barbarous type of labour, and the other workers it turns into machines. It produces intelligence—but for the worker idiocy, cretinism. (EPM, T 73)

Second, *the capitalist system alienates workers from their own productive activity*. "Labour produces not only commodities; it produces itself and the worker as a *commodity*" (EPM, T 71). When entering the workplace, I leave my humanity at the door, for I become identified as bolt tightener 3 on assembly line 22 of the graveyard shift of a factory that belongs to someone else. I am just as much of an interchangeable part as the parts of the machines I am using.

Third, *capitalism alienates the workers from their essential human nature*. Animals produce for their immediate needs, while human beings have the capacity to creatively transform the world into works of art, science, and technology to be shared by the whole human race. However, the capitalist system reduces the worker to a beast of burden. Ironically, the dehumanizing effects of the work environment cause the worker to dehumanize himself in his after-work hours, for he only feels freely engaged in life when reveling in the animal functions of eating, drinking, and sex (EPM, T 74).

Fourth, *the workers are alienated from each other*. Having been degraded themselves, they view others as degraded also. They see their employer as merely a source of money and see one another as competitors for jobs and wages. "The *increasing value* of the world of things," Marx notes, "proceeds in direct proportion the *devaluation* of the world of men" (EPM, T 71).

It is important to note that Marx is not calling for piecemeal adjustments in the way things are run. For example, he does not think a more equitable distribution of money is the solution. As he points out, an increase in wages would be "nothing but *better payment for the slave*, and would not conquer either for the worker or for labour their human status and dignity" (EPM, T 80). Hence, what is necessary is nothing less than a radical reorganization of the structure of power and economics in society.

ARE THERE TWO MARXISMS?

The discovery of the 1844 manuscripts attracted the attention of scholars with religious, humanistic, and existential concerns. This caused an interest in Marx to blossom in intellectual circles where it had not been present before. Marx's depiction of the alienation and loneliness of the modern age presented the more humane side of his philosophy, which was obscured by his ponderous economic theories and his cold, scientific socialism. For many, it was the early Marx who spoke most eloquently to the twentieth century. In contrast, the official position of Soviet scholars was that these early writings came from the immature thoughts of the young Marx and were meant to be superseded by his later, technical works. They considered the new interest in the early Marx a bourgeois attack on the theoretical foundations of communism that sought to replace the scientific, revolutionary Marx with the more innocuous philosophical Marx, who had not yet overcome his Hegelian hangover.

Perhaps it is not necessary to choose between the earlier or later Marx. Some see the early emphasis on alienation and the later emphasis on economic theory as complementary stages in one, large project. In this interpretation, the early works receive their fulfillment in the technical theories of the mature Marx, and the later works must be viewed in terms of the motivating passion of the younger Marx.

Historical Materialism

MATERIALISM

The name frequently given to Marx's philosophy is *historical materialism*.* Basically, this is a philosophy of history and a theory of economics based on a materialistic conception of reality and causation. In the hands of Marx's followers, the theory blossomed into a comprehensive worldview that had implications for the philosophies of every domain of human concern, including nature, science, art, religion, language, and literary criticism. Historical materialism claims that human beings are rooted in nature and that no other causal factors are at work in the world beyond physical laws and human activity. Most particularly, it rejects any reference to a "spiritual" dimension in reality. This sweeping rejection includes not only religious views, but also philosophical views such as those of Plato, Descartes, and Hegel.

THE MARXIAN DIALECTIC

To convert the study of history into a science, Marx needed a general law that would enable him to explain past events and predict future ones. Hegel's notion that history follows a dialectical development provided Marx with the solution he

---

*Marx never used this term himself, but it was coined by Engels, as was the label "scientific socialism." The Marxist system is also called "dialectical materialism," a term introduced by a Russian Marxist in 1891.

needed. Even though he sharply criticizes Hegel's idealism, Marx learned from Feuerbach that Hegel could be salvaged. Hegel's only problem was that he had turned things upside down with his mystical view that the world is the external unfolding of a rational, spiritual Idea. Instead, the opposite is true, Marx says, for the ideal world is nothing more than the material world as reflected in human consciousness:

> The mystification which dialectic suffers in Hegel's hands, by no means prevents him from being the first to present its general form of working in a comprehensive and conscious manner. With him it is standing on its head. It must be turned right side up again, if you would discover the rational kernel within the mystical shell. (CI, T 302)

According to the dialectical view of history, an internal logic to events guides their development. Marx saw that if one purged Hegel's dialectic of its spiritual fluff and replaced Hegel's struggle and opposition of ideas with the conflict of classes, Hegel's model could be taken over.

In the Marxist dialectic, an initial state of affairs (called the *thesis*) develops to a point where it produces its own contradiction (the *antithesis*). The two remain in tension until another state of affairs supersedes them (the *synthesis*). In each round of the dialectic, the deficiencies of one stage bring forth opposing forces to balance out what is lacking. Thus, conflict and struggle are an inevitable part of history.

There is an ambiguity in Marx's account of the laws of history. The tension is apparent in a single phrase in the preface to *Capital* where he refers to the laws of history as "tendencies working with iron necessity towards inevitable results" (CI, preface; T 296). The term "tendencies" implies a loose, general direction that events will probably take, all things being equal. However, the terms "iron necessity" and "inevitable results" can mean nothing less than that history is programmed by rigid, deterministic laws. Marx is always caught between his theory of historical determinism and his call for political activism. On the one hand, a deter-

AKG London

Vladimir Tatlin, Monument to the Third International, *1919–1929. In this model of his never-completed sculpture, the Russian artist Tatlin graphically represented the Marxist vision. The spiraling structure illustrates the twists and turns of the dialectic of history as it moves toward its culmination.*

ministic view of history makes possible a science of history in which future outcomes can be predicted. Furthermore, it provides a powerful psychological stimulus for the proletariat. The oppressed class does not need to hope for social justice as merely a tentative possibility, because the laws of history are on their side and guarantee the outcome. On the other hand, there needs to be some room for human freedom, for people need to believe they can affect history by their actions.

Marx tends to suggest a compromise. First, history is the sum total of the actions of individuals:

> History *does* nothing, it *"possesses no immense wealth,"* it *"wages no battles."* It is man, *real living man, that does all that, that possesses and fights;* "history" is not a person apart, using man as a *means* for its own *particular aims; history is nothing but the activity of man pursuing his aims.*[9]

Second, people's actions tend to take on a life of their own and have effects far beyond those intended. For example, the capitalists do not wish to create socialism, but in pursuing their own ends they give birth to the force that will cause their demise. Third, in creating history we also create ourselves. Marx says that "circumstances make men just as much as men make circumstances" (GI, T 165). In other words, once we set events in motion, their effects can turn back on us and determine our behavior. In the *Communist Manifesto,* Marx says the capitalist is "like the sorcerer, who is no longer able to control the powers of the nether world whom he has called up by his spells" (CM, T 478).

Although history is broadly determined, there is room for variations and contingencies within certain broad limits. Thus, the forces of history could be compared to a boulder someone has sent rolling down a mountain. Once set in motion, it becomes an independent force with its own momentum. Obstructions may be set in its path to slow it down, or obstacles may be minimized to speed up the boulder's descent. However, because of its mass and momentum, it cannot be stopped, and when it has passed through each stage of its descent it will finally reach its destination. Thus, Marx says that the necessary phases of social change cannot be leapt over nor removed by legislation, but must be endured. However, our political and revolutionary efforts can "shorten and lessen the birth-pangs" (CI, T 297).

THE ECONOMIC
INTERPRETATION OF HISTORY

In contrast to Hegel, and the entire philosophical tradition as well, Marx says that ideas play, at

best, a subsidiary role in causing historical changes. He begins with the undeniable truth that people cannot eat ideas, but must live on the material products of labor.* From this premise, Marx quickly concludes that economic conditions are the base on which all human history is built. Thus, Marx saw it as his task to set out a materialistic or "earthly" approach to understanding history (GI, T 156).

In one of his most famous passages, Marx outlines his conception of history:

> In the social production of their life, human beings enter into definite relations that are indispensable and independent of their will, relations of production which correspond to a definite stage of development of their material productive forces. The sum total of these relations of production constitutes the economic structure of society, the real foundation, on which rises a legal and political superstructure and to which correspond definite forms of social consciousness. (CCPE, T 4)

Here Marx introduces the three key elements of his economic theory of history. In any society we find that there are, first, *forces of production* (or material productive forces). Under this label falls anything that can be used to create products for the satisfaction of human needs and wants. The forces of production can be divided into two categories: the means of production (natural resources, tools, and machines) and human labor power. However, for the forces of production to be used, they require certain social and economic arrangements with regard to power, authority, and ownership. Thus, we also find (second) *relations of production*. These consist of the institutions and practices that govern the forces of production. According to Marx, when we seek to understand a period of history or a particular society we must ask, Who owns the means of

---

*If this sounds too much like a glib caricature, consider this statement by Marx: "The Middle Ages could not live on Catholicism, nor could the ancient world on politics. On the contrary, it is the manner in which they gained their livelihood which explains why in one case politics, in the other case Catholicism, played the chief part" (CI 176n).

production and controls the labor power? The collective total of these productive relationships is called the *economic structure*. The combination of these two factors in production, working together, is variously referred to as the *base*, the *mode of production*, or the *economic substructure*. Finally, in contrast to the economic substructure, there is (third) the *superstructure*. This consists of the official legal and political system, as well as the forms of social consciousness. This level of society is not engaged in economic production but in the production of ideas, legal and political theories, cultural expressions, philosophies, moral codes, religious views, and patterns of explanation. In short, the economic substructure consists of what we do, while the superstructure implicitly and explicitly reflects what we think our lives are all about.*

There is a very special relationship among these various elements. In the preceding passage, Marx says that the superstructure "rises" from and "corresponds" to the underlying economic structure. Commentators frequently refer to this thesis as *economic determinism*.[†] This label is applied because Marx claims that the economic structure of a society determines its legal, political, and cultural forms. At the lower level, the relations of production "correspond" to the stage of development of the forces of production. Thus, Marx says that "the wind-mill gives you society with the feudal lord; the steam-mill society with the industrial capitalist."[10] In other words, changes in the technology (forces of production) produce changes in the organization of society (relations of production). This thesis is often referred to as *technological determinism*. This claim, also, is discussed further, in a later section on revolution. The important point for now is that in Marx's economic interpretation of history any given society is an organic whole in which all power and causality flows from the eco-

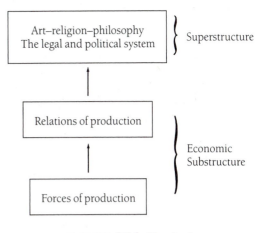

FIGURE 25-1 Marx's view
of the structure of society

nomic foundation up to the rest of the culture. This may be represented as in Figure 25-1.

IDEOLOGY

The top level of society or the superstructure represents all the ways in which people in a particular age tend to think of themselves and their activities. However, Marx points to the well-known fact that the way in which people think and speak of themselves is not always consistent with what they are and do. This sort of self-deceptive distortion is what we commonly call *rationalization*. However, individual people not only rationalize their own behavior, but as a group they rationalize the behavior of their society in order to maintain and justify the current social system. This sort of cultural "false consciousness" or self-imposed illusion is what Marx calls *ideology*. For the most part, people who promote an ideology are not hypocritically engaging in a conscious deception, for they really do believe that their distorted picture accurately represents the truth about their society. To summarize, ideologies are (1) cultural expressions that (2) represent a society's self-understanding, but that (3) present a distorted view of reality and (4) that serve to maintain and justify the power structure.

---

*Marx is not completely consistent nor clear in his use of this terminology. Thus, there are slight variations between commentators in how they define these terms.

[†]Marx does not seem to believe that individual behavior is determined. However, he does believe that the collective effects of many individuals' actions will produce an overall pattern.

Since ideology is a form of power, ideologies are necessarily the product of the dominant class:

The ideas of the ruling class are in every epoch the ruling ideas; . . . The class which has the means of material production at its disposal, has control at the same time over the means of mental production. (GI, T 172)

In Marx's view, philosophers are nothing but the unwitting tools of the reigning power structure. He refers to intellectuals as "active, conceptive ideologists, who make the perfecting of the illusions of the class about itself their chief source of livelihood" (GI, T 173). Because class-divided societies serve the interests of the privileged few, it is psychologically useful for the ruling class to convince the exploited group as well as to convince *themselves* that the social system is really serving the interests of all. For example, in the ideology of the American slave owners, the institution of slavery actually benefited the "primitive and pagan" African slaves, because it introduced them to the glories of civilization and Christianity.

Marx suggests that "in all ideology human beings and their circumstances appear upside down" (GI, T 154). In other words, ideologies present an inverted perspective because they distort reality and reverse the true direction of causality. Marx complains that the philosophers of his time like to flatter themselves by thinking that a society is formed by its ideas and that the rise of new ideas plays the major role in causing changes in the form of that society. While most philosophers would recognize that other cultural forces are involved, there is still the conviction that the change from, say, the Middle Ages to the Renaissance, was the product of some very significant intellectual changes. This thesis of the causal power of ideas is represented in Figure 25-2.

The first vertical arrow indicates that the form of society A is, to a large extent, the result of philosophy A. When this philosophy is replaced by another one (B), the form of the society also changes. Actually, the reverse is true, Marx says, for changes in the economic base produce changes in philosophy and the rest of intellectual life. Hence, Marx would redraw the picture as shown in Figure 25-3.

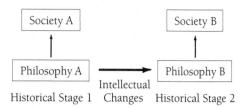

FIGURE 25-2 The traditional view that philosophy causes social changes

In this picture, the philosophy in one age does not bring about the philosophy of another age. Instead, the economic system changes, and this causes a change in philosophy. In other words, for Marx there really is no "history of philosophy," for the history of ideas is merely the by-product of the history of economic systems.

Morality, religion, metaphysics, all the rest of ideology and their corresponding forms of consciousness, thus no longer retain the semblance of independence. They have no history, no development; but men, developing their material production and their material intercourse, alter, along with this their real existence, their thinking and the products of their thinking. . . .

. . . Consciousness is therefore from the very beginning a social product, and remains so as long as men exist at all. (GI, T 118-19, 122)

Marx never gave a detailed account of how economic conditions can control people's ideas. At times he speaks as though art, religion, and philosophy were like the foam on top of a soft drink, produced by the forces below it bubbling to the surface. However, some Marxists say the mechanism is actually similar to Darwin's biological theory of natural selection.[11] Darwin said that only those species who successfully adapt to their environment will survive, while those who don't fit in with their material conditions will die out. Similarly, the Marxist says ideas will flourish, will be encouraged, will get a hearing, and will find a publisher, when they correspond with the prevailing economic system. Those that do not comply will be "blocked" or "selected out." Hence, ideas must find their place within an artificially limited

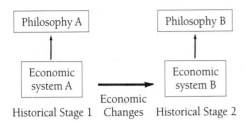

FIGURE 25-3 Marx's theory that
economic forces cause
philosophical changes

field of expression, and this guarantees that the prevailing ideology will always correspond to the economic structure of the society.

Examples of ideology are easy to find. In their political philosophies, the ruling classes imagine that their control of society is in accord with "the laws of nature," "God's will," "the General Will," "the Social Contract," or "eternal necessity." In the fixed economic system of the Middle Ages, pride, envy, and avarice were considered to be cardinal sins. However, with the rise of capitalism, and its need for insatiable consumerism and growth, these qualities were considered the mainsprings of economic life. Many a capitalist has inherited his wealth and depends on the government to nurture his economic interests, and yet considers himself a "self-made man" and espouses the myth of "rugged individualism."

Religion is a potent form of ideology, according to Marx. It advises people to endure their earthly suffering and to focus on their eternal destiny, where they will be walking on streets of gold. For this reason, Marx says, religion is the "opium of the people." Religion is frequently used to suggest that the social hierarchy is God-ordained. A line from a nineteenth-century Christian hymn says, "The rich man in his castle, / the poor man at his gate, / God made them high or lowly, / and ordered their estate."[12]

Finally, Marx says that philosophy is a tool of ideology. All philosophies from Plato to Hegel that emphasize the spiritual realm serve to draw attention away from the issues in the material realm. In the modern age, the epistemological individualism of Descartes and the political individualism of Locke obscured the way in which each person is tightly woven into the fabric of society and has no life apart from it.

The Marxist doctrine of ideology has found advocates in almost every discipline in the twentieth century. It is one form of what has come to be known as the "hermeneutics of suspicion." Hermeneutics is the science of interpretation. Hence, this sort of interpretive theory says that when analyzing a cultural expression you cannot trust what people think they are doing, you must look beneath the surface to find the implicit motives and causes that produced it. The Marxist advises that when you are seeking to understand a novel, a movie, a work of art, a philosophy, a religious concept, a news report, a law, or *any* theory, look beneath the surface for the economic motive.* The key questions to ask about any cultural product are, Whose interests does it represent? and How is it distorting reality to justify and promote the interests of a particular social group? This method of interpretation assumes there are no value-free or class-neutral cultural expressions, for economics and politics permeate every phase of culture. Everything in the superstructure represents the viewpoint of the group in power.

Marx's position on ideology is summarized in the following passage:

> The mode of production of material life conditions the social, political and intellectual life process in general. It is not the consciousness of human beings that determines their being, but, on the contrary, their social being that determines their consciousness. (CCPE, T 4)

The plausibility of Marx's view is affected by whether we emphasize the word "conditions" or "determines" in this quotation. If Marx is saying that (1) people must eat before they can think, wor-

---

*Other varieties of the hermeneutics of suspicion would look for different causes. The Freudian would look for suppressed sexual motives. The feminist would look for the way latent gender issues affect the surface phenomenon. Others look for racism as a disguised agenda in cultural works.

ship, or paint and (2) economic factors *condition* (or influence) the intellectual life of a culture, then this is a very qualified and uncontroversial claim. However, if Marx insists that (1) all ideas are *determined* by the economic foundation and (2) ideas never have an independent history of their own apart from economic changes, then this is a much stronger claim, open to a number of objections.

The first objection to the strong thesis is that even though Marx has no problem finding plenty of examples that support his case, he seems to ignore historical examples that falsify his thesis. Second, any claim that all ideas are ideological distortions produced by underlying social interests always boomerangs on the person making this claim. Thus, it could be charged that Marxism is itself an ideology that promotes the interests of the proletariat by distorting the facts of social reality. Third, ideas must not merely reflect the prevailing economic structures, but must also be able to critically turn back on those conditions if Marx's revolutionary ideas are to have any social effects. If Marx was able to unmask ideological distortions and see things clearly, why does he think it is impossible for other philosophers to do the same? If Marx's critics are correct, there is some degree of reciprocal causality between the economic foundation and the upper level of culture. In other words, the one-way arrows in Figure 25-3 that go from the economic foundation to philosophy should be replaced by arrows going in both directions.

THE THEORY OF REVOLUTION

The picture Marx has given us thus far is that society is an organic whole in which each element is related to all the others. However, if a society was perfectly coherent and satisfactorily meeting the needs of its members, there would be no reason for it to change. Thus, it is important for Marx to explain why history is endlessly restless and why well-established social orders pass away and give birth to their successors. The answer is found in the thesis of technological determinism.

During relatively stable times in the life of a historical era, the social order corresponds to the stage of technology that has developed. However, because humans have a drive to be creative and productive, they continually improve and develop the methods of production. For example, hand weaving was replaced by mechanical looms, and small family farms have given way to large agricultural complexes. However, as the forces of production develop, Marx says that the following mechanism of historical change will come into play:

> At a certain stage of their development, the material productive forces of society come into conflict with the existing relations of production, or—what is but a legal expression for the same thing—with the property relations within which they have been at work hitherto. From forms of development of the productive forces these relations turn into their fetters. Then begins an epoch of social revolution. (CCPE, T 4-5)

In other words, there reaches a point when the organization of a society no longer keeps pace with the changes in its technological base, and this prevents the full use and further development of the forces of production. This introduces a tension within the economic organization of the society, for it becomes like clothes that no longer fit their owner.

Society, of course, does not change itself. These changes are brought about by human agents. Thus, when the internal pressure on the current system is building up, the class in power is motivated to preserve the old order, while the class that is rising in power seeks to make changes. In this way, class conflicts are caused by these inevitable economic dynamics, and at this point a social revolution is in the making. In some cases, it may be violent, in others not. However, it will not occur until the forces of production have developed to the fullest extent possible within the existing relations of production and all piecemeal adjustments have failed. Then, like a larva developing within its cocoon until it becomes a butterfly that bursts from its shell, so the new form of society emerges from the shell of the old.

Marx claims that this process has been at work throughout all human history. In a number of his writings, he divides history into different epochs defined according to their dominant economic system. The five epochs are (1) primitive communal, (2) slave, (3) feudal, (4) capitalist, and (5) socialist communist. In each case, the transition from one stage to the next follows the dialectical pattern of economic development just discussed. According to Marx, we are now in the fourth stage where capitalism rules. We now need to see why he thinks it is producing its own negations and how the socialist or communist system inevitably arises from it.

Marx's Analysis of Capitalism

Marx's chief criticisms of capitalism revolve around his theory of surplus labor. He begins with what is known as the "labor theory of value," which was held by many of the economists of his day. This theory states that the value of any commodity is a function of the amount of labor that it took to produce it. In capitalism the worker's labor is a commodity, so the value of that labor is determined by its cost. What it takes to produce a worker's labor is what it takes to sustain him. Giving what he thinks is the most charitable account of capitalism, Marx assumes the product will be sold for its just price. However, this alone would leave the capitalist without any profit. So the capitalist must find some way to work profit into this scenario. He does so by forcing the worker to labor more hours than is necessary for his own survival. Marx theorizes that the worker's day can be divided into two parts. First, there are the hours that he spends producing products whose total value are equivalent to his wages (wages that are equal to what it takes to sustain the worker). The second part of the workday consists of the hours he spends producing commodities whose value is expropriated by the capitalist. Thus the capitalist makes a profit on this "surplus value."

For these reasons, Marx describes the capitalist as having a "vampire thirst for the living blood of labour" (CI 367). However, in his less emotional passages, Marx (who was fond of classical literature) presents the capitalists almost like the characters in Greek dramas, who are the helpless victims of Fate and who unwittingly bring about their own destruction. Although greed for profits drives the capitalist, this is not because he is a morally defective being. It is because the laws of his own economic system give him no rest and continually whisper in his ear, "Go on! Go on!" (T 213).[13] Thus, Marx describes the capitalists as victims of their own system:

> As capitalist, he is only capital personified. His soul is the soul of capital. But capital has one single life impulse, the tendency to create value and surplus-value, to make its constant factor, the means of production, absorb the greatest possible amount of surplus-labour. (CI, T 362)

A capitalist may desire to be compassionate, but if he is not competitive—if he doesn't race after profits, and, consequently, doesn't exploit the workers—he will not remain a capitalist for long.

The dynamics of the capitalist system will not last forever, for it is inevitably doomed. Marx describes capitalism as a precarious system whose dialectical laws determine that it will continually swing back and forth from economic booms to recessions. However, each cycle further weakens the system and strengthens its own negation until, finally, the system will self-destruct. As he looked at the development of capitalism in his day, Marx said that "a foreboding is dawning, that the present society is no solid crystal, but an organism capable of change, and is constantly changing" (CI, T 298). According to Marx, the course that capitalism will take can be set out in terms of the following dialectical development, which has all the necessity of a law of nature:

I. **Thesis: Capitalism**

Capitalism arises as a system in which a small class of people own and control the major forces of production as their private property and employ workers who have no economic resources but their own labor power.

A. *The Contradiction of Capitalism*

The ideology of capitalism is based on individualism and private property. However, the growth of capitalism will necessarily require a highly organized, socialized base with a continually

increasing size, complexity, and inter-
dependence.*

B. *The Dialectical Development of Capitalism*

(1) In the competitive struggle for profits,
a capitalist will introduce labor-saving
machinery and lay off workers. However, machines can't be exploited,
only workers can. Hence, the capitalist ends up cutting into the source of
surplus value and profits.

(2) When all the capitalists obtain the
new technology, it no longer provides a competitive edge. But with
more efficient means of production
and fewer employed workers to be
consumers, overproduction and a
decline in profits result.

(3) The smaller companies will go bank-
rupt, and their resources will become
the spoils of war of the surviving
companies.

C. *The Consequences of the Development of
Capitalism*

(1) Capitalism will become more monolithic. This results from (a) the
concentration of capital (it takes increasingly more capital to stay in the
game and, thus, the surviving firms
grow in size) and (b) the centraliza-
tion of capital (to maintain their economic power, companies merge and
the means of production are concentrated in fewer and fewer
hands).†

(2) The capitalists whose companies
have failed will no longer be capitalists but will be forced to join the
growing pool of the unemployed.

(3) The larger number of unemployed
workers will cause more competition
for wages, giving greater power to
the capitalists.

(4) In the quest for more power, greater
markets, and cheaper labor, companies will expand to an international
scale (thus increasing imperialism,
international conflicts, and wars).

II. *Antithesis: The Proletariat*

As capitalism develops, the wealthy will become wealthier and fewer in number at the
same time that the system produces its own
negation within itself: an embittered and
impoverished but unified class of proletarians. "What the bourgeoisie, therefore, produces, above all, is its own grave-diggers. Its
fall and the victory of the proletariat are
equally inevitable" (CM, T 483). Thus, capitalism will unintentionally produce the following results:

A. *The Rise of the Proletariat*

(1) Workers will become concentrated in
factories in large numbers where they
can form revolutionary associations.

(2) The size of the proletariat will
increase.

(3) The members of the working class
will become increasingly miserable,
which will raise their consciousness
and solidify them.

(4) Through the international expansion
of capitalism, the class of workers
will become an international class.

B. *The Inevitability of Revolution*

Following dialectical principles, constantly increasing quantitative change
will produce a qualitative change or a
revolution. Like a tire being inflated, it
will keep getting larger and larger until it

---

*Think of the many interdependent industries and groups of
laborers that support the manufacturing of automobiles and
how much the economy of the United States is affected by the
status of this one industry. For this reason, the government is
intimately involved in the support of large industries such as
this one.
†Think of how small corner grocery stores have been swallowed up by the large grocery chains. Similarly, local hospitals, banks, and small computer manufacturers have either
closed or merged with larger corporations.

reaches a point where it explodes. In this way, the growth of capitalism will be its undoing: "Centralisation of the means of production and socialisation of labour at last reach a point where they become incompatible with their capitalist integument [husk]. This integument is burst asunder. The knell of capitalist private property sounds. The expropriators are expropriated" (CI chap. 32, T 438).

III. Synthesis: Socialism

The new socioeconomic system of socialism will appear, to resolve the tensions in the old system. Eventually the socialist state will wither away, and socialism will give birth to true communism.

Communism: The New Humanity and the New Society

After capitalism has become yet one more obsolete system to join the junkpile of dialectical history, there will be a stage of transition that Marx calls "the dictatorship of the proletariat." This will be a necessarily grim time when the proletariat will use their political power to clean out the last remnants of capitalism. Next will come the first stage of communism, the stage now known as "socialism." Here the state takes over the means of production. However, this will eventually give way to the final stage of ultimate communism. At this stage, the people will control not only political decisions but also the economic life of the country.

Thus far, history has been moved forward by a continual succession of class conflicts. In each era, it has been the same ball game, only the teams have been changed. Under communism, Marx says, the nature of the game will have changed altogether. With no more private ownership of the means of production, society will no longer have the tensions and contradictions produced by class divisions. Without class conflict, history will change from a vicious competitive game to one of mutual cooperation, where there will no longer be winners and losers. Hence, the

dialectical struggles of history will come to rest, for the driving force of history, the struggle to achieve a rational society, will have achieved its goal. Human beings, having been the victims of a bad dream, will now be fully awake to take charge of their destiny for the first time. As Friedrich Engels describes it,

> The extraneous objective forces that have hitherto governed history pass under the control of man himself. Only from that time will man himself, more and more consciously, make his own history—only from that time will the social causes set in movement by him have, in the main and in a constantly growing measure, the results intended by him. It is the ascent of man from the kingdom of necessity to the kingdom of freedom. (T 715-16)[14]

Alienation will cease to be a problem because workers will not be separated from the products of their labor. There will no longer be any socioeconomic classes because there will no longer be masters and wage slaves. People will no longer be treated as commodities but will be able to rediscover their true selves and their dignity. The ethos will change from that of a dog-eat-dog competitive struggle to that of a family, the family of humanity. Marx says the communist society will inscribe on its banner: "From each according to his ability, to each according to his needs!" (T 531).[15] This is possible, he says, because character traits such as greed or selfishness are not intrinsic to human nature. Instead, these traits are nurtured within us by our society. By changing society, we also change human nature as we know it.

It would be nice to be able to describe the details of this society, but Marx provides only a general outline. The specific policies were to be hammered out when the time came. According to Marx's analysis of the human situation, communism would restore humanity to its true essence and things would just naturally fall into place. Communism is

> the genuine resolution of the conflict between man and nature and between man and man. . . . Communism is the riddle of history solved, and it knows itself to be this solution. (EPM, T 84)

Evaluation and Significance

It is hard to deny that many of Marx's comments about capitalism hit the target. One hundred years after the publication of *The Communist Manifesto*, Sidney Hook listed the features of capitalism described by Marx that are still ongoing concerns today:

> economic centralization and monopoly, the cycle of boom and depression, unemployment and the effects of technological change, political and economic class wars, excessive specialization and division of labor, the triumph of materialistic and money values on the rest of our culture.[16]

However, many of Marx's predictions were off the mark. Most significantly, he thought the collapse of the capitalist system was just around the corner. But capitalism seems to have a resiliency he could not have fathomed. The power of labor unions, the government's prosecution of monopolies, the extensive regulations governing the health and safety of workers, affirmative action programs, the increased leisure of workers, and numerous employee benefits are just a few of the developments in the twentieth-century workplace that Marx never imagined would develop within capitalism. He seemed to assume that the only alternatives were a total laissez-faire economy or a total collectivism and did not allow for the mixed economies of today's world.

A further problem is that Marx had a romantic view of human nature. He believed that the motivation of self-interest and the lust for power and control were exclusively the results of the capitalist system and would not carry over to humanity under a socialistic government. However, history has shown that the capitalist is not always driven by a blind instinct to maximize profits and that, for better or worse, some features of human nature will be the same in any economic system. Obviously, the fall of numerous Marxist governments in the latter part of the twentieth century is the most striking indictment of Marxist theory. However, those who have lived through this transition say that they have seen four things they had

never seen under socialism. On the one hand, they are experiencing the freedom to travel and intellectual freedom; on the other hand, unfortunately, unemployment and homelessness are emerging. Perhaps history's final verdict on Marxism is yet to come. What is clear is that the dialectic of history has further chapters that Marx did not envision.

It is easy to get caught up in the debate over the strengths and weaknesses of Marx's economic theories and political proposals and forget that, for him, these were really means to a much more lofty goal: the flourishing of each and every human being in society. Marx's critics can justly point to the way that capitalism continues to remedy its own evils. However, the Marxist can justly reply that the social conscience of capitalist societies has been raised as a result of Marx's exposure of the evils that the industrial age had created. Karl Popper, one of Marxism's most forceful critics, has written this tribute to his genius:

> [Marx] opened and sharpened our eyes in many ways. A return to pre-Marxian social science is inconceivable. All modern writers are indebted to Marx, even if they do not know it.[17]

As long as some people in society are disfranchised and as long as issues of social justice remain unresolved, Marxist themes will have some appeal. However, the applications of Marxism will probably be much more limited in the future, for it seems to fail as a comprehensive philosophy that offers answers to all the questions of human existence. Even if the light of Marxist theory has dimmed in the field of economics, many literary critics still find it useful to understand a work of literature by attending to its social context and by reading between the lines of the text to uncover the author's hidden ideological agenda.

In the twentieth century, as material prosperity has increased and the standard of living of the average person has risen far higher than Marx could ever have dreamed, the sense of alienation that people feel has not decreased. This suggests the possibility that alienation may not be a function of external conditions, but is more deeply embedded in human nature, a symptom of an internal malaise. This alternative diagnosis was explored by the two founders of existentialism, Søren Kierkegaard and Friedrich Nietzsche, the subjects of the next two chapters.

Questions for Understanding

1. What did Marx take as his task or mission in life?

2. What ideas, events, and circumstances influenced Marx's philosophy?

3. Why does Marx think that most people in his time were suffering from alienation?

4. In what ways does Marx's dialectic differ from Hegel's?

5. How does Marx attempt to reconcile his theory of historical determinism with his call for political activism?

6. What is economic determinism? How does Marx use this notion to explain society and the pattern of history?

7. What is ideology and how does Marx think it influences history?

8. Why does Marx say "religion is the opium of the people"?

9. Why is Marx critical of all previous philosophies?

10. Why does Marx think capitalism is doomed to fail?

11. What is Marx's view of the culmination of history?

Questions for Reflection

1. In what ways (if any) was your understanding or preconceptions of Marx's philosophy changed by this chapter?

2. What do you think of Marx's claim that human nature is not fixed but can be changed through a change in social conditions?

3. How would Marx use economics to explain the following features of modern life? To what degree is the Marxist analysis plausible in: (a) college and professional sports, (b) the movie and music industries, (c) university and college curriculums, (d) religious movements and institutions, (e) television news?

4. If you could eliminate poverty, homelessness, illiteracy, and provide universal medical care for everyone in your society, but could do so only by eliminating the accumulation of individual wealth, would you choose to do so? Why or why not?

5. If you had been born into completely different social and economic circumstances (your family was extremely wealthy or extremely poor) would your political and social views be any different than they are now?

Notes

1. All quotations from Marx and Engels, unless otherwise stated, have been taken from Robert C. Tucker, ed., *The Marx-Engels Reader*, 2d ed. (New York: Norton, 1978). References to this anthology, abbreviated as "T," appear in parentheses along with the appropriate page numbers. Because so many different sources of Marx's works are available, the work by Marx in which the quotation originally appeared is also indicated. In some cases, this appears in an endnote. However, when the work is frequently cited, its abbreviation precedes the Tucker reference. These abbreviations are as follows:

CCPE   Preface to *A Contribution to the Critique of Political Economy*.

CHPR   "Contribution to the Critique of Hegel's *Philosophy of Right*: Introduction."

CI   *Capital*, vol. 1, trans. Ben Fowkes (London: Penguin Books, 1990).

CM   *The Communist Manifesto*.

EPM   *Economic and Philosophic Manuscripts of 1844*.

GI   *The German Ideology*.

2. Letter to Arnold Ruge.

3. Quoted in A. James Gregor, *A Survey of Marxism* (New York: Random House, 1965), 6.

4. "On the Jewish Question."

5. Quoted in John Herman Randall, Jr., *The Making of the Modern Mind* (Cambridge, MA: Riverside Press, 1940), 384.

6. Letter to Arnold Ruge.

7. Speech at the graveside of Karl Marx.

8. "Theses on Feuerbach," XI.

9. *The Holy Family*, quoted in David Caute, ed., *Essential Writings of Karl Marx* (New York: Collier Books, 1967), 50.

10. *The Poverty of Philosophy* (Chicago: Kerr), 119.

11. See John McMurtry, *The Structure of Marx's World-View* (Princeton, NJ: Princeton University Press, 1978), chap. 7.

12. Cecil Frances Alexander, "All Things Bright and Beautiful" (1848), stanza 3.

13. *Wage Labour and Capital*, sec. 5.

14. Friedrich Engels, *Socialism: Utopian and Scientific*, sec. 3.

15. "Critique of the Gotha Program."

16. Sidney Hook, "*The Communist Manifesto* 100 Years After," *New York Times Magazine*, February 1, 1948, in *Molders of Modern Thought*, ed. Ben B. Seligman (Chicago: Quadrangle Books, 1970), 80.

17. Karl Popper, *The Open Society and Its Enemies*, vol. 2 (London: Routledge & Kegan Paul, 1966), 82.

26

Søren Kierkegaard:
The Founder of
Religious Existentialism

THE TWENTIETH CENTURY PHILOSOPHY NOW known as **existentialism** has its roots in the nineteenth century in the writings of Søren Kierkegaard and Friedrich Nietzsche. Kierkegaard is discussed in this chapter and Nietzsche in the next, but a preliminary comparison of the two will be useful at the outset. The two thinkers were radically different and yet very much alike. They differed in that Kierkegaard was a passionate Christian and Nietzsche was an equally passionate atheist. Yet despite this enormous difference, they shared some of the same philosophical convictions and some of the same criticisms of their age. Developing the themes that later characterized the existentialist movement, they both asserted the importance of passion over reason, subjectivity over objectivity, and the importance of the individual person over the abstract universal or the impersonal crowd.

Neither Kierkegaard nor Nietzsche had much impact on their own time compared with the interest and following that developed in the twentieth century around their ideas. For this reason, Kierkegaard has been called the "Danish time bomb" because his ideas lay quietly ticking until

they exploded several generations later. To express his sense that his age was not yet ready to understand his message, Nietzsche has one of his fictional creations exclaim,

> *I have come too early, . . . my time is not yet. . . . Lightning and thunder require time; the light of the stars requires time; deeds, though done, still require time to be seen and heard.*[1]

The nineteenth century was not yet ready to give up the notion that a scientific or rational analysis of human nature can tell us everything we need to know about ourselves, including how to conduct our lives. However, people in the twentieth century found this optimism wore thin as they tried to cope with the terror and inhumanity of two world wars, the depersonalizing effects of mass culture, and a sense of alienation and emptiness even as they were surrounded by the most wonderful, shining technology. Only after these disillusioning experiences were people ready to listen to Kierkegaard's and Nietzsche's accounts of the dark side of human nature, the importance of inwardness, and their critiques of modern culture.

Kierkegaard and Nietzsche are similar not only in their diagnoses of the human condition but also in their "therapies." Because they felt that truth could not be communicated directly through propositions, both philosophers employed an engaging literary style. They used every conceivable trick to seduce our imaginations so that the truth would sneak up on us from behind. In the old days, a safecracker would file his fingertips to make them painfully sensitive to the internal movements of the lock as he twisted the dial in search of the combination. Similarly, Kierkegaard and Nietzsche write to irritate you, to "rub you raw" so that you will be sensitive to the textures of your own existence. Instead of presenting philosophical arguments, they present existential possibilities and leave the choice up to you. It is easy to find flaws in their analysis. But just when you think you have successfully passed judgment on *their* writings, their words have a way of turning on you until you realize their writings are now judging *you*. In taunting you to react to them, Kierkegaard and Nietzsche force you to reveal yourself, along with your fears, your convictions, and your sacred idols. If they were successful in evoking this sort of self-honesty, they would have cared little about what you thought of their words.

The Stages in Kierkegaard's Life: From Passionate Playboy to Passionate Christian

Søren Kierkegaard was born on May 5, 1813, in Copenhagen. Nature had cursed him with a frail body, a curved spine, and a hoarse voice that frequently cracked when he spoke. He spoke of his body as a heavy weight dragging down a healthy spirit that longed to be free. When he was seventeen, he entered Copenhagen University. Initially, at his father's insistence he majored in theology, but he later changed to philosophy. Although his academic studies influenced his thought, the spirit of his writings arose from four turning points in his life. These were two relationships (with his father and his only female love affair) and two battles (with the press and with the Danish Church).

Kierkegaard's father had grown up as a poor peasant but through hard work and good luck became so successful in business that he was able to retire at age forty. He was a deeply religious Protestant, but his life was tortured by a morbid sense of guilt for all his moral failures. The result was that he gave his son a very stern, oppressive religious upbringing. Kierkegaard later described it as "crazy."

As a university student, Kierkegaard rebelled against the religious pressures of his childhood. He tried to squeeze out of life all the pleasure he could and worked hard at developing the reputation of being a happy-go-lucky, cultured, man-about-town. However, according to his journals, he was being eaten up by despair behind his carefree mask:

> I have just returned from a party of which I was the life and soul; wit poured from my lips, everyone laughed and admired me—but I went away—and the dash should be as long as the earth's orbit———and wanted to shoot myself. (KA 7)[2]

Just before his father's death, Kierkegaard became reconciled to him. The son realized that his father's harsh religious training was actually a loving attempt to spare him from the melancholy and guilt his father had experienced. With this new realization of his father's love, Kierkegaard began to understand God's love and turned back toward Christianity.

The second influential event in his life that had an impact on his philosophy was his engagement to Regina Olsen. It was a tortuous experience for Kierkegaard. He was passionately in love with her and yet felt that his melancholy personality would be like a lead weight that would drag her down. Furthermore, he felt he had a unique mission in life that would be subverted by the entanglements of marriage and a normal, middle-class existence. Both before and after the engagement was broken, Kierkegaard found that his love for her brought out the best in him and inspired the writer within him to emerge. However, he found it easier to revel in the abstract inspiration of this love than to be in her concrete, personal presence. The theme of the tension between the abstract and the concrete continued throughout all his writings.

The third influence on Kierkegaard was his lifelong war with the press. He worried that the press made individuals think of themselves as members of the anonymous, collective group known as "the public." His tensions with the press came to a head in his famous battle with *The Corsair*. This was a popular newspaper that loved to report the gossip of the day as well as provide witty, cynical book reviews. The newspaper had earlier praised the work of two of Kierkegaard's pseudonymous authors. However, in December 1845 it made some unfavorable comments about his *Stages on Life's Ways*. Kierkegaard now thought it was time to put the low-brow paper in its place. Referring back to the earlier favorable reviews, he claimed his reputation had been damaged by being praised by this disreputable paper. In his typical polemical style, Kierkegaard wrote a public letter to the journal, begging the editor to restore his dignity by repudiating him. The editor granted the request and began a series of editorial attacks on Kierkegaard and his work, as well as publishing cruel cartoons that ridiculed him. The crusade was successful, for it turned much of Copenhagen against Kierkegaard and made him the object of ridicule. Prior to this dispute, he had planned to retire from writing and work in a quiet, country church. Now, however, he felt the need to stand by his post and continue to criticize his culture.

Finally, Kierkegaard entered into a battle with the Danish State Church. His complaint was that to be a Christian in Denmark was a taken-for-granted, cultural event. In his view, the Church was a comfortable institution that had abandoned authentic Christianity long ago. He satirized the churchgoers of Denmark as bloated geese that met every Sunday to praise the Creator for giving them wings, but who had grown too fat to fly and reviled those that did use their wings. Although he was still battling "Christendom" in the name of Christianity, his health began to fail and he died on November 5, 1855. At his funeral, his brother Peter, a leading clergyman, apologized for Søren's attacks against the Church. However, a number of univer-

sity students, who admired Kierkegaard's iconoclastic writings, rose up to protest. This erupted into a small-scale riot. Appropriately, even as he was being laid in the grave, Kierkegaard was still causing controversy and forcing people to take a stand. He would have wanted it no other way.

Task: To Make Life More Difficult

Through the voice of one of his pseudonymous characters, Kierkegaard describes an afternoon sitting in a cafe, thinking about what his life's mission should be.* As he looked about his society, it seemed that everyone was hard at work trying to make life easier with new inventions and new technology. What he must do, he concludes, is to give people what they were missing but what they really needed. Thus, he says,

> Out of love for mankind, and out of despair at my embarrassing situation, seeing that I had accomplished nothing and was unable to make anything easier than it had already been made, and moved by a genuine interest in those who make everything easy, I conceived it as my task to create difficulties everywhere. (CUP 166)

But what is the point of trying to make life difficult? Kierkegaard could, perhaps, respond that life's greatest rewards come only to those who are willing to endure difficulties and even suffering. The labor pains of the mother bring forth new life, the perseverance and exertions of the athlete produce self-mastery and athletic records, and the creative struggles of the writer produce great novels. For Kierkegaard, the most important and most difficult goal in life is self-understanding. However, this is something we shrink from. We prefer to adopt a stance of detachment and view life as spectators. We are more comfortable with reason and analysis than passion and commitment. We have a

---

*Although it is not always safe to assume that the words of Kierkegaard's fictional characters reflect his own sentiments, in this case they repeat what Kierkegaard says many times over about himself.

smug complacency that prevents us from being painfully and fully honest with ourselves.

If self-knowledge were his whole concern, Kierkegaard would be the nineteenth-century predecessor of contemporary self-help—pop psychology. Kierkegaard had a larger goal in mind, however. He believed that the more honest we were with ourselves, the more despair we would experience, until we finally realized that we cannot become fully actualized selves apart from a relationship to God. As he revealed throughout *My Point of View for my Work as an Author*, his overriding goal was to understand what it means to be a Christian and then to prod himself and his reader to realize that in practice. To do this, however, he had to make us aware of the insufficiency of all our other attempts to find life's center. Therefore, while most philosophers sought to provide answers to our problems, Kierkegaard sought to provide problems for our comfortable answers. His goal was to destroy, one by one, every one of our cherished solutions, until in despair we would realize only one was left.

Kierkegaard's Method: Indirect Communication

If Kierkegaard had a religious message to convey, one might expect his works to take the form of religious discourses. However, most of his notable works are not ostensibly religious in their subject matter. In examining Kierkegaard's writings, it is significant to note that he wrote his master's thesis on the concept of irony in Socrates. With Socrates, Kierkegaard did not believe that he could communicate the truth to anyone. Thus he had to use a method of indirect communication that would lure his readers into discovering the truth for themselves. He uses various literary devices effectively, such as irony, humor, satire, parables, and thought experiments. However, the most interesting technique he uses is to present his works as the writings of various pseudonymous characters and himself as merely their neutral editor. Examples of some of his characters are a committed hedonist and seducer who has no sense of selfhood,

a moralist who has not yet discovered that the morally upright life does not lead to self-discovery, a writer on Christianity who is a sympathetic outsider, and a Christian whose faith reaches beyond that which Kierkegaard himself had attained.* The reader is enticed to view life through the lenses of these different outlooks and to draw his or her own conclusions about their adequacy. Kierkegaard's goal was to seduce your imagination and lead you down a path where you would suddenly find yourself staring in a mirror and be shocked into self-understanding. Kierkegaard's method is nicely depicted by Roger Shinn:

> Like a literary boxer, Kierkegaard jabs, feints, catches his reader off-balance. He drives you (for his writings are always directed at you) into a corner, pummels you, offers you a way out and dares you to take it. He makes you laugh as he turns his whiplike wit on someone, then agonize as the backlash catches you. He pours out sarcasms and invective, then instantaneously shifts to humble and reverent prayer.[3]

Although Kierkegaard addresses many standard philosophical problems, he had no use for *theories* of knowledge, reality, or morality. He thought that philosophers' fascination with them were as absurd as someone analyzing a menu in great detail when they were starving and needed the immediate nourishment of a real meal. For Kierkegaard, no intellectual issue can be understood in isolation from the type of people we are, the degree of self-honesty we have, how we are related to the truth, and how we participate in reality.† The contrast he felt between intellectual abstractions and his real need was set out in an 1835 journal entry:

> What I really lack is to be clear in my mind what I am to do, not what I am to know, except in so far as a certain understanding must precede every action. The thing is to understand myself, to see what God really wishes me to do; the thing is to find a

---

*These are found, respectively, in *Either/Or I*, *Either/Or II*, *Concluding Unscientific Postscript*, and *Training in Christianity*.
†Kierkegaard is very similar to Augustine in this regard. The Augustinian notion of the religious root of all philosophical speculation was acquired through the Augustinian spirit latent within the Lutheran theology of Kierkegaard's tradition.

truth which is true for me, *to find* the idea for which I can live and die. *(KA 4-5)*

Kierkegaard on Knowledge: Truth and Subjectivity

OBJECTIVE KNOWING VERSUS SUBJECTIVE KNOWING

For most modern philosophers, the main problem of epistemology was how to rise above our subjectivity in order to obtain objective truth. However, Kierkegaard turns the problem on its head. For him, the hardest task in life is to become subjective. Our natural tendency, he says, is to hide within the shelter of objectivity in order to shirk from the pain and crisis of making personal decisions (CUP 115). We will most fully understand our situation as knowers when we come to see that "truth is subjectivity."

Most of Kierkegaard's discussions of knowledge are an attempt to draw out the distinction between the two kinds of truths: objective truth and subjective truth. To understand what Kierkegaard is getting at, note that there are two meanings of the word *subjective*, one pejorative and the other neutral. The bad kind of subjectivity occurs when someone's personal interests interfere with his or her ability to see and judge things correctly. The word *subjective* in this sense is associated with the terms "arbitrary," "idiosyncratic," or "biased." If a professor gives high grades to his "pets" and low grades to the rest of the students, and there is no correlation between the students' grades and their performance, then his grading is subjective in the bad sense of the word.

Subjective can also mean "necessarily related to the subject." In this case (the one Kierkegaard is concerned with) to say that an outlook or decision is "subjective" means it is inescapably related to the agent's needs, interests, or values. The decisions you make concerning what career to pursue, whether or not you will marry, or what your ethical values shall be are choices that necessarily involve you as a person. You may seek advice from others and consider all the objective data

available, but in the final analysis it will be your decision. In confronting these sorts of issues, you bring to the decision your total development as a person up to that point and take a personal stance on what sort of person you now choose to *become*.

Kierkegaard has no problem with objective truth when we are talking about issues in logic, mathematics, science, or any area of knowledge that is not essential to one's subjective existence. The task of becoming a full person is not intrinsically affected by your possessing or lacking these sorts of truths. Consider the statement "2 + 2 = 4." It does not matter who says this, or what the circumstances are, for it is impersonal, objective information. In assenting to its truth, nothing of who you are as a person is at stake. But compare this mathematical statement with "I love you." Now it *does* matter who says this and the circumstances in which this is said. When you say "I love you" to a person, you are involving yourself in a commitment and you are affected and changed by it. If you are not sincere, you are involving yourself in a deception. Either way, your affirmation is self-involving and affects your development as a person.

KNOWING THE TRUTH VERSUS BEING IN THE TRUTH

This last example opens up an important distinction Kierkegaard makes between knowing the truth and being in the truth. We use phrases such as "Be true to yourself" or "Be true to your friend." Obviously, we are not talking about having true beliefs or speaking true propositions here. Instead, we are talking about being in a certain sort of relationship. This is what Kierkegaard is getting at when he talks about "being in the truth." His distinction between knowing and being expresses a radical disagreement with Socrates' ethics. In his ethical outlook, Socrates heavily emphasized knowing the good. However, in Kierkegaard's analysis, a person could intellectually embrace a very elevated moral theory, but be a scoundrel in actual practice. Such a person would objectively know the truth but not be subjectively living in its truth. In contrast, a person might espouse a degenerate moral theory and still be more morally sensitive in practice than his theory would allow.

In one of Kierkegaard's best-known passages, he compares two approaches to religious knowledge:

> *If one who lives in the midst of Christendom goes up to the house of God, the house of the true God, with the true conception of God in his knowledge, and prays, but prays in a false spirit; and one who lives in an idolatrous community prays with the entire passion of the infinite, although his eyes rest upon the image of an idol: where is there most truth? The one prays in truth to God though he worships an idol; the other prays falsely to the true God, and hence worships in fact an idol.* (CUP 179-180)

The first person knows the truth, for he has the correct objective knowledge about God. However, he is not related to this knowledge authentically. The second person has the correct subjective relation to the true God, even though his ideas about this God are false. According to Kierkegaard, only the second person can be said to be *in* the truth.

THE RESULT VERSUS THE PROCESS

The distinction between objectively knowing the truth and subjectively being in the truth is related to another distinction Kierkegaard makes between the result and the process. In some cases, I can acquire a certain result by relying on the efforts of others without having to go through the process of obtaining it myself. For example, I can look up the distance from the earth to the moon in a book. I do not need to calculate this myself, because some astronomer has already done the work for me. However, in other cases, one cannot have the results without going through a certain process. For example, I cannot give you physical fitness. That is something you can get only if you go through the process of obtaining it yourself. For Kierkegaard, the kinds of truths that really matter (self-knowledge, the way one should live, or religious understanding) are more similar to physical fitness than to mathematical information. The individual cannot have the result apart from the way to that result. *What* you know is bound up with *how* you know it. The journey to self-understanding is a tor-

tuous one that only you can take. For this reason, Kierkegaard felt it would be useless to try to communicate this sort of understanding directly. Instead, he used his method of indirect communication, allowing the reader to experience life through the eyes of different characters, in order to see where each approach leads.

RELIGIOUS BELIEF

Given everything that has been said thus far, you would be correct to guess that Kierkegaard sees reason as having very little to do with the making of religious choices. In fact, he was dismayed by the attempt of religious philosophers to make Christianity palatable to speculative reason. "For if the God does not exist it would of course be impossible to prove it; and if he does exist it would be folly to attempt it" (PF 49).

Since Kierkegaard believes God does exist, why does he think it is folly to attempt to demonstrate this to reason? His first complaint is that the theistic proofs are logically fallacious. With Hume and Kant, Kierkegaard believes that the type of *a priori* reasoning that works so well in logic and mathematics cannot be used to prove existence. His second concern is that religious proofs are detrimental to human freedom. For example, once I understand the proof of the Pythagorean theorem, I have no rational choice but to accept it. For this reason, it makes no sense to say I believe it or I have faith in it. Faith in God, however, must be freely chosen, it must result from a decisive act of the will.

> *Belief is not a form of knowledge but a free act, an expression of the will. . . . The conclusion of belief is not so much a conclusion as a resolution.* (PF 103-104)

Kierkegaard's third point is that objective knowledge cannot provide a foundation for the sort of commitment that faith requires. The objective approach can, at best, give us a hypothesis that is tentatively confirmed through a continual accumulation and weighing of evidence, or what Kierkegaard terms an "approximation process." Each piece of positive evidence we discover gives us more and more confidence in the hypothesis.

But there is always the possibility that some negative evidence will be introduced that will lessen its probability. It is appropriate for our commitment to a scientific or historical hypothesis to go up and down in proportion to the evidence. However, faith must be something I can stake my life on, without reservation. Kierkegaard gives a comical description of a man who thinks he can obtain faith through the objective approach. However, it only allows him to approximate the object of his intended faith, but prevents him from ever reaching it:

> Anything that is almost probable, or probable, or extremely and emphatically probable, is something he can almost know, or as good as know, or extremely and emphatically almost know—but it is impossible to believe. (CUP 189)

For this reason, Kierkegaard defines both subjective truth and faith as *"An objective uncertainty held fast in an appropriation-process of the most passionate inwardness is the truth,* the highest truth attainable for an *existing* individual" (CUP 182). Faith involves risk, it involves taking a leap—it involves committing myself without the security of indubitable, objective evidence:

> There is no other road to faith; if one wishes to escape risk, it is as if one wanted to know with certainty that he can swim before going into the water. (PF 103n)

The fourth point is that religious choices must be made with the whole person and not just with the intellect. For Kierkegaard, Christianity is not a set of doctrines to be understood but a divine person to be encountered. "God is a subject, and therefore exists only for subjectivity in inwardness" (CUP 178). Hence, a philosopher's proofs for the existence of God will not lead to faith. It will only leave one with logical syllogisms and dry, intellectual dust that will not quench anyone's spiritual thirst. There are reasons why a person may decide to believe, but these reasons are not to be found in an objective argument. Kierkegaard quotes an old saying, "Whatever is known, is known in the mode of the knower." As he goes on to say,

> In the case of a kind of observation where it is requisite that the observer should be in a specific condi-
> tion, it naturally follows that if he is not in this condition, he will observe nothing. (CUP 51)

Hence, religious truth can only be found if you are "in a specific condition"—that is, if you feel a spiritual thirst nothing finite can quench, and if you are willing to continue the lonely journey of self-understanding to its ultimate goal.

With all his talk on subjectivity, it is easy to get the impression (and many commentators have had this impression) that Kierkegaard is claiming any "truth" will do as long as it is held passionately. If this is what he means, then a passionate belief in the Wizard of Oz would be just as valid as a commitment to the God of Christianity. However, it is clear he believes Christianity is objectively true, at the same time that he is stressing that its truth must be subjectively appropriated. When he says, "Truth is subjectivity," he does not mean you and I can never be related to the same truth. Something can be known subjectively without it being subjective. In faith, the mode of knowing is person related but the object of that knowledge is not. "The inwardness of understanding consists precisely in each individual coming to understand it for himself" (CUP 71). In the passage mentioned previously, where he compares (1) a person who has the true conception of God, but worships him in a false spirit, and (2) one who worships an idol with all the passion of his or her being, it is important to note that Kierkegaard does distinguish between "the true God" and an idol. This indicates that he believes there is an objective, absolute God. However, he also suggests that one has a greater hold on the truth if one has a passionate faith and false concepts than with orthodox concepts held inauthentically and without passion.

Kierkegaard the Antimetaphysician: Existence, Time, Eternity

Kierkegaard is often described as an antimetaphysician, for with Kant he did not believe we can have logical, speculative knowledge of reality. Although he always expresses respect for Hegel's great mind, Kierkegaard concludes (with a great deal of irony) that Hegel's magnificent metaphysical system was not only intellectually mistaken, but also that it was a comedy of errors:

> If Hegel had written his whole logic and had written in the preface that it was only a thought-experiment, . . . he undoubtedly would have been the greatest thinker who has ever lived. As it is he is comic.[4]

In other words, Hegel's system can be admired for its magnitude and intricacy the way we would admire a very clever work of science fiction, even though it bore no relationship to reality. Kierkegaard never tires of attacking speculative metaphysicians such as Hegel.*

Kierkegaard's first criticism of any metaphysical system, such as Hegel's, is that it is too abstract. Nothing in it speaks to the concrete issues an individual faces in life:

> Most systemizers in relation to their systems are like a man who builds an enormous castle and himself lives alongside it in a shed; they themselves do not live in the enormous systematic building. But in the realm of mind and spirit this nonresidence is and remains a decisive objection. Spiritually understood, a man's thoughts must be the building in which he lives—otherwise the whole thing is deranged.[5]

Using a different metaphor, Kierkegaard says that looking for guidance from such a philosophy is like

> travelling in Denmark with the help of a small map of Europe, on which Denmark shows no larger than a steel pen-point—aye, it is still more impossible. (CUP 275)

In other words, while Hegel talks about "the human spirit" and "being," he does not speak to me as an individual and does not address the concrete features of my existence. I cannot find my unique situation in the metaphysician's generali-

ties any more than we could find our way through Denmark using the highly condensed map.

Kierkegaard's second complaint is that we can have a timeless *logical* system that is complete and finished, but it is impossible for there to be an *existential* system, for our existence is still ongoing. It was absurd for Hegel to think his system was able to capture and contain the whole of a reality that can never be embraced by a finite human being. Since God can see the whole, it is possible for existence to be a system for him. For us, however, we never achieve finality but continually face new choices. We are immersed in life and cannot distance ourselves from it to see it abstractly, the way we can a mathematical system.

For Kierkegaard, the word *existence* has special meaning. It is the process of realizing what it means to be a self through personal choices. It is what contemporary existentialists refer to as "authentic existence." For Hegel (at least as Kierkegaard interprets him), the goal of human life was to rise above one's particularity in the direction of greater universality. One does this by merging one's interests with those of the communal spirit and, finally, by achieving the level of absolute knowledge where all particulars are absorbed into one, universal perspective. But for Kierkegaard, the more universal something is, the more abstract and empty it is. The more you approach the description of a human-being-in-general, the more you shed the distinctives of your unique existence.

Kierkegaard believed that deep within us is a longing for eternity and the infinite that is in tension with the weight of our earthly, time-bound life. If we experience this tension, we will know what it means to exist passionately.

> It is impossible to exist without passion, unless we understand the word "exist" in the loose sense of a so-called existence. . . . And it is just this that it means to exist, if one is to become conscious of it. Eternity is the winged horse, infinitely fast, and time is a worn-out jade; the existing individual is the driver. That is to say, he is such a driver when his mode of existence is not an existence loosely so called; for then he is no driver but a drunken peasant who lies asleep in the wagon and lets the horses take care of themselves. To be sure, he also drives

---

*Keep in mind that philosophers sympathetic to Hegel complain that Kierkegaard frequently caricatures Hegel's position. Even if this is true, however, it is hard to disagree with Kierkegaard's claim that Hegel subordinates the individual to the forces of history and culture.

and is a driver, and so there are many who—also exist. (CUP 276)

The sleeping driver represents the person who is numb to his existence because he either hides himself within the community mind-set, the Hegelian flow of universal history, and philosophical abstractions or because he is pulled unreflectively by his impulses. Only the person who grabs the reins and struggles with the decisive choices in his own life can be said to "exist" in the fullest sense of the word.

Kierkegaard's notion of the self conflicts with two of the leading positions in the history of philosophy. For one group of philosophers, such as Descartes, the self was a fully existent, self-evident substance. It was as much a part of the furniture of the world as one's body. For another group of philosophers, such as Hume, there is no self beyond the passing flow of experiences. Kierkegaard's position is that Descartes and Hume were each partially correct. When we do not actively strive to be a self, our lives are as Hume described them, simply a passing flow of experiences with no unity and no center. However, this is not the whole story, for it is possible to become a self. In contrast, contrary to Descartes, being a self is not a given, for *becoming* a self is the major project of our life. "An existing individual is himself in process of becoming. . . . In existence the watchword is always *forward*" (CUP 368). Achieving existence is a task to be accomplished with a great deal of anxiety, fear, and trembling. All about me (and within me) are forces that would pull me away from authenticity and anesthetize me to my own existence. Like the sleepy passenger in the preceding passage, I am passively riding the wagon through life but am not consciously choosing the direction in which I am traveling. The route to becoming a self is set out in Kierkegaard's discussion of the stages in life.

Stages on Life's Way

According to Kierkegaard's analysis of human experience, every individual faces the option of choosing between three fundamental kinds of commitments: the aesthetic, the ethical, and the religious. In various places he calls them "views of life," "existential categories," "existence-spheres," "modes of existing," and "stages on life's way." Kierkegaard's "modes of existence" are similar to Hegel's "forms of consciousness" in the *Phenomenology of Spirit*, in that they represent different ways of perceiving and experiencing life. For Hegel, the movement from one viewpoint to another is a logical unfolding of the patterns of history. The process in which cultures and historical epochs pass through the different forms of consciousness exhibits an underlying rationality. Opposing conceptions and modes of life are continually mediated at a higher level, as history converges on an all-comprehensive, universal point of view. For Kierkegaard, in contrast, the movement through the different existence-spheres does not take place at the level of culture or history at all. It is an individual journey in which the tensions in one sphere of existence are overcome by an individual's passionate choice (or "leap") to an alternate form of life. The goal here is not a cognitively adequate conception, but an existentially adequate life, as the agent seeks to escape despair by becoming an integrated, authentic self.

According to Kierkegaard, the movement from one stage of existence to another cannot be based on logical reasons, but is based on existential reasons, rooted in one's personal life story. Choosing to live out of any one of the existence-spheres is a value choice because the choice is based on the answer to questions such as "What shall I become? Is this a way of life I can make my own?" There can be no impersonal, rational court of appeal for assessing the value of any such choice, because all values are rooted in one sphere or another, since they are all competing visions of what values are important in life. At the same time, this does not mean the choice is as arbitrary as a flip of the coin. The inadequacy of one stage of existence makes itself felt in the experience of despair, and this drives us on to the next stage.

Kierkegaard believes that as we progress through each stage, we will be moving in the direction of becoming a fully developed self, a goal that can only be found at the religious stage. Yet,

AKG London

Caspar David Friedrich, The Wanderer above the Mists. *According to Kierkegaard, the most important task in life was to achieve authentic, individual existence. As a young man, he wrote in his journal: "The thing is to understand myself, to see what God really wishes* me *to do; the thing is to find a truth which is true for* me, *to find the* idea *for which I can live and die."*

for all the subjectivity in these choices, it does not take away from the fact that a person can make the wrong decision (possibly because of a desire to avoid self-knowledge). Thus, there is no logical reason why one might not stay in despair and avoid the choice of having to make a leap to a new and more demanding way of life. A large part of Kierkegaard's discussion of the existence-spheres is carried out in his two-part work *Either/Or.* The title suggests that life involves decisive choices between mutually exclusive alternatives that cannot

be resolved in a "both/and" synthesis as Hegel supposed.*

THE AESTHETIC STAGE

The first existence-sphere is the aesthetic stage.† The aesthetic person lives at the level of the senses, impulses, and emotions with a sort of childlike immediacy. Life is a continual search for satisfying moments. The aesthetic category covers a wide range of personality types that includes the raw hedonist who wallows in base, sensual pleasures, as well as the romantic who revels in the enjoyment of the arts and literature, and even the intellectual who enjoys ideas as though they were fine wines, but without committing his life to any of them.

For the aesthetic person, the only two categories that matter are *boring* and *interesting.* Life is a frantic attempt to avoid boredom by filling one's plate with ever-new interesting experiences. Whereas Descartes said, "I think, therefore I am," the aesthete says, "I have interesting moments, therefore I am." For this type of person, "Boredom is the root of all evil" (EO 1.281). However, boredom has two weapons in its arsenal. First, boredom is a threat because of the transitory nature of all experiences. Just when the aesthetic person thinks her life is full of pleasure, the beautiful flower fades, the concert comes to an end, or the moment of passion passes and she is left once again with an inner emptiness. The second weapon of boredom is repetition. Too much of any pleasure eventually becomes tiresome, stale, and dis-

*Using his literary skills to their fullest, Kierkegaard presents this book as though it were a series of papers edited by someone named Victor Eremita. Each part is a first-person account written by yet another pseudonymous character. The first is a presentation of life lived at the aesthetic level, and the second is a series of letters written to the first author by a person recommending the ethical approach to life.

†The word *aesthetic* has come to be associated with art and beauty. This is part of the meaning of Kierkegaard's usage. However, Kierkegaard's use also includes the original Greek meaning, which is "to sense or perceive." (We still use *anaesthetic* to refer to anything that dulls the senses.) The Greek verb also has the same root as the words *theory* and *theater.* Thus, the aesthetic person for Kierkegaard is one who approaches life with a sense of detachment and who is an uninvolved spectator.

satisfying. To overcome this problem, one is driven to a frantic search for new experiences.

To make us experience the aesthetic life from the inside, Kierkegaard invents a set of papers allegedly written by an anonymous young man referred to as "A." The pseudonymous author of these papers is the purest example of an aesthete, for he tries to make the pursuit of interesting moments into a fine art. In a paper titled "The Rotation Method," the character A recommends that we vary our pleasures the same way a farmer rotates his crops:

> One tires of living in the country, and moves to the city; one tires of one's native land, and travels abroad; one is europamüde [tired of Europe], and goes to America, and so on; finally one indulges in a sentimental hope of endless journeyings from star to star. (EO 1.287)

According to A, the key to life is to keep in control and avoid commitments. Guard against friendship, but maintain a variety of social contacts. Marriage is dangerous, for you will lose the freedom and detachment necessary for the aesthetic life. However, it is good to spice up your life with a multitude of erotic engagements (but limit them to an hour, or a month at most). But when you start to fall in love, have the courage to break it off, for you will have everything to lose and nothing to gain. In general, avoid responsibilities. Make arbitrariness into an art, he says, for this will lead to unending amusement.

The papers of the pseudonymous character A fill the first book of *Either/Or* and run from a glorification of the fictional Don Juan (whose love affairs are legendary) to a piece called the "Diary of the Seducer." Throughout it all, A is joyously making his life's project the pursuit of pleasures, whether these are sexual, musical, literary, or intellectual (one must always keep rotating pleasures to avoid stagnation). However, as we dwell in his inner life, a sense of emptiness seems to pervade it. When he is reveling in a pleasurable moment, he seems to be lost in the sheer immediacy of it all. When he is engaged in scheming and planning his next interesting moment, he becomes detached and alienated from his life. The happy-go-lucky aesthetic person, for whom every moment has equal value, is merely the flip side of the cynic for whom nothing has value. A life driven by the pursuit of pleasure, even if these pleasures are of the highest intellectual and cultural types, is a life whose only center is a collection of fragmentary, spasmodic moments. The problem with the aesthetic person is that he does not have a self, for his choices are determined by his environment, his moods, and impulses. Thus, there is a natural, dialectical tendency to seek more, to seek some unified core of values, to seek one's self, a restless urge to find something stable to be committed to. If a person answers this call, he or she will make the leap up to the ethical stage of existence.

THE ETHICAL STAGE

Only at the ethical stage does the individual make choices. To exist at this stage does not mean that the person suddenly makes all the right moral choices. What makes this a new stage is that the morality of one's choices is even considered at all. In the ethical stage the world is divided into the dichotomy of good–bad. Although the decision to live in the ethical sphere is not one based on reason, once a person decides to be moral she can derive ethical principles rationally, just as Kant claimed we could. However, this is not simply a theorizing about ethics, because a person could play with ethical philosophies the way one might with a coin collection and still live life aesthetically. Instead, achieving the ethical means that one's existence is dominated by ethical concerns.

The second part of *Either/Or* is written under the pseudonym of Judge William (sometimes referred to as "B" to contrast him with his aesthetic counterpart). The book is largely a series of letters written to A in which the Judge recommends the ethical life to him. If the figure of Don Juan and the "Diary of the Seducer" are the metaphors of the aesthetic stage, the paradigm of the ethical stage is found in Socrates and the institution of marriage. Marriage is not a matter of being passively swept up in the passion of love, but it is a matter of making a significant commitment. However, to make a commitment requires some continuity within me from moment to moment. Thus, in making significant choices I am on the way to becoming a self that endures beyond the immediate moment. For the first time, I am choosing who I will be and am not just the collection of fragmentary impulses that make up the aesthetic life. As Kierkegaard says in another place, in the ethical life I achieve "the possibility of *gaining a history*" (CUP 227). The ethical person is characterized by *passion* (an important quality for Kierkegaard). However, this does not refer to the whimsical desires of the aesthetic person. To have passion is to care about something with all one's being, to embrace the motivating values that one consciously uses to guide one's life. The qualities of caring deeply about something, self-reflection, and principled choice are not possible for the aesthetic person.

Even though the ethical person is much further along the way to becoming a self, the goal has not yet been fully attained. There is no way within the ethical sphere to discover myself as an individual. I am serving universal moral principles and participating within the community of rational, moral agents, but I am not a fully self-aware individual yet. Kierkegaard describes a man who is living within the ethical sphere in this way:

> Outwardly he is completely "a real man." He is a university man, husband and father, an uncommonly competent civil functionary even, a respectable father, very gentle to his wife and carefulness itself with respect to his children. And a Christian? Well, yes, he is that too after a sort. (SD 197)

Although such a person has obviously gone far beyond the aesthetic stage, something is still missing. His identity is summed up by the series of universals that clothe him. He is nothing but a collection of social roles: husband, father, civil servant. The problem is that the preceding description could fit any number of people. The question is, Where is the unique, authentic self behind all these descriptions?

For these reasons, the ethical person has not achieved the self-fulfillment that is only possible at the religious stage, even though such a person, such as Judge William, may be a sincere church-

goer. However, such a religious stance is still at the level of Kant's *Religion within the Limits of Reason Alone*, where the religious outlook is derived from a rational understanding of the moral law. The ethical person, according to Kierkegaard, does not have any relation to God other than that of good moral conduct. At this stage, sin or moral failure is thought of as simply a human weakness that can be overcome through strength of will and a clearer intellectual understanding of the moral good. The ethical person, such as Socrates, has an attitude of moral self-sufficiency. But the realization of one's own sin and moral inadequacy is the antithesis to the ethical stage. The person who is comfortably situated within the ethical sphere strives to do what is morally required but is satisfied only to be just as good as the average person. To identify myself with the bland, mediocre norm of the human average, is to strive to be a person just like any other good person, but this is not the route to individual authenticity. However, the most fully developed ethical person will be one who clearly perceives the moral ideal and, paradoxically, will be most painfully aware of her failure to be an ethically developed person. This realization of one's inadequacy rips apart the self-sufficient attitude of the ethical stage and produces despair. Thus, pursuing the ethical to its maximum produces a dialectical tension that leads me beyond it. The only escape is through a leap to another stage of existence.

THE RELIGIOUS STAGE

At the religious stage a person discovers what it means to be a self. This stage is not characterized by the adoption of a set of religious doctrines, but is nothing less than an encounter with the living God. In the aesthetic and ethical spheres, I try to find fulfillment in terms of what I can control. However, in the religious sphere I give up my need to be autonomous and in control and my stance is one of simply being open to what I can't control, which is God's initiative. The sense of self within the ethical sphere is always measured by the standard of other finite persons, which gives one a limited understanding of selfhood. Only when an individual stands before an infinite God does she obtain a true sense of her authentic self:

> But this self acquires a new quality or qualification in the fact that it is the self directly in the sight of God. . . . And what an infinite reality this self acquires by being before God! (SD 210)

For this reason, Kierkegaard says that "the more conception of God, the more self; the more self, the more conception of God" (SD 211). An important factor here is that my individuality is only fully realized with the highest degree of self-honesty and this is possible only when confronted with my own inadequacy. "Here Christianity begins with the doctrine of sin, and therefore with the individual" (SD 251). When I encounter the living God, I stand naked, free of my socially defined roles and free of my masks. Stripped of every possibility of self-deception, I am able to know myself for the first time.

In his book, *Fear and Trembling*, Kierkegaard emphasizes the sharp contrast between the ethical and religious spheres by retelling the Old Testament story of Abraham. In this story, Abraham hears the voice of God, calling on him to sacrifice Isaac, his son. In deciding what to do, Abraham cannot fall back on universal, ethical norms, for the average person is expected to love and protect his or her children. Thus, he is caught between obeying the demands of the ethical or serving God. What he must realize is what Kierkegaard calls a "teleological suspension of the ethical" (FT 64-77). That is, his relationship to what is universal must be suspended for the sake of a higher goal, namely his individual relationship to God. Normally, the ethical and the religious do not conflict. However, Kierkegaard does not want us to think the two can be collapsed, as Kant supposed. By giving us an example where the two are in tension, he is pointing out that the individual's relationship to God is a higher priority than a rationally based universal ethics.

The crisis in Abraham's life illustrates that the difference between the "knight of faith" (as Kierkegaard calls him) and the ethically upright person is that the person of faith is not related to God by way of morality, but his commitment to morality derives from his relationship to God (and thus can be superseded by God). In less dramatic circumstances, the person at the ethical stage and one at the religious stage are indistinguishable from the standpoint of external appearances. If we were to follow around a knight of faith as the latter engages in the mundane events and pleasures of her daily life, we would find nothing extraordinary about her outward life. But inwardly there is all the difference in the world. The difference is that her relationship to anything finite and relative is always a relative commitment governed by her absolute commitment to the absolute God. Kierkegaard compares this to an adult who engages wholeheartedly in a game with children, but who still retains the adult understanding and commitments that transcend those of the child (CUP 370).

For Kierkegaard, the three existence-spheres are not like three separate circles that have nothing in common. Instead, they are like three concentric circles with the religious stage and authentic selfhood at the center. As I move inward from the periphery of life (from the aesthetic stage to the ethical), I do not leave life's pleasures behind, but now realize they are not absolute but are relative and subordinate to the higher principles within the ethical stage. For example, from within the sphere of the ethical, Judge William defends "the aesthetic validity of marriage." When I realize the religious stage, I can now place both life's moments of pleasure as well as ethical principles in context, as I live in relation with God. Seen in this way, Kierkegaard is actually reiterating Hegel's insight that each advance of the dialectic retains what was of value in the previous stages, but elevates it to a higher level.

Christianity as the Paradox and the Absurd

In the earlier discussion of subjective truth, I pointed out that the choice to become a Christian, according to Kierkegaard, is not one that can be based on reason. Nevertheless, Christianity is no more subjective than any other commitment. Almost arguing in the spirit of Hume, Kierkegaard insists that the sum total of the rationally grounded data is a collection too fragmentary and limited to tell us what commitments to make. Thus all ultimate choices require a kind of leap, based on our sheerly personal value commitments. Indeed, even the choice to be rational is not a choice reason can dictate, but is based on a decision as to what sort of persons we want to be.

But Kierkegaard is not interested in making it easy for us, for he is never content to rest with the moderate claim that reason is limited. Instead, he insists on stating his position in the most extreme rhetoric possible. Thus, he continually speaks of Christianity not only as beyond reason but as the supreme paradox and even as the absurd. Consider the following typical passages:

1. "For the absurd is the object of faith, and the only object that can be believed" (CUP 189).

2. "Christianity has declared itself to be the eternal essential truth which has come into being in time. It has proclaimed itself as the *Paradox*, and it has required of the individual the inwardness of faith in relation to that which stamps itself as . . . an absurdity to the understanding" (CUP 191).

3. Kierkegaard calls a person to "relinquish his understanding and his thinking, to keep his soul fixed upon the absurd" (CUP 495) and says we must achieve a "crucifixion of the understanding" (CUP 496).

There are two ways of interpreting Kierkegaard's hard sayings at this point. The first and most obvious reading would be to conclude that Kierkegaard believes that the person of faith must despise reason and that a religious commitment requires intellectual suicide. Based on this interpretation, his critics have rejected Kierkegaard's claims as unintelligible and have labeled him "the apostle of absurdity" and "an irrationalist." Some of Kierkegaard's admirers also agree with this interpretation because they believe faith and reason are mortal enemies.

A second, more subtle interpretation of Kierkegaard makes him appear less of a total irrationalist than he seems at first. Basically, this tradi-

tion sees Kierkegaard as claiming that Christianity is above reason but that it is not contrary to the laws of logic. This view stresses at least two, major points. First, in referring to Christianity as a "paradox," Kierkegaard is pointing out the limits of reason much as Kant did (and no one would call Kant an irrationalist). The infinite simply cannot be contained within the categories of our finite reason, it is claimed. Kierkegaard frequently contrasts the paradoxical nature of Christianity with straightforward logical contradictions.[6] Second, Kierkegaard is claiming that with respect to the ultimate issues in one's life, there are no bare, uninterpreted, objective, neutral facts. Everything is viewed from within one or another set of background beliefs. We come to experience with such notions as what is or is not likely, what is or is not plausible, what does or does not have value. These are partly the result of historical conditioning and partly the result of our attitudes, commitments, and our personal stance toward life. What will seem to "fit" and make sense from one standpoint will seem paradoxical and absurd from another.

To use an analogy from science, those scientists in the early part of the twentieth century who were working within the paradigm of Newtonian physics found Einstein's revolutionary ideas to be insane. As a matter of fact, in terms of Newton's understanding of space and time, there was no way to make sense out of what Einstein was saying. Gradually, physicists had to let go of their previous assumptions and see the universe in a new way. Similarly, it is claimed, Kierkegaard is not asking us to give up rationality altogether, but to give up certain features of our present way of understanding things that leave us closed to the option of faith.* When we do so, things look entirely different. "When the believer has faith, the absurd is not the absurd—faith transforms it."[7] Under ei-

*Almost every time Kierkegaard refers to Christianity as "absurd" it is through the voice of a pseudonymous character, usually one who is not a Christian himself, but one who is looking at Christianity from the outside. Rarely does Kierkegaard speak this way when he presents the text as his own writings. A computer analysis of Kierkegaard's texts confirms this. See Alastair MacKinnon, *The Kierkegaard Indices* (Leiden: Brill, 1970–1975), particularly volumes 3 and 4.

ther interpretation, it is clear Kierkegaard does not think that the content of Christianity can be translated into the propositions of speculative philosophy as Hegel thought, nor that rational knowledge is a sufficient basis for a meaningful, human life.

Evaluation and Significance

Kierkegaard's positions always seem to gravitate toward the extremes, making him an easy target for philosophical critics. However, Kierkegaard thought it was actually his culture that should be blamed for being out of balance. Hence, it was necessary to overcompensate for this by placing his weight far at the other end of center. His thought was not meant to be the standard for all time, but a standard that was most needed for his time. The Hegelian thought of the day exclusively focused on the objective, the propositional, the abstract, and the universal. In reaction, Kierkegaard stressed the subjective, the experiential, the concrete, and the individual. If the meal is too bland, he says, it needs a bit of spice:

> As a skillful cook says with regard to a dish in which already a great many ingredients are mingled: "It needs still just a little pinch of cinnamon". . . .
>
> A little pinch of spice! That is to say: Here a man must be sacrificed, he is needed to impart a particular taste to the rest.
>
> These are the correctives. It is a woeful error if he who is used for applying the corrective becomes impatient and would make the corrective normative for others. That is the temptation to bring everything to confusion.[8]

These qualifications having been made, however, some problems still remain in his discussions. First, Kierkegaard wants to distinguish between the paradox of Christianity that transcends our human ability to conceptually understand it and sheer nonsense on the other hand. However, since paradoxes and nonsense are both offensive to reason, how do we know which is which? In embracing what I think is a paradox, how do I know I am not embracing nonsense? Second, he tends to think that the objective

dimension of truth (*what* I believe) is not as significant as the subjective (*how* I am related to the truth). However, Christianity clearly does rest on certain claims about historical events and about the nature of the universe. Any sort of ultimate commitment must always involve more than intellectual assent to a proposition. Nevertheless, that commitment has value only to the extent that my objective beliefs are more or less correct. For example, your relationship to your life's partner requires unconditional trust and faith, but this faith in another person is misplaced if he or she is an imposter. Kierkegaard scholar Louis Pojman suggests that Kierkegaard's subjectivity–objectivity dichotomy may be exaggerated. "It presumes an impossibility of being impartial and passionate at the same time, and it assumes that objectivity and neutrality are somehow closely related or even near-synonyms." Instead, Pojman argues, "Reason can be very passionate" and "One can seek the best objective evidence by passionate inquiry."[9]

In the final analysis, Kierkegaard did not stem the tide of analytic and speculative thinking, for these approaches continued to characterize philosophy throughout the remainder of the nineteenth and twentieth centuries. However, he did give people pause and continues to serve as the nagging conscience of our age. He influenced those psychologists who think the human person cannot be studied with the same laboratory methods we use to study a rock or a rat. The notions that persons are self-creating beings, that alienation from one's self is our greatest malady, and that personal authenticity is the route to mental wholeness are Kierkegaardian themes that have found their way into some corners of psychology.

Perhaps Kierkegaard had his greatest impact in theology. At the beginning of the twentieth century, mainstream theology was permeated by a liberal, intellectualized, moralistic Christianity that had unlimited optimism about human moral progress and too easily identified a Hegelianized God with the prevailing social order. When the brutality, insanity, and alienation of that century began to reveal itself, many theologians abandoned their Hegelian rationalism in favor of Kierkegaard's outlook.

Finally, of course, Kierkegaard was one of the founders of the existentialist movement. In the writings of this intense Christian, even secular writers such as Jean-Paul Sartre, Martin Heidegger, and Albert Camus found ideas that reverberated with their own. Both directly and indirectly, Kierkegaard significantly influenced novelists, artists, and poets in the twentieth century.

Questions for Understanding

1. What did Kierkegaard take as his mission in life? Why did the think this was important?

2. What is meant by Kierkegaard's method of indirect communication? Why did he use such a method?

3. What are the two meanings of the word "subjective"? Which sense of the word is the focus of Kierkegaard's concern? What is his distinction between subjective truth and objective truth?

4. Explain Kierkegaard's distinction between knowing the truth and being in the truth.

5. According to Kierkegaard, what sorts of results can only be obtained by going through a certain process? In what sorts of cases can I have results without obtaining them myself? Why is Kierkegaard concerned with the relationship between what we know and how we know it?

6. What would Kierkegaard say about attempts to rationally prove the existence of God?

7. What are Kierkegaard's criticisms of metaphysical systems such as Hegel's?

8. How does Kierkegaard's view of the self differ from that of both Descartes and Hume?

9. Describe Kierkegaard's three stages of life. What causes a person to move from one stage to the next? Why does he think that one can fully become a self only in the religious stage?

10. What does Kierkegaard mean when he labels Christianity as "the absurd" and "the paradox"? Why are these positive and not negative evaluations for him?

Questions for Reflection

1. What do you think of Kierkegaard's distinction between knowing something objectively and knowing it subjectively? Has there been an occasion in your life when you had objective knowledge but lacked subjective knowledge? What are the strengths and limitations of each approach?

2. Do you agree or disagree with Kierkegaard's claim that it is both impious and impossible to construct rational arguments for the existence of God?

3. Provide examples from fiction (novels, TV, movies) of persons living at the aesthetic, ethical, and religious stages of life. Where would you place yourself in terms of these stages? Do you think Kierkegaard's three categories are adequate and complete for describing the different possible stances toward one's life?

4. Do you agree with Kierkegaard scholar Louis Pojman that Kierkegaard fails to realize that "Reason can be very passionate" and that "One can seek the best objective evidence by passionate inquiry"? Either support Pojman's point or defend Kierkegaard's view on these issues.

Notes

1. Friedrich Nietzsche, *The Gay Science*, trans. Walter Kaufmann (New York: Vintage Books, 1974), 182.

2. References to the works of Kierkegaard are abbreviated as follows:

CUP *Concluding Unscientific Postscript*, trans. David F. Swenson and Walter Lowrie (Princeton, NJ: Princeton University Press, 1941).

EO *Either/Or*, vol. 1, trans. David Swenson, Lillian Marvin Swenson, and Howard A. Johnson; vol. 2, trans. Walter Lowrie and Howard A. Johnson (Princeton, NJ: Princeton University Press, 1971).

FT *Fear and Trembling* in *Fear and Trembling and The Sickness unto Death*, trans. Walter Lowrie (Princeton, NJ: Princeton University Press, 1968).

KA *A Kierkegaard Anthology*, ed. Robert Bretall (New York: Modern Library, 1946).

PF *Philosophical Fragments or a Fragment of Philosophy*, trans. David Swenson and Howard V. Hong (Princeton, NJ: Princeton University Press, 1962).

SD   *The Sickness unto Death* in *Fear and Trembling and The Sickness unto Death*, trans. Walter Lowrie (Princeton, NJ: Princeton University Press, 1968).

3. Roger Shinn, *The Existentialist Posture*, rev. ed. (New York: Association Press, 1970), 44.

4. *Søren Kierkegaard's Journals and Papers*, vol. 2, trans. and ed. Howard and Edna Hong (Bloomington: Indiana University Press, 1967), no. 1605, p. 217.

5. *Søren Kierkegaard's Journals and Papers*, vol. 3, trans. and ed. Howard and Edna Hong (Bloomington: Indiana University Press, 1975), no. 3308, p. 519.

6. This point is argued by C. Stephen Evans in *Kierkegaard's "Fragments" and "Postscript": The Religious Philosophy of Johannes Climacus* (Atlantic Highlands, NJ: Humanities Press, 1983), 212–219.

7. *Søren Kierkegaard's Journals and Papers*, vol. 1, trans. and ed. Howard and Edna Hong (Bloomington: Indiana University Press, 1967), no. 10, p. 7.

8. From an 1852 journal entry, quoted in Walter Lowrie, *A Short Life of Kierkegaard* (Princeton, NJ: Princeton University Press, 1970), 259–260.

9. Louis P. Pojman, *The Logic of Subjectivity: Kierkegaard's Philosophy of Religion* (University: University of Alabama Press, 1984), 143.

27

Friedrich Nietzsche: The Founder of Secular Existentialism

A RANDOM SURVEY OF ADJECTIVES USED TO describe Friedrich Nietzsche would come up with a list such as "tragic, terrifying, strident, troubled, and mad" as well as "powerful, intense, intoxicating, charismatic, and prophetic." Anyone who reads Nietzsche finds him either infuriating or fascinating, but never boring. How could anyone have a bland reaction to a writer who said, "I am no man, I am dynamite"?[1] Nietzsche's place in history has been summarized thus:

> Widely rejected as a brilliant madman in the complacent atmosphere of pre-1914, a destructive and perverse genius who could not be taken really seriously, he stands today as the major prophet of the tortured twentieth century.[2]

The ideas he left behind are disturbing and difficult, just as the life he lived was tormented and burdensome.

Nietzsche's Life: The Lonely Prophet

Friedrich Nietzsche was born in 1844 in Prussian Saxony. His father and both his grandfathers were Lutheran ministers. However, his father died when Nietzsche was four, leaving him to be brought up by his sister, mother, grandmother, and two aunts. He was a brilliant student and distinguished himself at the universities of Bonn and Leipzig, where he studied classics and philology. Nietzsche was religiously devout in his younger years (we even have a number of examples of his devotional poetry). However, he gradually drifted away from his earlier piety and by the time he reached his early twenties he had embraced the spirited atheism that was one of the most distinguishing features of his philosophy.

At the early age of twenty-five, he was appointed professor of classical philology at the

University of Basel. He had not yet completed his doctoral degree, but had already attracted the attention of scholars through his published papers. In 1879, tired of academic life and suffering from the ill health that plagued him the rest of his life, he retired from teaching. Struggling with migraine headaches, nausea, insomnia, and bad eyesight, he traveled from one resort to another throughout Switzerland and Italy in an attempt to regain his health. Despite these problems, he wrote eighteen books and a lengthy unfinished manuscript during the years 1872 to 1888.

His final years were a time of deep loneliness. "A profound man has to have friends, unless he still has his god. But I have neither god nor friends!"[3] Eventually, both his physical and mental health deteriorated from what appeared to be a neurological disorder. In January 1889, he collapsed in the street while protecting a horse being beaten by its owner. For the remaining twelve years of his life, he was physically disabled and pathetically insane. After an unsuccessful treatment in a clinic, he was taken home to be cared for by his mother and later by his sister. By now, his writings were receiving a great deal of attention, but he was not lucid enough to enjoy his fame. Nietzsche spent his life forecasting the future cultural crises just over the horizon at a time when most in his century were oblivious to what lay ahead. Appropriately, as the twentieth century was coming into place, Nietzsche handed the torch over to his cultural offspring and died, on August 25, 1900.

Task: The Journey from Darkness to Daybreak

In the midst of the nineteenth century's optimism, Nietzsche saw storm clouds looming on the horizon. He thought the time would soon come when we would find all our dearest dreams shattered. The notions of God, truth, reality, objective values, and human progress would be exposed as empty illusions that were no longer viable. Would this crush us? How can we live without our illusions? We are about to be engulfed by the darkness of nihilism, the belief that there are no enduring values on which to build our lives. It would take a particular kind of person to lead us through the night to the dawn. What is needed is the ability to affirm life with open eyes and without the cosmic comforts of our philosophical and theological traditions. Nietzsche believes that Darwin's theory of evolution had showed we are not the crown of creation. We are a part of nature, and with the beasts we must survive by exercising power in a ruthless, brutal world. However, we are better than other animals because we can remake ourselves. The call to reinvent humanity is the persistent theme throughout Nietzsche's philosophy.

Like Kierkegaard, Nietzsche took it as his mission to criticize a culture he thought had reached an unprecedented low point. He said philosophers are surgeons who apply the scalpel of their thoughts "to the chest of the very *virtues of their time*" to understand and excise the pathological conditions that plague us (BGE §212).[4] A large part of his writings are destructive. He even speaks of "philosophizing with a hammer." His philosophical hammer functions like a tuning fork that taps the idols of our culture to show that they are hollow.[5] However, the useless idols must be smashed and this requires "the hardness of the hammer, the *joy even in destroying*."[6]

Nietzsche carries out his mission in a style that is sketchy, irritating, and slippery. Typically, he expresses himself in aphorisms or brief, pithy statements meant to provoke, shock, and challenge his reader. According to Nietzsche, the good writer handles

> his language like a flexible foil, feeling from his arm right down to his toe the dangerous bliss of the quivering razor-sharp blade, which is eager to bite, hiss, cut . . .

We will be frustrated if we search for formal answers to questions or straightforward statements of Nietzsche's points. In fact, he thought our desire for systematic answers showed a lack of integrity.[7] Disgusted with the graceless style of most philosophers, he sought to "dance" with concepts, words, and the pen.[8]

Nietzsche's Theory of Knowledge: Perspectives and Instincts

RADICAL PERSPECTIVISM

In one sense, Nietzsche's theory of knowledge can be stated quite simply: *we don't have any knowledge*. Lurking behind this claim is Nietzsche's adherence to the **correspondence theory of truth**. This is the view, accepted by many philosophers as well as the person-in-the-street, that reality has a certain independent and objective content and that a theory is true or false to the degree it correctly states that content. Nietzsche seems to assume this definition of truth and then argues that since we can't have this sort of relationship to reality, there is no such thing as truth (in the sense this notion has been traditionally understood). Against the philosopher who claims that the only things that exist are facts, Nietzsche counters,

> No, facts is precisely what there is not, only interpretations. We cannot establish any fact "in itself": perhaps it is folly to want to do such a thing. (WP §481)

There are no uninterpreted "facts" or "truths," for everything we encounter is seen from one perspective or another. This is what Nietzsche calls his theory of "perspectivism" (WP §481). According to Nietzsche, three things can be said about perspectives: they are unavoidable, they are false, and yet they are useful.

First, Nietzsche claims that perspectives are unavoidable. "There is *only* a perspective seeing, *only* a perspective 'knowing' " (GM 3.12). For example, consider the exterior of this book. If you want to know its title, you look at its cover. But if you need it to hold down some papers, you view it in terms of its bulk. If you viewed it as a graphic artist does, you would be interested in its design and color. If you are an editor, you would be concerned with its marketability. To an ant it would seem enormous, while to a bird in the sky it would appear as a speck. A baby might see it as something to chew on. Different observers will have different perspectives on the book, depending on their physiology, their values, or their purposes. In other words, "there are no 'facts-in-themselves,'

for a sense must always be projected into them before they can be facts" (WP §556). Even the sciences only give us reality as mediated through a particular perspective: "Physics, too, is only an interpretation and exegesis of the world" (BGE §14).

The second feature of perspectives is that they are lies and falsify reality. "Parmenides said, 'one cannot think of what is not';—we are at the other extreme, and say 'what can be thought of must certainly be a fiction' " (WP §539). Our perspectives are embodied in how we speak and think about things. We are under the illusion we can capture reality with the "net" of our words and concepts. However, rather than being a net, concepts are more like a filter that shapes and distorts the materials it processes.*

> Every concept originates through our equating what is unequal. No leaf ever wholly equals another, and the concept "leaf" is formed through an arbitrary abstraction from these individual differences, through forgetting the distinctions.[9]

The problem is that every item in the world and every experience is unique, but we seek to preserve the contents of an experience by relating it to similar ones and then applying verbal labels to the group. These labels become universal concepts and are added to our intellectual inventory so that they can be used again and again to refer to new experiences. However, universal concepts conceal the originality and individuality of each moment of reality. The dynamic, continuously flowing real world is chopped up into discrete, seemingly identical units that are turned into "concept-mummies" so that they may be shelved in the museum of the intellect.[10] In this way, language becomes a separate world unto itself, which we mistake for the real world (HAH §11).

Nietzsche's third (and most important) point about perspectives is that even though they do not depict reality itself, they do serve a purpose. Interpreting the world by means of a perspective is "the basic condition of all life" (BGE preface).

---

*Notice throughout this section how Nietzsche adopts but then radicalizes the Kantian notion of the constructive activity of the mind.

However, truth is not an issue here, for "a belief can be a condition of life and *nonetheless* be *false*" (WP §483). This is because our perspectives make the overwhelming chaos of the world manageable by making it seem simpler than it really is (GS §189, WP §515). By imposing our interpretations on the world, "we thereby create a world which is calculable, simplified, comprehensible, etc., for us" (WP §521). Finding the correspondence theory to be useless, Nietzsche proposes a new and paradoxical definition of truth:

> Truth is the kind of error without which a certain species of life could not live. The value for life is ultimately decisive. (WP §493)

For example, if a certain tribe believed a poisonous plant was dangerous because it contained demons, their belief would be false. But if this fiction caused them to avoid eating the plant, it would serve a life-preserving purpose.* What we call "truths" are simply those fictions that have had the most survival value throughout our evolutionary history:

> Over immense periods of time the intellect produced nothing but errors. A few of these proved to be useful and helped to preserve the species: those who hit upon or inherited these had better luck in their struggle for themselves and their progeny. (GS §110)†

ROMANTIC PRIMITIVISM

Normally, the development of perspectives is not carried out at the conscious level, for then we would be aware of the fact that all our cherished "truths" are lies and most people could not bear to face this. Instead, our perspectives arise from a very deep stratum within human consciousness.

Nietzsche's position has been called "romantic primitivism" because he emphasizes that our primary interaction with the world is in terms of feelings and instincts rather than ideas. All judgments arise out of our "instincts, likes, dislikes, experiences, and lack of experiences" (GS §335). Knowledge is "actually nothing but a *certain behavior of the instincts toward one another*" (GS §333).

By placing the instincts in the center stage of epistemology, Nietzsche implies that reason has little to do with the behavior of the human animal. In fact, it is just a name we use to disguise the underlying, primitive drive that fuels our cognitive life. Reading between the lines of philosophers he concludes that "most of the conscious thinking of a philosopher is secretly guided and forced into certain channels by his instincts" (BGE §3). Thus, there is no "drive to knowledge" behind philosophy but another drive that is disguising itself (BGE §6). This is a drive to overcome, to dominate my environment, to make my personal mark on the world, to create, to express myself. It is what he calls the *will to power*.

> "Truth" is therefore not something there, that might be found or discovered—but something that must be created and that gives a name to a process, or rather to a will to overcome that has in itself no end—introducing truth, as a *processus in infinitum, an active determining*—not a becoming-conscious of something that is in itself firm and determined. It is a word for the "will to power." (WP §552)

This will to power is the essence of life and is manifested as "the essential priority of the spontaneous, aggressive, expansive, form-giving forces that give new interpretations and directions" (GM 2.13).

Nietzsche's subjectivism carries through and radicalizes the progressive developments in epistemology that began with Kant. For Kant there is a

(1) *single* way of structuring experience, which is

(2) *universal* to all minds because

(3) it is the result of the mind's own, *rational* structure, by means of which

(4) we can obtain *objective, absolute* knowledge (within the phenomenal world of human experience).

---

*Nietzsche's notion that an idea is "true" if it works and enables us to live successful lives, anticipates the twentieth-century pragmatism of William James.

†In Western thought, these life-preserving errors have included believing "that there are things, substances, bodies; that a thing is what it appears to be; that our will is free; that what is good for me is also good in itself" (GS §110). Another type of useful error is found in geometry and science where we postulate theoretical entities that do not exist, such as "lines, planes, bodies, atoms, divisible time spans, divisible spaces" (GS §112).

Hegel disagrees with Kant by claiming that there are

(1) *multiple* ways of structuring experience, which are

(2) *relative* to the level of development in a given historical period. However, Hegel turns back toward Kant by making Kant's starting point into the goal of history, which is to develop

(3) increasingly more *rational* structures, which

(4) culminate in *objective, absolute* knowledge.

Kierkegaard (whom Nietzsche did not know) makes Hegel's picture even more subjective by claiming there are

(1) *multiple* ways of structuring experience, which are

(2) *relative* to each individual and are

(3) based on *nonrational*, existential choices, which

(4) do not give us objective knowledge, but do enable us to have *subjective* knowledge of an *Absolute God.*

Nietzsche completes this development by asserting that there are

(1) *multiple* ways of structuring experience, which are

(2) *relative* to each individual and are

(3) based on *nonrational* instincts, which

(4) are thoroughly *subjective* and *void of any absolute value.*

At this point an objection may justly be raised against Nietzsche. We might say to him, "Why should I accept your 'perspectivism'? Doesn't it follow from what you have said that your position is nothing more than *your* arbitrary perspective or interpretation?" However, Nietzsche gleefully anticipated this attack when he said, "Supposing that this also is only interpretation—and you will be eager to make this objection?—well, so much the better" (BGE §22).

He delights in your objections, because in seeking to refute Nietzsche you are only illustrat-

ing his thesis that philosophy is a struggle of wills. You are seeking to impose your own form on the world and make Nietzsche submit to your interpretation. The conflict of ideas produces "ferment, struggle, and lust for power" (GS §110). In the competition between interpretations, the strength and weaknesses of each is revealed. Nietzsche always turns the issue back on you. As his fictional character Zarathustra says, "This is *my* way; where is yours?"[11]

For Nietzsche, interpretations and their criticisms are symptomatic. They reveal as much about the speaker as they do the object of discourse. If you shrink from his conclusions, he would say that reveals you are a fearful person who cannot stand uncomfortable thoughts. As we will see shortly, Nietzsche did not suppose everyone would appreciate his writings. Trying to communicate to readers who are clinging to their illusions is like teaching the tone deaf to sing.

CRITERIA FOR EVALUATING PERSPECTIVES

If everything is a matter of subjective interpretation, does this mean "anything goes"? Apparently not, for Nietzsche says the philologist in him cannot resist pointing out bad modes of interpretation (BGE §22). However, if there is no objective truth, on what basis does he despise some interpretations and praise others? Nietzsche suggests two criteria for evaluating interpretations of the world. First, we can rank interpretations in terms of their *pragmatic value.* Even though an idea is not true, we may judge it in terms of how useful it is for accomplishing our purposes:

> *The falseness of a judgment is for us not necessarily an objection to a judgment; . . . The question is to what extent it is life-promoting, life-preserving, species-preserving, perhaps even species-cultivating.* (BGE §4)

When we face two contradictory judgments, we decide between them on the basis of their "higher or lower degree of *utility* for life" (GS §110). What we call *a priori* judgments—such as "the fictions of logic" and the "constant falsification of the world by means of numbers"—are simply those myths without which we could not live (BGE §4). Second, we may judge ideas in terms of their *aesthetic value*. Nietzsche considers philosophies like various works of art. They are the philosopher–artist's attempt to catch our attention and give us new and interesting outlooks. Nietzsche says that where ideas do not have utility, they still may provoke delight and may be "the expression of an intellectual play and impulse" (GS §110). For Nietzsche, the search for variety was a more important quest than Descartes's search for certainty:

> Deeply mistrustful of the dogmas of epistemology, I loved to look now out of this window, now out of that; I guarded against settling down with any of these dogmas, considered them harmful. (WP §410)

Unfortunately, instead of enjoying the multiple insights of different perspectives, we petrify our favorite ones with the label of "truth" and repeat them until they lose their power;

> What, then, is truth? A mobile army of metaphors, metonyms, and anthropomorphisms— . . . truths are illusions about which one has forgotten what they are; metaphors which are worn out and without sensuous power; coins which have lost their pictures and now matter only as metal, no longer as coins.[12]

PHILOSOPHY AS PATHOLOGY

Nietzsche was convinced that traditional philosophy is not simply the result of intellectual mistakes but is symptomatic of a deep-seated psychological disease of which we need to be cured. Paralleling Kierkegaard, Nietzsche finds that the major problem is a lack of honesty and a fear of our own subjectivity. The philosopher has an image of himself as one who simply mirrors reality in his thought, while deluding himself that he has stamped out any taint of his own personal commitments in his "objective" analyses (BGE §207). In contrast, Nietzsche says, "Gradually it has become clear to me what every great philosophy so far has been: namely the personal confession of its author and a kind of involuntary and unconscious memoir" (BGE §6). This discovery led him to look for the true motives behind each philosophy, "the *hidden*

history of the philosophers, the psychology of the great names."[13] In effect, Nietzsche has taken over Hegel's notion that each philosophy must be understood in the context in which it arose. Unlike Hegel, however, the context is not an objective, historical one, but a personal, psychological one.

PHILOSOPHY AS THERAPY

Can we live with a philosophy that says all our deepest "truths" are fictions and all our highest ideals are subjective projections? Like Hume, Nietzsche wonders if his skepticism is intolerable:

> Is it true, is all that remains a mode of thought whose outcome on a personal level is despair and on a theoretical level a philosophy of destruction? (HAH §34)

Nietzsche goes on to answer "No!" to his own question. Despair is not inevitable but is a choice we make or refuse to make. It all depends on our temperament. The facts of our situation have no meaning until we decide what meaning to give them. What is needed is a new type of spirit that will let us face this dismal picture and triumph over it. For Nietzsche, the hope for philosophy as well as for Western civilization rests in the fact that "a new species of philosopher is coming up over the horizon" (BGE §42). These thinkers will no longer rest comfortably in the illusion that values and truth are waiting out there in the world, ready to be plucked. Instead, these individuals will have the ego strength to realize that they must each create their own truth and their own values. For this reason, Nietzsche calls them "commanders and legislators" (BGE §211).

Because all we have are the array of human interpretations, Nietzsche calls for a spirit of "experimentalism." An interesting theory should not be thought of as a picture of objective reality, but it should be treated as an invitation to view life in a new way. Thus, the proper response to an idea is not to ask, "Is it true?" but to exclaim, "Let us try it!" (GS §51). A great thinker is one who "sees his own actions as experiments and questions" (GS §41). By "experiment" Nietzsche means testing an outlook by dwelling within it and seeing whether it enhances or diminishes one's life. The new philosophers have the courage to say, "We ourselves wish to be our experiments and guinea pigs" (GS §319). If no view is genuinely true, the philosophical experimenter will realize that to become entrenched in only one point of view robs life of its variety and possibilities:

> That the value of the world lies in our interpretation . . . that every elevation of man brings with it the overcoming of narrower interpretations; that every strengthening and increase of power opens up new perspectives and means believing in new horizons— this idea permeates my writings. (WP §616)

Living Without Metaphysical Hopes

It follows clearly from Nietzsche's epistemology that if all we have are interpretations, then we must abandon all hopes of a rational, metaphysical knowledge of the "true world" that lies beyond the world of appearance. In fact, he says,

> The "true" world—an idea which is no longer good for anything . . . an idea which has become useless and superfluous—consequently, a refuted idea: let us abolish it![14]

Even if it were meaningful to talk about reality-in-itself, it would not be relevant to the human situation:

> Knowledge of it would be the most useless of all knowledge: more useless even than knowledge of the chemical composition of water must be to a sailor in danger of shipwreck. (HAH §9)

Metaphysics grows out of human weakness, the need for certainty or something outside of us that we can lean on (GS §347). Appropriately, Nietzsche refers to himself as an "antimetaphysician" (GS §344). For the ancient Greek and the medieval monk, as well as the modern rationalist or empiricist, the universe was like a warm, comfortable home that nurtured and sustained our intellectual, moral, and spiritual quests as long as we approached it with the correct method. However, we can no longer enjoy the comforts of this picture.

The values that give life meaning have evaporated. The world has become colder, night is closing in, and humanity is left desolate and abandoned, without a cosmic home. Nietzsche continually uses the metaphor of "homelessness" to describe the human situation and says we are wanderers who must resign ourselves to "spiritual nomadism."[15]

THE DEATH OF GOD

Nietzsche's epistemology revolves around the notion that there is no objective truth, no standard apart from us by which our ideas may be measured, and thus our minds swim in a sea of personal interpretations. If Nietzsche's picture is accurate, then it logically follows there is no God. This is because if God existed, he would be an absolute standard of truth and value, but Nietzsche denies there are any absolutes. Hence, it is the lingering afterimage of theism that produces our most persistent illusions. But Nietzsche announces that there is a growing realization that this ideology is dead:

> The greatest recent event—that "God is dead," that the belief in the Christian god has become unbelievable—is already beginning to cast its first shadows over Europe. (GS §343)

Nietzsche is not suggesting the bizarre notion that an all-powerful, eternal being once existed and then died. Rather, he is describing a psychological and cultural event that is beginning to make itself evident. Although theism played a decisive role in the development of our civilization, he thinks we are moving into an age of secularism in which people will no longer find the notion of God relevant. However, the multitude do not fully realize this has happened; much less do they anticipate what lies beyond the horizon. Only those who are detached from their culture and are "waiting on the mountains" can see the cultural crisis coming in the distance:

> How much must collapse now that this faith has been undermined because it was built upon this faith, propped up by it, grown into it; for example, the whole of our European morality. (GS §343)

In proclaiming that the age of belief is over, Nietzsche provides no arguments for atheism and no refutations of the traditional arguments for God. Instead, he assumes theism is a hypothesis that is no longer viable, for it has served its purpose and, like a dead skin, must be cast off:

> Formerly it was sought to prove that there was no God—now it is shown how the belief that a God existed could have originated, *and by what means this belief gained authority and importance: in this way the counterproof that there is no God becomes unnecessary and superfluous.*[16]

Notice that Nietzsche thinks that if he can find the psychological origins of an idea, this is sufficient to discredit it. In his account, the God story arose because we are unable to have faith in ourselves and thus need to project something "out there" to which we can cling. Once we realize this, religious faith is no longer credible.

In spite of his antireligious conclusions, Nietzsche recognizes that there have been people in history who were religious and that religion has had some beneficial effects. This is illustrated by his ambivalence toward the founder of Christianity. Although Nietzsche despises the Sermon on the Mount, he admires Jesus' personal power. According to Nietzsche's account, what Jesus offered us was a model of the inner-directed person, not a set of doctrines or personal redemption. Jesus lived "not to 'redeem men' but to show how one must live" (AC 1, §35). Nietzsche distinguishes between what is admirable in Jesus and the doctrines and morality that Christendom has piled on top of him. For this reason, he says, "in truth, there was only *one* Christian, and he died on the cross" (AC 1, §39). However, he still insists that Christianity has mostly been motivated by weakness and that now humanity must become strong enough to do without its cosmic crutches. Ironically, Christianity's morality has been its own undoing. "The sense of truthfulness, developed highly by Christianity, is nauseated by the falseness and mendaciousness of all Christian interpretations of the world and history" (WP §2). Interestingly, Nietzsche's critique of Christianity is very similar to Søren Kierkegaard's critique of "Christendom."

They are both repelled by comfortable, passionless religion. However, while Kierkegaard sought to find an authentic Christianity, Nietzsche believes religion is irredeemable.*

In one of his most famous passages, in which he forecasts the loss of religious belief, Nietzsche puts his vision into the words of a madman who wanders into town:

> The madman jumped into their midst and pierced them with his glances. "Whither is God," he cried. "I shall tell you. We have killed him—you and I. All of us are his murderers." (GS §125)

Since these words come from the mouth of a madman, that might appear to suggest that the loss of God paves the road to insanity. But there is another message here. Copernicus, Galileo, and others who ripped away our conventional ideas were also considered mad by their societies. The one who is labeled mad is often the one whose creative vision is out of step with the conventional wisdom of society. The latter interpretation is truer to Nietzsche's spirit, for he sees the abandonment of theism as a cause for celebration.

> Indeed, we philosophers and "free spirits" feel, when we hear the news that "the old god is dead," as if a new dawn shone on us; our heart overflows with gratitude, amazement, premonitions, expectation. At long last the horizon appears free to us again, even if it should not be bright; at long last our ships may venture out again, venture out to face any danger; all the daring of the lover of knowledge is permitted again; the sea, our sea, lies open again; perhaps there has never yet been such an "open sea." (GS §343)

THE WILL TO POWER

As mentioned, Nietzsche did not believe there was such a thing as a "drive to knowledge." Instead, all our cognitive activities manifest a drive to achieve mastery and to exert personal power

---

*A friend once suggested to Nietzsche that he read Kierkegaard, but he never got around to it. It would have been interesting to see what he thought of this passionate Christian writer who was a kindred spirit with him in so many ways.

over our environment. Nietzsche views this principle, the will to power, as the fundamental psychological force in human life. All other drives are merely manifestations of this one, master obsession. The notion of "the will to power" has frequently been misinterpreted to mean only physical or military power. However, whether they are strong or weak, all people manifest the will to power, although it may express itself in many hidden and subtle ways. Nietzsche would say the will to power lurks behind the meaning-creating activities of the most diverse sorts of people: the saint who disciplines her body and mind through the rigors of fasting and meditation in order to achieve an ecstatic experience of the holy, the artist who struggles against poverty and criticism to impose his vision of the world on the mute materials of canvas and oil, the scientist who subdues a wide range of physical phenomena by reducing them to an elegant mathematical formula, the lover who risks rejection to win over the affections of the person he adores. All these are manifesting the will to power.

By means of a thought experiment, Nietzsche suggests that the will to power can be considered more than a principle of human psychology. If we view it as the fundamental drive in all of nature, this would let us explain everything on the basis of one, fundamental principle—the intrinsic drive to exercise power (BGE §36). He agrees with Darwin that nature is a brutal arena of struggle and war:

> Here we must beware of superficiality and get to the bottom of the matter, resisting all sentimental weakness: life itself is essentially appropriation, injury, overpowering of what is alien and weaker, suppression, hardness, imposition of one's own forms, incorporation, and at least, at its mildest, exploitation. (BGE §259)

However, he criticizes Darwin for thinking survival is the goal of all life forms. Instead, Nietzsche says that the goal is dominance and power. This is illustrated by the fact that some will risk self-preservation in the drive to expand their power (GS §349). In short, the model for all the sciences, whether it be physics, biology, or psychology, is that "all driving force is will to power, that there is no other physical, dynamic or psychic force except this" (WP §688).

Moral Values and Personality Types

An examination of Nietzsche's criticisms of metaphysicians leads us into a consideration of his comments about morality. This is because he believes that hidden beneath the veneer of philosophers' rational arguments we will find their true agenda, which flows from their personalities and subjective preferences:

> Indeed, if one would explain how the abstrusest metaphysical claims of a philosopher really came about, it is always well (and wise) to ask first: at what morality does all this (does he) aim? (BGE §6)

If this is good advice, then moral theory will need to look closely at how various personality types have produced the moralities that have arisen in history.

MASTER AND SLAVE MORALITY

According to Nietzsche, all morality is a manifestation of the will to power. However, it exhibits itself through two kinds of temperaments. One is driven by the will to power and revels in it, the other is driven by the will to power but attempts to deny this. Christianity is the supreme example of the latter, dishonest approach. The two main types of morality are what he calls "master morality" and "slave morality." Historically, they developed out of literal master–slave relationships (the Egyptians versus the Jews, or the Romans versus the early Christians, for example). Despite their historical origins, however, the terms "master" and "slave" actually represent two ideal types of personalities. For example, even though the proper, nineteenth-century European socialites were anything but literal slaves, Nietzsche viewed them as living examples of slave morality.

The term "master morality" refers to the values of psychologically powerful and strong-willed people. Nietzsche identifies these people as the higher, more noble, aristocratic, or elite segment of humanity. These adjectives do not refer to their actual social status, but to their abilities as creative achievers, whether their accomplishments are in art, politics, philosophy, or war. The noble types are characterized by a spontaneous overflowing of power. They are moral legislators or commanders in the sense that they determine their own values and are never at the mercy of the approval of others. Instead of resting comfortably on social convention, authority, metaphysical principles, or revelation, the only sanction they need for their values is the confidence to say, "My judgment is *my* judgment" (BGE §43).

For such people "good" refers to whatever leads to self-fulfillment and affirms one's sense of personal power. Thus, what they pronounce "good" are such values as nobility, strength, courage, power, and pride. In contrast, the notion of "bad" is defined relative to their good. They have no notion of "sin" (for this assumes something higher to which they are subject). Instead, "bad" designates what is contemptible, common, banal, pathetic, cowardly, timid, petty, and humble. In short, it is anything that restricts growth or accomplishment, and everything born of weakness.

The antithesis of master morality is slave morality. It is the morality that appeals to those who are downtrodden, uncertain of themselves, and weak-willed. Lacking the power to be creatively assertive, they have no values of their own. Their values arise out of a fearful, resentful reaction to the values of the strong. Since the weak lack the psychological resources of the noble person, they turn the tables and make the latter's strengths into vices. In turn, they define "good" as what makes life easier, safer, and justifies the existence of the weak. Thus, such qualities as patience, humility, pity, charity, abstinence, modesty, compassion, resignation, and submissiveness are considered virtuous. Slave morality is a "sour grapes" morality, a way of getting even. In an aphorism, Nietzsche sums up the hidden motive behind most traditional morality:

"I don't like him."—Why?—"I am not equal to him." (BGE §185)

Behind the gentle façade of slave morality really lies a desire for power. For example, these types comfort themselves with the notion "the meek shall inherit the earth." We could imagine Nietzsche replying, "Maybe so, but they will not be creative artists, leaders, philosophers, or even great lovers." Moral values are neither true nor false; we can classify them according to whether they diminish our humanity or enhance it:

Have they hitherto hindered or furthered human prosperity? Are they a sign of distress, of impoverishment, of the degeneration of life? Or is there revealed in them, on the contrary, the plenitude, force, and will of life, its courage, certainty, future? (GM preface, §3)

Despite their mediocrity, the slaves have the strength of numbers and through this they have been able to dominate the culture, leaving the master morality to be lived out by isolated individuals and social outcasts. For example, slave morality took root among oppressed people such as the ancient Jews and early Christians. Motivated by resentment, they made their weakness a virtue and viewed anyone who was powerful as evil. With the spread of Christianity and the conversion of the Romans under Constantine, the weak got their revenge and took control. They were so skillful at this that eventually the strong came to accept the slave morality, and became apologetic and disdainful of their own powers and excellence:

When the decadent type of man ascended to the rank of the highest type, this could only happen at the expense of its countertype, the type of man that is strong and sure of life. When the herd animal is irradiated by the glory of the purest virtue, the exceptional man must have been devaluated into evil.[17]

In this way, Western civilization accepted what Nietzsche considered the insipid lie of "equality," and promoted the group solidarity of the mediocre against the excellence and individual achievement of the select few. In response to both the democratic and socialistic ideals of his day, Nietzsche said, "*Morality in Europe today is herd animal morality*" (BGE §202).

It is important to understand that when Nietzsche refers to the strength of the master types, he is not speaking primarily of physical strength. Historically, the noble types often did express themselves by physical conquest, but Nietzsche says, "Their predominance did not lie mainly in physical strength but in strength of the soul—they were more *whole* human beings" (BGE §257). First and foremost, being a master type means exercising power over one's self, more than over others. This sort of power is exemplified in the self-discipline of the artist, the musician, or the athlete. Accordingly, more than 100 of the 125 examples of "higher men" mentioned in *Beyond Good and Evil* are writers rather than people noted for their military or political strength.[18]

For Nietzsche, whether an action represents slave or master morality is determined by its underlying psychological origins. The question is not what you do, but in what spirit you do it. For example, he considers pity one of the slave virtues, because it involves condescension and a veiled contempt for its recipient. Weak people pathetically affirm their own superiority by pitying someone more wretched than they are.[19] Noble human beings can help the less fortunate, but merely because they have an excess of power, not because they need to feel good about themselves (BGE §260). Nietzsche even goes so far as to say that "when the exceptional human being treats the mediocre more tenderly than himself and his peers, this is not mere politeness of the heart—it is simply his *duty*."[20] Nietzsche says that before you "love your neighbor as yourself," you must first love *yourself* (something the mediocre person has a hard time doing).[21]

Nietzsche is unique among moral theorists in that he does not exhort you to accept his vision of morality. In fact this is impossible, because everyone, by virtue of their temperament, is inescapably either a master type or a slave type. The eagle cannot cease to be an eagle, and a lamb cannot aspire to be an eagle. Some are irredeemably destined to be "sheep," "little gray people," and "shallow ponds."[22] Thus, Nietzsche's moral wisdom is not addressed to all humanity, but only to those in whom it strikes a resonate chord. He is calling forth the noble types to break through the windows of the petty morality that enclose them and to find their wings and let their spirits soar. As for the weak, Nietzsche has no problem with letting them quietly live out their dismal lives, for the noble ones can coexist with them as long as the worshipers of mediocrity do not seek to pull the excellent types down to their level.

REVALUATION OF VALUES

If our values do not have their foundation in God or the nature of the world but are rooted in our psychological makeup, it may seem as though there were no values worth embracing. However, Nietzsche believes this crisis of values has brought us, not to the edge of a nihilistic abyss, but instead to the threshold of a new form of human existence:

> Now that the shabby origin of these values is becoming clear, the universe seems to have lost value, seems "meaningless"—but that is only a transitional stage. (WP §7)

The next stage will involve what he calls the "revaluation of values." However, this is not the invention of a completely new set of values. In fact, the values he celebrates, such as honesty, courage, integrity, and self-discipline, can be found in Aristotle. Hence, the title of his book *Beyond Good and Evil* is not meant to imply that we should be completely amoral. Instead, he is declaring war on the taken-for-granted morality that suppressed everything good in humanity. "Good and evil" are the categories of the weak and represent the illusion that there are objective, moral facts in the world. To go beyond this morality means to embrace the categories of "good and bad," which refer to types of people: the noble and the contemptible. What Nietzsche finds at fault in traditional morality is not so much its values as the motives from which they spring. Hence, a Nietzschean morality does not focus on actions and rules, but on qualities of people. Its heroes are those courageous people who find the source of value in their own character and who do not hide behind the façade of a transcendent moral realm.

THE OVERMAN

Nietzsche summarizes his ideal of humanity in the image of the *Übermensch* or the "overman."* He does not have a particular individual in mind, but is describing a type of person that will realize, for the first time, all the unfulfilled potential within humanity: "The time has come for man to set himself a goal. The time has come for man to plant the seed of his highest hope."[23] The higher types that have appeared thus far have come close to realizing the ideal, but even they are still infected with the weight of their humanity:

> Never yet has there been an overman. Naked I saw both the greatest and the smallest man: they are still all-too-similar to each other. Verily, even the greatest I found all-too-human.[24]

The type of individual who fulfills the ideal of the overman will save humanity from its own psychological destruction. While Nietzsche compares humanity to a "polluted stream," he says the overman is like a great sea that can absorb the minuscule pollution without being corrupted by it.[25]

Parodying the medieval notion that humans stand on the scale of being between the animals and the angels, Nietzsche says that "man is a rope stretched between beast and overman—a rope over an abyss."[26] However, the biological process of evolution will not produce this new breed of humanity, for evolution is an unconscious process that only produces types of species and not the singularly unique sort of individual that Nietzsche envisions, who will rise above the herd. One becomes an overman by a process of self-cultivation, which can only be accomplished through an act of the will. Human nature, as we know it, is constituted by our biological inheritance and our cultural conditioning. It constitutes what we *are*, but Nietzsche is speaking to those who are concerned with what they shall *become*. What is needed is to redefine what it means to be human, by overcoming the limitations of human nature: "*I teach you the overman.* Man is something that shall be overcome. What have you done to overcome him?"[27]

Although he speaks of the overman as a powerful, commanding person, Nietzsche is not describing a tyrant. The overman is not one who conquers others as much as he is one who overcomes himself, for he masters the destructive drives within, the all-too-human passions and fears. Thus, despite his antireligious bias, Nietzsche can say that the higher men always admired the saint for his self-trial, self-discipline (BGE §51). However, while the Christian saints may get an A+ for discipline, they get an F- for failing the task of self-affirmation. The saint masters himself only by trying to stamp out the passions and ends by extinguishing any sense of his individual self. Instead, Nietzsche's ideal is a "union of spiritual superiority with well-being and an excess of strength" (WP §899). The fulfilled person combines "the Roman Caesar with Christ's soul" (WP §983). Although he admires the great conquerors in history, the kind of "strength" he admires in them is not their military power over others, but their psychological power and inner strength. For this reason, Nietzsche's ideal is more often found in the artist than in the military conqueror.

Nietzsche's ideal of the overman remains consistent with that expressed in his first book, *The Birth of Tragedy*. In that work, he took the Greek gods of Apollo and Dionysius as symbols of two forces at work in the human personality. Apollo was the god of light. He symbolizes order, moderation, form, and intellect. The Apollonian spirit was realized in the beauty of Greek sculpture and architecture. Dionysus was the god of wine and ecstasy. He symbolizes the passions, impulses, and instincts. By itself, the Dionysian force is savage and destructive. But the Apollonian spirit of self-control is useless if it lacks the Dionysian vitality and drive. Like a tightly strung bow, the human ideal is realized in the unity of reason and passion. In the healthy individual (to switch metaphors),

---

Übermensch has sometimes been translated as "superman," but because this term misleadingly implies Nietzsche is referring to the physical strength associated with the famous cartoon character, the more literal translation of "overman" is preferred.

the floodlike forces of passion and impulse are not denied or suppressed, but are channeled by the spirit of self-mastery and turned into creative energy. The creative artist has mastered this feat, and this is why he so often represents Nietzsche's hero. Nietzsche believes the greatness of Greek tragedy came to birth when the Greeks realized how to achieve a balanced tension of these two great forces in life.*

Although creating powerful plays and beautiful statues are fine, Nietzsche says, the truly creative person is one who has gone beyond producing external art objects and who now lives his own life as a work of art.[28] From his early work on the birth of tragedy to his vision of the overman, Nietzsche was haunted by a vision of the greatness possible for humanity. He says he and the German poet Goethe share the same vision of the human ideal. Nietzsche's description of their shared paradigm succinctly summarizes his job description for those applying to be an overman:

> A human being who would be strong, highly educated, skillful in all bodily matters, self-controlled, reverent toward himself, and who might dare to afford the whole range and wealth of being natural, being strong enough for such freedom; the man of tolerance, not from weakness but from strength, because he knows how to use to his advantage, even that from which the average nature would perish; the man for whom there is no longer anything that is forbidden—unless it be weakness, whether called vice or virtue.[29]

THE MYTH OF ETERNAL RECURRENCE

One of Nietzsche's most famous doctrines is that of the eternal recurrence. In his unpublished notes he gives the notion a metaphysical formulation. He starts with the premise that the world is a certain finite combination of units of force that are randomly interacting to produce various combinations. As in a cosmic dice game, every possible combination is realized at some time or another. Eventually, given an infinite amount of time, every combination and every sequence of combinations are repeated again and again (WP §1066). Critics have pointed out that this hypothesis contains a number of questionable assumptions and from a mathematical standpoint the conclusion is not inevitable. However, Nietzsche primarily used the notion of the eternal recurrence as a thought experiment. Taken simply as a psychological test, it still has value whether or not it really could occur. Nietzsche asks you to consider your emotional reaction to the following situation:

> This life as you now live it and have lived it, you will have to live once more and innumerable times more; and there will be nothing new in it, but every pain and every joy and every thought and sigh and everything unutterably small or great in your life will have to return to you, all in the same succession and sequence. (GS §341)

Honestly facing this possibility leads to either despair or celebration, depending on what sort of person you are. Thus, it serves as a sieve that sifts out the higher types from the lower. The Stoic, the Christian, the Hegelian, and even the Marxist can embrace the pains and struggles of life because they all have a teleological conception of history. In the long run, they say, all this will make sense, for there is a final meaning to it all. However, Nietzsche does not think the meaning of life depends on any historical or cosmic redemption somewhere over the rainbow. In contrast, the higher types are the only ones who are life affirming, for they accept reality as it is, without illusions. Even though the cosmos and one's own life do not have any ultimate purpose, such people still embrace it and love it.[†] Nietzsche refers to this attitude as that of "amor fati" or love of fate:

> My formula for greatness in a human being is amor fati: that one wants nothing to be different . . . not in

---

*In Nietzsche's later works, "Dionysus" becomes the symbol of the unity of the two forces.

[†]It is important to note that his call to love existence for its own sake was made after a decade in which he had been plagued by ill health, crippling physical pain, and a disappointing reception of his books.

all eternity. Not merely bear what is necessary, still less conceal it . . . but love it.[30]

This is a love for the immediate moment, seeing it as rich with value, even though it has no significance that transcends it. Anyone who can approach life with this attitude is an overman, for such people have overcome the human psychological need to find MEANING and are content to live with the smaller "meanings" they have created for themselves.

Evaluation and Significance

Nietzsche was more concerned with being brilliant and shocking than with being consistent. Nevertheless, even if he abandoned all hopes of a philosophy being "true," he did claim his outlook was in some sense "superior" to anything that had gone before. Hence, in an attempt to take his claim seriously, four critical comments follow. First, when Nietzsche says all we have are "perspectives," one can justifiably ask, "Perspectives on *what*?" The notion of "perspective" seems to logically require the notion of a nonperspectival, objective reality. Furthermore, to label philosophies as "errors," "lies," and "illusions" implies some standard of comparison against which our ideas may be measured. Thus, all his terminology assumes the "myth" of objective reality he wants to reject. Second, he distinguishes between the "higher" and "lower" types of people and showers the first with words of praise and describes the second with a multitude of negative adjectives. However, these sorts of value-laden judgments seem to assume the very objectivity of values he rejected. He could only avoid this conclusion if he acknowledged that his judgments are simply his personal preferences, similar to his likes or dislikes with respect to food. But obviously he believes his evaluations of different personality types are saying something important and true about human nature and are not simply a report of his own, emotional state. Third, Nietzsche presents the world as chaotic and meaningless but praises those who can still affirm the value of existence in the face of this. However, isn't this optimistic attitude actually a rejection of the

world as we find it, rather than an honest acceptance of it? Maybe nihilism, the denial of all value, is the more honest approach. Granted, nihilism is unlivable, but isn't Nietzsche's call to overcome nihilism by assigning meaning to our existence merely asking us to create another illusion in order to go on living?

Finally, a criticism could be made of his philosophical method. Too often, Nietzsche dismisses traditional philosophical ideas with a wave of the hand by merely demonstrating that these ideas have a psychological origin and fulfill subjective needs within us. However, this is an example of the genetic fallacy. The genetic fallacy is a type of argument that attempts to prove a belief is false on the basis of its origin. It would be just as easy (and just as fallacious) to explain away Nietzsche's philosophy by looking at the reasons why he had a psychological need for power and strength. Even if many of our beliefs arise from deep-seated psychological needs, this does not imply that the conditions that would meet these needs do not exist. For example, it is both *true* that we have built-in needs for food, friends, and sex, *and that* there are objective conditions in reality that fulfill these needs. Isn't it also possible that a belief in a rational world order or belief in God *both* fulfill subjective needs *and* correspond to an objective reality that could meet these needs? This, of course, does not prove there is a rational order or a God. But it does show that the fact that an idea is psychologically satisfying does not in itself constitute grounds for its rejection.

Despite the criticisms that have been made of Nietzsche's philosophical assumptions and arguments, he was very perceptive in anticipating the century that lay ahead. The rise of secularism, the crumbling of our culture into a divisive pluralism, the tendency of moral discourse to turn into power struggles, the growing sense of alienation, and the crisis of values are just a few of the trends in the twentieth century Nietzsche saw coming.

Furthermore, no one can deny the tremendous influence his thought has had in the century following his death. Unfortunately, a great deal of this influence has been based on a misinterpretation of his ideas. During World War I, as Nietzsche's popularity was rising in Germany, critics in England and the United States considered him the ideological expression of German ruthlessness. During World War II Hitler and the Nazis practically made him a patron saint. Hitler visited the Nietzsche archives several times and had his picture taken by the bust of the philosopher. The Nazis saw themselves in Nietzsche's passages on the "will to power" and "master morality." They thought they were the "overmen" who would save a degenerate European civilization. His words of praise for warriors, hardness, and heroism as well as disdain for democracy, conventional morality, and weakness were almost treated as biblical texts by the Nazis. However, as numerous commentators have pointed out, the Nazis failed to see that Nietzsche cannot always be taken literally and that he was glorifying spiritual strength and not physical brutality. This misinterpretation was fueled by the fact that Nietzsche's sister, Elizabeth, had married a vitriolic anti-Semite. After her brother's death she forged proto-Nazi manuscripts in his name and edited his manuscripts to make him sound like a racist and German nationalist. Typical of Nietzsche's actual sentiments, however, was his suggestion that "it might be useful and fair to expel the anti-Semite screamers from the country" (BGE §251). Furthermore, he referred to the Germans' "nationalism and race hatred" as "scabies of the heart and blood poisoning" (GS §377).

Nietzsche's writings influenced an enormous range of people. Numerous philosophers have written books on him and the philosophical outlooks of Albert Camus, Jean-Paul Sartre, Max Scheler, and Oswald Spengler show the impact of his thought. He influenced poets such as Rainer Maria Rilke and Stefan George, and his presence is felt in the novels of Thomas Mann, Hermann Hesse, André Gide, and André Malraux, as well as in the work of George Bernard Shaw and William Butler Yeats. Some literary theories such as deconstructionism have been built on Nietzsche's denial that there is a single, authoritative interpretation of a text apart from the multiple perspectives and projected meanings of its readers. Furthermore, Nietzsche's search for an author's underlying, hidden motives behind the text has been the model for feminist and Marxist readings of literature. Sigmund Freud's analysis of the unconscious drives within us were foreshadowed by Nietzsche's observations. At seventy-eight, Freud wrote concerning Nietzsche, "In my youth he signified a nobility which I could not attain." Although the novelist Ayn Rand despised Nietzsche's irrationalism, her novels *The Fountainhead* and *Atlas Shrugged* betray her youthful attraction to *Thus Spoke Zarathustra*. Her passionate contempt for the herd mentality and traditional Christian virtues as well as her glorification of egoism and the heroic, creative individual would have won Nietzsche's admiration. Inspired by Nietzsche's vision of the overman, Richard Strauss wrote the powerful and often heard concerto *Thus Spoke Zarathustra* in 1896. Ironically, Nietzsche also had an impact on a number of theologians, such as the Protestant writer Paul Tillich and the Jewish thinker Martin Buber.

Even though a century has passed since he wrote his last words, Nietzsche's voice has not lost its power. One writer has explained his continuing appeal thus:

It is not a matter of agreeing or disagreeing with his philosophical conclusions, but of having passed through his corrosives of metaphysical, moral, and psychological doubts. They leave a man scarred or purified; certainly changed.[31]

Questions for Understanding

1. How did Nietzsche describe his mission?
2. What is meant by Nietzsche's perspectivism?
3. Why has Nietzsche's position been called a "romantic primitivism"?
4. What criteria does Nietzsche provide for evaluating perspectives?
5. What does Nietzsche think of the attempt to find objective truth?
6. What does Nietzsche mean when he says that a great thinker will be an "experimenter"?
7. What is Nietzsche's assessment of metaphysics?

8. When Nietzsche refers to the "death of God," what does he mean?

9. According to Nietzsche, what is the "will to power"? Why does it not necessarily refer to physical power? What role does it play in human psychology? What role does it play in nature?

10. Describe the differences between master morality and slave morality.

11. What is the "overman"?

12. What is "eternal recurrence" and why does Nietzsche believe in it? What sort of attitude should we have toward it?

Questions for Reflection

1. If all philosophies are simply the author's "personal confession," as Nietzsche claims, does this undermine his implied claim that his philosophy is the best perspective on life? How would he respond to this criticism?

2. Choose one of the great philosophers in history and imagine how Nietzsche would analyze this thinker's ideas.

3. Do you agree with Nietzsche that we deal with the world in terms of our feelings and instincts rather than reason? If this is true, is it good or bad?

4. In what ways are Nietzsche and Kierkegaard similar? In what ways are they different?

5. Nietzsche thinks that the religious way of life is a form of weakness, whereas Kierkegaard thinks that a relationship to God is the way to authenticity. Choose one of these thinkers and imagine how he would respond to the other on this issue.

6. If our society were run according to Nietzsche's ideals, in what ways would it be different? In what ways might it be better? In what ways might it be worse?

Notes

1. Friedrich Nietzsche, *Ecce Homo*, "Why I Am a Destiny," §1, trans. Walter Kaufmann in *On the Genealogy of Morals and Ecce Homo*, ed. Walter Kaufmann (New York: Vintage Books, 1969).

2. Roland N. Stromberg, *An Intellectual History of Modern Europe* (New York: Appleton-Century-Crofts, 1966), 333–334.

3. Letter to his sister, July 8, 1886, quoted in Karl Jaspers, *Nietzsche: An Introduction to the Understanding of His Philosophical Activity*, trans. Charles F. Wallraff and Frederick J. Schmitz (Chicago: Regnery, 1965), 436.

4. Hereafter, the works by Nietzsche that are most frequently quoted are referenced within the text and further endnotes using the following abbreviations. To accommodate readers who have other editions, the numbers in the reference refer to sections, not pages. Many of the quotations from individual works were taken from the anthology *The Portable Nietzsche*, trans. and ed. Walter Kaufmann (New York: Viking Press, 1968).

AC   *The Antichrist* in *The Portable Nietzsche*.

BGE   *Beyond Good and Evil*, trans. Walter Kaufmann (New York: Vintage Books, 1966).

EH   *Ecce Homo*, trans. Walter Kaufmann in *On the Genealogy of Morals and Ecce Homo*, ed. Walter Kaufmann (New York: Vintage Books, 1969).

GM   *On the Genealogy of Morals*, trans. Walter Kaufmann and R. J. Hollingdale in *On the Genealogy of Morals and Ecce Homo*, ed. Walter Kaufmann (New York: Vintage Books, 1969). Quotations from this work are referenced using the essay number followed by the section number.

GS   *The Gay Science*, trans. Walter Kaufmann (New York: Vintage Books, 1974).

HAH   *Human, All Too Human*, trans. R. J. Hollingdale (Cambridge, England: Cambridge University Press, 1986).

TI   *Twilight of the Idols* in *The Portable Nietzsche*.

WP   *The Will to Power*, trans. Walter Kaufmann and R. J. Hollingdale (New York: Vintage Books, 1968).

Z   *Thus Spoke Zarathustra* in *The Portable Nietzsche*.

5. TI, preface.

6. EH, "Thus Spoke Zarathustra," §8.

7. TI, "Maxims and Arrows," §26.

8. TI, "What the Germans Lack," §7.

9. "On Truth and Lie in an Extra-Moral Sense" in *The Portable Nietzsche*, trans. and ed. Walter Kaufmann (New York: Viking Press, 1968), 46.

10. HAH, "The wanderer and his shadow," §11 and TI, "'Reason' in Philosophy," §1.

11. Z, pt. 3, "On the Spirit of Gravity," §2.

12. "On Truth and Lie in an Extra-Moral Sense," 46–47.

13. EH, preface, §3.

14. TI, "How the 'True World' Finally Became a Fable."

15. GS §377; HAH, "Assorted Opinions and Maxims," §211.

16. Friedrich Nietzsche, *The Dawn of Day*, trans. J. M. Kennedy (New York: Macmillan, 1913), §95.

17. EH, "Why I Am a Destiny," §5.

18. Robert C. Solomon, *Continental Philosophy since 1750: The Rise and Fall of the Self*, A History of Western Philosophy: 7 (Oxford, England: Oxford University Press, 1988), 112.

19. *Dawn of Day*, §224.

20. Friedrich Nietzsche, *The AntiChrist*, §57 in *The Portable Nietzsche*.

21. Z, pt. 3, "On Virtue That Makes Small," §3.

22. Z, pt. 4, "The Ugliest Man."

23. Z, "Zarathustra's Prologue," §5.

24. Z, pt. 2, "On Priests."

25. Z, "Zarathustra's Prologue," §3.

26. Z, "Zarathustra's Prologue," §4.

27. Z, "Zarathustra's Prologue," §3.

28. *The Birth of Tragedy and The Genealogy of Morals*, trans. Francis Golffing (Garden City, NY: Doubleday Anchor Books, 1956), 24.

29. TI, "Skirmishes of an Untimely Man," §49.

30. EH, "Why I Am So Clever," §10.

31. Werner Pelz, "Jesus and Nietzsche," *Listener*, May 3, 1962.

28

Nineteenth-Century Empiricism: Comte, Bentham, and Mill

KARL MARX DIVIDED INTELLECTUALS INTO THOSE who try to understand the world and those who try to change it. The three philosophers discussed in this chapter believed with Marx that the task for philosophers was to change the world. The nineteenth century was still feeling the impact of the French Revolution and the Industrial Revolution, both of which had begun with great ideals but ended up bringing enormous social problems in their wake. Tired of philosophies that simply tried to put things into perspective, a number of thinkers engaged their intellects with the project of radical social reform.

Among the most important of these social philosophers were Auguste Comte in France, who started the movement known as **positivism**, and the British philosophers Jeremy Bentham and John Stuart Mill, who gave birth to the movement known as **utilitarianism**. Although Comte and Bentham began writing before Marx, their lives overlapped his, and Mill and Marx were both writing on social philosophy in London during the same twenty-four-year period. However, even though Marx quotes his three contemporaries, his

own work did not reach a broad audience during his lifetime, and the founders of positivism and utilitarianism took no notice of his writings. Nevertheless, although their solutions are different, all four of these writers tried to develop a science of human behavior that would provide the basis for a new, more rational society.

Although there were significant differences between nineteenth-century positivism and utilitarianism, they shared a number of convictions. First, they were rigorous empiricists. Tracing their intellectual family tree backward, it bypassed Kant and was rooted in the philosophies of hard-core empiricists such as Hobbes and Hume. Although they agreed with Kant that all knowledge was confined to the world of spatial-temporal phenomena, they rejected the Kantian notion of an unknowable noumenon. Accordingly, their worldview was that of *scientism*. This ideology goes far beyond merely having respect for science. Instead, scientism is the belief that science is the *only* reliable source of knowledge and values. All areas of human concern, whether psychology, morals, politics, or religion were credible only to the degree that their principles could be derived from science. Since metaphysics typically deals with claims about reality that go beyond what is directly observed, the positivists and the utilitarians were outspoken anti-metaphysicians.

Second, they were all interested in developing moral and social theories that would lead to the reform of society. If ideas are not ladders to ultimate reality, as the metaphysicians thought, then ideas are to be valued for their usefulness in making our existence in the here-and-now world as successful as possible. Consistent with their initial assumptions, they believed that any changes in society had to be based on a scientific foundation. Human beings are a part of nature, and any moral and social claims or recommendations must be based on what is observable and measurable in human experience. Thus, Bentham said that an ethical theory should function like a "moral thermometer" in measuring what is of value. Comte said he wanted to develop a "social physics" and Mill spoke of a "science of human nature."

Their empiricism made them proudly practical minded in their moral theorizing. Kant said it was the purity of the will that had moral value, not the consequences of our actions. For the positivists and the utilitarians, however, what matters is what people *do*. After all, the horrors of the Industrial Revolution and the French Revolution began with the best of intentions and motives. Hence, it is how things turn out that should concern us and mo-

tives and intentions are of interest only in terms of what practical results they tend to produce.

Furthermore, their empiricism and faith in science made them cheerfully optimistic about the possibilities of social reform. If the mind is a blank tablet at birth, then what and how we think will be a product of our experiences and environment. By understanding the laws of physics, we can predict and control the behavior of the billiard ball. Similarly, by creating the right sort of society, based on the laws of psychology and sociology, we will be able to create the right sort of people to live out its ideals.

Third, they were secularists. Their antipathy toward metaphysics naturally made them suspicious of traditional religion. However, while they tended to be agnostics with respect to the existence of God, they recognized the sociological and pragmatic value of religious ideals. For this reason, Comte tried to develop a secular form of religion to provide emotional support for his social ideals, and Bentham recognized the power of religion for providing sanctions that encourage socially beneficial behavior. Mill was alone in stepping beyond sheer agnosticism. He was willing to acknowledge that there was some empirical evidence for the existence of a rather nontraditional, finite God. Nevertheless, he still saw the value of religion primarily in terms of the socially useful ideals it sets before us. Despite these philosophers' concessions to religious belief, they were basically secularists in temperament.

AUGUSTE COMTE

|||

Comte's Life: A Reformer of Science, Society, and Religion

Auguste Comte (1798–1857) was born in Montpellier, France. Although his parents were sincere Catholics, he announced at age fourteen that he had ceased believing in God. During the years 1814–1816, he studied at the École Polytechnique, a school whose approach to science was focused

on practical, technical applications. While he was there, his intense study of the work of famous scientists inspired his lifelong devotion to scientific knowledge. Beginning in 1817, Comte served for seven years as the secretary to Saint-Simon, the noted socialist. Although the relationship ended in bitter acrimony, Comte was decidedly influenced by his mentor and employer. Comte was never able to fulfill his dream of obtaining a satisfactory university position and survived mainly by tutoring in mathematics and from contributions of his friends and admirers. However, he began to achieve a measure of fame from a series of lectures he gave on his philosophical ideas that was attended by a number of prominent scientists. During the years 1830 to 1842, Comte published his major work, the six-volume *Course in Positive Philosophy*, which he developed from the lectures. It set out a vision of human knowledge and human society built on nothing but a rock-hard foundation of observable scientific facts.

His attempts to find a solid foundation for science was paralleled by a great deal of instability in his personal life. Throughout his life he suffered from emotional and physical distress. Two years after he dissolved a short-lived, unhappy marriage, Comte fell madly in love with a Mme. Clotilde de Vaux. This romance, which ended two years later with her tragic death, taught him the transforming power of love. He subsequently took a strange and radical turn in his thinking, moved beyond the rigid scientific philosophy of his earlier career, and attempted to invent a new, humanistic religion. Suffering from nervous exhaustion, he died in poverty and obscurity in 1857.

Comte's Task: Moving from Superstition to Positive Science

Comte devoted the bulk of his writings to developing a scientifically based philosophy that would be free of all speculation and anchored firmly in positive knowledge. For this reason, he called his philosophy "positivism" (a term he borrowed from Saint-Simon). The only claims the positivist would embrace are those that people have empirically verified. As he puts it, "No proposition that is not finally reducible to the enunciation of a fact, particular or general, can offer any real and intelligible meaning."[1] However, for Comte we are not to pursue knowledge for its own sake. The ultimate purpose of knowledge is to enable us to control our environment. To resolve our problems, what we need is not piecemeal social reforms, but a total overhaul of society. Although science has made

tremendous progress, we have not yet properly applied it to the issues that really matter, where it can improve the social, political, and moral spheres of human existence.

Comte advances a theory concerning the development of human history, which he calls the "Law of Three Stages." He believes the history of the race parallels the intellectual development of the individual human being. The first stage of human intellectual development was the theological stage. Comte says that this stage represented humanity in its infancy, for just as a child attributes intentions and personality to his teddy bear, so people at this stage assumed that the cosmos is governed by the actions of personal gods. This stage developed from fetishism or animism through polytheism, and culminated in monotheism, in which the world is viewed as a unified product of one deity. The second stage humanity has passed through is the metaphysical stage. Here, events were explained in terms of impersonal and hidden causes, using abstract notions such as forces, essences, or faculties. This represents humanity at the stage of adolescence. The third, and final stage, is that of positivism. At this stage, humanity has achieved adulthood, for the world is viewed scientifically.

Unfortunately, Comte's historical account reflects his own philosophical prejudices rather than a faithful rendering of the historical facts. Contrary to Comte's picture, there were antitheological scientific endeavors among the ancient Greeks, whereas the rise of modern science was brought about by men such as Newton who were both physicists and theologians. Furthermore, manifestations of the "adolescent" stage have followed the rise of the "adult" stage, since the grandiose, metaphysical speculations of Hegel developed centuries after the scientific theories of Newton. Nevertheless, although Comte is aware that modern science got its start with Newton, he still insists that Newton's theories were replete with extraneous metaphysical notions and thus had not achieved a fully mature scientific outlook. Despite its superficiality, Comte's account of intellectual history provides a good example of the nineteenth century's tendency to see history as progressing toward a rational, utopian ideal.

The positivist's view of science understands particular events as instances of the laws of nature. However, these laws are not metaphysical forces, but are simply the observed regularities within experience. Thus, science simply describes what is observed and does not postulate anything beyond the appearances. Comte says that we must abandon our dreams of having absolute knowledge. For this reason, he thinks science should not refer to "causes" but only to "observable sequences." For example, we must not ask, "What is gravity?" for this question is asking for a metaphysical essence. Instead, we should use the term "gravity" to refer to the relationship between successive appearances of a falling body, instead of using it to refer to some occult cause beyond the phenomena. Hence, Comte agrees with Kant in viewing science as simply an account of the phenomena of experience as opposed to a window that opens onto reality-in-itself.

To assist in carrying out his dream of putting human knowledge on a solid scientific foundation, Comte arranges the sciences in a logical order. He ranks the departments of knowledge on a continuum from the most simple and abstract to the most complex and concrete, in which each discipline depends on the ones preceding it. The order he gives of the traditional sciences is mathematics, astronomy, physics, chemistry, and physiology. At the apex of the sciences, he places a "new department," which had not yet been developed. He calls this new science "sociology." Consequently, from Comte's time on this has been the label for the scientific study of society. In Comte's vision, sociology would unify the sciences by putting them in the service of humanity and its needs. According to Comte's account, the progress of the human sciences has followed his historical model. The theological stage viewed human events as controlled by the gods. In the metaphysical stage the political philosophers referred to such unobservable and abstract notions as equality, rights, sovereignty, the general will, or the state of nature. With the dawning of positivism, however, human interactions are to be scientifically studied like any other natural phenomenon. Comte takes credit for being the first to elevate the study of society from the level of

metaphysics to that of a science. The goal of this new science is to find general laws that will enable us to predict and control human behavior. Thus, he proposes a sort of "social physics" that would set out the engineering principles for constructing the good society.

Comte's Scientific Religion

Originally, Comte's sociology included what we now call social psychology, economics, political theory, and history. Later, however, Comte made ethics the seventh science in the hierarchy. However, his notion of ethics was quite different from that of traditional moral theorists. For Comte, ethics was simply the application of the laws of human behavior to effective social planning. To make an effective society, however, he had to take into account not only the human intellect but also the emotions. How can people in the age of positive science be motivated to love and serve humanity without the support and inspiration of a Christian worldview? Comte's answer is to construct a new religion, the "Religion of Humanity." Given his disdain for theology and metaphysics, it may seem strange for Comte to fall back on religion, which he earlier said was part of humanity's infancy. However, although he does not think it meaningful to talk about God, he also rejects atheism as a dogmatic metaphysical position. Theism and atheism give different accounts of the nature of the cosmos and the ultimate causes of things, but there is no empirical way to test their claims. Nevertheless, from a strictly sociological point of view, Comte recognizes the power of religious ideals to bring out the best in people and to serve as the mortar in constructing a coherent community. What we need, Comte thinks, is a scientifically respectable religion that will have all the emotional appeal and motivating force of Christianity without its theological and metaphysical baggage. Its purpose will be to enable people to rise above egoism to embrace **altruism** (another word invented by Comte). His program for the Religion of Humanity is first set out in his *System of Positive Politics* (1851–1854). Having abandoned Roman Catholic Christianity in his youth, he now seeks to free it of its theological and metaphysical superstitions, while preserving the socially beneficial elements within it. This he accomplishes by redefining the essential concepts of Christianity. For example, discarding the notion of God, he proposes that the Supreme Being for the positivist should be Humanity. To this he added Earth and Space to complete the positivist's Trinity. The calendar will be reformed so that the significant dates no longer mark religious events but instead honor the great intellects in human history. Major figures such as Gutenberg, Shakespeare, and Descartes are used to name the months of the year, which would now be expanded to thirteen. There are nine secular sacraments or rites celebrating the great transitions in life from birth all the way to death. Plato said that philosophers should become kings; Comte's utopian vision is one where social engineers will be the rulers (he called them "scientific politicians"). Society will only be efficient if run by an intellectual, technological elite. Comte, like Plato, believed that allowing the general public to make political decisions was as absurd as allowing them to make decisions on technical matters in astronomy and physics.[2]

Evaluation and Significance of Comte's Ideas

Comte's attempt to limit science to a narrow empirical methodology encouraged those who wanted to sever science from any sort of metaphysical base. However, it is not clear that science could survive this positivist surgery. His pronouncement that any proposition should be rejected "that is not finally reducible to the enunciation of a fact" would sound the death knell of contemporary astronomy and nuclear physics where the observable facts can only be made intelligible in terms of unobservable, theoretical entities. However, Comte had nothing but ridicule for scientists who went beyond what was directly verifiable, scornfully comparing their theories to the belief in angels and genii.[3] Furthermore, his attempt to build a worldview, including a system of values, on this razor-thin empirical foundation was doomed to failure. A science re-stricted to Comtean limits could prescribe medicine to cure gout, but could not prescribe values by which to live. Even Comte himself seemed unable to live on the austere diet of verified facts he recommended. Although he claimed science as the source of his utopian vision, he continually smuggled unwarranted values and emotional preferences into the picture. The severe scientistic stance of his earlier period was overwhelmed by his love and virtual worship of Clotilde. He ended up saying that the intellect should be wholly subordinate to the feelings. Even though John Stuart Mill respected the scientific aspects of Comte's positivism, he regretfully admitted that "an irresistible air of ridicule" hovers over Comte's religion and mourned that "others may laugh, but we could far rather weep at this melancholy decadence of a great intellect."[4]

Despite these difficulties, Comte's positivism enjoyed a fair amount of influence. For example, Mill was influenced by the scientific aspects of positivism and actively promoted it. Comte's dream of making the study of humanity into a rigorous science has continued to be the goal for many in disciplines such as economics, psychology, and sociology. Furthermore, Comte, along with Hegel and Marx, contributed to the spirit of the nineteenth century with his claims that concepts should be studied in terms of their historical development and that historical progress follows a logical and inevitable pattern.

The later and more extravagant features of Comte's philosophy actually had the greatest impact. The Religion of Humanity struck a responsive chord within many people, for positivist societies sprung up in England and France that were devoted to the worship of the great minds in history. Positivism was even popular as far away as Latin America. Not only were churches established in Brazil, but the positivists put Comte's ideas to work in carrying out revolutionary political reform. To this day, the Brazilian flag carries the motto *"Ordem e Progreso"* ("Order and Progress"), the key phrase in all of Comte's writings.

By the end of the nineteenth century, the influence of Comte's social theory was eclipsed by the unashamedly metaphysical materialism of the

Marxists. Still, the spirit of positivism took on a life of its own and lived on beyond Comte's explicit doctrines. This methodological spirit remains an important force in the twentieth century among those who think we should stick purely with what can be empirically verified (in the most narrow sense of those words) and repudiate any metaphysical claims that go beyond the phenomena.

JEREMY BENTHAM

Bentham's Life: The Making of a Political Reformer

Jeremy Bentham (1748–1832) was born in London. He was the son of a London attorney who had ambitious plans for Jeremy to become famous in a career in law. Accordingly, at age twelve Jeremy was sent to Queen's College, Oxford. After graduating in 1763, he began the study of law, following in the footsteps of his father. However, he discovered that he had no interest in practicing the law but was interested in changing it. He was dissatisfied with both the prevailing theoretical foundations of the law and the actual applications of it in the courts. It was a pivotal time for one such as Bentham who was interested in social and political theory. He lived through the American Revolution, the French Revolution, the Napoleonic wars, and the rise of parliamentary government in England. He attributed the political instability of the times to the irrational and chaotic foundations of the current legal systems and social structures.

Bentham's solution was to develop a moral and political philosophy that would come to be known as *utilitarianism*. His writings attracted a great deal of attention and inspired the formation of a group of followers whose political ideas were radical for their time. With the help of funds supplied by Bentham, they published a journal that promoted his ideas. One of his most important disciples was James Mill, a writer and businessman. As a result of their friendship, Bentham became the godfather of James's eldest son, John Stuart Mill. The younger Mill would go on to refine and popularize Bentham's utilitarianism and make it one of the most influential ethical theo-

ries in history. Bentham died on June 6, 1832. He left his estate to the University of London, a school he helped to found. Furthermore, in his will he dictated that his body should be dissected for the benefit of science and that it should be preserved and remain on display at the University of London to remind people of his philosophy. His mummified body, dressed in his own clothes, is still on exhibit there today and according to the conditions of the will it must be present at each meeting of the board.

Bentham's Task: A Scientific Foundation for Morals and Politics

Bentham was drawn into philosophy by his extreme dissatisfaction with not only the current state of society but with the theories from which it had developed. He ferociously attacks standard pillars of social theory such as the belief in a natural moral law and the notion of innate, natural human rights. Since these are scientifically unobservable, he considers them to be fictitious entities. If you ask people to set out the dictates of the natural law or to list our natural rights, you will get numerous conflicting lists, a sign that these notions do not refer to anything objective but are merely subjective preferences. Although he was sympathetic to the American Revolution, he thought its philosophical foundation was confused. In a note at the end of his *Introduction to the Principles of Morals and Legislation*, he says about the American Declaration of Independence, "Who can help lamenting, that so rational a cause should be rested, upon reasons, so much fitter to beget objections than to remove them?" Having rejected the prevailing theories concerning the foundations of morals, society, and government, Bentham sets out a program to place them on a more scientific basis. He begins with a theory of psychology, from which he derives a theory of morality and then goes on to apply it to issues of government and social policy.

Bentham's Moral Philosophy: Pleasure Is the Only Source of Value

Bentham begins *An Introduction to the Principles of Morals and Legislation* with his fundamental premise:

> *Nature has placed mankind under the governance of two sovereign masters,* pain *and* pleasure. *It is for them alone to point out what we ought to do, as well as to determine what we shall do. On the one hand the standard of right and wrong, on the other the chain of causes and effects, are fastened to their throne. (PML 1.1)*[5]

This passage contains the thesis of **psychological hedonism**, which is a claim about the causes of human behavior, namely, that pain and pleasure "*determine* what we *shall* do." In other words, when we dig down to the root motive of every human action, we will find that ultimately we are always trying to pursue pleasure or avoid pain. This is an empirical claim and may be supported or refuted by an appeal to the facts of human behavior. It may seem to be easy to find counterexamples to this thesis. However, in every case, Bentham would maintain that our two "sovereign masters" are motivating the behavior. For example, the religious martyr dies for her faith because she believes that great will be her reward in heaven. The mother who lives in poverty to send her son to college gets pleasure from his accomplishments. The masochist who lives to be hurt simply gets emotional pleasure from things most of us would avoid. In addition to this psychological claim, the preceding passage asserts an **ethical hedonism** that main-

tains that the moral rightness or wrongness of an action is a function of the amount of pleasure or pain it produces. Thus, pleasure and pain alone "point out what we *ought* to do."

If pleasure and pain are the standards of morality, then actions must be evaluated in terms of their consequences. For this reason, utilitarianism is one variety of the ethical theory known as **consequentialism** or, more traditionally, it is called a **teleological ethics.*** The foundation of utilitarianism is the *principle of utility*. Bentham defines "utility" as follows:

> *By utility is meant that property in any object whereby it tends to produce benefit, advantage, pleasure, good, or happiness (all this in the present case comes to the same thing), or (what comes again to the same thing) to prevent the happening of mischief, pain, evil, or unhappiness to the party whose interest is considered. (PML 1.3)*

Given this definition, Bentham says that an action conforms to the principle of utility "when the tendency it has to augment the happiness of the community is greater than any it has to diminish it" (PML 1.6). In other words, the fundamental moral rule of utilitarianism is "Act always to promote the greatest happiness for the greatest number." Since utility or the ability to produce happiness is that which accounts for the value of anything else, it is foolish to ask for a defense of the value of utility. Hence, only an indirect proof of the principle of utility is possible. If we reject this principle, Bentham believes there are only two other alternatives.

The first alternative is the principle of asceticism. This states that an action is right if it denies pleasure. Although this is not an appealing ethical principle, there are historical examples of it, such as the ancient Stoics who repudiated pleasure and sought virtue, those medieval monks and mystics who abused their bodies in order to subdue the flesh and put it in the service of the spirit, and all forms of Puritanism that are suspicious of worldly pleasures. However, asceticism is inconsistent,

---

*As mentioned in earlier chapters, this word comes from the Greek word *telos*, which means end or goal. Teleological ethics evaluates actions in terms of their end or consequences.

Bentham claims. The ascetic does not deny himself pleasure because he thinks pain is good in itself, but because it is a means to the pleasures of moral or religious enlightenment and heavenly reward. Thus, the ascetic is assuming the principle of utility while denying it.

The second alternative Bentham calls the "principle of sympathy and antipathy." Basically, this is the principle proposed by all theories that base ethical judgments on intuition or some sort of inner, moral sense. However, these theories make ethics too subjective and arbitrary and lead to moral anarchy. When you and I have conflicting moral opinions, there is no way I can argue my moral sentiments are more correct than yours. Thus, Bentham concludes that all competing moral principles are either incoherent or reducible to utility. Tying *ought* to *pleasure* is the only way "the words *ought*, and *right* and *wrong*, and others of that stamp have a meaning: when otherwise, they have none" (PML 1.10).

Bentham consistently points out that there is no sensible meaning to the notion of "higher" or "lower" pleasures. Pleasures can only differ in their quantity. Bentham expresses this in a memorable quotation:

> *Prejudice apart, the game of pushpin is of equal value with the arts and sciences of music and poetry. If the game of pushpin furnish more pleasure, it is more valuable than either.*[6]*

Bentham provides a method to scientifically quantify and calculate the value of different pleasures (PML 4.1-8). This is commonly referred to as Bentham's "hedonic calculus." When considering any action, we should evaluate the amount of pleasure or pain it will produce according to the following seven dimensions:

1. *Intensity:* How strong is the pleasure?
2. *Duration:* How long will the pleasure last?

3. *Certainty or Uncertainty:* How likely or unlikely is it that the pleasure will occur?
4. *Propinquity or Remoteness:* How soon will the pleasure occur?
5. *Fecundity:* How likely is it that the proposed action will produce more sensations of the same kind (either pleasure or pain)?
6. *Purity:* Will it be followed by sensations of the opposite kind? (Will the pain be followed by pleasure or the pleasure by pain?)
7. *Extent:* How many other people will be affected?

To illustrate how these are applied, it is obvious that receiving $25 would not produce as much pleasure as receiving $30, so, assuming that all factors are equal, you would prefer the action whose outcome was $30. However, if the $25 would be given to you now when you need it for school expenses, but the $30 would not be received for another forty years, it might be rational to choose the action that leads to the lesser but more immediate pleasure. To take another example, while going to a party tonight would produce a high amount of immediate pleasure, if it caused you to flunk a medical school admissions test tomorrow, it would be an impure pleasure, for the long-range pain of not pursuing your career would outweigh the immediate pleasure. Thus, all these factors must be taken into account in calculating which action is best.

Even when we are faced with more complicated moral dilemmas, the process of calculation is simple. For each person affected by the action, add up the total amount of units of pleasure produced and compare that figure with the amount of pain produced. Merge the calculations for each individual into the sum total of pleasure and pain produced for the community. Do this for alternative courses of action. This will give you the final verdict on which action is morally superior. Thus, on Bentham's analysis, moral dilemmas are turned into problems of addition and subtraction, where decisions are made by looking at the final balance much as we would an accountant's ledger of credits and debits. Although the process looks

*Pushpin was a rather trivial eighteenth-century children's game. If he were writing today, Bentham might say, "If they produce the same amounts of pleasure, playing video games is as worthy a pleasure as reading poetry."

awkward and even bizarre, Bentham thinks it formalizes what we actually do in practice, for we are constantly assessing the pluses and minuses of the consequences of any course of action.

Notice that in all this there is never any discussion of what has intrinsic or ultimate value. To be desired or valued by someone is all that it takes for something to have genuine value for that person. Obviously, what gives me pleasure may differ from what produces pleasure for you. There is no absolute standard of value, it is all relative and subjective. However, each of us who is affected by an action has one vote in determining the worthiness of an action. Thus, ethics is not the search for some hidden, unobservable quality called "moral goodness." Ethical decisions are no more complicated or sublime than planning the menu for a dinner party in which I take into account my guests' likes and dislikes.

Bentham's hedonism is basically individualistic in its orientation because we are fundamentally motivated by our own pleasures and pains. Why then should I be interested in the last element of these criteria, the extent to which pleasure is distributed? The answer lies in enlightened self-interest. To be concerned about my own welfare requires me also to attend to the interests of others. For example, the aristocrats on the eve of the 1789 French Revolution were selfishly concerned only about their own interests. However, this was a foolish self-interest because the suffering of the mobs in the streets had fatal consequences for the well-being of the aristocrats. Bentham is convinced that, with the proper legislation, we can create a society in which the pursuit of personal happiness will produce those actions which lead to "the greatest good for the greatest number."

Bentham's Social Philosophy: A Scientific Guide for Reform

Bentham's principle of utility has a number of implications for the reform of society and the legal system. He outlines a series of practical projects for the practical reform of schools, laws, courts, and prisons. The questions to be asked about each social policy are What end does it accomplish? and Can the policy be improved so as to be more effective in maximizing the total happiness? Bentham insists on a hardheaded approach that would turn the management of society into a science. He urges social planners to discard metaphysical rubbish in politics and law, such as an appeal to "natural moral laws" and "innate rights." Instead, social legislation should be based on the empirical foundation of measurable human happiness. The formula to follow is this: gather the facts, calculate the utility produced by each proposed action, and then legislate accordingly. The job of the legislator is to so orchestrate society that my pursuit of my own self-interest coincides with the interests of society. In some cases, to ensure that an individual's interests coincide with those of the community, it is necessary to associate punishments with behavior harmful to the social good. Bentham provides an extensive theory of punishment that nicely illustrates the practical implications of his utilitarianism. Since punishment always inflicts pain (physical or mental), by itself it is an evil. However, it is morally justified if it promises to prevent some greater evil. In the following cases, according to Bentham, punishment is not justified:

1. Where it is *groundless*. There is no evil for it to prevent or there is certainty that compensation for the harm will be forthcoming.

2. Where it is *ineffective*. Where it cannot prevent evil. Cases of this sort would be where the penalty is established after the act is done, where insufficient steps were taken to make people aware of the law, or where the agent could not have been fully aware of what he was doing.

3. Where it is *unprofitable* or too *expensive*. Where it would produce more evil than it prevented.

4. Where it is *needless*. Where the evil will cease of itself or may be prevented with more economical means.

With many such applications, Bentham showed that the principle of utility could serve as an effective tool for social legislation. Accordingly,

Bentham and his followers, known as the "philosophical radicals," demanded parliamentary reform, prison reform, changes in the calculus of punishments, and other wide-sweeping changes in society. Bentham's philosophy was considered radical in his time, for it posed a threat to the power of the ruling classes. In the utilitarian calculus, each person "counts as one and none more," and thus one's wealth, class, and title do not gain any special political privileges. In this way, Bentham established the basis for a truly democratic society. Bentham's ideas not only changed social structures, they also enriched our vocabulary. In the quest for efficiency and precision in his speech, he coined hundreds of new words. Among those still in use are *minimize, maximize, deterioration, unilateral, dynamic, detachable, cross-examination, international, exhaustive,* and *codification.* Bentham laid the groundwork for utilitarianism; John Stuart Mill refined it and made it one of the most influential theories in the history of ethical and social philosophy.

JOHN STUART MILL

Mill's Life: Corporate Executive and Philosopher

John Stuart Mill (1806–1873) was born in London. He was the eldest son of the nine children of James Mill, a high official in the East India Company, as well as a philosopher, economist, historian, and disciple of Bentham. James Mill was an intellectually intense man, with a stern stoical personality, who had no use for feelings and sentiment. Although he had been trained to be a minister, the problem of suffering in the world drove him to become a lifelong agnostic. Beginning when John was three years old, his father subjected him to a rigorous educational experiment to show how the proper education could turn the blank mind of a child into a learned, rational machine. Accordingly, he began teaching John Greek and arithmetic at age three. When this precocious child reached the ripe old age of six and a half, he wrote a history of Rome, complete with footnotes. At age eleven he was taught Latin, geometry, and algebra, and he learned philosophy and logic when he was twelve. Although he never attended a university, it is said that when he was thirteen years old he was better educated than any university graduate of the time. Later, Mill modestly claimed his intellectual abilities were below average, making him a living testimony to what could be accomplished through a methodical program of education.

In 1823, Mill began a thirty-five-year career at the East India Company, the trading firm where his father was employed. He spent his free time writing and working in support of various liberal economic and political causes. However, when he was twenty, Mill's lack of a normal childhood and fatherly affection caught up with him, and he suffered from a mental crisis and severe depression. All his intellectual and political goals seemed to lead to inner emptiness. The utilitarian philosophy of Bentham and his father, which he had enthusiastically supported, now seemed barren and uninspiring. He described his crisis thus:

> The habit of analysis has a tendency to wear away the feelings. . . . I was thus, as I said to myself, left stranded at the commencement of my voyage, with a well-equipped ship and a rudder, but no sail.[7]

Although the experience was unsettling, he recovered from this breakdown several months later with a new outlook on life. First, he discovered that happiness cannot be the direct goal in life, but is the natural accompaniment of pursuing other worthy goals. Second, he realized that what his intellectual development had lacked was a cultivation of feeling and an appreciation for the arts. He began to fill in the gaps in his personality and his upbringing by studying art and reading the romantic poetry of Wordsworth, Coleridge, Goethe, and Carlyle (writers considered the antithesis of the Benthamites). In his own life and writings, he sought to synthesize the emphasis on analytic reason found in the French philosophers and Bentham with the English and German romantics' appreciation of the emotions.

In 1830 Mill met Harriet Taylor, a young woman of extraordinary beauty and intellect. Even though she was married and the mother of three, Mill developed a quite intimate relationship with her. Her husband died in 1849, and two years later Mill and she married. Her influence on him was profound. She was the joint author with him of such important works as *Principles of Political Economy* and *On Liberty*. In his *Autobiography*, he states that during their marriage as well as the twenty-one years of their confidential friendship "all my published writings were as much my wife's work as mine."[8] Although he was one of the most influential philosophers in modern history, he never held an academic position. Instead, he remained a businessman, while promoting his ideas in his writings and political activism. In 1856, two years before he retired, he was promoted to be the head officer of his company and received a substantial salary. In 1858 Harriet died in Avignon, France. Mill purchased a house near her grave, and for the rest of his life spent half of each year in Avignon. He was profoundly influenced by his wife's thinking and his admiration for her abilities led him to become a leader of the movement for women's rights. While serving a term in Parliament during the years 1865–1868, Mill unsuccessfully tried to amend the Reform Bill of 1867 to give the vote to women. Furthermore, he published *The Subjection of Women* in 1869, in which he argued for the political empowerment of women. Mill died in Avignon on May 8, 1873, and was buried there next to Harriet.

Mill's Refinement of Utilitarianism

In developing his moral philosophy, Mill accepts the main outlines of Bentham's hedonism. Happi-

ness (the experience of pleasure and the absence of pain) is the only thing desirable in itself. Consequently, the total sum of happiness or the greatest good of the greatest number is the criterion of morality. His argument for the validity of this hedonism is quite simple:

> The only proof capable of being given that an object is visible is that people actually see it. The only proof that a sound is audible is that people hear it: and so of the other sources of our experience. In like manner, I apprehend, the sole evidence it is possible to produce that anything is desirable is that people do actually desire it. (U 4)[9]

In other words, values are not objective entities lying out there in the world. They are an expression of people's preferences. This position is a form of *value relativism*.

Although Mill, like Bentham, begins his moral philosophy by pointing to the psychological fact that people always pursue pleasure or happiness, he differs from Bentham on several issues. The first issue is the criteria for evaluating pleasure. Bentham maintained a quantitative hedonism. However, Mill adds to this a qualitative hedonism, for he insists pleasures can differ in quality, not just in amount. He says that those pleasures that are the product of our intellectual and more refined capacities are higher and better than physical pleasures. But how can we determine that some pleasures are higher? Again, there is no standard beyond human experience:

> Of two pleasures, if there be one to which all or almost all who have experience of both give a decided preference, irrespective of any feeling of moral obligation to prefer it, that is the more desirable pleasure. (U 2)

In this passage he says that moral obligations must be set aside, because this is what we are trying to determine. Like Epicurus, Mill believed intellectual pleasures are superior to the pleasures of the body. Only those who have the capacity to experience the life of the intellect can make this assessment. Mill thinks that anyone who is in a position to make the comparison would agree that the higher but more elusive pleasures are superior to the easily acquired and plentiful pleasures of the fool or an animal. In an often quoted remark he says,

> It is better to be a human being dissatisfied than a pig satisfied; better to be Socrates dissatisfied than a fool satisfied. And if the fool, or the pig, are of a different opinion, it is because they only know their own side of the question. The other party to the comparison knows both sides. (U 2)

Mill criticizes Bentham for having too limited a view of human nature. Human beings, Mill insists, are more than pleasure-seeking organisms. In seeking pleasure they also seek to develop their "higher faculties" and to become "well-developed human beings" (U 2, L 3). Mill says that in Bentham's account,

> Man is never recognized by him as a being capable of pursuing spiritual perfection as an end; of desiring, for its own sake, the conformity of his own character to his standard of excellence, without hope of good or fear of evil from [any] other source than his own inward consciousness.[10]

However, in saying that we strive to realize our potential as human beings as an end in itself, Mill has moved away from the utilitarian doctrine of psychological hedonism and has come amazingly close to Aristotle's view of human nature.

The second issue on which Mill disagreed with Bentham concerned the question of whether self-interest was the basis for all our actions. Bentham did recognize that we sometimes experience personal pleasure from making others happy. He called this the "pleasure of benevolence." He also noted that attending to other people's interests is often the best way to promote our own interests. However, in the final analysis, Bentham tended toward an egoistic hedonism, for he thought that the most universal motive for action was always the individual's self-interest. In contrast, Mill emphasizes much more strongly that we naturally have social feelings for humanity and the desire for unity with our fellow creatures (U 3). Mill goes on to say that in a utilitarian calculation, your own happiness cannot be given any more weight than the happiness of another person.

> The happiness which forms the utilitarian standard of what is right in conduct, is not the agent's own happiness, but that of all concerned. As between his own happiness and that of others, utilitarianism requires him to be as strictly impartial as a disinterested and benevolent spectator. (U 2)

He thinks he can provide proof that general happiness is the supreme good by means of the following argument: "Each person's happiness is a good to that person, and the general happiness, therefore, a good to the aggregate of all persons" (U 4). What he appears to be saying is that if people voted on whose happiness should be supported, they would vote for themselves. If we tally up the votes, then each person would get an equal number of votes (namely, one), so it follows that the happiness of all people should be pursued equally.

Kant thought that one's motives were what made an action morally right or wrong, whereas the actual consequences of one's actions were irrelevant in determining their morality. However, the utilitarians reversed this formula and made the consequences of our actions (promoting happiness or not) the key principle in ethics. But surely our motives play some role in ethics? Mill would agree, but he says the motive of the agent is a test of the goodness of the agent and not of the goodness of that person's actions. We primarily value such things as morally worthy motives, virtue, or a good character, Mill claimed, not because they are good in themselves, but because they are a means to an end. A virtuous person is one who has a tendency to promote the happiness of others, and for this reason alone we value virtue. If a virtuous character did not increase the chances of producing actions with good consequences, it would be superfluous and without value.

Mill's Social Philosophy
The Importance of Liberty

Previous democratic thinkers had been so concerned to defend the rights of the citizens from the tyranny of the king that they had ignored the sort of tyranny that can arise in a democracy—the tyranny of the majority. Realizing this could be as oppressive as any monarch, Mill addressed this problem in *On Liberty*, published in 1859. From his standpoint, censorship, intolerance, and imposed conformity are some of the greatest dangers that a society can face, for unlike a foreign invader, they arise in the midst of a society and masquerade as defenders of the social good. However, Mill insists that within the sphere of our personal lives, we should have the fullest amount of freedom to do as we wish, provided that we do not harm others. Consequently, the principle that a good society should follow is

> *That the sole end for which mankind are warranted, individually or collectively, in interfering with the liberty of action of any of their number, is self-protection. That the only purpose for which power can be rightfully exercised over any member of a civilized community, against his will, is to prevent harm to others. (L 1)*

The sphere of individual liberty includes our inward life, in which there is the absolute right to freedom of thought and expression. It also includes our outward life, which involves our choices and actions.

Mill's discussion of the first realm of freedom, the right to free expression and discussion of ideas, has been enormously influential. He says society is harmed by the suppression of free speech regardless of whether the ideas in question are true or false. First, the unpopular idea that is suppressed may, in fact, be true. In this case, it will not get a fair hearing and society will be deprived of its need to correct its false beliefs. The case of Galileo showed that the majority are often wrong and the nonconformist is often right. Since we are not infallible, we need to be exposed to ideas that will make us check the soundness of our beliefs. Second, even if an idea is false, we still should let it be heard, to expose it to the light of free discussion so its errors may be revealed and so the outlines of the true opinion can be seen more clearly. Third, even when their ideas are false, dissenters from the ideological status quo make a contribution, for they prevent intellectual stagnation and force us to re-examine the grounds for the prevailing convic-

tions. Unless this is done, a true opinion will become "a dead dogma, not a living truth."

The only restriction on free speech Mill allowed was when it threatened to cause immediate harm. However, this is not really an exception to his rule, because his whole theory of personal liberty is based entirely on what will promote the social good and prevent harm. The example he provides is

> *An opinion that corn-dealers are starvers of the poor . . . ought to be unmolested when simply circulated through the press, but may justly incur punishment when delivered orally to an excited mob assembled before the house of a corn-dealer. (L 3)*

This principle found its way into the "clear and present danger" criterion that the U.S. Supreme Court uses to determine when free speech may be limited.

The second area of freedom, the liberty to act as I wish, was based on the utilitarians' undying conviction that, on the whole, individuals are the best judges of their own interest, but are not always the best judges of the interests of others. In particular cases, of course, someone's personal choices concerning his or her way of life may not actually be what is best for that person (for individuals do make foolish choices), but it is best to allow individuals this choice, simply because it is their own choice. Hence, personal autonomy is one of the highest social values in Mill's vision of society. As he states it,

> *The only part of the conduct of anyone, for which he is amenable to society, is that which concerns others. In the part which merely concerns himself, his independence is, of right, absolute. Over himself, over his own body and mind, the individual is sovereign. (L 1)*

Two points need to be made here. First, Mill excludes the application of this principle to minors who, for the most part, are not likely to have enough experience or maturity to make sound decisions about their lives. Second, consistent with his empiricism, Mill does not ground this principle on any notion of intrinsic, natural human "rights," as Locke might have done. A so-called natural right is an abstract notion that is not empirical and, hence, can't be verified. Instead, he argues that individuals should be free to perform any actions that do not harm others because this principle will maximize the general "well-being" of the community. Hence, in good empiricist fashion, the principle is justified in terms of its observable consequences.

The implications for legal theory are enormous if we adopt Mill's principle that society has no right to infringe on an individual's freedom except when that person's actions harm others. Some of the examples he provides of unjustifiable interference with personal liberty are the punishment of nonviolent drunkenness; the suppression of polygamy among Mormons; the prohibition of recreational drugs, gambling, and sexual relations between consenting adults (such as prostitution); restrictions on Sunday amusements; and restrictions on the sale of poisons. We may personally find these sorts of behavior repugnant, but the people who engage in them do not inflict harm on others. Hence, these are all examples of "victimless crimes" and should be tolerated.

With the right to freely engage in such behavior, however, comes the necessity of accepting its natural consequences. For example, although we are not allowed to prevent people from drinking, the offensive drunk may find that people shun his company. Critics of Mill have asked if we can draw the line so cleanly between actions that affect only the person engaging in them and actions that affect society. The person who gets drunk in the privacy of his own home may seem to be harming only himself, but what if this personal vice leaves his family to starve? Mill's response was that we may justly punish him for nonsupport, the only socially harmful act he has committed. We may urge the drunk, the prostitute, and the compulsive gambler to mend their ways, but society cannot otherwise interfere in their personal lifestyle choices. Mill's view is radically different from Kant's, for the latter did not think that morality was simply a matter of preventing harm to others. Kant maintained that even if you were isolated on a island you still had moral duties to *yourself* and that harming one's self through chronic idleness was immoral.

Despite the strong tone of political libertarianism that permeates Mill's writings, remember that personal liberty is not an intrinsic right but is always grounded in social utility. Thus, the government may always intervene in personal liberty when it serves the common good. In *On Liberty*, Mill says that when overpopulation threatens the economy, the state may legitimately forbid people to marry if they have insufficient means of supporting a family (L 5). He says other government limitations on liberty to protect society's interests might include requiring the registration of poisons (to guard against their criminal use), enforcing sanitary conditions, or restricting the location of a casino. In his later years, Mill began to abandon the economic individualism of his earlier work and saw a greater need for state control of the distribution of wealth. Speaking of himself and his wife, he said that "our ideal of ultimate improvement went far beyond Democracy, and would class us decidedly under the general designation of Socialists."[11]

Mill's Other Contributions

John Stuart Mill is best known for his ethical and social theories, which have had an extraordinary influence on twentieth-century thought. Nevertheless, his writings on logic, epistemology, and psychology have been of some interest also. He developed a theory of inductive logic, the sort of reasoning we use when we reason from what is true in several cases to what will be true of other cases of the same kind. His account of induction is still used in logic textbooks today. However, Mill went on to make the very controversial claim that *all* reasoning is of this sort. In other words, there is no a priori knowledge, and even the principles of logic and mathematics are generalizations from experience. In epistemology he tried to take seriously the Kantian claim that all we can know are the phenomena and not things-in-themselves. This led Mill to conclude that when we refer to external objects, we are merely referring to the "permanent possibility of sensations of a certain sort." Finally, he developed the theory that "a free action" is merely an action caused by the agent's own, inner desires. However, since no event is uncaused, it follows that our will, desires, and wishes are the products of deterministic causes. Thus, Mill maintained a form of psychological determinism.

Evaluation and Significance of Utilitarianism

Much in utilitarianism is appealing. Certainly it is a fundamental feature of human nature that we all want to be happy. By building their ethical theory on this premise, Bentham and Mill have given us an ethics consistent with our most basic inclinations rather than one that makes happiness and morality natural enemies. Furthermore, because people's happiness is something concrete and identifiable, utilitarianism gives us a definitive method for making moral decisions and adjudicating moral conflicts. If we are in doubt as to what our moral obligations are, we simply calculate the amount of human happiness produced by one action or another. Finally, some find utilitarianism more reasonable than Kant's unquestioning obedience to the stern demands of duty and total disregard for the consequences. What good is it, the utilitarian asks, to do our "duty" if we make everyone miserable and there are no positive consequences? How is it possible, they ask, for an action to be "immoral" if it produces pleasure for someone and harms no one else? Certainly much can be said in favor of making consequences an important feature in determining the desirability of actions.

Despite the strong points of utilitarianism, it has not been immune to criticism. Critics have asked, How can one base an ethical theory on psychological hedonism? Bentham and Mill claim pleasure is the criterion of value because we are always naturally driven to pursue pleasure. But if this is true, what sense does it make for the utilitarian to preach, "You ought to do what you desire"? However, if we sometimes pursue values other than pleasure, then it raises the question of why pleasure is the most important value. Fur-

thermore, most would agree with Mill that Bentham's hedonism is too vulgar. What conscientious person would affirm that living at the level of an animal and only pursuing the pleasures of the body is just as good as developing the life of the mind? Granted, using Bentham's calculus, we might decide the pleasures of the mind will be more fruitful and long lasting. Nevertheless, if "pushpin is as good as poetry" then Bentham's ethics would seem to find no moral fault with a concert pianist or great writer debasing himself by choosing to be a beach bum instead of enduring the pain and effort of developing his talents.

Certainly, Mill's modified version of hedonism is more appealing. However, how does he decide that one pleasure is "better" than another? To do so, we would have to use some criterion other than pleasure to judge the value of competing pleasures. Yet, if pleasure is the only criterion of value, then we cannot rank pleasures except in terms of their quantity, which puts us right back to Bentham's version.

Another problem is that sometimes there is a tension between the utilitarian goals of "creating the greatest amount of happiness" and "creating happiness for the greatest number." In case 1, suppose I could create the greatest total amount of pleasure over pain within a community of ten people by making four people supremely happy while six people were miserable. In case 2, I could make all ten people moderately happy, with none experiencing any misery. However, the total amount of happiness would not be as great as in the first case. If the total amount of pleasure over pain is what counts, then case 1 would be morally preferable. If creating happiness for the greatest number is what counts, then case 2 would be best. The problem is that there can be conflicts between the goals of (1) creating the greatest amount of happiness and (2) distributing it among the greatest number. Furthermore, the utilitarian concern for maximizing happiness does not seem to take into account the principle of justice. Critics point out that the principle of justice and the greatest happiness principle often lead to different social policies. Contemporary utilitarians and their critics continue to debate whether the utilitarian principle has the resources to solve these problems.

In addition to these general problems, critics claim there are fallacies in some of Mill's arguments. For example, in the passage quoted earlier in this chapter, Mill says "the sole evidence it is possible to produce that anything is desirable is that people do actually desire it." His argument for this goes something like this:

(1) Seeing, hearing, and desiring are similar in that they are ways that a subject is related to an object.
(2) Visible, audible, and desirable are similar in that they are subject-related properties of an object.
(3) So the relationship between the terms of each pair (seeing visible, hearing audible, desiring desirable) will be the same in each case.
(4) The fact that an object is seen is the only evidence possible that it is visible and the fact that a sound is heard is the only evidence possible that it is audible.
(5) Therefore, the fact that something is desired is the only evidence possible that it is desirable.

Premises 1, 2, and 3 are not explicitly stated, but are clearly what Mill assumes. The questionable part of the argument is the analogy in premise 3. It is true that "visible" means "capable of being seen." But does the analogy hold for desirability? What we ordinarily mean when we say something is "desirable" is not that "it is desired by someone," but that it is "what *ought* to be desired." The problem is, it does not seem that factual claims can entail a value judgment. The factual judgment that "people desire *X*" does not entail the value judgment that "*X* is desirable or good." For example, there was a time when many people approved of slavery (a factual claim), but we would not want to say that this provides evidence that the practice was desirable (a value judgment). However, the fact that something is *not* desired is compatible with the fact that it *ought* to be desired. There are monolithic and authoritarian societies where no one values the free discussion of ideas. Neverthe-

less, even if not valued, it is morally desirable and ought to be promoted.

Second, as discussed earlier, Mill believed that a rational person will seek not only his or her own happiness, but the happiness of everyone. His argument was

(1) Each person's happiness is a good to that person.
(2) Therefore, the general happiness is a good to the aggregate of all people.

However, this argument seems fallacious. To use an analogy, each runner in a race wants to win, but it does not follow from this that they all desire for everybody to win.* Therefore, some other argument is needed to get from psychological hedonism ("I desire my own pleasure") to Mill's universal hedonism ("We all desire—or should desire—the happiness of everyone").

The utilitarian theory did not end its development with Bentham and Mill. Utilitarians in the twentieth century have clarified or modified some of their principles and responded to the sorts of objections just mentioned. Likewise, antiutilitarians have continued to provide counterexamples and arguments to expose what they consider to be problems in the theory. Thus, utilitarianism continues to be a live, though controversial, option in ethics and social theory. A few moments' reflection will make clear how much Mill has influenced our contemporary thinking and practice in the moral and political spheres.

Questions for Understanding

1. What are some of the similarities between nineteenth-century positivism and utilitarianism?
2. What was Comte's mission as a philosopher?
3. Why does Comte call his philosophy "positivism"?

---

*Logicians call this "the fallacy of composition," because it reasons from what is true of each individual to what is true of them collectively.

4. According to Comte, what are the three stages of history?

5. What is Comte's view of science? What sorts of questions should scientists ask and what sorts of questions lie outside the boundaries of science?

6. What was Comte's view of traditional religion and what was his proposal for replacing it?

7. What was Bentham's task as a philosopher?

8. What was Bentham's quarrel with the philosophy of the American Revolution?

9. According to Bentham, what are the two "sovereign masters" in human motivation?

10. What is the difference between psychological and ethical hedonism?

11. Briefly define consequentialism or teleological ethics. What makes utilitarianism an example of this theory?

12. What is the fundamental moral rule of utilitarianism?

13. Why does Bentham claim that the notion of "higher" or "lower" pleasures is meaningless?

14. What are the seven criteria in Bentham's hedonic calculus?

15. Why does Bentham say it is right to be concerned with the interests of others?

16. According to Bentham, what is the justification of punishment? Under what conditions is punishment not justified?

17. According to Mill, what criteria do we use to determine that something is desirable?

18. What is the difference between quantitative hedonism and qualitative hedonism? In terms of this distinction, how does Mill differ from Bentham?

19. According to Mill, how can we decide which pleasures are higher than others?

20. Why does Mill say that each person should be concerned with the happiness of other people? How does his position differ from Bentham's on this point?

21. According to Mill, what is the role of motives in our moral assessments? How does he differ from Kant on this point?

22. In Mill's social philosophy, what are the only legitimate grounds for interfering with an individual's liberty?

23. What are the three arguments Mill gives for protecting freedom of speech? What is the one situation where free speech may be limited?

24. According to Mill, why is it wrong for society to interfere with a person's choices, even if those choices may be harmful to that individual? When is it legitimate for society to restrict a person's actions? What are some examples of "victimless crimes" that Mill says society should not regulate?

Questions for Reflection

1. Agree or disagree with Comte's belief that a scientific humanism can provide all the emotional inspiration of religion without the theological baggage.

2. Do you agree or disagree with Bentham's psychological hedonism? Briefly argue in support of your opinion.

3. Argue for or against Bentham's claim that pleasures may be distinguished only in terms of their quantity.

4. Think of an ethical decision that you had to make recently. What advice does Bentham give you on this issue? How adequate is his ethical theory in guiding behavior?

5. In what ways does utilitarian ethics disagree with Kant's ethics? Choose some contemporary moral issue and analyze it first in terms of Kantian ethics and then from the perspective of utilitarianism. On this particular issue, would the two positions agree or disagree as to what is the morally correct action?

6. According to Mill's theory of individual liberty, what restrictions (if any) would he place on obscene, racist, or sexist speech? What would his arguments be? State why you agree or disagree with his position.

7. If our lawmakers adopted Mill's philosophy, what activities would no longer be illegal? Do you think that putting Mill's views on liberty

into effect would make society better or worse? Why?

8. What are some criticisms that have been made of utilitarianism? How would either Bentham or Mill respond?

Notes

1 Auguste Comte, *Cours de philosophie positive*, 6.13, trans. Harriet Martineau as *The Positive Philosophy of Auguste Comte* (New York: Gowans, 1868), 799.

2. See his essays "Separation of Opinions and Aspirations" and "Plan of the Scientific Operations Necessary for Reorganizing Society" in *Auguste Comte and Positivism: The Essential Writings*, ed. Gertrud Lenzer (New York: Harper & Row, 1975), 6–8, 14.

3. *The Positive Philosophy of Auguste Comte*, 3.1, 201.

4. John Stuart Mill, *Auguste Comte and Positivism* (Ann Arbor: University of Michigan Press, 1961), 153, 199.

5. References to Bentham's work *An Introduction to the Principles of Morals and Legislation* are abbreviated as PML and reference numbers refer to the chapter and the section.

6. Jeremy Bentham, *The Rationale of Reward* in *The Works of Jeremy Bentham*, vol. 2, ed. John Bowring (Edinburgh: Tait, 1843), 253.

7. John Stuart Mill, *Autobiography* (Boston: Houghton Mifflin, 1969), 83–84.

8. *Autobiography*, 145.

9. Since there are so many readily available editions of Mill's works and because the chapters are relatively short, making passages easy to find, reference numbers refer to the chapter numbers where the quotations may be found. The following abbreviations refer to Mill's two major works:

   L   *On Liberty*.

   U   *Utilitarianism*.

10. John Stuart Mill, "Bentham," in *Collected Works of John Stuart Mill*, ed. J. M. Robson, vol. 10, *Essays on Ethics, Religion and Society* (Toronto: University of Toronto Press, 1969), 95.

11. *Autobiography*, 138.

IV

THE CONTEMPORARY PERIOD

CHAPTER

29

The Twentieth-Century Cultural Context: Science, Language, and Experience

THE TWENTIETH CENTURY HAS BEEN DESCRIBED in a number of ways. It has been called "the Age of Analysis," "the Age of Technology," and "the Information Age." These titles capture the global impact that science and technology have made on our sensibilities and the way we live. However, the happy notes sounded by these developments must be balanced by the discordant themes of two world wars, continuing threats of nuclear war, economic crises, environmental problems, social unrest, a sense of personal alienation, and . . . the list goes on. Hence another favorite title for the twentieth century has been "the Age of Anxiety."

Although these labels and others like them have their point to make, perhaps the safest generalization to make in terms of the history of philosophy is that this century has been "the Age of Plurality." At the same time that our information technology has turned our world into a global village, the explosion of perspectives has made our culture seem like a ship with multiple rudders and navigators, each trying to set a different course. The effect of this on philosophy was expressed by Edmund Husserl in 1931:

Instead of a unitary living philosophy, we have a philosophical literature growing beyond all bounds and almost without coherence. Instead of a serious discussion among conflicting theories that, in their very conflict, demonstrate the intimacy with which they belong together, the commonness of their underlying convictions, and an unswerving belief in a true philosophy, we have . . . a mere semblance of philosophizing seriously with and for one another. . . . To be sure, we still have philosophical congresses. The philosophers meet but, unfortunately, not the philosophies. [1]

One symptom that an age is in a state of crisis and transition is a recurring obsession with philosophical method and debates over the very nature of philosophy itself. In ancient Greece, we saw this in the conflicts between the Sophists and their culture, which led to Socrates and Plato's attempt at philosophical renewal. During the decline of the Middle Ages, the debate over the roles of faith and reason became a transforming cultural force. Likewise, at the beginning of the modern period the conflict between the rationalists and the empiricists was the manifestation of a culture trying to find its center.

Whenever there is a crisis in the foundations of culture and thought, there is a concerted effort to find a philosophical method that will put us on the right track. Consequently, all the philosophies in this century are characterized not only by their particular doctrines but by the fact that each one has a distinctive notion of the appropriate philosophical method to be employed. This concern is evident in the four major twentieth-century philosophical movements: pragmatism, process philosophy, analytic philosophy, and the intertwined movements of phenomenology and existentialism.

Living in Kant's Shadow

To set the stage of the twentieth century, it is important to remind ourselves that this is the post-Kantian era in philosophy. The themes and problems introduced by Kant continue to consciously or unconsciously set the agenda for philosophy. To review, Kant sought to set out the limits of knowledge. His conclusion was that what we can know is only the phenomena, or what appears within our spatially and temporally structured experience and can be understood scientifically. The corollary of this was that reality in itself, the noumenon, cannot be comprehended. However, Kant thought that we could not escape thinking in terms of "the big picture." Hence, he thought that "regulative ideas" guide thought, even if they cannot be objects of knowledge. These are the notions of the self, the cosmos as a totality, and God.

From these Kantian materials we can uncover three themes that reappear throughout all the twentieth-century philosophies. First, there is the issue of whether philosophy should focus on a detailed analysis of the phenomena or strive for a comprehensive outlook on the self, the cosmos, and God. This includes the question of whether or not the large-scale picture we construct conforms to the nature of reality itself or only traces the outlines of the human situation. Second, there are questions concerning the role of science in doing philosophy. Third, there are controversies concerning the respective roles that language and experience play in our philosophical investigations. We

will briefly discuss these issues and preview how each philosophical position addresses it.

Philosophy: Piecemeal Analysis or Grasping the Big Picture?

To begin with an analogy, there are two ways one can study a particular section of geographical terrain. One can approach it like a chemist, gathering soil samples, analyzing them in the laboratory, and making a detailed list of the elementary chemicals contained within this region of the earth. Or one can get in an airplane and fly high over it, trying to get a feel for the whole, how the region is put together, and the relationships between the different hills and fields within it. Who should the philosopher emulate: the chemist or the aerial surveyor? Should we search for detailed knowledge of the parts or for a comprehensive understanding of the whole? This admittedly rough analogy tries to capture a major divergence within contemporary philosophy: who has a better understanding of the terrain, the person with a knowledge of the parts or of the whole? In the case of the chemist versus the pilot, we would say that which method you should use depends on your goal. For example, do you want to know what crops to plant in the soil, or do you wish to make a map of the terrain? With philosophy, however, the question about the appropriate method cannot be answered by appealing to our goal because the question simply reasserts itself at a more fundamental level: what is the goal of philosophy? Unfortunately, there is no agreement on this question. Philosophy is the one discipline that includes itself within its own domain of questioning so that the question "What is philosophy?" is a central philosophical question.

Those who favor analysis believe that if we get the details right, we can then build up from them to the larger generalities. For want of a better term, we can say that the opposing side is searching for synthesis. They argue that the details have no meaning unless they are interpreted within the larger framework. Think of the two ways people

The Human Condition I (1933), René Magritte.
In a series of paintings, the French artist Magritte depicted the epistemological problem of the relationship between the mind and reality that philosophers from the time of Descartes to the twentieth century tried to solve. In the above work, our view of the outside world is obscured by the canvas in front of the window. However, the images on the painted canvas (symbolizing the mind and its contents) seem to represent what is in the outside world. According to Magritte, this is how we see the world, "we see it as being outside ourselves even though it is only a mental representation of it that we experience inside ourselves."

work a jigsaw puzzle. Some try to find individual pieces that fit together and continually build isolated collections of pieces, hoping they will all link up together eventually. Others start with the borders, on the theory that if they can get the main outline of the picture, they will know where the individual pieces belong.

Pragmatism represents a compromise position, because its individual members cover the scale from the analytic pole to the synthesis pole. The three pragmatists we will study are C. S. Peirce, William James, and John Dewey. C. S. Peirce was a scientifically trained philosopher who sought analytic clarity in our conceptions. Although William James was also trained in science, he always looked for the big picture that would make the best sense out of the details. James did not think that accumulating scientific facts would ever give us the guidance we needed for life. John Dewey kept close to the methods and the detailed outcomes of the sciences, but always wanted to trace out their implications for the large-scale issues within human life. Since the pragmatists believed that reason was limited and the world was constantly changing, they believed any picture of the whole always had to be tentative and constantly changing as our experience of the world changed.

Henri Bergson and A. N. Whitehead represent *process philosophy*. They thought that a comprehensive understanding of the cosmos and our place within it was the main goal of philosophy. Although Bergson appealed to biology for many of his ideas and Whitehead appealed to both biology and physics, they thought scientific data were just the grist for the metaphysician's mill. For Bergson, the method of metaphysics was intuition. For Whitehead, it took a combination of experience, imagination, and reason.

The *analytic philosophers*, as their very name suggests, were interested in analyzing the details. They said that philosophers should give up their grandiose hopes to know ultimate reality and should instead stay safely within the bounds of experience. However, the subject of their analysis was not the facts found through experience, for this endeavor can only be carried out by science. Instead, they believed the primary role of the philosopher is to analyze language. By getting clear on either the logical structure of language or how it functions, we can avoid many of the muddles that have kept metaphysicians in business. The analysts delegated the job of dealing with the ultimate meaning of things to the artists, poets, and novelists. Of course, the analysts also believed that the vision the artists give us merely consists of inspiring expressions of emotion, but nothing that we can sink our cogni-

The Bridgeman Art Library

tive teeth into. Bertrand Russell was always the analysts' best spokesperson. He said he aspired toward the same sort of advance in philosophy that Galileo introduced into physics, which is "the substitution of piecemeal, detailed, and verifiable results for large untested generalities recommended only by a certain appeal to imagination."[2]

In the first two-thirds of the twentieth century, phenomenology and existentialism were the leading movements within Continental philosophy. Edmund Husserl, the founder of *phenomenology*, definitely had an interest in analysis. He proposed phenomenology as a new discipline that would carry out a detailed analysis, not of scientific facts nor of language, but of the structures of consciousness and its objects. Like mountain climbers who will not advance until they have securely anchored themselves and tested the soundness of each foothold, Husserl's method was an agonizingly slow, detailed analysis of the domain of consciousness. The *existentialists* he inspired, however, were not so patient. Compared to Husserl, they moved very quickly to the big issues in human life. However, their "big picture" was much more modest than that of classical metaphysics. Perhaps their one point of agreement with the analysts was that we must accept the Kantian view of the limitations of reason. In contrast to all the other twentieth-century philosophers, they focused on the structures of human existence as it is subjectively lived.

The Role of Science in Philosophy

There is a fundamental divide between twentieth-century philosophers concerning where science should be placed with respect to the appearance–reality distinction. The *pragmatists* saw science as the basis for all our knowledge about the world. However, they had an extremely broad and humanistic view of the scientific method, thinking that it could give us not only the atomic weight of helium (for example), but also values. Hence they saw science as meshing perfectly with our deepest, human concerns. In the first half of the twentieth century, the *analytic philosophers* (for the most part) thought that science gives us the last word

on reality and that our prescientific, ordinary ways of viewing the world must be radically revised in the light of the latest discoveries in physics. For these philosophers, however, science was not as generous as the pragmatists supposed. Science could not guide us concerning values. Generally, the analysts believed ethical judgments lacked a factual basis, for they were simply emotive utterances on their view. In contrast, the *process philosophers* (Bergson and Whitehead) and the *phenomenologists* and *existentialists* (such as Husserl and Heidegger) insisted that science arises out of our ordinary ways of experiencing the world, but they claimed it simply gives us the world as viewed through the abstract grid of our quantitative methods.

The Role of Language and Experience in Philosophy

Twentieth-century philosophers can also be divided by the relative weights they give the role of language and experience in the philosophical enterprise. Although many have disagreed concerning the nature of philosophy, few would deny that language is crucial to the enterprise, for philosophy is an attempt to *speak* accurately and coherently about our deepest concerns. With the dawn of the twentieth century, however, many became convinced that all is not well with language. The philosopher and novelist Iris Murdoch expressed it well:

> We can no longer take language for granted as a medium of communication. Its transparency has gone. We are like people who for a long time looked out of a window without noticing the glass—and then one day began to notice this too.[3]

For those attracted to *analytic philosophy*, its methods seemed to provide a fruitful way to clarify our most abstract concepts by looking at the concrete ways in which we speak about them. Although they were empiricists, they believed a mute immersion within experience tells us nothing. Only when experience is described can we get clear on what has been presented. Hence, the propositions we use to make claims about our experience were the focus of their concern. For this reason, analytic philosophy is also called "linguistic philosophy."

Consider how you would answer this age-old philosophical question: What is knowledge? Such questions are likely to provoke a sense of paralysis and uncertainty about how to begin searching for an answer. Now consider these questions:

How do we use the *word* "knowledge"?

In what situations would we *say* that someone has knowledge?

When would we *say* that someone does not have knowledge?

With these sorts of questions, we know where to begin and how to proceed. Promising answers can be supported by examples, and inadequate answers can be rejected by citing counterexamples from our common fund of linguistic usage. Not all the analysts would approach an issue exactly this way. Nevertheless, the example illustrates the way questions of the form "What is *X*?" can be helpfully transformed into questions about language by asking, "What do we mean when we say '*X*'?" The approach of the analytic philosopher was illustrated by Bertrand Russell when he was challenged to explain what meaning life can have to an agnostic. Russell replied, "I feel inclined to answer by another question: What is the meaning of 'the meaning of life'?"[4]

When it came to analyzing statements about experience, the early analytic philosophers such as Bertrand Russell and the logical positivists, worked within the tradition of David Hume and saw experience as a collection of sense data. Hence, they sought an interpretation-free analysis of experience. However, the end result was that the only sort of statements that could be asserted with certainty were statements such as "redness here, now." To say, "I am experiencing a red book," introduces questionable entities such as the self and questionable inferences about the external world. This part of the analysts' program was never successful, for they were either left with totally useless certitudes or had to violate their methodological principles. The later ana-

lysts remedied the situation by developing broader notions of both language and experience.

Although the *pragmatists* did not think the analysis of language was the sole occupation of philosophy, they did think it was a first step to clarifying our concepts. They developed what was known as the "pragmatic theory of meaning," which insisted that the meaning of a term or concept be explicated in terms of the practical effects associated with the object of that conception. For the most part, the pragmatists looked to experience and not to language for the source of philosophical insight. However, their understanding of experience was much broader than that of the early analysts. John Dewey, for example, denied that we ever experience isolated sense data or even single objects and events. Instead, we experience contextual wholes that he called "situations." Experience is not made up of bits of data that bombard a passive mind, but is an arena for action in which we face practical problems, seek solutions, and carry out our projects and aims.

The process philosophers, phenomenologists, and existentialists were the most pessimistic about the insights that language could offer us, and they put the priority on experience, broadly understood. Bergson exemplified the approach that *process philosophy* took. He argued that concepts and the words that carry them are fragmenting, distorting instruments. By putting too much faith in our conceptual and linguistic categories, we try to force a flowing, unified experience into preformed containers that cannot hold it. Likewise, Whitehead complained that language only makes room for those thoughts that have been thought before. An original thought does not already have a home in our language, so our old language must be stretched or a new language created to accommodate novel ideas. He criticized the analytic philosophers for committing "the Fallacy of the Perfect Dictionary" with their assumption that philosophical insights can be gained by analyzing language as it currently stands.[5]

Since Husserl presented his *phenomenology* as a way of breaking free from our ordinary ways of approaching the world, he viewed his philosophical method as a particularly honest "seeing" of the way things are. Language played no role in this process other than to come in at the final phase to articulate and to share what the philosopher has discovered. When Husserl examined our pretheoretical level of experience, he did not find it to consist of a collection of independent sense data as the analysts claimed. Instead, he maintained that in addition to a display of sensory qualities, a faithful reading of experience revealed such contents as universals, meanings, values, moral duties, and aesthetic qualities. Furthermore, according to Husserl, the discrete sense data of the analysts were theoretical abstractions that obscured the rich, multilayered dimensions of experience as it is lived.

The *existentialists* agreed with Husserl in focusing on "lived experience" as opposed to a scientifically interpreted experience. But while Husserl tended to emphasize the way that the contents of experience are cognitively apprehended, the existentialists explored its subjective dimensions. Like their nineteenth-century predecessors Kierkegaard and Nietzsche, the experiences that really mattered to the twentieth-century existentialists were those revelatory of the human situation. These included the experience of our own, unbounded freedom, the experience of the contingency of all existence, and the deep, existential experiences of responsibility, anxiety, guilt, and our confrontation with the possibility of our own death.

Furthermore, the existentialists went much further than Husserl in depicting the role language plays in our intercourse with the world. Martin Heidegger, for example, contrasted ordinary language with the language of poetry. When we are immersed within our daily lives (what he called the mode of "everydayness"), we tend to allow authentic dialogue to degenerate into "idle talk." Idle talk is the detached, unthinking "chit-chat" that characterizes our life when it is lived inauthentically. Taken-for-granted, average points of view become solidified in idle talk and are passed on from one person to another like a worn coin whose distinctive markings have been rubbed smooth. The language of the poets, however, opens us up to reality and uncovers what has been concealed by our mundane, comfortable perspectives.

For Jean-Paul Sartre, another existentialist, the world is intrinsically meaningless in itself. It is simply there. What meaning we find within it is the meaning we create and project onto the world. Hence, language is just one way in which we break the world up into intelligible units and fashion it after our own image. However, it can create the illusion that when we use language to describe something we are really capturing its essence. In his novel *Nausea*, one of his characters, Roquetin, has the horrifying realization while riding a streetcar that words and reality are divorced. Words crystallize the meanings that he has imposed on the world, but the world itself simply exists and is nothing but a mute canvas on which he paints his own, subjective interpretations:

> This thing I'm sitting on, leaning my hand on, is called a seat. . . . I murmur: "It's a seat," a little like an exorcism. But the word stays on my lips: it refuses to go and put itself on the thing. . . . Things are divorced from their names. They are there, grotesque, headstrong, gigantic and it seems ridiculous to call them seats or say anything at all about them: I am in the midst of things, nameless things. Alone, without words, defenceless, they surround me, are beneath me, behind me, above me. They demand nothing, they don't impose themselves: they are there.[6]

Questions for Understanding

1. In what ways did Kant's philosophy influence the agenda of twentieth-century philosophy? What are the three major themes of twentieth-century philosophy?

2. What is the issue of analysis versus synthesis in twentieth-century philosophy? What philosophers or movements are representatives of each stance on this issue?

3. Where do the various philosophical movements stand on the role of science in philosophy?

4. What are the various stances that have been taken on the respective roles of language and experience in twentieth-century philosophy? What philosophers or movements are representatives of each stance?

Questions for Reflection

1. For each of the three issues discussed in this chapter, decide which position you find most plausible. Have you found yourself aligned with the same philosophers or movements in each of the three cases? Argue for one of the following two theses: (a) The three issues are not independent. The choice you make on any one of these issues commits you to a certain position on the other two. (b) The three issues are independent. You could be aligned with, say, the analysts on one issue, but could side with, for example, the process philosophers on another issue.

2. Pick a philosopher from each of the three previous historical periods (ancient, medieval, modern). Try to imagine the stance that each of these philosophers would take on the three issues discussed in this chapter.

Notes

1. Edmund Husserl, *Cartesian Meditations: An Introduction to Phenomenology*, trans. Dorion Cairns (The Hague: Nijhoff, 1960), 5.

2. Bertrand Russell, *Our Knowledge of the External World* (New York: New American Library, 1956), 12.

3. Iris Murdoch, *Sartre* (New Haven, CT: Yale University Press, 1953), 27.

4. Bertrand Russell, "What Is an Agnostic?" *Look Magazine* (1953), reprinted in *The Basic Writings of Bertrand Russell*, ed. R. E. Enger and L. E. Dennon (New York: Simon & Schuster, 1961), 582.

5. Alfred North Whitehead, *Modes of Thought* (New York: The Free Press, 1966), 173.

6. Jean-Paul Sartre, *Nausea*, trans. Lloyd Alexander (New York: New Directions, 1964), 168–169.

30

Pragmatism:
The Unity of
Thought and Action

The Origins of Pragmatism

The French writer De Tocqueville complained in his 1835 book *Democracy in America* that there was no country in the civilized world in which philosophy was taken less seriously than in America. This is not entirely true, for from the colonial period on, philosophy played an active role in American intellectual life. Throughout the nation's history, a number of American writers made original contributions to philosophy, ranging from political theory to philosophy of religion and metaphysics. It could be argued, however, that up until the latter part of the nineteenth century, a great deal of American philosophy was by and large a reflection of the philosophical movements that arose in Great Britain and Europe. However, with the development of the movement known as **pragmatism**, American thinkers made their most distinctive contribution to the world of philosophy.

People often say that pragmatism reflects the spirit of American culture. It is down-to-earth and shuns abstruse abstractions that have no "cash" value. It is oriented toward experience, action, and practical issues, the sort of characteristics that enabled a fledgling nation to come late onto the scene and shortly become a major cultural force in the world. Pragmatism views ideas as tools for getting a job done and values them only if they are successful when put to work. Furthermore, many people say that pragmatism fits in well with the spirit of science and technology and the enthusiasm for problem solving that Americans exemplify. However, while there is a measure of truth in all this, it is good to keep in mind that not all American philosophers have been pragmatists and not all pragmatists have been American. Furthermore, pragmatism has had a very deep impact not only on American culture but on the whole contemporary world as well. For example, Dewey's lectures in China and Japan were enthusiastically received.

In everyday contexts, people speak of a policy as being a "pragmatic" solution to a problem and politicians love to brag that they are "pragmatists." Thus, pragmatism ranks with cynicism, epicureanism, stoicism, and existentialism as a philosophy that so captured the public imagination that it found its way into popular discourse. However, fame is both a blessing and a curse. With most popular philosophies, such as pragmatism, the original versions propounded by the philosophers are more sophisticated and refined than the fashionable adaptations of them. For example, in popular usage, "pragmatic" is associated with "practical" and this is seen as contrasting with the "theoretical." However, nothing could be further from the teachings of the pragmatic philosophers, for they believed that the best theories will be practical and that nothing can be practical unless it is undergirded by sound theory.

Although typically thought of as a twentieth-century movement, pragmatism actually came to birth in the late nineteenth century. It began with a group of thinkers who met in Cambridge, Massachusetts, in the 1870s to read and debate philosophical papers. With both a sense of irony and defiance, they called themselves the "Metaphysical Club," for most of them were skeptical of the rationalistic and dogmatic metaphysics of the Hegelians. Among the better-known members of this circle were Charles Sanders Peirce, William James, and Oliver Wendell Holmes, a legal theorist who would later become the chief justice of the U.S. Supreme Court. The members of this group were by and large empiricists, and many were influenced by the writings of Bentham and Mill as well as Darwin's theory of evolution.

In 1878 Peirce introduced the term "pragmatism" to apply to this new outlook in philosophy. He derived the term from Kant's notion of *pragmatisch*, which refers to principles that are empirical or experimental, as opposed to *a priori*. Accordingly, Peirce was interested in developing a theory of inquiry and a theory of meaning that would primarily apply to our scientific conceptions. At the end of the nineteenth century, William James popularized the philosophy and expounded it as a theory of truth with applications to psychology, morality, and religion. Consistent with these interests, James traced his own use of the term "pragmatism" back to its roots in a Greek word that means "action," "deed," or "practice." John Dewey developed pragmatism further, making it a comprehensive philosophy with implications for our understanding of nature, knowledge, education, values, art, social issues, religion, and just about every area of human concern.

The pragmatists' ideas arose out of a dissatisfaction with all the other options in philosophy available in their day: rationalism, empiricism, Kantianism, and Hegelianism. They opposed the rationalist's notion that the ultimate truths are eternal and necessary and that there is a certain way the world *must* be that we can discern through pure logic. Instead, the pragmatists approached the world with a sense of openness and in a spirit of experimentalism. The truths that are the most unchanging, they said, are also the most abstract and will not give us knowledge of a concrete and changing world.

Although their rejection of rationalism obviously aligned them with empiricism, the pragmatists did not think the traditional versions of empiricism were any more adequate. Empiricists such as John Locke and David Hume sought to validate our ideas by tracing their origins back to original sensory impressions. Instead, the pragmatists said it was not the origin of our ideas but their future consequences that determine their truth and meaning. In criticizing the classical empiricists, John Dewey says the role of our general ideas is not that of "reporting and registering past experiences" but to serve as "the bases for organizing future observations and experiences."[1] Furthermore, the empiricists treated experience as a collection of isolated sense data. According to the pragmatists, however, sense data are artificial, selective abstractions from the rich, integrated field of experience. Dewey says that we do not first experience sensory impressions nor even objects, but we experience "situations" or contextual wholes within which particulars find their meaning.

The pragmatists faulted both the rationalists and the empiricists for conceiving the mind as a kind of container that holds ideas. Instead of viewing the mind as a static entity, they spoke of *mind* as a name for the many cognitive activities by means of which we come to terms with the world. Ideas, as well, are not simply mental furniture, but are tools that we actively employ for solving practical problems. They criticized what they called the "spectator view" of knowledge, which pictures the mind as passively contemplating the world from a distance. Instead, the pragmatists insisted that having a mental life means being actively engaged with the biological and cultural matrix out of which our experience emerges. They agreed with Kant that the mind is active and creative, but rejected his notion that our mental structures are innate and fixed. On the contrary, the pragmatists said, our conceptual categories arise through experience and are changed by it.

The pragmatists agreed with Hegel that our ideas and the world are continually developing, but rejected the notion that this process is simply the unfolding of a set, logical pattern. We are not pawns of history, for our decisions and actions affect the outcome of things. Hence, they emphasized the future and embraced, in the words of John Dewey, "the conception of a universe whose evolution is not finished, of a universe that is still, in James's term, 'in the making,' 'in the process of becoming,' of a universe up to a certain point still plastic" (PC 25).

CHARLES SANDERS PEIRCE

|||

The Obscure Founder of a Famous Philosophy

C. S. Peirce (1839–1914) was the son of Benjamin Peirce, a distinguished Harvard University mathematician.* Graduating from Harvard with a degree in chemistry, C. S. Peirce worked as a scientist for the U.S. Coast and Geodetic Survey from 1861 to 1891. During this time he also taught intermittently at Harvard and Johns Hopkins University. However, his nonconformist personality prevented him from securing a permanent academic position despite his wealthy friend William James's efforts on his behalf. He was forced to devote a great deal of time to writing book reviews and publishing in popular magazines to shore up his dwindling finances. Peirce spent his last years in poverty and was saved from total destitution only by the generosity of James. While Peirce wrote volumes of essays during his life, with the exception of a few articles, his work never saw the light of day until his papers were finally edited and published long after his death. Consequently, he remained a relatively obscure figure to his contemporaries, and his ideas had very little influence during his lifetime. Plagued by ill health, living the life of a recluse with only the care of his faithful French wife, Juliette, C. S. Peirce died in 1914. Relatively unknown during his lifetime, his philosophy has merited a great deal of interest in the latter half of the twentieth century. He has had an impact on the fields of logic, epistemology, and philosophy of science. Furthermore, his highly original contribution to the theory of signs has attracted the attention of those working in the areas of philosophy of language, information theory, and literary interpretation.

The Nature of Inquiry

In the late 1870s Peirce wrote a series of articles in *Popular Science Monthly* in which he presented

*Peirce pronounced his name as *Purse*.

some of his seminal ideas. This may seem a strange place for a philosopher to publish, but it gave his ideas a wide dissemination and illustrated his conviction that philosophy should be brought down out of the clouds and applied to issues of practical science. In one of these articles, "The Fixation of Belief" (1877), Peirce attacks traditional epistemology for construing thought as the detached acquisition of truth. In contrast, Peirce emphasizes that thought has the job of producing beliefs. Beliefs are not just pieces of mental furniture that reside in the mind nor are they momentary psychological states. Instead, "our beliefs guide our desires and shape our actions" (FB §371).[2] They affect action because beliefs are actually habits or dispositions to act in certain ways in certain circumstances. For example, if I believe that a drinking glass is a very expensive piece of fine crystal, I will expect it to be fragile and will treat it gently and even apprehensively. However, if I believe it is cheap, easily replaceable, and unbreakable, I will expect it to be immune from harm and will be much more careless in handling it. Undergirding every action is a series of beliefs. In contrast, a belief that does not have implications for action is empty and dead. For example, I once saw a team of policemen inspecting a classroom building in response to a phone call stating that a bomb was set to go off at 2 P.M. Concluding that it was a false alarm, they radioed to headquarters that the building was safe and its occupants did not need to be evacuated. However, a minute before 2 P.M., the bomb squad came running out of the building and took up a position from a safe distance. Peirce would say that if they genuinely believed the building was safe, their actions would have been quite different.

As long as our beliefs are successful, we do not need to engage in inquiry. The bulk of our daily lives are routine, and we can fall back on habitual beliefs and their corresponding patterns of behavior that have proven themselves. For example, as I casually switch on my computer each morning, I am acting on the implicit belief that since my computer was in good working condition yesterday, it will work for me today. However, suppose I turn on my computer one morning, just as I always do, and the screen remains blank. My routine has been disrupted. I cannot continue on as I usually do; now I have to search for some solution to this new problem. When a belief is called into question in this way, we are unsettled, we are not sure what to do. Peirce describes this as a state of doubt. Doubt is "an uneasy and dissatisfied state from which we struggle to free ourselves." Doubt stimulates us to action and seeks its own elimination by means of inquiry, which is a process of finding the way to a new and more adequate belief.

Just as there can be empty beliefs, so there can be empty doubts. Peirce has nothing but disdain for the sorts of doubts Descartes rehearsed in his *Meditations*. Inquiry has no purpose unless action is disrupted by real and living doubts. Such doubts must involve an uncertainty as to how to act based on a conflict between old beliefs and new experience. At the beginning of his *Meditations*, Descartes claimed to have doubted whether or not the physical world existed and even whether or not his body existed. Nevertheless, he still got up from his writings to stoke the stove and he avoided touching the flames. Peirce dismisses his doubting as "make-believe" doubt (WPI §416). The goal for Peirce is not to have certainty beyond all possible doubt (something we will never find), but to have beliefs that are free from all actual doubt. "Let us not pretend to doubt in philosophy what we do not doubt in our hearts" (SCFI §265).

There are many ways of escaping doubt and achieving belief. As long as we feel satisfied, does it matter how we arrived at a belief? Peirce says it does, for ends cannot be separated from the means we use to achieve them. He lists four ways to achieve belief of which only one will prove to be satisfactory. The first way of eliminating doubt is what Peirce calls the *method of tenacity*:

> If the settlement of opinion is the sole object of inquiry, and if belief is of the nature of a habit, why should we not attain the desired end, by taking as answer to a question any we may fancy, and constantly reiterating it to ourselves, dwelling on all which may conduce to that belief, and learning to turn with contempt and hatred from anything that might disturb it? (FB §377)

This method involves setting rationality aside and clinging to my opinions with determination and perseverance. This is the approach of someone who says, "I know what I believe, don't confuse me with the facts." Peirce admits that having such unwavering convictions leads to peace of mind. The problem is that it produces tensions with the "social impulse" within us. We will eventually find that reasonable people disagree with us, and this can cause doubt to arise. Although the method of tenacity would work for a hermit who never had to discuss his beliefs with others, for most of us our beliefs must be fixed with reference to the community.

The second way of fixing belief is the *method of authority*. This is the method employed by a community of believers who allow their beliefs to be dictated by an authority or by an institution. It corrects the problem of the first method, for this one will ensure that my beliefs are consistent with my community. Peirce says that great civilizations, such as ancient Egypt and medieval Europe, have been built on this method. It produces a comfortable belief system, but only for those who are content to be "intellectual slaves." In effect, it is the method of tenacity raised to the level of an entire culture. A culture based on this principle cannot tolerate diverse opinions or contact with other belief systems. However, in such a system the specter of doubt lies waiting, for some will realize that their opinions are socially conditioned if they see that other cultures entertain opinions contrary to their own.

Third, there is the *a priori method*. It is better than the first two methods, for the person arrives at beliefs after a process of reflection. By the *a priori* method, Peirce does not mean basing beliefs on logical necessity, but embracing beliefs because they are "agreeable to reason." However, what is "agreeable to reason" is very subjective, for it is based on personal inclinations and sentiments. Peirce thinks there is no settled opinion in metaphysics, because each thinker who uses the *a priori* method has different preferences about what he or she personally considers to be beyond doubt. Hence, a belief system based on this method can end up being nothing but well-entrenched intellectual prejudices.

The problems with the previous three methods illustrate that what is important is not just finding belief but finding it in a certain way. What is needed is a method of fixing belief that does not depend on our human idiosyncrasies but on some "external permanency. . . . The method must be such that the ultimate conclusion of every man shall be the same. Or would be the same if inquiry were sufficiently persisted in" (FB §384). To answer this need, Peirce proposes the fourth and final method, the *method of science*. By this Peirce does not necessarily mean what is done with test tubes, but instead what could be broadly considered an empirical procedure. The fundamental hypothesis underlying this method is

> There are real things, whose characters are entirely independent of our opinions about them; those realities affect our senses according to regular laws, and . . . by taking advantage of the laws of perception, we can ascertain by reasoning how things really and truly are. (FB §384)

Although the method of science cannot prove this hypothesis, Peirce says the method will never lead to doubts about its fundamental principle, as do the other methods. Furthermore, this method has been successful in helping us resolve doubts. Therefore, when applied the method will lead to its own confirmation. Although the other methods make it possible to maintain an internally coherent system, they do so at the expense of being immune from all correction. In contrast, the method of science is error revealing and self-corrective, since it is tested against what is independent of our cherished beliefs or wishes.

The Theory of Meaning

The beliefs we seek through inquiry will only be meaningful and useful if they are clear. Hence, in an 1878 article on "How to Make Our Ideas Clear," Peirce set out a technique for making our ideas clear by making clear the terms in which they are expressed. He begins by criticizing Descartes's account of meaning. Descartes thought we can directly grasp the meaning of a concept within the recesses of the mind in a mental intuition. Other theories have treated meaning as a kind of ghostly "halo" that hovered around a word or idea. But these views make meanings too illusive or private for them to ever be clarified.

In response to this problem, Peirce wants to explain meaning in terms of our interactions with the world and the publicly observable ways the world responds. Accordingly, he offers the following method for clarifying the intellectual content of our ideas:

> Consider what effects, that might conceivably have practical bearings we conceive the object of our conception to have. Then, our conception of these effects is the whole of our conception of the object. (HMIC §402)

Applying his criteria to a concrete case, Peirce examines what we mean when we say something is *hard*. We say something (such as a diamond) is hard if there are many things that will not scratch it. The meaning of "will not be scratched" refers to a certain operation that may be performed with certain anticipated results. However, we do not have to actually perform the action to understand the meaning of the term, we just have to conceive of what it would be.

If the entire meaning of an idea consists of its conceived effects, then two ideas or theories that cannot be translated into a difference in practice, either of how we expect the world to behave or how we will respond to it, are really not two different concepts at all. To use a well-known example, the claim that "the glass is half full" and the claim that "the glass is half empty" are really the same claim expressed in different words, for each one leads us to expect the same set of conditions with respect to the glass. If we apply Peirce's pragmatic theory of meaning to Bishop Berkeley's idealism and Thomas Hobbes's materialism, we will find no real difference between them, even though they seem to make radically different claims about the world. Berkeley says the objects we perceive are nothing but ideas in our minds whose source is God. Hobbes believes our experiences are caused by material substances. Whether I am an idealist or a materialist, when I experience a moving hammer making contact with my thumb, I will experience pain. To embrace one or the other of opposing metaphysical systems neither adds to

nor subtracts from what is experienced. Thus, if the practical effects of Berkeley's theory are no different from those of the materialist's theory, then there is no disagreement between them. This is because "there is no distinction of meaning so fine as to consist in anything but a possible difference in practice" (HMIC §400).

Truth and Reality

Thus far Peirce has given us a way of arriving at beliefs and a method for clarifying the meaning of our conceptions. However, it would seem that simply having clear and satisfactory beliefs is not enough. We also want to know if our beliefs are true and if they are related to reality. In addressing this issue, it is significant that Peirce talks about beliefs far more than he does knowledge or truth. His reason for emphasizing belief is simple. If we list all our beliefs and then make another list of what we think to be true, they would be the same list. In practical terms, as soon as we reach a satisfactory state of belief, inquiry comes to an end. We can no more jump outside our beliefs than outside our own skin. Not only are the notions of truth and belief inseparable, but the notions of truth and reality are intertwined as well. To think of the *true* conception of X and to think of X as *real* is simply to "regard one and the same thing from two different points of view; for the immediate object of thought in a true judgment *is* the reality" (CP 8.16).

Initially, this view seems problematic. True beliefs are consistent with reality, but we always understand reality in terms of our beliefs about reality. How can we ever escape this circle? In defining reality in terms of the ultimate object of our beliefs, Peirce did not want to embrace the sort of subjectivism that says "reality is whatever *I* believe it to be." This view makes reality completely dependent on my conceptions and collapses into the method of tenacity. Likewise, Peirce rejects Kantianism, for this makes reality (in the sense of reality-in-itself) so independent of the mind that we could never know it. Peirce's way of avoiding both subjectivism and Kant's position is to say reality is independent of the beliefs of *any particular* thinker but is not irretrievably beyond the limits of human thought altogether. The notion of "reality" is a kind of ideal located in the future such that it is the object of that "final opinion" the community of inquirers will converge on if the scientific method were applied for an indefinitely long period of time. In this way, Peirce gives us a joint definition of both truth and reality:

> *The opinion which is fated to be ultimately agreed to by all who investigate is what we mean by the truth, and the object represented in this opinion is the real. That is the way I would explain reality. (HMIC §407)*

By defining truth with reference to community opinion, Peirce is not saying it is all a matter of convention. Instead, he assumes the scientific method is error revealing and self-correcting, so that if continuously applied it successively approximates the perfect truth and the perfect conception of reality. There is no possibility of an error, which in principle could never be detected. Given his theory of meaning, an error that could have no conceivable practical effects, no matter how long inquiry continues, is a meaningless notion. Hence, while you or I can be mistaken in our beliefs, it is inconceivable that in the long run the whole of humanity could not get closer to the truth. In this way, Peirce rejects the Kantian notion of the thing-in-itself that forever eludes our grasp.*

Fallibilism

It follows from Peirce's definition of truth that we have no guarantee that any particular belief will ever be immune from the need to be revised. This position is known as *fallibilism*. Peirce once made the paradoxical claim that the only infallible statement is that all statements are fallible (CP 2.75). He had to emphasize this point, for if we ever think we have arrived at an infallible truth, this would put an end to inquiry, which is essential to the self-correcting nature of the scientific method. The end result of Peirce's epistemology is not full-blown certainty, but instead the reassurance that at any given time we can find (1) provisional beliefs that work in practice thus far, joined with (2) a method of proceeding on to better beliefs. Thus, instead of searching for the "TRUTH," the cognitive pursuits of humanity need no higher goal than "a state of belief unassailable by doubt" (WPI §416). By "doubt" here, Peirce means real doubt, not Descartes's imaginary doubts. Although we may never reach the destination of perfect knowledge, we can at least know we will be on the right road.

WILLIAM JAMES

|||

From Physician to Philosopher

William James (1842–1910) was born in New York into a family where intellectual and cultural debates were part of the dinner table conversation. His father was an eccentric, mystical theologian and his brother was the famous novelist, Henry James. From the time that he was a teenager, through his university years, James traveled extensively. He studied science, painting, and medicine in England, France, Switzerland, Germany, and the United States, finally earning his medical degree from Harvard in 1869. James started out as an instructor in physiology at Harvard but his interests broadened out into psychol-

---

*Peirce was aware of Hegel's influence on him. Both see thinking as a process of moving from half-truths to fuller truths, and both see the end of inquiry as a convergence on some final totality where truth and reality are one. However, Peirce deviated from Hegel in significant ways. Peirce's method was empirical and not rationalistic. Furthermore, he defines thought in behavioral terms and roots it in a concrete, biological environment.

ogy, a discipline that was still in its infancy as an experimental science. In 1890 he published *Principles of Psychology*, one of the first textbooks in experimental psychology. Eventually he made philosophy his full-time occupation and taught in Harvard's philosophy department alongside such notable figures as Josiah Royce, George Santayana, and, for a brief time, C. S. Peirce.

James and Peirce

Although James and Peirce were committed to the same general approach to philosophy, there were some significant differences between their expressions of pragmatism. In spite of the fact that James shared with Peirce a training in the sciences, the former's interests were primarily oriented around the broader issues of morality and practical living. As John Dewey put it, "Peirce wrote as a logician and James as a humanist."[3] James saw the value of a philosophy almost purely in terms of its contribution to life as it is lived:

> The whole function of philosophy ought to be to find out what definite difference it will make to you and me, at definite instants of our life, if this world-formula or that world-formula be the true one. (P 50)[4]

This practical, humanist emphasis made James in great demand as a speaker. In fact, Peirce's pragmatism never received much attention until James popularized it in a series of lectures. Although James thought he was doing Peirce a service, the originator of pragmatism was appalled at how badly James had distorted his thought. Consequently, Peirce abandoned the term and dubbed his own position "pragmaticism," remarking that this label "is ugly enough to be safe from kidnappers."

The differences between the two pragmatists went much deeper than their style. When Peirce spoke of the "practical consequences" and "usefulness" of our beliefs, he was speaking primarily of the sort of public, empirical observations that would lend themselves to scientific analysis. For James, however, the consequences of a belief were to be understood in terms of the personal and practical impact it has in the life of an individual. This tended toward a much more pluralistic and even relativistic outlook, for the same belief could be "workable" in terms of the needs, interests, and life situation of one person but not to another.

The Cash Value of Truth

At times, James's exposition sticks closely to Peirce's position when he insists that pragmatism is simply a method for clarifying the meaning of our conceptions. However, James deviated radically from Peirce (much to the latter's discomfort) when he additionally presented pragmatism as a theory of truth. James is best known for the extravagant metaphors he uses to define his theory of truth. He says theories are "instruments" that enable us to "handle" reality. True beliefs have the characteristic that "they pay" or have "practical cash value." He defines truth in terms of "what works," what "gives satisfaction," or the "practical consequences" of our beliefs. Many nonpragmatists would accept all this if James were simply setting forth a *pragmatic* test for truth, a way of finding out what propositions are true. But James is not content with saying that "workability" is an indicator that a belief is true. Instead, he seems to be saying "workability" is the *pragmatic definition* of what it means for a belief to be true. Just as a hammer is useful if it enables us to relate to the world in a certain way (driving nails), so a belief is useful (true) if it lets us relate to our experience satisfactorily. Truth is not a fact in the world, but is a quality of satisfactory belief when we put it to work in our interaction with facts. "The 'facts' themselves . . . are not *true*. They simply *are*. Truth is the function of the beliefs that start and terminate among them" (P 225). A crucial aspect of James's view is that the rational and the emotive, knowing and valuing, successful beliefs and successful living cannot be neatly divided. He explicitly links our cognitive and moral endeavors:

> Truth is one species of good, and not, as is usually supposed, a category distinct from good, and coordinate with it. The true is whatever proves itself to be good in the way of belief. (P 75–76)

> "The true" . . . is only the expedient in the way of our thinking, just as "the right" is only the expedient

in the way of our behaving. . . . Expedient . . . in the long run and on the whole. (P 222)

In one of his most startling statements, James says that "Truth *happens* to an idea. It *becomes* true, is *made* true by events" (P 201). He makes a number of applications of this notion. In some cases, a belief is not true unless I act to *make* it true. If I am trying to break an athletic record, rally my political forces to win an election, or win the affections of another person, the hoped-for outcome is not yet true, but can be made true by my acting with confidence. In science, a hypothesis is merely a conjecture until put to the test, which, if successful, makes the hypothesis a verified truth.

James gives his critics ammunition with the vague, constantly shifting way he expounds his doctrines. According to James, we can say of an idea, "It is useful because it is true," or we can say, "It is true because it is useful." What is problematic is his claim that "both these phrases mean exactly the same thing" (P 204). But are these two expressions really equivalent? The first statement seems unobjectionable, for if a belief is true, then usually it will be useful, in the sense of helping us deal with reality. The problem is that the second half of his formula does not seem as plausible. Just because a belief is useful does not mean it is true, contrary to what James supposes. For example, in a grave emergency it may be necessary to reassure a little child that nothing is wrong, that there is no danger, so that he will follow our directions without panicking. If his false belief that everything is under control causes him to calmly make his way to safety, then under the circumstances, his belief was useful though not true.

James was continually assailed by his critics for reducing truth to subjective satisfaction. Certainly in many passages he leaves himself open to this charge. However, he continually complained that these attacks never hit their target, for they misrepresented his point. When James says a true belief is one that "gives satisfaction" or "works," he was not referring simply to immediate, emotional satisfaction in the short run. I may find it emotionally satisfying to believe that my checking account has a positive balance, but this belief will not prove satisfactory when tested in practi-

cal action. Similarly, any false belief that seems to work will eventually be discovered as unworkable. As James puts it, "experience, as we know, has ways of *boiling over*, and making us correct our present formulas" (P 222).

James agrees with Peirce's fallibilism that "absolute truth" doesn't exist except as the ideal goal of inquiry and the most we can hope for are truths that continue to work for the time being until experience causes us to revise them. The anti-pragmatist's notion of truth, James would say, is a truth he does not have and never can have, so it is not a viable alternative to the pragmatist's conception. James says that discarded theories such as Ptolemaic astronomy "worked" in its day, in terms of the problems to be solved then. In our present situation, we now consider the theory false, although we could say it was "relatively true" or "true within those borders of experience" defined by its own time (P 223).

In response to charges that his view is too subjective, James tries to provide objective criteria for truth. "True ideas are those that we can assimilate, validate, corroborate, and verify. False ideas are those that we cannot" (MT v–vi). Furthermore, although James is much more subjective than Peirce when he speaks of the search for true ideas as a personal quest for ideas that work in an individual's life, he never neglects the larger context in which our beliefs and our lives are rooted. "As we humans are constituted in point of fact, we find that to believe in other men's minds, in independent physical realities, in past events, in eternal logical relations, is satisfactory" (MT 192).

The Subjective Justification of Beliefs

There is a significant contrast between Peirce and James concerning the issues to which they applied the pragmatic method. Peirce was interested in clarifying scientific language by providing operational definitions of such terms as "hardness" and "solubility." But James was interested in wide-ranging questions that penetrated to the core of human life as subjectively lived. We can get an insight into James's thought concerning the personal and practical character of philosophical ideas by examining how he resolved a personal crisis early in his life. As a result of his years of studying science and medicine, James became morbidly depressed by the thought that human beings might be nothing more than determined mechanisms doomed to live in a closed universe where nothing escapes the domination of physical laws.

James recorded his struggles in a diary entry written in 1870, when he was twenty-eight and one year out of medical school. He apparently found relief from his torments in the form of a decisive philosophic commitment of the sort that Kierkegaard, Nietzsche, and Dostoevsky would have appreciated. James resolved that if he was to go on living and find any sort of meaning at all in life, he would have to commit himself to the thesis that free will is not an illusion and base his actions on that conviction:

> My first act of free will shall be to believe in free will. . . . I will go a step further with my will, not only act with it, but believe as well; believe in my individual reality and creative power. . . . Life shall be built in doing and suffering and creating.[5]

Although this was a turning point in his life, it would be a mistake (and some have made this mistake) to suppose James is simply saying, "Believe what you find it pleasant to believe," without any further qualifications. Certainly, when logical or empirical considerations can decisively resolve an issue, James would say our beliefs must be subservient to reason and the facts. However, he says that in some issues of vital importance logic and science do not clearly guide us one way or another, because the objective facts are consistent with different interpretations. In these cases, James offers us the following rule:

> Of two competing views of the universe which in all other respects are equal, but of which the first denies some vital human need while the second satisfies it, the second will be favored by sane men for the simple reason that it makes the world seem more rational. (MT preface)

The general argument that James uses throughout his works may be formalized as follows:

(1) *The impossibility of the neutral standpoint:* There are significant issues in life about which we are forced to make a decision for one hypothesis or another.

(2) *The insufficiency of reason:* Most of the important decisions in life are ones in which none of the competing alternatives can be conclusively proven on rational grounds.

(3) *The reasonableness of subjective justifications:* Since we cannot avoid making a decision about ultimate issues, and are left without the guidance of objective criteria, it follows that we are justified in making the decision on the basis of subjective considerations.

This sort of reasoning is the basis of most of James's discussions on issues such as freedom of the will, morality, and religious belief.

Freedom and Determinism

As apparent from the diary entry, one philosophical issue that concerned James was that of freedom of the will. In his essay "The Dilemma of Determinism" (1884), James presents the issue as the choice between two large-scale conceptions of the universe: determinism and indeterminism:

> What does determinism profess? It professes that those parts of the universe already laid down absolutely appoint and decree what the other parts shall be. . . .

> Indeterminism, on the contrary, says that the parts have a certain amount of loose play on one another, so that the laying down of one of them does not necessarily determine what the others shall be. (DD 40–41)

Having set out the alternatives, James first argues for the impossibility of the neutral standpoint. The two possibilities are clear contradictories: "The truth *must* lie with one side or the other, and its lying with one side makes the other false" (DD 41). Hence, because the issue is a fundamental one, we find ourselves living as though one or the other of the beliefs is true. Second, he argues for the insufficiency of reason on this issue. Concerning a particular decision, for example, science only deals with facts, with what has happened—it cannot tell us whether the decision necessarily had to be this way or whether another decision would have been possible (DD 42).

Finally, James indicates reasons why determinism is subjectively unsatisfactory. His lengthy discussion may be distilled into this argument:

(1) There are many actions in this world, performed by ourselves or by others, that we *regret* (such as acts of murder or wanton cruelty).

(2) Determinism defines the universe as a place in which it is impossible for anything to be otherwise than it is.

(3) If everything is the inevitable result of previous causes, then determinism implies that judgments of regret are in error, for regret suggests that things could have been different from the way they are.

(4) However, this leads to the totally pessimistic position that evil actions, such as murders, are necessary and unavoidable and should not be regretted but accepted.

(5) A determinist can avoid this total pessimism by saying that acts of murder are actually good (because they were rationally necessary from all eternity and serve some greater good). But we can only avoid pessimism at the price of saying that regret is bad (because it is irrational). On the other hand, if regret is good, then murder is bad. But both types of events are supposed to have been determined. So, the world "must be a place of which either sin or error forms a necessary part."

(6) Therefore, if determinism is true, then "something must be fatally unreasonable, absurd, and wrong in the world" (DD 50).

Having set out the consequences of believing in determinism, James does the same for indeterminism. If we choose to believe there is freedom or indeterminism in the universe, then there are real possibilities and our actions can make a decisive difference as to whether good or evil will triumph:

That is what gives the palpitating reality to our moral life and makes it tingle . . . with so strange and elaborate an excitement. This reality, this excitement, are what the determinisms [of all varieties] . . . suppress by their denial that anything is decided here and now, and their dogma that all things were foredoomed and settled long ago. (DD 64)

It is important to realize that James never claims he has refuted determinism or proven indeterminism. He has simply set out the practical consequences of believing in one or the other. As was true in his own life, we have the option to choose which vision of the universe we find the most reasonable and fulfilling to assume.

The Will to Believe

James applies this same reasoning to the issue of religious belief in his essay "The Will to Believe" (1896). Many wrongly thought that in talking of "the will to believe" James meant we could believe anything we wanted to. He later said he should have expressed his principle as "the right to believe." James was responding to an article by W. K. Clifford titled "The Ethics of Belief," in which this philosopher discussed the conditions that give us the right to believe something and when it would be immoral to do so. Clifford argued that "it is wrong always, everywhere, and for every one, to believe anything upon insufficient evidence."[6] James's account of religious belief rests on the assumption that no compelling evidence either proves or disproves the religious hypothesis. Thus, whatever position we take will not be based on hard evidence. James attempts to counter Clifford's conclusions by arguing that even without sufficient evidence we must make a choice one way or another on this issue, and it is reasonable to choose religious faith.

James writes, "Let us call the decision between two hypotheses an *option*." Options may be living or dead, forced or avoidable, momentous or trivial. A live option is one in which each of the opposing alternatives "makes some appeal, however, small, to your belief." A forced option is one "based on a complete logical disjunction, with no possibility of not choosing." A momentous option is one where the choice has important consequences for the conduct of life as opposed to a trivial one where the stakes are insignificant or when the decision is reversible. For most people, the question of whether or not beings from another planet built the pyramids is a dead option. I do not need to consider this hypothesis seriously, because nothing about it seems plausible. It is not a forced option, because I can suspend judgment on the issue, refusing to commit myself one way or another. Finally, it is not a momentous option, because whether I believe one alternative or another would not seem to make much difference to my life.

In the religious option, however, subjective justification is appropriate. Since philosophers continue to debate the existence of God, it is clearly a live option for many people. Second, I will either live my life with a religious perspective on the world, or by default I will live as though there is no God. Hence it is a forced option. Finally, it is a momentous option, because which way I choose will influence how I approach my life. When an option meets these three criteria, then it is a *genuine* option. Contrary to Clifford, I have a right to believe what is subjectively and pragmatically appealing concerning a genuine option when the evidence is insufficient. "Our passional nature not only lawfully may, but must, decide an option be-

tween propositions, whenever it is a genuine option that cannot be decided on intellectual grounds" (WB 95). Since James, like David Hume, does not think that rational arguments for or against God's existence are persuasive, the grounds for belief are to be found in practical considerations. "On pragmatistic principles, if the hypothesis of God works satisfactorily in the widest sense of the word, it is 'true' " (P 299).

Despite his impassioned defense of religious belief, James never argued for any specific religious view. He was content to say that the evidence points toward "some form of superhuman life with which we may, unknown to ourselves, be co-conscious" (APU 309). However, when it came to the nature of this superhuman life, he took the unorthodox position that the amount of evil and imperfection in the world suggests that "there is a God, but that he is finite, either in power or in knowledge, or in both at once" (APU 311). Concerning the question of whether or not good will triumph over evil in the world, James was neither an optimist nor a pessimist. Instead, he took the middle position of *meliorism*. This position views the "salvation" of the world as neither necessary nor impossible but as a possibility to be achieved by the combination of divine and human efforts (P 285–286). Hence, we are not pawns in a vast, predetermined scheme, but how the world turns out may, in part, be up to us.

JOHN DEWEY

The Ambassador-at-Large of Pragmatism

John Dewey (1859–1952) was born in 1859 in Burlington, Vermont. He received his undergraduate education at the University of Vermont and went on to complete a doctorate in philosophy at the newly organized Johns Hopkins University (where Peirce was one of his professors). After teaching philosophy at the University of Michigan for ten years, he accepted a position at the University of Chicago

as the head of the department of philosophy, psychology, and education. At Chicago he developed his ideas into a theory of progressive education and created an experimental elementary school to serve as a laboratory for testing his educational theories. His theory of education was widely adopted and transformed American school systems. In 1904 Dewey ran into conflicts with the university administration over the laboratory school. As a result he resigned and went to Columbia University, where he remained until his retirement in 1929. He was not content to simply express his ideas in books, but was an evangelist of liberal approaches to education, going all over the world to gain the largest possible audience. He lectured in Japan, China, Turkey, Mexico, and the Soviet Union. Furthermore, his works have been translated into every major language.

Dewey's Task

A glance at the multitude of Dewey's writings would make it appear as though there were two Deweys. The first Dewey was interested in technical issues in the theory of knowledge, which were addressed by his theory of instrumentalism. The second Dewey was interested in the humanities and dealt with questions concerned with education, art, value theory, and social philosophy. However, in Dewey's mind these diverse areas were linked together in that the theory of pragmatism deals with the consequences of our ideas, which have implications for every area of human concern. In this way, Dewey's philosophy synthesized the logical and scientific concerns of Peirce with the moral and humanistic ideals of James. Throughout his life, Dewey believed the split between science and human values was "the greatest dualism which now weighs humanity down" (RP 173).[7] For this reason, he wrote the book *Reconstruction in Philosophy*, which proposed a new approach to old philosophical problems. His ability to synthesize the best in his predecessors, as well as the broad range of the issues he addressed, made Dewey the most influential of all the pragmatists.

Influences on Dewey's Thought

Dewey began his career under the influence of Hegelian idealism and neo-Kantianism. Although he eventually abandoned the explicit doctrines of both philosophies, some of their spirit remained throughout all his writings. The most important influence on Dewey's thought was the theory of biological evolution. He was born in 1859, the year Charles Darwin published his theory of evolution. Dewey built his philosophy on the notions that we are rooted in our biological environment and our intellectual life is the result of our attempts to adapt to the changing world around us. Darwin's evolutionary model enabled Dewey to retain Hegel's developmental perspective while discarding its metaphysical shell. Likewise, just as evolution never reaches a finished state of perfection, so Dewey taught that we continuously modify our ideas as they prove inadequate and replace them with fuller, richer conceptions—without, however, ending in any sort of Hegelian absolute knowledge. After going beyond neo-Kantianism, Dewey still maintained that cognition is not simply a passive mirroring of the world, but is a matter of actively constructing concepts that will make our experience intelligible.

Instrumentalism

Dewey called his theory of knowledge "instrumentalism," to distinguish it from the other versions of pragmatism. The term captures Dewey's emphasis that ideas are tools for solving problems and for shaping our environment to our ends. Throughout his works he battled the spectator view of knowledge, which presents the mind as a closed room detached from the world, containing ideas the way a museum contains pictures. This image of the mind and its contents existing in isolation from the external world led philosophers such as Descartes to wonder whether these pictures (ideas) correctly represented what was outside or even whether anything was outside the mind at all.

According to Dewey, the Cartesian kind of account completely misconstrues our situation. In the historical evolution of the species as well as in a person's development from infancy to adulthood, our cognitive skills develop in response to a world that makes demands on us. Hence, when we begin to reason we do so as biological organisms that have already wrestled with our environment:

> *The function of intelligence is therefore not that of copying the objects of the environment, but rather a taking account of the way in which more effective and more profitable relations with these objects may be established in the future. (DAP 30)*

Note that Dewey is very cautious with the term "mind." Much of the time he uses it in reference to positions he rejects, such as Descartes's. When discussing the issues in epistemology where the word *mind* would usually occur, Dewey prefers to use "intelligence," because this term refers to a capacity that manifests itself in interactions with concrete problems rather than a metaphysical substance.

The core of Dewey's instrumentalism is found in his theory of inquiry. According to Dewey, all inquiry takes place within a specific situation in which our ability to successfully interact with our environment has broken down. Inquiry is a transitional process between two stages: "a perplexed, troubled, or confused situation at the beginning and a cleared-up, unified, resolved situation at the close" (HWT 106). This account is very similar to Peirce's view that reasoning takes us from doubt to belief. However, whereas Peirce tended to treat doubt as a psychological state, Dewey was much more influenced by theories of biological evolution and so gave the environment a much larger role. It is not just our state of mind that is indeterminate, uncertain, unsettled, or disturbed, he says, but also the *situation* has these qualities. "*We* are doubtful because the situation is inherently doubtful" (LTI 105–106).

Dewey gives a rather simple example of how a perplexing situation leads to inquiry and experimentation, which is worth quoting in full:

Suppose you are walking where there is no regular path. As long as everything goes smoothly, you do not have to think about your walking; your already formed habit takes care of it. Suddenly you find a ditch in your way. You think you will jump it (supposition, plan); but to make sure, you survey it with your eyes (observation), and you find that it is pretty wide and that the bank on the other side is slippery (facts, data). You then wonder if the ditch may not be narrower somewhere else (idea), and you look up and down the stream (observation) to see how matters stand (test of idea by observation). You do not find any good place and so are thrown back upon forming a new plan. As you are casting about, you discover a log (fact again). You ask yourself whether you could not haul that to the ditch and get it across

the ditch to use as a bridge (idea again). You judge that idea is worth trying, and so you get the log and manage to put it in place and walk across (test and confirmation by overt action). (HWT 105)

All of this sounds pretty obvious and simplistic. However, Dewey's story is used to support an enormous philosophical claim. He believes *all* human inquiry follows this same model. This claim includes not only the most advanced theories of modern physics but all our wrestling with ethical and political problems as well. Hence, all thinking is problem solving and there is no absolute division between the pattern of inquiry in the sciences, common sense, and morality. In every case, thinking involves a problem, hypotheses, plans of action, observations, facts, testing, and confirmation.

The Concept of Truth

Thus far, Dewey has shown that reason is an instrument or an activity for solving problems. The question is, How does the notion of *truth* fit in here? Dewey makes a considerable effort to avoid using the word *truth* in discussing his theory of knowledge. For example, contrary to what we might expect, in an entire book on the nature of inquiry (*Logic: The Theory of Inquiry*) the word *truth* only occurs in a footnote. His avoidance of the term can be explained by the fact that the notion of truth is burdened with its history, in which it has traditionally been used to refer to a static property of a proposition. However, this approach to knowledge is a long way from Dewey's notion of the active, dynamic relationship between the knower and a changing, problematic world. When he does speak about truth, he often falls back on Peirce's and James's notions of "successfully guiding action," "satisfying the needs and conditions evoked by a problem," "working in action," and so on (RP 156–157).

Dewey typically explains the idea of knowledge in terms of the notion of "warranted assertibility" (LTI 9). This notion captures Dewey's conviction that there is no final end of inquiry where our ideas will be perfectly adequate and immune from the need for revision. Whether our knowledge is complete or adequate is always a relative matter. We can always ask, "Our knowledge is complete or adequate with respect to what goals?" To ask, "Is a hammer adequate?" is meaningless, because a hammer is adequate for some tasks but not for others. Similarly, Newton's physics was thought adequate and almost complete until the end of the nineteenth century. It was an adequate tool for calculating the paths of pendulums, cannon balls, and planets. It proved not to work for other situations, such as predicting certain kinds of subatomic and astronomical events. Inquiry is a continual process of adjusting means to ends. But as new ends arise within a changing world, we need new means, new ideas, and new theories. Theories, like instruments such as the slide rule, are not so much refuted as abandoned when we require new and more adequate instruments to meet our needs.

Ethics as Problem Solving

One problem that has haunted modern philosophy is the dichotomy between facts and values. One position often taken states that science studies facts while ethics studies values. But if facts are located in the spatiotemporal world, where are values located? One answer has been that they are simply subjective preferences located in our sentiments or existential choices. Those who reject this subjectivism often think the only other alternative is to assign some sort of mysterious, transcendent status to values such that they float far above the world of empirical facts (in the mind of God for the medieval or in pure reason for Kant). However, Dewey believes this "two worlds" view of facts and values will not do:

> The problem of restoring integration and cooperation between man's beliefs about the world in which he lives and his beliefs about values and purposes that should direct his conduct is the deepest problem of any philosophy that is not isolated from that life. (QC 255)

If we analyze our experience, we will find that facts and values appear separate only because we ourselves have ripped them apart through a process of abstraction, creating an artificial gulf between them. The truth is, we initially begin with a world we value before we make it an object of inquiry:

> Things are objects to be treated, used, acted upon and with, enjoyed and endured, even more than things to be known. They are things had before they are things cognized. (EN 21)

If we cannot separate facts and values, then it is a mistake to employ one method in the natural sciences and another in morality, for human life is a single project of adapting successfully to the environment. "Morals is as much a matter of interaction of a person with his social environment as walking is an interaction of legs with a physical environment" (HNC 318). Ethical reasoning both begins and is carried out in the same way as any inquiry:

> A moral situation is one in which judgment and choice are required antecedently to overt action. . . . There are conflicting desires and alternative apparent goods. What is needed is to find the right course of action, the right good. Hence inquiry is exacted. (RP 163–164)

Although insisting on the necessity of an empirical theory of value, Dewey criticizes the naivete of the utilitarians' approach. Mill believed that the fact something is *desired* is what we mean by calling it *desirable*. However, Dewey questions this glib identification, for he says that "the fact that something is desired only raises the *question* of its desirability; it does not settle it" (QC 260). For this reason, he distinguishes sharply between "the enjoyed and the enjoyable, the desired and the desirable, the satis*fying* and the satis*factory*" (QC 260).

How then do we distinguish between what is merely satisfying (a subjective fact) and what is satisfactory (the genuinely valuable)? Taking his usual approach, Dewey compares the task of making value judgments with that of making scientific judgments. First, while science begins with observations it is not content to rest on what is initially given in naive perception. Without further inquiry, the earth seems to be flat and moving objects always seem to come to rest. However, science seeks to develop coherent connections between one set of observations and the entire fabric of observations. Similarly, the process of moral reasoning is one of moving beyond what initially seems good to judgments of value that fit the whole of human experience.

Second, scientists accomplish their goals by proposing experimental hypotheses that guide future actions and let us make predictions. Hypotheses that prove successful in all situations to which they are applied are those we will continue to use. Similarly, Dewey says, mere enjoyments become values when intelligent inquiry identifies those attitudes and ways of acting that help humans flourish in the long run. If we took an experimental approach to values, then

> all tenets and creeds about good and goods, would be recognized to be hypotheses. Instead of being rigidly fixed, they would be treated as intellectual instruments to be tested and confirmed—and altered—through consequences effected by acting upon them. (QC 277)

Hence, in one sense we can test moral beliefs in the crucible of experience. In making moral decisions, we proceed just as we would when trying to cross a ditch in the woods. We analyze the situation, imaginatively project possible courses of action, and evaluate the consequences of these actions.

If value judgments are like well-confirmed but always tentative and revisable scientific hypotheses, then moral dogmatism and the search for fixed, eternal, and a priori ethical principles are mistaken:

> A moral law, like a law in physics, is not something to swear by and stick to at all hazards; it is a formula of the way to respond when specified conditions present themselves. (QC 278)

Significantly, one of Dewey's most important statements of his moral philosophy appears in a chapter titled "The Construction of Good" (QC chap. 10). He says the "good" is not an autonomous entity, existing independently of the human situation, like an undiscovered planet waiting for us to find it. Instead, to say that "X is good" or "one

ought to do X" is a constructive proposal for dealing with specific situations to achieve certain ends.

With this topic we return to Dewey's evolutionary theory. Values are just one of the adjustment mechanisms in our lives that let us direct our behavior to achieve the best consequences. Furthermore, just as the theory of evolution showed that all patterns in organic life are changeable, so there are no fixed ends that have unending value beyond the way they fulfill the concrete needs we happen to have. Since we live in a changing world and are changing along with it, there is always the open possibility that we will have to revise our value assessments at a future time.

This leads to Dewey's notion of the *means ends continuum*. Any means can itself come to be valued as an end, and any end we achieve may become a means to further ends. In the final analysis, there are no ends-in-themselves; nothing has intrinsic value except for the ongoing process of seeking better means to ever-increasing ends:

> Honesty, industry, temperance, justice, like health, wealth and learning, are not goods to be possessed as they would be if they expressed fixed ends to be attained. They are directions of change in the quality of experience. Growth itself is the only moral "end." (RP 177)

Education, Social Philosophy, and Religion

Like all the great systems of thought (Plato's, Aristotle's, and Hegel's, for example), Dewey's philosophy is attractive because of its power to illuminate all areas of human experience. For example, Dewey's perspective has had an enormous influence on American education. In his day, education consisted of the rote memorization of a mass of factual information and historical classics. Dewey, however, says the goal of education should be to help students develop effective problem-solving methods and skills for social interaction. Hence, the emphasis is on process and not content, on learning by doing. With Socrates, Dewey says that the role of the teacher is not to provide information but to bring the students to the point of discovering truths for themselves.

Dewey's pragmatism also has many implications for social philosophy. With Peirce, he believes inquiry cannot be an individual, subjective project, but will succeed most as a community effort. Science can only succeed in the context of free communication, free action, and mutual dialogue that includes as many points of view as possible. Thus this sort of structure will be valued in a society founded on scientific principles in the broadest sense. Accordingly, Dewey gives a pragmatic defense of the American ideal of a democracy dominated by the values of freedom, participation, and inclusiveness. Furthermore, the biological, organic model that guides all his thought implies that the health of the whole organism is a function of the health of its parts. Hence, his educational philosophy supports his social philosophy, for society has the need as well as the responsibility to help each member become an effective decision maker in a changing world.

Finally, Dewey developed a pragmatic approach to the religious dimension in human experience in a 1934 book titled *A Common Faith*. He says our age consists of two warring camps—those who embrace some sort of traditional religion (each claiming that theirs is the "true" one), and those who are antireligion secularists. Both share the belief that the religious is identified with supernaturalism. Dewey, however, argues for the importance of the religious quality of experience, while claiming it can be freed of all supernaturalistic baggage. The adjective *religious* can apply to any experience in which the self is directed toward an ideal that transcends a person's narrow concerns. Thus, we can encounter the religious dimension of life in aesthetic, scientific, or moral experience, as well as in relationships of friendship and love. Dewey's naturalistic faith retains the word *God* to refer to the active relation between the actual world and the ideals we seek to embody in it. In this way he hoped to move beyond the divisiveness of narrow sectarianism toward a perspective that would retain the religious spirit, harmonize with science, and be a "common faith" shared by all.

The Significance of Pragmatism

True to the spirit of pragmatism, Peirce, James, and Dewey would not claim their writings have completed the task of philosophy, but they would claim they have provided the only method for moving toward that goal. What is the goal of philosophy, according to pragmatism? Dewey summed it up nicely in expressing the crucial test for evaluating his and any other philosophy:

> There is . . . a first rate test of the value of any philosophy which is offered us: Does it end in conclusions which, when they are referred back to ordinary life-experiences and their predicaments, render them more significant, more luminous to us, and make our dealings with them more fruitful? (EN 9–10)

Few philosophers call themselves "pragmatists" today. But this is not because the essential features of pragmatism have been abandoned or discredited. Instead, its major insights have become integrated into most of twentieth-century philosophy, particularly in North America and Britain.

Questions for Understanding

1. What were the points of disagreement between the pragmatists and the rationalists? How did the pragmatists differ from traditional empiricism?

2. In what ways did the pragmatists both agree and disagree with Kant? On what points did they agree and disagree with Hegel?

3. According to Peirce, what is the relationship between beliefs and action?

4. Why does Peirce reject Descartes's method of doubt?

5. According to Peirce, what are the four methods of arriving at belief? Which one does he think we should use? Why? What are his criticisms of each of the other three methods?

6. What is Peirce's theory of meaning?

7. How is Peirce's theory of truth? In what way does it also provide a theory of reality?

8. What is fallibilism? Why does Peirce think it is important that we believe in it?

9. What are the differences between James's pragmatism and Peirce's?

10. What is the difference between a pragmatic test of truth and a pragmatic definition of truth? What is James's theory of truth?

11. What is James's argument for the acceptability of subjective justifications for one's beliefs?

12. How does James argue against pragmatism?

13. What is James's quarrel with W. K. Clifford's approach to belief?

14. According to James, under what conditions is a person's religious belief justified?

15. What did Dewey take as his philosophical task?

16. Why did Dewey label his philosophy "instrumentalism"?

17. What is Dewey's theory of inquiry?

18. Why does Dewey avoid the term "truth"? What phrase does he use in its place?

19. According to Dewey, what is the relation between facts and values? What implications does this have for ethics?

20. In Dewey's philosophy, what are the implications of pragmatism for education, social philosophy, and religion, respectively?

21. According to Dewey what is the criterion for evaluating a philosophy?

Questions for Reflection

1. Given Peirce's theory of reality, why would he reject the following two claims? (a) "Reality is whatever I believe it to be" and (b) "We can never know reality."

2. What are the similarities and differences between Peirce's notion of the "practical bearings" of our concepts and what James refers to as the "practical consequences" of our beliefs?

3. Descartes claimed that we should not accept a belief unless it is free of all possible doubts. How would James respond to this criterion for the acceptability of a belief? What reasons would he give for his position?

4. Some suppose that James claimed that we have a right to believe whatever we find it pleasant to believe. Do you think this is correct? What would James think of this statement of his position?

5. In what way does Dewey consider making an ethical decision to be similar to the approach that a scientist takes in testing a hypothesis? What are the strengths and weaknesses of this sort of approach to ethics?

Notes

1. John Dewey, "The Development of American Pragmatism," in *Philosophy and Civilization* (New York: Putnam's, 1931), 24–25.

2. References to C. S. Peirce's works are in terms of section numbers of the following editions:

   CP   *The Collected Papers of Charles Sanders Peirce*, 8 vols., vols. 1–6, ed. Charles Hartshorne and Paul Weiss, vols. 7 and 8, ed. Arthur W. Burks (Cambridge, MA: Harvard University Press, 1931–1958).

   FB   "The Fixation of Belief," in *Collected Papers*, vol. 5.

   HMIC "How to Make Our Ideas Clear," in *Collected Papers*, vol. 5.

   SCFI "Some Consequences of Four Incapacities," in *Collected Papers*, vol. 5.

   WPI "What Pragmatism Is," in *Collected Papers*, vol. 5.

3. Dewey, "The Development of American Pragmatism," 21.

4. References to the works of William James are made in terms of page numbers. The following abbreviations are used in the text:

   APU *A Pluralistic Universe* (New York: Longmans, Green, 1916).

   DD   "The Dilemma of Determinism," in William James, *Essays in Pragmatism*, ed. Alburey Castell (New York: Hafner Press, Macmillan, 1948).

   MT   *Meaning and Truth: A Sequel to "Pragmatism"* (New York: McKay, 1909; reprint, Westport, CT: Greenwood Press, 1968).

   P   *Pragmatism: A New Name for Some Old Ways of Thinking* (New York: Longmans, Green, 1947).

   WB   "The Will to Believe," in William James, *Essays in Pragmatism*.

5. *The Letters of William James*, ed. Henry James (Boston: Atlantic Monthly Press, 1920), 1:147–148.

6. W. K. Clifford, "The Ethics of Belief," quoted in William James, "The Will to Believe," 93.

7. References to John Dewey's books are in terms of their page numbers using the following abbreviations:

DAP　"The Development of American Pragmatism," chap. in *Philosophy and Civilization* (New York: Putnam's, 1931).

EN　*Experience and Nature*, 2d ed. (LaSalle, IL: Open Court, 1929).

HNC　*Human Nature and Conduct* (New York: The Modern Library, 1922).

HWT　*How We Think* (Boston: Heath, 1933).

LTI　*Logic: The Theory of Inquiry* (New York: Holt, Rinehart & Winston, 1938).

QC　*The Quest for Certainty* (New York: Capricorn Books, 1929).

RP　*Reconstruction in Philosophy*, enlarged ed. (Boston: Beacon Press, 1948).

CHAPTER

31

Process Philosophy: Bergson and Whitehead

IF WE POLLED THE KEY FIGURES IN PHILOSOPHY, from its very beginning up to the twentieth century, the majority opinion would be that reality consists of fundamental substances that remain identical throughout their temporal existence. There are many varieties of this basic theme; the general approach can be tagged with the generic label of "substance metaphysics." However, the nature of philosophy is to question all taken-for-granted assumptions and settled opinions. Consequently, critics who advocate a "process metaphysics" have opposed this prevailing tradition. This viewpoint stresses that reality is dynamic and consists of a series of processes or events. "Process" here means more than simply that reality consists of a succession of events. It also includes the claim that creativity is fundamental to the nature of things and that genuine novelties emerge within the process.

Heraclitus, Hegel, and Nietzsche are examples of philosophers covered in previous chapters who emphasized the priority of change and temporality over substances and essences. In the twentieth century, Henri Bergson succinctly stated the core of

process philosophy as follows: "There is change, but there are not things which change" (CM 177).[1] Similarly, Alfred North Whitehead proclaimed, "The flux of things is one ultimate generalization around which we must weave our philosophical system" (PR 317).[2]

Our language is stacked against process philosophy, for the subject of most sentences is a noun to which we attach properties or activities. This reflects Aristotle's metaphysical view that the subjects of discourse are substances in which qualities inhere and that maintain their identity through time, even while undergoing change. For example, we say, "The carpet is blue," or "The carpet is fading," suggesting that the carpet is a fundamental reality that exhibits a color or loses it.

But maybe things are not quite as simple as they seem. Consider these examples: "The weather is becoming humid," "Public opinion is changing," and "Their friendship is solid." Despite our grammar, "the weather," "public opinion," and a "friendship" really are not "things." Rather, they are shorthand and abstract ways of speaking about a collection of more primary and concrete events and activities.

Humidity does not inhere within the weather—the weather is an outcome of those events that create humidity. When one of these "entities" is changing, a set of dynamic conditions exhibiting one sort of pattern is giving way to another set of events with a different pattern. When these "entities" manifest ongoing properties, this is because the changing events exhibit repetitive patterns and similarities.

Perhaps we will better understand the objects in our experience (rocks, trees, people) when we see them as having a status similar to the weather than when we view them as Aristotelian substances. We say, "He is in love," not "Love is in him," suggesting that we find our identity within a larger complex of relationships and events rather than the other way around. Turning to nuclear physics, scientists tell us that material objects are really dynamic collections of subatomic events. This has certainly given new insight to Heraclitus's claim that "All things come into being through opposition and all are in flux, like a river."

If this makes any sense at all, then it is worth considering how Henri Bergson and Alfred North Whitehead, two of the leading process philosophers in the twentieth century, sought to parlay these insights into full-scale visions of the universe. Bergson and Whitehead swam against the stream of the history of philosophy by emphasizing a process view over a substance view. However, they also stood out among their contemporaries for trying to do speculative metaphysics in a time when not only was interest in it decreasing, but also many claimed that achieving a grand vision of reality was impossible. Nevertheless, they were both convinced the human mind could arrive at a coherent synthesis that pulled together our best understanding of knowledge, reality, and values. Both had a spiritual affinity with the romantic poets in sensing a unity between human experience and nature. At the same time, they also looked to the sciences of biology, psychology, and physics for clues to an adequate metaphysics.

HENRI BERGSON

The Philosopher of Creativity

Henri Bergson (1859–1941) was born in Paris on October 18, 1859, into a cosmopolitan Jewish family. It was a good year for producing philosophers: this year also saw the birth of John Dewey, the great American pragmatist, and Edmund Husserl, the founder of phenomenology. As a student Bergson distinguished himself in science, mathematics, and literature. He first received public attention at age eighteen when he won a mathematics competition with a solution good enough to be published in a professional mathematics journal. When the time came to decide on his goals for advanced education, he wavered between science and literature. In the end, he compromised by pursuing a degree in philosophy at the École Normale Supérieure, one of France's most famous schools.

After receiving his degree, Bergson taught at a series of schools and quickly gained a reputation for being an exciting teacher whose passion for ideas was contagious. For Bergson, philosophy was not a narrow academic discipline, but a way of illuminating every area of human experience. This is indicated by the fact that in 1900 he published one of the few philosophical works devoted to the topic of the meaning of laughter in human experience. His philosophical articles and books began to attract attention, leading to his appointment in 1900 to the chair of modern philosophy at the Collège de France, one of the most prestigious positions in the nation. Bergson remained there for the rest of his academic career.

With the appearance of *Creative Evolution* in 1907, he achieved international fame. His reputation brought academics and laypeople to Paris from all over the world to hear him lecture. Before long, he had even become the darling of the social set and his audiences were packed with those who snapped up the latest daring fashions—even in the world of ideas. He appealed to those who felt alienated from institutionalized religion and yet who had no appetite for the chilly materialism that had been offered as the only alternative. As science continued to reduce nature to lifeless particles in motion, Bergson responded with the vision of a rich and value-laden world. The human spirit, for so long alienated from a nature stripped of its enchantment, could now return home and find the world was still as the poets had described it. Over the next fourteen years, Bergson had lecture engagements in New York and throughout England and Europe. Yet this adulation did not seem to affect his naturally modest and unassuming personality.

In 1921, at the height of his career, exhausted by the demands of fame, and suffering from ill health, he resigned his position at the Collège de France. Even in his retirement, the public continued to bestow honors on him, including the Nobel Prize for literature in 1927. For a number of years, the public saw no evidence that he was still actively working. Most assumed he had made his last contribution to philosophy. However, during this period of retreat he was engaging in an intensive study of history, anthropology, and theology. This bore fruit in 1932 with the release of his final book, *The Two Sources of Religion and Morality.*

In the following years he meditated in seclusion, constantly in pain from arthritis, but continuing to follow through on the ideas introduced in his last work. Although of Jewish descent, Bergson became attracted to the Catholic religion and might have become a convert if it hadn't been for the growing wave of anti-Semitism that was sweeping Europe. In the face of this development, he felt obliged to remain identified with the suffering of his people.

When France was taken over by the Nazis in 1940, the new government imposed a series of restrictions on its Jewish citizens. Although Bergson was granted an exemption because of his international reputation, he refused any special treatment. Furthermore, he renounced all state honors

he had achieved, to disassociate himself from the current government. When all Jews were required to be registered with the government, Bergson was again exempted. But although he was now an eighty-one-year-old invalid, he left his bed and waited his turn in the registration line, held up by two attendants throughout the inclement weather. This silent protest turned out to be his last, eloquent message to the world. Bergson died a few days later, on January 4, 1941.

Two Ways of Knowing: Intellect and Intuition

According to Bergson, there are two fundamental ways of knowing the world: intellect and intuition. His entire philosophy is permeated by the division between these two, competing approaches to epistemology. When we approach reality from one side (intuition), reality is opened up to us in all its purity and richness. When we approach it from the other standpoint (intellect), we are left with the dry dust of empty abstractions and fragmentary images. Bergson says that in seeking to know something the intellect moves around the outside of the object, captures it in symbols, and only achieves a relative perspective. However, intuition enters into the object of knowledge, does not depend on symbols, and attains the absolute (IM 21). The difference between knowing something through the intellect versus knowing it intuitively is like the difference between trying to know Paris through a series of photographs as opposed to walking its streets, smelling its smells, feeling its textures, reveling in its spirit, and dwelling within it.

Intuition is a simple act of sympathy that directly grasps what is unique and inexpressible in its object. However, the intellect, which proceeds by means of analysis, must understand things in terms of concepts, categories, and symbols. There is a twofold problem with analysis. First, when it represents its object in terms of concepts and their associated symbols, it is translating the reality, or even worse, replacing it with a representation. Hence, thought and language stand as intermediaries and, therefore, barriers between us and reality. Second, by seeking to capture the object in concepts and language, the method of analysis must reduce it to those qualities that are universal. In this way it falsifies the reality and turns it into a barren abstraction by stripping it of its concrete, unique features.

Although he frequently speaks very harshly of the intellect, Bergson does not wish to discard it, but only to put it in perspective. He explains that the distinction between intuition and the intellect arose as a product of evolutionary processes. Historically, the intellect developed to enhance our ability to cope with the environment. In the history of the species, the instincts were originally our fundamental mode of dealing with the world. As the instincts became self-conscious and reflective, they developed into intuition. The intellect is only a very late development in our history. It is a tool that arose to meet practical needs:

> We do not aim generally at knowledge for the sake of knowledge, but in order to take sides, to draw profit—in short, to satisfy an interest. . . . To try to fit a concept on an object is simply to ask what we can do with object, and what it can do for us. To label an object with a certain concept is to mark in precise terms the kind of action or attitude the object should suggest to us. (IM 38 39)

Hence, to serve our practical needs, the intellect needs to divide reality into a series of static moments in order to create conceptually manageable units. We assign names and labels to these moments such as "the weather" or "my headache," ignoring for practical purposes the fact that these are really abstractions from a dynamic and seamless flow of experience.

Kant claimed the mind imposes its order on reality. From this he concluded that we can never know reality in itself. However, Bergson says that this conclusion is wrong. "But because we fail to reconstruct the living reality with stiff and ready-made concepts, it does not follow that we cannot grasp it in some other way" (IM 51). This other way, of course, is intuition. Bergson agrees with Kant that the mind pours experience into its categories. However, unlike Kant, he does not think

this is an *a priori* necessity. Instead, we can reverse the natural tendency of the intellect and enter into the fluid stream of reality, allowing the mind's categories to be shaped by this process. "In this way it will attain to fluid concepts, capable of following reality in all its sinuosities and of adopting the very movement of the inward life of things" (IM 51). Bergson consistently follows his own advice, expressing his philosophy in rich pictorial metaphors. This feature of his philosophy held his audiences spellbound, while exasperating his more logically inclined critics.

Bergson has such an extraordinary faith in the openness of intuition to reality itself, he says that if intuition could be prolonged beyond a few instants, philosophers would agree (CE 252). The problem is, philosophy cannot function by means of a mute immersion in reality. Instead, it must base itself within language while carrying out a never-ending "raid on the inarticulate / With shabby equipment always deteriorating" (as T. S. Eliot described the task of speaking). Nevertheless, although the imperfections of language necessarily burden the philosopher, Bergson insists that philosophical discourse can have no other source of confirmation than what we read from the experience of intuition.

Bergson was continually charged with "anti-intellectualism" and "irrationalism." This was due to the fact that his propensity toward vivid speech led him to make some rather extreme statements. However, although he frequently seems to be opposed to science, his more moderate passages make clear that only certain approaches to science bother him. He remarks, for example, that the development of the infinitesimal calculus represented the triumph of continuity and becoming over disconnected and static approaches (IM 52). Likewise, Galileo's principles of motion overcame the fixed categories of Aristotelian science (IM 54). Bergson attributes the greatest feats of science to intuitive insights into the continuity and mobility of reality. His own metaphysics sought to integrate philosophy with the current biology of his day. Rather than dismissing science altogether, he says that in their maturest forms, "science and meta-

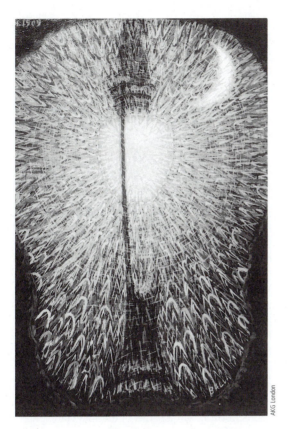

Giacomo Balla, Street Light *(1909). Influenced, in part, by the theories of Henri Bergson concerning the dynamic nature of reality, a group of Italian artists developed a movement known as Futurism. The Futurists' works were alive with motion and emphasized the dynamic relationship between objects and the environment and between the spectator and the work of art. In this painting, the artist Balla used multiple strokes of intense color to depict a dazzling shower of light rays, creating the illusion of pulsating energy.*

physics therefore come together in intuition" (IM 53–54).

Lurking in the background of Bergson's judgments about the adequate and inadequate ways of obtaining knowledge is a vision of the reality each method is trying to know. If philosophy can succeed only if it develops "flexible, mobile, almost fluid representations," this can only mean that re-

ality itself must be closer to a fluid than to a series of discrete units. Thus, Bergson's epistemology leads quite naturally into his metaphysics.

Metaphysics: Mechanism Versus Vitalism

The fundamental argument of all process philosophers is that if the basic units of reality are "things," we will never be able to explain how motion, much less novelty, are possible. Yet if process, spontaneity, and creativity are fundamental, then stability, order, and continuously existing objects can be understood as abstractions from this flux or repeated patterns within the dynamic flow.

If metaphysics is the study of reality, then it makes sense to begin with a look at that reality we know best. "There is one reality, at least, which we all seize from within, by intuition and not by simple analysis. It is our personality in its flowing—through time—our self which endures" (IM 24). If our own experience gives us a window to reality, then what sort of reality does it reveal to us?

> This reality is mobility. Not things made, but things in the making, not self-maintaining states, but only changing states, exist. Rest is never more than apparent, or, rather, relative. The consciousness we have of our own self in its continual flux introduces us to the interior of reality, on the model of which we must represent other realities. (IM 49–50)

Since Descartes, modern philosophy has wrestled with the problem of how we can know that our inner experience tells us about the outer world. Bergson believes that this problem gets off the ground by first assuming that we are islands of consciousness that are somehow isolated from the world at large. Obviously, however, we are a part of reality and there is a constant two-way flow between the inner and the outer. Contrary to the fragmenting perspective of the intellect, we find within our experience a *durée réelle* (real duration). When we intuitively make contact with our own duration, we are in touch with the larger stream of duration:

The matter and life which fill the world are equally within us; the forces which work in all things we feel within ourselves; whatever may be the inner essence of what is and what is done, we are of that essence. (CM 147)

Hence, contrary to Kant, Bergson thinks that there is no ultimate dichotomy between reality as we experience it and reality as it is in itself.

TIME AND DURATION

Bergson's theory of time and its implications for metaphysics was developed in his first work, *Time and Free Will* (French 1889, English version 1910). The phenomenon of time is the central thread throughout all Bergson's philosophy, for time seems to be the bridge that overcomes the dichotomy between the internal mind and the external world. In one sense, time is out there in the world, characterizing the existence of external objects, but it is also something we experience internally as characterizing our subjective experience. Ever alert to polar tensions within human experience, Bergson distinguishes two approaches to time: *scientific time* (also called "clock time"), and what he called *duration* (or "real time"). The first is time as an intellectual, scientific concept, and the second is time as we experience it and live it.

The abstract time of the sciences is thought of in spatial terms, as though it were an unbounded straight line whose points are temporal moments. When we try to appropriate time in language, we talk about "a point in time," "a length of time," "a short time." A future event is spoken of as something that will happen "further on down the line." In contrast, duration is lived time, it is known through intuition as an immediate datum of consciousness. Duration is not a succession of discrete moments but a flowing, indivisible continuum. Its phases "melt into one another and form an organic whole." For practical purposes, our intellect divides this flowing unity into distinct, measurable, conceptualized entities. Although this is useful, it becomes harmful when the artificially constructed, intellectualized world is confused with reality it-

self. The attempt to reduce the world to concepts is like filling buckets with water from the tumultuous, roaring ocean and supposing that if we just had enough buckets, we could capture and recreate the reality of the ocean.

THE EXPERIENCE OF BEING A SELF

Corresponding to these two ways of viewing time are two aspects of the self. There is the superficial self, a succession of psychological states, and there is the real self, which is an enduring and continuous self. These correlate loosely with Kant's empirical self and the noumenal self, but with one difference. Since Kant thought knowledge had to have sensory content and a conceptual form, he did not think it was possible to know the real self. We could only postulate it. However, Bergson does think we can know the real self through intuition by living in it, and thus we can apprehend it by a form of knowledge that eludes the senses as well as the intellect.

The behavioral sciences can study the self as a collection of discrete psychological states like an external object. The problem is that if we think the self is nothing but a series of distinct states, then we will think of the preceding state as causing the state that follows it, as though the moments within experience were like billiard balls setting each other in motion. In this way determinism follows from a faulty psychology. In contrast, if we view the self as a seamless totality, which is the way we experience it, then acts that flow from our whole personality are free actions. It is true that our actions emerge from what preceded them, for where else would they come from? However, each new moment synthesizes the past elements and adds to them, creating a novel unity that could not have been predicted:

Thus our personality shoots, grows and ripens without ceasing. Each of its moments is something new added to what was before. We may go further: it is not only something new, but something unforeseeable. Doubtless, my present state is explained by what was in me and by what was acting on me a moment ago.

In analyzing it I should find no other elements. But even a superhuman intelligence would not have been able to foresee the simple indivisible form which gives to these purely abstract elements their concrete organization. (CE 8–9)

Bergson acknowledges that freedom can't be proven because this would require analysis, a fragmenting process that would obscure the phenomenon of freedom. However, he thinks we will discover freedom in our own experience. When you study psychology, for example, it is easy to view *other people* as objects whose behavior is the product of causes operating on them. However, you cannot view yourself as a deterministic mechanism, because you experience yourself as a free, spontaneous agent who creatively responds to your experience of the external world. Having said this, however, it is possible to live at the level of the superficial self, passively allowing yourself to be acted on by social pressures or other determinants within your environment. But one can only become like an object by refusing to live out of the deepest, most authentic center of one's being.

EVOLUTION IN A NEW LIGHT

The year of Bergson's birth (1859) was the year that Charles Darwin published his theory of evolution in *The Origin of Species*. Obviously, Bergson's perspective has much in common with Darwin's notion that nature does not consist of fixed, static biological categories but is a continuous process in which one form of life evolves into another type of species. Bergson's 1907 book, *Creative Evolution*, was an attempt to build a theory of reality on the evolutionary model. However, he has a number of critical remarks to make regarding Darwin's approach. For example, Darwin's principle of natural selection claimed that random variations would produce changes in a species if they helped it adapt better to its environment. But any increase in complexity creates a greater degree of risk. If survival value were the only force at work, evolution would have stopped with the simplest of organisms (such

as the ant, perhaps). Furthermore, an integrated whole, such as the eye, could not have been produced by partial, random changes.

Although he rejected the mechanistic version of evolution, Bergson also rejected a teleological view that said species develop according to some predetermined plan, whether this is the plan of a Leibnizian God or a Hegelian Absolute Spirit. Evolution, Bergson argues, is neither mechanistic, in which events are pushed by deterministic causes from behind, nor is it teleological, in which events are pulled toward some future goal along tracks laid down in advance. Neither case accounts for the restless, creative striving of nature and the emergence of novelty. What harmony there is in the world is a harmony created on the run. It is a harmony continually in the making with the emergence of each new novelty.

To understand the process of evolution in nature, we can once again look to our inner experience for the key to reality. We find an *élan vital* (vital force) that is manifested in the self's continuous experience of duration. This vital impetus is present in all nature and is the cause of the emergence of novelty. Although the *élan vital* is ever surging and expressing its creative force, it encounters resistance from stable, inert matter and so must find new outlets through which to express itself. Like a vine that forces a crack in a wall to yield to its striving, the *élan vital* breaks through its limits and transcends the present stage of organization in which it finds itself.

As always, when he has done as much as possible to show that his theory corresponds to the facts, Bergson resorts to a metaphor to spark our intuitions. Bergson suggests we imagine a vessel full of steam at a high pressure in which some of the steam is escaping through a crack:

The steam thrown into the air is nearly all condensed into little drops which fall back, and this condensation and this fall represent simply the loss of something, an interruption, a deficit. But a small part of the jet of steam subsists, uncondensed, for some seconds; it is making an effort to raise the drops which are falling; it succeeds at most in retarding their fall.

So, from an immense reservoir of life, jets must be gushing out unceasingly, of which each, falling back, is a world. (CE 269)

Thus, reality is a dynamic process in which the inner spiritual core is the gushing, spontaneous, creative *élan vital* that provides novelty to the world. At the same time, a portion of this vital force "condenses" and leaves behind the world of order, stability, and matter as a residue. With respect to evolution, the emergence of novelties and new species are due to the creative, spiritual core of nature, while the perpetuation of ongoing species is the "falling back" process that results in continuity.

One might wonder if this vital force in nature can be thought of as a conscious activity. Bergson is cautious in answering this question, but he does speak at one point of "the consciousness, or rather supra-consciousness, that is at the origin of life." He even suggests the possibility of applying the term "God" to this creative force that is the source of all things. However, he never elaborates on these remarks, and not until his last publication on morality and religion did he work out their full meaning.

The Two Sources of Morality and Religion

Having exposed the opposition between the static and the dynamic in his epistemology and metaphysics, Bergson uses this contrast to illuminate morality and religion, the theme of his last important work, *The Two Sources of Morality and Religion*. When we look at the way in which morality has developed in history, Bergson says, we find two sets of phenomena: static morality and dynamic morality. One type of morality manifests itself as enduring moral traditions. This sort of morality provides the continuity essential for maintaining a stable community. This is static or closed morality. We find static morality in obligations and those structures that make society stable. A large portion of the self is a social self, so that even when society's direct pressures are absent, we internalize its values, which impinge on us.

The type of morality that is open and dynamic results from the moral genius and insights of creative people. Such individuals rise above the standard of their society to present a vision of a new, higher moral ideal. In so doing, they bring their society to a new level of moral awareness. Although dynamic morality originates in the great moral idealists and prophets, ultimately it flows from the creative source of life itself. "It is the mystic souls who draw and will continue to draw civilized societies in their wake" (TSMR 84). Whereas the morality of obligation makes its claims on us through social pressure, open morality solicits our convictions through appeal and aspiration. Open morality is the creative movement of life; closed morality is the fixed residue left behind. Static morality is propelled by the inertia of tradition and is largely something below the activity of reason, while dynamic morality transcends reason. Reason, therefore, mediates between the two.

Morality includes both "a system of *orders* dictated by *impersonal* social requirements and a series of *appeals* made to the conscience of each of us by *persons* who represent the best there is in humanity" (TSMR 84). They are constantly pulling in opposite directions, but intermingle in most societies, for society needs the strengths of each of them. Open morality infuses fresh life into the closed morality, while the latter makes the insights of the former a part of society's structures. In religion the same dynamics are at work. Religion presents itself as a historical and sociological phenomenon in which doctrines, traditions, and institutions prevail. Yet there is also the deeper, more personal level of extraordinary religious consciousness. The great mystics, prophets, and religious leaders represent this dynamic form of religion. The ultimate end of religious experience is

a contact, consequently of a partial coincidence, with the creative effort which life itself manifests. This effort is of God, if it is not God himself. The great mystic is to be conceived as an individual being, capable of transcending the limitations imposed on the species by its material nature, thus continuing and extending the divine action. (TSMR 220– 221)

A complete mysticism is a twofold movement that goes from a participation in the divine life to bringing this vision down to earth within the human community.

Bergson's Influence

Bergson's impact spread beyond the narrow domain of professional philosophy, and writers, social activists, and theologians all felt the impact of his ideas. However, though Bergson left behind a small number of disciples who carried on his philosophy, a well-defined Bergsonian movement never developed. For the most part, his influence was reflected in the writings of other philosophers who admired Bergson while eclipsing him, such as the pragmatists. Bergson anticipated themes that would find their way into different philosophies in the twentieth century. These include the priority of processes over things, a concern for the limits of reason and language, the role of evolution in explaining human nature, and the central importance of immediate experience.[3] Although the enormous fame Bergson enjoyed dwindled after his death, William James's congratulatory letter on the release of *Creative Evolution* indicates the admiration Bergson received from many of his contemporaries.

> *O my Bergson, you are a magician, and your book is a marvel, a real wonder in the history of philosophy.*[4]

ALFRED NORTH WHITEHEAD

|||

Although Bergson tried to integrate his philosophy with current scientific thinking, many philosophers still dismissed his ideas as hopelessly vague and poetic. However, process metaphysics surged forward with new vigor when Alfred North Whitehead (1861–1947) took up its defense. He had already established his fame in the field of mathematical logic, and when he turned to speculative metaphysics his colleagues were shocked to discover that this hardheaded logician had the soul of a romantic poet.

Whitehead's Life: From Mathematics to Metaphysics

Alfred North Whitehead was born on February 15, 1861, in Kent, England.[5] He received his university education at Trinity College, Cambridge, where, by his own admission, he never attended lectures on any topic other than mathematics. However, Whitehead says this was balanced out by the equally important education he received from after-dinner discussions with students and faculty on literature, history, religion, and philosophy. Later on, he said that it was his wife's "vivid life," her appreciation of beauty and capacity for love, that taught him to appreciate the moral and aesthetic values that lie beyond the domains of logic and science. After completing his studies, he stayed on at Trinity College to teach, and there he first became acquainted with Bertrand Russell, who was first his most distinguished pupil and later his colleague and friend.

Whitehead's intellectual career falls into three main periods. During the first period he worked on the foundations of mathematics. He and Russell found that they shared some of the same ideas, and this led to their coauthorship of *Principia Mathematica* (1910–1913). In this work they provided an elaborate demonstration that mathematics can be deduced from the principles of formal logic. It has been called "one of the great intellectual monuments of all time." In the second phase of his life, Whitehead moved to London in 1910 where he worked at the University of London and then became a professor of applied mathematics at the Imperial College of Science and Technology. Most of his work on the philosophy of science came out of this period. The third phase of Whitehead's life began in 1924. Although he was sixty-three, an age when most professors would be wrapping up their career, Whitehead started a new one and became a professor of philosophy at Harvard. In the early years of his career, his writings on mathematics, nature, and science were very technical in nature. However, his ideas gradually developed to the point where they could not be separated from philosophical concerns. During this remaining period of his life, he marched boldly into the center of philosophy, expanding his earlier ideas into a full-scale metaphysical vision of reality.

Whitehead's Task: Finding the Ultimate Categories

At a time when many of his contemporaries were growing skeptical of the possibility of attaining a grand vision of reality as a whole, Whitehead was a dauntless metaphysician. He sought to discover the ultimate categories that apply to all reality. His vision of philosophy was breathtaking in scope:

> Speculative Philosophy is the endeavour to frame a coherent, logical, necessary system of general ideas in terms of which every element of our experience can be interpreted. By this notion of "interpretation" I mean that everything of which we are conscious, as enjoyed, perceived, willed, or thought, shall have the character of a particular instance of the general scheme. . . .
>
> It will also be noticed that this ideal of speculative philosophy has its rational side and its empirical side. The rational side is expressed by the terms "coherent" and "logical." The empirical side is expressed by the terms "applicable" and "adequate." (PR 4–5)

Whitehead was not satisfied with any view that assumes the mind imposes patterns on the world that cannot be found within the world's own structure. Hence, he rejected both Nietzschian subjectivism and Kantian constructivism. Since science has been successful in finding general truths about nature, Whitehead argued, why not carry this process of generalization to its metaphysical completion?

The Method and Possibility of Metaphysics

METAPHYSICS AND THE IMAGINATION

The way to do metaphysics, Whitehead said, is to first start with a system of concepts that seem illuminating for some region of experience and then, using this "free imagination" and logical criteria, see if these concepts can be generalized and used to coherently interpret the other regions of experience:

> The true method of discovery is like the flight of an aeroplane. It starts from the ground of particular observation; it makes a flight in the thin air of imaginative generalization; and it again lands for renewed observation rendered acute by rational interpretation. (PR 7)

Whitehead started from several regions of experience from which he made his metaphysical generalizations. First, he was impressed with the developments in twentieth-century physics that made events and not particles the fundamental unit. Second, he took the dynamic, vital processes of biological organisms as a clue to the nature of reality. For this reason, he referred to his system as the "Philosophy of Organism" (PR v). Finally, his most common point of reference was our own, immediate experience. With Bergson, he believed that if we could have an accurate picture of what goes on in the flow of experience, we would have a window to the larger world of which it is a part.

To those, such as the positivists who doubted whether metaphysical speculation was useful or even possible, Whitehead countered that metaphysics is unavoidable. The only alternatives we have are either a metaphysics that is self-critical or one that is naively assumed:

All constructive thought, on the various topics of scientific interest, is dominated by some such [metaphysical] scheme, unacknowledged, but no less influential in guiding the imagination. The importance of philosophy lies in its sustained effort to make such schemes explicit and thereby capable of criticism and improvement. (PR x)

Whitehead believed that a metaphysical system had to adhere to the logical principles of coherence and consistency, but he also believed that intuition, not argument, is the final court of appeal. In effect, he enjoined his reader to "try on" his scheme, to view the world through the lens of his metaphysics, and see if it made sense of things.

METAPHYSICS AND LANGUAGE

One problem facing the metaphysician is the limits of language. This problem has burdened all creative thinkers, for, as Whitehead said, the history of ideas has been the constant "struggle of novel thought with the obtuseness of language" (AI 120). For this reason, many readers find that their first attempt to understand Whitehead's terminology is strenuous, if not frustrating. The problem is that Whitehead thought the concepts and their associated terms we have used for thousands of years to think and speak about reality have given us a misleading picture of its structure. This is because our conceptual equipment is infected with questionable philosophical assumptions and contains the sediment of philosophical ideas that have made their mark on culture. To use an analogy, it is as though Whitehead sees reality as circular in nature, but our current conceptual categories and terms are made to hold only triangular shapes. To overcome this problem, Whitehead had to create his own technical terms, using such peculiar words as "prehension," "nexus," and "superject." He also stretched ordinary terms far beyond their customary usages. For example, he said electrons have "feelings" and things such as chairs are "societies." However, these sorts of linguistic oddities are inevitable if philosophy is the "attempt to express the infinity of the universe in terms of the limitations of language."[6]

The Fallacies of Scientific Materialism

One factor that motivated Whitehead to shift his emphasis from science to metaphysics was that he believed classical physics was built on a questionable metaphysical outlook he called "scientific materialism." According to Whitehead, this view consists of the following fallacious doctrines. (1) *The irrelevance of time to the essence of things*: the physical universe consists of particles of matter whose essential identity and characteristics remain the same throughout their temporal duration. (2) *The thesis of external relations*: the characteristics of each particle are self-contained such that its essential nature is independent of its relationship to any other particles. (3) *The thesis of simple location*: at any given moment each particle has a definite location within space and time. (4) *Determinism*: the state of a given particle at a particular time is completely determined by its antecedent causes.

Whitehead was aware that developments in twentieth-century physics cast doubts on every one of these principles.* However, he was concerned not only to develop a metaphysics that would fit with contemporary science, but one that would also heal our sense of alienation from nature that began with the rise of the modern outlook in the sixteenth century. Hence, he attacked what he called "the bifurcation of nature." This results from the distinction that Galileo and Locke (among others) made between (1) the world of immediate experience, a world consisting of sounds, scents, colors, tastes, celebrated by the poets, and (2) the world of science in which "nature is a dull affair, soundless, scentless, colourless; merely the hurrying of material, endlessly, meaninglessly" (SMW 54). This dichotomy results, according to Whitehead, from the "Fallacy of Misplaced Concreteness"

---

*For example, a discovery known as "Heisenberg's indeterminacy principle" suggested that there is spontaneity in nature. This caused problems for classical determinism and forced physicists to formulate their discoveries in terms of probability laws instead of deterministic laws. Furthermore, the theory of relativity showed the interrelatedness of space and time, making time as much an essential feature of things as their spatial dimensions.

(SMW 51). This is the fallacy of taking the abstract entities of science (such as material particles) and mistaking them for what is most concrete and real. After quoting the romantic poets he says,

> We forget how strained and paradoxical is the view of nature which modern science imposes on our thoughts. . . . Is it not possible that the standardised concepts of science are only valid within narrow limitations, perhaps too narrow for science itself? (SMW 84)

Consequently, an adequate philosophy overcomes the dichotomies of mind-matter, subjective-objective, and human experience-science by recognizing that "the red glow of the sunset should be as much part of nature as are the molecules and electric waves by which men of science would explain the phenomenon" (CN 29).

Metaphysics: The Philosophy of Organic Process

EVENTS AS THE PRIMARY REALITIES

In contrast to the emphasis on substance in the history of philosophy, Whitehead starts with the conviction that *process* is the fundamental feature of all reality. To be actual, he says, is to be in process. Things that appear permanent and unmoving are really abstractions from the basic reality. To use an analogy, suppose you see what appears to be a log lazily floating on a pond. On closer inspection you discover it is actually a dense school of fish rapidly swimming together in one location. In your initial judgment you committed the "Fallacy of Misplaced Concreteness," for what you thought was a single, large, motionless mass was actually a very superficial appearance of the primary reality that was a collection of rapidly moving, individual fish circling around one point in the lake.

Even though reality is a temporal process, it is not one, indivisible flow. Whitehead's philosophy is atomistic, in that he thinks basic, irreducible, discrete units make up reality. However, these units are not the bits of matter of scientific materialism, but are *events* or momentary happenings. White-

head calls them "actual entities" or "actual occasions." Even God is to be understood in terms of this basic category. "God is an actual entity, and so is the most trivial puff of existence in far-off empty space" (PR 28).* A particular event or actual occasion could be, for example, a single vibration of an electron that is one among the many momentary vibrations that make up the series of events we collectively call "the electron." Again, another type of actual occasion could be a single, momentary event in your stream of consciousness (a twinge of pain or the perception of a flash of light).

According to scientific materialism, the spatial extension of an entity is crucial to its identity, but its temporal extension is not. However, Whitehead disagrees. To take an example from our common experience, the ultimate entities that make up reality are more like a sneeze, in that their temporal extension is just as important a feature of their identity as is their spatial extension.[†] If we consider half the time period it takes a sneeze to occur, we do not have a sneeze lasting half as long. Instead, we have only half a sneeze. The sneeze is not a complete entity lasting through several moments of time. Instead, its existence is possible only if it has a certain temporal duration. The fundamental units of reality, actual entities, have this same feature. "*How* an actual entity *becomes* constitutes *what* that actual entity *is*. . . . Its 'being' is constituted by its 'becoming' " (PR 34-35).

FEELINGS: HOW EVENTS ARE RELATED TO ONE ANOTHER

Descartes divided the world into two kinds of realities, minds and bodies. However, the problem with his dualism was that the two realities were so different it was not clear how they were related. The materialists argued that this showed

---

*The sense in which God (and other persons) are changing aspects of the world's process, and yet endure through time, is discussed in a later section.

[†]This illuminating example was suggested by William Alston in *Readings in Twentieth-Century Philosophy*, ed. William P. Alston and George Nakhnikian (New York: The Free Press of Glencoe, Macmillan, 1963), 117.

we need a unified theory of reality in which there are no breaks in nature. Hence, they reduced all reality to a collection of physical particles in motion and tried to explain mental events as particular kinds of material motions.

Whitehead agrees we need a unified picture of nature, but says the materialist has started with the wrong model. If you start with inert hunks of matter, having no interior life, you will never be able to explain the phenomenon of subjective feelings. However, maybe our metaphysics will be more successful if we start with our own experience of being subjective centers of feeling and then view entities such as electrons or crystals as rather low-level examples. Whitehead draws the extraordinary conclusion that *no entity in reality is devoid of subjective experience*. Accordingly, he describes actual entities as brief but unified, "drops of experience."

Returning back to our own experience, any particular human feeling can fall on a continuum ranging from those feelings we are fully conscious of (a headache) to those we are only dimly aware of and that are recessed in the background of our conscious experience (our feelings of our general bodily state), all the way down to unconscious feelings (the bodily experiences we have when asleep). Other sorts of organisms (such as a worm or an amoeba) have very low levels of feeling. Still, at a very low level, they are active, feeling, and valuing subjects. Even though they have no conscious awareness, they respond to their environment and seek out conditions conducive to their survival. Do feelings fade out entirely at any point in nature? Whitehead thinks not, for even electrons feel their environment and respond to it. Electrons are not passive entities mechanically imposed on by external forces. Instead, they are active centers of energy whose characteristics are substantially affected by the way in which they incorporate their environment and respond to it by becoming "excited," "agitated," "attracted," and "repelled." Thus the difference between the entities the psychologist studies and those the physicist studies is only a difference of degree. "The energetic activity considered in physics is the emotional intensity entertained in life" (MT 168).

This view is sometimes called **panpsychism**, the claim that everything in reality has some degree of mental life. There are obvious similarities between Whitehead and Leibniz on this point.*

The technical term Whitehead uses for an entity's perception of its environment is "prehension." This notion is similar to apprehension, except that prehending is a lower-level way of relating to the world that does not involve conscious awareness. Prehensions include all the modes by which one actual entity is affected by another, from human ways of experiencing down to the electromagnetic energy transmitted from one electron to another. A positive prehension is identical with a feeling, for it is the activity by which an actual entity includes a datum within itself. A negative prehension is that activity within an entity's self-creation in which it excludes data. To use an analogy, a block of marble is creatively transformed into a statue by chipping away some of the pieces (corresponding to negative prehensions) so as to reveal a new form within the marble that is preserved (corresponding to positive prehensions).

Contrary to the mechanistic picture of the world in which things are what they are, independent of how they are related to other things, Whitehead says that the unique character of each entity in the universe is a function of its relationship to everything else. Physicists tell us that each electron is affected by the energy transmitted by every other particle in the universe, although the intensity of a particle's effect, of course, is diminished the further away we get from it. Hence, the causal relationship between events is not an external one, but it is a relationship in which one event enters into the experience of another event:

> In a certain sense, everything is everywhere at all times. For every location involves an aspect of itself

---

*In fact, Whitehead was impressed with Leibniz's writings and continually came back to Bertrand Russell's book on this seventeenth-century logician and metaphysician. The main difference between their positions is that, contrary to Leibniz's view, Whitehead's actual occasions are not "windowless." They are open to the world and enter into one another's experience.

in every other location. Thus every spatio-temporal standpoint mirrors the world. (SMW 91)

For this reason, Whitehead rejects "the thesis of simple location" and claims that reality is a web of interconnected events.

CREATIVITY: THE ULTIMATE CATEGORY

Any metaphysical theory must account for the phenomena of causality and freedom, continuity and spontaneity, and multiplicity and unity. For Whitehead, the ultimate metaphysical category that characterizes everything that exists is the category of *creativity*. Creativity characterizes not only the activity of the artist, but also describes the activity of an amoeba, a plant, and an electron as well. Each new entity comes into existence by emerging out of a background of previous events, and forms itself by unifying its causes in a novel way, bringing a new synthesis into the world.

In Whitehead's metaphysics, *concrescence* is the temporal process that constitutes the existence of an actual occasion. "Concrescence" is derived from Latin words that mean "growing together" and "becoming concrete." This process of becoming a concrete actuality consists of the following phases:

1. As a new actual occasion emerges, it *prehends its immediate past.** Hence, every occasion is partly the result of causes acting on it in which it is influenced (but not determined) by previous events. The events that have just become past are the objective "data" to which the emerging event must conform.

2. As an entity emerges out of the immediate past, there is a process of *self-creation*. Even though the past moment shapes its successor, there are alternative ways in which the emerging present event can incorporate its inheritance. The objective content of a prehension is *what* is felt, while the "subjective form" is *how* it is felt. There

are many species of subjective forms, "such as emotions, valuations, purposes, adversions, aversions, consciousness, etc." (PR 35). As an actual entity takes into account the data of its past, it unifies them in a novel, unique way. In this way it produces a new synthesis that is not simply the blind, logical outcome of the initial ingredients.

3. When this state of "satisfaction" has been achieved, the activity of self-creation has reached its culmination and the actual entity simply is what it is. It has realized its unique identity as a distinct moment in the universe related to yet different from everything else. However, nothing is static in the universe, and as soon as the present moment is achieved it immediately gives itself over to its offspring. Hence, there is a creative urge within everything to thrust itself into the future as a cause of further events.

4. Finally, while presenting itself as an objective datum for the next occasion, the event fades into the past and perishes. However, the past is never completely dead and gone, for it has made a difference to the universe and in this way everything that happens achieves what Whitehead calls "objective immortality." These successive phases characterize the life span of every temporal event, including the most trivial physical event as well as the moments within our own stream of consciousness.

THE REALM OF POSSIBILITIES: ETERNAL OBJECTS

Thus far, we have a picture of the world as a continuous process, a rhythm in which actual occasions come to be for a brief duration and then perish as the next event emerges from them. But something is missing. For change to occur, possibilities must be actualized. Furthermore, we need a principle of definiteness, for we can say about any actuality that it is *this* but not *that*. We can speak about the world because things that are actual always manifest intelligible and repeatable forms and characteristics. To fill in this gap, Whitehead says there must be "eternal objects" or "forms of definiteness." These are somewhat like Platonic forms in that they are universals such as colors, shapes, and numbers that may be concep-

---

*To give a rough indication of what he means by "immediate past," Whitehead says "it is that portion of our past lying between a tenth of a second and a half second ago" (AI 181).

tually intuited. The process of becoming actual involves the selection and exclusion of forms from among this domain of possibilities. Hence, some forms become part of an event and others not. Whitehead says that eternal objects "ingress" into actual entities (a concept similar to Plato's notion of "participation"). Since an actual entity may be simultaneously definite in many ways, it must be able to manifest more than one eternal object.

ENDURING OBJECTS: SOCIETIES OF ACTUAL ENTITIES

The important question that now arises is, How do we get from the spatially and temporally minute actual entities making up reality to the everyday objects that we see around us? The answer is that the larger entities that make up our commonsense world (rocks, chairs, trees, dogs, human beings) are not irreducible individual entities, but are groups or "societies" of actual entities. Contrary to common sense, they are not "things" but are continuing, repeated patterns within the temporal process. At any given point in time, a physical object (a rock) is the collection of subatomic events that are occurring within it, whereas a biological organism (a tree or human) is an organized collection of many individual cells, each with their own individual experiences and activities. From the temporal perspective, an object that endures through a span of time is really a series of actual occasions who come into being and perish while maintaining a stream of continuity by passing on their characteristics to the next emerging occasion.

The difference between organic and inorganic objects is the way they are organized. A rock is simply an aggregate. There is only a loose connection between its parts. In contrast, a plant, such as a tree, is like a democracy (AI 206). Its parts are mutually interdependent and what happens to one part will affect the whole society. A high-level organism, such as a human being, is more like a monarchy, for it is an intimately related society of cells organized and directed by a dominant actual entity (the mind) that imparts its subjective aims throughout the smaller entities composing the organism.

THE MIND–BODY PROBLEM

Whitehead offers a distinctive solution to the classic mind–body problem. Previously, the main options were dualism, materialism, and idealism: the mind and body were viewed as two completely different substances (Descartes), or the mind was reduced to bodily motions (Hobbes), or physical bodies were reduced to mental ideas (Berkeley). In Whitehead's view, however, there are neither pure mental substances nor pure physical substances. These are abstractions from the more fundamental reality, which is the series of actual occasions, each of which is a continuum having a mental pole and a physical pole.

> No actual entity is devoid of either pole; though their relative importance differs in different actual entities. . . .

> Thus, an actual entity is essentially dipolar, with its physical and mental poles; and even the physical world cannot be properly understood without reference to its other side, which is the complex of mental operations. (PR 366)

In other words, in each part of reality there is that aspect (the physical pole) that tends to conform to the patterns of its immediate past, is passive, and causally determined. There is also that aspect (the mental pole) that is creative, active, and self-determining.

In nonliving beings, the mental pole is negligible, for it is "canalized into slavish conformity. It is merely the appetition towards, or from, whatever in fact already is" (FR 33). For example, the primary mental activity of a crystal consists of resisting the intrusion of novelty by continuing the patterns of the past (the crystal simply persists) or allowing them to fade away (the crystal disintegrates), but it does not introduce anything new. The apparent stability of physical objects results from the fact that they are collections of events whose diversity is averaged out at the level of the totality.

In complex organisms such as humans, the mental pole predominates. This allows us to creatively and subjectively respond to our causal influences, giving us the capacity to respond to a wider range of possibilities, and thereby producing greater amounts of diversity. If the mental and the physical are two poles of the same continuum, then nature is not divided into separate compartments (mind matter, organic inorganic), but is a unified reality.

> In a sense, the difference between a living organism and the inorganic environment is only a question of degree; but it is a difference of degree which makes all the difference—in effect, it is a difference of quality. (PR 271)

Whitehead's Natural Theology

GOD AND THE HARMONY OF THE WORLD

Although many of the aspects of nature can be explained by the categories introduced thus far, Whitehead believes something is still missing. There must be a principle of order. If all actualities exercise some degree of freedom, their unbridled creativity would produce a tumult of random occurrences without any direction or coherence. For this reason, Whitehead introduces a version of the teleological argument (the argument from design). The harmony in the world is explained by the activity of God. "The immanence of God gives reason for the belief that pure chaos is intrinsically impossible" (PR 169). To achieve a definite form, each emerging actual occasion must draw on the realm of possibilities (the eternal objects). But possibilities are abstract and provide no agency for introducing themselves into the actual world. God is the agency that mediates between the sphere of possibilities and the process of the world.

A GOD IN PROCESS

Whitehead's God is very different from the God of classical theism we find in philosopher-theologians such as Augustine, Aquinas, and Leibniz. Historically, the development of Christian theology drew not only on the biblical tradition, but also on Greek conceptions. The Greeks (Plato is a prime example) tended to depreciate becoming. What was immutable and free of influence from others was considered superior to what was changing and affected by others. In assimilating this Greek prejudice, traditional Christian theism held that God was a radically different sort of being from the world, for he was thought to be completely independent, fully actualized, and, therefore, unchanging. Whitehead, however, says that God has the same metaphysical character as any other entity. "God is not to be treated as an exception to all metaphysical principles, invoked to save their collapse. He is their chief exemplification" (PR 521).

God's nature is dipolar, consisting of two aspects. First, there is his *primordial nature*. This aspect of God is eternal, fully complete, unchanging, and the ground of all the possibilities in the world. This sphere of possibilities, the realm of eternal objects, exists in the sense that it is comprehended by God as part of his nature. Hence, God "does not create eternal objects; for his nature requires them in the same degree that they require him" (PR 392). But Whitehead says that if this was the whole of God's nature, then he would be static, wholly apart from the world, and unable to value, to love, or to interact creatively with a changing world. Traditional Christian theists would agree that the world is in process and that God relates to it, but at the same time they try to hold onto God's immutability and independence. According to Whitehead, however, this is a contradiction, for to relate to something is to be affected by it. Hence, in knowing the world and loving it, God is affected by it and changes as it changes.

The God of process philosophy is immanent within the world's process and intimate with it. This temporal, relative, dependent, and changing aspect of God is what Whitehead calls God's *consequent nature*. To say that God has an unchanging primordial nature and a changing, consequent nature is not to say that God is divided into parts. Imagine a circle on a computer screen that maintains its shape while changing color from red to blue to green as you press the keys on the keyboard. One aspect of the figure, its circularity, is unchanging and unaffected by your input. But this abstract, unchanging aspect is actualized and manifested through the successive changes of color in response to your activities. The fact that the world and God are interactive means that "it is as true to say that God creates the World, as that the World creates God" (PR 528).

Whitehead says the consequent nature of God is enriched by his prehensions of the temporal world. He is the repository of all value achieved in this world. No event is ever totally lost even though it perishes into the past, for every event achieves "objective immortality" by contributing to God's being. "The consequent nature of God is his judgment on the world. He saves the world as it passes into the immediacy of his own life" (PR 525).

Strictly speaking, Whitehead's view is not theism, for he denies that God is transcendent to the world. "[God] is not *before* all creation, but *with* all creation" (PR 521). Nor is his view pantheism—the claim that God and the world are identical. In contrast to pantheism, Whitehead's God is an independent entity that interacts with the world. Instead, Whitehead's position is commonly called **panentheism**. This is the view that God includes the world in his being (since he is affected by every event within it) at the same time that he is more than the events in the world (God has his own unique aims and actions). Thus, we can consider the world "God's body." Looked at in this way, God's experience is analogous to yours, for your experience includes the experiences of all the cells in your body. At the same time, Whitehead would say that your thoughts, values, decisions are something more than the physical processes in your body.

GOD'S INFLUENCE ON THE WORLD

Whitehead provides a unique account of how God causally influences the world. A key feature of Whitehead's position is the conviction that God cannot violate the integrity or the freedom of his creatures. He cannot use his sheer power to impose his will on the world, for then every creature's actions (including human actions) would no longer belong to that creature but would simply be God's actions. Whitehead proposes that instead of controlling events through brute force, God allows the world to feel his influence through persuasion. "He is the poet of the world, with tender patience leading it by his vision of truth, beauty, and goodness" (PR 526).

God is an immanent presence in the emergence of every actual entity. "Thus each temporal occasion embodies God, and is embodied in God" (PR 529). In every moment within the history of an electron or a human being, we are continually prehending God, even though we are not fully aware of this (except, perhaps, in moments of mystical insight). As an actual entity is being formed, God presents to it those possibilities or eternal objects that are relevant to its situation and that will maximize the realization of its potential. Thus, when a snowflake forms it can represent an unlimited number of geometrical forms, but a snowflake will never take the shape of a kangaroo. In this way, there is both order and spontaneity in the changing world as the result of God selecting and presenting possibilities for each entity to realize. In doing so, each emerging actual occasion "receives that initial aim from which its self-causation starts" (PR 374):

> [God] is the lure for feeling, the eternal urge of desire. His particular relevance to each creative act, as it arises from its own conditioned standpoint in the world, constitutes him the initial "object of desire" establishing the initial phase of each subjective aim. (PR 522)

Thus, although Whitehead's God does not transcend the world, he does transcend every other actual entity within the world.

THE PROBLEM OF EVIL

Every metaphysical system that postulates God's existence must come to terms with the problem of evil. Whitehead does not try to explain the problem away by saying that evil is only "apparent" or that it is always a stepping-stone on the way to a greater good. For him, evil is an irreducibly real presence in the world. God is continually enticing the world to fulfill his purposes, which always involves producing the greatest intensity of enjoyment and value. However, as discussed, finite actualities are not compelled to conform to his will. Thus, each entity, from a human being to a biological cell, has the freedom to resist God's persuasion and can fail to conform to his aims. "So far as the conformity is incomplete, there is evil in the world" (RM 60). The problem is, a greater capacity for good is always correlated with a greater capacity for evil. If there were no conscious beings, there would be no suffering in the world. However, such a world would be of minimal value compared to ours. When God seeks to maximize the good by supporting his creatures' capacity for freedom and creativity, he risks that they will use their powers to resist his desire for harmony. Nevertheless, God is not the passive spectator of the world, he is a God in process. "God is the great companion—the fellow-sufferer who understands" (PR 532). He is actively involved in his creation and is working with us to increase both his and our fullest satisfaction. However, "there is no totality which is the harmony of all perfections" (AI 276). There is always more for God and us to do, and there will always be values that have not yet been realized.

The Impact of Process Philosophy

Many philosophers (as well as writers, scientists, artists, historians, sociologists, and others) were inspired by the majestic vision, if not the details of Bergson's and Whitehead's philosophies. The process philosophers had much in common with the pragmatists in viewing philosophy as the search for a unifying perspective that would incorporate the full range of human experience. Both groups of philosophers tried to give us a sense of the whole and our relationship to it, which can serve as a basis for integrating our aesthetic, moral, and spiritual values into the nature of the universe. Particularly Whitehead sought to do this in a way consistent with contemporary physics.

Bergson and Whitehead boldly kept alive the project of speculative metaphysics in a time when it had fallen into disrepute. However, while appreciating this point, more traditional metaphysicians argued that the process view that reality is a flow of momentary events did not provide the stability necessary to make the world intelligible. On an even more practical level, critics claimed that process philosophy does not provide the category

of "person" with enough continuity through time to account for the notion of moral responsibility. Traditional philosophical theologians accused Whitehead's God of being a mere "godling," a relatively weak, finite deity, buffeted about by causal influences while bobbing in the flow of time, and lacking the sovereignty, power, and transcendence of the God of traditional theism.

A group of philosophers who composed the movement known as *analytic philosophy* did not quibble over the details of process philosophy, for they thought the quest to know the ultimate nature of reality was doomed from the start. They claimed that philosophy simply cannot answer all our questions and that we must lower our expectations, seeking only to establish humble bits of truth that can be decisively verified through the methods of logic and science. The analysts thought Bergson's method of intuition and Whitehead's "play of a free imagination" did not give us the ultimate categories for understanding our world. Instead, these metaphysicians provided inspiring but cognitively barren, emotional poetry. Even Bertrand Russell, who had collaborated with Whitehead on the logical foundations of mathematics, said about his friend's later work, "I must confess that the metaphysical speculations of Whitehead are somewhat strange to me."[7] In the next chapter, on analytic philosophy, therefore, we must shift gears and look at a radically different conception of the goals of philosophy.

Questions for Understanding

1. What is the main difference between substance metaphysics and process metaphysics?

2. What are the two ways of knowing the world, according to Bergson? How are they different?

3. According to Bergson, what is the one reality that we know directly or "seize from within"? What does this window to reality reveal to us?

4. What distinction does Bergson make between "scientific time" and "duration"?

5. What are the two aspects of the self in Bergson's philosophy? How is this distinction similar to and different from the one Kant

makes? What is Bergson's view of psychological determinism?

6. In what way is Bergson's metaphysics similar to yet different from Charles Darwin's evolutionary view?

7. What is the *élan vital*? What sorts of phenomena does it explain?

8. What is the difference between static morality and dynamic morality in Bergson's ethics? Why are both important?

9. In your own words, describe what Whitehead took to be the task of speculative philosophy.

10. According to Whitehead, what is the role of the imagination in metaphysics?

11. What are the four fallacies of scientific materialism according to Whitehead?

12. What does Whitehead mean by the "Fallacy of Misplaced Concreteness"?

13. What are actual occasions and why does Whitehead think they are the primary units of reality?

14. How does Whitehead attempt to avoid Descartes's dualism without lapsing into scientific materialism?

15. What is panpsychism? Why is this an apt name for Whitehead's metaphysics? What is his surprising thesis concerning feelings?

16. What does Whitehead mean by "prehension"?

17. What does "concrescence" mean? What are the four phases of becoming a concrete actuality?

18. What are eternal objects? What role do they play in the world?

19. What are some examples of "societies" of actual objects?

20. What is Whitehead's unique solution to the mind-body problem?

21. What is Whitehead's argument for God?

22. What does Whitehead mean by his distinction between God's primordial nature and his consequent nature?

23. How is Whitehead's panentheism different from both theism and pantheism?

24. What is Whitehead's view of how God causally influences the world?

25. How does Whitehead address the problem of evil?

Questions for Reflection

1. Using Bergson's categories, which do you trust more, intuition or intellect? Why?

2. Do you agree or disagree with Bergson that the self as studied by science is an abstraction or distortion of the self that is lived through in subjective experience?

3. In what way is it true to say "Both Bergson and Whitehead view the world on the model of biology than on the model of a machine"?

4. In what ways is Whitehead's philosophy an attempt to reconcile the scientific and romantic views of the world?

5. Do you think Whitehead's view that our subjective experience and relation to the world differs only in degree from that of an electron is plausible?

6. What does Whitehead mean when he says "it is as true to say that God creates the World as that the World creates God"?

7. Do you think that Bergson's and Whitehead's project of trying to arrive at a comprehensive metaphysical vision of the universe is possible or worthwhile?

Notes

1. References to Henri Bergson's works are made using the following abbreviations:

CE   *Creative Evolution*, trans. A. Mitchell (New York: Holt, Rinehart & Winston, 1911).

CM   *The Creative Mind*, trans. Mabelle L. Andison (New York: Philosophical Library, 1946).

IM   *Introduction to Metaphysics*, trans. T. E. Hulme, rev. ed. (Indianapolis: Library of Liberal Arts, Bobbs-Merrill, 1955).

TFW   *Time and Free Will*, trans. F. L. Pogson (New York: Macmillan, 1913).

TSMR *The Two Sources of Morality and Religion*, trans. R. Ashley Audra and Cloudesley Brereton (Notre Dame: University of Notre Dame Press, 1977).

2. Quotations from the works by Whitehead are referenced within the text using the following abbreviations. The numbers in the reference refer to page numbers.

   AI *Adventures of Ideas* (New York: The Free Press, 1961).

   CN *The Concept of Nature* (Cambridge, England: Cambridge University Press, 1964).

   FR *The Function of Reason* (Boston: Beacon Press, 1958).

   MT *Modes of Thought* (New York: The Free Press, 1966).

   PR *Process and Reality*, corrected ed., ed. David Ray Griffin and Donald W. Sherburne (New York: The Free Press, 1978). The page numbers of this work are given using the pagination of the original 1957 Macmillan edition, which are also provided in brackets in the 1978 corrected version.

   RM *Religion in the Making* (Cleveland: Meridian Books, World Publishing, 1954).

   SMW *Science and the Modern World* (New York: The Free Press, 1953).

3. These points have been made by William Alston in *Readings in Twentieth-Century Philosophy*, ed. William P. Alston and George Nakhnikian (New York: The Free Press, Macmillan, 1963), 56.

4. *The Letters of William James*, ed. by Henry James (Boston: Atlantic Monthly Press, 1920), 2:290.

5. A personal account of Whitehead's life can be found in his brief autobiographical sketch in the first chapter of *Essays in Science and Philosophy* (New York: Greenwood Press, 1968).

6. *Essays in Science and Philosophy*, 14.

7. Bertrand Russell, *Wisdom of the West* (London: Crescent Books, 1959), 297.

32

Analytic Philosophy and the Linguistic Turn

The Turn to Language and Analysis

In the early part of the twentieth century and continuing on today, a group of philosophers united around the conviction that clarifying language is the most pressing, if not the sole, task of philosophy. This movement is known as **analytic philosophy** or **linguistic philosophy**. These labels signify the fact that, in spite of their diversity, the philosophers within this movement believe that analysis is the correct approach to philosophy and that language is its primary subject matter. There are at least two reasons for this "linguistic turn" in philosophy. First, these philosophers felt science had taken over much of the territory formerly occupied by philosophy. The questions of metaphysics had been inherited by physics, they said, those of epistemology and philosophy of mind were now being answered by physiology and psychology, and the concerns of social and political philosophy were better left to sociology and political science. If the mission of acquiring knowledge about our world has been taken over by science, then the only task that remained for philosophy was to clarify linguistic meaning. As Moritz Schlick, an early member of the analytic movement, put it, "Science should be defined as the '*pursuit of truth*' and Philosophy as the '*pursuit of meaning.*' "[1] Second, new and more powerful methods of logic had been developed in the twentieth century that promised to shed new light on some of the old, philosophical stalemates. With these logical techniques, expressions that appeared to be meaningful propositions, but that were actually vague, equivocal, misleading, or nonsensical, could be exposed and eliminated by careful analysis.

Although the analytic philosophers proposed many different theories of language and methods of attacking philosophical problems, they all embraced three fundamental doctrines: (1) philosophical puzzles, problems, and contradictions are not found in the world, but in the things we say about the world; (2) philosophical problems can first be clarified and then solved or dissolved by either analyzing or reforming the way that language works; and (3) if any problems remain that cannot be resolved in this way, they are pseudo-problems and are not worth worrying about.

Analytic philosophy can be divided up into five stages or movements.[2] The first stage was *early realism and analysis*, introduced by G. E. Moore and Bertrand Russell in his early period. They reacted against the grandiose metaphysics of the Hegelians and brought British philosophy back to the search for clarity by means of a piecemeal analysis of particular propositions.

Second, the philosophy of *logical atomism* was developed in the work of Russell from 1914–1919 and in Ludwig Wittgenstein's early work, represented by his *Tractatus Logico-Philosophicus* (1921). During this period, Russell and Wittgenstein saw the task of philosophy as constructing a logically perfect language whose syntax would mirror the metaphysical structure of the world. By applying new techniques in logic, they hoped to find the fundamental, "atomistic" units of language that relate to the corresponding units that compose the world of facts.

Third, *logical positivism* arose in the 1920s and early 1930s. This widespread movement included a number of significant thinkers. Like the logical atomists, these philosophers tried to construct a logically perfect language. However, while the first two movements made metaphysics one of their concerns, the logical positivists claimed that metaphysical statements were meaningless. Hence, their ideal language would be able to articulate clearly all scientific and logical truths, while making it impossible to express any metaphysical claims.

The fourth stage in the analytic movement could be called *ordinary language philosophy: the Wittgensteinian model*. This movement resulted from the radical shift in direction taken by Wittgenstein in his later period. Repudiating the assumptions of stages 2 and 3, including his own work, he now thought there was no such thing as a logically perfect language. Ordinary language was now said to be perfectly adequate as it is. Philosophical problems arise, however, when philosophers become confused about how language functions, and therefore they get caught in a tangle of pseudo-problems. The unique feature of this stage of analysis was that Wittgenstein thought that the linguistic analyst, like a therapist, merely "cures" philosophers of their distortions. Philosophical problems are not solved but are dissolved by taking a more careful look at how language works. Once this is done, there is no more need of philosophy.

The fifth stage, which we will call *ordinary language philosophy: conceptual analysis*, was initiated by such thinkers as Gilbert Ryle and John Austin. They and many other heirs of the analytic movement turned Wittgenstein's linguistic "therapies" into a positive method for doing philosophy. Unlike Wittgenstein, they did not see language analysis as simply a way to cure philosophers of their philosophical pathology. Instead, they engaged in systematic explorations of traditional philosophical topics, using ordinary language as a guide for mapping the regions of our conceptual landscape.

BERTRAND RUSSELL

Russell's Life: Mathematician, Philosopher, Reformer

Bertrand Russell (1872–1970) was born into an aristocratic British family. (He inherited the title of Earl Russell in 1931.) He was the godson of John Stuart Mill, "so far as is possible in a non-religious sense," as Russell put it. His parents died

when he was three and even though they were freethinkers, he ended up being raised by his fervently religious grandmother. When he was a teenager, he wrestled intensely with the intellectual credibility of theism and abandoned it by the time he was eighteen. The rest of his life he was an outspoken critic of all forms of religious belief. He studied mathematics and philosophy at

Cambridge and went on to become a lecturer in philosophy at Trinity College. Russell was never reticent about speaking his mind, and throughout his life his iconoclastic and liberal opinions caused a stir wherever he went. He was fired from two academic positions because of his controversial views on politics and sexual morality. His confrontational political protests also landed him in jail several times. Even at the age of eighty-nine, he was still going strong and was jailed for leading a protest against nuclear arms in London.

In spite of these troubles, Russell was a respected international figure because of his groundbreaking work in logic and philosophy. Although he held several academic positions in England and America for short periods of time, he supported himself on his writings and public lectures for most of his life. Throughout his long career, Russell received many distinguished honors, including the Nobel Prize for literature in 1950. In addition to numerous articles, he wrote over ninety books, both technical and popular, on a wide range of topics. Russell died in 1970, two years short of living a century.

Background: The Revolt Against Hegelianism

BRITISH IDEALISM

During Bertrand Russell's student days, a form of Hegelianism known as British Idealism was the prevailing orthodoxy. The two most famous spokesmen of this outlook were F. H. Bradley and J. M. E. McTaggart. Russell enthusiastically read Bradley's books and sat in on McTaggart's lectures at Cambridge. The captivating vision of their philosophies caused the young Russell to become a Hegelian himself. The Idealists taught a form of monism in which reality was viewed as a single, eternal, all-comprehensive, experiencing being (sort of an atemporal version of Hegel's Absolute Spirit). Consequently, no particular could be understood on its own, for everything is merely an aspect of the whole. Eventually, Russell came to realize this contradicted the principles of mathe-

matics, where we first study isolated, fundamental units and then learn about their relations to other units. Consequently, he rebelled against Hegelian philosophy and asserted that reality is a plurality of fundamentally independent particular things.

G. E. MOORE

Russell was supported in his rebellion against Idealism by his fellow student G. E. Moore (1873–1958). Moore was upset by the way in which the British Idealists violated common sense. They claimed that particular physical objects are not real but are merely appearances, that nothing exists that is not related to a mind, and that time is unreal. In reaction to the Idealists, Moore and Russell affirmed a form of **realism** that asserted that the components of reality exist on their own, independent of their relationship to minds, that time is real, and that things can be known apart from their relationship to anything else. In their early period, their realism was somewhat Platonic, for they believed in the full reality not only of particular things such as minds and material objects, but also of universals such as redness, numbers, and equality.

In responding to the Idealists, Moore developed a new method for analyzing the meanings of philosophical questions and answers. Guiding his method was the conviction that our fundamental concepts and the linguistic meanings that express those concepts arise out of common sense and ordinary language. Most philosophical perplexities, he believed, result from philosophers using concepts and terms in peculiar ways.

In one of his most famous analyses, which has become an important position in ethical theory, Moore examined the concept of goodness. He argued that good is an indefinable notion (in the same sense that "yellow" cannot be given a purely verbal definition). Good is a property that cannot be reduced to any nonethical natural quality such as pleasure or desirability, but can only be known through an intellectual intuition. He argued that the attempt to reduce ethical claims to factual, empirical claims commits a logical error that he called the **naturalistic fallacy**.

Moore's persistent search for clarity and his detailed dissection and analysis of the meanings of philosophical propositions provided a model for the analytic philosophers after him. In particular, Moore's appeal to ordinary language had an impact on the later stages of analytic philosophy's development. While Moore and Russell both started out as Hegelians and then converted to anti-Hegelian realism, their philosophical interests gradually grew further apart. Moore continued to engage in piecemeal analyses of the meanings of perplexing philosophical statements, while Russell attempted a large-scale reconstruction of our ways of speaking and thinking about reality.

Russell's Task: Developing a Logically Perfect Language

Russell tells us that the "constant preoccupation" of his life was "to discover how much we can be said to know and with what degree of certainty or doubtfulness."[3] "I wanted certainty in the kind of way in which people want religious faith."[4] Accordingly, Russell did not value achieving finality in his thinking as much as he valued being correct. Thus he was his own, harshest critic, and throughout his career he continually revised or abandoned positions he had earlier defended vigorously.

Russell was one of the twentieth century's greatest minds in logic and mathematics and the whole of his philosophy reflects the work he did in these disciplines. Particularly important to Russell was the groundbreaking work he did with Alfred North Whitehead on the foundations of mathematics and logic. Together they wrote the three-volume classic of modern logic, *Principia Mathematica*, published in the years 1910–1913. This work demonstrated that the whole of mathematics could be reduced to a set of fundamental statements in logic in which numbers did not appear. This remarkable discovery served as the key to the whole of Russell's philosophical program, for he continually tried to show that what is complex can be reduced to a collection of elementary units.

Russell's central assumption through most of his life was that there was a necessary link between the nature of language and the truths of metaphysics. Since language is capable of describing the world and expressing true propositions about it, then there must be, he argued, some correspondence between the logical structure of language and the necessary structure of reality. Although the later analysts would be decidedly antimetaphysical, Russell enthusiastically believed that the new, powerful tools of modern logic he had developed would let us put metaphysics on a sound foundation at last.

Russell's Logical Atomism

Russell called his philosophical perspective **logical atomism**. This label expresses his conviction that the logical analysis of language would show it consisted of a relatively small number of irreducible, "atomistic" linguistic units that would, of necessity, correspond to the basic entities within the world. As with all the analytic philosophers, he begins with the conviction that many of the muddles in philosophy result from confusions about our ordinary language.

Russell's concern can be made clear with an example. Consider the following argument:

(1a) There is a fire in my kitchen.
(2a) My kitchen is in my house.
(3a) Therefore, there is a fire in my house.

Now compare that argument with this one:

(1b) There is a pain in my foot.
(2b) My foot is in my shoe.
(3b) Therefore, there is a pain in my shoe.[5]

In the first example, there seems to be no problem. But something has gone wrong in the second argument. Although the second argument is valid and its premises are relatively unproblematic, the conclusion (3b) is absurd when interpreted literally. Since the corresponding statements in the two arguments seem grammatically identical, what is the source of the problem? The problem, Russell would say, is that the syntax of ordinary language does not represent the true logical form of statements. Although statements (1a) and (1b) are *grammatically* similar, they are *logically* quite different. The sense in which a fire is "in" my kitchen is a straightforward spatial notion, leading to the conclusion in (3a). However, the sense in which a pain is "in" my foot does not let us transfer this property to the larger spatial context of my shoe.

The task, therefore, according to Russell, is to reformulate ordinary language statements in terms of an ideal language whose syntax would be logically precise. This ideal language would serve two purposes:

> First, to prevent inferences from the nature of language to the nature of the world, which are fallacious because they depend upon the logical defects of language; secondly, to suggest, by inquiring what logic requires of a language which is to avoid contradiction, what sort of structure we may reasonably suppose the world to have.[6]

In this way, a logically ideal language would both prevent and solve problems in metaphysics.

To begin with Russell's theory of language, he assumes the primary function of language is to represent facts. Thus, a proposition will be true if it corresponds to a fact and false if it doesn't. What is needed is an improved language where this correspondence can be set out clearly.

> In a logically perfect language the words in a proposition would correspond one by one with components of the corresponding fact, with the exception of such words as 'or', 'not', 'if', 'then', which have a different function.[7]

This correspondence is revealed by the parallel activities of analyzing complex propositions down to their simplest components (called "atomic propositions") and likewise analyzing facts down to their simplest components (which he called "atomic facts").*

---

*In referring to "atomic facts," Russell is not talking about anything that has to do with nuclear physics. Instead, he is talking about whatever is logically and metaphysically fundamental. As we will see, Russell's position implies that even our concepts of the elementary particles postulated by physics (electrons, neutrinos, and so on) are actually constructions from elements in our experience that are logically, epistemologically, and metaphysically more primary.

An atomic proposition ascribes a simple property to an individual or asserts a relation among two or more individuals. Examples of each of these cases are "This is red" and "This is taller than that." Atomic propositions can be combined to form complex propositions called *molecular propositions*. These compounds are created by using logical operators such as "and," "or," "not," "if . . . then." An example of a molecular proposition is "This is red, and that is blue." However, Russell believed there were no complex or molecular facts, so the conditions that would make this statement true are *two* atomic facts, namely the first thing being red and the second being blue. Russell thinks this analysis provides us with the logical skeleton of any meaningful language. English, German, and all other ordinary languages are imperfect and confused versions of this logically precise language.

All this seems very straightforward. However, Russell's theory of language is packed with a number of metaphysical implications. Since the truth or falsity of atomic propositions are independent of one another, the world they describe must be made up of wholly independent, discrete entities. Hence, from one fact we cannot logically infer another fact. Furthermore, since there is no logical necessity to the contents of the world, whether or not a particular statement corresponds to a fact in the world is wholly an empirical matter to be decided by scientific observation. So, while the logical structure of language provides us with the logical form of the world, a metaphysics of this sort cannot tell us what particular things exist. This can be accomplished only by an appeal to experience. As we will see, the more Russell tried to get clear on the sort of facts we can actually know, his position became increasingly radical.

How Language Connects with the World

So far, we have a general overview of how Russell thinks language and the world are structured. However, we need to say more about how to determine the meaning of a proposition. Russell's theory of meaning follows from two fundamental principles. First, Russell believes every word has a meaning: the entity to which it refers. This is often called the "referential" or "naming theory of meaning."* Second, this definition of meaning implies that "if we can understand what a sentence means, it must be composed entirely of words denoting things with which we are acquainted or definable in terms of such words."[8] A word that directly refers to a particular entity with which we are acquainted is a "logically proper name." Since we cannot analyze an atomic proposition any further, it must describe a particular fact in the world, and therefore the subject of an atomic proposition must be a logically proper name. You might suppose that the name of your best friend is a proper name, since you *are* acquainted with this person. However, Russell makes the startling claim that, in the logically precise sense, you *do not* have direct acquaintance with your best friend nor with familiar physical objects such as your favorite chair. Rather than being proper names or denoting terms, the terms you use to refer to your friend or your chair are actually descriptions of complicated systems of sense data. To make this puzzling notion clear, let's look at Russell's account of logical constructions.

Russell's Theory of Logical Constructions

Russell embraced the methodological principle known as Ockham's razor (after the fourteenth-century logician). This principle advises us that "explanatory entities are not to be multiplied without necessity." In other words, "Keep your explanations as simple as possible." As Russell says,

> I always wish to get on in philosophy with the smallest possible apparatus, partly because . . . you run less risk of error the fewer entities you assume.[9]

Russell's philosophical development was a continuous quest for those elements of the world that were absolutely simple and fundamental and that could be known with absolute certainty based on our direct acquaintance with them. These particulars with which we are directly acquainted are what Russell called "hard data." The problem is that a good number of our beliefs concern "soft data," which are inferred entities. Russell's task is to show that a great deal of the soft data can be reinterpreted as constructions from the indubitable hard data. To achieve this goal, he formulated another methodological principle: "Whenever possible, logical constructions are to be substituted for inferred entities."[10]

Consider your experience of a chair. A chair appears within your visual field as a series of color patches whose size and shape vary, depending on the angle and the distance from which you view it. Each distinct, particular sense datum you experience at a given moment is a piece of hard data, for you cannot doubt that what is directly appearing to you is a series of rectangular patches of a certain color. However, by psychological habit and for practical purposes, you group these particular patches of color data together and treat them as parts of a class you refer to as "the chair." This is not something you *consciously* do, but if Russell's atomistic empiricism is correct then this is what you *actually* do.

In this way, Russell thinks, science and ordinary experience can be set on a rock-solid foundation. Instead of making the word *chair* refer to an inferred entity outside of experience as the seventeenth-century empiricist John Locke would have, Russell reduces the word *chair* to a class term referring to a collection of "hard," sensory data that we directly experience. Russell does not deny that there could be a "chair substance" beneath all the appearances, he just concludes we cannot know it and don't need to postulate it to speak meaningfully about the chair. If the notion of a "chair" is a logical construction from our immediate sense data, it is even more obvious that scientific objects such as electrons and protons are logical constructions. Of course, the same sort of analysis applies to your experience of your friend. The friend's

---

*Although this theory of meaning appeals to common sense, it is controversial. The ordinary language philosophers, whom we encounter later in this chapter, contend this account of meaning is inadequate.

name is actually a class term for the collection of sense data you associate with him or her.

When he first started working on these ideas, Russell thought we directly experience three sorts of things: particular sense data, universals, and our self. However, he came to doubt we have direct knowledge of the self, and claimed it, too, was a logical construction from the particular data of experience. In his later work, the only logically proper name Russell would allow was the word *this*. Thus, propositions such as "This is red," said when referring to a certain sense datum, are the only sort of solid claims we can make about the world. To prevent someone from thinking that "this" refers to some sort of metaphysical substance, he preferred to state "This is red," as "Redness is here."

This account of experience—as a flow of sense data grouped together under class names such as "chair"—does not seem a sufficient basis for ordinary life or science. If we don't have a basis for asserting the existence of enduring physical objects nor for believing in causal relations, how can we make inferences and predictions from the sense data? Since logical atomism rejects the claim that there are logically necessary relationships between facts, we will not be able to make deductive inferences about anything in the world. However, Russell says that we can make cautious nondeductive inferences from our experiences. Therefore, he tentatively proposes a set of five postulates that provide minimum foundation for science and practical living. The nature of his postulates may be illustrated by quoting one of them, "the postulate of quasi-permanence." He says we can use this postulate "to replace the common-sense notion of 'thing' and 'person' in a manner not involving the concept of 'substance.' " This postulate states that

> Given any event A, it happens very frequently that, at any neighboring time, there is at some neighboring place an event very similar to A.[11]

Thus, if I have chairlike or personlike appearances in one moment, I am reasonable to expect experiences "very similar" in the next moment without appealing to a metaphysical substance.

Still, we may ask, What is the justification for these postulates? The only answer Russell comes up with is that they are acquired habits or "animal inferences" rooted in our biological nature.[12]

This shows that, despite his complicated conceptual apparatus, when we get down to the basis of Russell's position he has made very little progress beyond David Hume's skepticism. Even worse, in the final analysis, he speaks as though everything rested on a subjective choice.

> If we are to hold that we know anything of the external world, we must accept the canons of scientific knowledge. Whether . . . an individual decides to accept or reject these canons, is a purely personal affair, not susceptible to argument.[13]

There is tremendous irony here. Russell began with a Cartesian search for absolute certainty, but in the end it seems all we can know about the world are such barren truths as "Redness is here." To get beyond this level, we have to place our trust in the canons of scientific knowledge, but this requires a Kierkegaardian leap of faith in which "an individual decides to accept or reject these canons."

Russell says that at the beginning of his career, he had hoped to find in philosophy an intellectually and emotionally satisfying substitute for religion. However, at age seventy-one he concluded that "my intellectual journeys have been, in some respects, disappointing."[14] Even though Russell's philosophical labors did not accomplish all he hoped they would, his contributions were enormous. Particularly in the area of logic, Russell expanded and sharpened one of our most important philosophical tools.

The difficulties in the logical atomists' attempt to base a metaphysical theory on an analysis of language led later analytic philosophers to lower their sights, giving up all expectations that philosophy tells us anything about ultimate reality or that it provides the meaning of human life. Instead, they put philosophy to work on a much more humble task, that of clarifying the expressions we use to speak about the world. Logical positivism, the third phase of analytic philosophy, represents this chastened, antimetaphysical turn in philosophy.

LOGICAL POSITIVISM

In the 1920s and early 1930s a group of philosophers took it as their mission to search for a body of positive knowledge based on science, much as Auguste Comte did a century earlier. They called their position **logical positivism** (or *logical empiricism*, as it was also known) to distinguish their specific program from earlier positivisms, as well as to indicate that logical analysis was the core of their method. This movement originated with a group called the Vienna Circle. The most influential members of the Circle were Rudolf Carnap, Otto Neurath, Herbert Feigl, Friedrich Waismann, and Kurt Gödel. A. J. Ayer attended a number of the sessions and introduced logical positivism to England in his classic book *Language, Truth and Logic*. Hans Reichenbach led a similar group in Berlin. Their goal of rebuilding philosophy on a sound logical and scientific foundation was very appealing. Because they vigorously promoted their philosophy at international congresses and through their publications, logical positivism became an international movement that spread throughout most of Europe and became very powerful in the English-speaking countries.

The logical positivists were strongly influenced by the logical atomism of Bertrand Russell and Ludwig Wittgenstein. Although they disagreed with some of the details of logical atomism, the positivists carried forward the vision of a logically ideal language and the attempt to anchor the meaning of terms in irreducible sense data. They were also influenced by David Hume's empiricism and sought to provide an updated version of it. Although they joined with many of their contemporaries in the attack on metaphysical systems such as Hegel's, they thought philosophy needed stronger logical artillery to vanquish metaphysics once and for all.

The logical positivists had three main goals: (1) to develop a logically adequate theory of language that would provide a criterion of linguistic meaning, (2) to use this criterion as a sieve to separate meaningful scientific statements from meaningless metaphysical statements, and (3) to use this theory of language to set out the epistemological and logical foundations of science.

The spirit of logical positivism is captured by Hume's famous statement:

> *When we run over libraries, persuaded of these principles, what havoc must we make? If we take in our hand any volume; of divinity or school metaphysics, for instance; let us ask,* Does it contain any abstract reasoning concerning quantity or number? *No.* Does it contain any experimental reasoning concerning matter of fact and existence? *No. Commit it then to the flames: for it can contain nothing but sophistry and illusion.*[15]

Like Hume, the logical positivists believed that all genuine knowledge falls within the two realms of science: (1) the formal sciences of logic and mathematics and (2) the empirical sciences. The first sort of knowledge is expressed in what are called analytic propositions. The truth or falsity of these sorts of statements is based on the logical form of language or on the definitions of words. Thus "All lemons are lemons," "2 + 2 = 4," and "All bachelors are unmarried" are examples of true analytic statements. Wittgenstein called such statements **tautologies**.* A false analytic statement, such as "John is an unmarried bachelor," is identified by the fact that it contains a contradiction. Since tautologies are always true and contradictions are always false, no matter what is the case, analytic statements do not give us any factual knowledge about the way the world is.

---

*Such statements express what Hume called "relations of ideas" and what Kant called "analytic *a priori* judgments." Kant, however, treated mathematical statements differently, claiming they fell into the class of "synthetic *a priori* judgments." Neither Hume nor the logical positivists acknowledged the existence of such a category.

The second category of statements consists of empirical statements.* Statements such as "Lemons are yellow" or "The sun rises in the east" are true, empirical statements. In contrast, "The moon is made out of green cheese" is a meaningful empirical statement, even though it is false. Unlike analytic statements, both true and false empirical statements do, of course, make claims about the way the world is. Since analytic and empirical statements are the only sorts of meaningful statements there are, any proposition that does not fall into either category is not simply false, nor is it merely unknowable, it is *meaningless*. Plato's metaphysical claim that "beyond individual human beings there exists the nonphysical Form of Humanity" makes no more sense than the following pieces of nonsense: "Is the number 7 holy?" or "Which numbers are more athletic, the even or the odd ones?"

The Verifiability Principle

The rules of logic and language give us clear-cut methods for determining the meaning of analytic statements. However, to carry out their program the logical positivists also needed a definitive method for separating meaningful empirical statements from meaningless pseudo-statements. They therefore developed the **verifiability principle**, and this criterion of meaning became the centerpiece of their program. Note that they were not trying to decide whether a given statement about the world was true or not, for this is the task of science. The role of philosophy is to decide what it means to say that a statement has *cognitive* meaning. A cognitively meaningful statement is one that provides information about the world. (As we will see, they acknowledged there may be noncognitive meaning as well.)

The verifiability principle can be stated thus: *a factual statement is meaningful if it can be verified in experience*. The corollary of this principle is the

*Hume said these statements express "matters of fact," and Kant said they express "synthetic *a posteriori* judgments."

meaning of a factual statement is the method of its verification. Suppose, for example, someone claims that "it is raining outside." This claim (whether true or false) is meaningful because I can specify concrete experiences that would verify it. The entire meaning of the claim can be translated into a series of sentences referring directly to possible sense experiences. These were sometimes called "protocol statements." In our example, the meaning of the claim could be captured by sentences such as "If I look out the window, I will see water falling" or "If I stand outside, I will feel water droplets."

The logical positivists found themselves continually modifying the verifiability principle in the attempt to remedy problems that kept arising. First, they said we may not be able to actually verify a statement, but it must be verifiable *in principle* to be meaningful. In other words, we must be able to state what sorts of experiences would count for or against the claim, even if we cannot subject it to the test. This allows historical statements to be meaningful even if we cannot verify or falsify them. An example would be "Julius Caesar had breakfast the day he died." Also, verification in principle allowed statements to be meaningful that cannot be actually verified because we lack the technology to do so. Statements about an unexplored planet would be such a case.

Second, the positivists originally dictated that for a statement to be factually meaningful, it must be capable of being *conclusively* verified by experience. This was later called "strong verification." However, a great many important statements in science would fail this test. Statements expressing large-scale scientific theories are only indirectly and incompletely supported by particular observations. For example, a collection of observation statements such as "this rock is falling to the earth" will not verify Newton's theory of gravitation. Also, universal statements such as "all oxygen is combustible" cannot be conclusively verified, because there is always the possibility that the next experiment will produce a counterexample. Therefore, the logical positivists decided that it is enough if a statement can be "weakly verified." Roughly, the principle of weak verification declares that a statement is cognitively meaningful if experience can render it probable. The logical positivists thought this revised version would draw the boundaries of cognitive meaning so as to include scientific statements, while excluding the philosophical statements they wished to reject.

THE DEMISE OF METAPHYSICS AND THEOLOGY

What made the logical positivists unique in the history of philosophy was that, unlike previous critics of metaphysics, they did not simply say metaphysical statements are false or unfounded. Instead, they insisted all metaphysical statements, in principle, are totally nonsensical. Consider the statement "Blue ideas sleep furiously." It doesn't violate any rules of English grammar, but is obviously a piece of nonsense. It is not so obvious that metaphysical statements are nonsense. Yet under the logical positivists' analysis these statements are a form of disguised nonsense and are just as empty of cognitive content as the statement about blue ideas. To make this point, A. J. Ayer quotes a statement from the Neo-Hegelian F. H. Bradley: "The Absolute enters into, but is itself incapable of, evolution and progress." Applying the verifiability principle, Ayer remarks, "One cannot conceive of an observation which would enable one to determine whether the Absolute did, or did not, enter into evolution and progress."[16] Similarly, statements such as "all reality is material" go beyond the bounds of experience and therefore are neither true not false, but are pseudo-propositions.*

Since theological statements make claims about ultimate reality, the logical positivist would say they also are unverifiable and meaningless. For example, the statement "there is a loving God" cannot be translated into any observation statements. Religious people still maintain there is a loving God even when their lives are filled with

suffering and arbitrary, cruel misfortunes. This demonstrates that claims about God do not have anything to do with what we will or will not experience. Of course, it follows that the denial of any metaphysical claim will have no empirical content either. So the atheist's assertion that "there is no God" is also an example of an unverifiable and meaningless claim. At best, metaphysical and theological statements express our feelings about the world. As Rudolf Carnap expressed it, metaphysical propositions "are, like laughing, lyrics, and music, expressive."[17]

The Status of Ethics

Traditionally, ethics was an important branch of philosophy. Ethical statements make claims about how people ought to act and what sorts of things have intrinsic value. However, logical positivism cast them in a new light. The positivists made several different kinds of responses to ethics. Moritz Schlick said that ethical statements are factual claims about how people use the word *good* and why a person approves of this or that action. Hence, ethics can be understood as a division within psychology. Of course, if ethics is merely a type of behavioral science, it cannot make normative pronouncements about what the word "good" *should* mean nor can it provide an absolute justification of ethical norms.

Rudolf Carnap and A. J. Ayer represented the majority opinion on ethics within the positivist's camp. Their ethical theory came to be known as *emotivism*. In their analysis, ethical statements do not make factual claims capable of being verified and, therefore, they have no cognitive meaning. However, ethical statements do have *emotive* meaning. They are best understood as verbal ways of expressing certain attitudes of approval or disapproval. Thus, when someone says, "You acted wrongly in stealing that money," this does not make a factual claim about stealing, because no sense data corresponds to the quality of "moral wrongness." Instead, when a person morally condemns an act of stealing, what they are actually doing is (1) stating a fact plus (2) expressing an

---

*Insofar as Russell's logical atomism made claims about the structure of reality, these claims would be rejected by the logical positivists' criterion as meaningless intellectual baggage.

emotion or attitude toward it such as "You stole the money!—Ugh, Boo, Hiss!" Carnap and Ayer also believed that moral claims may be used to influence the attitudes and behavior of others. In this case, the statement "It is your moral duty to tell the truth" means nothing more than "I recommend you tell the truth."[18]

The final verdict rendered by the logical positivists is that philosophy cannot be a source of truth. Knowledge comes to us only through the formal propositions of mathematics and logic or through the empirically verified observations of science. As Carnap said, "We give no answer to philosophical questions and instead reject all *philosophical questions*, whether of metaphysics, ethics or epistemology. For our concern is with *logical analysis*."[19] Nevertheless, because philosophy is the activity of clarifying language, the logical positivists believed philosophers, as the caretakers of language, could still make three contributions. First, philosophers could be put in charge of the "environmental quality" of the intellectual realm. They could use the verifiability test to clear our intellectual discourse of the verbal pollution of meaningless statements. Second, the philosopher could be an "efficiency expert" who clarifies complex and murky scientific statements by analyzing them into the clean and crisp statements of direct observation. Third, the philosopher could be an "organizational administrator" who tries to realize the dream of the unity of the science. Here, philosophers could use their logical techniques to show how all the sciences may be reduced to physics, the most fully developed and well-grounded of the sciences.

Problems with Logical Positivism

As with a leaky ship at sea, problems with logical positivism were continually being discovered, and its advocates spent much time patching its leaks instead of carrying out their positive program. First, as mentioned, the verifiability principle went through a number of modifications. If the principle was made very narrow (strong verifiability), it eliminated a good deal of science. Scientific state-

ments expressing general laws or referring to unobservable entities such as electrons cannot be conclusively and directly verified. According to the strong verifiability principle, such statements would have to be classified as meaningless. In other words, the logical positivists found, as Russell had, that conclusively verifiable observation statements such as "Redness here now" provide too thin a foundation on which to build knowledge. To remedy this problem, the logical positivists made the principle more liberal (weak verifiability). Under this version, statements about unobservable subatomic entities are meaningful because observations are relevant to assessing their truth. The problem was that by preserving the more theoretical regions of science, weak verifiability allowed some metaphysical statements to creep back in. For example, many arguments in natural theology use observations about the world as evidence that the existence of God is probable. Hence, by the standards of the weaker principle, statements about God, Plato's Forms, and Hegel's Absolute were cognitively meaningful.

Second, critics were quick to drag the logical positivist's principle of verification before its own tribunal of judgment. Let's consider this statement of the verifiability principle: "A meaningful statement will either be analytic or empirically verifiable." We may ask, Is this itself a meaningful statement? It doesn't seem to be an analytic statement based on a rule of logic or a definition. However, it doesn't seem to be an empirical statement, either. What sort of sense data could possibly verify it? Pressed up against the wall, many logical positivists had to admit the principle is simply a recommendation they were making about how to use the terms "meaningful" and "meaningless." But this response reduces their theory of language to simply a matter of subjective, personal preference.

Somewhere between 1930 and 1940 logical positivism lost its momentum. As a movement it is now dead, although some philosophers still retain some of the spirit of this philosophy. Their interest in the philosophy of science brought this area of philosophy into prominence. Ironically, the model of scientific language they set forth was an ideal refuted by a closer look at the empirical facts of how scientific theories actually develop.* Eventually, analytic philosophers found that the major shortcoming of logical positivism was that it assumed all meaningful language had to conform to the model of scientific language. In 1959 A. J. Ayer, one of the most famous of the logical positivists, repented of his earlier one-sided perspective. Speaking of what the logical positivists had accomplished, he said,

> The most that has been proved is that metaphysical statements do not fall into the same category as the laws of logic, or as scientific hypotheses, or as historical narratives, or judgments of perception, or any other common sense descriptions of the "natural" world. Surely it does not follow that they are neither true nor false, still less that they are nonsensical.[20]

Similarly, Ludwig Wittgenstein, a guiding light of logical atomism and logical positivism, discovered that his original position was misguided and that a new way of looking at language was needed. Wittgenstein took analytic philosophy to the next stage of its development. However, before we can look at how he changed the course of analytic philosophy, we must follow the path of his earlier ideas to see why they led to a dead end.

LUDWIG WITTGENSTEIN

Wittgenstein's Life: From Engineer to Philosopher

Ludwig Wittgenstein (1889–1951) was born in Vienna into a family that was not only financially wealthy, but rich in intellectual and artistic talents as well. The composer Johannes Brahms was a close friend of the Wittgenstein family and a frequent visitor to their home. Wittgenstein's father was a Jewish convert to Protestantism, but Wittgenstein himself was raised in his mother's faith, Roman Catholicism.

Wittgenstein began his university education at the University of Manchester, where he studied engineering and researched aeronautical design. His work toward a career in engineering ended when he became interested in pure mathematics and then in the philosophical foundations of mathematics. Pursuing this, he discovered the work of Bertrand Russell and enrolled in Trinity College at Cambridge in 1912 to study with Russell. Very quickly, Russell realized his student's great genius and told Wittgenstein's sister he believed the next great advance in philosophy would be made by her brother. Russell became one of Wittgenstein's closest friends and had an important influence on his career, even though they came to differ on a number of issues. Like many great geniuses, Wittgenstein was an extraordinarily intense person, and this intensity, combined with his thirst for personal and intellectual honesty, tormented him his whole life. His sister says that when he was pursuing a career as an engineer,

> he was suddenly seized so strongly and so completely against his will by philosophy, i.e., by reflections about philosophical problems, that he suffered severely. . . . One of several transformations which he was to undergo in his life had come over him and shaken his whole being.[21]

From this intensity came the fulfillment of Russell's prediction, for in the 1920s Wittgenstein's ideas reverberated throughout the halls of philosophy departments. However, Russell underestimated the genius of his student, for Wittgenstein initiated not one, but two revolutions in philoso-

*See Thomas Kuhn, *The Structure of Scientific Revolutions*, 2d ed., enlarged (Chicago: University of Chicago Press, 1970), for the classic work on the history of science that undermined the logical positivists' view of science when it first appeared in 1962.

phy. Approximately ten years after he had made his first impact, Wittgenstein's driving demand for intellectual honesty forced him to repudiate the ideas that had made him famous and led him to chart a new course in philosophy.

The two periods in Wittgenstein's intellectual life center on his two major works. His early philosophy is represented by the *Tractatus Logico-Philosophicus*, published in 1921. His later philosophy was stated in the *Philosophical Investigations*, published in 1953. The two books differ radically in style as well as in their conceptions of philosophy and language. In his later period, when he attacks his earlier theories, Wittgenstein refers to the mistakes of "the author of the *Tractatus*" as though he were speaking about a completely different person. Although Wittgenstein's general approach to language in his early period has been covered in our discussion of logical atomism, we must sketch out some of the features of the *Tractatus* to understand the radical shift he made.

The Early Wittgenstein: From Logic to Mysticism

THE TASK OF THE *TRACTATUS*

The *Tractatus* was written before Wittgenstein was thirty years old. Running fewer than eighty pages in length, it consists of a series of short, numbered statements. The composition of the book and its range of topics is very unusual. Although most of the book is a collection of very precise statements on the nature of logic, the last four pages take a very strange shift in direction and consist of poetical and mystical utterances. The philosophy of language Wittgenstein developed during this period linked Russell's logical atomism and logical positivism. Despite their differences, all these philosophies united around three common projects: (1) the repudiation of traditional metaphysics, (2) the attempt to reduce language to a series of elementary propositions that would correspond with observable facts, and (3) the attempt to develop a theory of language that would establish the boundaries of meaning. In Wittgenstein's

case, his project takes the form of a "linguistic Kantianism." Kant tried to set out the limits of reason by distinguishing what, in principle, is knowable from what is unknowable. Since Wittgenstein believes whatever can be thought can be spoken, it follows that the limits of thought can be set out by determining the limits of language. This will give us the limits of what can be intelligible.

THE PICTURE THEORY OF LANGUAGE

Russell believed the world was a collection of atomic facts. Using the term "states of affairs" for "atomic facts," Wittgenstein gives us a similar account of the world.

(1)   The world is all that is the case.

(1.1)   The world is the totality of facts, not of things.

-
-
-

(2)   What is the case—a fact—is the existence of states of affairs.

(2.01)   A state of affairs (a state of things) is a combination of objects (things).[22]

Similar to Russell's logical atomism, Wittgenstein took for granted that the function of language is to represent states of affairs in the world. This was known as his "picture theory of language":

(4.01)   A proposition is a picture of reality.
A proposition is a model of reality as we imagine it.

Obviously, a proposition does not give us a spatial representation of a situation. Instead, the logical relationships among the elements of a proposition represent the logical relationships among objects in the world. A proposition has a sense if it describes a specific, possible situation within the world; otherwise, it is meaningless. The logical positivists considered this a statement of their principle of verification. Consequently, they wrongly

Penn Station, New York City, 1934. The skeletal structures produced by modern arthitects provide a visual image of Ludwig Wittgenstein's early philosophy of language. Wittgenstein attempted to get below the surface of our language to reveal the logical structure of any possible language. However, just as the unbounded sky can be seen through the confining framework of the building, Wittgenstein stressed that there is much that is beyond the boundaries of language: "There are, indeed, things that cannot be put into words. They make themselves manifest. They are what is mystical."

assumed Wittgenstein was one of them. However, Wittgenstein did agree with them on at least three points. First, he claims that the only meaningful language is the fact-stating language of the natural sciences. "The totality of true propositions is the whole of natural science" (T 4.11). Second, Wittgenstein also agrees a correct understanding of the logic of language would eliminate most traditional philosophy:

(4.003) Most of the propositions and questions to be found in philosophical works are not false but nonsensical. Consequently we cannot give any answer to questions of this kind, but can only establish that they are nonsensical. Most of the propositions and questions of philosophers arise from our failure to understand the logic of our language.

Third, like the logical positivists, Wittgenstein believes philosophy does not give us any information about reality. Its job is simply to straighten up our thought and language by removing misunderstandings. "Philosophy is not a body of doctrine but an activity. . . . Philosophy does not result in 'philosophical propositions', but rather in the clarification of propositions" (T 4.112).

WITTGENSTEIN'S MYSTICISM

Thus far, the doctrines of the *Tractatus* simply seem to repeat the main ideas of logical atomism and logical positivism, adding a few, unique flourishes. However, what makes this work so fascinating is the startling set of implications Wittgenstein draws from his position and the ways he deviated radically from his contemporaries. Following the example of Kant once again, Wittgenstein said that if we can draw a boundary, then something must be on both sides of the boundary. Within the boundary of meaningful language is nothing but the propositions of science. But what lies beyond the limits of language? It would, of course, be something inexpressible. The positivists thought what is inexpressible could never be anything more than sheer nonsense. However, Wittgenstein believed something transcends the limits of language, which he called "the mystical." "There are, indeed, things that cannot be put into words. They *make themselves manifest*. They are what is mystical" (T 6.522).

Paradoxically, among the inexpressible things are the propositions of the *Tractatus* itself. Wittgenstein came to this conclusion by reasoning as follows. The doctrine he and Russell embraced was "A proposition is meaningful only if it can be analyzed down into one or more elementary propositions each of which refer to an atomic fact." According to this theory, the relationship between a proposition and the world is one of "referring to" or "picturing" and can be illustrated with the following diagram:

Proposition ⟶ Atomic fact

But given this picture, what is the status of Russell and Wittgenstein's proposition? Clearly, it does not make a claim about some particular fact in the world. Instead, this proposition and the others Wittgenstein expresses describe the relationship between propositions and facts or, to put it more generally, they are making claims about the relationship between language and the world. This may be diagrammed in this way:

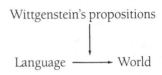

Wittgenstein's propositions

Language ⟶ World

The problem is that according to his own theory of language, Wittgenstein's propositions stand outside the domain of meaningful language. Wittgenstein "bit the bullet" and accepted this conclusion. For this reason, he acknowledges,

(6.54)   My propositions serve as elucidations in the following way: anyone who understands me finally recognizes them as nonsensical, when he has used them—as steps—to climb up beyond them. (He must, so to speak, throw away the ladder, after he has climbed up it.)

In other words, Wittgenstein's propositions are attempting to say the unsayable (and this applies to those of Russell and the logical positivists as well). Nevertheless, these propositions are "elucidations" for they can help trigger an insight into the nature of the world, even though this insight cannot be expressed.

Another aspect of the mystical is the realm of ethical and spiritual values. Wittgenstein says we will not find values among the facts of the world, for everything just is what it is (T 6.41). Therefore, the sense of the world, what constitutes its value, must lie outside the world. It cannot be one more mundane fact among the scientifically observable facts in the world. Consequently, "ethics cannot be put into words. Ethics is transcendental" (T 6.421). A little bit later he says,

(6.432)   *How* things are in the world is a matter of complete indifference for what is higher. God does not reveal himself *in* the world.

Wittgenstein closes his discussion of the mystical and ends the *Tractatus* with proposition 7, his final, oracular statement:

(7) What we cannot speak about we must pass over in silence.

At first glance, this seems a truism and the logical positivists took it as such. But Wittgenstein is actually making the significant point that there is *something* to be silent about. He once wrote to a friend concerning the *Tractatus*, "My work consists of two parts: the one presented here plus all that I have *not* written. And it is precisely this second part that is the important one."[23] Eventually, through meetings with Wittgenstein, the logical positivists realized with horror that the man who had inspired their antimetaphysical polemics really wasn't one of them. Wittgenstein agreed with them that it is hopeless to "thrust against the limits of language," at the same time he insisted, "the tendency, the thrust, *points to something*."[24]

The Later Wittgenstein: The Turn to Ordinary Language

In the preface to the *Tractatus*, Wittgenstein claimed his conclusions seemed "unassailable and definitive" and he had found "the final solution of the problems" (T 5). After showing that scientific statements constitute the whole of what we can think and say—and that the rest, what can only be shown but not spoken, is left to mysticism—Wittgenstein concluded that the task of philosophy was finished. Ending his work with the summons to philosophical silence, he followed his own advice and stopped doing philosophy. First he became an elementary school teacher in an Austrian village from 1920 to 1926; then he served as a gardener's assistant in a monastery for several months. After that, he spent two years using his architectural skills to design a house for one of his sisters. Gradually Wittgenstein began to think about philosophy again. He had a gnawing suspicion that, somehow, he had not gotten it right in his early work and he needed to rethink his whole approach.

Wittgenstein returned to Cambridge in 1929 to do research in philosophy and eventually was made a Fellow of Trinity College. In 1930 he began giving informal lectures to a carefully, screened group of advanced students. Actually, they could hardly be called *lectures*, for Wittgenstein was really thinking out loud about various philosophical problems in front of his students, without the benefit of notes. In the midst of this extemporaneous philosophizing, he frequently engaged in intense, question-and-answer dialogues with his students, much like Socrates. During two of the years he taught, Wittgenstein dictated his thoughts to his inner circle of students, who then circulated transcripts of these meetings around Cambridge. After Wittgenstein's death, these notes were published as *The Blue and Brown Books* (referring to the original covers of the typewritten copies). Finally, Wittgenstein retired from teaching in 1947 in order to devote his time and energies to his research. After a period of ill health, he died on April 29, 1951. Two years after Wittgenstein's death, the *Philosophical Investigations*, the most significant work of his later period, was published. Through the impact of Wittgenstein's lectures and his later writings, analytic philosophy took off in a completely new direction.

There are a number of striking differences between the *Tractatus* and the *Investigations*. First, the *Tractatus* used an *a priori*, logical method. The early Wittgenstein thought the results of his analysis showed that language necessarily *must* conform to the logician's ideals. In contrast, the *Investigations* uses an empirical, descriptive method. He now cautions, "One cannot guess how a word functions. One has to *look at* its use and learn from that" (PI §340).[25] The *Tractatus* had a linear, logical format, each proposition fitting neatly into its appointed place. The later book, however, has neither a beginning nor end. When you start reading it, you are thrust into the middle of a rambling album of sketches, remarks, questions, descriptions, dialogues, jokes, stories, and confessions that unfold in almost a stream-of-consciousness style.

It is easy to find contrasts between Wittgenstein's earlier and later work. However, there is also a sense in which he was wrestling with the same questions in both periods, albeit with different methods and assumptions.* In the *Tractatus* he said that philosophical problems arise because "the logic of our language is misunderstood" (T, preface). In the *Investigations* he says we have these problems because "we do not *command a clear view* of the use of our words" (PI §122). In both works he was concerned to find the limits of legitimate language and to confront the problems that arise when these boundaries are violated. However, there is a considerable change from his earlier writings in how Wittgenstein conceives the method of clarifying language and his notion of the limits and boundaries of language.

LANGUAGE-GAMES

One of the most important analogies Wittgenstein draws in his later work is that between language and games. He captures this comparison with his notion of "language-games." He makes numerous uses of the metaphor of language-games; three will be discussed here. First, the term "language-games" is used to emphasize the plurality of our ways of speaking. To get the analogy off the ground, consider the many kinds of games and the ways they differ in purposes, rules, and the kinds of action response interactions that characterize them. Wittgenstein asks the following question concerning games:

> What is common to them all?—Don't say: "There must be something common, or they would not be called 'games' "—but look and see whether there is anything common to all.—For if you look at them you will not see something that is common to all, but similarities, relationships, and a whole series of them at that. (PI §66)

Similar to the diversity of literal games, our multiple ways of speaking (language-games) do not

conform to a single model. Wittgenstein's repeated insistence on this was meant to refute "the author of the *Tractatus*" (as Wittgenstein sometimes referred to his earlier phase). The earlier theory had supposed the sole function of a word was to name an object. In response to this theory, Wittgenstein says we do use words in this way in some language-games, but this does not describe the whole of language:

> It is as if someone were to say: "A game consists in moving objects about on a surface according to certain rules . . ." —and we replied: You seem to be thinking of board games, but there are others. You can make your definition correct by expressly restricting it to those games. (PI §3)

In contrast to the one-dimensional "naming" theory of language of the *Tractatus*, Wittgenstein gives a random list of language-games to illustrate their diversity. He includes giving orders and obeying them; describing the appearance of an object; speculating about an event; making a joke; translating from one language into another; asking, thanking, cursing, greeting, praying (PI §23). To illustrate the relationship of language-games to one another, Wittgenstein uses yet another analogy. He says the different uses of language are like "family resemblances" (PI §67). The people at a family reunion will share many similar features, such as eye color, temperament, hair, facial structure, and build. However, there will be no one particular feature that they all share in common. A daughter may have her father's eyes, her mother's hair, and her aunt's smile. With this analogy, Wittgenstein is attacking the theory of essentialism, which is the Platonic thesis that for things to be classed together they must share some essence. Wittgenstein's point, however, is that while our modes of discourse are all examples of *language*, the fact that they belong to the same category does not imply there is a single essence they all possess. Instead, the different language-games "are *related* to one another in many different ways" (PI §65).

A second reason why Wittgenstein compares the use of language to the playing of different games is to emphasize that the speaking of language is

---

*Wittgenstein is reported to have said that "the *Tractatus* was not *all* wrong: it was not like a bag of junk professing to be a clock, but like a clock that did not tell you the right time." Reported by G. E. M. Anscombe in *An Introduction to Wittgenstein's Tractatus*, 2d ed., rev. (New York: Harper & Row, Harper Torchbooks, 1959), 78.

an *activity*. As he says, "the whole, consisting of language and the actions into which it is woven, [is] the 'language-game' " (PI §7). For example, the problem with the "naming theory" of language is not only that there are other uses of language besides naming objects, but also that the act of naming objects plays no role unless it is an activity within the context of a particular language-game (PI §49). Suppose I point to a piece of furniture and say "chair." So far, I have done nothing other than uttering a sound. However, in the right sort of circumstances it could be a move in a language-game. For example, if I am teaching you English, you would point to the object and repeat "chair." If I am drilling you on your German, you would try to respond with the correct German equivalent. If I am rearranging the living room, you might respond to the word by bringing the chair to me. Apart from the linguistic responses and activities that make up such language-games, my saying "chair" would make no sense. We don't simply speak—we do things by means of speaking.

Third, Wittgenstein used the notion of language-games to illustrate that we run into confusion when we aren't aware that the way in which words function will vary from one language-game to another. In literal games, for example, catching the ball in one's hands is important in basketball, but in soccer if someone other than the goalie uses hands to catch the ball that is an illegitimate move. With respect to language, the logical positivists treated scientific discourse as the only language-game and judged all other ways of speaking (religious and ethical discourse) to be meaningless. But this is like supposing that ducks are the only kind of fowl there are and, therefore, like judging swans to be deficient and malformed ducks. According to Wittgenstein, language-games (like ducks and swans) must be judged on their own terms, by their own standards.

Not paying attention to the different ways in which language functions is the cause of many traditional philosophical problems. Wittgenstein thinks the proper role of the philosopher is not to propose new and exotic theories but to remove "misunderstandings concerning the use of words, caused, among other things, by certain analogies

between the forms of expression in different regions of language" (PI §90). To illustrate Wittgenstein's point, consider whether or not the questions "Where was it lost?" and "Can I help you find it?" would be appropriate responses to each of the following statements: (1) I lost my contact lens. (2) He lost consciousness. (3) I lost my train of thought. (4) I lost my job. (5) I lost my faith. The preceding questions clearly apply in some of these cases and not in others; and in some of the cases, whether the questions make sense or not might depend on the context. Even in situations where one or the other question does apply, the questions have a different sense from one context to another. Clearly, losing a lens differs from losing consciousness. Although we could try to find the lens, it would be senseless to try to find the consciousness. The reason for this difference, of course, is not because consciousness is so much harder to detect than a lens. The point of the examples is that the language-games in which we speak of physical objects follow different rules (have a different grammar, Wittgenstein would say) from the language-games in which we talk of mental states, abilities, relationships, religious commitments, and so on. To use one of Wittgenstein's own examples, if you *know* the height of Mont Blanc you know a certain proposition that can be stated. But you can *know* how a clarinet sounds without being able to say it (PI §78). Again, this is because the word *know* functions in different ways.

It would be misleading to leave the impression that Wittgenstein is saying that the boundaries of language-games are clear-cut, hard-and-fast lines. Boundaries are drawn for special purposes, and they may vary depending on our purposes (PI §499). The general purpose of the language-games metaphor was not to catalogue linguistic usages but to remove confusions. Wittgenstein says that the language-games serve as

> objects of comparison *which are meant to throw light on the facts of our language by way not only of similarities, but also of dissimilarities.* (PI §130)

The mistake of the *Tractatus* was to impose on language the standards of "the crystalline purity of logic" as though human language were some sort of calculus (PI §107). However, to suppose that the inexactness of our language is a defect would be like supposing that the light from a reading lamp is not a real light because it has no sharp boundary (BB 27).

MEANING AND USE

In his earlier work, Wittgenstein explained meaning in terms of the logical relations between a name and its object or between a proposition and a fact. Gradually, however, he came to understand that words and sentences do not have meanings all by themselves, for they have the meanings we give to them. They are intimately tied to human purposes and activities, and in this context they have their life. Some have speculated that Wittgenstein received a new appreciation of how language functions from his experience as an elementary school teacher. Little children do not acquire new words by learning formal, exact definitions, but by learning how a word performs a job within an particular kind of context. To make us aware of the close relationship between meaning and use, Wittgenstein offers the following, tentative definition: "For a *large* class of cases—though not for all—in which we employ the word 'meaning' it can be defined thus: the meaning of a word is its use in the language" (PI §43). To emphasize the point that "use" can mean many sorts of things, Wittgenstein compares words to tools, each having a distinctive function (PI §11).

FORMS OF LIFE

The *Tractatus* account views language as an autonomous system of symbols in which the human speaker is mysteriously absent. In striking contrast, Wittgenstein now emphasizes that speaking is one sort of activity that takes place within the broader, concrete circumstances of human life. Wittgenstein uses the notion of "form of life" to capture this insight:

> To imagine a language means to imagine a form of life. (PI §19)

> Here the term "language-game" is meant to bring into prominence the fact that the speaking of language is part of an activity, or of a form of life. (PI §23)

Linguists have been able to decode long-dead ancient languages because there is something universal within human life.

> The common behaviour of mankind is the system of reference by means of which we interpret an unknown language. (PI §206)

In contrast to his earlier views, Wittgenstein does not think there is anything logically necessary about the ways in which our language is structured. At the same time, our ways of speaking are not completely arbitrary, either. They are intimately tied into the common human practices, needs, interests, goals, and understandings we seem to have. That language only has meaning within this broader context implies that simply uttering meaningful English sounds (such as a parrot does) is not yet to speak *our* language. In one of his typically striking epigrams, Wittgenstein says, "If a lion could talk we would not understand him" (PI II, p. 223). If the lion said, "I'm going to see a lawyer," while still behaving like a typical lion, basking in the sun, his words would not be serving a purpose within the activities or contexts where they have meaning for us.

Philosophers such as Descartes supposed a philosophical justification had to be given for every belief we have. However, Wittgenstein thinks this is a hopeless and useless task. There is simply a point where justifications come to an end:

> If I have exhausted the justifications I have reached bedrock, and my spade is turned. Then I am inclined to say: "This is simply what I do." (PI §217)

> What has to be accepted, the given is—so one could say—forms of life. (PI II, p. 226)

What makes possible our agreements in the forms of our language and practice? There seems to be no basis apart from human practice to ensure we will so agree. As Stanley Cavell puts it,

> That on the whole we do [agree] is a matter of our sharing routes of interest and feeling, modes of response, senses of humor and of significance and of fulfillment, of what is outrageous, of what is similar to what else, what a rebuke, what forgiveness, of when an utterance is an assertion, when an appeal,

when an explanation—all the whirl of organism Wittgenstein calls "forms of life." Human speech and activity, sanity and community, rest upon nothing more, but nothing less, than this.[26]

There can be no justification for our most basic concepts and ways of viewing the world because "what people accept as a justification—is shewn by how they think and live" (PI §325).

ORDINARY LANGUAGE VERSUS PHILOSOPHICAL LANGUAGE

One of the most important features of Wittgenstein's later philosophy is the distinction he makes between ordinary uses of language and philosophical uses. Previous philosophers had thought our understanding of terms such as "knowledge," "goodness," "mind," "time," and "reality" was confused. Hence, they tried to develop new definitions and theories to replace our ordinary conceptions. However, is it conceivable people never knew what they meant by these words? By what other standard than our ordinary practices could we critique our use of these terms? To say generations of people did not know what they meant when they said, "I know *X*," is like saying the rules of baseball we have used since the beginning of the game are wrong. The philosopher may come up with a new conception of knowledge, but would it improve our pre-philosophical understanding of knowledge? We seem to communicate and understand one another when we use the term "know" in ordinary discourse. Speaking about our ordinary ways of speaking, Wittgenstein says,

> *Is this language somehow too coarse and material for what we want to say? Then how is another one to be constructed?" (PI §120)*

Philosophers such as Russell created an ideal language against which our ordinary language was to be judged. According to Wittgenstein, the judge and the defendant should be reversed. The technical ways in which philosophers analyze and use ordinary terms create pseudo-problems because language has been taken out of the practical contexts where it is functioning just fine:

> *For philosophical problems arise when language goes on holiday. (PI §38)*

> *The confusions which occupy us arise when language is like an engine idling, not when it is doing its work. (PI §132)*

> *It is wrong to say that in philosophy we consider an ideal language as opposed to our ordinary one. For this makes it appear as though we thought we could improve on ordinary language. But ordinary language is all right. (BB 28)*

PHILOSOPHY AS THERAPY

If traditional philosophical problems result from the misuse of ordinary language, then the role of the Wittgensteinian philosopher is to show the source of the puzzlement:

> *When philosophers use a word—"knowledge", "being", "object", "I", "proposition", "name"—and try to grasp the* essence *of the thing, one must always ask oneself: is the word ever actually used in this way in the language-game which is its original home?—. (PI §116)*

If the answer to this question is no, then the remedy is to "bring words back from their metaphysical to their everyday use" (PI §116). Wittgenstein speaks of traditional philosophy as though it were a pathology. For example, he describes the philosopher's search for essences as "our craving for generality" (BB 17). To heal this deep discomfort, therefore, what is needed is a sort of "linguistic therapy" that will cure us of our search for Platonic perfection and that will make us feel at home in the ambiguous world of ordinary life and discourse. It was the purpose of Wittgenstein's work to accomplish this healing. "There is not *a* philosophical method, though there are indeed methods, like different therapies" (PI §133).

Just as the *Tractatus* ended in philosophical silence and Wittgenstein went on to pursue other things, so in his later period he hoped that once we saw things clearly, there would be no more need for philosophical theories and explanations and we could return to the peace of philosophical silence again:

Philosophy simply puts everything before us, and neither explains nor deduces anything.—Since everything lies open to view there is nothing to explain. (PI §126)

The real discovery is the one that makes me capable of stopping doing philosophy when I want to.—The one that gives philosophy peace, so that it is no longer tormented by questions which bring itself in question. (PI §133)

That Wittgenstein never accomplished this goal in his personal life nor in his culture, and that others used his methods to carry on the task of philosophy, leaves the haunting feeling that maybe philosophical questioning is just inextricably a part of our human form of life. Perhaps Wittgenstein, in spite of himself, realized this when he said that philosophical problems are "deep disquietudes; their roots are as deep in us as the forms of our language and their significance is as great as the importance of our language" (PI §111).

THE IMPACT OF WITTGENSTEIN'S LATER PHILOSOPHY

Wittgenstein once wrote, "Our language continually ties new knots in our thinking. And philosophy is never done with disentangling them."[27] This quote illustrates Wittgenstein's conviction that philosophy has only a negative, therapeutic mission. It also illustrates the fact that he did not think there was any way to systematically do philosophy. When trying to untangle the knots in a fishing line, one can start just about anywhere, attacking the problem first at this point and then at that one. For this reason, Wittgenstein's later writings are a loose collection of rambling remarks, dealing with a multitude of philosophical tangles. However, a number of philosophers who were inspired by Wittgenstein's example believed his techniques could be used to produce sustained and systematic analyses of traditional philosophical topics. Hence, many of the later ordinary language philosophers did not agree with him that philosophy simply attacks confusions. They saw his method of linguistic analysis as a positive method for doing philosophy of mind, epistemology, philosophy of religion, ethics, and so on.

This new method of doing philosophy benefited from the fresh, new way of looking at language that Wittgenstein provided. Previously, the logical positivists had banished religious, ethical, and aesthetic language from the realm of meaningful discourse. However, Wittgenstein showed that there are other kinds of discourse besides scientific reports and descriptions of sense data. The philosopher cannot improve on our ways of speaking, much less condemn language-games that have a function. The cardinal rule is "Philosophy may in no way interfere with the actual use of language; it can in the end only describe it" (PI §124). Although Wittgenstein did motivate a return to some of the traditional topics in philosophy, those who used his method still refrained from producing elaborate theories, and they remained skeptical of speculative metaphysics. Instead, analytic philosophy in the Wittgensteinian tradition engaged in the much more humble task of "mapping" the geography of our linguistic concepts. This new approach to language and philosophy is best described by looking at some representatives of post-Wittgensteinian analytic philosophy who labored at the task of conceptual analysis.

CONCEPTUAL ANALYSIS

|||

Gilbert Ryle

Gilbert Ryle (1900–1976) was educated at Oxford and taught there until his retirement. He was a powerful influence on philosophy in the English-speaking world. In 1949, four years before the publication of Wittgenstein's *Philosophical Investigations*, Ryle published *The Concept of Mind*. Many of his contemporaries called it one of the major events of philosophy in the postwar years. It was the first sustained investigation of a classical philosophical problem (the mind–body problem) that used the new techniques of ordinary language analysis. Ryle shared Wittgenstein's conviction that philosophical problems are not to be solved as much as they are to be dissolved. In other words, a proper analysis of the terminology of a problem area in philosophy will show that what initially appeared to be a problem was only a pseudo-problem. Thus, Ryle claimed he was not putting forth any philosophical theories, but was trying to make us attentive to the features of our linguistic terrain we have misconstrued:

> The philosophical arguments which constitute this book are intended not to increase what we know about minds, but to rectify the logical geography of the knowledge which we already possess. (CM 7)[28]

CATEGORY MISTAKES

The organizing principle Ryle uses for mapping our conceptual terrain is that of "categories." He says that "the logical type or category to which a concept belongs is the set of ways in which it is logically legitimate to operate with it" (CM 8). According to Ryle, a typical source of philosophical perplexity is that philosophers tend to confuse the differences between categories in their thought and language. Ryle gives the following example of a category mistake (CM 16). Suppose a visitor to the Oxford University campus is shown the libraries, playing fields, museums, laboratories, residences, the administration building, and so on. After com-

pleting the tour he or she now says, "I have seen all the classroom buildings, research centers, and dormitories, but when are you going to show me the university?" This person has committed what Ryle calls a category mistake. He or she has placed the university in the wrong category, assuming that the university is another particular thing, along with the buildings on the campus. The university, however, is not one more part within the whole, but the way in which all the parts are organized to form a whole. This sort of mistake occurs frequently in philosophy, Ryle claims, when we suppose that what we refer to with words such as "mind" and "body" belong to the same conceptual category, when they are actually serving different logical functions.

DESCARTES'S MYTH

Ryle believes Descartes made a similar sort of category mistake when he analyzed the mind–body problem. Descartes said the mechanical theories of Galileo apply to physical bodies but do not apply to minds. Therefore, since minds are not physical things governed by mechanical laws, he concluded that minds must be nonphysical, nonspatial sorts of things whose activities are mysterious, nonmechanical processes. It follows from Descartes's view that every person is a divided being. Some of a person's activities are bodily events that are in space and are publicly observable. Running parallel to these are mental events that are internal and private. Ryle describes Descartes's view of the mind as that of "the dogma of the Ghost in the Machine." This image trapped Descartes into asking questions about how and where a nonphysical mind can interact with a physical body. This picture has been so influential that Ryle says it is "the official doctrine" on the nature of the mind.

Ryle's solution is to argue that mental conduct words and physical thing words belong to different categories such that trying to figure out the relationship between mental events and bodily events is as absurd as asking if Oxford University is east or west of the chemistry building. The problem is, when we encounter a noun (such as "mind"), we tend to suppose it refers to some sort of distinct *thing*, even if a ghostly thing. To use an example (this one is not Ryle's), if you say, "He gives me the creeps," it would be a mistake for me to ask, "How many creeps does he give you?" We know what was meant by the first statement, and it didn't mean to imply that some sort of transferable entity exists called a "creep."

The thesis of Ryle's book is that "*the* mind" is a misleading term that can best be translated into the manifold mental conduct terms we use to describe certain aspects of one another's public activities. Thus, he tries to make clear what we are doing when we talk about thinking, understanding, and willing or when we say something was done intelligently, carelessly, purposefully, and so on. It is important to note that, as an ordinary language philosopher, Ryle does not intend to rob us of any of the ways we normally speak:

> I am not, . . . denying that there occur mental processes. Doing long division is a mental process and so is making a joke. But I am saying that the phrase "there occur mental processes" does not mean the same sort of thing as "there occur physical processes", and, therefore that it makes no sense to conjoin or disjoin the two. (CM 22)

In other words, he wants to describe how language functions and not reform it. His problem is not with how we use mental terms but with philosophers' *theories* about mental activities.

RYLE'S ANALYSIS OF MENTAL TERMS

Typical of Ryle's method is his analysis of the notion of intelligence. The official doctrine says that acting intelligently consists of two activities: (1) doing something and (2) thinking what one is doing while doing it. It is true we often deliberate before we do something, as in playing chess, but deliberation is not a necessary feature of intelligent performances. When we drive a car, make a humorous response in a conversation, or address a letter, we usually do not mentally rehearse our

intended action. Furthermore, if intelligence is defined in terms of a hidden, private process that occurs behind the scenes, then we could never know if someone was intelligent, for we would not have access to the private theater of the mind. Similarly, we could not know a host of other things we do know about people, such as that they are vain, creative, conscientious, or observant. The correct analysis, Ryle believes, is to view an attribute such as intelligence as a kind of competence or skill similar to knowing how to tie a knot or play a musical instrument. Hence, "overt intelligent performances are not clues to the workings of minds; they are those workings" (CM 58). Ryle points out that dispositional properties are a different sort of property from properties such as color or shape. For example, being brittle is a dispositional property. When we say a glass is brittle, we are saying that under certain circumstances the glass will break. Similarly, when we say Smith is intelligent (or devious, or cautious, and so on), we mean that in certain sorts of circumstances he will tend to respond in certain sorts of ways.

One problem with the view that bodily activities are directed by mental acts is that it leads to an infinite regress. If acting intelligently requires the bodily action to be preceded by some sort of intellectual operation, then for these mental activities themselves to be intelligent, their execution must be preceded by another prior act of theorizing, and so on. Similarly, if we say a bodily action is voluntary if it originated in an act of the will, then if that mental action of willing is to be voluntary, it must have itself been preceded by yet another volition, and so on endlessly. Ryle argues that "voluntary" does not refer to a mental act that precedes or accompanies an action, but indicates the manner in which it was done.

One argument that Descartes and other dualists use to defend their position is based on the phenomenon of self-knowledge. We have privileged access to the private theater of our minds, they claim, in ways other people do not. In critiquing this thesis, Ryle points out that we do not have a totally unique, privileged access to our own mental life because (1) we are often wrong in interpreting our own motives and emotional states and (2) people sometimes understand us better than we do ourselves. For the most part, however, "the sorts of things that I can find out about myself are the same as the sorts of things that I can find out about other people" (CM 155). To illustrate this, he asks us to consider the answer to the following sorts of questions:

> How do I discover that I am more unselfish than you; that I can do long division well, but differential equations only badly; that you suffer from certain phobias and tend to shirk facing certain sorts of facts; that I am more easily irritated than most people but less subject to panic, vertigo, or morbid conscientiousness? (CM 169)

To answer such questions, I do not "peep into a windowless chamber, illuminated by a very peculiar sort of light" (CM 168–169). In knowing how to answer such questions about myself as well as others, I observe the activities of the person in question, his or her tendencies, dispositions, and patterns of behavior in certain circumstances. Finally, if the mind is not a private arena of mental states, the dualist asks, how can the hypocrite be outwardly contrite while he remains inwardly unrepentant? Ryle says we judge that someone is contrite from his or her gestures, accents, words, and deeds. If we were not usually correct in making inferences from such behavior, the hypocrite could not deceive us by simulating this behavior. To conclude, Ryle would, perhaps, say that whether or not you consider his own philosophical intellect to be brilliant or mediocre, you did not find this out by peering into the hidden recesses of his mind. Any judgments you make about a philosopher's intellectual powers are necessarily made on the basis of the publicly available data of his or her scholarly achievements.

John Austin

John Austin (1911–1960) was a professor of moral philosophy at Oxford University from 1952 until his death in 1960. He once said that early in his career he had to choose between publishing as much as possible or devoting the major portion of his time to teaching. He chose to concentrate on

training students in the philosophical method he had developed and so did not publish as much as some of his contemporaries. Nevertheless, the few journal articles he published during his lifetime created a stir because of the new techniques he had developed for analyzing concepts. Happily, several books published after his death enabled the philosophical community to benefit from the labors of this great mind. The essays he wrote were collected under the title *Philosophical Papers* (1961). A reconstruction of Austin's lectures and notes on the theory of perception were published, as *Sense and Sensibilia* (1964). Finally, a series of lectures he gave at Harvard University in 1955 were published, as *How to Do Things with Words* (1962). All three books have since become classics within analytic philosophy.

AUSTIN'S PHILOSOPHICAL METHOD

Unlike Wittgenstein, Austin believes philosophy can make a positive contribution to the understanding of our language and concepts rather than simply serving as a therapy to our linguistic pathology. In response to the question "How many kinds of sentence are there?" Wittgenstein gave the inexact reply "There are *countless* kinds" (PI §23). However, Austin thinks we can classify various forms of expression much as a botanist classifies species of flowers, producing an orderly array. He thinks that analyzing and cataloguing the rich and diverse varieties of linguistic phenomena is worthwhile in itself, independently of the practical results of eliminating conceptual confusions. Austin does not claim the analysis of ordinary language is the only method that should be used in philosophy, but he insists it is a useful one. As he says, "Ordinary language is *not* the last word: in principle it can everywhere be supplemented and improved upon and superseded. Only remember, it is the *first* word" (PE 386).[29]

Austin lists several reasons why the analysis of ordinary language is important to philosophy. First, "words are our tools, and, as a minimum, we should use clean tools: we should know what we mean and what we do not, and we must forearm ourselves against the traps that language sets us." Second, since our ways of speaking (like biological species) have evolved over a long period of time, those that have endured are likely to be the most effective ones. As Austin expresses it,

> Our common stock of words embodies all the distinctions men have found worth drawing, and the connexions they have found worth marking, in the lifetimes of many generations: these surely are likely to be more numerous, more sound, since they have stood up to the long test of the survival of the fittest, and more subtle, at least in all ordinary and reasonably practical matters, than any that you or I are likely to think up in our arm-chairs of an afternoon—the most favoured alternative method. (PE 383–384)

Finally, linguistic analysis is not simply words about words, even though words and things must not be confused. Careful attention to words can give us insight into the world of experience:

> When we examine what we should say when, what words we should use in what situations, we are looking again not merely at words (or "meanings," whatever they may be) but also at the realities we use the words to talk about: we are using a sharpened awareness of words to sharpen our perception of, though not as the final arbiter of, the phenomena. (PE 384)

AUSTIN'S ANALYSIS OF EXCUSES

Austin's seminal essay "A Plea for Excuses" gives us a paradigm example of the method of conceptual analysis. Instead of offering us a full-scale ethical theory, Austin uses his conceptual microscope to focus in on one, manageable area of ethical discourse, namely, those situations where we offer excuses for our actions. Nevertheless, he is convinced this sort of microanalysis will be useful for ethics because it will help clarify the nature of action, the differences between permissible and prohibited acts, as well as the notions of responsibility, blame, and freedom. When we want to offer an excuse for an action we performed that was unacceptable in some way, we use such words as "involuntarily," "inadvertently," "accidentally," "unwillingly," "unintentionally," and so on. He notices that some words come paired in positive and negative forms, such as "voluntarily" and "involuntarily," but some

words do not have these dual forms. For example, I can knock over the teacup *inadvertently* when I pass the butter. But if I did not upset the cream jug, I did not avoid it *advertently*. Furthermore, he argues that contrary to appearances, "voluntarily" and "involuntarily" are not true opposites. When we did not do something voluntarily, we did not do it involuntarily either, but we did it under constraint, under duress, or in some other way were compelled by factors that impinged on us. However, the opposite of an involuntarily action is one done deliberately, on purpose, or the like. Furthermore, these terms do not exhaust the possibilities, for when I do something routine such as eating breakfast, we do not say I did it either voluntarily or involuntarily unless some extraordinary circumstances require one of these descriptions. In this way, Austin shows the connections, the differences, and the subtle nuances among these important words in our moral vocabulary.

HOW TO DO THINGS WITH WORDS

Wittgenstein employed the notion of "language-games" to indicate that speaking is not simply making sounds but is a type of activity. Similarly, in his important work *How to Do Things with Words*, Austin introduces the notion of "speech acts." Whenever someone says something, a number of distinguishable acts are performed. First, the *locutionary act* is simply the act *of* uttering (or writing) a set of words with a certain meaning. Second, the *illocutionary act* is what a person intentionally does *in* performing the locutionary act (such as reporting, warning, confessing, suggesting, ordering). Third, the *perlocutionary act* consists of the actual response on the part of the listener the speaker hopes to bring about *by* performing the illocutionary act (for example, persuade, deceive, frighten, inspire, and so on).

To illustrate Austin's analysis, I can say, "It is raining outside" (locutionary act). In saying this, there are several possibilities as to what action I am actually performing (illocutionary act): reporting a fact, expressing dismay at the weather, suggesting that you stay, telling a lie, and so on. Let us suppose I am simply reporting a fact. Then, by means of this act, there is some effect on the listener I am intending to bring about (perlocutionary act). For example, I could be trying to get the listener to *believe* correctly it is raining, *distract* the listener from her self-pity, *cause* the listener to realize that the driving will be dangerous, and so on. As a result of Austin's investigations, speech act theory has blossomed into a very complex but fruitful approach to understanding language. From this brief account it is clear the theory of language has come a long way from Russell's view that the function of language is simply to refer to a fact in the world.

The Significance of Analytic Philosophy

The analytic movement has provided philosophy with new methods, new tools, and new territories for philosophical exploration. It has made philosophers aware of the importance of language both as a philosophical resource and as an impediment to clear understanding. Its importance is signified by such slogans as "the linguistic turn in philosophy" and "the revolution in philosophy" that have been used to describe its impact. Analytic philosophy, in all its different varieties, has become dominant in the English-speaking world and has produced many brilliant practitioners of the method as well as a wealth of illuminating, twentieth-century philosophical classics. No one can be a serious student of philosophy today without giving careful attention to the accomplishments of this movement.

Despite the influence of analytic philosophy, however, it has had its detractors. For the most part, Marxist philosophers have never been fond of it. Herbert Marcuse, a contemporary Marxist theorist, describes it as "one-dimensional philosophy."[30] He claims that ordinary language contains the sedimented ideology of the prevailing power structures. Hence Wittgenstein's assurance that philosophy "leaves everything as it is" prevents any sort of radical critique and change of the status quo. Those within the Continental (European) movements of phenomenology and existentialism

charge that an analysis of language is irrelevant because our current ways of speaking may obscure rather than reveal the rich dimensions of our lived experience, which they think is the proper subject of philosophical exploration. The last few decades of the twentieth century, however, have seen signs of increased understanding between the proponents of these diverse philosophical movements. Some have made attempts to build bridges from both sides of the gulf between analytic and Continental philosophy in order to learn from the insights of the opposing camp.

Questions for Understanding

1. What are three fundamental points of agreement among analytic philosophers?

2. What are the five stages of analytic philosophy?

3. Why did Russell call his philosophy "logical atomism"?

4. Why did Russell believe there was a need to construct an ideal language?

5. In Russell's ideal language, what are atomic propositions and molecular propositions and how are these related to atomic facts?

6. What sorts of things are logical constructions, according to Russell?

7. According to Russell, what is the nature of a logically proper name? In his later work, what was the only expression he would have recognized as a logically proper name?

8. What were the three main goals of the logical positivists?

9. What are the two kinds of genuine knowledge according to the logical positivists?

10. What are tautologies?

11. What is the verifiability principle? Why was it modified several times and in what ways?

12. Why did the logical positivists say the statements of metaphysics and theology are not simply false but meaningless?

13. What were the two different ways logical positivists explained ethical statements?

14. What was the task of Wittgenstein's *Tractatus*?

15. What was the earlier Wittgenstein's picture theory of language?

16. What were the implications of Wittgenstein's *Tractatus* for traditional philosophy?

17. Why did Wittgenstein call his own propositions in the *Tractatus* "nonsensical"?

18. In the *Tractatus*, why does Wittgenstein refer to "the mystical"?

19. In what ways was Wittgenstein's philosophy different in his later period?

20. In spite of all the differences, what were the common concerns in both Wittgenstein's earlier and later work?

21. What features of language is Wittgenstein drawing our attention to in using the expression "language-games"?

22. What is Wittgenstein's point concerning "family resemblances"?

23. What does Wittgenstein suggest is a good way to view the meaning of a word?

24. What does Wittgenstein mean by "forms of life"? What does he say about their justification?

25. Why does the later Wittgenstein think there is no need for a special philosophical language or an ideal language?

26. Why does Wittgenstein speak of philosophy as a kind of therapy in his later period?

27. What does Gilbert Ryle mean by "category mistakes"? What are some examples?

28. According to Ryle, what is Descartes's "myth"? What is Ryle's remedy to Descartes's way of talking about the mind?

29. What account does Ryle give of each of the following: acting intelligently, acting voluntarily, self-knowledge? In what way do his explanations attempt to undermine Descartes's notion that the mind is a separate entity in which special mental activities take place?

30. What is J. L. Austin's philosophical method?

31. What is the distinction Austin makes between locutionary, illocutionary, and perlocutionary acts? How does his account of language differ from the view that the purpose of language is simply to refer to a fact in the world?

Questions for Reflection

1. Take a philosophical problem that you have encountered previously. How might an analytic philosopher translate that problem into one concerning the meaning and use of our terms?

2. Browse through the previous chapters and find philosophical claims that would be rejected as meaningless by the logical positivists. Do you agree with their verdict on these claims?

3. What are the strengths and weaknesses of the verifiability principle?

4. Taking the standpoint of the later Wittgenstein, Ryle, or Austin, argue against the thesis that the purpose of language is simply to name objects in the world.

5. Think of examples that illustrate Wittgenstein's and Ryle's claim that philosophical pseudo-problems can result from misunderstanding the use of a word.

Notes

1. Moritz Schlick, "The Future of Philosophy," in *The Linguistic Turn: Recent Essays in Philosophical Method*, ed. Richard Rorty (Chicago: University of Chicago Press, 1967), 48.

2. This method of organizing the positions is taken from Barry R. Gross, *Analytic Philosophy: An Historical Introduction* (New York: Pegasus, 1970), 13–14.

3. Bertrand Russell, *My Philosophical Development* (New York: Simon & Schuster, 1959), 11.

4. Bertrand Russell, *Portraits from Memory and Other Essays* (London: Allen & Unwin, 1956), 53.

5. This example was taken from Jerrold J. Katz, *The Underlying Reality of Language and Its Philosophical Import* (New York: Harper Torchbooks, Harper & Row, 1971), 6.

6. Bertrand Russell, "Logical Atomism," in *Contemporary British Philosophy*, vol. 1, ed. J. H. Muirhead (London: Allen & Unwin, 1924), 377.

7. Bertrand Russell, *The Philosophy of Logical Atomism*, ed. David Pears (La Salle, IL: Open Court, 1985), 58.

8. Russell, *My Philosophical Development*, 169.

9. Russell, *The Philosophy of Logical Atomism*, 86.

10. Bertrand Russell, "The Relation of Sense-Data to Physics," in his *Mysticism and Logic* (Garden City, NY: Doubleday Anchor Books, 1957), 150.

11. Bertrand Russell, *Human Knowledge, Its Scope and Limits* (New York: Simon & Schuster, 1948), 488.

12. Russell, *Human Knowledge*, 495.

13. Bertrand Russell, "Reply to Criticisms," in *The Philosophy of Bertrand Russell*, The Library of Living Philosophers, vol. 5, ed. Paul A. Schilpp (Evanston, IL: Northwestern University, 1944), 719.

14. Bertrand Russell, "My Mental Development," in *The Philosophy of Bertrand Russell*, 19.

15. David Hume, *An Enquiry Concerning Human Understanding*, sec. 12, pt. 3.

16. A. J. Ayer, *Language, Truth and Logic* (New York: Dover, n.d.), 36.

17. Rudolf Carnap, *Philosophy and Logical Syntax*, in *Readings in Twentieth-Century Philosophy*, ed. William P. Alston and George Nakhnikian (New York: The Free Press of Glencoe, Macmillan, 1963), 432.

18. A. J. Ayer, 107–108.

19. Rudolf Carnap, "The Physical Language as the Universal Language of Science," in *Readings in Twentieth-Century Philosophy*, 393–394.

20. A. J. Ayer, "Editor's Introduction," in *Logical Positivism*, ed. A. J. Ayer (New York: The Free Press, 1959), 15–16.

21. Hermine Wittgenstein, "My Brother Ludwig," trans. Bernhard Leitner in *Ludwig Wittgenstein: Personal Recollections*, ed. Rush Rhees (Totowa, NJ: Rowman & Littlefield, 1981), 2.

22. Ludwig Wittgenstein, *Tractatus Logico-Philosophicus*, trans. D. F. Pears and B. F. McGuinness (London: Routledge & Kegan Paul, 1961). Block quotations from this work place the paragraph numbers in the left margin as in the original. Short quotations within the text place the paragraph numbers at the end in parentheses, and the abbreviation "T" indicates the *Tractatus*.

23. Quoted in Paul Engelmann, *Letters from Ludwig Wittgenstein, with a Memoir*, ed. B. F. McGuinness, trans. L. Furtmüller (New York: Horizon Press, 1974), 144.

24. Ludwig Wittgenstein, "Wittgenstein's Lecture on Ethics," *The Philosophical Review*, 74, no. 1 (January 1965), 13.

25. The following abbreviations are used to refer to works from Wittgenstein's later period.

   BB   "The Blue Book" in *The Blue and Brown Books* (New York: Harper & Row, Harper Torchbooks, 1958). Numbers in the citation refer to page numbers.

   PI   *Philosophical Investigations*, trans. G. E. M. Anscombe (New York: Macmillan, 1953). Numbers in the citation refer to section numbers, except when the passage is from part II of the book, in which case the numbers are page numbers.

26. Stanley Cavell, "The Availability of Wittgenstein's Later Philosophy," *The Philosophical Review*, 71 (1962), reprinted in *Wittgenstein: The Philosophical Investigations*, ed. George Pitcher (New York: Anchor Books, Doubleday, 1966), 160–161.

27. Quoted in Garth Hallett, *A Companion to Wittgenstein's "Philosophical Investigations"* (Ithaca, NY: Cornell University Press, 1977), 195.

28. Gilbert Ryle, *The Concept of Mind* (New York: Barnes & Noble, 1949). References to this work are abbreviated "CM," and the numbers refer to page numbers.

29. John Austin, "A Plea for Excuses," *Proceedings of the Aristotelian Society*, n.s., 57 (1956–1957), reprinted in *Classics of Analytic Philosophy*, ed. Robert R. Ammerman (New York: McGraw-Hill, 1965). References to this work are abbreviated "PE."

30. Herbert Marcuse, *One-Dimensional Man* (Boston: Beacon Press, 1964), chap. 7.

33

Phenomenology and Existentialism

WHEN WE TURN FROM THE ANALYTIC PHILOSO- phy that flourished on British and American ter- rain, to the philosophies that developed on European soil in the twentieth century, we find ourselves in an entirely different world. The Con- tinental movements of phenomenology and exis- tentialism were concerned with questions such as "What is consciousness?" and "What does it mean to be a person?" However, the phenomenologists and existentialists saw no use in analyzing how we use the *words* "consciousness" or "person," for this would only give us the unclarified assumptions and residues of our historical traditions. Instead, they believed we must look to the *experience* of being a conscious person to answer these ques- tions. However, it will be clear that the notion of "experience" that underlies their investigations is a far cry from the analytical, scientific model of classical empiricism.

Although their roots go back to such nineteenth-century figures as Søren Kierke- gaard, Friedrich Nietzsche, and Fyodor Dostoev- sky, most of the twentieth-century Continental thinkers cannot be understood apart from the work of Edmund Husserl, the founder of phe- nomenology. Many seminal figures in twentieth- century Continental thought either studied with Husserl or studied his writings. There is a great deal of irony in Husserl's impact, however, for his philosophical offspring were influenced as much by the insights of his philosophy as they were by those features they considered dead wrong. The existentialists, for example, gave philosophy a new agenda by focusing on the dark, shadowy side of human existence with their analyses of such phe- nomena as anxiety, dread, guilt, and death. They were equally at home expressing their philosophy in terms of poetry, novels, and plays and writing ponderously worded philosophical essays. In striking contrast, Husserl, their intellectual men- tor, received his training in mathematics and took it as his goal to make philosophy into a "rigorous science." It is an interesting case study of philo- sophical "genetics," therefore, to find the seed in Husserl's philosophy and method that gave birth to such unlikely offspring.

EDMUND HUSSERL

|||

The Life of a Perpetual Beginner

Edmund Husserl (1859–1938) was born the same year in which Bergson and Dewey were born. He studied physics, astronomy, and mathematics at the University of Leipzig, continued his education in Berlin, and finally earned his doctorate at the University of Vienna in 1883 with a dissertation on mathematical theory. The turning point in his life occurred when he attended the lectures of the German philosopher and psychologist Franz Brentano in Vienna from 1884 to 1886. Under Brentano's influence, Husserl discovered that his true calling was philosophy. After several teaching appointments, he settled in at the University of Freiburg in 1916 where he remained until his retirement in 1928.

Although Husserl was Jewish, he had converted to Protestant Christianity in his twenties. Nevertheless, when the Nazis rose to power, this did not exempt him from their anti-Semitism. After 1933 Husserl was forbidden to engage in academics. He published several major works and numerous, lengthy articles. In addition, he left behind a massive collection of 45,000 pages of handwritten manuscript, recorded in shorthand and preserved in the Husserl Archives in Louvain, Belgium. His working notes are so extensive because he described himself as a "perpetual beginner" who had to continually rethink everything he had done before. In 1938 Edmund Husserl died at the age of seventy-nine, sparing him from the worst of the Nazi terrors to come.

Husserl's Task: Developing Philosophy into a Rigorous Science

The driving force throughout Husserl's career was the quest for certainty. As he noted in his diary,

> I have been through enough torments from lack of clarity and doubt that wavers back and forth. . . . Only one need absorbs me: I must win clarity, else I

cannot live; I cannot bear life unless I believe that I shall achieve it.[1]

Husserl believed that Western culture was in a state of crisis because we have lost our belief that we can attain rational certainty. Among other consequences, this led to irrationalism in the social and political realm, an irrationalism that would eventually produce the bitter fruit of Nazism. Furthermore, by neglecting the foundations of our knowledge, the theoretical sciences were drifting, having ignored their roots in the activities of consciousness that produced them. As his thought developed, Husserl realized that the crisis of rational certainty was also a crisis of meaning. The sciences had severed themselves from their origins in pretheoretical experience (called the "life-world") where all meaning is constituted.

As Husserl saw it, a major cause of the crisis of the modern world was an outlook known as naturalism. **Naturalism** claims that physical nature encompasses everything real and that all reality can be exhaustively explained by the natural sciences.* But this implies that consciousness itself is just another item of nature that can be explained by the laws of physics, chemistry, and biology. Husserl argued, however, that if consciousness and our beliefs are simply products of blind and irrational physical causes, then we cannot have rational, justified beliefs (including the belief in naturalism). Dismissing these theories that undermine the foundations of knowledge, Husserl began the search for rational certainty where Descartes before him had sought it, by looking within to consciousness. Accordingly, he titled one of his books

---

*In the early years of his career, Husserl himself had embraced a form of naturalism known as *psychologism*. His first book, *The Philosophy of Arithmetic*, was an attempt to base the foundations of arithmetic on certain generalizations about human psychology. However, through the criticisms of the mathematician and logician Gottlob Frege, Husserl came to see that logic and mathematics contain *a priori*, necessary truths that cannot be reduced to the empirical truths of psychology.

Cartesian Meditations and closed it with a line from Augustine: "Do not wish to go out; go back into yourself. Truth dwells in the inner man." But if consciousness is to provide us with the foundations of knowledge, Husserl thought it must be approached in a special way. Hence, he spent his life charting a new course for philosophy.

Phenomenology as a Science of Experience

Husserl proposes a *method*, the method of phenomenology, which not only guides us in discovering new truths but also enables us to test the rational adequacy of any truth claim. Husserl's understanding of phenomenology has affinities with Hegel's massive work *The Phenomenology of Spirit*. For Hegel and Husserl alike, phenomenology is a systematic study of the phenomena, or of what appears within experience. By denying that any meaningful content exists in the notion of a reality that is, in principle, inaccessible to reason, both wish to avoid the trap Kant fell into when he postulated the unknowable "things in themselves." They both argue that once we suppose there is such a gap between the phenomena and reality, then skepticism is unavoidable.

Husserl's goal is to find an approach to philosophical truth that will be "presuppositionless." Minimally, Husserl meant by this claim that philosophers should not use any assumptions in their investigations that have not been thoroughly examined, clarified, and justified. The fundamental philosophical rule is to accept only what is directly evident. As Husserl puts it, there can be no higher justification for the truth of a claim than "I see that it is so" (I 76).[2]

The uniqueness of phenomenology is indicated by the fact that it can be characterized as both a type of rationalism and a radical empiricism. It is a rationalism because it searches for *a priori* principles and essences that are more than inductive generalizations and are known through rational intuition. Yet it is also a form of empiricism because it justifies its claims by reference to experience. It is a "radical" empiricism because

phenomenologists claim they are more empirical, more faithful to experience, than those who traditionally have called themselves *empiricists*. Phenomenology has a richer, broader, and deeper notion of experience than the British empiricists and most of the twentieth-century analysts. According to phenomenology, the content of experience includes more than the sensory impressions that come through the five senses. For example, Husserl claims we may also "experience" numbers, geometrical figures, ideal entities, universals, the meanings of propositions, values, moral duties, aesthetic qualities, and (perhaps) religious phenomena.* Furthermore, Husserl claims that perceptual experience is not the collection of discrete, unrelated sensations Hume talked about. According to Husserl, this picture is not what experience presents to us, but is the result of imposing onto experience the empiricists' *theory* of what they think experience *must* be like. Nobody experiences Hume's units of red-spherical-sweet sense data. Instead, we experience such things as apples, tomatoes, and cherries. At best, such sense data are abstractions artificially lifted out of certain moments within the complex unity of experience.

The Phenomenological Method

THE THESIS OF THE NATURAL STANDPOINT

According to Husserl, the phenomenological method involves taking a certain stance toward experience. All experiencing prior to our phenomenological investigations is characterized by what Husserl calls the "natural standpoint" or the "natural attitude." This is a particular way of viewing the world that is based on a number of unquestioned and implicit assumptions. The most basic assumption is that the external world is a

---

*Husserl himself never applied the phenomenological method to religious experience. However, besides the fact that he became a Protestant, his view of philosophy was such that he was as open to religious phenomena as he was to any genuine experience. Some thinkers who came after him did try to develop a phenomenology of religion.

spatiotemporal realm that exists independently of our consciousness and consists of objects that experience reveals to us (chairs, coffee cups, books, trees, and so on). Among the items in this world there are minds: my mind, your mind, and our neighbors' minds. In our everyday life we are immersed in our practical concerns and carry on our commerce with people and things in terms of this standpoint. To free us from this taken-for-granted standpoint, Husserl developed a number of techniques that would allow us to get back to pure experience, freeing it of the overlays and theories that philosophers have imported into experience.

BRACKETING THE WORLD

The point of departure for the phenomenological method is the "bracketing" of the world. This is done by initiating a shift of attention in which we take up a different stance from that of our everyday dealings with the world to clarify the sense and the structure of the world and our engagements with it. Husserl also called this procedure the phenomenological reduction or *epoche*.* This means that the world and its objects, as well as our beliefs about them, are put in mental brackets so that we can view this panorama of phenomena with a sense of objectivity and detachment. Besides initiating this shift of attention, bracketing also includes suspending judgment about the existence of the world as well as any theories about the causes of phenomena that appear within it.

Husserl's technique of withholding or disconnecting our beliefs about the world was inspired by Descartes's method of doubt. Unlike Descartes, however, Husserl is not asking us to doubt the existence of the world or our prephilosophical beliefs. Instead, the phenomenological reduction leaves everything within the natural standpoint as it was, except now we put our beliefs "out of action" and do not use them in describing experience. In other words, I do not cease believing in the world, but now I see it as "a-world-that-is-believed-in."

Epoche was the term used by the Greek skeptics when they recommended we withhold our commitment and suspend judgment about things that were uncertain.

Whereas previous philosophers theorized about experience, leading to a number of distortions, Husserl proposes a disciplined method of pure description. Phenomenological description explains the layers and strata within experience by making thematic what is operative and making explicit what is implicit, without adding to or subtracting from the phenomena:

> This cannot be emphasized often enough—*phenomenal explication does nothing but* explicate the sense this world has for us all prior to any philosophizing, *and obviously gets solely from our experience*—a sense which philosophy can uncover but never alter. (CM 151)

The basic thrust of Husserl's entire philosophy could be encapsulated in his famous slogan "To the things themselves!"

CONSCIOUSNESS AS INTENTIONALITY

One significant result of stepping back from the world and putting it in brackets is that consciousness is no longer submerged in the background of experience, but comes to the forefront of my reflective awareness. Ordinarily, when I am engaged with the world in the natural attitude, I have relatively little self-awareness, because I mainly attend to the objects of experience. However, when the world is put in brackets, when I am no longer straightforwardly engaged in it, I discover consciousness is at work in all my experiences. The next step in phenomenology is to uncover what we find when we bring consciousness to the center stage of our investigation.

Unlike Descartes, Husserl finds that when we examine consciousness, we do not discover some sort of metaphysical substance. Consciousness does not have the qualities of a thing—not even a ghostly thing. At the same time, Hume and the empiricists were wrong to suppose we find nothing but a flow of sensations. What we do find, Husserl insists, is a certain structure that we can describe independently of its particular contents. The turn to consciousness discloses not an entity but a series of acts of awareness that are always correlated with some object. This, then, is the essential feature of consciousness. Consciousness is always a consciousness-*of* some object or another. This is known as Husserl's "doctrine of intentionality." Here "intentionality" does *not* mean the purpose of an action, as when we ask, "Did you intend to harm your opponent?" Instead, "intentionality" refers to that feature of consciousness characterized as tending toward, pointing to, or directedness toward an object. Since these two poles of experience are always correlated, the intentional act (the experiencing) is called the *noetic correlate*, and the object of that act (what is experienced) is the *noematic correlate*.

Two qualifications are necessary to understand Husserl's notion of intentionality. First, even though consciousness is essentially referential, its objects do not need to exist; for example, I can think of a unicorn or the perfect society. Second, the objects of consciousness are not always *physical* objects (real or imagined). For example, I can doubt a proposition, think about a prime number, worry about the emotional tone of a meeting, admire the values of another culture, desire moral goodness, or recognize the universal of redness as something different from red objects.

THE DISCOVERY OF ESSENCES

Husserl is not interested in simply an empirical, psychological description of various kinds of experiences. The search for certainty requires that we discover the essential features of the phenomena. Hence, the next step in Husserl's phenomenological method is what he calls the *eidetic reduction*. This is the process of reducing the phenomena to essences. The essence of something is its defining characteristics, what makes it the sort of thing it is. Essences are not discovered by means of empirical generalizations or abstractions from particulars, but through direct intuition. Suppose, for example, the phenomenon I am examining is perception and I begin by considering the specific case of my-seeing-an-apple. For the phenomenologist, the ultimate focus is not on the particular features of this concrete experience but on the essence of each of the three elements of the

experience. In other words, the phenomenologist uses this experience to examine what it means to be (1) a consciousness for whom there can be perceived objects, (2) an act of perceiving, and (3) a perceptual object. Through an exhaustive series of phenomenological investigations, Husserl hoped to uncover the sense that phenomena have for us, those acts through which the phenomena are revealed, and the ground of all meanings and human engagements in consciousness.

Transcendental Phenomenology

Husserl became increasingly radical in his later writings as he placed more emphasis on the role of consciousness in experience. Talk of consciousness as an activity became transformed into talk about a "transcendental ego" that is identical throughout its acts. Husserl had hoped to find a middle road between realism and idealism. However, there was always an ambiguity or a tension in Husserl's phenomenology that he could not resolve and that drove him, according to some interpreters, into the ranks of the idealists.

The tension in Husserl's position comes out in the following passage:

> Objects exist for me, and are for me what they are, only as objects of actual and possible consciousness. (CM 65)

The moderate interpretation of this would be that only through consciousness are things present to us as meaningful entities. The more radical interpretation is that things depend entirely on consciousness for their existence. The problem is, once we have bracketed the world to study what appears to consciousness, can we find some basis for asserting the world's objectivity and independence from the mind, apart from slipping back into the natural attitude?

This problem emerges as Husserl's understanding of the relation between consciousness and objects develops. In his earlier writings, he says the objects we experience are *given* in intuition (experience). Here, consciousness plays a partially passive role as the various aspects and structures of the phenomena reveal themselves to us. In his later writings, Husserl speaks of the phenomena as *constituted* by consciousness. For example, it is through the activities of a constituting consciousness that my experience of someone begins to take shape, from the initial perceptual data, to my observations of his or her behavior, then to the further level of the style and content of their speech, and so on. Layer by layer, "sedimentations" of meanings build up as consciousness constitutes the objects within experience. The process by which the many dimensions of a phenomenon take shape and are constituted in consciousness is studied by means of what Husserl called "genetic phenomenology." The question that remains throughout all this concerns the extent to which consciousness is active or passive in apprehending the phenomena and whether the objects constitute themselves or are constituted by consciousness.

Even some of Husserl's admirers worried that his later position had elevated the active role of the transcendental ego to the point that he had surrendered to idealism. There seemed to be a fine and fast-disappearing line between the notion of consciousness *constituting* the objects of experience and the transcendental ego *constructing* them. The following example illustrates how this issue arises. As I type this, I am perceiving a nearby coffee mug. However, it does not seem to depend on my mind, but seems to be an object existing across the room, sitting on the table by the window. Yet, for Husserl, we cannot escape the fact that when we call something "an objective and independently existing object" we are referring to an intentional object whose appearance has the aspect of *being-independent-of-me*, and this aspect is nothing more than the sense and meaning it has for consciousness. All our talk about realities apart from consciousness is always talk about one way in which objects can appear *to* consciousness. In the final analysis it seems that consciousness reigns supreme throughout the world.

The Shift to the Life-World

Toward the end of his life, Husserl moved from talking of the transcendental individual ego to focusing on the intersubjective community of individuals along with a social conception of cognition. Although we can only speculate on the causes of this shift, we can argue that it follows from his own view of consciousness. I do not simply experience the coffee mug, but I experience it as being on the table, which is by the window, which is located in my office, and so on. This process of the continually expanding horizons of any experience eventually leads to a sense of the totality or the horizon of all horizons. This all-inclusive region of ordinary experience, out of which all meanings must emerge, is what Husserl called the life-world (*Lebenswelt*). It is the total background of our pretheoretical experience. Yet Husserl discovered that even the world of everyday lived-experience has *a priori* structures for the phenomenologist to discover and explicate.

Since the Enlightenment, people had been increasingly convinced that it is science that truly reveals reality to us and that all other ways of comprehending our experience must be subservient to the scientific outlook. Husserl observes, however, that scientists are first and foremost human beings living in the world of everyday experience before they formulate their theories. Behind the objective, scientific account of the world is the scientist as a center of subjective consciousness, who is engaging in the mental activities of observing, counting, calculating, hypothesizing, theorizing, and explaining. But naturalism either ignores this fact or explains it away by supposing that these conscious acts of the scientist herself are just one more set of objective events in the world.

Notice that in scientific journals the subject is mysteriously missing in the report of an experiment. A laboratory report may say, "The test tube was heated, and a white precipitate formed." A more accurate account would say, instead, "*I* heated the test tube and waited with expectation until *I* observed a white precipitate forming, at which point *I* bubbled with excitement as *I* realized that *my* theory had been confirmed." For this reason, scientists are what Husserl called "self-forgetful theorizers." Everything a scientist does, whether reading her instruments, proposing hypotheses, or formulating theories, is an abstraction from what is first given in the concrete experiences within the life-world.

Many philosophers (Bertrand Russell, for example) believe the scientific outlook has replaced or invalidated the perspective of the life-world. In Husserl's account, however, the life-world is now revealed as the source of all meaning and concepts from which scientists begin their task:

> The investigator of nature, however, does not make it clear to himself that the constant foundation of his admittedly subjective thinking activity is the environing world of life. The latter is constantly presupposed as the basic working area, in which alone his questions and his methodology make sense. (PCEM 185)

According to Husserl, science gives us an "idealized and naively objectivized nature." He does not discount the fruitfulness of such an abstract, mathematical reformulation of the world, for he says science is "a triumph of the human spirit." Instead, Husserl simply insists we must remember that the world science presents us is an artificially structured world and that only by means of the conscious acts of the scientist as a subject has such a world been constituted.

Husserl's Significance

THE INFLUENCE OF PHENOMENOLOGY

The methods Husserl developed to understand the structures of experience have had a lasting influence on philosophy as well as the other disciplines. He helped spark a movement within the social sciences among those who believed the human subject cannot be understood on the same terms as the objects of the other sciences. Psychologists and sociologists who have been influenced by phenomenology claim that the human subject lives life from the inside out. Simply focusing on empirical facts, physical stimuli, and external causes will not explain human behavior, they say. Instead, the human sciences must understand how experience is structured by the subject and must chart the structures of the life-world in terms of which the data are interpreted and made meaningful by the experiencing subject.

THE TRANSITION TO EXISTENTIAL PHENOMENOLOGY

The existentialists whom Husserl influenced, such as Martin Heidegger and Jean-Paul Sartre, modified the key features of his method. Two major points of disagreement arise between Husserl's conception of phenomenology and its existentialist versions. First, Husserl's focus on consciousness is too intellectualized, the existentialists claim. We are not simply cognitive spectators, holding the world at a distance as an object of contemplation. Hence Heidegger says we first engage with the world through concern and care, and only later do we intellectualize it. The existentialists focused on the experiences of anxiety, dread, guilt, aloneness, choosing, and the confrontation with the possibility of our own death as revelatory of the human situation. To translate these experiences into Husserlian terms of a conscious ego glaring at its intentional objects does not capture the reality of the human situation. Thus Husserl's notion of "intentionality" is broadened into a more general sort of precognitive engagement with the world.

Second, the existentialists who learned from Husserl dropped his method of bracketing the world. We are immersed in the world, they said, and cannot disconnect ourselves from it, as though it were nothing but a virtual reality displayed on the computer screen of the mind. As William Barrett expresses the problem that led Heidegger to reject Husserl's version of phenomenology,

> Husserl tells us we are to put within brackets absolutely everything that is given; but where does the given end, and suppose the reality of the world, as well as its appearance, is given? . . . The brackets bulge and break, the mass of the world is too great to be contained by them.[3]

MARTIN HEIDEGGER

Heidegger's Life

Martin Heidegger (1889–1976) was born in a small town in southwest Germany in the region of the Black Forest. In the early part of his education he studied Catholic theology, preparing to enter the priesthood. While studying at the University of Freiburg, however, Heidegger became increasingly interested in philosophy and his change of focus became solidified under the influence of Edmund Husserl, then a professor at Freiburg. After receiving his doctorate, Heidegger worked for five years as Husserl's assistant. In 1923 he left to fill a chair in philosophy at the University of Marburg. In 1927 his extraordinarily influential work, *Being and Time*, appeared, dedicated to Husserl. On Husserl's recommendation, Heidegger was elected as his teacher's successor to the chair of philosophy in Freiburg in 1929.

When Hitler came to power in 1933, Heidegger joined the Nazi Party. Shortly after Hitler set up his new regime, Heidegger was appointed rector of the University of Freiburg, but resigned this post early in 1934. Although Heidegger made a number of statements supporting the Nazi movement, scholars continue to debate how long and to what degree he enthusiastically supported this ideology. Furthermore, scholars continue to differ on whether or not his philosophical ideas can be separated from his political views and whether the one naturally leads to the other.

After the war, Heidegger never completed the promised second volume of *Being in Time*. Instead his thought seemed to shift, and he published a number of shorter works, in which he turned to poetry as a way of revealing what our ordinary ways of speaking and approaching the world have concealed. Even though he was married and had three children, he was reclusive by nature. He spent his last years in seclusion in a mountain retreat in the Black Forest, emerging only occasionally to give a public lecture. Martin Heidegger died in 1976.

Heidegger's Task: Understanding the Meaning of Being

Acknowledging his debt to Husserl, Heidegger writes in the frontispiece of *Being and Time* that the book is dedicated to his teacher "in friendship and admiration." However, the contents of the book make a radical break with Husserl's philosophy. The difference is illustrated by the fact that Husserl thought "The wonder of all wonders is the pure ego and pure consciousness."[4] By way of contrast, Heidegger says, "Man alone of all existing things . . . experiences the wonder of all wonders: that there are things-in-being."[5] While Husserl bracketed the world to focus on consciousness, Heidegger responds that there is no "pure consciousness." Consequently, he turns to wonder at the world. Heidegger's deviation from his teacher and the sensation caused by his new approach mark the beginnings of existentialism as a distinctive philosophical movement.

Unlike Husserl, Heidegger engages in **ontology**, the science of Being. To understand this, we must recognize the distinction Heidegger makes between beings (or particular objects) and Being (what is manifested in anything that is). As an example of the first case, we can say a dog is a being. To illustrate the second case, when a suicidal Hamlet says, "To be or not to be—that is the question," he is trying to decide between Being or non-Being (Be-ing or not Be-ing).* We live in a world of plural beings: people, trees, cars, carrots, stars, kittens—the list is endless. Specific beings come into existence and pass out of it. What characterizes the Being of things? It is important to understand that Being is not an entity, for this would make it simply one being alongside other beings. For this reason, Heidegger denies that Being is to be identified

---

*Other languages, such as Greek, Latin, French, and German, make a distinction absent in English between "the thing that is" and "the Being of the thing that is."

with God. He believes that in traditional theology God is considered simply the highest among beings. Falling back on metaphors, he says Being is the light that illumines everything else.[6]

We can get a glimpse of Being in that experience of wonder that provokes us to ask, "Why is there anything at all, rather than nothing?" (IM 1).[7] The broad appeal of this question is indicated by the fact that it has been asked by professional philosophers such as Leibniz as well as by four-year-olds. To wonder at Being is to be open to the presence of Being. But we quickly lose this sense of wonder and return back to the crush of daily life, becoming wrapped up in the objects and tasks around us.

Heidegger thinks the early Greeks knew how to wonder at Being. But with the rise of Greek science and philosophy they quickly began to isolate things from their encompassing background in order to submit them to rational analysis. This yielded many wonderful and practical results, but Western thought forgot Being. The task for Heidegger, therefore, is to deconstruct the whole history of Western metaphysics to recover a kind of thinking that is responsive to Being.

Heidegger's Radical Conception of Phenomenology

Following his teacher Husserl, Heidegger uses the method of phenomenology to carry out his project. Accordingly, we will find very little in Heidegger's writings that resembles a philosophical argument. Instead, he tries to draw our attention to features of our experience, revealing what we have missed, covered up, or ignored. His only method of convincing us is to trigger a disclosure experience within us that will make his conclusions evident.*

*Heidegger's method can be compared to that of the later Wittgenstein, who said that "the work of the philosopher consists in assembling reminders" and that "philosophy simply puts everything before us, and neither explains nor deduces anything." Ludwig Wittgenstein, *Philosophical Investigations*, trans. G. E. M. Anscombe (New York: Macmillan, 1953), §§ 127, 126.

With Husserl, Heidegger describes phenomenology as "the science of phenomena." However, Heidegger disagrees with Husserl's attempt to bracket the world and peel back the layers of experience until we are left with an intuition of pure consciousness. As we will see, Heidegger claims Being cannot be bracketed or doubted, but can only be forgotten, for it is the fundamental phenomenon in which all others (including our own existence) are grounded and from which they derive their meaning. Heidegger's modification of Husserl's method was so radical that it split the phenomenological movement in two. It is now necessary to distinguish Husserlian phenomenology and Heideggerian existential phenomenology, the latter giving birth to twentieth-century existentialism.

Our Existence as a Window to Being

The problem in studying Being is not with the scarcity of the data, but with their abundance. Everything we encounter is a manifestation of Being. So where do we start if we want to study Being? Heidegger's answer is to pick out a particular disclosure of Being that will best illuminate it. Accordingly, he proposes that we begin ontology with a study of our existence. To disassociate his philosophy from previous treatments of the topic, Heidegger uses the term *Dasein* as a technical term to stand for our being. The German word *Dasein* literally means "being there."† We are characterized as "being there" in the sense that we are always situated or related to the world in a certain way. Unlike other entities (and unlike previous discussions of human "nature"), Dasein cannot be defined in terms of a set of fixed properties. Instead, we each are characterized as a set of possibilities and we have the responsibility of choosing what we will be. For this reason, Heidegger says an object "is," but only humans *exist*.

†To retain the unique content of Heidegger's concept, *Dasein* is not translated in most English versions of Heidegger's texts. This text follows this convention, and henceforth we will treat the word as a technical term in English.

What about our existence makes it a privileged standpoint for studying Being? We are unique in that we are the only kind of entity in the world able to raise questions about what it means to be. Accordingly, Heidegger says Dasein is not one object among others, but a clearing in the midst of the otherwise dense forest of Being. A clearing is an opening where the light can stream in. Thus, Dasein represents the region in Being where the latter is most fully revealed. Although Heidegger gives a very perceptive analysis of human existence, it is important to understand that this is not his ultimate goal. His hope is always that an analysis of what it means to be the sort of beings we are will open a window onto the larger issue. "The analytic of Dasein . . . is to prepare the way for the problematic of fundamental ontology—*the question of the meaning of Being in general*" (BT 227).

Heidegger refers to the basic *a priori* features of human existence as existential structures or *existentialia* (we will translate this as *existentials*). Since Heidegger is trying to draw our attention to what has been forgotten, our ordinary language is inadequate. Thus, he has to construct a unique vocabulary to speak about the extraordinary. There are, then, two levels about which he speaks. The *ontic* level refers to particular, ordinary facts within daily life. "In the last year, I have begun to care more about the environment" is an ontic fact. However, the *ontological* level refers to the fundamental structures of human existence that provide the framework within which mundane, ontic facts appear. Hence, when Heidegger refers to such things as care, anxiety, guilt, or death, he is not speaking about ordinary ontic events, but is speaking ontologically. For example, Heidegger does not speak of *care* as a particular attitude of a particular individual. Instead, it is the basic relationship we have to our existence.

Heidegger begins his analysis of Dasein at the most generic level of human existence, the realm of average, everyday experience. This is the world in which we all live prior to any philosophical speculation. Yet even at this level we implicitly understand Being. By unpacking this understanding through interpretation (hermeneutic phenomenology), we can move from our naive immersion in the world to a fully ontological appreciation of what is the ground and meaning of all things. In so doing, Heidegger introduces a complex set of interrelated *existentials* that characterize our mode of existence. For our purposes, the *existentials* we need to discuss are Being-in-the-world, concern, facticity, Being-ahead, and fallenness.

Being-in-the-World

Heidegger radically breaks with the philosophical tradition, which tended to separate the knowing subject and the object of knowledge and treat them as distinct entities. Descartes, for example, identified himself with his consciousness and then worried about how he could know that this consciousness was related to an external world. Husserl, likewise, bracketed the world in order to focus on the nature of pure consciousness. However, Heidegger considers this the first step to skepticism, for once we assume consciousness can be meaningfully considered in isolation from the world, they become difficult to reunite. In modern philosophy this is sometimes known as "the problem of the subject–object dichotomy."

Heidegger sweeps aside the whole problem with a single, fundamental concept. He refers to Dasein as *Being-in-the-world*. The hyphens in this phrase indicate that Dasein cannot be separated from the world, for our existence is a world-embedded existence.* Hence, Being-in-the-world is a fundamental structure of human existence. To clarify this phrase, we will discuss, in turn, the phenomena of "Being-in" and "the world," and then explain Heidegger's fundamental epistemological category of "concern."

---

*In reading the English translations of Heidegger, you may get the impression that if his typewriter didn't have hyphens he couldn't philosophize. There are two reasons for this excessive use of hyphens. First, the German language has the facility for connecting many words to create one big word. Translating such words into individual English words without hyphens would lose the sense that the German word is expressing one, unified concept. Second, because Heidegger is trying to get at phenomena that are ignored by our ordinary ways of thinking, he sometimes must manufacture words in this way to express original ideas for which there is no standard term.

BEING-IN

The notion of Being-in when applied to human existence differs from that of "being contained in." We are in the world in a different sense from the sense in which water is in a glass. Dasein is not a thinglike entity spatially juxtaposed with other objects. Instead, we *dwell* in the world, we are taken up with it, we are absorbed in it. Being-in-the-world is not a spatial notion, for it is closer to what we mean when we talk about "being in love" or "being in college." In these cases I am talking about a situation in which I am involved, which is tied to my interests, aspirations, and projects. Hence, the most important feature of the world is not the *what* (a collection of objects), but the *how* (the manner in which things present themselves to me).

THE WORLD

Next, we need to examine the notion of "world" phenomenologically. From the fact that he could doubt the existence of any particular object, Descartes mistakenly concluded he could doubt the world itself. However, it is only in terms of the total background of the world that we can resolve questions concerning the existence or nonexistence of a particular object. According to Heidegger, we are not Cartesian minds isolated within our private, inner rooms peering out at an alien, external reality (BT 89). Instead, we are "out there" dealing with a world that is familiar and meaningful.

When Heidegger says we "belong to a world," he is not referring to a collection of objects such as planets, trees, buildings, or chairs. Instead, he is using the term much as we speak of "the world of Shakespeare," "the nineteenth-century world," "the world of sports," "the world of the artist," or "the world of the corporate executive." We speak of people (such as an artist, or an executive) as being "worlds apart," or say, "They live in different worlds," even though they may live and work on the same street. Ultimately, of course, we sense that these regional worlds overlap with a larger, public world. When the world is understood in this way, then it can never be doubted, for it is a fundamental feature of our existence.

Although the world is not a collection of objects, we do relate to particular entities in the world. What does a phenomenological analysis reveal about the objects within our experience? First and foremost, it reveals that we do not encounter "things." A thing is a spatially extended object we can describe in terms of its geometrical properties. When an object is present as an explicit object of consciousness to be analyzed in a detached way, Heidegger says it is *present-at-hand*. However, this sort of relationship is an intellectualized mode of apprehension derived from our more fundamental encounters with the world. What we first and foremost encounter are not present-at-hand things but meaningful *ready-at-hand* items. Heidegger refers to things that are ready-at-hand with a term (*Zeug*) that means "equipment," "utensils," "tools," "gear," or "instruments." Something is equipment when its mode of presence is that of being used in my practical engagements.

To illustrate the way objects are present to us as ready-at-hand, Heidegger analyzes the experience of using a hammer to do a task, as opposed to treating it as an object for cognitive inspection. However, any of the thousands of moments in our daily life when we are engaged with a "tool" (such as a pen, a musical instrument, one's eyeglasses, a tennis racquet, or a car) can serve equally as well to make his point. For example, when you start your car, you don't have to explicitly think to yourself, "This is my car—this is the steering wheel—I will now turn the key and start the engine." Instead, the car is like an extension of your body. The familiar routine of starting the engine and pulling out of the driveway is carried out with the same unreflective ease that your hand reaches for a nearby cup of coffee. The car is "equipment" (in Heidegger's technical sense). It is not in the forefront of your attention. Instead, you are probably focusing on your intended destination.

Contrary to classical empiricism, we encounter things first and foremost not as collections of sensations nor as members of logical categories, but as instruments within our lived-space that are available for our projects and needs. Normally, objects in themselves are "transparent" to us, for they are experienced exclusively in relationship to their functions. In other words, we relate to an object as a "something-in-order-to" or a "for-the-sake-of-which."* Only when there is some interruption or breakdown in our normal precognitive Being-in-the-world (the car will not start) do we consciously focus on our equipment, turning them into objects that are present-at-hand to be inspected and considered in terms of their properties.

CONCERN

An implicit theme that has run through this discussion can now come to center stage. Heidegger complains that our philosophical tradition has given us a one-sided and artificial account of our primary relationship to the world. "The phenomenon of Being-in has for the most part been represented exclusively by a single exemplar—knowing the world" (BT 86). If knowing is not our primary way of relating to the world, then what is? The clue to Heidegger's alternative to traditional epistemology is found in our everyday dealings with things.

> The kind of dealing which is closest to us is . . . not a bare perceptual cognition, but rather that kind of concern which manipulates things and puts them to use; and this has its own kind of "knowledge." (BT 95)

Hence, concern is what characterizes our Being-in-the-world. Knowing, in contrast, is a second-level activity derived from our original encounter with the world. This original relationship to the world is found in practical relationships such as

> having to do with something, producing something, attending to something and looking after it, making use of something, giving something up and letting it go, undertaking, accomplishing, evincing, interrogating, considering, discussing, determining. (BT 83)

I can minimize this attitude of concern by relating to things by means of "leaving undone, ne-

---

*This is the cause of the humorous situation in which people frantically search for their glasses but forget that the only reason they can see well enough to search for anything is that they are already looking through the glasses! Looking for the glasses is to treat them as present-at-hand, while seeing with the glasses is to use them as ready-at-hand.

glecting, renouncing." But even in these cases, I never reach a completely neutral cognitive state, free of concern, for I am still expressing an attitude toward the things I encounter.

Heidegger's notion of "concern" could be viewed as a replacement for Husserl's notion of "intentionality." Both terms seek to describe how we are related to the world. However, Husserl tended to focus on acts of cognition such as perceiving, believing, asserting, judging, recalling, or thinking. For Heidegger, however, these more intellectual operations arise out of the precognitive level of concern. Descartes had it all wrong when he said, "I think, therefore I am." If Heidegger is correct, then the slogan should be "I am, therefore I think." What this means is that our brute immersion in the world precedes all cognitive activities.

Modes of Dasein

FACTICITY AND THROWNNESS

Heidegger says our existence is characterized by "facticity." By this he means we always find ourselves in a situation where certain "givens" structure our existence. Some are the result of past choices (for example, choosing to be a student places you within a certain set of structures). Other givens are thrust on you by the features of your personal history that you did not choose, such as the century in which you live and your place of birth, race, gender, intelligence, and personality. Your facticity makes you the you that you are. Related to facticity is the concept of "thrownness." Because there is no reason or purpose for the fact that you exist and exist as this person in this situation, it is almost as though you have been thrown into the world.

Heidegger says this sense of alienation is a mood that discloses our facticity and thrownness. Moods are forms of disclosure, because we do not engage the world only with the cerebral cortex of the brain, but with our whole being. We do not first see the world and then assign a value to it. Instead, we encounter the world as something "attuned" to our mood. A person we are dating is fascinating, the movie is boring, the icy road is threatening, the chocolate dessert is enticing, the dreary weather is depressing. These moods are not experienced simply as subjective states within us but as aspects of our relationship to the world itself. "A mood assails us. It comes neither from 'outside' nor from 'inside', but arises out of Being-in-the-world, as a way of such Being" (BT 176). Hence, cognition and our affective states cannot be divorced, for our moods disclose the character of the world to us. As we will see later, Heidegger believes the most important mood is anxiety or dread.

BEING-AHEAD-OF-MYSELF

Human beings, unlike billiard balls, do not relate only to what exists in their present environment. We are always living-ahead in the sense that our here-and-now is oriented toward future possibilities. A future possibility presents itself as something-I-can-be, but realizing this possibility constitutes part of what I am now. Your present life may be oriented around completing a degree, and mine toward finishing this book. Heidegger calls this feature of Dasein's existence "Being-ahead-of-itself." This is why Heidegger and the existentialists influenced by him do not believe there is such a thing as human nature. We do not have a static essence, for we are always "on the way," creating ourselves by realizing this possibility and not that one. As Kierkegaard discovered, the question to ask is not "Who am I?" but "What shall I become?"

FALLENNESS

Another aspect of our Being-in-the-world is fallenness. Heidegger sometimes speaks of it as Being-along-with-the-entities-in-the-world.* Although this tends to lead to an inauthentic way of relating to existence, Heidegger seems to suggest it also can be simply a neutral aspect of our everydayness. In this sense, we are necessarily and continually

*I have used "Being-along-with" to express the sense of intimacy that is lost in the phrase "Being-alongside" used in the published English translation.

"falling in with" the things in the world that elicit our concern. Heidegger also says this immersion in the world involves coexistence with other people. "The world is always the one that I share with Others. The world of Dasein is a with-world. Being-in is a Being-with Others" (BT 155). Once again, Heidegger rejects the Cartesian notion that we are private, isolated minds for whom the existence of the world and others becomes a philosophical problem. On the contrary, we can become selves only in interaction with other selves.

Although falling in with and being involved with the things and people in my situation is an inescapable feature of my Being-in-the-world, I can lose myself in my situation and fall away from my authentic self. In this sort of fallenness we become preoccupied with the world of objects, but lose ourselves in the whirlpool of endless activity. Furthermore, instead of authentic relationships with other people, we identify ourselves with the anonymous, impersonal entity that Heidegger calls the "they" or the "one." The "they" becomes the authority, the standard of the way things are and is created by the voices of gossip and social pressure, as in the statements, "You know what they say about her . . ." or "One doesn't do that here." Within this inauthentic version of the public world, "Everyone is the other, and no one is himself" (BT 165). When we identify ourselves with the anonymous world of the "other," we interpret our experience in terms of the pregiven understandings that reside in our society:

> We take pleasure and enjoy ourselves as they take pleasure; we read, see, and judge about literature and art as they see and judge; likewise we shrink back from the "great mass" as they shrink back; we find "shocking" what they find shocking. (BT 164)

There is a "leveling off" or a "dimming down" of my possibilities "to what lies within the range of the familiar, the attainable, the respectable—that which is fitting and proper" (BT 239). For this reason, "the Self of everyday Dasein is the they-self." Heidegger says this is different from "the authentic Self—that is, from the Self which has been taken hold of in its own way" (BT 167).

The Fundamental Division: Authentic Versus Inauthentic Existence

Having analyzed our Being-in-the-world within the mode of everydayness, Heidegger now considers the possible ways in which we can relate to it. To summarize and reorganize his findings:

1. Dasein is *already-in-a-world*. We find ourselves "thrown" into a particular situation. This refers to our *facticity*, the unique deposit of given facts that makes up each person's *past*.

2. Dasein is *Being-along-with-the-world*. We engage with things that are ready-to-hand within the world as well as with other human beings. However, we tend to become absorbed into our situation, losing ourselves in the world of the impersonal, anonymous "they." We experience this *fallenness* within our *present* situation.

3. Dasein is *Being-ahead-of-itself*. Our past and present do not sum up what we are, for we are a field of possibilities that offer us choices in each moment of our existence. This existential structure of *possibility* includes the fact that our orientation toward the *future* provides part of the structure of who we are in the present.

This analysis indicates the importance of temporality to Dasein. My relationship to time is different from that of, say, a pencil, which simply is what it is within each isolated slice of time. However, I cannot understand my existence apart from what I have been, what I am, and what I will be. Heidegger says these three aspects of our existence are so interrelated that they form a single, unified phenomenon characterized as *care* (BT 237). This word is used both in the sense of (1) "I really *care* for her" and (2) "proceed with *care*." In other words, the phenomenon of care indicates both that (1) I am intimately involved with my Being and (2) how I respond to it is laden with consequences of great significance.

Previously, Heidegger said that "concern" is one of the *existentials*. But within the sphere of everydayness, this manifests concern for this or

that particular thing (my health, my career, my love life). By way of contrast, care is a "primordial structural totality" that lies before every specific attitude or situation.* It is not something I choose, for it is the *a priori* ground of all choices. Both our practical and our theoretical engagements arise out of care.

As human beings we make choices because we care about our existence. Unlike the busy ant following out the dictates of its biological programming, we are beings who are structured by our possibilities and whose existence necessarily involves making choices. The difficulty is, there are two ways of choosing:

> *Dasein always understands itself in terms of its existence—in terms of a possibility of itself: to be itself or not itself. Dasein has either chosen these possibilities itself, or got itself into them, or grown up in them already. Only the particular Dasein decides its existence, whether it does so by taking hold or by neglecting.* (BT 33)

If I consider my choices to be pregiven and just accept the situation I have drifted into or grown up with, as though I had no possibilities, I will live inauthentically. In this mode of existence, I am mired in my fallenness. In contrast, living authentically means that, in the face of my thrownness, I recognize I am the one who has to make choices and realize my possibilities. Authenticity is taking hold of my self in my own way (BT 167).

In a number of controversial passages, Heidegger repeatedly insists he is not interested in ethics. His discussions of the authentic or inauthentic modes of existence, he claims, merely provide ontological descriptions of Dasein and do not offer moral advice.† Yet aren't the terms "authentic" and "inauthentic" value laden? It would seem that authenticity is something to strive for and inauthenticity something to avoid. Heideg-

---

*It is worth noting that John Dewey was interested in Heidegger's thought, particularly in the notion of care (*Sorge*). Reported in Herbert Spiegelberg, *The Phenomenological Movement*, 2d ed. (The Hague, Netherlands: Nijhoff, 1965), 1:272.

†Jean-Paul Sartre adopted the terms "authentic" and "inauthentic" and, in contrast to Heidegger, used them for explicitly ethical purposes.

ger's reply is that fallenness and its accompanying inauthenticity are inevitable features of Dasein's condition. Hence, this level of existence is not condemned as morally deficient, for it is not something we can either choose or totally avoid.

If this is our natural condition, how, then, do we become open to the possibilities of our existence in an authentic way? The answer is that this new mode of existence comes on us "against all expectation and against our will" in a way that is "never planned, prepared, or willingly accomplished by ourselves" (BT 320). Heidegger says that the doorway to authentic existence is opened to us by the experience of dread or anxiety. Carrying forward the insights of Kierkegaard, Heidegger's discussion of anxiety has made it central to the twentieth-century existentialist's understanding of the human condition.

ANXIETY

According to Heidegger, anxiety differs from the experience of fear. Fear always has a specific object. I am fearful about an upcoming test, I fear going to the dentist, and so on. However, anxiety has ontological dimensions. Anxiety is not about this or that particular fact but is experienced with respect to what it means to be human. "That in the face of which one has anxiety is Being-in-the-world as such" (BT 230). Anxiety arises when we realize our whole system of meanings and our values have no ultimate ground other than that this is how our historical tradition has developed. This makes us realize that what we are is not what we could choose to be. We look around for some signposts to give us direction and discover we must invent the signposts. We have no absolute values to fall back on, no directions, no limits, no paths are laid out for us in advance to follow. We must make choices because we are finite and cannot realize all our possibilities. Hence, in the experience of anxiety we are forced to come face to face with our finitude. Our finitude is most concretely manifested in the fact that someday we will die. Our mortality, our Being-towards-death is one of the most important *existentials* that characterize Dasein.

BEING-TOWARDS-DEATH

Heidegger finds that facing the inevi‌ death is a key to authenticity. For Kierkegaard, it was religious experience that individualizes me, that makes me aware of the "me-ness" of me. For Heidegger, however, realizing I am a "Being-towards-death" opens up this awareness. There is a big difference between entertaining the generalization "All people are mortal" and concretely realizing that "I will die."* In this sort of experience I become aware that one among my many possibilities is the termination of all possibilities. But in facing this possibility I become intimately acquainted with my own existence through realizing its boundaries and uniqueness.

In everything else in life (my job, my relationships) someone else can replace me. But no one can fill in the slot designated as "my death." That is the one role in life reserved for me alone. This perspective liberates me from my immersion in the mundane details of my life that ensnare me, and it snatches me out of the web of "comfortableness, shirking, and taking things lightly," so that I can begin to fully *exist* (BT 435). For this reason, Heidegger refers to it as "freedom towards death" (BT 311). A number of popular literary works have explored how a person's life would look to the person if he or she could look back on it after death. Others have depicted people who had a brush with death and returned to life with a new sense of who they were.†

CONSCIENCE

Since we can deny our own mortality and continually turn our minds away from it, even our attitude toward our own death can be inauthentic. What calls us to authenticity? Heidegger says it is

---

*In a footnote, Heidegger refers to Tolstoy's story, *The Death of Ivan Illyich*. In the character of Ivan, Tolstoy gives a powerful description of how an ordinary, average person moves from the abstract to the existential way of dealing with death.
†Thornton Wilder's play *Our Town* and Jean-Paul Sartre's play *No Exit* explore the first situation. Charles Dickens's classic *A Christmas Carol* and Frank Capra's sentimental film *It's a Wonderful Life* depict the second situation.

the voice of *conscience*. Obviously, conscience can be an ontic event, as when I feel a nagging guilt when I don't volunteer my time to someone who needs me. However, it should be clear by now that in Heidegger's analysis these passing ontic experiences are the surface of something deeper. Hence, the call of conscience Heidegger is pointing to is an ontological feature of human existence. As such, it is neither a product of our social conditioning, nor is it the voice of God, for the possibility of everyday experiences of guilt is grounded in the fundamental *existential* of conscience. What is the source of this call? "*In conscience Dasein calls itself*" (BT 320). Conscience is the self making itself aware of its own potential.

Conscience opens me to my own freedom by making me realize that neither my society nor my current identity (student, teacher, author) necessarily determines what I shall do or become. I have to take responsibility for my choices. Heidegger sums up authenticity as *resoluteness*. "When the call of conscience is understood, lostness in the 'they' is revealed. Resoluteness brings Dasein back to its ownmost potentiality-for-Being-its-Self" (BT 354). It is important to realize that authenticity is not achieved by retreating from life and becoming a mystical hermit living in the desert. Heidegger says "*authentic* existence is not something which floats above falling everydayness; existentially, it is only a modified way in which such everydayness is seized upon" (BT 224). Heidegger's philosophy may seem a burdensome, morbid obsession with anxiety, death, and guilt, but it has an optimistic strain. "Along with the sober anxiety which brings us face to face with our individualized potentiality-for-Being, there goes an unshakable joy in the possibility" (BT 358).

The Call of Being

To many readers, the heart of *Being and Time* is Heidegger's very perceptive phenomenological descriptions of human existence. His account of what it means to be an authentic human being has had an enormous influence on existentialists such as

Jean-Paul Sartre. However, Heidegger continually insisted that he was not an existentialist and that his earlier analysis of human existence was only a stepping-stone on the way to revealing the nature of Being itself. He never finished the promised second part of his project and, instead, he spent the last part of his life publishing essays and lectures on a number of topics. There is a definite change in style in his later period, for he becomes even more cryptic and mystical. The turning point in his thought seemed to occur in the early 1930s, when he began to view poetry as the field within human experience that Being reveals itself. In his later period, the focus on Dasein becomes secondary and Being comes to center stage.

There are considerable differences of opinion as to whether Heidegger began developing a completely new philosophy or whether the early and later Heidegger form a coherent whole. Some see the later work as a "turn," a change in direction, and others see it as a fulfillment of his original project. Heidegger himself claimed he never abandoned the project of *Being and Time*, but merely discovered that he had to approach the problem differently. Despite of his best efforts, he realized that his earlier work was too metaphysical, subjectivistic, and humanistic. It tried to clear a path to Being, but became entangled with our human understanding of Being. In his later work he no longer sees Being as something that must be approached, but as something to be listened to.

THE QUESTION OF TRUTH

An essential part of Heidegger's later work is his discussion of truth. We will first look at how he discussed it in his early work and then trace his understanding of truth as it emerges in his later discussions of language and poetry. In *Being and Time*, Heidegger starts by examining the traditional **correspondence theory of truth**. According to this theory, an assertion is true if it corresponds with its object. For example, the statement "The ball is red" is true if indeed the ball is red. However, it is not clear what we mean if we say that the string of words forming the preceding statement is related to some physical entity in the world, such as a ball.* To locate truth within the mind still raises the problem of how mental contents can "be like" an entirely different sort of entity.

To solve this problem, Heidegger changes the whole notion of truth as follows: "To say that an assertion 'is *true*' signifies that it uncovers the entity as it is in itself. Such an assertion asserts, points out, 'lets' the entity 'be seen' " (BT 261). Heidegger points out that the Greek word for truth is *aletheia*, which he translates literally as "unhiddenness" (BT 265).[†] This suggests that there can be truth only if something is disclosed, discovered, or revealed that was already present but hidden.[‡]

THE PROBLEM OF LANGUAGE

If truth is unhiddenness, what causes Being to be hidden in the first place? One answer is that in our fallenness we turn away from Being. A corollary is that language conspires with us to conceal Being. When functioning authentically, language discloses and makes things manifest. However, when we become lost within everydayness, our speaking becomes inauthentic and becomes simply a vehicle for our taken-for-granted perspectives:

> Words and language are not wrappings in which things are packed for the commerce of those who write and speak. It is in words and language that things first come into being and are. For this reason the misuse of language in idle talk, in slogans and phrases, destroys our authentic relation to things. (IM 11)

---

*We saw a very good example of the correspondence theory in Bertrand Russell's and Ludwig Wittgenstein's logical atomism discussed in Chapter 32. When Wittgenstein says in the *Tractatus* that thoughts or propositions "picture" facts, this metaphor makes the problem scream out at us rather than explaining anything.

[†]In Greek mythology, the river of forgetfulness was Lethe. Hence, the negative prefix in *aletheia* suggests that truth is an unforgetting of what was hidden.

[‡]Notice that in English we have the following words: (1) "discover," (2) "disclose," (3) "reveal." Taking these words in turn, their literal meanings are (roughly): (1) "to reverse the process of covering," (2) "to open" (undoing a closing), (3) "to draw back the veil."

Even when we try to speak philosophically, as Heidegger discovered in writing *Being and Time*, we must use a language overladen with conceptions deposited by twenty-five centuries of metaphysical thought. What we need is a kind of speaking that will open us up to Being rather than following the well-trodden paths of tradition. Heidegger discovers this in the language of the poets.

THE TASK OF THE POET

Heidegger rejects the notion that the poet simply says what everyone already knows, but says it in a colorful way. Instead, the poet brings into language and makes explicit what is so close to us that we do not notice it:

> Poetry is the inaugural naming of being and of the essence of all things—not just any speech, but that particular kind which for the first time brings into the open all that which we then discuss and deal with in everyday language. (HEP 283)

Thus, the poetic mode of speaking is the most fundamental form of language and the one that reunites us with the forgotten ground of our existence. It follows that literal language is derivative. It is a tool created by closing off the possibilities of language, making it uniform and necessarily dull. Instead of treating language like a tool we manipulate, Heidegger says we should see it is our dwelling place, as something toward which we have special responsibilities. "Language is the house of Being. In its home man dwells. Whoever thinks or creates in words is a guardian of this dwelling" (LH 193).[§]

[§]The comparisons that can be made between Wittgenstein and Heidegger are interesting. Wittgenstein ended his first book with the "mystical" and with the silence of what can be shown but cannot be said. In his later period, he thought we could recover our humanity by returning to everydayness and ordinary language. Heidegger, in contrast, finds that it is ordinary language that supports inauthenticity and in his later period says we must turn to the mystical, extraordinary language of the poet to rediscover our authenticity within what cannot be said but only shown.

LETTING-BE

Throughout the history of philosophy, the philosopher's task was frequently seen as a holy crusade, using the sharpened weapons of reason to assault the castle of truth to bring back its treasures. A particularly nice example is found in Hegel's inaugural lecture at the University of Berlin:

> The nature of the Universe, hidden and closed to start with, has no power to withstand the boldness of man's search for knowledge; it must open itself before him and disclose to his eyes its riches and its depths, offering them for his gratification.[8]

Heidegger himself, in *Being and Time*, had spoken of the appropriation of truth as a kind of "robbery" in which truth is "wrested" from entities (BT 265). However, Heidegger's study of Nietzsche in the late 1930s made him realize that Nietzsche's will-to-power was only the nihilistic version of an attitude toward truth that had driven metaphysics in the Western tradition from the time of Plato. However, he now understands this has been the problem all along. Finding an opening to Being is not something we do by our willing, but something we receive as a gift.

In his later period Heidegger now sees that dwelling in the presence of truth requires the *freedom to let-be* (ET 305-312). What he means by "freedom" here is something like being free of what would interfere with our ability to be open. Truth as an unconcealing results not from what we do, but from what we undo. It is a "letting-be of what-is." The poet cannot command inspiration to come to him, but must wait until it happens. In contrast, our Western approach to knowledge has been one of possessing, controlling, and manipulating in an attempt to wrestle the world into submission. In place of the Western tradition of epistemology, Heidegger proposes a way of thinking that revolves around the notions of being-available, listening, surrendering, and obeying. "Obedient to the voice of Being, thought seeks the Word through which the truth of Being may be expressed" (WM 360). Renouncing the humanism that began with the Greeks and was reborn in the Renaissance, Heidegger says, "Man is not the master of beings. Man

is the shepherd of Being" (LH 210). In the difference between mastering and shepherding, we have the difference between technology and poetry.

REDISCOVERING THE HOLY

In Heidegger's later work, Being is spoken of in very anthropomorphic terms as something that "calls" us, "conceals" itself from us, and "reveals" itself to us. At the same time, Heidegger rejects the attempt to identify Being with any sort of traditional notion of a divine person. The ambiguities in Heidegger's thought are indicated by the fact that both atheistic existentialists and Christian theologians have found resources for their thought in his writings.* Heidegger clearly is not a theist in the sense of believing in a transcendent, supernatural being. At the same time, if his outlook is a secular one, it is one surrounded with the aura of the sacred and inspired by an appreciation for the mysteries of Being that are both concealed and revealed in the visible world. For this reason, some have referred to Heidegger's philosophy as a "godless theology."

Our age is the culmination of 2,500 years of attempts to conceptualize the world metaphysically. However, according to Heidegger, after making technology possible, philosophy has run its course. Our age is now one in which we have been "given" the scientific and technological way of appropriating reality. We do not choose how things appear to us, any more than the medievals voluntarily decided to see everything as manifesting God. In our age, however, the sense of awe, mystery, sacredness, and reverence has been replaced by a fascination with atoms, quarks, black holes, and intelligent computers. For us, Heidegger believes, God is silent.

The supreme mistake would be to suppose that ours is the only way to view the world or that it will always remain our way of viewing the world. Our time is "the time of the gods that have fled *and*

---

*The difficulties we run up against in interpreting Heidegger are the same ones we encountered in Chapter 24 with Hegel's notion of Spirit. These two thinkers can be read in both secular and religious lights.

of the god that is coming" (HEP 289). Does Heidegger really believe a new revelation of the divine is possible? He says it is useless to ask that question unless we first rediscover the one dimension where this question can be asked, which is

The dimension of the holy, which even as dimension, remains closed unless the openness of Being is cleared and in its clearing is close to man. Perhaps the distinction of this age consists in the fact that the dimension of grace has been closed. Perhaps this is its unique disgrace. (LH 216)

Although technology can conceal Being from us, Being is never far away. Heidegger believes that in our fascination with technology, we lose sight of what comes to presence in it. To remedy this, Heidegger calls us to step back from viewing the world technologically, to viewing ourselves as viewing-the-world-technologically. Once we understand technology as simply one way that the world is present to us today, it will have released its hold on us. "Thus the coming to presence of technology harbors in itself what we least suspect, the possible arising of the saving power" (QCT 32). Whether or not we will experience a new sense of the whole or the holy arising within the age of technology, and whether or not the voice of Being will call to us through Heidegger's writings, only the future will tell.

Heidegger's Significance

It is difficult to give a philosophical critique of Heidegger, for where no arguments have been provided, none can be refuted. A phenomenologist believes that the fundamental truths he sees cannot be revealed by analyzing language or deducing conclusions from premises that themselves need grounding. Hence, the only means of persuasion he has at his disposal is to be as illuminating in his descriptions of experience as possible, hoping that the phenomena will be disclosed to you as well. Naturally, many have looked in their experience where Heidegger tells us to look and have found that his insights have been illuminating. Others, particularly the analytic philosophers, deny he is doing philosophy at all. From the standpoint of his later thought, Heidegger would not deny the charge. "Future thought is no longer philosophy, because it thinks more originally than metaphysics" (LH 224). He thinks philosophy is so burdened with metaphysics it is unsalvageable. (He would add that the antimetaphysical analytic philosophers have not escaped metaphysics.) This assumes that Western philosophy has run its course and the only remedy is to break out of the structures that have alienated us from Being. Of course, this conclusion is more radical than many are willing to accept.

If a philosopher's significance can be measured in terms of the number of diverse disciplines he or she has influenced, then Heidegger certainly deserves his reputation as one of the most significant thinkers in the twentieth century. Existentialist phenomenologists such as Jean-Paul Sartre and Maurice Merleau-Ponty developed their thought in the light he had cast. Furthermore, Heidegger contributed to the development of existential theology. The foremost existentialist theologians Rudolf Bultmann and Paul Tillich were colleagues with Heidegger at Marburg. Their theological project was to make the Christian message relevant for our age by lifting it out of the ancient metaphysical categories in which it was first presented, in order to translate it into Heidegger's existential categories. Heidegger's thought also influenced the existentialist revolt against scientism and behaviorism within psychiatry and psychology. Psychiatrists Ludwig Binswanger and R. D. Laing were particularly influenced by Heidegger. Finally, Heidegger is alive and well among literary theorists. His writings on poetry, language, culture, and his notion that human experience is a text that needs to be interpreted, have all played a role in the literary theory known as *deconstructionism*.

JEAN-PAUL SARTRE

|||

A Life Lived Amidst Books

Jean-Paul Sartre (1905–1980) was born in Paris. His father died when Sartre was fifteen months old, and young Jean-Paul and his mother moved in with her parents. In his autobiography titled *The Words*, Sartre says he hated his childhood because of the suffocating atmosphere of his grandparents' household. Tutored at home, he was isolated and deprived of association with children his own age. Sartre's only friends were the books that filled his grandfather's study. "I began my life," Sartre says, "as I shall no doubt end it: amidst books." In his philosophy, Sartre describes the way we live out our lives by choosing projects in an attempt to define who we are. He says about himself, "I keep creating myself; I am the giver and the gift." As the title of his autobiography suggests, Sartre decided his life's project would revolve around words. As he puts it, "I was prepared at an early age to regard teaching as a priesthood and literature as a passion."

Pursuing his calling, Sartre received his university education at the prestigious École Normale Supérieure, after which he began his career teaching philosophy at a number of *lycées* (advanced high schools). During the academic year 1933–1934, he was a research student in Germany, where he studied the phenomenology of Husserl and Heidegger. In 1938 he published *Nausea*, his first novel. It became a surprising best-seller. Reading it in the light of his later work, it was an early statement of many of the existentialist themes that pervaded Sartre's literary and philosophical works for the remainder of his life. With the outbreak of World War II, Sartre was called into military service, but was captured and imprisoned by the Nazis for approximately a year. Pleading poor health, he was allowed to return to his life in Paris as a citizen. However, he became active in the underground movement of the French Resistance. Here he came to know Albert Camus, who went on to be a famous novelist and writer with affini-

ties to existentialism. Another member of Sartre's intellectual resistance group was Maurice Merleau-Ponty, who became a famous existential phenomenologist. Both of these friends eventually bitterly fell out with Sartre when they became disillusioned with the Communist Party and Sartre continued to sympathize with it.

Sartre's philosophical masterpiece, *Being and Nothingness: An Essay of Phenomenological Ontology*, came out in 1943. The work was clearly influenced by Heidegger's thought even though the latter was not pleased with the way Sartre used his ideas to articulate an existentialist humanism. As his fame spread, Sartre was able to live on his literary income alone. In his philosophical essays, novels, plays, and short stories, he put words to the experiences of both alienation and hope that characterized the twentieth century. His fictional works both stand on their own literary merit and brilliantly illustrate his philosophical and psychological insights into the human situation. Sartre was awarded the Nobel Prize for Literature in 1964, but he refused to accept the honor and the $53,000 prize money, because he did not want to become a tool of the establishment.

Consistent with the extreme individualism of his philosophy, Sartre lived a very unconventional life. He lived his adult life out of hotel rooms and had few personal possessions. When an interviewer asked to see a copy of Sartre's latest book, he confessed he didn't own one. While a university student, he met Simone de Beauvoir. They became lifelong companions, while avoiding the "bourgeois snares of matrimony." De Beauvoir became a world-famous author herself and contributed to French existentialism and political thought through her short stories, novels, and essays. Sartre and de Beauvoir did much of their writing in the Left Bank sidewalk cafés of Paris, particularly the Café de Flore and the Café des Deux Magots. The Paris café has traditionally been a gathering place for artists, intellectuals, and political radicals of all persuasions. Situated at his favorite table, Sartre was able to be a detached observer of the human situation while immersed in the hustle and bustle of daily life taking place on the sidewalks of Paris.

In the latter part of his life, Sartre's interests shifted toward social and political thought, and he tried to build a bridge between existentialism and Marxism. In very poor health throughout his life, he steadily declined in his later years. On April 15, 1980, Jean-Paul Sartre died of acute heart failure. As the hearse bearing his body drove to the cemetery, a crowd of about 50,000 people, most of them students, accompanied it through the streets of Paris.

Sartre's Task: A Human-Centered Ontology

Sartre's task, as evident from the subtitle of his major work, is to develop a phenomenological ontology. Phenomenology, as we have seen, is the study of the way the world is revealed through the structures of consciousness. Sartre believes this will also provide us with an ontology or an account of what the world must be like for experience to be the way it is. However, while ontology can describe the structures of being, it cannot answer metaphysical questions, such as why this particular world exists. Hence, Sartre tries to provide descriptive answers to "How?" and "What?" questions from within the scope of human consciousness, but with Kant he says it is meaningless to ask "why" questions that refer beyond the limits of reality as we experience it. All we can say is that "being is without reason, without cause, and without necessity" (BN 788).[9]

Sartre's philosophy owes more to Heidegger than to any other thinker. However, there were significant differences between the two.[*] For Sartre, the standpoint of the human subject is the beginning and the end of his philosophy. There is never any hint of Heidegger's Being that calls to us through the poets and in terms of which we

can find a "saving power." On the contrary, for Sartre human consciousness confronts a totality of being that is alien and meaningless. Sartre's writings return to the emphasis on human willing and action. Going along with this is the sort of subjectivism Heidegger tried so hard to avoid. According to Sartre, we must make our way in the world by subjectively creating meaning, rather than having it flood in on us by the "letting-be of what-is," as Heidegger proposed.

Two Kinds of Reality: Objects and Persons

Sartre says that when we analyze what appears to us, we discover two modes of being. First of all, one sort of being is manifested in objects. This is called the *in-itself* (*l'en-soi*). The term "in-itself" signifies that objects are self-contained or self-identical. Nothing in them transcends what they currently are. A table simply is what it is. The second sort of being is what characterizes human consciousness. Sartre calls this form of being the *for-itself* (*le pour-soi*). The term "for-itself" signifies that such beings are conscious and self-aware. Rather than being determined by external causes, we are bursting with spontaneous freedom and live our lives in terms of future possibilities. Unlike the table, we do not have static identities, for we are continually self-projecting beings. We are always incomplete, ongoing projects that are never finished, always being recreated anew by our own choices.

Descartes supposed a person's conscious acts are rooted in some sort of mental substance. But Sartre says consciousness is a nothingness. He is referring to the "no-thingness" of consciousness, the fact that it is not a thing. Instead, it is totally transparent, existing only as a consciousness of some object. We become aware of our own consciousness by being aware of the gap between ourselves and the world of causally determined objects. Like a bubble moving through a liquid, consciousness introduces nothingness into the world. Being-in-itself is simply there, without gaps, without possibilities, without any deficiencies, without the presence of any negations. When consciousness

---

[*]Recall that Heidegger continually tried to disassociate himself from Sartre's existential humanism.

Actual

is present, however, "nothingness" is introduced into the world. Sartre speaks of coming to a café and finding that his friend Pierre is not there. In this awareness, consciousness introduces a negation, "the absence of Pierre," into the continuous, solid being of the café and its material objects. Similarly, consciousness looks at the world about it and sees not simply what is there, but also what it lacks, or possibilities that could be realized but that are not yet actual. Only the for-itself can become separate from the bare existence of things in the causal order in this way. As we shall see, the nothingness that is consciousness, its ability to separate from things and to live in the "what-is-not" (the realm of possibilities), makes us totally free. Since phenomenology only studies what appears to consciousness, Sartre never asks how the world divided into these two categories of being or how consciousness appeared in the midst of physical things. With Kant, Sartre believes that such metaphysical questions are unanswerable from within the human situation.

An Empty Universe

A fundamental feature of Sartre's philosophy is his outspoken atheism. As he describes his philosophy, "existentialism is nothing else but an attempt to draw the full conclusions from a consistently atheistic position" (EH 310). He provides at least two reasons why he rejects the theistic standpoint. The first reason takes the form of a syllogism:

(1) If a sovereign God existed, then persons would not be free agents.
(2) Persons are free agents.
(3) Therefore, a sovereign God does not exist.

Why does he assert the first premise? Apparently he agrees with Leibniz that a God who created the world would fill it with creatures having certain, given natures. If so, then everything a person does would simply be determined by the sort of nature that God had given people as part of his plan. As for the second claim that we are, indeed, free, Sartre believes that the anxiety we face when we

have to make a crucial choice shows that the decision is not already programmed into either our divinely created nature, our genes, or our social conditioning. Furthermore, Sartre says that even if God could create genuinely free creatures apart from himself, to have this sort of freedom would mean we would not depend on God nor be determined by him. Hence, what we chose to become would be the result of our own, sovereign choices, and for all practical purposes it would not make any difference, to the structures of human existence, how we came into the world (BN 26–27).

His second argument for atheism is based on the claim that the concept of God is contradictory, for it merges the two, incompatible types of beings. On the one hand, Sartre agrees with the medievals that a being such as God would have to be a fully realized, complete, unchanging, and absolute being. He could not have plans or desires, for these would imply he had unfulfilled potentialities. But this would mean he was a being-in-itself, the sort of being that characterizes objects. At the same time, the religious concept of God is the concept of a person. But, according to Sartre's analysis, a person is a being who has goals, values, projects. To be a person is to be incomplete because we are continually transcending our present by projecting ourselves into a still-unfinished future. Indeed, much of the religious language in the Bible describes God this way. Furthermore, to be a person is to be self-aware. But in self-awareness we step back from our being and become both a subject and an object for ourselves. Hence, unlike the table, if I have consciousness I never fully coincide with what I am. Therefore everything is either a fully complete being (in-itself) or a being continually transcending itself (for-itself)—but nothing (including God) can be both. Hence, the concept of a God that is an in-itself and for-itself is self-contradictory.

Existence Precedes Essence

In his most famous essay, "Existentialism is a Humanism" (1946), Sartre introduces the memorable statement, "Existence precedes essence." The essence of something is the set of its defining properties, what makes it the sort of thing it is. Sartre says an entity's essence precedes its existence only if it is a manufactured article. With respect to manufactured articles, we can ask, "What is it?" or "What is it for?" The initial idea of the statue in the artist's mind or the architect's blueprint are examples of how the essence of created things precede their actual existence. However, if we are not divinely created beings, then there was no plan and no blueprint for what we were intended to be. "Man first of all exists, encounters himself, surges up in the world—and defines himself afterwards" (EH 290). Sartre faults previous atheists for supposing they could remove the concept of God from their systems and still go on talking about human nature and objective values. Instead, "there is no human nature, because there is no God to have a conception of it. . . . Man is nothing else but that which he makes of himself" (EH 290–291).

One may wonder how Sartre can go on to philosophize about human existence if there is no common human nature. Sartre's answer is that nothing at the core of persons defines what they are. We cannot describe humans as naturally selfish, aggressive, good, social, rational, nor can we appeal to any other sort of defining essence. We are only social, say, if we choose to engage in social activities, but this does not define what we are. However, while there is no universal human nature, there is a common *human condition*. We face the same challenges, the same questions, and the same limitations. The existential structures of human existence are the same, but within these structures each person responds in his or her own, unique way.

CONDEMNED TO FREEDOM

Philosophers have debated for centuries about whether or not we have freedom. However, Sartre has the most radical and totalistic view of human freedom ever put forth in the history of thought. He says we do not *have* freedom, we *are* freedom. Freedom is not one property among many, but is intrinsic to the sort of beings we are, for at each moment of our existence we are creating ourselves anew. Most have assumed that having free will

would be a welcome condition, but in one of his most striking comments, Sartre says, "We are condemned to freedom" (EH 295). He wants to impress on us what an overwhelming burden it is that we cannot escape our freedom. He quotes Dostoevsky's pronouncement "If God does not exist, everything would be permitted" (EH 294). We want some direction in making decisions, we want to fall back on some objective realm of values that will assure us we are making the right choice. However, the fact is that

> we have neither behind us, nor before us in a luminous realm of values, any means of justification or excuse. We are left alone, without excuse. (EH 295)

Sartre tells about a Jesuit priest he met while they were both in a Nazi prison. Initially, this man's life was a total failure. He was orphaned, impoverished, had a disastrous love affair, and was denied a military career because he failed an exam. He took all these events as a sign that he was not destined for secular success but was being called to serve God. Sartre says this is the meaning that this individual *chose* to assign to these experiences. However, he could have just as easily decided that they meant he should become a revolutionary (EH 298). The crux of Sartre's position is that bare facts have no meaning until an individual assigns them a meaning.

FACTICITY

You might think that there are a number of obvious limits on freedom caused by past events over which we had no control. For example, I was born an American male and was raised in a middle-class home. These sorts of inescapable features of our existence Sartre calls our *facticity*. However, if facts do not have intrinsic meaning but are things to which we assign meaning, then to state the features of our facticity is, as such, to say very little. Our true freedom becomes clear in the ways in which we respond to our facticity. I was born an American. What does that mean to me today? Do I see it as a source of nationalistic pride? Or do I feel guilty over my country's affluence when compared to the rest of the world? Should I renounce my citizenship or even become a traitor, or should I be a flag-waving patriot? These are all choices I have to make. The same is true of my gender. In the latter part of the twentieth century, there has been a great deal of discussion and debate over what it means to be a female or a male. Should a man show his emotions? Should a woman be assertive? To be female or male as a biological fact tells us nothing about what it *means* to be this or that gender. Hence, scientific facts tell us very little about how to live our lives. As we face the bare givens of our facticity, we face an overwhelming amount of freedom in deciding what meaning these have for us.

THE PARADOX OF HUMAN EXISTENCE

In one of his typically enigmatic phrases, Sartre says that a feature of human existence is that *I-am-what-I-am-not* and *I-am-not-what-I-am* (BN 196, 798; EP 65). At first glance, this assertion seems contradictory if not completely impenetrable. However, a great deal of Sartre's philosophy can be unpacked from this brief formula. The first half of the statement ("I-am-what-I-am-not") refers to the quality of transcendence (which is the opposite of facticity). This means that we are always oriented toward the future.* Our possibilities, our freedom, the things we are striving for but have not yet realized are what shape our present life. My current life is oriented around the goal of finishing this book. Thus *I am* (someone trying to be) *what I am not* (a published author). To be a "being-for-itself" is always to be striving, always to be on the way. Our ongoing projects, those activities in which we seek to transcend what we are now, continually define us. "What we mean to say is that a man is no other than a series of undertakings, that he is the sum, the organization, the set of relations that constitute these undertakings" (EH 301).

The other half of the formula ("I-am-not-what-I-am") refers to the roles that we are playing out,

*Note how often we hear echoes of Heidegger in Sartre's descriptions of human existence.

but that do not fully define us. Someone labeling me might say I am a husband, a father, a philosopher, and a professor. However, these identities are not woven into my being. In one sense, I am not fully and completely a teacher, but I am striving to be one (with various degrees of success). Furthermore, being a teacher (or any of the other labels) is not part of my essence, because it is something I am continually *choosing* to be or can choose not to be. A table is completely identified with being a table, because it has no choice about it. However, I choose to identify myself with one role or another. It might be thought that my being a father is a biological fact about my past I cannot change. Insofar as this is part of my facticity, that is true. But how I see this role makes an enormous difference to how I live my life and relate to my family. Furthermore, I can choose to identify myself with what it means to be a father or I can refuse to accept this role as part of who I am. Thus, *I am not* (essentially and unchangeably identified with) *what I am* (the roles and labels that I adopt for myself).

BAD FAITH VERSUS AUTHENTICITY

Sartre cautions us against falling into the trap of labeling ourselves, for this is simply an attempt to deny our freedom. I might say, "I am a loser" or "I can't change, because this is just the way I am." Labels become our identity only because we make them so. In his biography of the famous playwright Jean Genet, Sartre tells us that Genet stole something when he was a boy. When caught, he was told, "Jean, you *are* a thief!" He naively accepted this as his identity and ended up becoming a professional thief in his early adulthood. In many such ways we inauthentically identify ourselves with this or that role and think we are not free to be anything else. Consistent with his own philosophy, Sartre refused to identify his free, spontaneous self with the public's attempt to lock him into the identity of being a famous writer. In response to an interviewer's question, Sartre says,

> *You know, the fame seems to go on in someone else's life, it has happened to someone else. There is me and then there is the other person. The other person*

has written books and is read. . . . He exists, I know, but he doesn't bother me; I use him . . . but I do not think of him as being me.[10]

Sartre uses the term *bad faith* to refer to the attempt to deny our freedom, to see ourselves as products of our circumstances, or the attempt to identify ourselves with our past choices while closing off our future possibilities. We feel a need to be an "in-itself," a being that is defined, that has an identity. But this is because, as Heidegger pointed out, facing our freedom brings with it the burden of responsibility and the experiences of anxiety, anguish, and despair. It is all up to us, for there is no meaning to the world or our lives but the meaning we create. When a young man came to Sartre seeking ethical advice, the only advice Sartre would give him was "You are free, therefore choose—that is to say, invent" (EH 297-298). Only when we take responsibility for the meaning of our past and present, and self-consciously choose our future, will we achieve *authenticity*, the one value Sartre seems to embrace in an otherwise valueless universe.

Alienation and Other People

What are the implications of Sartre's philosophy for our relationship to others? Try this thought experiment: look up, down, to the left, to the right, forward, and behind you. You have just demonstrated that you are the *center* of your lived-world. All the directions in the universe radiate out from you. If Sartre is correct in saying we cannot escape playing a godlike role in assigning meanings and values to our world, then each of us is sovereign in our own lived-world. The problem is, there are as many lived-worlds as individuals. However, there can only be one universe, with one God, and one center. Hence, there is an inevitable conflict among human beings.

I determine what meaning *you* have in *my* world. Are you interesting? dull? beautiful? plain? threatening? innocuous? *I* decide what value and meaning you have, for you are but one item in *my* world. Of course, others are doing the same for me. Hence, we are involved in a "war of the

Giraudon/Art Resource, NY

Alberto Giacometti, The Forest, Seven Figures and a Head *(1950). The stark, elongated figures in Giacometti's sculpture reside forever in their individual spaces. Though in close proximity, they are forever alone. These figures provide an image of Sartre's philosophy and his emphasis on our experiences of alienation and anxiety as well as individual autonomy and personal dignity.*

worlds." Sartre talks about the feeling of discomfort we feel when someone stares at us. You are enjoying a moment of solitude in the park, thinking you are alone. You feel in control of your space. But then you become uncomfortably aware someone is staring at you. The presence of another consciousness means you have just become an item in someone else's world. Like water rushing to the drain of a bathtub when the plug has been pulled out, my whole world seems to drain toward that other center of consciousness. What is he thinking of me? What judgments is he making about me? The stare of another person is unsettling because it means you no longer fully control your psychological space. You continually struggle to be a fully subjective consciousness, giving meaning to the items in your world. But this means others can only be objects for *your* consciousness. Of course, the reverse is true as the other tries to absorb you within his or her conscious experience.

For such reasons, Sartre does not believe we can really share our experience with another, because individual autonomy is an inescapable feature of our way of experiencing the world. At best, a friendship can be like two separate ships moving in the same direction. As one of Sartre's characters says at the end of his play *No Exit*, "Hell is—other people."

Optimism in the Midst of Alienation

According to Sartre's analysis, there is something fundamentally absurd about human existence. Living in a universe without God, it is up to each one of us to answer questions about meaning and value. At the same time, we cannot fall back on any sort of rational order, for our lives are grounded in pure, subjective freedom. For this reason, Sartre says, "The existentialist . . . finds it extremely embarrassing that God does not exist, for there disappears with Him all possibility of finding values in an intelligible heaven" (EH 294). In practical terms, each of us must fill the slot occupied by God in previous philosophical systems. We also try to be like God in our efforts to find some sort of stable identity. Suffering from the anguish of always deciding, always being on the way, we thirst for completion and fulfillment. For this reason, Sartre says, "the best way to conceive of the fundamental project of human reality is to say that man is the being whose project is to become God" (EP 66). Yet Sartre has already argued that the idea of God is contradictory. Therefore, it follows that "man is a useless passion" (EP 199).

Despite all the negative features of Sartre's philosophy, he still thinks it is the most optimistic outlook possible. Unlike either theism or deterministic scientific philosophies, the future is not already decided, according to Sartrean existentialism. We face genuine possibilities, we are free,

we can choose, we are in control. This philosophy gives us dignity and a hope that we can make ourselves what we decide to be. Neither nature, nor the gods, nor society have the last word, for each individual writes the next chapter of their own autobiography.

Sartre's Turn to Marxism

The ideas outlined thus far account for Sartre's enormous impact on existentialism, literature, and psychology. However, in the later part of his life he tried to weave his existentialism together with Marxism. Sartre felt lifelong regret over being a man of ideas instead of a man of action. Although never denying that freedom is inescapable, he began to focus on the way in which society limits people's ability to express their freedom. He hoped existentialism would make Marxism less dogmatic and deterministic.

Sartre's turn toward Marxism is expressed in his 1960 book *The Critique of Dialectical Reason*. In the beginning of the book he states, "Marxism is the inescapable philosophy of our time." Differing from orthodox Marxism, and the Hegelianism on which it is founded, Sartre does not believe Marxism is inescapable because history is determined. Instead, he is making the more modest claim that Marxism best expresses the human situation in our time. Sartre discusses two ways in which several individuals can relate together. One is the "serial collective," which would characterize a collection of isolated individuals waiting in line for a bus. They have no sense of unity, for each is engaged in his or her own projects and knows nothing of the other's concerns. The second type of plurality is a "group-in-fusion." In this case, people find that they face a common situation and that their individual projects can be merged, making them capable of concerted historical action, as in the French Revolution. Under capitalism, the individual workers are a serial collective in which they see themselves as powerless, oppressed, and alienated individuals. Realizing their shared alienation, and the fact that they are viewed by their bosses as just objects to be exploited, they begin to see themselves as an "Us-object." In turn, the oppressors become a "Them." With this new level of awareness, the workers can transform themselves from a collection of objects into a "We-subject." At this point, they define their aspirations toward individual freedom in terms of collective liberation and they can work together for a more humane society.

Sartre never was a true Marxist, for he always resisted the deterministic view of history that is intrinsic to Marxism. At the same time, many believe that by emphasizing the power of social structures and introducing the notion of collective identity, Sartre abandoned his existentialism. Sartre hoped, nevertheless, that existentialism would humanize Marxism, leading to a transformation of the human condition:

> As soon as there will exist for everyone *a margin of real freedom beyond the production of life, Marxism will have lived out its span; a philosophy of freedom will take its place. But we have no means, no intellectual instrument, no concrete experience which allows us to conceive of this freedom or of this philosophy.*[11]

The Significance of Existentialism

Critics of existentialism, who preferred a more analytic and scientific approach to things, complained that existentialism was simply an emotional reaction to the dark side of human existence and did not offer anything of cognitive value. As one analytic philosopher said to me, "Everyone is an existentialist at 3 A.M. on a sleepless night." Nevertheless, existentialism, as a way of approaching the human condition, was enormously influential and found adherents in any field that touched on distinctively human concerns, such as art, literature, psychology, theology. Although existentialism as a movement is not as strong today as when Sartre was in his prime, the existentialist spirit will always be alive. It is a spirit of revolt against the pretensions of reason, against the dehumanizing conditions of modern life, and against the attempts of the sciences to reduce persons to simply one more type of object among others in nature.

Questions for Understanding

1. In the context of this chapter, what is naturalism and why does Husserl reject it?

2. What does Husserl mean by "phenomenology"?

3. In what sense is Husserl's phenomenology a rationalism and in what sense is it a radical form of empiricism?

4. According to Husserl, what is the natural standpoint?

5. What does Husserl mean by "bracketing" or epoche? How does it differ from Descartes's method of doubt? Why does Husserl think it is important to do this?

6. What is Husserl's view of consciousness? What does he mean by "intentionality"?

7. What is the life-world, according to Husserl? What is its relation to the scientific account of the world?

8. How did philosophers such as Heidegger and Sartre modify Husserl's philosophy to transform it into an existential phenomenology?

9. In Heidegger's philosophy, what is meant by "ontology"?

10. What is the distinction Heidegger makes between beings and Being? According to him, how did Western thought lose sight of Being?

11. What does the German word Dasein mean? Why does Heidegger use it to refer to human existence? Why does Heidegger think the study of ontology should begin with an analysis of our existence?

12. How does Heidegger's notion of Being-in-the-world differ from Descartes's approach to human existence?

13. What unique meaning does Heidegger give to the notion of "world."

14. What is the difference Heidegger observes between an object being "present-at-hand" and "ready-at-hand"?

15. Why does Heidegger say that knowing is not our most basic relationship to the world? What does he think is our more fundamental way of relating to the world?

16. What do the following expressions mean in Heidegger's philosophy: "facticity," "thrownness," "Being-ahead-of-itself," "fallenness," "anxiety," "Being-towards-death," "conscience"?

17. According to Heidegger, what constitutes the difference between authentic and inauthentic existence?

18. How does Heidegger define "truth" in his later work?

19. What is the problem of language according to Heidegger? What is the remedy?

20. According to Heidegger, what problems for our relationship to the world have been caused by technology? What is the solution?

21. According to Sartre, what are the two kinds of reality? How does he describe each of them?

22. What are the two arguments Sartre uses to defend his atheism?

23. What does Sartre mean by saying "existence precedes essence"? Why does it imply that there is no human nature?

24. What does Sartre mean by "facticity" and "transcendence"? How do these concepts illuminate his slogan "I-am-what-I-am-not and I-am-not-what-I-am"?

25. What does Sartre mean by "bad faith"? How does it contrast with his notion of "authenticity"?

26. What are the implications of Sartre's philosophy for our relationship to others?

27. Why does Sartre say that human existence is "a useless passion"? In the light of this, why does Sartre consider himself to be an optimist?

28. What is the significance of Sartre's turn toward Marxism? Is it consistent with his earlier philosophy?

Questions for Reflection

1. Make an attempt to try out Husserl's method of bracketing. Stand back from being naively involved with the world and try to be attentive to the acts of consciousness in terms of which the world is given to you or constituted by you. What do you find when you take this perspective?

2. Do you think Husserl's point is plausible, that consciousness cannot be treated as just another natural object within the world?

3. In what ways is Heidegger's view of experience different than that of the British empiricists?

4. Do you agree with Heidegger's claim that poetry is more revelatory than other, more objective forms of speech?

5. Argue for or against Sartre's claim that if God existed, then humans would not be free.

6. Do you think Sartre is correct in claiming that "existence precedes essence"? What are some of the implications of embracing this principle for one's life?

7. List some features of your life that Sartre would describe as your "facticity." Now, for each one, list some of the choices you have for deciding the meaning of that fact.

Notes

1. Quoted in Herbert Spiegelberg, *The Phenomenological Movement*, 2d ed. (The Hague, Netherlands: Nijhoff, 1965), 1:82.

2. Throughout this chapter, the works of Edmund Husserl are referenced by means of their page numbers, using the following abbreviations:

   CM   *Cartesian Meditations*, trans. Dorion Cairns (The Hague, Netherlands: Nijhoff, 1960).

   I   *Ideas: General Introduction to Pure Phenomenology*, trans. W. R. Boyce Gibson (New York: Collier Books, 1962).

   PCEM   "Philosophy and the Crisis of European Man," in *Phenomenology and the Crisis of Philosophy*, trans. Quentin Lauer (New York: Harper & Row, 1965).

3. William Barrett, *What Is Existentialism?* (New York: Grove Press, 1964), 82.

4. Quoted in Spiegelberg, *The Phenomenological Movement*, 1:284.

5. Ibid.

6. Martin Heidegger, "The Way Back into the Ground of Metaphysics," in *Existentialism from Dostoevsky to Sartre*, trans. and ed. Walter Kaufmann (New York: New American Library, 1956), 207.

7. The works of Martin Heidegger are referenced in terms of the pages of their English editions using the following abbreviations:

    BT   *Being and Time*, trans. John Macquarrie and Edward Robinson (London: SCM Press, 1962).

    ET   "On the Essence of Truth," trans. R. F. C. Hull and Alan Crick, in Martin Heidegger, *Existence and Being*, ed. Werner Brock (Chicago: Regnery, 1949).

    HEP "Hölderlin and the Essence of Poetry," trans. Douglas Scott, in Martin Heidegger, *Existence and Being*.

    IM   *Introduction to Metaphysics*, trans. Ralph Manheim (Garden City, NY: Anchor Books, Doubleday, 1959).

    LH   "Letter on Humanism," trans. Edgar Lohner, in *Philosophy in the Twentieth Century*, Vol. 3: *Contemporary European Thought*, ed. William

Barrett and Henry D. Aiken (New York: Harper & Row, 1962).

    QCT "The Question Concerning Technology," in Martin Heidegger, *The Question Concerning Technology and Other Essays*, trans. William Lovitt (New York: Harper & Row, 1977).

    WM   "What Is Metaphysics?" trans. R. F. C. Hull and Alan Crick, in Martin Heidegger, *Existence and Being*.

8. Quoted in J. L. Mehta, *Martin Heidegger: The Way and the Vision* (Honolulu: University Press of Hawaii, 1976), 336.

9. Quotations from Jean-Paul Sartre's works are referenced by their page numbers, using the following abbreviations:

    BN   *Being and Nothingness*, trans. Hazel Barnes (New York: Washington Square Press, 1956).

    EH   "Existentialism Is a Humanism," trans. Philip Mairet, in *Existentialism from Dostoevsky to Sartre*, ed. Walter Kaufmann (New York: Meridian Books, New American Library, 1956).

    EP   *Existential Psychoanalysis*, trans. Hazel E. Barnes (New York: Philosophical Library, 1953).

10. "What's Jean-Paul Sartre Thinking Lately? An Interview by Pierre Bénichou," trans. Patricia Southgate, *Esquire*, December 1972, 286.

11. Jean-Paul Sartre, *Search for a Method*, trans. Hazel E. Barnes (New York: Vintage Books, Random House, 1963), 34.

34

Recent Issues in Philosophy

WHERE IS PHILOSOPHY NOW, AND WHERE IS IT going? If the history of philosophy has taught us anything, it is that it would be risky to answer this question in too much detail. Thirty years ago, when I was an undergraduate philosophy major, no one could have anticipated some of the issues philosophers are writing about today. Likewise, it is hard to predict which philosophers in our own time will have the most lasting influence in the decades and centuries to come. Philosophers who were unappreciated by their contemporaries often get rediscovered hundreds of years later.

Perhaps Jean-Paul Sartre was right—the past is never finished but is continually receiving its meaning in terms of the present moment. Furthermore, Sartre, as well as the pragmatists and process philosophers, emphasized that the future is always open. From our stance within the present, we are continually deciding what the future will become. The most I will try to do in this final chapter, therefore, is to say a few words about what new issues and movements are currently creating philosophical commotion, as well as briefly mentioning a few names to guide the reader who wants to study philosophy's present in more detail.

Rethinking Empiricism

One significant development in the latter part of the twentieth century has been a radical reassessment of the fundamental assumptions of modern empiricism. Although this is not a recent turn of events, it has influenced the philosophical environment that produced many of our current philosophical movements. From Francis Bacon on, the empiricists claimed to have provided the philosophical foundations of science. Subsequently, as scientists developed their methods and theories through the centuries, they accepted the empiricists' story of what scientists were doing. When classical empiricism came into question, it required a rethinking of what scientific knowledge is all about. Furthermore, many philosophers who still remained within the empiricist tradition had to radically revise the nature of empiricism.

W. V. O. QUINE

One of the most influential philosophers leading the charge against traditional empiricism has been Willard Van Orman Quine (1908–2000).* His classic essay "Two Dogmas of Empiricism" (1953) shook the foundations of empiricism.[1] The first "dogma" of empiricism he attacks is the traditional distinction between **analytic** and **synthetic** statements.† The assumption that we can make this sharp distinction has been a fundamental pillar of modern empiricism, from John Locke to the logical empiricists. Quine, however, makes the startling statement that the distinction between analytic and synthetic statements is "an unempirical dogma of empiricists, a metaphysical article of faith." He makes his case by systematically chipping away at every attempt to formulate the difference between analytic and synthetic statements.

One traditional way to define "analyticity" is to say that a statement is analytic if it can be reduced to a logical truth based on the logical law of identity, "A is A." Take, for example, the statement "All bachelors are unmarried." We presume that the analytic nature of this statement can be demonstrated if we turn it into a logical truth by substituting one synonym for another. Since "unmarried man" is a synonym for "bachelor," we can translate the original sentence into the logical truth "All unmarried men are unmarried."

The problem here, Quine argues, is that this definition of analytic statements assumes we can explain what we mean when we say one word is *synonymous* with another. To show that this is problematic, he first considers the suggestion that

the synonymy of "bachelor" and "unmarried male" might be explained by saying that this is how we define these terms or that people normally use these words interchangeably. Quine replies that this reference to people's linguistic behavior is a sociological observation and does not help explain why the analytic-synthetic distinction is thought to be a *logical* one.

Second, in a series of complex arguments I will not reproduce here, he argues that all attempts to define analytic statements end up defining "analyticity" in terms of "synonymy" and defining "synonymy" in terms of "analyticity." Hence, without a defining criteria that is clear and noncircular, empiricism cannot maintain a logical distinction between analytic and synthetic statements.

The second "dogma" of empiricism Quine attacks is that of "reductionism." This is the belief that a statement is meaningful if and only if it can be translated completely into statements about immediate experience. This assumption is contained in the logical positivist's **verifiability principle**. Even in its weakest forms, reductionism supposes that an individual statement can be confirmed or disconfirmed in isolation from other statements. This assumption lies at the foundation of analytic philosophy, for only if it is possible to consider our beliefs one by one can we subject them to piecemeal analysis.

In opposing reductionism, Quine argues that "our statements about the external world face the tribunal of sense experience not individually but only as a corporate body." In other words, whether we consider an individual statement to be proven or disproven depends on our entire belief system, including background assumptions about what experiences should be accepted or disregarded, how we should interpret them, and what we see their implications to be.‡ Furthermore, Quine says the two dogmas are really the same. Lurking in the analytic-synthetic distinction is the notion that the

---

*W. V. O. Quine was an important American philosopher who taught for many decades at Harvard University. He made many contributions to the theory of logic and its application to epistemology and metaphysics, which created considerable turmoil within the philosophical community. His work was influenced by both the analytic and pragmatic traditions.

†To review, analytic truths are those whose truth is based on the meanings of the terms, such as "All mothers are parents." A synthetic statement is one whose predicate adds information that cannot be deduced by analyzing the subject term, such as "All mothers are under 20 feet tall."

‡This thesis is a development of the position of the great French historian and philosopher of science, Pierre Duhem. Hence, it is sometimes referred to as the "Duhem-Quine thesis."

truth of synthetic statements depends on experience, while analytic statements are logically different because they are true no matter what we find in experience.

In contrast to the traditional empiricist's distinction, Quine says that "any statement can be held true come what may" and that "no statement is immune to revision." This means that whether or not we treat a statement as analytic or synthetic will depend on (1) the degree to which we are inclined to embrace it no matter what counterevidence arises, as opposed to (2) our willingness to revise it if it conflicts with new experiences. Furthermore, this choice is a practical one and not one dictated by logic.

Quine says the totality of our knowledge, ranging from our commonsense beliefs to the laws of logic, is "a man-made fabric which impinges upon experience only along the edges." In other words, the beliefs on the periphery of our belief system are the ones we would abandon most willingly if experience conflicted with them. This is because we can discard the beliefs on the edge without making major changes to the rest of our beliefs. Other beliefs, particularly the laws of science, mathematics, and logic, are deeply embedded in the interior of our belief systems. It is improbable that an everyday experience would cast them in doubt. Furthermore, because they have so many connections to the rest of our beliefs, we would be inclined to doubt our observations rather than abandon these central beliefs.

Despite the centrality of our scientific, mathematical, and logical beliefs, Quine believes there could be situations when even one of these would have to be modified, to preserve the coherence of the rest of our beliefs. For example, the logical principle known as the "law of excluded middle" states: either P or Not-P is true—there is no third possibility. Because of this logical law, we consider the statement "Either John is married or he is not married" to be true no matter what the facts about John may be. However, experimental results in an area of physics known as *quantum mechanics* have led some scientists to doubt the law of ex-

cluded middle. Others, who think it would be disastrous to abandon this principle, reinterpret the evidence to preserve the logical law. Quine says that the history of science shows us that even the most central assumptions of our belief systems are open to revision. For example, Ptolemy's assumptions were replaced by Kepler, Newton's by Einstein, and Aristotle's assumptions were overthrown by Darwin.*

To summarize, Quine has changed the hard-and-fast logical distinction of the empiricists between analytic and synthetic statements into a distinction made on the basis of pragmatic considerations. He has also challenged the notion that there can be any direct empirical verification or falsification of a single statement. Quine says the radical effects of abandoning these two dogmas include that of "blurring the supposed boundary between speculative metaphysics and natural science." The modern physicist's belief in physical objects and the ancient Greek's belief in Homer's gods are simply two beliefs that find their place within different sorts of belief systems. "In point of epistemological footing the physical objects and the gods differ only in degree and not in kind," Quine says. However, he retreats from total relativism and embraces pragmatism because he thinks we can argue for the practical superiority of one belief and its supporting assumptions over another belief. As Quine says,

> The myth of physical objects is epistemologically superior to most in that it has proved more efficacious than other myths as a device for working a manageable structure into the flux of experience.

---

*Thomas Kuhn, a philosopher and historian of science, applies Quine's notion that a proposition is accepted or rejected in terms of how it fits in with our entire network of beliefs to explain the process of scientific inquiry. Kuhn shows the way scientists interpret their experience to maintain their current theories and documents the fact that scientific revolutions are not produced by the discovery of new data, but by large-scale displacements of the reigning scientific paradigm. This is developed in his book, *The Structure of Scientific Revolutions*, 2d ed., enlarged (Chicago: University of Chicago Press, 1970).

Rethinking Philosophy: Postmodernism

A relatively recent event in philosophy has been the rise of **postmodernism**. Postmodernists are a loose-knit group of thinkers united around the belief that they are the pallbearers of the modern tradition that originated in the Enlightenment. The tradition of modernism they reject includes the following beliefs: (1) there is one true picture of reality, (2) it is possible to obtain universal, objective knowledge, (3) science is a superior form of knowledge, (4) the history of modern thought has been a cumulative progression of increasingly better theories about reality, and (5) the autonomous, knowing subject is the source of all ideas.

Postmodernists join with Nietzsche and Heidegger in unmasking the pretensions of reason and the illusions of metaphysics. According to these thinkers, the dream of finding a central theme or set of categories for understanding reality is now over. There are no essences or certitudes on which we can pin our hopes. We must now face our stark, uncharted waking experience for the first time. We are the products of history, and history is nothing but an aimless play of shifting social forces. What is left for us to do is to analyze or "deconstruct" the dream of reason, to see how it arose and why it seemed so real, or else to revel in the endless play of interpretations and perspectives, realizing that it is a game without a final goal. For these reasons, postmodernists frequently allude to the death of epistemology, the death of metaphysics, and even the death of philosophy, at least as it has traditionally been understood. The most frequently discussed postmodernists in current philosophy are Michel Foucault, Jacques Derrida, and Richard Rorty.

MICHEL FOUCAULT

Frequently spoken of as the most important French thinker since Sartre, Michel Foucault (1926–1984) has been one of the central figures in postmodernism.* The works of Foucault's first period are *Madness and Civilization*, *The Birth of the Clinic: An Archaeology of Medical Perception*, *The Order of Things: An Archaeology of the Human Sciences*, and *The Archaeology of Knowledge*, all originally published in the 1960s. The word "archaeology" in most of the titles indicates how he conceived his task at that time. He was digging down beneath the surface of our social-intellectual traditions to uncover the strata of various historical eras. The "strata" he examines are called *epistemes*.[†] An *episteme* is the dominant conceptual framework of a given historical period. It makes no sense to ask which one is "true," for any notion of *truth* is the product of a particular *episteme*. As Foucault expresses it, " 'Truth' is to be understood as a system of ordered procedures for the production, regulation, distribution, circulation and operation of statements."[2] Embracing a form of relativism, Foucault believes the notion of one, universal truth is no longer viable, since it belongs to the *episteme* of an earlier age.

An *episteme* consists of a number of discursive practices (or structured linguistic patterns). The discursive practices Foucault is interested in are those that have been awarded the status of truth by society and that, in turn, effectively control that society. Hence, he looks at the normative discourses of medicine, psychiatry, law, and morality for his data. The dominant discursive practices of an era define what it makes sense to say, what is excluded from discourse, what questions are meaningful, and how behaviors are to be described. They create a social reality in their own image by indicating (implicitly or explicitly) how the world should be divided up according to such categories as

---

*Throughout his academic career, Michel Foucault lectured in universities around the world, including a number of American universities. At the time of his death he held a distinguished chair of the history and systems of thought at France's most prestigious institution, the Collège de France.
[†]*Episteme* is the Greek word for "knowledge." However, Foucault pluralizes the term, indicating that he believes there is a plurality of "knowledges."

true–false, madness–sanity, rational–irrational, moral–immoral, or normal–perverse.

Foucault rejects the referential view of language, which is the theory that the meaning of a word is the object to which it refers. Instead, he claims that words receive their meaning from their role within the whole network of discourse and practices. Employing what appears to be a sort of linguistic Kantianism, Foucault points out that words do not refer to objects as much as they constitute them. Although it is obvious that words cannot literally create a tree, we know things (including a tree) *as* this or that sort of thing—that is, in terms of some description or other.*

Reversing the Enlightenment assumption that philosophers' ideas create society, Foucault maintains that an *episteme* is a system of external social structures that determine our ideas. Hence, the Enlightenment *episteme* created the Enlightenment intellectuals, the intellectuals did not create their age. Even though Foucault speaks of "rules of production" that govern the discursive practices of a society, these rules have not been consciously invented and are never explicitly formulated by their participants. Each historical period is an unconscious play of forces that Foucault seeks to understand by "decoding" their patterns. The notion that human institutions and history exhibit rationality and continuity is attacked as an illusion. Instead, history is a purposeless series of ruptures, gaps, transformations, and displacements, as socially created realities come and go without order or reason.

After the May 1968 student uprisings in the Paris universities, Foucault came to a greater appreciation of the role of power structures. Instead of discourse being primary in the constitution of social reality, he now saw it as merely one outcome of an ever-expanding institutionalized social power. In this stage of his work, the term "genealogy" looms large. It is a term Nietzsche used when he discussed how the "will to power" expressed itself in covert ways. Foucault frequently uses the phrase "power/knowledge" to indicate that the two always go together. He says we must realize

> that power and knowledge directly imply one another; that there is no power relation without the correlative constitution of a field of knowledge, nor any knowledge that does not presuppose and constitute at the same time power relations.[3]

For Foucault, intellectual history is nothing more than a display of the way in which the notion of "truth" has been used to mask the will to power operating beneath the surface. In the following statement, notice how he wraps the notion of "truth" in political phrases: "Each society has its own régime of truth, its 'general politics' of truth: that is, the type of discourse which it accepts and makes function as true."[4]

This stage of Foucault's research is best exemplified in his 1975 work, *Discipline and Punish: The Birth of the Prison*. This study discusses the way in which the historically evolving architecture, policies, and practices of prisons in the nineteenth century exemplified the mechanisms of power and control. Although the concern for "technologies of control" may seem a necessary feature of a prison system, Foucault cites historical documents to show how the same mechanisms and ideology were applied to the organization of armies, schools, hospitals, and factories. In all these institutions, power and control were exercised under the guise of scientific, enlightened, humanitarian social reform. Through its "régimes of truth," society imposes its historically relative ideals on individuals, whether they are criminals, students, patients, or workers.

Consistently, Foucault recognized that his relativistic view implied that his own work was not an objective march toward universal truth. He applied to himself his claim that discourse is not the product of an autonomous subject but reflects the *episteme* of the time. Speaking about his book *The Order of Things*, he said,

---

*To roughly illustrate Foucault's point, think of words such as *credit*, *wife*, *sin*, *success*. Their meanings are not made clear by pointing to a certain object or action. Instead, to understand what is being described, you have to understand the complex network of words and practices that create the worlds of economics, social institutions, religion, and social ideals.

my book is a pure and simple "fiction": . . . it is not I who invented it; it is the relation of our epoch and its epistemological configuration to a whole mass of utterances. So, although the subject is in effect present in the totality of the book, it is an anonymous "someone" who speaks today in everything which is said.[5]

JACQUES DERRIDA

Another of the leading French postmodernists is Jacques Derrida (1930–).* The influence of Derrida's writings is matched only by the magnitude of their difficulty. The main project of his work is to deflate the pretensions of reason that are manifested throughout the history of thought. According to Derrida, the entire history of philosophy is a series of variations on "the myth of presence." In other words, every philosophy starts by assuming some central presence that is the axis around which the whole system revolves. This center may be Plato's Forms, Aristotle's substance, the medievals' God, Descartes's self, Newton's material particles, Kant's moral law, and so forth. In each system, this central reality (whatever it may be) is thought to be the rock-solid certitude that serves as the key for unlocking all the secrets of reality. As Derrida says,

The function of this center was not only to orient, balance, and organize the structure . . . but above all to make sure that the organizing principle would limit what we might call the play *of the structure.*[6]

By "play" Derrida means an openness to unexplored possibilities and novel approaches. In seeking to anchor thought and language in a "center," the philosopher limits and freezes our modes of in-

terpretation, seeking security in a foundation that will not fail us. Derrida's strategy is not to refute these claims, but to unmask them by exposing the underlying motives and illusions that animate them all. He calls for an approach "which is no longer turned toward the origin, affirms play," and that abandons the dream of "full presence, the reassuring foundation, the origin and the end of play."[7] Derrida calls this process "deconstruction" and its result is a "decentering" of our systems of thought.

With Nietzsche and Foucault, Derrida rejects "logocentrism" or the notion that language refers to an order of meaning and truth, an order that is based in a reality that exists independently of our historically relative perspectives. However, if there is no certainty, no possibility of finding *the* center, no meanings or universals external to the language we invent, then everything is interpretation. The logical conclusion of this position is that all we ever achieve are reinterpretations of interpretations. As Derrida states it,

Reading . . . cannot legitimately transgress the text toward something other than it, toward the referent (a reality that is metaphysical, historical, psychobiographical, etc.) or toward a signifier outside the text whose content could take place, could have taken place outside of language, that is to say, in the sense that we give here to that word, outside of writing in general. . . . There is nothing outside of the text.[8]

Assuming that language cannot refer beyond itself, Derrida concludes that the meaning of a term is a function of the place it occupies within a system of linguistic concepts.[†] More specifically, terms receive their meanings from the role they play in differentiating one category of things from another.[‡] For example, nature does not present us

*Jacques Derrida was first a student and later a critic of both Husserl and Heidegger. He taught philosophy at the École Normale Supérieure in France from 1965 to 1984. From 1960 to 1964, he taught at the Sorbonne in Paris. Since the early 1970s he has divided much of his time between Paris and the United States, where he has lectured at such universities as Johns Hopkins, Yale, Cornell, and the University of California at Irvine.

[†]Some have supported Derrida's point by noting that a dictionary explains a word by associating it or contrasting it with other words.
[‡]Derrida's thesis is a radical interpretation of a position known as "structuralism," which was based on the thought of linguist Ferdinand de Saussure and anthropologist Claude Lévi-Strauss.

with any absolute divisions corresponding to the terms "warm" or "hot," any more than it does for the contrasting terms of masculine–feminine or normal–abnormal. Instead, Derrida says, all such terms receive their meanings from the distinctions that are created within language. From the premise that language has no absolute, external point of reference, Derrida concludes that language is arbitrary, imposing no limits on the play of meanings and interpretations readers may find in a text.* Deconstructionists seek to reveal the incoherencies within texts, for from the conflict of multiple interpretations new possibilities of interpretation are generated.

To provide a concrete summary of the preceding points, Derrida creates a French pun with the word *différance*. This has the double meaning of "differ" and "defer." Because words do not have a fixed, positive meaning, but meaning emerges from the way they *differ*, then we have to continually *defer* any final interpretation or assignment of meaning. To undermine the seriousness of language and to underscore the element of "play," Derrida sprinkles his writings with puns, plays on words, unlikely metaphors, amusing allusions, and phonic and typographical tricks.[†]

Derrida realizes that even his own language is infected with metaphysical pretensions. The words "essence," "existence," "experience," "consciousness," "subject," and "object" carry with them the baggage of thousands of years of philosophical speculation and inescapably reflect the metaphysics of presence. Finding it impossible to critique philosophy without employing the traditional terms of philosophy, Derrida uses them, as he says, "under erasure." Thus, when he writes a word such as *thing*, he literally crosses it out, indicating that in using it he is not taking it seriously.

This brief glimpse of Derrida's thought is enough to give the flavor of his iconoclastic undermining of all traditional notions of truth, logic, rationality, objectivity, language, and interpretation. His deconstructionism has had its major impact in the field of literature where, in the last few decades of the twentieth century, it has become one of the most important movements within literary theory.

RICHARD RORTY

Within American philosophy, Richard Rorty (1931–) has been the most influential advocate of postmodernism.[‡] Rorty started out as a doctrinaire analytic philosopher but eventually became disillusioned, concluding that analytic philosophy was far from the revolutionary philosophy it aspired to be. Although analytic philosophers were innovative in their use of linguistic methods, he said, they were still pursuing the age-old project of finding the universal foundations of knowledge that animated the Descartes-Locke-Kant tradition. Questioning the validity of this project, Rorty scandalized his analytic colleagues by rejecting this tradition and turning to Dewey's pragmatism instead. As Rorty's pragmatism became increasingly radical, he continued to cause a stir by developing his nontraditional vision of philosophy from the ideas of the unlikely combination of Dewey, Wittgenstein, and Heidegger. Consequently, Rorty has been a leading force in building bridges between Anglo-American philosophy and European Continental thought.

In his book *Philosophy and the Mirror of Nature*, Rorty attacks traditional epistemology and

---

*Critics often point out that deconstructionists inconsistently object when they believe the "true" meaning of their own texts have been wrongly interpreted. See Derrida's essay "Signature, Event, Context" in *Glyph* 1 (1977), 172–197, and John Searle's response "Reiterating the Differences: A Reply to Derrida" in the same issue, 198–208. In Derrida's retort, "Limited, Inc. abc" in *Glyph* 2 (1977), 162–254, Derrida complains that Searle misunderstood his position.

†The element of "play" in Derrida's view of language (referring to both the lack of restraint and the lack of seriousness) has been the target of criticism. Some Marxists and feminists accuse him of an escapism that lacks any serious political agenda. Similarly, conservatives and traditionalists accuse him of **nihilism**.

‡Richard Rorty spent most of his philosophical career as a faculty member in the philosophy department at Princeton. Beginning in 1983, he held the position of professor of humanities at the University of Virginia. After retiring there, he became a professor of comparative literature at Stanford University in 1998.

its attempt to set out the conditions that enable us to grasp "how things really are."[9] As the title of his book suggests, Rorty contends that traditional philosophy views the mind as a mirror that "reflects" the external world. Since the surface of the mirror was thought to be hazy or uneven, traditional philosophers tried to produce more accurate representations by "inspecting, repairing, and polishing the mirror" (PMN 12). Drawing on Dewey's insights, Rorty opposes traditional philosophy with four theses: the mind does not mirror nature, statements are simply tools for accomplishing certain tasks, an idea is true if it works, and there are no final ends in either philosophy or life.

The radical nature of Rorty's philosophy is captured by his call to abandon the project of epistemology. Epistemology is based on the notion that we can arrive at ideas or statements that will give us the one, true picture of reality. However, drawing on the insights of Quine and the philosopher of science T. S. Kuhn, Rorty argues that our beliefs and statements are always components of large-scale systems of practices that are chosen for practical reasons. If, as Dewey said, beliefs and statements are tools, then their effectiveness for our tasks is the issue and not their correspondence to reality. Referring to Wittgenstein and Heidegger, Rorty says that

> they do not think that when we say something we must necessarily be expressing a view about a subject. We might just be saying something—participating in a conversation rather than contributing to an inquiry. Perhaps saying things is not always saying how things are. (PMN 371)

What is the purpose of philosophical discourse if it is not that of "saying how things are"? Rorty's answer is that philosophy is "edifying discourse." The purpose of edifying philosophy is "finding new, better, more interesting, more fruitful ways of speaking" and "to keep the conversation going rather than to find objective truth" (PMN 360, 377). Rorty agrees with Jean-Paul Sartre that human beings are not fixed like objects, but we are always on the way, continually remaking ourselves:

> To see keeping a conversation going as a sufficient aim of philosophy, to see wisdom as consisting in the ability to sustain a conversation, is to see human beings as generators of new descriptions rather than beings one hopes to be able to describe accurately. (PMN 378)

If the mind does not mirror reality and our statements do not correspond to what is out there, is there any place at all for the notion of "truth"? In his essay "Solidarity or Objectivity?" Rorty repeats William James's statement that truth is "what it is good for *us* to believe" (SO 22).[10] But this notion of truth means it can never be conceived as some sort of final destination, for it is continually being reinvented. Rorty suggests we replace the epistemologist's static goal of "objectivity" with the pragmatist's goal of "intersubjective agreement" or "solidarity." The problem is, how can we agree if there is no objective reality about which we can agree? From Rorty's standpoint, the only possible answer is that our lives overlap, we engage in common projects, and we have similar needs and sentiments. Out of these common bonds, we create cohesive communities and a sense of solidarity. Hence, "truth" and "rationality" are inescapably social notions, for they cannot be discussed apart from "descriptions of the familiar procedures of justification that a given society—*ours*—uses in one or another area of inquiry" (SO 23).* Rorty says some are repelled by this view because it is hard for them to admit that we exist in a "lonely provincialism" and that "we are just the historical moment that we are" (SO 30). Nevertheless, even if we abandon the belief that there can be a final philosophy or an objective, universal picture of the world, we can still strive to break down the barriers between communities.

> For pragmatists, the desire for objectivity is not the desire to escape the limitations of one's community, but simply the desire for as much intersubjective

---

*Rorty's position has similarities to that of the later Wittgenstein (Chapter 32), who claimed our beliefs and ways of speaking are not grounded in logic but in our "form of life." "What people accept as a justification—is shewn by how they think and live," Wittgenstein said.

agreement as possible, the desire to extend the reference of "us" as far as we can. (SO 23)

Rethinking Philosophy: Feminism

Feminism is another contemporary movement that is seeking to rethink philosophy.* Since this is a movement and not a doctrine-laden school of thought, there are many conceptions among its adherents as to what constitutes feminist philosophy. Generally, feminist philosophers stress the role of gender in shaping the patterns of thought, society, and history. Furthermore, feminists focus on the ways in which our male-dominated historical traditions have excluded women from the intellectual and political realms. Consequently, feminists make it their goal not only to describe the world but also to change it, producing a society that recognizes women and men as both different and equal.

It is obvious that the history of philosophy, like that of most of our disciplines, has been shaped by men. This does not mean that there have not been women philosophers. In fact, we can find women philosophers all the way back to ancient Greece.† It does mean, however, that opportunities for women to have their voices heard have been limited. A work on the history of philosophy, such as this one, necessarily focuses on those thinkers in the past who have been most *influential*. A book exclusively devoted to those philosophers whose ideas have been the most sound or the most deserving of an audience would include women and men who are not included in standard histories, while others

would be dropped from their position of historical prominence.

A few male philosophers throughout history have criticized the exclusion of women. Plato in his *Republic* and John Stuart Mill in *The Subjection of Women* both argued that women of superior intellect and abilities should take their place with their male peers in providing intellectual and political leadership. Too often, however, Aristotle's attitude has prevailed. He asserted that only the free adult male is qualified to rule society, for only he is invested by nature with full rational capacity.[11] Furthermore, some feminists argue that when philosophers such as Kant discuss the political rights and equality of all "men," they often are not talking about human beings in general, but specifically about *males*.[12] For such reasons, feminists tend to agree with thinkers such as Marx, Nietzsche, and Foucault that "objective thought" often disguises underlying interests and power structures.

In addition to developing theories about the role of gender and power in the history of ideas, feminist philosophers focus attention on topics of particular concern to women, such as issues concerning equality, rights, sex roles, the family, and social structures. For this reason, the feminists have done a great deal of work in ethics and social philosophy.

Feminists are divided into two categories. The first category consists of (what are variously called) "equity," "liberal," or "first wave" feminists. The equity feminists want to retain the current social structures and the intellectual tradition of the Enlightenment. Their concern is that women be given full intellectual and political participation in society. Thus, they want to open up society, correct the distortions in our traditions, and modify our intellectual disciplines. The second group of feminists is called "gender," "radical," or "second wave" feminists. Gender feminists claim that the fundamental structures, assumptions, methods, and discourse of our Western heritage reflect the fact that it has been controlled by men. Using their own term, the gender feminists' approach is much more "subversive," for instead of making piecemeal corrections to the Western tradition, they

---

*In addition to the many books and anthologies that are now available, *Hypatia: A Journal of Feminist Philosophy* provides many examples of what this movement is about. (Hypatia was a fifth-century female leader of the Neoplatonist movement who was condemned to death as a heretic and died a brutal death at the hands of Christian fanatics.)

†For a comprehensive survey of women in the history of philosophy, see *A History of Women Philosophers*, ed. Mary Ellen Waithe, 4 vols. (Dordrecht, Netherlands: Kluwer Academic, 1987–1994). This series covers women philosophers from ancient Greece through the twentieth century.

Simone de Beauvoir (1908–1986) is best known for her novels and essays which made her one of France's most celebrated twentieth-century writers. Her book The Second Sex *became an influential document in the feminist movement and contained the often quoted words, "one is not born a woman but becomes one." She was the life-long companion of existentialist Jean-Paul Sartre.*

want to bring the validity of that whole tradition into question and to devise alternatives.

The notion of "gender" is, itself, one of the most controversial topics within the feminist movement. A distinction is frequently made between sex and gender. Sex is a biological category that refers to the obvious physical differences between males and females. Gender, however, is a social-psychological category. It includes (but is not limited to) the notions of masculine-feminine, social roles, sexuality, and the apparent psychological differences between men and women. Some feminists are *essentialists*, claiming that there is a distinct and essential female nature. Some essentialists are biological determinists who see female nature as rooted in women's unique biology. Looser versions of essentialism claim that the

properties constituting the female gender are rather stable, although created through the unique and common features of female experience. Feminists who are *nonessentialists* or *nominalists* deny that gender characteristics are fixed in any way at all, viewing them as purely social constructs that are open to change and redefinition. Rejecting both extreme essentialism and nominalism, Simone de Beauvoir expresses a mediating position in her famous quote "One is not born, but rather becomes, a woman."[13] Briefly, her view is that gender characteristics are not biologically determined, but they can be either socially imposed or subjectively chosen. The role gender plays in feminist thought can be illustrated by a brief and selective look at ways feminists are attempting to remap the terrains of epistemology and ethics.

FEMINIST APPROACHES TO EPISTEMOLOGY

According to gender feminists, traditional theories of knowledge have been based on the following assumptions:

1. There is one, universal, human nature. Hence, epistemology is the attempt to describe the fundamental cognitive structures of the generic human being.

2. The particular identity of a knower (including gender, race, class, and social-political-historical circumstances) is irrelevant to the production and assessment of that person's knowledge claims.

3. It is possible to obtain knowledge that is purely objective, value-free, and politically neutral.

In contrast to these assumptions, gender feminists claim that (1) there is no universal human nature, (2) knowledge is always related to the standpoint of a particular knower, and (3) knowledge claims reflect the dominant values and political structures of a society. Feminists claim that the picture of generic humanity has actually made men's experiences and interests the paradigm. Other points of view and characteristics, particularly those of women, that deviate from the standard picture have been excluded or marginalized for being too subjective, idiosyncratic, or unconventional. Traditional epistemologists seek for universal standards of rationality; feminists ask, "Standard and rational for whom?" This concern is expressed in the title of Sandra Harding's book *Whose Science? Whose Knowledge?*[14] Similarly, in criticizing a recent book on rationality that enthrones traditional notions of reason, Lorraine Code asserts, "Critics must ask for whom this epistemology exists; whose interests it serves; and whose it neglects or suppresses in the process."[15]

Most feminist writers contend that women's experiences and ways of thinking differ from those that have been the basis of traditional (male) epistemologies. Just as the standards used to evaluate oranges do not apply to apples, grapes, and lemons, so there cannot be one paradigm for epistemology. Feminists appeal to empirical research on children, which has provided interesting data on gender-specific ways of knowing. Boys tend to organize the world in terms of independent, manipulable, discrete units. Girls, in contrast, perceive the world in terms of functional, relational characteristics and interdependent connections. If there are these sorts of differences, then there cannot be one, generic theory of knowledge.

A major topic within feminist epistemology is the nature of rationality and its relation to the emotions. The majority position in Western tradition, feminists charge, has defined rationality in a way that devalued the emotions. Addressing this issue in an essay titled "The Man of Reason," Genevieve Lloyd discusses this traditional ideal of rationality.[16] She has an easy task demonstrating that the standard equations throughout history have been "male = rational" and "female = nonrational." Descartes's dualism aggravated the problem by creating the following divisions: intellect versus the emotions, reason versus imagination, mind versus the body. The consequence of Descartes's divisions was that the emotions, the imagination, and the sensuous dimension were assigned to women as their special area of responsibility, while excluding them from the realm of reason.

According to Lloyd's analysis, "If women's minds are less rational than men's, it is because the limits of reason have been set in a way that excludes qualities that are then assigned to women."[17] Furthermore, this ideal of rationality has political consequences. "Exclusion from reason has meant exclusion from power."[18] In rejecting our traditional definition of rationality, Lloyd also rejects the romantics' solution, for they accepted the preceding polarities such as intellect versus emotions and then went on to exclusively embrace the second half of each dichotomy. Instead, she calls for a broader notion of reason that seeks for the unity beneath the divisions, which have been the basis of illegitimate sexual stereotypes.

Taking a different approach from Lloyd, Alison Jaggar is willing to accept that women have a richer emotional life than men, but argues that this makes women better knowers.[19] While recognizing that emotions such as love and hate can undermine critical reflection, she still insists that the emotions may be helpful and even necessary to the construction of knowledge. Referring to work in the epistemology of science, Jaggar argues that all observation is selective. As part of this selection process, our values, motivations, and interests direct our cognitive pursuits, shape what we know, and help determine its significance. Yet these subjective factors that influence cognition are heavily imbued with emotional dimensions.* Jaggar argues that the emotions of marginalized people (such as women) make them epistemologically privileged. For example, the pain and anger women feel in response to subtle sexual harassment or injustice allows them to perceive features of the prevailing social structures that are invisible to men.

FEMINIST APPROACHES TO ETHICS

Feminists apply the same sorts of analyses in ethics that they do in epistemology. Traditionally,

---

*Jaggar suggests, for example, that Jane Goodall's important scientific contributions to our understanding of chimpanzee behavior was made possible only by her love and empathy for these animals.

ethical theory has been presented as though the topic were objective and neutral. As a matter of fact, feminist critics charge, the theories have contained pervasive gender biases. In 1982, Harvard psychologist Carol Gilligan published *In a Different Voice: Psychological Theory and Women's Development*.[20] This book ended up being one of the most influential books in feminist ethics.* Gilligan noted that empirical research on the development of moral reasoning was carried out primarily by males and on mostly male subjects. The result was that psychological theories about this topic took male reasoning as the norm.

According to Gilligan's research, males and females solve ethical dilemmas with different sets of criteria. Males tend to employ a "judicial" model, which emphasizes equality, justice, rights, impartiality, objectivity, universal principles, and logic. In contrast, females tend to approach ethics in a more person-centered way, stressing care, compassion, trust, mercy, forgiveness, preventing harm, and feelings. Gilligan concludes that these two separate ethical perspectives are products of the different ways that males and females are socialized. The problem is that traditional theories of moral development characterize the judicial (male) approach as the highest stage and characterize more relational (female) approaches as less mature stages of development.† However, Gilligan says these two approaches cannot be ranked on the same scale, for they are different ways of achieving moral maturity. Furthermore, she says each approach has its strengths and weaknesses,

suggesting the need for a more adequate ethical perspective that includes both dimensions.

Other feminists start with the uniqueness of the female approach to ethics and go on from there to argue for its superiority over traditional (male) morality.‡ However, many are not sure that this is a good strategy. Feminist critics say that narrowing feminist ethics to the "ethics of caring" reinforces gender stereotypes and supports the traditional dogma that women are best suited to be mothers and nurses, rather than lawyers and executives. Furthermore, critics charge, downgrading the principles of impartiality, autonomy, and justice found in traditional moral theories undermines women's drive for equality.

To summarize, feminists have raised important questions, such as, How do power structures and social conditions shape and limit the development of ideas? To what extent are our personal identities formed by biological factors, to what extent are they constructed by social forces, and to what extent do we freely choose them? To what degree is knowledge relative to the situation of the knower? In our personal lives and in our theories, how do we find a balance between reason and emotion or justice and caring? Although these sorts of questions arose out of women's attempts to rethink history and their own experience and identities, the impact of these questions goes far beyond issues that are exclusively concerned with women.

Philosophy in a Global Village

The feminists' attempt to rethink our philosophical tradition has been paralleled by a new interest in non-Western philosophical traditions. Just as

---

*At least since Kant, many traditional philosophers have tended to say that empirical psychology has no relevance to issues concerning standards and foundations in epistemology and ethics. Thus, they would see Gilligan's book on psychology as irrelevant to philosophy. Many feminists, however, see disciplinary boundaries as artificial structures that are used to fragment human experience and maintain control over the sorts of questions that may be raised. They claim that our psychological structures, gender, values, politics, social patterns, relationships of power, knowledge, and conceptions of reality are all intertwined in making our experience the way it is.

†Gilligan illustrates her point by analyzing the work of Lawrence Kohlberg, one of the leading researchers in the area of moral development.

‡See, for example, Annette Baier, *Postures of the Mind: Essays on Mind and Morals* (Minneapolis: University of Minnesota Press, 1985), Nel Noddings, *Caring: A Feminist Approach to Ethics and Moral Education* (Berkeley: University of California Press, 1984); Sara Ruddick, *Maternal Thinking: Toward a Politics of Peace* (Boston: Beacon Press, 1989); and Margaret Walker, "Moral Understandings: Alternative 'Epistemology' for a Feminist Ethics," *Hypatia: A Journal of Feminist Philosophy* 4, no. 2 (Summer 1989).

feminists sought to make room within philosophy for the "different voice" represented by women's experiences, so has there been a growing concern to open up Western philosophy to include the perspectives of other cultures. More and more, multicultural approaches are being explored in order to broaden our outlook on traditional philosophical questions. Because of space limitations, this book has covered only Western philosophy. However, becoming aware of the hidden assumptions solidified in Western history can be a broadening rather than a limiting experience if it makes us more discerning in our dialogue with other traditions.

New Issues in Philosophy of Mind

The development of computer technology, particularly artificial intelligence research, has raised new questions and suggested new methods and directions within the area of philosophy of mind. In fact, a new interdisciplinary field has emerged called *cognitive science*, which is a hybrid of the disciplines of artificial intelligence, philosophy, psychology, neuroscience, and linguistics. A basic feature of this new approach is the "computational model of the mind," which assumes that the analogy between computers and human cognition will be a fruitful one. This is an attempt to fulfill La Mettrie's vision that he set out in his 1747 work, *Man the Machine*. The philosophers working in this field hope that an increased understanding of how to make computers intelligent will give us a better understanding of human cognition, and a better understanding of human cognition will help us make computers more intelligent.

Although many researchers in this area think that the psychology of information processing will answer our philosophical questions about our mental life, other philosophers insist that we must get down to an even more fundamental level to explore the biological basis of thought. If we understand the details of how the brain works, they say, we will resolve the mysteries of human cognition. Two important philosophers in this movement are Patricia Churchland, with her aptly titled book *Neurophilosophy* (1986), and her

husband, Paul Churchland, who wrote the influential book *Matter and Consciousness* (1984). If their approach is correct, an adequate scientific understanding of the brain will eliminate the need for such terms as "mind," "self," "beliefs," "thoughts," "desires," or "intentions." Instead, all future talk about human cognition will be cast in terms of brain states. If this happens, then the traditional discipline of philosophy of mind that uses these epistemological terms will be cast aside as "folk psychology," just as medical science has unseated many theories of folk medicine. As it stands now, the neurological approach to philosophical psychology is a research program that is still in its beginning stages. The critics of this approach have revived Edmund Husserl's arguments against naturalism, claiming we will never be able to consistently develop a theory that does away with the knowing subject who did the theorizing in the first place.

New Issues in Ethics

Another development that has come to the forefront of philosophy in recent decades is *applied ethics*. Unlike the previous movements mentioned in this chapter, applied ethics is not a particular philosophy or point of view. Instead, it is a new application of ethical theory to practical ethical problems, particularly as they are found in the various professions. The best-known example of this new topic is the field of medical ethics. The issues that make the headlines (and the law courts) are, typically, abortion, euthanasia, physician-assisted suicides, surrogate motherhood, and genetic engineering. However, there are many, more subtle ethical issues in medicine dealing with such topics as autonomy–paternalism, the physician–patient relationship, consent, disclosure, and issues concerning privacy or confidentiality. Although some of these issues were unheard of fifty years ago, the relevance of the history of philosophy is indicated by the fact that such names as Immanuel Kant and John Stuart Mill continually occur in contemporary discussions of current problems. In addition to medical ethics, there has also been a growing demand for philosophers to clarify the ethical dimensions of professions such as business, accounting, journalism, and engineering, as well as the issues arising out of our environmental concerns.

A Parting Word

With all this emphasis in these last six chapters on the new movements in philosophy, it should not be thought that the traditional positions have been abandoned. Plenty of thinkers still believe that Plato, Aristotle, Augustine, Aquinas, or one or more of the moderns from Descartes to Hegel got at least part of the picture right. For example, I have a colleague in law and one in mathematics who are Hegelians. I also know physicists who think that metaphysical idealism makes a lot of sense. Philosophy is a unique discipline in that its theories have more enduring value than those of any other field. There is still much to be learned from positions that are centuries old.

I can think of no better way to end this book than by returning to a quote from Martin Heidegger. He addresses the accusation that "you can't do anything with philosophy." Heidegger acknowledges that this claim is true. Certainly (to elaborate on his remarks), philosophy will not get us to the farthest planets, it will not lead to a cure for any fatal disease, nor will it help us make a killing on the stock market. However, Heidegger cautions that this is not the last word on philosophy. "Granted that *we* cannot do anything with philosophy, might not philosophy, if we concern ourselves with it, do something *with us*?"[21] I hope that you have found this to be the outcome of reading this book.

Questions for Understanding

1. What two "dogmas of empiricism" does Quine attack? What arguments does he use in his attack?

2. What is meant by "modernism"? How has it been attacked by postmodernism?

3. What does *episteme* mean? In his epistemology, why does Foucault replace it with the plural term *epistemes*?

4. According to Foucault, what is the relationship between power and knowledge?

5. What does Derrida mean by the following terms: *the myth of presence, deconstruction,* and *logocentrism*?

6. What is Derrida's account of the meaning of a word?

7. What four theses does Rorty assert in his critique of traditional philosophy?

8. According to Rorty, what is the purpose of philosophical discourse?

9. Rorty replaces the notion of "objectivity" in traditional epistemology with what goal?

10. What are the differences between "first wave" feminists and "second wave" feminists?

11. What is the distinction feminists make between sex and gender?

12. What is the difference between feminists who are essentialists and those who are nonessentialists?

13. According to gender feminists, what are the three assumptions of traditional theories of knowledge and why do they reject them?

14. What is Genevieve Lloyd's thesis about rationality?

15. What does Alison Jaggar say about the role of the emotions in knowledge?

16. What does Carol Gilligan say about the role of gender in the development of moral reasoning?

17. What is cognitive science?

18. What is meant by the "computational model of the mind"?

19. Why do philosophers such as Patricia and Paul Churchland think that notions such as "mind" or "belief" should be eliminated? What notions will they use to replace them?

20. Why has applied ethics become such an important topic recently?

Questions for Reflection

1. According to Quine, how are modern physics and Greek mythology epistemologically similar? If they are similar in this way, why does he prefer modern physics as a way of understanding the world? Is he rational in this preference?

2. To what degree do you agree or disagree with Foucault that power defines what will be accepted as knowledge? Think of some examples in the past or the present that he could use to illustrate this point.

3. If everyone accepted Rorty's claim that solidarity and not objectivity is the goal of thought, how would this change the activity of philosophy? How might society be different? What problems would be solved by this point of view? What problems might be created?

4. If female thinkers had predominated throughout the history of philosophy, would it have developed differently? How so?

5. Is our outlook on the world or our philosophy affected by our gender? How so? What are the implications of your answer for the doing of philosophy?

6. Is there, ideally, one true philosophy or are there necessarily only many philosophies? If there is no possibility of any particular perspective being the correct one, what is the value of doing philosophy? How would Rorty or a feminist respond?

7. What are some of the issues on which the feminists disagree with each other? In each case, which feminists do you think have the most plausible view?

8. Do you think research on the brain will solve our epistemological questions? Why or why not? What philosophical questions (if any) do you think will not be illuminated, much less solved, by further scientific research?

Notes

1. Willard Van Orman Quine, "Two Dogmas of Empiricism," in *From a Logical Point of View*, rev. ed. (New York: Harper Torchbooks, Harper & Row, 1961).

2. Michel Foucault, *Power/Knowledge: Selected Interviews and Other Writings, 1972–1977*, ed. Colin Gordon, trans. Colin Gordon, Leo Marshall, John Mepham, and Kate Soper (New York: Pantheon Books, 1980), 133.

3. Michel Foucault, *Discipline and Punish: The Birth of the Prison*, trans. Alan Sheridan (New York: Vintage Books, Random House, 1977), 27.

4. Foucault, "Truth and Power," in *Power/Knowledge*, 131.

5. Quoted in Pamela Major-Poetzl, *Michel Foucault's Archaeology of Western Culture* (Chapel Hill: University of California Press, 1983), 19.

6. Jacques Derrida, "Structure, Sign, and Play in the Discourse of the Human Sciences," chapter in his *Writing and Difference*, trans. Alan Bass (Chicago: University of Chicago Press, 1978), 278.

7. Ibid., 292.

8. Jacques Derrida, *Of Grammatology*, trans. Gayatri Chakravorty Spivak (Baltimore: Johns Hopkins University Press, 1976), 158.

9. Richard Rorty, *Philosophy and the Mirror of Nature* (Princeton, NJ: Princeton University Press, 1979). This work is cited in the text using the abbreviation PMN.

10. Richard Rorty, "Solidarity or Objectivity," chapter in his *Objectivity, Relativism, and Truth*, Philosophical Papers, vol. 1 (Cambridge, England: Cambridge University Press, 1991). This essay is cited in the text using the abbreviation SO.

11. Aristotle, *Politics*, bk. 1.

12. Susan Mendus, "Kant: An Honest But Narrow-Minded Bourgeois?" in *Women in Western Political Philosophy: Kant to Nietzsche*, ed. Ellen Kennedy and Susan Mendus (New York: St. Martin's Press, 1987).

13. Simone de Beauvoir, *The Second Sex*, trans. H. M. Parshley (New York: Knopf, 1975), 267.

14. Sandra Harding, *Whose Science? Whose Knowledge?* (Ithaca, NY: Cornell University Press, 1991).

15. Lorraine Code, "Taking Subjectivity into Account," in Linda Alcoff and Elizabeth Potter, eds., *Feminist Epistemologies* (New York: Routledge, 1993), 23.

16. Genevieve Lloyd, "The Man of Reason," in *Women, Knowledge, and Reality: Explorations in Feminist Philosophy*, ed. Ann Garry and Marilyn Pearsall (Boston: Unwin Hyman, 1989), 111–128. Originally published in *Metaphilosophy* 10, no. 1 (January 1979): 18–37. See also, the book-length treatment, Genevieve Lloyd, *The Man of Reason: "Male" and "Female" in Western Philosophy* (Minneapolis: University of Minnesota Press, 1984).

17. Ibid., 124.

18. Ibid., 127.

19. Alison M. Jaggar, "Love and Knowledge: Emotion in Feminist Epistemology," in *Women, Knowledge, and Reality: Explorations in Feminist Philosophy*, ed. Ann Garry and Marilyn Pearsall (Boston: Unwin Hyman, 1989), 129–155. Previously published in *Inquiry: An Interdisciplinary Journal of Philosophy* (June 1989) and in *Gender/Body/Knowledge: Feminist Reconstructions of Being and Knowing*, ed. Alison M. Jaggar and Susan R. Bordo (New Brunswick, NJ: Rutgers University Press, 1989).

20. Carol Gilligan, *In a Different Voice: Psychological Theory and Women's Development* (Cambridge, MA: Harvard University Press, 1982).

21. Martin Heidegger, *An Introduction to Metaphysics*, trans. Ralph Manheim (Garden City, NY: Anchor Books, Doubleday, 1959), 10.

This Glossary contains all the terms set out in bold in the preceding chapters. Terms set out in bold within the definitions are defined elsewhere in the glossary. The chapter in which the term is introduced as well as those in which it plays a central role are indicated in parentheses.

Aesthetics (or esthetics)—An area of philosophy that pursues questions concerning art, including the nature and role of art, the standards for evaluating art, and the nature of beauty. (Introduction chapter)

Agnosticism—With respect to a particular issue, the claim that nothing can be known, one way or another, because the evidence is thought to be insufficient to provide us with any knowledge. Hence, the agnostic argues that we must suspend judgment on the issue. Typically, agnosticism refers to the position that the existence of God can neither be affirmed nor denied. (Chap. 21)

Altruism—The claim that people either are or ought to be motivated to serve the interests of others. The opposite of **egoism**. (Chap. 24)

Analytic judgment—A knowledge claim expressed by an **analytic statement**. (Chap. 22)

Analytic philosophy—A twentieth-century movement in philosophy, particularly strong in America and Britain, that approaches philosophical problems primarily through an analysis of language. Also called *linguistic philosophy*. (Chap. 32)

Analytic statement—A statement in which the predicate is contained within the subject (its truth is based on the meaning and relationship of its terms) and its denial results in a logical contradiction, e.g., "All mothers are parents." Contrasted with synthetic statements. (Chaps. 22, 32)

Antinomy—A pair of seemingly reasonable conclusions that flatly contradict each other and hence cannot both be true. Kant used antinomies to argue that reason contradicts itself when it reaches beyond its proper limits in attempting to answer traditional metaphysical questions about the nature of reality. (Chap. 22)

A posteriori—A type of knowledge, statement, or concept whose content and truth are derived from experience. For example, "Water freezes at 32°F" is an *a posteriori* truth. Contrasted with **a priori**. (Chaps. 13, 22)

Appearance—The way in which something presents itself to the senses which is different from how it is in reality. For example, a straight stick in water appears to be bent, even though it really is not. (Chaps. 2, 3, 6, 22, 23)

A priori—A type of knowledge, statement, or concept whose content and truth can be known prior to or independently of experience. For example, some philosophers believe that "two plus two equals four" and "every event has a cause" are *a priori* truths which cannot be proven by experience. Contrasted with **a posteriori**. (Chaps. 13, 22)

Argument—An attempt to establish the truth of a statement (the conclusion) by showing that it follows from, or is supported by, the truth of one or more other statements (the premises). (Introduction chapter, Chap. 5)

Atomism—A metaphysical position originating with the ancient Greeks that claims that reality is made up of numerous, indivisible particles of matter moving in a void. (Chap. 2)

Autonomy—Being one's own authority or rule giver, as opposed to being subject to external authority. In Kant's ethics this is an essential condition for rational morality. (Chap. 22)

Categorical imperative—According to Kant, a command that is binding on all rational persons at all times, which generates universal moral laws. It commands us to always act in such a way that we could rationally wish that everyone followed the principle governing that action. Contrasted with hypothetical imperatives, in which the command applies only under certain conditions. (Chap. 22)

Cogent argument—An **inductive argument** that is (a) inductively strong and (b) has all true premises. (Introduction chapter)

Cognition—Knowledge or the act of knowing.

Cognitive meaning—The informative content of a statement that asserts a claim that may be either true or false. The cognitive meaning of a statement is sometimes contrasted with its emotive meaning, or the emotional attitude it expresses or evokes. (Chap. 32)

Coherence theory of truth—The theory that a true assertion or belief is one that coheres with our entire system of interconnected and mutually supporting beliefs. (Chap. 24)

Compatibilism—The theory that human beings are *both* determined and free as long as their actions proceed from their own, inner choices and are not compelled by an external cause. (Chap. 17)

Conceptualism—The claim that **universals** are mental concepts obtained by abstracting the common qualities appearing in similar particular objects. See **Nominalism** and **Realism**. (Chap. 10)

Consequentialism—See **Teleological ethics**.

Contingent—A contingent event is one that is not logically necessary, for whether it occurs or not is dependent on other events. Similarly, a contingent statement is one whose truth is not logically necessary. It may be denied without asserting a contradiction. (Chaps. 12, 13, 16, 17)

Correspondence theory of truth—The theory that a true assertion or belief is one that corresponds with the fact or state of affairs in reality to which it refers. (Chaps. 27, 33)

Cosmological argument—An argument for the existence of God based on the claim that the universe requires a cause for its existence. (Chap. 11)

Deduction—The form of reasoning we use when we attempt to argue from the truth of one proposition or set of propositions to a conclusion that necessarily follows from those propositions. (Introduction chapter)

Deductively valid—See **Valid**.

Deism—A religious outlook, based on reason, that acknowledges the existence of God and his creation of the world, but denies that God intervenes in the world either in the form of miracles or revelation. Deists argue that the divinely ordered natural laws and reason make both nature and humanity self-sufficient. (Chap. 19)

Deontological ethics—From the Greek word *deon*, meaning "duty" or "obligation." Deontological ethics defines the moral rightness or wrongness of an act in terms of the intrinsic value of the act. According to this theory, our duty to perform an action (or to refrain from doing it) is based on the nature of the act itself and not on its consequences. Kant was a leading proponent of this theory. Contrasted with **teleological ethics**. (Chap. 22)

Determinism—The metaphysical position that claims every event (including human actions) follows necessarily from previous events. (Chaps. 14, 17, 30)

Dialectic—(1) For Socrates, a conversational method for progressing toward the truth, by continually examining proposed answers to a question, repeatedly replacing inadequate answers with more refined and adequate ones. (2) For Plato, it was the philosophical method of rising above particulars and hypotheses to achieve the highest form of knowledge. (3) For Hegel, it is a historical process in which both thought and reality develop as oppositions and tensions are resolved at a higher stage. (4) Marx adopted Hegel's historical dialectic, but changed it into the conflict and development of material forces. (Chaps. 3, 4, 24, 25)

Dogmatism—Asserting a position without providing adequate reasons for its truth.

Dualism—A theory that asserts that there are two irreducible realities, such as mind and body, spirit and matter, or good and evil. (Chaps. 2, 4, 15)

Egoism—(1) Psychological egoism is a descriptive theory that claims people always pursue what they perceive to be their own best interests. (2) Ethical egoism is a prescriptive theory that claims people *ought* to always act according to their own best interests. The opposite of **altruism**. (3) In both of the preceding types of egoism, egoistic **hedonism** identifies pleasure with one's best interests. (Chaps. 6, 14, 27, 28)

Empirical—Related to sense experience.

Empiricism—The theory that knowledge is obtained solely from sense experience. (Chaps. 2, 13, 19, 20, 21, 28, 32)

Epicureanism—A version of **hedonism**, based on the philosophy of Epicurus (341–271 B.C.), which claims that (1) only pleasure is intrinsically good and (2) all pleasures are not to be desired equally, the more prudent and sedate pleasures being the ones that lead to true happiness. (Chap. 6)

Epistemology—An area of philosophy that pursues questions concerning truth and knowledge. (Introduction chapter)

Essence—The defining characteristic of something. That property or set of properties without which it would not be the sort of thing that it is. (Chaps. 5, 11)

Ethical egoism—See **Egoism**.

Ethical hedonism—See **Hedonism**.

Ethics—An area of philosophy that reasons about morality, particularly the meaning and justification of claims concerning right or wrong actions, obligation, moral rules, rights, virtue, the good life, and the possibility of objective morality. (Introduction chapter)

Existentialism—A nineteenth- and twentieth-century philosophy that focuses on the nature and meaning of human existence as understood from the subjective standpoint of the subject. Repudiating the notion of a fixed human nature, existentialists claim that we are continually creating the self. They stress the priority of subjective choosing over objective reasoning, concrete experience over intellectual abstractions, individuality over mass culture, human freedom over determinism, and authentic living over inauthenticity. (Chaps. 23, 26, 27, 29, 33)

Feminism—A movement within philosophy and other disciplines that (1) stresses the role of gender in shaping the patterns of thought, society, and history, (2) focuses on the ways in which women have been assigned roles throughout history that excluded them from the intellectual and political realms, and (3) strives to produce a society that recognizes women and men as both different and equal. (Chap. 34)

Forms—According to Plato, the Forms are the ultimate realities and objects of genuine knowledge. Forms are nonphysical, eternal, known only through reason, and impart intelligibility and reality to things in the physical world that imitate them. For example, Plato believes all circular things (rings, hoops, wreathes) are imperfect representations of the Form of Circularity. (Chap. 4)

Hedonism—The position that claims pleasure is the only thing that has intrinsic value. (1) Psychological hedonism claims that it is a psychological fact that people always strive to pursue pleasure and avoid pain. (2) Ethical hedonism claims that pleasure is what people *ought* to pursue. (Chaps. 2, 6, 14, 28)

Historicism—The theory that everything human is affected by the processes of history, such that any idea cannot be understood apart from its historical context and is valid only for a particular time, place, and community. (Chaps. 23, 24)

Idea—(1) In general, any object of thought. (2) For Plato, Ideas were another term for the **Forms** (e.g., the Idea of Justice, the Idea of Circularity). (3) For Descartes and Locke an idea was any mental content, which could include sensations (redness, sweetness, heat) or the mind's mental states (doubting, imagining, believing). (4) For Berkeley, ideas and the minds that contained them were the whole of reality. (5) For Hume, an idea was a copy of an original sensation (called an *impression*) that was recalled in memory or the imagination. (Chaps. 4, 15, 19, 20, 22)

Idealism—The theory that reality is ultimately mental or of the nature of a mind. Idealism characterizes the philosophies of Leibniz, Berkeley, and Hegel. Contrasted with **materialism** and contemporary forms of **realism**. (Chaps. 17, 20, 23, 24)

Indeterminism—The theory that some events in the world (particularly human choices) are not the necessary result of previous causes, because these events are either random or the products of free will. (Chap. 30)

Induction—The form of reasoning we use when we argue from what is true of one set of facts to what is probably true of further facts of the same kind. An inductive argument either concludes something about a new case, based on what was true of similar cases, or it arrives at a generalization concerning all cases similar to those that have been observed. (Introduction chapter, Chap. 21)

Inductively strong argument—A successful inductive argument in which the premises, if true, would make the conclusion highly probable. (Introduction chapter)

Innate ideas or knowledge—Mental contents that are inborn or part of the natural content of the human mind and not derived from experience. Their existence is defended by most rationalists and attacked by empiricists. (Chaps. 3, 4, 15, 17, 19)

Intellectualism—The theory that the intellect is prior to or superior to the will. Accordingly, it is claimed that the intellect or reason perceives that certain ends or goals are desirable and then directs the will to achieve them. Theological intellectualism claims that God's intellect first knows that certain actions are either intrinsically good or evil and then he wills that they should be done or avoided. The opposite of **voluntarism**. (Chap. 10)

Intuition—(1) Knowledge that is directly and immediately known by the mind, rather than being the product of reasoning or inference; or (2) the object of such knowledge. According to Kant, humans can have only sensory intuitions. (Chap. 22, 31)

Linguistic philosophy—See **Analytic philosophy**.

Logical atomism—The philosophy of Russell and the early Wittgenstein, which claimed that the structure of language and reality are the same, since language is reducible to elementary units corresponding to the fundamental units that compose the world of facts. (Chap. 32)

Logical positivism—A twentieth-century version of **empiricism** and a version of **analytic philosophy**, which states that (1) logical and mathematical statements are logically necessary statements (**tautologies**) that do not provide information about the world and (2) factual statements are meaningful only if they are capable of being verified in sense experience (**verifiability principle**). (Chap. 32)

Logos—A particularly rich Greek term that has a large number of related meanings: speech, discourse, word, explanation, reason, order. It is the source of many English words such as "logic," "logo," "biology," "psychology." Heraclitus believed that *logos* was the rational principle that permeated all things. The Stoics identified it with God, Providence, Nature, or Fate. Christian writers identified it with God or Christ. (Chaps. 2, 6, 7)

Marxism—The philosophy based on the writings of Karl Marx, which asserts that (1) reality is material, (2) history follows a dialectical pattern controlled by economic forces, (3) each era of history is characterized by conflict between opposing economic classes, (4) history is a **dialectic** in which each economic stage produces its own contradictions, giving way to its successor, and (5) the present stage of capitalism will be overcome by socialism, leading to the final stage of pure communism in which class conflict will be abolished. (Chap. 25)

Materialism—The metaphysical position that claims matter is the only reality. Also called *material monism*. (Chaps. 2, 14, 25)

Material monism—See **Materialism**.

Metaphysical dualism—See **Dualism**.

Metaphysics—An area of philosophy that pursues questions about the nature of reality. (Introduction chapter)

Monism—Any metaphysical position that asserts that there is only one kind of reality. **Materialism** claims that matter is the only reality, while **idealism** claims that it is mental. (Chap. 2)

Monotheism—The belief that there is only one God.

Moral relativism—See **Relativism**.

Naive realism—The belief that the properties we perceive objects to have are the properties that they really do have in the external world. (Chap. 20)

Naturalism—The metaphysical position that claims that physical nature encompasses everything that is real and that all of reality can be completely explained by the natural sciences. (Chap. 33)

Naturalistic fallacy—The fallacy of attempting to derive ethical claims (what we ought to do) from factual claims (what is the case). (Chap. 32)

Natural law—In ethics, the claim that there is an objective moral law, transcending human conventions, which may be discerned by examining human nature. (Chaps. 3, 6, 10, 11)

Natural theology—A discipline within philosophy that attempts to prove conclusions about God based on our natural reason and experience without appealing to revelation. (Chap. 11)

Nihilism—From the Latin word for nothing; the belief that there is no knowledge or truth and, particularly, that nothing has any genuine value, meaning, or purpose. (Chap. 27)

Nominalism—The claim that there are no real, independently existing **universals** and that uni-

versal terms refer only to collections of particular things. See **Conceptualism**, **Realism**. (Chaps. 10, 12, 14, 20)

Noumena—Things as they really are in themselves, as opposed to how they appear in experience. Kant claimed that the noumena were unknowable. They are the opposite of **appearances** or **phenomena**. (Chaps. 22, 23)

Occasionalism—The claim that there is no causal relationship between mental events and physical events, but that certain mental events always seem to occur simultaneously with certain physical events only because the occurrence of one is the occasion on which God produces the other. (Chap. 15)

Ockham's razor—The principle that our explanations should always be as simple as possible, avoiding the postulation of unnecessary entities. Named after William of Ockham (c. 1270–1350), whose formulation of this principle was very influential, particularly in scientific methodology. (Chap. 12)

Ontological argument—An argument for the existence of God based on the concept of God's perfection and unsurpassable greatness. The argument was defended by Anselm, Descartes, Spinoza, and Leibniz and attacked by Kant, among others. (Chaps. 10, 15, 16, 22)

Ontology—The study of the generic features of being, as opposed to the study of the particular things that exist. Ontology is concerned with questions such as "What is most fundamentally real?" "What does it mean to exist?" and "What is the structure of reality?" Some writers virtually identify ontology and **metaphysics**, while others view it as a subdivision of metaphysics. Other philosophers, such as Heidegger and Sartre, distinguish their ontology from metaphysics in order to avoid the latter's association with questions about God, substance, and the origin of the universe. (Chap. 33)

Panentheism—The belief that God's being includes that of the world but is not limited to it. (Chap. 31)

Panpsychism—A form of **idealism** that maintains that all of reality consists of multiple centers of experience, such as minds or souls, who have various degrees of awareness. Leibniz called them "monads," and Whitehead referred to them as "actual occasions." (Chaps. 17, 31)

Pantheism—The belief that God and the world are identical. (Chap. 16)

Parallelism—The claim that there is no direct causal relationship between mental and physical events, but that the two series run parallel to each other. Essentially the same as Leibniz's **pre-established harmony** doctrine. (Chap. 15)

Phenomena—Things as they appear within experience, in contrast to how they are in reality. Kant said that this is all that we could know about the world. They are the opposite of **noumena**. (Chaps. 22, 23)

Phenomenalism—The doctrine that all statements about material objects can be completely analyzed into statements about sense data without making reference to any reality external to sensation. This position is the contrary of **representative realism**. (Chap. 20)

Phenomenology—The attempt to describe the structure and contents of consciousness in a way that is free of presuppositions and that does not go beyond what appears to consciousness. Versions were set out by Hegel, Husserl, and Heidegger. (Chaps. 24, 33)

Pluralism—The metaphysical position that claims that there are many kinds of reality. (Chap. 2)

Positivism—The view that all knowledge claims must be limited to observable facts, that only science provides genuine knowledge, and that the role of philosophy is to apply the findings of the sciences to problems of human conduct and social organization. Positivism rejects all metaphysical claims and any inquiry not reducible to scientific method. Advocated by Auguste Comte and John Stuart Mill. The movement was a predecessor of **logical positivism**. (Chap. 28)

Postmodernism—A movement that arose in the late twentieth century, that was influenced by Nietzsche and Heidegger and that embraces **relativism** and **historicism**. Postmodernists seek to unmask what they consider to be the pretensions of reason and the illusions of metaphysics. They repudiate the Enlightenment ideal of seeking for objective, rational truth and they replace the notion of one, true picture of reality with that of multiple, ongoing interpretations. Postmodernism has been particularly influential in literary studies. (Chap. 34)

Pragmatism—A philosophy that stresses the intimate relationship between thought and action. Pragmatists claim, for example, that the meaning of a concept is identical to the practical effects of the object of our conception. Likewise, a true belief is defined as one that will effectively guide action in the long run. (Chap. 30)

Pre-established harmony—The doctrine that events in the world, particularly the activities of the mind and body, do not causally interact, but have been arranged by God from the beginning of time to work in unison like two independent clocks that keep the same time. Leibniz was its most important proponent. (Chap. 17)

Primary qualities—Those qualities of an object that may be represented mathematically such as size, shape, number, quantity, motion, and location. According to Galileo and the early modern philosophers, such as Descartes and Locke, primary qualities represent the world as it really is. Contrasted with **secondary qualities**. (Chaps. 13, 15, 19)

Psychological egoism—See **Egoism**.

Psychological hedonism—See **Hedonism**.

Rationalism—The theory that at least some knowledge is obtained by the mind independently of experience. (Chaps. 2, 4, 13, 15, 16, 17)

Realism—(1) In its contemporary usage, the thesis that reality exists independently of our consciousness of it, in contrast to **idealism**. (2) In ancient and medieval thought: (a) Platonic or extreme realism refers to the claim that **universals** have an objective, independent existence apart from the minds that know them or the individuals that exemplify them; (b) moderate realism claims that universals are abstracted by the mind from objective features of individuals, but that they do not have any reality apart from minds or individuals. (This is sometimes called Aristotelian realism or equated with **conceptualism**.) All medieval versions of realism are in opposition to **nominalism**. (Chap. 10, 32)

Relativism—(1) In epistemology, the claim that there is no absolute knowledge, because different individuals, cultures, or historical periods have different opinions on the truth and all opinions are equally valid. (2) Likewise, in ethics, the claim that there are no objective moral truths, for all moral judgments are said to be relative to the knowing subject and equally correct. (Chaps. 3, 4)

Representative realism—The epistemological claim that the mind is directly acquainted only with its own ideas, but that these ideas are caused by and represent objects external to the mind. (Chap. 19)

Scholasticism—The dominant philosophy of the medieval period in which logic was used to demonstrate the harmony of philosophy and the authoritative writings of the religious tradition. (Chap. 10)

Secondary qualities—According to the early modern philosophers, these are the subjective sensations (colors, tastes, odors, sounds, temperature) produced within us by the **primary qualities** of an object. (Chaps. 13, 15, 19)

Sense data—A term used to refer to the particular, individual impressions received in sensation, such as particular colors, tastes, sounds, odors, and textures. Reference to sense data need not presuppose anything about their cause. (Chap. 32)

Skepticism—The claim that it is impossible to know anything to be absolutely true. (Chaps. 2, 3, 6, 21)

Social contract theory—The theory that the justification of government is based on an explicit or implicit agreement made by individuals among themselves or with a sovereign power (Hobbes, Locke, and Rousseau). (Chaps. 3, 14, 19)

Solipsism—The view that nothing can be known apart from my self and the contents of my conscious experience, usually leading to the conclusion that "only I exist." Finding solipsism to be implausible, philosophers such as Descartes were motivated to find demonstrations of the external world or other minds. (Chaps. 15, 20)

Sophists—A group of educators in fifth-century Athens who taught the skills of rhetoric and argumentation, usually to prepare people for political careers. Most of the Sophists were advocates of **skepticism** and **relativism**. (Chap. 3)

Sound argument—A deductive argument that is (1) **valid** and (2) has all true premises. (Introduction chapter)

Stoicism—The view that we will find happiness only if we resign ourselves to accept whatever may happen in life. Historically, this view was based on the belief that the universe is fulfilling the benevolent purposes of divine providence and that every event is inevitable. (Chap. 6)

Substance—A fundamental and independently existing reality that supports or underlies the various qualities or properties we perceive. Various philosophers who believe in substances disagree over how many kinds there are and what sorts of things qualify as substances. The concept was particularly important in the philosophies of the Pre-Socratics, Aristotle, Descartes, Spinoza, Leibniz, and Locke. (Chaps. 2, 5, 15, 16, 17, 19, 21, 22)

Synthetic judgment—A knowledge claim expressed by a **synthetic statement**. (Chap. 22)

Synthetic statement—A statement in which the predicate adds information to the subject that is not logically contained within it and in which its denial (even if false) does not result in a logical contradiction, e.g., "All mothers are under fifty feet tall" is a synthetic statement. Contrasted with **analytic statements**. (Chap. 22)

Tautology—A statement that is true because of its logical form; e.g., "X is identical to X." (Chap. 32)

Teleological argument—An argument for the existence of God based on the evidence of purpose and design in the world; e.g., Aquinas's fifth argument for God. (Chap. 11)

Teleological ethics—Any ethical theory that defines moral rightness or wrongness in terms of the desirability or undesirability of an action's consequences. Contrasted with **deontological ethics**. (Chaps. 11, 22, 28)

Teleological explanation—An explanation of an event or thing in terms of the end, goal, or purpose it tends to achieve. (Chaps. 4, 13)

Teleology (or teleological)—From the Greek word *telos*, meaning "purpose" or "end." A teleological metaphysics claims that nature exhibits purpose; i.e., events in the world are directed to the fulfillment of some goal. (Chaps. 4, 5, 11)

Theism—The belief that there is one God, who transcends the world.

Things-in-themselves—According to Kant, the contents of reality as they are, independent of the mind's apprehension of them. Identical to the **noumena**. (Chap. 22)

Transcendental—Refers to conditions within the knower which makes knowledge or action possible. Kant's critical philosophy tried to set out the transcendental conditions that enable us to be knowers and agents. (Chap. 22)

Universal—(1) Any general term or concept that refers to a number of particular things that are members of the same group; e.g., "human" is a universal that applies to each member of the human race. Since the time of Plato, there has been a controversy as to whether universals exist in reality, or whether they are mere concepts or words. See **Conceptualism**, **Nominalism**, and **Realism**. (Chap. 4, 10) (2) As an adjective, it designates that which applies to all persons, at all times, in all circumstances, e.g., universal truths, universal moral rules. (Chap. 4, 22)

Utilitarianism—A theory of ethics and a political philosophy built around the claim that a good action is one that creates the greatest amount of good for the greatest number over any other alternative action. (Chap. 28)

Valid argument—A successful deductive argument whose form is such that if the premises are true, the conclusion necessarily must be true. (Introduction chapter)

Verifiability principle—The criterion of meaning developed by the **logical positivists** stating that (1) a factual statement has **cognitive meaning** only if sense experience can provide evidence of its truth and (2) the experiences that would demonstrate its truth are identical to its meaning. (Chap. 32, 34)

Voluntarism—The theory that the will is prior to or superior to the intellect or reason. Accordingly, reason is viewed as merely an instrument for achieving the ends or goals that the will voluntarily chooses. Theological voluntarism claims that God declares an action to be morally good or evil solely on the basis of his free choice, for he is not compelled to do so because of any intrinsic property in the action itself. The opposite of **intellectualism**. (Chap. 10, 12)

INDEX